CHILTON BOOK COMPANY
REPAIR MANUAL

FORD PICK–UPS and BRONCO 1987–90

Covers all models of F–150, F–250, F–350, F–Super Duty, Bronco, Chassis/Cab, Stripped Commercial Chassis, Motorhome Chassis • 2– and 4–Wheel Drive • Gasoline and Diesel Engines

President GARY INGERSOLL
Senior Vice President, Book Publishing and Research RONALD A. HOXTER
Publisher KERRY A. FREEMAN, S.A.E.
Editor–in–Chief DEAN F. MORGANTINI, S.A.E.
Senior Editor RICHARD J. RIVELE, S.A.E.

CHILTON BOOK COMPANY
Radnor, Pennsylvania
19089

CONTENTS

GENERAL INFORMATION and MAINTENANCE

ENGINE PERFORMANCE and TUNE-UP

ENGINE and ENGINE OVERHAUL

EMISSION CONTROLS

FUEL SYSTEM

CHASSIS ELECTRICAL

DRIVE TRAIN

SUSPENSION and STEERING

BRAKES

BODY

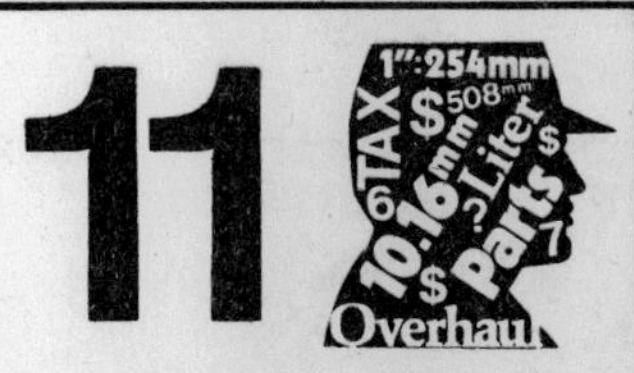

MECHANIC'S DATA

SAFETY NOTICE

Proper service and repair procedures are vital to the safe, reliable operation of all motor vehicles, as well as the personal safety of those performing repairs. This book outlines procedures for servicing and repairing vehicles using safe, effective methods. The procedures contain many NOTES, CAUTIONS and WARNINGS which should be followed along with standard safety procedures to eliminate the possibility of personal injury or improper service which could damage the vehicle or compromise its safety.

It is important to note that repair procedures and techniques, tools and parts for servicing motor vehicles, as well as the skill and experience of the individual performing the work vary widley. It is not possible to anticipate all of the conceivable ways or conditions under which vehicles may be serviced, or to provide cautions as to all of the possible hazards that may result. Standard and accepted safety precautions and equipment should be used during cutting, grinding, chiseling, prying, or any other process that can cause material removal or projectiles

Some procedures require the use of tools specially designed for a specific purpose. Before substituting another tool or procedure, you must be completly satisfied that neither your personal safety, nor the performance of the the vehicle will be endangered.

Although the information in this guide is based on industry sources and is as complete as possible at the time of publication, the possibility exists that the manufacturer made later changes which could not be included here. While striving for total accuracy, Chilton Book Company cannot assume responsibility for any errors, changes, or omissions that may occur in the compilation of this data.

PART NUMBERS

Part numbers listed in this reference are not recommendations by Chilton for any product by brand name. They are references that can be used with interchange manuals and aftermarket supplier catalogs to locate each brand supplier's discrete part number.

SPECIAL TOOLS

Special tools are recommended by the vehicle manufacturer to perform their specific job. Use has been kept to a minimum, but where absolutely necessary, they are referred to in the text by the part number of the tool manufacturer. These tools can be purchased, under the appropriate part number, from Owatonna Tool Co., Owatonna, MN 55060, or an equivalent tool can be purchased locally from a tool supplier or parts outlet. Before substituting any tool for the one recommended, read the SAFETY NOTICE at the top of this page.

ACKNOWLEDGMENTS

Chilton Book Company expresses appreciation to Ford Motor Co., Ford Parts and Service Division. Service Technical Communications Department, Dearborn, MI for their generous assistance.

Published in Radnor, Pennsylvania 19089, by Chilton Book Company

Manufactured in the United States of America
1234567890 9876543210

Chilton's Repair Manual: Ford Pick–ups and Bronco 1987–90
ISBN 0–8019–8137–9 pbk.
Library of Congress Caatalog Card No. 90–056128

General Information and Maintenance

1

HOW TO USE THIS BOOK

Chilton's Repair Manual for 1987–90 Ford Pickups, Bronco, Super Duty and Motor Home chassis is intended to help you learn more about the inner workings of your vehicle and save you money on its upkeep and operation.

The first two chapters will be the most used, since they contain maintenance and tune-up information and procedures. Studies have shown that a properly tuned and maintained truck can get at least 10% better gas mileage than an out-of-tune truck. The other chapters deal with the more complex systems of your truck. Operating systems from engine through brakes are covered to the extent that the average do-it-yourselfer becomes mechanically involved. This book will not explain such things as rebuilding the differential for the simple reason that the expertise required and the investment in special tools make this task uneconomical. It will give you detailed instructions to help you change your own brake pads and shoes, replace spark plugs, and do many more jobs that will save you money, give you personal satisfaction, and help you avoid expensive problems.

A secondary purpose of this book is a reference for owners who want to understand their truck and/or their mechanics better. In this case, no tools at all are required.

Before removing any bolts, read through the entire procedure. This will give you the overall view of what tools and supplies will be required. There is nothing more frustrating than having to walk to the bus stop on Monday morning because you were short one bolt on Sunday afternoon. So read ahead and plan ahead. Each operation should be approached logically and all procedures thoroughly understood before attempting any work.

All chapters contain adjustments, maintenance, removal and installation procedures, and repair or overhaul procedures. When repair is not considered practical, we tell you how to remove the part and then how to install the new or rebuilt replacement. In this way, you at least save the labor costs. Backyard repair of such components as the alternator is just not practical.

Two basic mechanic's rules should be mentioned here. One, whenever the left side of the truck or engine is referred to, it is meant to specify the driver's side of the truck. Conversely, the right side of the truck means the passenger's side. Secondly, most screws and bolt are removed by turning counterclockwise, and tightened by turning clockwise.

Safety is always the most important rule. Constantly be aware of the dangers involved in working on an automobile and take the proper precautions. (See the section in this chapter Servicing Your Vehicle Safely and the SAFETY NOTICE on the acknowledgement page.)

Pay attention to the instructions provided. There are 3 common mistakes in mechanical work:

1. Incorrect order of assembly, disassembly or adjustment. When taking something apart or putting it together, doing things in the wrong order usually just costs you extra time; however, it CAN break something. Read the entire procedure before beginning disassembly. Do everything in the order in which the instructions say you should do it, even if you can't immediately see a reason for it. When you're taking apart something that is very intricate (for example, a carburetor), you might want to draw a picture of how it looks when assembled at one point in order to make sure you get everything back in its proper position. (We will supply exploded view whenever possible). When making adjustments, especially tune-up adjustments, do them in order; often, one ad-

justment affects another, and you cannot expect even satisfactory results unless each adjustment is made only when it cannot be changed by any order.

2. Overtorquing (or undertorquing). While it is more common for over-torquing to cause damage, undertorquing can cause a fastener to vibrate loose causing serious damage. Especially when dealing with aluminum parts, pay attention to torque specifications and utilize a torque wrench in assembly. If a torque figure is not available, remember that if you are using the right tool to do the job, you will probably not have to strain yourself to get a fastener tight enough. The pitch of most threads is so slight that the tension you put on the wrench will be multiplied many, many times in actual force on what you are tightening. A good example of how critical torque is can be seen in the case of spark plug installation, especially where you are putting the plug into an aluminum cylinder head. Too little torque can fail to crush the gasket, causing leakage of combustion gases and consequent overheating of the plug and engine parts. Too much torque can damage the threads, or distort the plug which changes the spark gap.

There are many commercial products available for ensuring that fasteners won't come loose, even if they are not torqued just right (a very common brand is Loctite®). If you're worried about getting something together tight enough to hold, but loose enough to avoid mechanical damage during assembly, one of these products might offer substantial insurance. Read the label on the package and make sure the products is compatible with the materials, fluids, etc. involved before choosing one.

3. Crossthreading. This occurs when a part such as a bolt is screwed into a nut or casting at the wrong angle and forced. Cross threading is more likely to occur if access is difficult. It helps to clean and lubricate fasteners, and to start threading with the part to be installed going straight in. Then, start the bolt, spark plug, etc. with your fingers. If you encounter resistance, unscrew the part and start over again at a different angle until it can be inserted and turned several turns without much effort. Keep in mind that many parts, especially spark plugs, used tapered threads so that gentle turning will automatically bring the part you're treading to the proper angle if you don't force it or resist a change in angle. Don't put a wrench on the part until its's been turned a couple of turns by hand. If you suddenly encounter resistance, and the part has not seated fully, don't force it. Pull it back out and make sure it's clean and threading properly.

Always take your time and be patient; once you have some experience, working on your truck will become an enjoyable hobby.

TOOLS AND EQUIPMENT

Naturally, without the proper tools and equipment it is impossible to properly service you vehicle. It would be impossible to catalog each tool that you would need to perform each or any operation in this book. It would also be unwise for the amateur to rush out and buy an expensive set of tool on the theory that he may need on or more of them at sometime.

The best approach is to proceed slowly gathering together a good quality set of those tools that are used most frequently. Don't be misled by the low cost of bargain tools. It is far better to spend a little more for better quality. Forged wrenches, 6- or 12-point sockets and fine tooth ratchets are by far preferable to their less expensive counterparts. As any good mechanic can tell you, there are few worse experiences than trying to work on a truck with bad tools. Your monetary savings will be far outweighed by frustration and mangled knuckles.

Begin accumulating those tools that are used most frequently; those associated with routine maintenance and tune-up.

In addition to the normal assortment of screwdrivers and pliers you should have the following tools for routine maintenance jobs:

1. SAE (or Metric) or SAE/Metric wrenches-

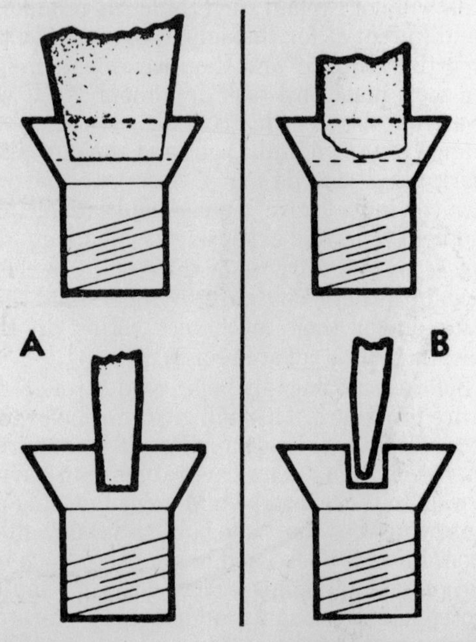

Keep screwdrivers in good shape. They should fit the slot as shown 'A'. If they look like those in 'B', they need grinding or replacing.

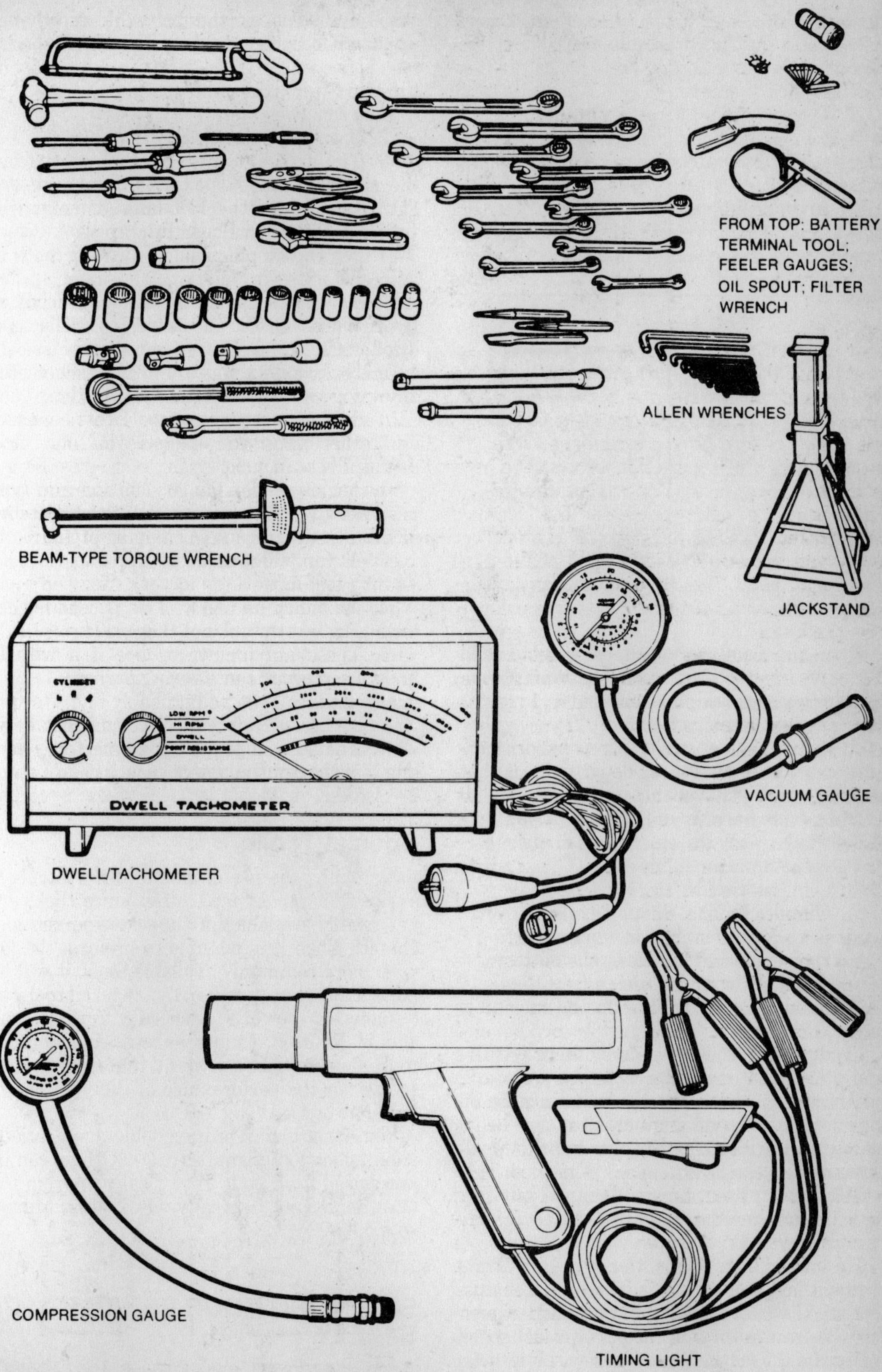

This basic collection of tools and test instruments is all you need for most maintenance on your truck.

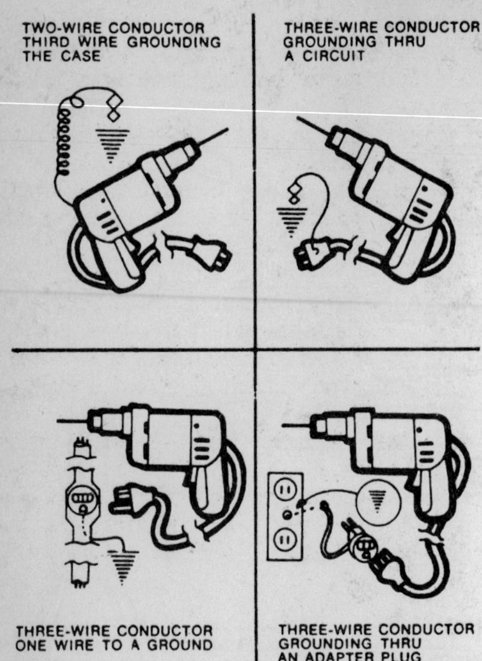

When using electric tools, make sure they are properly grounded.

sockets and combination open end-box end wrenches in sizes from 1/8 in. (3mm) to 3/4 in. (19mm) and a spark plug socket (13/16 in. or 5/8 in. depending on plug type).

If possible, buy various length socket drive extensions. One break in this department is that the metric sockets available in the U.S. will all fit the ratchet handles and extensions you may already have (1/4 in., 3/8 in., and 1/2 in. drive).

2. Jackstands for support.
3. Oil filter wrench.
4. Oil filler spout for pouring oil.
5. Grease gun for chassis lubrication.
6. Hydrometer for checking the battery.
7. A container for draining oil.
8. Many rags for wiping up the inevitable mess.

In addition to the above items there are several others that are not absolutely necessary, but handy to have around. these include oil dry, a transmission funnel and the usual supply of lubricants, antifreeze and fluids, although these can be purchased as needed. This is a basic list for routine maintenance, but only your personal needs and desire can accurately determine you list of tools.

The second list of tools is for tune-ups. While the tools involved here are slightly more sophisticated, they need not be outrageously expensive. There are several inexpensive tach/dwell meters on the market that are every bit as good for the average mechanic as a $100.00 professional model. Just be sure that it goes to a least 1,200–1,500 rpm on the tach scale and that it works on 4, 6, 8 cylinder engines. (A special tach is needed for diesel engines). A basic list of tune-up equipment could include:

1. Tach/dwell meter.
2. Spark plug wrench.
3. Timing light (a DC light that works from the truck's battery is best, although an AC light that plugs into 110V house current will suffice at some sacrifice in brightness).
4. Wire spark plug gauge/adjusting tools.
5. Set of feeler blades.

Here again, be guided by your own needs. A feeler blade will set the points as easily as a dwell meter will read well, but slightly less accurately. And since you will need a tachometer anyway. . . well, make your own decision.

In addition to these basic tools, there are several other tools and gauges you may find useful. These include:

1. A compression gauge. The screw-in type is slower to use, but eliminates the possibility of a faulty reading due to escaping pressure.
2. A manifold vacuum gauge.
3. A test light.
4. An induction meter. This is used for determining whether or not there is current in a wire. These are handy for use if a wire is broken somewhere in a wiring harness.

As a final not, you will probably find a torque wrench necessary for all but the most basic work. The beam type models are perfectly adequate, although the newer click type are more precise.

Special Tools

Normally, the use of special factory tools is avoided for repair procedures, since these are not readily available for the do-it-yourself mechanic. When it is possible to preform the job with more commonly available tools, it will be pointed out, but occasionally, a special tool was designed to perform a specific function and should be used. Before substituting another tool, you should be convinced that neither your safety nor the performance of the vehicle will be compromised.

Some special tools are available commercially from major tool manufacturers. Others can be purchased from your Ford Dealer or from the Owatonna Tool Company, Owatonna, Minnesota 55060.

SERVICING YOUR VEHICLE SAFELY

It is virtually impossible to anticipate all of the hazards involved with automotive maintenance and service but care and common sense will prevent most accidents.

The rules of safety for mechanics range from "don't smoke around gasoline" to "use the proper tool for the job." The trick to avoiding injuries is to develop safe work habits and take every possible precaution.

Do's

• Do keep a fire extinguisher and first aid kit within easy reach.

• Do wear safety glasses or goggles when cutting, drilling, grinding, or prying, even if you have 20/20 vision. If you wear glasses for the sake of vision, then they should be made of hardened glass that can serve also as safety glasses, or wear safety glasses over your regular glasses.

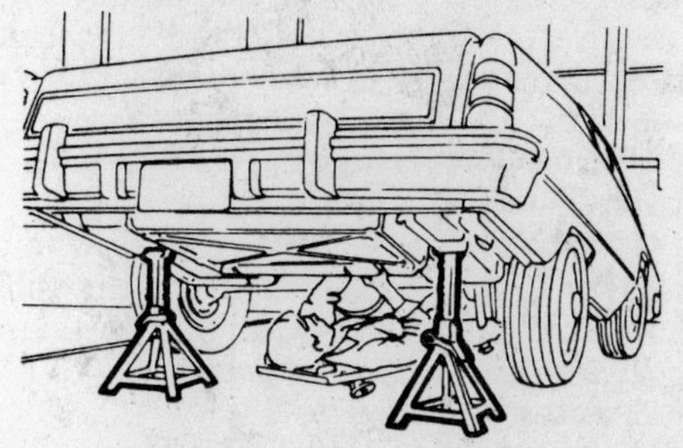

Always use jackstands when working under your truck.

• Do shield your eyes whenever you work around the battery. Batteries contain sulphuric acid; in case of contact with the eyes or skin, flush the area with water or a mixture of water and baking soda and get medical attention immediately.

• Do use safety stands for any under-truck service. Jacks are for raising vehicles; safety stands are for making sure the vehicle stays raised until you want it to come down. Whenever the vehicle is raised, block the wheels remaining on the ground and set the parking brake.

• Do use adequate ventilation when working with any chemicals. Like carbon monoxide, the asbestos dust resulting from brake lining wear can be poisonous in sufficient quantities.

• Do disconnect the negative battery cable when working on the electrical system. The primary ignition system can contain up to 40,000 volts.

• Do follow manufacturer's directions whenever working with potentially hazardous materials. Both brake fluid and antifreeze are poisonous if taken internally.

• Do properly maintain your tools. Loose hammerheads, mushroomed punches and chisels, frayed or poorly grounded electrical cords, excessively worn screwdrivers, spread wrenches (open end), cracked sockets, slipping ratchets, or faulty droplight sockets can cause accidents.

• Do use the proper size and type of tool for the job being done.

• Do when possible, pull on a wrench handle rather than push on it, and adjust your stance to prevent a fall.

• Do be sure that adjustable wrenches are tightly adjusted on the nut or bolt and pulled so that the face is on the side of the fixed jaw.

• Do select a wrench or socket that fits the nut or bolt. The wrench or socket should sit straight, not cocked.

• Do strike squarely with a hammer. Avoid glancing blows.

• Do set the parking brake and block the drive wheels if the work requires that the engine be running.

Don't's

• Don't run an engine in a garage or anywhere else without proper ventilation – EVER! Carbon monoxide is poisonous; it takes a long time to leave the human body and you can build up a deadly supply of it in your system by simply breathing in a little every day. You may not realize you are slowly poisoning yourself. Always use proper vents, window, fans or open the garage door.

• Don't work around moving parts while wearing a necktie or other loose clothing. Short sleeves are much safer than long, loose sleeves and hard-toed shoes with neoprene soles protect your toes and give a better grip on slippery surfaces. Jewelry such as watches, fancy belt buckles, beads or body adornment of any kind is not safe working around a truck. Long hair should be hidden under a hat or cap.

• Don't use pockets for toolboxes. A fall or bump can drive a screwdriver deep into your body. Even a wiping cloth hanging from the back pocket can wrap around a spinning shaft or fan.

• Don't smoke when working around gasoline, cleaning solvent or other flammable material.

• Don't smoke when working around the battery. When the battery is being charged, it gives off explosive hydrogen gas.

• Don't use gasoline to wash your hands; there are excellent soaps available. Gasoline may contain lead, and lead can enter the body through a cut, accumulating in the body until you are very ill. Gasoline also removes all the natural oils from the skin so that bone dry hands will such up oil and grease.

• Don't service the air conditioning system

unless you are equipped with the necessary tools and training. The refrigerant, R-12, is extremely cold and when exposed to the air, will instantly freeze any surface it comes in contact with, including your eyes. Although the refrigerant is normally non-toxic, R-12 becomes a deadly poisonous gas in the presence of an open flame. One good whiff of the vapors from burning refrigerant can be fatal.

• Don't ever use a bumper jack (the jack that comes with the vehicle) for anything other than changing tires! If you are serious about maintaining your truck yourself, invest in a hydraulic floor jack of at least $1^1/_2$ ton capacity. It will pay for itself many times over through the years.

SERIAL NUMBER IDENTIFICATION

Vehicle

The vehicle identification number is located on the left side of the dash panel behind the windshield.

A seventeen digit combination of numbers

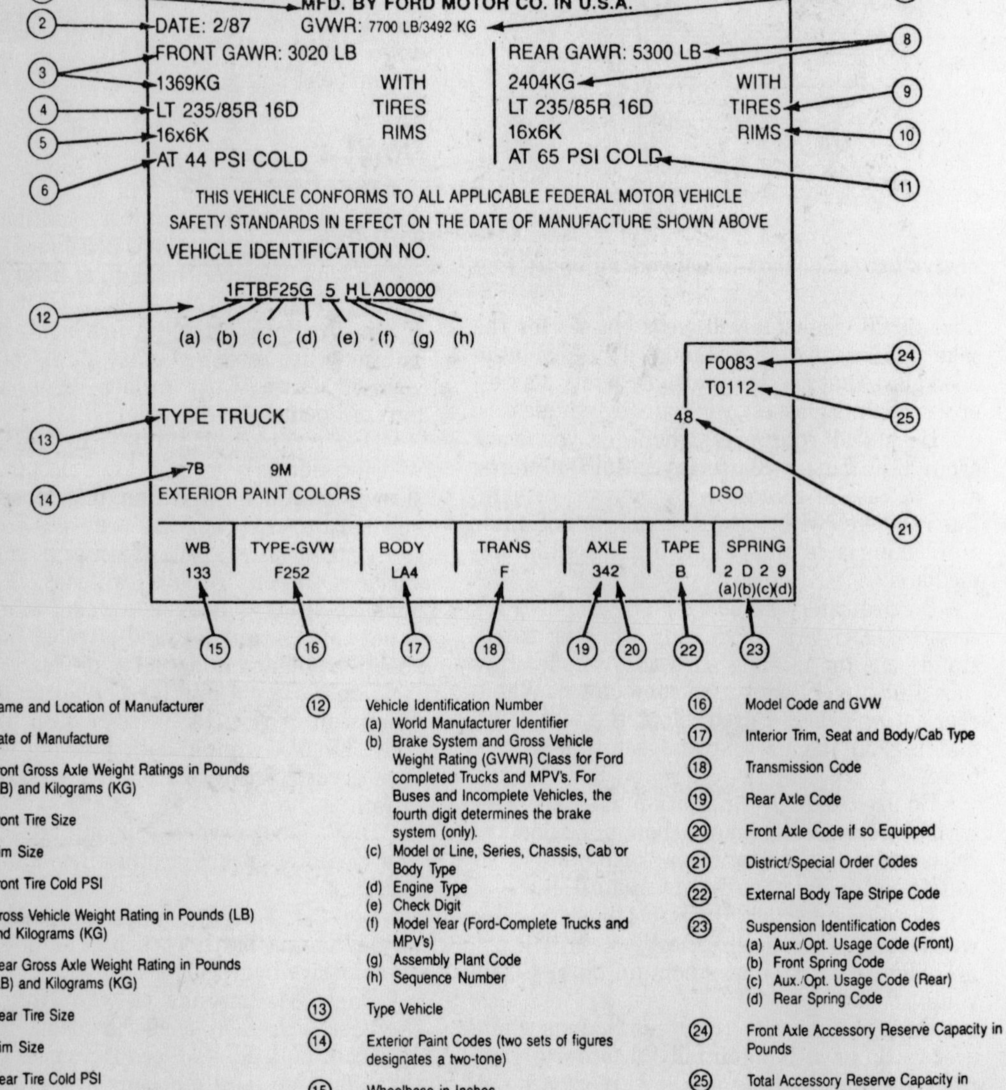

1. Name and Location of Manufacturer
2. Date of Manufacture
3. Front Gross Axle Weight Ratings in Pounds (LB) and Kilograms (KG)
4. Front Tire Size
5. Rim Size
6. Front Tire Cold PSI
7. Gross Vehicle Weight Rating in Pounds (LB) and Kilograms (KG)
8. Rear Gross Axle Weight Rating in Pounds (LB) and Kilograms (KG)
9. Rear Tire Size
10. Rim Size
11. Rear Tire Cold PSI
12. Vehicle Identification Number
    - (a) World Manufacturer Identifier
    - (b) Brake System and Gross Vehicle Weight Rating (GVWR) Class for Ford completed Trucks and MPV's. For Buses and Incomplete Vehicles, the fourth digit determines the brake system (only).
    - (c) Model or Line, Series, Chassis, Cab or Body Type
    - (d) Engine Type
    - (e) Check Digit
    - (f) Model Year (Ford-Complete Trucks and MPV's)
    - (g) Assembly Plant Code
    - (h) Sequence Number
13. Type Vehicle
14. Exterior Paint Codes (two sets of figures designates a two-tone)
15. Wheelbase in Inches
16. Model Code and GVW
17. Interior Trim, Seat and Body/Cab Type
18. Transmission Code
19. Rear Axle Code
20. Front Axle Code if so Equipped
21. District/Special Order Codes
22. External Body Tape Stripe Code
23. Suspension Identification Codes
    - (a) Aux./Opt. Usage Code (Front)
    - (b) Front Spring Code
    - (c) Aux./Opt. Usage Code (Rear)
    - (d) Rear Spring Code
24. Front Axle Accessory Reserve Capacity in Pounds
25. Total Accessory Reserve Capacity in Pounds

Truck safety compliance certification label

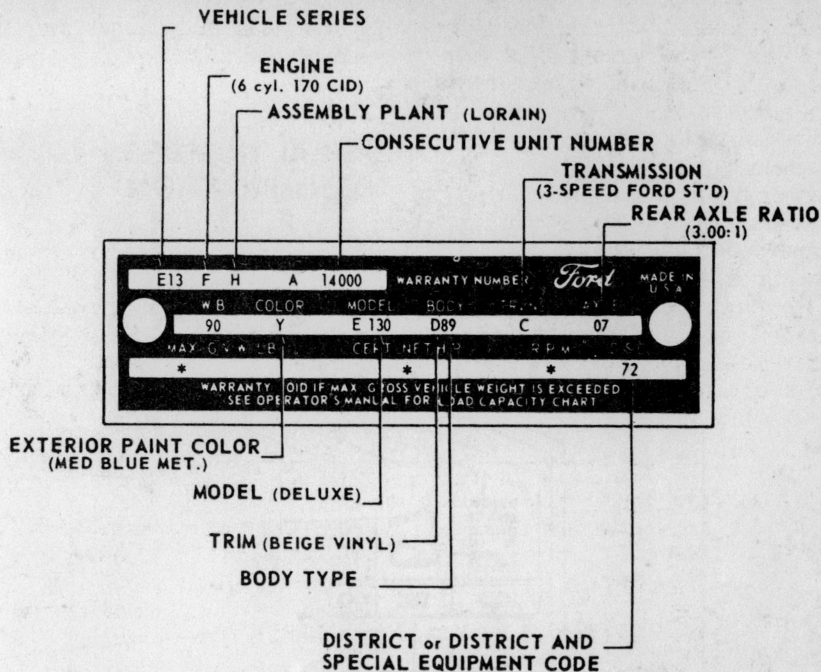

Vehicle Identification Plate

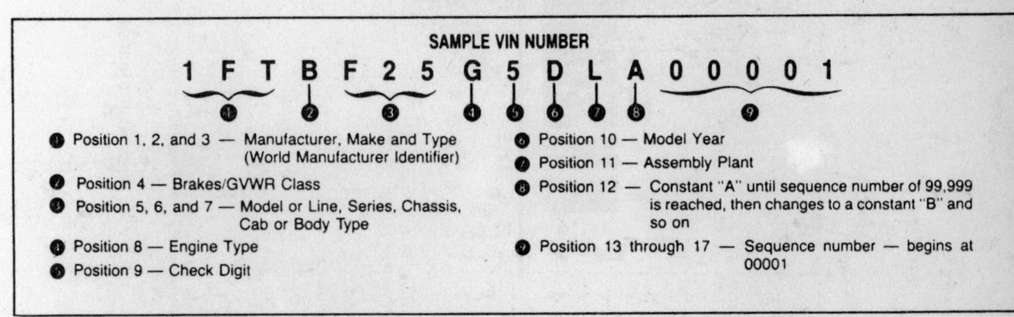

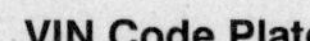
VIN Code Plate

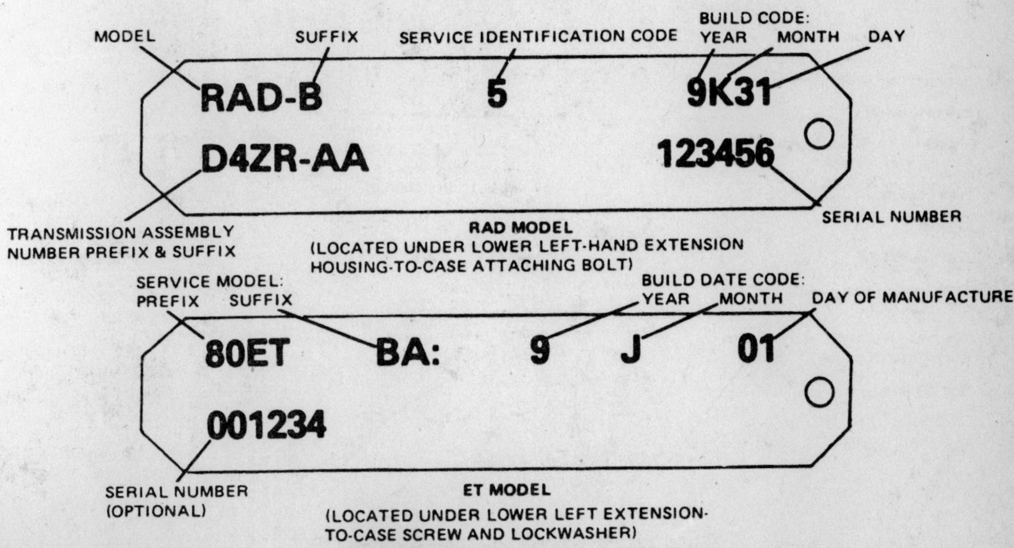

Diesel fuel filter removal

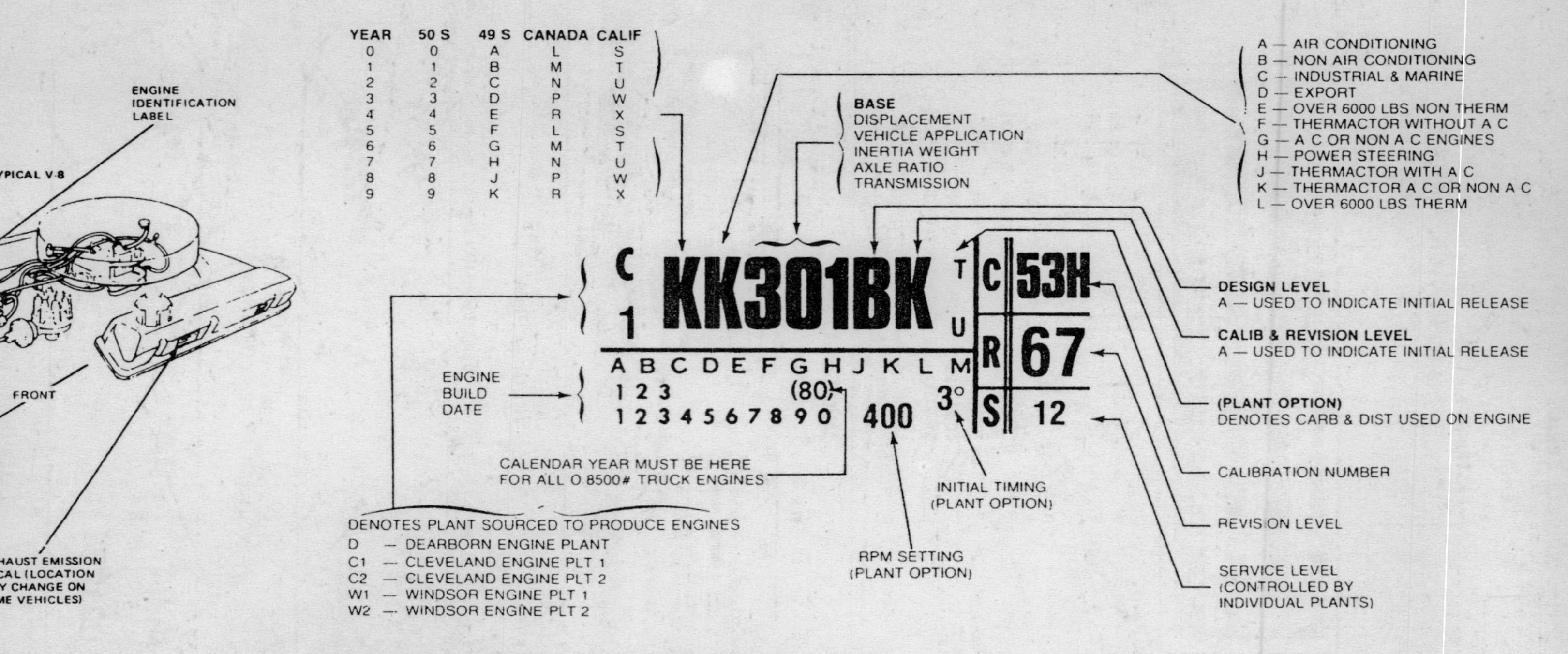

Diesel air cleaner

VIN Code	Year
H	1987
J	1988
K	1989
L	1990

Vehicle model year is the 10th position

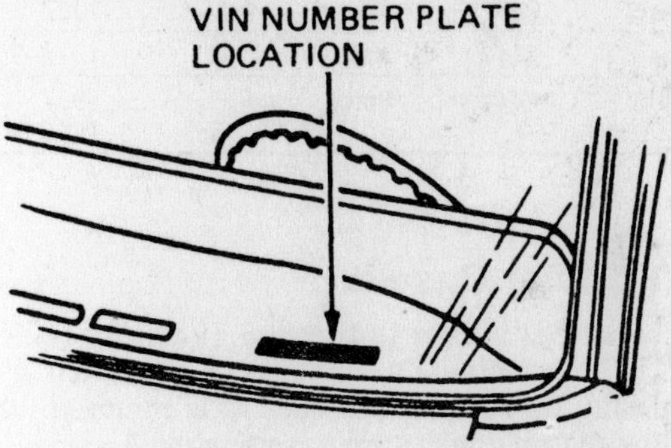

The VIN plate is located on the driver's side of the dash

and letters forms the Vehicle Identification Number (VIN). Refer to the illustration for VIN details.

Vehicle Safety Compliance Certification Label

The label is attached to the driver's door lock pillar. The label contains the name of the manufacturer, the month and year of the vehicle, certification statement and VIN. The label also contains gross vehicle weight and tire data.

Engine

The engine identification tag identifies the cubic inch displacement of the engine, the model year, the year and month in which the engine was built, where it was built and the change level number. The change level is usually the number one (1), unless there are parts on the engine that will not be completely interchangeable and will require minor modification.

The engine identification tag is located under the ignition coil attaching bolt on all engines except the 6.9L and 7.3L diesels. The diesel engine I.D. number is stamped on the front of the block in front of the left cylinder head.

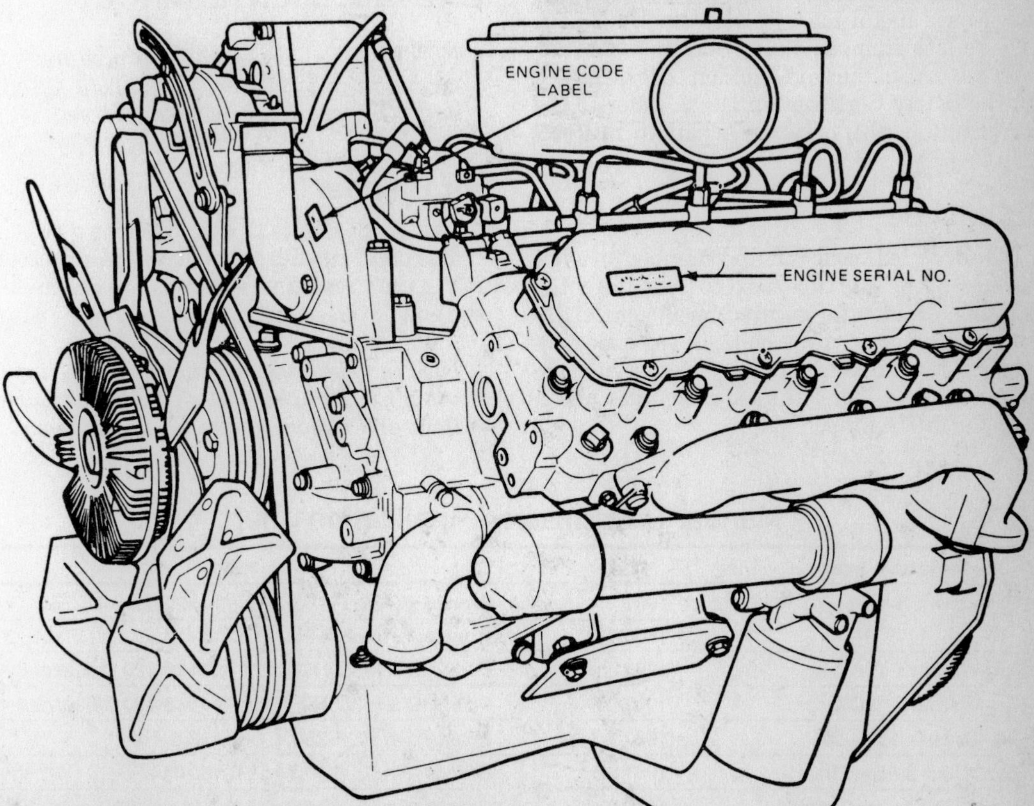

ENGINE CODE LABEL

ENGINE SERIAL NO.

Diesel engine serial number and identification label locations

Engine Application Chart

No. of Cylinders and Cu. In. Displacement	Actual Displacement Cu. In.	CC	Liters	Fuel System	Type	Built by	Engine Code	Years
6-300	300.1	4,917.5	4.9	EFI EFI	OHV	Ford	B Y	1987 1988–90
8-302	301.5	4,942.2	5.0	4-bbl EFI	OHV	Ford	G N	1987 1987–90
8-351W	351.9	5,765.9	5.8	4-bbl EFI	OHV	Ford	H H	1987 1988–90
8-420	420.2	6,886.1	6.9	Diesel	OHV	Nav.	1	1987
8-444	443.6	7,270.0	7.3	Diesel	OHV	Nav.	M	1988–90
8-460	459.8	7,535.5	7.5	4-bbl EFI	OHV	Ford	L G	1987 1988–90

Nav.: Navistar International Corp.

The engine identification code is located in the VIN at the eighth digit. The VIN can be found in the safety certification decal and the VIN plate at the upper left side of the dash panel. Refer to the "Engine Application" chart for engine VIN codes.

Transmission

The transmission identification letter is located on a metal tag or plate attached to the case or it is stamped directly on the transmission case. Also, the transmission code is located on the Safety Certification Decal. Refer to the "Transmission Application" chart in this section.

Drive Axle

The drive axle code is found stamped on a flat surface on the axle tube, next to the differential housing, or, on a tag secured by one of the differential housing cover bolts. A separate limited-slip tag is attached to the differential housing cover bolt. The letters L-S signifies a limited-slip differential.

Transfer Case

A tag is affixed to the case mounting bolts. The information on the tag is needed when ordering service parts. If the tag is removed for any reason, make sure it is reinstalled.

ROUTINE MAINTENANCE

NOTE: *All maintenance procedures included in this chapter refer to both gasoline and diesel engines except where noted.*

Air Cleaner

The air cleaner is a paper element type.

The paper cartridge should be replaced according to the Preventive Maintenance Schedule at the end of this chapter.

NOTE: *Check the air filter more often if the vehicle is operated under severe dusty conditions and replace or clean it as necessary.*

Manual Transmission Application Chart

Transmission Types	Years	Models
Borg-Warner T-18 4-sp	1987	Bronco; F-150, F-250, VF-350 4x2 and 4x4
	1989–90	Bronco; F-150 & F-250 4x2 and 4x4
Borg-Warner T-19A 4-sp	1987	F-250HD & F-350HD 4x2 & 4x4 w/8-420 Diesel or 8-460
Borg-Warner T-19C 4-sp	1987	F-250HD & F-350HD 4x2 & 4x4 w/8-420 Diesel or 8-460
New Process 435 4-sp	1987	Bronco; F-150, F-250, F-350 4x2 & 4x4
Ford TOD 4-sp Overdrive	1987	Bronco; F-150, F-250 4x2; F-150 4x4
Mazda M50D 5-sp Overdrive	1988–90	Bronco; F-150 4x2 & 4x4 w/6-300 or 8-302
ZF S5-42 5-speed Overdrive	1988–90	F-250, F-250HD, F-350, F-Super Duty; Bronco

Transfer Case Application Chart

Transfer Case Types	Years	Models
Borg-Warner 1356 Manual Shift	1987–90	All
Borg-Warner 1356 Electronic Shift	1987–90	Bronco w/auto. trans.
Borg-Warner 1345	1987–90	All

Automatic Transmission Application Chart

Transmission	Years	Models
Ford C6 3-speed	1987–90	All models; all engines
Ford AOD 4-speed	1987	All models with 6-300 or 8-302
	1988–90	F-150, F-250 w/6-300 or 8-302 Bronco w/8-302
Ford E4OD	1989–90	F-150 & F-250 under 8500 lb. GVW w/V8 F-250 & F-350 over 8500 lb. GVW w/V8 All F-Super Duty

Front Drive Axle Application Chart

Axle	Model	Years
Dana 44 IFS	F-150, Bronco	1987–90
Dana 44 IFS-HD	F-250	1987–90
Dana 44 IFS-HD	F-250	1987–90
Dana 50 IFS	F-250 HD	1987–90
Dana 60 Monobeam	F-350, F-Super Duty	1987–90

Rear Drive Axle Application Chart

Axle	Model	Years
Ford 8.8 inch	F-150, Bronco	1987–90
Ford 10.25 inch	F-250, F-350	1987–90
Dana 80	F-Super Duty	1988–90

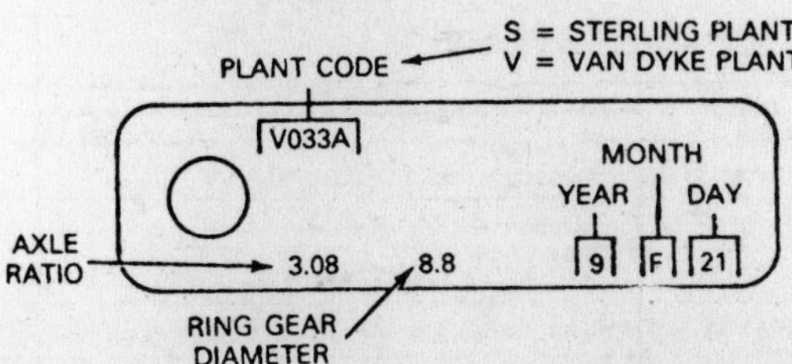

Differential identification tag. Limited slip units have as separate tag secured by a cover bolt

REPLACEMENT

Carbureted Engines

1. Open the engine compartment hood.
2. Remove the wing nut holding the air cleaner assembly to the top of the carburetor.
3. Disconnect the crankcase ventilation hose at the air cleaner and remove the entire air cleaner assembly from the carburetor.
4. Remove and discard the old filter element, and inspect the condition of the air cleaner mounting gasket. Replace the gasket as necessary.

NOTE: *A crankcase ventilation filter is located in the side of the air cleaner body. The*

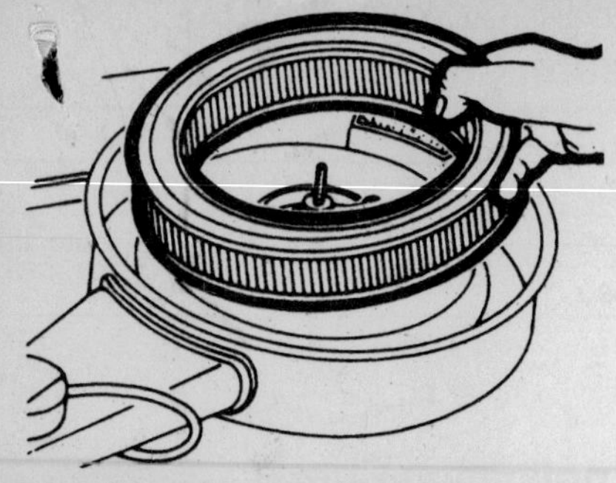

Removing the carburetor air cleaner element

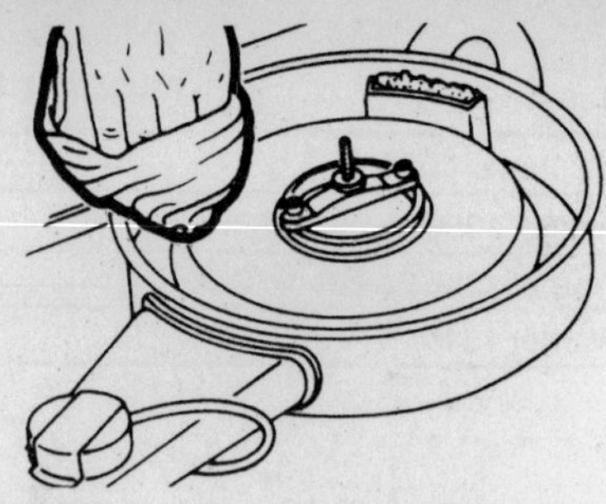

Clean out the air cleaner body before installing the new filter

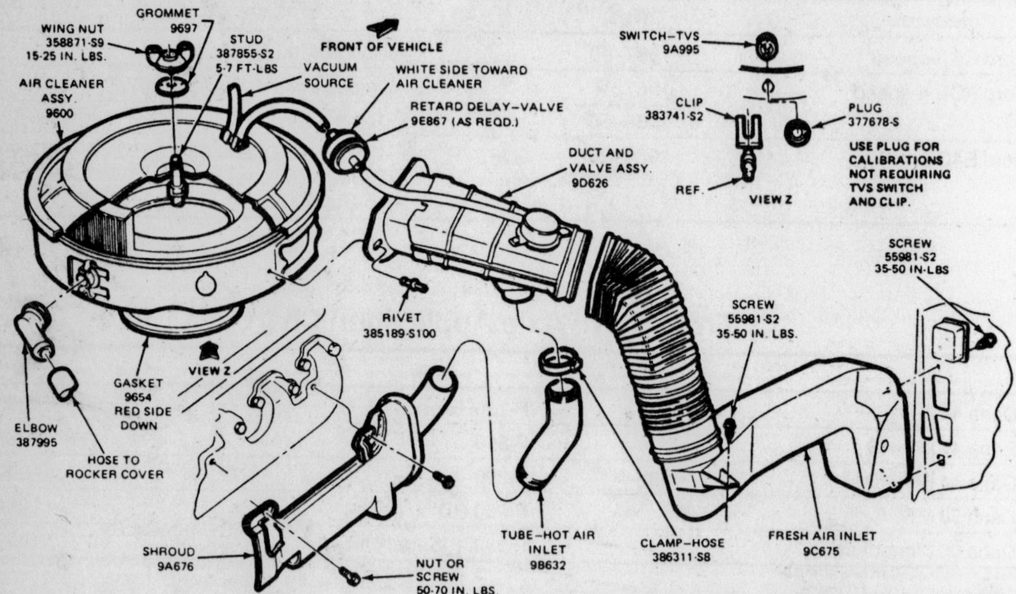

Carbureted V8 air cleaner

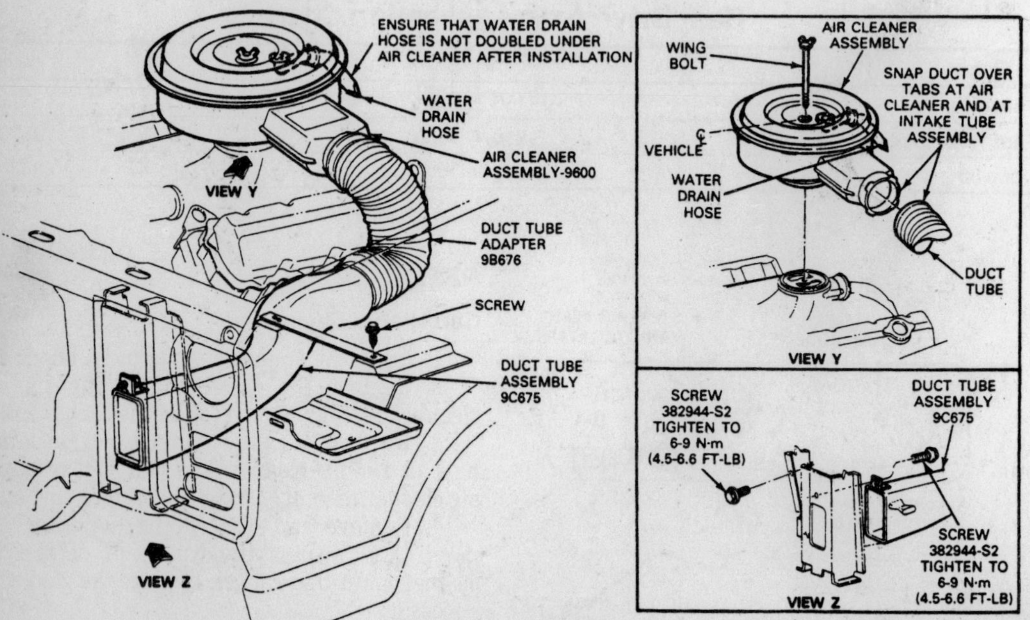

Diesel air cleaner

AIR CLEANER ASSY
9600
SCREW AND WASHER ASSY
386144-S8 2.3-3.3 N·m (20-30 IN-LBS)
GROMMET
9697
SCREW-40920-S2
2.3-3.9 N·m (20-35 IN-LBS)
SCREW-55981-S2
35-50 IN-LBS
SCREW 55981-S2
4.0-5.6 N·m
(35-50 IN-LBS)
CLAMP
386311-S8
SCREW-40920-S2
2.3-3.9 N·m
(20-35 IN-LBS)
TUBE-HOT AIR
INLET-93632
SCREW AND WASHER ASSY.
57633-S2
14-21 N·m (11-16 FT-LBS)
FRESH AIR
INLET 9C675
FRONT OF ENGINE
FRONT OF ENGINE
BRACKET-9C670
NUT-385165-S2
5.7-7.9 N·m (50-70 IN-LBS)
NUT-34664-S2
30-43 N·m (22-32 IN-LBS)
SHROUD-9A607
BRACKET-SUPPORT
9E613
NUT
382802-S2

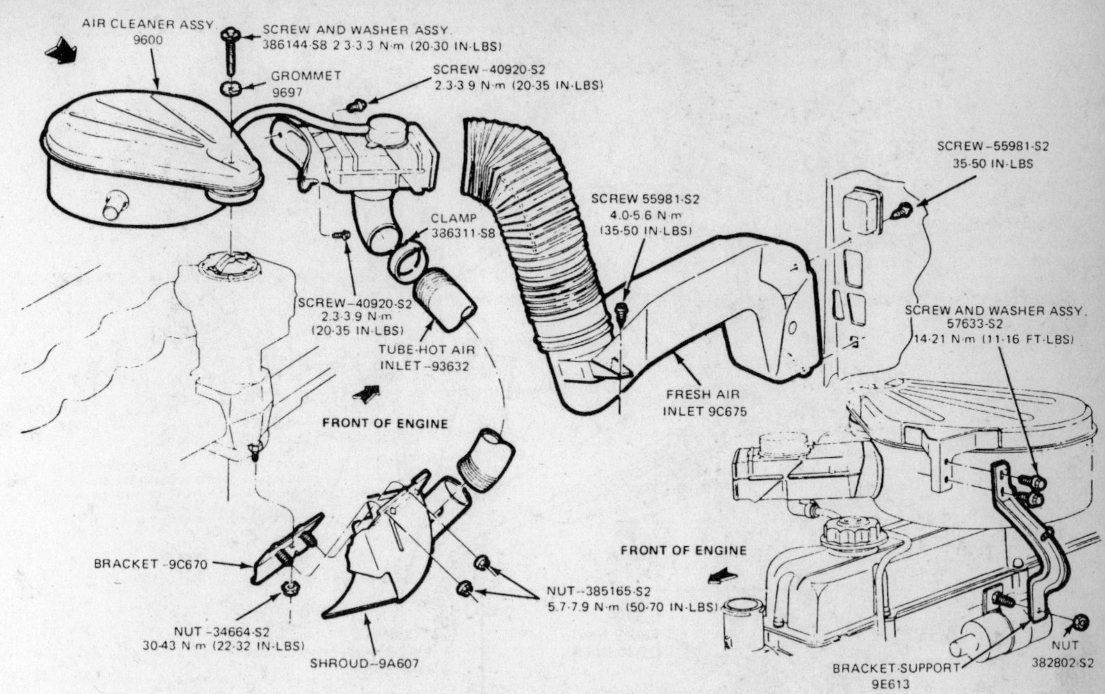

Carbureted 6–4.9L air cleaner

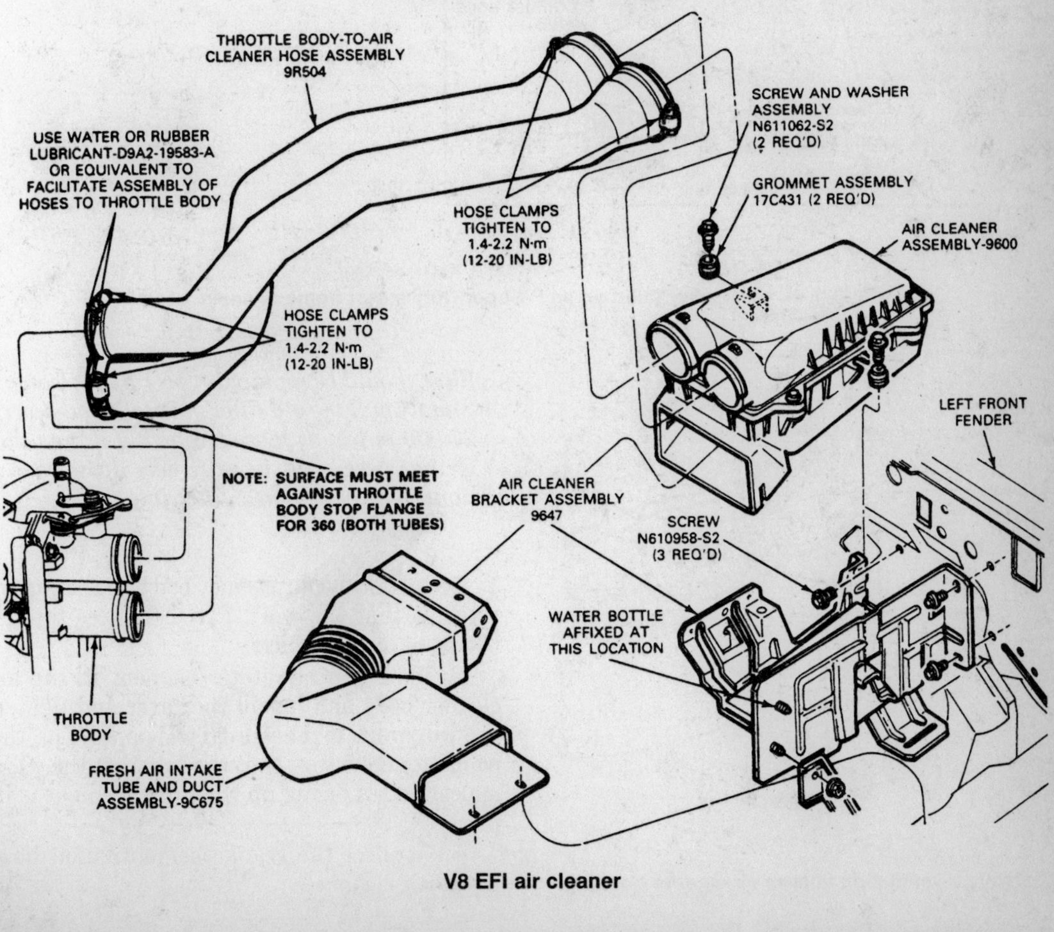

THROTTLE BODY-TO-AIR
CLEANER HOSE ASSEMBLY
9R504
USE WATER OR RUBBER
LUBRICANT-D9A2-19583-A
OR EQUIVALENT TO
FACILITATE ASSEMBLY OF
HOSES TO THROTTLE BODY
SCREW AND WASHER
ASSEMBLY
N611062-S2
(2 REQ'D)
GROMMET ASSEMBLY
17C431 (2 REQ'D)
HOSE CLAMPS
TIGHTEN TO
1.4-2.2 N·m
(12-20 IN-LB)
AIR CLEANER
ASSEMBLY-9600
HOSE CLAMPS
TIGHTEN TO
1.4-2.2 N·m
(12-20 IN-LB)
LEFT FRONT
FENDER
NOTE: SURFACE MUST MEET
AGAINST THROTTLE
BODY STOP FLANGE
FOR 360 (BOTH TUBES)
AIR CLEANER
BRACKET ASSEMBLY
9647
SCREW
N610958-S2
(3 REQ'D)
WATER BOTTLE
AFFIXED AT
THIS LOCATION
THROTTLE
BODY
FRESH AIR INTAKE
TUBE AND DUCT
ASSEMBLY-9C675

V8 EFI air cleaner

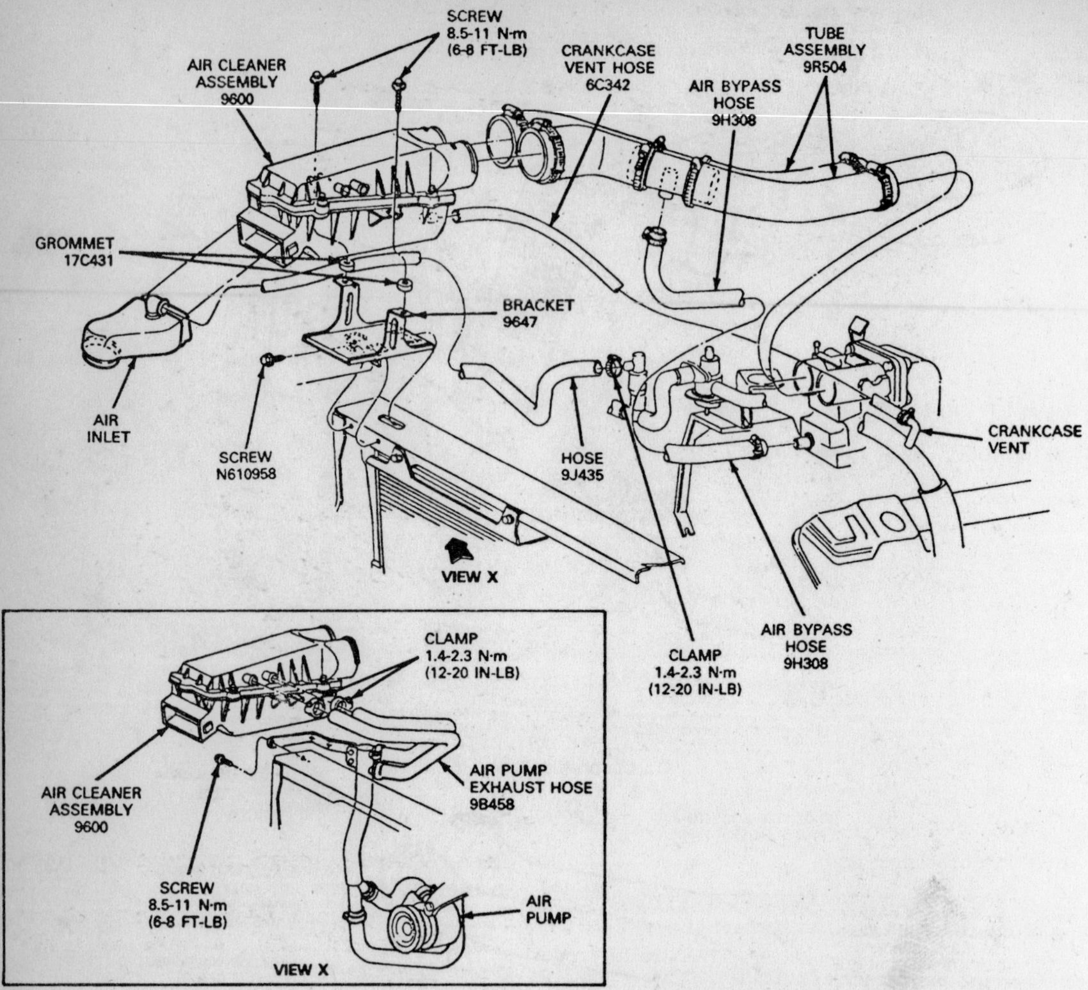

SCREW
8.5-11 N·m
(6-8 FT-LB)
AIR CLEANER
ASSEMBLY
9600
CRANKCASE
VENT HOSE
6C342
TUBE
ASSEMBLY
9R504
AIR BYPASS
HOSE
9H308
GROMMET
17C431
BRACKET
9647
AIR
INLET
SCREW
N610958
HOSE
9J435
CRANKCASE
VENT
VIEW X
CLAMP
1.4-2.3 N·m
(12-20 IN-LB)
AIR BYPASS
HOSE
9H308
CLAMP
1.4-2.3 N·m
(12-20 IN-LB)
AIR CLEANER
ASSEMBLY
9600
AIR PUMP
EXHAUST HOSE
9B458
SCREW
8.5-11 N·m
(6-8 FT-LB)
AIR
PUMP
VIEW X

8–7.5L air cleaner used on an F-Super Duty motor home chassis

FILTER PACK
FILTER RETAINER
AIR CLEANER
SHELL (REF.)
RETAINER
CLIP
PCV
HOSE
ELBOW

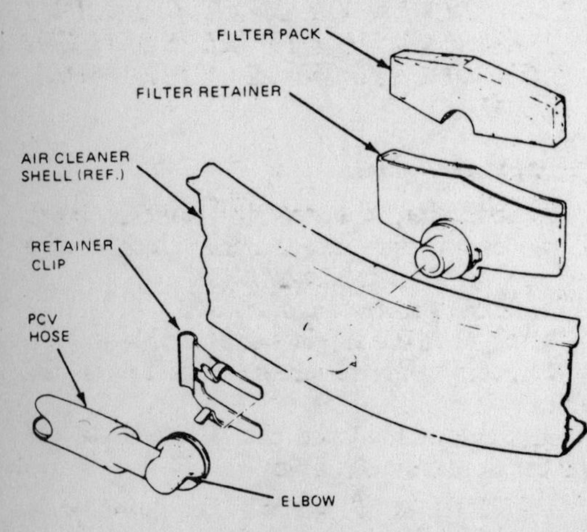

Crankcase ventilation filter in air cleaner housing

filter should be replaced rather than cleaned. Simply pull the old filter out of the body every 20,000 miles (or more frequently if the vehicle has been used in extremely dusty conditions) and push a new filter into place.

5. Install the air cleaner body on the carburetor so that the word **FRONT** faces toward the front of the vehicle.

6. Place the new filter element in the air cleaner body and install the cover and tighten the wing nut. If the word **TOP** appears on the element, make sure that the side that the word appears on is facing up when the element is in place.

7. Connect the crankcase ventilation hose to the air cleaner.

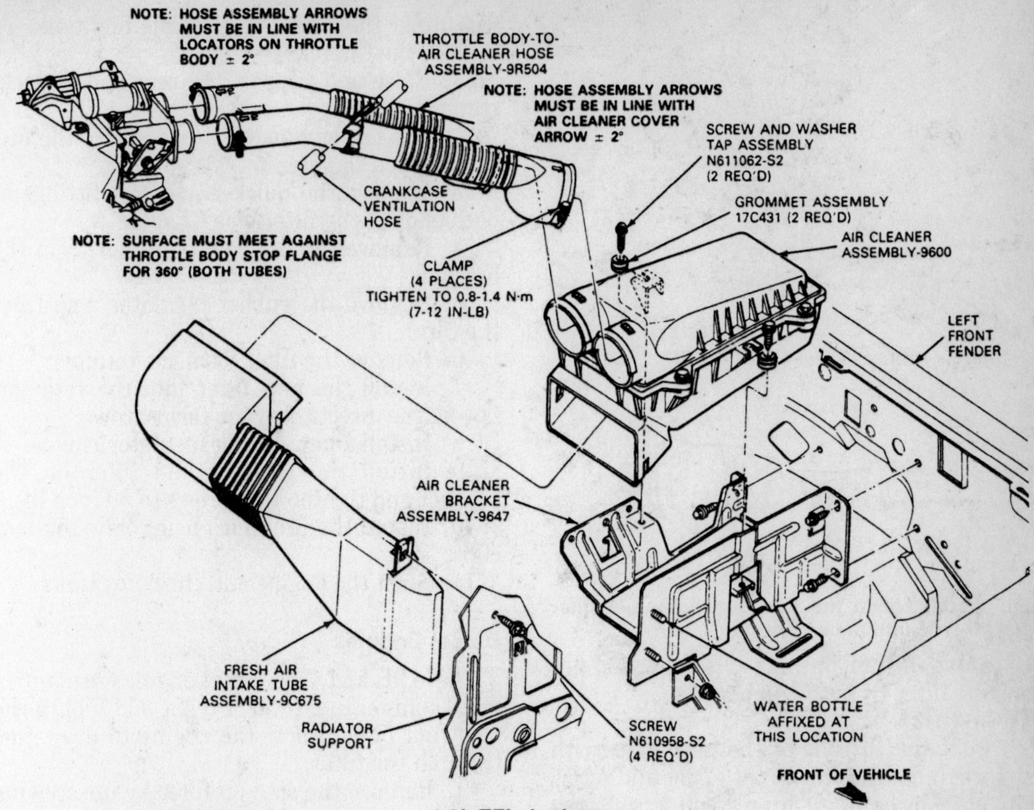

4.9L EFI air cleaner

Fuel Injected Engines

1. Loosen the two clamps that secure the hose assembly to the air cleaner.
2. Remove the two screws that attach the air cleaner to the bracket.
3. Disconnect the hose and inlet tube from the air cleaner.
4. Remove the screws attaching the air cleaner cover.
5. Remove the air filter and tubes.

To install:

1. Install the air filter and tubes.
2. Install the screws attaching the air cleaner cover. Don't over tighten the hose clamps! A torque of 12–15 inch lbs. is sufficient.
3. Connect the hose and inlet tube to the air cleaner.
4. Install the two screws that attach the air cleaner to the bracket.
5. Tighten the two clamps that secure the hose assembly to the air cleaner.

Diesel Engines

1. Open the engine compartment hood.
2. Remove the wing nut holding the air cleaner assembly.
3. Remove and discard the old filter element, and inspect the condition of the air cleaner mounting gasket. Replace the gasket as necessary.
4. Place the new filter element in the air cleaner body and install the cover and tighten the wing nut.

Fuel Filter

REPLACEMENT

CAUTION: *NEVER SMOKE WHEN WORKING AROUND OR NEAR GASOLINE! MAKE SURE THAT THERE IS NO IGNITION SOURCE NEAR YOUR WORK AREA!*

Carbureted Engines

A carburetor mounted gas filter is used. These filters screw into the float chamber. To replace one of these filters:

1. Wait until the engine is cold.
2. Remove the air cleaner assembly.
3. Place some absorbent rags under the filter.
4. Remove the hose clamp and slide the rubber hose from the filter.

CAUTION: *It is possible for gasoline to spray in all directions when removing the hose! This rarely happens, but it is possible, so protect your eyes!*

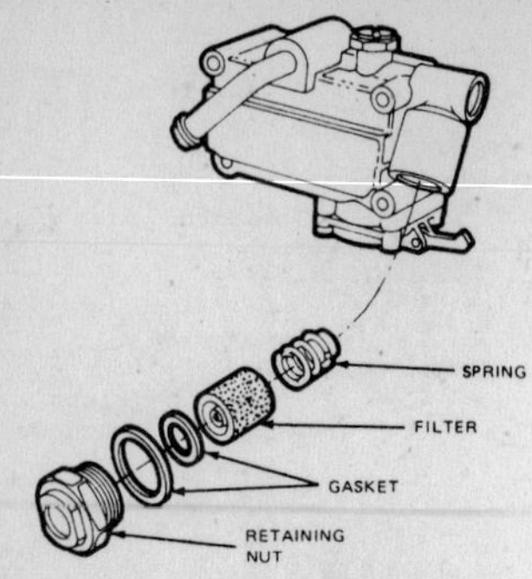

Fuel filter – Holley model 4180C 4BBL

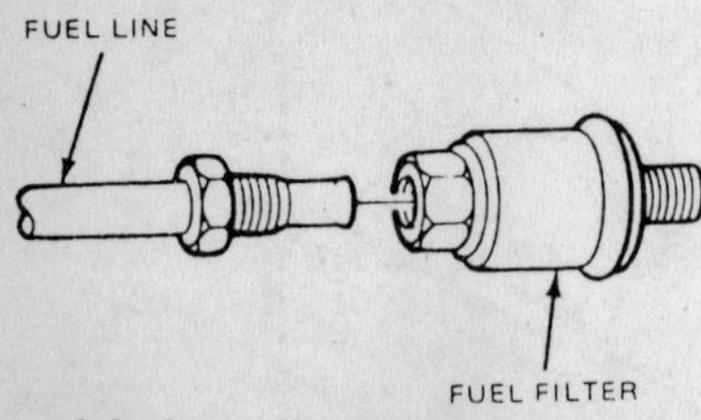

Some models have the screw-in type fuel filter which threads into the carburetor

5. Move the fuel line out of the way and unscrew the filter from the carburetor.

To install:

6. Coat the threads of the new filter with non-hardening, gasoline-proof sealer and screw it into place by hand. Tighten it snugly with the wrench.

WARNING: *Do not over tighten the filter! The threads in the carburetor bowl are soft metal and are easily stripped! You don't want to damage these threads!!*

7. Connect the hose to the new filter. Most replacement filters come with a new hose and clamps. Use them.

8. Remove the fuel-soaked rags, wipe up any spilled fuel and start the engine. Check the filter connections for leaks.

Fuel Injected Gasoline Engines

The inline filter is mounted on the same bracket as the fuel supply pump on the frame rail under the truck, back by the fuel tank. To replace the filter:

1. Raise and support the rear end on jackstands.
2. With the engine off, depressurize the fuel system. See Chapter 5.
3. Remove the quick-disconnect fittings at both ends of the filter. See Chapter 5.
4. Remove the filter and retainer from the bracket.
5. Remove the rubber insulator ring from the filter.
6. Remove the filter from the retainer.
7. Install the new filter into the retainer, noting the direction of the flow arrow.
8. Install a new rubber insulator ring.
9. Install the retainer and filter on the bracket and tighten the screws to 60 inch lbs.
10. Install the fuel lines using new retainer clips.
11. Start the engine and check for leaks.

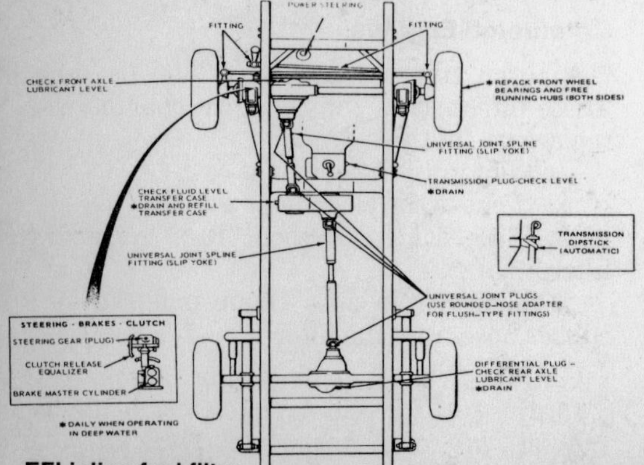

EFI inline fuel filter

Diesel Engines

The 6.9L and 7.3L diesel engines use a one-piece spin-on fuel filter. Do not add fuel to the new fuel filter. Allow the engine to draw fuel through the filter.

1. Remove the spin-on filter by unscrewing

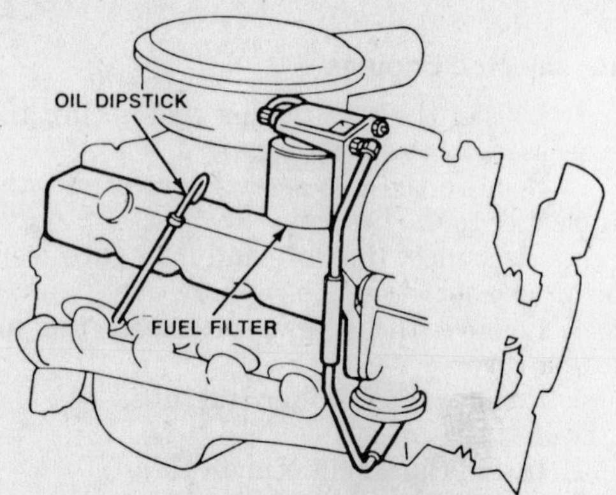

Diesel fuel filter location; filter screws on

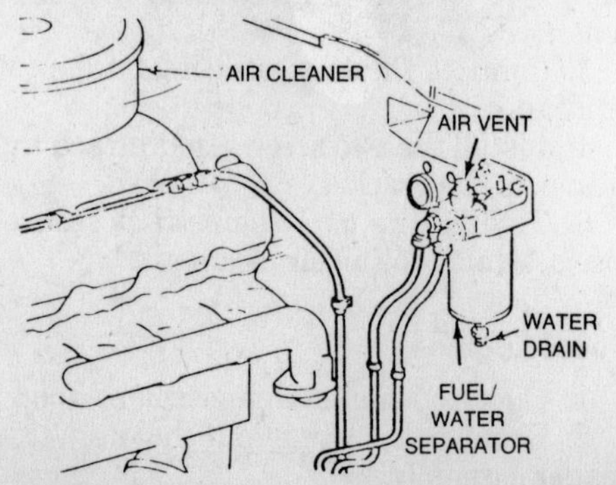

Open the drain screw on the bottom of the water separator to drain

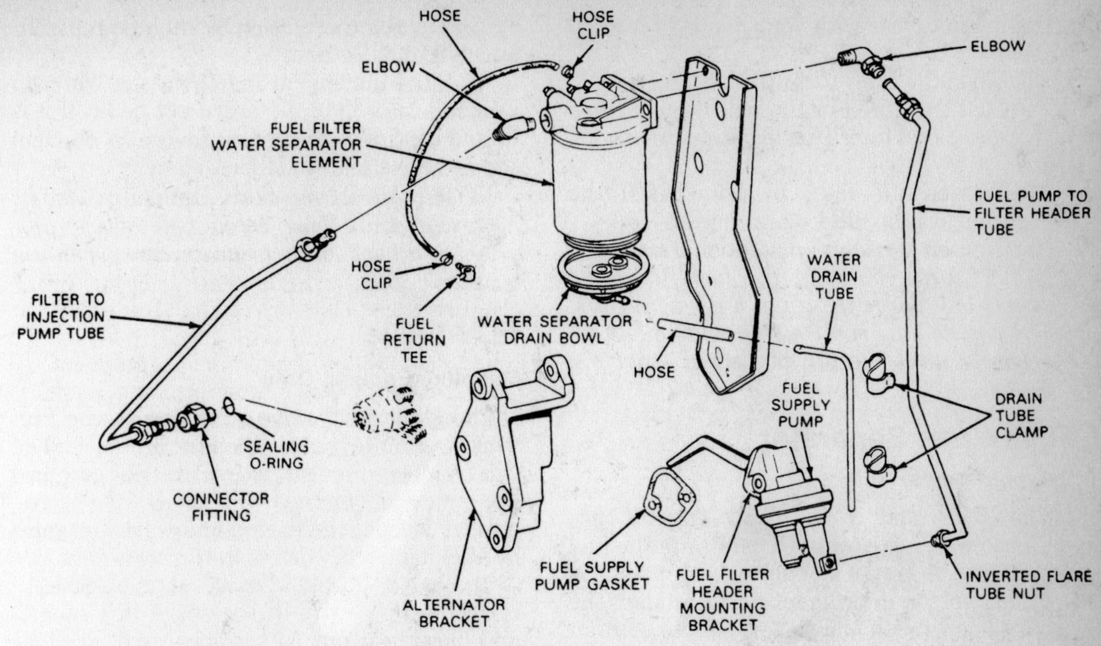

HOSE
HOSE CLIP
ELBOW
ELBOW
FUEL FILTER WATER SEPARATOR ELEMENT
FUEL PUMP TO FILTER HEADER TUBE
HOSE CLIP
WATER DRAIN TUBE
FILTER TO INJECTION PUMP TUBE
FUEL RETURN TEE
WATER SEPARATOR DRAIN BOWL
HOSE
FUEL SUPPLY PUMP
DRAIN TUBE CLAMP
SEALING O-RING
CONNECTOR FITTING
FUEL SUPPLY PUMP GASKET
FUEL FILTER HEADER MOUNTING BRACKET
INVERTED FLARE TUBE NUT
ALTERNATOR BRACKET

Diesel fuel filter/water separator

FILTER/WATER SEPARATOR HEADER
ELBOW
ELBOW
FUEL RETURN HOSE (IN PHANTOM)
FUEL PUMP TO FILTER TUBE
FILTER TO INJECTION PUMP TUBE
WATER DRAIN HOSE
INJECTION PUMP
ALTERNATOR BRACKET
CONNECTOR NUT
CONNECTOR FITTING
WATER DRAIN TUBE CLAMP (2 PLACES)
WATER DRAIN TUBE
FUEL SUPPLY PUMP
INVERTED FLARE TUBE NUT
FILTER HEADER MOUNTING HARDWARE:
(2) 3 8-16 × 1-3/8" BOLTS
(4) HARDENED WASHERS
(2) HEX NUTS
FUEL RETURN HOSE (LEAK OFF)
HEADER MOUNTING BRACKET
FUEL PUMP TO FILTER TUBE
℄ ENGINE
INJECTION PUMP
3/8-16 × 3 1/2" FLANGE HEAD BOLT
3/8-16 × 1-1/4" FLANGE HEAD BOLT
4.50 (REF.)
ALTERNATOR BRACKET
FUEL SUPPLY PUMP
INVERTED FLARE TUBE NUT
℄ CRANKSHAFT
RIGHT SIDE VIEW
FRONT VIEW

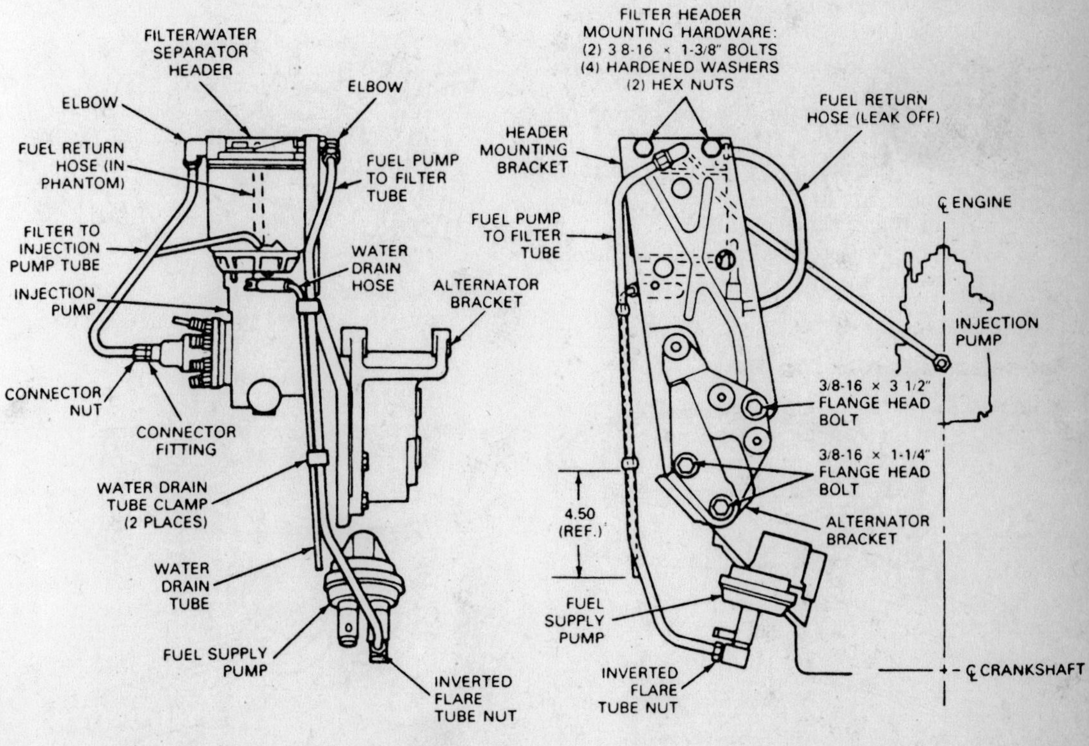

Diesel fuel filter removal

it counterclockwise with your hands or a strap wrench.

2. Clean the filter mounting surface.

3. Coat the gasket or the replacement filter with clean diesel fuel. This helps ensure a good seal.

4. Tighten the filter by hand until the gasket touches the filter mounting surface.

5. Tighten the filter an additional 1/2 turn.

NOTE: *After changing the fuel filter, the engine will purge the trapped air as it runs. The engine may run roughly and smoke excessively until the air is cleared from the system.*

Fuel/Water Separator

Diesel Engines

The 6.9L and 7.3L diesel engines are equipped with a fuel/water separator in the fuel supply line. A Water in Fuel indicator light is provided on the instrument panel to alert the driver. The light should glow when the ignition switch is in the Start position to indicate proper light and water sensor function. If the light glows continuously while the engine is running, the water must be drained from the separator as soon as possible to prevent damage to the fuel injection system.

1. Shut off the engine. Failure to shut the engine off before draining the separator will cause air to enter the system.

2. Unscrew the vent on the top center of the separator unit 2 1/2 to 3 turns.

3. Unscrew the drain screw on the bottom of the separator 1 1/2 to 2 turns and drain the water into an appropriate container.

4. After the water is completely drained, close the water drain fingertight.

5. Tighten the vent until snug, then turn it an additional 1/4 turn.

6. Start the engine and check the Water in Fuel indicator light; it should not be lit. If it is lit and continues to stay so, there is a problem somewhere else in the fuel system.

NOTE: *All but very early production models have a drain hose connected to separator which allows water to drain directly into a container placed underneath the vehicle.*

PCV Valve

Gasoline Engines Only

Check the PCV valve according to the Preventive Maintenance Schedule at the end of this chapter to see if it is free and not gummed up, stuck or blocked. To check the valve, remove it from the engine and work the valve by sticking a screwdriver in the crankcase side of the valve. It should move. It is possible to clean the PCV valve by soaking it in a solvent and blowing it out with compressed air. This

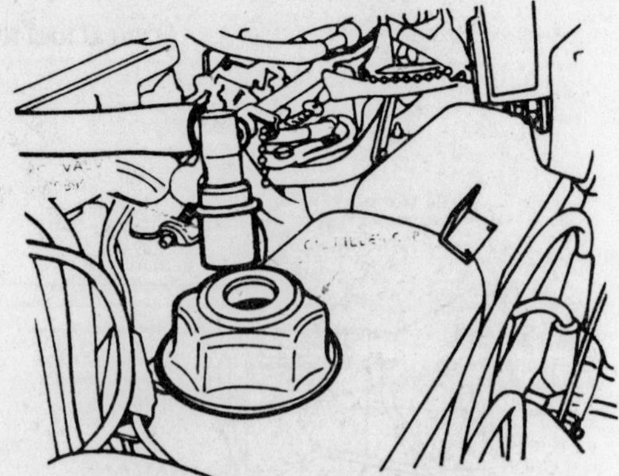

V8 PCV valve location

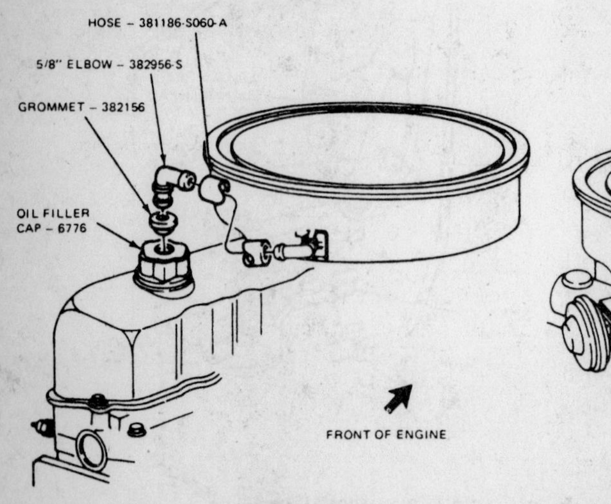

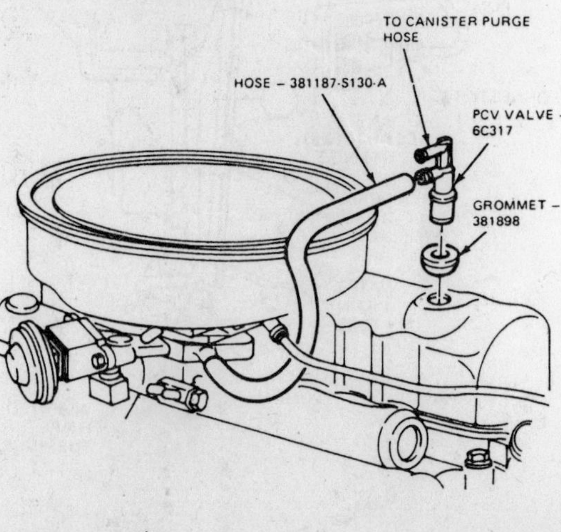

6–4.9L PCV valve location

can restore the valve to some level of operating order. This should be used only as an emergency measure. Otherwise the valve should be replaced.

Evaporative Canister

Gasoline Engines Only

The fuel evaporative emission control canister should be inspected for damage or leaks at the hose fittings every 24,000 miles. Repair or replace any old or cracked hoses. Replace the canister if it is damaged in any way. The canister is located under the hood, to the right of the engine.

For more detailed canister service, see Chapter 4.

Battery

Loose, dirty, or corroded battery terminals are a major cause of "no-start." Every 3 months or so, remove the battery terminals and clean them, giving them a light coating of petroleum jelly when you are finished. This will help to retard corrosion.

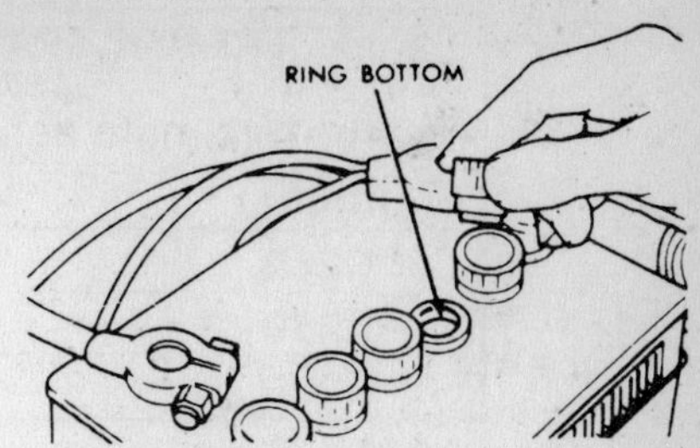

Fill each battery cell to the bottom of the split ring with distilled water

Battery State of Charge at Room Temperature

Specific Gravity Reading	Charged Condition
1.260–1.280	Fully Charged
1.230–1.250	¾ Charged
1.200–1.220	½ Charged
1.170–1.190	¼ Charged
1.140–1.160	Almost no Charge
1.110–1.130	No Charge

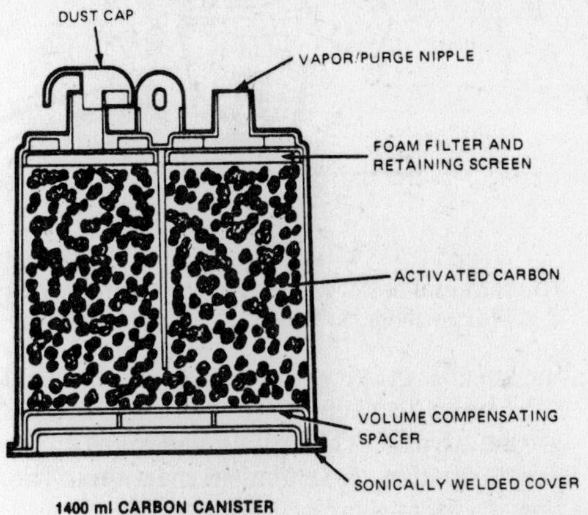

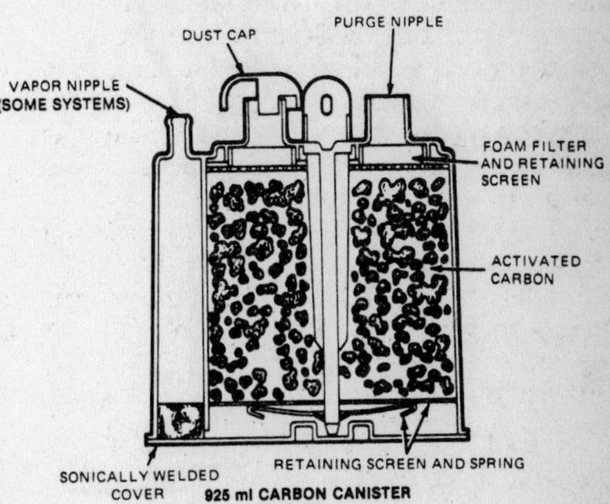

Carbon canister cross-sections

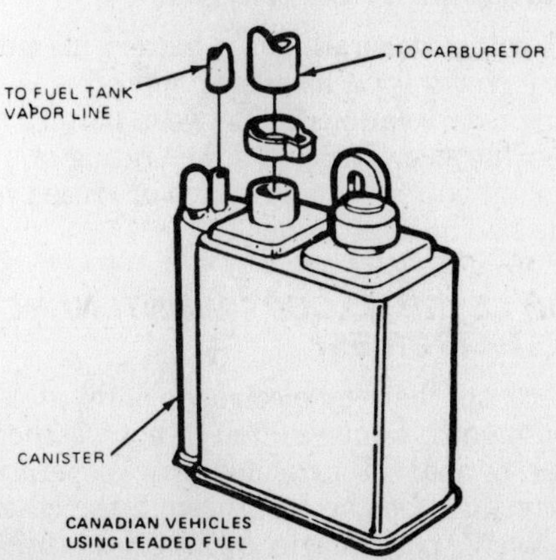

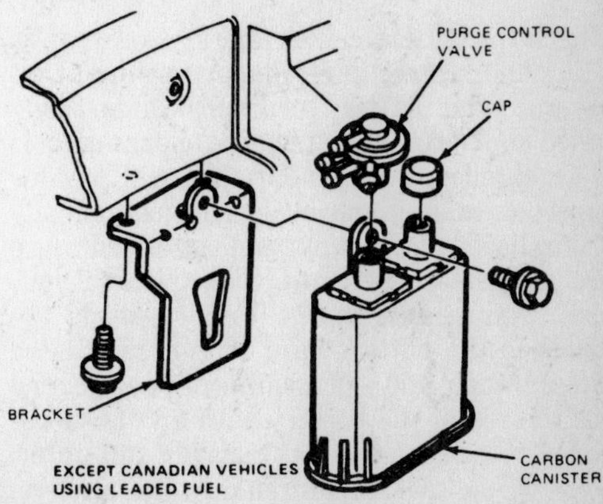

Carbon canisters are mounted on the inner fender

SPECIFIC GRAVITY (@ 80°F.) AND CHARGE Specific Gravity Reading (use the minimum figure for testing)	
Minimum	**Battery Charge**
1.260	100% Charged
1.230	75% Charged
1.200	50% Charged
1.170	25% Charged
1.140	Very Little Power Left
1.110	Completely Discharged

Battery specific gravity. Some testers have colored balls which correspond to the numerical values in the left column

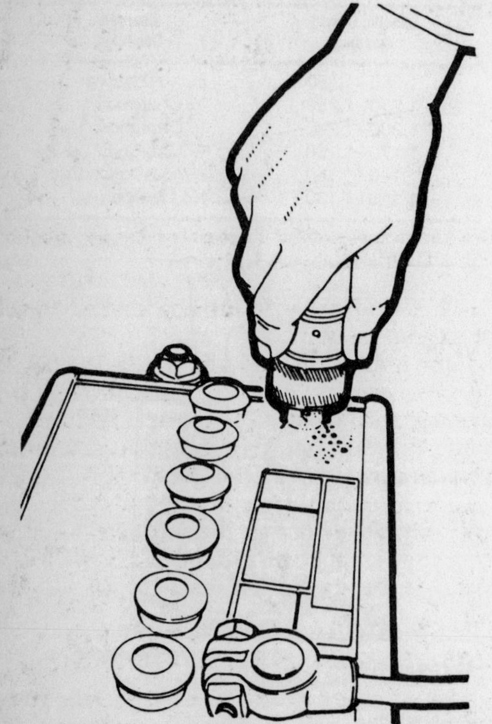

Clean the battery posts with a wire terminal cleaner

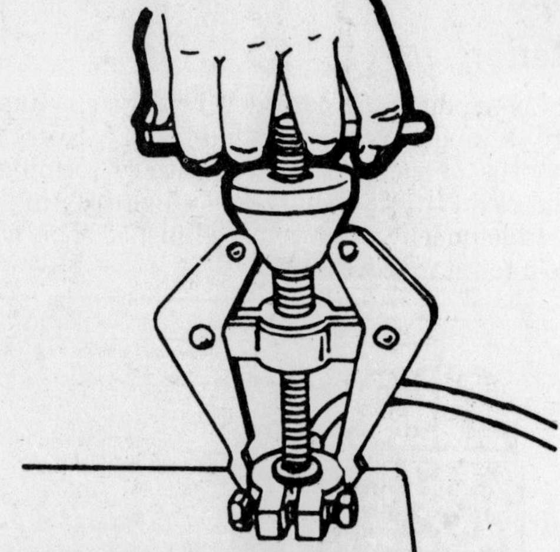

Top terminal battery cables are easily removed with this inexpensive puller

Check the battery cables for signs of wear or chafing and replace any cable or terminal that looks marginal. Battery terminals can be easily cleaned and inexpensive terminal cleaning tools are an excellent investment that will pay for themselves many times over. They can usually be purchased from any well-equipped auto store or parts department. Side terminal batteries require a different tool to clean the threads in the battery case. The accumulated white powder and corrosion can be cleaned from the top of the battery with an old toothbrush and a solution of baking soda and water.

Unless you have a maintenance-free battery, check the electrolyte level (see Battery under Fluid Level Checks in this chapter) and check the specific gravity of each cell. Be sure that the vent holes in each cell cap are not blocked by grease or dirt. The vent holes allow hydrogen gas, formed by the chemical reaction in the battery, to escape safely.

REPLACEMENT BATTERIES

The cold power rating of a battery measures battery starting performance and provides an approximate relationship between battery size and engine size. The cold power rating of a replacement battery should match or exceed your engine size in cubic inches.

FLUID LEVEL (EXCEPT MAINTENANCE FREE BATTERIES)

Check the battery electrolyte level at least once a month, or more often in hot weather or during periods of extended truck operation. The level can be checked through the case on translucent polypropylene batteries; the cell caps must be removed on other models. The electrolyte level in each cell should be kept filled to

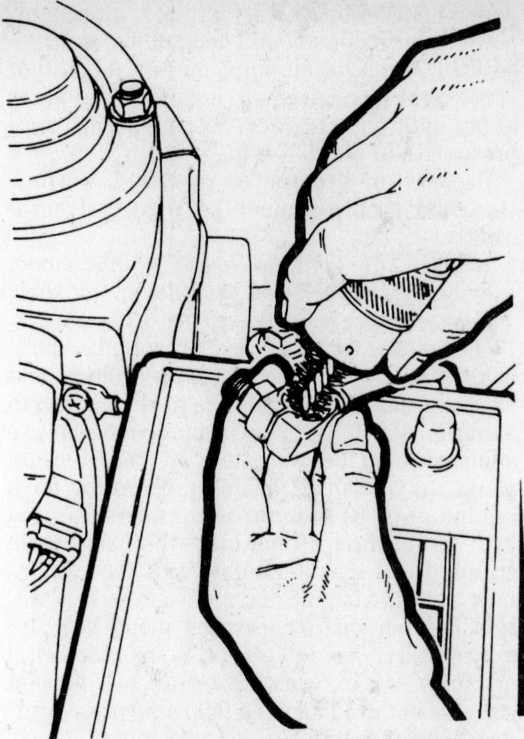

Clean the cable ends with a stiff cable cleaning tool (male end)

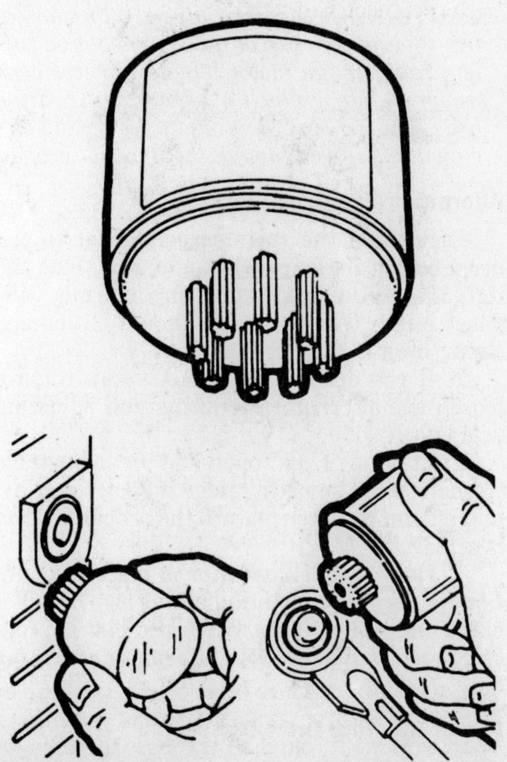

Side terminal batteries require a special wire brush for cleaning

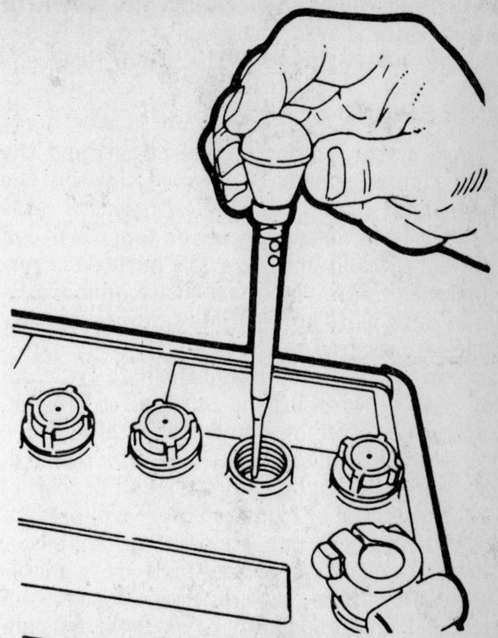

The specific gravity of the battery can be checked with a simple float-type hydrometer

the split ring inside, or the line marked on the outside of the case.

If the level is low, add only distilled water, or colorless, odorless drinking water, through the opening until the level is correct. Each cell is completely separate from the others, so each must be checked and filled individually.

If water is added in freezing weather, the truck should be driven several miles to allow the water to mix with the electrolyte. Otherwise, the battery could freeze.

SPECIFIC GRAVITY (EXCEPT MAINTENANCE FREE BATTERIES)

At least once a year, check the specific gravity of the battery. It should be between 1.20 in.Hg and 1.26 in.Hg at room temperature.

The specific gravity can be check with the use of an hydrometer, an inexpensive instrument available from many sources, including auto parts stores. The hydrometer has a squeeze bulb at one end and a nozzle at the other. Battery electrolyte is sucked into the hydrometer until the float is lifted from its seat. The specific gravity is then read by noting the position of the float. Generally, if after charging, the specific gravity between any two cells varies more than 50 points (0.50), the battery is bad and should be replaced.

It is not possible to check the specific gravity in this manner on sealed (maintenance free) batteries. Instead, the indicator built into the top of the case must be relied on to display any signs of battery deterioration. If the indicator is dark, the battery can be assumed to be OK. If the indicator is light, the specific gravity is low, and the battery should be charged or replaced.

CABLES AND CLAMPS

Once a year, the battery terminals and the cable clamps should be cleaned. Loosen the clamps and remove the cables, negative cable first. On batteries with posts on top, the use of a puller specially made for the purpose is recommended. These are inexpensive, and available in auto parts stores. Side terminal battery cables are secured with a bolt.

Clean the cable lamps and the battery terminal with a wire brush, until all corrosion, grease, etc., is removed and the metal is shiny. It is especially important to clean the inside of the clamp thoroughly, since a small deposit of foreign material or oxidation there will prevent a sound electrical connection and inhibit either starting or charging. Special tools are available for cleaning these parts, one type for conventional batteries and another type for side terminal batteries.

Before installing the cables, loosen the battery holddown clamp or strap, remove the battery and check the battery tray. Clear it of any debris, and check it for soundness. Rust should be wire brushed away, and the metal given a coat of anti-rust paint. Replace the battery and tighten the holddown clamp or strap securely, but be careful not to over tighten, which will crack the battery case.

After the clamps and terminals are clean, reinstall the cables, negative cable last; do not hammer on the clamps to install. Tighten the clamps securely, but do not distort them. Give the clamps and terminals a thin external coat of grease after installation, to retard corrosion.

Check the cables at the same time that the terminals are cleaned. If the cable insulation is cracked or broken, or if the ends are frayed, the cable should be replaced with a new cable of the same length and gauge.

CAUTION: *Keep flame or sparks away from the battery; it gives off explosive hydrogen gas. Battery electrolyte contains sulphuric acid. If you should splash any on your skin or in your eyes, flush the affected area with plenty of clear water. If it lands in your eyes, get medical help immediately.*

Belts

Once a year or at 12,000 mile intervals, the tension (and condition) of the alternator, power steering (if so equipped), air conditioning (if so equipped), and Thermactor air pump drive belts should be checked, and, if necessary, adjusted. Loose accessory drive belts can lead to poor engine cooling and diminish alternator, power steering pump, air conditioning compressor or Thermactor air pump output. A belt that is too tight places a severe strain on the water pump, alternator, power steering pump, compressor or air pump bearings.

Replace any belt that is so glazed, worn or stretched that it cannot be tightened sufficiently.

NOTE: *The material used in late model drive belts is such that the belts do not show wear. Replace belts at least every three years.*

On vehicles with matched belts, replace both belts. New $^1/_2$ in. (13mm), $^3/_8$ in. (10mm) and $^{15}/_{32}$ in. (12mm) wide belts are to be adjusted to a tension of 140 lbs.; $^1/_4$ in. (6mm)wide belts are adjusted to 80 lbs., measured on a belt tension gauge. Any belt that has been operating for a minimum of 10 minutes is considered a used belt. In the first 10 minutes, the belt should stretch to its maximum extent. After 10 minutes, stop the engine and recheck the belt tension. Belt tension for a used belt should be maintained at 110 lbs. (all except $^1/_4$ in. wide belts) or 60 lbs. ($^1/_4$ in. wide belts). If a belt tension gauge is not available, the following procedures may be used.

ADJUSTMENTS FOR ALL EXCEPT THE SERPENTINE (SINGLE) BELT

CAUTION: *On models equipped with an electric cooling fan, disconnect the negative battery cable or fan motor wiring harness connector before replacing or adjusting drive belts. The fan may come on, under certain circumstances, even though the ignition is off.*

Alternator (Fan Drive) Belt

1. Position the ruler perpendicular to the drive belt at its longest straight run. Test the tightness of the belt by pressing it firmly with your thumb. The deflection should not exceed $^1/_4$ in. (6mm).
2. If the deflection exceeds $^1/_4$ in. (6mm), loosen the alternator mounting and adjusting arm bolts.
3. Place a 1 in. open-end or adjustable wrench on the adjusting ridge cast on the body, and pull on the wrench until the proper tension is achieved.
4. Holding the alternator in place to maintain tension, tighten the adjusting arm bolt. Recheck the belt tension. When the belt is properly tensioned, tighten the alternator mounting bolt.

Power Steering Drive Belt

6–4.9L

1. Hold a ruler perpendicularly to the drive belt at its longest run, test the tightness of the

HOW TO SPOT WORN V-BELTS

V-Belts are vital to efficient engine operation—they drive the fan, water pump and other accessories. They require little maintenance (occasional tightening) but they will not last forever. Slipping or failure of the V-belt will lead to overheating. If your V-belt looks like any of these, it should be replaced.

Cracking or weathering

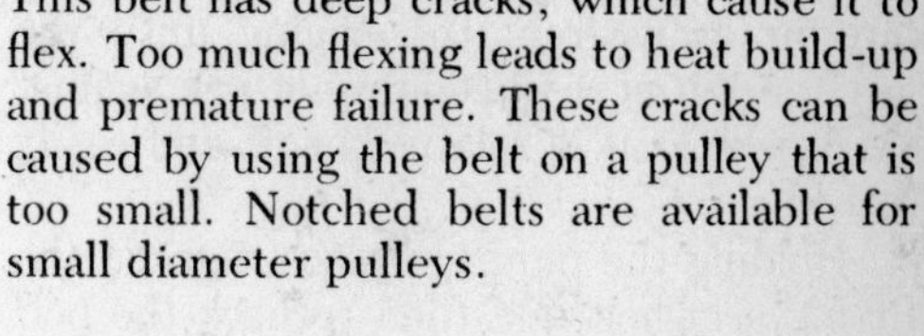

This belt has deep cracks, which cause it to flex. Too much flexing leads to heat build-up and premature failure. These cracks can be caused by using the belt on a pulley that is too small. Notched belts are available for small diameter pulleys.

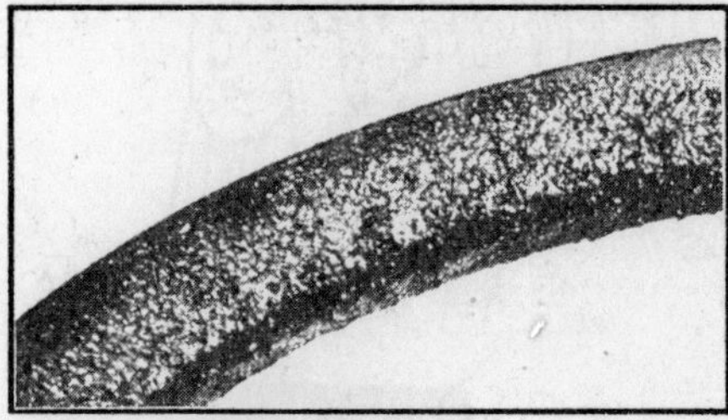

Softening (grease and oil)

Oil and grease on a belt can cause the belt's rubber compounds to soften and separate from the reinforcing cords that hold the belt together. The belt will first slip, then finally fail altogether.

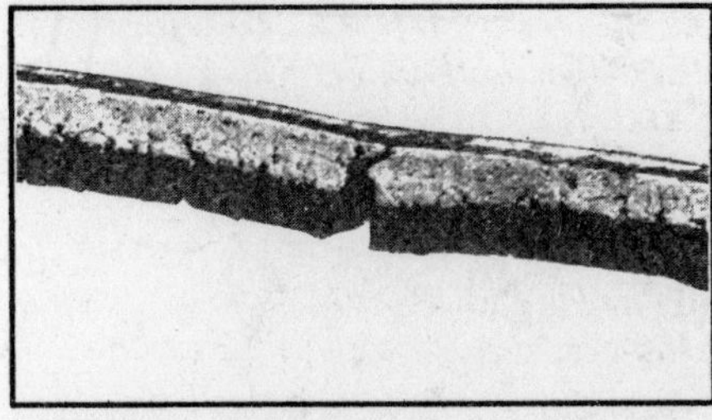

Glazing

Glazing is caused by a belt that is slipping. A slipping belt can cause a run-down battery, erratic power steering, overheating or poor accessory performance. The more the belt slips, the more glazing will be built up on the surface of the belt. The more the belt is glazed, the more it will slip. If the glazing is light, tighten the belt.

Worn cover

The cover of this belt is worn off and is peeling away. The reinforcing cords will begin to wear and the belt will shortly break. When the belt cover wears in spots or has a rough jagged appearance, check the pulley grooves for roughness.

Separation

This belt is on the verge of breaking and leaving you stranded. The layers of the belt are separating and the reinforcing cords are exposed. It's just a matter of time before it breaks completely.

belt by pressing it firmly with your thumb. The deflection should not exceed 1/4 in. (6mm).

2. To adjust the belt tension, loosen the adjusting and mounting bolts on the front face of the steering pump cover plate (hub side).

3. Using a pry bar or broom handle on the pump hub, move the power steering pump toward or away from the engine until the proper tension is reached. Do not pry against the reservoir as it is relatively soft and easily deformed.

4. Holding the pump in place, tighten the adjusting arm bolt and then recheck the belt

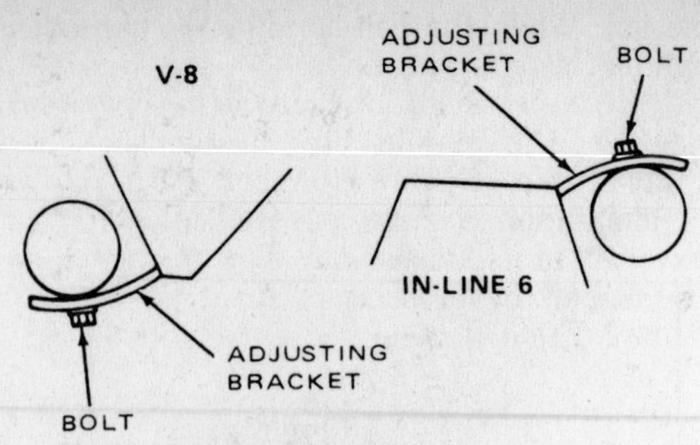

Air pump adjustment points

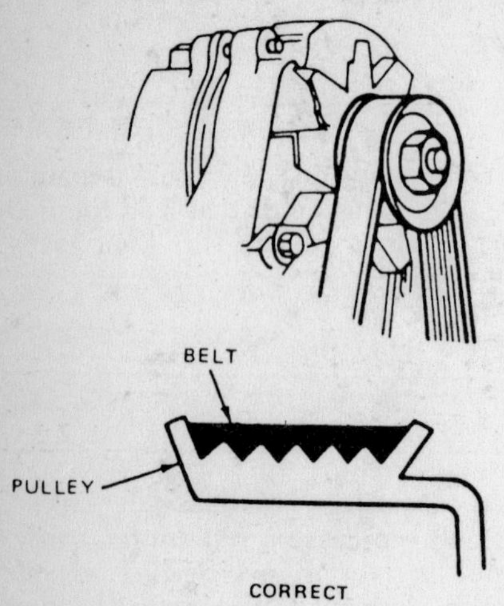

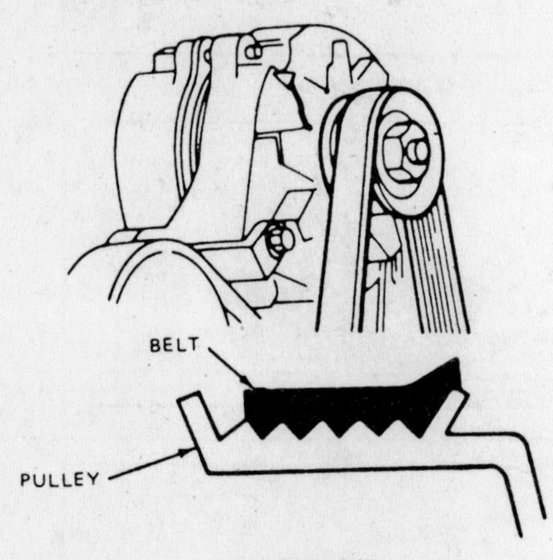

Serpentine belt installation

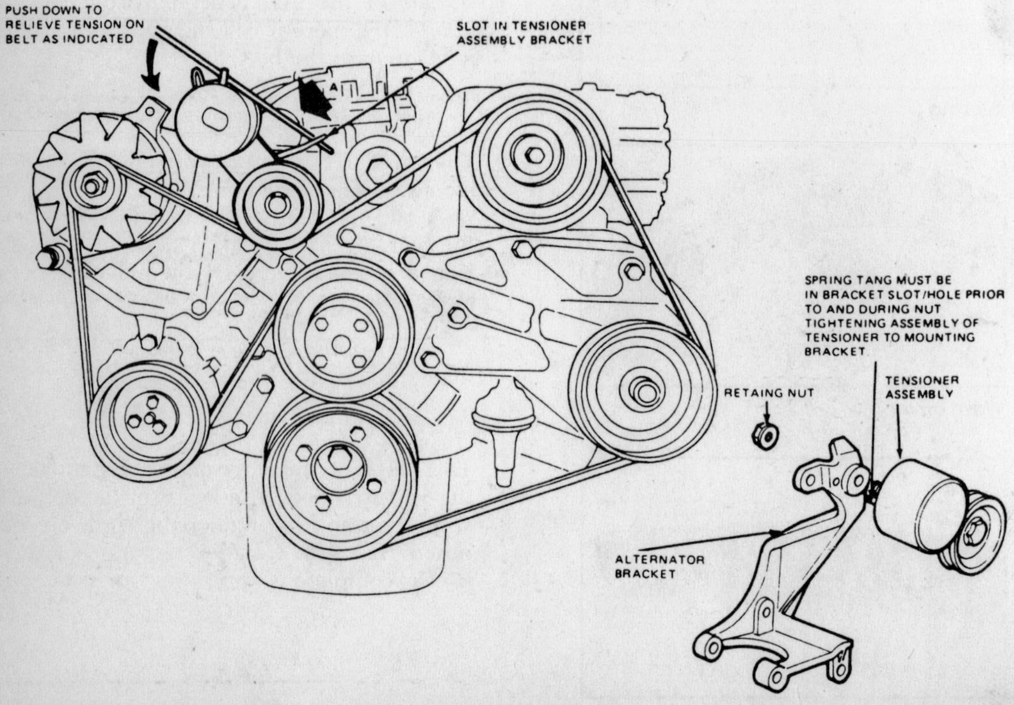

Serpentine belt adjustment

tension. When the belt is properly tensioned tighten the mounting bolts.

V8 MODELS

1. Position a ruler perpendicular to the drive belt at its longest run. Test the tightness of the belt by pressing it firmly with your thumb. The deflection should be about 1/4 in. (6mm).

2. To adjust the belt tension, loosen the three bolts in the three elongated adjusting

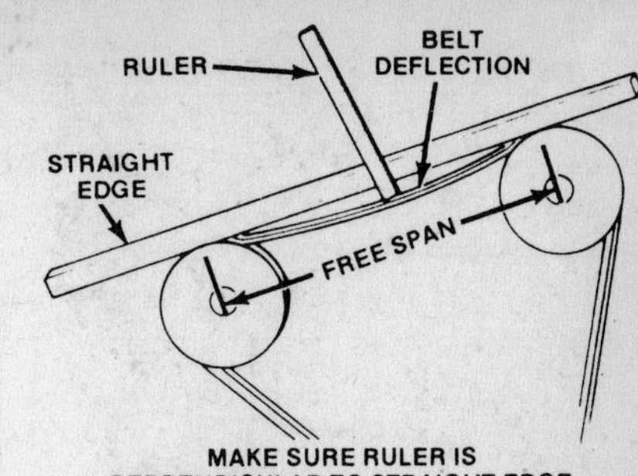

Measuring belt deflection

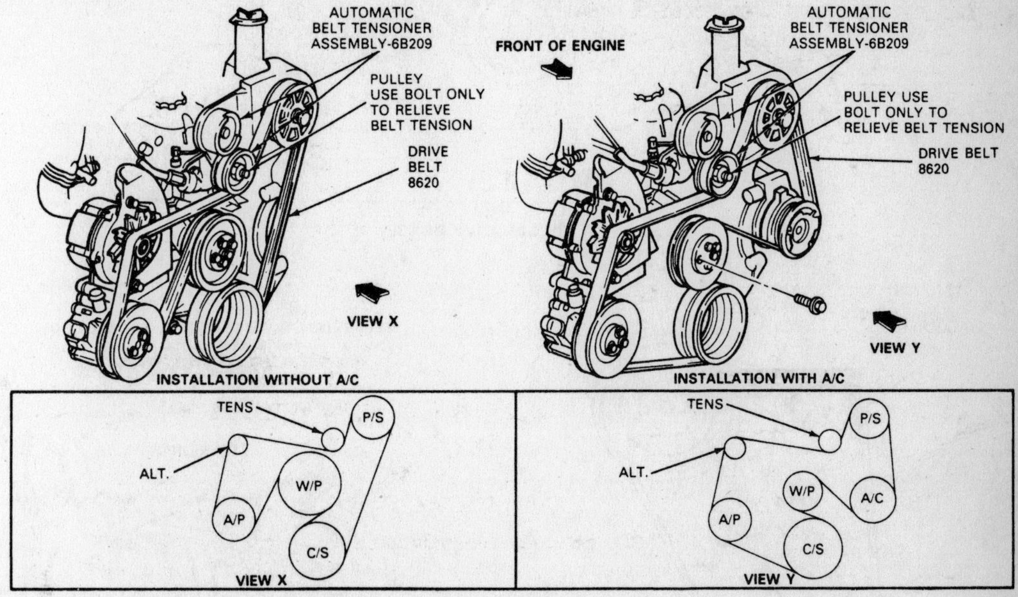

4.9L EFI drive belts

NOTE: THE SINGLE BELT, SERPENTINE DRIVE ARRANGEMENT OF THE 4.9L, 5.0L AND 5.8L EFI ENGINES USE AN AUTOMATIC BELT TENSIONER. NO BELT TENSION ADJUSTMENT IS REQUIRED.

SPECIAL INSTRUCTIONS:

1. LIFT AUTO TENSIONER PULLEY BY APPLYING TORQUE TO IDLER PULLEY PIVOT BOLT WITH WRENCH AND SOCKET
2. INSTALL DRIVE BELT OVER PULLEYS PER APPROPRIATE BELT ROUTING
3. CHECK BELT TENSION. REFERENCE TENSION CODE (4.9L), (5.0L) OR (5.8L)
4. IF BELT TENSION IS TOO LOW CHECK WITH NEW BELT BEFORE REPLACING TENSIONER.
5. IF TENSION IS NOT WITHIN SPECIFICATION INSTALL A NEW AUTOMATIC TENSIONER. LOCATE PIN AS SHOWN IN VIEW A.

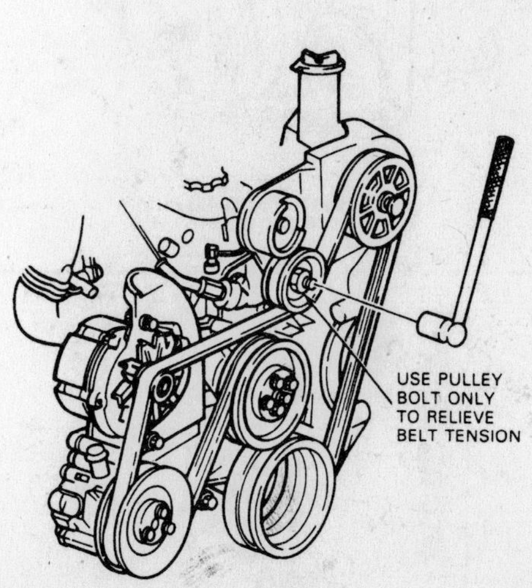

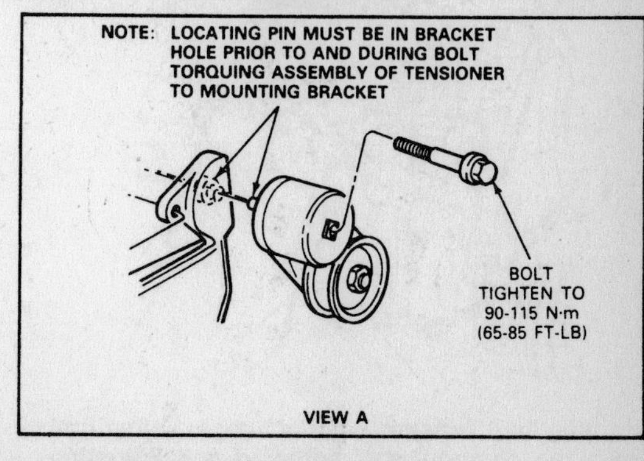

Drive belt adjustments on the 6–4.9L, 8–5.0L and 8–5.8L EFI engines

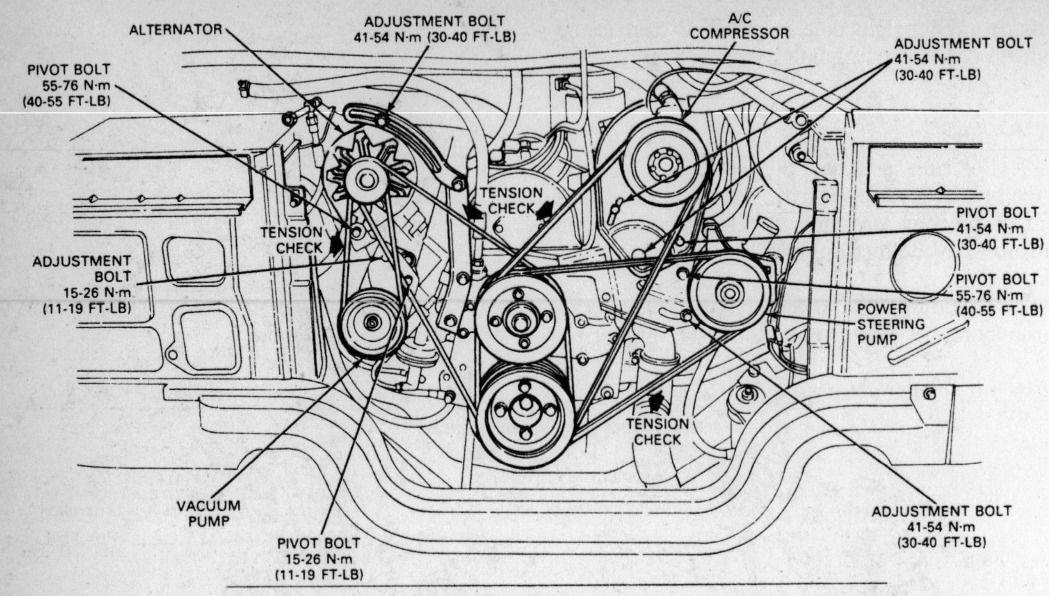

7.3L diesel drive belts

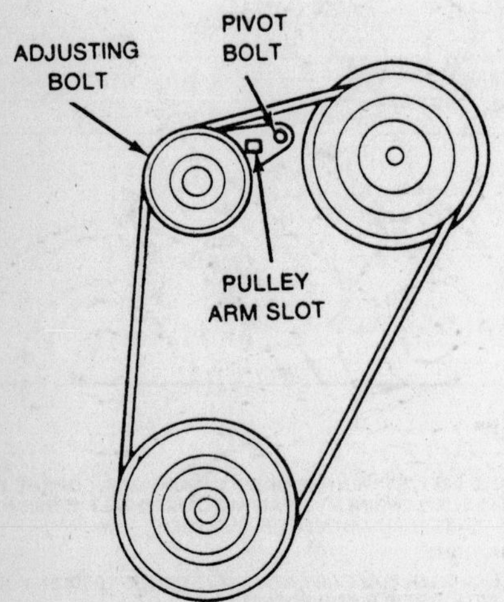

Some pulleys have a rectangular slot to aid in moving the accessory to be tightened

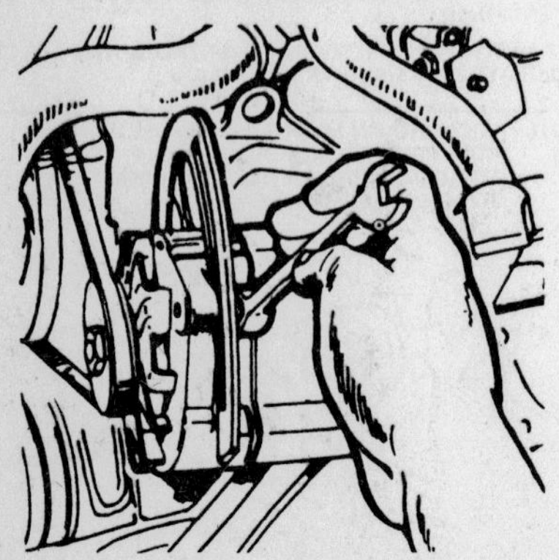

To adjust belt tension or to change belts, first loosen the component's mounting and adjusting bolts slightly

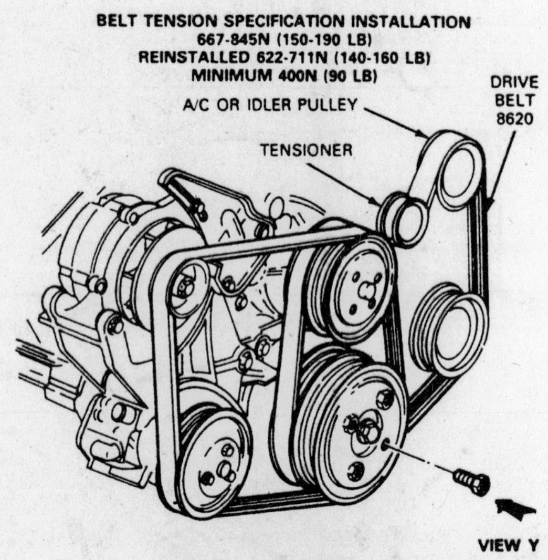

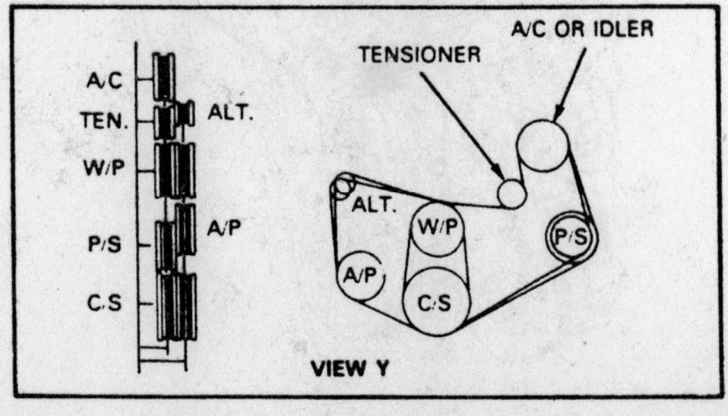

8–7.5L EFI drive belts

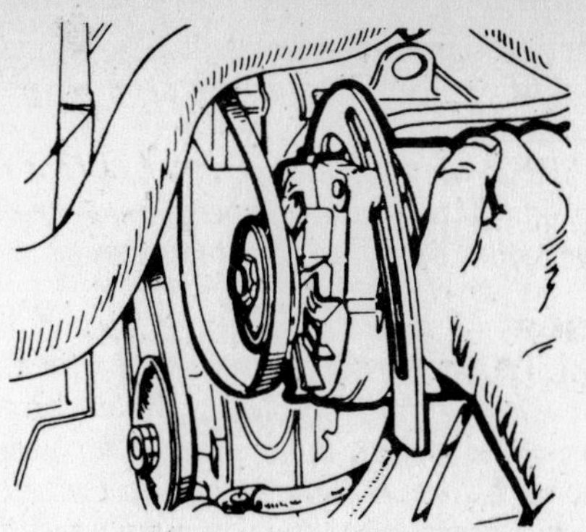

Push the component towards the engine and slip off the belt.

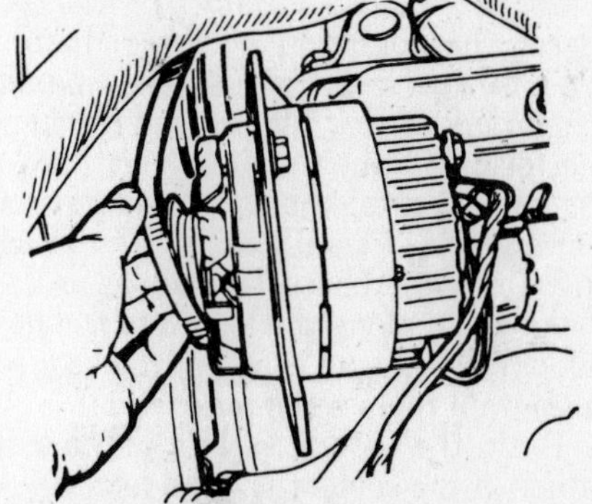

Slip the new belt over the pulley

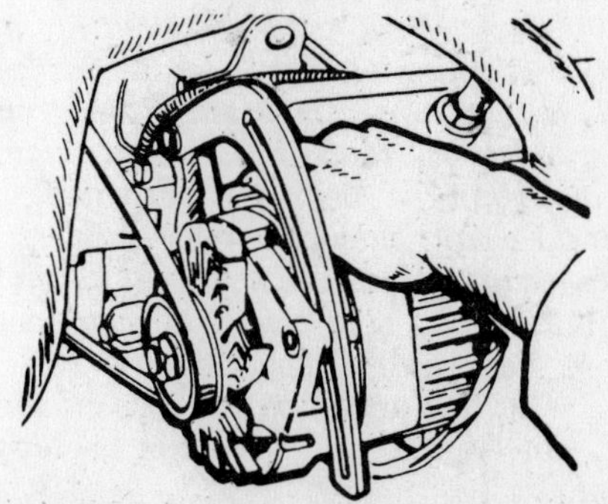

Pull outward on the component and tighten the mounting bolts

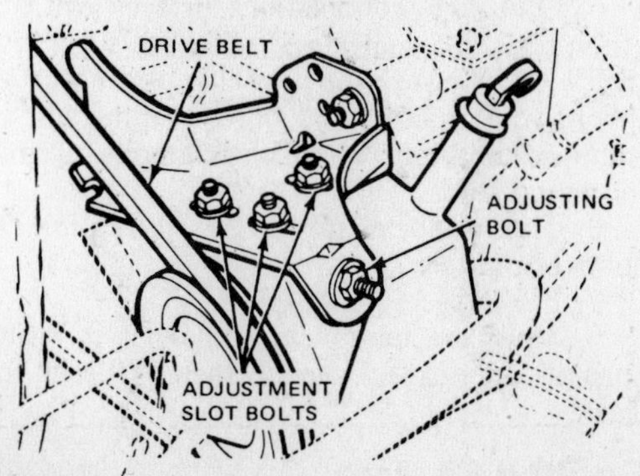

Power steering pump adjustment

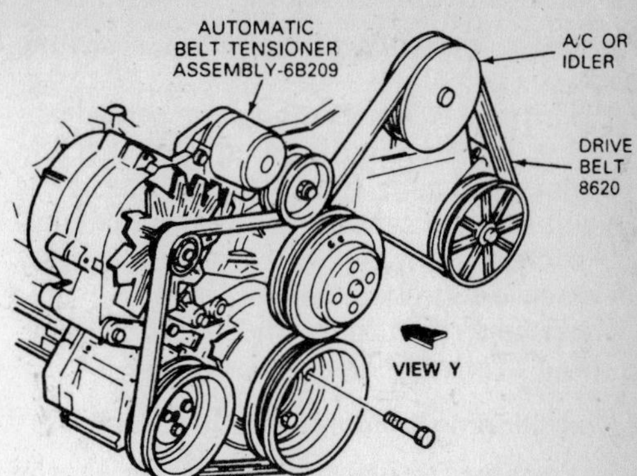

INSTALLATION WITH THERMACTER AIR PUMP

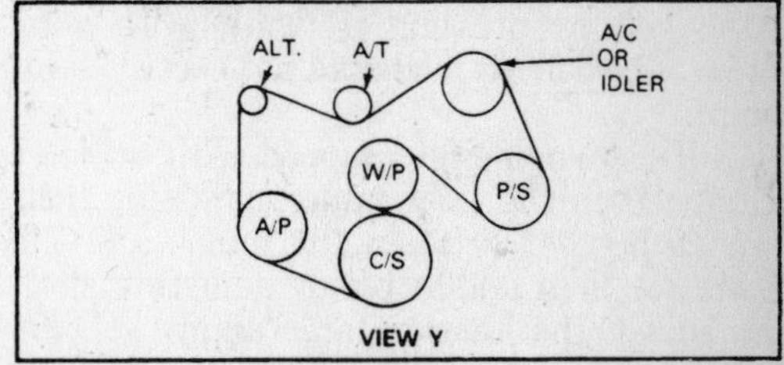

8–5.0L, 8–5.8L drive belts

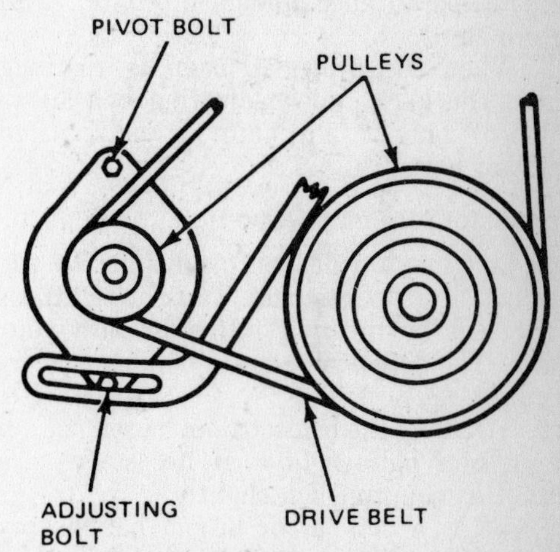

Alternator belt adjustment

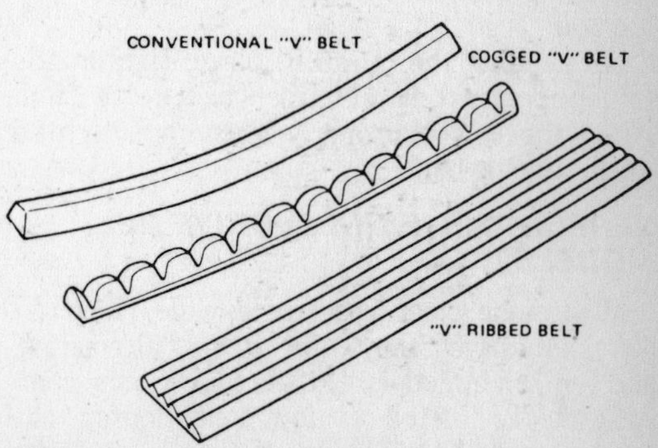

Power Steering Drive Belt

slots at the power steering pump attaching bracket.

3. Turn the steering pump drive belt adjusting nut as required until the proper deflection is obtained. Turning the adjusting nut clockwise will increase tension and decrease deflection; counterclockwise will decrease tension and increase deflection.

4. Without disturbing the pump, tighten the three attaching bolts.

Air Conditioning Compressor Drive Belt

1. Position a ruler perpendicular to the drive belt at its longest run. Test the tightness of the belt by pressing it firmly with your thumb. The deflection should not exceed $^1/_4$ in. (6mm).

2. If the engine is equipped with an idler pulley, loosen the idler pulley adjusting bolt, insert a pry bar between the pulley and the engine (or in the idler pulley adjusting slot), and adjust the tension accordingly. If the engine is not equipped with an idler pulley, the alternator must be moved to accomplish this adjustment, as outlined under Alternator (Fan Drive) Belt.

3. When the proper tension is reached, tighten the idler pulley adjusting bolt (if so equipped) or the alternator adjusting and mounting bolts.

Thermactor Air Pump Drive Belt

1. Position a ruler perpendicular to the drive belt at its longest run. Test the tightness of the belt by pressing it firmly with your thumb. The deflection should be about $^1/_4$ in. (6mm).

2. To adjust the belt tension, loosen the adjusting arm bolt slightly. If necessary, also loosen the mounting belt slightly.

3. Using a pry bar or broom handle, pry against the pump rear cover to move the pump toward or away from the engine as necessary.

CAUTION: *Do not pry against the pump housing itself, as damage to the housing may result.*

4. Holding the pump in place, tighten the adjusting arm bolt and recheck the tension. When the belt is properly tensioned, tighten the mounting bolt.

SERPENTINE (SINGLE) DRIVE BELT MODELS

Most models feature a single, wide, ribbed V-belt that drives the water pump, alternator, and (on some models) the air conditioner compressor. To install a new belt, loosen the bracket lock bolt, retract the belt tensioner with a pry bar and slide the old belt off of the pulleys. Slip on a new belt and release the tensioner and tighten the lock bolt. The spring powered tensioner eliminates the need for periodic adjustments.

WARNING: *Check to make sure that the V-ribbed belt is located properly in all drive pulleys before applying tensioner pressure.*

Hoses

CAUTION: *On models equipped with an electric cooling fan, disconnect the negative battery cable, or fan motor wiring harness connector before replacing any radiator/heater hose. The fan may come on, under certain circumstances, even though the ignition is Off.*

REPLACEMENT

Inspect the condition of the radiator and heater hoses periodically. Early spring and at the beginning of the fall or winter, when you are performing other maintenance, are good times. Make sure the engine and cooling system are cold. Visually inspect for cracking, rotting or collapsed hoses, replace as necessary. Run your hand along the length of the hose. If a weak or swollen spot is noted when squeezing the hose wall, replace the hose.

1. Drain the cooling system into a suitable container (if the coolant is to be reused).

CAUTION: *When draining the coolant, keep in mind that cats and dogs are attracted by the ethylene glycol antifreeze, and are quite likely to drink any that is left in an uncovered container or in puddles on the ground. This will prove fatal in sufficient quantity. Always drain the coolant into a sealable container. Coolant should be reused unless it is contaminated or several years old.*

2. Loosen the hose clamps at each end of the hose that requires replacement.

3. Twist, pull and slide the hose off the radiator, water pump, thermostat or heater connection.

4. Clean the hose mounting connections. Position the hose clamps on the new hose.

5. Coat the connection surfaces with a water resistant sealer and slide the hose into position. Make sure the hose clamps are located beyond the raised bead of the connector (if equipped) and centered in the clamping area of the connection.

6. Tighten the clamps to 20–30 inch lbs. Do not over tighten.

7. Fill the cooling system.

8. Start the engine and allow it to reach normal operating temperature. Check for leaks.

Cooling System

CAUTION: *Never remove the radiator cap under any conditions while the engine is run-*

HOW TO SPOT BAD HOSES

Both the upper and lower radiator hoses are called upon to perform difficult jobs in an inhospitable environment. They are subject to nearly 18 psi at under hood temperatures often over 280°F., and must circulate nearly 7500 gallons of coolant an hour—3 good reasons to have good hoses.

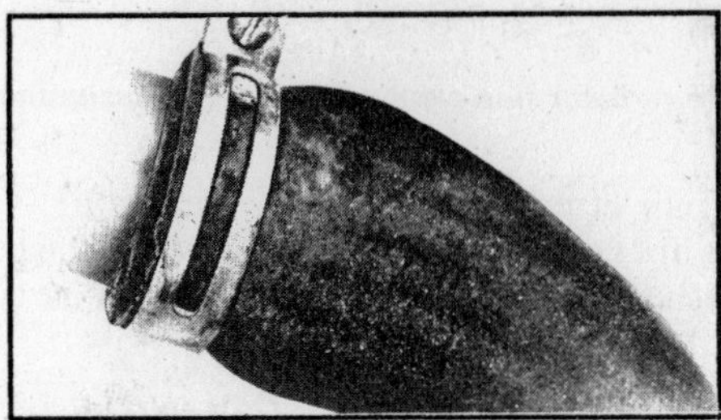

Swollen hose

A good test for any hose is to feel it for soft or spongy spots. Frequently these will appear as swollen areas of the hose. The most likely cause is oil soaking. This hose could burst at any time, when hot or under pressure.

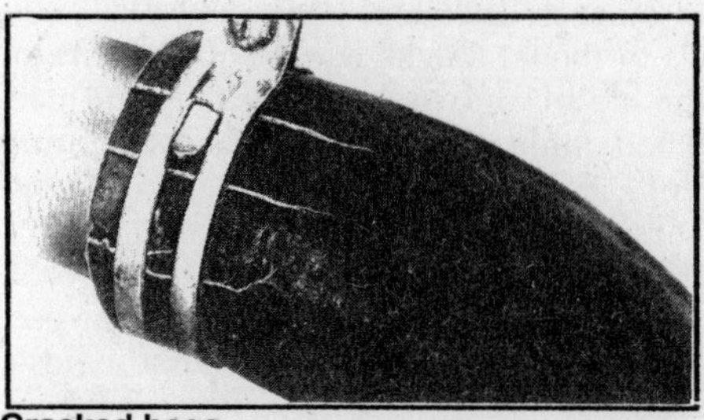

Cracked hose

Cracked hoses can usually be seen but feel the hoses to be sure they have not hardened; a prime cause of cracking. This hose has cracked down to the reinforcing cords and could split at any of the cracks.

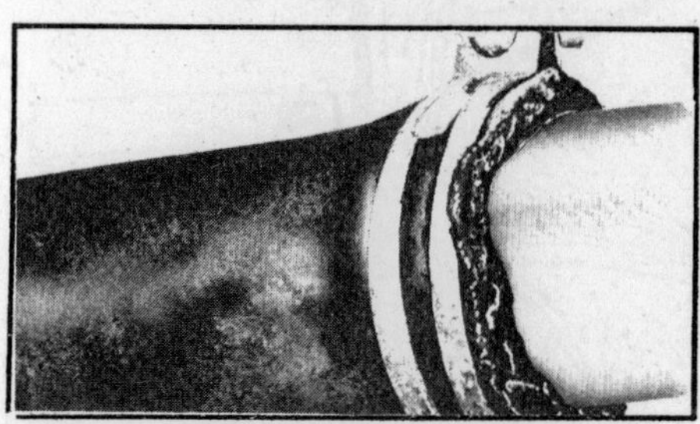

Frayed hose end (due to weak clamp)

Weakened clamps frequently are the cause of hose and cooling system failure. The connection between the pipe and hose has deteriorated enough to allow coolant to escape when the engine is hot.

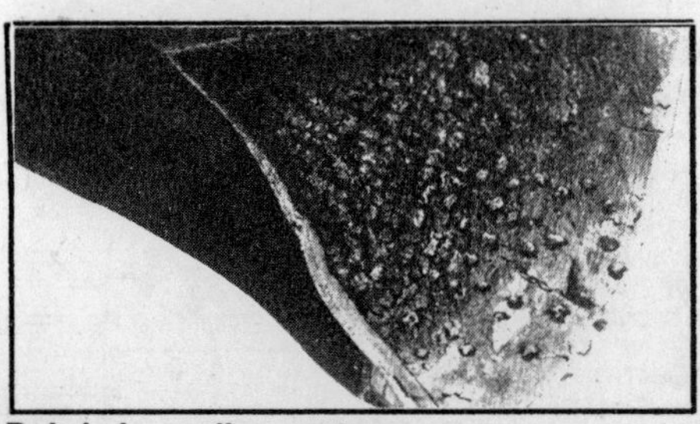

Debris in cooling system

Debris, rust and scale in the cooling system can cause the inside of a hose to weaken. This can usually be felt on the outside of the hose as soft or thinner areas.

ning! Failure to follow these instructions could result in damage to the cooling system or engine and/or personal injury. To avoid having scalding hot coolant or steam blow out of the radiator, use extreme care when removing the radiator cap from a hot radiator. Wait until the engine has cooled, then wrap a thick cloth around the radiator cap and turn it slowly to the first stop. Step back while the pressure is released from the cooling system. When you are sure the pressure has been released, press down on the radiator cap (still have the cloth in position) turn and remove the radiator cap.

At least once every 2 years, the engine cooling system should be inspected, flushed, and refilled with fresh coolant. If the coolant is left in the system too long, it loses its ability to prevent rust and corrosion. If the coolant has too much water, it won't protect against freezing.

The pressure cap should be looked at for signs of age or deterioration. Fan belt and other drive belts should be inspected and adjusted to the proper tension. (See checking belt tension).

Hose clamps should be tightened, and soft or cracked hoses replaced. Damp spots, or accumulations of rust or dye near hoses, water pump or other areas, indicate possible leakage, which must be corrected before filling the system with fresh coolant.

CHECK THE RADIATOR CAP

While you are checking the coolant level, check the radiator cap for a worn or cracked gasket. It the cap doesn't seal properly, fluid will be lost and the engine will overheat.

Worn caps should be replaced with a new one.

CLEAN RADIATOR OF DEBRIS

Periodically clean any debris – leaves, paper, insects, etc. – from the radiator fins. Pick the large pieces off by hand. The smaller pieces can be washed away with water pressure from a hose.

Carefully straighten any bent radiator fins

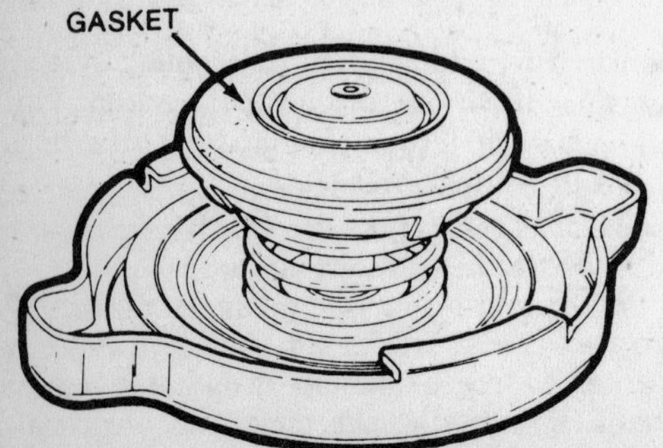

Check the radiator cap gasket for cracks or wear

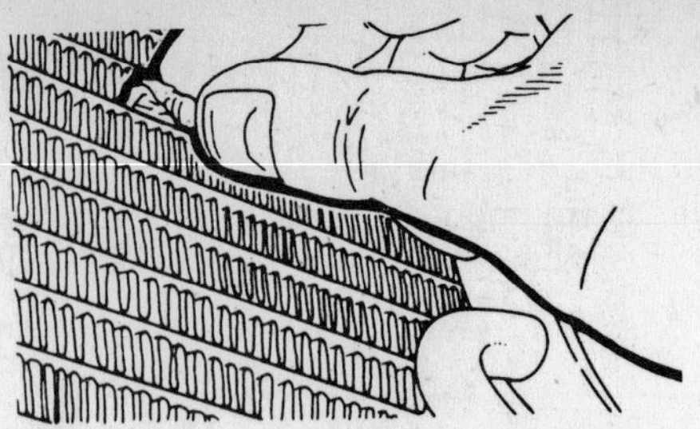

Keep the radiator fins clear of debris for maximum cooling

with a pair of needle nose pliers. Be careful – the fins are very soft. Don't wiggle the fins back and forth too much. Straighten them once and try not to move them again.

DRAIN AND REFILL THE COOLING SYSTEM

Completely draining and refilling the cooling system every two years at least will remove accumulated rust, scale and other deposits. Coolant in late model trucks is a 50/50 mixture of ethylene glycol and water for year round use. Use a good quality antifreeze with water pump lubricants, rust inhibitors and other corrosion inhibitors along with acid neutralizers.

1. Drain the existing antifreeze and coolant. Open the radiator and engine drain petcocks, or disconnect the bottom radiator hose, at the radiator outlet.

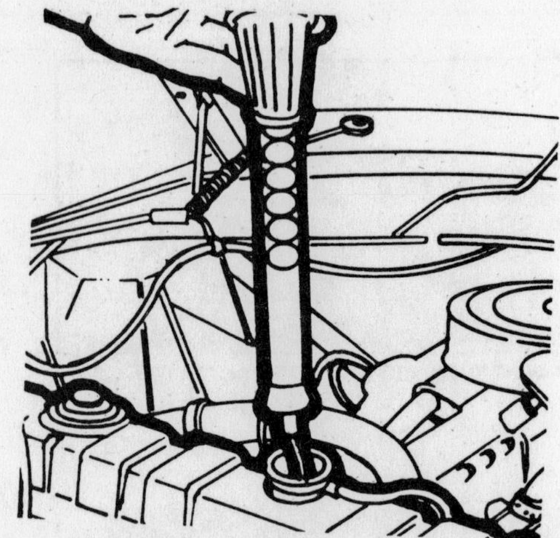

Check antifreeze protection with an inexpensive tester

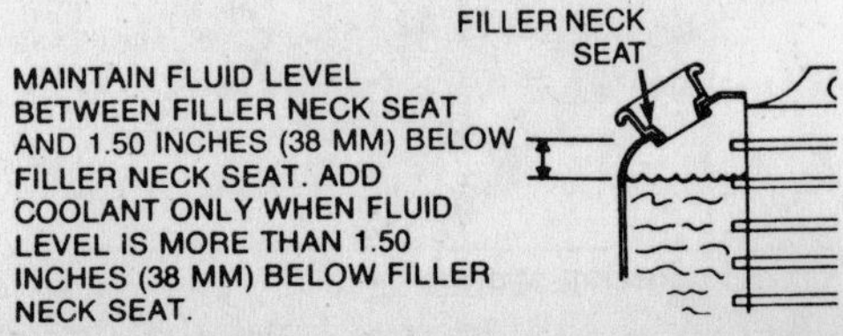

Coolant level check

Open the radiator petcock to drain the cooling system. Spray first with penetrating oil

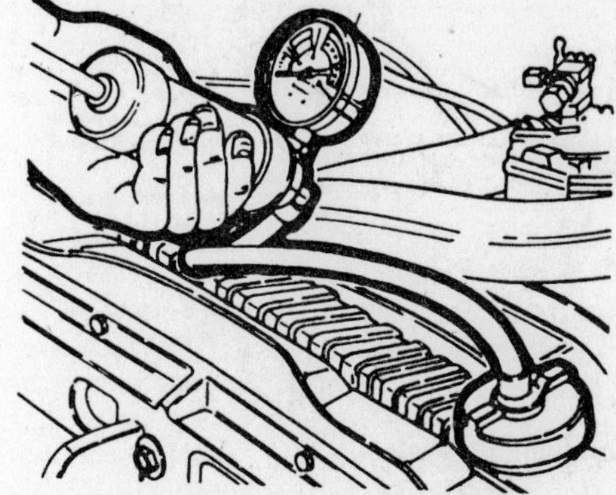

The system should be pressure tested once a year

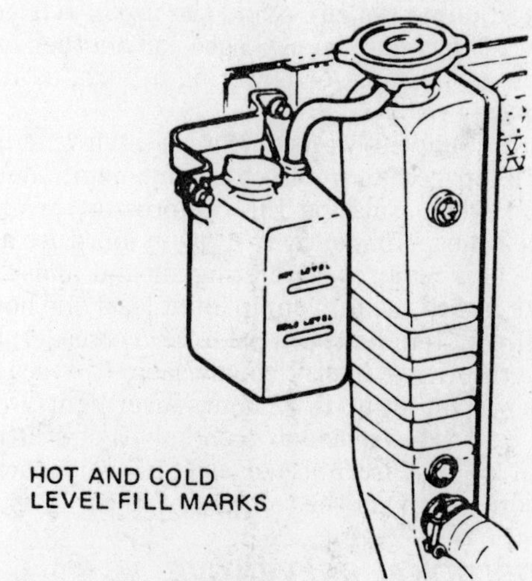

Coolant recovery system

NOTE: *Before opening the radiator petcock, spray it with some penetrating lubricant.*

2. Close the petcock or reconnect the lower hose and fill the system with water.
3. Add a can of quality radiator flush.
4. Idle the engine until the upper radiator hose gets hot.
5. Drain the system again.
6. Repeat this process until the drained water is clear and free of scale.
7. Close all petcocks and connect all the hoses.
8. If equipped with a coolant recovery system, flush the reservoir with water and leave empty.
9. Determine the capacity of your coolant system (see capacities specifications). Add a 50/50 mix of quality antifreeze (ethylene glycol) and water to provide the desired protection.
10. Run the engine to operating temperature.
11. Stop the engine and check the coolant level.
12. Check the level of protection with an antifreeze tester, replace the cap and check for leaks.

Air Conditioning

GENERAL SERVICING PROCEDURES

The most important aspect of air conditioning service is the maintenance of pure and adequate charge of refrigerant in the system. A refrigeration system cannot function properly if a significant percentage of the charge is lost. Leaks are common because the severe vibration encountered in an automobile can easily cause a sufficient cracking or loosening of the air conditioning fittings. As a result, the extreme operating pressures of the system force refrigerant out.

The problem can be understood by considering what happens to the system as it is operated with a continuous leak. Because the expansion valve regulates the flow of refrigerant to the evaporator, the level of refrigerant there is fairly constant. The receiver/drier stores any excess of refrigerant, and so a loss will first appear there as a reduction in the level of liquid. As this level nears the bottom of the vessel, some refrigerant vapor bubbles will begin to appear in the stream of liquid supplied to the expansion valve. This vapor decreases the capacity of the expansion valve very little as the valve opens to compensate for its presence. As the quantity of liquid in the condenser decreases, the operating pressure will drop there and throughout the high side of the system. As the R-12 continues to be expelled, the pressure available to force the liquid through the expansion valve will continue to decrease, and, eventually, the valve's orifice will prove to be too much of a restriction for adequate flow even with the needle fully withdrawn.

At this point, low side pressure will start to drop, and severe reduction in cooling capacity, marked by freeze-up of the evaporator coil, will result. Eventually, the operating pressure of the evaporator will be lower than the pressure of the atmosphere surrounding it, and air will

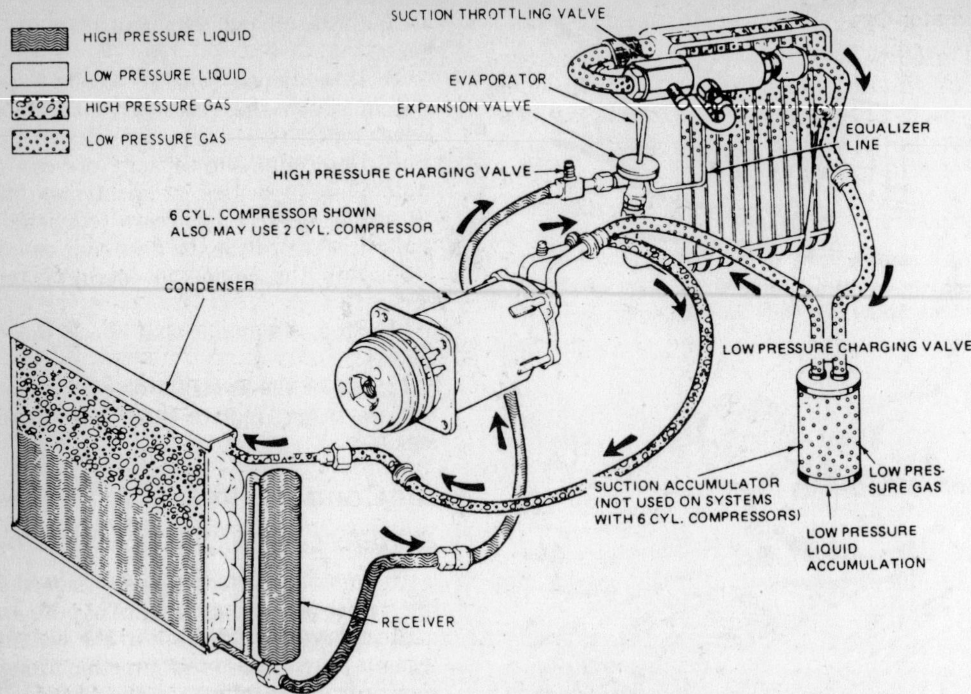

Flow diagram of a typical air conditioning system

be drawn into the system wherever there are leaks in the low side.

Because all atmospheric air contains at least some moisture, water will enter the system and mix with the R-12 and the oil. Trace amounts of moisture will cause sludging of the oil, and corrosion of the system. Saturation and clogging of the filter/drier, and freezing of the expansion valve orifice will eventually result. As air fills the system to a greater and greater extend, it will interfere more and more with the normal flows of refrigerant and heat.

A list of general precautions that should be observed while doing this follows:

1. Keep all tools as clean and dry as possible.
2. Thoroughly purge the service gauges and hoses of air and moisture before connecting them to the system. Keep them capped when not in use.
3. Thoroughly clean any refrigerant fitting before disconnecting it, in order to minimize the entrance of dirt into the system.
4. Plan any operation that requires opening the system beforehand in order to minimize the length of time it will be exposed to open air. Cap or seal the open ends to minimize the entrance of foreign material.
5. When adding oil, pour it through an extremely clean and dry tube or funnel. Keep the oil capped whenever possible. Do not use oil that has not been kept tightly sealed.
6. Use only refrigerant 12. Purchase refrigerant intended for use in only automotive air conditioning system. Avoid the use of refrigerant 12 that may be packaged for another use, such as cleaning, or powering a horn, as it is impure.
7. Completely evacuate any system that has been opened to replace a component, other than when isolating the compressor, or that has leaked sufficiently to draw in moisture and air. This requires evacuating air and moisture with a good vacuum pump for at least one hour.

If a system has been open for a considerable length of time it may be advisable to evacuate the system for up to 12 hours (overnight).

8. Use a wrench on both halves of a fitting that is to be disconnected, so as to avoid placing torque on any of the refrigerant lines.

ADDITIONAL PREVENTIVE MAINTENANCE CHECKS

Antifreeze

In order to prevent heater core freeze-up during A/C operation, it is necessary to maintain permanent type antifreeze protection of +15°F (-9°C) or lower. A reading of -15°F (-26°C) is ideal since this protection also supplies sufficient corrosion inhibitors for the protection of the engine cooling system.

WARNING: *Do not use antifreeze longer than specified by the manufacturer.*

Radiator Cap

For efficient operation of an air conditioned truck's cooling system, the radiator cap should have a holding pressure which meets manufacturer's specifications. A cap which fails to hold these pressure should be replaced.

Condenser

Any obstruction of or damage to the condenser configuration will restrict the air flow which is essential to its efficient operation. It is therefore, a good rule to keep this unit clean and in proper physical shape.

NOTE: *Bug screens are regarded as obstructions.*

Condensation Drain Tube

This single molded drain tube expels the condensation, which accumulates on the bottom of the evaporator housing, into the engine compartment.

If this tube is obstructed, the air conditioning performance can be restricted and condensation buildup can spill over onto the vehicle's floor.

SAFETY PRECAUTIONS

Because of the importance of the necessary safety precautions that must be exercised when working with air conditioning systems and R-12 refrigerant, a recap of the safety precautions are outlined.

1. Avoid contact with a charged refrigeration system, even when working on another part of the air conditioning system or vehicle. If a heavy tool comes into contact with a section of copper tubing or a heat exchanger, it can easily cause the relatively soft material to rupture.
2. When it is necessary to apply force to a fitting which contains refrigerant, as when checking that all system couplings are securely tightened, use a wrench on both parts of the fitting involved, if possible. This will avoid putting torque on the refrigerant tubing. (It is advisable, when possible, to use tube or line wrenches when tightening these flare nut fittings.)
3. Do not attempt to discharge the system by merely loosening a fitting, or removing the service valve caps and cracking these valves. Precise control is possibly only when using the service gauges. Place a rag under the open end of the center charging hose while discharging the system to catch any drops of liquid that might escape. Wear protective gloves when connecting or disconnecting service gauge hoses.
4. Discharge the system only in a well ventilated area, as high concentrations of the gas can exclude oxygen and act as an anesthetic. When leak testing or soldering this is particularly important, as toxic gas is formed when R-12 contacts any flame.
5. Never start a system without first verifying that both service valves are backseated, if equipped, and that all fittings are throughout the system are snugly connected.
6. Avoid applying heat to any refrigerant line or storage vessel. Charging may be aided by using water heated to less than 125°F (52°C) to warm the refrigerant container. Never allow a refrigerant storage container to sit out in the sun, or near any other source of heat, such as a radiator.
7. Always wear goggles when working on a system to protect the eyes. If refrigerant contacts the eye, it is advisable in all cases to see a physician as soon as possible.
8. Frostbite from liquid refrigerant should be treated by first gradually warming the area with cool water, and then gently applying petroleum jelly. A physician should be consulted.
9. Always keep refrigerant can fittings capped when not in use. Avoid sudden shock to the can which might occur from dropping it, or from banging a heavy tool against it. Never carry a refrigerant can in the passenger compartment of a truck.
10. Always completely discharge the system before painting the vehicle (if the paint is to be baked on), or before welding anywhere near the refrigerant lines.

TEST GAUGES

Most of the service work performed in air conditioning requires the use of a set of two gauges, one for the high (head) pressure side of the system, the other for the low (suction) side.

The low side gauge records both pressure and vacuum. Vacuum readings are calibrated

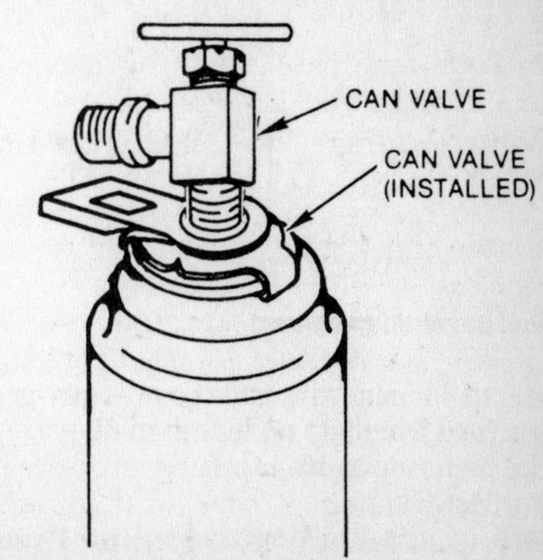

One pound R-12 can with opener valve connected

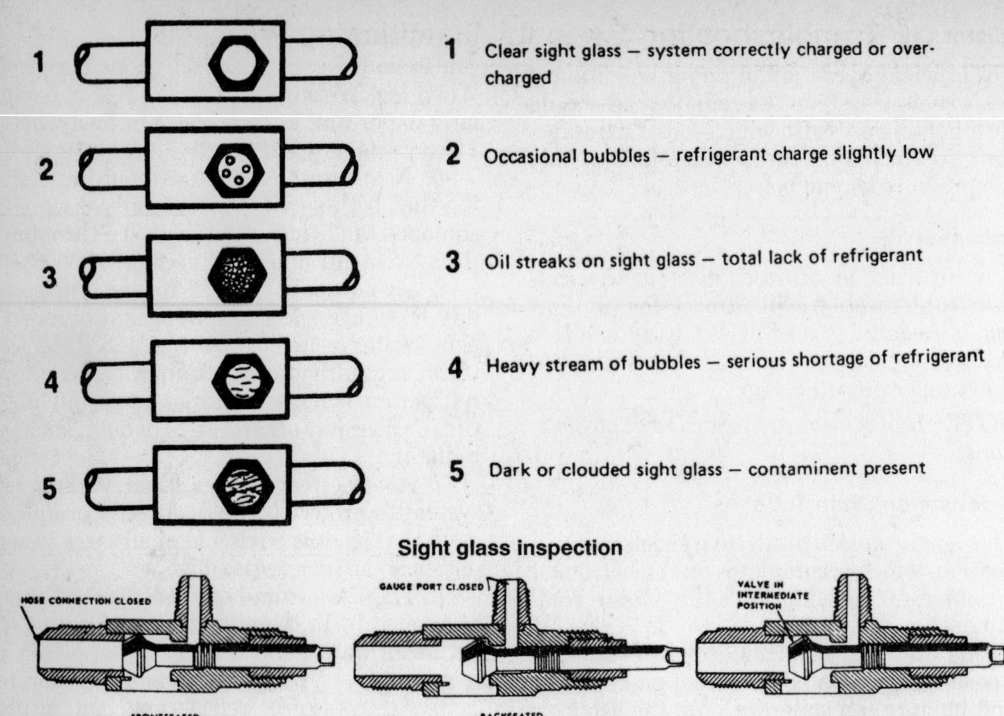

Sight glass inspection

Manual service valve positions

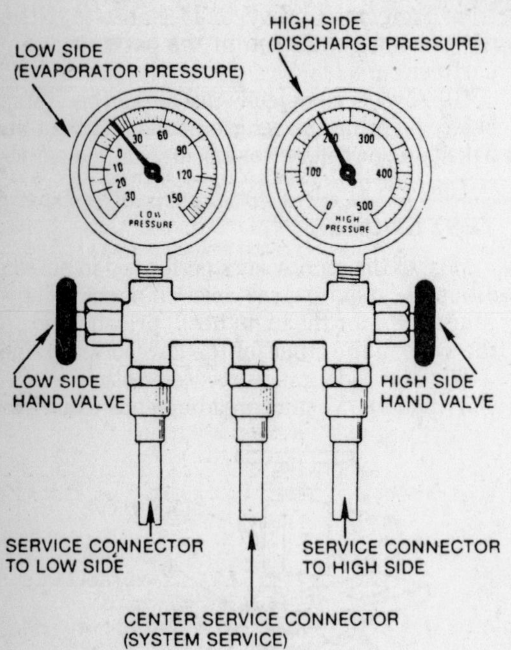

Typical manifold gauge set

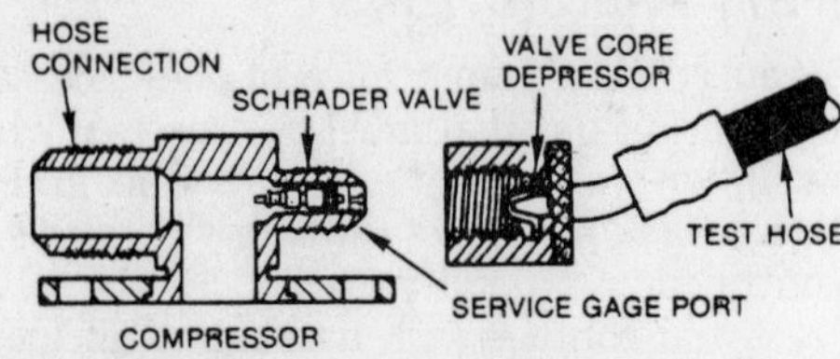

Schrader valve

from 0 to 30 inches Hg and the pressure graduations read from 0 to no less than 60 psi.

The high side gauge measures pressure from 0 to at last 600 psi.

Both gauges are threaded into a manifold that contains two hand shut-off valves. Proper manipulation of these valves and the use of the attached test hoses allow the user to perform the following services:

1. Test high and low side pressures.
2. Remove air, moisture, and contaminated refrigerant.
3. Purge the system (of refrigerant).
4. Charge the system (with refrigerant).

The manifold valves are designed so that they have no direct effect on gauge readings, but serve only to provide for, or cut off, flow of refrigerant through the manifold. During all testing and hook-up operations, the valves are kept in a close position to avoid disturbing the refrigeration system. The valves are opened only to purge the system or refrigerant or to charge it.

INSPECTION

CAUTION: *The compressed refrigerant used in the air conditioning system expands into the atmosphere at a temperature of –21.7°F (–30°C) or lower. This will freeze any surface, including your eyes, that it contacts.*

Troubleshooting Basic Air Conditioning Problems

Problem	Cause	Solution
There's little or no air coming from the vents (and you're sure it's on)	• The A/C fuse is blown • Broken or loose wires or connections • The on/off switch is defective	• Check and/or replace fuse • Check and/or repair connections • Replace switch
The air coming from the vents is not cool enough	• Windows and air vent wings open • The compressor belt is slipping • Heater is on • Condenser is clogged with debris • Refrigerant has escaped through a leak in the system • Receiver/drier is plugged	• Close windows and vent wings • Tighten or replace compressor belt • Shut heater off • Clean the condenser • Check system • Service system
The air has an odor	• Vacuum system is disrupted • Odor producing substances on the evaporator case • Condensation has collected in the bottom of the evaporator housing	• Have the system checked/repaired • Clean the evaporator case • Clean the evaporator housing drains
System is noisy or vibrating	• Compressor belt or mountings loose • Air in the system	• Tighten or replace belt; tighten mounting bolts • Have the system serviced
Sight glass condition		
Constant bubbles, foam or oil streaks	• Undercharged system	• Charge the system
Clear sight glass, but no cold air	• No refrigerant at all	• Check and charge the system
Clear sight glass, but air is cold	• System is OK	
Clouded with milky fluid	• Receiver drier is leaking dessicant	• Have system checked
Large difference in temperature of lines	• System undercharged	• Charge and leak test the system
Compressor noise	• Broken valves • Overcharged • Incorrect oil level • Piston slap • Broken rings • Drive belt pulley bolts are loose	• Replace the valve plate • Discharge, evacuate and install the correct charge • Isolate the compressor and check the oil level. Correct as necessary. • Replace the compressor • Replace the compressor • Tighten with the correct torque specification
Excessive vibration	• Incorrect belt tension • Clutch loose • Overcharged • Pulley is misaligned	• Adjust the belt tension • Tighten the clutch • Discharge, evacuate and install the correct charge • Align the pulley
Condensation dripping in the passenger compartment	• Drain hose plugged or improperly positioned • Insulation removed or improperly installed	• Clean the drain hose and check for proper installation • Replace the insulation on the expansion valve and hoses
Frozen evaporator coil	• Faulty thermostat • Thermostat capillary tube improperly installed • Thermostat not adjusted properly	• Replace the thermostat • Install the capillary tube correctly • Adjust the thermostat
Low side low—high side low	• System refrigerant is low • Expansion valve is restricted	• Evacuate, leak test and charge the system • Replace the expansion valve
Low side high—high side low	• Internal leak in the compressor—worn	• Remove the compressor cylinder head and inspect the compressor. Replace the valve plate assembly if necessary. If the compressor pistons, rings or

Troubleshooting Basic Air Conditioning Problems (cont.)

Problem	Cause	Solution
Low side high—high side low (cont.)		cylinders are excessively worn or scored replace the compressor
	• Cylinder head gasket is leaking	• Install a replacement cylinder head gasket
	• Expansion valve is defective	• Replace the expansion valve
	• Drive belt slipping	• Adjust the belt tension
Low side high—high side high	• Condenser fins obstructed	• Clean the condenser fins
	• Air in the system	• Evacuate, leak test and charge the system
	• Expansion valve is defective	• Replace the expansion valve
	• Loose or worn fan belts	• Adjust or replace the belts as necessary
Low side low—high side high	• Expansion valve is defective	• Replace the expansion valve
	• Restriction in the refrigerant hose	• Check the hose for kinks—replace if necessary
	• Restriction in the receiver/drier	• Replace the receiver/drier
	• Restriction in the condenser	• Replace the condenser
Low side and high side normal (inadequate cooling)	• Air in the system	• Evacuate, leak test and charge the system
	• Moisture in the system	• Evacuate, leak test and charge the system

In addition, the refrigerant decomposes into a poisonous gas in the presence of a flame. Do not open or disconnect any part of the air conditioning system.

Sight Glass Check

You can safely make a few simple checks to determine if your air conditioning system needs service. The tests work best if the temperature is warm (about 70°F [21.1°C]).

NOTE: *If your vehicle is equipped with an aftermarket air conditioner, the following system check may not apply. You should contact the manufacturer of the unit for instructions on systems checks.*

1. Place the automatic transmission in Park or the manual transmission in Neutral. Set the parking brake.
2. Run the engine at a fast idle (about 1,500 rpm) either with the help of a friend or by temporarily readjusting the idle speed screw.
3. Set the controls for maximum cold with the blower on High.
4. Locate the sight glass in one of the system lines. Usually it is on the left alongside the top of the radiator.
5. If you see bubbles, the system must be recharged. Very likely there is a leak at some point.
6. If there are no bubbles, there is either no refrigerant at all or the system is fully charged. Feel the two hoses going to the belt driven compressor. If they are both at the same temperature, the system is empty and must be recharged.
7. If one hose (high pressure) is warm and the other (low pressure) is cold, the system may be all right. However, you are probably making these tests because you think there is something wrong, so proceed to the next step.
8. Have an assistant in the truck turn the fan control on and off to operate the compressor clutch. Watch the sight glass.
9. If bubbles appear when the clutch is disengaged and disappear when it is engaged, the system is properly charged.
10. If the refrigerant takes more than 45 seconds to bubble when the clutch is disengaged, the system is overcharged. This usually causes poor cooling at low speeds.

WARNING: *If it is determined that the system has a leak, it should be corrected as soon as possible. Leaks may allow moisture to enter and cause a very expensive rust problem.*

Exercise the air conditioner for a few minutes, every two weeks or so, during the cold months. This avoids the possibility of the compressor seals drying out from lack of lubrication.

TESTING THE SYSTEM

1. Park the truck in the shade, at least 5 feet from any walls.
2. Connect a gauge set.
3. Close (clockwise) both gauge set valves.
4. Start the engine, set the parking brake, place the transmission in NEUTRAL and establish an idle of 1,100–1,300 rpm.

5. Run the air conditioning system for full cooling, in the MAX or COLD mode.

6. The low pressure gauge should read 5–20 psi; the high pressure gauge should indicate 120–180 psi.

WARNING: *These pressures are the norm for an ambient temperature of 70–80°F (21–27°C). Higher air temperatures along with high humidity will cause higher system pressures. At idle speed and an ambient temperature of 110°F (43°C), the high pressure reading can exceed 300 psi. Under these extreme conditions, you can keep the pressures down by directing a large electric floor fan through the condenser.*

DISCHARGING THE SYSTEM

1. Remove the caps from the high and low pressure charging valves in the high and low pressure lines.

2. Turn both manifold gauge set hand valves to the fully closed (clockwise) position.

3. Connect the manifold gauge set.

4. If the gauge set hoses do not have the gauge port actuating pins, install fitting adapters T71P–19703–S and R on the manifold gauge set hoses. If the truck does not have a service access gauge port valve, connect the gauge set low pressure hose to the evaporator service access gauge port valve. A special adapter, T77L–19703–A, is required to attach the manifold gauge set to the high pressure service access gauge port valve.

5. Place the end of the center hose away from you and the truck.

6. Open the low pressure gauge valve slightly and allow the system pressure to bleed off.

7. When the system is just about empty, open the high pressure valve very slowly to avoid losing an excessive amount of refrigerant oil. Allow any remaining refrigerant to escape.

EVACUATING THE SYSTEM

NOTE: *This procedure requires the use of a vacuum pump.*

1. Connect the manifold gauge set.

2. Discharge the system.

3. Make sure that the low pressure gauge set hose is connected to the low pressure service gauge port on the top center of the accumulator/drier assembly and the high pressure hose connected to the high pressure service gauge port on the compressor discharge line.

4. Connect the center service hose to the inlet fitting of the vacuum pump.

5. Turn both gauge set valves to the wide open position.

6. Start the pump and note the low side gauge reading.

7. Operate the pump until the low pressure gauge reads 25–30 in.Hg. Continue running the vacuum pump for 10 minutes more. If you've replaced some component in the system, run the pump for an additional 20–30 minutes.

8. Leak test the system. Close both gauge set valves. Turn off the pump. The needle should remain stationary at the point at which the pump was turned off. If the needle drops to zero rapidly, there is a leak in the system which must be repaired.

LEAK TESTING

Some leak tests can be performed with a soapy water solution. There must be at least a 1/2 lb. charge in the system for a leak to be detected. The most extensive leak tests are performed with either a Halide flame type leak tester or the more preferable electronic leak tester.

In either case, the equipment is expensive, and, the use of a Halide detector can be **extremely** hazardous!

CHARGING THE SYSTEM

CAUTION: *NEVER OPEN THE HIGH PRESSURE SIDE WITH A CAN OF REFRIGERANT CONNECTED TO THE SYSTEM! OPENING THE HIGH PRESSURE SIDE WILL OVER PRESSURIZE THE CAN, CAUSING IT TO EXPLODE!*

1. Connect the gauge set.

2. Close (clockwise) both gauge set valves.

3. Connect the center hose to the refrigerant can opener valve.

4. Make sure the can opener valve is closed, that is, the needle is raised, and connect the valve to the can. Open the valve, puncturing the can with the needle.

5. Loosen the center hose fitting at the pressure gauge, allowing refrigerant to purge the hose of air. When the air is bled, tighten the fitting.

CAUTION: *IF THE LOW PRESSURE GAUGE SET HOSE IS NOT CONNECTED TO THE ACCUMULATOR/DRIER, KEEP THE CAN IN AN UPRIGHT POSITION!*

6. Disconnect the wire harness snap-lock connector from the clutch cycling pressure switch and install a jumper wire across the two terminals of the connector.

7. Open the low side gauge set valve and the can valve.

8. Allow refrigerant to be drawn into the system.

9. When no more refrigerant is drawn into the system, start the engine and run it at about 1,500 rpm. Turn on the system and operate it at the full high position. The compressor will

operate and pull refrigerant gas into the system.

NOTE: *To help speed the process, the can may be placed, upright, in a pan of warm water, not exceeding 125°F (52°C).*

10. If more than one can of refrigerant is needed, close the can valve and gauge set low side valve when the can is empty and connect a new can to the opener. Repeat the charging process until the sight glass indicates a full charge. The frost line on the outside of the can will indicate what portion of the can has been used.

CAUTION: *NEVER ALLOW THE HIGH PRESSURE SIDE READING TO EXCEED 240 psi.*

11. When the charging process has been completed, close the gauge set valve and can valve. Remove the jumper wire and reconnect the cycling clutch wire. Run the system for at least five minutes to allow it to normalize. Low pressure side reading should be 4–25 psi; high pressure reading should be 120–210 psi at an ambient temperature of 70–90°F (21–32°C).

12. Loosen both service hoses at the gauges to allow any refrigerant to escape. Remove the gauge set and install the dust caps on the service valves.

NOTE: *Multi-can dispensers are available which allow a simultaneous hook-up of up to four 1 lb. cans of R-12.*

CAUTION: *Never exceed the recommended maximum charge for the system. The maximum charge for systems is 3 lb.*

Windshield Wipers

Intense heat from the sun, snow, and ice, road oils and the chemicals used in windshield washer solvent combine to deteriorate the rubber wiper refills. The refills should be replaced about twice a year or whenever the blades begin to streak or chatter.

WIPER REFILL REPLACEMENT

Normally, if the wipers are not cleaning the windshield properly, only the refill has to be replaced. The blade and arm usually require replacement only in the event of damage. It is not necessary (except on new Tridon® refills) to remove the arm or the blade to replace the refill (rubber part), though you may have to position the arm higher on the glass. You can do this turning the ignition switch on and operating the wipers. When they are positioned where they are accessible, turn the ignition switch off.

There are several types of refills and your vehicle could have any kind, since aftermarket blades and arms may not use exactly the same type refill as the original equipment.

Most Anco® styles use a release button that is pushed down to allow the refill to slide out of the yoke jaws. The new refill slides in and locks in place.

Some Trico® refills are removed by locating where the metal backing strip or the refill is wider. Insert a small screwdriver blade between the frame and metal backing strip. Press down to release the refill from the retaining tab.

Other Trico® blades are unlocked at one end by squeezing 2 metal tabs, and the refill is slid out of the frame jaws. When the new refill is installed, the tabs will click into place, locking the refill.

The polycarbonate type is held in place by a locking lever that is pushed downward out of the groove in the arm to free the refill. When the new refill is installed, it will lock in place automatically.

The Tridon® refill has a plastic backing strip with a notch about 1 in. (25mm) from the end. Hold the blade (frame) on a hard surface so that the frame is tightly bowed. Grip the tip of the backing strip and pull up while twisting counterclockwise. The backing strip will snap out of the retaining tab. Do this for the remaining tabs until the refill is free of the arm. The length of these refills is molded into the end and they should be replaced with identical types.

No matter which type of refill you use, be sure that all of the frame claws engage the refill. Before operating the wipers, be sure that no part of the metal frame is contacting the windshield.

Tires and Wheels

The tires should be rotated as specified in the Maintenance Intervals Chart. Refer to the accompanying illustrations for the recommended rotation patterns.

The tires on your truck should have built-in tread wear indicators, which appear as $^1/_2$ in. (13mm) bands when the tread depth gets as low as $^1/_{16}$ in. (1.5mm). When the indicators appear in 2 or more adjacent grooves, it's time for new tires.

For optimum tire life, you should keep the tires properly inflated, rotate them often and have the wheel alignment checked periodically.

Some late models have the maximum load pressures listed in the V.I.N. plate on the left door frame. In general, pressure of 28–32 psi would be suitable for highway use with moderate loads and passenger truck type tires (load range B, non-flotation) of original equipment size. Pressures should be checked before driving, since pressure can increase as much as 6 psi due to heat. It is a good idea to have an accu-

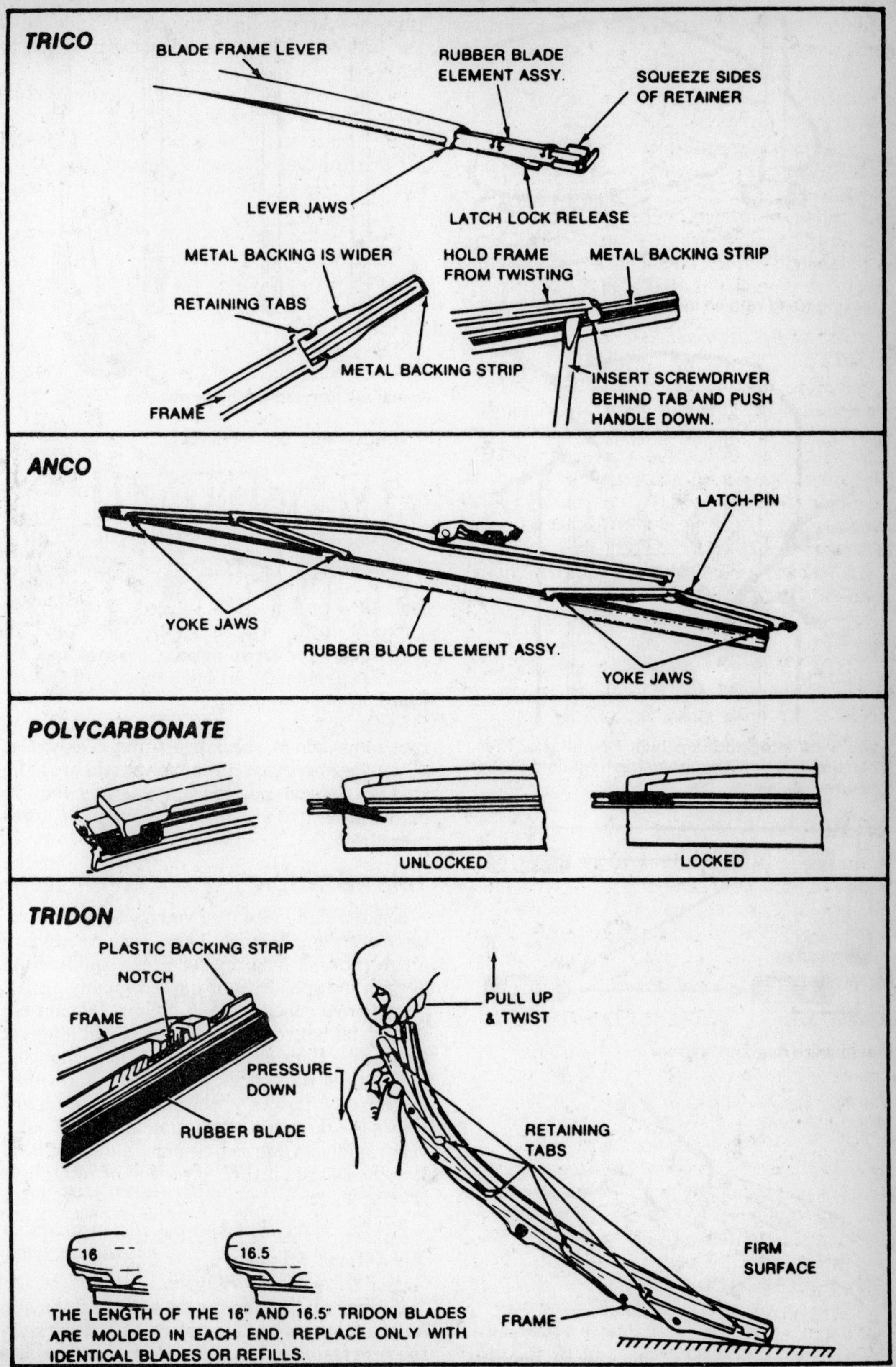

Popular styles of wiper refills

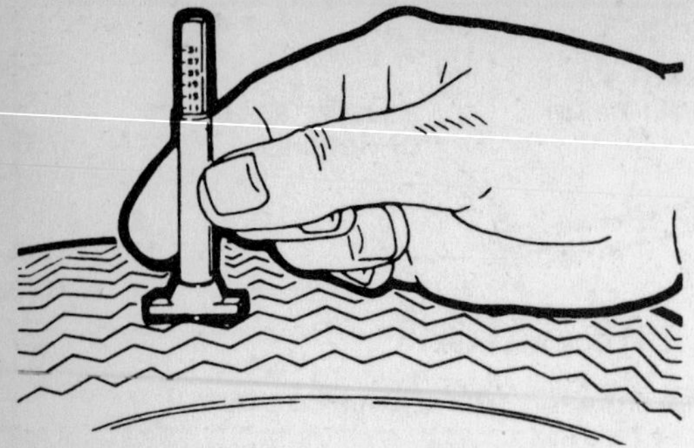

Checking tread with an inexpensive depth gauge

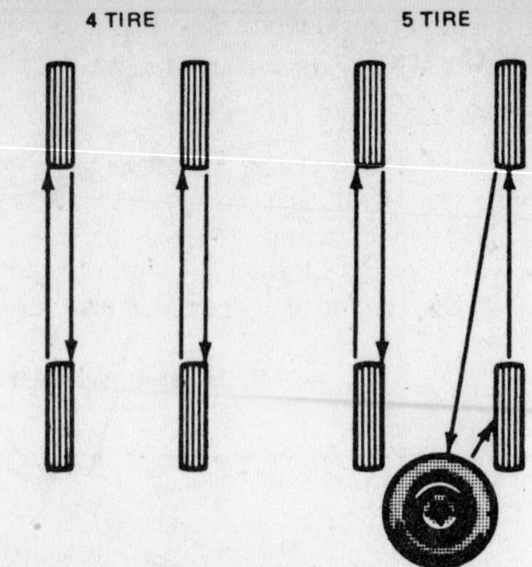

Radial-ply tire rotation diagram

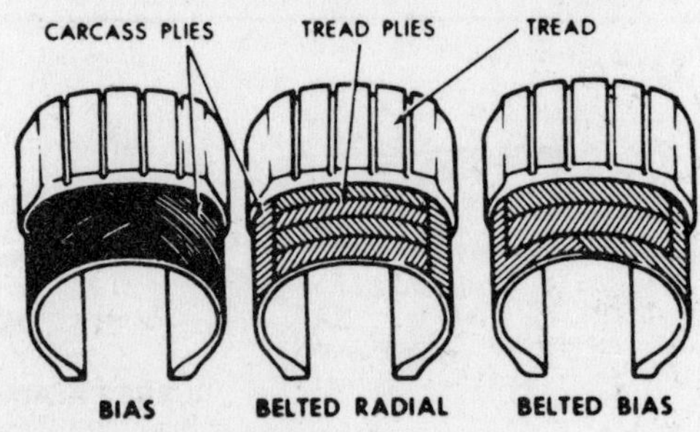

Types of tire construction

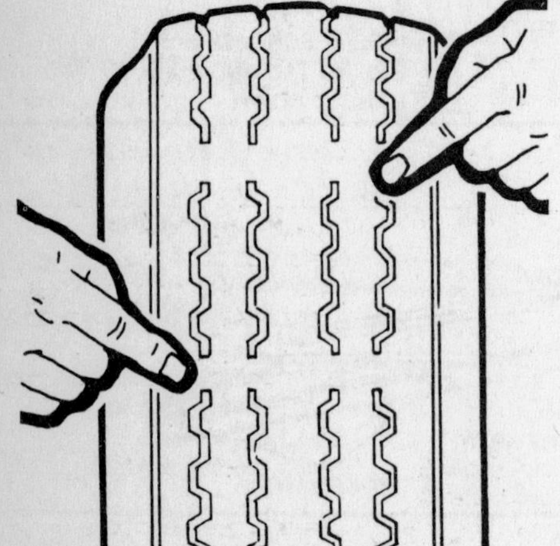

Tread wear indicators are built into all new tires. When they appear, it's time to trash that old rubber for some new skins

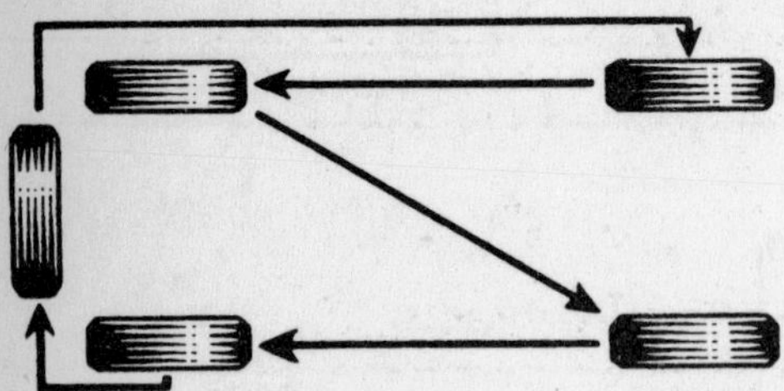

Bias-ply tire rotation diagram

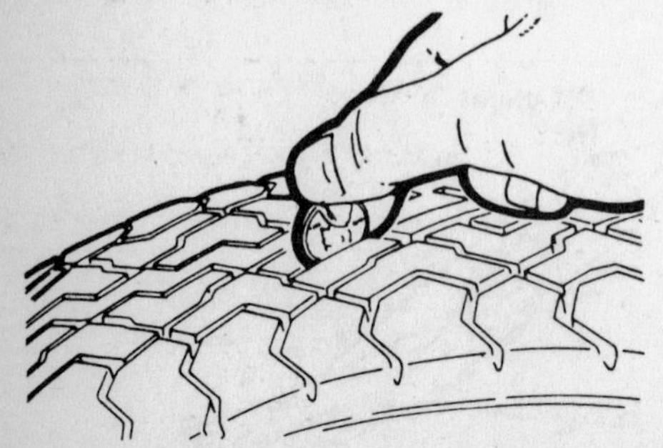

Tread depth can be checked with a penny; when the top of Lincoln's head is visible, it's time for new tires

rate gauge and to check pressures weekly. Not all gauges on service station air pumps are to be trusted. In general, truck type tires require higher pressures and flotation type tires, lower pressures.

TIRE ROTATION

It is recommended that you have the tires rotated every 6,000 miles. There is no way to give a tire rotation diagram for every combination of tires and vehicles, but the accompanying diagrams are a general rule to follow. Radial tires should not be cross-switched; they last longer if their direction of rotation is not changed. Truck tires sometimes have directional tread, indicated by arrows on the sidewalls; the arrow shows the direction of rotation. They will wear very rapidly if reversed. Studded snow tires will lose their studs if their direction of rotation is reversed.

NOTE: *Mark the wheel position or direction of rotation on radial tires or studded snow tires before removing them.*

If your truck is equipped with tires having different load ratings on the front and the rear, the tires should not be rotated front to rear. Rotating these tires could affect tire life (the tires with the lower rating will wear faster, and could become overloaded), and upset the handling of the truck.

TIRE USAGE

The tires on your truck were selected to provide the best all around performance for normal operation when inflated as specified. Oversize tires (Load Range D) will not increase the maximum carrying capacity of the vehicle, although they will provide an extra margin of tread life. Be sure to check overall height before using larger size tires which may cause interference with suspension components or wheel wells. When replacing conventional tire sizes with other tire size designations, be sure to check the manufacturer's recommendations. Interchangeability is not always possible because of differences in load ratings, tire dimensions,

Troubleshooting Basic Wheel Problems

Problem	Cause	Solution
The car's front end vibrates at high speed	• The wheels are out of balance • Wheels are out of alignment	• Have wheels balanced • Have wheel alignment checked/adjusted
Car pulls to either side	• Wheels are out of alignment • Unequal tire pressure • Different size tires or wheels	• Have wheel alignment checked/adjusted • Check/adjust tire pressure • Change tires or wheels to same size
The car's wheel(s) wobbles	• Loose wheel lug nuts • Wheels out of balance • Damaged wheel • Wheels are out of alignment • Worn or damaged ball joint • Excessive play in the steering linkage (usually due to worn parts) • Defective shock absorber	• Tighten wheel lug nuts • Have tires balanced • Raise car and spin the wheel. If the wheel is bent, it should be replaced • Have wheel alignment checked/adjusted • Check ball joints • Check steering linkage • Check shock absorbers
Tires wear unevenly or prematurely	• Incorrect wheel size • Wheels are out of balance • Wheels are out of alignment	• Check if wheel and tire size are compatible • Have wheels balanced • Have wheel alignment checked/adjusted

Troubleshooting Basic Tire Problems

Problem	Cause	Solution
The car's front end vibrates at high speeds and the steering wheel shakes	• Wheels out of balance • Front end needs aligning	• Have wheels balanced • Have front end alignment checked
The car pulls to one side while cruising	• Unequal tire pressure (car will usually pull to the low side) • Mismatched tires • Front end needs aligning	• Check/adjust tire pressure • Be sure tires are of the same type and size • Have front end alignment checked
Abnormal, excessive or uneven tire wear See "How to Read Tire Wear"	• Infrequent tire rotation • Improper tire pressure • Sudden stops/starts or high speed on curves	• Rotate tires more frequently to equalize wear • Check/adjust pressure • Correct driving habits
Tire squeals	• Improper tire pressure • Front end needs aligning	• Check/adjust tire pressure • Have front end alignment checked

Tire Size Comparison Chart

"Letter" sizes			Inch Sizes	Metric-inch Sizes		
"60 Series"	"70 Series"	"78 Series"	1965–77	"60 Series"	"70 Series"	"80 Series"
			5.50-12, 5.60-12	165/60-12	165/70-12	155-12
		Y78-12	6.00-12			
		W78-13	5.20-13	165/60-13	145/70-13	135-13
		Y78-13	5.60-13	175/60-13	155/70-13	145-13
			6.15-13	185/60-13	165/70-13	155-13, P155/80-13
A60-13	A70-13	A78-13	6.40-13	195/60-13	175/70-13	165-13
B60-13	B70-13	B78-13	6.70-13	205/60-13	185/70-13	175-13
			6.90-13			
C60-13	C70-13	C78-13	7.00-13	215/60-13	195/70-13	185-13
D60-13	D70-13	D78-13	7.25-13			
E60-13	E70-13	E78-13	7.75-13			195-13
			5.20-14	165/60-14	145/70-14	135-14
			5.60-14	175/60-14	155/70-14	145-14
			5.90-14			
A60-14	A70-14	A78-14	6.15-14	185/60-14	165/70-14	155-14
	B70-14	B78-14	6.45-14	195/60-14	175/70-14	165-14
	C70-14	C78-14	6.95-14	205/60-14	185/70-14	175-14
D60-14	D70-14	D78-14				
E60-14	E70-14	E78-14	7.35-14	215/60-14	195/70-14	185-14
F60-14	F70-14	F78-14, F83-14	7.75-14	225/60-14	200/70-14	195-14
G60-14	G70-14	G77-14, G78-14	8.25-14	235/60-14	205/70-14	205-14
H60-14	H70-14	H78-14	8.55-14	245/60-14	215/70-14	215-14
J60-14	J70-14	J78-14	8.85-14	255/60-14	225/70-14	225-14
L60-14	L70-14		9.15-14	265/60-14	235/70-14	
	A70-15	A78-15	5.60-15	185/60-15	165/70-15	155-15
B60-15	B70-15	B78-15	6.35-15	195/60-15	175/70-15	165-15
C60-15	C70-15	C78-15	6.85-15	205/60-15	185/70-15	175-15
	D70-15	D78-15				
E60-15	E70-15	E78-15	7.35-15	215/60-15	195/70-15	185-15
F60-15	F70-15	F78-15	7.75-15	225/60-15	205/70-15	195-15
G60-15	G70-15	G78-15	8.15-15/8.25-15	235/60-15	215/70-15	205-15
H60-15	H70-15	H78-15	8.45-15/8.55-15	245/60-15	225/70-15	215-15
J60-15	J70-15	J78-15	8.85-15/8.90-15	255/60-15	235/70-15	225-15
	K70-15		9.00-15	265/60-15	245/70-15	230-15
L60-15	L70-15	L78-15, L84-15	9.15-15			235-15
	M70-15	M78-15				255-15
		N78-15				

Note: Every size tire is not listed and many size comparisons are approximate, based on load ratings. Wider tires than those supplied new with the vehicle, should always be checked for clearance.

wheel well clearances, and rim size. Also due to differences in handling characteristics, 70 Series and 60 Series tires should be used only in pairs on the same axle; radial tires should be used only in sets of four.

The wheels must be the correct width for the tire. Tire dealers have charts of tire and rim compatibility. A mismatch can cause sloppy handling and rapid tread wear. The old rule of thumb is that the tread width should match the rim width (inside bead to inside bead) within an inch. For radial tires, the rim width should be 80% or less of the tire (not tread) width.

The height (mounted diameter) of the new tires can greatly change speedometer accuracy, engine speed at a given road speed, fuel mileage, acceleration, and ground clearance. Tire manufacturers furnish full measurement specifications. Speedometer drive gears are available for correction.

NOTE: *Dimensions of tires marked the same size may vary significantly, even among tires from the same manufacturer.*

The spare tire should be usable, at least for low speed operation, with the new tires.

TIRE DESIGN

For maximum satisfaction, tires should be used in sets of five. Mixing or different types (radial, bias-belted, fiberglass belted) should be avoided. Conventional bias tires are constructed so that the cords run bead-to-bead at an angle. Alternate plies run at an opposite angle. This type of construction gives rigidity to both tread and sidewall. Bias-belted tires are similar in construction to conventional bias ply tires. Belts run at an angle and also at a 90° angle to the bead, as in the radial tire. Tread life is improved considerably over the conventional bias tire. The radial tire differs in construction, but instead of the carcass plies running at an angle of 90° to each other, they run at an angle of 90° to the bead. This gives the tread a great deal of rigidity and the sidewall a great deal of flexibility and accounts for the characteristic bulge associated with radial tires.

Radial tire are recommended for use on all Ford trucks. If they are used, tire sizes and wheel diameters should be selected to maintain ground clearance and tire load capacity equivalent to the minimum specified tire. Radial tires should always be used in sets of five, but in an emergency radial tires can be used with caution on the rear axle only. If this is done, both tires on the rear should be of radial design.

NOTE: *Radial tires should never be used on only the front axle.*

FLUIDS AND LUBRICANTS

Oil and Fuel Recommendations

Gasoline Engines

All 1987–90 Ford pickups and Broncos must use lead-free gasoline.

The recommended oil viscosities for sustained temperatures ranging from below 0°F (–18°C) to above 32°F (0°C) are listed in this chapter. They are broken down into multiviscosities and single viscosities. Multiviscosity oils are recommended because of their wider range of acceptable temperatures and driving conditions.

When adding oil to the crankcase or changing the oil or filter, it is important that oil of an equal quality to original equipment be used in your truck. The use of inferior oils may void the warranty, damage your engine, or both.

The SAE (Society of Automotive Engineers) grade number of oil indicates the viscosity of the oil (its ability to lubricate at a given temperature). The lower the SAE number, the lighter

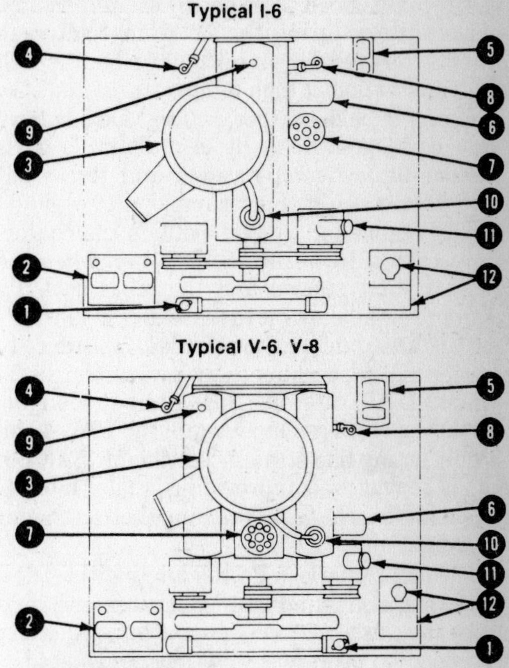

1. Radiator filler cap
2. Battery
3. Air cleaner
4. Automatic transmission dipstick
5. Brake master cylinder
6. Engine oil filter
7. Distributor
8. Engine oil dipstick
9. PCV valve
10. Engine oil filler cap
11. Power steering reservoir
12. Windshield washer reservoir and radiator overflow bottle

Engine compartment service points

The top of the oil can will tell you all you need to know about the oil

the oil; the lower the viscosity, the easier it is to crank the engine in cold weather but the less the oil will lubricate and protect the engine in high temperatures. This number is marked on every oil container.

Oil viscosities should be chosen from those oils recommended for the lowest anticipated temperatures during the oil change interval. Due to the need for an oil that embodies both good lubrication at high temperatures and easy cranking in cold weather, multigrade oils have been developed. Basically, a multigrade oil is thinner at low temperatures and thicker at high temperatures. For example, a 10W–40 oil (the W stands for winter) exhibits the characteristics of a 10 weight (SAE 10) oil when the truck is first started and the oil is cold. Its lighter weight allows it to travel to the lubricating surfaces quicker and offer less resistance to starter motor cranking than, say, a straight 30 weight (SAE 30) oil. But after the engine reaches operating temperature, the 10W–40 oil begins acting like straight 40 weight (SAE 40) oil, its heavier weight providing greater lubrication with less chance of foaming than a straight 30 weight oil.

The API (American Petroleum Institute) designations, also found on the oil container, indicates the classification of engine oil used under certain given operating conditions. Only oils designated for use Service SF/SG heavy duty detergent should be used in your truck. Oils of the SF/SG type perform may functions inside the engine besides their basic lubrication. Through a balanced system of metallic detergents and polymeric dispersants, the oil prevents high and low temperature deposits and also keeps sludge and dirt particles in suspension. Acids, particularly sulphuric acid, as well as other by-products of engine combustion are neutralized by the oil. If these acids are allowed to concentrate, they can cause corrosion and rapid wear of the internal engine parts.

CAUTION: *Non-detergent motor oils or straight mineral oils should not be used in your Ford gasoline engine.*

Diesel Engines

Diesel engines require different engine oil from those used in gasoline engines. Besides doing the things gasoline engine oil does, diesel oil must also deal with increased engine heat and the diesel blow-by gases, which create sulphuric acid, a high corrosive.

Under the American Petroleum Institute (API) classifications, gasoline engine oil codes begin with an **S**, and diesel engine oil codes begin with a **C**. This first letter designation is followed by a second letter code which explains what type of service (heavy, moderate, light) the oil is meant for. For example, the top of a typical oil can will include: API SERVICES SG, CD. This means the oil in the can is a superior, heavy duty engine oil when used in a diesel engine.

Many diesel manufacturers recommend an oil with both gasoline and diesel engine API classifications.

NOTE: *Ford specifies the use of an engine oil conforming to API service categories of both SG and CD. DO NOT use oils labeled as only SG or only CD as they could cause engine damage.*

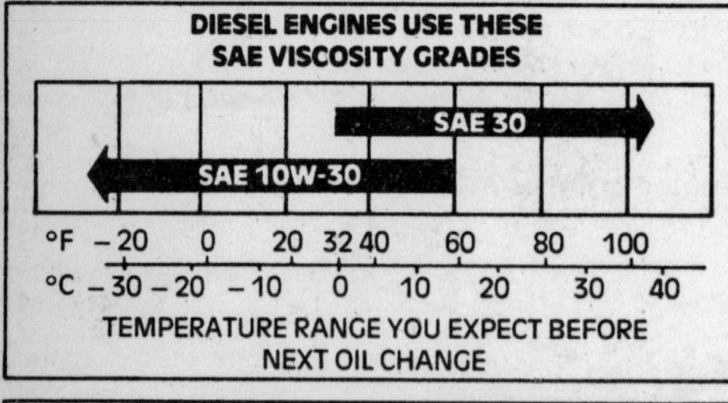

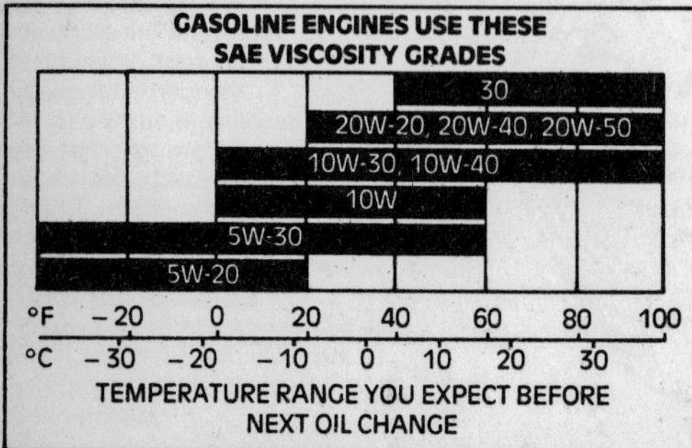

Engine oil viscosities

FUEL

Fuel makers produce two grades of diesel fuel, No. 1 and No. 2, for use in automotive diesel engines. Generally speaking, No. 2 fuel is recommended over No. 1 for driving in temperatures above 20°F (–7°C). In fact, in many areas, No. 2 diesel is the only fuel available. By comparison, No. 2 diesel fuel is less volatile than No. 1 fuel, and gives better fuel economy. No. 2 fuel is also a better injection pump lubricant.

Two important characteristics of diesel fuel are its cetane number and its viscosity.

The cetane number of a diesel fuel refers to the ease with which a diesel fuel ignites. High cetane numbers mean that the fuel will ignite with relative ease or that it ignites well at low temperatures. Naturally, the lower the cetane number, the higher the temperature must be to ignite the fuel. Most commercial fuels have cetane numbers that range from 35 to 65. No.

1 diesel fuel generally has a higher cetane rating than No. 2 fuel.

Viscosity is the ability of a liquid, in this case diesel fuel, to flow. Using straight No. 2 diesel fuel below 20°F (–7°C) can cause problems, because this fuel tends to become cloudy, meaning wax crystals begin forming in the fuel. 20°F (–7°C) is often call the cloud point for No. 2 fuel. In extremely cold weather, No. 2 fuel can stop flowing altogether. In either case, fuel flow is restricted, which can result in no start condition or poor engine performance. Fuel manufacturers often winterize No. 2 diesel fuel by using various fuel additives and blends (no. 1 diesel fuel, kerosene, etc.) to lower its winter time viscosity. Generally speaking, though, No. 1 diesel fuel is more satisfactory in extremely cold weather.

NOTE: *No. 1 and No. 2 diesel fuels will mix and burn with no ill effects, although the engine manufacturer recommends one or the other. Consult the owner's manual for information.*

Depending on local climate, most fuel manufacturers make winterized No. 2 fuel available seasonally.

Many automobile manufacturers publish pamphlets giving the locations of diesel fuel stations nationwide. Contact the local dealer for information.

Do not substitute home heating oil for automotive diesel fuel. While in some cases, home heating oil refinement levels equal those of diesel fuel, many times they are far below diesel engine requirements. The result of using dirty home heating oil will be a clogged fuel system, in which case the entire system may have to be dismantled and cleaned.

One more word on diesel fuels. Don't thin diesel fuel with gasoline in cold weather. The lighter gasoline, which is more explosive, will cause rough running at the very least, and may cause extensive damage to the fuel system if enough is used.

OIL LEVEL CHECK

Check the engine oil level every time you fill the gas tank. The oil level should be above the ADD mark and not above the FULL mark on the dipstick. Make sure that the dipstick is inserted into the crankcase as far as possible and that the vehicle is resting on level ground. Also, allow a few minutes after turning off the engine for the oil to drain into the pan or an inaccurate reading will result.

1. Open the hood and remove the engine oil dipstick.
2. Wipe the dipstick with a clean, lint-free rag and reinsert it. Be sure to insert it all the way.
3. Pull out the dipstick and note the oil level. It should be between the **SAFE** (MAX) mark and the **ADD** (MIN) mark.
4. If the level is below the lower mark, replace the dipstick and add fresh oil to bring the level within the proper range. Do not overfill.
5. Recheck the oil level and close the hood.

NOTE: *Use a multi-grade oil with API classification SG.*

OIL AND FILTER CHANGE

NOTE: *The engine oil and oil filter should be changed at the same time, at the recommended intervals on the maintenance schedule chart.*

The oil should be changed more frequently if the vehicle is being operated in very dusty areas. Before draining the oil, make sure that the engine is at operating temperature. Hot oil will hold more impurities in suspension and will flow better, allowing the removal of more oil and dirt.

Loosen the drain plug with a wrench, then, unscrew the plug with your fingers, using a rag to shield your fingers from the heat. Push in on

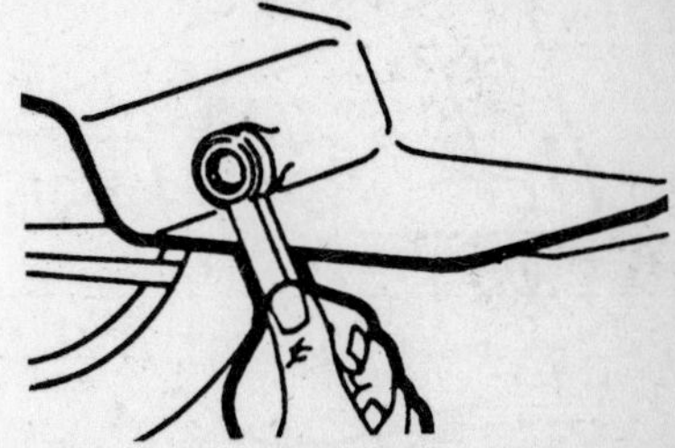

Loosen, but do not remove, the drain plug on the bottom of the oil pan. Get your drain pan ready

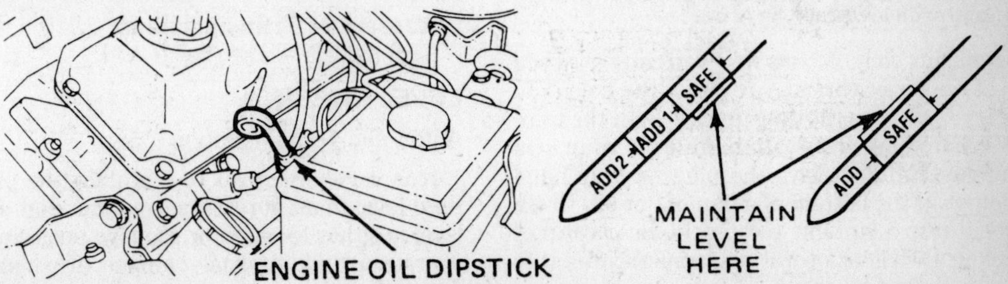

Checking engine oil level

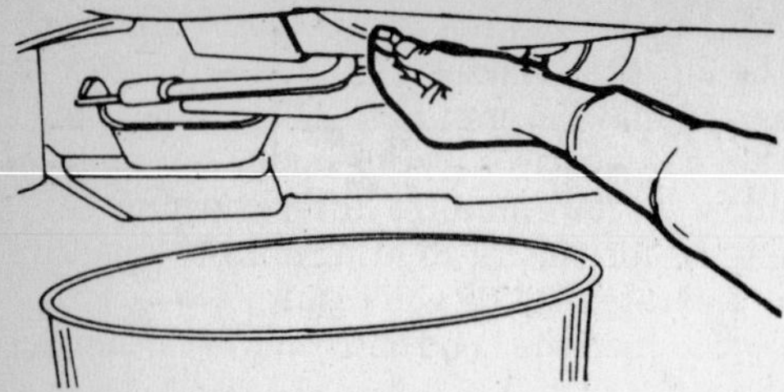

Unscrew the plug by hand. Keep an inward pressure on the plug as you unscrew it, so the oil won't escape until you pull the plug away.

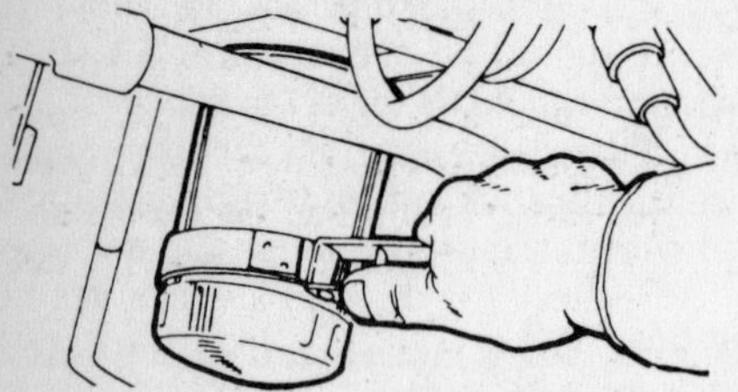

Move the drain pan underneath the oil filter. Use a strap wrench to remove the filter – remember it is still filled with about a quart of hot, dirty oil

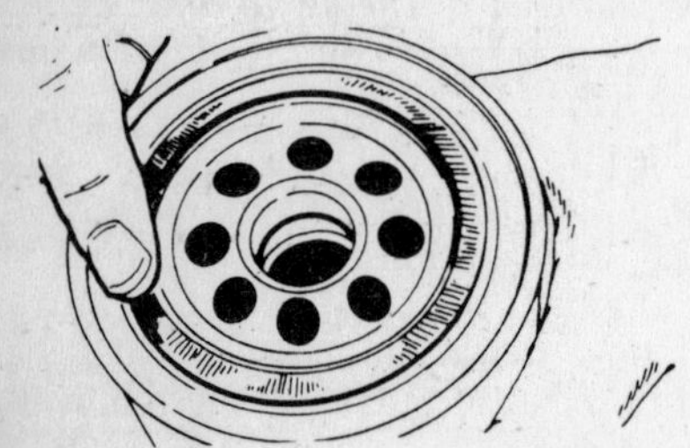

Wipe clean engine oil around the rubber gasket on the new filter. This helps ensure a good seal

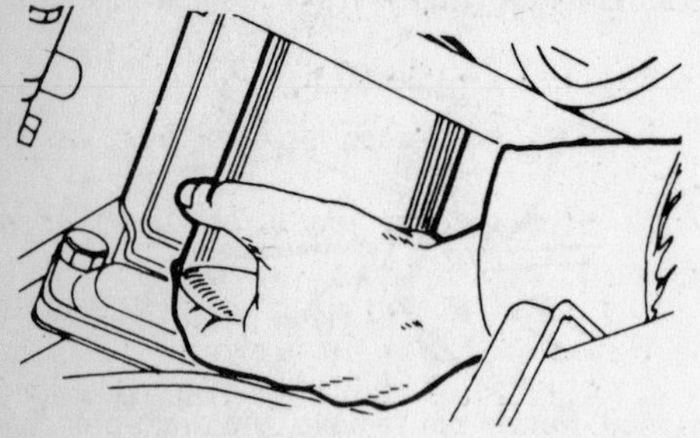

Install the new filter by hand only; DO NOT use a strap wrench to install

the plug as you unscrew it so you can feel when all of the screw threads are out of the hole. You can then remove the plug quickly with the minimum amount of oil running down your arm and you will also have the plug in your hand and not in the bottom of a pan of hot oil. Drain the oil into a suitable receptacle. Be careful of the oil. If it is at operating temperatures it is hot enough to burn you.

The oil filter is located on the left side of all

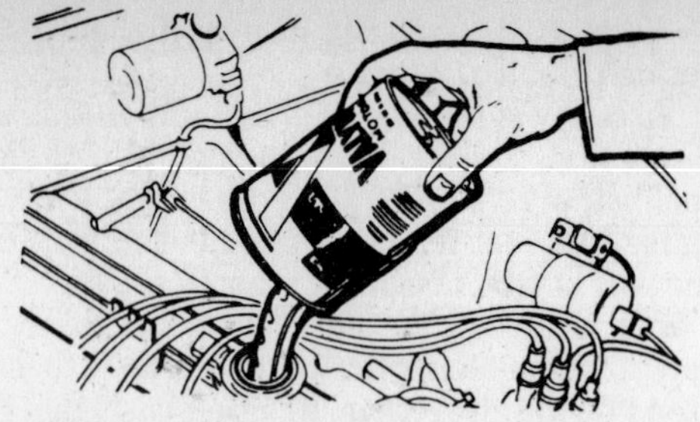

Don't forget to install the drain plug before refilling the engine with fresh oil

the engines installed in Ford trucks, for longest engine life, it should be changed every time the oil is changed. To remove the filter, you may need an oil filter wrench since the filter may have been fitted too tightly and the heat from the engine may have made it even tighter. A filter wrench can be obtained at an auto parts store and is well worth the investment, since it will save you a lot of grief. Loosen the filter with the filter wrench. With a rag wrapped around the filter, unscrew the filter from the boss on the side of the engine. Be careful of hot oil that will run down the side of the filter. Make sure that you have a pan under the filter before you start to remove it from the engine; should some of the hot oil happen to get on you, you will have a place to dump the filter in a hurry. Wipe the base of the mounting boss with a clean, dry cloth. When you install the new filter, smear a small amount of oil on the gasket with your finger, just enough to coat the entire surface, where it comes in contact with the mounting plate. When you tighten the filter, rotate if only a half turn after it comes in contact with the mounting boss.

Transmission

FLUID RECOMMENDATIONS

Manual Transmissions:

- All 1987 models – SAE 85W/90
- All 1988 models – Dexron®II ATF
- 1989–90 4-speed models – SAE 85W/90
- 1989–90 5-speed models – Dexron®II ATF

Automatic Transmissions:

- All models – Dexron®II ATF

LEVEL CHECK

Automatic Transmissions

It is very important to maintain the proper fluid level in an automatic transmission. If the level is either too high or too low, poor shifting operation and internal damage are likely to occur. For this reason a regular check of the fluid level is essential.

1. Drive the vehicle for 15–20 minutes to allow the transmission to reach operating temperature.

2. Park the truck on a level surface, apply the parking brake and leave the engine idling. Shift the transmission and engage each gear, then place the gear selector in **P** (PARK).

3. Wipe away any dirt in the areas of the transmission dipstick to prevent it from falling into the filler tube. Withdraw the dipstick, wipe it with a clean, lint-free rag and reinsert it until it seats.

4. Withdraw the dipstick and note the fluid

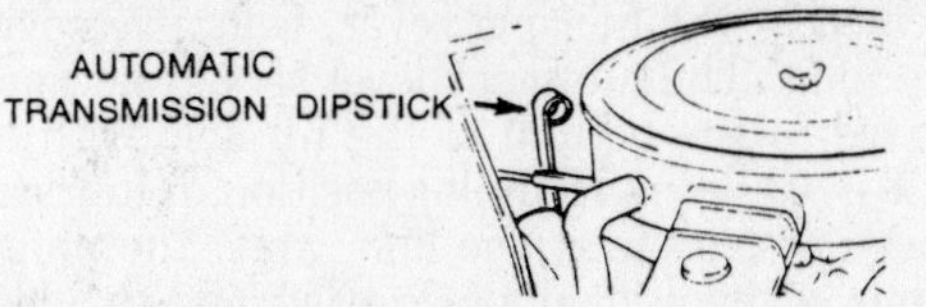

Automatic transmission dipstick is found towards the rear of the engine

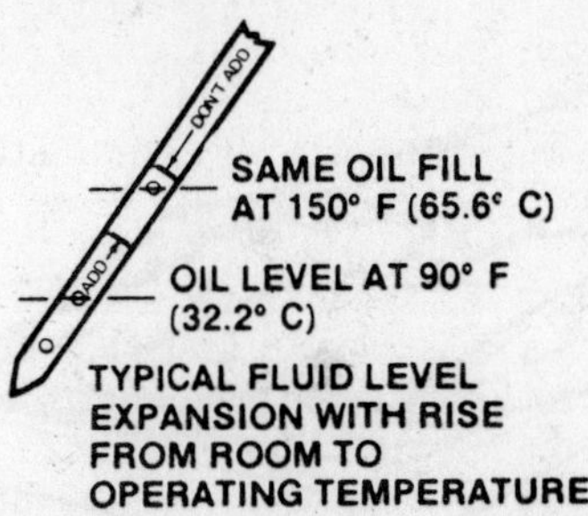

Checking automatic transmission fluid level. Check transmission when it is warmed to operating temperature

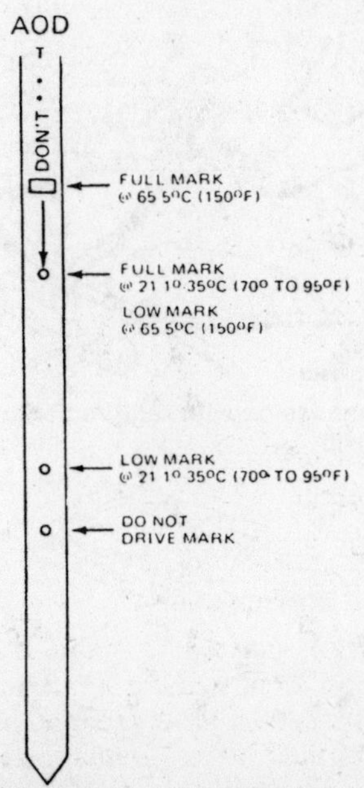

AOD dipstick marks

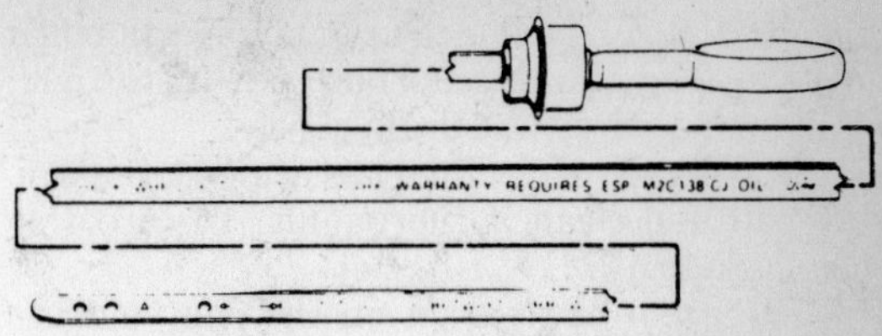

C6 automatic transmission dipstick (note the special fluid designation)

level. It should be between the upper (FULL) mark and the lower (ADD) mark.

5. If the level is below the lower mark, use a funnel and add fluid in small quantities through the dipstick filler neck. Keep the engine running while adding fluid and check the level after each small amount. Do not overfill.

Manual Transmission

The fluid level should be checked every 6 months/6,000 miles, whichever comes first.

1. Park the truck on a level surface, turn off the engine, apply the parking brake and block the wheels.

2. Remove the filler plug from the side of the transmission case with a proper size wrench. The fluid level should be even with the bottom of the filler hole.

3. If additional fluid is necessary, add it through the filler hole using a siphon pump or squeeze bottle.

4. Replace the filler plug; do not over tighten.

DRAIN AND REFILL

Automatic Transmission

1. Raise the truck and support on jackstands.

2. Place a drain pan under the transmission.

3. Loosen the pan attaching bolts and drain the fluid from the transmission.

4. When the fluid has drained to the level of

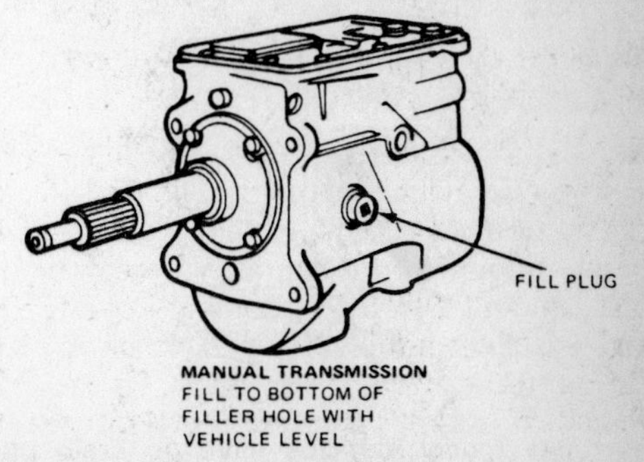

Manual transmission filler location

the pan flange, remove the remaining pan bolts working from the rear and both sides of the pan to allow it to drop and drain slowly.

5. When all of the fluid has drained, remove the pan and clean it thoroughly. Discard the pan gasket.

6. Place a new gasket on the pan, and install the pan on the transmission. Tighten the attaching bolts to 12–16 ft. lbs.

7. Add three 3 quarts of fluid to the transmission through the filler tube.

8. Lower the vehicle. Start the engine and move the gear selector through shift pattern. Allow the engine to reach normal operating temperature.

9. Check the transmission fluid. Add fluid, if necessary, to maintain correct level.

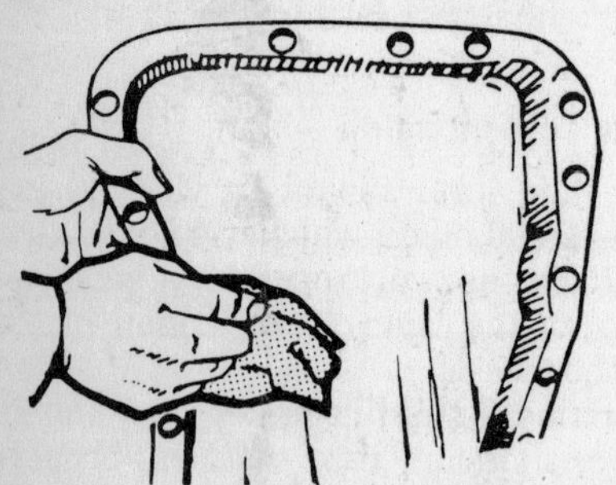

Clean the pan thoroughly with a safe solvent and allow it to air dry

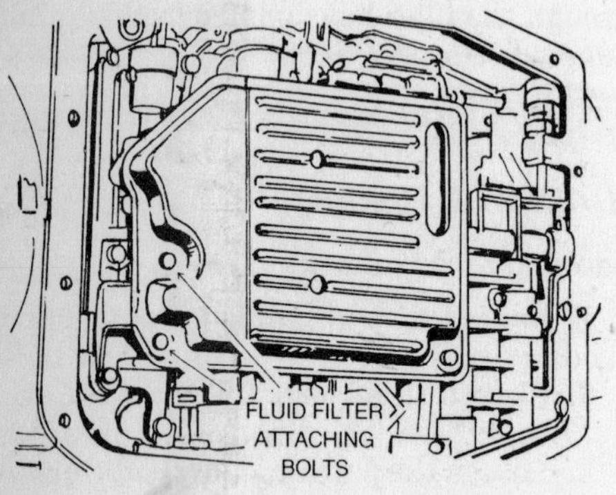

Fluid filter, automatic overdrive (AOD)

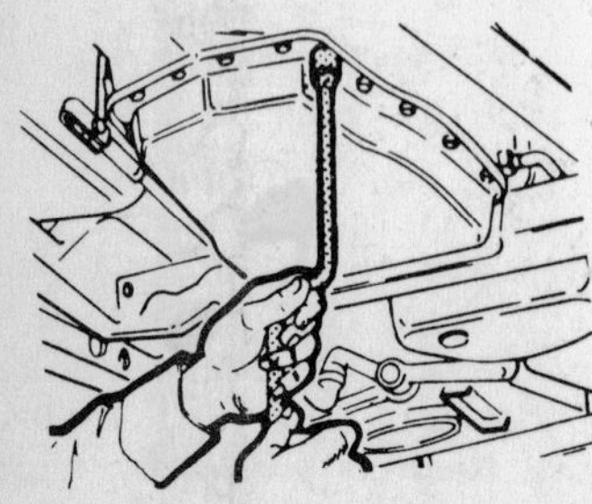

Many late model vehicles have no drain plug. Loosen the pan bolts and allow one corner of the pan to hang, so that the fluid will drain out

Manual Transmission

1. Place a suitable drain pan under the transmission.

2. Remove the drain plug and allow the gear lube to drain out.

3. Replace the drain plug, remove the filler plug and fill the transmission to the proper level with the required fluid.

4. Reinstall the filler plug.

Front (4WD) and Rear Axles

FLUID LEVEL CHECK

Clean the area around the fill plug, which is located in the housing cover, before removing the plug. The lubricant level should be maintained to the bottom of the fill hole with the axle in its normal running position. If lubricant does not appear at the hole when the plug is removed, additional lubricant should be added. Use hypoid gear lubricant SAE 80 or 90.

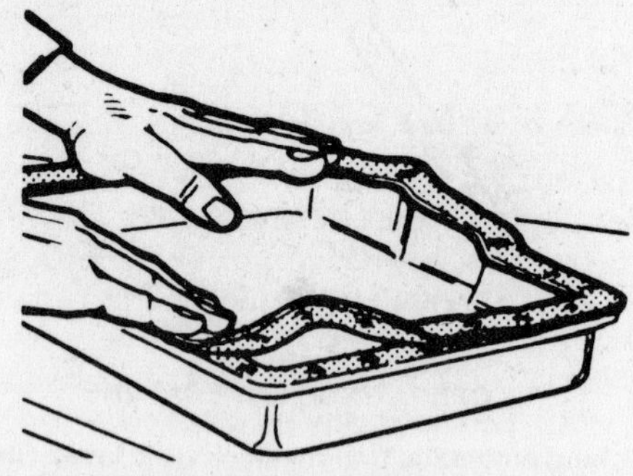

Install a new pan gasket

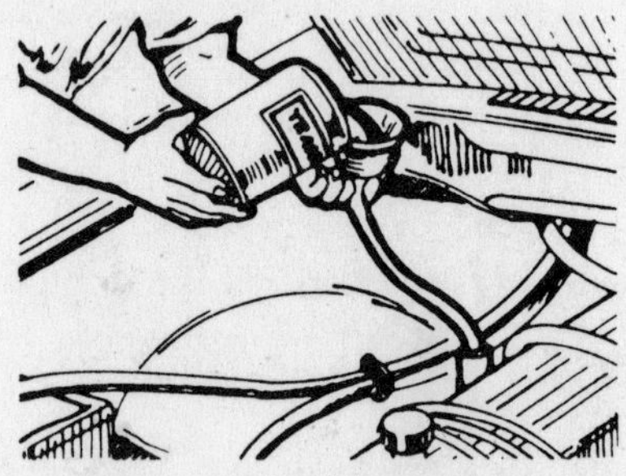

Fill the transmission with required amount of fluid. Do not overfill

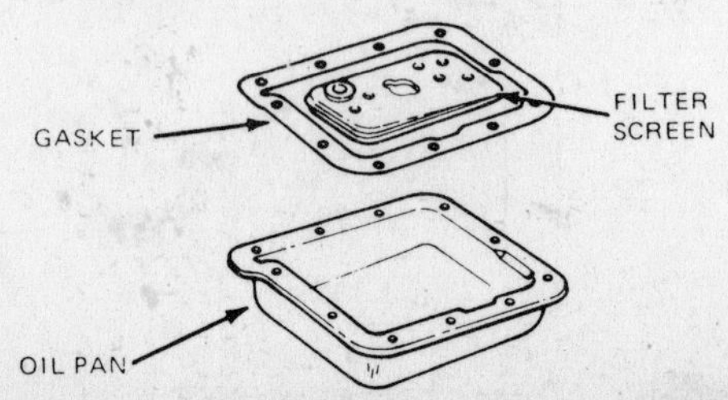

Automatic transmission filters are found above the transmission oil pan

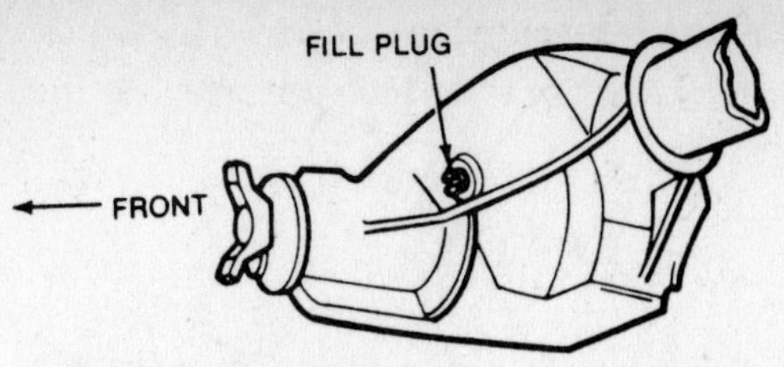

Differential fill plug location, 2-wheel drive shown. 4×4 front axle similar

NOTE: *If the differential is of the limited slip type, be sure and use special limited slip differential additive.*

DRAIN AND REFILL

Drain and refill the front and rear axle housing every 24,000 miles, or every day if the vehicle is operated in deep water. Remove the oil with a suction gun. Refill the axle housings with the proper oil. Be sure and clean the area around the drain plug before removing the plug. See the section on level checks.

Brake Master Cylinder

The master cylinder reservoir is located under the hood, on the left side firewall. Before removing the master cylinder reservoir cap, make sure the vehicle is resting on level ground and clean all dirt away from the top of the master cylinder. Pry off the retaining clip or unscrew the holddown bolt and remove the cap. The brake fluid level should be within $^1/_4$ in. (6mm) of the top of the reservoir.

If the level of the brake fluid is less than half the volume of the reservoir, it is advised that you check the brake system for leaks. Leaks in the hydraulic brake system most commonly occur at the wheel cylinder.

There is a rubber diaphragm in the top of the master cylinder cap. As the fluid level lowers in the reservoir due to normal brake shoe wear or leakage, the diaphragm takes up the space. This is to prevent the loss of brake fluid out the vented cap and contamination by dirt. After filling the master cylinder to the proper level with heavy duty brake fluid, but before replacing the cap, fold the rubber diaphragm up into the cap, then replace the cap in the reservoir and tighten the retaining bolt or snap the retaining clip into place.

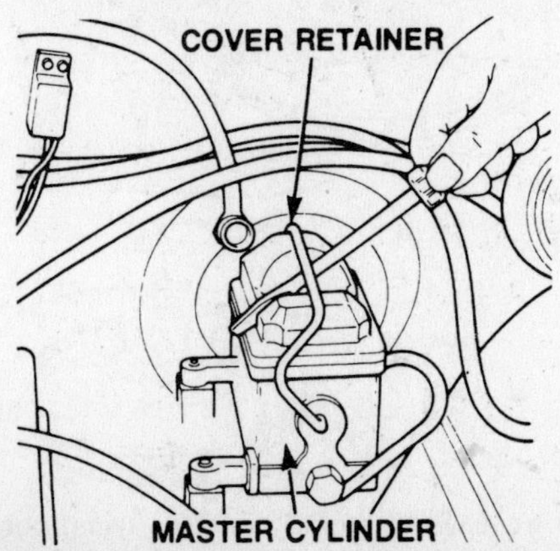

Prying off the master cylinder retaining wire

Hydraulic Clutch Reservoir

The hydraulic fluid reservoirs on these systems are mounted on the firewall. Fluid level checks are performed like those on the brake hydraulic system. The proper fluid level is indicated by a step on the reservoir. Keep the reservoir topped up with Ford Heavy-Duty Brake fluid or equivalent; do not overfill.

CAUTION: *Carefully clean the top and sides of the reservoir before opening, to prevent contamination of the system with dirt, etc. Remove the reservoir diaphragm before adding fluid, and replace after filling.*

See the illustration of the hydraulic clutch assembly in Chapter 7.

Steering Gear

2-Wheel Drive

1. Center the steering wheel.
2. Remove the steering gear housing filler plug.
3. Remove the lower cover-to-housing attaching bolt.
4. With a clean punch or similar object, clean out or push the loose lubricant in the filler plug hole and cover-to-housing attaching bolt hole inward.
5. Slowly turn the steering wheel to the left until the linkage reaches its stop. Lubricant should rise within the cover lower bolt hole.
6. Slowly turn the steering wheel to the right until the linkage reaches its stop. Lubricant should rise within the filler plug hole.
7. If lubricant does not rise in both of the holes, add steering gear lubricant until it comes out both the holes during the check.
8. Install the lower cover-to-housing attaching bolt and the filler plug.

4-Wheel Drive

1. Remove the filler plug from the sector shaft cover.
2. Check to see if the lubricant level is visible in the filler plug tower. If the lubricant is visible, install the filler plug. If the lubricant is not visible, add steering gear lubricant until the lubricant is visible about 1 in. (25mm) from the top of the hole in the filler plug tower.
3. Replace the filler plug.

Power Steering Reservoir

Position the vehicle on level ground. Run the engine until the fluid is at normal operating temperature. Turn the steering wheel all the way to the left and right several times. Position the wheels in the straight ahead position, then shut off the engine. Check the fluid level on the dipstick which is attached to the reservoir cap. The level should be between the ADD and FULL marks on the dipstick. Add fluid accordingly. Do not overfill. Use power steering fluid.

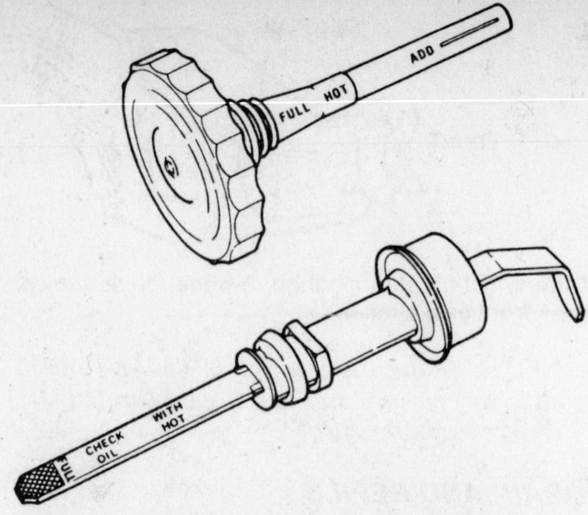

Typical power steering pump reservoir dipsticks

Transfer Case

FLUID LEVEL CHECK

Position the vehicle on level ground. Remove the transfer case fill plug located on the left side of the transfer case. The fluid level should be up to the fill hole. If lubricant doesn't run out when the plug is removed, add lubricant until it does run out and then replace the fill plug. Use SAE 50 lubricant when the air temperature averages above 10°F and SAE 30 lubricant when the air temperature averages below 10°F.

DRAIN AND REFILL

The transfer case is serviced at the same time and in the same manner as the transmission. Clean the area around the filler and drain plugs and remove the filler plug on the side of the transfer case. Remove the drain plug on the bottom of the transfer case and allow the lubricant to drain completely.

Clean and install the drain plug. Add the proper lubricant. See the section on level checks.

Chassis Greasing

The lubrication chart indicates where the grease fittings are located. The vehicle should be greased according to the intervals in the Preventive Maintenance Schedule at the end of this chapter.

2-Wheel Drive Front Wheel Bearings

ADJUSTMENT

The front wheels each rotate on a set of opposed, tapered roller bearings as shown in the accompanying illustration. The grease retainer at the inside of the hub prevents lubricant from leaking into the brake drum.

F-150, F-250, F-350
F-Super Duty Chassis/Cab

1. Raise and support the front end on jackstands.
2. Remove the grease cap and remove excess grease from the end of the spindle.
3. Remove the cotter pin and nut lock shown in the illustration.
4. Rotate the wheel, hub and drum assembly while tightening the adjusting nut to 17–25 ft. lbs. in order to seat the bearings.
5. Back off the adjusting nut 1/2, then retighten the adjusting nut to 10–15 inch lbs.
6. Locate the nut lock on the adjusting nut so that the castellations on the lock are lined up with the cotter pin hole in the spindle.
7. Install the new cotter pin, bending the ends of the cotter pin around the castellated flange of the nut lock.

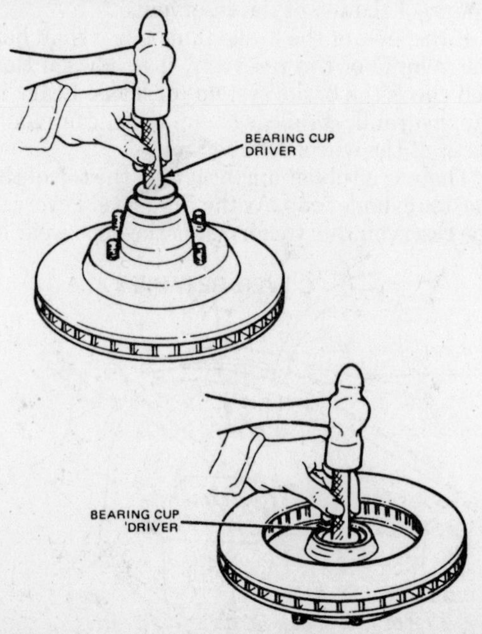

2WD front wheel bearing removal using bearing driver

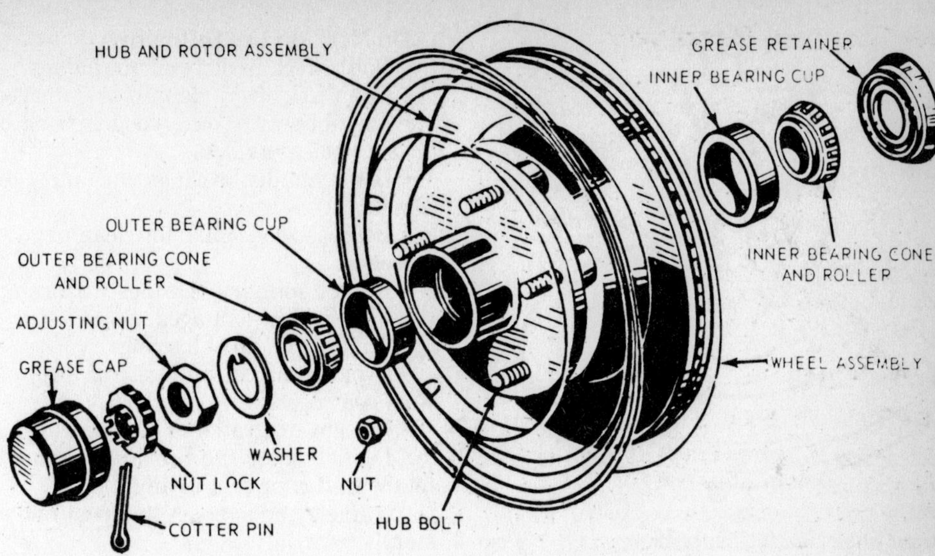

Front hub, bearing, and grease seal with disc brakes — 2WD

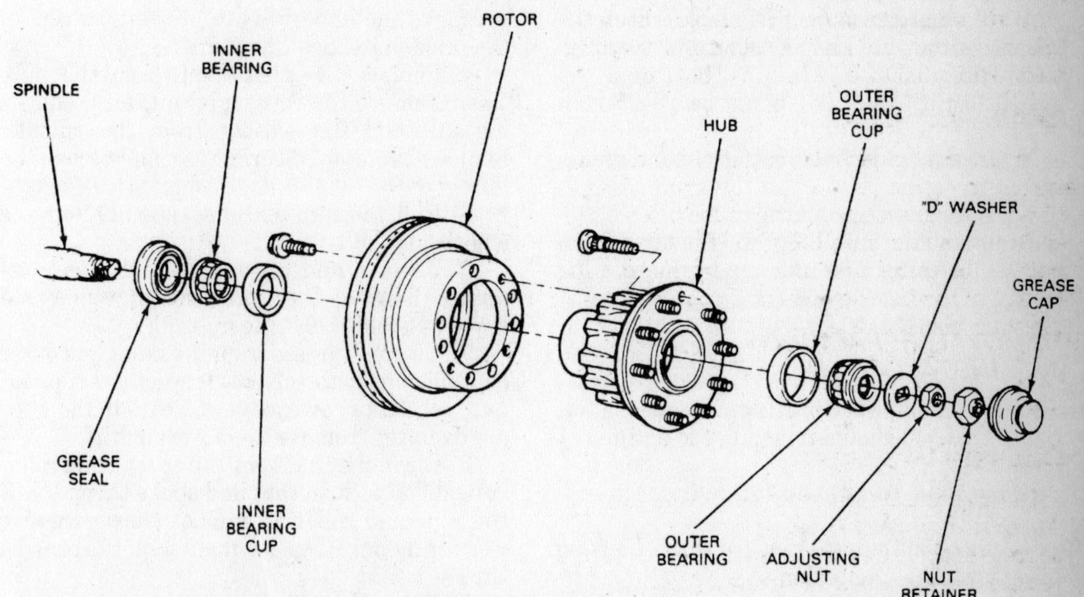

Front hub, rotor, bearings and related parts for the F-Super Duty

8. Check the wheel for proper rotation, then install the grease cap. If the wheel still does not rotate properly, inspect and clean or replace the wheel bearings and cups.

F-Super Duty Stripped Chassis Motor Home Chassis

1. Raise and support the front end on jackstands.
2. Remove the grease cap and remove excess grease from the end of the spindle.
3. Remove the cotter pin and nut lock shown in the illustration.
4. Loosen the adjusting nut 3 full turns. Obtain a clearance between the brake rotor and brake pads by rocking the wheel in and out several times to push the pads away from the rotor. If that doesn't work, you'll have to remove the caliper (see Chapter 9). The rotor must turn freely.

5. Tighten the adjusting nut to 17–25 ft. lbs. while rotating the rotor in the opposite direction.

6. Back off the adjusting nut 120–180° (1/3–1/2 turn).

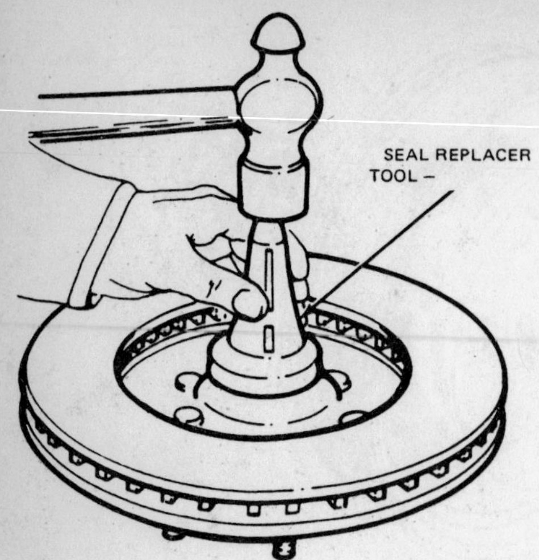

2WD front wheel bearing installation

7. Tighten the adjusting nut to 18–20 inch lbs. while rotating the rotor.

8. If a dial indicator is available, check the endplay at the hub. Endplay should be 0.00024–0.0050 in. (0.006–0.127mm). The torque required to turn the hub should be 10–25 inch lbs.

9. Install the locknut, cotter pin and grease cap.

10. If removed, install the caliper.

11. Install the wheel. Torque the lug nuts to 140 ft. lbs. After 500 miles, retorque the lug nuts.

REMOVAL, REPACKING, AND INSTALLATION

Before handling the bearings, there are a few things that you should remember to do and not to do.

Remember to DO the following:

- Remove all outside dirt from the housing before exposing the bearing.
- Treat a used bearing as gently as you would a new one.
- Work with clean tools in clean surroundings.
- Use clean, dry canvas gloves, or at least clean, dry hands.
- Clean solvents and flushing fluids are a must.
- Use clean paper when laying out the bearings to dry.
- Protect disassembled bearings from rust and dirt. Cover them up.
- Use clean rags to wipe bearings.
- Keep the bearings in oil-proof paper when they are to be stored or are not in use.
- Clean the inside of the housing before replacing the bearing.

Do NOT do the following:

- Don't work in dirty surroundings.
- Don't use dirty, chipped or damaged tools.
- Try not to work on wooden work benches or use wooden mallets.
- Don't handle bearings with dirty or moist hands.
- Do not use gasoline for cleaning; use a safe solvent.
- Do not spin-dry bearings with compressed air. They will be damaged.
- Do not spin dirty bearings.
- Avoid using cotton waste or dirty cloths to wipe bearings.
- Try not to scratch or nick bearing surfaces.
- Do not allow the bearing to come in contact with dirt or rust at any time.

1. Raise and support the front end on jackstands.

2. Remove the wheel cover. Remove the wheel.

3. Remove the caliper from the disc and wire it to the underbody to prevent damage to the brake hose. See Chapter 9

4. Remove the grease cap from the hub. Then, remove the cotter pin, nut lock, adjusting nut and flat washer from the spindle. Remove the outer bearing assembly from the hub.

5. Pull the hub and disc assembly off the wheel spindle.

6. Remove and discard the old grease retainer. Remove the inner bearing cone and roller assembly from the hub.

7. Clean all grease from the inner and outer bearing cups with solvent. Inspect the cups for pits, scratches, or excessive wear. If the cups are damaged, remove them with a drift.

8. Clean the inner and outer cone and roller assemblies with solvent and shake them dry. If the cone and roller assemblies show excessive wear or damage, replace them with the bearing cups as a unit.

9. Clean the spindle and the inside of the hub with solvent to thoroughly remove all old grease.

10. Covering the spindle with a clean cloth, brush all loose dirt and dust from the brake assembly. Remove the cloth carefully so as to not get dirt on the spindle.

11. If the inner and/or outer bearing cups were removed, install the replacement cups on the hub. Be sure that the cups seat properly in the hub.

12. It is imperative that all old grease be removed from the bearings and surrounding surfaces before repacking. The new lithium-based grease is not compatible with the sodium base grease used in the past.

13. Install the hub and disc on the wheel spin-

dle. To prevent damage to the grease retainer and spindle threads, keep the hub centered on the spindle.

14. Install the outer bearing cone and roller assembly and the flat washer on the spindle. Install the adjusting nut.

15. Adjust the wheel bearings by torquing the adjusting nut to 17–25 ft. lbs. with the wheel rotating to seat the bearing. Then back off the adjusting nut 1/2 turn. Retighten the adjusting nut to 10–15 inch lbs. Install the locknut so that the castellations are aligned with the cotter pin hole. Install the cotter pin. Bend the ends of the cotter pin around the castellations of the locknut to prevent interference with the radio static collector in the grease cap. Install the grease cap.

WARNING: *New bolts must be used when servicing floating caliper units. The upper bolt must be tightened first. For caliper service see Chapter 9.*

16. Install the wheels.

17. Install the wheel cover.

Manual Free Running Hub

REMOVAL AND INSTALLATION

1. To remove hub, first separate cap assembly from body assembly by removing the six (6) socket head capscrews from the cap assembly and slip apart.

2. Remove snapring (retainer ring) from the end of the axle shaft.

3. Remove the lock ring seated in the groove of the wheel hub. The body assembly will now slide out of the wheel hub. If necessary, use an appropriate puller to remove the body assembly.

4. Install hub in reverse order of removal. Torque socket head capscrews to 30–35 inch lbs.

Automatic Locking Hubs

REMOVAL AND INSTALLATION

1. Remove the 5 capscrews (Torx® bit TX25) and remove the hub cap assembly from the hub.

NOTE: *Take care to avoid dropping the spring, ball bearing, bearing race or retainer!*

2. Remove the rubber seal.

3. Remove the seal bridge (a small metal stamping) from the retainer ring space.

4. Remove the lock ring, seated in the groove of the wheel hub, by compressing the ends with a needle nosed pliers, while pulling the hub lock from the hub body. If the body assembly does not slide out easily, you'll have to use a puller.

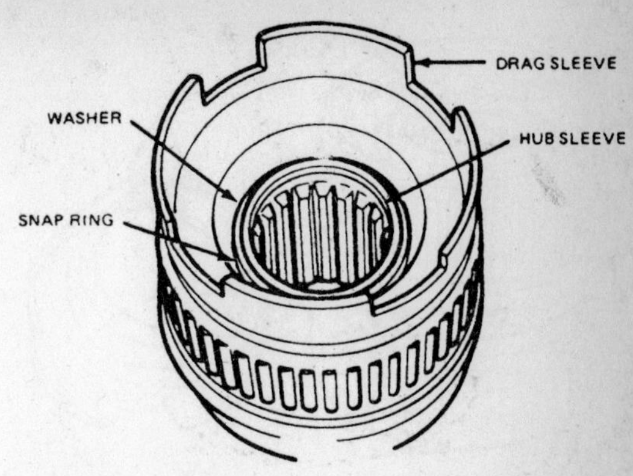

Washer and snap ring

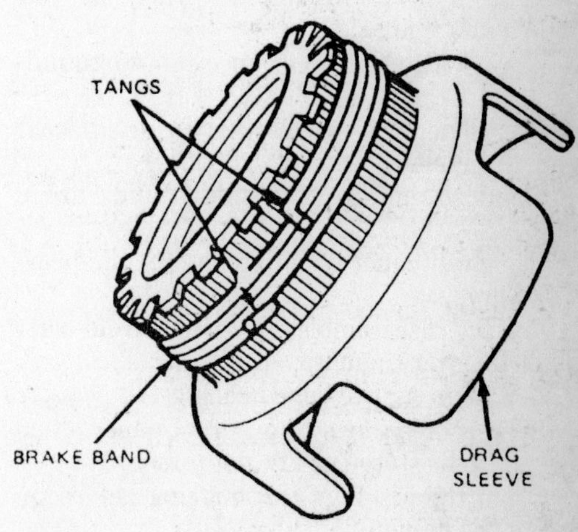

Drag sleeve and brake band

5. If the hub and spindle are being removed:

   a. Remove the C-washer from the groove in the stub shaft

   b. Remove the splined spacer from the shaft

   c. Remove the outer locknut, locking washer and inner bearing locknut.

   d. Pull the hub and bearings from the spindle.

6. See the Wheel Bearing procedures, below, for cleaning and packing the bearings.

4-Wheel Drive Front Wheel Bearings

REPLACEMENT OR REPACKING

Before handling the bearings, there are a few things that you should remember to do and not to do.

Remember to DO the following:

• Remove all outside dirt from the housing before exposing the bearing.

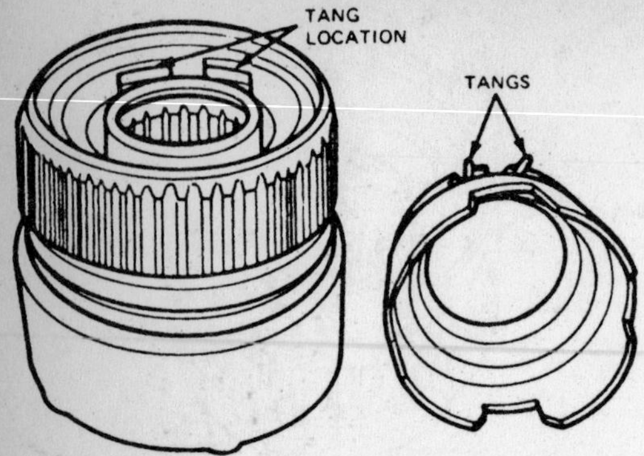

Brake band and drag sleeve assembly to body assembly installation

• Treat a used bearing as gently as you would a new one.
• Work with clean tools in clean surroundings.
• Use clean, dry canvas gloves, or at least clean, dry hands.
• Clean solvents and flushing fluids are a must.
• Use clean paper when laying out the bearings to dry.
• Protect disassembled bearings from rust and dirt. Cover them up.
• Use clean rags to wipe bearings.
• Keep the bearings in oil-proof paper when they are to be stored or are not in use.
• Clean the inside of the housing before replacing the bearing.

Do NOT do the following:

• Don't work in dirty surroundings.
• Don't use dirty, chipped or damaged tools.
• Try not to work on wooden work benches or use wooden mallets.
• Don't handle bearings with dirty or moist hands.
• Do not use gasoline for cleaning; use a safe solvent.
• Do not spin-dry bearings with compressed air. They will be damaged.
• Do not spin dirty bearings.
• Avoid using cotton waste or dirty cloths to wipe bearings.
• Try not to scratch or nick bearing surfaces.
• Do not allow the bearing to come in contact with dirt or rust at any time.

With Manual Locking Hubs

1. Raise and support the front end on jackstands.
2. Remove the hubs.
3. On Bronco, F-150 and F-250 LD with the Dana 44 axle: apply inward pressure on the bearing adjusting nut, using a socket made for that purpose available at most auto parts stores, to disengage the adjusting nut locking splines, while turning it counterclockwise to remove it.

On the F-250 HD (Dana 50 axle) and F-350, use the hub nut tool to unscrew the outer locking nut. Then, remove the lock ring from the bearing adjusting nut. This can be done with your finger tips or a screwdriver. Use the tool to remove the bearing adjusting nut.

4. Remove the caliper and suspend it out of the way. See Chapter 9.
5. Slide the hub and disc assembly off of the spindle. The outer wheel bearing will slide out as the hub is removed, so be prepared to catch it.
6. Lay the hub on a clean work surface. Carefully drive the inner bearing cone and grease seal out of the hub using Tool T69L-1102-A, or equivalent.
7. Inspect the bearing cups for pits or

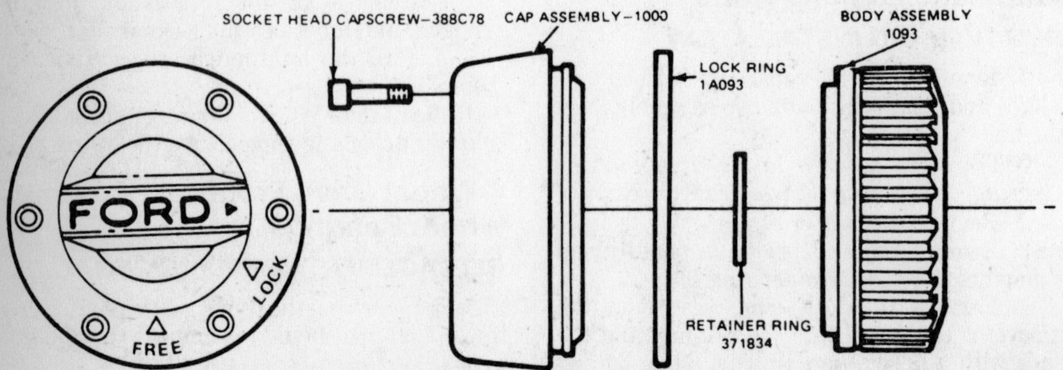

Manual locking hubs

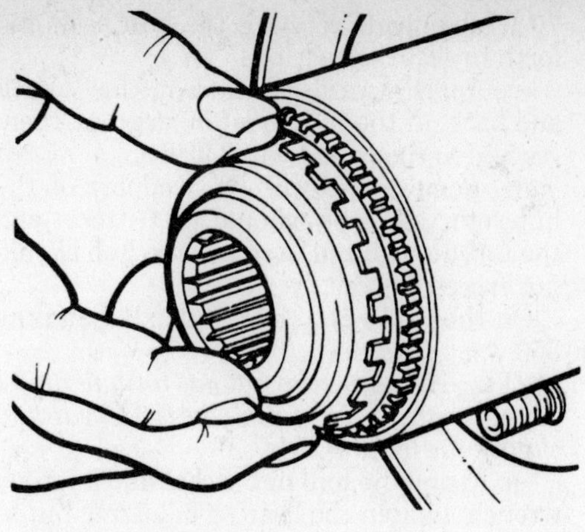

Axle shift sleeve and ring, and inner clutch ring installation

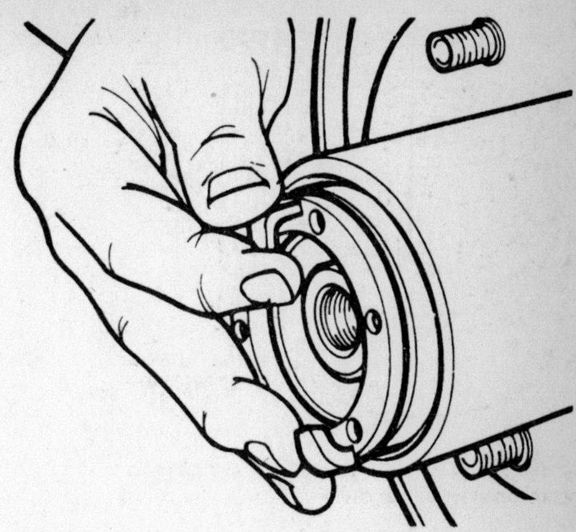

Installing the cam body ring into the clutch retaining ring

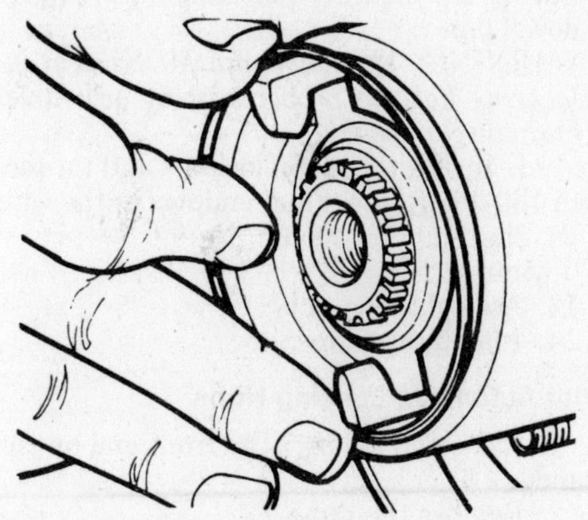

Installing the internal snap ring

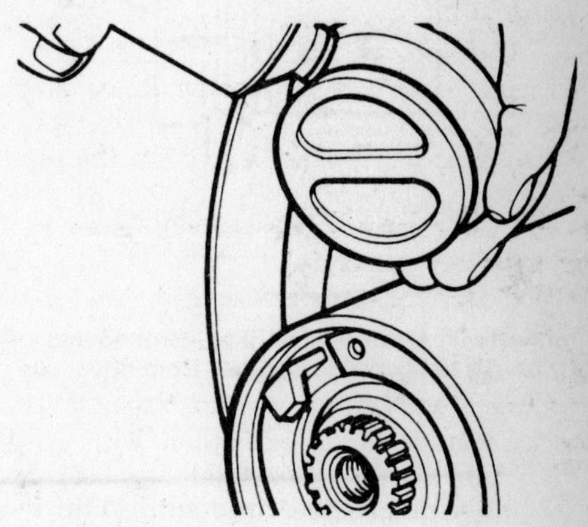

Lubricating the selector knob

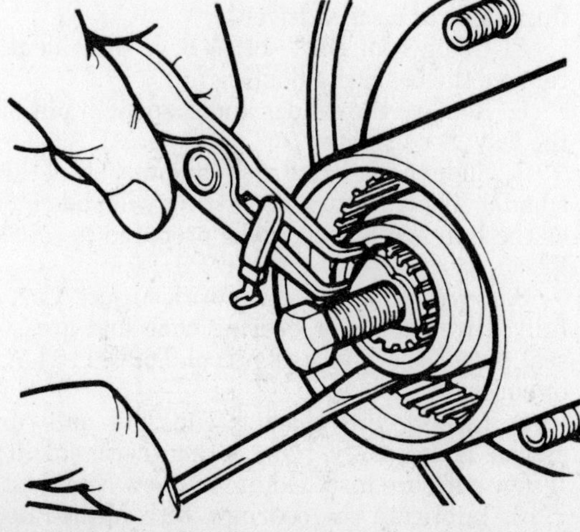

Installing the axle shaft snap ring

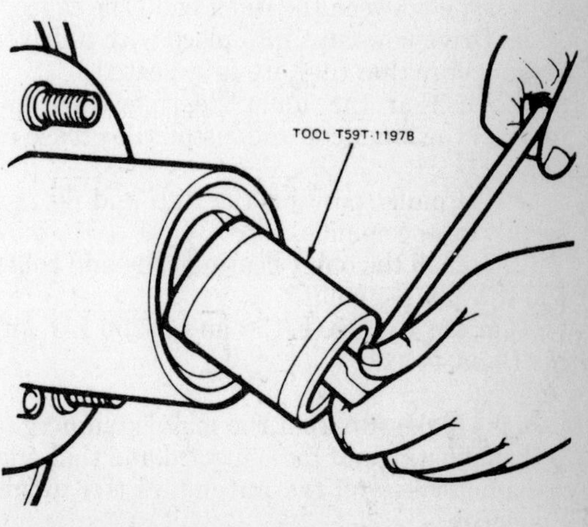

Lock nut, lock ring and adjusting nut removal

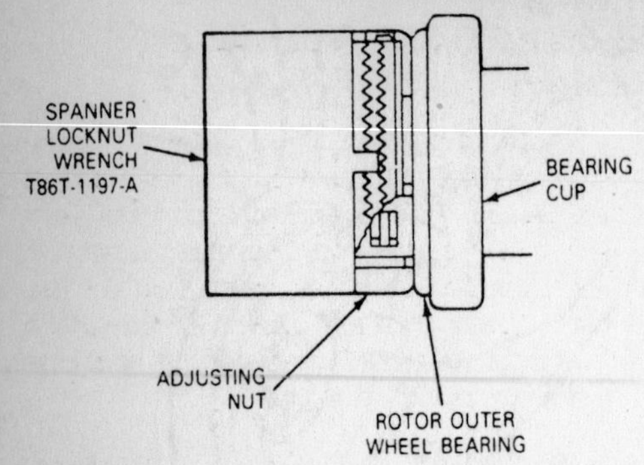

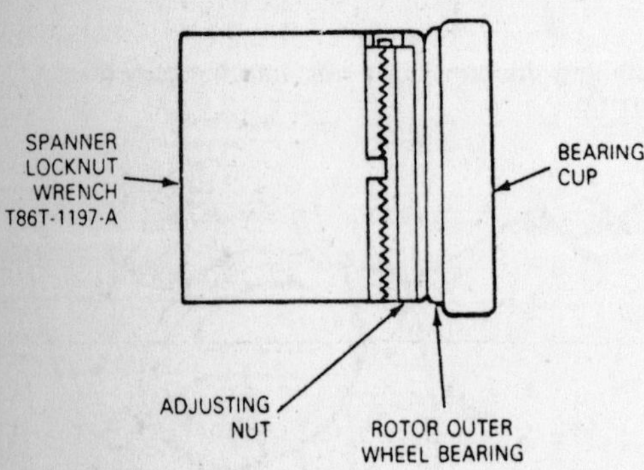

Front wheel bearing Adjustment – Bronco and F-150 – F-250 (4x4) with Dana 44 front drive axle

cracks. If necessary, remove them with a drift. If new cups are installed, install new bearings.

8. Lubricate the bearings with Multi-Purpose Lubricant Ford Specification, ESA-MIC7-B or equivalent. Clean all old grease from the hub. Pack the cones and rollers. If a bearing packer is not available, work as much lubricant as possible between the rollers and the cages.

9. Drive new cups into place with a driver, making sure that they are fully seated.

10. Position the inner bearing cone and roller in the inner cup and install the grease retainer.

11. Carefully position the hub and disc assembly on the spindle.

12. Install the outer bearing cone and roller, and the adjusting nut.

On the Bronco, F-150 and F-250 LD with the Dana 44 axle:

a. Make sure that the metal stamping on the adjusting nut faces inward and the inner diameter key on the nut enters the spindle keyway.

b. Apply inward pressure with the hub nut wrench and tighten the adjusting nut to 70 ft. lbs. while rotating the hub back and forth to seat the bearings.

c. Apply inward pressure on the wrench and back off the nut about 90 degrees, then, re-tighten the nut to 15-20 ft. lbs.

d. Remove the wrench. Endplay of the hub/rotor assembly should be 0 (zero) and the torque required to rotate the hub should not exceed 20 inch lbs.

On the F-250 HD (Dana 50 axle) and the F-350

NOTE: *The adjusting nut has a small dowel on one side. This dowel faces outward to engage the locking ring.*

a. Using the hub nut socket and a torque wrench, tighten the bearing adjusting nut to 50 ft. lbs., while rotating the hub back and forth to seat the bearings.

b. Back off the adjusting nut about 90 degrees.

c. Install the locking ring by turning the nut to the nearest hole and inserting the dowel pin.

WARNING: *The dowel pin MUST seat in a lockring hole for proper bearing adjustment and wheel retention!*

d. Install the outer locknut and torque it to 160-205 ft. lbs. Final endplay of the wheel on the spindle should be 0-0.004 in. (0-0.15mm).

13. Assemble the hub.

14. Install the caliper.

With Automatic Locking Hubs

1. Raise and support the front end on jackstands.

2. Remove the hubs.

3. Remove the wheel bearing lock nut, using Tool T59T–1197–B, or equivalent.

4. Remove the lock ring from the bearing adjusting nut. This can be done with your finger tips or a screwdriver.

5. Using Tool T59T–1197–B, or equivalent, remove the bearing adjusting nut.

6. Remove the caliper and suspend it out of the way. See Chapter 9.

7. Slide the hub and disc assembly off of the spindle. The outer wheel bearing will slide out as the hub is removed, so be prepared to catch it.

8. Lay the hub on a clean work surface. Carefully drive the inner bearing cone and grease seal out of the hub using Tool T69L–1102–A, or equivalent.

9. Inspect the bearing cups for pits or cracks. If necessary, remove them with a drift. If new cups are installed, install new bearings.

10. Lubricate the bearings with Multi-Purpose Lubricant Ford Specification, ESA–MIC7–B or equivalent. Clean all old grease from the

hub. Pack the cones and rollers. If a bearing packer is not available, work as much lubricant as possible between the rollers and the cages.

11. Drive new cups into place with a driver, making sure that they are fully seated.

12. Position the inner bearing cone and roller in the inner cup and install the grease retainer.

13. Carefully position the hub and disc assembly on the spindle.

14. Install the outer bearing cone and roller, and the adjusting nut.

NOTE: *The adjusting nut has a small dowel on one side. This dowel faces outward to engage the locking ring.*

15. Using Tool T59T–1197–B and a torque wrench, tighten the bearing adjusting nut to 50 ft. lbs., while rotating the wheel back and forth to seat the bearings.

16. Back off the adjusting nut approximately 90°.

17. Install the lock ring by turning the nut to the nearest hole and inserting the dowel pin.

NOTE: *The dowel pin must seat in a lock ring hole for proper bearing adjustment and wheel retention.*

18. Install the outer lock nut and tighten to 160–205 ft. lbs. Final end play of the wheel on the spindle should be 0–0.004 in. (0–0.15mm).

19. Assemble the hub parts.

20. Install the caliper.

21. Remove the safety stands and lower the vehicle.

F-250 and F-350 Rear Axle Bearings

The wheel bearings on the F-250 and F-350 full floating rear axle are packed with wheel bearing grease. Axle lubricant can also flow into the wheel hubs and bearings, however, wheel bearing grease is the primary lubricant. The wheel bearing grease provides lubrication until the axle lubricant reaches the bearings during normal operation.

1. Set the parking brake and loosen the axle shaft bolts.

2. Raise the rear wheels off the floor and place jackstands under the rear axle housing so that the axle is parallel with the floor.

3. Remove the axle shaft bolts.

4. Remove the axle shaft and gaskets.

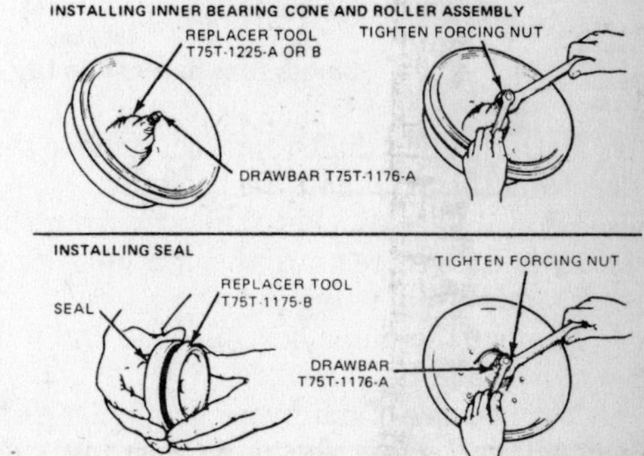

Rear wheel bearing and seal installation. Seal installation tools are very helpful here

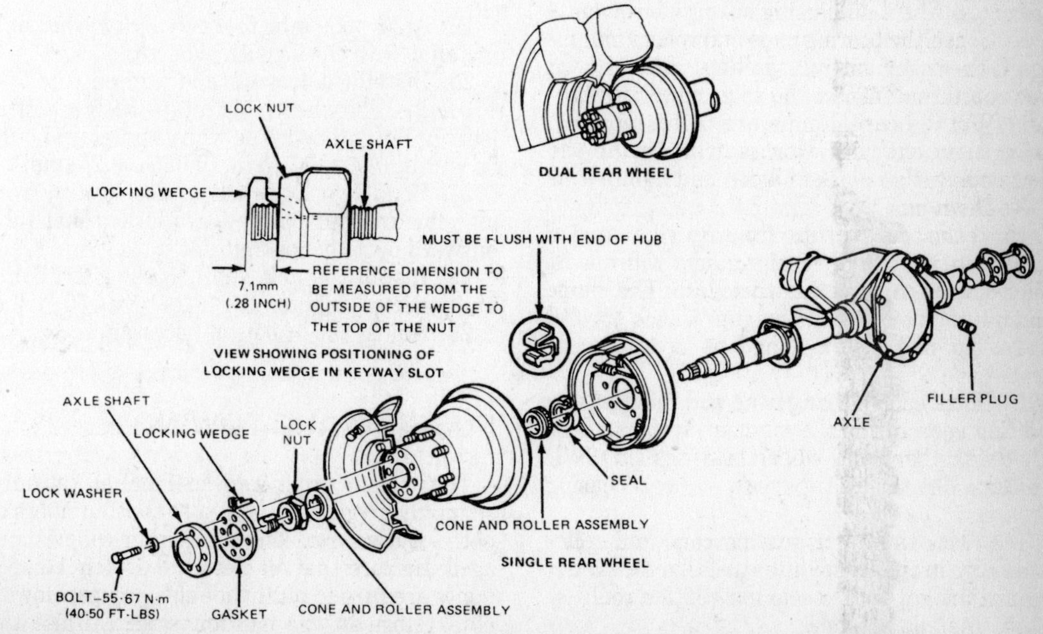

Rear wheel hub showing wedge positioning—F350 4×2 with dual rear wheels shown

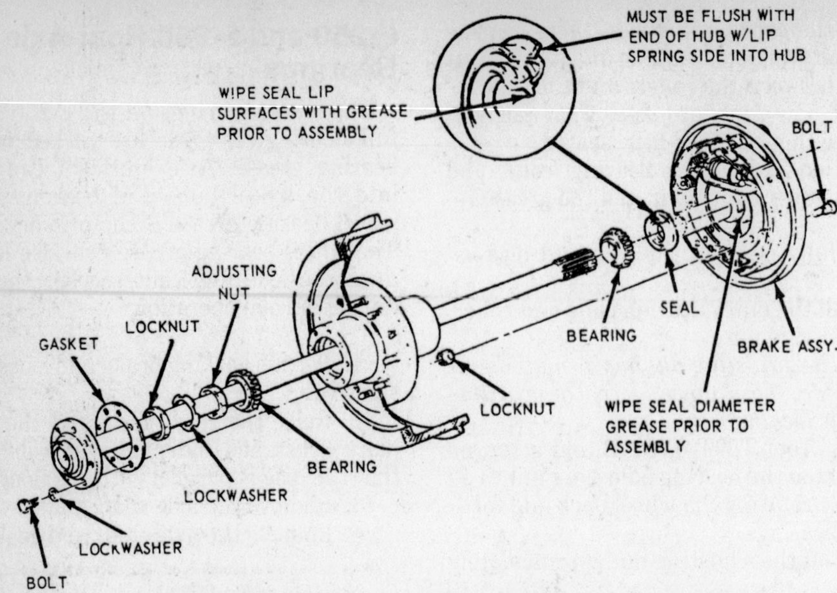

Single rear hub assembly with full-floating axles, F-250 only

5. With the axle shaft removed, remove the gasket from the axle shaft flange studs.

6. Bend the lockwasher tab away from the locknut, and then remove the locknut, lockwasher, and the adjusting nut.

7. Remove the outer bearing cone and pull the wheel straight off the axle.

8. With a piece of hardwood or a brass drift which will just clear the outer bearing cup, drive the inner bearing cone and inner seal out of the wheel hub.

9. Wash all the old grease or axle lubricant out of the wheel hub, using a suitable solvent.

10. Wash the bearing cups and rollers and inspect them for pitting, galling, and uneven wear patterns. Inspect the roller for end wear.

11. If the bearing cups are to be replaced, drive them out with a brass drift. Install the new cups with a block of wood and hammer or press them in.

12. if the bearing cups are properly seated, a 0.0015 in. (0.038mm) feeler gauge will not fit between the cup and the wheel hub. The gauge should not fit beneath the cup. Check several places to make sure the cups are squarely seated.

13. Pack each bearing cone and roller with a bearing packer or in the manner previously outlined for the front wheel bearings on 2WD trucks. Use a multi-purpose wheel bearing grease.

14. Place the inner bearing cone and roller assembly in the wheel hub. Install a new inner seal in the hub with a seal installation tool.

15. Install the wheel.

16. Install and tighten the bearing adjusting nut to 50–80 ft.lbs. while rotating the wheel.

17. Back off (loosen) the adjusting nut $^3/_8$ of a turn.

18. Position the locking wedge in the keyway slot and carefully drive the wedge into position. The wedge must be bottomed against the shoulder of the adjusting nut when fully installed.

NOTE: *The locking wedge and the adjusting nut can be used over again, as long as the locking wedge cut a new groove in the nylon retainer material within the $^1/_8$ to $^3/_8$ turn specified. The wedge must not be pressed into the previously cut groove.*

19. Apply axle lube to a new lockwasher and install it with the smooth side out.

20. Install the locknut and tighten it to 90–110 ft. lbs. The wheel must rotate freely after the locknut if tightened. The wheel end-play should be within 0.001–0.010 in. (0.0254–0.254mm).

21. Bend two lockwasher tabs inward over an adjusting nut flat and two lockwasher tabs outward over the locknut flat.

22. Install the axle shaft, gasket, lockbolts, and washers. Tighten the bolts to 40–50 ft. lbs.

23. Adjust the brakes, if necessary.

PUSHING AND TOWING

To push-start your vehicle, (manual transmission only), check to make sure that bumpers of both vehicles are aligned so neither will be damaged. Be sure that all electrical system components are turned off (headlight, heater, blower, etc.). Turn on the ignition switch. Place the shift lever in Third or Fourth and push in the clutch pedal. At about 15 mph, signal the driver of the pushing vehicle to fall back, depress the accelerator pedal, and release the clutch pedal slowly. The engine should start.

When you are doing the pushing, make sure that the two bumpers match so you won't damage the vehicle you are to push. Another good idea is to put an old tire between the two vehicles. Try to keep your truck right up against the other vehicle while you are pushing. If the two vehicles do separate, stop and start over again instead of trying to catch up and ramming the other vehicle. Also try, as much as possible, to avoid riding or slipping the clutch.

If your truck has to be towed by a tow truck, it can be towed forward for any distance with the driveshaft connected as long as it is done fairly slowly. Otherwise disconnect the driveshaft at the rear axle and tie it up. On and F-250, the rear axle shafts can be removed and the hub covered to prevent lubricant loss. If your 4-wheel drive truck has to be towed backward, remove the front axle driving hubs, or disengage the lock-out hubs to prevent the front differential from rotating. If the drive hubs are removed, improvise a cover to keep out dust and dirt.

JACKING AND HOISTING

It is very important to be careful about running the engine, on vehicles equipped with limited slip differentials, while the vehicle is up on the jack. This is because when the drive train is engaged, power is transmitted to the wheel with the best traction and the vehicle will drive off the jack if one drive wheel is in contact with the floor, resulting in possible damage or injury.

Jack a Ford truck from under the axles, radius arms, or spring hangers and the frame. Be sure and block the diagonally opposite wheel. Place jackstands under the vehicle at the points mentioned or directly under the frame when you are going to work under the vehicle.

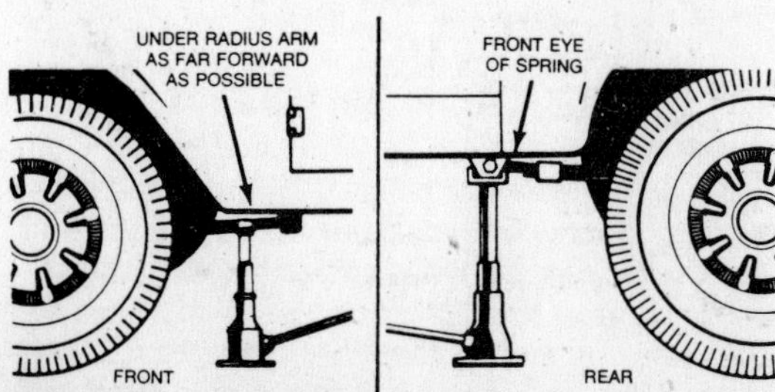

Proper jack placement

JUMP STARTING A DUAL-BATTERY DIESEL

Ford pickups equipped with the 420 cid or 444 cid (6.9L and 7.3L) V8 diesel utilize two 12 volt batteries, one on either side of the engine compartment. The batteries are connected in a parallel circuit (positive terminal to positive terminal, negative terminal to negative terminal). Hooking the batteries up in parallel circuit increases battery cranking power without increasing total battery voltage output. Output remains at 12 volts. On the other hand, hooking two 12 volt batteries up in a series circuit (positive terminal to negative terminal, positive terminal to negative terminal) increases total battery output to 24 volts (12 volts plus 12 volts).

CAUTION: *NEVER hook the batteries up in a series circuit or the entire electrical system will go up in smoke, especially the starter.*

In the event that a diesel pickup needs to be jump started, use the following procedure.

1. Turn all lights off.
2. Turn on the heater blower motor to remove transient voltage.
3. Connect one jumper cable to the passenger side battery positive (+) terminal and the other cable clamp to the positive (+) terminal to the booster (good) battery.
4. Connect one end of the other jumper cable to the negative (–) terminal of the booster (good) battery and the other cable clamp to an engine bolt head, alternator bracket or other solid, metallic point on the diesel engine. DO NOT connect this clamp to the negative (–) terminal of the bad battery.

CAUTION: *Be very careful to keep the jumper cables away from moving parts (cooling fan, belts, etc.) on both engines.*

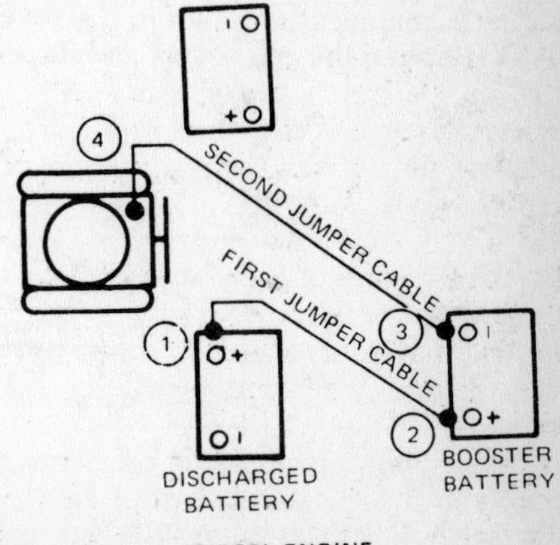

Diesel dual-battery jump starting diagram

JUMP STARTING A DEAD BATTERY

The chemical reaction in a battery produces explosive hydrogen gas. This is the safe way to jump start a dead battery, reducing the chances of an accidental spark that could cause an explosion.

Jump Starting Precautions

1. Be sure both batteries are of the same voltage.
2. Be sure both batteries are of the same polarity (have the same grounded terminal).
3. Be sure the vehicles are not touching.
4. Be sure the vent cap holes are not obstructed.
5. Do not smoke or allow sparks around the battery.
6. In cold weather, check for frozen electrolyte in the battery. Do not jump start a frozen battery.
7. Do not allow electrolyte on your skin or clothing.
8. Be sure the electrolyte is not frozen.

CAUTION: *Make certain that the ignition key, in the vehicle with the dead battery, is in the OFF position. Connecting cables to vehicles with on-board computers will result in computer destruction if the key is not in the OFF position.*

Jump Starting Procedure

1. Determine voltages of the two batteries; they must be the same.
2. Bring the starting vehicle close (they must not touch) so that the batteries can be reached easily.
3. Turn off all accessories and both engines. Put both cars in Neutral or Park and set the handbrake.
4. Cover the cell caps with a rag—do not cover terminals.
5. If the terminals on the run-down battery are heavily corroded, clean them.
6. Identify the positive and negative posts on both batteries and connect the cables in the order shown.
7. Start the engine of the starting vehicle and run it at fast idle. Try to start the car with the dead battery. Crank it for no more than 10 seconds at a time and let it cool off for 20 seconds in between tries.
8. If it doesn't start in 3 tries, there is something else wrong.
9. Disconnect the cables in the reverse order.
10. Replace the cell covers and dispose of the rags.

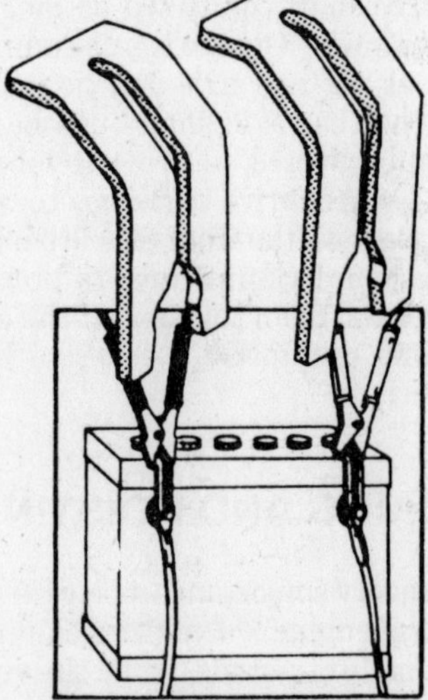

Side terminal batteries oc casionally pose a problem when connecting jumper cables. There frequently isn't enough room to clamp the cables without touching sheet metal .Side terminal adaptors are available to alleviate this problem and should be removed after use.

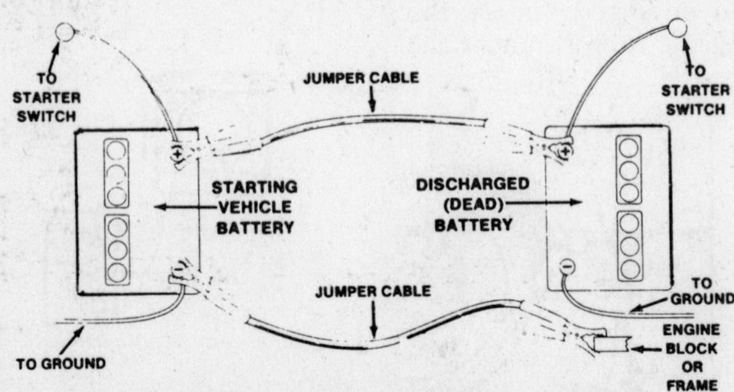

Make sure vehicles do not touch

This hook–up for negative ground cars only

5. Start the engine of the donor truck and run it at moderate speed.

6. Start the engine of the diesel.

7. When the diesel starts, remove the cable from the engine block before disconnecting the positive terminal.

TRAILER TOWING

Factory trailer towing packages are available on most trucks. However, if you are installing a trailer hitch and wiring on your truck, there are a few thing that you ought to know.

Trailer Weight

Trailer weight is the first, and most important, factor in determining whether or not your vehicle is suitable for towing the trailer you have in mind. The horsepower-to-weight ratio should be calculated. The basic standard is a ratio of 35:1. That is, 35 pounds of GVW for every horsepower.

To calculate this ratio, multiply you engine's rated horsepower by 35, then subtract the weight of the vehicle, including passengers and luggage. The resulting figure is the ideal maximum trailer weight that you can tow. One point to consider: a numerically higher axle ratio can offset what appears to be a low trailer weight. If the weight of the trailer that you have in mind is somewhat higher than the weight you just calculated, you might consider changing your rear axle ratio to compensate.

Hitch Weight

There are three kinds of hitches: bumper mounted, frame mounted, and load equalizing.

Bumper mounted hitches are those which attach solely to the vehicle's bumper. Many states prohibit towing with this type of hitch, when it attaches to the vehicle's stock bumper, since it subjects the bumper to stresses for which it was not designed. Aftermarket rear step bumpers, designed for trailer towing, are acceptable for use with bumper mounted hitches.

Frame mounted hitches can be of the type which bolts to two or more points on the frame, plus the bumper, or just to several points on the frame. Frame mounted hitches can also be

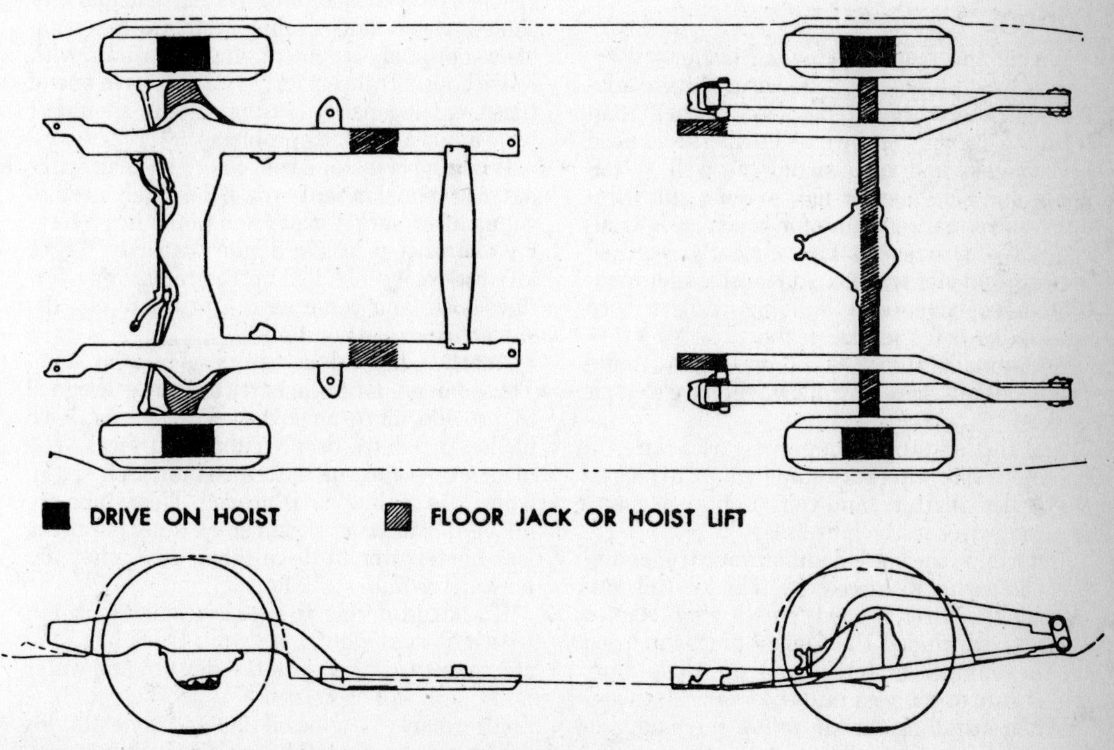

Vehicle hoisting and jacking points

of the tongue type, for Class I towing, or, of the receiver type, for Classes II and III.

Load equalizing hitches are usually used for large trailers. Most equalizing hitches are welded in place and use equalizing bars and chains to level the vehicle after the trailer is hooked up.

The bolt-on hitches are the most common, since they are relatively easy to install.

Check the gross weight rating of your trailer. Tongue weight is usually figured as 10% of gross trailer weight. Therefore, a trailer with a maximum gross weight of 2,000 lb. will have a maximum tongue weight of 200 lb. Class I trailers fall into this category. Class II trailers are those with a gross weight rating of 2,000–3,500 lb., while Class III trailers fall into the 3,500–6,000 lb. category. Class IV trailers are those over 6,000 lb. and are for use with fifth wheel trucks, only.

When you've determined the hitch that you'll need, follow the manufacturer's installation instructions, exactly, especially when it comes to fastener torques. The hitch will subjected to a lot of stress and good hitches come with hardened bolts. Never substitute an inferior bolt for a hardened bolt.

Wiring

Wiring the truck for towing is fairly easy. There are a number of good wiring kits available and these should be used, rather than trying to design your own. All trailers will need brake lights and turn signals as well as tail lights and side marker lights. Most states require extra marker lights for overly wide trailers. Also, most states have recently required backup lights for trailers, and most trailer manufacturers have been building trailers with backup lights for several years.

Additionally, some Class I, most Class II and just about all Class III trailers will have electric brakes.

Add to this number an accessories wire, to operate trailer internal equipment or to charge the trailer's battery, and you can have as many as seven wires in the harness.

Determine the equipment on your trailer and buy the wiring kit necessary. The kit will contain all the wires needed, plus a plug adapter set which included the female plug, mounted on the bumper or hitch, and the male plug, wired into, or plugged into the trailer harness.

When installing the kit, follow the manufacturer's instructions. The color coding of the wires is standard throughout the industry.

One point to note, some domestic vehicles, and most imported vehicles, have separate turn signals. On most domestic vehicles, the brake lights and rear turn signals operate with the same bulb. For those vehicles with separate turn signals, you can purchase an isolation unit so that the brake lights won't blink whenever the turn signals are operated, or, you can go to your local electronics supply house and buy four diodes to wire in series with the brake and turn signal bulbs. Diodes will isolate the brake and turn signals. The choice is yours. The isolation units are simple and quick to install, but far more expensive than the diodes. The diodes, however, require more work to install properly, since they require the cutting of each bulb's wire and soldering in place of the diode.

One final point, the best kits are those with a spring loaded cover on the vehicle mounted socket. This cover prevents dirt and moisture from corroding the terminals. Never let the vehicle socket hang loosely. Always mount it securely to the bumper or hitch.

Cooling

ENGINE

One of the most common, if not THE most common, problem associated with trailer towing is engine overheating.

With factory installed trailer towing packages, a heavy duty cooling system is usually included. Heavy duty cooling systems are available as optional equipment on most trucks, with or without a trailer package. If you have one of these extra-capacity systems, you shouldn't have any overheating problems.

If you have a standard cooling system, without an expansion tank, you'll definitely need to get an aftermarket expansion tank kit, preferably one with at least a 2 quart capacity. These kits are easily installed on the radiator's overflow hose, and come with a pressure cap designed for expansion tanks.

Another helpful accessory is a Flex Fan. These fan are large diameter units are designed to provide more airflow at low speeds, with blades that have deeply cupped surfaces. The blades then flex, or flatten out, at high speed, when less cooling air is needed. These fans are far lighter in weight than stock fans, requiring less horsepower to drive them. Also, they are far quieter than stock fans.

If you do decide to replace your stock fan with a flex fan, note that if your truck has a fan clutch, a spacer between the flex fan and water pump hub will be needed.

Aftermarket engine oil coolers are helpful for prolonging engine oil life and reducing overall engine temperatures. Both of these factors increase engine life.

While not absolutely necessary in towing Class I and some Class II trailers, they are rec-

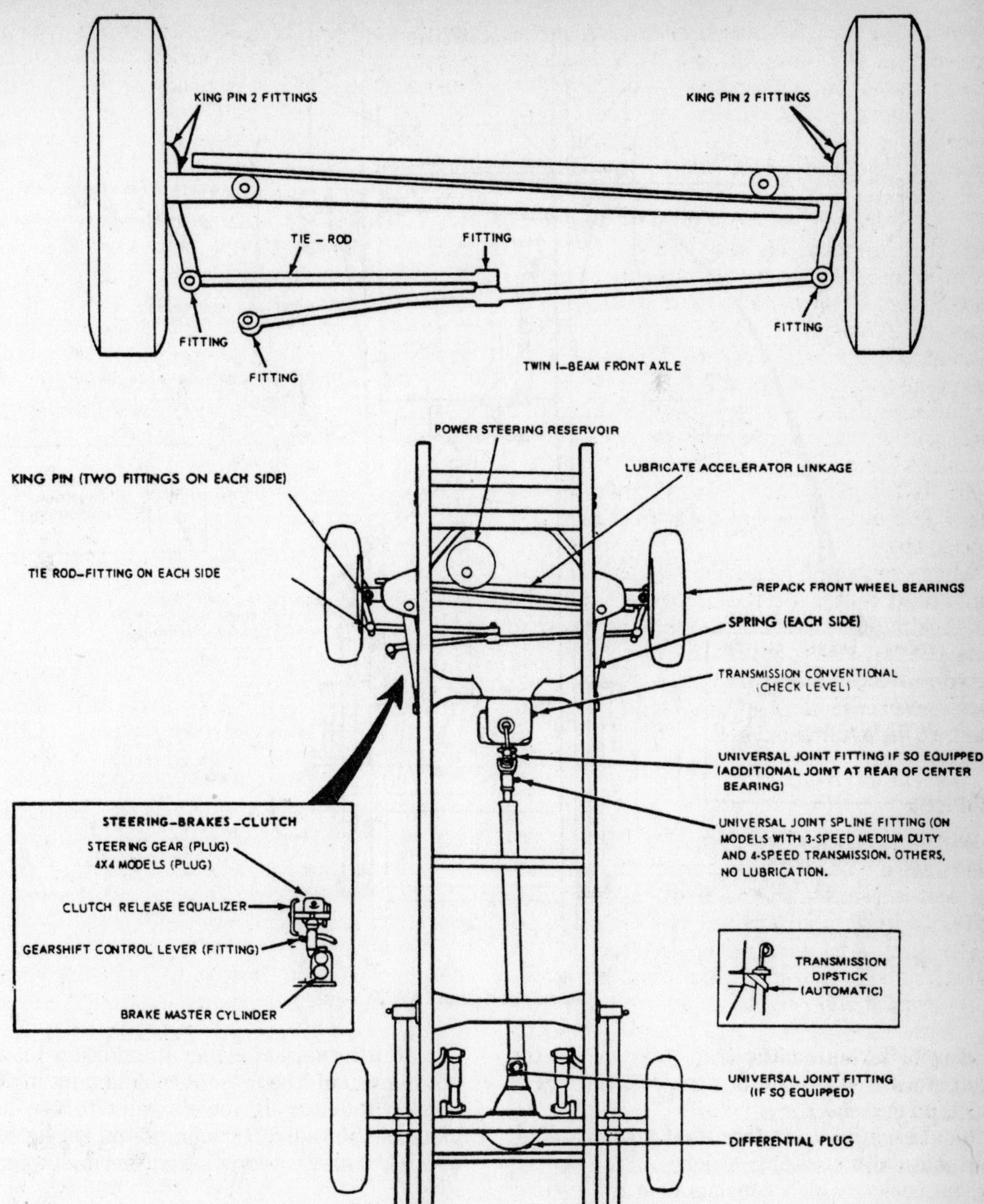

Lubrication chart 2WD

ommended for heavier Class II and all Class III towing.

Engine oil cooler systems consist of an adapter, screwed on in place of the oil filter, a remote filter mounting and a multi-tube, finned heat exchanger, which is mounted in front of the radiator or air conditioning condenser.

TRANSMISSION

An automatic transmission is usually recommended for trailer towing. Modern automatics have proven reliable and, of course, easy to operate, in trailer towing.

The increased load of a trailer, however, causes an increase in the temperature of the automatic transmission fluid. Heat is the worst

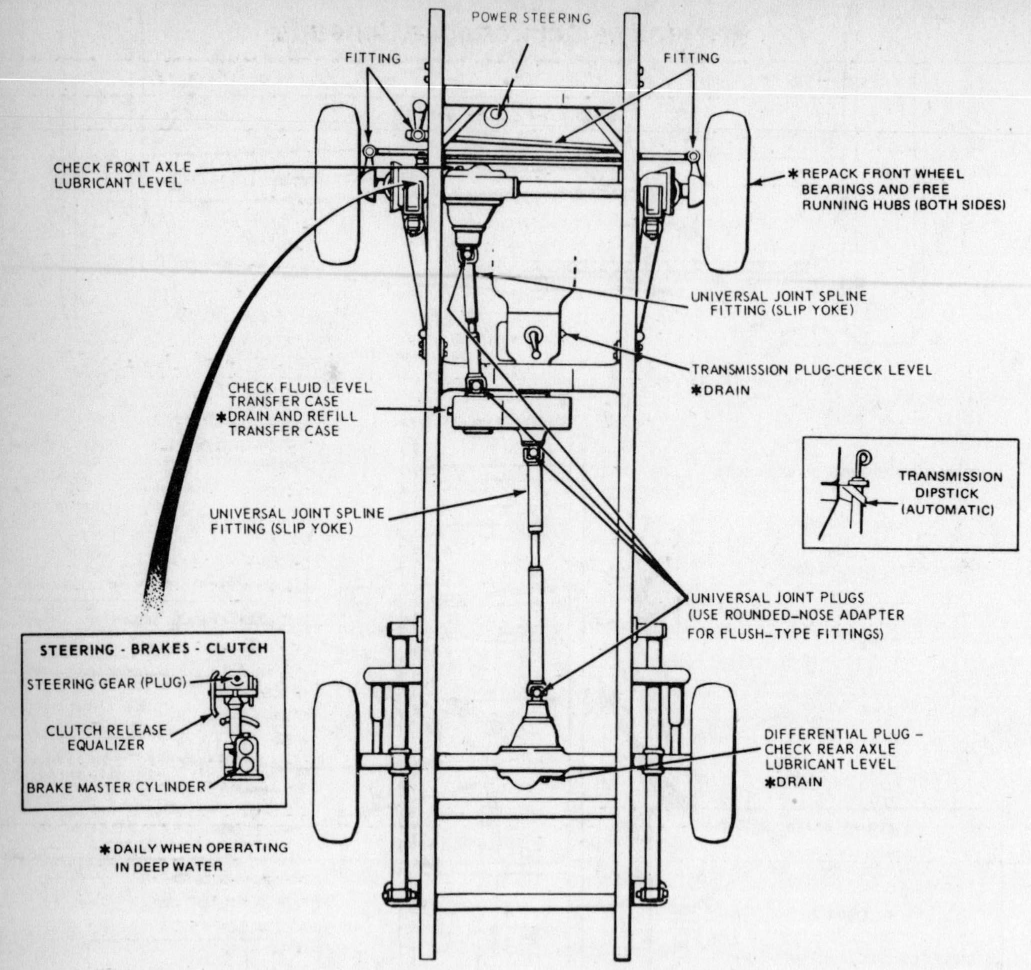

Lubrication chart 4WD

enemy of an automatic transmission. As the temperature of the fluid increases, the life of the fluid decreases.

It is essential, therefore, that you install an automatic transmission cooler.

The cooler, which consists of a multi-tube, finned heat exchanger, is usually installed in front of the radiator or air conditioning compressor, and hooked inline with the transmission cooler tank inlet line. Follow the cooler manufacturer's installation instructions.

Select a cooler of at least adequate capacity, based upon the combined gross weights of the truck and trailer.

Cooler manufacturers recommend that you use an aftermarket cooler in addition to, and not instead of, the present cooling tank in your truck's radiator. If you do want to use it in place of the radiator cooling tank, get a cooler at least two sizes larger than normally necessary.

NOTE: *A transmission cooler can, sometimes, cause slow or harsh shifting in the transmission during cold weather, until the fluid has a chance to come up to normal operating temperature. Some coolers can be purchased with or retrofitted with a temperature bypass valve which will allow fluid flow through the cooler only when the fluid has reached operating temperature, or above.*

Preventive Maintenance Schedule

Model/Interval	Item	Service
	Gasoline Engine Models	
Every 6 months or 6,000 miles	Crankcase	change oil & filter
	Cooling system	change coolant
	Idle speed and TSP-off speed	adjust
	Ignition timing	adjust
	Decel throttle control system	check
	Chassis fittings	lubricate
	4 x 4 power cylinder	lubricate
	Clutch linkage	inspect and oil
	Exhaust system heat shields	inspect
	Transmission, automatic	adjust bands, check level
Every 15 months or 15,000 miles	Spark plugs	replace
	Exhaust control valve	check & lubricate
	Drive belts	check and adjust
	Air cleaner temperature control	check
	Choke system	check
	Thermactor system	check
	Crankcase breathe cap	clean
	EGR system	clean and inspect
	PCV system	clean and inspect
Every 30 months or 30,000 miles	PCV valve	replace
	Air cleaner element	replace
	Air cleaner crankcase filter	replace
	Fuel vapor system	replace
	Brake master cylinder	check
	Brakes	inspect
	Free-running hubs	clean and repack
	Front wheel bearings	clean and repack
	Rear wheel bearings, Dana axles	clean and repack
	Diesel Engine Models	
Every 6 months or 5,000 miles	Crankcase	change oil and filter
	Idle speed	check and adjust
	Throttle linkage	check operation
	Fuel/water separator	drain water
	U-joints	lubricate
	Front axle spindles	lubricate
Every 6 months or 15,000 miles	Fuel filter	replace
	Drive belts	check/adjust
	Steering linkage	lubricate
Every year	Coolant	check condition/replace
	Cooling hoses, clamps	check condition/replace

Capacities Chart—Pick-Ups

Years	Engine Liters	Crankcase Incl. Filter (qt.)	Transmission (pt.) 4-sp	5-sp	Auto	Transfer Case (pts.)	Drive Axle (pt.) Front	Rear	Fuel Tank (gal.)	Cooling System (qt.) w/AC	wo/AC
1987	6-4.9	6.0	②	—	③	4.0	④	⑤	⑥	①	①
	8-5.0	6.0	②	—	③	4.0	④	⑤	⑥	18.0	15.0
	8-5.8W	6.0	②	—	26.75	4.0	④	⑤	⑥	17.0	17.0
	8-6.9	10.0	②	—	26.75	4.0	④	⑤	⑥	29.0	29.0
	8-7.5	6.0	—	—	26.75	4.0	④	⑤	⑥	18.0	18.0
1988–90	6-4.9	6.0	⑯	⑦	⑧	4.0	⑩	⑪	⑫	⑬	13.0
	8-5.0	6.0	⑯	7.6	⑨	4.0	⑩	⑪	⑫	⑭	13.0
	8-5.8W	6.0	—	6.8	⑨	4.0	⑩	⑪	⑫	⑮	15.0
	8-7.3	10.0	—	6.8	⑨	4.0	⑩	⑪	⑫	31.0	31.0
	8-7.5	6.0	—	6.8	⑨	4.0	⑩	⑪	⑫	18.0	18.0

① Standard cooling with manual transmission: 13.0
Standard cooling with automatic transmission: 14.0
With air conditioning: 17.0
With extra cooling and without air conditioning: 14.0

② Warner T-18 and T-19B; 7.0
NP-435 with extension housing: 7.0
NP-435 without extension housing: 6.5
4-Speed overdrive: 5.0

③ C-6: 23.5
AOD: 24.0

④ Dana 60-7F: 6.0
Dana 50-IFS: 4.1
Dana 44-IFS: 3.8

⑤ Dana 61-1: 6.0
Dana 61-2: 6.0
Dana 70: 7.0
Dana 70HD: 7.4

⑥ 1987 F-100 2-wheel drive regular cab: 16.5 standard
1987 F-100 2-wheel drive regular cab: 19.0 optional behind axle
1987 F-150 2-wheel drive Crew Cab: 16.5 standard
1987 F-150 2-wheel drive Crew Cab: 19.0 optional behind axle
1987 F-150 4x4 regular cab: 16.5 standard
1987 F-150 4x4 regular cab: 19.0 optional behind axle
1987 F-250 2-wheel drive Crew Cab: 16.5 standard
1987 F-250 2-wheel drive Crew Cab: 19.0 optional behind axle
1987 F-150 2-wheel drive regular cab: 16.5 standard
1987 F-150 2-wheel drive regular cab: 19.0 optional behind axle
1987 F-250 2-wheel drive regular cab: 19.0 standard
1987 F-250 2-wheel drive regular cab: 19.0 optional behind axle
1987 F-150 all 4x4: 19.0 standard
1987 F-250 all 4x4: 19.0 optional behind axle
1987 F-350 all models: 19.0 standard
1987 F-350 all models: 19.0 optional behind axle

⑦ Mazda 5-sp OD: 7.6
ZF 5-sp Heavy Duty OD: 6.8

⑧ C6 3-sp: 24.5 w/2-wheel drive
27.5 w/4-wheel drive
AOD 4-sp: 24.0

⑨ 1988 2-wheel drive: 24.5
4-wheel drive: 27.5
1989–90 C6 2-wheel drive: 24.0
4-wheel drive: 27.0
AOD: 24.6
E40D 2-wheel drive: 31.0
4-wheel drive: 32.0

⑩ F-150 and F-250: 3.6
F-350 w/Dana 50-IFS: 3.8
F-350 w/Dana 60 Monobeam: 5.4

⑪ F-150: 5.5
F-250, F-350: 7.5
F-Super Duty: 8.25

⑫ F-150 Standard Cab:
116.8 in. wb—Standard 18.2; optional 16.5
133.0 in. wb—Standard 19.0; optional 18.2
F-250, F-350 Standard Cab:
Standard—19.0 w/gasoline engine; 20.9 w/diesel engine
Option—F-250 4x2 and 4x4 and F-250 HD 4x4, 17.5
Optional—F-250 HD 4x2 and F-350 4x2, 18.2
F-150, F-250 SuperCab:
138.8 in. wb—Standard dual tanks 34.7
155.0 in. wb—Standard dual tanks 37.2
F-350 Crew Cab: 27.2
F-350 Chassis Cab and F-Super Duty:
133.0 in wb—Standard 19.0 w/gasoline engine; 20.0 w/diesel engine
136.8 & 160.8 in. wb—Optional 19.0

⑬ With air conditioning or Super Cooling: 14.0
With air conditioning and Super Cooling, (MT) 15.0
With Super Cooling, (AT) 14.0

⑭ With air conditioning: 15.0
With Super Cooling: 14.0

⑮ With air conditioning and/or Super Cooling: 16.0

⑯ 1989–90 T-18: 3.5

Capacities Chart—Bronco

Years	Engine Liters	Crankcase Incl. Filter (qt.)	Transmission (pt.) 4-sp	Transmission (pt.) 5-sp	Transmission (pt.) Auto	Transfer Case (pts.)	Drive Axle (pt.) Front	Drive Axle (pt.) Rear	Fuel Tank (gal.)	Cooling System (qt.) w/AC	Cooling System (qt.) wo/AC
1987	6-4.9	6.0	⑥	—	27.0	4.0	3.6	5.5	32.0	③	③
	8-5.0	6.0	⑥	—	②	4.0	3.6	5.5	32.0	④	④
	8-5.8	6.0	—	—	27.0	4.0	3.6	5.5	32.0	⑤	⑤
1988–90	6-4.9	6.0	—	①	27.0	4.0	3.6	5.5	32.0	③	③
	8-5.0	6.0	—	7.6	②	4.0	3.5	5.5	32.0	④	④
	8-5.8	6.0	—	—	27.0	4.0	3.6	5.5	32.0	⑤	⑤

① Mazda M50D: 7.6
ZF S5-42: 6.8

② C6 and E4OD: 27.0
AOD: 24.6

③ Standard cooling: 13.0
Manual Transmission w/AC or Super Cooling: 14.0
Automatic Transmission w/Super Cooling: 14.0
Man. Tran. or Auto Tran. w/AC and Super Cooling: 15.0
Auto. Trans. w/AC: 15.0

④ Man. Tran. w/Standard Cooling: 13.0
Auto. Tran. w/Standard Cooling: 14.0
Man. Tran. or Auto Tran. w/AC: 14.0
Man. Tran. or Auto Tran. w/AC or w/AC and Super Cooling: 15.0

⑤ With Standard Cooling or AC: 16.0
With Super Cooling or Super Cooling and Air Conditioning: 17.0

⑥ Warner T-18: 7.0
NP-435 with extension housing: 7.0
Ford 4-Speed overdrive: 5.0

Engine Performance and Tune-Up

2

TUNE-UP PROCEDURES

In order to extract the full measure of performance and economy from your engine it is essential that it be properly tuned at regular intervals. A regular tune-up will keep your vehicle's engine running smoothly and will prevent the annoying minor breakdowns and poor performance associated with an untuned engine.

A complete tune-up should be performed every 12,000 miles or twelve months, whichever comes first. This interval should be halved if the vehicle is operated under severe conditions, such as trailer towing, prolonged idling, continual stop and start driving, or if starting or running problems are noticed. It is assumed that the routine maintenance described in Chapter 1 has been kept up, as this will have a decided effect on the results of a tune-up. All of the applicable steps of a tune-up should be followed in order, as the result is a cumulative one.

If the specifications on the tune-up sticker in the engine compartment disagree with the Tune-Up Specifications chart in this chapter, the figures on the sticker must be used. The sticker often reflects changes made during the production run.

Spark Plugs

A typical spark plug consists of a metal shell surrounding a ceramic insulator. A metal electrode extends downward through the center of the insulator and protrudes a small distance. Located at the end of the plug and attached to the side of the outer metal shell is the side electrode. The side electrode bends in at a 90° angle so that its tip is even with, and parallel to, the tip of the center electrode. The distance between these two electrodes (measured in thousandths of an inch) is called the spark plug gap. The spark plug in no way produces a spark but merely provides a gap across which the current can arc. The coil produces anywhere from 20,000 to 40,000 volts which travels to the distributor where it is distributed through the spark plug wires to the spark plugs. The current passes along the center electrode and jumps the gap to the side electrode, and, in do doing, ignites the air/fuel mixture in the combustion chamber.

SPARK PLUG HEAT RANGE

Spark plug heat range is the ability of the plug to dissipate heat. The longer the insulator (or the farther it extends into the engine), the hotter the plug will operate; the shorter the insulator the cooler it will operate. A plug that absorbs little heat and remains too cool will quickly accumulate deposits of oil and carbon since it is not hot enough to burn them off. This leads to plug fouling and consequently to misfiring. A plug that absorbs too much heat will have no deposits, but, due to the excessive heat, the electrodes will burn away quickly and in some instances, pre-ignition may result. Pre-ignition takes place when plug tips get so hot that they glow sufficiently to ignite the fuel/air

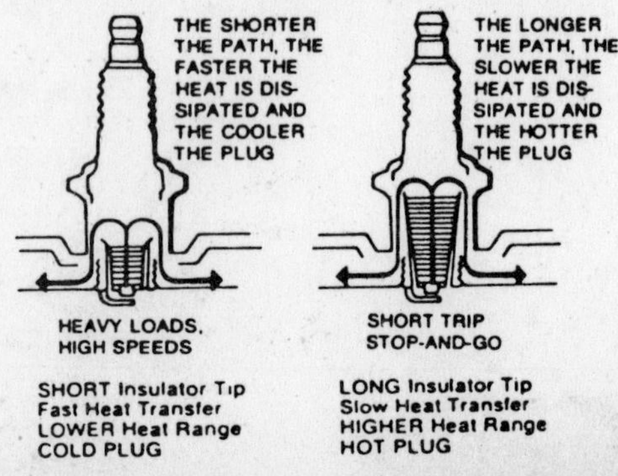

Spark plug heat range

Troubleshooting Engine Performance

Problem	Cause	Solution
Hard starting (engine cranks normally)	• Binding linkage, choke valve or choke piston	• Repair as necessary
	• Restricted choke vacuum diaphragm	• Clean passages
	• Improper fuel level	• Adjust float level
	• Dirty, worn or faulty needle valve and seat	• Repair as necessary
	• Float sticking	• Repair as necessary
	• Faulty fuel pump	• Replace fuel pump
	• Incorrect choke cover adjustment	• Adjust choke cover
	• Inadequate choke unloader adjustment	• Adjust choke unloader
	• Faulty ignition coil	• Test and replace as necessary
	• Improper spark plug gap	• Adjust gap
	• Incorrect ignition timing	• Adjust timing
	• Incorrect valve timing	• Check valve timing; repair as necessary
Rough idle or stalling	• Incorrect curb or fast idle speed	• Adjust curb or fast idle speed
	• Incorrect ignition timing	• Adjust timing to specification
	• Improper feedback system operation	• Refer to Chapter 4
	• Improper fast idle cam adjustment	• Adjust fast idle cam
	• Faulty EGR valve operation	• Test EGR system and replace as necessary
	• Faulty PCV valve air flow	• Test PCV valve and replace as necessary
	• Choke binding	• Locate and eliminate binding condition
	• Faulty TAC vacuum motor or valve	• Repair as necessary
	• Air leak into manifold vacuum	• Inspect manifold vacuum connections and repair as necessary
	• Improper fuel level	• Adjust fuel level
	• Faulty distributor rotor or cap	• Replace rotor or cap
	• Improperly seated valves	• Test cylinder compression, repair as necessary
	• Incorrect ignition wiring	• Inspect wiring and correct as necessary
	• Faulty ignition coil	• Test coil and replace as necessary
	• Restricted air vent or idle passages	• Clean passages
	• Restricted air cleaner	• Clean or replace air cleaner filler element
	• Faulty choke vacuum diaphragm	• Repair as necessary
Faulty low-speed operation	• Restricted idle transfer slots	• Clean transfer slots
	• Restricted idle air vents and passages	• Clean air vents and passages
	• Restricted air cleaner	• Clean or replace air cleaner filter element
	• Improper fuel level	• Adjust fuel level
	• Faulty spark plugs	• Clean or replace spark plugs
	• Dirty, corroded, or loose ignition secondary circuit wire connections	• Clean or tighten secondary circuit wire connections
	• Improper feedback system operation	• Refer to Chapter 4
	• Faulty ignition coil high voltage wire	• Replace ignition coil high voltage wire
	• Faulty distributor cap	• Replace cap
Faulty acceleration	• Improper accelerator pump stroke	• Adjust accelerator pump stroke
	• Incorrect ignition timing	• Adjust timing
	• Inoperative pump discharge check ball or needle	• Clean or replace as necessary
	• Worn or damaged pump diaphragm or piston	• Replace diaphragm or piston

Tune-Up Specifications
Gasoline Engines

Years	Engine Liters	Spark Plugs Type	Spark Plugs Gap (in.)	Distributor Point Gap (in.)	Distributor Dwell (deg.)	Ignition timing (deg.) Man. Trans.	Ignition timing (deg.) Auto. Trans.	Valve Clearance In.	Valve Clearance Exh.	Idle Speed Man. Trans.	Idle Speed Auto. Trans.
1987	6-4.9	BSF-42	0.044	Electronic		①	①	Hyd.	Hyd.	①	①
	8-5.0	ASF-42	0.044	Electronic		①	①	Hyd.	Hyd.	①	①
	8-5.8W	ASF-32	0.044	Electronic		—	①	Hyd.	Hyd.	—	①
	8-7.5	ASF-42	0.044	Electronic		—	①	Hyd.	Hyd.	—	①
1988–90	6-4.9	BSF-44C	0.044	Electronic		①	①	Hyd.	Hyd.	①	①
	8-5.0	ASF-42C	0.044	Electronic		①	①	Hyd.	Hyd.	①	①
	8-5.8	ASF-32C	0.044	Electronic		①	①	Hyd.	Hyd.	①	①
	8-7.5	ASF-42C	0.044	Electronic		①	①	Hyd.	Hyd.	①	①

① See underhood sticker

Tune-Up Specifications
Diesel Engines

Years	Engine Liters	Static Timing	Dynamic Timing	Nozzle Opening Pressure (psi)	Curb Idle Speed (rpm)	Fast Idle Speed (rpm)	Maximum Compression Pressure (psi)
1987	8-6.9	Index	①	1,850	650–700	850–900	440
1988–90	8-7.3	Index	①	1,850	650–700	850–900	440

Static timing is set by aligning the index mark on the pump mounting flange with the index mark on the pump mounting adapter.

① Cetane rating of 38–42: Up to 3,000 ft.—6° ATDC ± 1°
Over 3,000 ft.—7° ATDC ± 1°
Cetane rating of 43–46: Up to 3,000 ft.—5° ATDC ± 1°
Over 3,000 ft.—6° ATDC ± 1°
Cetane rating of 47–50: Up to 3,000 ft.—4° ATDC ± 1°
Over 3,000 ft.—5° ATDC ± 1°

Twist and pull on the rubber boot to remove the spark wires; never pull on the wire itself

mixture before the actual spark occurs. This early ignition will usually cause a pinging during low speeds and heavy loads.

The general rule of thumb for choosing the correct heat range when picking a spark plug is: if most of your driving is long distance, high speed travel, use a colder plug; if most of your driving is stop and go, use a hotter plug. Original equipment plugs are compromise plugs, but most people never have occasion to change their plugs from the factory-recommended heat range.

REPLACING SPARK PLUGS

A set of spark plugs usually requires replacement after about 20,000 to 30,000 miles, depending on your style of driving. In normal operation, plug gap increases about 0.001 in. (0.025mm) for every 1,000–2,500 miles. As the gap increases, the plug's voltage requirement

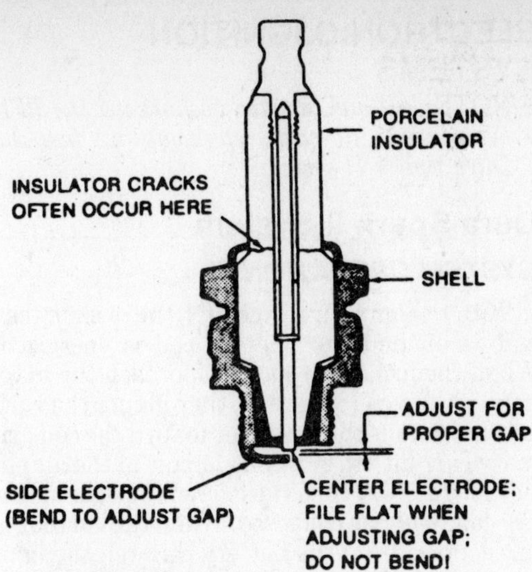

Cross section of a spark plug

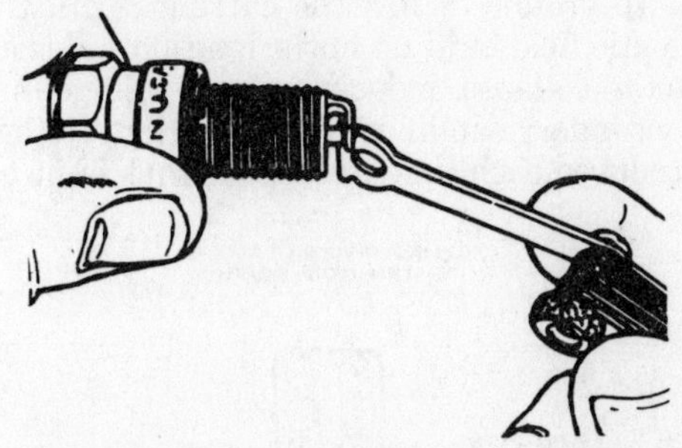

Adjust the electrode gap by bending the electrode

1 2 3 4 5
R 4 5 T S X

1 – R--INDICATES RESISTOR-TYPE PLUG.
2 – "4" INDICATES 14 mm THREADS.
3 – HEAT RANGE
4 – TS--TAPERED SEAT
S--EXTENDED TIP
5 – SPECIAL GAP

Spark plug type number chart, using the R45TSX as an example

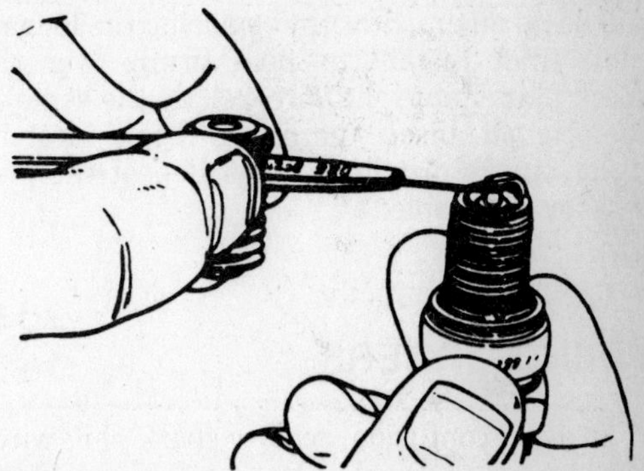

Always use a wire gauge to check the electrode gap; a flat feeler gauge may not give the proper reading.

also increases. It requires a greater voltage to jump the wider gap and about two to three times as much voltage to fire a plug at high speeds than at idle.

When you're removing spark plugs, you should work on one at a time. Don't start by removing the plug wires all at once, because unless you number them, they may become mixed up. Take a minute before you begin and number the wires with tape. The best location for numbering is near where the wires come out of the cap.

NOTE: *On models equipped with electronic ignition, apply a small amount of silicone dielectric compound (D7AZ–19A331–A or the equivalent) to the inside of the terminal boots whenever an ignition wire is disconnected from the plug, or coil/distributor cap connection.*

1. Twist the spark plug boot and remove the boot and wire from the plug. Do not pull on the wire itself as this will ruin the wire.

2. If possible, use a brush or gag to clean the area around the spark plug. Make sure that all the dirt is removed so that none will enter the cylinder after the plug is removed.

3. Remove the spark plug using the proper size socket. Truck models use either a $^5/_8$ in. or $^{13}/_{16}$ in. size socket depending on the engine. Turn the socket counterclockwise to remove the plug. Be sure to hold the socket straight on the plug to avoid breaking the plug, or rounding off the hex on the plug.

4. Once the plug is out, check it against the plugs shown in the Color section to determine engine condition. This is crucial since plug readings are vital signs of engine condition.

5. Use a round wire feeler gauge to check the plug gap. The correct size gauge should pass through the electrode gap with a slight drag. If you're in doubt, try one size smaller and one larger. The smaller gauge should go through easily while the larger one shouldn't go through at all. If the gap is incorrect, use the electrode bending tool on the end of the gauge to adjust the gap. When adjusting the gap, always bend the side electrode. The center electrode is non-adjustable.

6. Squirt a drop of penetrating oil on the threads of the new plug and install it. Don't oil the threads too heavily. Turn the plug in clockwise by hand until it is snug.

7. When the plug is finger tight, tighten it with a wrench. If you don't have a torque wrench, tighten the plug as shown.

8. Install the plug boot firmly over the plug. Proceed to the next plug.

CHECKING AND REPLACING SPARK PLUG CABLES

Visually inspect the spark plug cables for burns, cuts, or breaks in the insulation. Check the spark plug boots and the nipples on the distributor cap and coil. Replace any damaged wiring. If no physical damage is obvious, the wires can be checked with an ohmmeter for excessive resistance. (See the tune-up and troubleshooting section).

When installing a new set of spark plug cables, replace the cables on at a time so there will be no mixup. Start by replacing the longest cable first. Install the boot firmly over the spark plug. Route the wire exactly the same as the original. Insert the nipple firmly into the tower on the distributor cap. Repeat the process for each cable.

FIRING ORDERS

To avoid confusion, replace spark plug wires one at a time.

ELECTRONIC IGNITION SYSTEMS

NOTE: *All fuel injected engines use the TFI-IV system. All carbureted engines use the Dura Spark II system.*

Dura Spark II System

SYSTEM OPERATION

With the ignition switch **ON**, the primary circuit is on and the ignition coil is energized. When the armature spokes approach the magnetic pickup coil assembly, they induce the voltage which tells the amplifier to turn the coil primary current off. A timing circuit in the amplifier module will turn the current on again after the coil field has collapsed. When the current is on, it flows from the battery through the ignition switch, the primary windings of the ignition coil, and through the amplifier module circuits to ground. When the current is off, the magnetic field built up in the ignition coil is allowed to collapse, inducing a high voltage into the secondary windings of the coil. High voltage is produced each time the field is thus built up

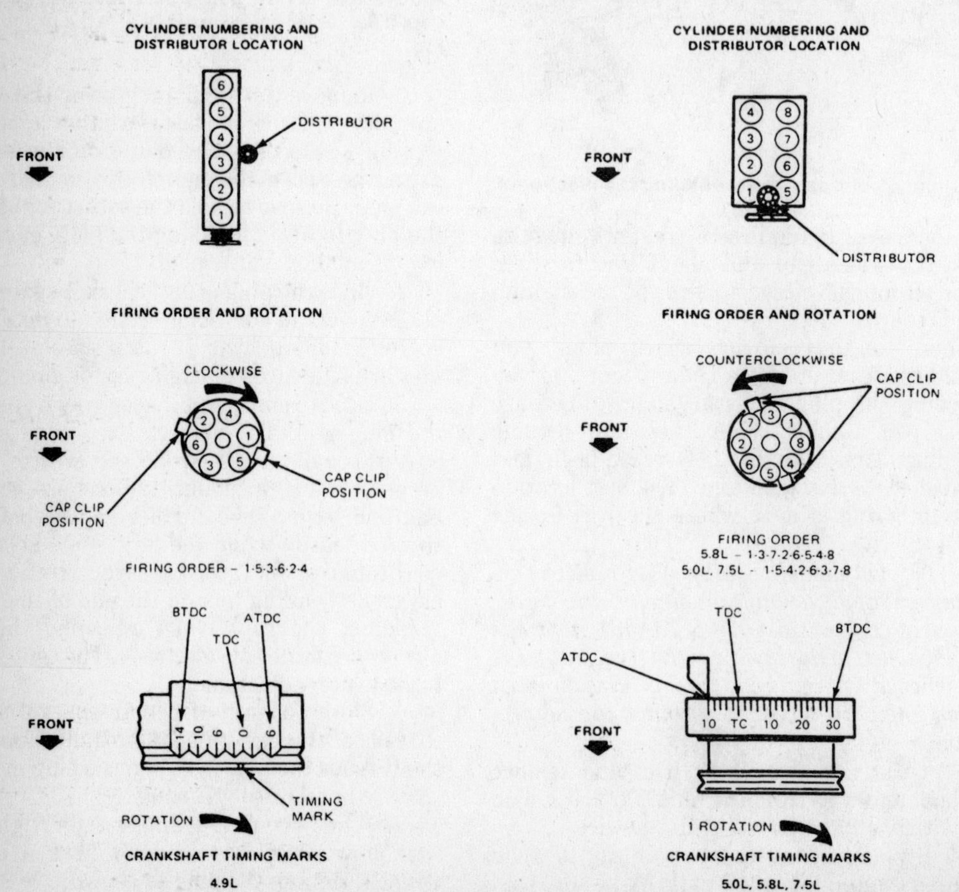

Engine firing orders

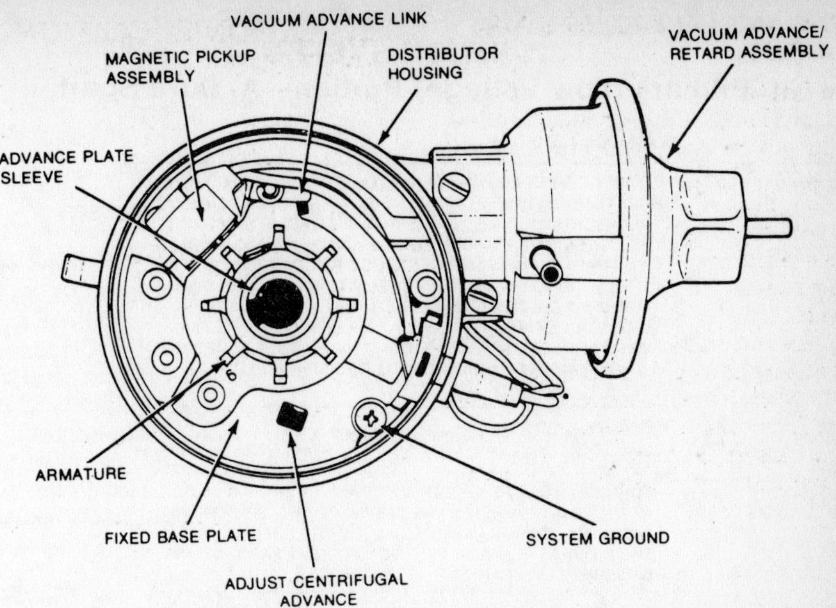

V8 type electronic distributor components

and collapsed. When DuraSpark is used in conjunction with the EEC, the EEC computer tells the DuraSpark module when to turn the coil primary current off or on. In this case, the armature position is only a reference signal of engine timing, used by the EEC computer in combination with other reference signals to determine optimum ignition spark timing.

The high voltage flows through the coil high tension lead to the distributor cap where the rotor distributes it to one of the spark plug terminals in the distributor cap. This process is repeated for every power stroke of the engine.

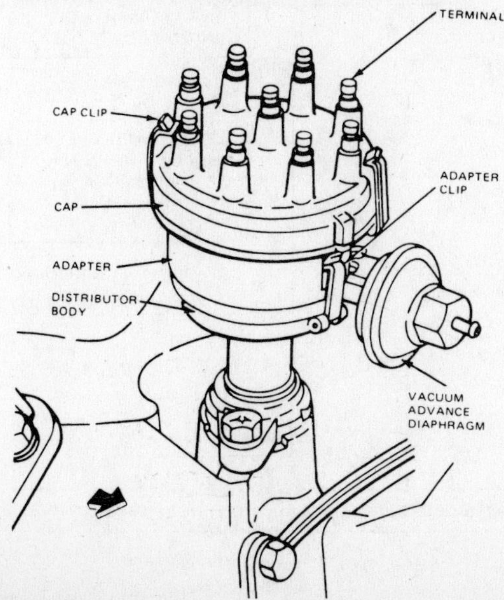

Distributor assembly

Ignition system troubles are caused by a failure in the primary and/or the secondary circuit; incorrect ignition timing; or incorrect distributor advance. Circuit failures may be caused by shorts, corroded or dirty terminals, loose connections, defective wire insulation, cracked distributor cap or rotor, defective pick-up coil assembly or amplifier module, defective distributor points or fouled spark plugs.

If an engine starting or operating trouble is attributed to the ignition system, start the engine and verify the complaint. On engines that will not start, be sure that there is gasoline in the fuel tank and the fuel is reaching the carburetor. Then locate the ignition system problem using the following procedures.

TROUBLESHOOTING DURASPARK II

The following procedures can be used to determine whether the ignition system is working or not. If these procedures fail to correct the problem, a full troubleshooting procedure should be performed.

Preliminary Checks

1. Check the battery's state of charge and connections.
2. Inspect all wires and connections for breaks, cuts, abrasions, or burn spots. Repair as necessary.
3. Unplug all connectors one at a time and inspect for corroded or burned contacts. Repair and plug connectors back together. DO NOT remove the dielectric compound in the connectors.
4. Check for loose or damaged spark plug or

IGNITION SYSTEM
II. Primary (Low Voltage) Portion—A. Dura Spark II

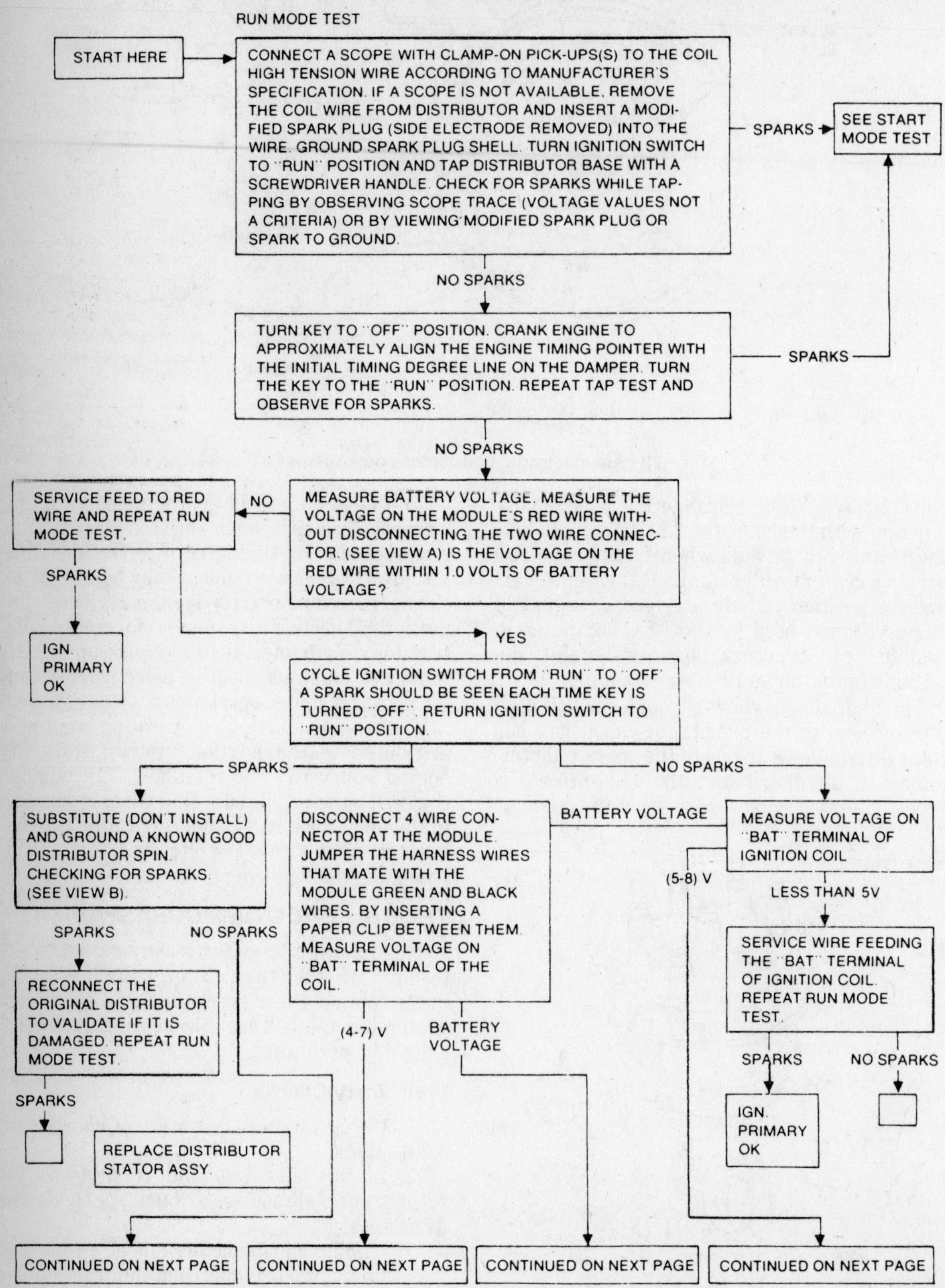

IGNITION SYSTEM (CONTINUED)
II. Primary (Low Voltage) Portion (continued)
A. Dura Spark II (continued)

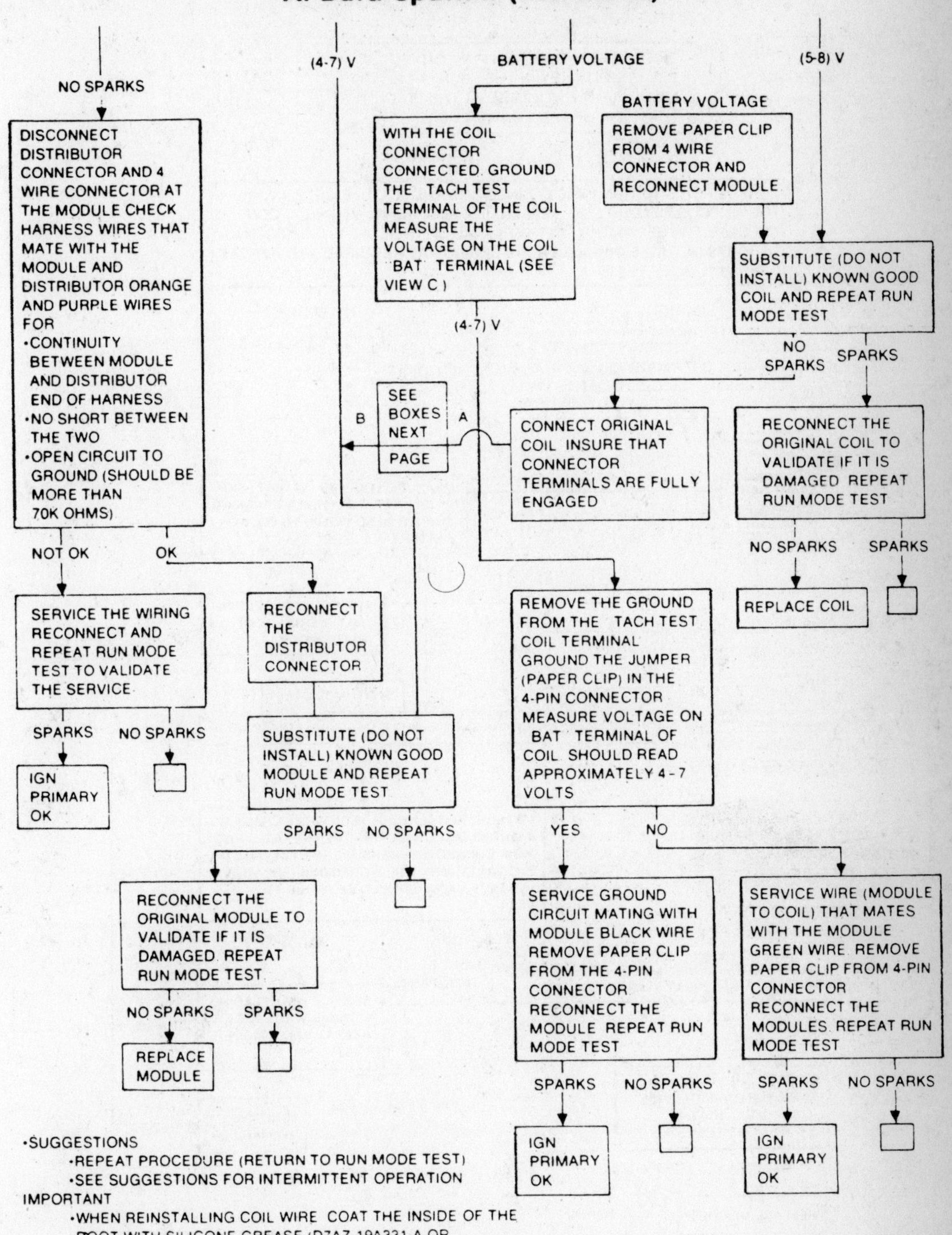

•SUGGESTIONS
- •REPEAT PROCEDURE (RETURN TO RUN MODE TEST)
- •SEE SUGGESTIONS FOR INTERMITTENT OPERATION

IMPORTANT
- •WHEN REINSTALLING COIL WIRE COAT THE INSIDE OF THE BOOT WITH SILICONE GREASE (D7AZ-19A331-A OR EQUIVALENT) USING SMALL CLEAN SCREWDRIVER BLADE

IGNITION SYSTEM (CONTINUED)
II. Primary (Low Voltage) Portion (Continued)
A. Dura Spark II (continued)

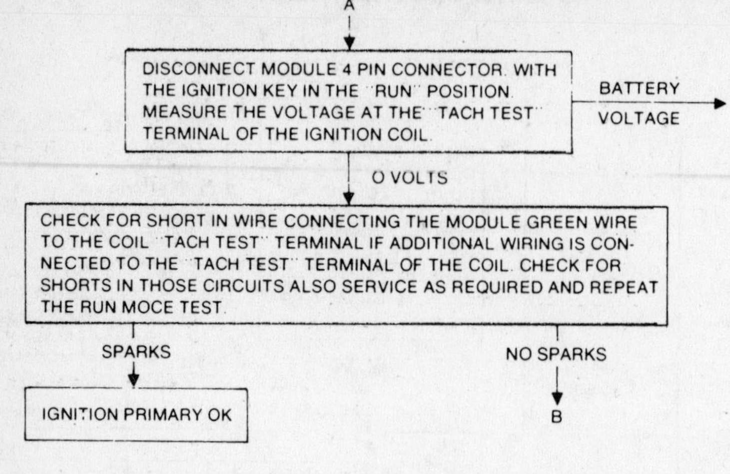

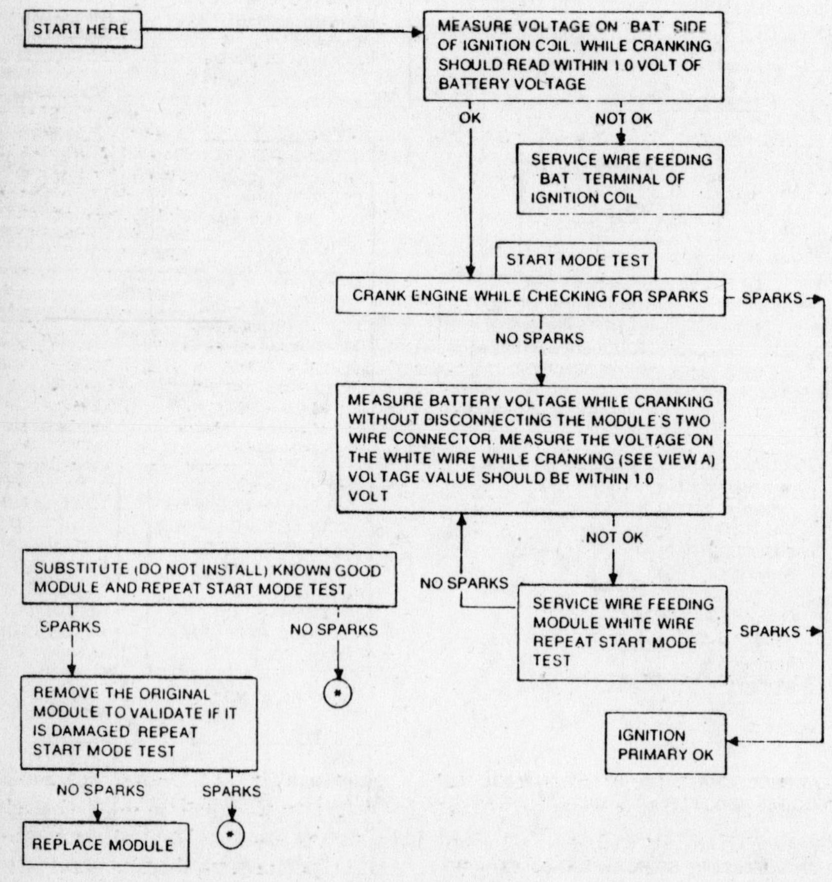

(*) SUGGESTIONS

- REPEAT PROCEDURE (RETURN TO RUN MODE TEST)
- SEE SUGGESTIONS FOR INTERMITTENT OPERATION

IMPORTANT

- WHEN REINSTALLING COIL WIRE. COAT THE INSIDE OF THE BOOT WITH SILICONE GREASE (D7AZ-19A331-A OR EQUIVALENT DOW 111 OR GE-G627) USING A SMALL. CLEAN SCREWDRIVER BLADE.

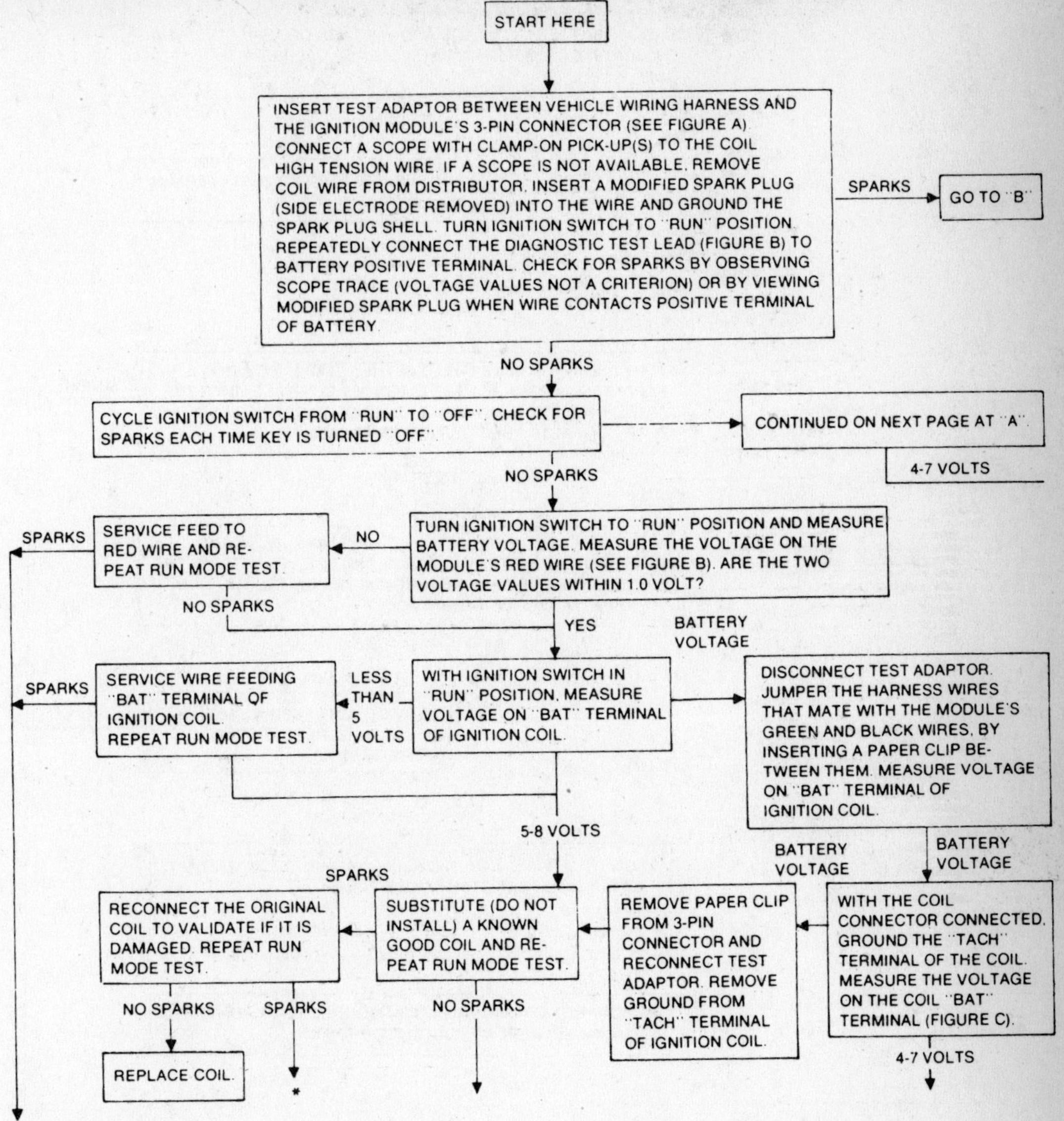

coil wires. A wire resistance check is given at the end of this section. If the boots or nipples are removed on 8mm ignition wires, reline the inside of each with new silicone dielectric compound (Motorcraft WA-10).

Special Tools

To perform the following tests, two special tools are needed; the ignition test jumper shown in the illustration and a modified spark plug. Use the illustration to assembly the ignition test jumper. The test jumper must be used when performing the following tests. The modified spark plug is basically a spark plug with the side electrode removed. Ford makes a special tool called a Spark Tester for this purpose, which besides not having a side electrode is equipped with a spring clip so that it can be

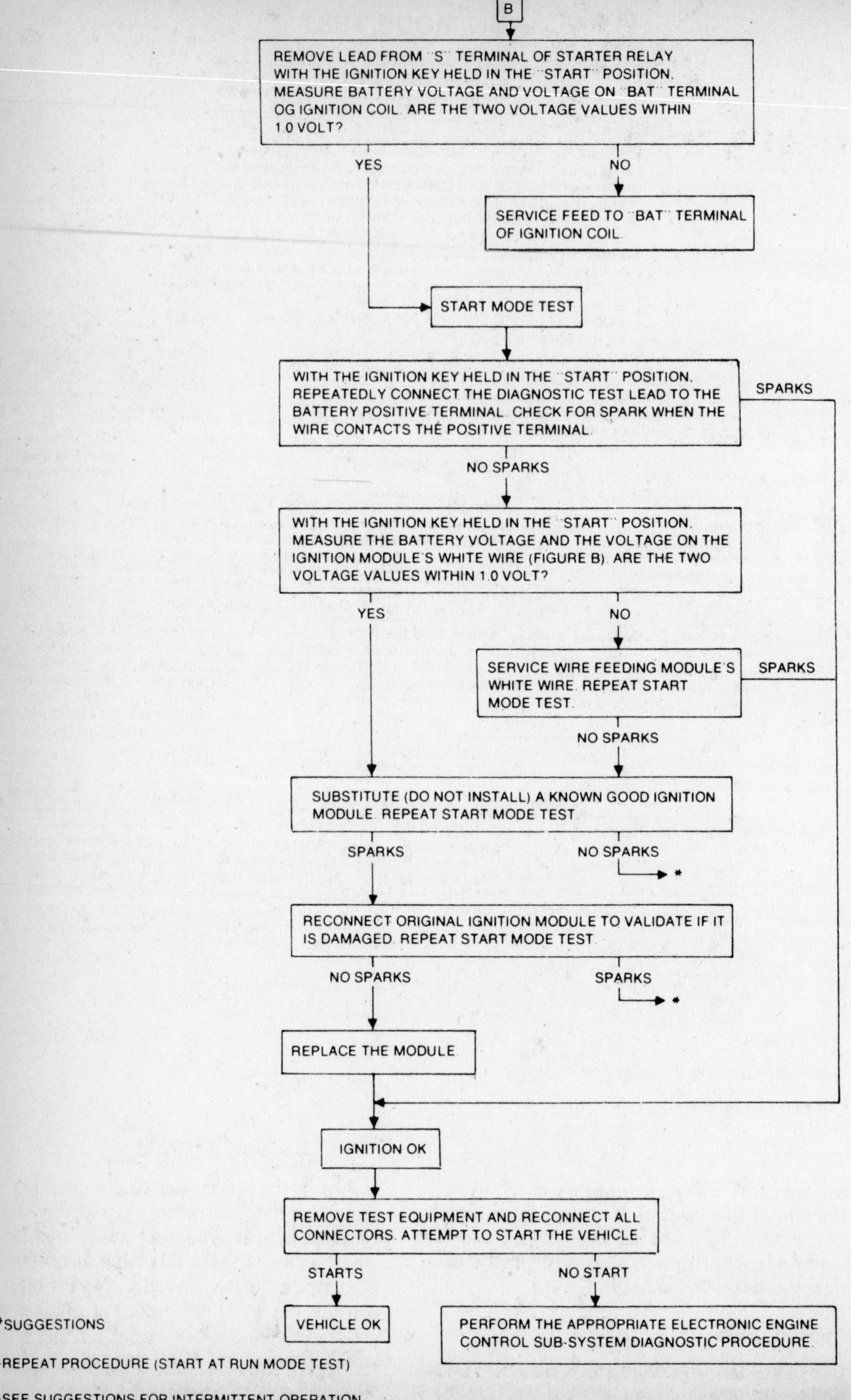
B
REMOVE LEAD FROM "S" TERMINAL OF STARTER RELAY WITH THE IGNITION KEY HELD IN THE "START" POSITION. MEASURE BATTERY VOLTAGE AND VOLTAGE ON "BAT" TERMINAL OG IGNITION COIL. ARE THE TWO VOLTAGE VALUES WITHIN 1.0 VOLT?
YES
NO
SERVICE FEED TO "BAT" TERMINAL OF IGNITION COIL.
START MODE TEST
WITH THE IGNITION KEY HELD IN THE "START" POSITION, REPEATEDLY CONNECT THE DIAGNOSTIC TEST LEAD TO THE BATTERY POSITIVE TERMINAL. CHECK FOR SPARK WHEN THE WIRE CONTACTS THE POSITIVE TERMINAL.
SPARKS
NO SPARKS
WITH THE IGNITION KEY HELD IN THE "START" POSITION. MEASURE THE BATTERY VOLTAGE AND THE VOLTAGE ON THE IGNITION MODULE'S WHITE WIRE (FIGURE B). ARE THE TWO VOLTAGE VALUES WITHIN 1.0 VOLT?
YES
NO
SERVICE WIRE FEEDING MODULE'S WHITE WIRE. REPEAT START MODE TEST.
SPARKS
NO SPARKS
SUBSTITUTE (DO NOT INSTALL) A KNOWN GOOD IGNITION MODULE. REPEAT START MODE TEST.
SPARKS
NO SPARKS
*
RECONNECT ORIGINAL IGNITION MODULE TO VALIDATE IF IT IS DAMAGED. REPEAT START MODE TEST.
NO SPARKS
SPARKS
*
REPLACE THE MODULE.
IGNITION OK
REMOVE TEST EQUIPMENT AND RECONNECT ALL CONNECTORS. ATTEMPT TO START THE VEHICLE.
STARTS
NO START
VEHICLE OK
PERFORM THE APPROPRIATE ELECTRONIC ENGINE CONTROL SUB-SYSTEM DIAGNOSTIC PROCEDURE.
*SUGGESTIONS
•REPEAT PROCEDURE (START AT RUN MODE TEST)
•SEE SUGGESTIONS FOR INTERMITTENT OPERATION

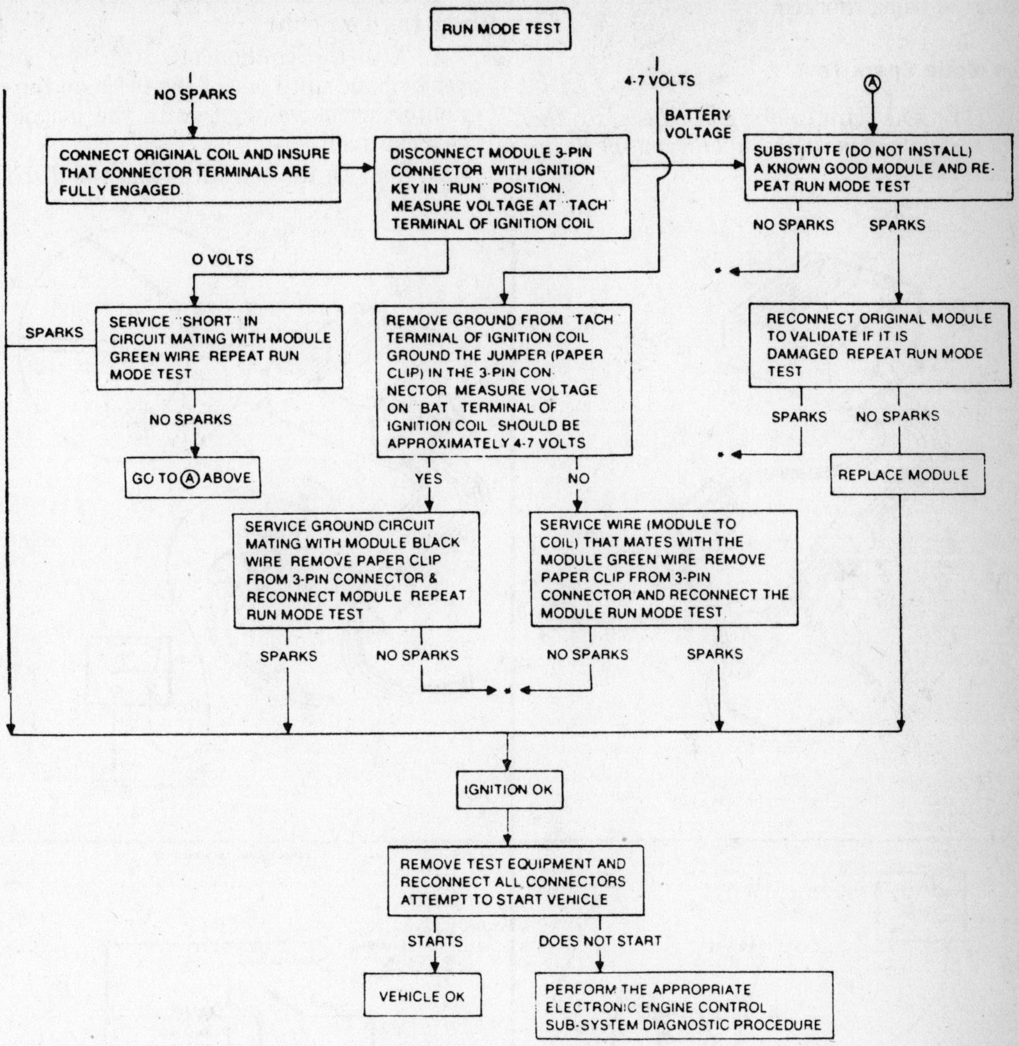

RUN MODE TEST
NO SPARKS
CONNECT ORIGINAL COIL AND INSURE THAT CONNECTOR TERMINALS ARE FULLY ENGAGED
DISCONNECT MODULE 3-PIN CONNECTOR WITH IGNITION KEY IN "RUN" POSITION. MEASURE VOLTAGE AT "TACH" TERMINAL OF IGNITION COIL
4-7 VOLTS
BATTERY VOLTAGE
Ⓐ
SUBSTITUTE (DO NOT INSTALL) A KNOWN GOOD MODULE AND REPEAT RUN MODE TEST
NO SPARKS
SPARKS
0 VOLTS
SPARKS
SERVICE "SHORT" IN CIRCUIT MATING WITH MODULE GREEN WIRE REPEAT RUN MODE TEST
REMOVE GROUND FROM "TACH" TERMINAL OF IGNITION COIL GROUND THE JUMPER (PAPER CLIP) IN THE 3-PIN CONNECTOR MEASURE VOLTAGE ON "BAT" TERMINAL OF IGNITION COIL SHOULD BE APPROXIMATELY 4-7 VOLTS
RECONNECT ORIGINAL MODULE TO VALIDATE IF IT IS DAMAGED REPEAT RUN MODE TEST
NO SPARKS
SPARKS
NO SPARKS
GO TO Ⓐ ABOVE
YES
NO
REPLACE MODULE
SERVICE GROUND CIRCUIT MATING WITH MODULE BLACK WIRE REMOVE PAPER CLIP FROM 3-PIN CONNECTOR & RECONNECT MODULE REPEAT RUN MODE TEST
SERVICE WIRE (MODULE TO COIL) THAT MATES WITH THE MODULE GREEN WIRE REMOVE PAPER CLIP FROM 3-PIN CONNECTOR AND RECONNECT THE MODULE RUN MODE TEST
SPARKS
NO SPARKS
NO SPARKS
SPARKS
IGNITION OK
REMOVE TEST EQUIPMENT AND RECONNECT ALL CONNECTORS ATTEMPT TO START VEHICLE
STARTS
DOES NOT START
VEHICLE OK
PERFORM THE APPROPRIATE ELECTRONIC ENGINE CONTROL SUB-SYSTEM DIAGNOSTIC PROCEDURE

*SUGGESTIONS

•REPEAT PROCEDURE (START AT RUN MODE TEST)

•SEE SUGGESTIONS FOR INTERMITTENT OPERATION

IGNITION CONDENSER
(0.25-0.35 MFD)
FROM STANDARD
BREAKER POINT
IGNITION SYSTEM
ALLIGATOR CLIP
ALLIGATOR CLIP
14 GAUGE WIRE
14 GAUGE WIRE
SWITCH
10 AMP
110 VOLT

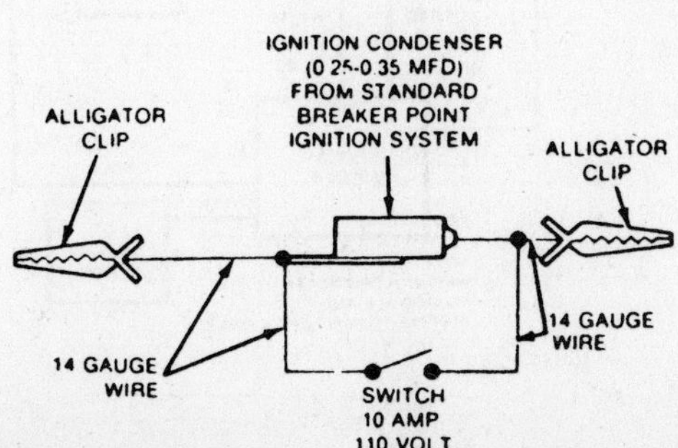

Test jumper wire switch used for testing Dura Spark ignition systems

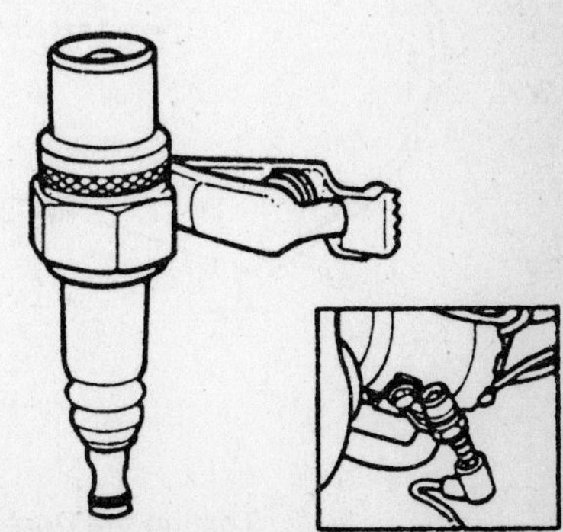

Spark plug tester; actually a modified spark plug (side electrode removed) with a spring for ground

grounded to engine metal. It is recommended that the Spark Tester be used as there is less change of being shocked.

Run Mode Spark Test

NOTE: *The wire colors given here are the main colors of the wires, not the dots or hashmarks.*

STEP 1

1. Remove the distributor cap and rotor from the distributor.

2. With the ignition off, turn the engine over by hand until one of the teeth on the distributor armature aligns with the magnet in the pickup coil.

3. Remove the coil wire from the distribu-

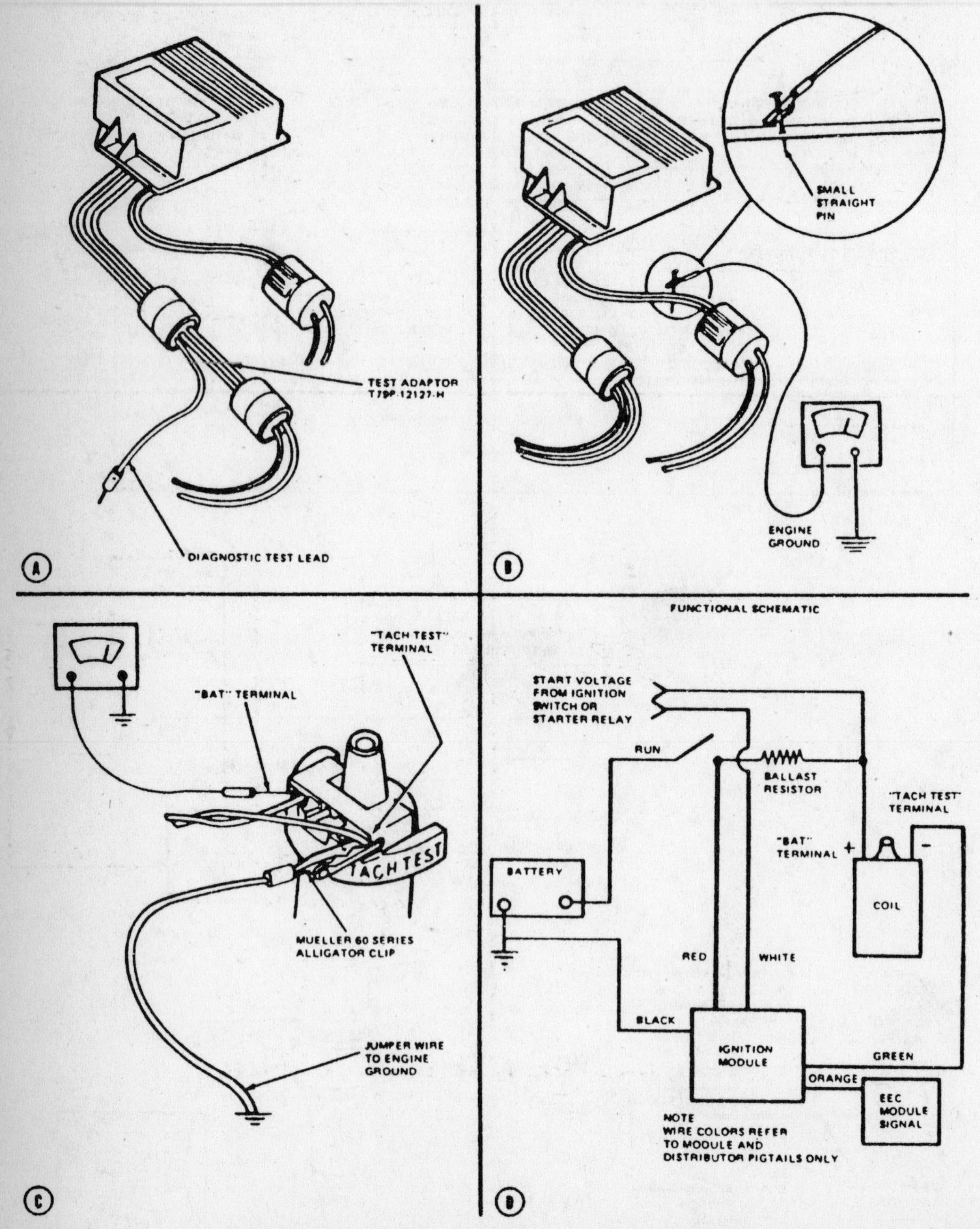

Testing the Dura Spark ignition on models with EEC

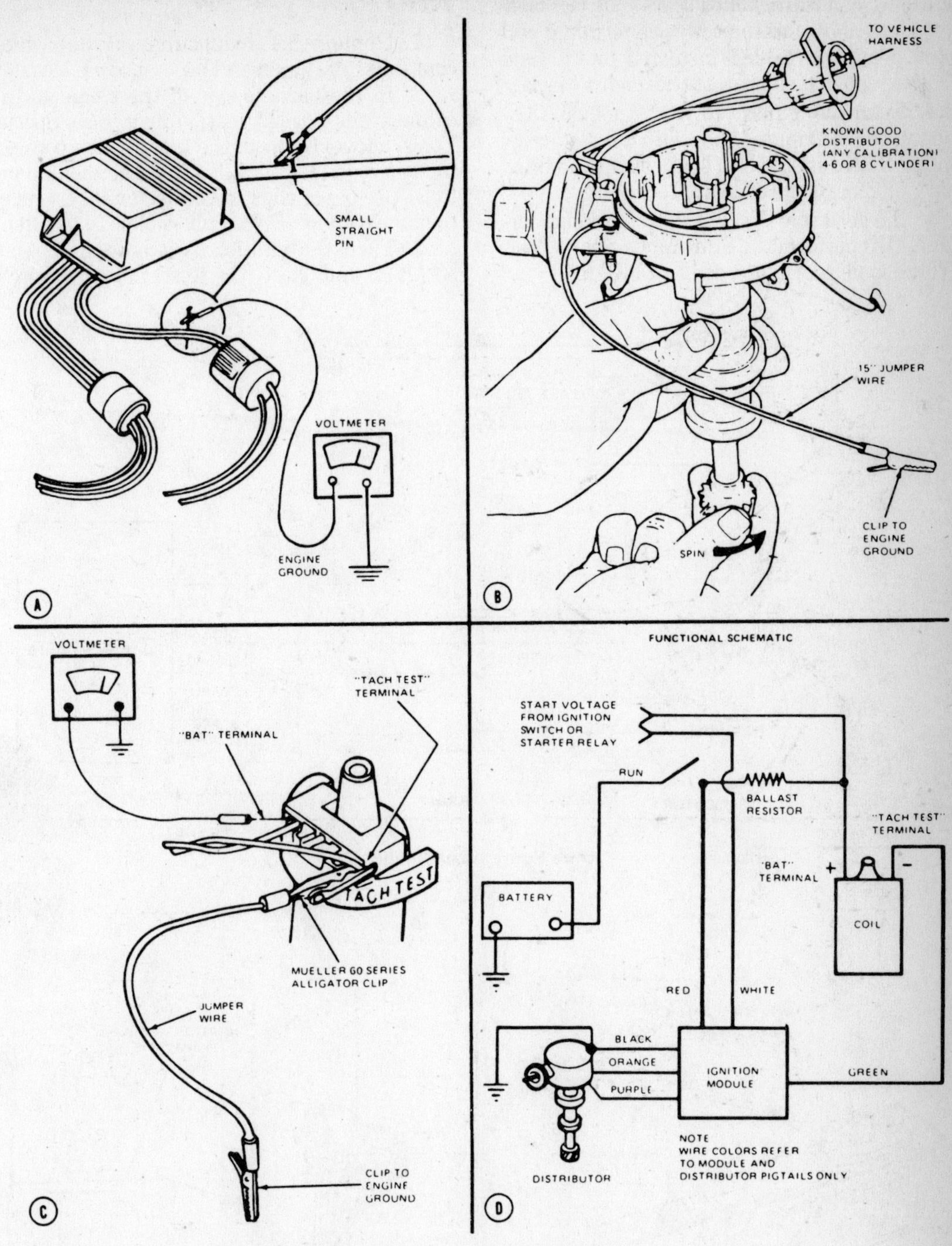

Testing the Dura Spark ignition on models without EEC

tor cap. Install the modified spark plug (see Special Tools, above) in the coil wire terminal and using heavy gloves and insulated pliers, hold the spark plug shell against the engine block.

4. Turn the ignition to RUN (not START) and tap the distributor body with a screwdriver handle. There should be a spark at the modified spark plug or at the coil wire terminal.

5. If a good spark is evident, the primary circuit is OK: perform the Start Mode Spark Test. If there is no spark, proceed to STEP 2.

STEP 2

1. Unplug the module connector(s) which contain(s) the green and black module leads.

2. In the harness side of the connector(s), connect the special test jumper (see Special Tools, above) between the leads which connect to the green and black leads of the module pig tails. Use paper clips on connector socket holes to make contact. Do not allow clips to ground.

3. Turn the ignition switch to RUN (not START) and close the test jumper switch.

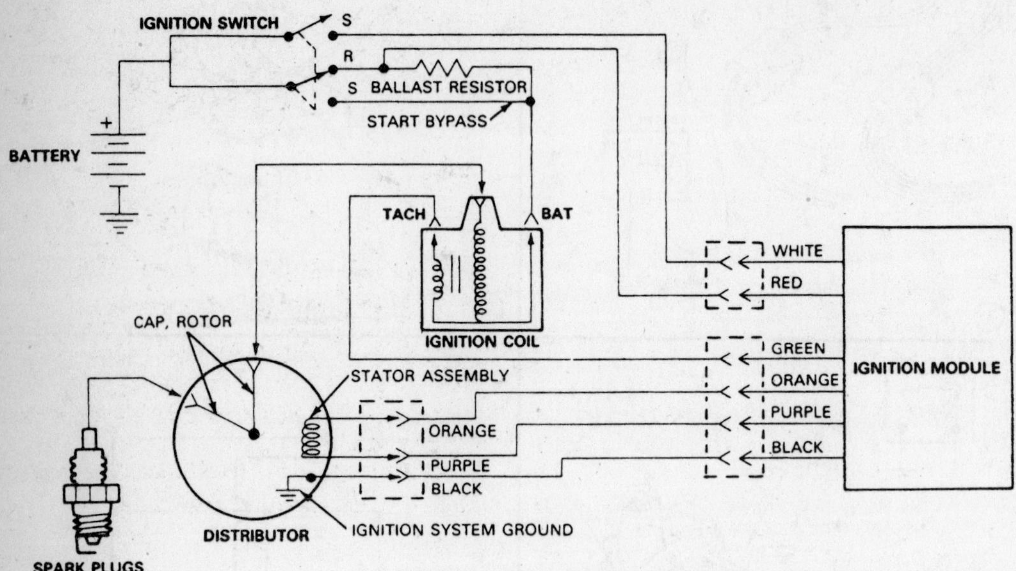

Dura Spark II schematic

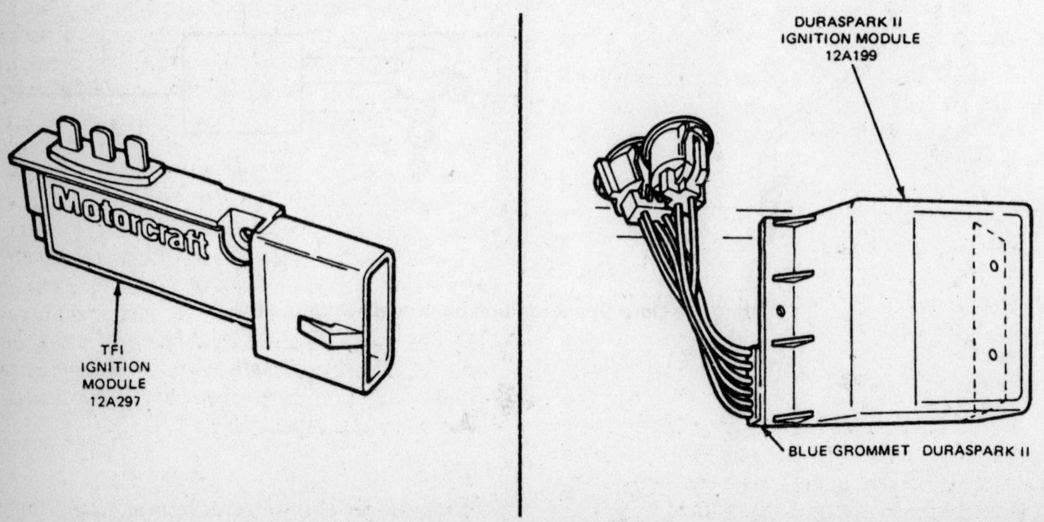

Ignition modules

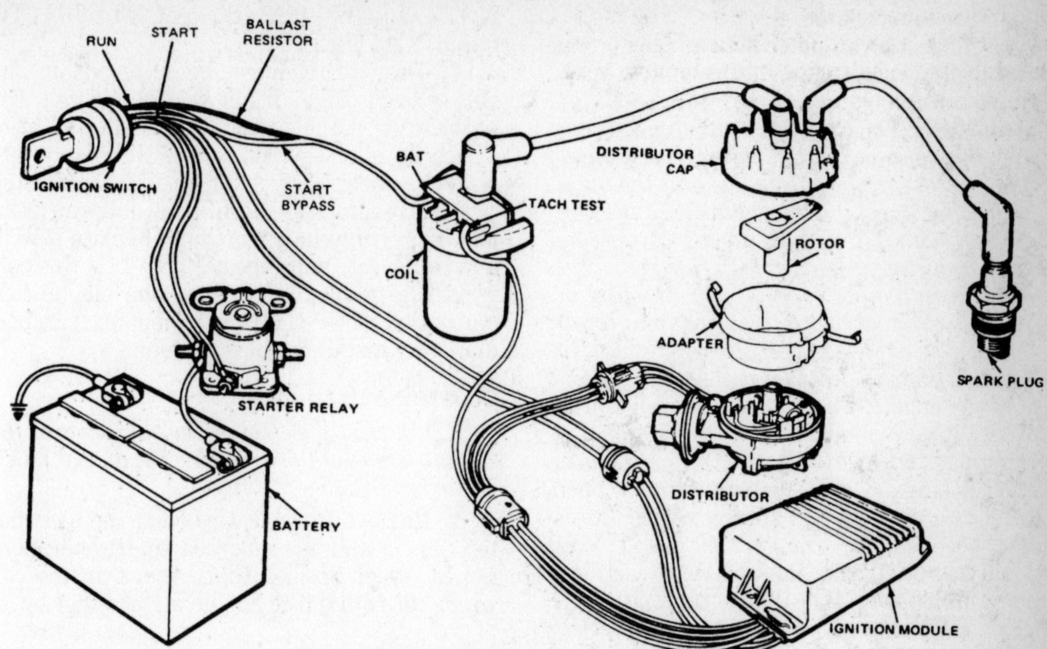

Dura Spark II components

Leave closed for about 1 second, then open. Repeat several times. There should be a spark each time the switch is opened.

4. If there is no spark, the problem is probably in the primary circuit through the ignition switch, the coil, the green lead or the black lead, or the ground connection in the distributor; Perform STEP 3. If there is a spark, the primary circuit wiring and coil are probably OK. The problem is probably in the distributor pick-up, the module red wire, or the module: perform STEP 6.

STEP 3

1. Disconnect the test jumper lead from the black lead and connect it to a good ground. Turn the test jumper switch on and off several times as in STEP 2.

2. If there is no spark, the problem is probably in the green lead, the coil, or the coil feed circuit: perform STEP 5.

3. If there is spark, the problem is probably in the black lead or the distributor ground connection: perform STEP 4.

STEP 4

1. Connect an ohmmeter between the black lead and ground. With the meter on its lowest scale, there should be no measurable resistance in the circuit. If there is resistance, check the distributor ground connection and the black lead from the module. Repair as necessary, remove the ohmmeter, plug in all connections and repeat STEP 1.

2. If there is no resistance, the primary ground wiring is OK: perform STEP 6.

STEP 5

1. Disconnect the test jumper from the green lead and ground and connect it between the TACH-TEST terminal of the coil and a good ground to the engine.

2. With the ignition switch in the RUN position, turn the jumper switch on. Hold it on for about 1 second then turn it off as in Step 2. Repeat several times. There should be a spark each time the switch in turned off. If there is no spark, the problem is probably in the primary circuit running through the ignition switch to the coil BAT terminal, or in the coil itself. Check coil resistance (test given later in this section), and check the coil for internal shorts or opens. Check the coil feed circuit for opens, shorts, or high resistance. Repair as necessary, reconnect all connectors and repeat STEP 1. If there is spark, the coil and its feed circuit are OK. The problem could be in the green lead between the coil and the module. Check for an open or short, repair as necessary, reconnect all connectors and repeat STEP 1.

STEP 6

To perform this step, a voltmeter which is not combined with a dwell meter is needed. The slight needle oscillations ($^1/_2$v) you'll be looking for may not be detectable on the combined voltmeter/dwell meter unit.

1. Connect a voltmeter between the orange and purple leads on the harness side of the module connectors.

CAUTION: *On catalytic converter equipped cars, disconnect the air supply line between the Thermactor by-pass valve and the manifold before cranking the engine with the ignition off. This will prevent damage to the catalytic converter. After testing, run the engine for at least 3 minutes before reconnecting the by-pass valve, to clear excess fuel from the exhaust system.*

2. Set the voltmeter on its lowest scale and crank the engine. The meter needle should oscillate slightly (about 1/2v). If the meter does not oscillate, check the circuit through the magnetic pick-up in the distributor for open, shorts, shorts to ground and resistance. Resistance between the orange and purple leads should be 400–1,000Ω, and between each lead and ground should be more than 70,000Ω. Repair as necessary, reconnect all connectors and repeat STEP 1.

If the meter oscillates, the problem is probably in the power feed to the module (red wire) or in the module itself: proceed to STEP 7.

STEP 7

1. Remove all meters and jumpers and plug in all connectors.

2. Turn the ignition switch to the RUN position and measure voltage between the battery positive terminal and engine ground. It should be 12 volts.

3. Next, measure voltage between the red lead of the module and engine ground. To mark this measurement, it will be necessary to pierce the red wire with a straight pin and connect the voltmeter to the straight pin and to ground. DO NOT ALLOW THE STRAIGHT PIN TO GROUND ITSELF!

4. The two readings should be within one volt of each other. If not within one volt, the problem is in the power feed to the red lead. Check for shorts, open, or high resistance and correct as necessary. After repairs, repeat Step 1. If the readings are within one volt, the problem is probably in the module. Replace it with a good module and repeat STEP 1. If this corrects the problem, reconnect the old module and repeat STEP 1. If the problem returns, permanently install the new module.

Start Mode Spark Test

NOTE: *The wire colors given here are the main colors of the wires, not the dots or hashmarks.*

1. Remove the coil wire from the distributor cap. Install the modified spark plug mentioned under Special Tools, above, in the coil wire and ground it to engine metal either by its

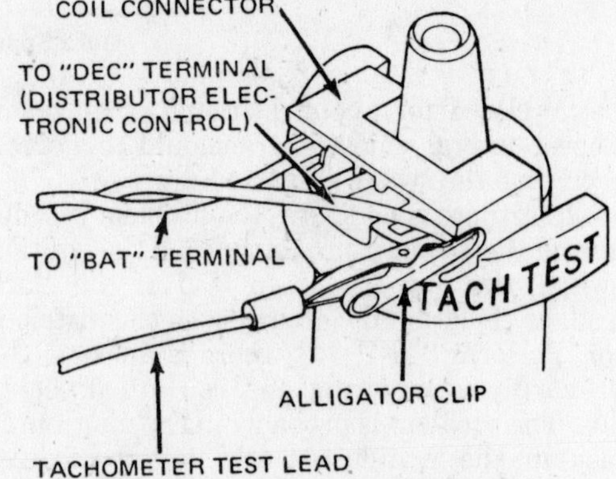

Attaching a tachometer to the coil

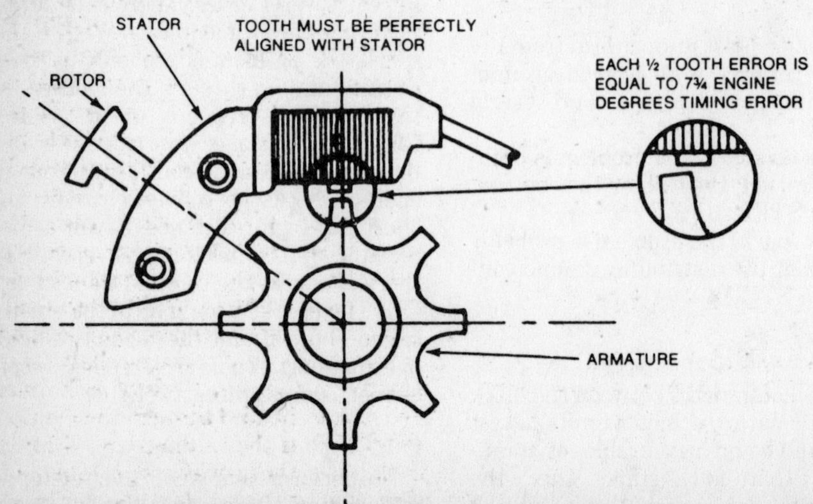

V8 electronic distributor, static timing position

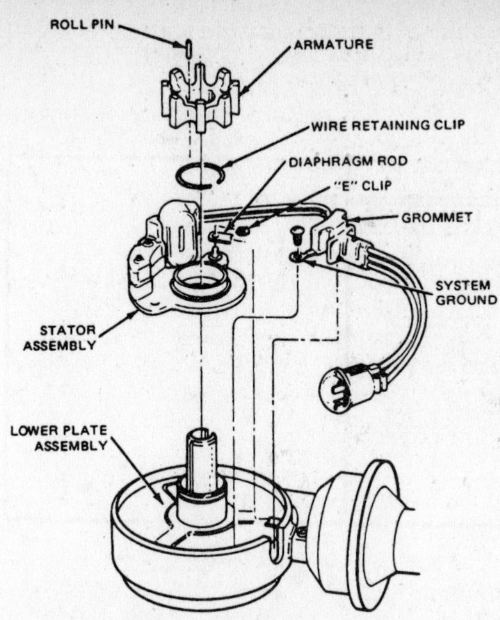

Dura Spark II stator replacement

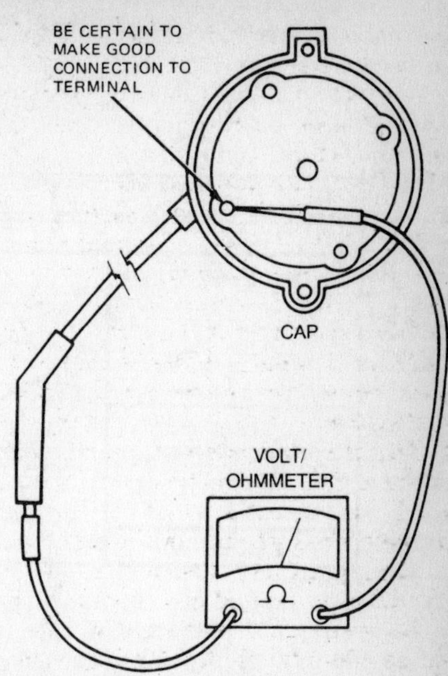

Checking ignition wire resistance

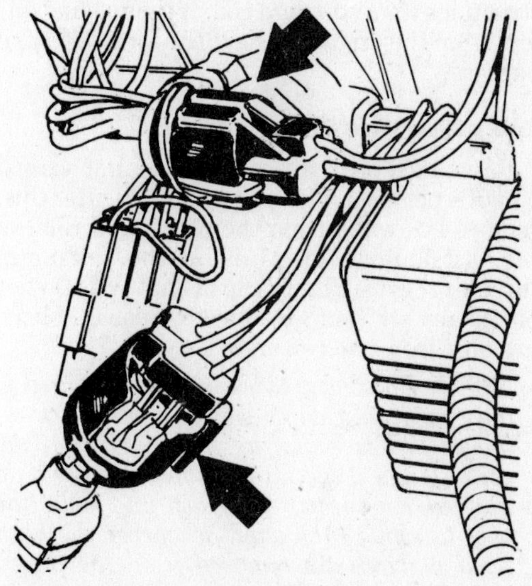

When you're working on the electronic ignition, unplug the module connectors here. Leave the module side alone or you'll short out the module (shown on right)

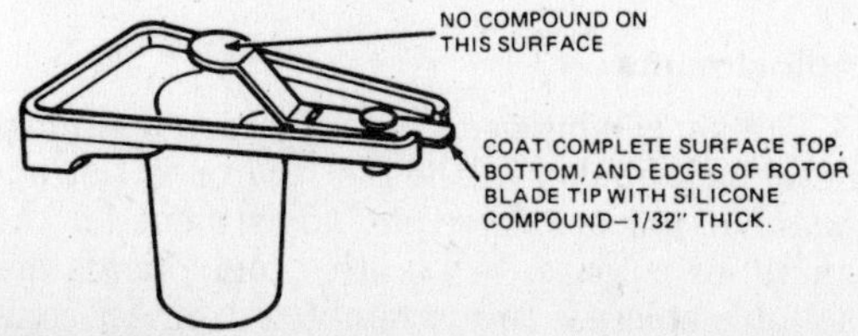

Silicone-compound application to distributor rotor

spring clip (Spark Tester) or by holding the spark plug shell against the engine block with insulated pliers.

NOTE: *See CAUTION under STEP 6 of Run Mode Spark Test, above.*

2. Have an assistant crank the engine using the ignition switch and check for spark. If there is good spark, the problem is probably in distributor cap, rotor, ignition cables or spark plugs. If there is no spark, proceed to Step 3.

3. Measure the battery voltage. Next, measure the voltage at the white wire of the module while cranking the engine. To mark this measurement, it will be necessary to pierce the white wire with a straight pin and connect the voltmeter to the straight pin and to ground. DO NOT ALLOW THE STRAIGHT PIN TO GROUND ITSELF. The battery voltage and the voltage at the white wire should be within 1 volt of each other. If the readings are not within 1 volt of each other, check and repair the feed through the ignition switch to the white wire. Recheck for spark (Step 1). If the readings are within 1 volt of each other, or if there is still no spark after the power feed to white wire is repaired, proceed to Step 4.

4. Measure the coil BAT terminal voltage while cranking the engine. The reading should be within 1 volt of battery voltage. If the readings are not within 1 volt of each other, check and repair the feed through the ignition switch to the coil. If the readings are within 1 volt of each other, the problem is probably in the ignition module. Substitute another module and repeat the test for spark (Step 1).

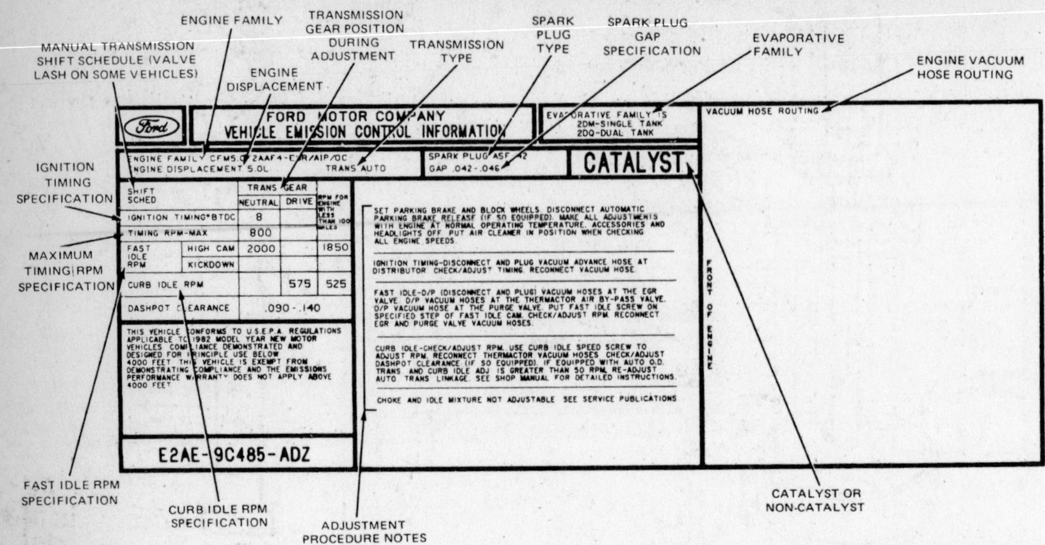

TFI-IV System

SYSTEM OPERATION

The TFI-IV ignition system features a universal distributor using no centrifugal or vacuum advance. The distributor has a die cast base which incorporates an integrally mounted TFI (Thick Film Integrated) ignition module, a "Hall Effect" vane switch stator assembly and provision for fixed octane adjustment. The TFI system uses an E-Core ignition coil in lieu of the Dura Spark coil. No distributor calibration is required and initial timing is not a normal adjustment, since advance etc. is controlled by the EEC-IV system.

GENERAL TESTING

Ignition Coil Test

The ignition coil must be diagnosed separately from the rest of the ignition system.

1. Primary resistance is measured between the two primary (low voltage) coil terminals, with the coil connector disconnected and the ignition switch off. Primary resistance should be 0.3–1.0Ω.

2. On Dura Spark ignitions, the secondary resistance is measured between the BATT and high voltage (secondary) terminals of the ignition coil with the ignition off, and the wiring from the coil disconnected. Secondary resistance must be 8,000–11,500Ω.

3. If resistance tests are okay, but the coil is still suspected, test the coil on a coil tester by following the test equipment manufacturer's instructions for a standard coil. If the reading differs from the original test, check for a defective harness.

Spark Plug Wire Resistance

Resistance on these wires must not exceed 5,000Ω per foot. To properly measure this, remove the wires from the plugs, and remove the distributor cap. Measure the resistance through the distributor cap at that end. Do not pierce any ignition wire for any reason. Measure only from the two ends.

NOTE: *Silicone grease must be re-applied to the spark plug wires whenever they are removed. When removing the wires from the spark plugs, a special tool should be used. do not pull on the wires. Grasp and twist the boot to remove the wire. Whenever the high tension wires are removed from the plugs, coil, or distributor, silicone grease must be applied to the boot before reconnection. Use a clean small screwdriver blase to coat the entire interior surface with Ford silicone grease D7AZ–19A331–A, Dow Corning #111, or General Electric G–627.*

Adjustments

The air gap between the armature and magnetic pick-up coil in the distributor is not adjustable, nor are there any adjustment for the amplifier module. Inoperative components are simply replaced. Any attempt to connect components outside the vehicle may result in component failure.

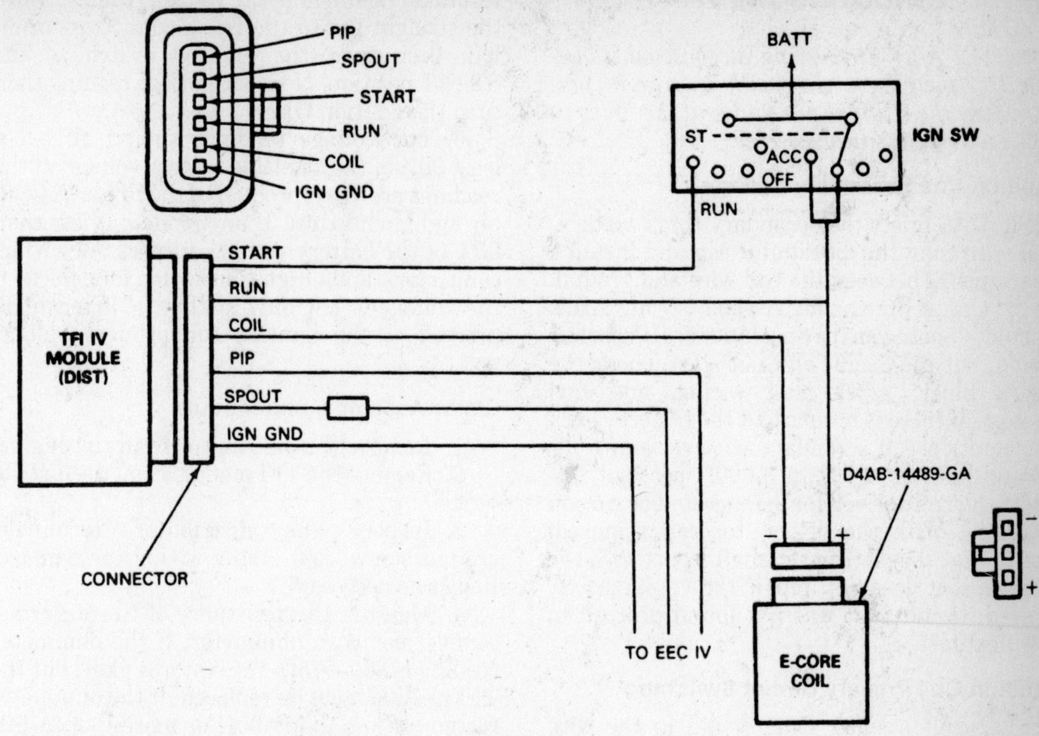

TFI schematic

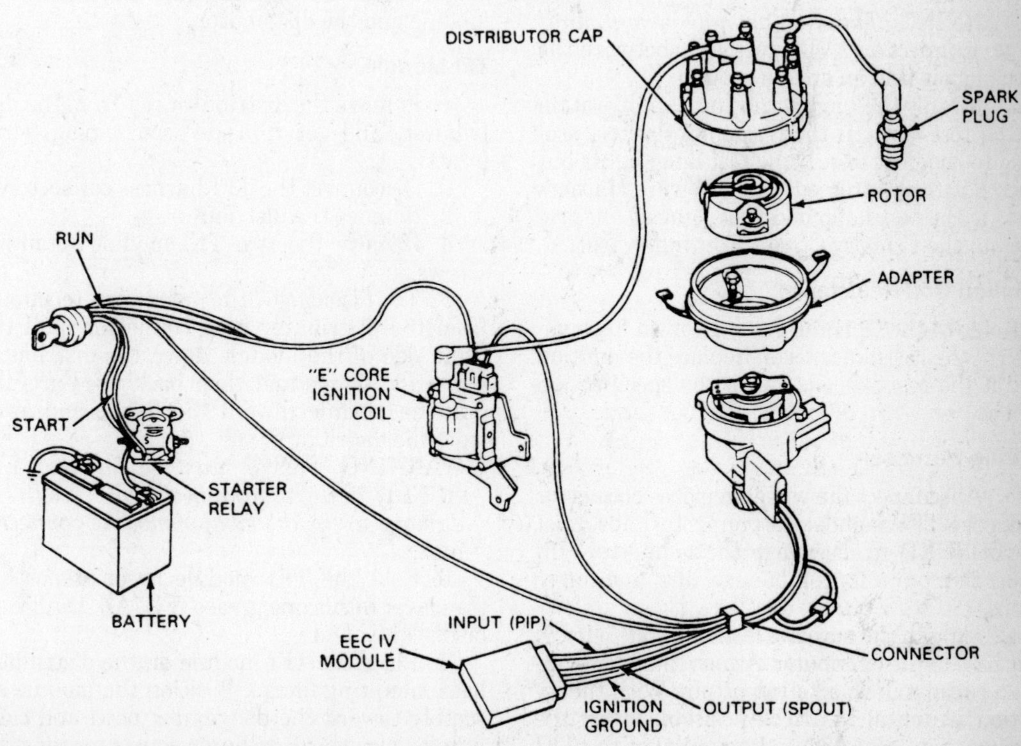

TFI components

TROUBLESHOOTING THE TFI-IV SYSTEM

NOTE: *After performing any test which requires piercing a wire with a straight pin, remove the straight pin and seal the holes in the wire with silicone sealer.*

Ignition Coil Secondary Voltage

1. Disconnect the secondary (high voltage) coil wire from the distributor cap and install a spark tester between the coil wire and ground.
2. Crank the engine. A good, strong spark should be noted at the spark tester. If spark is noted, but the engine will not start, check the spark plugs, spark plug wiring, and fuel system. If there is no spark at the tester: Check the ignition coil secondary wire resistance; it should be no more than 5,000Ω per foot. Inspect the ignition coil for damage and/or carbon tracking. With the distributor cap removed, verify that the distributor shaft turns with the engine; if it does not, repair the engine as required. If the fault was not found proceed to the next test.

Ignition Coil Primary Circuit Switching

1. Insert a small straight pin in the wire which runs from the coil negative (–) terminal to the TFI module, about 1 in. (25mm) from the module.

WARNING: *The pin must not touch ground!*

2. Connect a 12 VDC test lamp between the straight pin and an engine ground.
3. Crank the engine, noting the operation of the test lamp. If the test lamp flashes, proceed to the next test. If the test lamp lights but does not flash, proceed to the Wiring Harness test. If the test lamp does not light at all, proceed to the Primary Circuit Continuity test.

Ignition Coil Resistance

Refer to the General Testing for an explanation of the resistance tests. Replace the ignition coil if the resistance is out of the specification range.

Wiring Harness

1. Disconnect the wiring harness connector from the TFI module; the connector tabs must be PUSHED to disengage the connector. Inspect the connector for damage, dirt, and corrosion.
2. Attach the negative lead of a voltmeter to the base of the distributor. Attach the other voltmeter lead to a small straight pin. With the ignition switch in the RUN position, insert the straight pin into the No. 1 terminal of the TFI module connector. Note the voltage reading. With the ignition switch in the RUN position, move the straight pin to the No. 2 connector terminal. Again, note the voltage reading. Move the straight pin to the No. 3 connector terminal, then turn the ignition switch to the START position. Note the voltage reading then turn the ignition OFF.
3. The voltage readings should all be at least 90% of the available battery voltage. If the readings are okay, proceed to the Stator Assembly and Module test. If any reading is less than 90% of the battery voltage, inspect the wiring, connectors, and/or ignition switch for defects. if the voltage is low only at the No. 1 terminal, proceed to the ignition coil primary voltage test.

Stator Assembly and Module

1. Remove the distributor from the engine.
2. Remove the TFI module from the distributor.
3. Inspect the distributor terminals, ground screw, and stator wiring for damage. Repair as necessary.
4. Measure the resistance of the stator assembly, using an ohmmeter. If the ohmmeter reading is 800–975Ω, the stator is okay, but the TFI module must be replaced. If the ohmmeter reading is less than 800Ω or more than 975Ω; the TFI module is okay, but the stator module must be replaced.
5. Repair as necessary and install the TFI module and the distributor.

TFI Module

1. Remove the distributor cap from the distributor, and set it aside (spark plug wires intact).
2. Disconnect the TFI harness connector.
3. Remove the distributor.
4. Remove the two TFI module retaining screws.
5. To disengage the modules terminals from the distributor base connector, pull the right side of the module down the distributor mounting flange and then back up. Carefully pull the module toward the flange and away from the distributor.

WARNING: *Step 5 must be followed EXACTLY; failure to do so will result in damage to the distributor module connector pins.*

6. Coat the TFI module baseplate with a thin layer of silicone grease (FD7AZ–19A331–A or its equivalent).
7. Place the TFI module on the distributor base mounting flange. Position the module assembly toward the distributor bowl and carefully engage the distributor connector pins. Install and torque the two TFI module retaining screws to 9–16 inch lbs.
8. Install the distributor assembly.

9. Install the distributor cap and check the engine timing.

Primary Circuit Continuity

This test is performed in the same manner as the previous Wiring Harness test, but only the No. 1 terminal conductor is tested (ignition switch in Run position). If the voltage is less than 90% of the available battery voltage, proceed to the coil primary voltage test.

Ignition Coil Primary Voltage

1. Attach the negative lead of a voltmeter to the distributor base.
2. Turn the ignition switch ON and connect the positive voltmeter lead to the negative (–) ignition coil terminal. Note the voltage reading and turn the ignition OFF. If the voltmeter reading is less than 90% of the available battery voltage, inspect the wiring between the ignition module and the negative (–) coil terminal, then proceed to the last test, which follows.

Ignition Coil Supply Voltage

1. Attach the negative lead of a voltmeter to the distributor base.
2. Turn the ignition switch ON and connect the positive voltmeter lead to the positive (+) ignition coil terminal. Note the voltage reading then turn the ignition OFF. If the voltage reading is at least 90% of the battery voltage, yet the engine will still not run; first, check the ignition coil connector and terminals for corrosion, dirt, and/or damage; second, replace the ignition switch if the connectors and terminal are okay.
3. Connect any remaining wiring.

IGNITION TIMING

Ignition timing is the measurement, in degrees of crankshaft rotation, of the point at which the spark plugs fire in each of the cylinders. It is measured in degrees before or after Top Dead Center (TDC) of the compression stroke.

Ideally, the air/fuel mixture in the cylinder will be ignited by the spark plug just as the piston passes TDC of the compression stroke. If this happens, the piston will be beginning the power stroke just as the compressed and ignited air/fuel mixture starts to expand. The expansion of the air/fuel mixture then forces the piston down on the power stroke and turns the crankshaft.

Because it takes a fraction of a second for the spark plug to ignite the mixture in the cylinder, the spark plug must fire a little before the piston reaches TDC. Otherwise, the mixture will not be completely ignited as the piston passes TDC and the full power of the explosion will not be used by the engine.

The timing measurement is given in degrees of crankshaft rotation before the piston reaches TDC (BTDC, or Before Top Dead Center). If the setting for the ignition timing is 5°BTDC, each spark plug must fire 5° before each piston reaches TDC. This only holds true, however, when the engine is at idle speed.

As the engine speed increases, the piston go faster. The spark plugs have to ignite the fuel even sooner if it is to be completely ignited when the piston reaches TDC.

With the Dura Spark II system, the distributor has a means to advance the timing of the spark as the engine speed increases. This is accomplished by centrifugal weights within the distributor and a vacuum diaphragm mounted on the side of the distributor. It is necessary to disconnect the vacuum lines from the diaphragm when the ignition timing is being set.

With the TFI-IV system, ignition timing is calculated at all phases of vehicle operation by the TFI module.

If the ignition is set too far advanced (BTDC), the ignition and expansion of the fuel in the cylinder will occur too soon and tend to force the piston down while it is still traveling up. This causes engine ping. If the ignition spark is set too far retarded after TDC (ATDC), the piston will have already passed TDC and started on its way down when the fuel is ignited. This will cause the piston to be forced down for only a portion of its travel. This will result in poor engine performance and lack of power.

The timing is best checked with a timing light. This device is connected in series with the No. 1 spark plug. The current that fires the spark plug also causes the timing light to flash.

There is a notch on the crankshaft pulley on all 6-cyl. engines. A scale of degrees of crankshaft rotation is attached to the engine block in such a position that the notch will pass close by the scale. On the V8 engines, the scale is located on the crankshaft pulley and a pointer is attached to the engine block so that the scale will pass close by. When the engine is running, the timing light is aimed at the mark on the crankshaft pulley and the scale.

IGNITION TIMING ADJUSTMENT

With the Dura Spark II system, only an initial timing adjustment is possible. Ignition timing is not considered to be a part of tune-up or routine maintenance.

With the TFI-IV system no ignition timing

adjustment is possible and none should be attempted.

IGNITION TIMING CHECK

Dura Spark II Systems

1. Locate the timing marks on the crankshaft pulley and the front of the engine.
2. Clean the timing marks so that you can see them.
3. Mark the timing marks with a piece of chalk or with paint. Color the mark on the scale that will indicate the correct timing when it is aligned with the mark on the pulley or the pointer. It is also helpful to mark the notch in the pulley or the tip of the pointer with a small dab of color.
4. Attach a tachometer to the engine.
5. Attach a timing light according to the manufacturer's instructions. If the timing light has three wires, one is attached to the No. 1 spark plug with an adapter. The other wires are connected to the battery. The red wire goes to the positive side of the battery and the black wire is connected to the negative terminal of the battery.
6. Disconnect the vacuum line to the distributor at the distributor and plug the vacuum line. A golf tee does a fine job.
7. Check to make sure that all of the wires clear the fan and then start the engine.
8. Adjust the idle to the correct setting.
9. Aim the timing light at the timing marks. if the marks that you put on the flywheel or pulley and the engine are aligned with the light flashes, the timing is correct. Turn off the engine and remove the tachometer and the timing light. If the mark are not in alignment, replace the ignition module.

IDLE SPEED ADJUSTMENT

Carbureted Engines

1. Block the wheels and apply parking brake.
2. Run engine until normal operating temperature is reached.
3. Place the vehicle in Park or Neutral, A/C in Off position, and set parking brake.
4. Remove air cleaner.
5. Disconnect and plug decel throttle control kicker diaphragm vacuum hose.
6. Connect a slave vacuum hose from an engine manifold vacuum source to the decel throttle control kicker.
7. Run engine at approximately 2,500 rpm for 15 seconds, then release the throttle.
8. If decel throttle control rpm is not within ± 50 rpm of specification, adjust the kicker.
9. Disconnect the slave vacuum hose and allow engine to return to curb idle.
10. Adjust curb idle, if necessary, using the curb idle adjusting screw.
11. Rev the engine momentarily, recheck curb idle and adjust if necessary.
12. Reconnect the decel throttle control vacuum hose to the diaphragm.
13. Reinstall the air cleaner.

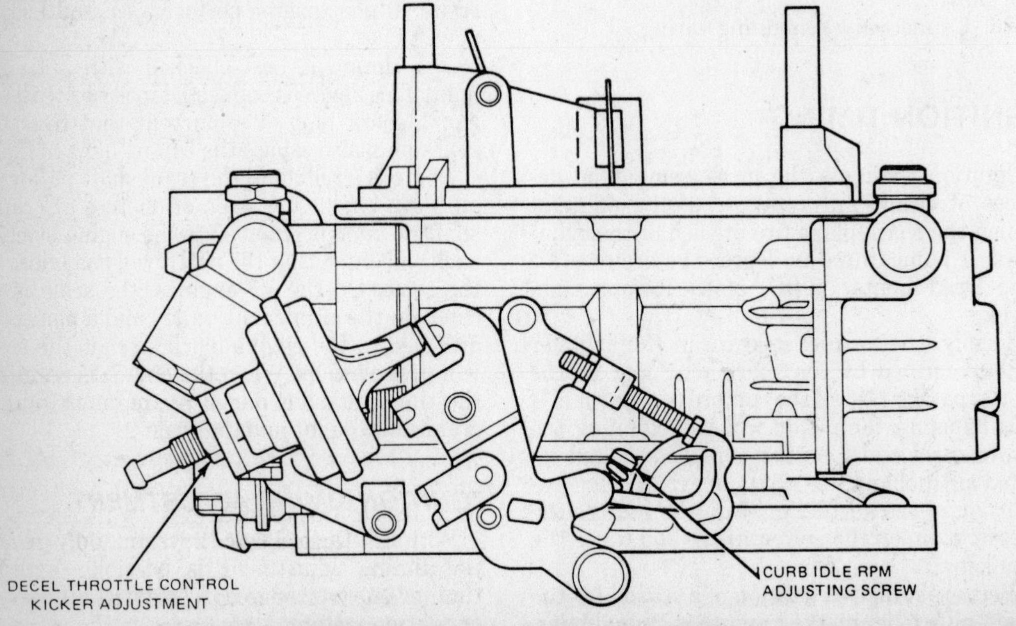

Curb idle screw locations for the 4180C

Fuel Injected Engines

These engines have idle speed controlled by the TFI-IV/EEC-IV system and no adjustment is possible.

6.9L and 7.3L V8 Diesel

CURB IDLE ADJUSTMENT

1. Place the transmission in neutral or park.
2. Bring the engine up to normal operating temperature.
3. Idle speed is measured with manual transmission in neutral and automatic transmission in Drive with the wheels blocked and parking brake ON.
4. Check the curb idle speed, using a magnetic pickup tachometer suitable for diesel engines. The part number of the Ford tachometer is Rotunda 99–0001. Adjust the idle speed to 600–700 rpm.

NOTE: *Always check the underhood emissions control information sticker for the latest idle and adjustment specifications.*

5. Place the transmission in neutral or park and momentarily speed up the engine. Allow the rpm to drop to idle and recheck the idle speed. Readjust if necessary.

FAST IDLE ADJUSTMENT

1. Place the transmission in neutral or park.
2. Start the engine and bring up to normal operating temperatures.
3. Disconnect the wire from the fast idle solenoid.
4. Apply battery voltage to activate the solenoid plunger.

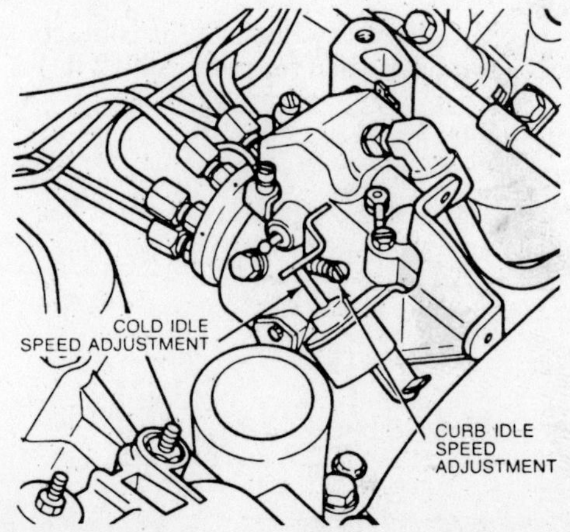

Diesel injection pump showing idle speed adjustment. Pump is mounted on top (front) of the intake manifold

5. Speed up the engine momentarily to set the plunger.
6. The fast idle should be between 850–900 rpm. Adjust the fast idle by turning the solenoid plunger in or out.
7. Speed up the engine momentarily and recheck the fast idle. Readjust if necessary.
8. Remove the battery voltage from the solenoid and reconnect the solenoid wire.

Valve Lash

Valve adjustment determines how far the valves enter the cylinder and how long they stay open and closed.

If the valve clearance is too large, part of the lift of the camshaft will be used in removing the excessive clearance. Consequently, the valve will not be opening as far as it should. This condition has two effects: the valve train components will emit a tapping sound as they take up the excessive clearance and the engine will perform poorly because the valves don't open fully and allow the proper amount of gases to flow into and out of the engine.

If the valve clearance is too small, the intake valve and the exhaust valves will open too far and they will not fully seal on the cylinder head when they close. When a valve seats itself on the cylinder head, it does two things: it seals the combustion chamber so that none of the gases in the cylinder escape and it cools itself by transferring some of the heat it absorbs from the combustion in the cylinder to the cylinder head and to the engine's cooling system. If the valve clearance is too small, the engine will run poorly because of the gases escaping from the combustion chamber. The valves will also become overheated and will warp, since they cannot transfer heat unless they are touching the valve seat in the cylinder head.

NOTE: *While all valve adjustments must be made as accurately as possible, it is better to have the valve adjustment slightly loose than slightly tight as a burned valve may result from overly tight adjustments.*

ADJUSTMENT

6–4.9L

1. Crank the engine until the TDC mark on the crankshaft damper is aligned with timing pointer on the cylinder front cover.
2. Scribe a mark on the damper at this point.
3. Scribe two more marks on the damper, each equally spaced from the first mark (see illustration).
4. With the engine on TDC of the compression stroke, (mark A aligned with the pointer) back off the rocker arm adjusting nut until

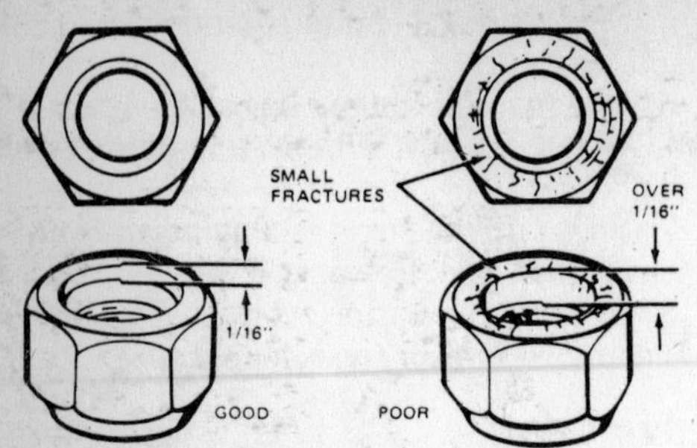

Checking the rocker stud nut

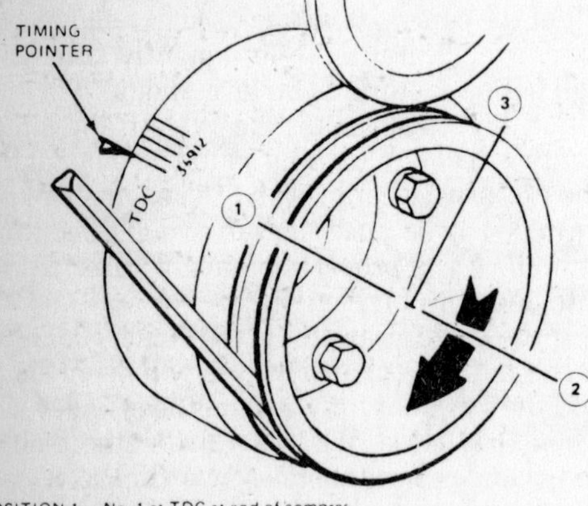

Position of the crankshaft and adjustment valve clearance on the V8

there is end-play in the pushrod. Tighten the adjusting nut until all clearance is removed, then tighten the adjusting nut one additional turn. To determine when all clearance is removed from the rocker arm, turn the pushrod with the fingers. When the pushrod can no longer be turned, all clearance has been removed.

5. Repeat this procedure for each valve, turning the crankshaft 1/3 turn to the next mark each time and following the engine firing order of 1–5–3–6–2–4.

8–5.0L
8–5.8L
8–7.5L

1. Crank the engine until the No. 1 cylinder is at TDC of the compression stroke and the timing pointer is aligned with the mark on the crankshaft damper.

2. Scribe a mark on the damper at this point.

3. Scribe two additional marks on the damper (see illustration).

4. With the timing pointer aligned with mark 1 on the damper, tighten the following valves on the specified torque:

- 5.0L and 7.5L: Nos. 1, 7 and 8 Intake; Nos. 1, 5 and 4 Exhaust
- 5.8L: Nos. 1, 4 and 8 Intake; Nos. 1,3 and 7 Exhaust

5. Rotate the crankshaft 180° to point 2 and tighten the following valves:

- 5.0L and 7.5L: Nos. 5 and 4 Intake; Nos. 2 and 6 Exhaust
- 5.8L: Nos. 3 and 7 Intake; Nos. 6 and 6 Exhaust

6. Rotate the crankshaft 270° to point 3 and tighten the following valves:

- 5.0L and 7.5L: Nos. 2, 3 and 6 Intake; Nos. 7, 3 and 8 Exhaust
- 5.8L: Nos. 2, 5 and 6 Intake; Nos. 4, 5 and 8 Exhaust

7. Rocker arm tightening specifications are:

- 5.0L and 5.8L: tighten the nut until it contacts the rocker shoulder, then torque to 18–20 ft. lbs.
- 7.5L: tighten the nut until it contacts the rocker shoulder, then torque to 18–22 ft. lbs.

Engine and Engine Overhaul

3

ENGINE ELECTRICAL

Understanding the Engine Electrical System

The engine electrical system can be broken down into three separate and distinct systems:

1. The starting system.
2. The charging system.
3. The ignition system.

BATTERY AND STARTING SYSTEM

Basic Operating Principles

The battery is the first link in the chain of mechanisms which work together to provide cranking of the automobile engine. In most modern cars, the battery is a lead/acid electrochemical device consisting of six 2v subsections connected in series so the unit is capable of producing approximately 12v of electrical pressure. Each subsection, or cell, consists of a series of positive and negative plates held a short distance apart in a solution of sulfuric acid and water. The two types of plates are of dissimilar metals. This causes a chemical reaction to be set up, and it is this reaction which produces current flow from the battery when its positive and negative terminals are connected to an electrical appliance such as a lamp or motor. The continued transfer of electrons would eventually convert the sulfuric acid in the electrolyte to water, and make the two plates identical in chemical composition. As electrical energy is removed from the battery, its voltage output tends to drop. Thus, measuring battery voltage and battery electrolyte composition are two ways of checking the ability of the unit to supply power. During the starting of the engine, electrical energy is removed from the battery. However, if the charging circuit is in good condition and the operating conditions are normal, the power removed from the bat-

General Engine Specifications

Engine Liters	Years	Fuel System Type	SAE net Horsepower @ rpm	SAE net Torque ft. lbs. @ rpm	Bore × Stroke (in.)	Comp. Ratio	Oil Pres. (psi.) @ 2000 rpm
6-4.9	**1987**	EFI	120 @ 3,200	245 @ 1,600	4.00 × 3.98	8.4:1	40–60
	1988–90	EFI	150 @ 3,400	265 @ 2,000	4.00 × 3.98	8.8:1	40–60
8-5.0	**1987**	EFI	170 @ 3,800	275 @ 2,800	4.00 × 3.00	8.9:1	40–60
		4-bbl	225 @ 3,600	280 @ 2,800	4.00 × 3.00	9.0:1	40–60
	1988–90	EFI	185 @ 3,800	270 @ 2,400	4.00 × 3.00	9.0:1	40–60
8-5.8W	**1987**	4-bbl	210 @ 4,000	305 @ 2,800	4.00 × 3.50	8.3:1	40–60
	1988–90	EFI	210 @ 3,800	315 @ 2,800	4.00 × 3.50	8.8:1	40–60
8-6.9	**1987**	Diesel	170 @ 3,300	315 @ 1,400	4.00 × 4.18	21.5:1	40–60
8-7.3	**1988–90**	Diesel	180 @ 3,300	345 @ 1,400	4.11 × 4.18	21.5:1	40–70
8-7.5	**1987**	4-bbl	225 @ 4,000	365 @ 2,800	4.36 × 3.85	8.0:1	40–65
	1988–90	EFI	245 @ 4,000	380 @ 2,800	4.36 × 3.85	8.5:1	40–65

EFI: Electronic fuel injection

Valve Specifications

Engines Liters	Years	Seat Angle (deg)	Face Angle (deg)	Spring Test Pressure (lbs. @ in.)	Spring Installed Height (in.)	Stem-to-Guide Clearance (in.) Intake	Stem-to-Guide Clearance (in.) Exhaust	Stem Diameter (in.) Intake	Stem Diameter (in.) Exhaust
6-4.9	**1987–90**	45	44	①	②	0.0010–0.0027	0.0010–0.0027	0.3416–0.3423	0.3416–0.3423
8-5.0	**1987**	45	44	③	⑤	0.0010–0.0027	0.0015–0.0032	0.3416–0.3423	0.3411–0.3418
	1988–90	45	44	③	④	0.0010–0.0027	0.0015–0.0032	0.3416–0.3423	0.3411–0.3418
8-5.8W	**1987**	45	44	200 @ 1.20	⑥	0.0010–0.0027	0.0015–0.0032	0.3416–0.3423	0.3411–0.3418
	1988–90	45	44	200 @ 1.20	⑥	0.0010–0.0027	0.0015–0.0032	0.3416–0.3423	0.3411–0.3428
8-6.9	**1987**	⑦	⑦	80 @ 1.833	⑧	0.0012–0.0029	0.0012–0.0029	0.3717–0.3724	0.3717–0.3724
8-7.3	**1988–90**	⑦	⑦	80 @ 1.833	⑧	0.0055	0.0055	0.3717–0.3724	0.3717–0.3724
8-7.5	**1987–90**	45	44	229 @ 1.330	1.813	0.0010–0.0027	0.0010–0.0027	0.3415–0.3423	0.3415–0.3723

① Intake: 166–184 @ 1.240
Exhaust: 166–184 @ 1.070
② Intake: 1.640
Exhaust: 1.470
③ Intake: 1.96–212 @ 1.360
Exhaust: 190–210 @ 1.200
④ Intake: 1.78
Exhaust: 1.60
⑤ Intake: 1.6885
Exhaust: 1.594
⑥ Intake: 1.782
Exhaust: 1.594
⑦ Intake: 30
Exhaust: 37.5
⑧ Intake: 1.767
Exhaust: 1.833

Piston and Ring Specifications

(All specifications in inches)

Engines Liters	Years	Ring Gap #1 Compr.	Ring Gap #2 Compr.	Ring Gap Oil Control	Ring Side Clearance #1 Compr.	Ring Side Clearance #2 Compr.	Ring Side Clearance Oil Control	Piston-to-Bore Clearance
6-4.9	**1987–90**	0.0100–0.0200	0.0100–0.0200	0.015–0.055	0.0019–0.0036	0.0020–0.0040	snug	0.0010–0.0018
8-5.0	**1987–88**	0.0100–0.0200	0.0100–0.0200	0.015–0.055	0.0013–0.0033	0.0020–0.0040	snug	0.0013–0.0030
8-5.8W	**1987–90**	0.0100–0.0200	0.0100–0.0200	0.015–0.055	0.0013–0.0033	0.0020–0.0040	snug	0.0013– ① 0.0030
8-6.9	**1987**	0.0140–0.0240	0.0600–0.0700	0.0100–0.0240	0.0020–0.0040	0.0020–0.0040	0.0010–0.0030	0.0055–0.0065
8-7.3	**1988–90**	0.0140– ② 0.0240	0.0600– ③ 0.0700	0.0100–0.0240	0.0020–0.0040	0.0020–0.0040	0.0010–0.0030	0.0055– ④ 0.0065
8-7.5	**1987–90**	0.0100–0.0200	0.0100–0.0200	0.010–0.035	0.0025–0.0045	0.0025 0.0045	snug	0.0022–0.0030

① 1989–90: 0.0018–0.0026
② 1989–90: 0.013–0.045
③ 1989–90: 0.060–0.085
④ 1989–90:
Nos. 1-6: 0.0055–0.0085
Nos. 7, 8: 0.0060–0.0085

Torque Specifications

(All specifications in ft. lb.)

Engine Liters	Years	Cyl. Head	Conn. Rod	Main Bearing	Crankshaft Damper	Flywheel	Manifold	
							Intake	Exhaust
6-4.9	**1987–90**	①	40–45	60–70	130–150	75–85	22–32	22–32
8-5.0	**1987–90**	②	19–24	60–70	70–90	75–85	23–25	18–24
8-5.8W	**1987–90**	③	40–45	95–105	70–90	75–85	23–25	18–24
8-6.9	**1987**	④	⑤	⑥	90	44–50	⑦	⑧
8-7.3	**1988–90**	⑨	⑤	⑥	90	44–50	⑦	⑧
8-7.5	**1987–90**	⑫	45–50	95–105	70–90	75–85	⑪	⑩

① Step 1: 50–55 ft. lb.
Step 2: 60–65 ft. lb.
Step 3: 70–85 ft. lb.
② Step 1: 55–65 ft. lb.
Step 2: 65–72 ft. lb.
③ Step 1: 85 ft. lb.
Step 2: 95 ft. lb.
Step 3: 105–112 ft. lb.
④ Step 1: 40 ft. lb.
Step 2: 70 ft. lb.
Step 3: 80 ft. lb.
Step 4: Run the engine to normal operating temperature
Step 5: Retorque to 80 ft. lb. hot
⑤ Step 1: 38 ft. lb.
Step 2: 48–53 ft. lb.
⑥ Step 1: 75 ft. lb.
Step 2: 95 ft. lb.
⑦ Step 1: Tighten to 24 ft. lb.
Step 2: Run engine to normal operating temperature
Step 3: Retorque to 24 ft. lb. hot
⑧ Step 1: Tighten to 35 ft. lb.
Step 2: Run engine to normal operating temperature
Step 3: Retorque to 35 ft. lb. hot
⑨ Step 1: 65 ft. lb.
Step 2: 90 ft. lb.
Step 3: 100 ft. lb.
⑩ 1987: 28–33
1988–90: 22–30
⑪ Step 1: 8–12 ft. lb.
Step 2: 12–22 ft. lb.
Step 3: 22–35 ft. lb.
⑫ Step 1: 70–80 ft. lb.
Step 2: 100–110 ft. lb.
Step 3: 130–140 ft. lb.

Crankshaft and Connecting Rod Specifications

(All specifications in inches)

Engines Liters	Years	Crankshaft				Connecting Rod		
		Main Bearing Journal Dia.	Main Bearing Oil Clearance	Shaft End Play	Thrust on No.	Journal Dia.	Oil Clearance	Side Clearance
6-4.9	**1987–90**	2.3982–2.3990	0.0008–0.0015	0.004–0.008	5	2.1228–2.1236	0.0008–0.0015	0.0060–0.0130
8-6.0	**1987–90**	2.2482–2.2490	①	0.004–0.008	3	2.1228–2.1236	0.0008–0.0015	0.0100–0.0200
8-5.8W	**1987–90**	2.9994–3.0002	0.0008–0.0015	0.004–0.008	3	2.3103–2.3111	0.0008–0.0015	0.0100–0.0200
8-6.9	**1987**	3.1228–3.1236	0.0018–0.0036	0.0020–0.0090	3	2.4980–2.4990	0.0011–0.0026	0.0120–0.0240
8-7.3	**1988–90**	3.1228–3.1236	0.0018–0.0036	0.0020–0.0090	3	2.4980–2.4990	0.0011–0.0026	0.0120–0.0240
8-7.5	**1987–90**	2.9994–3.0002	0.0008–0.0015	0.004–0.008	3	2.4992–2.5000	0.0008–0.0015	0.0100–0.0200

① #1: 0.0001–0.0015
All others: 0.0005–0.0015

Camshaft Specifications

(All specifications in inches)

Engine Liters	Journal Diameter 1	2	3	4	5	Bearing Clearance	Lobe Lift Int.	Exh.	End Play
6-4.9	2.0175	2.0175	2.0175	2.0175	—	0.0020	0.2490 ①	0.2490 ①	0.004
8-5.0	2.0810	2.0660	2.0510	2.0360	2.0210	0.0020	0.2375	0.2474	0.004
8-5.8W	2.0810	2.0660	2.0510	2.0360	2.0210	0.0020	0.2600 ②	0.2600 ②	0.004
8-6.9	2.0995	2.0995	2.0995	2.0995	2.0995	0.0030	0.2535	0.2535	0.005
8-7.3	2.0995	2.0995	2.0995	2.0995	2.0995	0.0025	0.2535	0.2530	0.005
8-7.5	2.1243	2.1243	2.1243	2.1243	2.1243	0.0020	0.2520	0.2780	0.004

① 1989–90 F-150 4x2 w/2.47:1 or 2.75:1 axle & man. trans. 49S: 0.2470
② 1989–90 intake: 0.2780; exhaust: 0.2830

tery will be replaced by the generator (or alternator) which will force electrons back through the battery, reversing the normal flow, and restoring the battery to its original chemical state.

The battery and starting motor are linked by very heavy electrical cables designed to minimize resistance to the flow of current. Generally, the major power supply cable that leaves the battery goes directly to the starter, while other electrical system needs are supplied by a smaller cable. During starter operation, power flows from the battery to the starter and is grounded through the car's frame and the battery's negative ground strap.

The starting motor is a specially designed, direct current electric motor capable of producing a very great amount of power for its size. One thing that allows the motor to produce a great deal of power is its tremendous rotating speed. It drives the engine through a tiny pinion gear (attached to the starter's armature), which drives the very large flywheel ring gear at a greatly reduced speed. Another factor allowing it to produce so much power is that only intermittent operation is required of it. This, little allowance for air circulation is required, and the windings can be built into a very small space.

The starter solenoid is a magnetic device which employs the small current supplied by the starting switch circuit of the ignition switch. This magnetic action moves a plunger which mechanically engages the starter and electrically closes the heavy switch which connects it to the battery. The starting switch circuit consists of the starting switch contained within the ignition switch, a transmission neutral safety switch or clutch pedal switch, and the wiring necessary to connect these in series with the starter solenoid or relay.

A pinion, which is a small gear, is mounted to a one-way drive clutch. This clutch is splined to the starter armature shaft. When the ignition switch is moved to the **start** position, the solenoid plunger slides the pinion toward the flywheel ring gear via a collar and spring. If the teeth on the pinion and flywheel match properly, the pinion will engage the flywheel immediately. If the gear teeth butt one another, the spring will be compressed and will force the gears to mesh as soon as the starter turns far enough to allow them to do so. As the solenoid plunger reaches the end of its travel, it closes the contacts that connect the battery and starter and then the engine is cranked.

As soon as the engine starts, the flywheel ring gear begins turning fast enough to drive the pinion at an extremely high rate of speed. At this point, the one-way clutch begins allowing the pinion to spin faster than the starter shaft so that the starter will not operate at excessive speed. When the ignition switch is released from the starter position, the solenoid is de-energized, and a spring contained within the solenoid assembly pulls the gear out of mesh and interrupts the current flow to the starter.

Some starter employ a separate relay, mounted away from the starter, to switch the motor and solenoid current on and off. The relay thus replaces the solenoid electrical switch, buy does not eliminate the need for a solenoid mounted on the starter used to mechanically engage the starter drive gears. The relay is used to reduce the amount of current the starting switch must carry.

THE CHARGING SYSTEM

Basic Operating Principles

The automobile charging system provides electrical power for operation of the vehicle's ignition and starting systems and all the electrical accessories. The battery services as an electrical surge or storage tank, storing (in chemical form) the energy originally produced by the engine driven generator. The system also provides a means of regulating generator output to protect the battery from being overcharged and to avoid excessive voltage to the accessories.

The storage battery is a chemical device incorporating parallel lead plates in a tank containing a sulfuric acid/water solution. Adjacent plates are slightly dissimilar, and the chemical reaction of the two dissimilar plates produces electrical energy when the battery is connected to a load such as the starter motor. The chemical reaction is reversible, so that when the generator is producing a voltage (electrical pressure) greater than that produced by the battery, electricity is forced into the battery, and the battery is returned to its fully charged state.

The vehicle's generator is driven mechanically, through V-belts, by the engine crankshaft. It consists of two coils of fine wire, one stationary (the stator), and one movable (the rotor). The rotor may also be known as the armature, and consists of fine wire wrapped around an iron core which is mounted on a shaft. The electricity which flows through the two coils of wire (provided initially by the battery in some cases) creates an intense magnetic field around both rotor and stator, and the interaction between the two fields creates voltage, allowing the generator to power the accessories and charge the battery.

There are two types of generators: the earlier is the direct current (DC) type. The current produced by the DC generator is generated in the armature and carried off the spinning armature by stationary brushes contacting the commutator. The commutator is a series of smooth metal contact plates on the end of the armature. The commutator is a series of smooth metal contact plates on the end of the armature. The commutator plates, which are separated from one another by a very short gap, are connected to the armature circuits so that current will flow in one directions only in the wires carrying the generator output. The generator stator consists of two stationary coils of wire which draw some of the output current of the generator to form a powerful magnetic field and create the interaction of fields which generates the voltage. The generator field is wired in series with the regulator.

Newer automobiles use alternating current generators or alternators, because they are more efficient, can be rotated at higher speeds, and have fewer brush problems. In an alternator, the field rotates while all the current produced passes only through the stator winding. The brushes bear against continuous slip rings rather than a commutator. This causes the current produced to periodically reverse the direction of its flow. Diodes (electrical one-way switches) block the flow of current from traveling in the wrong direction. A series of diodes is wired together to permit the alternating flow of the stator to be converted to a pulsating, but unidirectional flow at the alternator output. The alternator's field is wired in series with the voltage regulator.

The regulator consists of several circuits. Each circuit has a core, or magnetic coil of wire, which operates a switch. Each switch is connected to ground through one or more resistors. The coil of wire responds directly to system voltage. When the voltage reaches the required level, the magnetic field created by the winding of wire closes the switch and inserts a resistance into the generator field circuit, thus reducing the output. The contacts of the switch cycle open and close many times each second to precisely control voltage.

While alternators are self-limiting as far as maximum current is concerned, DC generators employ a current regulating circuit which responds directly to the total amount of current flowing through the generator circuit rather than to the output voltage. The current regulator is similar to the voltage regulator except that all system current must flow through the energizing coil on its way to the various accessories.

Ignition Coil

REMOVAL AND INSTALLATION

1. Disconnect the battery ground.
2. Disconnect the two small and one large wires from the coil.
3. Disconnect the condenser connector from the coil, if equipped.
4. Unbolt and remove the coil.
5. Installation is the reverse of removal.

Ignition Module

REMOVAL AND INSTALLATION

Removing the module, on all models, is a matter of simply removing the fasteners that attach it to the fender or firewall and pulling apart the connectors. When unplugging the connectors, pull them apart with a firm, straight pull. NEVER PRY THEM APART! To pry them will cause damage. When reconnecting them, coat the mating ends with silicone dielectric grease to waterproof the connection. Press the connectors together firmly to overcome any vacuum lock caused by the grease.

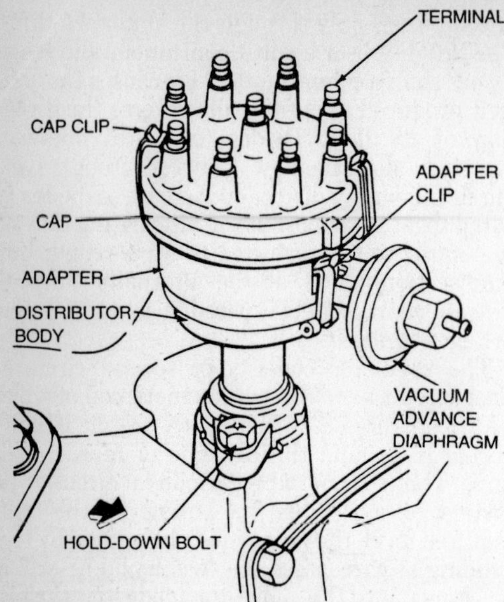

Distributor assembly. Arrow points to front

NOTE: *If the locking tabs weaken or break, don't replace the unit. Just secure the connection with electrical tape or tie straps.*

Distributor

REMOVAL

Carbureted Engines (DuraSpark II)

1. Remove the air cleaner assembly, taking note of the hose locations.
2. Disconnect the distributor wiring connector from the vehicle wiring harness.
3. Noting the position of the vacuum line(s) on the distributor diaphragm, disconnect the lines at the diaphragm. Unsnap the two distributor cap retaining clamps and remove the cap, rotor and adapter.

   NOTE: *If it is necessary to disconnect ignition wires from the cap to get enough room to remove the distributor, make sure to label every wire and the cap for easy and accurate reinstallation.*
4. Rotate the engine to align any pole on the armature with the pole on the stator.
5. Install the rotor. Using chalk or paint, carefully mark the position of the distributor rotor in relation to the distributor housing and mark the position of the distributor housing in relation to the engine block. When this is done, you should have a line on the distributor housing directly in line with the tip of the rotor and another line on the engine block directly in line with the mark on the distributor housing. This is very important because the distributor must be installed in the exact same location from which it was removed, if correct ignition timing is to be maintained.
6. Remove the distributor holddown bolt and clamp. Remove the distributor from the engine. Make sure that the oil pump (intermediate) driveshaft does not come out with the distributor. If it does, remove it from the distributor shaft, coat its lower end with heavy grease, and reinsert it, making sure that it fully engages the oil pump drive.

   NOTE: *Do not disturb the engine while the distributor is removed. If you turn the engine over with the distributor removed, you will have to retime the engine.*

INSTALLATION ENGINE NOT ROTATED

Carbureted Engines (DuraSpark II)

1. If the engine was not cranked (disturbed) when the distributor was removed, position the distributor in the block with the armature and stator poles aligned, the rotor aligned with the mark previously scribed on the distributor body and the marks on the distributor body and cylinder block in alignment. Install the distributor holddown bolt and clamp finger tight.
2. If the stator and armature poles cannot be aligned by rotating the distributor, pull the distributor out just far enough to disengage the drive gear and rotate the distributor shaft to engage a different gear tooth.
3. Install the distributor cap and wires.
4. Connect the distributor wring connector to the wiring harness. Tighten the holddown bolt.
5. Install the air cleaner, if removed.
6. Check the ignition timing as outlined in Chapter 2.

INSTALLATION CRANKSHAFT OR CAMSHAFT ROTATED

Carbureted Engines (DuraSpark II)

If the engine is cranked (disturbed) with the distributor removed, it will now be necessary to retime the engine.

1. Rotate the engine so that No.1 piston is at TDC of the compression stroke.
2. Align the timing marks to the correct initial timing shown on the underhood decal.
3. Install the distributor with the rotor in the No.1 firing position and any armature pole aligned with the stator pole.

   NOTE: *Make sure that the oil pump intermediate shaft properly engages the distributor shaft. It may be necessary to crank the engine after the distributor gear is partially engaged in order to engage the oil pump intermediate shaft and fully seat the distributor in the block.*

4. If it was necessary to rotate the engine to align the oil pump, repeat Steps 1, 2 and 3.
5. Install the holddown bolt finger tight.
6. Install the distributor cap and wires.
7. Connect the distributor wring connector to the wiring harness. Tighten the holddown bolt.
8. Install the air cleaner, if removed.
9. Check the ignition timing as outlined in Chapter 2.
10. When everything is set, tighten the holddown bolt to 25 ft. lbs.

REMOVAL

Fuel Injected Engines (TFI-IV Systems)

1. Disconnect the primary wiring connector from the distributor.
2. Mark the position of the cap's No.1 terminal on the distributor base.
3. Unclip and remove the cap. Remove the adapter.
4. Remove the rotor.
5. Remove the TFI connector.
6. Matchmark the distributor base and engine for installation reference.
7. Remove the holddown bolt and lift out the distributor.

INSTALLATION

Fuel Injected Engines (TFI-IV System)

1. Rotate the engine so that the No.1 piston is at TDC of the compression stroke.
2. Align the timing marks so that the engine is set at the initial timing shown on the underhood sticker.
3. Install the rotor on the shaft and rotate the shaft so that the rotor tip points to the No.1 mark made on the distributor base.
4. Continue rotating the shaft so that the leading edge of the vane is centered on the vane switch assembly.
5. Position the distributor in the block and rotate the distributor body to align the leading edge of the vane and vane switch. Verify that the rotor tip points to the No.1 mark on the body.

NOTE: *If the vane and vane switch cannot be aligned by rotating the distributor body in the engine, pull the distributor out just far enough to disengage the gears and rotate the shaft to engage a different gear tooth. Repeat Steps 3, 4 and 5.*

6. Install and finger tighten the holddown bolt.
7. Connect the TFI and primary wiring.
8. Install the rotor, if not already done.

NOTE: *Coat the brass portions of the rotor with a $^1/_{32}$ in. (0.8mm) thick coating of silicone dielectric compound.*

9. Install the cap and adapter (as necessary). Install the wires and start the engine.
10. Check and set the initial timing.
11. Tighten the holddown bolt to 25 ft. lbs.

Alternator

The alternator charging system is a negative (–) ground system which consists of an alternator, a regulator, a charge indicator, a storage battery and wiring connecting the components, and fuse link wire.

The alternator is belt-driven from the engine. Energy is supplied from the alternator/regulator system to the rotating field through two brushes to two slip-rings. The slip-rings are mounted on the rotor shaft and are connected to the field coil. This energy supplied to the rotating field from the battery is called excitation current and is used to initially energize the field to begin the generation of electricity. Once the alternator starts to generate electricity, the excitation current comes from its own output rather than the battery.

The alternator produces power in the form of alternating current. The alternating current is rectified by 6 diodes into direct current. The direct current is used to charge the battery and power the rest of the electrical system.

When the ignition key is turned on, current flows from the battery, through the charging system indicator light on the instrument panel, to the voltage regulator, and to the alternator. Since the alternator is not producing any current, the alternator warning light comes on. When the engine is started, the alternator begins to produce current and turns the alternator light off. As the alternator turns and produces current, the current is divided in two ways: part to the battery to charge the battery and power the electrical components of the vehicle, and part is returned to the alternator to enable it to increase its output. In this situation, the alternator is receiving current from the battery and from itself. A voltage regulator is wired into the current supply to the alternator to prevent it from receiving too much current which would cause it to put out too much current. Conversely, if the voltage regulator does not allow the alternator to receive enough current, the battery will not be fully charged and will eventually go dead.

The battery is connected to the alternator at all times, whether the ignition key is turned on or not. If the battery were shorted to ground, the alternator would also be shorted. This would damage the alternator. To prevent this, a fuse link is installed in the wiring between the battery and the alternator. If the battery is shorted, the fuse link is melted, protecting the alternator.

ALTERNATOR PRECAUTIONS

To prevent damage to the alternator and regulator, the following precautions should be taken when working with the electrical system.

1. Never reverse the battery connections.
2. Booster batteries for starting must be connected properly: positive-to-positive and negative-to-ground.
3. Disconnect the battery cables before using a fast charger; the charger has a tendency to force current through the diodes in the opposite direction for which they were designed. This burns out the diodes.
4. Never use a fast charger as a booster for starting the vehicle.
5. Never disconnect the voltage regulator while the engine is running.
6. Avoid long soldering times when replacing diodes or transistors. Prolonged heat is damaging to AC generators.
7. Do not use test lamps of more than 12 volts (V) for checking diode continuity.
8. Do not short across or ground any of the terminals on the AC generator.
9. The polarity of the battery, generator, and regulator must be matched and considered before making any electrical connections within the system.
10. Never operate the alternator on an open circuit. make sure that all connections within the circuit are clean and tight.
11. Disconnect the battery terminals when performing any service on the electrical system. This will eliminate the possibility of accidental reversal of polarity.
12. Disconnect the battery ground cable if arc welding is to be done on any part of the car.

CHARGING SYSTEM TROUBLESHOOTING

There are many possible ways in which the charging system can malfunction. Often the source of a problem is difficult to diagnose, requiring special equipment and a good deal of experience. This is usually not the case, however, where the charging system fails completely and causes the dash board warning light to come on or the battery to become dead. To troubleshoot a complete system failure only two pieces of equipment are needed: a test light, to determine that current is reaching a certain point; and a current indicator (ammeter), to determine the direction of the current flow and its measurement in amps. This test works under three assumptions:

1. The battery is known to be good and fully charged.
2. The alternator belt is in good condition and adjusted to the proper tension.
3. All connections in the system are clean and tight.

NOTE: *In order for the current indicator to give a valid reading, the car must be equipped with battery cables which are of the same gauge size and quality as original equipment battery cables.*

1. Turn off all electrical components on the car. Make sure the doors of the car are closed. If the car is equipped with a clock, disconnect the clock by removing the lead wire from the rear of the clock. Disconnect the positive battery cable from the battery and connect the ground wire on a test light to the disconnected positive battery cable. Touch the probe end of the test light to the positive battery post. The test light should not light. If the test light does light, there is a short or open circuit on the car.
2. Disconnect the voltage regulator wiring harness connector at the voltage regulator. Turn on the ignition key. Connect the wire on a test light to a good ground (engine bolt). Touch the probe end of a test light to the ignition wire connector into the voltage regulator wiring connector. This wire corresponds to the **I** terminal on the regulator. If the test light goes on, the charging system warning light circuit is complete. If the test light does not come on and the warning light on the instrument panel is on, either the resistor wire, which is parallel with the warning light, or the wiring to the voltage regulator, is defective. If the test light does not come on and the warning light is not on, either the bulb is defective or the power supply wire form the battery through the ignition switch to the bulb has an open circuit. Connect the wiring harness to the regulator.
3. Examine the fuse link wire in the wiring harness from the starter relay to the alternator. If the insulation on the wire is cracked or split, the fuse link may be melted. Connect a test light to the fuse link by attaching the ground wire on the test light to an engine bolt and touching the probe end of the light to the bottom of the fuse link wire where it splices into the alternator output wire. If the bulb in the test light does not light, the fuse link is melted.
4. Start the engine and place a current indicator on the positive battery cable. Turn off all electrical accessories and make sure the doors are closed. If the charging system is working properly, the gauge will show a draw of less than 5 amps. If the system is not working properly, the gauge will show a draw of more than 5 amps. A charge moves the needle toward the battery, a draw moves the needle away from the battery. Turn the engine off.

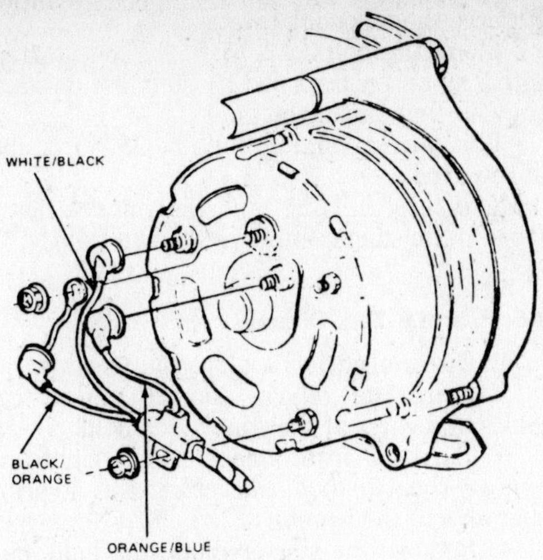

Rear terminal alternator

5. Disconnect the wiring harness from the voltage regulator at the regulator at the regulator connector. Connect a male spade terminal (solderless connector) to each end of a jumper wire. Insert one end of the wire into the wiring harness connector which corresponds to the **A** terminal on the regulator. Insert the other end of the wire into the wiring harness connector which corresponds to the **F** terminal on the regulator. Position the connector with the jumper wire installed so that it cannot contact any metal surface under the hood. Position a current indicator gauge on the positive battery cable. Have an assistant start the engine. Observe the reading on the current indicator. Have your assistant slowly raise the speed of the engine to about 2,000 rpm or until the current indicator needle stops moving, whichever comes first. Do not run the engine for more than a short period of time in this condition. If the wiring harness connector or jumper wire becomes excessively hot during this test, turn off the engine and check for a grounded wire in the regulator wiring harness. If the current indicator shows a charge of about three amps less than the output of the alternator, the alternator is working properly. If the previous tests showed a draw, the voltage regulator is defective. If the gauge does not show the proper charging rate, the alternator is defective.

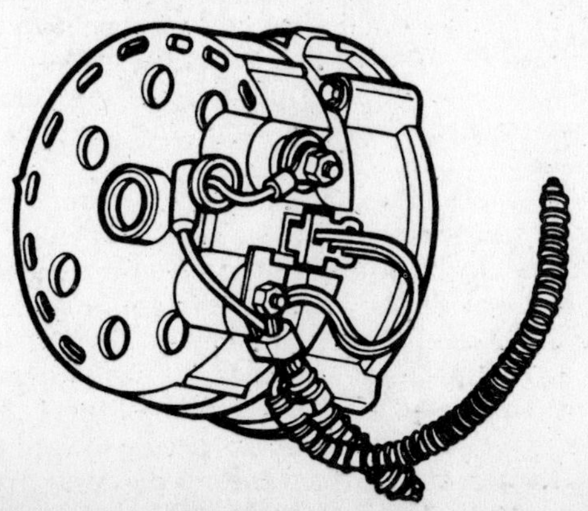

Side terminal alternator

REMOVAL AND INSTALLATION

While internal alternator repairs are possible, they require specialized tools and training. Therefore, it is advisable to replace a defective alternator, or have it repaired by a qualified shop.

1. Open the hood and disconnect the battery ground cable.
2. Remove the adjusting arm bolt.
3. Remove the alternator through-bolt. Remove the drive belt from the alternator pulley and lower the alternator.

NOTE: *Some engines are equipped with a ribbed, K-section belt and automatic tensioner. A special tool must be made to remove the tension from the tensioner arm. Loosen the idler pulley pivot and adjuster bolts before using the tool. See the accompanying illustration for tool details.*

4. Label all of the leads to the alternator so that you can install them correctly and disconnect the leads from the alternator.
5. Remove the alternator from the vehicle.
6. To install, reverse the above procedure. Observe the following torques:

- Pivot bolt: 58 ft. lbs.
- Adjusting bolt: 25 ft. lbs.
- Wire terminal nuts: 60–90 inch lbs.

BELT TENSION ADJUSTMENT

The fan belt drives the alternator and water pump. if the belt is too loose, it will slip and the alternator will not be able to produce it rated current. Also, the water pump will not operate efficiently and the engine could overheat.

Check the tension of the belt by pushing your thumb down on the longest span of the belt, midway between the pulleys. Belt deflection should be approximately $^1/_2$ in. (13mm). To adjust the belt tension, proceed as follows:

1. Loosen the alternator mounting bolt and the adjusting arm bolts.
2. Apply pressure on the alternator front housing only, moving the alternator away from the engine to tighten the belt. Do not apply pressure to the rear of the cast aluminum housing of an alternator; damage to the housing could result.
3. Tighten the alternator mounting bolt and the adjusting arm bolts when the correct tension is reached.

Starter Motor

REMOVAL AND INSTALLATION

Except Diesel

1. Disconnect the negative battery cable.
2. Raise the front of the truck and install jackstands beneath the frame. Firmly apply the parking brake and place blocks in back of the rear wheels.
3. Tag and disconnect the wiring at the starter.
4. Turn the front wheels fully to the right. On some later models it will be necessary to remove the frame brace. On many models, it will be necessary to remove the two bolts retaining the steering idler arm to the frame to gain access to the starter.
5. Remove the starter mounting bolts and remove the starter.
6. Reverse the above procedure to install.

Observe the following torques:

- Mounting bolts: 12–15 ft. lbs. on starters with 3 mounting bolts and 15–20 ft. lbs. on starters with 2 mounting bolts.
- Idler arm retaining bolts to 28–35 ft. lbs. (if removed).

Make sure that the nut securing the heavy cable to the starter is snugged down tightly.

8-6.9L and 8-7.3L Diesel

1. Disconnect the battery ground cable.
2. Raise the vehicle and disconnect the cables and wires at the starter solenoid.
3. Turn the front wheels to the right and remove the two bolts attaching the steering idler arm to the frame.
4. Remove the starter mounting bolts and remove the starter.
5. Installation is the reverse of removal. Torque the mounting bolts to 20 ft. lbs.

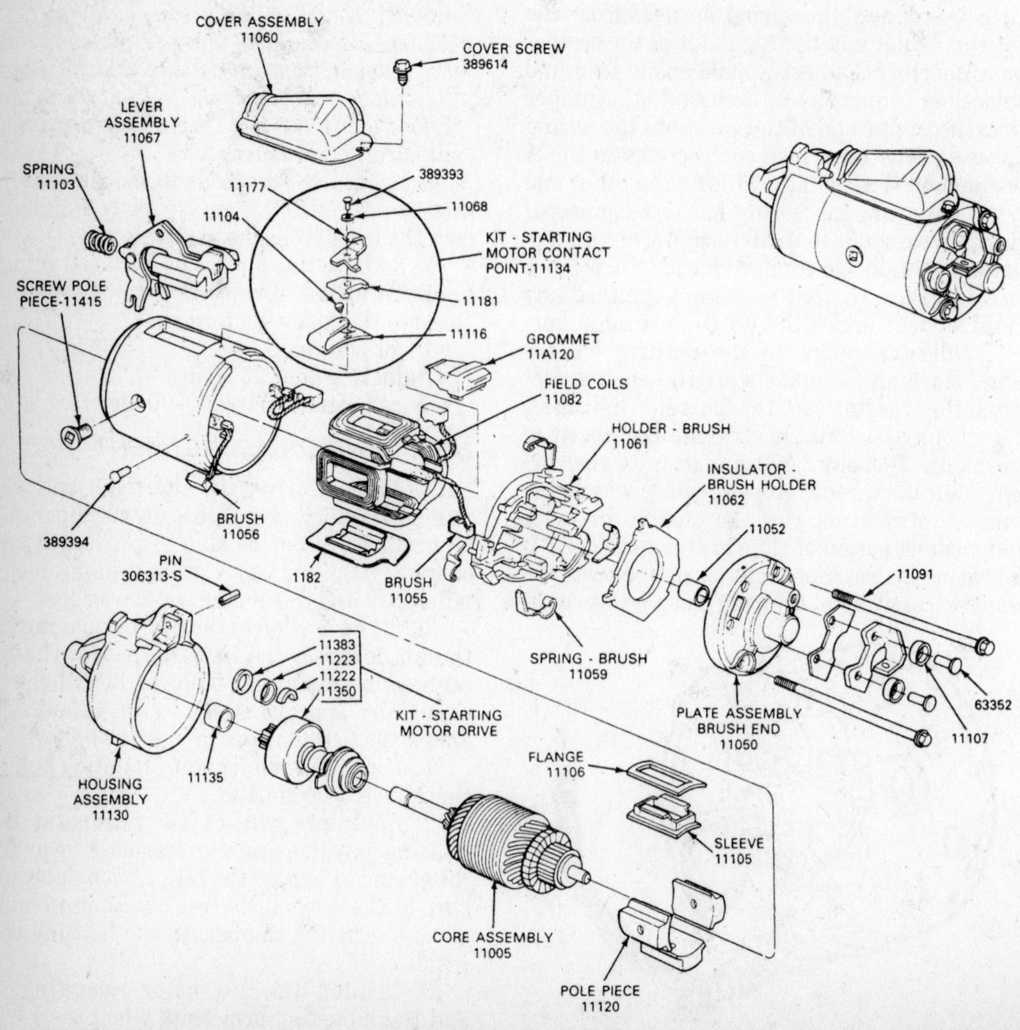

6–4.9L and 8–5.0L starter

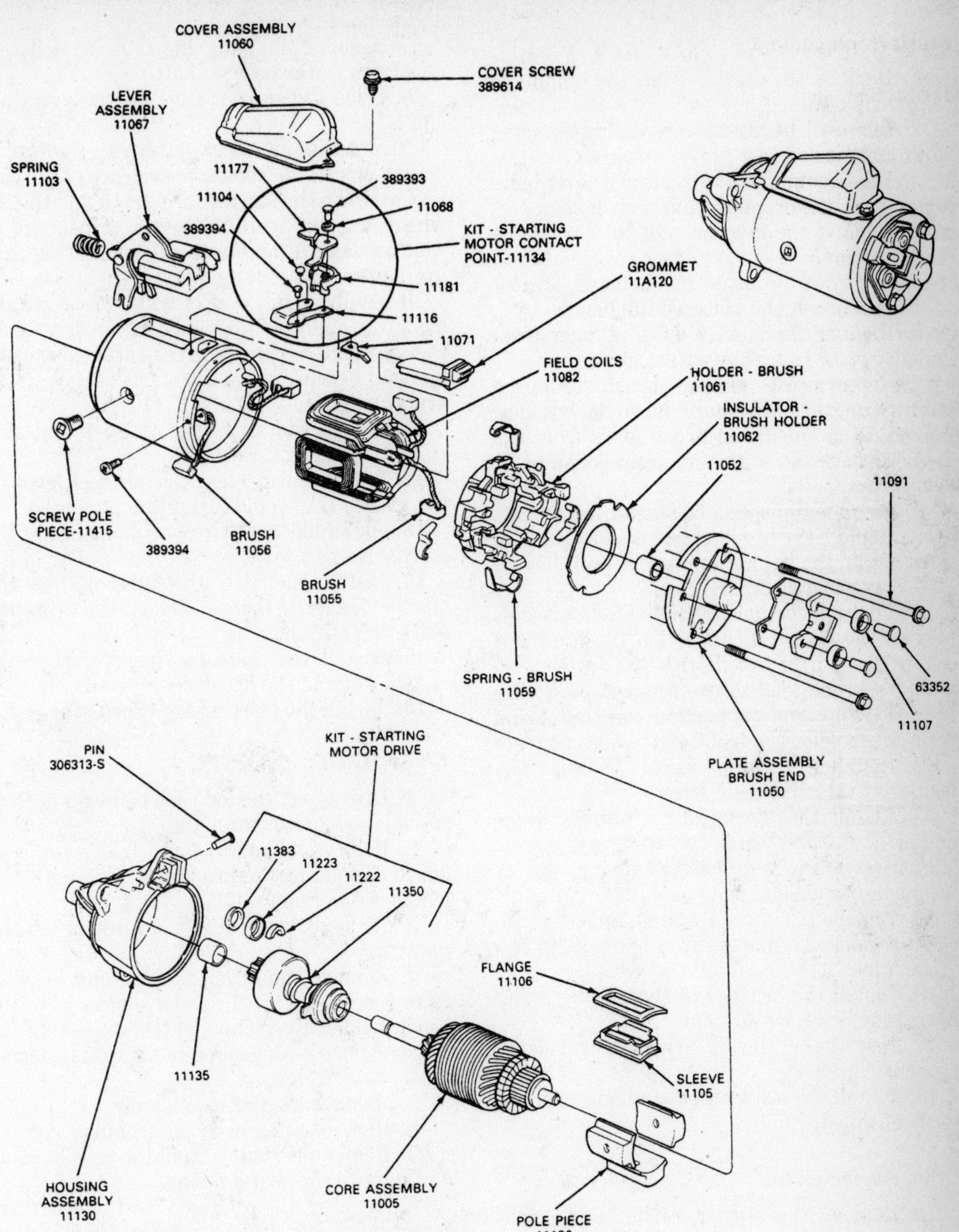

8–5.8L and 8–7.5L starter

OVERHAUL – EXCEPT DIESEL

Brush Replacement

1. Remove the starter from the engine as previously outlined.
2. Remove the starter drive plunger lever cover and gasket.
3. Loosen and remove the brush cover band and remove the brushes from their holder.
4. Remove the two through-bolts from the starter frame.
5. Separate the drive end housing, starter frame and brush end plate assemblies.
6. Remove the starter drive plunger lever and pivot pin, and remove the armature.
7. Remove the ground brush retaining screws from the frame and remove the brushes.
8. Cut the insulated brush leads from the field coils, as close to the field connection point as possible.
9. Clean and inspect the starter motor.
10. Replace the brush end plate if the insulator between the field brush holder and the end plate is cracked or broken.
11. Position the new insulated field brushes lead on the field coil connection. Position and crimp the clip provided with the brushes to hold the brush lead to the connection. Solder the lead, clip, and connection together using resin core solder. Use a 300 watt soldering iron.
12. Install the ground brush leads to the frame with the retaining screws.
13. Install the starter drive plunger lever and pivot pin, and install the armature.
14. Assemble the drive end housing, starter frame and brush end plate assemblies.
15. Install the two through-bolts in the starter frame. Torque the through-bolts to 55–75 inch lbs.
16. Install the brushes in their holders and install the brush cover band.
17. Install the starter drive plunger lever cover and gasket.
18. Install the starter on the engine as previously outlined.

Drive Replacement

1. Remove the starter as outlined previously.
2. Remove the starter drive plunger lever and gasket and the brush cover band.
3. Remove the two through-bolts from the starter frame.
4. Separate the drive end housing from the starter frame.
5. The starter drive plunger lever return spring may fall out after detaching the drive end housing. If not, remove it.
6. Remove the pivot pin which attaches the starter drive plunger lever to the starter frame and remove the lever.
7. Remove the stop ring retainer and stop ring from the armature shaft.
8. Slide the starter drive off the armature shaft.
9. Examine the wear pattern on the starter drive teeth. There should be evidence of full contact between the starter drive teeth and the flywheel ring gear teeth. If there is evidence of irregular wear, examine the flywheel ring gear for damage and replace if necessary.
10. Apply a thin coat of white grease to the armature shaft before installing the drive gear. Place a small amount of grease in the drive end housing bearing. Slide the starter drive on the armature shaft.
11. Install the stop ring retainer and stop ring on the armature shaft.
12. Install the starter drive plunger lever on the starter frame and install the pin.
13. Assemble the drive end housing on the starter frame.
14. install the two through-bolts in the starter frame. Tighten the starter through bolts to 55–75 inch lbs.
15. Install the starter drive plunger lever and gasket and the brush cover band.
16. Install the starter as outlined previously.

OVERHAUL – DIESEL

1. Disconnect the field coil connection from the solenoid motor terminal.
2. Remove the solenoid attaching screws, solenoid and plunger return spring. Rotate the solenoid 90° to remove it.
3. Remove the through-bolts and brush end plate.
4. Remove the brush springs and brushes from the plastic brush holder and remove the brush holder. Keep track of the location of the brush holder with regard to the brush terminals.
5. Remove the frame assembly.
6. Remove the armature assembly.
7. Remove the screw from the gear housing and remove the gear housing.
8. Remove the plunger and lever pivot screw and remove the plunger and lever.
9. Remove the gear, output shaft and drive assembly.
10. Remove the thrust washer, retainer, drive stop ring and slide the drive assembly off of the output shaft.

WARNING: *Don't wash the drive because the solvent will wash out the lubricant, causing the drive to slip. Use a brush or compressed air to clean the drive, field coils, armature, gear and housing.*

11. Inspect the armature windings for broken or burned insulation, and open connections at the commutator. Check for any signs of grounding.

12. Check the commutator for excessive runout. If the commutator is rough or more than 0.127mm out-of-round, replace it or correct the problem as necessary.

13. Check the plastic brush holder for cracks or broken pads. Replace the brushes if worn to a length less than 1/4 in. (6mm) in length. Inspect the field coils and plastic bobbins for burned or damaged areas. Check the continuity of the coil and brush connections. A brush replacement kit is available. Any other worn or damaged parts should be replaced.

14. Apply a thin coating of Lubriplate 777®, or equivalent on the output shaft splines. Slide the drive assembly onto the shaft and install a new stopring, retainer and thrust washer. Install the shaft and drive assembly into the drive end housing.

15. Install the plunger and lever assembly making sure that the lever notches engage the flange ears of the starter drive. Attach the lever pin screw and tighten it to 10 ft. lbs.

16. Lubricate the gear and washer. Install the gear and washer on the end of the output shaft.

17. Install the gear housing and tighten the mounting screw to 84 inch lbs.

18. After lubricating the pinion, install the armature and washer on the end of the shaft.

19. Position the grommet around the field lead and press it into the starter frame notch. Install the frame assembly on the gear housing, making sure that the grommet is positioned in the notch in the housing.

20. Install the brush holder on the end of the frame, lining up the notches in the brush holder with the ground brush terminals. The brush holder is symmetrical and can be installed with either notch and brush terminal.

21. Install the brush springs and brushes. The positive brush leads must be placed in their respective slots to prevent grounding.

22. Install the brush endplate, making sure that the insulator is properly positioned. Install and tighten the through-bolts to 84 inch lbs.

NOTE: *The brush endplate has a threaded hole in the protruding ear which must be oriented properly so the starter-to-vacuum pump support bracket can be installed.*

23. Install the return spring on the solenoid plunger and install the solenoid. Attach the 2 solenoid attaching screws and tighten them to 84 inch lbs. Apply a sealing compound to the

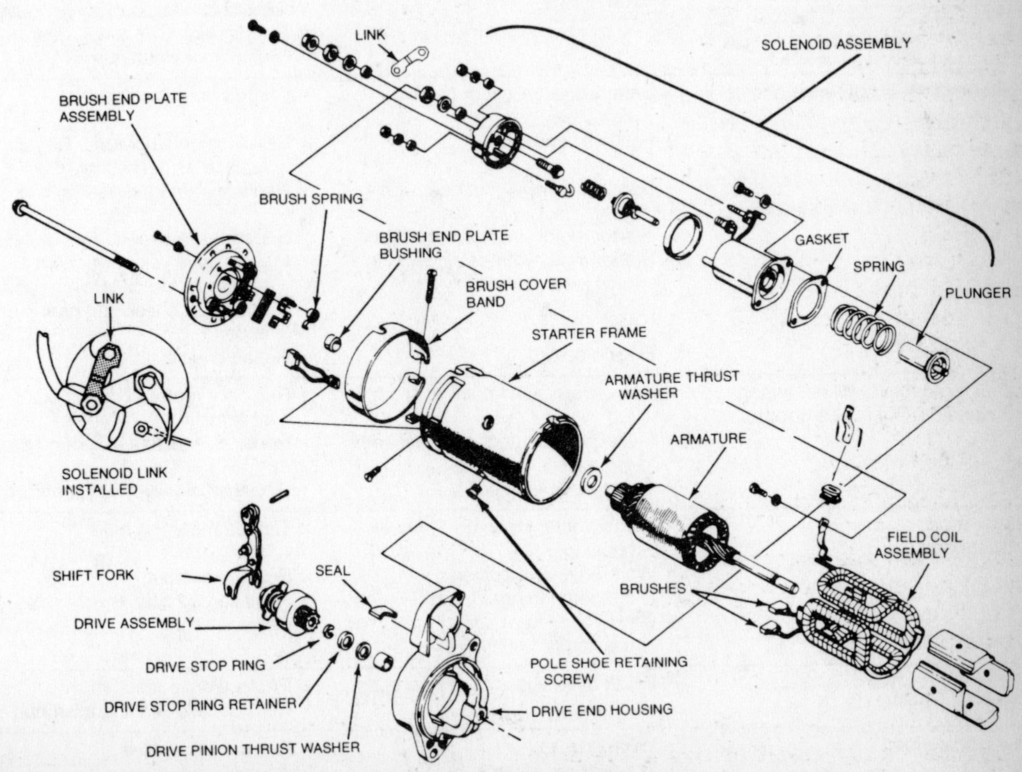

Solenoid actuated type starter

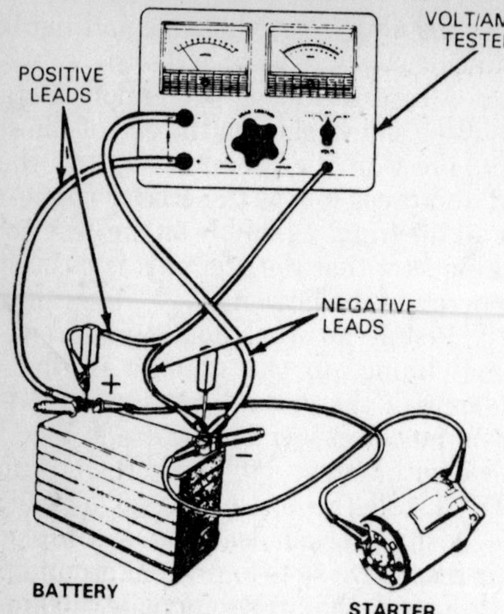

Starter no-load test with starter on test bench

junction of the solenoid case flange, gear and drive end housings.

24. Attach the motor field terminal to the **M** terminal of the solenoid, and tighten the fasteners to 30 inch lbs.

25. Check the starter no-load current draw. Maximum draw should be 190 amps.

Starter Relay

REMOVAL AND INSTALLATION

Gasoline Engines

1. Disconnect the positive battery cable from the battery terminal. With dual batteries, disconnect the connecting cable at both ends.

2. Remove the nut securing the positive battery cable to the relay.

3. Remove the positive cable and any other wiring under that cable.

Troubleshooting Basic Starting System Problems

Problem	Cause	Solution
Starter motor rotates engine slowly	• Battery charge low or battery defective	• Charge or replace battery
	• Defective circuit between battery and starter motor	• Clean and tighten, or replace cables
	• Low load current	• Bench-test starter motor. Inspect for worn brushes and weak brush springs.
	• High load current	• Bench-test starter motor. Check engine for friction, drag or coolant in cylinders. Check ring gear-to-pinion gear clearance.
Starter motor will not rotate engine	• Battery charge low or battery defective	• Charge or replace battery
	• Faulty solenoid	• Check solenoid ground. Repair or replace as necessary.
	• Damage drive pinion gear or ring gear	• Replace damaged gear(s)
	• Starter motor engagement weak	• Bench-test starter motor
	• Starter motor rotates slowly with high load current	• Inspect drive yoke pull-down and point gap, check for worn end bushings, check ring gear clearance
	• Engine seized	• Repair engine
Starter motor drive will not engage (solenoid known to be good)	• Defective contact point assembly	• Repair or replace contact point assembly
	• Inadequate contact point assembly ground	• Repair connection at ground screw
	• Defective hold-in coil	• Replace field winding assembly
Starter motor drive will not disengage	• Starter motor loose on flywheel housing	• Tighten mounting bolts
	• Worn drive end busing	• Replace bushing
	• Damaged ring gear teeth	• Replace ring gear or driveplate
	• Drive yoke return spring broken or missing	• Replace spring
Starter motor drive disengages prematurely	• Weak drive assembly thrust spring	• Replace drive mechanism
	• Hold-in coil defective	• Replace field winding assembly
Low load current	• Worn brushes	• Replace brushes
	• Weak brush springs	• Replace springs

Troubleshooting Engine Mechanical Problems

Problem	Cause	Solution
External oil leaks	• Fuel pump gasket broken or improperly seated	• Replace gasket
	• Cylinder head cover RTV sealant broken or improperly seated	• Replace sealant; inspect cylinder head cover sealant flange and cylinder head sealant surface for distortion and cracks
	• Oil filler cap leaking or missing	• Replace cap
	• Oil filter gasket broken or improperly seated	• Replace oil filter
	• Oil pan side gasket broken, improperly seated or opening in RTV sealant	• Replace gasket or repair opening in sealant; inspect oil pan gasket flange for distortion
	• Oil pan front oil seal broken or improperly seated	• Replace seal; inspect timing case cover and oil pan seal flange for distortion
	• Oil pan rear oil seal broken or improperly seated	• Replace seal; inspect oil pan rear oil seal flange; inspect rear main bearing cap for cracks, plugged oil return channels, or distortion in seal groove
	• Timing case cover oil seal broken or improperly seated	• Replace seal
	• Excess oil pressure because of restricted PCV valve	• Replace PCV valve
	• Oil pan drain plug loose or has stripped threads	• Repair as necessary and tighten
	• Rear oil gallery plug loose	• Use appropriate sealant on gallery plug and tighten
	• Rear camshaft plug loose or improperly seated	• Seat camshaft plug or replace and seal, as necessary
	• Distributor base gasket damaged	• Replace gasket
Excessive oil consumption	• Oil level too high	• Drain oil to specified level
	• Oil with wrong viscosity being used	• Replace with specified oil
	• PCV valve stuck closed	• Replace PCV valve
	• Valve stem oil deflectors (or seals) are damaged, missing, or incorrect type	• Replace valve stem oil deflectors
	• Valve stems or valve guides worn	• Measure stem-to-guide clearance and repair as necessary
	• Poorly fitted or missing valve cover baffles	• Replace valve cover
	• Piston rings broken or missing	• Replace broken or missing rings
	• Scuffed piston	• Replace piston
	• Incorrect piston ring gap	• Measure ring gap, repair as necessary
	• Piston rings sticking or excessively loose in grooves	• Measure ring side clearance, repair as necessary
	• Compression rings installed upside down	• Repair as necessary
	• Cylinder walls worn, scored, or glazed	• Repair as necessary
	• Piston ring gaps not properly staggered	• Repair as necessary
	• Excessive main or connecting rod bearing clearance	• Measure bearing clearance, repair as necessary
No oil pressure	• Low oil level	• Add oil to correct level
	• Oil pressure gauge, warning lamp or sending unit inaccurate	• Replace oil pressure gauge or warning lamp
	• Oil pump malfunction	• Replace oil pump
	• Oil pressure relief valve sticking	• Remove and inspect oil pressure relief valve assembly
	• Oil passages on pressure side of pump obstructed	• Inspect oil passages for obstruction

Troubleshooting Engine Mechanical Problems (cont.)

Problem	Cause	Solution
No oil pressure (cont.)	• Oil pickup screen or tube obstructed • Loose oil inlet tube	• Inspect oil pickup for obstruction • Tighten or seal inlet tube
Low oil pressure	• Low oil level • Inaccurate gauge, warning lamp or sending unit • Oil excessively thin because of dilution, poor quality, or improper grade • Excessive oil temperature • Oil pressure relief spring weak or sticking • Oil inlet tube and screen assembly has restriction or air leak • Excessive oil pump clearance • Excessive main, rod, or camshaft bearing clearance	• Add oil to correct level • Replace oil pressure gauge or warning lamp • Drain and refill crankcase with recommended oil • Correct cause of overheating engine • Remove and inspect oil pressure relief valve assembly • Remove and inspect oil inlet tube and screen assembly. (Fill inlet tube with lacquer thinner to locate leaks.) • Measure clearances • Measure bearing clearances, repair as necessary
High oil pressure	• Improper oil viscosity • Oil pressure gauge or sending unit inaccurate • Oil pressure relief valve sticking closed	• Drain and refill crankcase with correct viscosity oil • Replace oil pressure gauge • Remove and inspect oil pressure relief valve assembly
Main bearing noise	• Insufficient oil supply • Main bearing clearance excessive • Bearing insert missing • Crankshaft end play excessive • Improperly tightened main bearing cap bolts • Loose flywheel or drive plate • Loose or damaged vibration damper	• Inspect for low oil level and low oil pressure • Measure main bearing clearance, repair as necessary • Replace missing insert • Measure end play, repair as necessary • Tighten bolts with specified torque • Tighten flywheel or drive plate attaching bolts • Repair as necessary
Connecting rod bearing noise	• Insufficient oil supply • Carbon build-up on piston • Bearing clearance excessive or bearing missing • Crankshaft connecting rod journal out-of-round • Misaligned connecting rod or cap • Connecting rod bolts tightened improperly	• Inspect for low oil level and low oil pressure • Remove carbon from piston crown • Measure clearance, repair as necessary • Measure journal dimensions, repair or replace as necessary • Repair as necessary • Tighten bolts with specified torque
Piston noise	• Piston-to-cylinder wall clearance excessive (scuffed piston) • Cylinder walls excessively tapered or out-of-round • Piston ring broken • Loose or seized piston pin • Connecting rods misaligned • Piston ring side clearance excessively loose or tight • Carbon build-up on piston is excessive	• Measure clearance and examine piston • Measure cylinder wall dimensions, rebore cylinder • Replace all rings on piston • Measure piston-to-pin clearance, repair as necessary • Measure rod alignment, straighten or replace • Measure ring side clearance, repair as necessary • Remove carbon from piston

Troubleshooting Engine Mechanical Problems (cont.)

Problem	Cause	Solution
Valve actuating component noise	• Insufficient oil supply	• Check for: (a) Low oil level (b) Low oil pressure (c) Plugged push rods (d) Wrong hydraulic tappets (e) Restricted oil gallery (f) Excessive tappet to bore clearance
	• Push rods worn or bent	• Replace worn or bent push rods
	• Rocker arms or pivots worn	• Replace worn rocker arms or pivots
	• Foreign objects or chips in hydraulic tappets	• Clean tappets
	• Excessive tappet leak-down	• Replace valve tappet
	• Tappet face worn	• Replace tappet; inspect corresponding cam lobe for wear
	• Broken or cocked valve springs	• Properly seat cocked springs; replace broken springs
	• Stem-to-guide clearance excessive	• Measure stem-to-guide clearance, repair as required
	• Valve bent	• Replace valve
	• Loose rocker arms	• Tighten bolts with specified torque
	• Valve seat runout excessive	• Regrind valve seat/valves
	• Missing valve lock	• Install valve lock
	• Push rod rubbing or contacting cylinder head	• Remove cylinder head and remove obstruction in head
	• Excessive engine oil (four-cylinder engine)	• Correct oil level

Troubleshooting Basic Charging System Problems

Problem	Cause	Solution
Noisy alternator	• Loose mountings • Loose drive pulley • Worn bearings • Brush noise • Internal circuits shorted (High pitched whine)	• Tighten mounting bolts • Tighten pulley • Replace alternator • Replace alternator • Replace alternator
Squeal when starting engine or accelerating	• Glazed or loose belt	• Replace or adjust belt
Indicator light remains on or ammeter indicates discharge (engine running)	• Broken fan belt • Broken or disconnected wires • Internal alternator problems • Defective voltage regulator	• Install belt • Repair or connect wiring • Replace alternator • Replace voltage regulator
Car light bulbs continually burn out—battery needs water continually	• Alternator/regulator overcharging	• Replace voltage regulator/alternator
Car lights flare on acceleration	• Battery low • Internal alternator/regulator problems	• Charge or replace battery • Replace alternator/regulator
Low voltage output (alternator light flickers continually or ammeter needle wanders)	• Loose or worn belt • Dirty or corroded connections • Internal alternator/regulator problems	• Replace or adjust belt • Clean or replace connections • Replace alternator or regulator

Troubleshooting the Cooling System

Problem	Cause	Solution
High temperature gauge indication—overheating	• Coolant level low	• Replenish coolant
	• Fan belt loose	• Adjust fan belt tension
	• Radiator hose(s) collapsed	• Replace hose(s)
	• Radiator airflow blocked	• Remove restriction (bug screen, fog lamps, etc.)
	• Faulty radiator cap	• Replace radiator cap
	• Ignition timing incorrect	• Adjust ignition timing
	• Idle speed low	• Adjust idle speed
	• Air trapped in cooling system	• Purge air
	• Heavy traffic driving	• Operate at fast idle in neutral intermittently to cool engine
	• Incorrect cooling system component(s) installed	• Install proper component(s)
	• Faulty thermostat	• Replace thermostat
	• Water pump shaft broken or impeller loose	• Replace water pump
	• Radiator tubes clogged	• Flush radiator
	• Cooling system clogged	• Flush system
	• Casting flash in cooling passages	• Repair or replace as necessary. Flash may be visible by removing cooling system components or removing core plugs.
	• Brakes dragging	• Repair brakes
	• Excessive engine friction	• Repair engine
	• Antifreeze concentration over 68%	• Lower antifreeze concentration percentage
	• Missing air seals	• Replace air seals
	• Faulty gauge or sending unit	• Repair or replace faulty component
	• Loss of coolant flow caused by leakage or foaming	• Repair or replace leaking component, replace coolant
	• Viscous fan drive failed	• Replace unit
Low temperature indication—undercooling	• Thermostat stuck open	• Replace thermostat
	• Faulty gauge or sending unit	• Repair or replace faulty component
Coolant loss—boilover	• Overfilled cooling system	• Reduce coolant level to proper specification
	• Quick shutdown after hard (hot) run	• Allow engine to run at fast idle prior to shutdown
	• Air in system resulting in occasional "burping" of coolant	• Purge system
	• Insufficient antifreeze allowing coolant boiling point to be too low	• Add antifreeze to raise boiling point
	• Antifreeze deteriorated because of age or contamination	• Replace coolant
	• Leaks due to loose hose clamps, loose nuts, bolts, drain plugs, faulty hoses, or defective radiator	• Pressure test system to locate source of leak(s) then repair as necessary
	• Faulty head gasket	• Replace head gasket
	• Cracked head, manifold, or block	• Replace as necessary
	• Faulty radiator cap	• Replace cap
Coolant entry into crankcase or cylinder(s)	• Faulty head gasket	• Replace head gasket
	• Crack in head, manifold or block	• Replace as necessary
Coolant recovery system inoperative	• Coolant level low	• Replenish coolant to FULL mark
	• Leak in system	• Pressure test to isolate leak and repair as necessary
	• Pressure cap not tight or seal missing, or leaking	• Repair as necessary
	• Pressure cap defective	• Replace cap
	• Overflow tube clogged or leaking	• Repair as necessary
	• Recovery bottle vent restricted	• Remove restriction

Troubleshooting the Cooling System (cont.)

Problem	Cause	Solution
Noise	• Fan contacting shroud • Loose water pump impeller • Glazed fan belt • Loose fan belt • Rough surface on drive pulley • Water pump bearing worn • Belt alignment	• Reposition shroud and inspect engine mounts • Replace pump • Apply silicone or replace belt • Adjust fan belt tension • Replace pulley • Remove belt to isolate. Replace pump. • Check pulley alignment. Repair as necessary.
No coolant flow through heater core	• Restricted return inlet in water pump • Heater hose collapsed or restricted • Restricted heater core • Restricted outlet in thermostat housing • Intake manifold bypass hole in cylinder head restricted • Faulty heater control valve • Intake manifold coolant passage restricted	• Remove restriction • Remove restriction or replace hose • Remove restriction or replace core • Remove flash or restriction • Remove restriction • Replace valve • Remove restriction or replace intake manifold

NOTE: *Immediately after shutdown, the engine enters a condition known as heat soak. This is caused by the cooling system being inoperative while engine temperature is still high. If coolant temperature rises above boiling point, expansion and pressure may push some coolant out of the radiator overflow tube. If this does not occur frequently it is considered normal.*

Chilton's Three "C's" Diesel Engine Diagnosis Procedure

Condition	Cause	Correction
Rough Idle	Improper adjustment	Adjust idle
	Accelerator control cable binding	Repair or lubricate
	Air or water in the fuel system	Clear air or water from fuel system
	Injection nozzle clogged	Check and clean injector nozzles
	Injection pump malfunction	Check injection pump
Poor Performance	Air cleaner clogged	Check element
	Accelerator control cable binding	Check control cable for free movement
	Restricted fuel flow (water or air)	Check lines and filter
	Incorrect injection timing	Check injection timing
	Injection nozzle clogged	Check and clean injector nozzles
	Injection pump malfunction	Replace injection pump
Excessive Exhaust Smoke	Restricted air cleaner	Check element
	Air or water in fuel filter	Remove air or water from fuel system
	Improper grade fuel	Check fuel in tank
	Incorrect injection timing	Check injection timing
	Injection pump malfunction	Replace injection pump
	Injection nozzle stuck open	Check injector nozzles
Excessive Fuel Consumption	Restricted air cleaner	Check element
	Leak in fuel lines	Check for leaks
	Incorrect idle speed	Check idle
	Restricted exhaust system	Check exhaust
	Improper grade of fuel	Check fuel in tank
	Injection pump malfunction	Check injection pump operation
Loud Knocking in Engine	Detective fuel injector	Replace fuel injector

Note: If the problem persists after performing these preliminary checks, disassembly and inspection of internal engine components may be necessary for further diagnosis.

Troubleshooting the Serpentine Drive Belt

Problem	Cause	Solution
Tension sheeting fabric failure (woven fabric on outside circumference of belt has cracked or separated from body of belt)	• Grooved or backside idler pulley diameters are less than minimum recommended • Tension sheeting contacting (rubbing) stationary object • Excessive heat causing woven fabric to age • Tension sheeting splice has fractured	• Replace pulley(s) not conforming to specification • Correct rubbing condition • Replace belt • Replace belt
Noise (objectional squeal, squeak, or rumble is heard or felt while drive belt is in operation)	• Belt slippage • Bearing noise • Belt misalignment • Belt-to-pulley mismatch • Driven component inducing vibration • System resonant frequency inducing vibration	• Adjust belt • Locate and repair • Align belt/pulley(s) • Install correct belt • Locate defective driven component and repair • Vary belt tension within specifications. Replace belt.
Rib chunking (one or more ribs has separated from belt body)	• Foreign objects imbedded in pulley grooves • Installation damage • Drive loads in excess of design specifications • Insufficient internal belt adhesion	• Remove foreign objects from pulley grooves • Replace belt • Adjust belt tension • Replace belt
Rib or belt wear (belt ribs contact bottom of pulley grooves)	• Pulley(s) misaligned • Mismatch of belt and pulley groove widths • Abrasive environment • Rusted pulley(s) • Sharp or jagged pulley groove tips • Rubber deteriorated	• Align pulley(s) • Replace belt • Replace belt • Clean rust from pulley(s) • Replace pulley • Replace belt
Longitudinal belt cracking (cracks between two ribs)	• Belt has mistracked from pulley groove • Pulley groove tip has worn away rubber-to-tensile member	• Replace belt • Replace belt
Belt slips	• Belt slipping because of insufficient tension • Belt or pulley subjected to substance (belt dressing, oil, ethylene glycol) that has reduced friction • Driven component bearing failure • Belt glazed and hardened from heat and excessive slippage	• Adjust tension • Replace belt and clean pulleys • Replace faulty component bearing • Replace belt
"Groove jumping" (belt does not maintain correct position on pulley, or turns over and/or runs off pulleys)	• Insufficient belt tension • Pulley(s) not within design tolerance • Foreign object(s) in grooves • Excessive belt speed • Pulley misalignment • Belt-to-pulley profile mismatched • Belt cordline is distorted	• Adjust belt tension • Replace pulley(s) • Remove foreign objects from grooves • Avoid excessive engine acceleration • Align pulley(s) • Install correct belt • Replace belt
Belt broken (Note: identify and correct problem before replacement belt is installed)	• Excessive tension • Tensile members damaged during belt installation • Belt turnover • Severe pulley misalignment • Bracket, pulley, or bearing failure	• Replace belt and adjust tension to specification • Replace belt • Replace belt • Align pulley(s) • Replace defective component and belt

Troubleshooting the Serpentine Drive Belt (cont.)

Problem	Cause	Solution
Cord edge failure (tensile member exposed at edges of belt or separated from belt body)	• Excessive tension • Drive pulley misalignment • Belt contacting stationary object • Pulley irregularities • Improper pulley construction • Insufficient adhesion between tensile member and rubber matrix	• Adjust belt tension • Align pulley • Correct as necessary • Replace pulley • Replace pulley • Replace belt and adjust tension to specifications
Sporadic rib cracking (multiple cracks in belt ribs at random intervals)	• Ribbed pulley(s) diameter less than minimum specification • Backside bend flat pulley(s) diameter less than minimum • Excessive heat condition causing rubber to harden • Excessive belt thickness • Belt overcured • Excessive tension	• Replace pulley(s) • Replace pulley(s) • Correct heat condition as necessary • Replace belt • Replace belt • Adjust belt tension

4. Tag and remove the push-on wires from the front of the relay.
5. Remove the nut and disconnect the cable from the starter side of the relay.
6. Remove the relay attaching bolts and remove the relay.
7. Installation is the reverse of removal.

Battery

REMOVAL AND INSTALLATION

1. Loosen the nuts which secure the cable ends to the battery terminals. Lift the negative battery cables from the terminals first with a twisting motion, then the positive cables. If there is a battery cable puller available, make use of it.

WARNING: *On vehicles with dual batteries, take great care to avoid ground the disconnected end of the positive cable linking the two batteries, before the other end is disconnected.*

2. Remove the holddown nuts from the battery holddown bracket and remove the bracket and the battery. Lift the battery straight up and out of the vehicle, being sure to keep the battery level to avoid spilling the battery acid.
3. Before installing the battery in the vehicle, make sure that the battery terminals are clean and free from corrosion. Use a battery terminal cleaner on the terminals and on the inside of the battery cable ends. If a cleaner is not available, use coarse grade sandpaper to remove the corrosion. A mixture of baking soda and water poured over the terminals and cable ends will help remove and neutralize any acid buildup.

WARNING: *Take great care to avoid getting any of the baking soda solution inside the battery. If any solution gets inside the battery a violent reaction will take place and/or the battery will be damaged.*

4. Before installing the cables onto the terminals, cut a piece of felt cloth, or something similar into a circle about 3 in. (76mm) across. Cut a hole in the middle about the size of the battery terminals at their base. Push the cloth pieces over the terminals so that they lay flat on the top of the battery. Soak the pieces of cloth with oil. This will keep oxidation to a minimum.
5. Place the battery in the vehicle. Install the cables onto the terminals.

WARNING: *On vehicles with dual batteries, take great care to avoid grounding the disconnected end of the positive cable linking the two batteries, after the other end is connected.*

6. Tighten the nuts on the cable ends.

NOTE: *See Chapter 1 for battery maintenance illustrations.*

7. Smear a light coating of grease on the cable ends and tops of the terminals. This will further prevent the buildup of oxidation on the terminals and the cable ends.
8. Install and tighten the nuts of the battery holddown bracket.

ENGINE MECHANICAL

Engine Overhaul Tips

Most engine overhaul procedures are fairly standard. In addition to specific parts replacement procedures and complete specifications for your individual engine, this section also is a guide to accept rebuilding procedures. Examples of standard rebuilding practice are shown and should be used along with specific details concerning your particular engine.

Competent and accurate machine shop services will ensure maximum performance, reliability and engine life.

In most instances it is more profitable for the do-it-yourself mechanic to remove, clean and inspect the component, buy the necessary parts and deliver these to a shop for actual machine work.

On the other hand, much of the rebuilding work (crankshaft, block, bearings, piston rods, and other components) is well within the scope of the do-it-yourself mechanic.

TOOLS

The tools required for an engine overhaul or parts replacement will depend on the depth of your involvement. With a few exceptions, they will be the tools found in a mechanic's tool kit. More in-depth work will require any or all of the following:

- a dial indicator (reading in thousandths) mounted on a universal base
- micrometers and telescope gauges
- jaw and screw-type pullers
- scraper
- valve spring compressor
- ring groove cleaner
- piston ring expander and compressor
- ridge reamer
- cylinder hone or glaze breaker
- Plastigage®
- engine stand

The use of most of these tools is illustrated in this section. Many can be rented for a one-time use from a local parts jobber or tool supply house specializing in automotive work.

Occasionally, the use of special tools is called for. See the information on Special Tools and Safety Notice in the front of this book before substituting another tool.

INSPECTION TECHNIQUES

Procedures and specifications are given in this section for inspecting, cleaning and assessing the wear limits of most major components. Other procedures such as Magnaflux® and Zyglo® can be used to locate material flaws and stress cracks. Magnaflux® is a magnetic process applicable only to ferrous materials. The Zyglo® process coats the material with a fluorescent dye penetrant and can be used on any material Check for suspected surface cracks can be more readily made using spot check dye. The dye is sprayed onto the suspected area, wiped off and the area sprayed with a developer. Cracks will show up brightly.

OVERHAUL TIPS

Aluminum has become extremely popular for use in engines, due to its low weight. Observe the following precautions when handling aluminum parts:

- Never hot tank aluminum parts (the caustic hot tank solution will eat the aluminum.
- Remove all aluminum parts (identification tag, etc.) from engine parts prior to the tanking.
- Always coat threads lightly with engine oil or anti-seize compounds before installation, to prevent seizure.
- Never over torque bolts or spark plugs especially in aluminum threads.

Stripped threads in any component can be repaired using any of several commercial repair kits (Heli-Coil®, Microdot®, Keenserts®, etc.).

When assembling the engine, any parts that will be frictional contact must be prelubed to provide lubrication at initial start-up. Any product specifically formulated for this purpose can be used, but engine oil is not recommended as a prelube.

When semi-permanent (locked, but removable) installation of bolts or nuts is desired, threads should be cleaned and coated with Loctite® or other similar, commercial non-hardening sealant.

REPAIRING DAMAGED THREADS

Several methods of repairing damaged threads are available. Heli-Coil® (shown here), Keenserts® and Microdot® are among the most widely used. All involve basically the same principle – drilling out stripped threads, tapping the hole and installing a prewound insert – making welding, plugging and oversize fasteners unnecessary.

Two types of thread repair inserts are usually supplied: a standard type for most Inch Coarse, Inch Fine, Metric Course and Metric Fine thread sizes and a spark lug type to fit most spark plug port sizes. Consult the individual manufacturer's catalog to determine exact

Drill out the damaged threads with specified drill. Drill completely through the hole or to the bottom of a blind hole

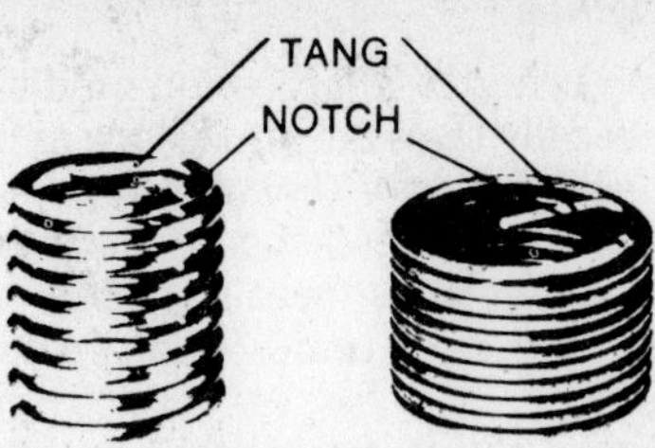

Standard thread repair insert (left) and spark plug thread insert (right)

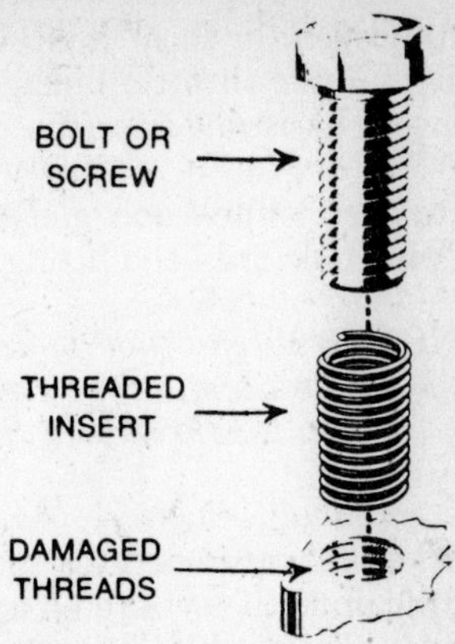

Damaged bolt holes can be repaired with thread

applications. Typical thread repair kits will contain a selection of prewound threaded inserts, a tap (corresponding to the outside diameter threads of the insert) and an installation tool. Spark plug inserts usually differ because they require a tap equipped with pilot threads and a combined reamer/tap section. Most manufacturers also supply blister-packed thread repair inserts separately in addition to a master kit containing a variety of taps and inserts plus installation tools.

Before effecting a repair to a threaded hole, remove any snapped, broken or damaged bolts or studs. Penetrating oil can be used to free frozen threads. The offending item can be removed with locking pliers or with a screw or stud extractor. After the hole is clear, the thread can be repaired, as shown in the series of accompanying illustrations.

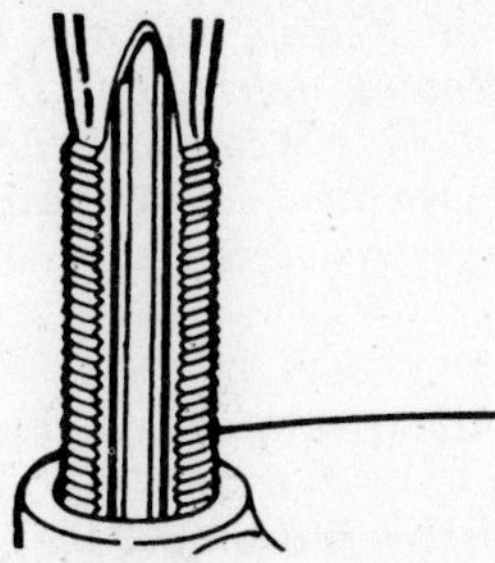

With the tap supplied, tap the hole to receive the thread insert. Keep the tap well oiled and back it out frequently to avoid clogging the threads

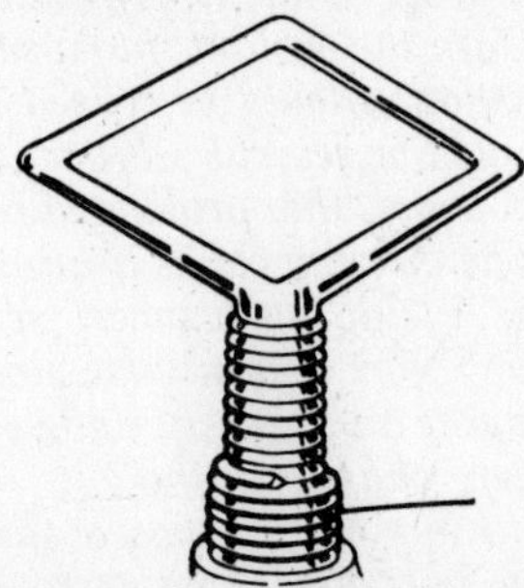

Screw the threaded insert onto the installation tool until the tang engages the slot. Screw the insert into the tapped hole until it is $^1/_4$–$^1/_2$ turn below the top surface, after installation break off the tang with a hammer and punch

Checking Engine Compression

A noticeable lack of engine power, excessive oil consumption and/or poor fuel mileage measured over an extended period are all indicators of internal engine war. Worn piston rings, scored or worn cylinder bores, blown head gaskets, sticking or burnt valves and worn valve seats are all possible culprits here. A check of each cylinder's compression will help you locate the problems.

As mentioned earlier, a screw-in type compression gauge is more accurate that the type you simply hold against the spark plug hole, although it takes slightly longer to use. It's worth it to obtain a more accurate reading. Follow the procedures below.

Gasoline Engines

1. Warm up the engine to normal operating temperature.
2. Remove all the spark plugs.
3. Disconnect the high tension lead from the ignition coil.

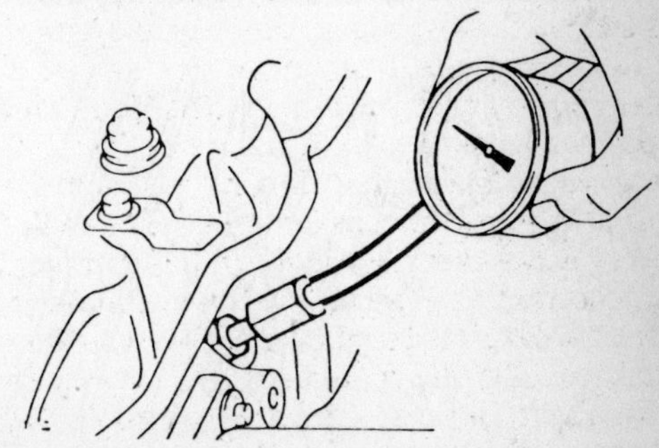

The screw-in type compression gauge is more accurate

4. On fully open the throttle either by operating the carburetor throttle linkage by hand or by having an assistant floor the accelerator pedal.

5. Screw the compression gauge into the no.1 spark plug hole until the fitting is snug.

WARNING: *Be careful not to crossthread the plug hole. On aluminum cylinder heads use extra care, as the threads in these heads are easily ruined.*

6. Ask an assistant to depress the accelerator pedal fully on both carbureted and fuel injected vehicles. Then, while you read the compression gauge, ask the assistant to crank the engine two or three times in short bursts using the ignition switch.

7. Read the compression gauge at the end of each series of cranks, and record the highest of these readings. Repeat this procedure for each of the engine's cylinders. Compare the highest reading of each cylinder to the compression pressure specification in the Tune-Up Specifications chart in Chapter 2. The specs in this chart are maximum values.

A cylinder's compression pressure is usually acceptable if it is not less than 80% of maximum. The difference between any two cylinders should be no more than 12–14 pounds.

8. If a cylinder is unusually low, pour a tablespoon of clean engine oil into the cylinder through the spark plug hole and repeat the compression test. If the compression comes up after adding the oil, it appears that the cylinder's piston rings or bore are damaged or worn. If the pressure remains low, the valves may not be seating properly (a valve job is needed), or the head gasket may be blown near that cylinder. If compression in any two adjacent cylinders is low, and if the addition of oil doesn't help the compression, there is leakage past the head gasket. Oil and coolant water in the combustion chamber can result from this problem. There may be evidence of water droplets on the engine dipstick when a head gasket has blown.

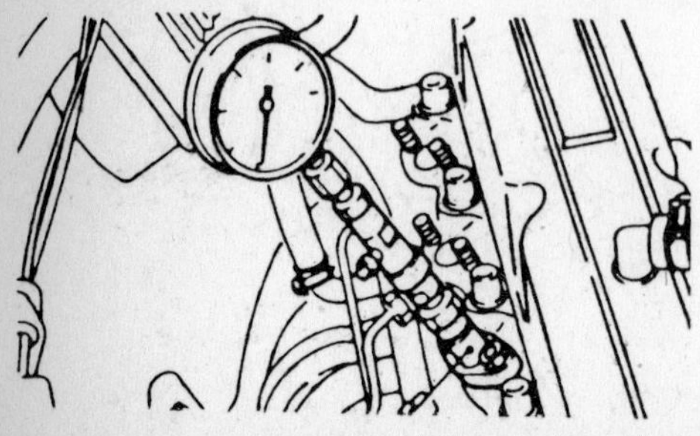

Diesel engines require a special compression gauge adaptor

Diesel Engines

Checking cylinder compression on diesel engines is basically the same procedure as on gasoline engines except for the following:

1. A special compression gauge adaptor suitable for diesel engines (because these engines have much greater compression pressures) must be used.

2. Remove the injector tubes and remove the injectors from each cylinder.

WARNING: *Don't forget to remove the washer underneath each injector. Otherwise, it may get lost when the engine is cranked.*

3. When fitting the compression gauge adaptor to the cylinder head, make sure the bleeder of the gauge (if equipped) is closed.

4. When reinstalling the injector assemblies, install new washers underneath each injector.

Engine

REMOVAL AND INSTALLATION

WARNING: *Disconnect the negative battery cable(s) before beginning any work. Always label all disconnected hoses, vacuum lines and wires, to prevent incorrect reassembly. Do not disconnect any air conditioning lines unless you are thoroughly familiar with air conditioning systems and the hazards involved; escaping refrigerant (Freon®) will freeze any surface it contacts, including skin and eyes. Have the system discharged professionally before required repairs are started.*

6–4.9L

1. Drain the cooling system and the crankcase.

CAUTION: *When draining the coolant, keep in mind that cats and dogs are attracted by the ethylene glycol antifreeze, and are quite likely to drink any that is left in an uncovered container or in puddles on the ground. This will prove fatal in sufficient quantity. Always drain the coolant into a sealable container. Coolant should be reused unless it is contaminated or several years old.*

The EPA warns that prolonged contact with used engine oil may cause a number of skin disorders, including cancer! You should make every effort to minimize your exposure to used engine oil. Protective gloves should be worn when changing the oil. Wash your hands and any other exposed skin areas as soon as possible after exposure to used engine oil. Soap and water, or waterless hand cleaner should be used.

2. Remove the hood.

3. Remove the throttle body inlet tubes.

4. Disconnect the positive battery cable.

5. Discharge the air conditioning system. See Chapter 1.
6. Disconnect the refrigerant lines at the compressor. Cap all openings at once.
7. Remove the compressor.
8. Disconnect the refrigerant lines at the condenser. Cap all openings at once.
9. Remove the condenser.
10. Disconnect the heater hose from the water pump and coolant outlet housing.
11. Disconnect the flexible fuel line from the fuel pump.
12. Remove the radiator.
13. Remove the fan, water pump pulley, and fan belt.
14. Disconnect the accelerator cable.
15. Disconnect the brake booster vacuum hose at the intake manifold.
16. On trucks with automatic transmission, disconnect the transmission kickdown rod at the bellcrank assembly.
17. Disconnect the exhaust pipe from the exhaust manifold.
18. Disconnect the Electronic Engine Control (EEC) harness from all the sensors.
19. Disconnect the body ground strap and the battery ground cable from the engine.
20. Disconnect the engine wiring harness at the ignition coil, the coolant temperature sending unit, and the oil pressure sensing unit. Position the wiring harness out of the way.
21. Remove the alternator mounting bolts and position the alternator out of the way.
22. Remove the power steering pump from the mounting brackets and move it to one side, leaving the lines attached.
23. Raise and support the truck on jackstands.
24. Remove the starter.
25. Remove the automatic transmission filler tube bracket, if so equipped.
26. Remove the rear engine plate upper right bolt.
27. On manual transmission equipped trucks:
   a. Remove the flywheel housing lower attaching bolts.
   b. Disconnect the clutch return spring.
28. On automatic transmission equipped trucks:
   a. Remove the converter housing access cover assembly.
   b. Remove the flywheel-to-converter attaching nuts.
   c. Secure the converter in the housing.
   d. Remove the transmission oil cooler lines from the retaining clip at the engine.
   e. Remove the lower converter housing-to-engine attaching bolts.
29. Remove the nut from each of the two front engine mounts.
30. Lower the vehicle and position a jack under the transmission and support it.
31. Remove the remaining bellhousing-to-engine attaching bolts.
32. Attach an engine lifting device and raise

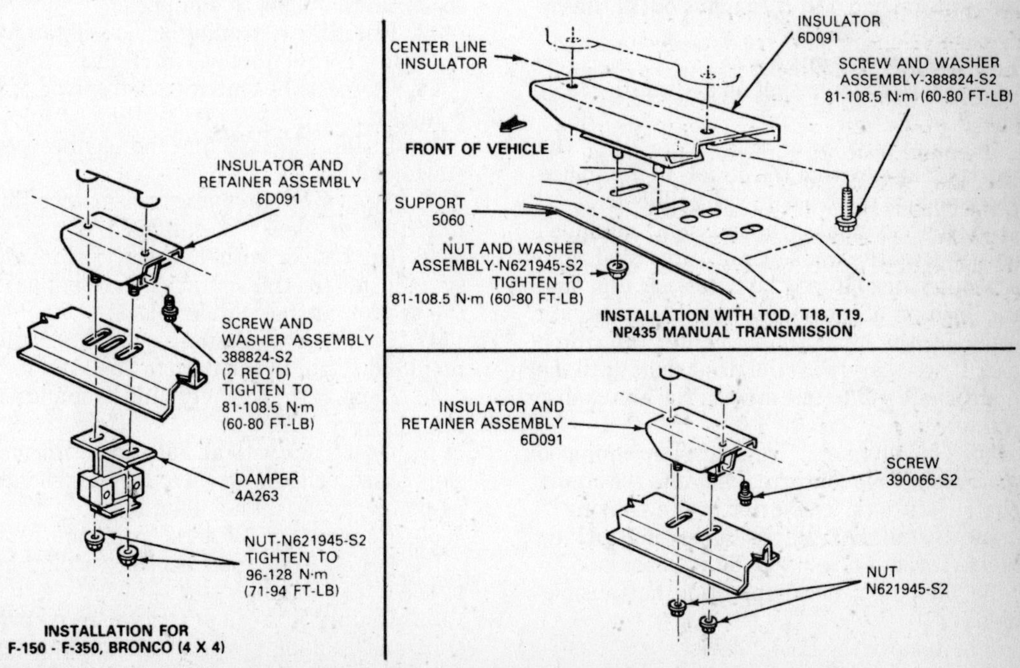

Engine rear mounts for the F-150, 250, 350 and Bronco w/6–4.9L

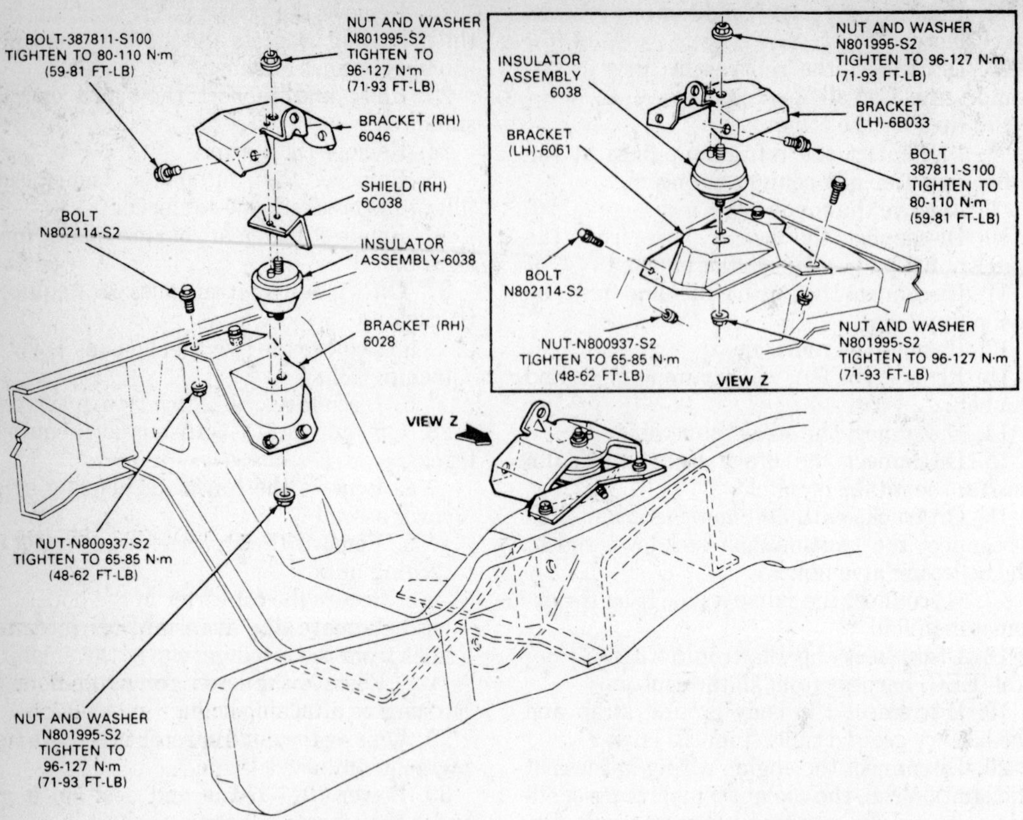

Engine front mounts for the F-150, 250 and Bronco w/6–4.9L

the engine slightly and carefully pull it from the transmission. Lift the engine out of the vehicle.

To install the engine:

33. Place a new gasket on the muffler inlet pipe.

34. Carefully lower the engine into the truck. Make sure that the dowels in the engine block engage the holes in the bellhousing.

35. On manual transmission equipped trucks, start the transmission input shaft into the clutch disc. It may be necessary to adjust the position of the engine or transmission in order for the input shaft to enter the clutch disc. If necessary, turn the crankshaft until the input shaft splines mesh with the clutch disc splines.

36. On automatic transmission equipped trucks, start the converter pilot into the crankshaft. Secure the converter in the housing.

37. Install the bellhousing upper attaching bolts. Torque the bolts to 50 ft. lbs.

38. Remove the jack supporting the transmission.

39. Remove the lifting device.

40. Install the engine mount nuts and tighten them to 70 ft. lbs.

41. Install the automatic transmission coil cooler lines bracket, if equipped.

42. Install the remaining bellhousing attaching bolts. Torque them to 50 ft. lbs.

43. Connect the clutch return spring, if so equipped.

44. Install the starter and connect the starter cable.

45. Attach the automatic transmission fluid filler tube bracket, if so equipped.

46. On trucks with automatic transmissions, install the transmission oil cooler lines in the bracket at the cylinder block.

47. Connect the exhaust pipe to the exhaust manifold. Tighten the nuts to 25–35 ft. lbs.

48. Connect the engine ground strap and negative battery cable.

49. On a truck with an automatic transmission, connect the kickdown rod to the bellcrank assembly on the intake manifold.

50. Connect the accelerator linkage.

51. Connect the brake booster vacuum line to the intake manifold.

52. Connect the coil primary wire, oil pressure and coolant temperature sending unit wires, fuel line, heater hoses, and the battery positive cable.

53. Connect the EEC sensors.
54. Install the alternator on its mounting bracket.
55. Install the power steering pump on its bracket.
56. Install the water pump pulley, spacer, fan, and fan belt. Adjust the belt tension.
57. Install the air conditioning compressor. Connect the refrigerant lines.
58. Install the radiator.
59. Install the condenser and connect the refrigerant lines.
60. Charge the refrigerant system. See Chapter 1.
61. Connect the upper and lower radiator hoses to the radiator and engine.
62. Connect the automatic transmission oil cooler lines, if so equipped.
63. Install and adjust the hood.
64. Fill the cooling system.
65. Fill the crankcase.
66. Start the engine and check for leaks.
67. Bleed the cooling system.
68. Adjust the clutch pedal free-play or the automatic transmission control linkage.
69. Install the air cleaner.

8–5.0L
8–5.7L

1. Remove the hood.
2. Drain the cooling system and crankcase.

CAUTION: *When draining the coolant, keep in mind that cats and dogs are attracted by the ethylene glycol antifreeze, and are quite likely to drink any that is left in an uncovered container or in puddles on the ground. This will prove fatal in sufficient quantity. Always drain the coolant into a sealable container. Coolant should be reused unless it is contaminated or several years old.*

The EPA warns that prolonged contact with used engine oil may cause a number of skin disorders, including cancer! You should make every effort to minimize your exposure to used engine oil. Protective gloves should be worn when changing the oil. Wash your hands and any other exposed skin areas as soon as possible after exposure to used engine oil. Soap and water, or waterless hand cleaner should be used.

3. Disconnect the battery and alternator cables.
4. On carbureted engines, remove the air cleaner and intake duct assembly, plus the crankcase ventilation hose. On fuel injected engines, remove the air intake hoses, PCV tube and carbon canister hose.
5. Disconnect the upper and lower radiator hoses.

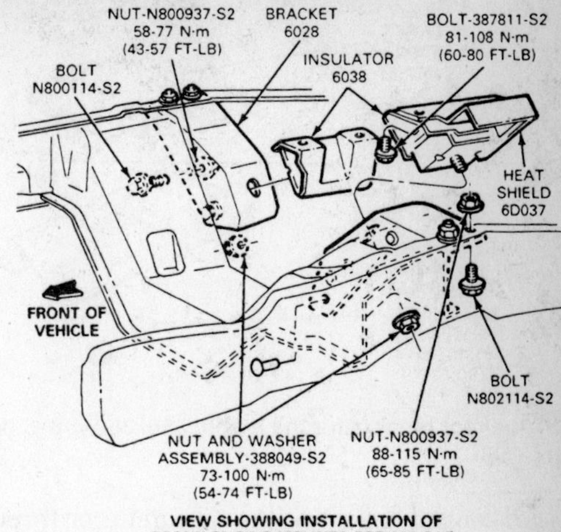

Engine front mounts for the F-150, 250, 350 and Bronco w/8–5.0L, 5.8L

6. Discharge the air conditioning system. See Chapter 1.
7. Disconnect the refrigerant lines at the compressor. Cap all openings immediately.
8. If so equipped, disconnect the automatic transmission oil cooler lines.
9. Remove the fan shroud and lay it over the fan.
10. Remove the radiator and fan, shroud, fan, spacer, pulley and belt.
11. Remove the alternator pivot and adjusting bolts. Remove the alternator.
12. Disconnect the oil pressure sending unit lead from the sending unit.
13. Disconnect the fuel tank-to-pump fuel line at the fuel pump and plug the line.
14. On trucks with EFI, disconnect the chassis fuel line at the fuel rails.
15. Disconnect the accelerator linkage and

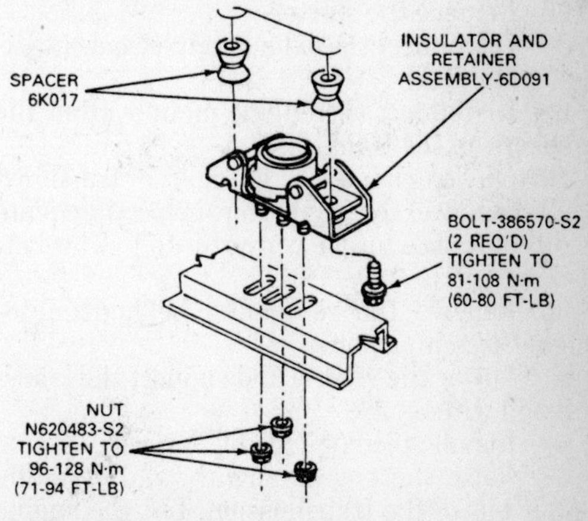

Engine rear mounts for the Bronco w/8–5.0L, 5.8L

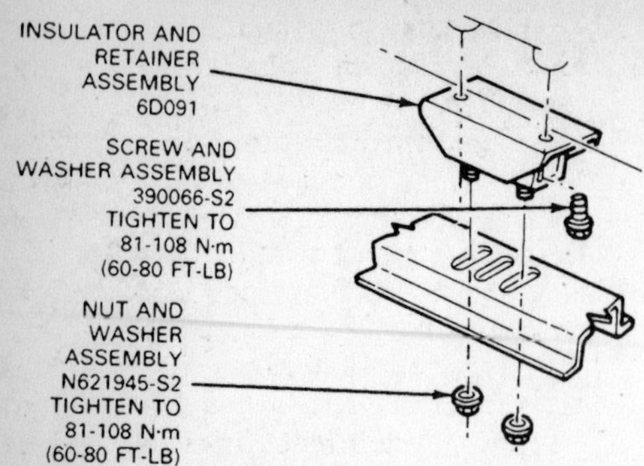

Engine rear mounts for the F-150, 250, 350 w/8–5.0L or 8–5.8L

speed control linkage at the carburetor or throttle body.

16. Disconnect the automatic transmission kick-down rod and remove the return spring, if so equipped.

17. Disconnect the power brake booster vacuum hose.

18. On EFI models, disconnect the throttle bracket from the upper intake manifold and swing it out of the way with the cables still attached.

19. Disconnect the heater hoses from the water pump and intake manifold or tee (EFI).

20. Disconnect the temperature sending unit wire from the sending unit.

21. Remove the upper bellhousing-to-engine attaching bolts.

22. Remove the wiring harness from the left rocker arm cover and position the wires out of the way.

23. Disconnect the ground strap from the cylinder block.

24. Disconnect the air conditioning compressor clutch wire.

25. Raise the front of the truck and disconnect the starter cable from the starter.

26. Remove the starter.

27. Disconnect the exhaust pipe from the exhaust manifolds.

28. Disconnect the engine mounts from the brackets on the frame.

29. On trucks with automatic transmissions, remove the converter inspection plate and remove the torque converter-to-flywheel attaching bolts.

30. Remove the remaining bellhousing-to-engine attaching bolts.

31. Lower the vehicle and support the transmission with a jack.

32. Install an engine lifting device.

33. Raise the engine slightly and carefully pull it out of the transmission. Lift the engine out of the engine compartment.

34. Lower the engine carefully into the transmission. Make sure that the dowel in the engine block engage the holes in the bellhousing through the rear cover plate. If the engine hangs up after the transmission input shaft enters the clutch disc (manual transmission only), turn the crankshaft with the transmission in gear until the input shaft splines mesh with the clutch disc splines.

35. Install the engine mount nuts and washers. Torque the nuts to 80 ft. lbs.

36. Remove the engine lifting device.

37. Install the lower bellhousing-to-engine attaching bolts. Torque the bolts to 50 ft. lbs.

38. Remove the transmission support jack.

39. On trucks with automatic transmissions, install the torque converter-to-flywheel attaching bolts. Torque the bolts to 30 ft. lbs.

40. Install the converter inspection plate. Torque the bolts to 60 inch lbs.

41. Connect the exhaust pipe to the exhaust manifolds. Tighten the exhaust pipe-to-exhaust manifold nuts to 25–35 ft. lbs.

42. Install the starter. Torque the mounting bolts to 20 ft. lbs.

43. Connect the starter cable to the starter.

44. Lower the truck.

45. Install the upper bellhousing-to-engine attaching bolts. Torque the bolts to 50 ft. lbs.

46. Connect the wiring harness at the left rocker arm cover.

47. Connect the ground strap to the cylinder block.

48. Connect the air conditioning compressor clutch wire.

49. Connect the heater hoses at the water pump and intake manifold or tee (EFI).

50. Connect the temperature sending unit wire at the sending unit.

51. Connect the accelerator linkage and speed control linkage at the carburetor or throttle body.

52. Connect the automatic transmission kick-down rod and install the return spring, if so equipped.

53. Connect the power brake booster vacuum hose.

54. On EFI models, connect the throttle bracket to the upper intake manifold.

55. Connect the fuel tank-to-pump fuel line at the fuel pump. On trucks with EFI, disconnect the chassis fuel line at the fuel rails.

56. Connect the oil pressure sending unit lead to the sending unit.

57. Install the alternator.

58. Connect the refrigerant lines to the compressor.

59. Install the radiator and fan, shroud, fan, spacer, pulley and belt.

60. Connect the upper and lower radiator

hoses, and, if so equipped, the automatic transmission oil cooler lines.

61. On carbureted engines, install the air cleaner and intake duct assembly, plus the crankcase ventilation hose. On fuel injected engines, install the air intake hoses, PCV tube and carbon canister hose.

62. Connect the battery and alternator cables.

63. Fill the cooling system and crankcase.

64. Charge the air conditioning system. See Chapter 1.

65. Install the hood.

If the torque for a particular fastener was not mentioned above, use the following torque values as a guide:

- 1/4 in.–20: 6–9 ft. lbs.
- 5/16 in.–18: 12–18 ft. lbs.
- 3/8 in.–16: 22–32 ft. lbs.
- 7/16 in.–14: 45–57 ft. lbs.
- 1/2 in.–13: 55–80 ft. lbs.
- 9/16 in.: 85–120 ft. lbs.

8–7.5L

1. Remove the hood.

2. Drain the cooling system.

CAUTION: *When draining the coolant, keep in mind that cats and dogs are attracted by the ethylene glycol antifreeze, and are quite likely to drink any that is left in an uncovered container or in puddles on the ground. This will prove fatal in sufficient quantity. Always drain the coolant into a sealable container. Coolant should be reused unless it is contaminated or several years old.*

3. Disconnect the negative battery cable from the block.

4. Remove the air cleaner assembly.

5. Remove the crankcase ventilation hose.

6. Remove the canister hose.

7. Disconnect the upper and lower radiator hoses.

8. Disconnect the transmission oil cooler lines from the radiator.

9. Disconnect the engine oil cooler lines at the oil filter adapter.

WARNING: *Don't disconnect the lines at the quick-connect fittings behind or at the oil cooler. Disconnecting them may permanently damage them.*

10. Discharge the air conditioning system. See Chapter 1.

11. Disconnect the refrigerant lines at the compressor. Cap the openings at once!

12. Disconnect the refrigerant lines at the condenser. Cap the openings at once!

13. Remove the condenser.

14. Remove the fan shroud from the radiator and position it up, over the fan.

15. Remove the radiator.

16. Remove the fan shroud.

17. Remove the fan, belts and pulley from the water pump.

18. Remove the compressor.

19. Remove the power steering pump from the engine, if so equipped, and position it to one side. Do not disconnect the fluid lines.

20. Disconnect the fuel pump inlet line from the pump and plug the line.

21. Disconnect the oil pressure sending unit wire at the sending unit.

22. Remove the alternator drive belts and disconnect the alternator from the engine, positioning it aside.

23. Disconnect the ground cable from the right front corner of the engine.

24. Disconnect the heater hoses.

25. Remove the transmission fluid filler tube attaching bolt from the right side valve cover and position the tube out of the way.

26. Disconnect all vacuum lines at the rear of the intake manifold.

27. Disconnect the speed control cable at the carburetor, if so equipped.

28. Disconnect the accelerator rod and the transmission kickdown rod and secure them out of the way.

29. Disconnect the engine wiring harness at the connector on the fire wall. Disconnect the primary wire at the coil.

30. Remove the upper flywheel housing-to-engine bolts.

31. Raise the vehicle and disconnect the exhaust pipes at the exhaust manifolds.

32. Disconnect the starter cable and remove the starter. Bring the starter forward and rotate the solenoid outward to remove the assembly.

33. Remove the access cover from the converter housing and remove the flywheel-to-converter attaching nuts.

34. Remove the lower the converter housing-to-engine attaching bolts.

35. Remove the engine mount through bolts attaching the rubber insulator to the frame brackets.

36. Lower the vehicle and place a jack under the transmission to support it.

37. Remove the converter housing-to-engine block attaching bolts (left side).

38. Remove the coil and bracket assembly from the intake manifold.

39. Attach an engine lifting device and carefully take up the weight of the engine.

40. Move the engine forward to disengage it from the transmission and slowly lift it from the truck.

41. Lower the engine slowly into the truck.

42. Slide the engine rearward to engage it

with the transmission and slowly lower it onto the supports.

43. Install the engine support nuts and torque them to 74 ft. lbs.

44. Remove the engine lifting device.

45. Install the converter housing-to-engine block upper and left side attaching bolts. Torque the bolts to 50 ft. lbs.

46. Install the coil and bracket assembly on the intake manifold.

47. Remove the jack from under the transmission.

48. Lower the truck.

49. Install the upper converter housing-to-engine attaching bolts. Torque the bolts to 50 ft. lbs.

50. Install the flywheel-to-converter attaching nuts. Torque the nuts to 34 ft. lbs.

51. Install the access cover on the converter housing. Torque the bolts to 60–90 inch lbs.

52. Install the starter.

53. Connect the starter cable.

54. Raise the vehicle and connect the exhaust pipes at the exhaust manifolds.

55. Connect the engine wiring harness at the connector on the fire wall.

56. Connect the primary wire at the coil.

57. Connect the accelerator rod and the transmission kickdown rod.

58. Connect the speed control cable.

59. Connect all vacuum lines at the rear of the intake manifold.

60. Install the transmission fluid filler tube attaching bolt from the right side valve cover and position the tube out of the way.

61. Connect the heater hoses.

62. Connect the ground cable at the right front corner of the engine.

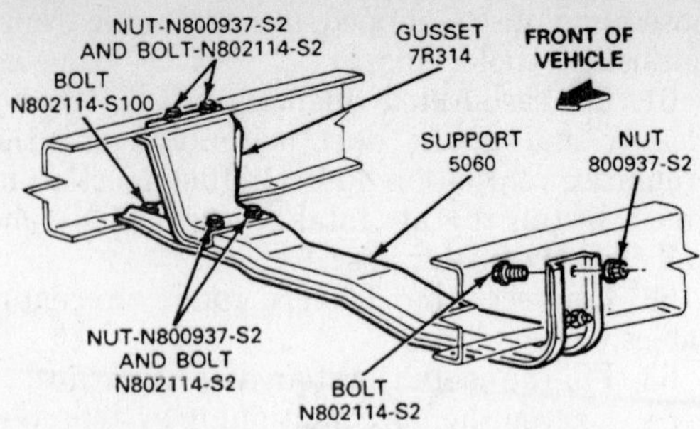

Engine rear mounts for the F-350 4×4

63. Install the alternator and drive belts.

64. Connect the oil pressure sending unit wire at the sending unit.

65. Connect the fuel pump inlet line at the pump and plug the line.

66. Install the power steering pump and belt.

67. Install air conditioning compressor. Connect the refrigerant lines.

68. Install the fan, belts and pulley on the water pump.

69. Position the fan shroud over the fan.

70. Install the radiator.

71. Attach the fan shroud.

72. Install the condenser.

73. Connect the refrigerant lines at the condenser.

74. Charge the air conditioning system. See Chapter 1.

75. Connect the engine oil cooler lines at the oil filter adapter.

76. Connect the transmission oil cooler lines at the radiator.

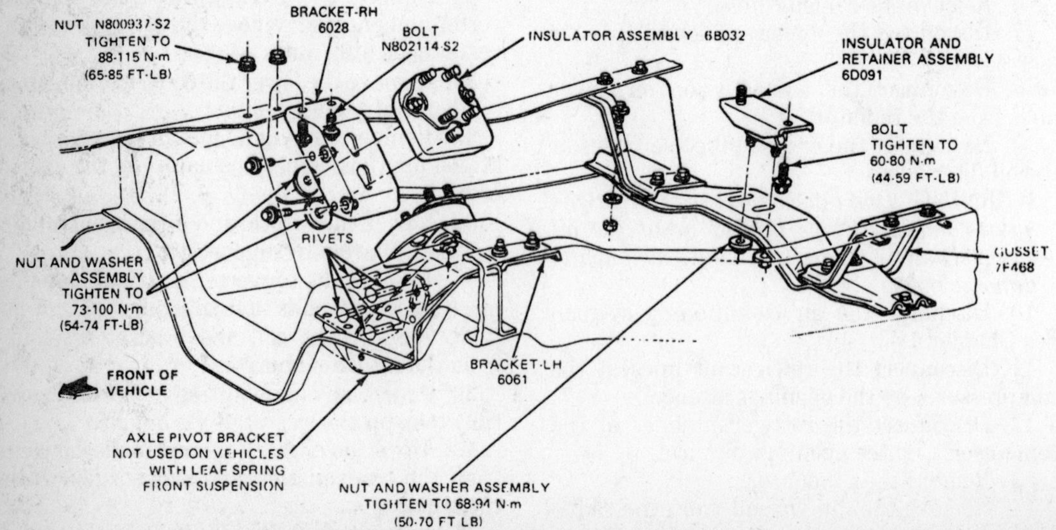

Engine supports for the F-250 and F-350 w/8–7.5L

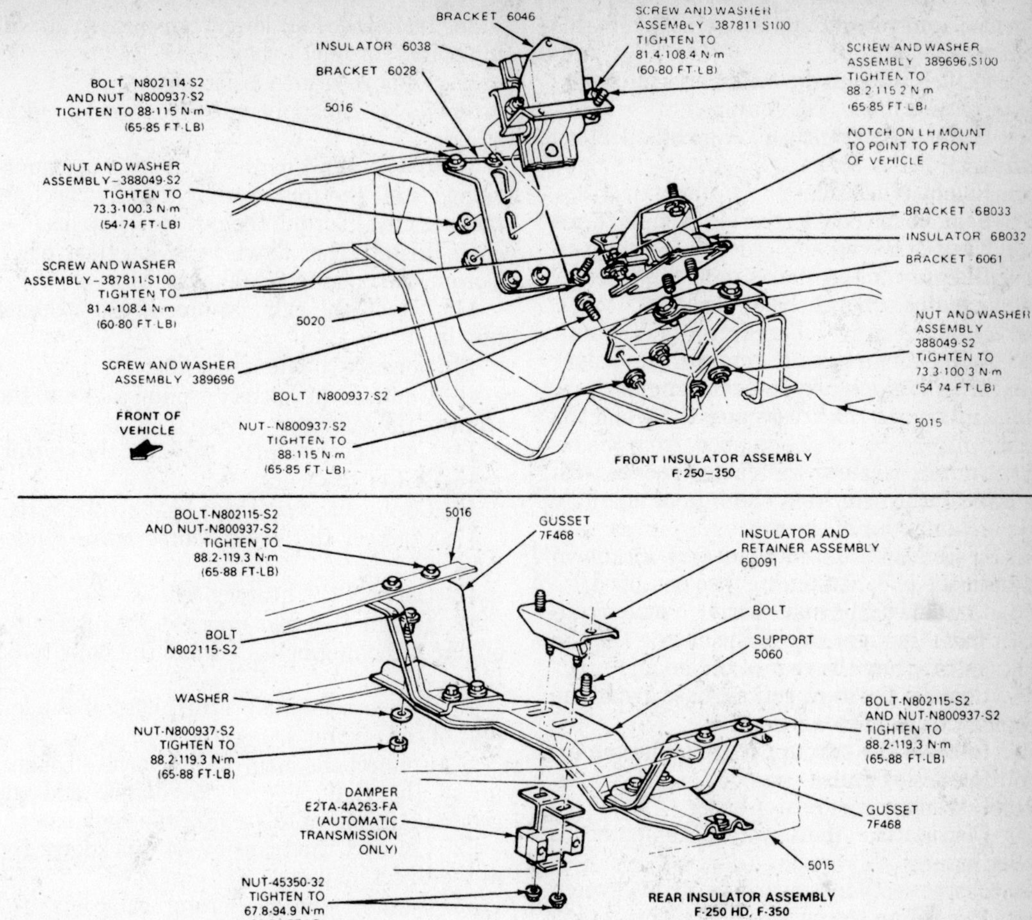

Engine supports for the F-250, 350 w/diesel

77. Connect the upper and lower radiator hoses.
78. Connect the canister hose.
79. Connect the crankcase ventilation hose.
80. Connect the negative battery cable from the block.
81. Fill the cooling system.
82. Install the air cleaner assembly.
83. Install the hood.

If the torque for a particular fastener was not mentioned above, use the following torque values as a guide:

- 1/4 in.–20: 6–9 ft. lbs.
- 5/16 in.–18: 12–18 ft. lbs.
- 3/8 in.–16: 22–32 ft. lbs.
- 7/16 in.–14: 45–57 ft. lbs.
- 1/2 in.–13: 55–80 ft. lbs.
- 9/16 in.: 85–120 ft. lbs.

6.9L and 7.3L Diesel Engines

1. Remove the hood.
2. Drain the coolant.

CAUTION: *When draining the coolant, keep in mind that cats and dogs are attracted by the ethylene glycol antifreeze, and are quite likely to drink any that is left in an uncovered container or in puddles on the ground. This will prove fatal in sufficient quantity. Always drain the coolant into a sealable container. Coolant should be reused unless it is contaminated or several years old.*

3. Remove the air cleaner and intake duct assembly and cover the air intake opening with a clean rag to keep out the dirt.
4. Remove the upper grille support bracket and upper air conditioning condenser mounting bracket.
5. On vehicles equipped with air conditioning, the system MUST be discharged to remove the condenser.

WARNING: *DO NOT attempt to do this yourself, unless you are familiar with air conditioning repair. See Chapter 1.*

6. Remove the radiator fan shroud halves.
7. Remove the fan and clutch assembly as

described under water pump removal in this chapter.

8. Detach the radiator hoses and the transmission cooler lines, if so equipped.

9. Remove the condenser. Cap all openings at once!

10. Remove the radiator.

11. Remove the power steering pump and position it out of the way.

12. Disconnect the fuel supply line heater and alternator wires at the alternator.

13. Disconnect the oil pressure sending unit wire at the sending unit, remove the sender from the firewall and lay it on the engine.

14. Disconnect the accelerator cable and the speed control cable, if so equipped, from the injection pump. Remove the cable bracket with the cables attached, from the intake manifold and position it out of the way.

15. Disconnect the transmission kickdown rod from the injection pump, if so equipped.

16. Disconnect the main wiring harness connector from the right side of the engine and the ground strap from the rear of the engine.

17. Remove the fuel return hose from the left rear of the engine.

18. Remove the two upper transmission-to-engine attaching bolts.

19. Disconnect the heater hoses.

20. Disconnect the water temperature sender wire.

21. Disconnect the overheat light switch wire and position the wire out of the way.

22. Raise the truck and support on it on jackstands.

23. Disconnect the battery ground cables from the front of the engine and the starter cables from the starter.

24. Remove the fuel inlet line and plug the fuel line at the fuel pump.

25. Detach the exhaust pipe at the exhaust manifold.

26. Disconnect the engine insulators from the no. 1 crossmember.

27. Remove the flywheel inspection plate and the four converter-to-flywheel attaching nuts, if equipped with automatic transmission.

28. Remove the jackstands and lower the truck.

29. Supporting the transmission on a jack.

30. Remove the four lower transmission attaching bolts.

31. Attach an engine lifting sling and remove the engine from the truck.

32. Lower the engine into truck.

33. Align the converter to the flex plate and the engine dowels to the transmission.

34. Install the engine mount bolts and torque them to 80 ft. lbs.

35. Remove the engine lifting sling.

36. Install the four lower transmission attaching bolts. Torque the bolts to 65 ft. lbs.

37. Remove transmission jack.

38. Raise and support the front end on jackstands.

39. If equipped with automatic transmission, install the four converter-to-flywheel attaching nuts. Torque the nuts to 34 ft. lbs.

40. Install the flywheel inspection plate. Torque the bolts to 60–90 inch lbs.

41. Attach the exhaust pipe at the exhaust manifold.

42. Connect the fuel inlet line.

43. Connect the battery ground cables to the front of the engine.

44. Connect the starter cables at the starter.

45. Lower the truck.

46. Connect the overheat light switch wire.

47. Connect the water temperature sender wire.

48. Connect the heater hoses.

49. Install the two upper transmission-to-engine attaching bolts. Torque the bolts to 65 ft. lbs.

50. Connect the fuel return hose at the left rear of the engine.

51. Connect the main wiring harness connector at the right side of the engine and the ground strap from the rear of the engine.

52. Connect the transmission kickdown rod at the injection pump, if so equipped.

53. Connect the accelerator cable and the speed control cable, if so equipped, at the injection pump.

54. Install the cable bracket with the cables attached, to the intake manifold.

55. Install the oil pressure sending unit.

56. Connect the oil pressure sending unit wire at the sending unit.

57. Connect the fuel supply line heater and alternator wires at the alternator.

58. Install the power steering pump.

59. Install the radiator.

60. Install the condenser.

61. Connect the radiator hoses and the transmission cooler lines, if so equipped.

62. Install the fan and clutch assembly as described under water pump removal in this chapter.

63. Install the radiator fan shroud halves.

64. On vehicles equipped with air conditioning, charge the system. See Chapter 1.

65. Install the upper grille support bracket and upper air conditioning condenser mounting bracket.

66. Install the air cleaner and intake duct assembly.

67. Fill the cooling system.

68. Install the hood.

Rocker Studs

REMOVAL AND INSTALLATION

6–4.9L
8–5.0L

Rocker arm studs which are broken or have damaged threads may be replaced with standard studs. Studs which are loose in the cylinder head must be replaced with oversize studs which are available for service. The amount of oversize and diameter of the studs are as follows:

- 0.006 in. (0.152mm) oversize: 0.3774–0.3781 in. (9.586–9.604mm)
- 0.010 in. (0.254mm) oversize: 0.3814–0.3821 in. (9.688–9.705mm)
- 0.015 in. (0.381mm) oversize: 0.3864–0.3871 in. (9.815–9.832mm)

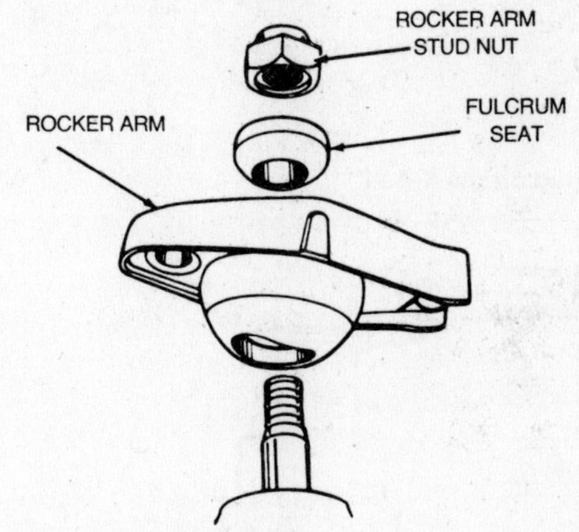

6–4.9L rocker arm assembly

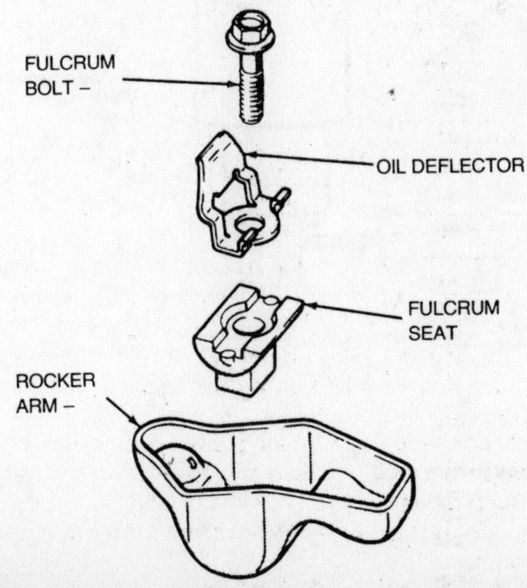

8–7.5L rocker arm assembly

Use a silicone sealant when reinstalling the valve covers

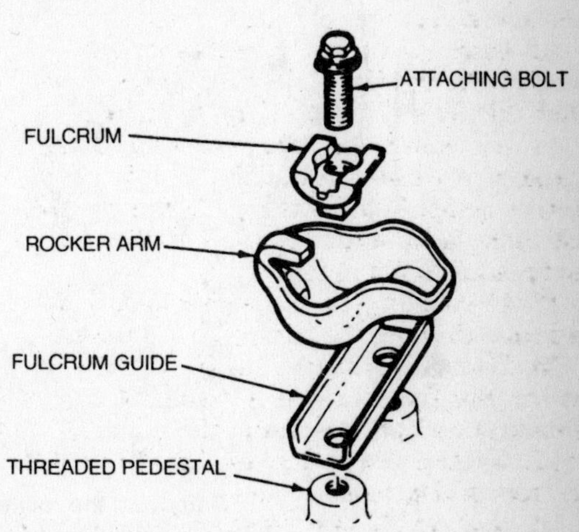

8–5.0L, 8–5.8L rocker arm assembly

A tool kit for replacing the rocker studs is available and contains a stud remover and two oversize reamers: one for 0.006 in. (0.152mm) and one for 0.015 in. (0.381mm) oversize studs. For 0.010 in. (0.254mm) oversize studs, use reamer tool T66P–6A527–B. to press the replacement studs into the cylinder head, use the stud replacer tool T69P–6049–D. Use the smaller reamer tool first when boring the hole for oversize studs.

1. Remove the valve rocker cover(s) by moving all hoses aside and unbolting the cover(s). Position the sleeve of the rocker arm stud remover over the stud with the bearing end down. When working on a 5.0L V8, cut the threaded part of the stud off with a hacksaw. Thread the puller into the sleeve and over the stud until it is fully bottomed. Hold the sleeve with a wrench and rotate the puller clockwise to remove the stud.

An alternate method of removing the rocker studs without the special tool is to put spacers over the stud until just enough threads are left showing at the top so a nut can be screwed onto the top of the rocker arm stud and get a full bite. Turn the nut clockwise until the stud is removed, adding spacers under the nut as necessary.

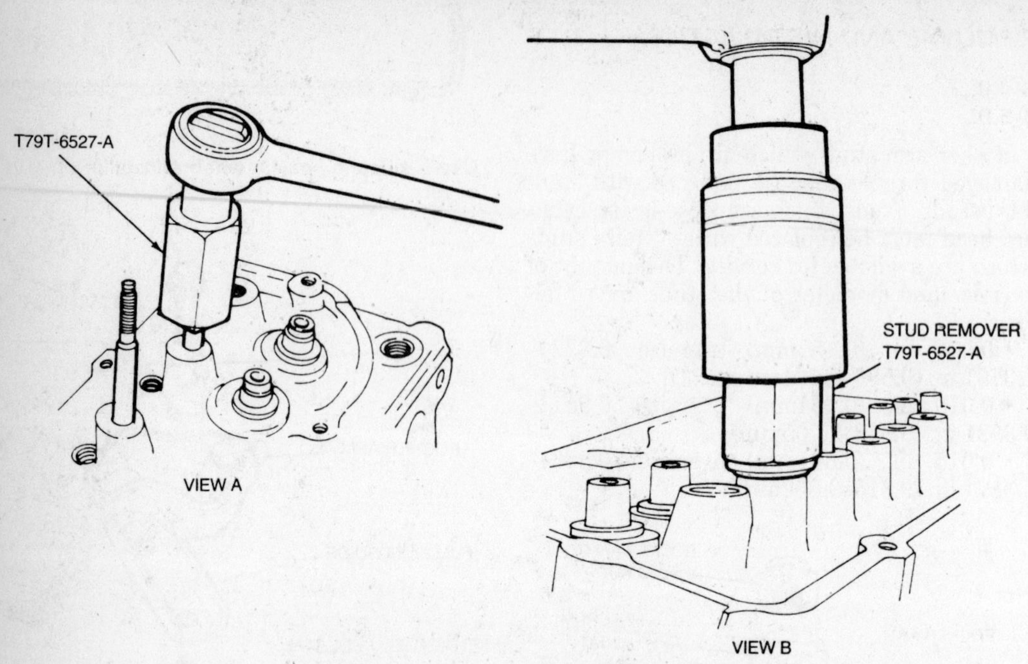

Removing the rocker arm stud on the 6–4.9L

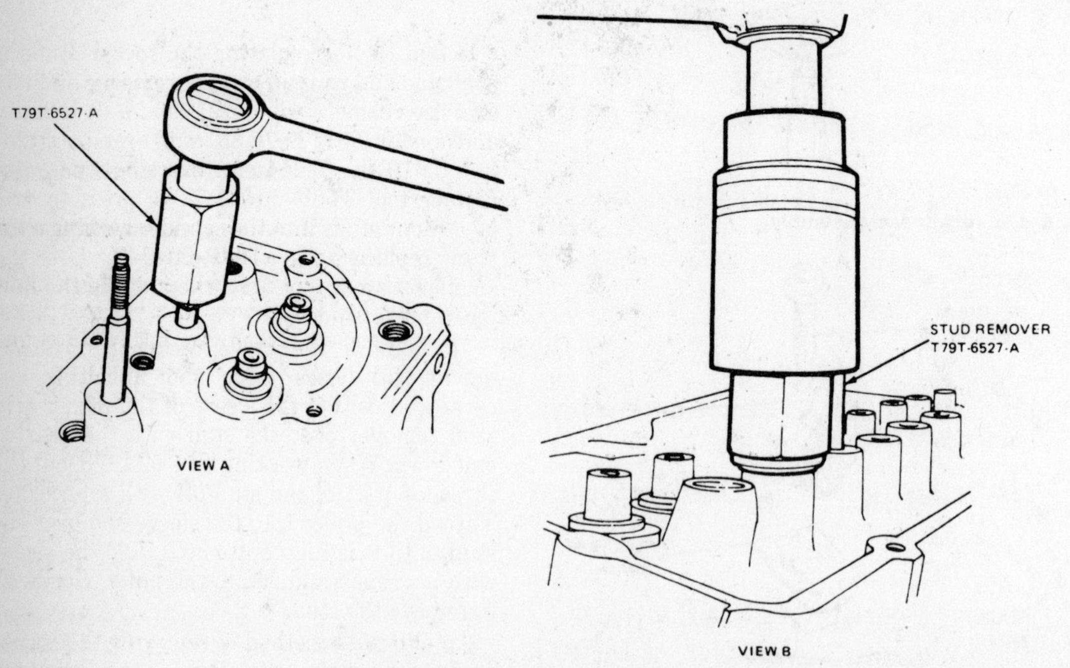

Installing a new rocker arm stud

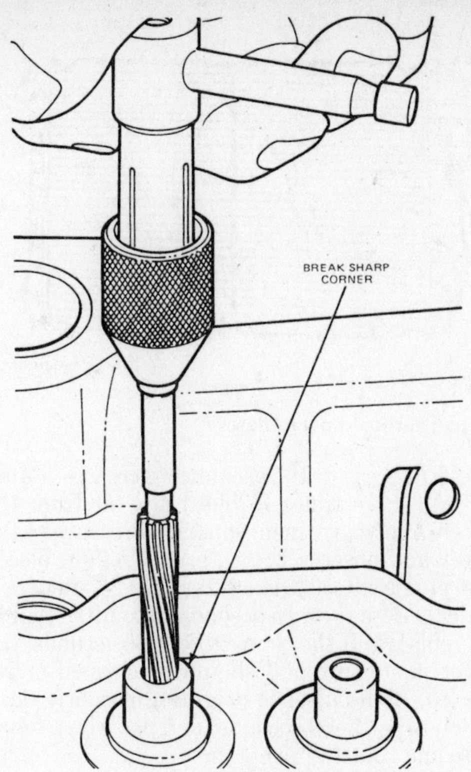

Reaming the rocker arm stud holes

NOTE: *If the rocker stud was broken off flush with the stud boss, use an easy-out tool to remove the broken off part of the stud from the cylinder head.*

2. If a loose rocker arm stud is being replaced, ream the stud bore for the selected oversize stud.

NOTE: *Keep all metal particles away from the valves.*

3. Coat the end of the stud with Lubriplate®. Align the stud and installer with the stud bore and top the sliding driver until it bottoms. When the installer contacts the stud boss, the stud is installed to its correct height.

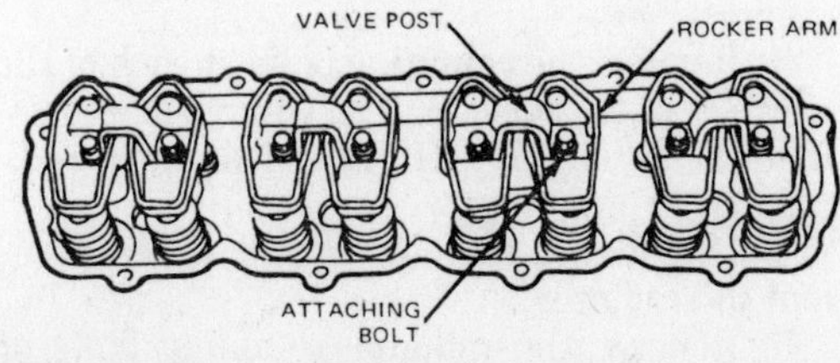

Diesel V8 rocker arm assembly

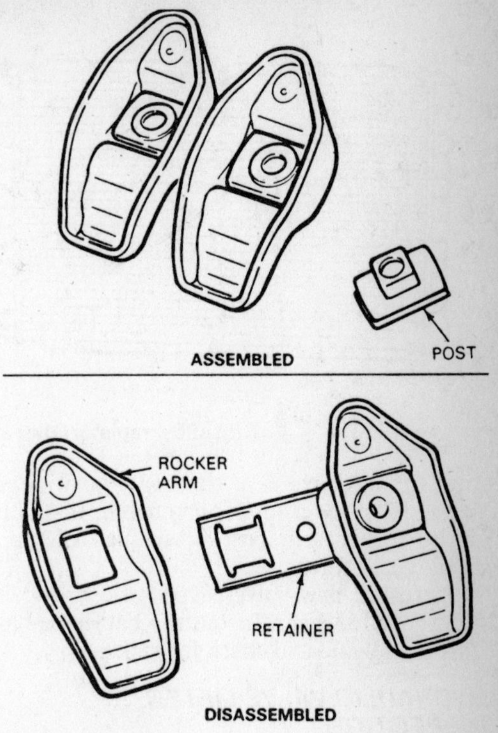

ASSEMBLED

POST

ROCKER
ARM

RETAINER

DISASSEMBLED

Diesel rocker arms

Rocker Arms

REMOVAL AND INSTALLATION

6.9L and 7.3L Diesel V8

1. Disconnect the ground cables from both batteries.
2. Remove the valve cover attaching screws and remove both valve cover.
3. Remove the valve rocker arm post mounting bolts. Remove the rocker arms and posts in order and mark them with tape so they can be installed in their original positions.
4. If the cylinder heads are to be removed, then the pushrods can now be removed. Make a holder for the pushrods out of a piece of wood or cardboard, and remove the pushrods in order. It is very important that the pushrods be re-installed in their original order. The pushrods can remain in position if no further disassembly is required.
5. If the pushrods were removed, install them in their original locations. make sure they are fully seated in the tappet seats.

NOTE: *The copper colored end of the pushrod goes toward the rocker arm.*

6. Apply a polyethylene grease to the valve stem tips. Install the rocker arms and posts in their original positions.
7. Turn the engine over by hand until the

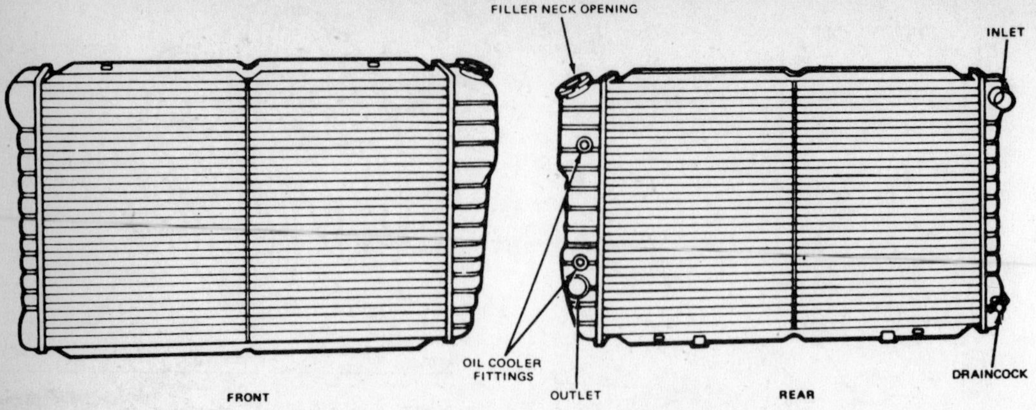

Crossflow radiator. Diesel models use vertical-flow radiator

valve timing mark is at the 11:00 position, as viewed from the front of the engine. Install all of the rocker arm post attaching bolts and torque to 27 ft.lbs.

8. Install new valve cover gaskets and install the valve cover. Install the battery cables, start the engine and check for leaks.

HYDRAULIC VALVE LIFTER INSPECTION

NOTE: *The lifters used on diesel engines require a special test fluid, kerosene is not satisfactory.*

Remove the lifters from their bores and remove any gum and varnish with safe solvent. Check the lifters for concave wear. If the bottom of the lifter is worn concave or flat, replace the lifter. Lifters are built with a convex bottom, flatness indicates wear. If a worn lifter is detected, carefully check the camshaft for wear.

To test lifter leak down, submerge the lifter in a container of kerosene. Chuck a used pushrod or its equivalent into a drill press. Position the container of kerosene so the pushrod acts on the lifter plunger. Pump the lifter with the drill press until resistance increases. Pump several more times to bleed any air from the lifter. Apply very firm, constant pressure to the lifter and observe the rate which fluid bleeds out of the lifter. If the lifter bleeds down very quickly (less than 15 seconds), the lifter should be replaced. If the time exceeds 60 seconds, the lifter is sticking and should be cleaned or replaced. If the lifter is operating properly (leak down time 15–60 seconds) and not worn, lubricate and reinstall in engine.

NOTE: *Always inspect the valve pushrods for wear, straightness and oil blockage. Damaged pushrods will cause erratic valve operation.*

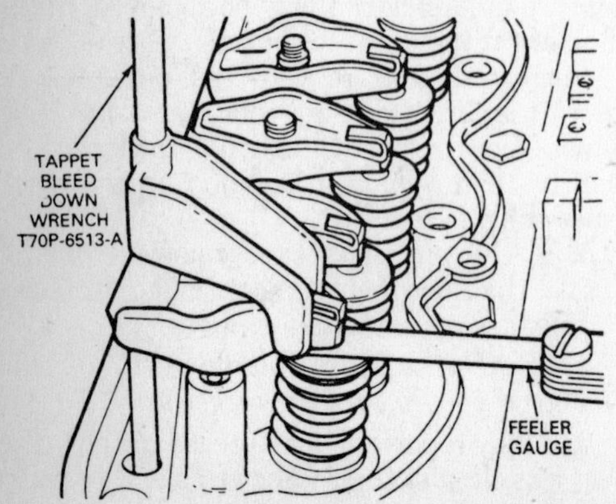

Valve clearance check

Radiator

REMOVAL AND INSTALLATION

1. Drain the cooling system.

CAUTION: *When draining the coolant, keep in mind that cats and dogs are attracted by the ethylene glycol antifreeze, and are quite likely to drink any that is left in an uncovered container or in puddles on the ground. This will prove fatal in sufficient quantity. Always drain the coolant into a sealable container. Coolant should be reused unless it is contaminated or several years old.*

2. Disconnect the transmission cooling lines from the bottom of the radiator, if so equipped.
3. Remove the retaining bolts at each of the 4 corners of the shroud, if so equipped, and position the shroud over the fan, clear of the radiator.
4. Disconnect the upper and lower hoses from the radiator.
5. Remove the radiator retaining bolts or the upper supports and lift the radiator from the vehicle.
6. Install the radiator in the reverse order

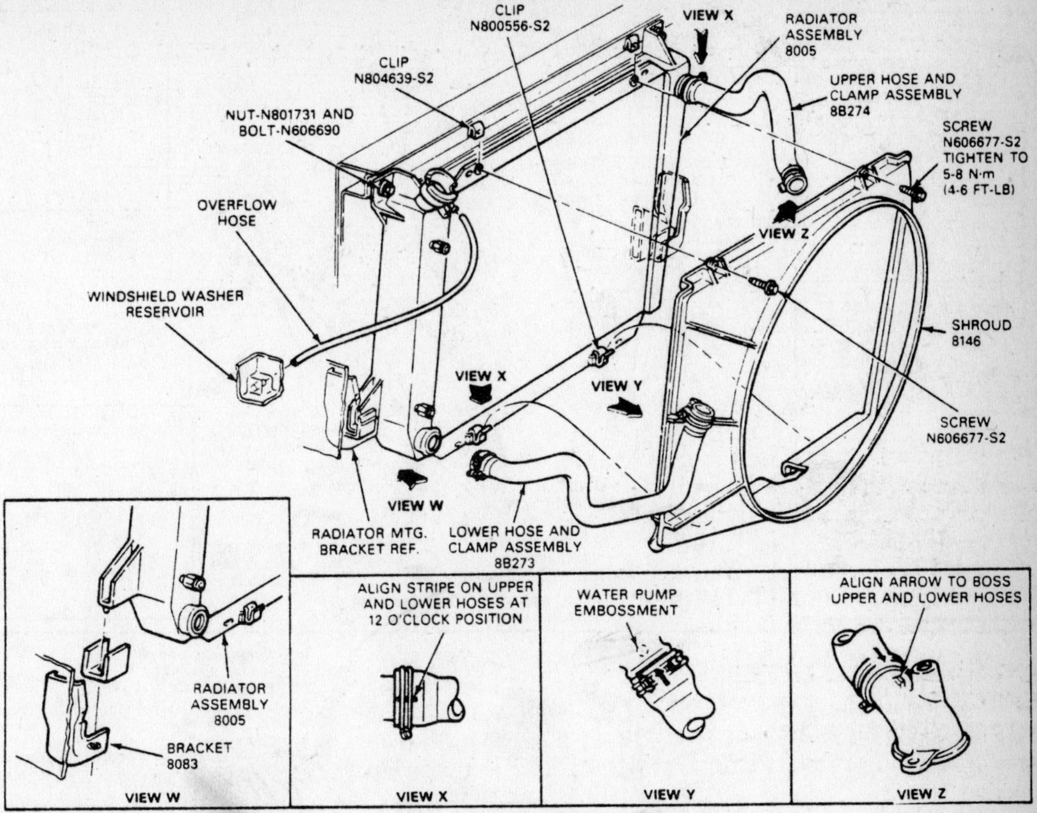

CLIP
N800556-S2
VIEW X
RADIATOR
ASSEMBLY
8005
CLIP
N804639-S2
UPPER HOSE AND
CLAMP ASSEMBLY
8B274
NUT-N801731 AND
BOLT-N606690
SCREW
N606677-S2
TIGHTEN TO
5-8 N·m
(4-6 FT-LB)
OVERFLOW
HOSE
VIEW Z
WINDSHIELD WASHER
RESERVOIR
SHROUD
8146
VIEW X
VIEW Y
SCREW
N606677-S2
VIEW W
RADIATOR MTG.
BRACKET REF.
LOWER HOSE AND
CLAMP ASSEMBLY
8B273
RADIATOR
ASSEMBLY
8005
BRACKET
8083
VIEW W
ALIGN STRIPE ON UPPER
AND LOWER HOSES AT
12 O'CLOCK POSITION
VIEW X
WATER PUMP
EMBOSSMENT
VIEW Y
ALIGN ARROW TO BOSS
UPPER AND LOWER HOSES
VIEW Z

8–7.5L radiator

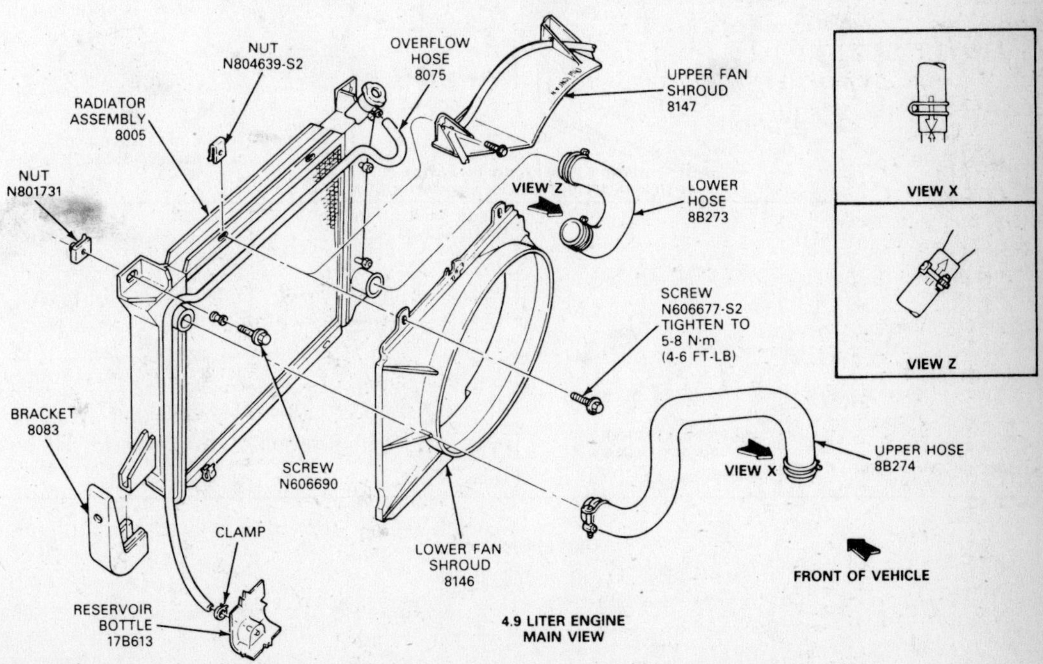

6–4.9L radiator

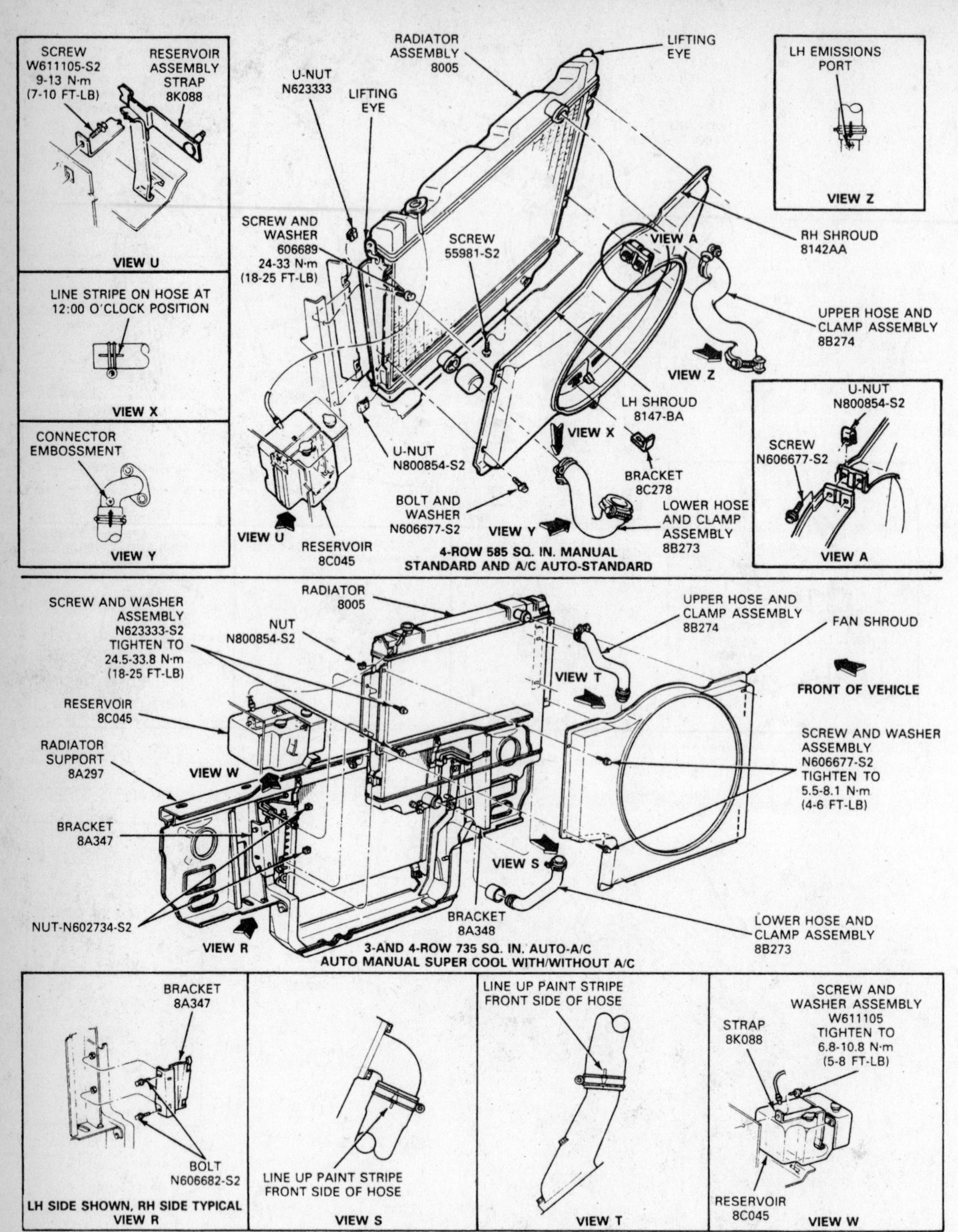

Diesel radiators

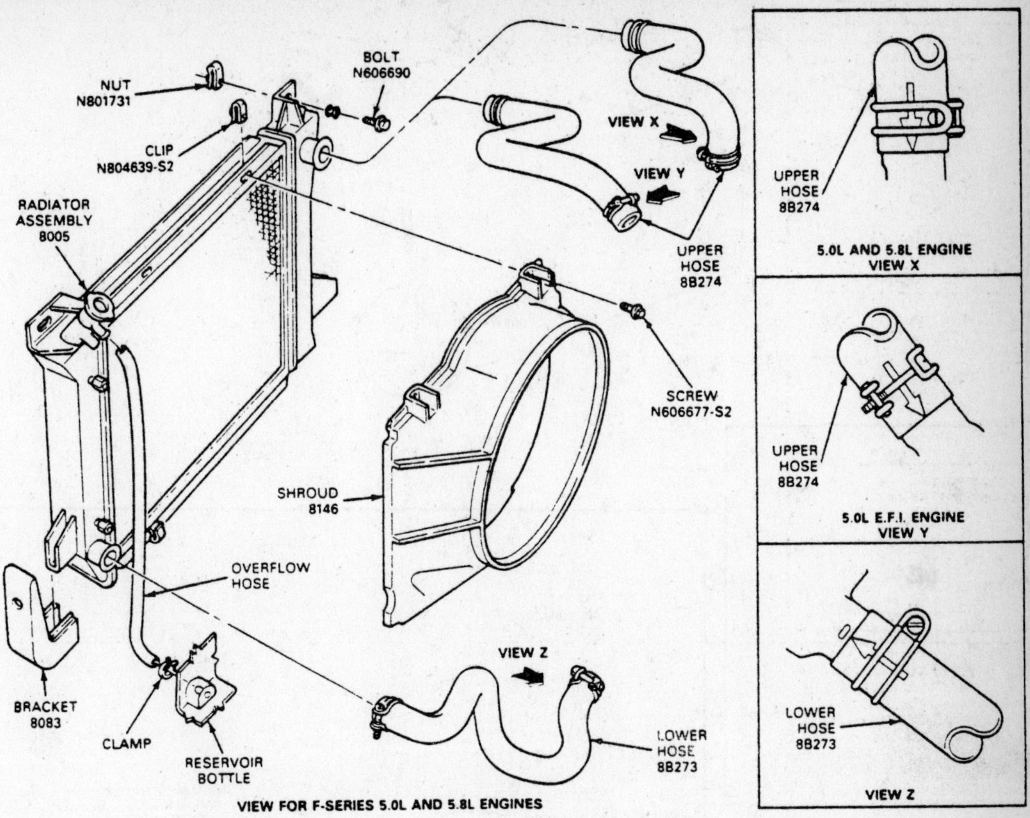

NUT
N801731
BOLT
N606690
CLIP
N804639-S2
RADIATOR
ASSEMBLY
8005
VIEW X
VIEW Y
UPPER
HOSE
8B274
SCREW
N606677-S2
SHROUD
8146
OVERFLOW
HOSE
BRACKET
8083
CLAMP
RESERVOIR
BOTTLE
VIEW Z
LOWER
HOSE
8B273
VIEW FOR F-SERIES 5.0L AND 5.8L ENGINES
UPPER
HOSE
8B274
5.0L AND 5.8L ENGINE
VIEW X
UPPER
HOSE
8B274
5.0L E.F.I. ENGINE
VIEW Y
LOWER
HOSE
8B273
VIEW Z

8–5.0L, 5.8L radiator

UPPER
RADIATOR
SUPPORT
OIL COOLER
AND BRACKET
ASSEMBLY
6C615
OIL COOLER
INLET HOSE
6K834
(YELLOW)
MATCH AND ALIGN
COLOR CODES
BOTH HOSES
OIL COOLER
OUTLET HOSE
6K834
(RED)
FRONT OF ENGINE
INLET
(YELLOW)
OUTLET
(RED)
OIL FILTER
ADAPTER
LOWER
RADIATOR
SUPPORT
USE OF SECOND (BACK-UP)
WRENCH MANDATORY ON ADAPTER
FITTING DURING HOSE REMOVAL
AND INSTALLATION TIGHTEN TO
48-61 N·m (35-45 FT-LB)(BOTH HOSES)

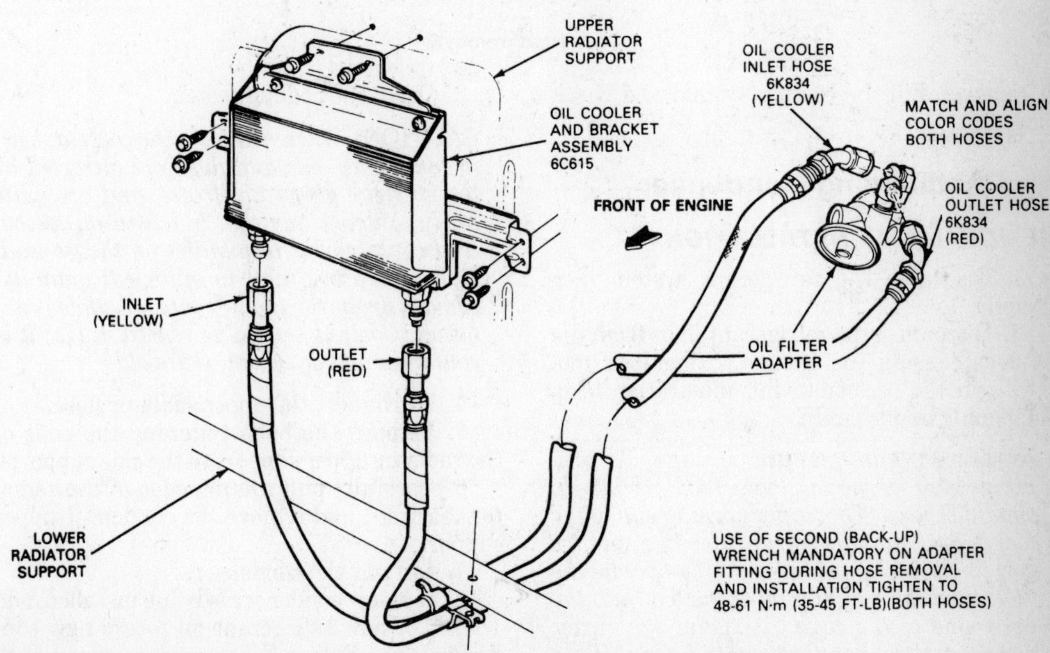

8–7.5L oil cooler

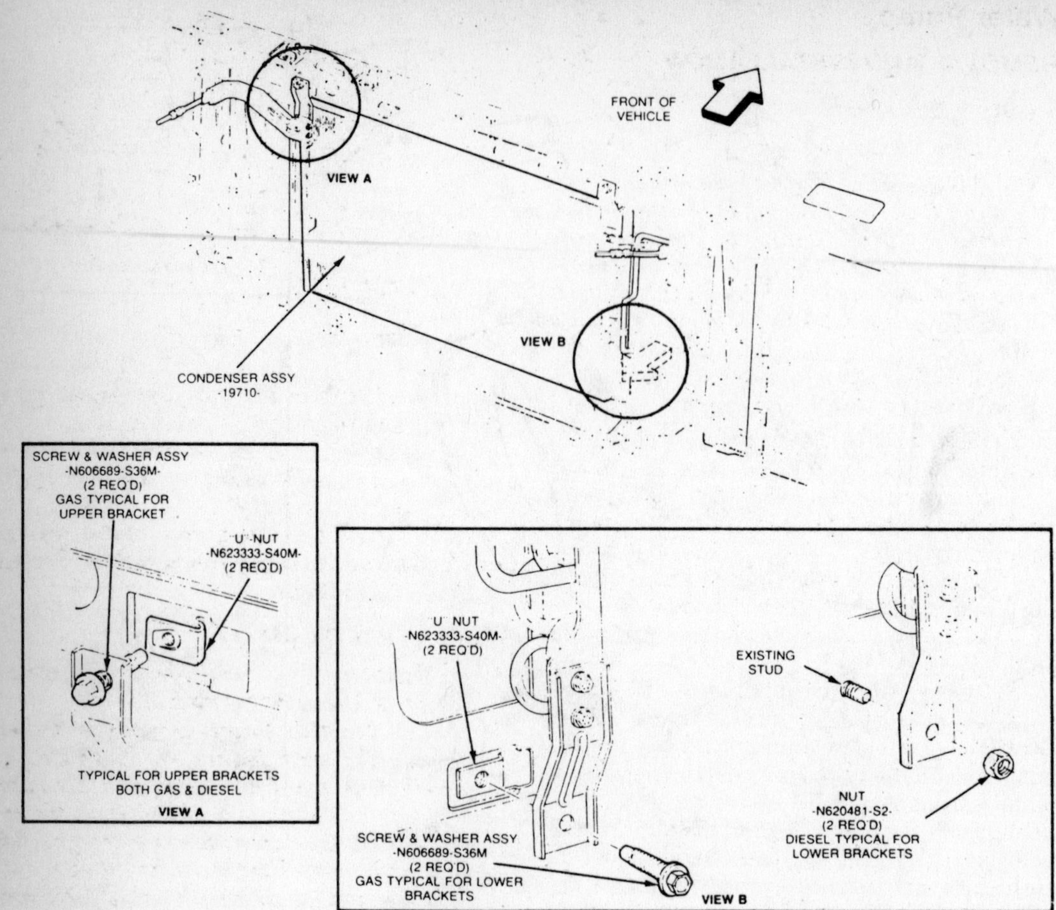

Condenser removal

of removal. Fill the cooling system and check for leaks.

Air Conditioning Condenser

REMOVAL AND INSTALLATION

1. Discharge the refrigerant system. See Chapter 1.
2. Disconnect the refrigerant lines from the condenser using the proper spring lock tool shown in the accompanying illustration. Cap all opening immediately!

NOTE: *The fittings are spring-lock couplings and a special tool, T81P–19623–G, should be used. The larger opening end of the tool is for 1/2 in. discharge lines; the smaller end for 3/8 in. liquid lines. To operate the tool, close the tool and push the tool into the open side of the cage to expand the garter spring and release the female fitting. If the tool is not inserted straight, the garter spring will cock and not release. After the garter spring is released, pull the fittings apart.*

3. Drain the cooling system.

CAUTION: *When draining the coolant, keep in mind that cats and dogs are attracted by the ethylene glycol antifreeze, and are quite likely to drink any that is left in an uncovered container or in puddles on the ground. This will prove fatal in sufficient quantity. Always drain the coolant into a sealable container. Coolant should be reused unless it is contaminated or several years old.*

4. Disconnect the upper radiator hose.
5. Remove the bolts retaining the ends of the radiator upper support to the side supports.
6. Carefully pull the top edge of the radiator rearward and remove the condenser upper support.
7. Lift out the condenser.
8. If a new condenser is being installed, add 1 fl.oz. of new refrigerant oil to the new condenser. Installation is the reverse of removal. Always use new O-rings coated with clean refrigerant oil on the line fittings. Evacuate, charge and leak test the system.

Water Pump

REMOVAL AND INSTALLATION

6–4.9L

1. Drain the cooling system.

CAUTION: *When draining the coolant, keep in mind that cats and dogs are attracted by the ethylene glycol antifreeze, and are quite likely to drink any that is left in an uncovered container or in puddles on the ground. This will prove fatal in sufficient quantity. Always drain the coolant into a sealable container. Coolant should be reused unless it is contaminated or several years old.*

2. Disconnect the lower radiator hose from the water pump.
3. Remove the drive belt, fan, fan spacer, fan shroud, if so equipped, and water pump pulley.
4. Remove the alternator pivot arm from the pump.
5. Disconnect the heater hose at the water pump.
6. Remove the water pump.
7. Before installing the old water pump, clean the gasket mounting surfaces on the pump and on the cylinder block. If a new water pump is being installed, remove the heater hose fitting from the old pump and install it on the new one. Coat the new gaskets with sealer on both sides and install the water pump in the reverse order of removal. Torque the mounting bolts to 18 ft. lbs.

8–5.0L
8–5.8L
8–7.5L

1. Drain the cooling system.

CAUTION: *When draining the coolant, keep in mind that cats and dogs are attracted by the ethylene glycol antifreeze, and are quite likely to drink any that is left in an uncovered container or in puddles on the ground. This will prove fatal in sufficient quantity. Always drain the coolant into a sealable container. Coolant should be reused unless it is contaminated or several years old.*

2. Remove the bolts securing the fan shroud to the radiator, if so equipped, and position the shroud over the fan.
3. Disconnect the lower radiator hose, heater hose and by-pass hose at the water pump. Remove the drive belts, fan, fan spacer and pulley. Remove the fan shroud, if so equipped.
4. Loosen the alternator pivot bolt and the bolt attaching the alternator adjusting arm to the water pump. Remove the power steering pump bracket from the water pump and position it out of the way.
5. Remove the bolts securing the water pump to the timing chain cover and remove the water pump.
6. Install the water pump in the reverse order of removal, using a new gasket. Torque the bolts to 18 ft. lbs.

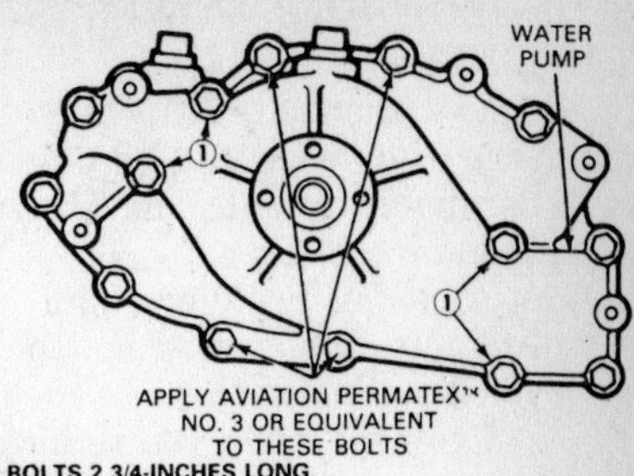

Diesel water pump

6.9L and 7.3L Diesels

1. Disconnect both battery ground cables.
2. Drain the cooling system.

CAUTION: *When draining the coolant, keep in mind that cats and dogs are attracted by the ethylene glycol antifreeze, and are quite likely to drink any that is left in an uncovered container or in puddles on the ground. This will prove fatal in sufficient quantity. Always drain the coolant into a sealable container. Coolant should be reused unless it is contaminated or several years old.*

3. Remove the radiator shroud halves.
4. Remove the fan clutch and fan.

NOTE: *The fan clutch bolts are left hand thread. Remove them by turning them clockwise.*

5. Remove the power steering pump belt.
6. Remove the air conditioning compressor belt.
7. Remove the vacuum pump drive belt.
8. Remove the alternator drive belt.
9. Remove the water pump pulley.
10. Disconnect the heater hose at the water pump.
11. If you're installing a new pump, remove the heater hose fitting from the old pump at this time.
12. Remove the alternator adjusting arm and bracket.
13. Unbolt the air conditioning compressor and position it out of the way. DO NOT DISCONNECT THE REFRIGERANT LINES!
14. Remove the air conditioning compressor brackets.
15. Unbolt the power steering pump and bracket and position it out of the way. DO NOT

DISCONNECT THE POWER STEERING FLUID LINES!

16. Remove the bolts attaching the water pump to the front cover and lift off the pump.
17. Thoroughly clean the mating surfaces of the pump and front cover.
18. Get a hold of two dowel pins - anything that will fit into 2 mounting bolt holes in the front cover. You'll need these to ensure proper bolt hole alignment when you're installing the water pump.
19. Using a new gasket, position the water pump over the dowel pins and into place on the front cover.
20. Install the attaching bolts. The 2 top center and 2 bottom center bolts must be coated with RTV silicone sealant prior to installation. See the illustration. Also, the 4 bolts marked No.1 in the illustration are a different length than the other bolts. Torque the bolts to 14 ft. lbs.
21. Install the water pump pulley.
22. Wrap the heater hose fitting threads with Teflon® tape and screw it into the water pump. Torque it to 18 ft. lbs.
23. Connect the heater hose to the pump.
24. Install the power steering pump and bracket. Install the belt.
25. Install the air conditioning compressor bracket.
26. Install the air conditioning compressor. Install the belt.
27. Install the alternator adjusting arm and install the belt.
28. Install the vacuum pump drive belt.
29. Adjust all the drive belts.
30. Install the fan and clutch. Remember that the bolts are left hand thread. Turn them counterclockwise to tighten them. Torque them to 45 ft. lbs.
31. Install the fan shroud halves.
32. Fill and bleed the cooling system.
33. Connect the battery ground cables.
34. Start the engine and check for leaks.

Thermostat

NOTE: *It is a good practice to check the operation of a new thermostat before it is installed in an engine. Place the thermostat in a pan of boiling water. If it does not open more than 1/4 in. (6mm), do not install it in the engine.*

REMOVAL AND INSTALLATION

6–4.9L

1. Drain the cooling system below the level of the coolant outlet housing. Use the petcock valve at the bottom of the radiator to drain the system. It is not necessary to remove any of the hoses.

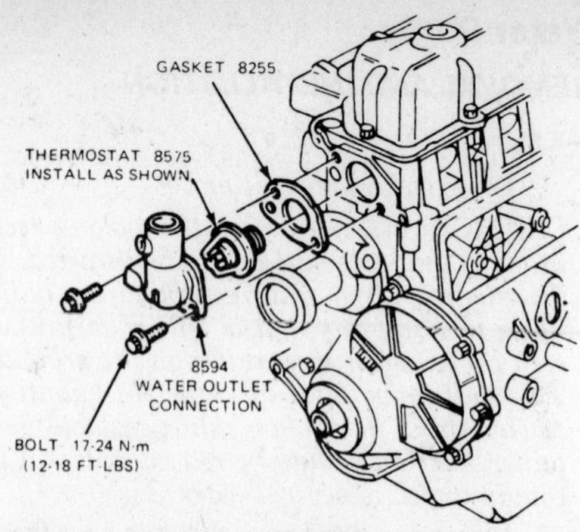

6–4.9L thermostat installation. V8 thermostat mounted vertically on front of engine, diesel is on side of front of intake manifold

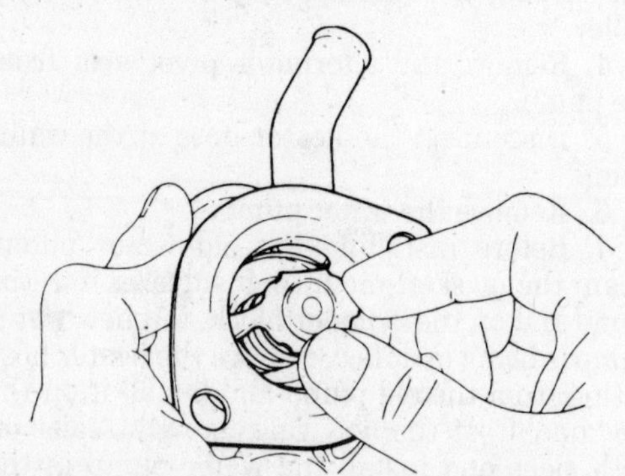

On all gasoline engines, turn the thermostat clockwise to lock it into position on the flats in the outlet elbow

CAUTION: *When draining the coolant, keep in mind that cats and dogs are attracted by the ethylene glycol antifreeze, and are quite likely to drink any that is left in an uncovered container or in puddles on the ground. This will prove fatal in sufficient quantity. Always drain the coolant into a sealable container. Coolant should be reused unless it is contaminated or several years old.*

2. Remove the coolant outlet housing retaining bolts and slide the housing with the hose attached to one side.
3. Remove the thermostat and gasket from the cylinder head and clean both mating surfaces.
4. To install the thermostat, coat a new gasket with water resistant sealer and position it on the outlet of the engine. The gasket must be in place before the thermostat is installed.
5. Install the thermostat with the bridge (op-

posite end of the spring) inside the elbow connection.

6. Position the elbow connection onto the mounting surface of the outlet, so that the thermostat flange is resting on the gasket and install the retaining bolts. Torque the bolts to 15 ft. lbs.

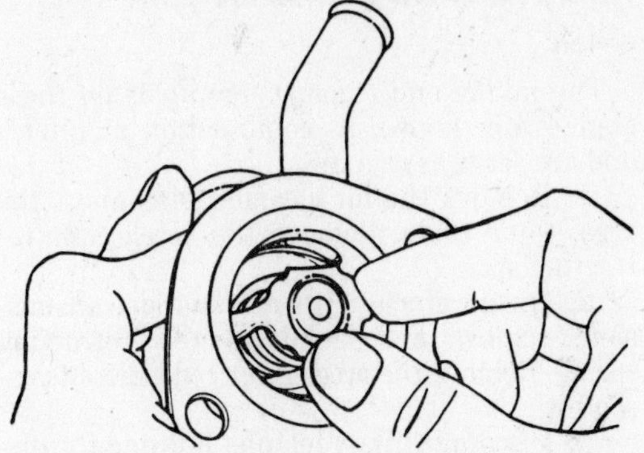

Thermostat spring always faces 'down' in all engines

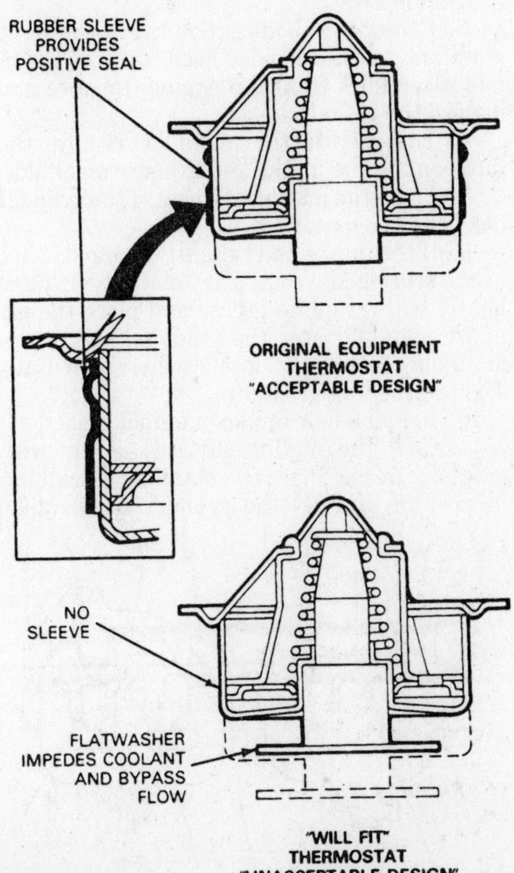

Thermostat positioning

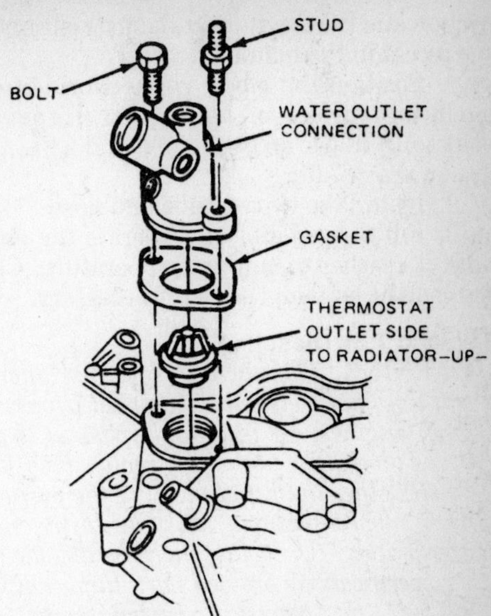

Thermostat installation for the V8

7. Fill the radiator and operate the engine until it reaches operating temperature. Check the coolant level and adjust if necessary.

8-5.0L
8-5.8L
8-7.5L

1. Drain the cooling system below the level of the coolant outlet housing. Use the petcock valve at the bottom of the radiator to drain the system. It is not necessary to remove any of the hoses.

CAUTION: *When draining the coolant, keep in mind that cats and dogs are attracted by the ethylene glycol antifreeze, and are quite likely to drink any that is left in an uncovered container or in puddles on the ground. This will prove fatal in sufficient quantity. Always drain the coolant into a sealable container. Coolant should be reused unless it is contaminated or several years old.*

2. Disconnect the bypass hoses at the water pump and intake manifold.
3. Remove the bypass tube.
4. Remove the coolant outlet housing retaining bolts, bend the hose and lift the housing with the hose attached to one side.
5. Remove the thermostat and gasket from the intake manifold and clean both mating surfaces.
6. To install the thermostat, coat a new gasket with water resistant sealer and position it on the outlet of the engine. The gasket must be in place before the thermostat is installed.
7. Install the thermostat with the bridge (opposite end of the spring) inside the elbow con-

nection and the thermostat flange positioned in the recess in the manifold.

8. Position the elbow connection onto the mounting surface of the outlet. Torque the bolts to 18 ft. lbs. on the 8–5.0L and 5.8L; 28 ft. lbs. on the 8–7.5L.

9. Install the bypass tube and hoses.

10. Fill the radiator and operate the engine until it reaches operating temperature. Check the coolant level and adjust if necessary.

6.9L and 7.3L Diesel

WARNING: *The factory specified thermostat does not contain an internal bypass. On these engines, an internal bypass is located in the block. The use of any replacement thermostat other than that meeting the manufacturer's specifications will result in engine overheating! Use only thermostats meeting the specifications of Ford part number E5TZ–8575–C or Navistar International part number 1807945–C1.*

1. Disconnect both battery ground cables.
2. Drain the coolant to a point below the thermostat housing.

CAUTION: *When draining the coolant, keep in mind that cats and dogs are attracted by the ethylene glycol antifreeze, and are quite likely to drink any that is left in an uncovered container or in puddles on the ground. This will prove fatal in sufficient quantity. Always drain the coolant into a sealable container. Coolant should be reused unless it is contaminated or several years old.*

3. Remove the alternator and vacuum pump belts
4. Remove the alternator.
5. Remove the vacuum pump and bracket.
6. Remove all but the lowest vacuum pump/alternator mounting casting bolt.
7. Loosen that lowest bolt and pivot the casting outboard of the engine.
8. Remove the thermostat housing attaching bolts, bend the hose and lift the housing up and to one side.
9. Remove the thermostat and gasket.
10. Clean the thermostat housing and block surfaces thoroughly.
11. Coat a new gasket with waterproof sealer and position the gasket on the manifold outlet opening.
12. Install the thermostat in the manifold opening with the spring element end downward and the flange positioned in the recess in the manifold.
13. Place the outlet housing into position and install the bolts. Torque the bolts to 20 ft. lbs.
14. Reposition the casting.
15. Install the vacuum pump and bracket.
16. Install the alternator.
17. Adjust the drive belts.
18. Fill and bleed the cooling system.
19. Connect both battery cables.
20. Run the engine and check for leaks.

Intake Manifold

REMOVAL AND INSTALLATION

6–4.9L

The intake and exhaust manifolds on these engines are known as combination manifolds and are services as a unit.

1. Remove the air cleaner. Disconnect the accelerator cable. Remove the accelerator retracting spring.
2. On a vehicle with automatic transmission, remove the kickdown rod retracting spring. Remove the accelerator rod bellcrank assembly.
3. Disconnect the fuel inlet line and the distributor vacuum line.
4. Disconnect the muffler inlet pipe from the exhaust manifold.
5. Disconnect the power brake vacuum line, if so equipped.
6. Remove the bolts and nuts attaching the manifolds to the cylinder head. Lift the manifold assemblies from the engine. Remove and discard the gaskets.
7. To separate the manifold, remove the nuts joining the intake and exhaust manifolds.
8. Clean the mating surfaces of the cylinder head and the manifolds.
9. If the intake and exhaust manifolds have been separated, coat the mating surfaces lightly with graphite grease and place the exhaust manifold over the studs on the intake manifold. Install the lock washers and nuts. Tighten them finger tight.
10. Install a new intake manifold gasket.
11. Coat the mating surfaces lightly with graphite grease. Place the manifold assemblies in position against the cylinder head. Make

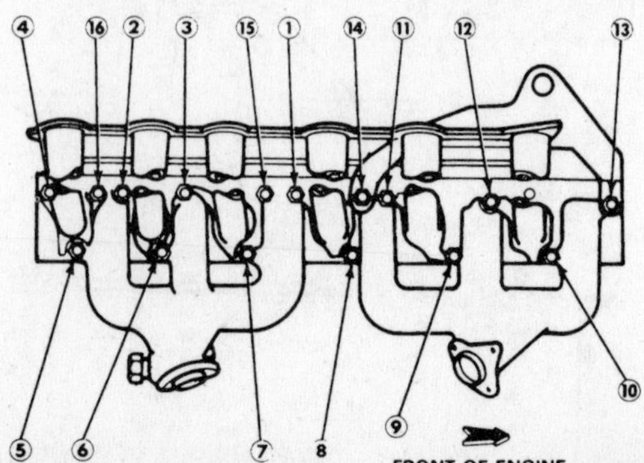

6–4.9L EFI intake and exhaust manifold bolt torque sequence

sure that the gaskets have not become dislodged. Install the attaching nuts and bolts in the proper sequence to 26 ft.lbs. If the intake and exhaust manifolds were separated, tighten the nuts joining them.

12. Position a new gasket on the muffler inlet pipe and connect the inlet pipe to the exhaust manifold.

13. Connect the crankcase vent hose to the intake manifold inlet tube and position the hose clamp.

14. Connect the fuel inlet line and the distributor vacuum line.

15. Connect the accelerator cable and install the retracting spring.

16. On a vehicle with an automatic transmission, install the bellcrank assembly and the kickdown rod retracting spring. Adjust the transmission control linkage.

17. Install the air cleaner.

Gasoline V8 Except 7.5L and EFI Models

1. Drain the cooling system, remove the air cleaner and the intake duct assembly.

CAUTION: *When draining the coolant, keep in mind that cats and dogs are attracted by the ethylene glycol antifreeze, and are quite likely to drink any that is left in an uncovered container or in puddles on the ground. This will prove fatal in sufficient quantity. Always drain the coolant into a sealable container. Coolant should be reused unless it is contaminated or several years old.*

2. Disconnect the accelerator rod from the carburetor and remove the accelerator retracting spring. Disconnect the automatic transmission kickdown rod at the carburetor, if so equipped.

3. Disconnect the high tension lead and all other wires from the ignition coil.

4. Disconnect the spark plug wires from the spark plugs by grasping the rubber boots and twisting and pulling at the same time. Remove the wires from the brackets on the rocker covers. Remove the distributor cap and spark plug wire assembly.

5. Remove the carburetor fuel inlet line and the distributor vacuum line from the carburetor.

6. Remove the distributor lockbolt and remove the distributor and vacuum line. See Distributor Removal and Installation.

7. Disconnect the upper radiator hose from the coolant outlet housing and the temperature sending unit wire at the sending unit. Remove the heater hose from the intake manifold.

8. Loosen the clamp on the water pump bypass hose at the coolant outlet housing and slide the hose off the outlet housing.

9. Disconnect the PCV hose at the rocker cover.

10. If the engine is equipped with the Thermactor® exhaust emission control system, remove the air pump to cylinder head air hose at the air pump and position it out of the way. Also remove the air hose at the backfire suppressor valve. Remove the air hose bracket from the valve rocker arm cover and position the air hose out of the way.

11. Remove the intake manifold and carburetor as an assembly. It may be necessary to pry the intake manifold from the cylinder head.

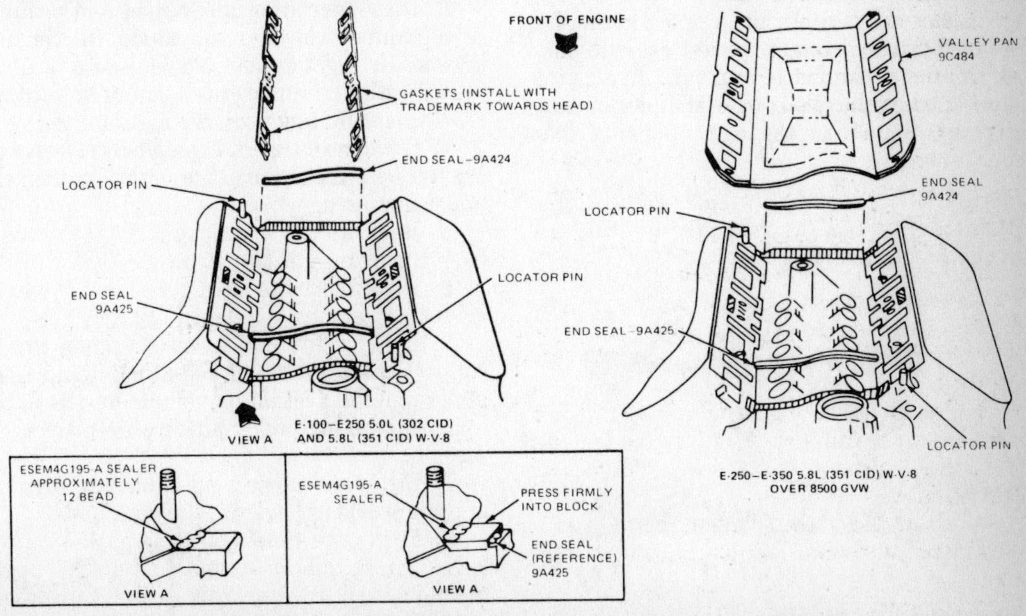

Carbureted 8–5.0L and 8–5.8L intake manifold sealing and gaskets

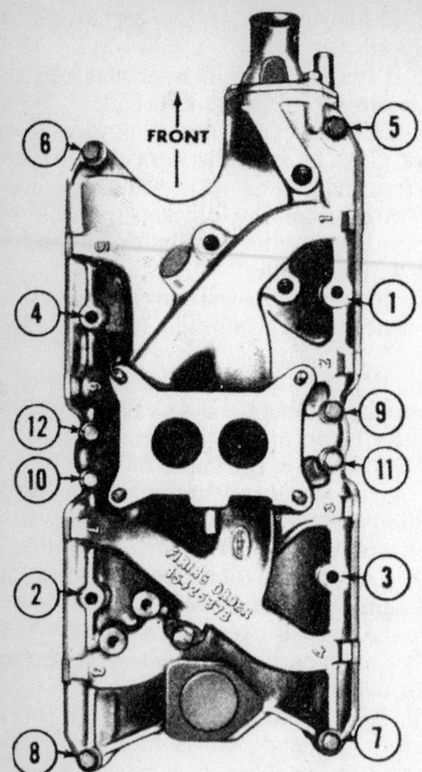

Carbureted 8–5.0L intake manifold bolt tightening sequence

Remove all traces of the intake manifold-to-cylinder head gaskets and the two end seals from both the manifold and the other mating surfaces of the engine.

Installation is as follows:

1. Clean the mating surfaces of the intake manifold, cylinder heads, and block with lacquer thinner or similar solvent. Apply a 1/8 in. (3mm) bead of silicone-rubber RTV sealant at the points shown in the accompanying diagram.

WARNING: *Do not apply sealer to the waffle portions of the seals as the sealer will rupture the end seal material.*

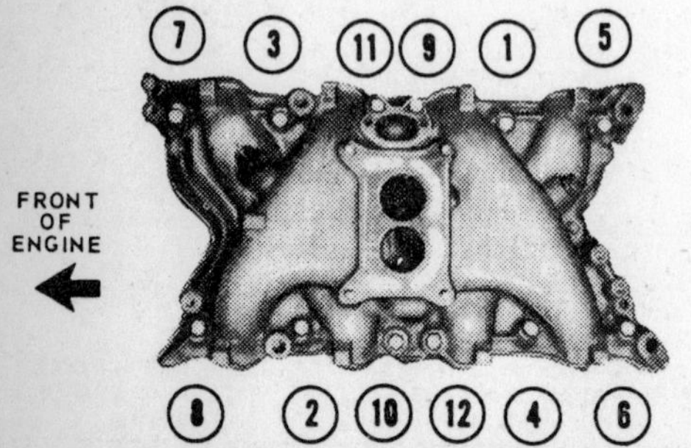

Carbureted 8–5.8L intake manifold bolt tightening sequence

2. Position new seals on the block and press the seal locating extensions into the holes in the mating surfaces.
3. Apply a 1/16 in. (1.5mm) bead of sealer to the outer end of each manifold seal for the full length of the seal (4 places). As before, do not apply sealer to the waffle portion of the end seals.

NOTE: *This sealer sets in about 15 minutes, depending on brand, so work quickly but carefully. DO NOT DROP ANY SEALER INTO THE MANIFOLD CAVITY. IT WILL FORM AND SET AND PLUG THE OIL GALLERY.*

4. Position the manifold gasket onto the block and heads with the alignment notches under the dowels in the heads. Be sure gasket holes align with head holes.
5. Install the manifold and related equipment in reverse order of removal.

Fuel Injected Engines

NOTE: *Discharge fuel system pressure before starting any work that involves disconnecting fuel system lines. See Fuel Supply Manifold removal and installation procedures (Gasoline Fuel System section).*

1. To remove the upper manifold: Remove the air cleaner. Disconnect the electrical connectors at the air bypass valve, throttle position sensor and EGR position sensor.
2. Disconnect the throttle linkage at the throttle ball and the AOD transmission linkage from the throttle body. Remove the bolts that secure the bracket to the intake and position the bracket and cables out of the way.
3. Disconnect the upper manifold vacuum fitting connections by removing all the vacuum lines at the vacuum tree (label lines for position identification). Remove the vacuum lines to the EGR valve and fuel pressure regulator.
4. Disconnect the PCV system by disconnecting the hose from the fitting at the rear of the upper manifold.
5. Remove the two canister purge lines from the fittings at the throttle body.
6. Disconnect the EGR tube from the EGR valve by loosening the flange nut.
7. Remove the bolt from the upper intake support bracket to upper manifold. Remove the upper manifold retaining bolts and remove the upper intake manifold and throttle body as an assembly.
8. Clean and inspect all mounting surfaces of the upper and lower intake manifolds.
9. Position a new mounting gasket on the lower intake manifold and install the upper manifold in the reverse order of removal. Mounting bolts are torqued to 12–18 ft. lbs.
10. To remove the lower intake manifold:

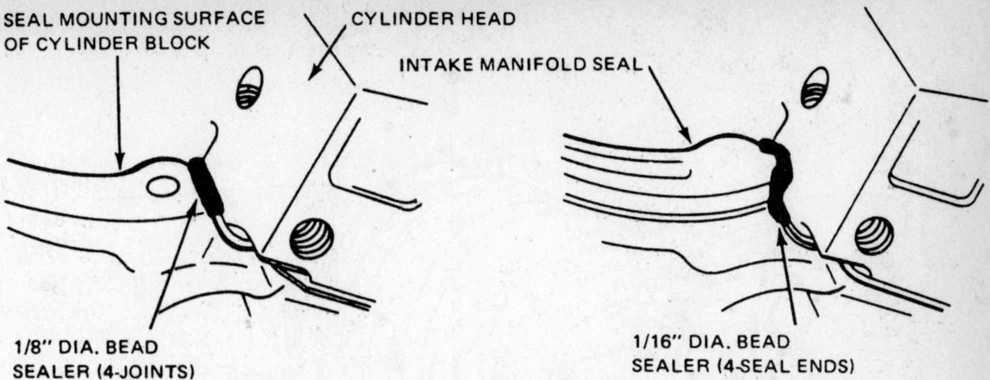

Sealer application area for intake manifold installation on all V8s except 7.5L

Upper manifold and throttle body must be removed first.

11. Drain the cooling system.

CAUTION: *When draining the coolant, keep in mind that cats and dogs are attracted by the ethylene glycol antifreeze, and are quite likely to drink any that is left in an uncovered container or in puddles on the ground. This will prove fatal in sufficient quantity. Always drain the coolant into a sealable container. Coolant should be reused unless it is contaminated or several years old.*

12. Remove the distributor assembly, cap and wires.

13. Disconnect the electrical connectors at the engine, coolant temperature sensor and sending unit, at the air charge temperature sensor and at the knock sensor.

14. Disconnect the injector wiring harness from the main harness assembly. Remove the ground wire from the intake manifold stud. The ground wire must be installed at the same position it was removed from.

LOWER INTAKE MANIFOLD ASSEMBLY 9J447

CYLINDER HEAD

FRONT OF ENGINE

NOTE: LOWER INTAKE MANIFOLD ASSEMBLY SHOWN SIMPLIFIED TO CLARIFY INSTALLATION

8–7.5L EFI intake manifold torque sequence

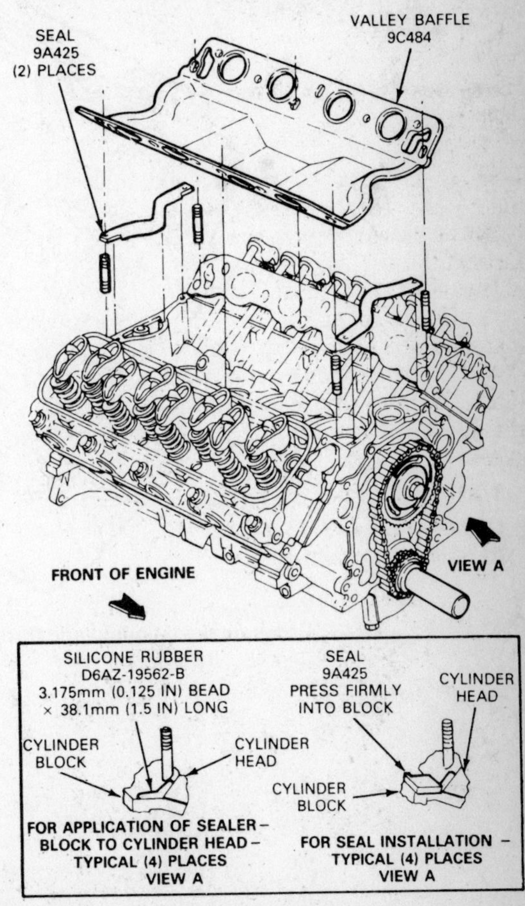

8–7.5L EFI lower intake manifold installation

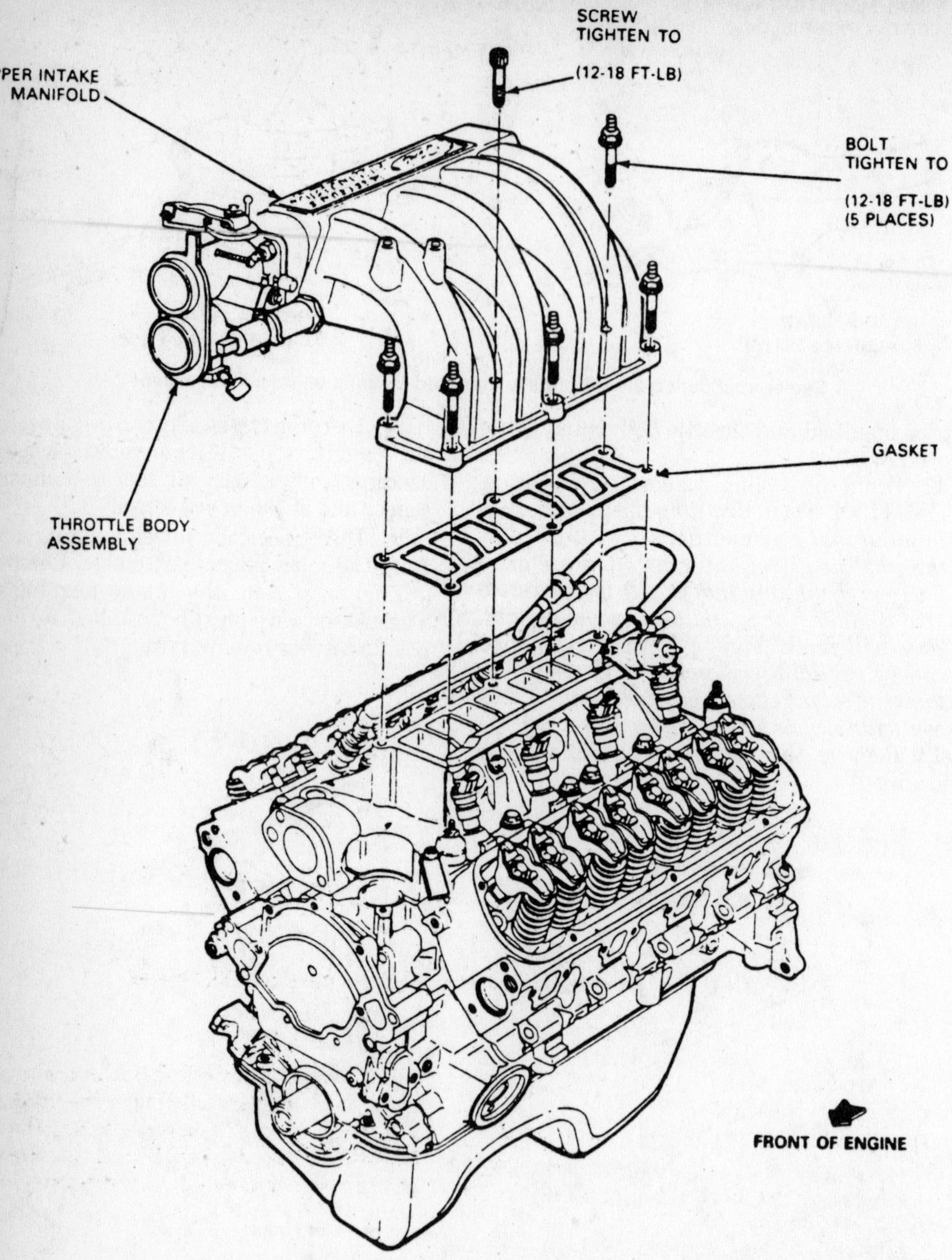

Upper intake manifold and throttle body for the 8–5.0L and 8–5.8L

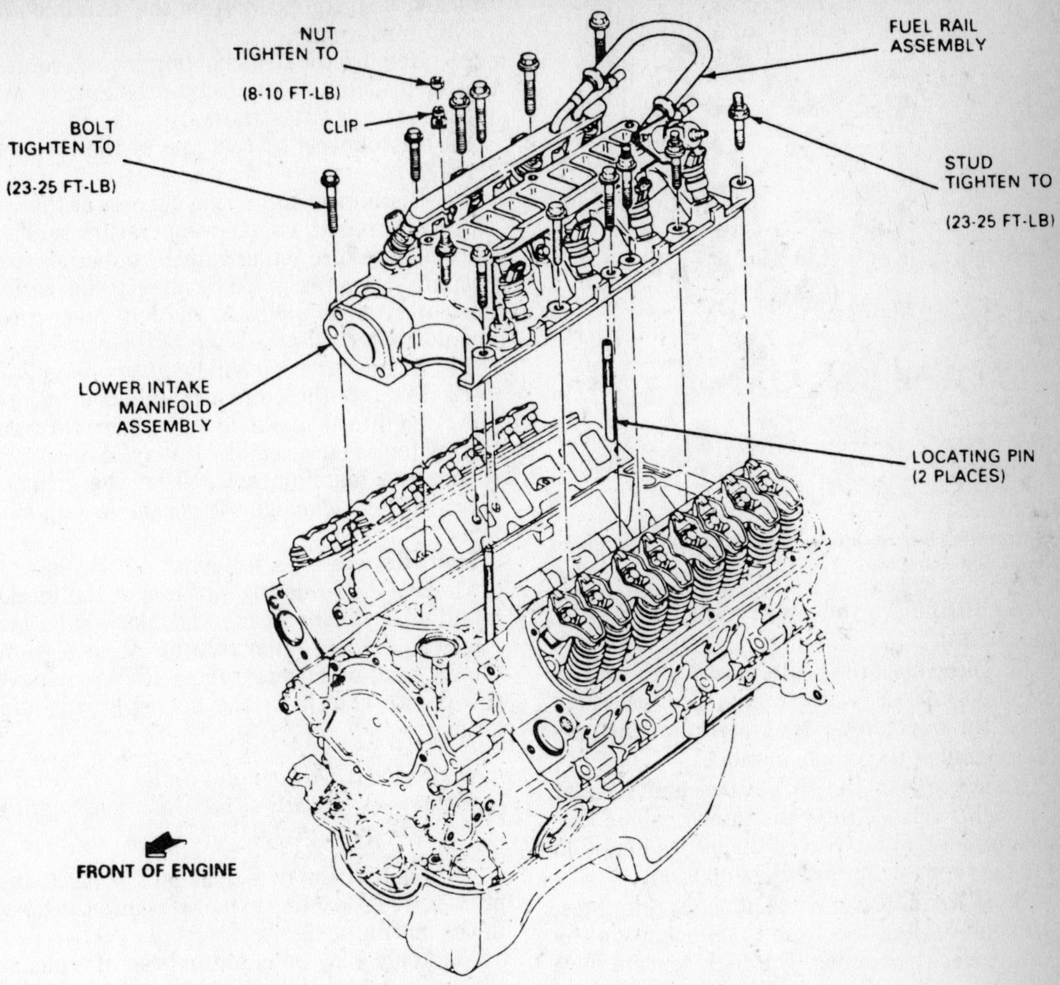

Lower intake manifold and throttle body for the 8–5.0L and 8–5.8L

15. Disconnect the fuel supply and return lines from the fuel rails.

16. Remove the upper radiator hose from the thermostat housing. Remove the bypass hose. Remove the heater outlet hose at the intake manifold.

17. Remove the air cleaner mounting bracket. Remove the intake manifold mounting bolts and studs. Pay attention to the location of the bolts and studs for reinstallation. Remove the lower intake manifold assembly.

18. Clean and inspect the mounting surfaces of the heads and manifold.

19. Apply a $^1/_{16}$ in. (1.5mm) bead of RTV sealer to the ends of the manifold seal (the junction point of the seals and gaskets). Install the end seals and intake gaskets on the cylinder heads. The gaskets must interlock with the seal tabs.

20. Install locator bolts at opposite ends of each head and carefully lower the intake manifold into position. Install and tighten the mounting bolts and studs to 23–25 ft. lbs. Install the remaining components in the reverse order of removal.

8–7.5L w/4-bbl

1. Drain the cooling system and remove the air cleaner assembly.

CAUTION: *When draining the coolant, keep in mind that cats and dogs are attracted by the ethylene glycol antifreeze, and are quite likely to drink any that is left in an uncovered container or in puddles on the ground. This will prove fatal in sufficient quantity. Always drain the coolant into a sealable container. Coolant should be reused unless it is contaminated or several years old.*

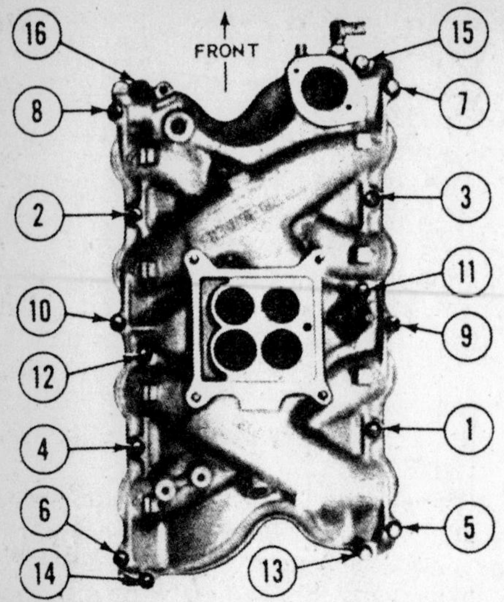

Carbureted 8–7.5L intake manifold bolt tightening sequence

2. Disconnect the upper radiator hose at the engine.

3. Disconnect the heater hoses at the intake manifold and the water pump. Position them out of the way. Loosen the water pump by-pass hose clamp at the intake manifold.

4. Disconnect the PCV valve and hose at the right valve cover. Disconnect all of the vacuum lines at the rear of the intake manifold and tag them for proper reinstallation.

5. Disconnect the wires at the spark plugs, and remove the wires from the brackets on the valve cover. Disconnect the high tension wire from the coil and remove the distributor cap and wires as an assembly.

6. Disconnect all of the distributor vacuum lines at the carburetor and vacuum control valve and tag them for proper installation. Remove the distributor and vacuum lines as an assembly.

7. Disconnect the accelerator linkage at the carburetor. Remove the speed control linkage bracket, if so equipped, from the manifold and carburetor.

8. Remove the bolts holding the accelerator linkage bellcrank and position the linkage and return springs out of the way.

9. Disconnect the fuel line at the carburetor.

10. Disconnect the wiring harness at the coil battery terminal, engine temperature sending unit, oil pressure sending until, and other connections as necessary. Disconnect the wiring harness from the clips at the left valve cover and position the harness out of the way.

11. Remove the coil and bracket assembly.

12. Remove the intake manifold attaching bolts and lift the manifold and carburetor from the engine as an assembly. It may be necessary to pry the manifold away from the cylinder heads. Do not damage the gasket sealing surfaces.

Installation is as follows:

1. Clean the mating surfaces of the intake manifold, cylinder heads and block with lacquer thinner or similar solvent. Apply a $^1/_8$ in. (3mm) bead of silicone-rubber RTV sealant at the points shown in the accompanying diagram.

WARNING: *Do not apply sealer to the waffle portions of the seals as the sealer will rupture the end seal material.*

2. Position the new seals on the block and press the seal locating extensions into the holes in the mating surfaces.

3. Apply a $^1/_{16}$ in. (1.5mm) bead of sealer to the outer end of each manifold seal for the full length of the seal (4 places). As before, do not apply sealer to the waffle portion of the end seals.

NOTE: *This sealer sets in about 15 minutes, depending on brand, so work quickly but carefully. DO NOT DROP ANY SEALER INTO THE MANIFOLD CAVITY. IT WILL FORM AND SET AND PLUG THE OIL GALLERY.*

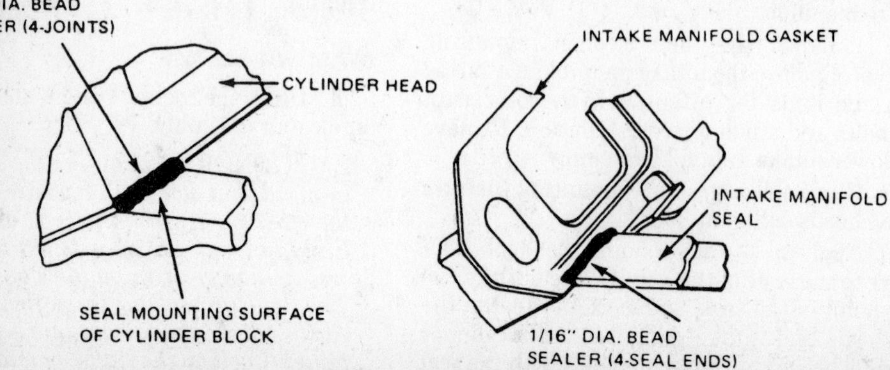

Sealer application areas for intake manifold installation of on 7.5L V8

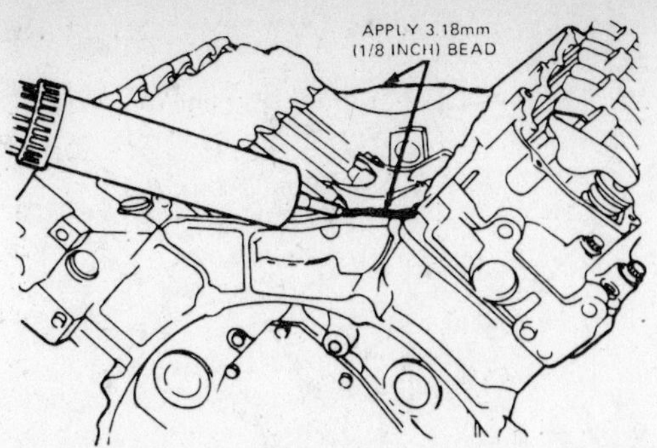

Apply sealer to the diesel cylinder block-to-intake manifold mating surfaces on each end

4. Position the manifold gasket onto the block and heads with the alignment notches under the dowels in the heads. Be sure gasket holes align with head holes.

5. Install the manifold and related equipment in reverse order of removal.

6.9L and 7.3L Diesel

1. Open the hood and remove both battery ground cables.

2. Remove the air cleaner and install clean rags into the air intake of the intake manifold. It is important that no dirt or foreign objects get into the diesel intake.

3. Remove the injection pump as described in Chapter 5 under Diesel Fuel Systems.

4. Remove the fuel return hose from No. 7 and No. 8 rear nozzles and remove the return hose to the fuel tank.

5. Label the positions of the wires and remove the engine wiring harness from the engine.

NOTE: *The engine harness ground cables must be removed from the back of the left cylinder head.*

6. Remove the bolts attaching the intake manifold to the cylinder heads and remove the manifold.

7. Remove the CDR tube grommet from the valley pan.

8. Remove the bolts attaching the valley pan strap to the front of the engine block, and remove the strap.

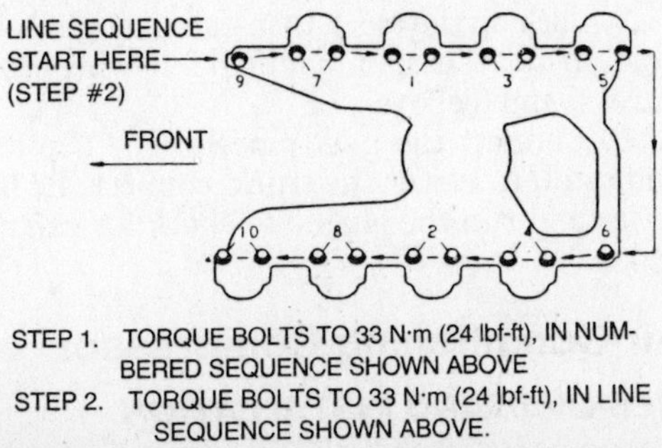

9. Remove the valley pan drain plug and remove the valley pan.

10. Apply a 1/8 in. (3mm) bead of RTV sealer to each end of the cylinder block as shown in the accompanying illustration.

NOTE: *The RTV sealer should be applied immediately prior to the valley pan installation.*

11. Install the valley pan drain plug, CDR tube and new grommet into the valley pan.

12. Install a new O-ring and new back-up ring on the CDR valve.

13. Install the valley pan strap on the front of the valley pan.

14. Install the intake manifold and torque the bolts to 24 ft. lbs. using the sequence shown in the illustration.

15. Reconnect the engine wiring harness and the engine ground wire located to the rear of the left cylinder head.

16. Install the injection pump using the procedure shown in Chapter 5 under Diesel fuel Systems.

17. Install the no. 7 and no. 8 fuel return hoses and the fuel tank return hose.

18. Remove the rag from the intake manifold and replace the air cleaner. Reconnect the battery ground cables to both batteries.

19. Run the engine and check for oil and fuel leaks.

NOTE: *If necessary, purge the nozzle high pressure lines of air by loosening the connector one half to one turn and cranking the engine until solid stream of fuel, devoid of any bubbles, flows from the connection.*

CAUTION: *Keep eyes and hands away from the nozzle spray. Fuel spraying from the nozzle under high pressure can penetrate the skin.*

20. Check and adjust the injection pump timing, as described in Chapter 5 under Diesel Fuel Systems.

LINE SEQUENCE
START HERE
(STEP #2)
FRONT
9 7 1 3 5
10 8 2 4 6

STEP 1. TORQUE BOLTS TO 33 N·m (24 lbf-ft), IN NUMBERED SEQUENCE SHOWN ABOVE
STEP 2. TORQUE BOLTS TO 33 N·m (24 lbf-ft), IN LINE SEQUENCE SHOWN ABOVE.

Diesel intake manifold bolt tightening sequence

Exhaust Manifold

REMOVAL AND INSTALLATION

6–4.9L

The intake and exhaust manifolds on these engines are known as combination manifolds and are serviced as a unit. See Intake Manifold Removal and Installation.

Gasoline V8

1. Remove the air cleaner if the manifold being removed has the carburetor heat stove attached to it.

2. On the 8–5.0L, remove the dipstick bracket.

3. Disconnect the exhaust pipe or catalytic

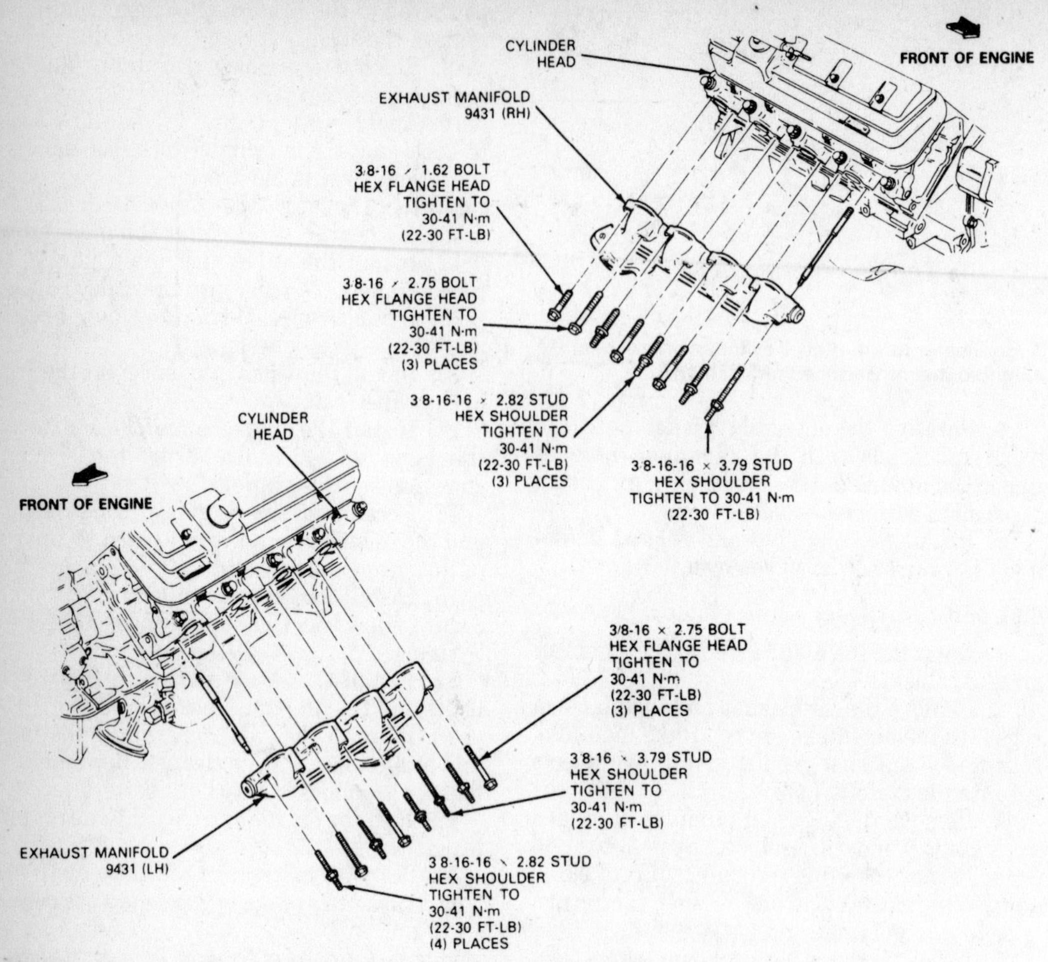

8–7.5L EFI exhaust manifold torque sequence

converter from the exhaust manifold. Remove and discard the doughnut gasket.

4. Remove the exhaust manifold attaching screws and remove the manifold from the cylinder head.

5. Install the exhaust manifold in the reverse order of removal. Apply a light coat of graphite grease to the mating surface of the manifold. Install and tighten the attaching bolts, starting from the center and working to both ends alternately. Tighten to the proper specifications.

6.9L and 7.3L Diesel

1. Disconnect the ground cables from both batteries.

2. Jack up the truck and safely support it with jackstands.

3. Disconnect the muffler inlet pipe from the exhaust manifolds.

4. Lower the truck to remove the right manifold. When removing the left manifold, jack the tuck up. Bend the tabs on the manifold attaching bolts, then remove the bolts and manifold.

5. Before installing, clean all mounting surfaces on the cylinder heads and the manifold. Apply an anti-seize compound on the manifold both threads and install the left manifold, using a new gasket and new locking tabs.

6. Torque the bolts to specifications and bend the tabs over the flats on the bolt heads to prevent the bolts from loosening.

7. Jack up the truck to install the right manifold. Install the right manifold following procedures 5 and 6 above.

8. Connect the inlet pipes to the manifold and tighten. Lower the truck, connect the batteries and run the engine to check for exhaust leaks.

Air Conditioning Compressor

REMOVAL AND INSTALLATION

NOTE: *An FS-6 6-cylinder axial compressor is standard on air conditioned Bronco and*

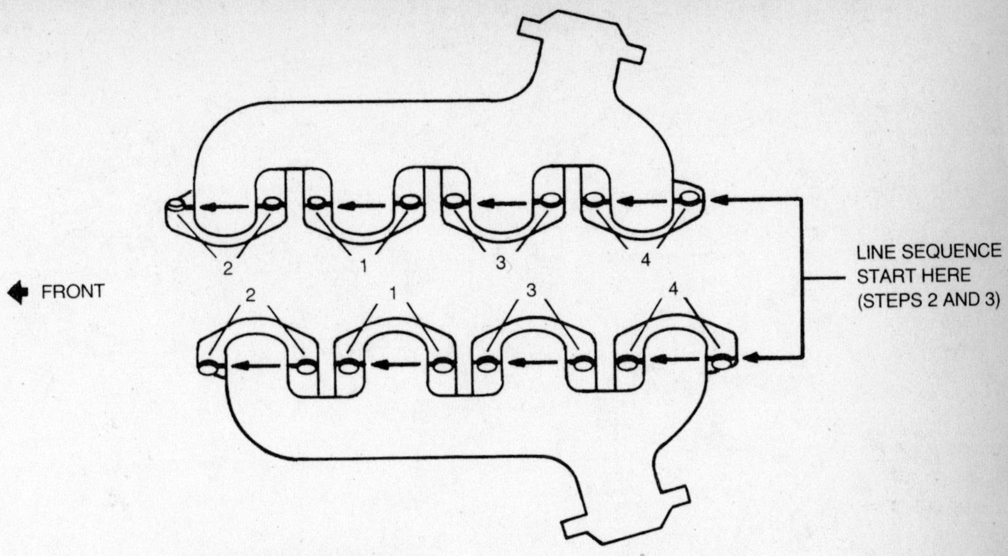

FRONT
2
1
3
4
2
1
3
4
LINE SEQUENCE
START HERE
(STEPS 2 AND 3)
EXHAUST MANIFOLD BOLTS
STEP 1. TORQUE BOLTS TO 41 NM (30 FT. LBS.) IN NUMBERED SEQUENCE SHOWN ABOVE.
STEP 2. TORQUE BOLTS TO 41 NM (30 FT. LBS.) IN LINE SEQUENCE SHOWN ABOVE.

Diesel exhaust manifold bolt tightening sequence

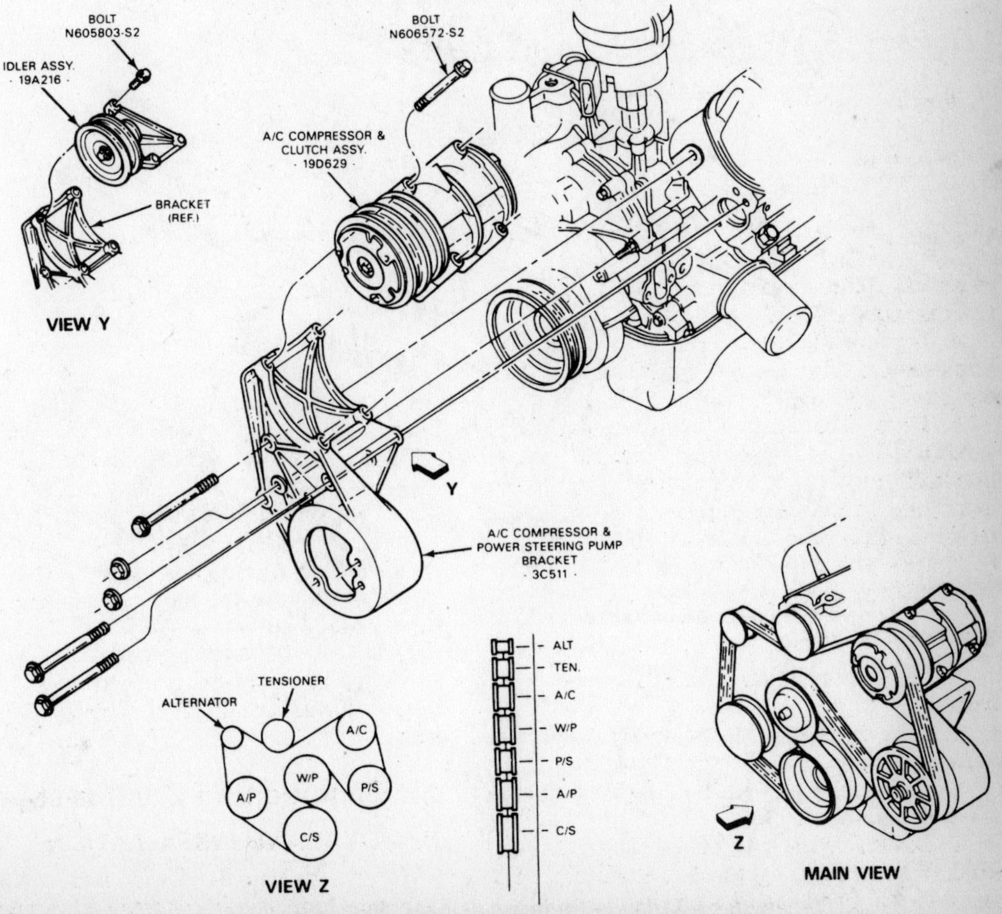

BOLT
N605803-S2
IDLER ASSY.
- 19A216 -
BRACKET
(REF.)
VIEW Y
BOLT
N606572-S2
A/C COMPRESSOR &
CLUTCH ASSY.
- 19D629 -
Y
A/C COMPRESSOR &
POWER STEERING PUMP
BRACKET
- 3C511 -
TENSIONER
ALTERNATOR
A/C
W/P
P/S
A/P
C/S
VIEW Z
ALT
TEN.
A/C
W/P
P/S
A/P
C/S
Z
MAIN VIEW

Compressor installation for the 8–5.0L and 8–5.8L EFI

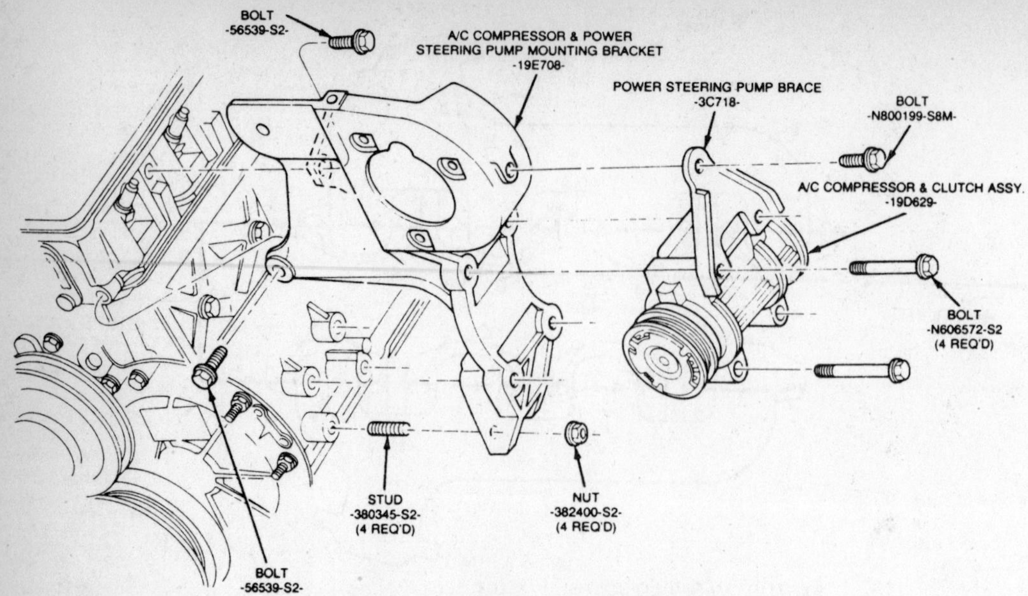

BOLT
-56539-S2-
A/C COMPRESSOR & POWER
STEERING PUMP MOUNTING BRACKET
-19E708-
POWER STEERING PUMP BRACE
-3C718-
BOLT
-N800199-S8M-
A/C COMPRESSOR & CLUTCH ASSY.
-19D629-
BOLT
-N606572-S2
(4 REQ'D)
STUD
-380345-S2-
(4 REQ'D)
NUT
-382400-S2-
(4 REQ'D)
BOLT
-56539-S2-

Compressor installation for the 6–4.9L EFI

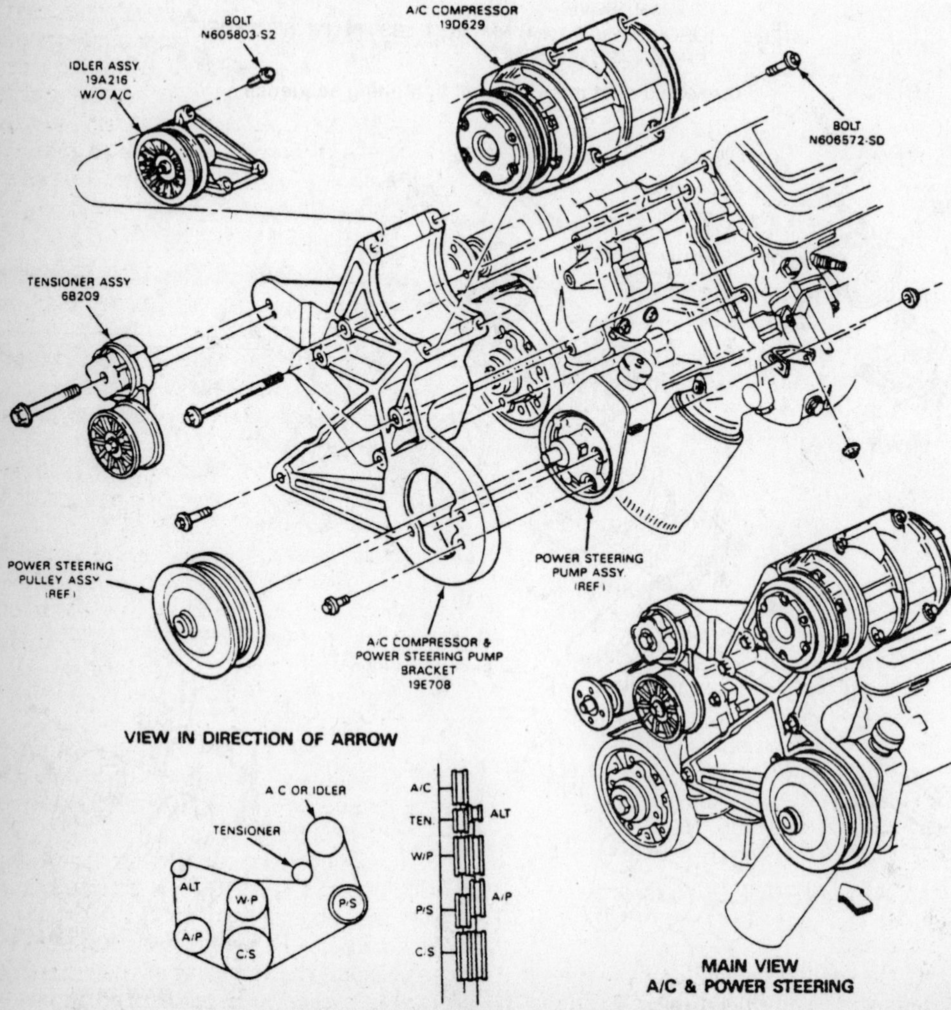

A/C COMPRESSOR
19D629
BOLT
N605803 S2
IDLER ASSY
19A216
W/O A/C
BOLT
N606572 SD
TENSIONER ASSY
6B209
POWER STEERING
PULLEY ASSY
(REF)
POWER STEERING
PUMP ASSY
(REF)
A/C COMPRESSOR &
POWER STEERING PUMP
BRACKET
19E708
VIEW IN DIRECTION OF ARROW
A C OR IDLER
TENSIONER
ALT
W/P
P/S
A/P
C/S
A/C
TEN.
W/P
P/S
C/S
ALT
A/P
MAIN VIEW
A/C & POWER STEERING

Compressor installation for the 8–7.5L

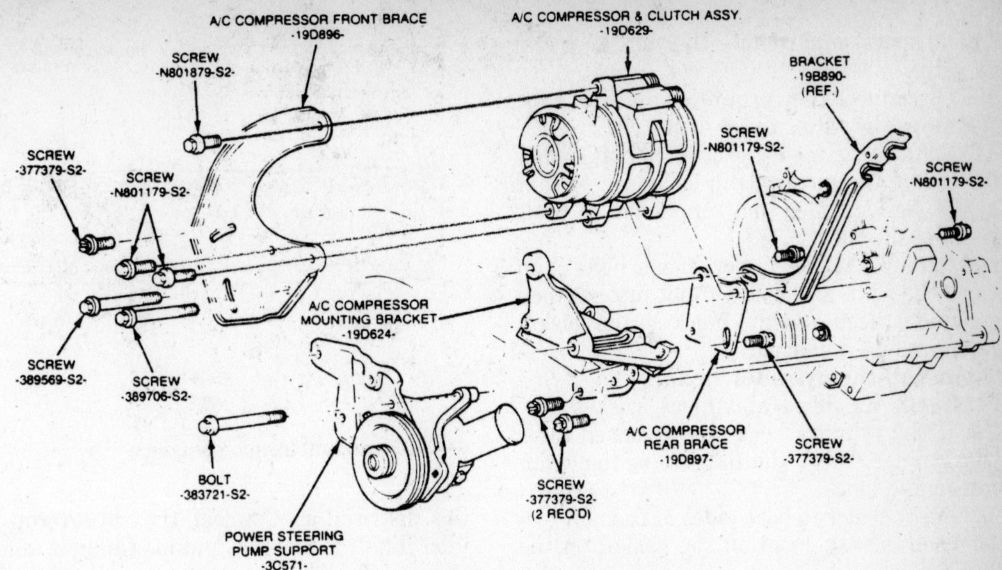

Compressor installation for the diesel

F-Series pick-ups. The 6E171 6-cylinder axial compressor is optional on the Bronco.

1. Discharge the refrigerant system. See ROUTINE MAINTENANCE in Chapter 1 for the proper procedure.
2. Disconnect the two refrigerant lines from the compressor. Cap the openings immediately!
3. Remove tension from the drive belt. Remove the belt
4. Disconnect the clutch wire at the connector.
5. Remove the bolt attaching the support brace to the front brace and the nut attaching the support brace to the intake manifold. Remove the support brace.
6. Remove the two bolts attaching the rear support to the bracket.
7. Remove the bolt attaching the compressor tab to the front brace and the two bolts attaching the compressor front legs to the bracket.
8. Remove the compressor.
9. Installation is the reverse of removal. Use new O-rings coated with clean refrigerant oil at all fittings. New, replacement compressors contain 10 oz. of refrigerant oil. Prior to installation, pour off 4 oz. of oil. This will maintain the oil charge in the system. Evacuate, charge and leak test the system.

Cylinder Head

REMOVAL AND INSTALLATION

6–4.9L

1. Drain the cooling system. Remove the air cleaner. Remove the oil filler tube. Disconnect the battery cable at the cylinder had.

CAUTION: *When draining the coolant, keep in mind that cats and dogs are attracted by the ethylene glycol antifreeze, and are quite likely to drink any that is left in an uncovered container or in puddles on the ground. This will prove fatal in sufficient quantity. Always drain the coolant into a sealable container. Coolant should be reused unless it is contaminated or several years old.*

2. Disconnect the muffler inlet pipe at the exhaust manifold. Pull the muffler inlet pipe down. Remove the gasket.
3. Disconnect the accelerator rod and cable retracting spring. Disconnect the choke control cable if applicable and the accelerator rod at the carburetor.
4. Disconnect the transmission kickdown rod. Disconnect the accelerator linkage at the bellcrank assembly.
5. Disconnect the fuel inlet line at the fuel filter hose, and the distributor vacuum line at the carburetor. Disconnect other vacuum lines as necessary for accessibility and identify them for proper connection.
6. Remove the radiator upper hose at the coolant outlet housing.
7. Disconnect the distributor vacuum line at the distributor. Disconnect the carburetor fuel inlet line at the fuel pump. Remove the lines as an assembly.
8. Disconnect the spark plug wires at the spark plugs and the temperature sending unit wire at the sending unit.
9. Grasp the PCV vent hose near the PCV valve and pull the valve out of the grommet in the valve rocker arm cover. Disconnect the PCV vent hose at the hose fitting in the intake

manifold spacer and remove the vent hose and PCV valve.

10. Disconnect the carburetor air vent tube and remove the valve rocker arm cover.

11. Remove the valve rocker arm shaft assembly. Remove the pushrods in sequence so that they can be identified and reinstalled in their original positions.

12. Remove the cylinder head bolts and remove the cylinder head. Do not pry between the cylinder head and the block as the gasket surfaces maybe damaged.

To install the cylinder head:

1. Clean the head and block gasket surfaces. If the cylinder head was removed for a gasket change, check the flatness of the cylinder head and block.

2. Apply sealer to both sides of the new cylinder head gasket. Position the gasket on the cylinder block.

3. Install a new gasket on the flange of the muffler inlet pipe.

4. Lift the cylinder head above the cylinder block and lower it into position using two head bolts installed through the head as guides.

5. Coat the threads of the no. 1 and 6 bolts for the right side of the cylinder head with a small mount of water-resistant sealer. Oil the threads of the remaining bolts. Install, but do not tighten, tow bolts at the opposite ends of the head to hold the head and gasket in position.

6. The cylinder head bolts are tightened in 3 progressive steps. Torque them (in the proper sequence):

- Step 1: 55 ft. lbs.
- Step 2: 65 ft. lbs.
- Step 3: 75 ft. lbs.

7. Apply Lubriplate to both ends of the pushrods and install them in their original positions.

8. Install the valve rocker arm shaft assembly.

9. Adjust the valves, as necessary.

10. Install the muffler inlet pipe lockwasher and attaching nuts.

11. Connect the radiator upper hose at the coolant outlet housing.

12. Position the distributor vacuum line and the carburetor fuel inlet line on the engine. Connect the fuel line at the fuel filter hose and install a new clamp. Install the distributor vacuum line at the carburetor. Connect the accelerator linkage at the bellcrank assembly. Connect the transmission kickdown rod.

13. Connect the accelerator rod retracting spring. Connect the choke control cable (if applicable) and the accelerator rod at the carburetor.

14. Connect the distributor vacuum line at

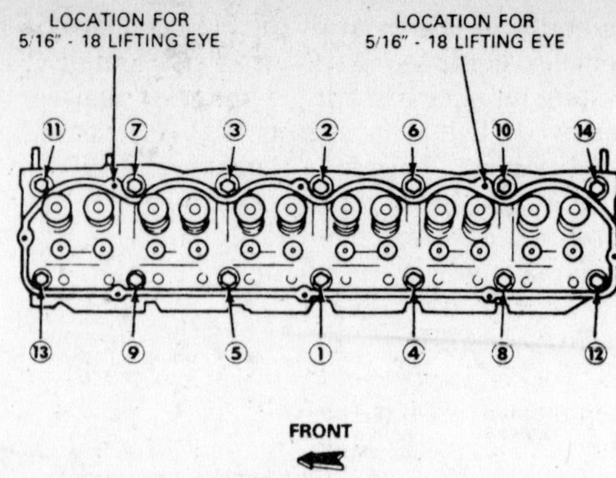

6-4.9L head bolt torque sequence

the distributor. Connect the carburetor fuel inlet line at the fuel pump. Connect all the vacuum lines using their previous identification for proper connection.

15. Connect the temperature sending unit wire at the sending unit. Connect the spark plug wires. Connect the battery cable at the cylinder head.

16. Fill the cooling system.

17. Install the valve rocker cover. Connect the carburetor air vent tube.

18. Connect the PCV vent hose at the carburetor spacer fitting. Insert the PCV valve with the vent hose attached, into the valve rocker arm cover grommet. Install the air cleaner, start the engine and check for leaks.

Gasoline V8 Except 8-7.5L

1. Remove the intake manifold, carburetor or EFI.

2. Remove the rocker arm cover(s).

3. If the right cylinder head is to be removed, loosen the alternator adjusting arm bolt and remove the alternator mounting bracket bolt and spacer. Swing the alternator down and out of the way. Remove the air cleaner inlet duct from the right cylinder head assembly.

If the left cylinder head is being removed, remove the bolts fastening the accelerator shaft

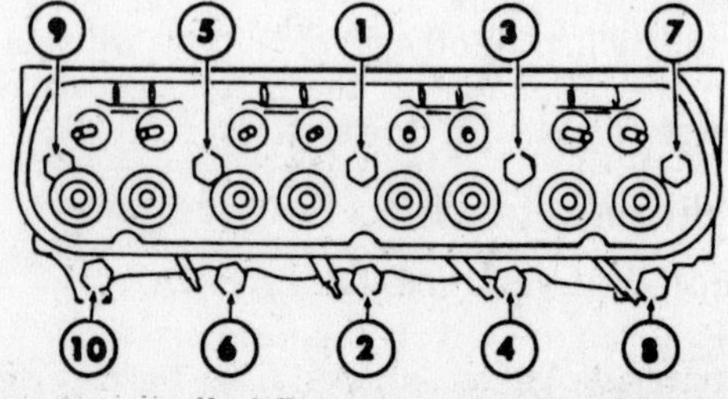

Cylinder head bolt torque sequence, all gasoline V8s

assembly at the front of the cylinder head. On vehicles equipped with air conditioning, the system must be discharged and the compressor removed. The procedure is best left to an air conditioning specialist. Persons not familiar with air conditioning systems can be easily injured when working on the systems.

4. Disconnect the exhaust manifold(s) from the muffler inlet pipe(s).

5. Loosen the rocker arm stud nuts so that the rocker arms can be rotated to the side. Remove the pushrods and identify them so that they can be reinstalled in their original positions.

6. Remove the cylinder head bolts and lift the cylinder head from the block.

To install the cylinder head(s):

1. Clean the cylinder head, intake manifold, the valve cover and the head gasket surfaces.

2. A specially treated composition head gasket is used. Do not apply sealer to a composition gasket. Position the new gasket over the locating dowels on the cylinder block. Then, position the cylinder head on the block and install the attaching bolts.

3. The cylinder head bolts are tightened in progressive steps. Tighten all the bolts in the proper sequence to:

8–5.0L

- Step 1: 55–65 ft.lbs.
- Step 2: 66–72 ft. lbs.

8–5.8L

- Step 1: 85 ft. lbs.
- Step 2: 95 ft. lbs.
- Step 3: 105–112 ft. lbs.

4. Clean the pushrods. Blow out the oil passage in the rods with compressed air. Check the pushrods for straightness by rolling them on a piece of glass. Never try to straighten a pushrod; always replace it.

5. Apply Lubriplate® to the ends of the pushrods and install them in their original positions.

6. Apply Lubriplate® to the rocker arms and their fulcrum seats and install the rocker arms. Adjust the valves.

7. Position a new gasket(s) on the muffler inlet pipe(s) as necessary. Connect the exhaust manifold(s) at the muffler inlet pipe(s).

8. If the right cylinder head was removed, install the alternator, ignition coil and air cleaner duct on the right cylinder head. Adjust the drive belt. If the left cylinder head was removed, install the accelerator shaft assembly at the front of the cylinder head.

9. Clean the valve rocker arm cover and the cylinder head gasket surfaces. Place the new gaskets in the covers, making sure that the tabs of the gasket engage the notches provided in the cover. Install the compressor, evaluate, charge and leak test the system. Let an air conditioning specialist do this.

10. Install the intake manifold and related parts.

8–7.5L

1. Remove the intake manifold and carburetor as an assembly.

2. Disconnect the exhaust pipe from the exhaust manifold.

3. Loosen the air conditioning compressor drive belt, if so equipped.

4. Loosen the alternator attaching bolts and remove the bolt attaching the alternator bracket to the right cylinder head.

5. Disconnect the air conditioning compressor from the engine and move it aside, out of the way. Do not discharge the air conditioning system.

6. Remove the bolts securing the power steering reservoir bracket to the left cylinder head. Position the reservoir and bracket out of the way.

7. Remove the valve rocker arm covers. Remove the rocker arm bolts, rocker arms, oil deflectors, fulcrums and pushrods in sequence so that they can be reinstalled in their original positions.

8. Remove the cylinder head bolts and lift the head and exhaust manifold off the engine. If necessary, pry at the forward corners of the cylinder head against the casting bosses provided on the cylinder block. Do not damage the gasket mating surfaces of the cylinder head and block by prying against them.

9. Remove all gasket material from the cylinder head and block. Clean all gasket material from the mating surfaces of the intake manifold. If the exhaust manifold was removed, clean the mating surfaces of the cylinder head and exhaust manifold. Apply a thin coat of graphite grease to the cylinder head exhaust port areas and install the exhaust manifold.

10. Position two long cylinder head bolts in the two rear lower bolt holes of the left cylinder head. Place a long cylinder head bolt in the rear lower bolt hole of the right cylinder head. Use rubber bands to keep the bolts in position until the cylinder heads are installed on the cylinder block.

11. Position new cylinder head gaskets on the cylinder block dowels. Do not apply sealer to the gaskets, heads, or block.

12. Place the cylinder heads on the block, guiding the exhaust manifold studs into the exhaust pipe connections. Install the remaining cylinder head bolts. The longer bolts go in the lower row of holes.

13. Tighten all the cylinder head attaching bolts in the proper sequence in three stages: 75

ft. lbs., 105 ft.lbs., and finally to 135 ft. lbs. When this procedure is used, it is not necessary to retorque the heads after extended use.

14. Make sure that the oil holes in the pushrods are open and install the pushrods in their original positions. Place a dab of Lubriplate to the ends of the pushrods before installing them.

15. Lubricate and install the valve rockers. Make sure that the pushrods remain seated in their lifters.

16. Connect the exhaust pipes to the exhaust manifolds.

17. Install the intake manifold and carburetor assembly. Tighten the intake manifold attaching bolts in the proper sequence to 25–30 ft. lbs.

18. Install the air conditioning compressor to the engine.

19. Install the power steering reservoir to the engine.

20. Apply oil-resistant sealer to one side of the new valve cover gaskets and lay the cemented side in place in the valve cover. Install the covers.

21. Install the alternator to the right cylinder head and adjust the alternator drive belt tension.

22. Adjust the air conditioning compressor drive belt tension.

23. Fill the radiator with coolant.

24. Start the engine and check for leaks.

6.9L and 7.3L Diesel

1. Open the hood and disconnect the negative cables from both batteries.

2. Drain the cooling system and remove the radiator fan shroud halves.

CAUTION: *When draining the coolant, keep in mind that cats and dogs are attracted by the ethylene glycol antifreeze, and are quite likely to drink any that is left in an uncovered container or in puddles on the ground. This will prove fatal in sufficient quantity. Always drain the coolant into a sealable container. Coolant should be reused unless it is contaminated or several years old.*

3. Remove the radiator fan and clutch assembly using special tool T83T–6312–A and B. This tool is available through the Owatonna Tool Co. whose address is listed in the front of this boot, or through Ford Dealers. It is also available through many tool rental shops.

NOTE: *The fan clutch uses a left hand thread and must be removed by turning the nut clockwise.*

4. Label and disconnect the wiring from the alternator.

5. Remove the adjusting bolts and pivot bolts from the alternator and the vacuum pump and remove both units.

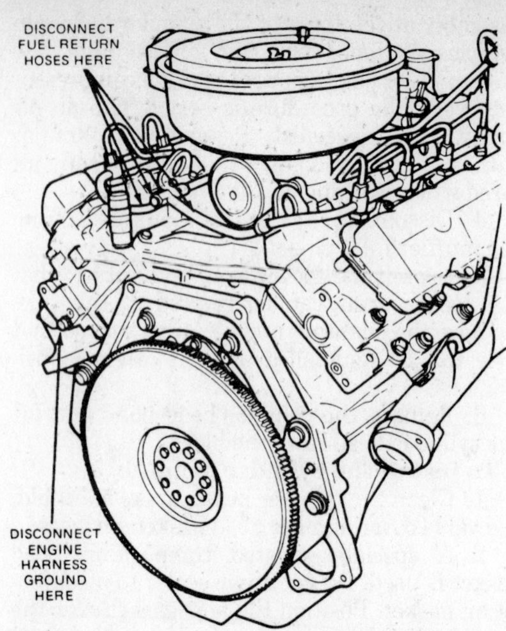

Diesel fuel hose and engine ground harness connections

6. Remove the fuel filter lines and cap to prevent fuel leakage.

7. Remove the alternator, vacuum pump, and fuel filter brackets with the fuel filter attached.

8. Remove the heater hose from the cylinder head.

9. Remove the fuel injection pump as described in Chapter 5 under Diesel Fuel Systems.

10. Remove the intake manifold and valley cover.

11. Jack up the truck and safely support it with jackstands.

12. Disconnect the exhaust pipes from the exhaust manifolds.

13. Remove the clamp holding the engine oil dipstick tube in place and the bolt attaching the transmission oil dipstick to the cylinder head.

14. Lower the truck.

15. Remove the engine oil dipstick tube.

16. Remove the valve covers, rocker arms and pushrods. Keep the pushrods in order so they can be returned to their original positions.

17. Remove the nozzles and glow plugs as described in Chapter 5 under Diesel Fuel Systems.

18. Remove the cylinder head bolts and attach lifting eyes, using special tool T70P–6000 or equivalent, to each end of the cylinder heads.

19. Carefully lift the cylinder heads out of

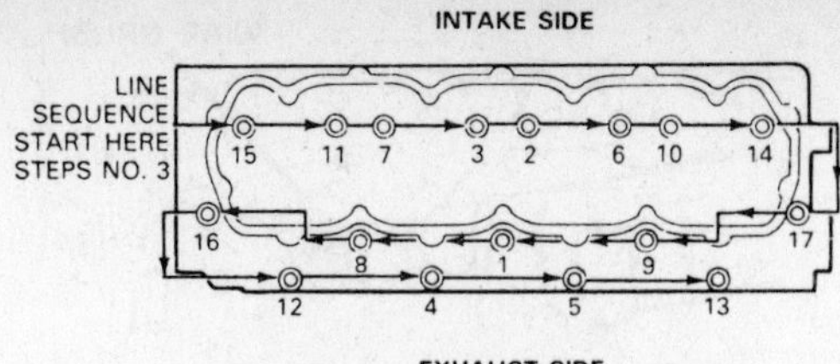

STEP 1. TIGHTEN BOLTS TO 88 N·m (65 FT-LB) IN NUMBERED SEQUENCE SHOWN ABOVE.
STEP 2. TIGHTEN BOLTS TO 115 N·m (85 FT-LB) IN NUMBERED SEQUENCE SHOWN ABOVE.
STEP 3. TIGHTEN BOLTS TO 136 N·m (100 FT-LB) IN LINE SEQUENCE SHOWN ABOVE.
STEP 4. REPEAT STEP NO. 3.

7.3L diesel head bolt torque sequence

the engine compartment and remove the head gaskets.

NOTE: *The cylinder head prechambers may fall out of the heads upon removal.*

To install:

20. Position the cylinder head gasket on the engine block and carefully lower the cylinder head in place.

NOTE: *Use care in installing the cylinder heads to prevent the prechambers from falling out into the cylinder bores.*

21. Install the cylinder head bolt and torque in 4 steps using the sequence shown in the illustration.

NOTE: *Lubricate the threads and the mating surfaces of the bolt heads and washers with engine oil.*

22. Dip the pushrod ends in clean engine oil and install the pushrods with the copper colored ends toward the rocker arms, making sure the pushrods are fully seated in the tappet pushrod seats.

23. Install the rocker arms and posts in their original positions. Apply Lubriplate® grease to the valve stem tips. Turn the engine over by hand until the timing mark is at the 11 o'clock position as viewed from the front. Install the rocker arm posts, bolts, and torque to 27 ft. lbs. Install the valve covers.

24. Install the valley pan and the intake manifold.

25. Install the fuel injection pump as described in Chapter 5 under Diesel Fuel Systems.

26. Connect the heater hose to the cylinder head.

27. Install the fuel filter, alternator, vacuum pump, and their drive belts.

28. Install the engine oil and transmission dip stick.

29. Connect the exhaust pipe to the exhaust manifolds.

30. Reconnect the alternator wiring harness and replace the air cleaner. Connect both battery ground cables.

31. Refill and bleed the cooling system.

32. Run the engine and check for fuel, coolant and exhaust leaks.

NOTE: *If necessary, purge the high pressure fuel lines of air by loosening the connector one half to one turn and cranking the engine until a solid stream of fuel, free from any bubbles, flows from the connections.*

33. Check the injection pump timing. Refer to Chapter 5 for these procedures.

34. Install the radiator fan and clutch assem-

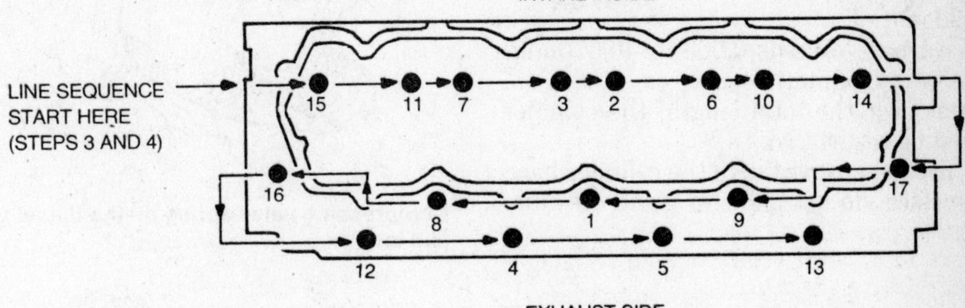

CYLINDER HEAD BOLTS

STEP 1. TORQUE BOLTS TO 40 FT. LBS. IN NUMBERED SEQUENCE SHOWN ABOVE.
STEP 2. TORQUE BOLTS TO 65 FT. LBS. IN NUMBERED SEQUENCE SHOWN ABOVE.
STEP 3. TORQUE BOLTS TO 75 FT. LBS. IN LINE SEQUENCE SHOWN ABOVE.
STEP 4. REPEAT STEP 3.

6.9L diesel cylinder head bolt tightening sequence

bly using special tools T83T–6312A and B or equivalent.

NOTE: *The fan clutch uses a left hand thread. Tighten by turning the nut counterclockwise. Install the radiator fan shroud halves.*

CLEANING AND INSPECTION

1. With the valves installed to protect the valve seats, remove deposits from the combustion chambers and valve heads with a scraper and a wire brush. Be careful not to damage the cylinder head gasket surface. After the valves are removed, clean the valve guide bores with a valve guide cleaning tool. Using cleaning solvent to remove dirt, grease and other deposits, clean all bolts holes; be sure the oil passage is clean (V8 engines).
2. Remove all deposits from the valves with a fine wire brush or buffing wheel.
3. Inspect the cylinder heads for cracks or excessively burned areas in the exhaust outlet ports.
4. Check the cylinder head for cracks and inspect the gasket surface for burrs and nicks. Replace the head if it is cracked.
5. On cylinder heads that incorporate valve seat inserts, check the inserts for excessive wear, cracks, or looseness.

RESURFACING

Cylinder Head Flatness

When the cylinder head is removed, check the flatness of the cylinder head gasket surfaces.

1. Place a straightedge across the gasket surface of the cylinder head. Using feeler gauges, determine the clearance at the center of the straightedge.
2. If warpage exceeds 0.003 in. (0.076mm) in a 6 in. (152mm) span, or 0.006 in. (0.152mm) over the total length, the cylinder head must be resurfaced.
3. If necessary to refinish the cylinder head gasket surface, do not plane or grind off more than 0.254mm (0.010 in.) from the original gasket surface.

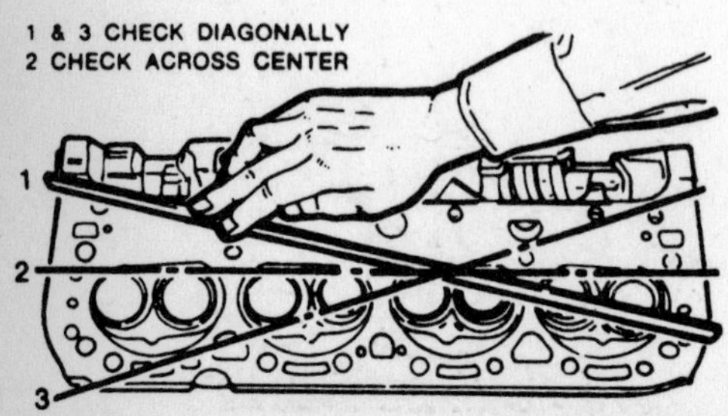

Checking the cylinder head for warpage

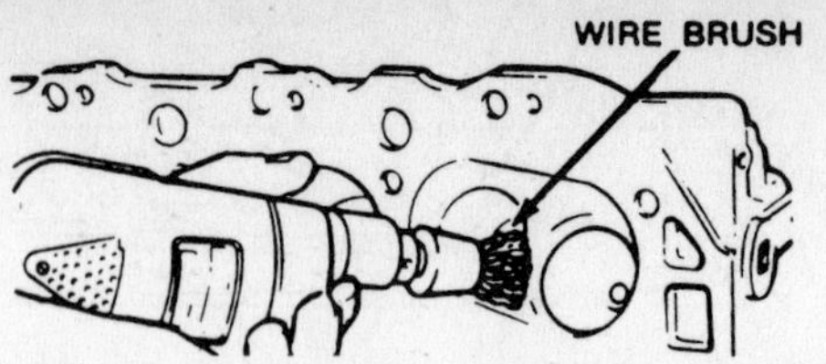

Remove combustion chamber carbon from the cylinder head with a wire brush and electric drill. Make sure all carbon is removed and not just burnished

NOTE: *When milling the cylinder heads of V8 engines, the intake manifold mounting position is altered, and must be corrected by milling the manifold flange a proportionate amount. Consult an experienced machinist about this.*

Valves and Springs

REMOVAL AND INSTALLATION

1. Block the head on its side, or install a pair of head-holding brackets made especially for valve removal.
2. Use a socket slightly larger than the valve stem and keepers, place the socket over

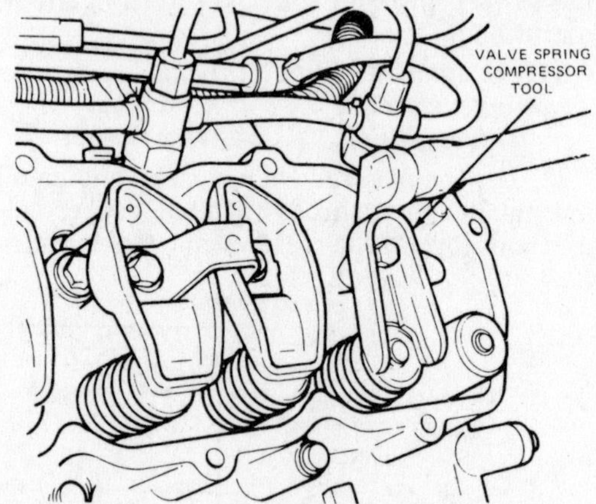

Compressing valve spring on the diesel using special tool

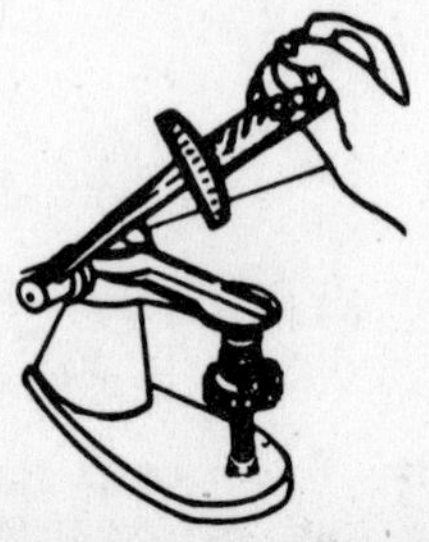

Have the valve spring test pressure checked at a machine shop. Make sure the readings are within specifications

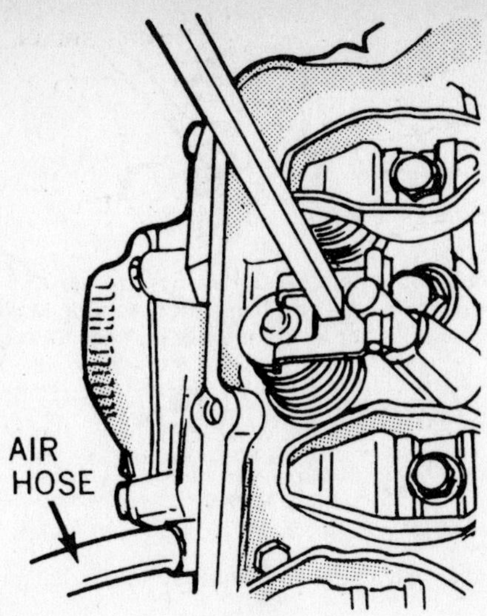

Compressing gasoline engine valve spring. Note spring compressor position and air hose. Cylinder at TDC

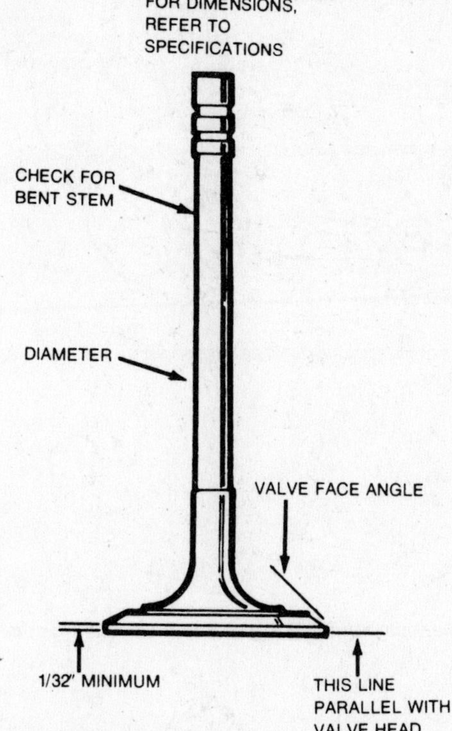

Critical valve dimensions

the valve stem and gently hit the socket with a plastic hammer to break loose any varnish buildup.

3. Remove the valve keepers, retainer, spring shield and valve spring using a valve spring compressor (the locking C-clamp type is the easiest kind to use).

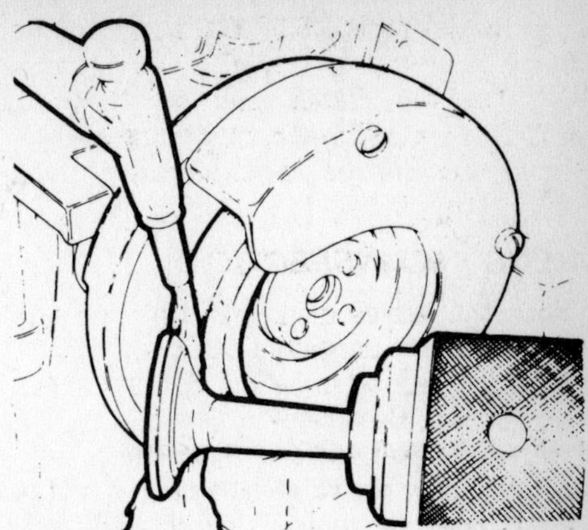

A well-equipped machine shop can handle valve refacing jobs

4. Put the parts in a separate container numbered for the cylinder being worked on; do not mix them with other parts removed.

5. Remove and discard the valve stem oil seals. A new seal will be used at assembly time.

6. Remove the valves from the cylinder head and place them, in order, through numbered holes punched in a stiff piece of cardboard or wood valve holding stick.

NOTE: *The exhaust valve stems, on some engines, are equipped with small metal caps. Take care not to lose the caps. Make sure to reinstall them at assembly time. Replace any caps that are worn.*

7. Use an electric drill and rotary wire brush to clean the intake and exhaust valve ports, combustion chamber and valve seats. In some cases, the carbon will need to be chipped away. Use a blunt pointed drift for carbon chipping. Be careful around the valve seat areas.

8. Use a wire valve guide cleaning brush and safe solvent to clean the valve guides.

9. Clean the valves with a revolving wires brush. Heavy carbon deposits may be removed with the blunt drift.

NOTE: *When using a wire brush to clean carbon on the valve ports, valves etc., be sure*

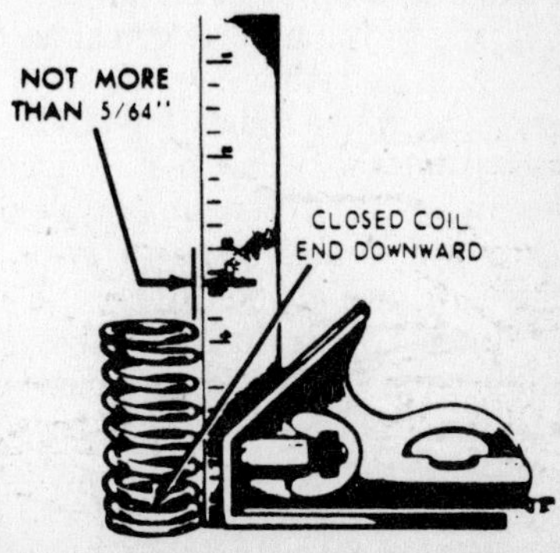

Check the valve spring free length and squareness

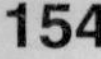

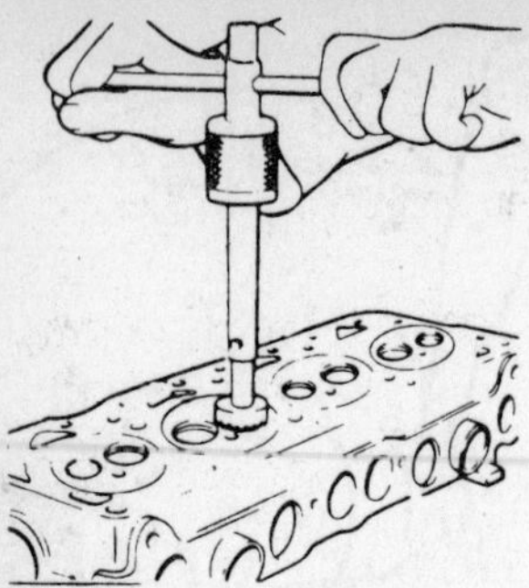

Reaming valve seat with a hand reamer

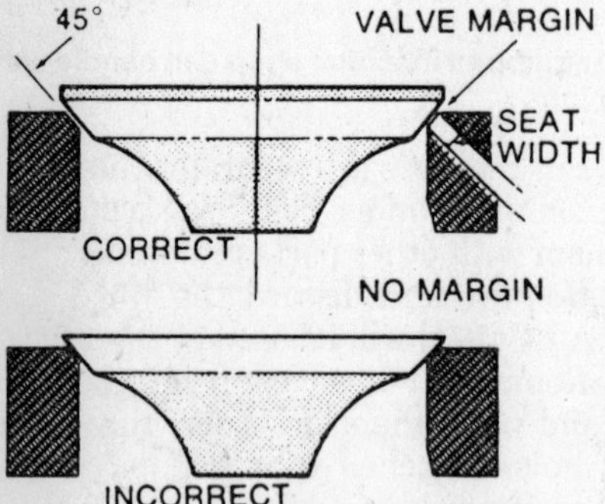

Valve seat width and centering after proper reaming

that the deposits are actually removed, rather than burnished.

10. Wash and clean all valve springs, keepers, retaining caps etc., in safe solvent.
11. Clean the head with a brush and some safe solvent and wipe dry.
12. Check the head for cracks. Cracks in the cylinder head usually start around an exhaust valve seat because it is the hottest part of the combustion chamber. If a crack is suspected but cannot be detected visually have the area checked with dye penetrant or other method by the machine shop.
13. After all cylinder head parts are reasonably clean, check the valve stem-to-guide clearance. If a dial indicator is not on hand, a visual inspection can give you a fairly good idea if the guide, valve stem or both are worn.
14. Insert the valve into the guide until slight away from the valve seat. Wiggle the valve sideways. A small amount of wobble is normal, excessive wobble means a worn guide or valve stem. If a dial indicator is on hand, mount the indicator so that the stem of the valve is at 90° to the valve stem, as close to the valve guide as possible. Move the valve off the seat, and measure the valve guide-to-stem clearance by rocking the stem back and forth to actuate the dial indicator. Measure the valve stem using a micrometer and compare to speci-

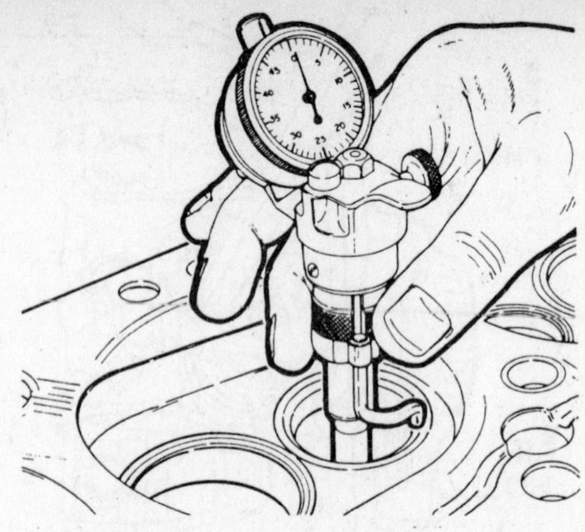

Checking valve seat concentricity with a dial gauge

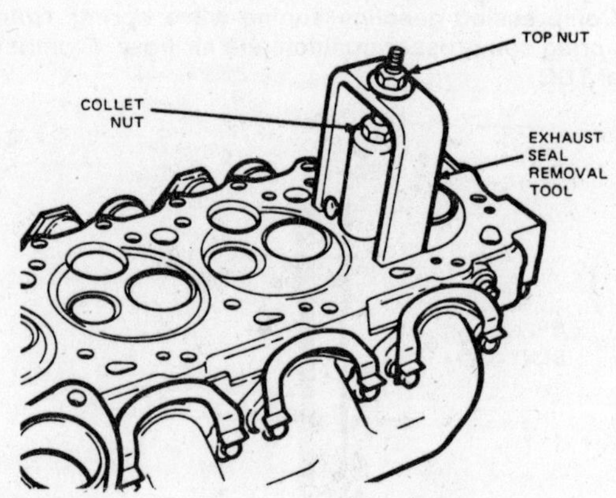

Diesel exhaust valve seat insert removal using special tool

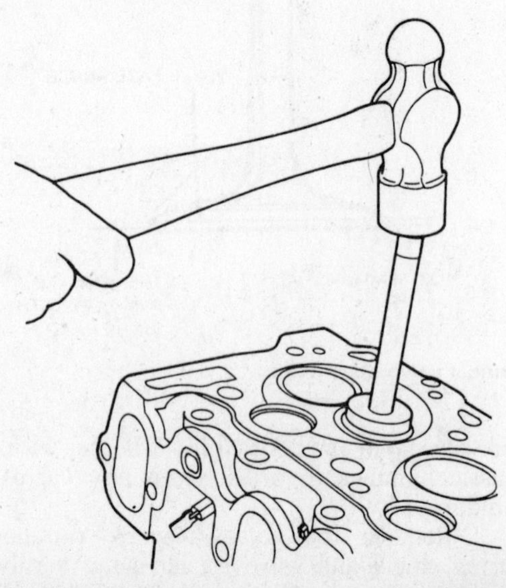

Installing diesel exhaust valve seats using special tool

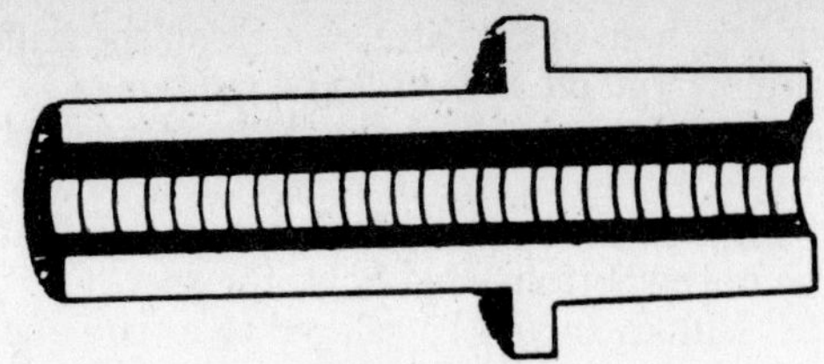
Cross-section of a knurled valve guide

Lapping the valves by hand. When done, the finish on both valve faces the seats should be smooth and evenly shiny

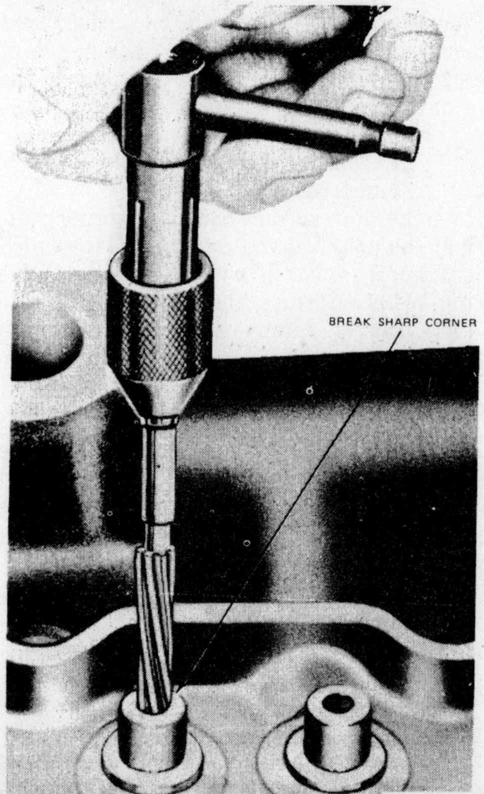

Reaming valve guides

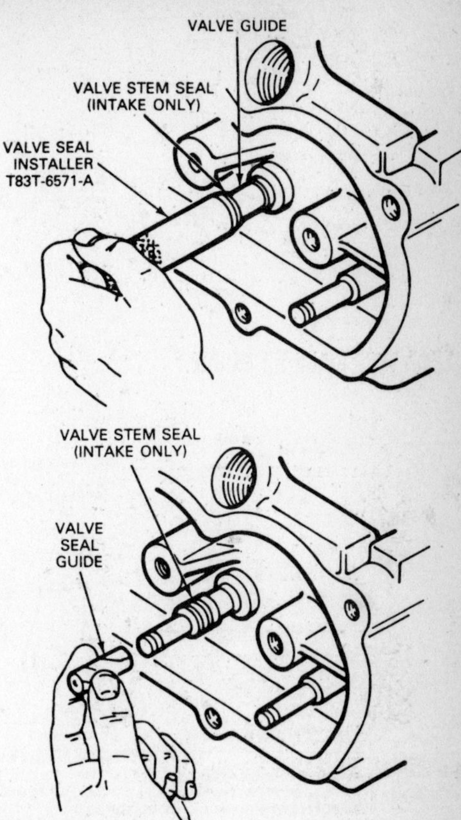

Installing the valve stem seals on the diesel

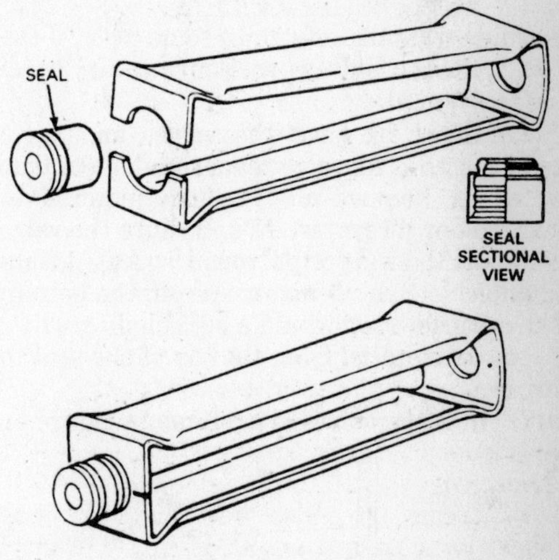

Valve stem seal installation tool for the 8–7.5L

fications to determine whether stem or guide wear is causing excessive clearance.

15. The valve guide, if worn, must be repaired before the valve seats can be resurfaced. Ford supplies valves with oversize stems to fit valve guides that are reamed to oversize for repair. The machine shop will be able to handle

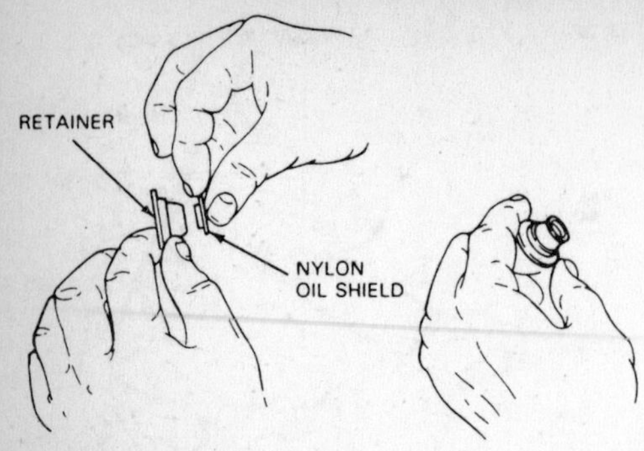

Installing the nylon oil shield

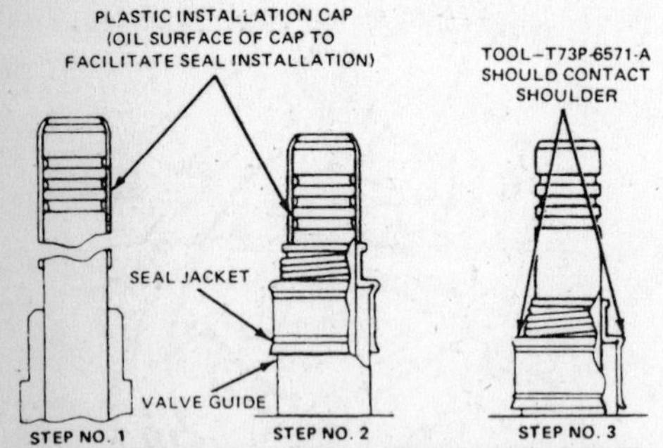

Valve stem seal installation

the guide reaming for you. In some cases, if the guide is not too badly worn, knurling may be all that is required.

16. Reface, or have the valves and valve seats refaced. The valve seats should be a true 45° angle. Remove only enough material to clean up any pits or grooves. Be sure the valve seat is not too wide or narrow. Use a 60° grinding wheel to remove material from the bottom of the seat for raising and a 30° grinding wheel to remove material from the top of the seat to narrow.

17. After the valves are refaced by machine, hand lap them to the valve seat. Clean the grinding compound off and check the position of face-to-seat contact. Contact should be close to the center of the valve face. If contact is close to the top edge of the valve, narrow the seat; if too close to the bottom edge, raise the seat.

18. Valves should be refaced to a true angle of 44°. Remove only enough metal to clean up the valve face or to correct runout. If the edge of a valve head, after machining, is $\frac{1}{32}$ in. (0.8mm) or less replace the valve. The tip of the valve stem should also be dressed on the valve grinding machine, however, do not remove more than 0.010 in. (0.254mm).

19. After all valve and valve seats have been machined, check the remaining valve train parts (springs, retainers, keepers, etc.) for wear. Check the valve springs for straightness and tension.

20. Install the valves in the cylinder head and metal caps.

21. Install new valve stem oil seals.

22. Install the valve keepers, retainer, spring shield and valve spring using a valve spring compressor (the locking C-clamp type is the easiest kind to use).

23. Check the valve spring installed height, shim or replace as necessary.

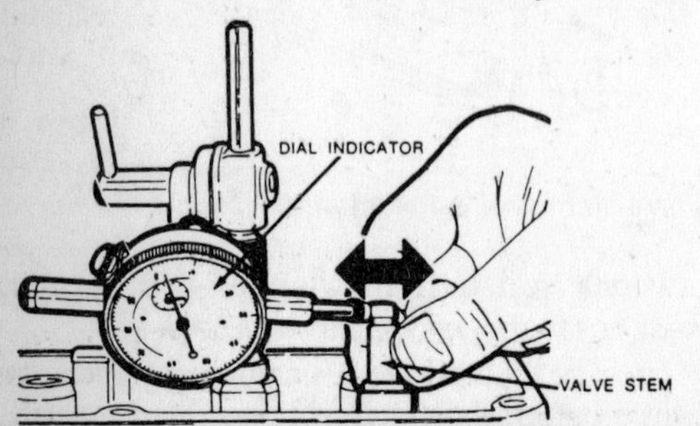

Measuring valve stem-to-guide clearance. Make sure the indicator is mounted at 90° to the valve stem and as close to the guide as possible

CHECKING VALVE SPRINGS

Place the valve spring on a flat surface next to a carpenter's square. Measure the height of the spring, and rotate the spring against the edge of the square to measure distortion. If the spring height varies (by comparison) by more than $\frac{1}{16}$ in. (1.5mm) or if the distortion exceeds $\frac{1}{16}$ in. (1.5mm), replace the spring.

Have the valve springs tested for spring pressure at the installed and compressed (installed height minus valve lift) height using a valve spring tester. Springs should be within one pound, plus or minus each other. Replace springs as necessary.

VALVE SPRING INSTALLED HEIGHT

After installing the valve spring, measure the distance between the spring mounting pad and the lower edge of the spring retainer. Compare the measurement to specifications. If the installed height is incorrect, add shim washers between the spring mounting pad and the spring. Use only washers designed for valve springs, available at most parts houses.

VALVE STEM OIL SEALS

When installing valve stem oil seals, ensure that a small amount of oil is able to pass the seal to lubricate the valve stems and guide walls, otherwise, excessive wear will occur.

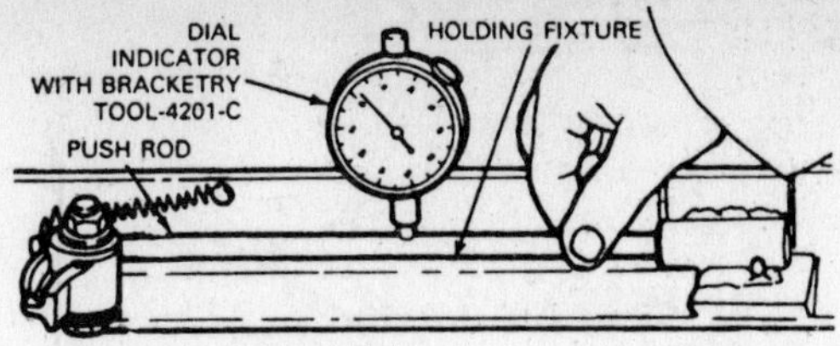

Checking pushrod runout

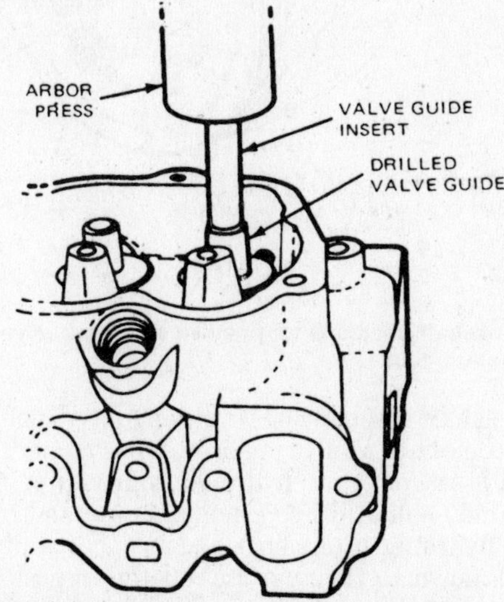

Installing the valve guide inserts on the diesel

VALVE SEATS

If the valve seat is damaged or burnt and cannot be serviced by refacing, it may be possible to have the seat machined and an insert installed. Consult an automotive machine shop for their advice.

VALVE GUIDES

Worn valve guides can, in most cases, be reamed to accept a valve with an oversized stem. Valve guides that are not excessively worn or distorted may, in some cases, be knurled rather than reamed. However, if the valve stem is worn reaming for an oversized

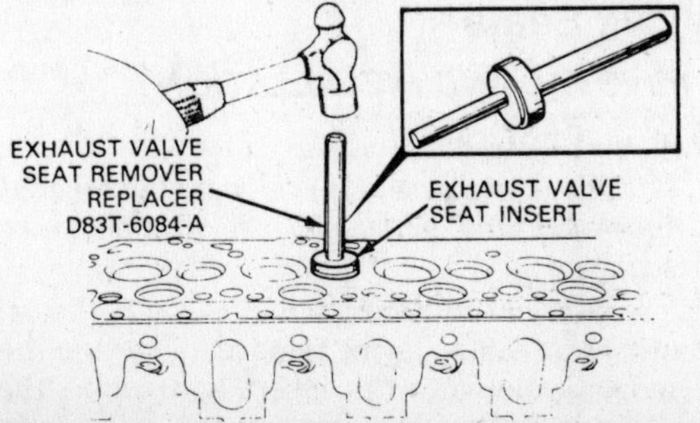

Installing the exhaust seat inserts on the diesel

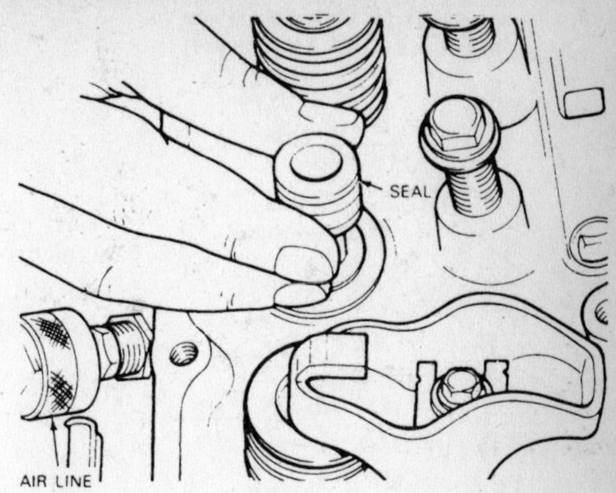

Removing or installing the valve stem seal on the 6–4.9L

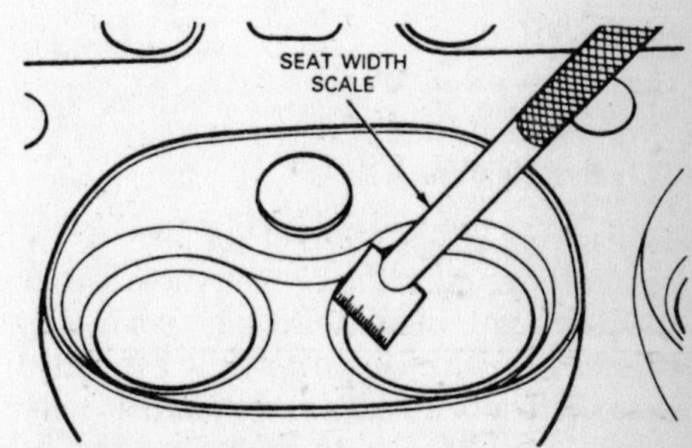

Checking valve seat width

valve stem is the answer since a new valve would be required.

Knurling is a process in which metal is displaced and raised, thereby reducing clearance. Knurling also produces excellent oil control. The possibility of knurling instead of reaming the valve guides should be discussed with a machinist.

HYDRAULIC VALVE CLEARANCE

Hydraulic valve lifters operate with zero clearance in the valve train, and because of this the rocker arms are nonadjustable. The only means by which valve system clearances can be altered is by installing over or undersize pushrods; but, because of the hydraulic lifter's natural ability to compensate for slack in the valve train, all components of all the valve system should be checked for wear if there is excessive play in the system.

When a valve in the engine is in the closed position, the valve lifter is resting on the base circle of the camshaft lobe and the pushrod is in its lowest position. To remove this additional clearance from the valve train, the valve lifter expands to maintain zero clearance in the valve system. When a rocker arm is loosened or removed from the engine, the lifter expands to it

STEP 1 - SET NO. 1 PISTON ON T.D.C. AT END OF COMPRESSION STROKE ADJUST NO. 1 INTAKE AND EXHAUST

STEP 4 - CHECK NO. 6 INTAKE AND EXHAUST

STEP 2 - CHECK NO. 5 INTAKE AND EXHAUST

STEP 3 - CHECK NO. 3 INTAKE AND EXHAUST

STEP 5 - CHECK NO. 2 INTAKE AND EXHAUST

STEP 6 - CHECK NO. 4 INTAKE AND EXHAUST

6–4.9L valve clearance

With No. 1 at TDC at end of compression stroke make a chalk mark at points 2 and 3 approximately 90 degrees apart

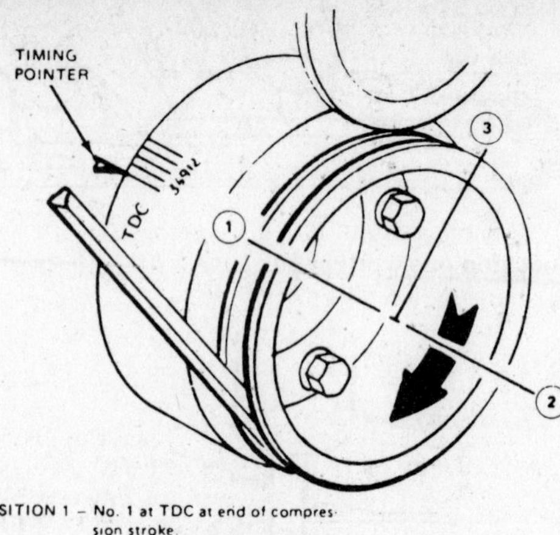

POSITION 1 – No. 1 at TDC at end of compression stroke.

POSITION 2 – Rotate the crankshaft 180 degrees (one half revolution) clockwise from POSITION 1.

POSITION 3 – Rotate the crankshaft 270 degrees (three quarter revolution clockwise from POSITION 2

Crankshaft positions for positive stop-type valve adjustment, 5.0L

fullest travel. When the rocker arm is reinstalled on the engine, the proper valve setting is obtained by tightening the rocker arm to a specified limit. But with the lifter fully expanded, if the camshaft lobe is on a high point it will require excessive torque to compress the lifter and obtain the proper setting. Because of this, when any component of the valve system has been removed, a preliminary valve adjustment procedure must be followed to ensure that when the rocker arm is reinstalled on the engine and tightened, the camshaft lobe for that cylinder is in the low position.

To determine whether a shorter or loner push rod is necessary, make the following check:

Mark the crankshaft pulley as described under Preliminary Valve Adjustment procedure. Follow each step in the procedure. As each valve is positioned, mount a suitable hydraulic lifter compressor tool on the rocker arm. Slowly apply pressure to bleed down the lifter until the plunger is completely bottomed. Take care to avoid excessive pressure that might bend the pushrod. Hold the lifter in bottom position and check the available clearance between the rocker arm and the valve stem tip with a feeler gauge. If the clearance is less than specified, install an undersized pushrod. If the clearance is greater than specified, install an oversized pushrod. When compressing the valve spring to remove the pushrods, be sure the piston in the individual cylinder is below TDC to avoid contact between the valve and the piston. To replace a pushrod, it will be necessary to remove the valve rocker arm shaft assembly on inline engines. Upon replacement of a valve pushrod, valve rocker arm shaft assembly or hydraulic valve lifter, the engine should not be cranked or rotated until the hydraulic lifters have had an opportunity to leak down to their normal operation position. The leak down rate can be accelerated by using the tool shown on the valve rocker arm and applying pressure in a direction to collapse the lifter.

Collapsed tappet gap

V8 Engines

- 8–5.0L

  Allowable: 0.071–0.193 in. (2.260–4.902mm)

  Desired: 0.096–0.165 in. (2.438–4.140mm)
- 8–5.8L

  Allowable: 0.098–0.198 in. (2.50–5.002mm)

  Desired: 0.123–0.173 in. (3.1–4.4mm)
- 8–7.5L

  Allowable: 0.075–0.175 in. (1.9–4.4mm)

  Desired: 0.100–0.150 in. (2.5–3.8mm)

Valve Seats

REMOVAL AND INSTALLATION

6.9L and 7.3L Diesel

NOTE: *The diesel is the only engine covered in this guide which has removable valve seats.*

1. Using Ford Rotunda tool 14–0309 the exhaust valve seats may be removed. Position the remover collet into the insert and rotate the collet nut clockwise to expand the collet jaws under the lip of the seat insert.

2. Rotate the top nut clockwise to remove the insert.

NOTE: *If an oversize seat insert is required, the cylinder head should be sent out to a qualified machine shop.*

3. To install a new exhaust valve seat, drive the seat in place using Rotunda tool 14–0309 and a hammer.

Valve seat inserts are supplied for service in standard size, 0.015 in. (0.381mm) oversize and 0.030 in. (0.762mm) oversize.

Valve Guides

REAMING VALVE GUIDES

If it becomes necessary to ream a valve guide to install with an oversize stem, a reaming kit is available which contains a oversize reamers and pilot tools.

When replacing a standard size valve with an oversize valve always use the reamer in sequence (smallest oversize first, then next smallest, etc.) so as not to overload the reamers. Always reface the valve seat after the valve guide has been reamed, and use a suitable scraper to brake the sharp corner at the top of the valve guide.

KNURLING

Valve guides which are not excessively worn or distorted may, in some cases, be knurled rather than reamed. Knurling is a process in which metal inside the valve guide bore is displaced and raised (forming a very fine cross-hatch pattern), thereby reducing clearance. Knurling also provides for excellent oil control. The possibility of knurling rather than reaming the guides should be discussed with a machinist.

STEM-TO-GUIDE CLEARANCE

Valve stem-to-guide clearance should be checked upon assembling the cylinder head, and is especially necessary if the valve guides have been reamed or knurled, or if oversize valve have been installed. Excessive oil consumption often is a result of too much clearance between the valve guide and valve stem.

1. Clean the valve stem with lacquer thinner or a similar solvent to remove all gum and varnish. Clean the valve guides using solvent and an expanding wire-type valve guide cleaner (a rifle cleaning brush works well here).

2. Mount a dial indicator so that the stem is 90° to the valve stem and as close to the valve guide as possible.

3. Move the valve off its seat, and measure the valve guide-to-stem clearance by rocking the stem back and forth to actuate the dial indicator. Measure the valve stems using a micrometer and compare to specifications, to determine whether stem or guide wear is responsible for excessive clearance.

VALVE LAPPING

The valve must be lapped into their seats after resurfacing, to ensure proper sealing. Even if the valve have not been refaced, they should be lapped into the head before reassembly.

Set the cylinder head on the workbench, combustion chamber side up. Rest the head on wooden blocks on either end, so there are 2–3 in. (51–76mm) between the tops of the valve guides and the bench.

1. Lightly lube the valve stem with clean engine oil. Coat the valve seat completely with valve grinding compound. Use just enough compound so that the full width and circumference of the seat are covered.

2. Install the valve in its proper location in the head. Attach the suction cup end of the valve lapping tool to the valve head. It usually helps to put a small amount of saliva into the suction cup to aid it sticking to the valve.

3. Rotate the tool between the palms, changing position and lifting the tool often to prevent grooving. Lap the valve in until a smooth, evenly polished seat and valve face are evident.

4. Remove the valve from the head. Wipe away all traces of grinding compound from the valve face and seat. Wipe out the port with a solvent soaked rag, and swab out the valve guide with a piece of solvent soaked rag to make sure there are no traces of compound grit inside the guide. This cleaning is very important, as the engine will ingest any grit remaining when started.

5. Proceed through the remaining valves, one at a time. Make sure the valve faces, sets, cylinder ports and valve guides are clean before reassembling the valve train.

Crankshaft Pulley (Vibration Damper)

REMOVAL AND INSTALLATION

1. Remove the fan shroud, as required. If necessary, drain the cooling system and remove the radiator.

Remove drive belts from pulley.

CAUTION: *When draining the coolant, keep in mind that cats and dogs are attracted by the ethylene glycol antifreeze, and are quite likely to drink any that is left in an uncovered container or in puddles on the ground. This will prove fatal in sufficient quantity. Always drain the coolant into a sealable container. Coolant should be reused unless it is contaminated or several years old.*

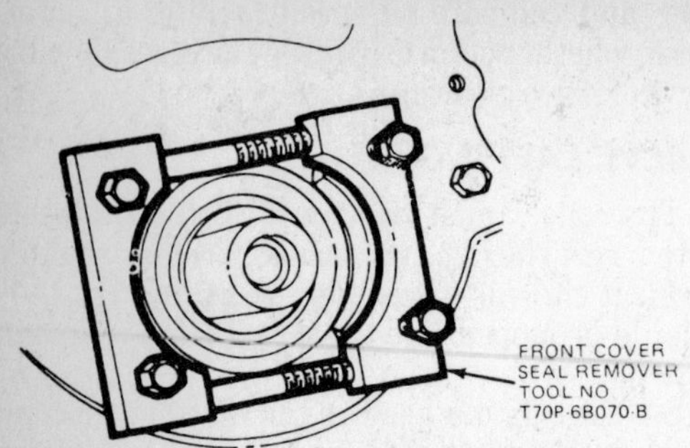

Removing the front crankshaft seal on gasoline V8s

2. On those engines with a separate pulley, remove the retaining bolts and separate the pulley from the vibration damper.

3. Remove the vibration damper/pulley retaining bolt from the crankshaft end.

4. Using a puller, remove the damper/pulley from the crankshaft.

5. Upon installation, align the key slot of the pulley hub to the crankshaft key. Complete the assembly in the reverse order of removal.

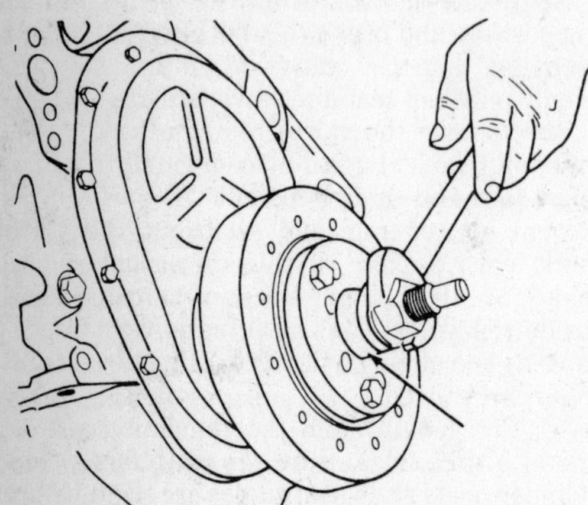
Vibration damper installation on gasoline V8s

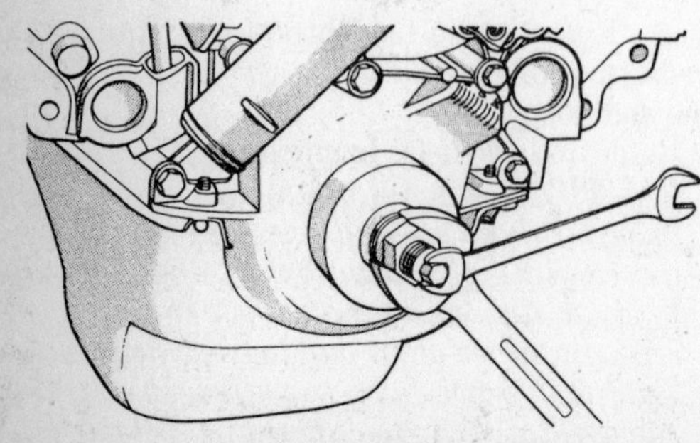
Installing the front crankshaft seal on gasoline V8s

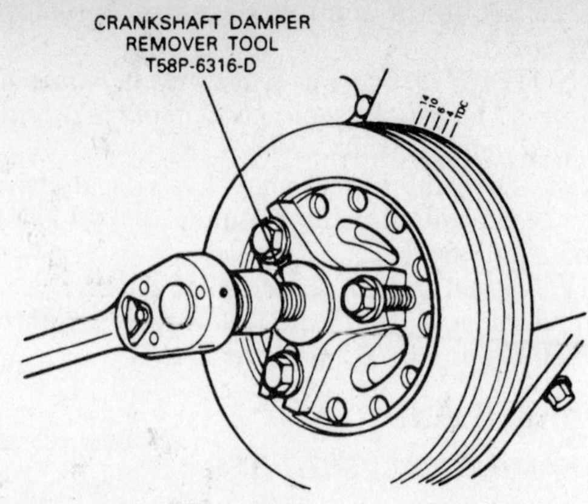

Removing the 6–4.9L crankshaft damper

Torque the retaining bolts to the specifications found in the Torque Specifications Chart.

Oil Pan

REMOVAL AND INSTALLATION

6–4.9L

1. Drain the crankcase and also drain the cooling system.

CAUTION: *When draining the coolant, keep in mind that cats and dogs are attracted by the ethylene glycol antifreeze, and are quite likely to drink any that is left in an uncovered container or in puddles on the ground. This will prove fatal in sufficient quantity. Always drain the coolant into a sealable container. Coolant should be reused unless it is contaminated or several years old.*

2. Remove the radiator.

3. Raise the vehicle on a hoist.

4. Remove the engine front support insulator to support bracket nuts and washers on both supports. Raise the front of the engine with a transmission jack and wood block and place 1 in. (25mm) thick wood blocks between the front support insulators and support brackets. Lower the engine and remove the transmission jack.

5. Remove the oil pan attaching bolts and lower the pan to the crossmember. Remove the 2 oil pump inlet tube and screw assembly bolts and drop the assembly in the pan. Remove the oil pan. Remove the oil pump inlet tube attaching bolts. Remove the inlet tube and screen assembly from the oil pump and leave it in the bottom of the oil pan. Remove the oil pan gaskets. Remove the inlet tube and screen from the oil pan.

6. Clean the gasket surfaces of the oil pump, oil pan and cylinder block. Remove the rear main bearing cap to oil pan seal and cylin-

der front cover to oil pan seal. Clean the seal grooves.

7. Apply oil-resistant sealer in the cavities between the bearing cap and cylinder block. Install a new seal in the rear main bearing cap and apply a bead of oil-resistant sealer to the tapered ends of the seal.

8. Install new side gaskets on the oil pan with oil-resistant sealer. Position a new oil pan to cylinder front cover seal on the oil pan.

9. Clean the inlet tube and screen assembly and place it in the oil pan.

10. Position the oil pan under the engine. Install the inlet tube and screen assembly on the oil pump with a new gasket. Tighten the screws to 5–7 ft. lbs. Position the oil pan against the cylinder block and install the attaching bolts. Tighten the bolts in sequence to 10–12 ft. lbs.

11. Raise the engine with a transmission jack and remove the wood blocks from the engine front supports. Lower the engine until the front support insulators are positioned on the support brackets. Install the washers and nuts on the insulator studs and tighten the nuts.

12. Install the starter and connect the starter cable.

13. Lower the vehicle. Install the radiator.

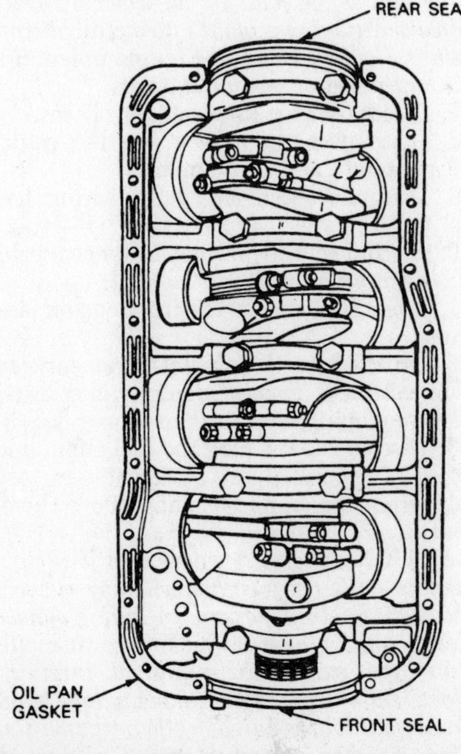

8–5.0L, 5.8L oil pan gaskets and seals

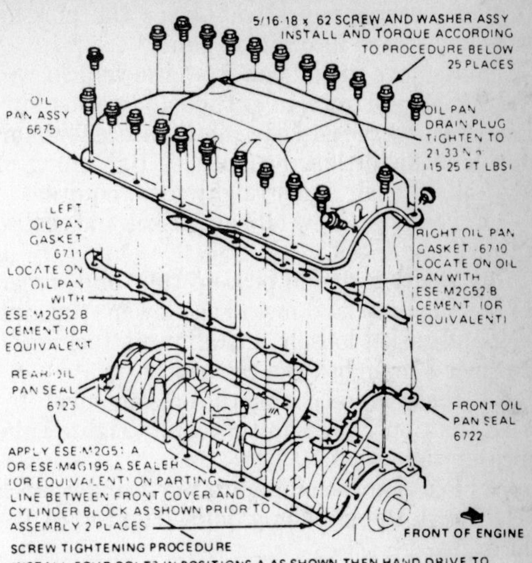

6–4.9L oil pan installation

14. Fill the crankcase and cooling system.

15. Start the engine and check for coolant and oil leaks.

8–5.0L
8–5.8L

1. Remove the oil dipstick (on pan entry models only).

2. Remove the bolts attaching the fan shroud to the radiator and position the shroud over the fan.

3. Remove the nuts and lock washers attaching the engine support insulators to the chassis bracket.

4. If equipped with an automatic transmission, disconnect the oil cooler line at the left side of the radiator.

5. Raise the engine and place wood blocks under the engine supports.

6. Drain the crankcase.

CAUTION: *The EPA warns that prolonged contact with used engine oil may cause a number of skin disorders, including cancer! You should make every effort to minimize your exposure to used engine oil. Protective gloves should be worn when changing the oil. Wash your hands and any other exposed skin areas as soon as possible after exposure to used engine oil. Soap and water, or waterless hand cleaner should be used.*

7. Remove the oil pan attaching bolts and lower the oil pan onto the crossmember.

8. Remove the two bolts attaching the oil pump pickup tube to the oil pump. Remove nut attaching oil pump pickup tube to the number

3 main bearing cap stud. Lower the pick-up tube and screen into the oil pan.

9. Remove the oil pan from the vehicle.

10. Clean oil pan, inlet tube and gasket surfaces. Inspect the gasket sealing surface for damages and distortion due to over tightening of the bolts. Repair and straighten as required.

11. Position a new oil pan gasket and seal to the cylinder block.

12. Position the oil pick-up tube and screen to the oil pump, and install the lower attaching bolt and gasket loosely. Install nut attaching to number 3 main bearing cap stud.

13. Place the oil pan on the crossmember. Install the upper pick-up tube bolt. Tighten the pick-up tube bolts.

14. Position the oil pan to the cylinder block and install the attaching bolts. Tighten to 10–12 ft. lbs.

8–7.5L

1. Raise and support the truck on jackstands. Remove the oil dipstick.

2. Remove the bolts attaching the fan shroud and position it over the fan.

3. Remove the engine support insulators-to-chassis bracket attaching nuts and washers. Disconnect the exhaust pipe at the manifolds.

4. If the vehicle is equipped with an automatic transmission, disconnect the oil cooler line at the left side of the radiator.

5. Raise the engine with a jack placed under the crankshaft damper and a block of wood to act as a cushion. Place wood blocks under the engine supports.

6. Drain the crankcase. Remove the oil filter.

CAUTION: *The EPA warns that prolonged contact with used engine oil may cause a number of skin disorders, including cancer! You should make every effort to minimize your exposure to used engine oil. Protective gloves should be worn when changing the oil. Wash your hands and any other exposed skin areas as soon as possible after exposure to used engine oil. Soap and water, or waterless hand cleaner should be used.*

7. Remove the oil pan attaching screws and lower the oil pan onto the crossmember. Remove the two bolts attaching the oil pump pick-up tube to the oil pump. Lower the assembly from the oil pump. Leave it on the bottom of the oil pan. Remove the oil pan and gaskets. Remove the inlet tube and screen from the oil pan.

8. In preparation for installation, clean the gasket surfaces of the oil pump, oil pan and cylinder block. Remove the rear main bearing cap-to-oil pan seal and engine front cover-to-oil pan seal. Clean the seal grooves.

9. Position the oil pan front and rear seal on the engine front cover and the rear main bearing cap, respectively. Be sure that the tabs on the seals are over the oil pan gasket.

10. Clean the inlet tube and screen assembly and place it in the oil pan.

11. Position the oil pan under the engine and install the inlet tube and screen assembly on the oil pump with a new gasket. Position the oil pan against the cylinder block and install the retaining bolts.

12. Assemble the rest of the engine in the reverse order of disassembly, starting with Step 7. Fill the crankcase with oil.

8–6.9, 8–7.3L Diesel

1. Disconnect both battery ground cables.

2. Remove the engine oil dipstick.

3. Remove the transmission oil dipstick.

4. Remove the air cleaner and cover the intake opening.

5. Remove the fan and fan clutch.

NOTE: *The fan uses left hand threads. Remove them by turning them clockwise.*

6. Drain the cooling system.

CAUTION: *When draining the coolant, keep in mind that cats and dogs are attracted by the ethylene glycol antifreeze, and are quite likely to drink any that is left in an uncovered container or in puddles on the ground. This will prove fatal in sufficient quantity. Always drain the coolant into a sealable container. Coolant should be reused unless it is contaminated or several years old.*

7. Disconnect the lower radiator hose.

8. Disconnect the power steering return hose and plug the line and pump.

9. Disconnect the alternator wiring harness.

10. Disconnect the fuel line heater connector from the alternator.

11. Raise and support the front end on jackstands.

12. On trucks with automatic transmission, disconnect the transmission cooler lines at the radiator and plug them.

13. Disconnect and plug the fuel pump inlet line.

14. Drain the crankcase and remove the oil filter.

CAUTION: *The EPA warns that prolonged contact with used engine oil may cause a number of skin disorders, including cancer! You should make every effort to minimize your exposure to used engine oil. Protective gloves should be worn when changing the oil. Wash your hands and any other exposed skin areas as soon as possible after exposure to used engine oil. Soap and water, or waterless hand cleaner should be used.*

15. Remove the engine oil filler tube.
16. Disconnect the exhaust pipes at the manifolds.
17. Disconnect the muffler inlet pipe from the muffler and remove the pipe.
18. Remove the upper inlet mounting stud from the right exhaust manifold.
19. Unbolt the engine from the No.1 crossmember.
20. Lower the vehicle.
21. Install lifting brackets on the front of the engine.
22. Raise the engine until the transmission contact the body.
23. Install wood blocks – 2 3/4 in. (70mm) on the left side; 2 in. (50mm) on the right side – between the engine insulators and crossmember.
24. Lower the engine onto the blocks.
25. Raise and support the front end on jackstands.
26. Remove the flywheel inspection plate.
27. Position fuel pump inlet line No.1 rearward of the crossmember and position the oil cooler lines out of the way.
28. Remove the oil pan bolts.
29. Lower the oil pan.

NOTE: *The oil pan is sealed to the crankcase with RTV silicone sealant in place of a gasket. It may be necessary to separate the pan from the crankcase with a utility knife.*

CHILTON TIP: *The crankshaft may have to be turned to allow the pan to clear the crankshaft throws.*

30. Clean the pan and crankcase mating surfaces thoroughly.

To install:

31. Apply a 1/8 in. (3mm) bead of RTV silicone sealant to the pan mating surfaces, and a 1/4 in. (6mm) bead on the front and rear covers and in the corners. You have 15 minutes within which to install the pan!
32. Install locating dowels (which you supply) into position as shown.
33. Position the pan on the engine and install the pan bolts loosely.
34. Remove the dowels.
35. Torque the pan bolts to 7 ft. lbs. for 1/4 in.-20 bolts; 14 ft. lbs. for 5/16 in.-18 bolts; 24 ft.lb for 3/8 in.-16 bolts.
36. Install the flywheel inspection cover.
37. Lower the truck.
38. Raise the engine and remove the wood blocks.
39. Lower the engine onto the crossmember and remove the lifting brackets.
40. Raise and support the front end on jackstands.
41. Torque the engine-to-crossmember nuts to 70 ft. lbs.
42. Install the upper inlet pipe mounting stud.
43. Install the inlet pipe, using a new gasket.
44. Install the transmission oil filler tube, using a new gasket.
45. Install the oil pan drain plug.
46. Install a new oil filter.
47. Connect the fuel pump inlet line. Make sure that the clip is installed on the crossmember.
48. Connect the transmission cooler lines.
49. Lower the truck.
50. Connect all wiring.
51. Connect the power steering return line.
52. Connect the lower radiator hose.
53. Install the fan and fan clutch.

NOTE: *The fan uses left hand threads. Install them by turning them counterclockwise.*

54. Remove the cover and install the air cleaner.
55. Install the dipsticks.
56. Fill the crankcase.
57. Fill and bleed the cooling system.
58. Fill the power steering reservoir.
59. Connect the batteries.
60. Run the engine and check for leaks.

Oil Pump

REMOVAL AND INSTALLATION

Gasoline Engines

1. Remove the oil pan.
2. Remove the oil pump inlet tube and screen assembly.
3. Remove the oil pump attaching bolts and remove the oil pump gasket and intermediate driveshaft.
4. Before installing the oil pump, prime it by filling the inlet and outlet port with engine

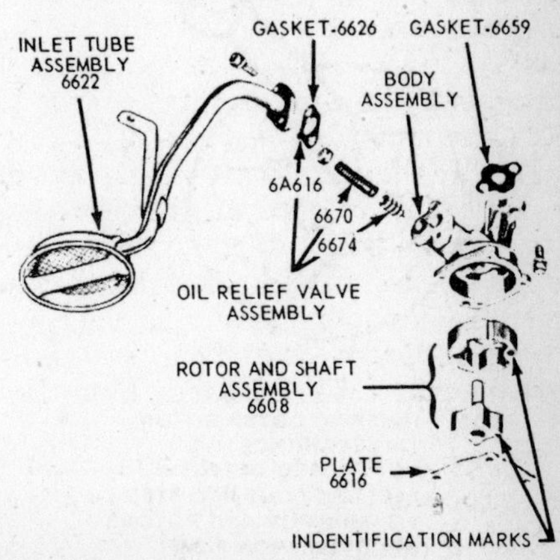

Exploded view of the V8 oil pump

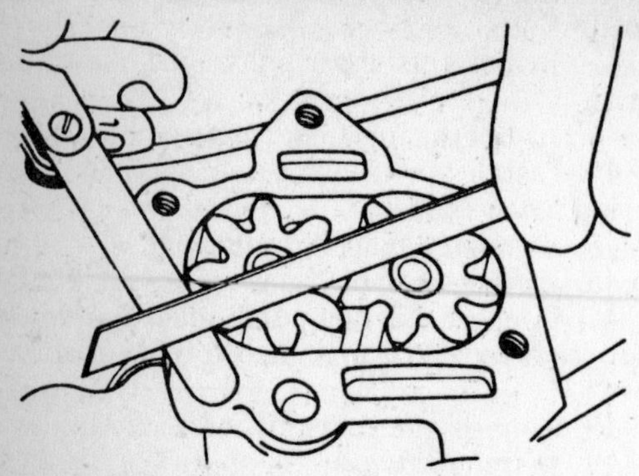

Checking rotor end play

oil and rotating the shaft of the pump to distribute it.

5. Position the intermediate driveshaft into the distributor socket.

6. Position the new gasket on the pump body and insert the intermediate driveshaft into the pump body.

7. Install the pump and intermediate driveshaft as an assembly. Do not force the pump if it does not seal readily. The driveshaft may be misaligned with the distributor shaft. To align it, rotate the intermediate driveshaft into a new position.

8. Install the oil pump attaching bolts and torque them to 12–15 ft. lbs. on the inline sixes and to 20–25 ft. lbs. on the V8s.

Diesel Engines

1. Remove the oil pan.
2. Remove the oil pick-up tube from the pump.
3. Unbolt and remove the oil pump.

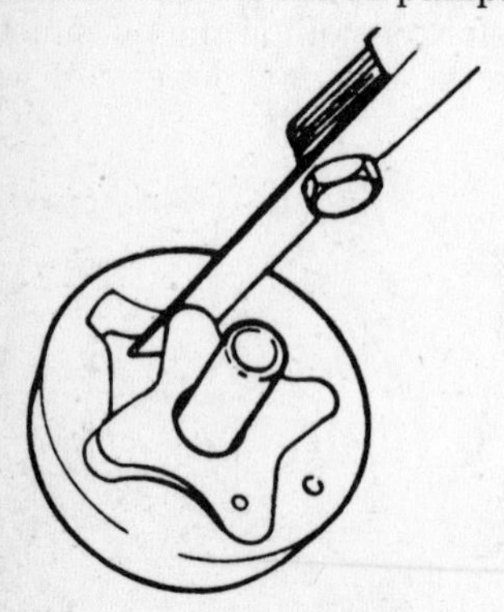

NOTE: INNER TO OUTER ROTOR TIP CLEARANCE MUST NOT EXCEED .012 WITH FEELER GAUGE INSERTED 1/2" MINIMUM AND ROTORS REMOVED FROM PUMP HOUSING.

Checking inner rotor tip clearance

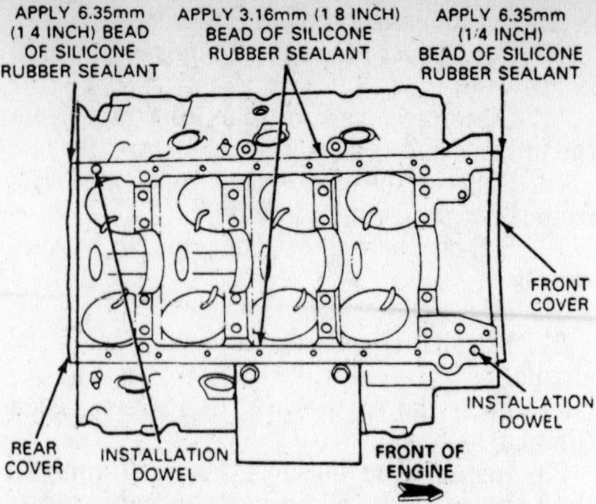

RTV sealant and dowel location for the diesel oil pan

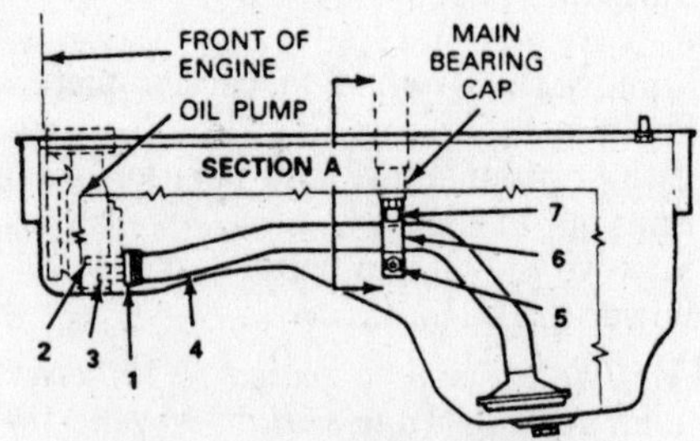

1. OIL PICK-UP TUBE MOUNTING GASKET
2. 5/16"-18 × 2" BOLT AND 5/16" HARDENED WASHER
3. 5/16"-18 × 1-1/2" BOLT AND 5/16" HARDENED WASHER
4. OIL PICK-UP TUBE ASSEMBLY
5. 5/16"-18 × 0.930 BOLT W/WASHER
6. OIL TUBE BRACKET
7. 5/16"-18 NUT AND 5/16" LOCK AND HARDENED WASHERS

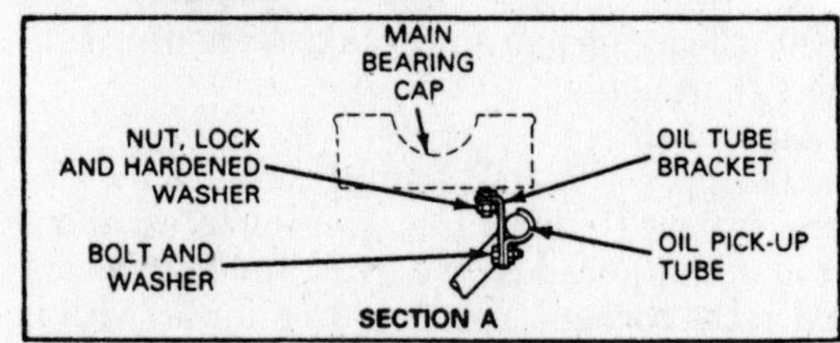

Diesel oil pick-up tube installation

4. Assemble the pick-up tube and pump. Use a new gasket.

5. Install the oil pump and torque the bolts to 14 ft. lbs.

OVERHAUL

1. Wash all parts in solvent and dry them thoroughly with compressed air. Use a brush to clean the inside of the pump housing and the pressure relief valve chamber. Be sure all dirt and metal particles are removed.

2. Check the inside of the pump housing and the outer race and rotor for damage or excessive wear or scoring.

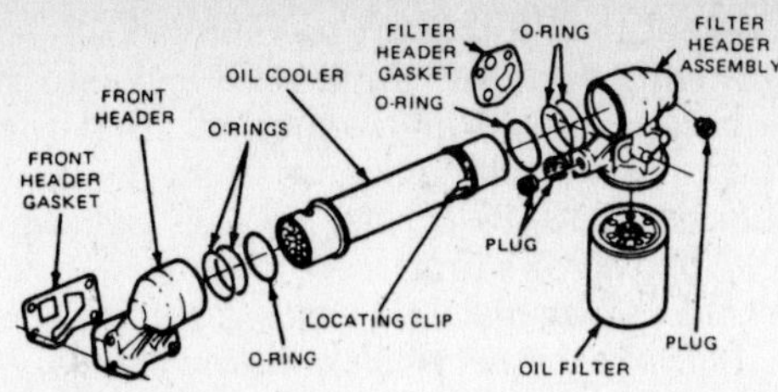

Diesel oil cooler

3. Check the mating surface of the pump cover for wear. If the cover mating surface is worn, scored, or grooved, replace the pump.

4. Measure the inner rotor tip clearance.

5. With the rotor assembly installed in the housing, place a straight edge over the rotor assembly and the housing. Measure the clearance (rotor end play) between the straight edge and the rotor and the outer race.

6. Check the drive shaft to housing bearing clearance by measuring the OD of the shaft and the ID of the housing bearing.

7. Components of the oil pump are not serviced. If any part of the pump requires replacement, replace the complete pump assembly.

8. Inspect the relief valve spring to see if it is collapsed or worn.

9. Check the relief valve piston for scores and free operation in the bore.

Oil Cooler

REMOVAL AND INSTALLATION

6.9L and 7.3L Diesel

The diesel oil cooler should be disassembled if the cooler O-rings begin to leak.

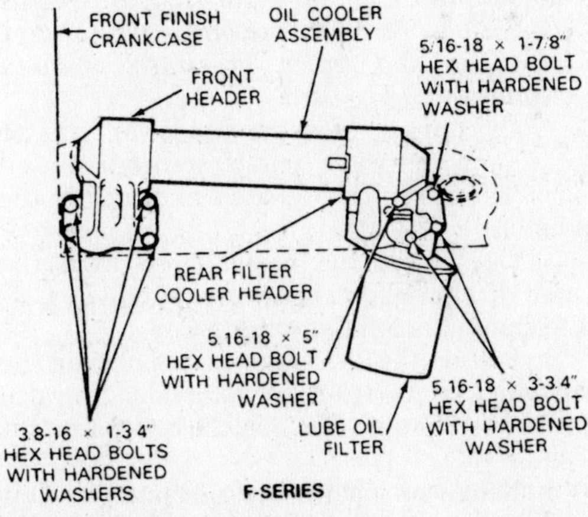

1988–90 diesel oil cooler

1. Gently rap the front and oil cooler headers to loosen the O-rings. Carefully twist the oil cooler apart.

2. Using a suitable solvent, thoroughly clean the oil cooler and the front and filter headers.

3. Always use new O-rings when reassembling. Lubricate the new rings and all O-ring mating surfaces with clean engine oil. Install the two narrow O-rings into their respective grooves inside the front and filter headers.

4. Place the large O-ring over the oil cooler shell.

5. Press the assembly together, making sure the locating clips align with the slots.

Timing Gear or Chain Front Cover and Oil Seal

REMOVAL AND INSTALLATION

6–4.9L

1. Drain the cooling system and disconnect the radiator upper hose at the coolant outlet elbow and remove the two upper radiator retaining bolts.

CAUTION: *When draining the coolant, keep in mind that cats and dogs are attracted by the ethylene glycol antifreeze, and are quite likely to drink any that is left in an uncovered container or in puddles on the ground. This will prove fatal in sufficient quantity.*

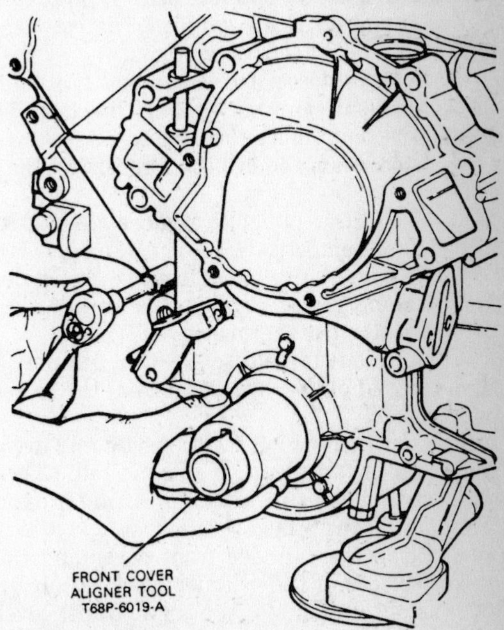

Aligning the front timing cover

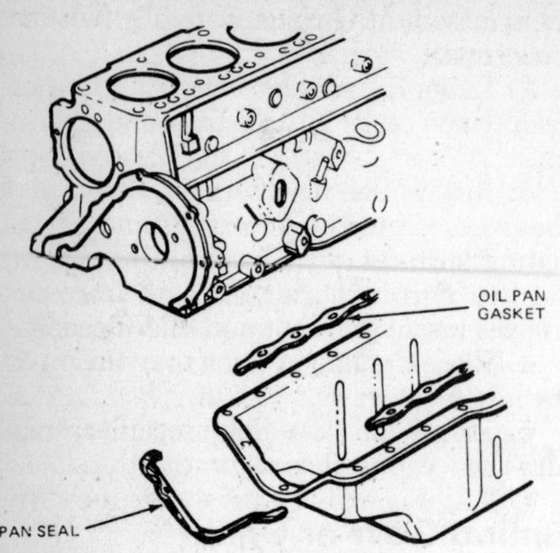

Front pan/cover seal, 6–4.9L engines

Always drain the coolant into a sealable container. Coolant should be reused unless it is contaminated or several years old.

2. Raise the vehicle and drain the crankcase.

CAUTION: *The EPA warns that prolonged contact with used engine oil may cause a number of skin disorders, including cancer! You should make every effort to minimize your exposure to used engine oil. Protective gloves should be worn when changing the oil. Wash your hands and any other exposed skin areas as soon as possible after exposure to used engine oil. Soap and water, or waterless hand cleaner should be used.*

3. Remove the splash shield and the automatic transmission oil cooling lines, if so equipped, then remove the radiator.
4. Loosen and remove the fan belt, fan and pulley.
5. Use a gear puller to remove the crankshaft pulley damper.
6. Remove the cylinder front cover retaining bolts and gently pry the cover away from the block. Remove the gasket.
7. Drive out the old seal with a pin punch from the rear of the cover. Clean out the recess in the cover.
8. Coat the new seal with grease and drive it into the cover until it is fully seated. Check the seal to make sure that the spring around the seal is in the proper position.
9. Clean the cylinder front cover and the gasket surface of the cylinder block. Apply an oil-resistant sealer to the new front cover gasket and install the gasket onto the cover.
10. Position the front cover assembly over the end of the crankshaft and against the cylinder block. Start, but do not tighten, the cover and pan attaching screws. Slide a front cover alignment tool (Ford part no. T68P–6019–A or equivalent) over the crank stub and into the seal bore of the cover. Tighten all front cover and oil pan attaching screws to 12–18 ft. lbs. front cover; 10–15 ft. lbs. oil pan, tightening the oil pan screws first.

NOTE: *Trim away the exposed portion of the old oil pan gasket flush with the front of the engine block. Cut and position the required portion of a new gasket to the oil pan and apply sealer to both sides.*

11. Lubricate the hub of the crankshaft damper pulley with Lubriplate® to prevent damage to the seal during installation or on initial starting of the engine.
12. Install and assemble the remaining components in the reverse order of removal, starting from Step 4. Start the engine and check for leaks.

Gasoline V8 Except 8–7.5L

1. Drain the cooling system and the crankcase.

CAUTION: *When draining the coolant, keep in mind that cats and dogs are attracted by the ethylene glycol antifreeze, and are quite likely to drink any that is left in an uncovered container or in puddles on the ground. This will prove fatal in sufficient quantity. Always drain the coolant into a sealable container. Coolant should be reused unless it is contaminated or several years old. The EPA warns that prolonged contact with used engine oil may cause a number of skin disorders, including cancer! You should make every effort to minimize your exposure to used engine oil. Protective gloves should be worn when changing the oil. Wash your hands and any other exposed skin areas as soon as possible after exposure to used engine oil. Soap and water, or waterless hand cleaner should be used.*

2. Disconnect the upper and lower radiator hoses from the water pump, transmission oil cooler lines from the radiator, and remove the radiator.
3. Disconnect the heater hose from the water pump. Slide the water pump by-pass hose clamp toward the water pump.
4. Loosen the alternator pivot bolt and the bolt which secures the alternator adjusting arm to the water pump. Position the alternator out of the way.
5. Remove the power steering pump and air conditioning compressor from their mounting brackets, if so equipped.
6. Remove the bolts holding the fan shroud to the radiator, if so equipped. Remove the fan, spacer, pulley and drive belts.
7. Remove the crankshaft pulley from the

crankshaft damper. Remove the damper attaching bolt and washer and remove the damper with a puller.

8. Disconnect the fuel pump outlet line at the fuel pump. Disconnect the vacuum inlet and outlet lines from the fuel pump. Remove the fuel pump attaching bolts and lay the pump to one side with the fuel inlet line still attached.

9. Remove the oil level dipstick and the bolt holding the dipstick tube to the exhaust manifold on the 8–5.0L.

10. Remove the oil pan-to-cylinder front cover attaching bolts. Use a sharp, thin cutting blade to cut the oil pan gasket flush with the cylinder block. Remove the front cover and water pump as an assembly.

11. Discard the front cover gasket.

12. Place the front seal removing tool (Ford part no. T70P–6B070–A or equivalent) into the front cover plate and over the front of the seal as shown in the illustration. Tighten the two through bolts to force the seal puller under the seal flange, then alternately tighten the four puller bolts a half turn at a time to pull the oil seal from the cover.

13. Coat a new front cover oil seal with Lubriplate® or equivalent and place it onto the front oil seal alignment and installation tool (Ford part no. T70P–6B070–A or equivalent) as shown in the illustration. Place the tool and the seal onto the end of the crankshaft and push it toward the engine until the seal starts into the front cover.

14. Place the installation screw, washer, and nut onto the end of the crankshaft, then thread the screw into the crankshaft. Tighten the nut against the washer and tool to force the seal into the front cover plate. Remove the tool.

15. Apply Lubriplate® or equivalent to the oil seal rubbing surface of the vibration damper inner hub to prevent damage to the seal. Coat the front of the crankshaft with engine oil for damper installation.

16. To install the damper, line up the damper keyway with the key on the crankshaft, then install the damper onto the crankshaft. Install the cap screw and washer, and tighten the screw to 80 ft. lbs. Install the crankshaft pulley.

17. Assemble the rest of the engine in the reverse order of disassembly.

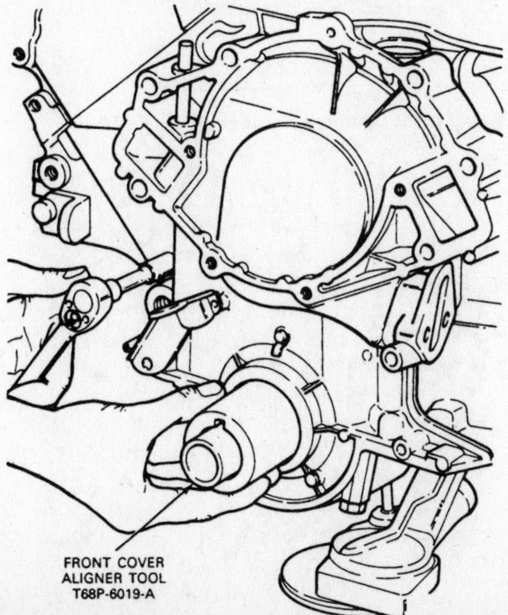

Aligning the front cover on the 8–7.5L

8–7.5L

1. Drain the cooling system and crankcase.

CAUTION: *When draining the coolant, keep in mind that cats and dogs are attracted by the ethylene glycol antifreeze, and are quite likely to drink any that is left in an uncovered container or in puddles on the ground. This will prove fatal in sufficient quantity. Always drain the coolant into a sealable container. Coolant should be reused unless it is contaminated or several years old. The EPA warns that prolonged contact with used engine oil may cause a number of skin disorders, including cancer! You should make every effort to minimize your exposure to used engine oil. Protective gloves should be worn when changing the oil. Wash your hands and any other exposed skin areas as soon as possible after exposure to used engine oil. Soap and water, or waterless hand cleaner should be used.*

2. Remove the radiator shroud and fan.

3. Disconnect the upper and lower radiator

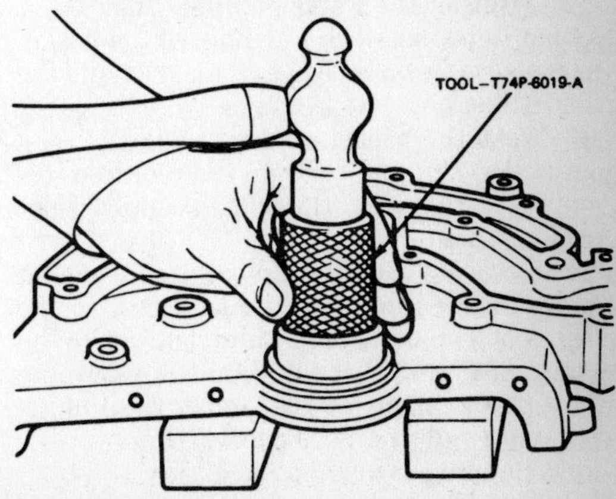

Installing oil seal into 7.5L V8 front cover. Tool makes it easier to drive in seal evenly

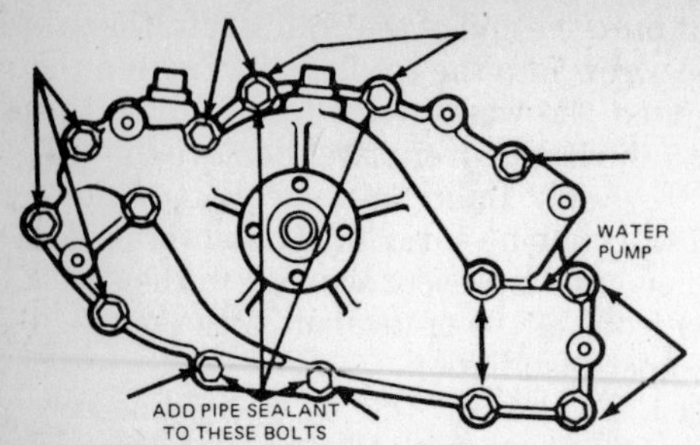

Water pump-to-front cover installation, diesel. The two top pump bolts must be no more then 1¼ in. long

hoses, and the automatic transmission oil cooler lines from the radiator.

4. Remove the radiator upper support and remove the radiator.

5. Loosen the alternator attaching bolts and air conditioning compressor idler pulley and remove the drive belts with the water pump pulley. Remove the bolts attaching the compressor support to the water pump and remove the bracket (support), if so equipped.

6. Remove the crankshaft pulley from the vibration damper. Remove the bolt and washer attaching the crankshaft damper and remove the damper with a puller. Remove the woodruff key from the crankshaft.

7. Loosen the by-pass hose at the water pump, and disconnect the heater return tube at the water pump.

8. Disconnect and plug the fuel inlet and outlet lines at the fuel pump, and remove the fuel pump.

9. Remove the bolts attaching the front cover to the cylinder block. Cut the oil pan seal flush with the cylinder block face with a thin knife blade prior to separating the cover from the cylinder block. Remove the cover and water pump as an assembly. Discard the front cover gasket and oil pan seal.

10. Transfer the water pump if a new cover is going to be installed. Clean all of the gasket sealing surfaces on both the front cover and the cylinder block.

11. Coat the gasket surface of the oil pan with sealer. Cut and position the required sections of a new seal on the oil pan. Apply sealer to the corners.

12. Drive out the old front cover oil seal with a pin punch. Clean out the seal recess in the cover. coat a new seal with Lubriplate® or equivalent grease. Install the seal, making sure the seal spring remains in the proper position. A front cover seal tool, Ford part no. T72J–117 or equivalent, makes installation easier.

13. Coat the gasket surfaces of the cylinder block and cover with sealer and position the new gasket on the block.

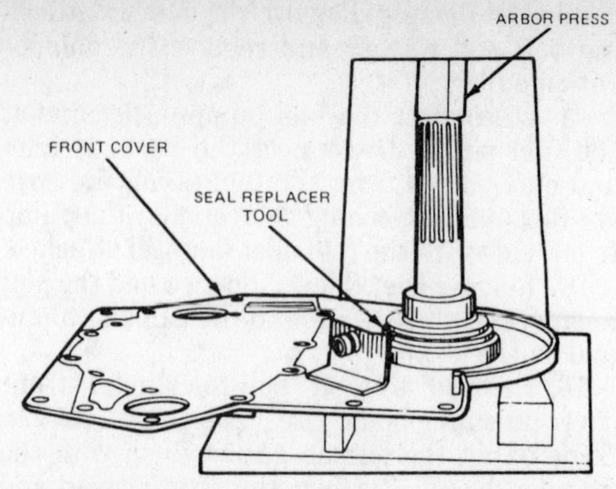

Diesel front oil seal removal and installation using an arbor press

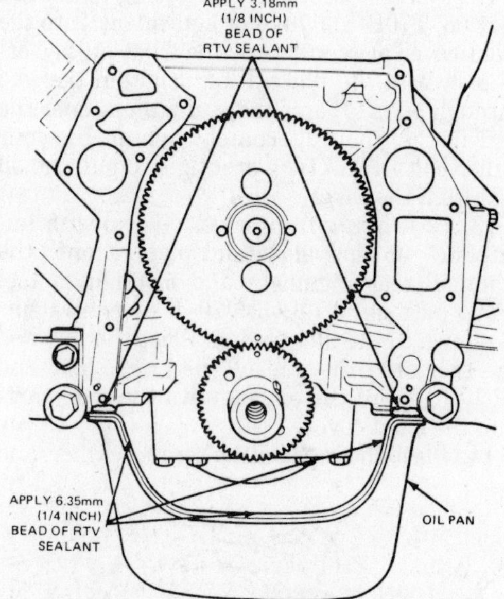

Diesel front cover sealer location

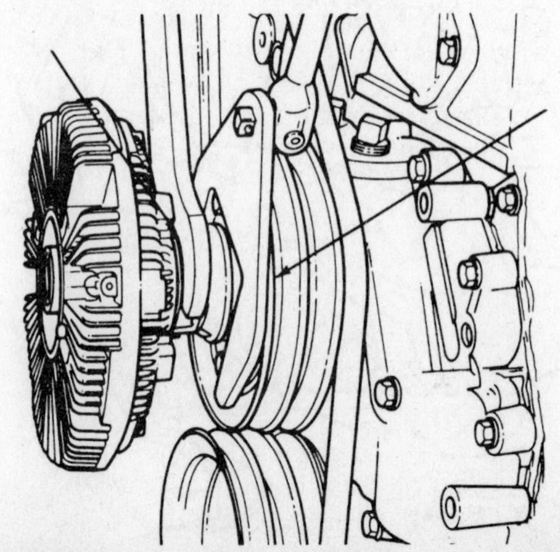
Removing the diesel fan clutch using a puller (arrows)

14. Position the front cover on the cylinder block. Use care not to damage the seal and gasket or misplace them.

15. Coat the front cover attaching screws with sealer and install them.

NOTE: *It may be necessary to force the front cover downward to compress the oil pan seal in order to install the front cover attaching bolts. Use a screwdriver or drift to engage the cover screw holes through the cover and pry downward.*

16. Assemble and install the remaining components in the reverse order of removal. Tighten the front cover bolts to 15–20 ft. lbs., the water pump attaching screws to 12–15 ft. lbs., the crankshaft damper to 70–90 ft. lbs., the crankshaft pulley to 35–50 ft. lbs., fuel pump to 19–27 ft. lbs., the oil pan bolts to 9–11 ft. lbs. for the $^5/_{16}$ in. screws and to 7–9 ft. lbs. for the $^1/_4$ in. screws, and the alternator pivot bolt to 45–57 ft. lbs.

6.9L and 7.3L Diesel

1. Disconnect both battery ground cables. Drain the cooling system.

CAUTION: *When draining the coolant, keep in mind that cats and dogs are attracted by the ethylene glycol antifreeze, and are quite likely to drink any that is left in an uncovered container or in puddles on the ground. This will prove fatal in sufficient quantity. Always drain the coolant into a sealable container. Coolant should be reused unless it is contaminated or several years old.*

2. Remove the air cleaner and cover the air intake on the manifold with clean rags. Do not allow any foreign material to enter the intake.
3. Remove the radiator fan shroud halves.
4. Remove the fan and fan clutch assembly. You will need a puller or ford tool No. T83T-6312-A for this.

NOTE: *The nut is a left hand thread; remove by turning the nut clockwise.*

5. Remove the injection pump as described in Chapter 5 under Diesel Fuel Systems.
6. Remove the water pump.

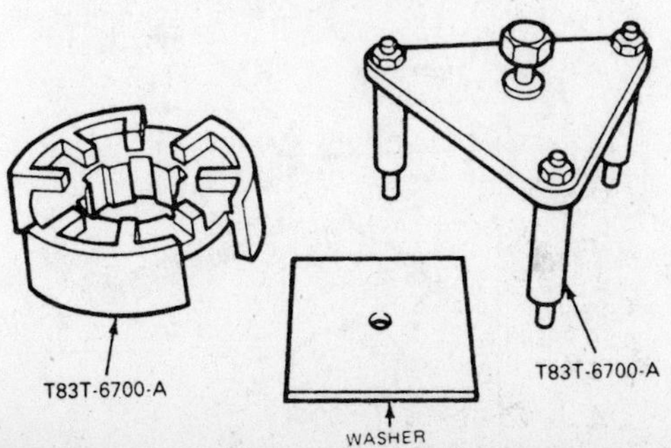

Tools for replacing the diesel front seal

7. Jack up the truck and safely support it with jackstands.
8. Remove the crankshaft pulley and vibration damper as described in this chapter.
9. Remove the engine ground cables at the front of the engine.
10. Remove the five bolts attaching the engine front cover to the engine block and oil pan.
11. Lower the truck.
12. Remove the front cover.

NOTE: *The front cover oil seal on the diesel must be driven out with an arbor press and a $3^1/_4$ in. (82.5mm) spacer. Take the cover to a qualified machinist or engine specialist for this procedure. See also steps 14 and 15.*

13. Remove all old gasket material from the front cover, engine block, oil pan sealing surfaces and water pump surfaces.
14. Coat the new front oil seal with Lubriplate® or equivalent grease.
15. The new seal must be installed using a seal installation tool, Ford part no. T83T-6700-A or an arbor press. A qualified machinist or engine specialist can handle seal installation as well as removal. When the seal bottoms out on the front cover surface, it is installed at the proper depth.
16. Install alignment dowels into the engine block to align the front cover and gaskets.

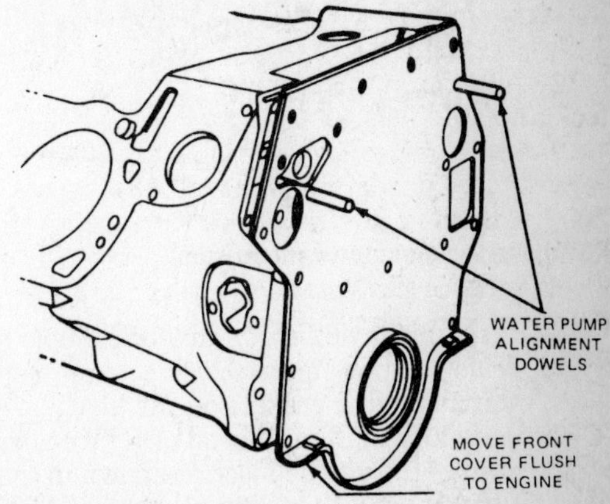

Front cover installation on diesel, showing alignment dowels

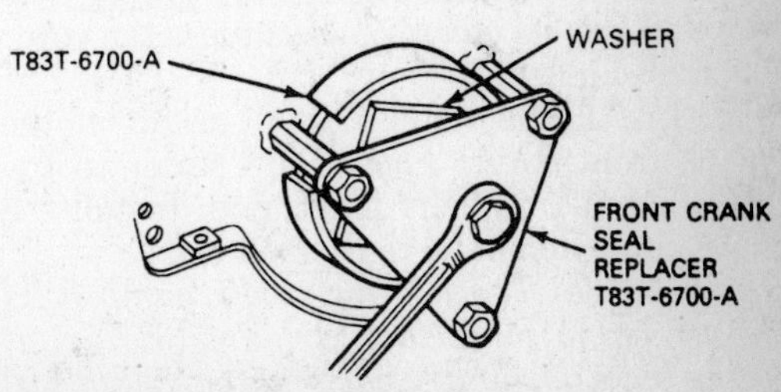

Diesel front seal installation

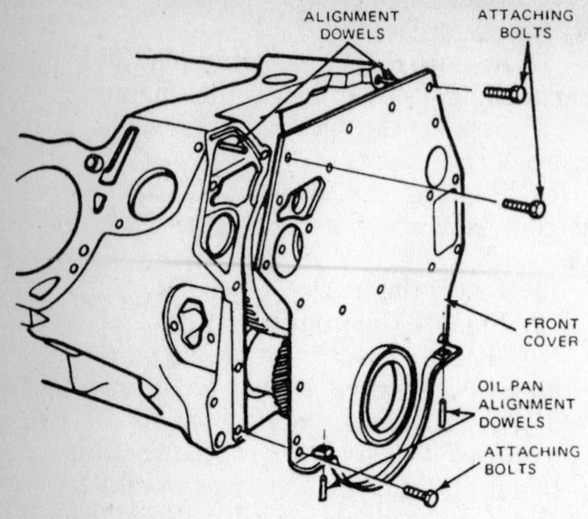

7.3L diesel front cover alignment dowels

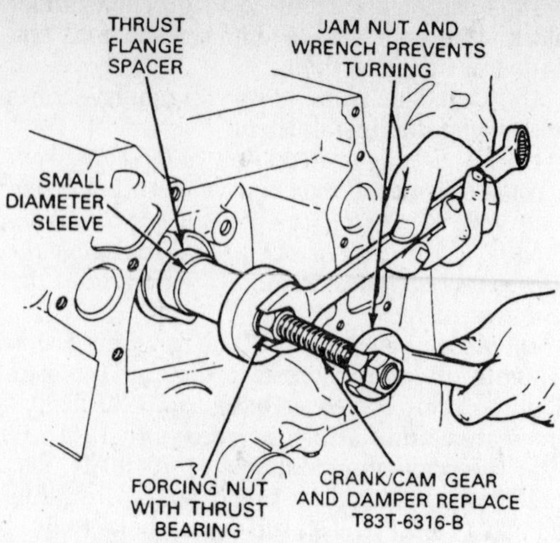

Installing the thrust flange spacer on the diesel

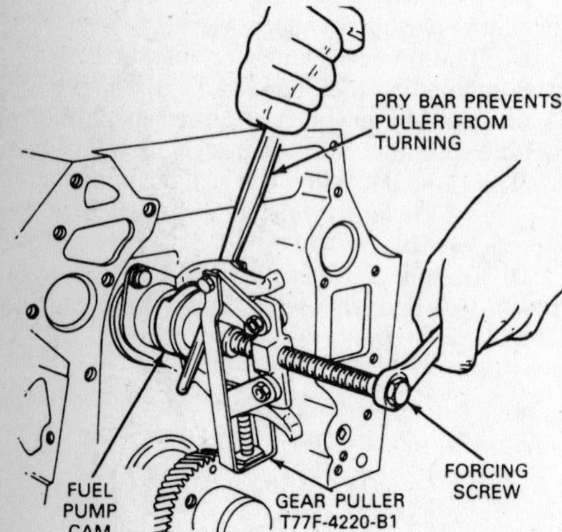

Removing the diesel fuel pump cam

These can be made out of round stock. Apply a gasket sealer to the engine block sealing surfaces, then install the gaskets on the block.

17. Apply a 1/8 in. (3mm) bead of RTV sealer on the front of the engine block as shown in the illustration. Apply a 1/4 in. (6mm) bead of RTV sealer on the oil pan as shown.

18. Install the front cover immediately after applying RTV sealer. The sealer will begin to cure and lose its effectiveness unless the cover is installed quickly.

19. Install the water pump gasket on the engine front cover. Apply RTV sealer to the four water pump bolts illustrated. Install the water pump and hand tighten all bolts.

WARNING: *The two top water pump bolts must be no more than 1¼ in. (31.75mm) long bolts any longer will interfere with (hit) the engine drive gears.*

20. Torque the water pump bolts to 19 ft. lbs. Torque the front cover bolts to specifications according to bolt size (see Torque Specifications chart).

21. Install the injection pump adaptor and injection pump as described in Chapter 5 under Diesel Fuel System.

22. Install the heater hose fitting in the pump using pipe sealant, and connect the heater hose to the water pump.

23. Jack up the truck and safely support it with jackstands.

24. Lubricate the front of the crankshaft with clean engine oil. Apply RTV sealant to the engine side of the retaining bolt washer to prevent oil seepage past the keyway. Install the crankshaft vibration damper using Ford Spe-

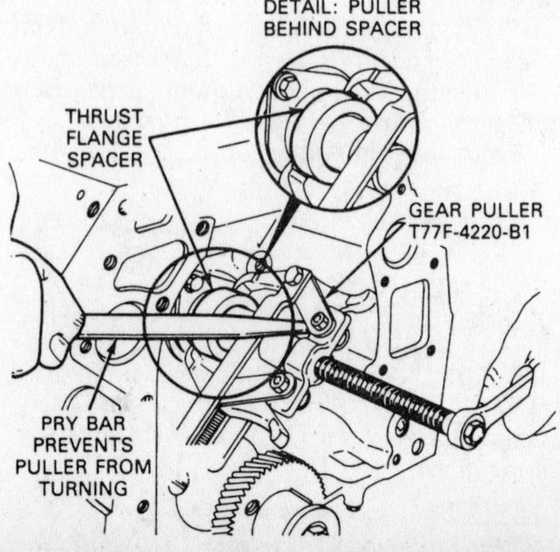

Removing the thrust flange spacer on the diesel

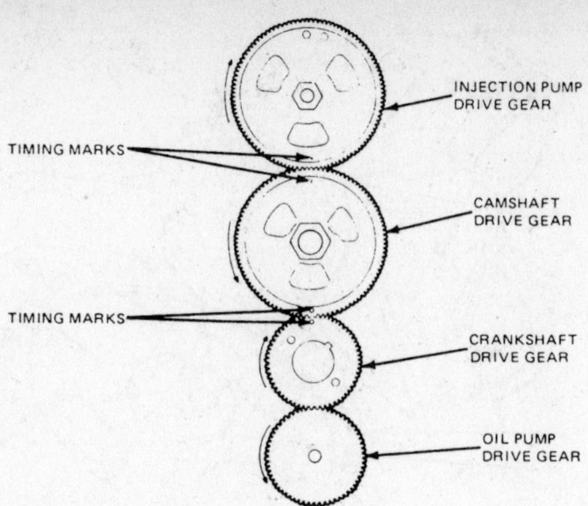

Diesel timing gear alignment

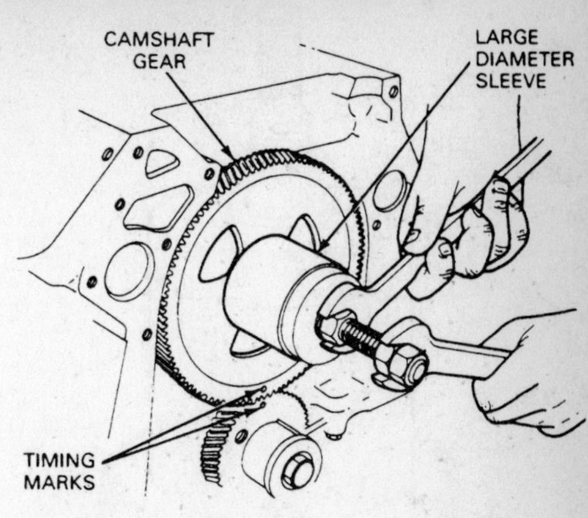

Installing the diesel camshaft gear

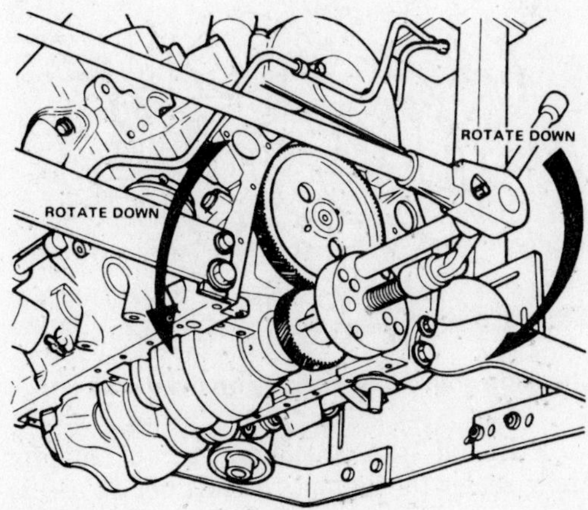

Diesel crankshaft drive gear removal; engine out of truck

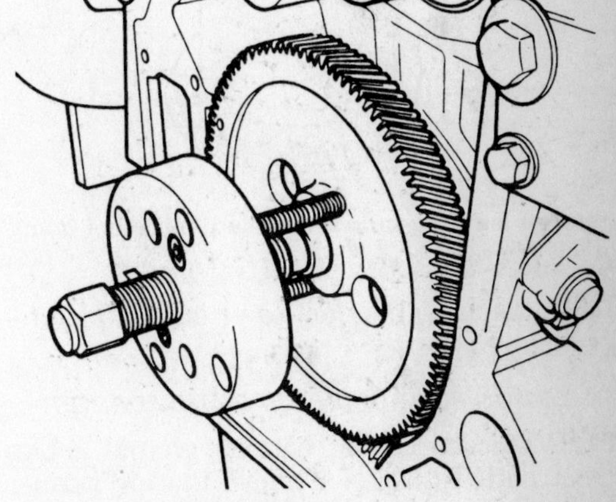

Removing the diesel camshaft timing gear

cial tools T83T–6316B. Torque the damper-to-crankshaft bolt to 90 ft. lbs.

25. Install the remaining engine components in the reverse order of removal.

CRANKSHAFT DRIVE GEAR

1. Complete the front cover removal procedures.
2. Install the crankshaft drive gear remover Tool T83T–6316–A, and using a breaker bar to prevent crankshaft rotation, or flywheel holding Tool T74R–6375–A, remove the crankshaft gear.
3. Install the crankshaft gear using Tool T83T–6316–B aligning the crankshaft drive gear timing mark with the camshaft drive gear timing mark.

NOTE: *The gear may be heated to 300–350°F (149–260°C) for ease of installation. Heat it in an oven. Do not use a torch.*

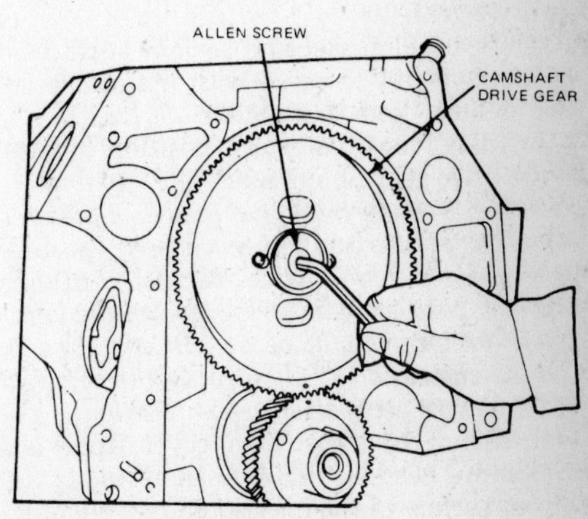

V8 diesel camshaft timing gear installation

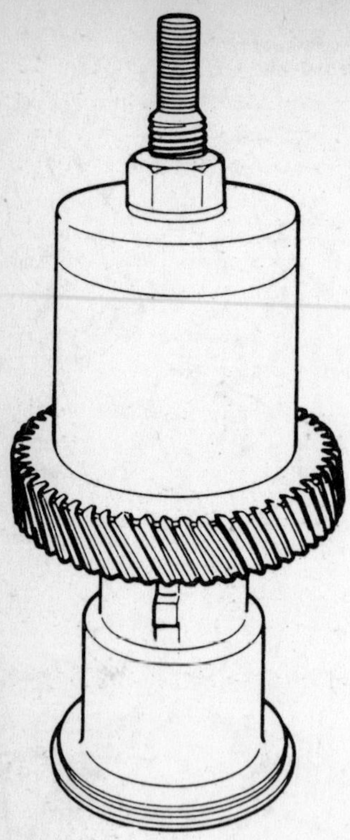

Special installation tool installed on diesel crankshaft drive gear

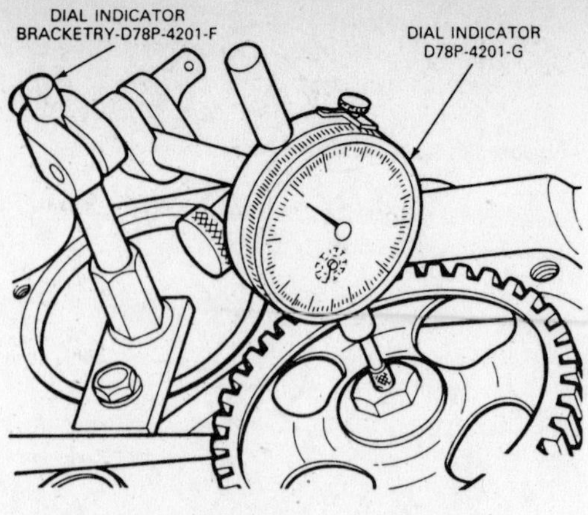

Checking camshaft endplay on the diesel

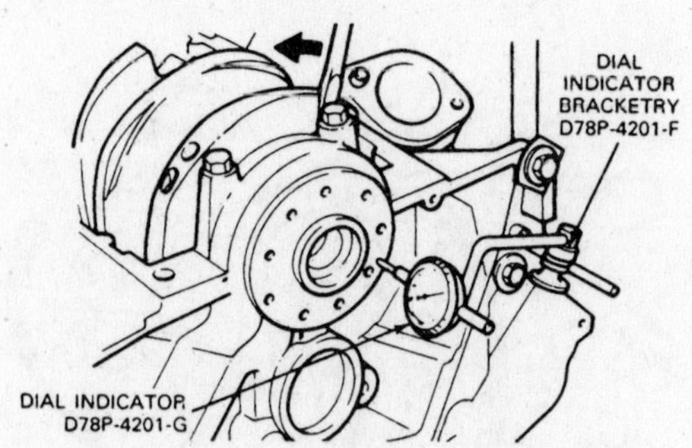

Checking crankshaft endplay on the diesel

4. Complete the front cover installation procedures.

INJECTION PUMP DRIVE GEAR AND ADAPTER

1. Disconnect the battery ground cables from both batteries. Remove the air cleaner and install an intake opening cover.
2. Remove the injection pump. Remove the bolts attaching the injection pump adapter to the engine block, and remove the adapter.
3. Remove the engine front cover. Remove the drive gear.
4. Clean all gasket and sealant surfaces of the components removed with a suitable solvent and dry them thoroughly.
5. Install the drive gear in position, aligning all the drive gear timing marks.

NOTE: *To determine that the No. 1 piston is at TDC of the compression stroke, position the injection pump drive gear dowel at the 4 o'clock position. The scribe line on the vibration damper should be at TDC. Use extreme care to avoid disturbing the injection pump drive gear, once it is in position.*

6. Install the engine front cover. Apply a 1/8 in. (3mm) bead of RTV Sealant along the bottom surface of the injection pump adapter.

NOTE: *RTV should be applied immediately prior to adapter installation.*

7. Install the injection pump adaptor. Apply sealer to the bolt threads before assembly.

NOTE: *With the injection pump adapter installed, the injection pump drive gear cannot jump timing.*

8. Install all removed components. Run the engine and check for leaks.

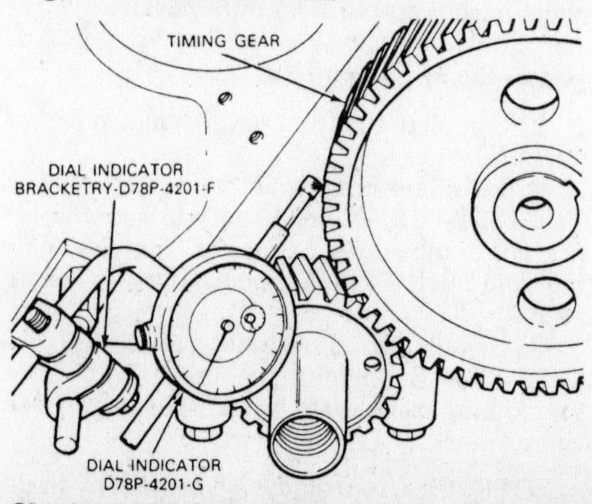

Checking drive gear backlash on the diesel

NOTE: *If necessary, purge the high pressure fuel lines of air by loosening the connector one half to one turn and crank the engine until a solid flow of fuel, free of air bubbles, flows from the connection.*

CAMSHAFT DRIVE GEAR, FUEL PUMP CAM, SPACER AND THRUST PLATE

1. Complete the front cover removal procedures.
2. Remove the camshaft allen screw.
3. Install a gear puller, Tool T83T–6316–A and remove the gear. Remove the fuel supply pump, if necessary.
4. Install a gear puller, Tool T77E–4220–B and shaft protector T83T–6316–A and remove the fuel pump cam and spacer, if necessary.
5. Remove the bolts attaching the thrust plate, and remove the thrust plate, if necessary.
6. Install a new thrust plate, if removed.
7. Install the spacer and fuel pump cam against the camshaft thrust flange, using installation sleeve and replacer Tool T83T–6316–B, if removed.
8. Install the camshaft drive gear against the fuel pump cam, aligning the timing mark with the timing mark on the crankshaft drive gear, using installation sleeve and replacer Tool T83T–6316–B.
9. Install the camshaft allen screw and tighten to 18 ft. lbs.
10. Install the fuel pump, if removed.
11. Install the front cover, following the previous procedure.

CHECKING TIMING CHAIN DEFLECTION

To measure timing chain deflection, rotate the crankshaft clockwise to take up slack on the left side of chain. Choose a reference point and measure the distance from this point and the chain. Rotate the crankshaft in the opposite direction to take up slack on the right side of the chain. Force the left (slack) side of the chain out and measure the distance to the reference point chosen earlier. The difference between the two measurements is the deflection.

The timing chain should be replaced if the deflection measurement exceeded the specified

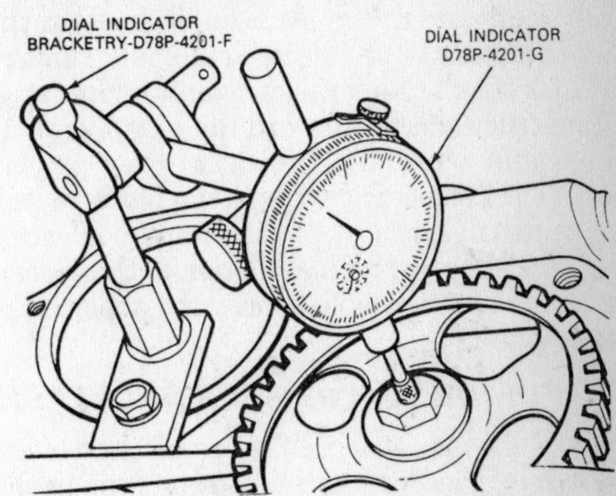

Checking camshaft endplay on gasoline V8s

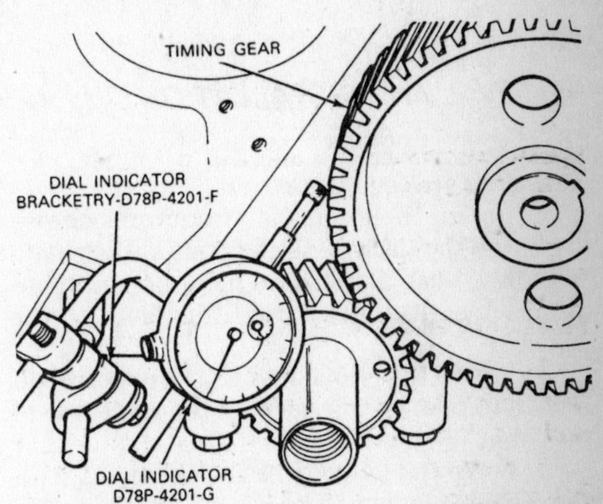

Checking timing gear backlash on the diesel

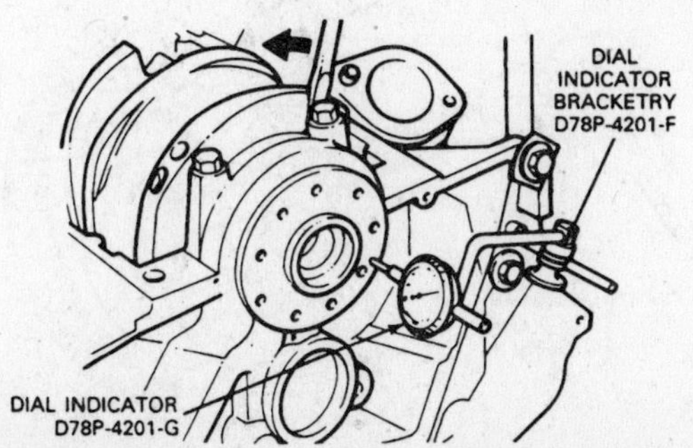

Checking crankshaft endplay on the diesel

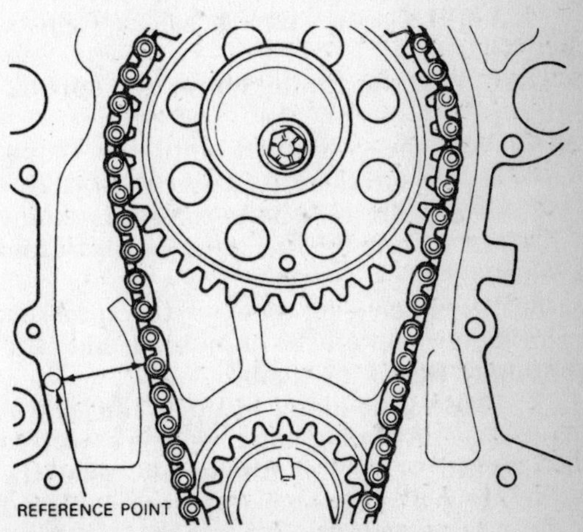

Checking V8 timing chain deflection

limit. The deflection measurement should not exceed 1/2 in. (13mm).

CAMSHAFT ENDPLAY MEASUREMENT

The camshaft gears used on some engines are easily damaged if pried upon while the valve train load is on the camshaft. Loosen the rocker arm nuts or rocker arm shaft support bolts before checking the camshaft endplay.

Push the camshaft toward the rear of engine, install and zero a dial indicator, then pry between the camshaft gear and the block to pull the camshaft forward. If the endplay is excessive, check for correct installation of the spacer. If the spacer is installed correctly, replace the thrust plate.

MEASURING TIMING GEAR BACKLASH

Use a dial indicator installed on block to measure timing gear backlash. Hold the gear firmly against the block while making the measurement. If excessive backlash exists, replace both gears.

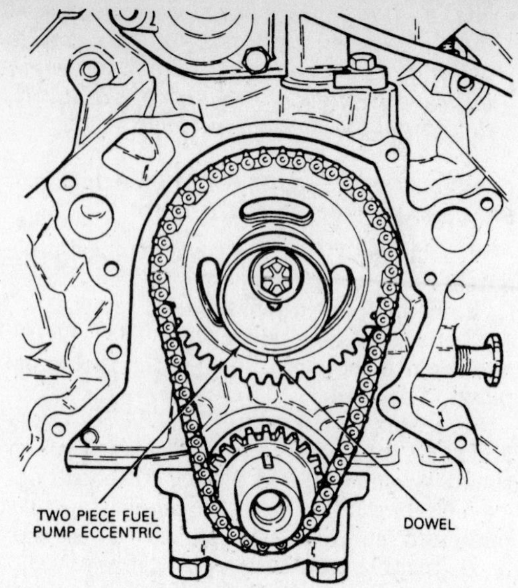

Fuel pump eccentric installed on the 8–5.0L and 8–5.8L

Timing Chain

REMOVAL AND INSTALLATION

V8 Gasoline Engines

1. Remove the front cover.
2. Rotate the crankshaft counterclockwise to take up the slack on the left side of the chain.
3. Establish a reference point on the cylinder block and measure from this point to the chain.
4. Rotate the crankshaft in the opposite direction to take up the slack on the right side of the chain.
5. Force the left side of the chain out with your fingers and measure the distance between the reference point and the chain. The timing chain deflection is the difference between the two measurements. If the deflection exceeds 1/2 in. (13mm), replace the timing chain and sprockets.

To replace the timing chain and sprockets:

6. Turn the crankshaft until the timing marks on the sprockets are aligned vertically.
7. Remove the camshaft sprocket retaining screw and remove the fuel pump eccentric and washers.
8. Alternately slide both of the sprockets and timing chain off the crankshaft and camshaft until free of the engine.
9. Position the timing chain on the sprockets so that the timing marks on the sprockets are aligned vertically. Alternately slide the sprockets and chain onto the crankshaft and camshaft sprockets.
10. Install the fuel pump eccentric washers

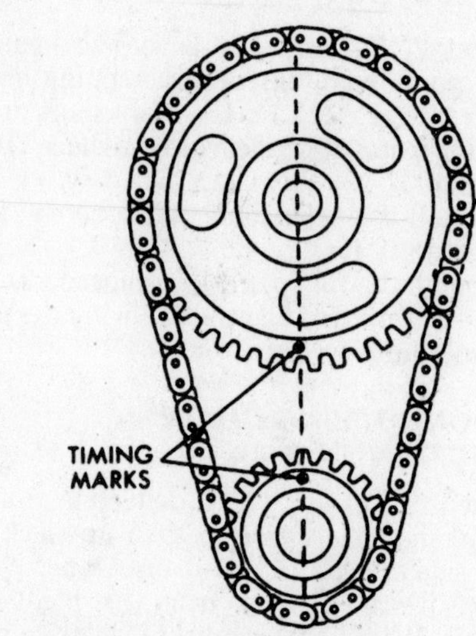

V8 timing chain installation

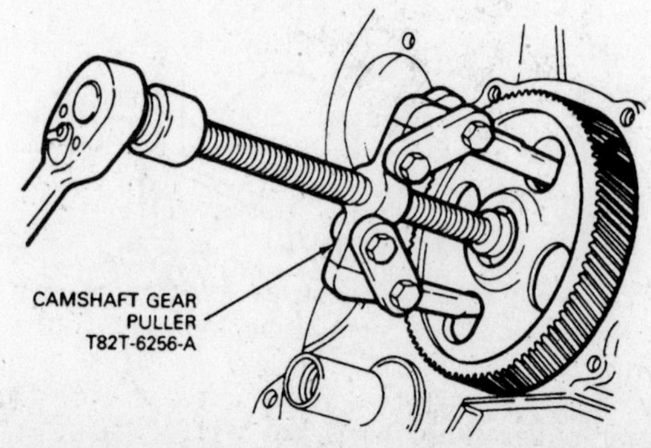

Removing the camshaft gear from the 6–4.9L

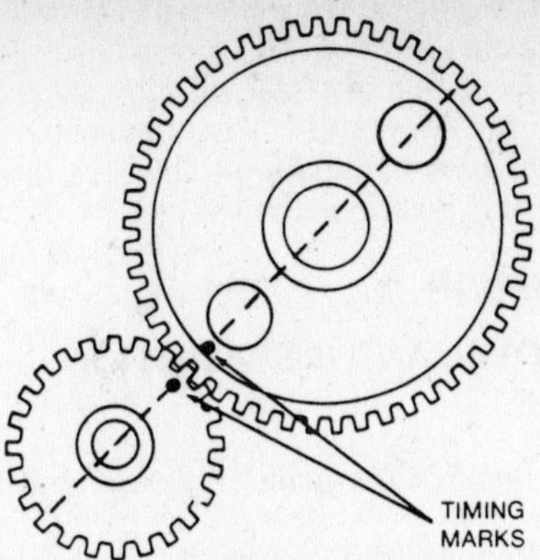

6–4.9L timing gear mark alignment

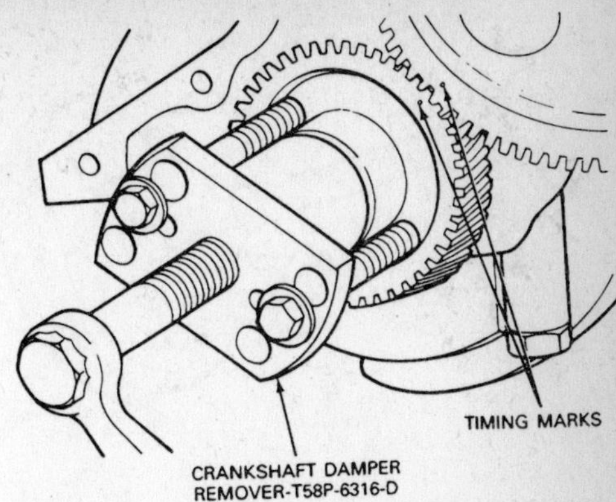

Removing the crankshaft gear from the 6–4.9L

and attaching bolt on the camshaft sprocket. Tighten to 40–45 ft. lbs.

11. Install the front cover.

Timing Gears

REMOVAL AND INSTALLATION

6–4.9L

1. Drain the cooling system and remove the front cover.

CAUTION: *When draining the coolant, keep in mind that cats and dogs are attracted by the ethylene glycol antifreeze, and are quite likely to drink any that is left in an uncovered container or in puddles on the ground. This will prove fatal in sufficient quantity. Always drain the coolant into a sealable container. Coolant should be reused unless it is contaminated or several years old.*

2. Crank the engine until the timing marks on the camshaft and crankshaft gears are aligned.
3. Use a gear puller to removal both of the timing gears.
4. Before installing the timing gears, be sure that the key and spacer are properly installed. Align the gear key way with the key and install the gear on the camshaft. Be sure that the timing marks line up on the camshaft and the crankshaft gears and install the crankshaft gear.
5. Install the front cover, and assemble the rest of the engine in the reverse order of disassembly. Fill the cooling system.

6.9L and 7.3L Diesel

1. Follow the procedures for timing gear cover removal and installation, and remove the front cover.
2. To remove the crankshaft gear, install gear puller (Ford part) no. T83T–6316–A or equivalent, and using a breaker bar to prevent the crankshaft from rotating, remove the crankshaft gear. To install the crankshaft gear use tool (Ford part) no. T83T–6316–B or equivalent while aligning the timing marks as shown in the illustration, and press the gear into place.
3. The camshaft gear may be removed by taking out the Allen screw and installing a gear

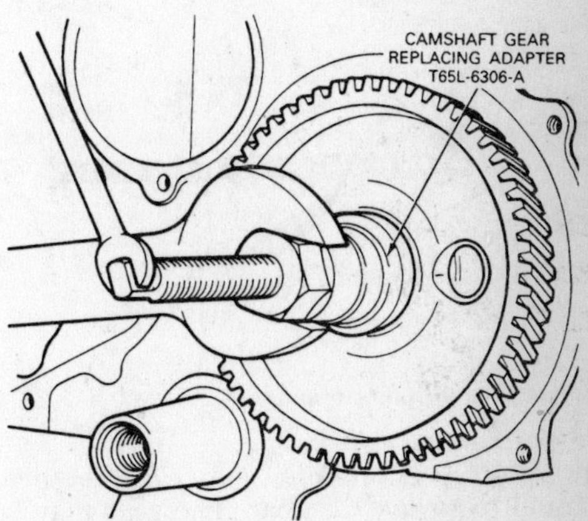

Installing the camshaft gear on the 6–4.9L

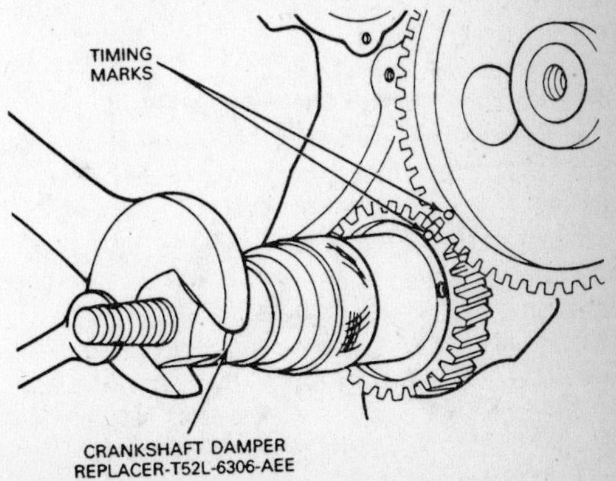

Installing the crankshaft gear on the 6–4.9L

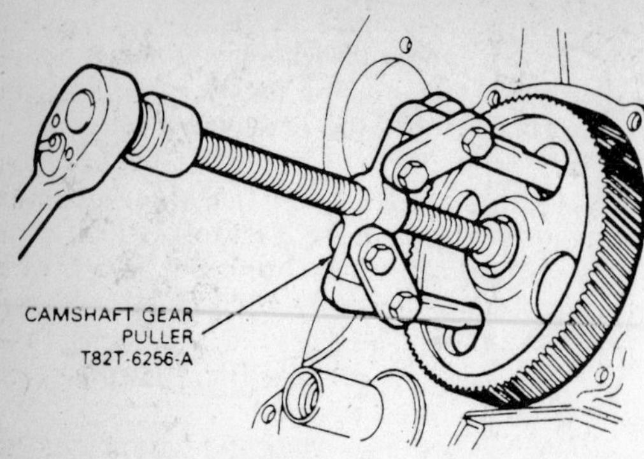

6–4.9L camshaft gear removal

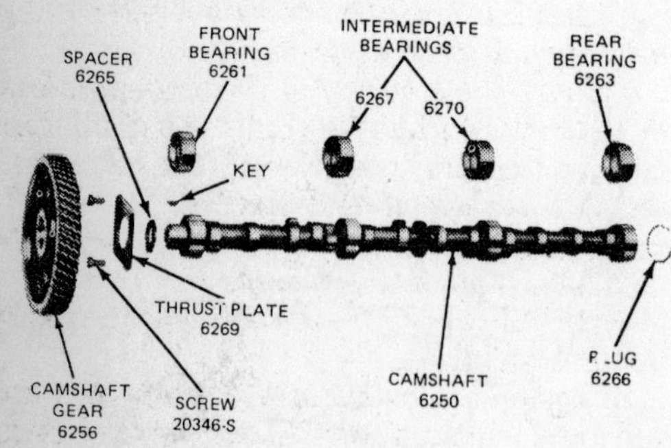

6–4.9L camshaft components

puller, Ford part no. T83T–6316–A or equivalent and removing the gear. The gear may be replaced by using tool (Ford part) no. T83T–6316–B or equivalent. Torque the Allen screw to 12–18 ft. lbs.

Front Cover Oil Seal

REMOVAL AND INSTALLATION

It is recommended to replace the cover seal any time the front cover is removed.

1. With the cover removed from the car, drive the old seal from the rear of cover with a pin punch. Clean out the recess in the cover.
2. Coat the new seal with grease and drive it into the cover until it is fully seated. Check the seal after installation to be sure the spring is properly positioned in the seal.

Camshaft

REMOVAL AND INSTALLATION

6–4.9L

1. Remove the grille, radiator, and timing cover.
2. Remove the distributor, fuel pump, oil pan and oil pump.
3. Align the timing marks. Unbolt the camshaft thrust plate, working through the holes in the camshaft gear.
4. Loosen the rocker arms, remove the pushrods, take off the side cover and remove the valve lifter with a magnet.
5. Remove the camshaft very carefully to prevent nicking the bearings.
6. Oil the camshaft bearing journals and use Lubriplate® or something similar on the lobes. Install the camshaft, gear, and thrust plate, aligning the gear marks. Tighten down the thrust plate. Make sure that the camshaft end-play is not excessive.
7. The last item to be replaced is the distributor. The rotor should be at the firing position for no. 1 cylinder, with the timing gear marks aligned.

V8 Including Diesel

NOTE: *Ford recommends removing the diesel engine for camshaft removal.*

1. Remove the intake manifold and valley pan, if so equipped.
2. Remove the rocker covers, and either remove the rocker arm shafts or loosen the rockers on their pivots and remove the pushrods.

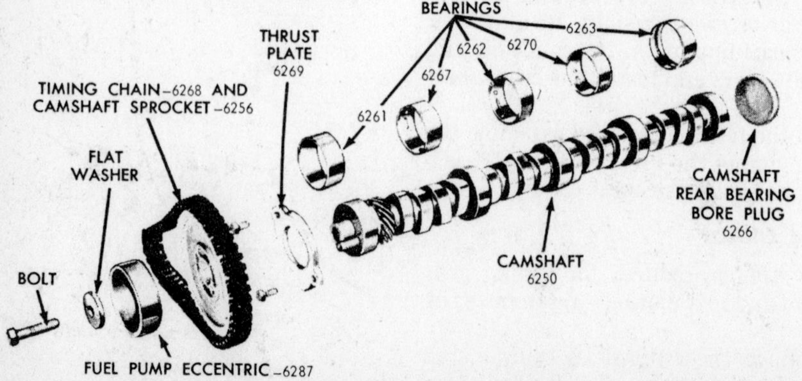

V8 camshaft and related parts

The pushrods must be reinstalled in their original positions.

3. Remove the valve lifters in sequence with a magnet. They must be replaced in their original positions.

4. Remove the timing gear cover and timing chain (timing gear on V8 diesel) and sprockets.

5. In addition to the radiator and air conditioning condenser, if so equipped, it may be necessary to remove the front grille assembly and the hook lock assembly to gain the necessary clearance to code the camshaft out of the front of the engine.

NOTE: *A camshaft removal tool, Ford part no. T65L–6250–A and adaptor 14–0314 are needed to remove the diesel camshaft.*

6. Coat the camshaft with engine oil liberally before installing it. Slide the camshaft into the engine very carefully so as not to scratch the bearing bores with the camshaft lobes. Install the camshaft thrust plate and tighten the attaching screws to 9–12 ft. lbs. Measure the camshaft end-play. If the end-play is more than 0.009 in. (0.228mm), replace the thrust plate. Assemble the remaining components in the reverse order of removal.

CHECKING CAMSHAFT

Camshaft Lobe Lift

Check the lift of each lobe in consecutive order and make a note of the reading.

1. Remove the fresh air inlet tube and the air cleaner. Remove the heater hose and crankcase ventilation hoses. Remove valve rocker arm cover(s).

2. Remove the rocker arm stud nut or fulcrum bolts, fulcrum seat and rocker arm.

3. Make sure the pushrod is in the valve tappet socket. Install a dial indicator D78P–4201–B or equivalent. so that the actuating point of the indicator is in the push rod socket (or the indicator ball socket adaptor tool 6565–AB is on the end of the push rod) and in the same plane as the push rod movement.

4. Disconnect the I terminal and the S terminal at the starter relay. Install an auxiliary starter switch between the battery and S terminals of the start relay. Crank the engine with the ignition switch off. Turn the crankshaft over until the tappet is on the base circle of the camshaft lobe. At this position, the push rod will be in its lowest position.

5. Zero the dial indicator. Continue to rotate the crankshaft slowly until the push rod is in the fully raised position.

6. Compare the total lift recorded on the dial indicator with the specification shown on the Camshaft Specification chart.

To check the accuracy of the original indicator reading, continue to rotate the crankshaft until the indicator reads zero. If the left on any lobe is below specified wear limits listed, the camshaft and the valve tappet operating on the worn lobe(s) must be replaced.

7. Install the dial indicator and auxiliary starter switch.

8. Install the rocker arm, fulcrum seat and stud nut or fulcrum bolts. Check the valve clearance. Adjust if required (refer to procedure in this chapter).

9. Install the valve rocker arm cover(s) and the air cleaner.

Camshaft End Play

NOTE: *On all gasoline V8 engines, prying against the aluminum-nylon camshaft sprocket, with the valve train load on the camshaft, can break or damage the sprocket. Therefore, the rocker arm adjusting nuts must be backed off, or the rocker arm and shaft assembly must be loosened sufficiently*

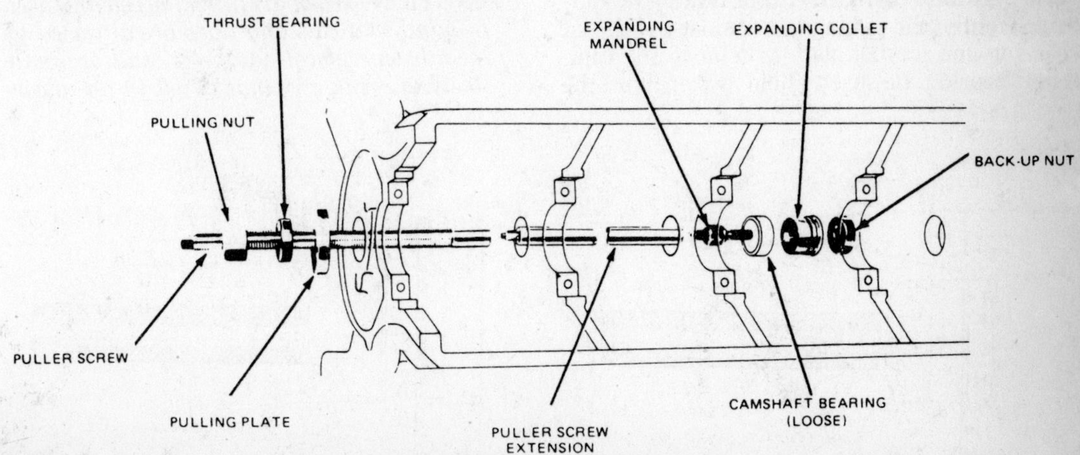

Camshaft bearing replacement

to free the camshaft. After checking the camshaft end play, check the valve clearance. Adjust if required (refer to procedure in this chapter).

1. Push the camshaft toward the rear of the engine. Install a dial indicator (Tool D78P–4201–F, –G or equivalent so that the indicator point is on the camshaft sprocket attaching screw.
2. Zero the dial indicator. Position a prybar between the camshaft gear and the block. Pull the camshaft forward and release it. Compare the dial indicator reading with the specifications.
3. If the end play is excessive, check the spacer for correct installation before it is removed. If the spacer is correctly installed, replace the thrust plate.
4. Remove the dial indicator.

CAMSHAFT BEARING REPLACEMENT

1. Remove the engine following the procedures in this chapter and install it on a work stand.
2. Remove the camshaft, flywheel and crankshaft, following the appropriate procedures. Push the pistons to the top of the cylinder.
3. Remove the camshaft rear bearing bore plug. Remove the camshaft bearings with Tool T65L–6250–A or equivalent.
4. Select the proper size expanding collet and back-up nut and assemble on the mandrel. With the expanding collet collapsed, install the collet assembly in the camshaft bearing and tighten the back-up nut on the expanding mandrel until the collet fits the camshaft bearing.
5. Assemble the puller screw and extension (if necessary) and install on the expanding mandrel. Wrap a cloth around the threads of the puller screw to protect the front bearing or journal. Tighten the pulling nut against the thrust bearing and pulling plate to remove the camshaft bearing. Be sure to hold a wrench on the end of the puller screw to prevent it from turning.
6. To remove the front bearing, install the puller from the rear of the cylinder block.
7. Position the new bearings at the bearing bores, and press them in place with tool T65L–6250–A or equivalent. Be sure to center the pulling plate and puller screw to avoid damage to the bearing. Failure to use the correct expanding collet can cause severe bearing damage. Align the oil holes in the bearings with the oil holes in the cylinder block before pressing bearings into place.

   NOTE: *Be sure the front bearing is installed 0.020–0.035 in. (0.508–0.889mm) for the inline six cylinder engines, 0.005–0.020 in. (0.127–0.508mm) for the gasoline V8, 0.040–0.060 in. (1.016–1.524mm) for the diesel V8, below the front face of the cylinder block.*
8. Install the camshaft rear bearing bore plug.
9. Install the camshaft, crankshaft, flywheel and related parts, following the appropriate procedures.
10. Install the engine in the truck, following procedures described earlier in this chapter.

Core (Freeze) Plugs

REPLACEMENT

Core plugs need replacement only if they are found to be leaking, are excessively rusty, have popped due to freezing or, if the engine is being overhauled.

If the plugs are accessible with the engine in the truck, they can be removed as-is. If not, the engine will have to be removed.

1. If necessary, remove the engine and mount it on a work stand. If the engine is being left in the truck, drain the engine coolant and engine oil

   CAUTION: *When draining the coolant, keep in mind that cats and dogs are attracted by the ethylene glycol antifreeze, and are quite likely to drink any that is left in an uncov-*

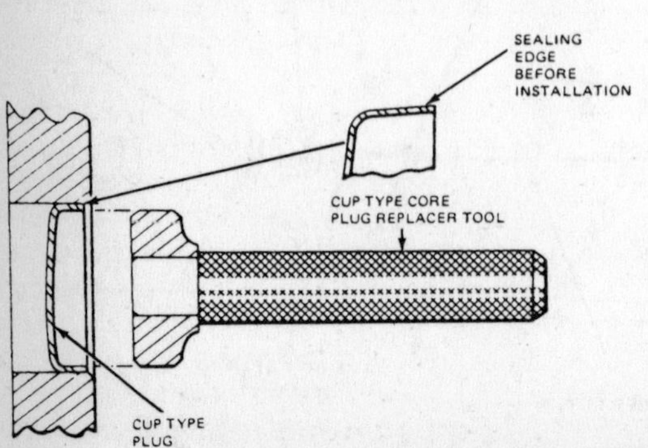

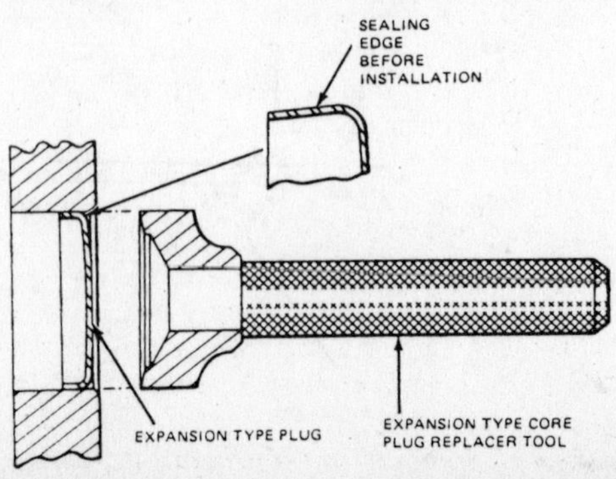

Core plugs and installation tools

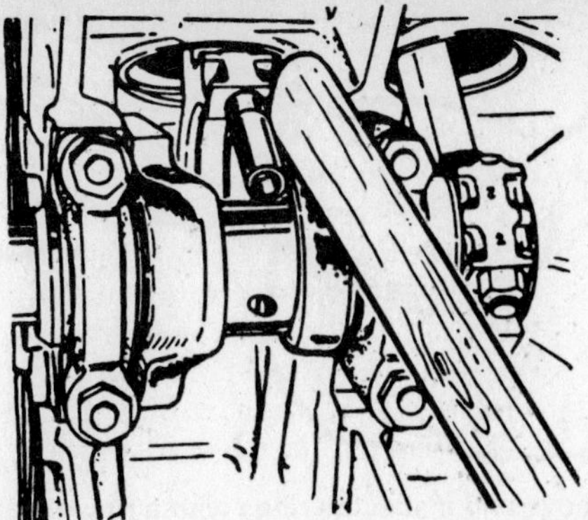

Push the piston assembly out with a hammer handle

ered container or in puddles on the ground. This will prove fatal in sufficient quantity. Always drain the coolant into a sealable container. Coolant should be reused unless it is contaminated or several years old.

2. Remove anything blocking access to the plug or plugs to be replaced.
3. Drill or center-punch a hole in the plug.
4. Using a slide-hammer, thread a machine screw adapter or insert 2-jawed puller adapter into the hole in the plug. Pull the plug from the block.
5. Thoroughly clean the opening in the block, using steel wool or emery paper to polish the hole rim.
6. Coat the outer diameter of the new plug with sealer and place it in the hole. Carefully and evenly, drive the new plug into place.
7. Install any removed parts and, if necessary, install the engine in the truck.
8. Refill the cooling system and crankcase.
9. Start the engine and check for leaks.

Pistons and Connecting Rods

REMOVAL AND INSTALLATION

6–4.9L

1. Drain the cooling system and the crankcase.

CAUTION: *When draining the coolant, keep in mind that cats and dogs are attracted by the ethylene glycol antifreeze, and are quite likely to drink any that is left in an uncovered container or in puddles on the ground. This will prove fatal in sufficient quantity. Always drain the coolant into a sealable container. Coolant should be reused unless it is contaminated or several years old.*

The EPA warns that prolonged contact with used engine oil may cause a number of skin disorders, including cancer! You should make every effort to minimize your exposure to used engine oil. Protective gloves should be worn when changing the oil. Wash your hands and any other exposed skin areas as soon as possible after exposure to used engine oil. Soap and water, or waterless hand cleaner should be used.

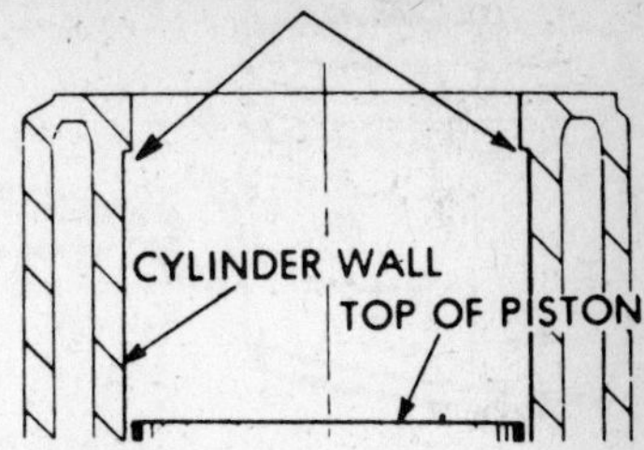

Ridge caused by cylinder wear

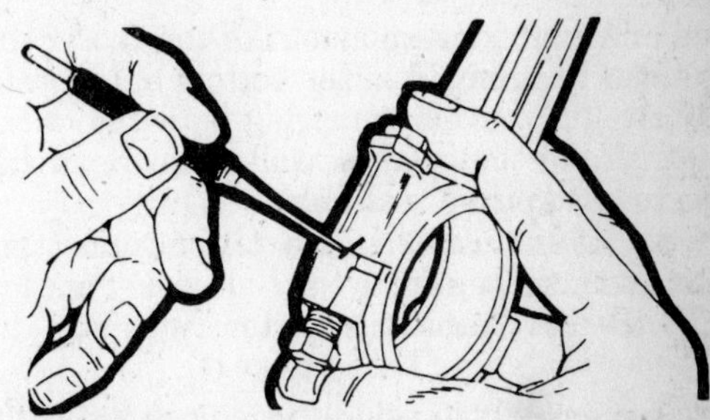

Match the connecting rods to their caps with a scribe mark for reassembly

2. Remove the cylinder head.
3. Remove the oil pan, the oil pump inlet tube and the oil pump.
4. Turn the crankshaft until the piston to be removed is at the bottom of its travel and place a cloth on the piston head to collect filings. Using a ridge reaming tool, remove any ridge of carbon or any other deposit from the upper cylinder walls where piston travel ends. Do not cut into the piston ring travel area more than $\frac{1}{32}$ in. (0.8mm) while removing the ridge.
5. Mark all of the connecting rod caps so that they can be reinstalled in the original positions from which they are removed and remove the connecting rod bearing cap. Also identify the piston assemblies as they, too, must be reinstalled in the same cylinder from which removed.
6. With the bearing caps removed, the connecting rod bearing bolts are potentially damaging to the cylinder walls during removal. To guard against cylinder wall damage, install 4 in. (101.6mm) or 5 in. (127mm) lengths of $^3/_8$ in. (9.5mm) rubber tubing onto the connecting rod bolts. These will also protect the crankshaft journal from scratches when the connecting rod is installed, and will serve as a guide for the rod.
7. Squirt some clean engine oil into each cylinder before removing the pistons. Using a wooden hammer handle, push the connecting

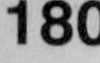

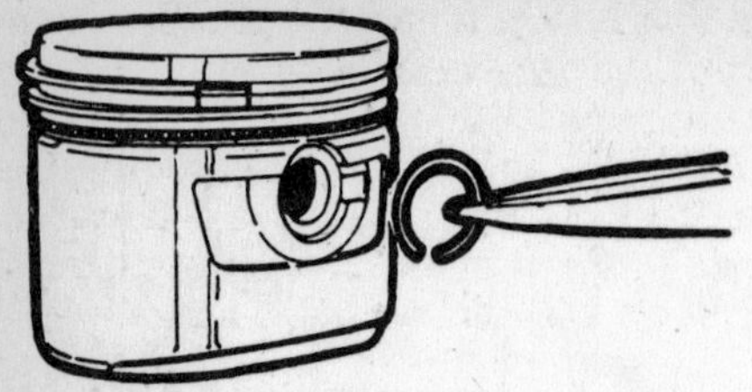

Use needle-nose or snapring pliers to remove the piston pin clips

rod and piston assembly out of the top of the cylinder (pushing from the bottom of the rod). Be careful to avoid damaging both the crank journal and the cylinder wall when removing the rod and piston assembly.

8. Before installing the piston/connecting rod assembly, be sure to clean all gasket mating surfaces, oil the pistons, piston rings and the cylinder walls with light engine oil.

9. Be sure to install the pistons in the cylinders from which they were removed. The connecting rod and bearing caps are numbered from 1 to 6 beginning at the front of the engine. The numbers on the connecting rod and bearing cap must be on the same side when installed in the cylinder bore. If a connecting rod is ever transposed from one engine or cylinder to another, new bearings should be fitted and the connecting rod should be numbered to correspond with the new cylinder number. The notch on the piston head goes toward the front of the engine.

10. Make sure the ring gaps are properly spaced around the circumference of the piston. Make sure rubber hose lengths are fitted to the

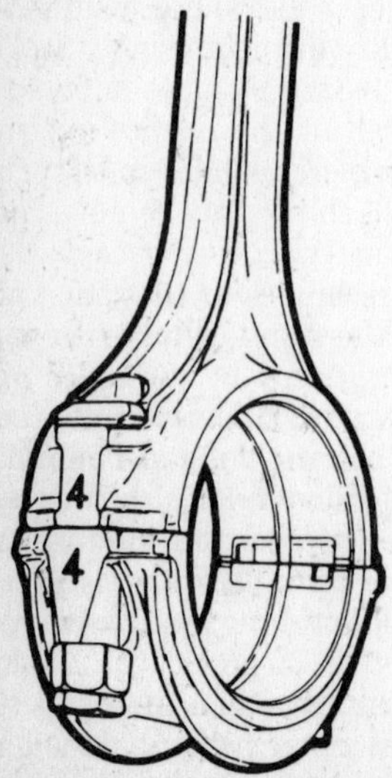

Number each rod and cap with its cylinder number for correct assembly

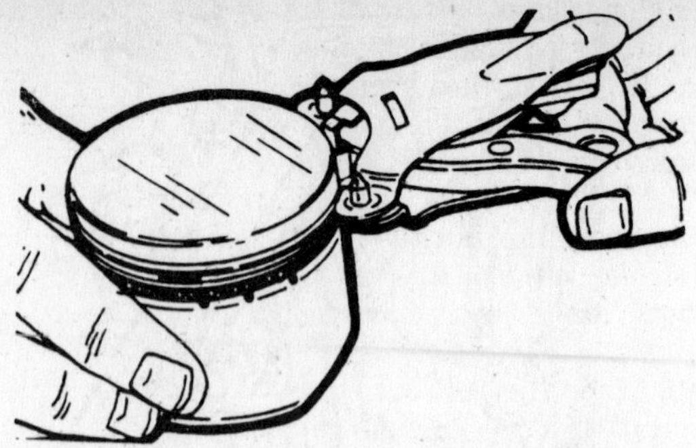

Remove and install the rings with a ring expander

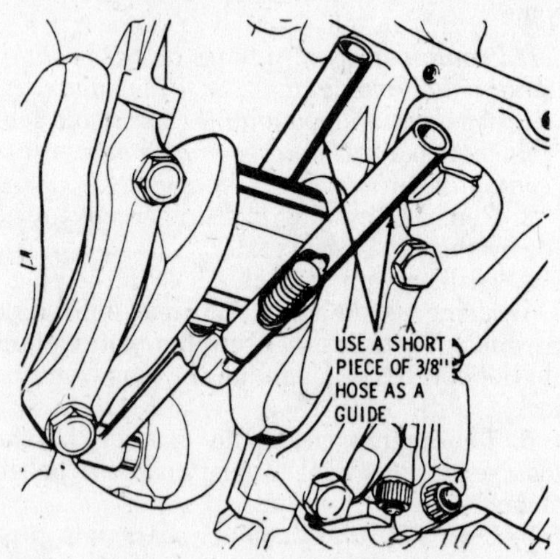

Make connecting rod bolt guides out of rubber tubing; these also protect the cylinder walls and crank journal from scratches

rod bolts. Fit a piston ring compressor around the piston and slide the piston and connecting rod assembly down into the cylinder bore, pushing it in with the wooden hammer handle. Push the piston down until it is only slightly below the top of the cylinder bore. Guide the connecting rods onto the crankshaft bearing journals carefully, using the rubber hose lengths, to avoid damaging the crankshaft.

11. Check the bearing clearance of all the

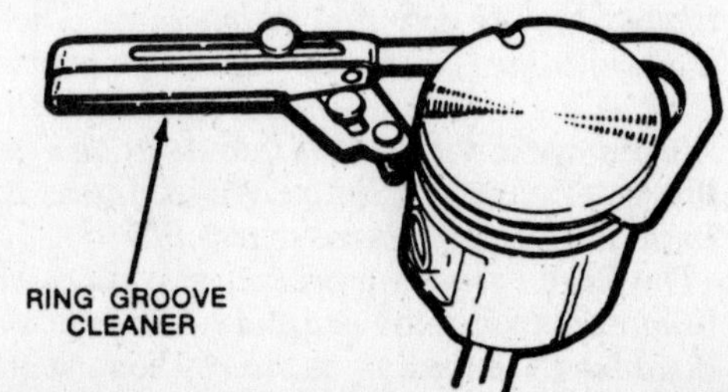

Clean the ring grooves with this tool or the edge of an old ring

rod bearings, fitting them to the crankshaft bearing journals.

12. After the bearings have been fitted, apply a light coating of engine oil to the journals and bearings.

13. Turn the crankshaft until the appropriate bearing journal is at the bottom of its stroke, then push the piston assembly all the way down until the connecting rod bearing seats on the crankshaft journal. Be careful not to allow the bearing cap screws to strike the crankshaft bearing journals and damage them.

14. After the piston and connecting rod assemblies have been installed, check the connecting rod side clearance on each crankshaft journal.

15. Prime and install the oil pump and the oil pump intake tube, then install the oil pan.

16. Reassemble the rest of the engine in the reverse order of disassembly.

V8 Engines Including Diesel

1. Drain the cooling system and the crankcase.

CAUTION: *When draining the coolant, keep in mind that cats and dogs are attracted by the ethylene glycol antifreeze, and are quite likely to drink any that is left in an uncovered container or in puddles on the ground. This will prove fatal in sufficient quantity. Always drain the coolant into a sealable container. Coolant should be reused unless it is contaminated or several years old.*

The EPA warns that prolonged contact with used engine oil may cause a number of skin disorders, including cancer! You should make every effort to minimize your exposure to used engine oil. Protective gloves should be worn when changing the oil. Wash your hands and any other exposed skin areas as soon as possible after exposure to used engine oil. Soap and water, or waterless hand cleaner should be used.

2. Remove the intake manifold.
3. Remove the cylinder heads.
4. Remove the oil pan.
5. Remove the oil pump.
6. Turn the crankshaft until the piston to be removed is at the bottom of its travel, then place a cloth on the piston head to collect filings.
7. Remove any ridge of deposits at the end of the piston travel from the upper cylinder bore, using a ridge reaming tool. Do not cut into the piston ring travel area more than $\frac{1}{32}$ in. (0.8mm) when removing the ridge.
8. Make sure that all of the connecting rod bearing caps can be identified, so they will be reinstalled in their original positions.
9. Turn the crankshaft until the connecting rod that is to be removed is at the bottom of its stroke and remove the connecting rod nuts and bearing cap.
10. With the bearing caps removed, the connecting rod bearing bolts are potentially damaging to the cylinder walls during removal. To guard against cylinder wall damage, install four or five inch lengths of $^3/_8$ in. (0.8mm) rubber tubing onto the connecting rod bolts. These will also protect the crankshaft journal from scratches when the connecting rod is installed, and will serve as a guide for the rod.
11. Squirt some clean engine oil into each cylinder before removing the piston assemblies. Using a wooden hammer handle, push the connecting rod and piston assembly out of the top of the cylinder (pushing from the bottom of the rod). Be careful to avoid damaging both the crank journal and the cylinder wall when removing the rod and piston assembly.
12. Remove the bearing inserts from the connecting rod and cap if the bearings are to be replace, and place the cap onto the piston/rod assembly from which it was removed.
13. Install the piston/rod assemblies in the same manner as that for the 6-cylinder engines. See the procedure given for 6-cylinder engines.

NOTE: *The connecting rod and bearing caps are numbered from 1 to 4 in the right bank and from 5 to 8 in the left bank, beginning at the front of the engine. The numbers on the rod and cap must be on the same side when they are installed in the cylinder bore. Also, the largest chamfer at the bearing end of the rod should be positioned toward the crank pin thrust face of the crankshaft and the notch in the head of the piston faces toward the front of the engine.*

14. See the appropriate component procedures to assemble the engine.

Piston Ring and Wrist Pin

REMOVAL

All of the Ford gasoline engines covered in this guide utilize pressed-in wrist pins, which can only be removed by an arbor press. The diesel pistons are removed in the same way, only the pistons are heated before the wrist pins are pressed out. On both gasoline and diesel engines, the piston/connecting rod assemblies should be taken to an engine specialist or qualified machinist for piston removal and installation.

A piston ring expander is necessary for removing the piston rings without damaging them; any other method (screwdriver blades, pliers, etc.) usually results in the rings being bent, scratched or distorted, or the piston itself being damaged. When the rings are removed, clean the ring grooves using an appropriate ring groove cleaning tool, using care not to cut too deeply. Thoroughly clean all carbon and varnish from the piston with solvent.

WARNING: *Do not use a wire brush or caustic solvent (acids, etc.) on pistons.*

Inspect the pistons for scuffing, scoring, cracks, pitting, or excessive ring groove wear. If these are evident, the piston must be replaced.

The piston should also be checked in relation to the cylinder diameter. Using a telescoping gauge and micrometer, or a dial gauge, measure the cylinder bore diameter perpendicular (90%) to the piston pin, $2^1/2$ in. (64mm) below the cylinder block deck (surface where the block mates with the heads). Then, with the micrometer, measure the piston, perpendicular to its wrist pin on the skirt. the difference between the two measurements is the piston clearance. If the clearance is within specifications or slightly below (after the cylinders have been bored or hones), finish honing is all that is necessary. If the clearance is excessive, try to obtain a slightly larger piston to bring clearance to within specifications. If this is not possible, obtain the first oversize piston and hone (or if necessary, bore) the cylinder to size. Generally, if the cylinder bore is tapered 0.005 in. (0.127mm) or more or is out-of-round 0.003 in. (0.076mm) or more, it is advisable to rebore for the smallest possible oversize piston and rings.

After measuring, mark pistons with a felt tip pen for reference and for assembly.

NOTE: *Cylinder honing and/or boring should be performed by a reputable, professional mechanic with the proper equipment. In some cases, clean-up honing can be done*

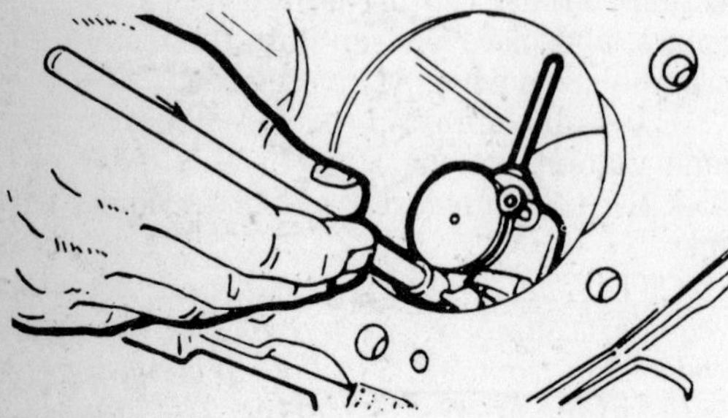

Measuring cylinder bore with a dial gauge

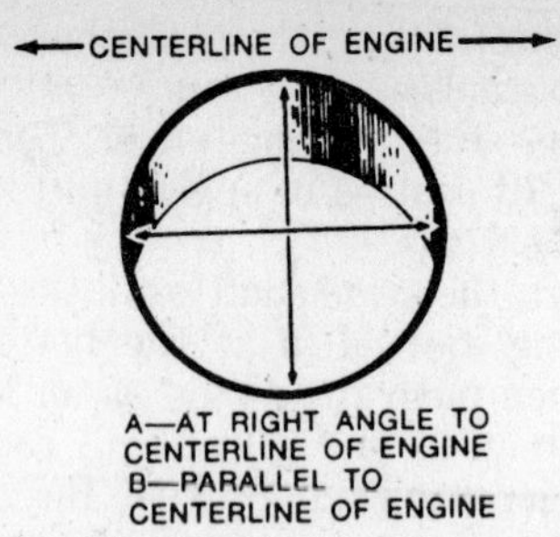

Cylinder bore measuring points. Take top measurement 1/2 in. below top of block deck, bottom measurement 1/2 in. above top of piston when piston is at BDC

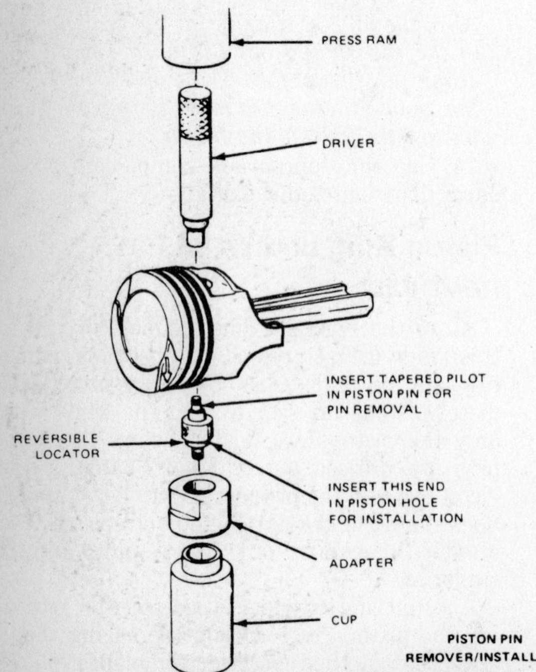

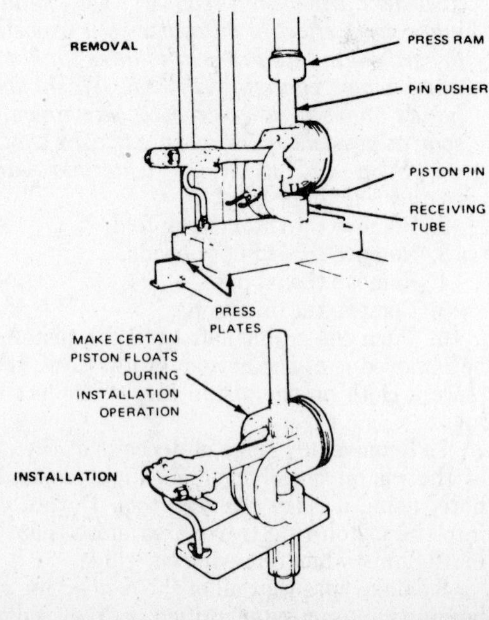

Have the wrist pins pressed in and out with an arbor press. This applies to all engines covered in this guide

with the cylinder block in the car, but most excessive honing and all cylinder boring must be done with the block stripped and removed from the car. Before honing the diesel cylinders, the piston oil cooling jets must be removed. this procedure should be handled by a diesel specialist, as special tools are needed. Jets cannot be reused; new jets should be fitted.

MEASURING THE OLD PISTONS

Check used piston-to-cylinder bore clearance as follows:

1. Measure the cylinder bore diameter with a telescope gauge.
2. Measure the piston diameter. When measuring the pistons for size or taper, measurements must be made with the piston pin removed.
3. Subtract the piston diameter from the cylinder bore diameter to determine piston-to-bore clearance.
4. Compare the piston-to-bore clearances obtained with those clearances recommended. Determine if the piston-to-bore clearance is in the acceptable range.
5. When measuring taper, the largest reading must be at the bottom of the skirt.

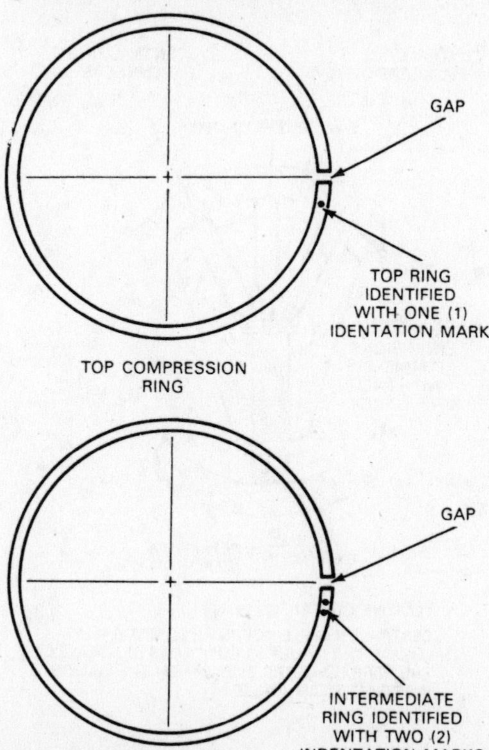

Diesel piston ring identification

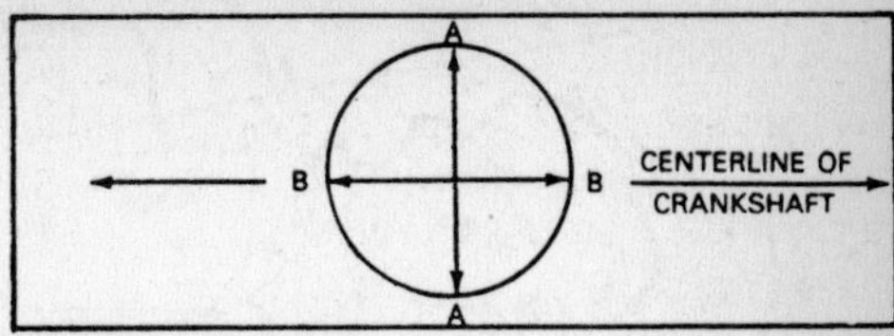

A - At Right angle to center line of engine
B - Parallel to center line of engine

Top Measurement: Make 12.70mm (1/2 inch) below top of block deck

Bottom Measurement: Make within 12.70mm (1/2 inch) above top of piston - when piston is at its lowest travel (B.D.C)

Bore Service Limit: Equals the average of "A" and "B" when measured at the center of the piston travel.

Taper: Equals difference between "A" top and "A" bottom.

Out-of-Round: Equals difference between "A" and "B" when measured at the center of piston travel.

Cylinder bore measurement

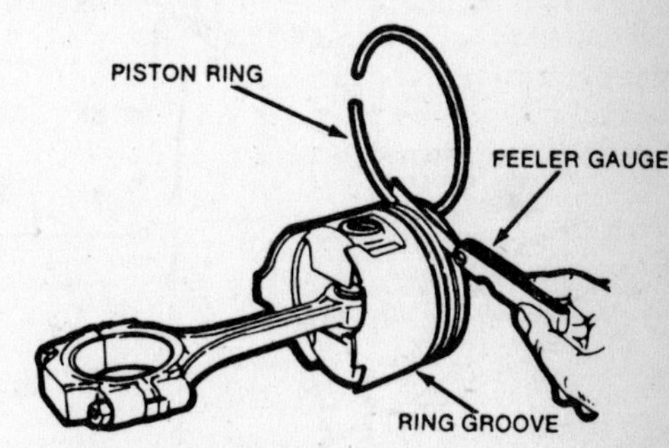

Checking ring side clearance

SELECTING NEW PISTONS

1. If the used piston is not acceptable, check the service piston size and determine if a new piston can be selected. (Service pistons are available in standard, high limit and standard oversize.

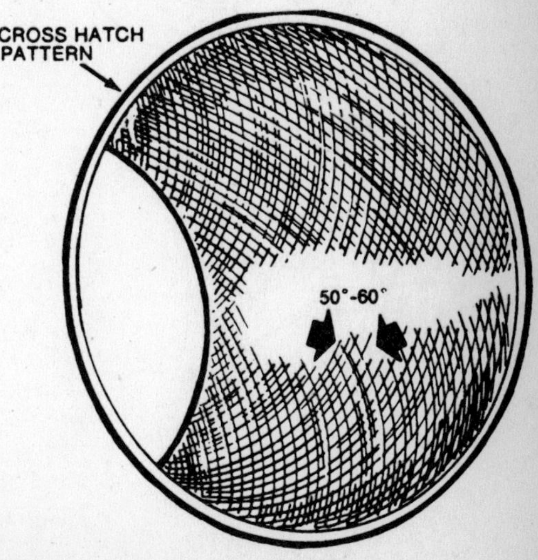

Proper cylinder bore cross-hatching after honing

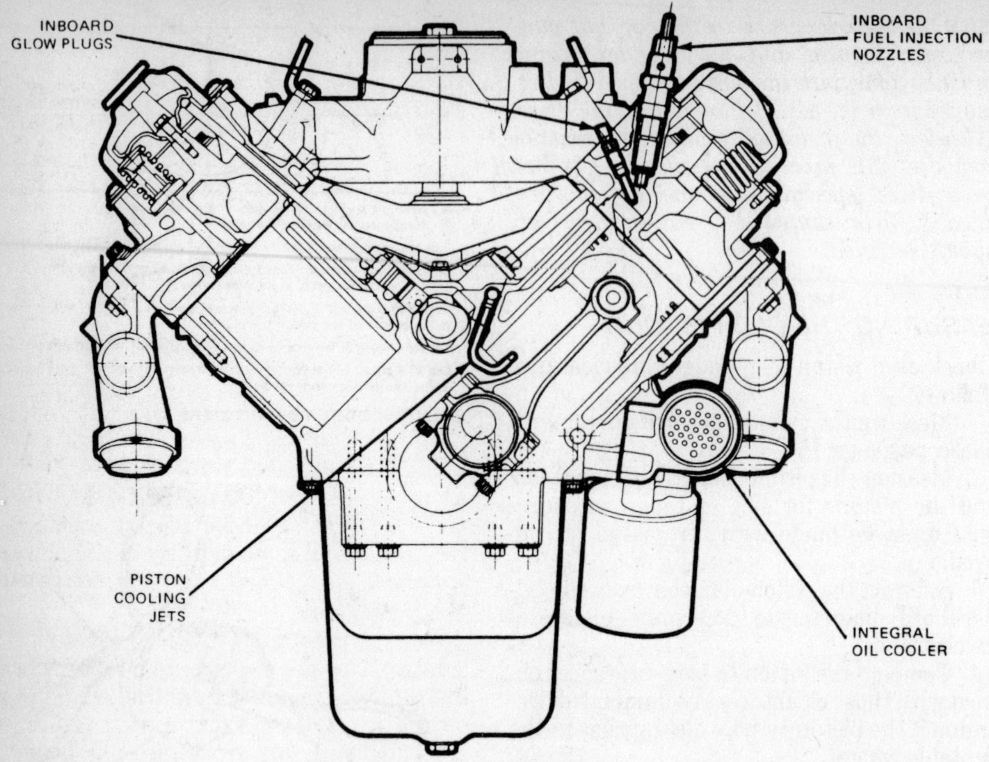

Diesel V8 cross-section

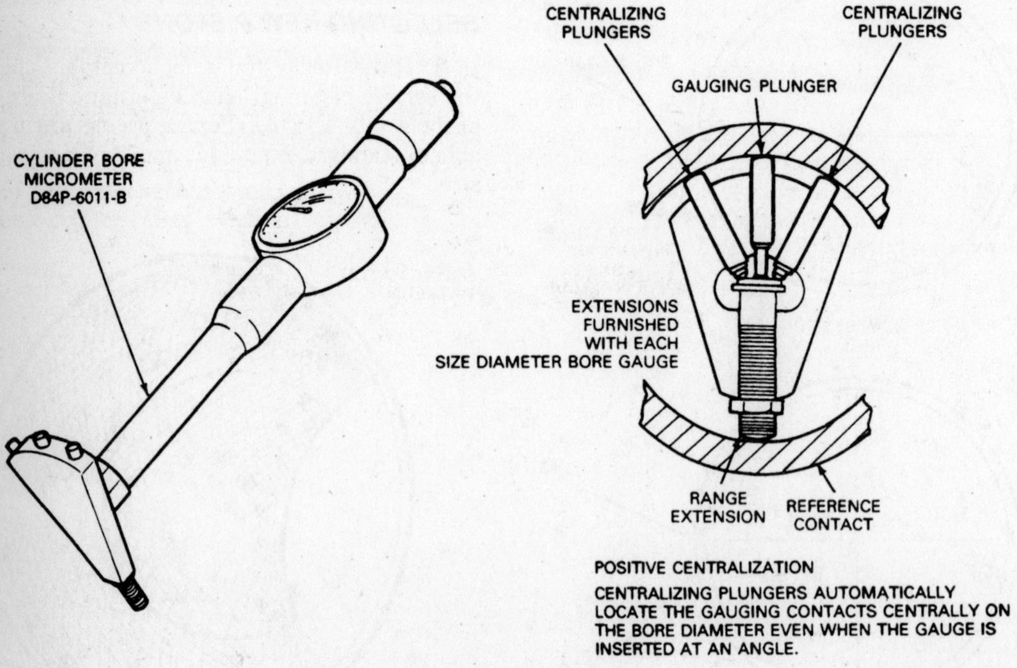

Cylinder bore micrometer

2. If the cylinder bore must be reconditioned, measure the new piston diameter, then hone the cylinder bore to obtain the preferred clearance.

3. Select a new piston and mark the piston to identify the cylinder for which it was fitted. (On some vehicles, oversize pistons may be found. These pistons will be 0.254mm [0.010 in.] oversize).

CYLINDER HONING

1. When cylinders are being honed, follow the manufacturer's recommendations for the use of the hone.

2. Occasionally, during the honing operation, the cylinder bore should be thoroughly cleaned and the selected piston checked for correct fit.

3. When finish-honing a cylinder bore, the hone should be moved up and down at a sufficient speed to obtain a very fine uniform surface finish in a cross-hatch pattern of approximately 45–65° included angle. The finish marks should be clean but not sharp, free from embedded particles and torn or folded metal.

4. Permanently mark the piston for the cylinder to which it has been fitted and proceed to hone the remaining cylinders.

WARNING: *Handle the pistons with care. Do not attempt to force the pistons through the cylinders until the cylinders have been honed to the correct size. Pistons can be distorted through careless handling.*

5. Thoroughly clean the bores with hot water and detergent. Scrub well with a stiff bristle brush and rinse thoroughly with hot water. It is extremely essential that a good cleaning operation be performed. If any of the abrasive material is allowed to remain in the cylinder bores, it will rapidly wear the new rings and cylinder bores. The bores should be swabbed several times with light engine oil and a clean cloth and then wiped with a clean dry cloth. CYLINDERS SHOULD NOT BE CLEANED WITH KEROSENE OR GASOLINE! Clean the remainder of the cylinder block to remove the excess material spread during the honing operation.

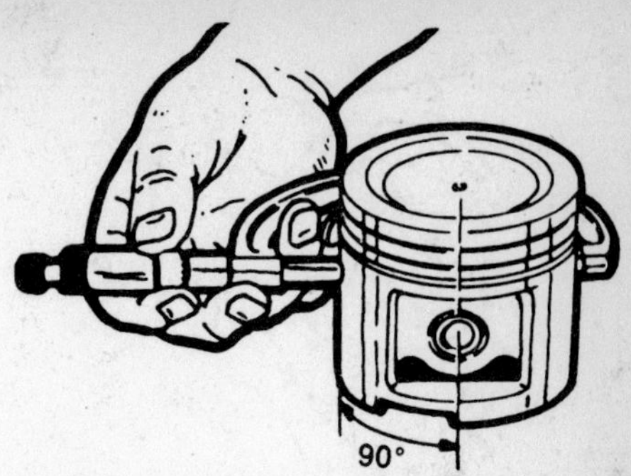

Check piston diameter at these points with a micrometer

PISTON RING END GAP

Piston ring end gap should be checked while the rings are removed from the pistons. Incorrect end gap indicates that the wrong size rings are being used; ring breakage could occur.

Compress the piston rings to be used in a cylinder, one at a time, into that cylinder. Squirt clean oil into the cylinder, so that the rings and the top 2 in. (51mm) of cylinder wall are coated. Using an inverted piston, press the rings approximately 1 in. (25mm) below the deck of the block (on diesels, measure ring gap clearance with the ring positioned at the bottom of ring travel in the bore). Measure the ring end gap with the feeler gauge, and compare to the Ring Gap chart in this chapter. Carefully pull the ring out of the cylinder and file the ends

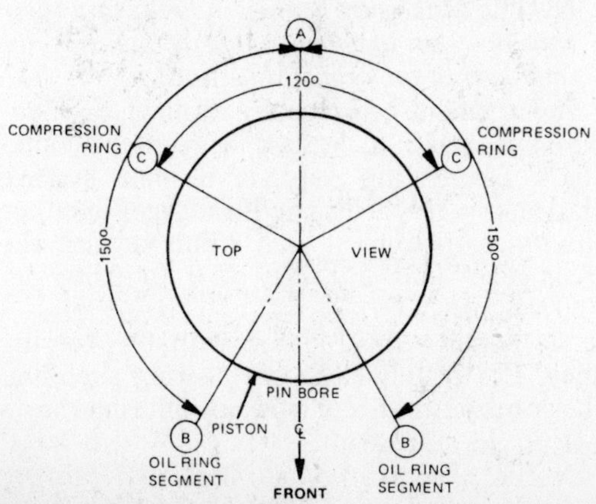

Diesel piston ring spacing

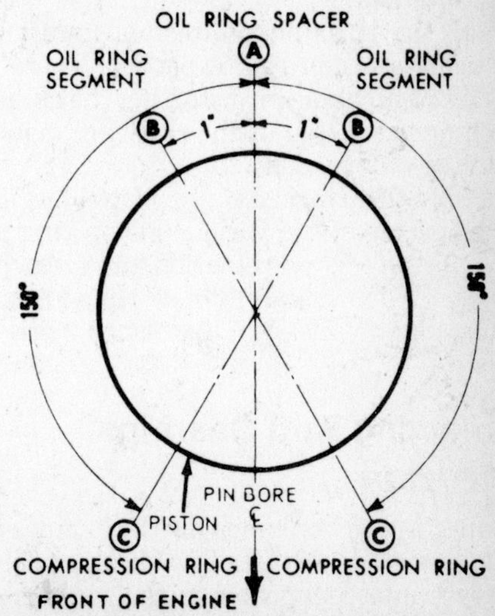

Proper spacing of the piston ring gaps around the circumference of the piston for gasoline engines

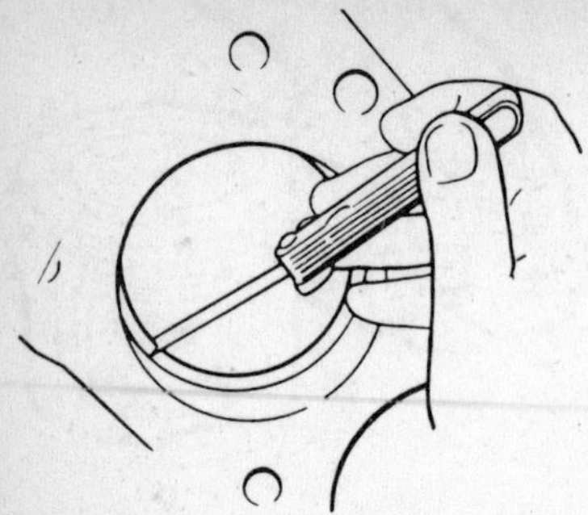

Check piston ring end gap with a feeler gauge, with the ring positioned in the cylinder one inch below the deck of the block

squarely with a fine file to obtain the proper clearance.

PISTON RING SIDE CLEARANCE CHECK AND INSTALLATION

Check the pistons to see that the ring grooves and oil return holes have been properly cleaned. Slide a piston ring into its groove, and check the side clearance with a feeler gauge. On gasoline engines, make sure you insert the gauge between the ring and its lower land (lower edge of the groove), because any wear that occurs forms a step at the inner portion of the lower land. On diesels, insert the gauge between the ring and the upper land. If the piston grooves have worn to the extend that relatively high steps exist on the lower land, the piston grooves have worn to the extent that relatively high steps exist on the lower land, the piston should be replaced, because these will interfere with the operation of the new rings and ring clearance will be excessive. Piston rings are not furnished in oversize widths to compensate for ring groove wear.

Install the rings on the piston, lowest ring first, using a piston ring expander. There is a high risk of breaking or distorting the rings, or scratching the piston, if the rings are installed by hand or other means.

Position the rings on the piston as illustrated; spacing of the various piston ring gaps is crucial to proper oil retention and even cylinder wear. When installing new rings, refer to the installation diagram furnished with the new parts.

Connecting Rod Bearings

INSPECTION

Connecting rod bearings for the engines covered in this guide consist of two halves or shells which are interchangeable in the rod and cap. when the shells are placed in position, the ends extend slightly beyond the rod and cap surfaces so that when the rod bolts are torqued the shells will be clamped tightly in place to insure positive seating and to prevent turning. A tang holds the shells in place.

NOTE: *The ends of the bearing shells must never be filed flush with the mating surfaces of the rod and cap.*

If a rod bearing becomes noisy or is worn so that its clearance on the crank journal is sloppy, a new bearing of the correct undersize must be selected and installed since there is a provision for adjustment.

WARNING: *Under no circumstances should the rod end or cap be filed to adjust the bearing clearance, nor should shims of any kind be used.*

Inspect the rod bearings while the rod assemblies are out of the engine. If the shells are scored or show flaking, they should be replaced. If they are in good shape, check for proper clearance on the crank journal (see below). Any scoring or ridges on the crank journal means the crankshaft must be reground and fitted with undersized bearings, or replaced.

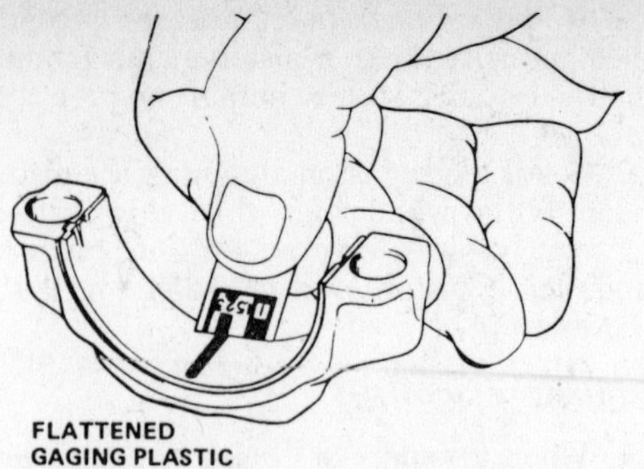

Checking rod bearing clearance with Plastigage® or equivalent

CHECKING BEARING CLEARANCE AND REPLACING BEARINGS

NOTE: *Make sure connecting rods and their caps are kept together, and that the caps are installed in the proper direction.*

Replacement bearings are available in standard size, and in undersizes for reground crankshaft. Connecting rod-to-crankshaft bearing clearance is checked using Plastigage® at either the top or bottom of each crank journal. the Plastigage® has a range of 0 to 0.003 in. (0.076mm).

1. Remove the rod cap with the bearing shell. Completely clean the bearing shell and the crank journal, and blow any oil from the oil hole in the crankshaft.

NOTE: *The journal surfaces and bearing shells must be completely free of oil, because Plastigage® is soluble in oil.*

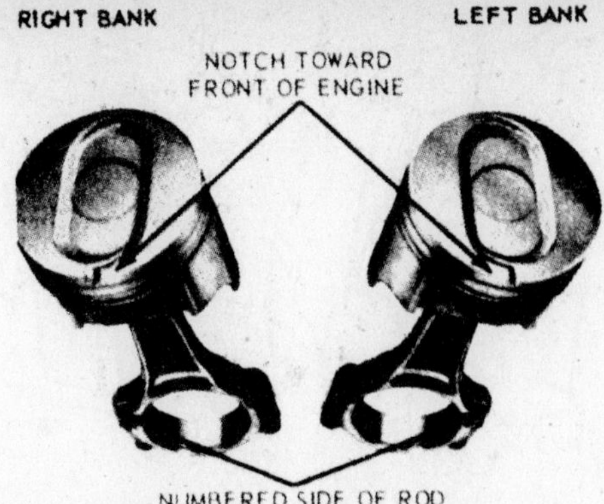

7.5L V8 piston and rod installation

2. Place a strip of Plastigage® lengthwise along the bottom center of the lower bearing shell, then install the cap with shell and torque the bolt or nuts to specification. DO NOT TURN the crankshaft with the Plastigage® installed in the bearing.

3. Remove the bearing cap with the shell. The flattened Plastigage® will be found sticking to either the bearing shell or crank journal. Do not remove it yet.

4. Use the printed scale on the Plastigage® envelope to measure the flattened material at its widest point. The number within the scale which most closely corresponds to the width of the Plastigage® indicated bearing clearance in thousandths of an inch.

5. Check the specifications chart in this chapter for the desired clearance. It is advisable to install a new bearing if clearance exceeds 0.003 in. (0.076mm); however, if the bearing is in good condition and is not being checked because of bearing noise, bearing replacement is not necessary.

6. If you are installing new bearings, try a standard size, then each undersize in order until one is found that is within the specified limits when checked for clearance with Plastigage®. Each under size has its size stamped on it.

7. When the proper size shell is found, clean off the Plastigage® material from the shell, oil the bearing thoroughly, reinstall the cap with its shell and torque the rod bolt nuts to specification.

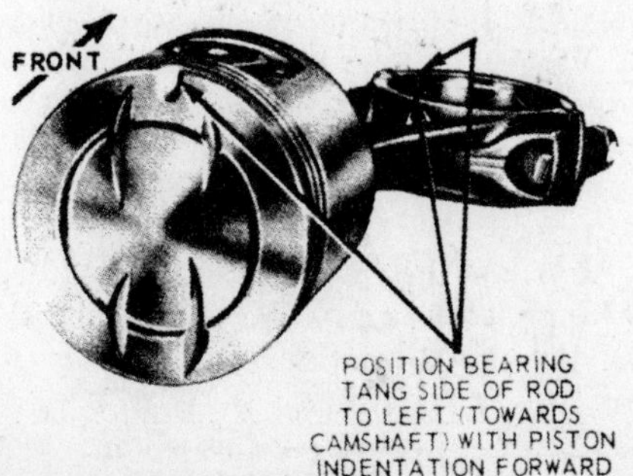

6-4.9L rod and piston assembly

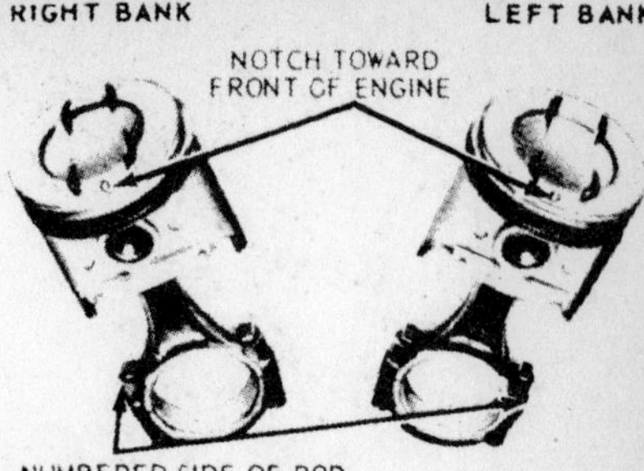

8-5.0L and 8-5.8L piston and rod assemblies

NOTE: *With the proper bearing selected and the nuts torqued, it should be possible to move the connecting rod back and forth freely on the crank journal as allowed by the specified connecting rod end clearance. If the rod cannot be moved, either the rod bearing is too far undersize or the rod is misaligned.*

Piston and Connecting Rod

ASSEMBLY AND INSTALLATION

Install the connecting rod to the piston making sure piston installation notches and any marks on the rod are in proper relation to one another. Lubricate the wrist pin with clean engine oil and install the pin into the rod and piston assembly by using an arbor press as re-

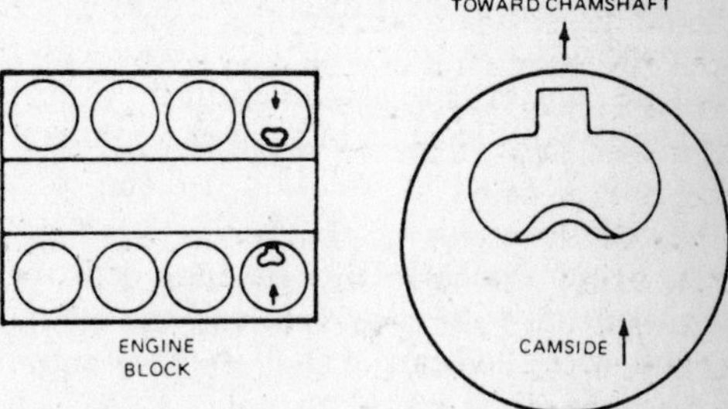

Diesel piston positioning

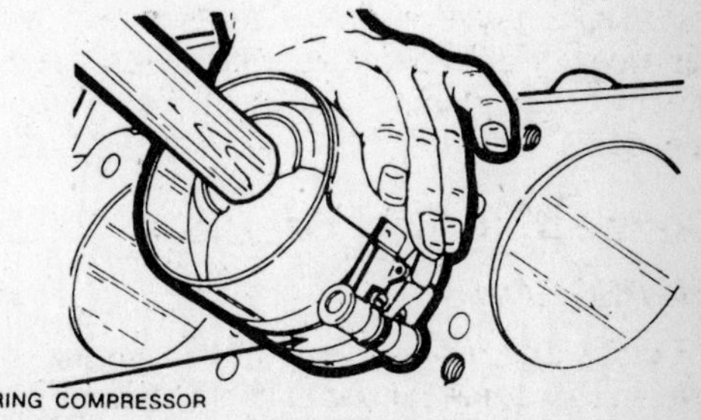

Tap the piston assembly into the cylinder with a wooden hammer handle. Notches on piston crown face the front of the engine

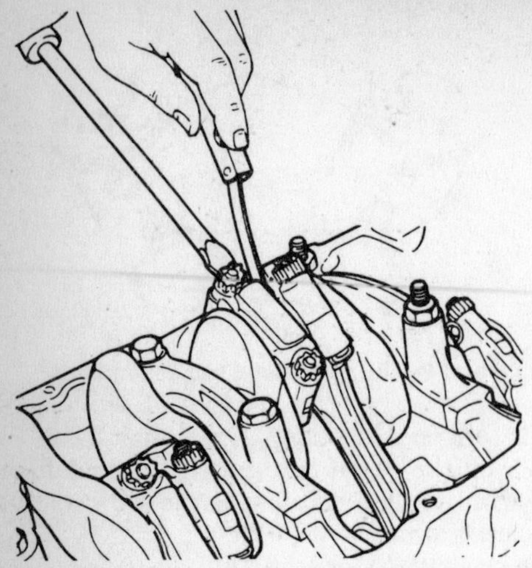

Checking connecting rod side clearance with a feeler gauge. Use a small pry bar to spread the connecting rods

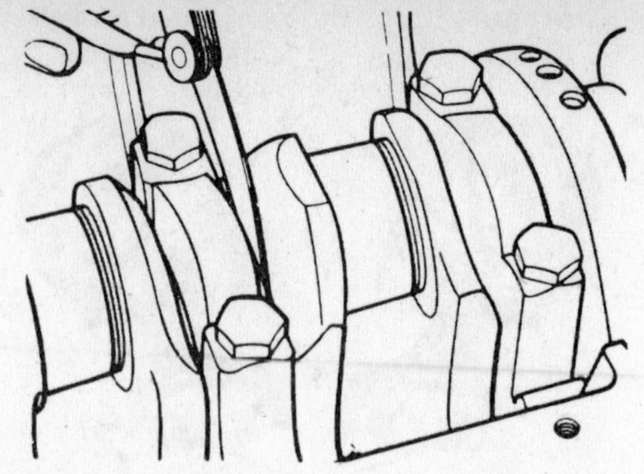

Crankshaft end play can also be checked with a feeler gauge

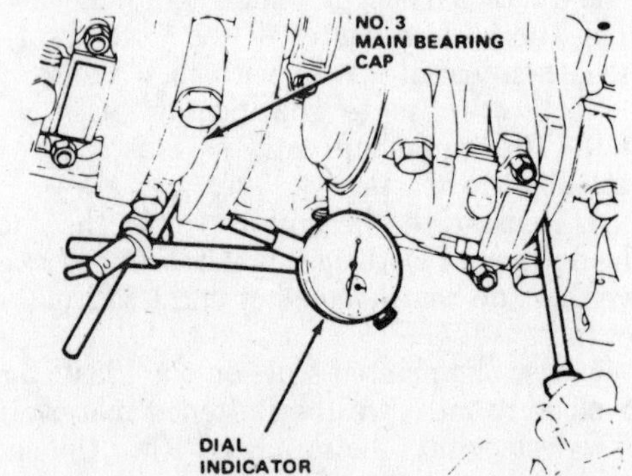

Checking crankshaft end-play with a dial indicator

quired. Install the wrist pin snaprings if equipped, and rotate them in their grooves to make sure they are seated. To install the piston and rod assemblies:

1. Make sure the connecting rod big bearings (including end cap) are of the correct size and properly installed.

2. Fit rubber hoses over the connecting rod bolt to protect the crankshaft journals, as in the Piston Removal procedure. Coat the rod bearings with clean oil.

3. Using the proper ring compressor, insert the piston assembly into the cylinder so that the notch in the top of the piston faces the front of the engine (this assumes that the dimple(s) or other markings on the connecting rods are in correct relation to the piston notch(s)).

4. From beneath the engine, coat each crank journal with clean oil. Pull the connecting rod, with the bearing shell in place, into position against the crank journal.

5. Remove the rubber hoses. Install the bearing cap and cap nuts and torque to specification.

NOTE: *When more than one rod and piston assembly is being installed, the connecting rod cap attaching nuts should only be tightened enough to keep each rod in position until all have been installed. This will ease the installation of the remaining piston assemblies.*

6. Check the clearance between the sides of the connecting rods and the crankshaft using a feeler gauge. Spread the rods slightly with a screwdriver to insert the gauge. If clearance is below the minimum tolerance, the rod may be machined to provide adequate clearance. If clearance is excessive, substitute an unworn rod, and recheck. If clearance is still outside specifi-

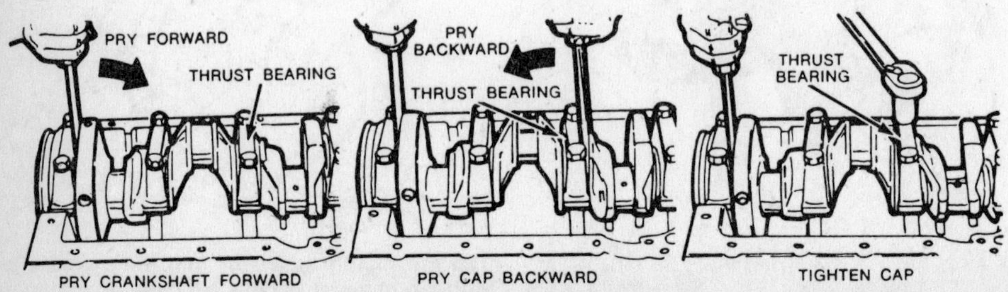

Crankshaft thrust bearing alignment

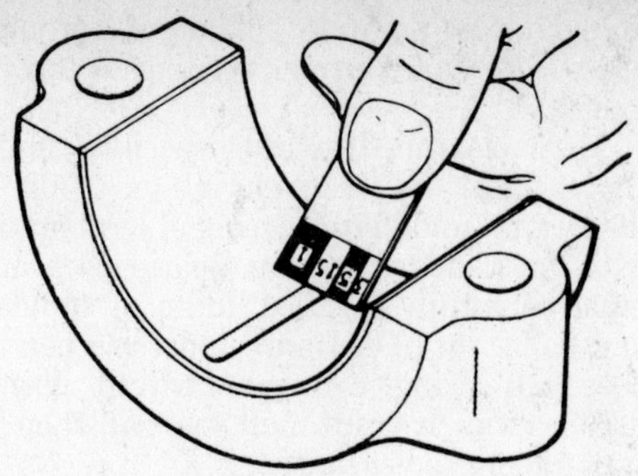

Checking main bearing clearance with Plastigage®

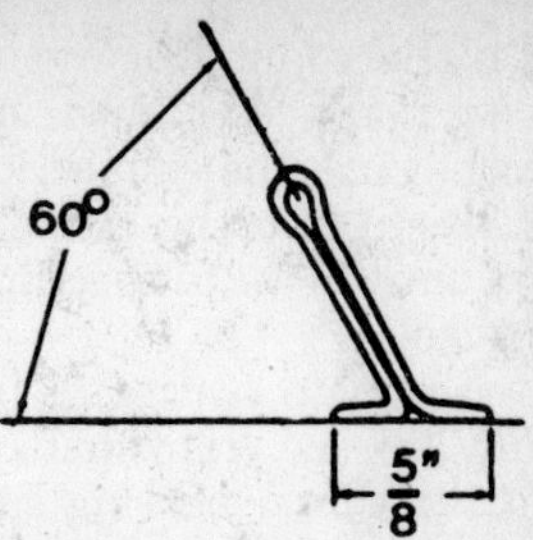

Make a bearing roll-out pin from a cotter pin

cations, the crankshaft must be welded and reground, or replaced.

7. Replace the oil pump if removed, and the oil pan.

8. Install the cylinder head(s) and intake manifold.

Crankshaft and Main Bearings.

REMOVAL AND INSTALLATION

Engine Removed

1. With the engine removed from the vehicle and placed in a work stand, disconnect the spark plug wires from the spark plugs and remove the wires and bracket assembly from the attaching stud on the valve rocker arm cover(s) if so equipped. Disconnect the coil to distributor high tension lead at the coil. Remove the distributor cap and spark plug wires as an assembly. Remove the spark plugs to allow easy rotation of the crankshaft.

2. Remove the fuel pump and oil filter. Slide the water pump by-pass hose clamp (if so equipped) toward the water pump. Remove the alternator and mounting brackets.

3. Remove the crankshaft pulley from the crankshaft vibration damper. Remove the capscrew and washer from the end of the crankshaft. Install a universal puller, Tool T58P–6316–D or equivalent on the crankshaft vibration damper and remove the damper.

4. Remove the cylinder front cover and crankshaft gear, refer to Cylinder Front Cover and Timing Chain in this chapter.

5. Invert the engine on the work stand. Remove the clutch pressure plate and disc (manual shift transmission). Remove the flywheel and engine rear cover plate. Remove the oil pan and gasket. Remove the oil pump.

6. Make sure all bearing caps (main and connecting rod) are marked so that they can be installed in their original locations. Turn the

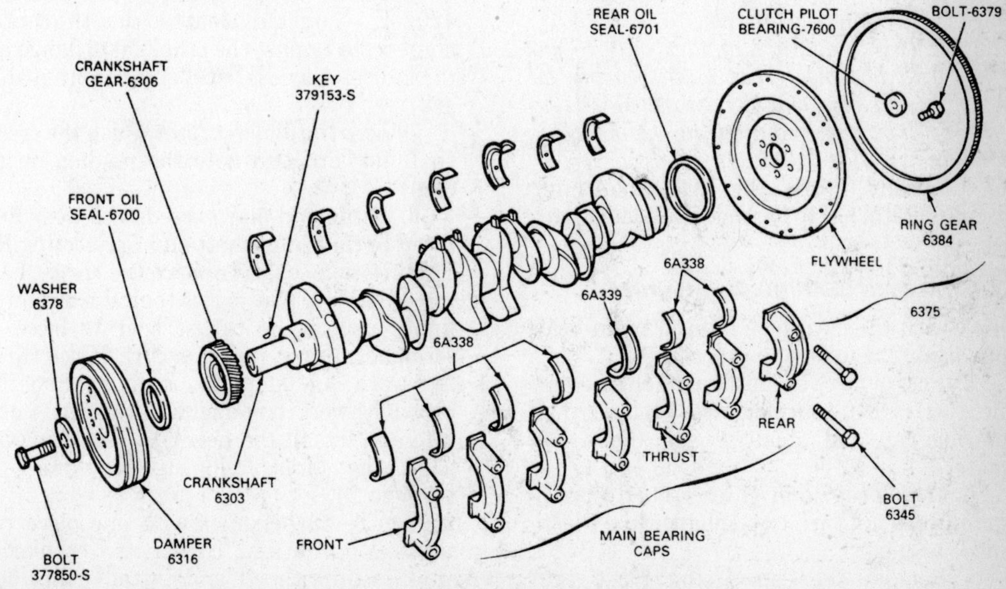

6–4.9L crankshaft and bearings

crankshaft until the connecting rod from which the cap is being removed is down, and remove the bearing cap. Push the connecting rod and piston assembly up into the cylinder. Repeat this procedure until all the connecting rod bearing caps are removed.

7. Remove the main bearings caps.

8. Carefully lift the crankshaft out of the block so that the thrust bearing surfaces are not damaged. Handle the crankshaft with care to avoid possible fracture to the finished surfaces.

9. Remove the rear journal seal from the block and rear main bearing cap.

10. Remove the main bearing inserts from the block and bearing caps.

11. Remove the connecting rod bearing inserts from the connecting rods and caps.

12. If the crankshaft main bearing journals have been refinished to a definite undersize, install the correct undersize bearings. Be sure the bearing inserts and bearing bores are clean. Foreign material under the inserts will distort the bearing and cause a failure.

13. Place the upper main bearing inserts in position in the bores with the tang fitting in the slot. Be sure the oil holes in the bearing inserts are aligned with the oil holes in the cylinder block.

14. Install the lower main bearing inserts in the bearing caps.

15. Clean the rear journal oil seal groove and the mating surfaces of the block and rear main bearing cap.

16. Dip the lip-type seal halves in clean engine oil. Install the seals in the bearing cap and block with the undercut side of the seal toward the front of the engine.

NOTE: *This procedure applies only to engines with two piece rear main bearing oil seals. those having one piece seals (6–4.9L engines) will be installed after the crankshaft is in place.*

17. Carefully lower the crankshaft into place. Be careful not to damage the bearing surfaces.

CHECKING MAIN BEARING CLEARANCES

18. Check the clearance of each main bearing by using the following procedure:

a. Place a piece of Plastigage® or its equivalent, on bearing surface across full width of bearing cap and about 1/4 in. (6mm) off center.

b. Install cap and tighten bolts to specifications. Do not turn crankshaft while Plastigage® is in place.

c. Remove the cap. Using Plastigage® scale, check width of Plastigage® at widest point to get the minimum clearance. Check at narrowest point to get maximum clearance. Difference between readings is taper of journal.

d. If clearance exceeds specified limits, try a 0.001 in. (0.0254mm) or 0.002 in. (0.051mm) undersize bearing in combination with the standard bearing. Bearing clearance must be within specified limits. If standard and 0.002 in. (0.051mm) undersize bearing does not bring clearance within desired limits, refinish crankshaft journal, then install undersize bearings.

NOTE: *Refer to Rear Main Oil Seal removal and installation, for special instructions in applying RTV sealer to rear main bearing cup.*

19. Install all the bearing caps except the thrust bearing cap (no. 3 bearing on all except the 6–4.9L which use the no. 5 as the thrust bearing). BE sure the main bearing caps are installed in their original locations. Tighten the bearing cap bolts to specifications.

21. install the thrust bearing cap with the bolts finger tight.

22. Pry the crankshaft forward against the thrust surface of the upper half of the bearing.

23. hold the crankshaft forward and pry the thrust bearing cap to the rear. This will align the thrust surfaces of both halves of the bearing.

24. Retain the forward pressure on the crankshaft. Tighten the cap bolts to specifications.

25. Check the crankshaft end play using the following procedures:

a. Force the crankshaft toward the rear of the engine.

b. Install a dial indicator (tools D78P–4201–F, –G or equivalent) so that the contact point rests against the crankshaft flange and the indicator axis is parallel to the crankshaft axis.

c. Zero the dial indicator. Push the crankshaft forward and note the reading on the dial.

d. If the end play exceeds the wear limit listed in the Crankshaft and Connecting Rod Specifications chart, replace the thrust bearing. If the end play is less than the minimum limit, inspect the thrust bearing faces for scratches, burrs, nicks, or dirt. If the thrust faces are not damaged or dirty, then they probably were not aligned properly. Lubricate and install the new thrust bearing and align the faces following procedures 21 through 24.

26. On 6–4.9L engines with one piece rear main bearing oil seal, coat a new crankshaft rear oil seal with oil and install using Tool T65P–6701–A or equivalent. Inspect the seal to be sure it was not damaged during installation.

27. Install new bearing inserts in the connecting rods and caps. Check the clearance of each bearing, following the procedure (18a through 18d).

28. After the connecting rod bearings have been fitted, apply a light coat of engine oil to the journals and bearings.

29. Turn the crankshaft throw to the bottom of its stroke. Push the piston all the way down until the rod bearing seats on the crankshaft journal.

30. Install the connecting rod cap. Tighten the nuts to specification.

31. After the piston and connecting rod assemblies have been installed, check the side clearance with a feeler gauge between the connecting rods on each connecting rod crankshaft journal. Refer to Crankshaft and Connecting Rod specifications chart in this chapter.

32. Install the timing chain and sprockets or gears, cylinder front cover and crankshaft pulley and adapter, following steps under Cylinder Front Cover and Timing Chain Installation in this chapter.

Engine in the Truck

1. With the oil pan, oil pump and spark plugs removed, remove the cap from the main bearing needing replacement and remove the bearing from the cap.

2. Make a bearing roll-out pin, using a bent cotter pin as shown in the illustration. Install the end of the pin in the oil hole in the crankshaft journal.

3. Rotate the crankshaft clockwise as viewed from the front of the engine. This will roll the upper bearing out of the block.

4. Lube the new upper bearing with clean engine oil and insert the plain (un-notched) end between the crankshaft and the indented or notched side of the block. Roll the bearing into place, making sure that the oil holes are aligned. Remove the roll pin from the oil hole.

5. Lube the new lower bearing and install it in the main bearing cap. Install the main bearing cap onto the block, making sure it is positioned in proper direction with the matchmarks in alignment.

6. Torque the main bearing cap to specification.

NOTE: *See Crankshaft Installation for thrust bearing alignment.*

CRANKSHAFT CLEANING AND INSPECTION

NOTE: *handle the crankshaft carefully to avoid damage to the finish surfaces.*

1. Clean the crankshaft with solvent, and blow out all oil passages with compressed air. On the 6–4.9L engine, clean the oil seal contact surface at the rear of the crankshaft with solvent to remove any corrosion, sludge or varnish deposits.

2. Use crocus cloth to remove any sharp edges, burrs or other imperfections which might damage the oil seal during installation or cause premature seal wear.

NOTE: *Do not use crocus cloth to polish the seal surfaces. A finely polished surface may produce poor sealing or cause premature seal wear.*

3. Inspect the main and connecting rod journals for cracks, scratches, grooves or scores.

4. Measure the diameter of each journal at least four places to determine out-of-round, taper or undersize condition.

5. On an engine with a manual transmission, check the fit of the clutch pilot bearing in the bore of the crankshaft. A needle roller bearing and adapter assembly is used as a clutch pilot bearing. It is inserted directly into the engine crank shaft. The bearing and adapter assembly cannot be serviced separately. A new bearing must be installed whenever a bearing is removed.

6. Inspect the pilot bearing, when used, for roughness, evidence of overheating or loss of lubricant. Replace if any of these conditions are found.

7. On the 6–4.9L engine, inspect the rear oil seal surface of the crankshaft for deep grooves, nicks, burrs, porosity, or scratches which could damage the oil seal lip during installation. Remove all nicks and burrs with crocus cloth.

Main Bearings

1. Clean the bearing inserts and caps thoroughly in solvent, and dry them with compressed air.

NOTE: *Do not scrape varnish or gum deposits from the bearing shells.*

2. Inspect each bearing carefully. Bearings that have a scored, chipped, or worn surface should be replaced.

3. The copper-lead bearing base may be visible through the bearing overlay in small localized areas. This may not mean that the bearing is excessively worn. It is not necessary to replace the bearing if the bearing clearance is within recommended specifications.

4. Check the clearance of bearings that appear to be satisfactory with Plastigage® or its equivalent. Fit the new bearings following the procedure Crankshaft and Main Bearings removal and installation, they should be reground to size for the next undersize bearing.

5. Regrind the journals to give the proper clearance with the next undersize bearing. If the journal will not clean up to maximum un-

dersize bearing available, replace the crankshaft.

6. Always reproduce the same journal shoulder radius that existed originally. Too small a radius will result in fatigue failure of the crankshaft. Too large a radius will result in bearing failure due to radius ride of the bearing.

7. After regrinding the journals, chamfer the oil holes, then polish the journals with a #320 grit polishing cloth and engine oil. Crocus cloth may also be used as a polishing agent.

COMPLETING THE REBUILDING PROCESS

Fill the oil pump with oil, to prevent cavitating (sucking air) on initial engine start up. Install the oil pump and the pickup tube on the engine. Coat the oil pan gasket as necessary, and install the gasket and the oil pan. Mount the flywheel and the crankshaft vibration damper or pulley on the crankshaft.

NOTE: *Always use new bolts when installing the flywheel. Inspect the clutch shaft pilot bushing in the crankshaft. If the bushing is excessively worn, remove it with an expanding puller and a slide hammer, and tap a new bushing into place.*

Position the engine, cylinder head side up. Lubricate the lifters, and install them into their bores. Install the cylinder head, and torque it as specified. Insert the pushrods (where applicable), and install the rocker shaft(s) (if so equipped) or position the rocker.

Install the intake and exhaust manifolds, the carburetor(s), the distributor and spark plugs. Mount all accessories and install the engine in the car. Fill the radiator with coolant, and the crankcase with high quality engine oil.

BREAK-IN PROCEDURE

Start the engine, and allow it to run at low speed for a few minutes, while checking for leaks. Stop the engine, check the oil level, and fill as necessary. Restart the engine, and fill the cooling system to capacity. Check and adjust the ignition timing. Run the engine at low to medium speed (800–2,500 rpm) for approximately 1/2 hour, and retorque the cylinder head bolts. Road test the car, and check again for leaks.

NOTE: *Some gasket manufacturers recommend not retorquing the cylinder head(s) due to the composition of the head gasket. Follow the directions in the gasket set.*

Flywheel/Flex Plate and Ring Gear

NOTE: *Flex plate is the term for a flywheel mated with an automatic transmission.*

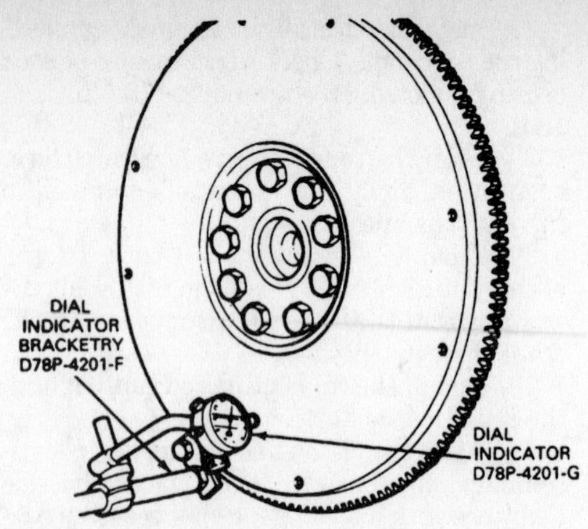

Checking flywheel runout

REMOVAL AND INSTALLATION

All Engines

NOTE: *The ring gear is replaceable only on engines mated with a manual transmission. Engines with automatic transmissions have ring gears which are welded to the flex plate.*

1. Remove the transmission and transfer case.
2. Remove the clutch, if equipped, or torque converter from the flywheel. The flywheel bolts should be loosened a little at a time in a cross pattern to avoid warping the flywheel. On cars with manual transmissions, replace the pilot bearing in the end of the crankshaft if removing the flywheel.
3. The flywheel should be checked for cracks and glazing. It can be resurfaced by a machine shop.
4. If the ring gear is to be replaced, drill a hole in the gear between two teeth, being careful not to contact the flywheel surface. Using a cold chisel at this point, crack the ring gear and remove it.
5. Polish the inner surface of the new ring gear and heat it in an oven to about 600°F (316°C). Quickly place the ring gear on the flywheel and tap it into place, making sure that it is fully seated.

WARNING: *Never heat the ring gear past 800°F (426°C), or the tempering will be destroyed.*

6. Position the flywheel on the end of the crankshaft. Torque the bolts a little at a time, in a cross pattern, to the torque figure shown in the Torque Specifications Chart.
7. Install the clutch or torque converter.
8. Install the transmission and transfer case.

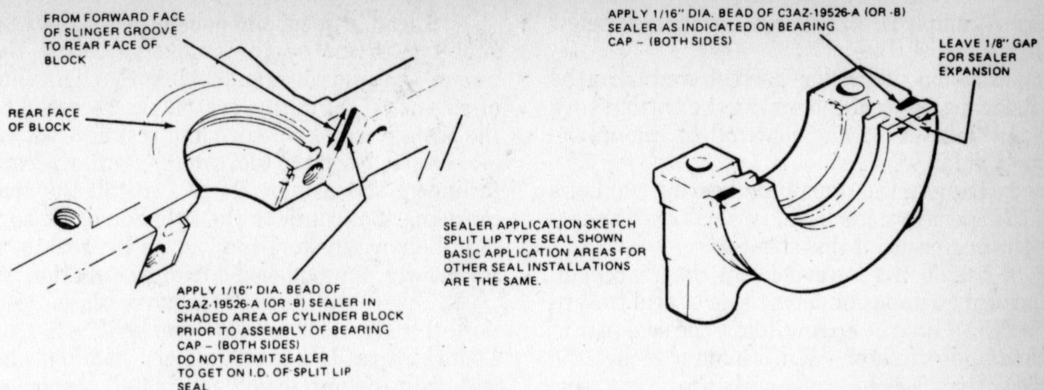

RTV sealant application on the main bearing cap of all gasoline V8s

Rear Main Oil Seal

REPLACEMENT – TWO PIECE SEAL

Gasoline V8

1. Remove the oil pan and the oil pump (if required).

2. Loosen all the main bearing cap bolts, thereby lowering the crankshaft slightly but not to exceed $\frac{1}{32}$ in. (0.8mm).

3. Remove the rear main bearing cap, and remove the oil seal from the bearing cap and cylinder block. On the block half of the seal use a seal removal tool, or install a small metal screw in one end of the seal, and pull on the screw to remove the seal. Exercise caution to prevent scratching or damaging the crankshaft seal surfaces.

4. Remove the oil seal retaining pin from the bearing cap if so equipped. The pin is not used with the split-lip seal.

5. Carefully clean the seal groove in the cap and block with a brush and solvent such as lacquer thinner, spot remover, or equivalent, or trichlorethylene. Also, clean the area thoroughly, so that no solvent touches the seal.

6. Dip the split lip-type seal halves in clean engine oil.

7. Carefully install the upper seal (cylinder block) into its groove with undercut side of the seal toward the FRONT of the engine, by rotating it on the seal journal of the crankshaft until

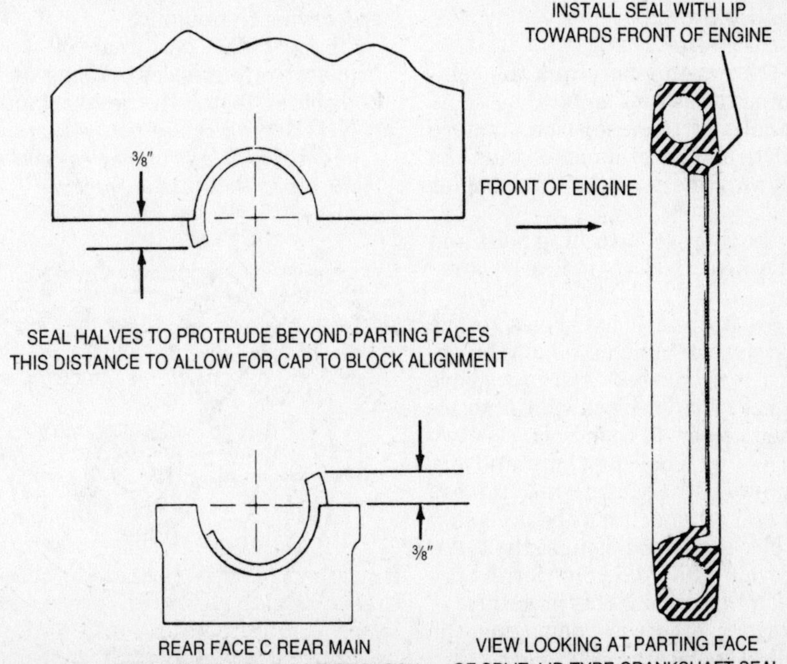

2-piece rear main seal installation on all V8s

approximately 3/8 in. (9.5mm) protrudes below the parting surface.

Be sure no rubber has been shaved from the outside diameter of the seal by the bottom edge of the groove. Do not allow oil to get on the sealer area.

8. Tighten the remaining bearing cap bolts to the specifications listed in the Torque chart at the beginning of this chapter.

9. Install the lower seal in the rear main bearing cap under undercut side of seal toward the FRONT of the engine, allow the seal to protrude approximately 3/8 in. (9.5mm) above the parting surface to mate with the upper seal when the cap is installed.

10. Apply an even 1/16 in. (1.6mm) bead of RTV silicone rubber sealer, to the areas shown, following the procedure given in the illustration.

11. Install the rear main bearing cap. Tighten the cap bolts to specifications.

12. Install the oil pump and oil pan. Fill the crankcase with the proper amount and type of oil.

13. Operate the engine and check for oil leaks.

6–4.9L

If the crankshaft rear oil seal replacement is the only operation being performed, it can be done in the vehicle as detailed in the following procedure. If the oil seal is being replaced in conjunction with a rear main bearing replacement, the engine must be removed from the vehicle and install on a work stand.

1. Remove the starter.
2. Remove the transmission from the vehicle, following procedures in Chapter 6.
3. On manual shift transmission, remove the pressure plate and cover assembly and the clutch disc following the procedure in Chapter 7.
4. Remove the flywheel attaching bolts and remove the flywheel and engine rear cover plate.
5. Use an awl to punch two holes in the crankshaft rear oil seal. Punch the holes on opposite sides of the crankshaft and just above the bearing cap to cylinder block split line. Install a sheet metal screw in each hole. Use two large screwdrivers or small pry bars and pry against both screws at the same time to remove the crankshaft rear oil seal. It may be necessary to place small blocks of wood against the cylinder block to provide a fulcrum point for the pry bars. Use caution throughout this procedure to avoid scratching or otherwise damaging the crankshaft oil seal surface.
6. Clean the oil seal recess in the cylinder block and main bearing cap.
7. Clean, inspect and polish the rear oil seal rubbing surface on the crankshaft. Coat the new oil seal and the crankshaft with a light film of engine oil. Start the seal in the recess with the seal lip facing forward and install it with a seal driver. Keep the tool straight with the centerline of the crankshaft and install the seal until the tool contacts the cylinder block surface. Remove the tool and inspect the seal to be sure it was not damaged during installation.
8. Install the engine rear cover plate. Position the flywheel on the crankshaft flange. Coat the threads of the flywheel attaching bolts with oil-resistant sealer and install the bolts. Tighten the bolts in sequence across from each other to the specifications listed in the Torque chart at the beginning of this Chapter.
9. On a manual shift transmission, install the clutch disc and the pressure plate assembly following the procedure in Chapter 7.
10. Install the transmission, following the procedure in Chapter 7.

6.9L and 7.3L Diesel

1. Remove the transmission, clutch and flywheel assemblies.
2. Remove the engine rear cover.
3. Using an arbor press and a 4 1/8 in. (104.775mm) diameter spacer, press out the rear oil seal from the cover.
4. To install, clean the rear cover and engine block surfaces. Remove all traces of old RTV sealant from the oil pan and rear cover sealing surface by cleaning with a suitable solvent and drying thoroughly.
5. Coat the new rear oil seal with Lubriplate® or equivalent. Using an arbor press and spacer, install the new seal into the cover.

NOTE: *The seal must be installed from the engine block side of the rear cover, flush with the seal bore inner surface.*

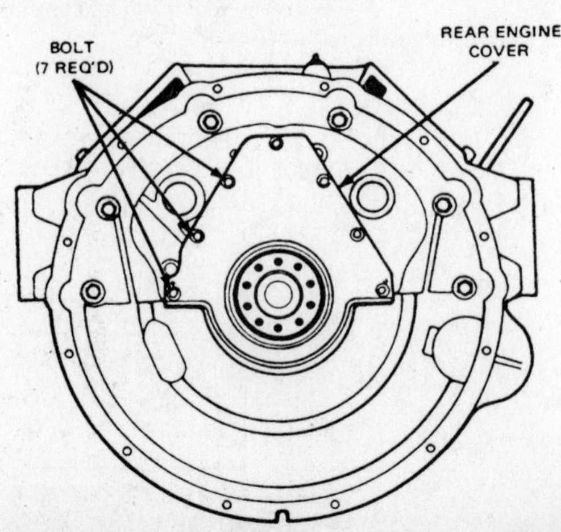

Diesel rear cover removal

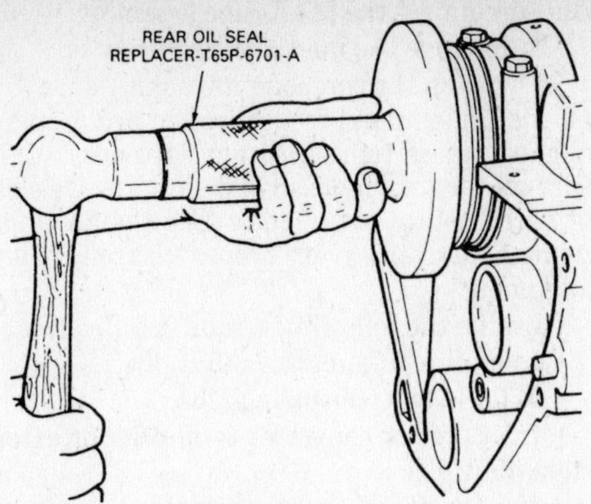

Installing the 1-piece main seal on gasoline engines

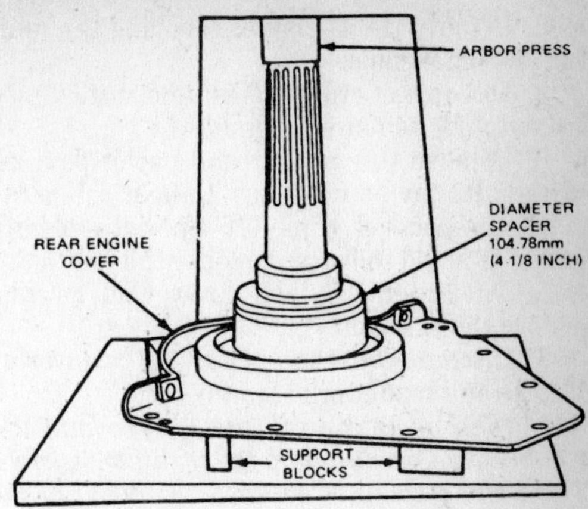

1-piece diesel rear main seal removal or installation

6. Install a seal pilot, ford part no. T83T–6701B or equivalent onto the crankshaft.

7. Apply gasket sealant to the engine block gasket surfaces, and install the rear cover gasket to the engine.

8. Apply a 1/4 in. (6mm) bead of RTV sealant onto the oil pan sealing surface, immediately after rear cover installation.

9. Push the rear cover into position on the engine and install the cover bolts. Torque to specification.

10. Position the flywheel on the crankshaft flange. Coat the threads of the flywheel attaching bolts with sealant and install the bolts and flexplate, if equipped. Torque the bolts to specification, alternating across from each bolt.

11. Install the clutch and transmission. Run the engine and check for oil leaks.

REPLACEMENT – ONE PIECE SEAL

1. Remove the transmission, clutch assembly or converter and flywheel.

2. (See Step 7 for diesel engines). Lower the oil pan if necessary for working room.

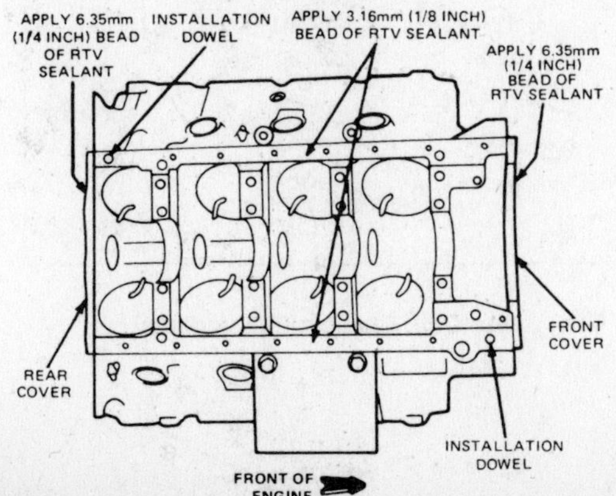

Diesel oil pan sealer application

3. On gasoline engines, use an awl to punch two small holes on opposite sides of the seal just above the split between the main bearing cap and engine block. Install a sheet metal screw in each hole. Use two small pry bars and pry evenly on both screws using two small blocks of wood as a fulcrum point for the pry bars. Use caution throughout to avoid scratching or damage to the oil seal mounting surfaces.

4. When the seal has been removed, clean the mounting recess.

5. Coat the seal and block mounting surfaces with oil. Apply white lube to the contact surface of the seal and crankshaft. Start the seal into the mounting recess and install with seal mounting tool Ford number T82L–6701–A or equivalent.

6. Install the remaining components in the reverse.

7. On the diesel engines, the oil seal is one piece but mounted on a retaining plate. Remove the mounting plate from the rear of the engine and replace the seal. Reinstall in reverse order of removal.

EXHAUST SYSTEM

CAUTION: *When working on exhaust systems, ALWAYS wear protective goggles! Avoid working on a hot exhaust system!*

Muffler, Catalytic Converter, Inlet and Outlet Pipes

REMOVAL AND INSTALLATION

NOTE: *The following applies to exhaust systems using clamped joints. Some models, use welded joints at the muffler. These joints will, of course, have to be cut.*

1. Raise and support the truck on jackstands.

2. Remove the U-clamps securing the muffler and outlet pipe.

3. Disconnect the muffler and outlet pipe bracket and insulator assemblies.

4. Remove the muffler and outlet pipe assembly. It may be necessary to heat the joints to get the parts to come off. Special tools are available to aid in breaking loose the joints.

5. On Super Cab and Crew Cab models, remove the extension pipe.

6. Disconnect the catalytic converter bracket and insulator assembly.

NOTE: *For rod and insulator type hangers, apply a soap solution to the insulator surface and rod ends to allow easier removal of the insulator from the rod end. Don't use oil-based or silicone-based solutions since they will allow the insulator to slip back off once it's installed.*

7. Remove the catalytic converter.

8. On models with Managed Thermactor Air, disconnect the MTA tube assembly.

9. Remove the inlet pipe assembly.

10. Install the components making sure that all the components in the system are properly aligned before tightening any fasteners. Make sure all tabs are indexed and all parts are clear of surrounding body panels. See the accompanying illustrations for proper clearances and alignment.

Observe the following torque specifications:

- Inlet pipe-to-manifold: 35 ft. lbs.
- MTA U-bolt: 60–96 inch lbs.
- Inlet pipe or converter-to-muffler or extension: 45 ft. lbs.
- Hanger bracket and insulator-to-frame: 24 ft. lbs.
- Bracket and insulator-to-exhaust: 15 ft. lbs.
- Flat flange bolts (8–7.5L and diesel) 30 ft. lbs.

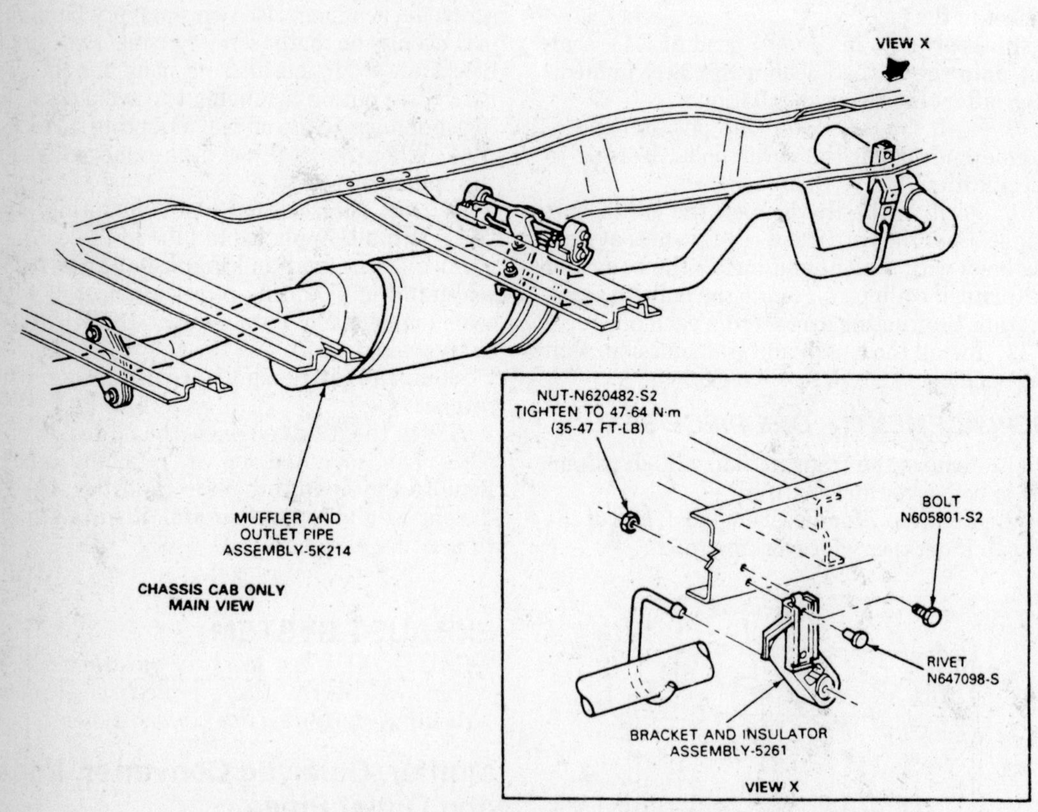

Exhaust system on the F-250HD, 350 Regular Cab, Super Cab, Chassis Cab w/diesel

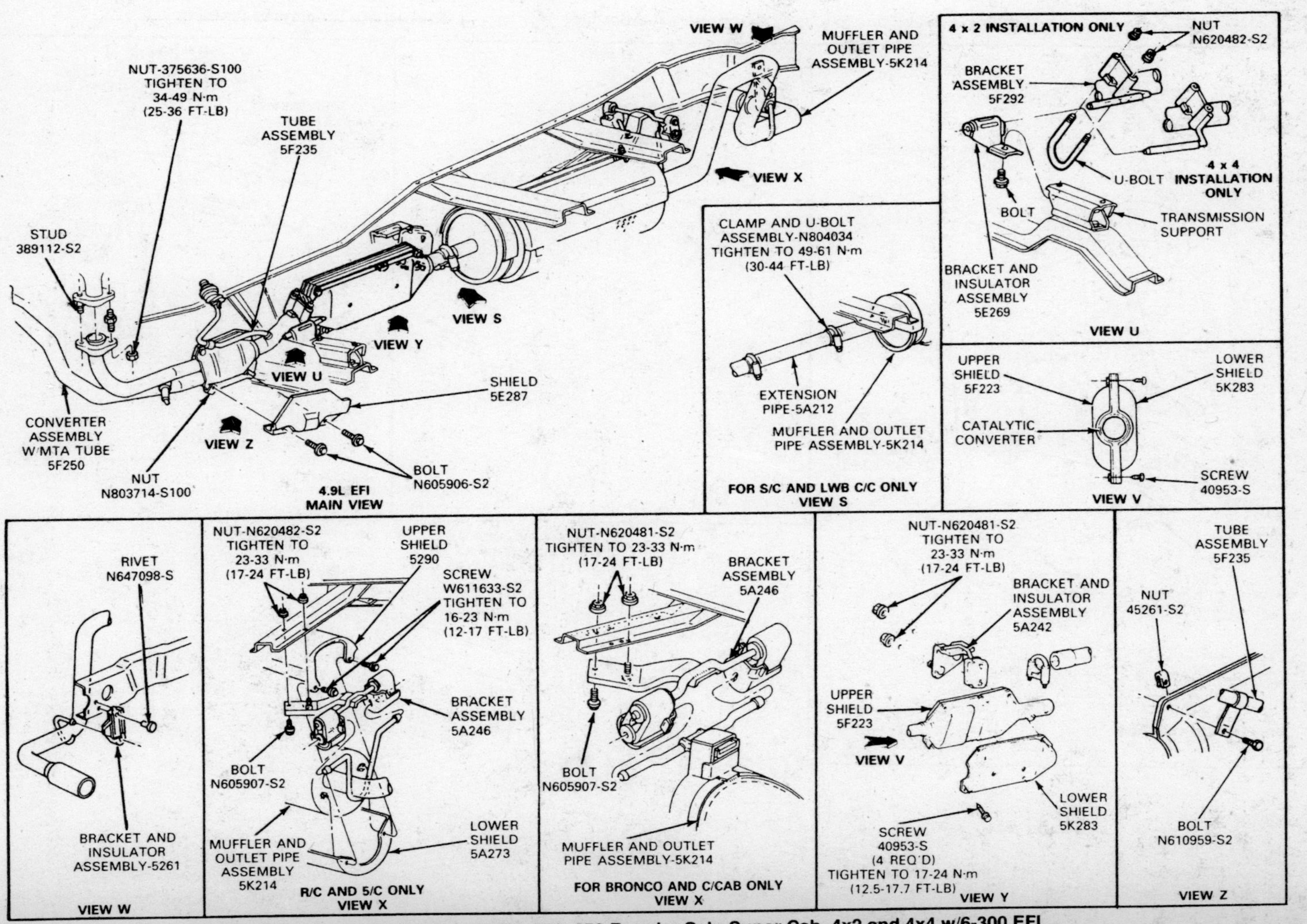

Exhaust system on the Bronco, F-150, 250, 350 Regular Cab, Super Cab, 4x2 and 4x4 w/6-300 EFI

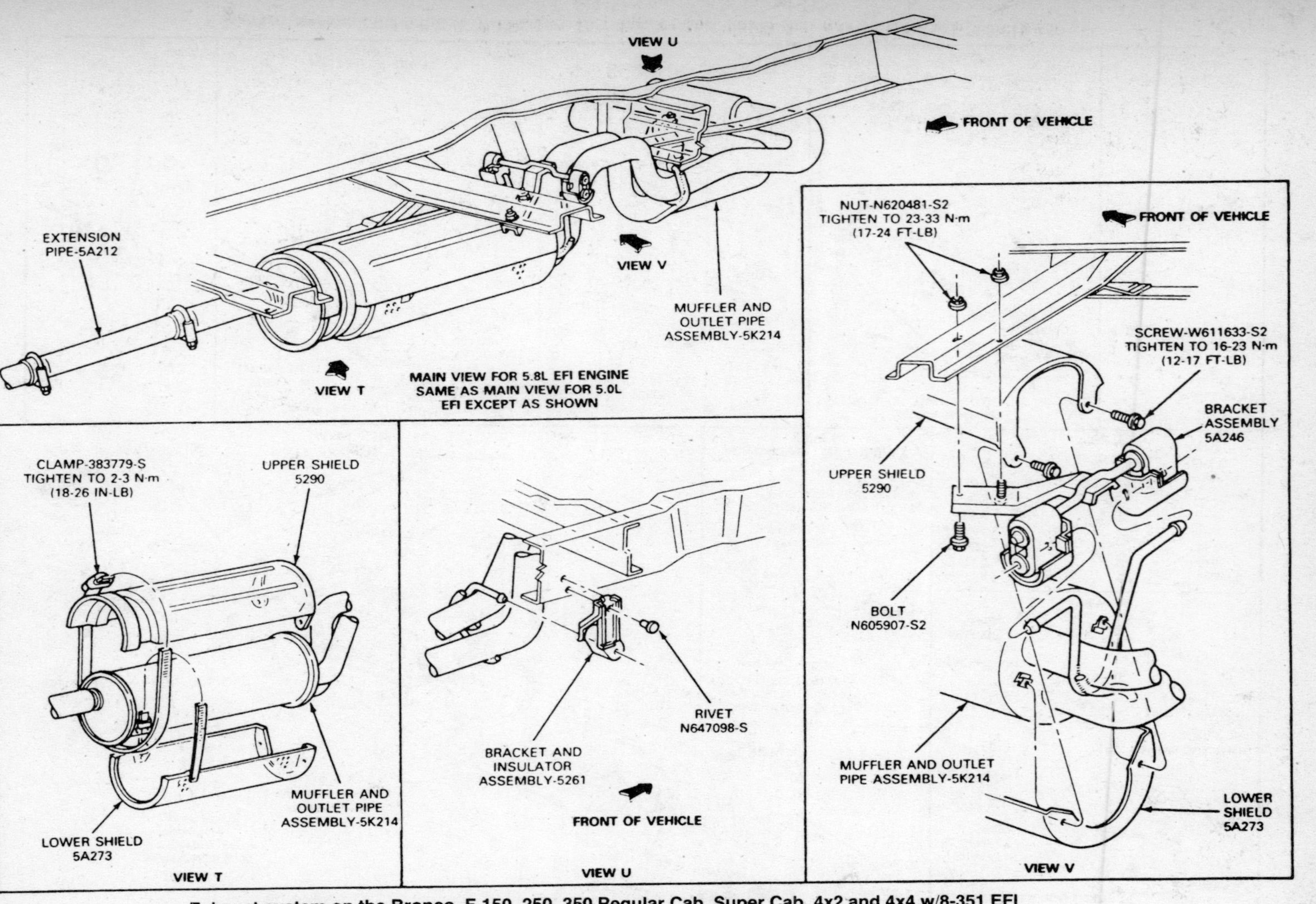

Exhaust system on the Bronco, F-150, 250, 350 Regular Cab, Super Cab, 4x2 and 4x4 w/8-351 EFI

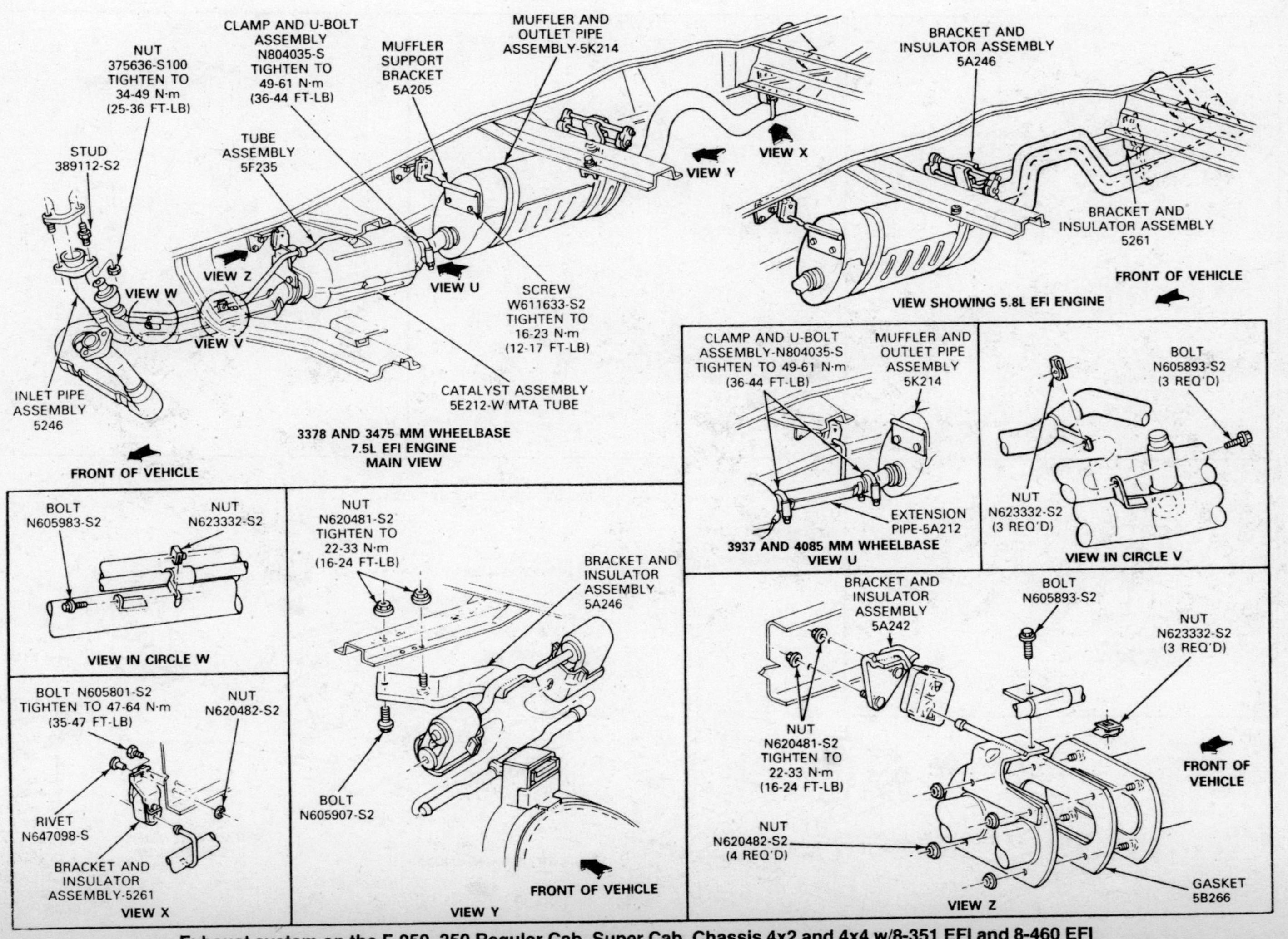

Exhaust system on the F-250, 350 Regular Cab, Super Cab, Chassis 4x2 and 4x4 w/8-351 EFI and 8-460 EFI

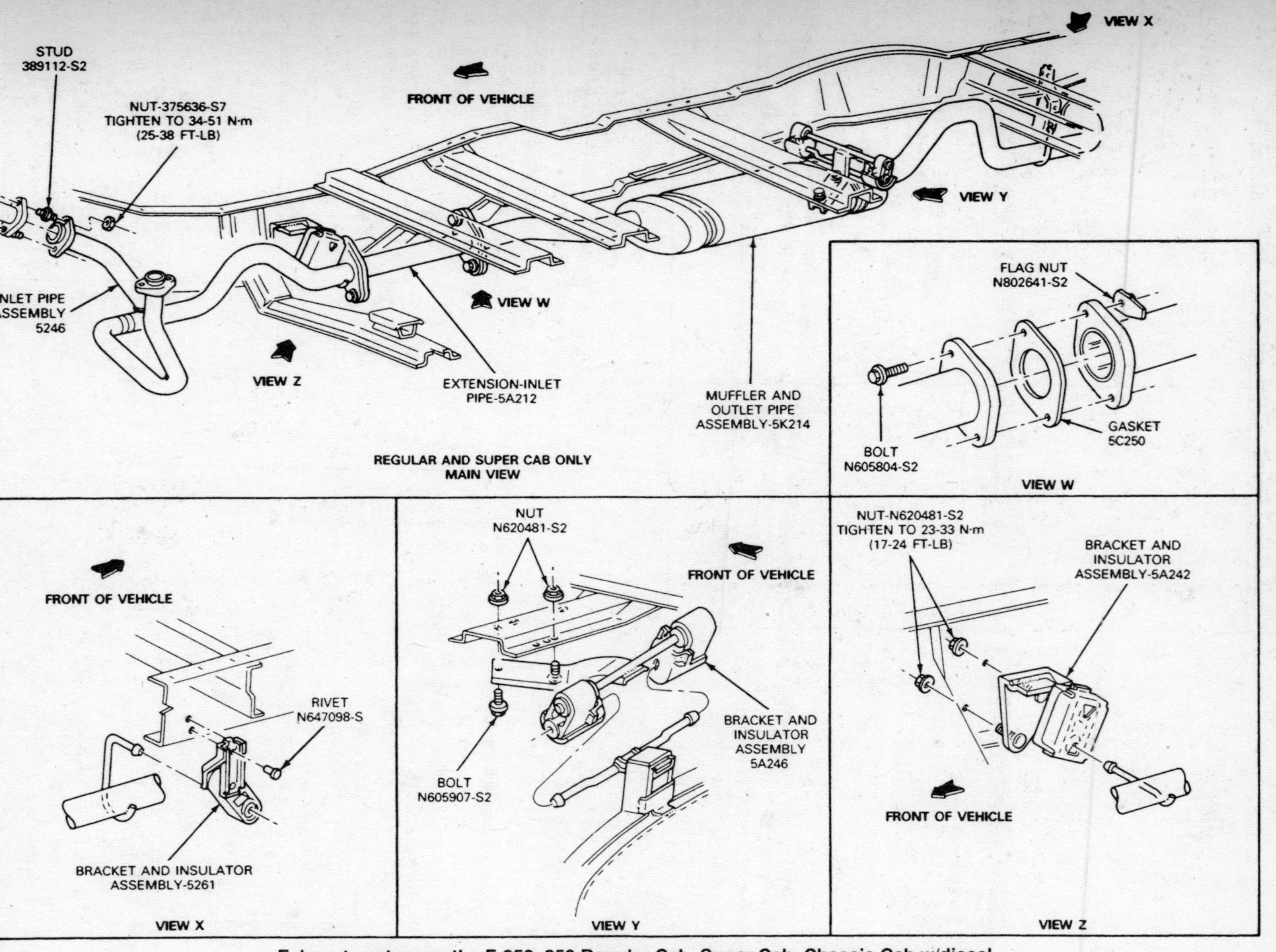

Exhaust system on the F-250, 350 Regular Cab, Super Cab, Chassis Cab w/diesel

Emission Controls

4

EMISSION CONTROLS APPLICATIONS

6–4.9L:
Positive Crankcase Ventilation system (PCV)
Evaporative Emission system (canister)
Three-way Catalyst (TWC)
Conventional Oxidation Catalyst (COC)
Electronic Fuel Injection Fuel System (EFI)
Electronic Engine Control IV system (EEC-IV)
Electronic (Sonic)
Exhaust Gas Recirculation (EEGR)
Managed Thermactor Air system (MTA)
Air Management 1 system (AM1)
Air Management 2 system (AM2)
Thick Film Ignition system (TFI-IV)
Bypass Air idle speed control (BPA)
8–5.0L 8–5.8L w/Fuel Injection:
Positive Crankcase Ventilation system (PCV)
Evaporative Emission system (canister)
Three-way Catalyst (TWC)
Conventional Oxidation Catalyst (COC)
Electronic Fuel Injection Fuel System (EFI)
Electronic Engine Control IV system (EEC-IV)
Electronic (Sonic)
Exhaust Gas Recirculation (EEGR)
Managed Thermactor Air system (MTA)
Air Management 1 system (AM1)
Air Management 2 system (AM2)
Thick Film Ignition system (TFI-IV)
Bypass Air idle speed control (BPA)
8–5.8L w/4-bbl Carburetor:
Positive Crankcase Ventilation system (PCV)
Evaporative Emission system (canister)
Three-way Catalyst (TWC)
Conventional Oxidation Catalyst (COC)
Holley 4180C 4-bbl carburetor Integral backpressure EGR valve (IBP)
Managed Thermactor Air System (MTA)
Dura Spark II Ignition System (DS-II)
8–7.5L w/4-bbl Carburetor:
Positive Crankcase Ventilation system (PCV)
Evaporative Emission system (canister)
Holley 4180C 4-bbl carburetor Exhaust Gas Recirculation system (EGR)
Managed Thermactor Air System (MTA)
Dura Spark II Ignition System (DS-II)
8–7.5L w/Fuel Injection: Positive Crankcase Ventilation system (PCV)
Evaporative Emission system (canister)
4 Reduction-Oxidation Catalysts (REDOX)
Electronic Fuel Injection fuel system (EFI)
Electronic Engine Control IV system (EEC-IV)
Electronic (Sonic)
Exhaust Gas Recirculation (EEGR)
Managed Thermactor Air System (MTA)
Thick Film Ignition ignition system (TFI-IV)
Bypass Air idle speed control (BPA)

Positive Crankcase Ventilation System

The crankcase emission control equipment consists of a positive crankcase ventilation (PCV) valve, a closed oil filler cap and the hoses that connect this equipment.

When the engine is running, a small portion of the gases which are formed in the combustion chamber leak by the piston rings and enter the crankcase. Since these gases are under pressure they tend to escape from the crankcase and enter into the atmosphere. If these gases are allowed to remain in the crankcase for any length of time, they would contaminate the engine oil and cause sludge to build up. If the gases are allowed to escape into the atmosphere, they would pollute the air, as they contain unburned hydrocarbons. The crankcase emission control equipment recycles these gases back into the engine combustion chamber, where they are burned.

Crankcase gases are recycled in the following manner. While the engine is running, clean filtered air is drawn into the crankcase through the intake air filter and then through a hose

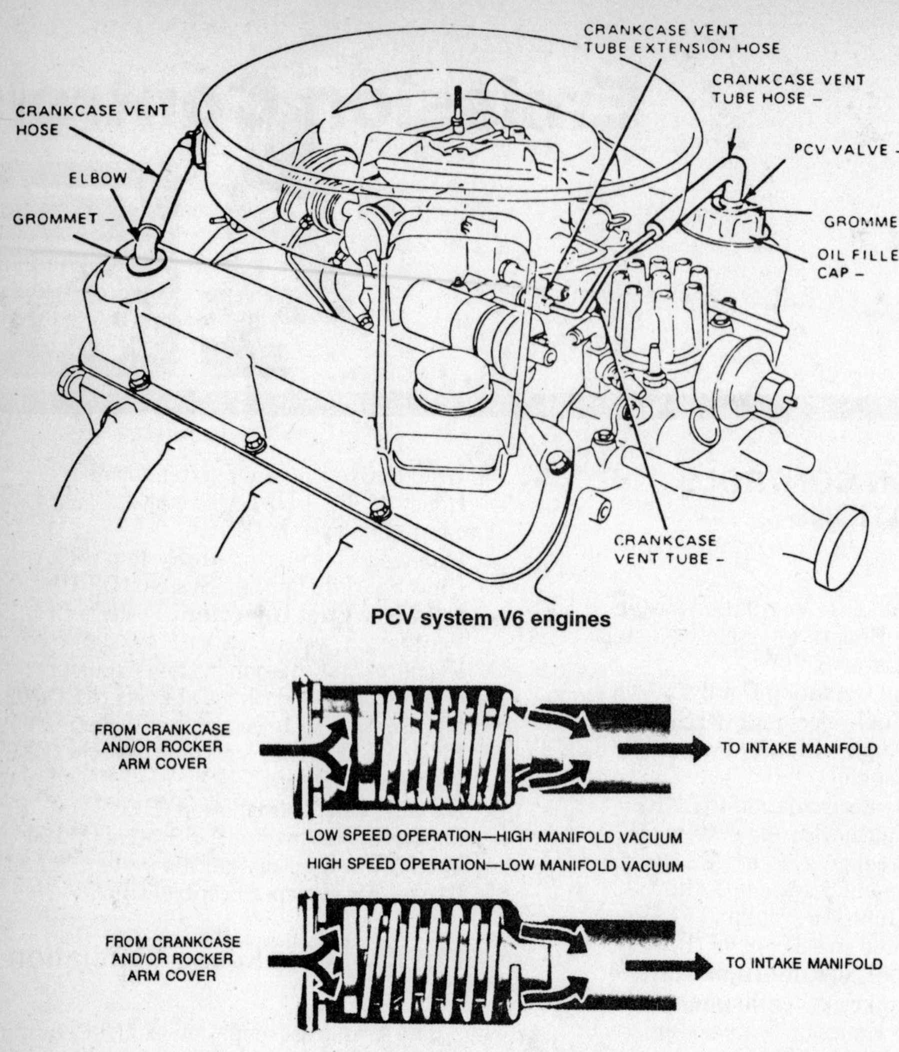

PCV system V6 engines

Cutaway of a PCV valve

leading to the oil filler cap. As the air passes through the crankcase it picks up the combustion gases and carries them out of the crankcase, up through the PCV valve and into the intake manifold. After they enter the intake manifold they are drawn into the combustion chamber and are burned.

The most critical component of the system is the PCV valve. This vacuum-controlled valve regulates the amount of gases which are recycled into the combustion chamber. At low engine speeds the valve is partially closed, limiting the flow of gases into the intake manifold. As engine speed increases, the valve opens to admit greater quantities of the gases into the intake manifold. If the valve should become blocked or plugged, the gases will be prevented from escaping the crankcase by the normal route. Since these gases are under pressure, they will find their own way out of the crankcase. This alternate route is usually a weak oil seal or gasket in the engine. As the gas escapes by the gasket, it also creates an oil leak. Besides causing oil leaks, a clogged PCV valve also allows these gases to remain in the crankcase for an extended period of time, promoting the formation of sludge in the engine.

The above explanation and the troubleshooting procedure which follows applies to all of the gasoline engines installed in Ford trucks, since all are equipped with PCV systems.

TROUBLESHOOTING

With the engine running, pull the PCV valve and hose from the valve rocker cover rubber grommet.

A hissing noise should be heard as air passes through the valve and a strong vacuum should be felt when you place a finger over the valve inlet if the valve is working properly. While you

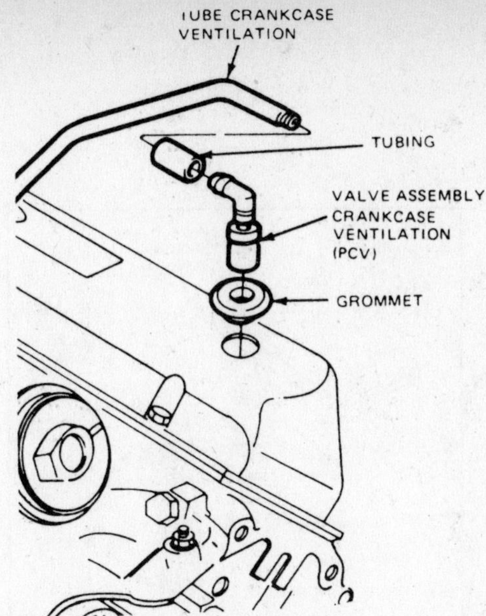

V8 PCV valve components

have your finger over the PCV valve inlet, check for vacuum leaks in the hose and at the connections.

When the PCV valve is removed from the engine, a metallic licking noise should be heard when it is shaken. This indicates that the metal check ball inside the valve is still free and is not gummed up.

REPLACEMENT

1. Pull the PCV valve and hose from the rubber grommet in the rocker cover.
2. Remove the PCV valve from the hose. Inspect the inside of the PCV valve. If it is dirty, disconnect it from the intake manifold and clean it in a suitable, safe solvent.

To install, proceed as follows:

1. If the PCV valve hose was removed, connect it to the intake manifold.
2. Connect the PCV valve to its hose.
3. Install the PCV valve into the rubber grommet in the valve rocker cover.

Evaporative Emission Controls

Changes in atmospheric temperature cause fuel tanks to breathe; that is, the air within the tank expands and contracts with outside temperature changes. As the temperature rises, air escapes through the tank vent tube or the vent in the tank cap. The air which escapes contains gasoline vapors. In a similar manner on carbureted engines, the gasoline which fills the carburetor float bowl expands when the engine is stopped. Engine heat causes this expansion. The vapors escape through the air cleaner.

The Evaporative Emission Control System provides a sealed fuel system with the capability to store and condense fuel vapors. The system has three parts: a fill control vent system; a vapor vent and storage system; and a pressure and vacuum relief system (special fill cap).

The fill control vent system is a modification to the fuel tank. It uses a dome air space within the tank which is 10–12% of the tank's volume. The air space is sufficient to provide for the thermal expansion of the fuel. The space also serves as part of the in-tank vapor vent system.

The in-tank vent system consists of the domed air space previously described and a vapor separator assembly. The separator assembly is mounted to the top of the fuel tank and is secured by a cam-lockring, similar to the one which secures the fuel sending unit. Foam material fills the vapor separator assembly. The foam material separates raw fuel and vapors, thus retarding the entrance of fuel into the vapor line.

The vapor separator is an orifice valve located in the dome of the tank. The restricted size of the orifice, 0.050 in. (1.27mm) tends to allow only vapor to pass out of the tank. The orifice valve is connected to the vent line which runs forward to the carbon filled canister in the engine compartment.

The sealed filler cap has a pressure-vacuum relief valve. Under normal operating conditions, the filler cap operates as a check valve, allowing air to enter the tank to replace the fuel

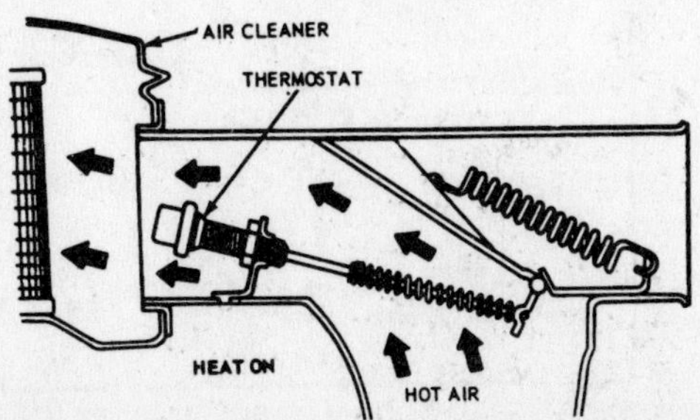

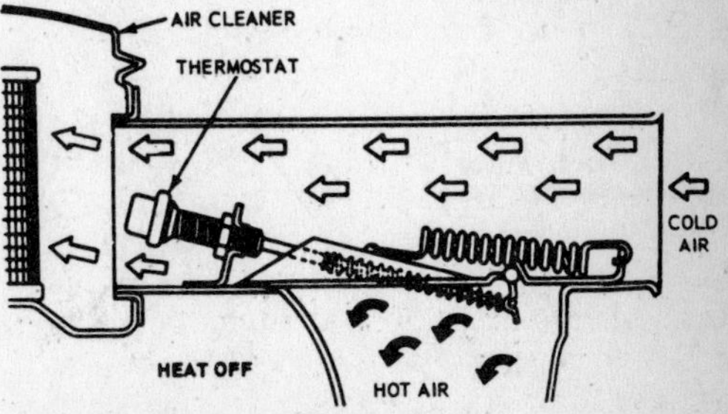

Operation of the thermostatically-controlled air cleaner

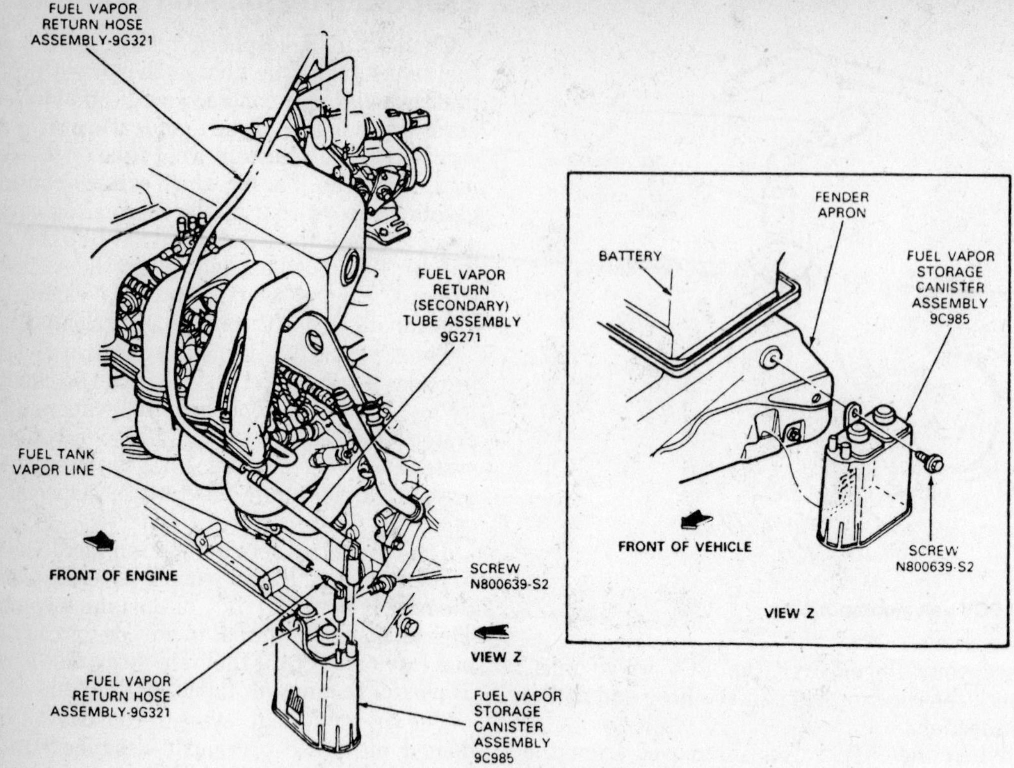

6–4.9L evaporative emission system

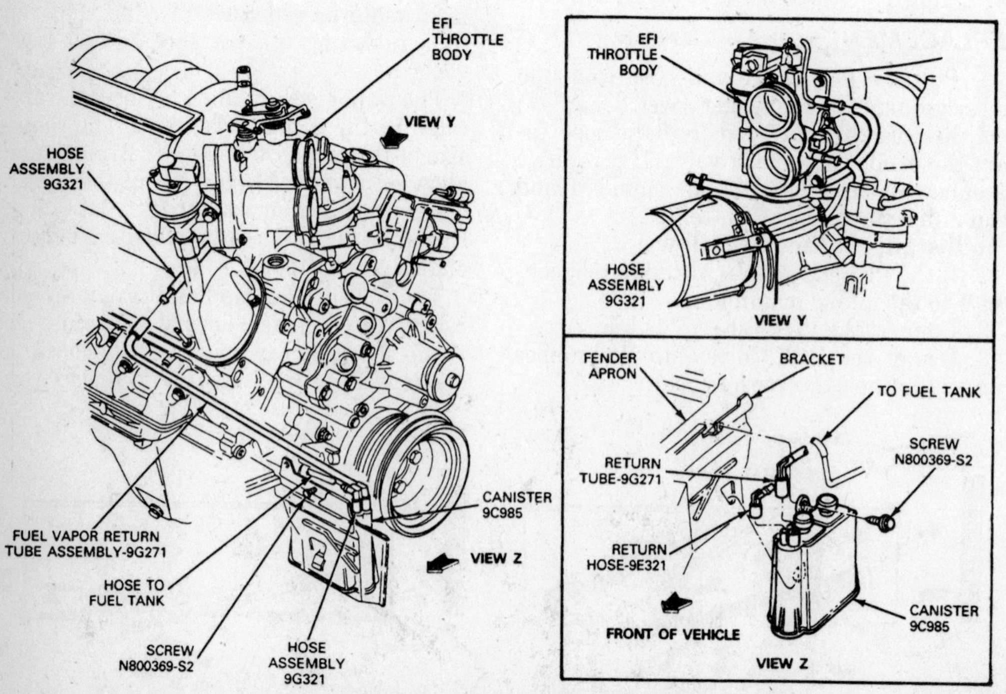

8–5.0L evaporative emission system

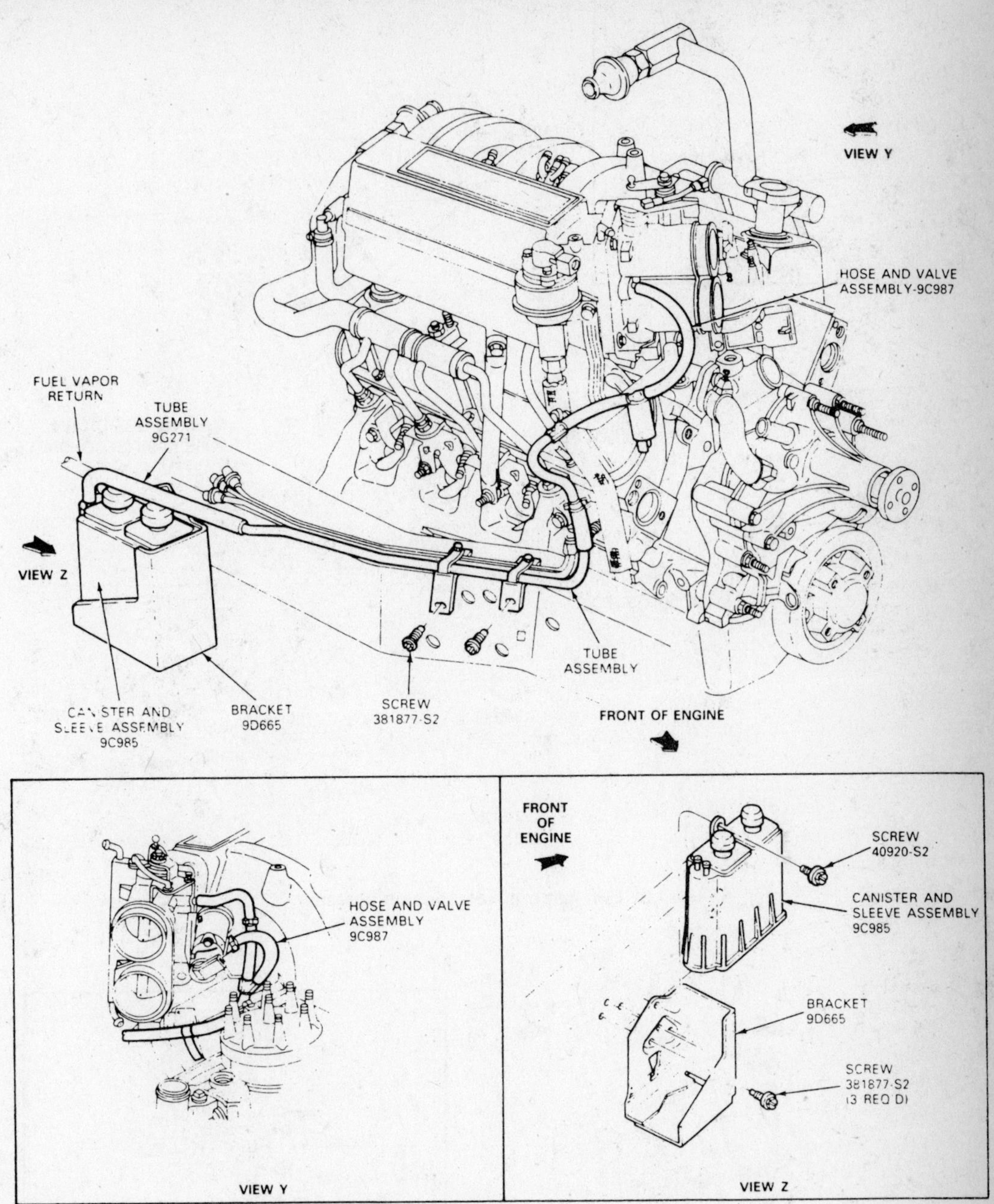

1987 8–5.8L evaporative emission system

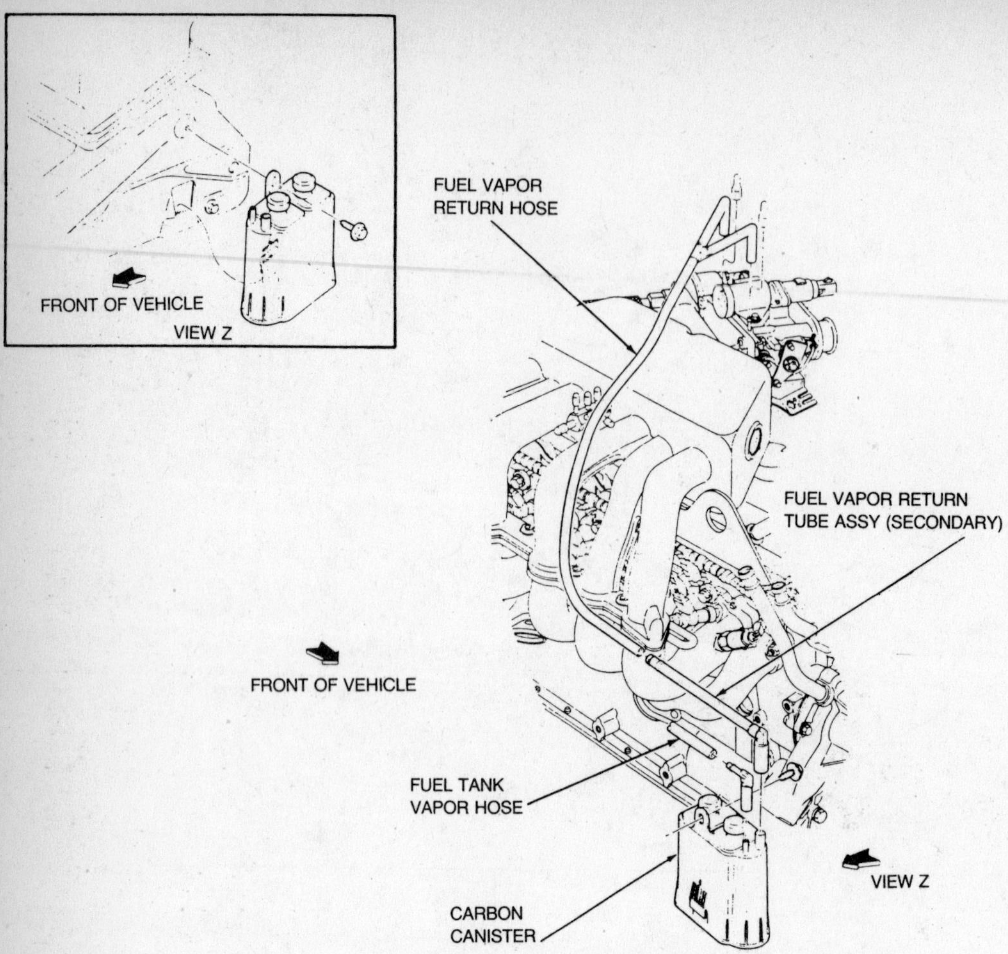

FRONT OF VEHICLE
VIEW Z
FUEL VAPOR RETURN HOSE
FUEL VAPOR RETURN TUBE ASSY (SECONDARY)
FRONT OF VEHICLE
FUEL TANK VAPOR HOSE
VIEW Z
CARBON CANISTER

6–4.9L EFI evaporative emission system

TUBE ASSEMBLY FUEL VAPOR RETURN
FRONT OF VEHICLE
FUEL TANK VAPOR HOSE
VIEW Z
FENDER APRON
TUBE ASSEMBLY FUEL VAPOR RETURN
THROTTLE BODY
AIR PUMP
FRONT OF VEHICLE
FRONT OF VEHICLE
BRACKET
VIEW Z

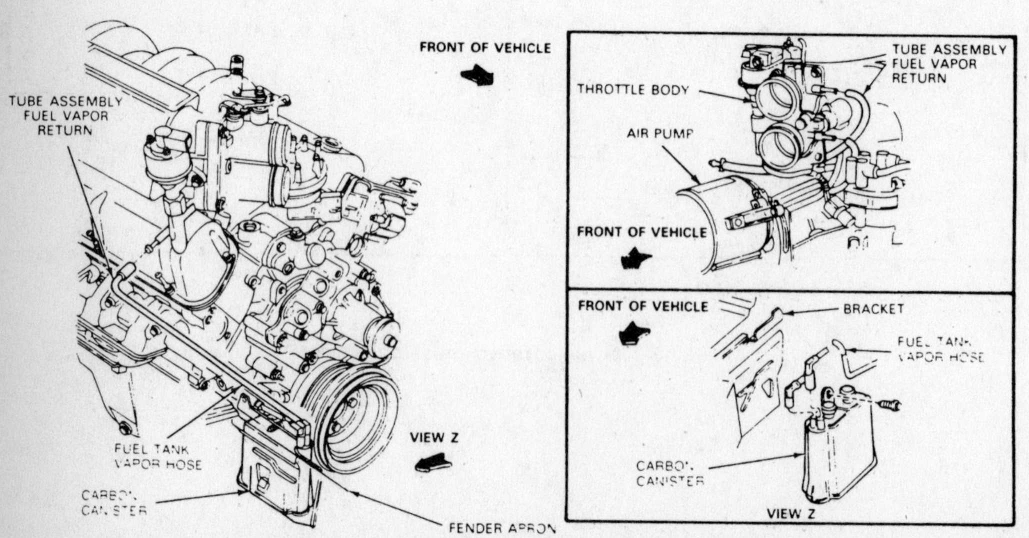

8–5.0L evaporative emission system

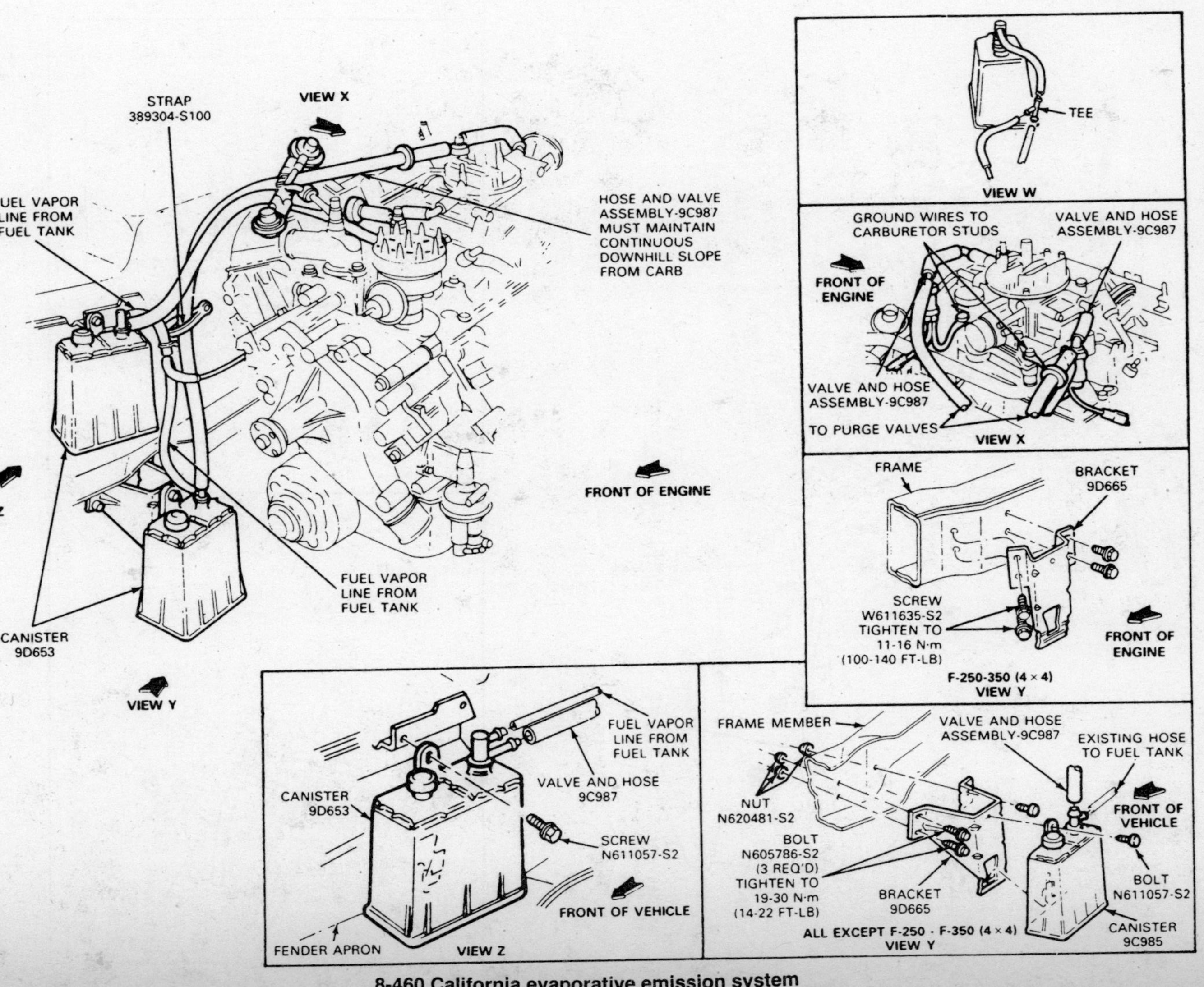

8-460 California evaporative emission system

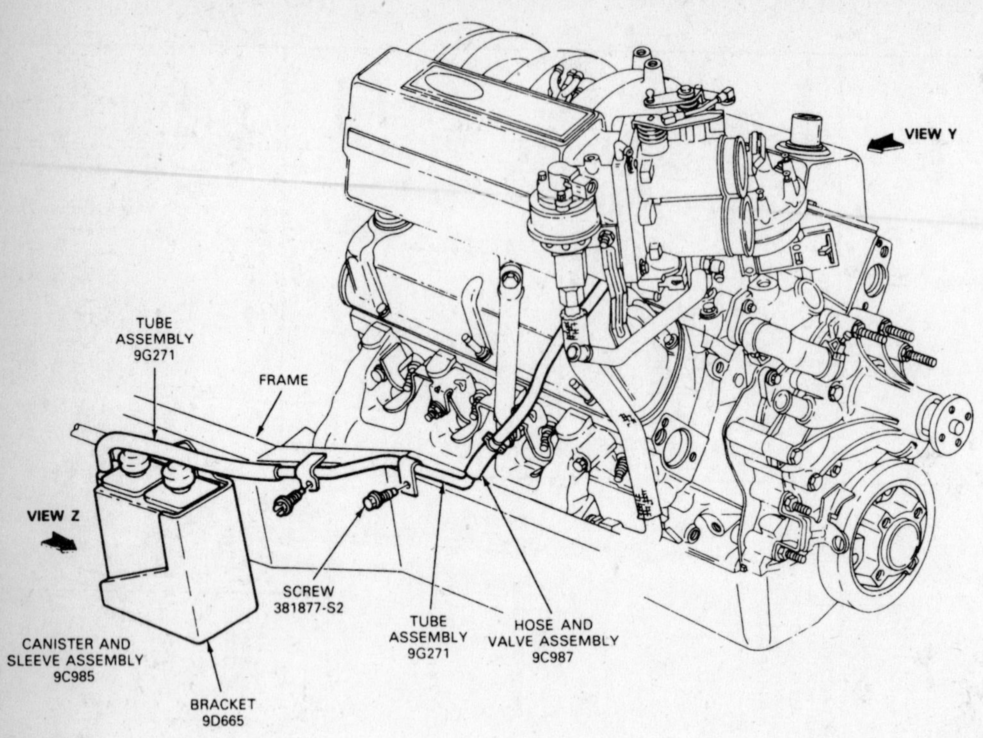

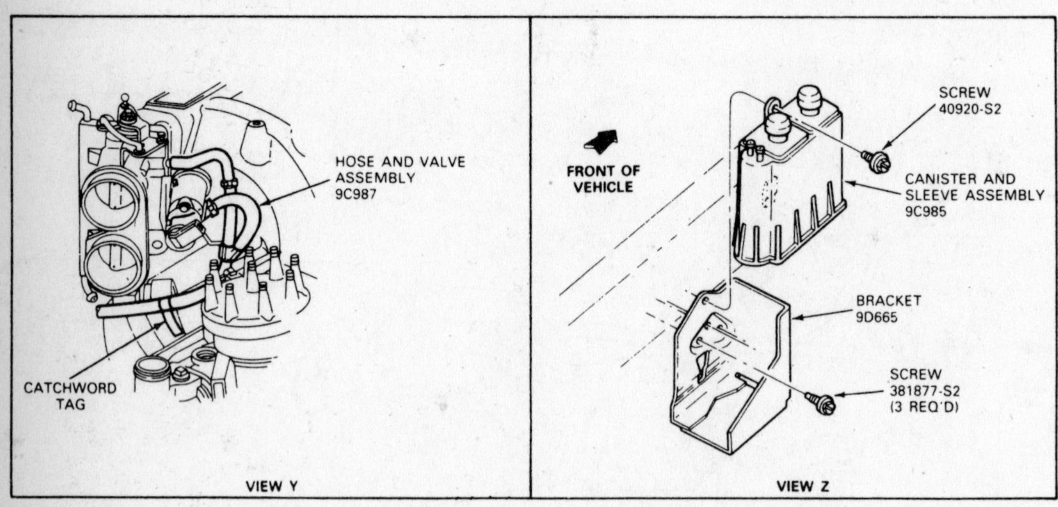

1988–90 8–5.8L evaporative emission system

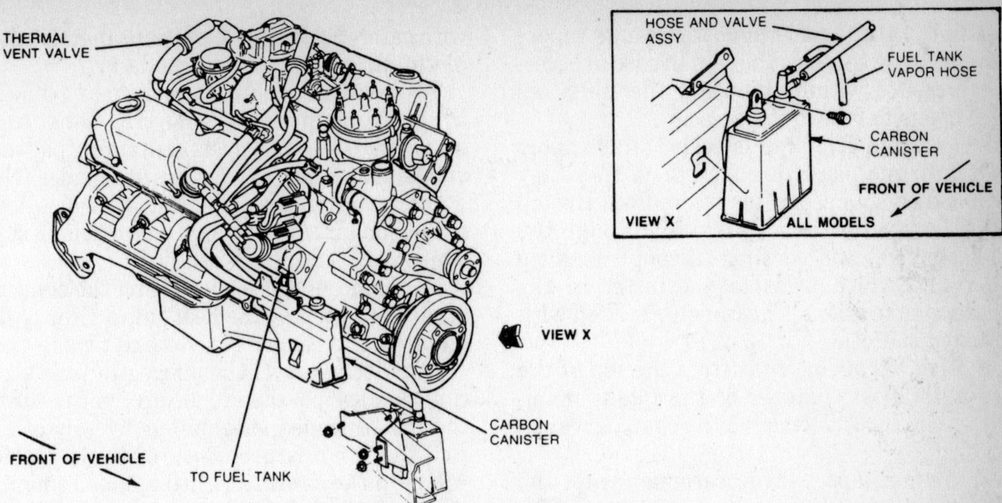

8–5.8L 4 bbl evaporative emission system

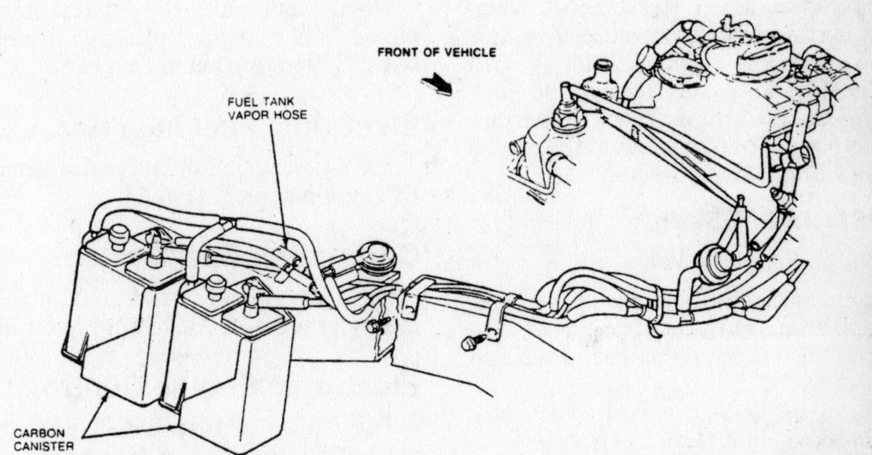

8–5.8L 4 bbl Heavy Duty Truck evaporative emission system, except California

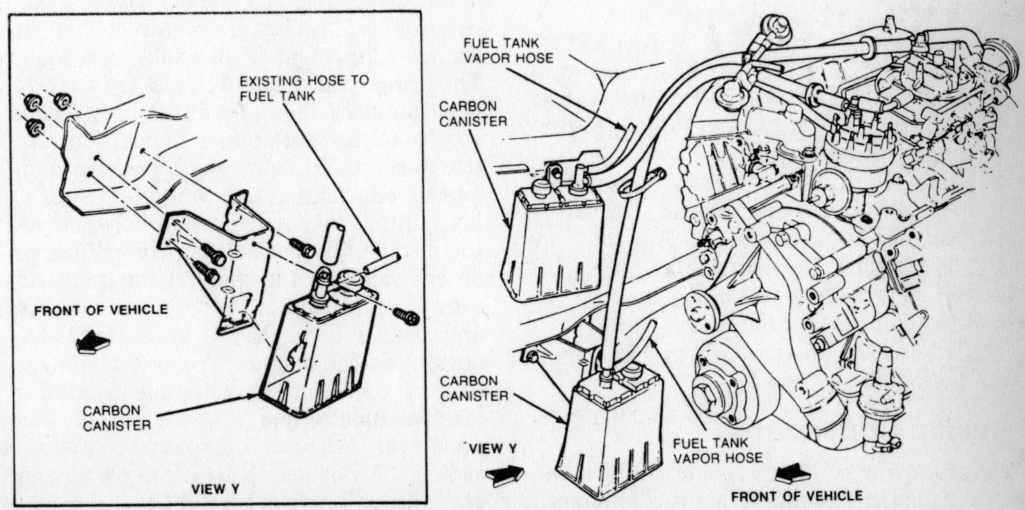

8–7.5L California and Canada Heavy Duty Truck evaporative emission system

consumed. At the same time, it prevents vapors from escaping through the cap. In case of excessive pressure within the tank, the filler cap valve opens to relieve the pressure.

Because the filler cap is sealed, fuel vapors have only one place through which they may escape: the vapor separator assembly at the top of the fuel tank. The vapors pass through the foam material and continue through a single vapor line which leads to a canister in the engine compartment. The canister is filled with activated charcoal.

Another vapor line runs from the top of the carburetor float chamber or the intake manifold, or the throttle body, to the charcoal canister.

As the fuel vapors (hydrocarbons), enter the charcoal canister, they are absorbed by the charcoal. The air is dispelled through the open bottom of the charcoal canister, leaving the hydrocarbons trapped within the charcoal. When the engine is started, vacuum causes fresh air to be drawn into the canister from its open bottom. The fresh air passes through the charcoal picking up the hydrocarbons which are trapped there and feeding them into the engine for burning with the fuel mixture.

DIAGNOSIS AND TESTING

Canister Purge Regulator Valve

1. Disconnect the hoses at the purge regulator valve. Disconnect the electrical lead.
2. Connect a vacuum pump to the vacuum source port.
3. Apply 5 in.Hg to the port. The valve should hold the vacuum. If not, replace it.

Canister Purge Valve

1. Apply vacuum to port **A**. The valve should hold vacuum. If not, replace it.
2. Apply vacuum to port **B**. Valves E5VE–AA, E4VE–AA and E77E–AA should show a slight vacuum leak-down. All other valves should hold vacuum. If the valve doesn't operate properly, replace it.
3. Apply 16 in.Hg to port **A** and apply vacuum to port **B**. Air should pass. On valves E5VE–AA, E4VE–AA and E77E–AA, the flow should be greater than that noted in Step 2.

NOTE: *Never apply vacuum to port C. Doing so will damage the valve.*

4. If the valve fails to perform properly in any of these tests, replace it.

Catalytic Converters

The catalytic converter, mounted in the trucks exhaust system is a muffler-shaped device containing a ceramic honeycomb shaped material coated with alumina and impregnated with catalytically active precious metals such as platinum, palladium and rhodium.

The catalyst's job is to reduce air pollutants by oxidizing hydrocarbons (HC) and carbon monoxide (CO). Catalysts containing palladium and rhodium also oxidize nitrous oxides (NOx).

On some trucks, the catalyst is also fed by the secondary air system, via a small supply tube in the side of the catalyst.

No maintenance is possible on the converter, other than keeping the heat shield clear of flammable debris, such as leaves and twigs.

Other than external damage, the only significant damage possible to a converter is through the use of leaded gasoline, or by way of a too rich fuel/air mixture. Both of these problems will ruin the converter through contamination of the catalyst and will eventually plug the converter causing loss of power and engine performance.

When this occurs, the catalyst must be replaced. For catalyst replacement, see the Exhaust System section in Chapter 3.

Electronic Fuel Injection

For a description of and maintenance to the EFI systems, see Chapter 5.

Carbureted Fuel System

For a description of and maintenance to the Holley 4180C 4-bbl carburetor, see Chapter 5.

Electronic Engine Controls

The Universal Distributor (EEC-IV) has a die cast base which incorporates an externally mounted TFI-IV ignition module, and contains a Hall Effect vane switch stator assembly and provision for fixed octane adjustment. No distributor calibration is required and initial timing adjustment is normally not required. The primary function of the EEC-IV Universal Distributor system is to direct high secondary voltage to the spark plugs. In addition, the distributor supplies crankshaft position and frequency information to a computer using a profile Ignition Pickup. The Hall Effect switch in the distributor consists of a Hall Effect device on one side and a magnet on the other side. A rotary cup which has windows and tabs rotates and passes through the space between the device and the magnet. When a window is between the sides of the switch the magnetic path is not completed and the switch is Off, sending no signal. When a tab passes between the switch the magnetic path is completed and the Hall Effect Device is turned On and a signal is sent. The voltage pulse (signal) is used by is EEC-IV system for sensing crankshaft position

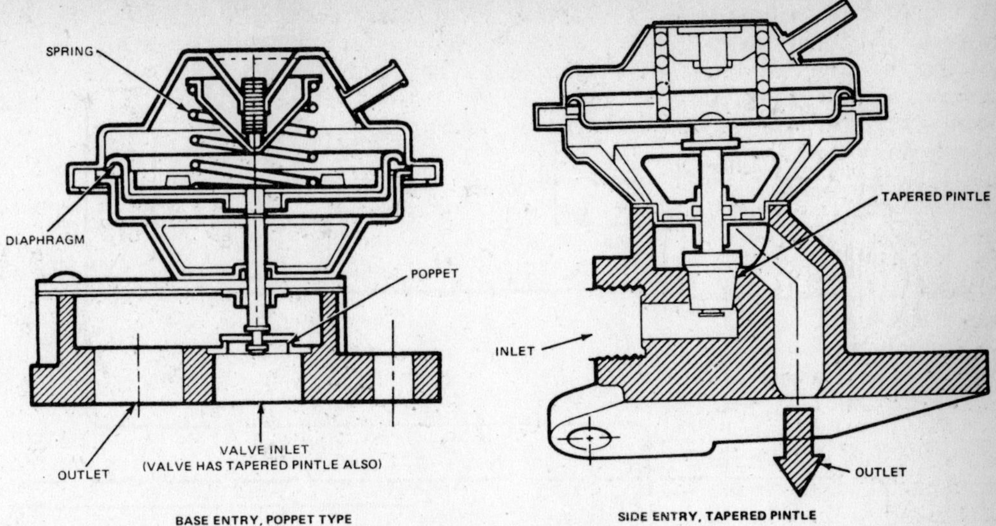

Vacuum-type EGR valve cutaways

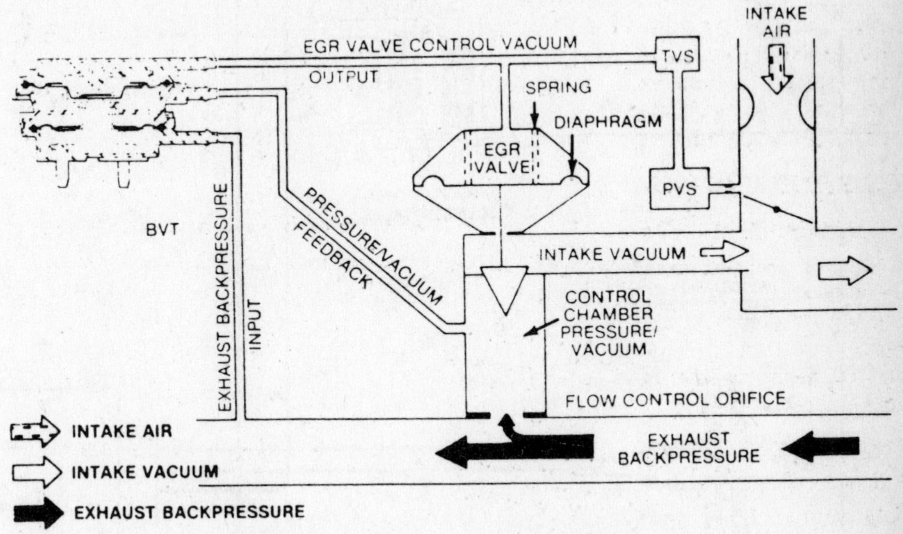

Backpressure Variable Transducer schematic

and computing the desired spark advance based on engine demand and calibration.

The heart of the EEC-IV system is a microprocessor called the Electronic Control Assembly (ECA). The ECA receives data from a number of sensors, switches and relays. The ECA contains a specific calibration for peak fuel economy, drivability and emissions control. Based on information stored in its memory, the ECA generates signals to control the various engine functions.

The ECA calibration module is located inside the ECA assembly. On all pick-ups and Broncos, the ECA is located inside the truck on the left of the firewall, behind the kick panel.

Exhaust Gas Recirculation

EEGR

The Electronic EGR system (EEGR) is found in all systems in which EGR flow is controlled according to computer commands by means of an EGR valve position sensor (EVP) attached to the valve.

The EEGR valve is operated by a vacuum signal from the dual EGR Solenoid Valves, or the electronic vacuum regulator which actuates the valve diaphragm.

As supply vacuum overcomes the spring load, the diaphragm is actuated lifting the pintle off of its seat allowing the exhaust gas to flow. The

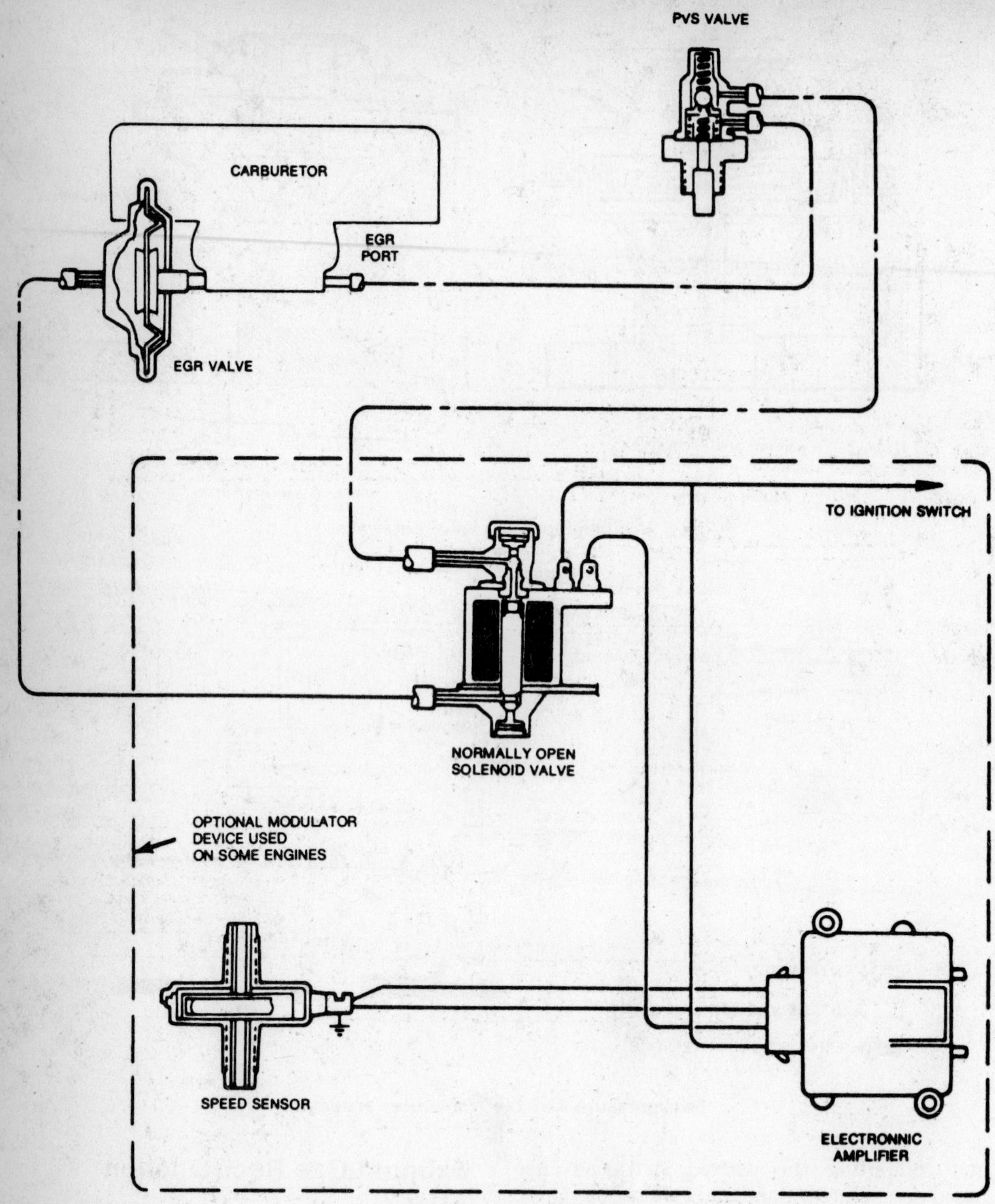

EGR system schematic

amount of flow is directly proportional to the pintle position. The EVP sensor sends an electrical signal notify the EEC of its position.

The EEGR valve is not serviceable. The EVP sensor must be serviced separately.

IBP EGR

The Integral Backpressure (IBP) EGR system combines inputs of EGR port vacuum and backpressure into one unit. The valve requires both inputs for proper operation. The valve won't operate on vacuum alone.

There are two types of backpressure valves: the poppet type and the tapered pintle type.

Ported EGR

The ported EGR valve is operated by engine vacuum alone. A vacuum signal from the carburetor activates the EGR valve diaphragm. As the vacuum signal increase it gradually opens the valve pintle allowing exhaust gases to flow.

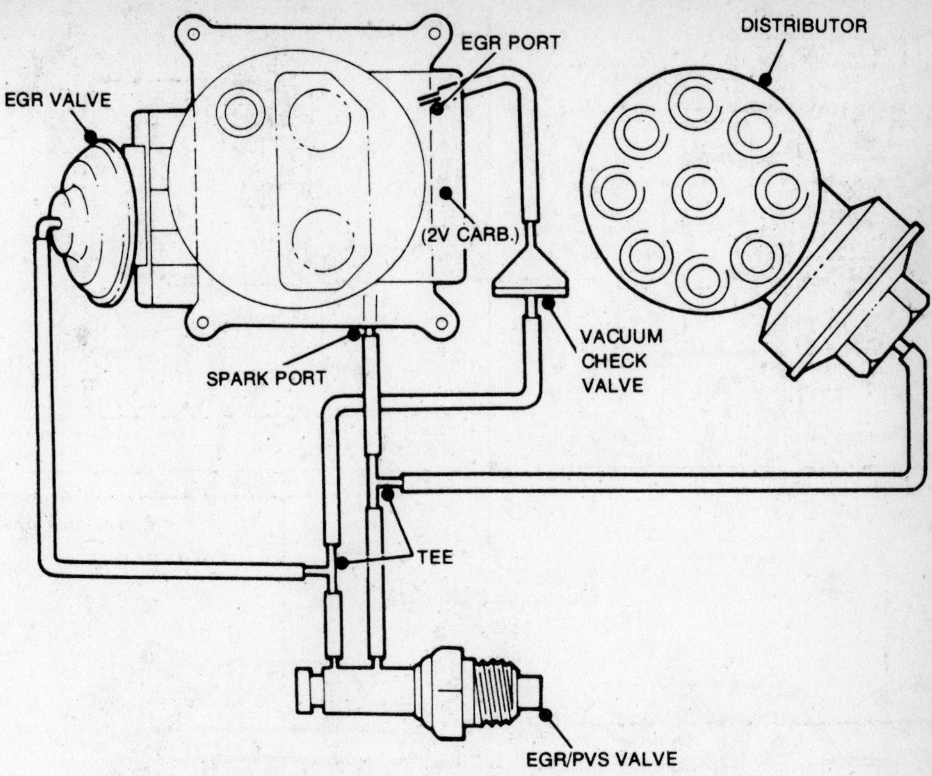

EGR valves are located adjacent to the carburetor

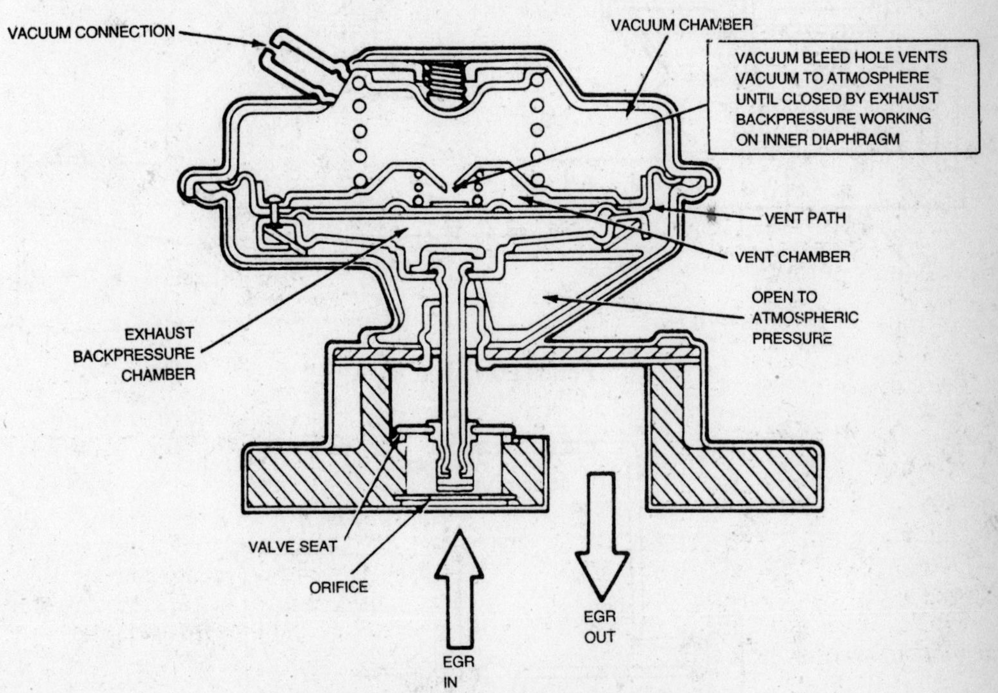

Integral backpressure transducer EGR valve

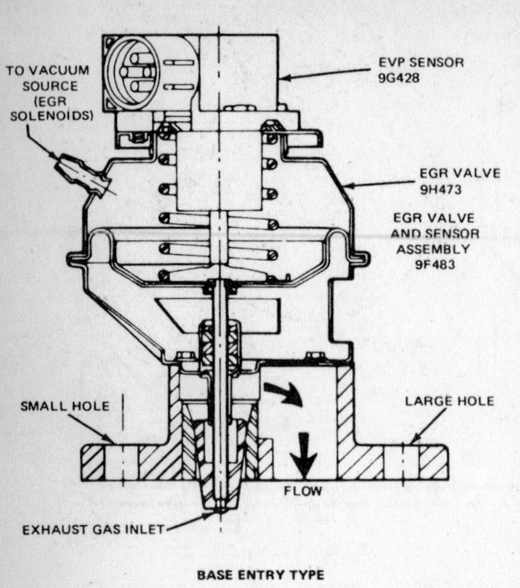

BASE ENTRY TYPE

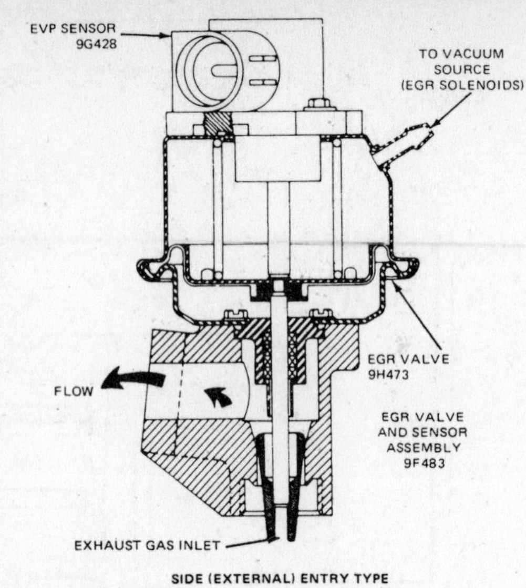

SIDE (EXTERNAL) ENTRY TYPE

Electronic EGR valve

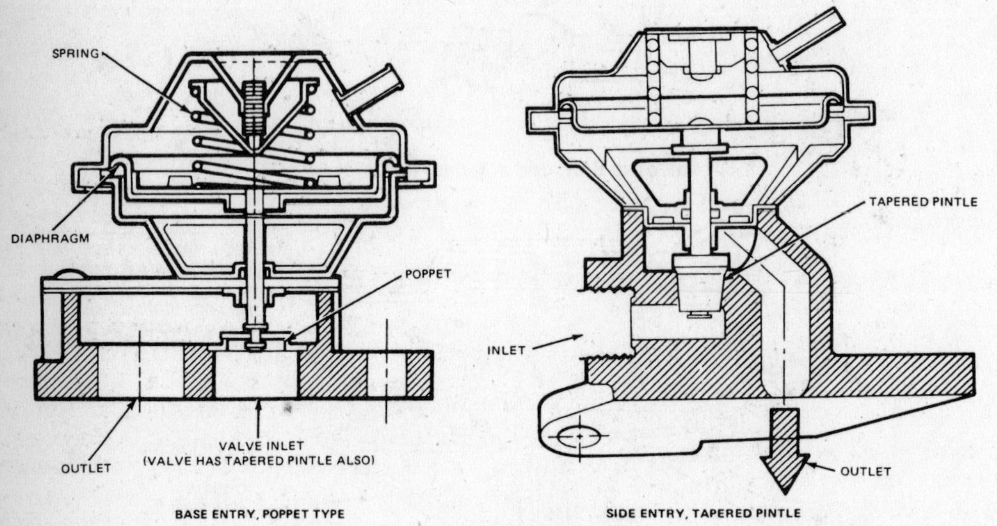

BASE ENTRY, POPPET TYPE

SIDE ENTRY, TAPERED PINTLE

Ported EGR valve

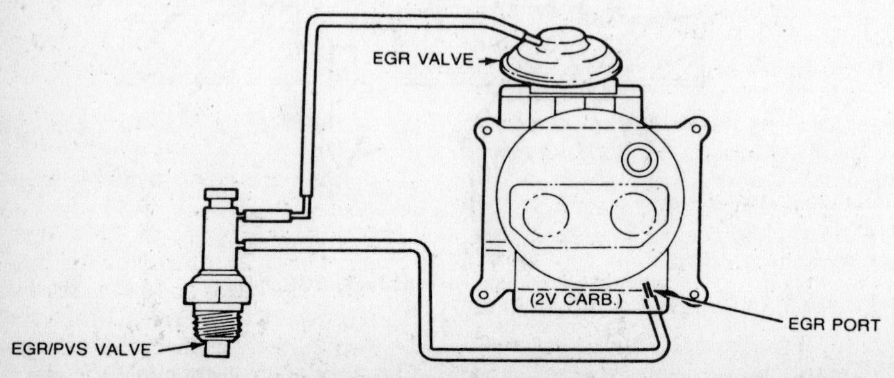

Vacuum operated EGR schematic

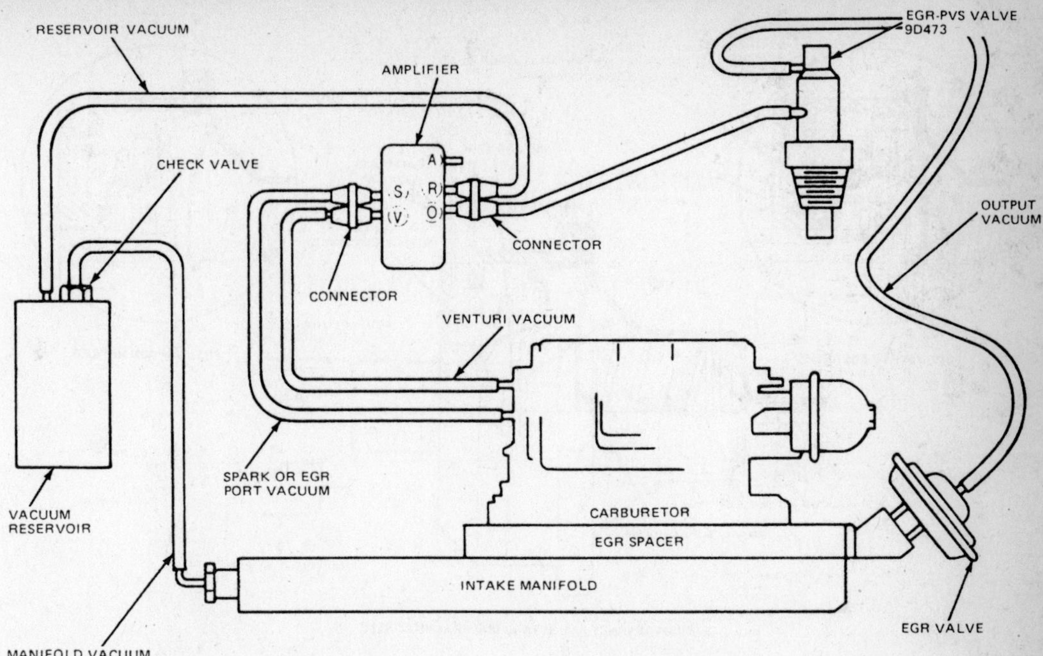

EGR system with venturi vacuum amplifier

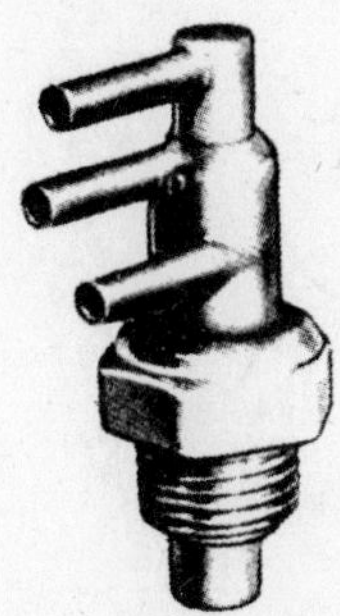

A ported vacuum switch

The amount of flow is directly proportional to the pintle position.

Managed Thermactor Air System

The MTA system is used to inject fresh air into the exhaust manifolds or catalytic converters via an air control valve. Under some operating conditions, the air can be dumped back into the atmosphere via an air bypass valve. On some applications the two valves are combined into one unit. The air bypass valve can be either the normally closed type, when the valves are separate, or the normally open type, when the valves are combined.

Normally Closed Air Bypass Valve Functional Test

1. Disconnect the air supply hose at the valve.
2. Run the engine to normal operating temperature.
3. Disconnect the vacuum line and make sure vacuum is present. If no vacuum is present, remove or bypass any restrictors or delay valves in the vacuum line.
4. Run the engine at 1,500 rpm with the vacuum line connected. Air pump supply air should be heard and felt at the valve outlet.
5. With the engine still at 1,500 rpm, disconnect the vacuum line. Air at the outlet should shut off or dramatically decrease. Air pump supply air should now be felt or heard at the silencer ports.
6. If the valve doesn't pass each of these tests, replace it.

Normally Open Air Bypass Valve Functional Test

1. Disconnect the air supply hose at the valve.
2. Run the engine to normal operating temperature.
3. Disconnect the vacuum lines from the valve.
4. Run the engine at 1,500 rpm with the vacuum lines disconnected. Air pump supply air should be heard and felt at the valve outlet.
5. Shut off the engine. Using a spare length of vacuum hose, connect the vacuum nipple of the valve to direct manifold vacuum.
6. Run the engine at 1,500 rpm. Air at the

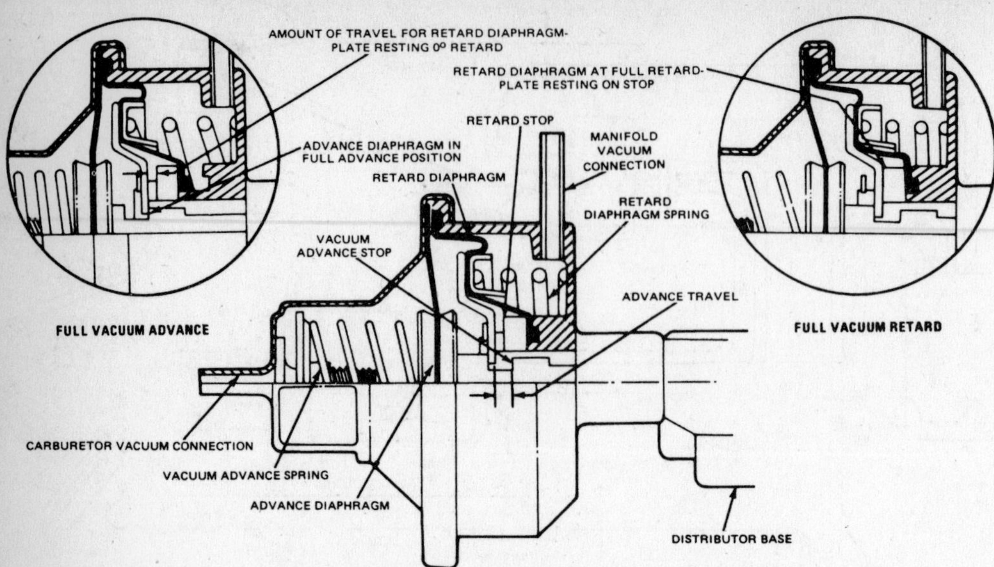

Dual diaphragm vacuum advance and retard mechanism for the distributor

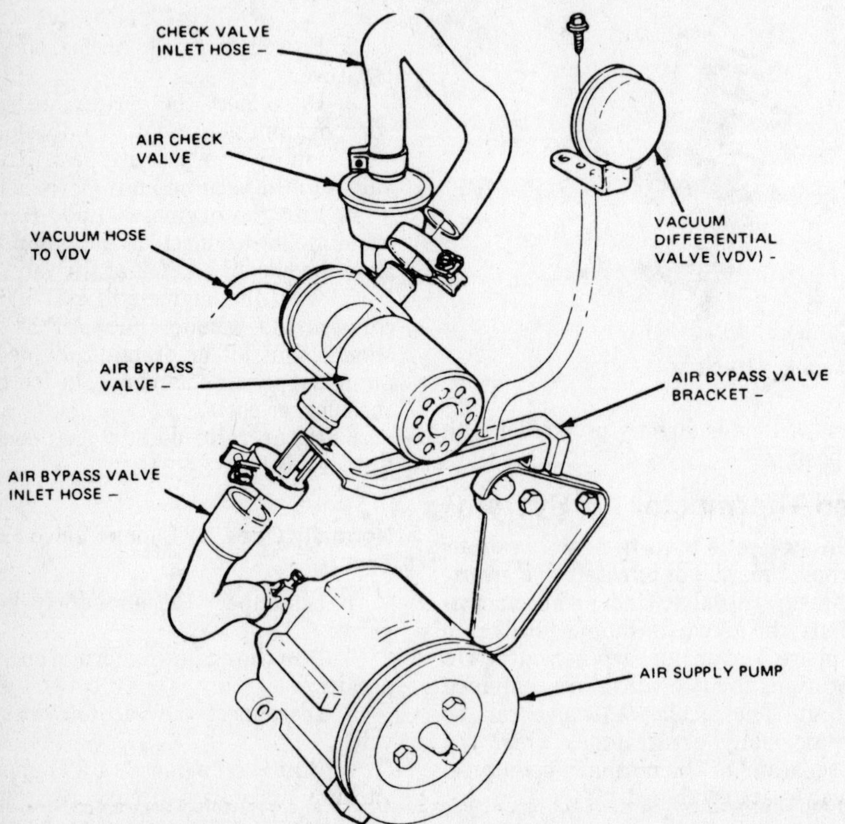

Thermactor® air pump system components. Locations vary slightly among engines

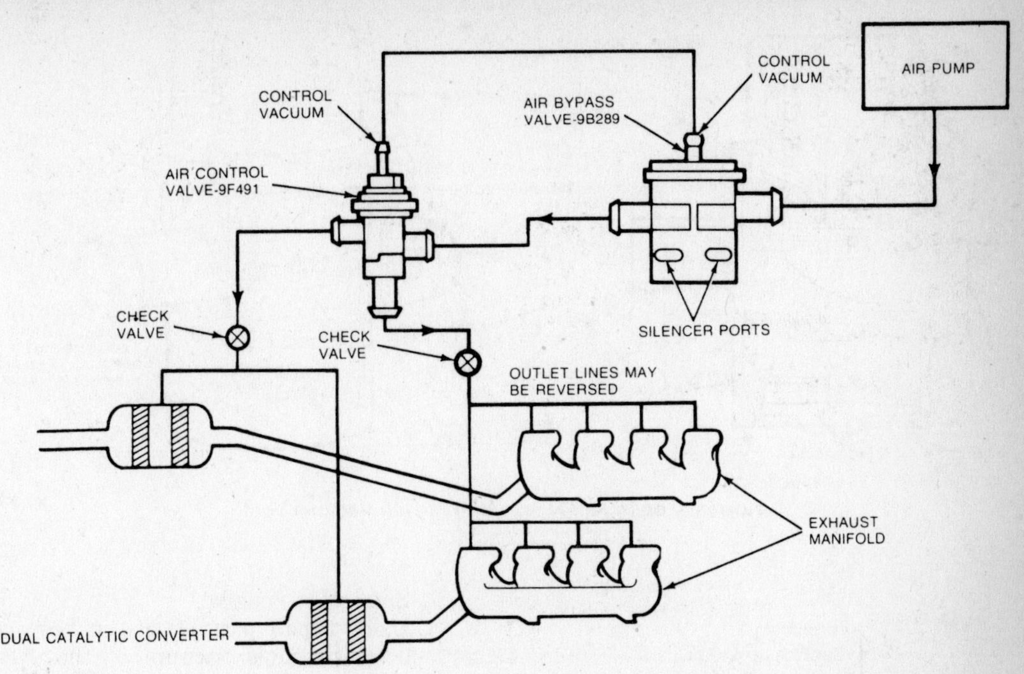

Managed Air Thermactor® System schematic

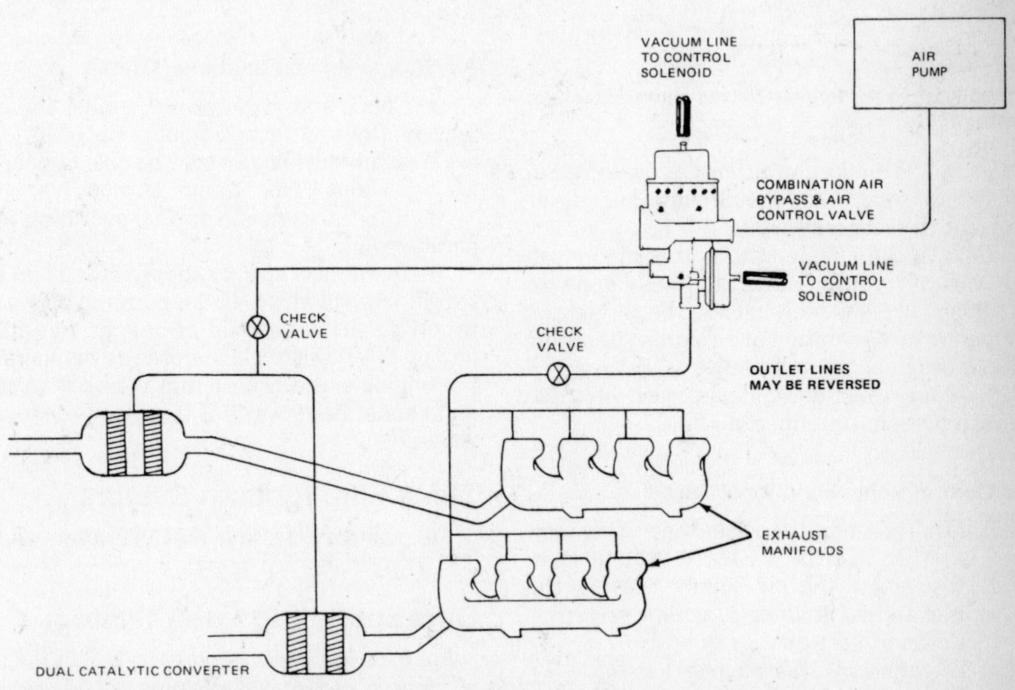

Managed Air Thermactor® System schematic with Electronically controlled bypass/control valve

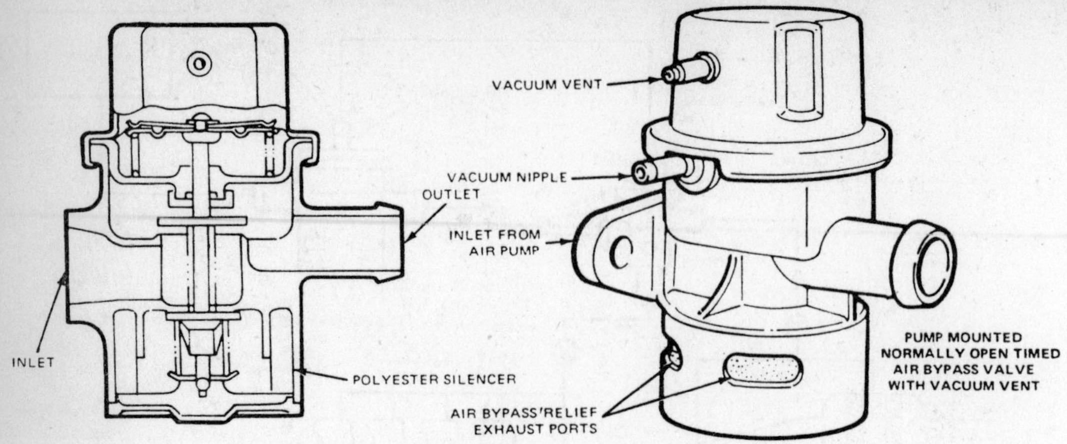

Normally open Air Bypass Valves with Vacuum Vent

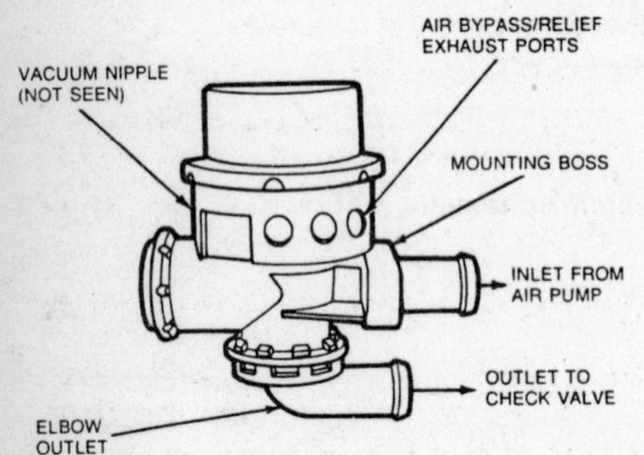

Normally open Air Bypass Valves without Vacuum Vent

outlet should shut off or dramatically decrease. Air pump supply air should now be felt or heard at the silencer ports.

7. With the engine still in this mode, cap the vacuum vent. Accelerate the engine to 2,000 rpm and suddenly release the throttle. A momentary interruption of air pump supply air should be felt at the valve outlet.

8. If the valve doesn't pass each of these tests, replace it. Reconnect all lines.

Air Control Valve Functional Test

1. Run the engine to normal operating temperature, then increase the speed to 1,500 rpm.
2. Disconnect the air supply hose at the valve inlet and verify there is airflow present.
3. Reconnect the air supply hose.
4. Disconnect both air supply hoses.
5. Disconnect the vacuum hose from the valve.
6. With the engine running at 1,500 rpm, airflow should be felt and heard at the outlet on the side of the valve, with no airflow heard or felt at the outlet opposite the vacuum nipple.
7. Shut off the engine.
8. Using a spare piece of vacuum hose, connect direct manifold vacuum to the valve's vacuum fitting. Airflow should be heard and felt at the outlet opposite the vacuum nipple, and no airflow should be present at the other outlet.
9. If the valve is not functioning properly, replace it.

Air Supply Pump Functional Check

1. Check and, if necessary, adjust the belt tension. Press at the mid-point of the belt's longest straight run. You should be able to depress the belt about $^1/_2$ in. (13mm) at most.
2. Run the engine to normal operating temperature and let it idle.
3. Disconnect the air supply hose from the bypass control valve. If the pump is operating properly, airflow should be felt at the pump outlet. The flow should increase as you increase the engine speed. The pump is not servicable and should be replaced if it is not functioning properly.

Thick Film Ignition System

For complete testing and operation of the TFI-IV system, see Chapter 2.

DuraSpark II Ignition System

For complete testing and operation of the DuraSpark II system, see Chapter 2.

Bypass Air Idle Speed Control

The air bypass solenoid is used to control the engine idle speed and is operated by the EEC module.

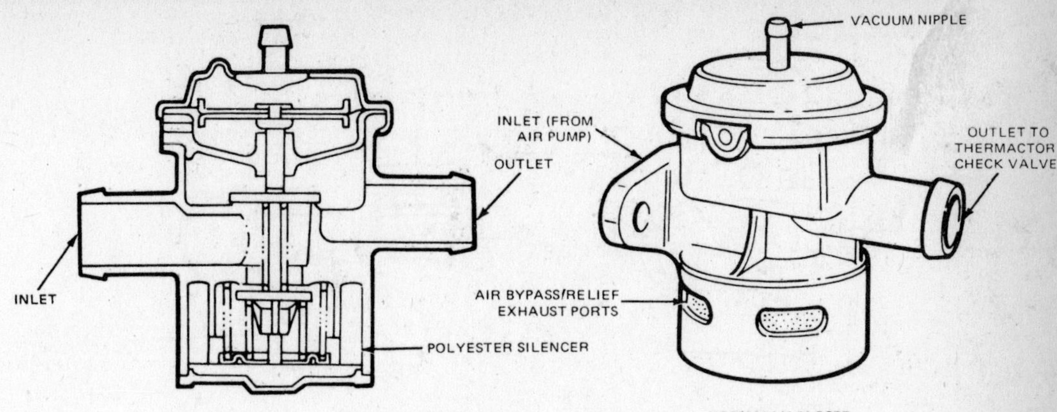

Normally closed Air Bypass Valve

The valve allows air to pass around the throttle plates to control:

- Cold engine fast idle
- Cold starting
- Dashpot operation
- Over-temperature idle boost
- Engine load correction

The valve is not servicable and correction is by replacement only.

Emissions Maintenance Warning Light (EMW)

DESCRIPTION

All gasoline engined light trucks built for sale outside of California employ this device.

The EMW consists of an instrument panel mounted amber light imprinted with the word EGR, EMISS, or EMISSIONS. The light is connected to a sensor module located under the instrument panel. The purpose is the warn the driver that the 60,000 mile emission system maintenance is required on the vehicle. Specific emission system maintenance requirements are listed in the truck's owner's manual maintenance schedule.

RESETTING THE LIGHT

1. Turn the key to the OFF position.
2. Lightly push a Phillips screwdriver through the 0.2 in. (5mm) diameter hole labeled RESET, and lightly press down and hold it.
3. While maintaining pressure with the screwdriver, turn the key to the RUN position. The EMW lamp will light and stay lit as long as you keep pressure on the screwdriver. Hold the screwdriver down for about 5 seconds.
4. Remove the screwdriver. The lamp should go out with 2–5 seconds. If not, repeat Steps 1–3.
5. Turn the key OFF.
6. Turn the key to the RUN position. The lamp will light for 2–5 seconds and then go out. If not, repeat the rest procedure.

NOTE: *If the light comes on between 15,000 and 45,000 miles or between 75,000 and 105,000 miles, you'll have to replace the 1,000 hour pre-timed module.*

Oxygen Sensor

An oxygen sensor is used on most models and is mounted in the exhaust manifold. The sensor protrudes into the exhaust stream and monitors the oxygen content of the exhaust hoses. The difference between the oxygen content of the exhaust gases and that of the outside air generates a voltage signal to the ECM. The ECM monitors this voltage and, depending upon the value of the signal received, issues a command to adjust for a rich or a lean condition.

No attempt should ever be made to measure the voltage output of the sensor. The current drain of any conventional voltmeter would be

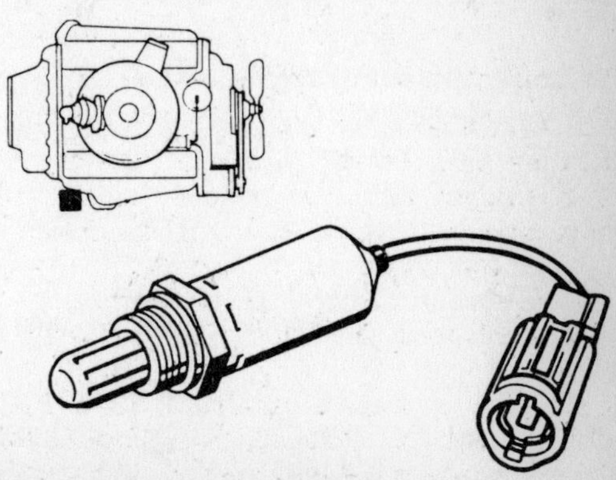

Exhaust Gas Oxygen Sensor

TO AIR CLEANER OR REM. SILENCER
VACUUM VENT
VACUUM VENT
VACUUM NIPPLE
AIR BYPASS RELIEF EXHAUST PORT(S)
INLET FROM AIR PUMP
INLET FROM AIR PUMP
MOUNTING BOSS
OUTLET TO CHECK VALVE
TEE TO CHECK VALVES

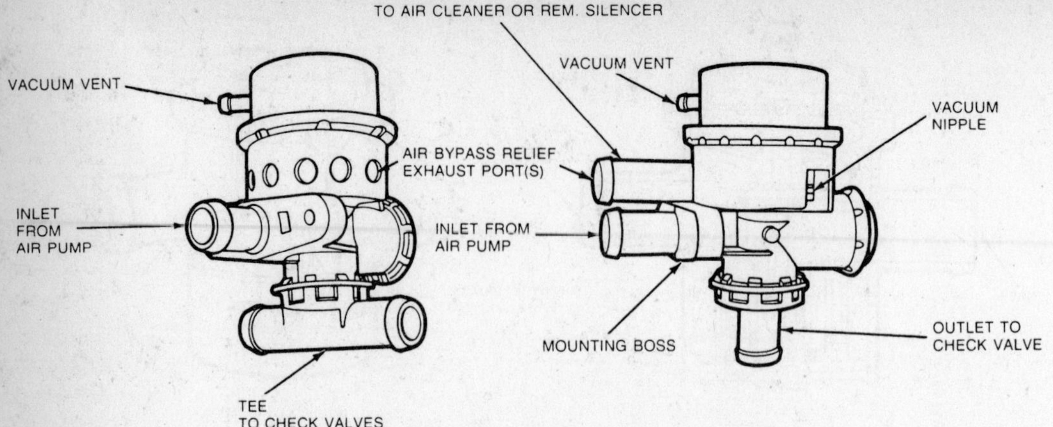

Heavy Duty truck Normally open Air Bypass Valves

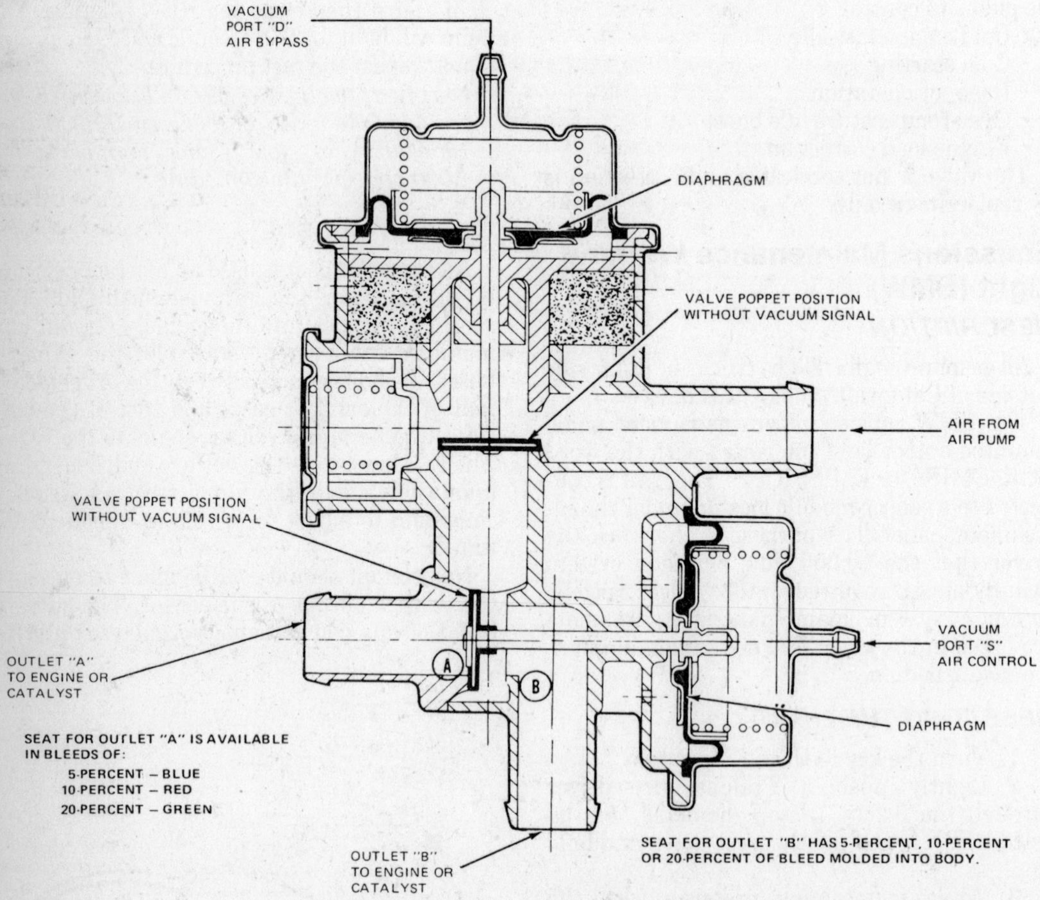

VACUUM PORT "D" AIR BYPASS
DIAPHRAGM
VALVE POPPET POSITION WITHOUT VACUUM SIGNAL
AIR FROM AIR PUMP
VALVE POPPET POSITION WITHOUT VACUUM SIGNAL
VACUUM PORT "S" AIR CONTROL
OUTLET "A" TO ENGINE OR CATALYST
A
B
DIAPHRAGM
SEAT FOR OUTLET "A" IS AVAILABLE IN BLEEDS OF:
5-PERCENT – BLUE
10-PERCENT – RED
20-PERCENT – GREEN
SEAT FOR OUTLET "B" HAS 5-PERCENT, 10-PERCENT OR 20-PERCENT OF BLEED MOLDED INTO BODY.
OUTLET "B" TO ENGINE OR CATALYST

Normally closed exhaust air supply control valve w/bleed

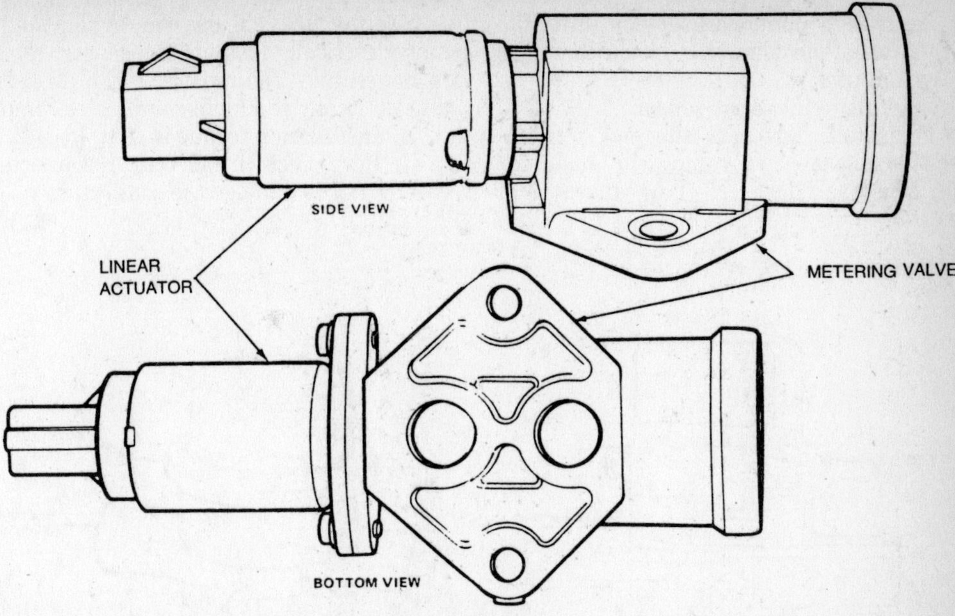

Air Bypass Valve

such that it would permanently damage the sensor. No jumpers, test leads or any other electrical connections should ever be made to the sensor. Use these tools ONLY on the ECM side of the wiring harness connector AFTER disconnecting it from the sensor.

REMOVAL AND INSTALLATION

The oxygen sensor must be replaced every 48,000 km (30,000 miles). The sensor may be difficult to remove when the engine temperature is blow 120°F (48°C). Excessive removal force may damage the threads in the exhaust manifold or pipe; follow the procedure carefully.

1. Locate the oxygen sensor. It protrudes from the center of the exhaust manifold and looks somewhat like a spark plug.
2. Disconnect the electrical connector from the oxygen sensor.

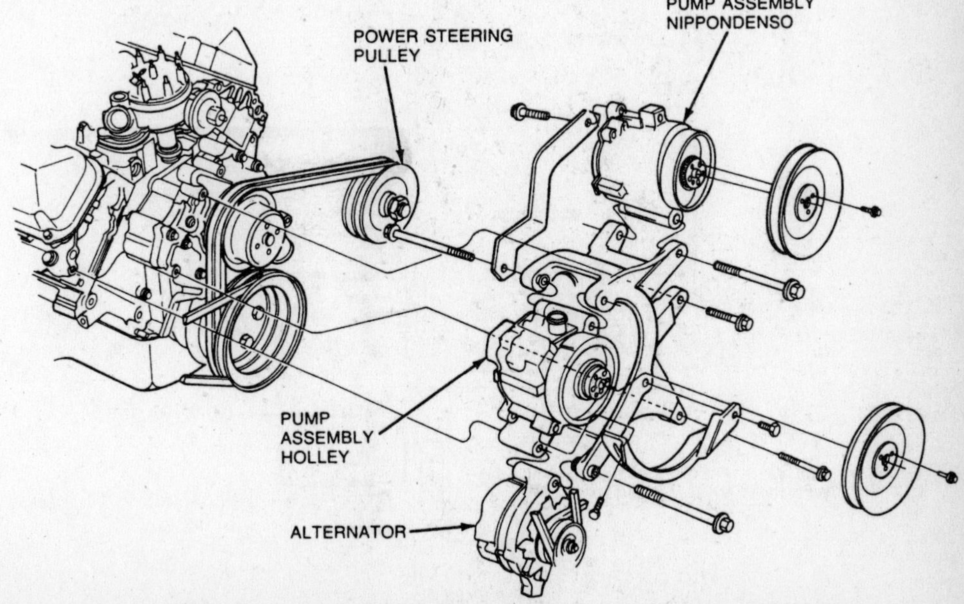

Dual air pump system on 8–5.8L 4-bbl and 8–7.5L 4-bbl, except California

3. Spray a commercial solvent onto the sensor threads and allow it to soak in for at least five minutes.

4. Carefully remove the sensor.

5. To install, first coat the new sensor's threads with anti-seize compound made for oxygen sensors. This is NOT a conventional anti-seize paste. The use of a regular compound may electrically insulate the sensor, rendering it inoperative. You must coat the threads with an electrically conductive anti-seize compound.

6. Installation torque is 30 ft. lbs. (42 Nm.).

7. Reconnect the electrical connector. Be careful not to damage the connector.

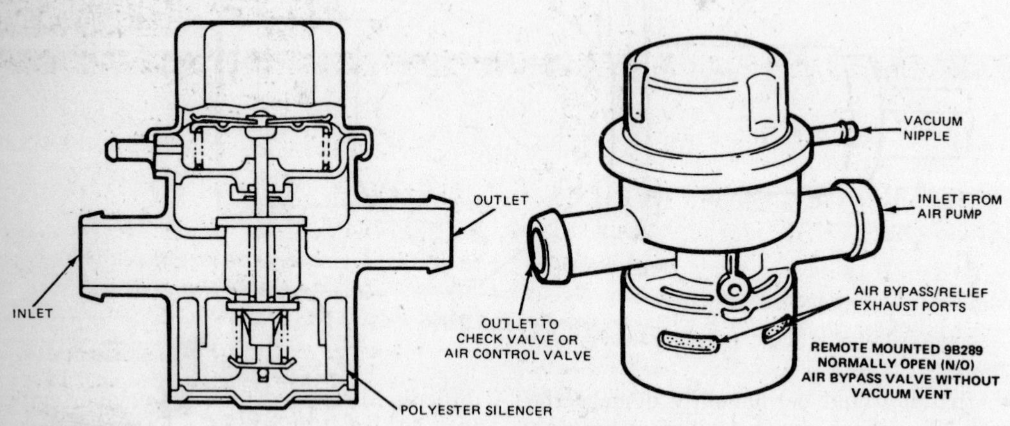

Normally open Air Bypass Valves without Vacuum Vent

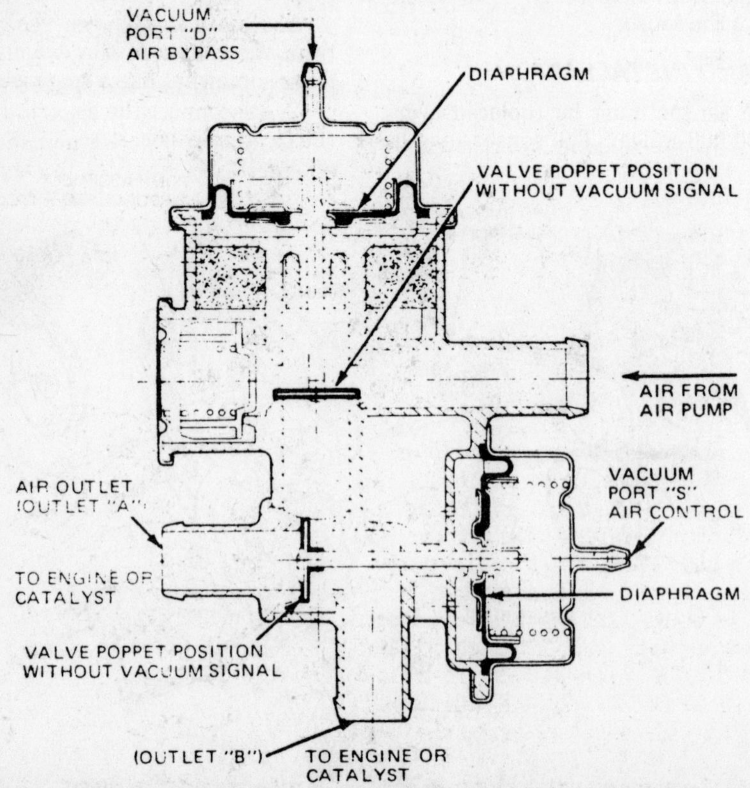

Normally closed exhaust air supply control valve wo/bleed

Fuel System 5

GENERAL FUEL SYSTEM COMPONENTS

Mechanical Fuel Pump

A mechanical pump is used on all carbureted engines, except the 8–7.5L. The mechanical fuel pump is camshaft eccentric-actuated and located on the left side of the front cover on V8 engines.

REMOVAL

CAUTION: *Never smoke when working around gasoline! Avoid all sources of sparks or ignition. Gasoline vapors are EXTREMELY volatile!*

1. Disconnect the fuel inlet and outlet lines at the fuel pump. Discard the fuel inlet retaining clamp.
2. Remove the pump retaining bolts then remove the pump assembly and gasket from the engine. Discard the gasket.

INSTALLATION

1. If a new pump is to be installed, remove the fuel line connector fitting from the old pump and install it in the new pump.
2. Remove all gasket material from the mounting pad and pump flange. Apply oil resistant sealer to both sides of a new gasket.
3. Position the new gasket on the pump flange and hold the pump in position against the mounting pad. make sure that the rocker arm is riding on the camshaft eccentric.
4. Press the pump tight against the pad, install the retaining bolts and alternately torque them to 20–24 ft. lbs. on the 8–5.0L; 14–20 on the 8–5.8L; 19–27 ft. lbs. on the 8–7.5L. Connect the fuel lines. Use a new clamp on the fuel inlet lines.
5. Operate the engine and check for leaks.

TESTING

CAUTION: *Never smoke when working around gasoline! Avoid all sources of sparks or ignition. Gasoline vapors are EXTREMELY volatile!*

Incorrect fuel pump pressure and low volume (flow rate) are the two most likely fuel pump troubles that will affect engine performance. Low pressure will cause a lean mixture and fuel starvation at high speeds and excessive pressure will cause high fuel consumption and carburetor flooding.

To determine that the fuel pump is in satisfactory operating condition, tests for both fuel pump pressure and volume should be performed.

The test are performed with the fuel pump installed on the engine and the engine at normal operating temperature and at idle speed.

Before the test, make sure that the replacea-

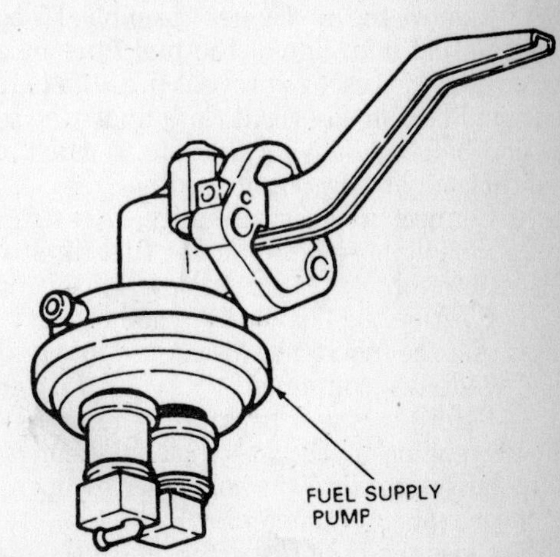

Carbureted V8 fuel pump

Troubleshooting Basic Fuel System Problems

Problem	Cause	Solution
Engine cranks, but won't start (or is hard to start) when cold	• Empty fuel tank • Incorrect starting procedure • Defective fuel pump • No fuel in carburetor • Clogged fuel filter • Engine flooded • Defective choke	• Check for fuel in tank • Follow correct procedure • Check pump output • Check for fuel in the carburetor • Replace fuel filter • Wait 15 minutes; try again • Check choke plate
Engine cranks, but is hard to start (or does not start) when hot—(presence of fuel is assumed)	• Defective choke	• Check choke plate
Rough idle or engine runs rough	• Dirt or moisture in fuel • Clogged air filter • Faulty fuel pump	• Replace fuel filter • Replace air filter • Check fuel pump output
Engine stalls or hesitates on acceleration	• Dirt or moisture in the fuel • Dirty carburetor • Defective fuel pump • Incorrect float level, defective accelerator pump	• Replace fuel filter • Clean the carburetor • Check fuel pump output • Check carburetor
Poor gas mileage	• Clogged air filter • Dirty carburetor • Defective choke, faulty carburetor adjustment	• Replace air filter • Clean carburetor • Check carburetor
Engine is flooded (won't start accompanied by smell of raw fuel)	• Improperly adjusted choke or carburetor	• Wait 15 minutes and try again, without pumping gas pedal • If it won't start, check carburetor

ble fuel filter has been changed at the proper mileage interval. If in doubt, install a new filter.

Pressure Test

1. Remove the air cleaner assembly. Disconnect the fuel inlet line of the fuel filter at the carburetor. Use care to prevent fire, due to fuel spillage. Place an absorbent cloth under the connection before removing the line to catch any fuel that might flow out of the line.
2. Connect a pressure gauge, a restrictor and a flexible hose between the fuel filter and the carburetor.
3. Position the flexible hose and the restrictor so that the fuel can be discharged into a suitable, graduated container.
4. Before taking a pressure reading, operate the engine at the specified idle rpm and vent the system into the container by opening the hose restrictor momentarily.
5. Close the hose restrictor, allow the pressure to stabilize and note the reading. The pressure should be 5 psi.

If the pump pressure is not within 4–6 psi and the fuel lines and filter are in satisfactory condition, the pump is defective and should be replaced.

If the pump pressure is within the proper range, perform the test for fuel volume.

Volume Test

1. Operate the engine at the specified idle rpm.
2. Open the hose restrictor and catch the fuel in the container while observing the time it takes to pump 1 pint. 1 pint should be pumped in 20 seconds. If the pump does not pump to specifications, check for proper fuel tank venting or a restriction in the fuel line leading from the fuel tank to the carburetor before replacing the fuel pump.

Electric Fuel Pump

Carbureted 7.5L Engine

Models equipped with the 7.5L carbureted engines use a single low pressure pump mounted in the fuel tank.

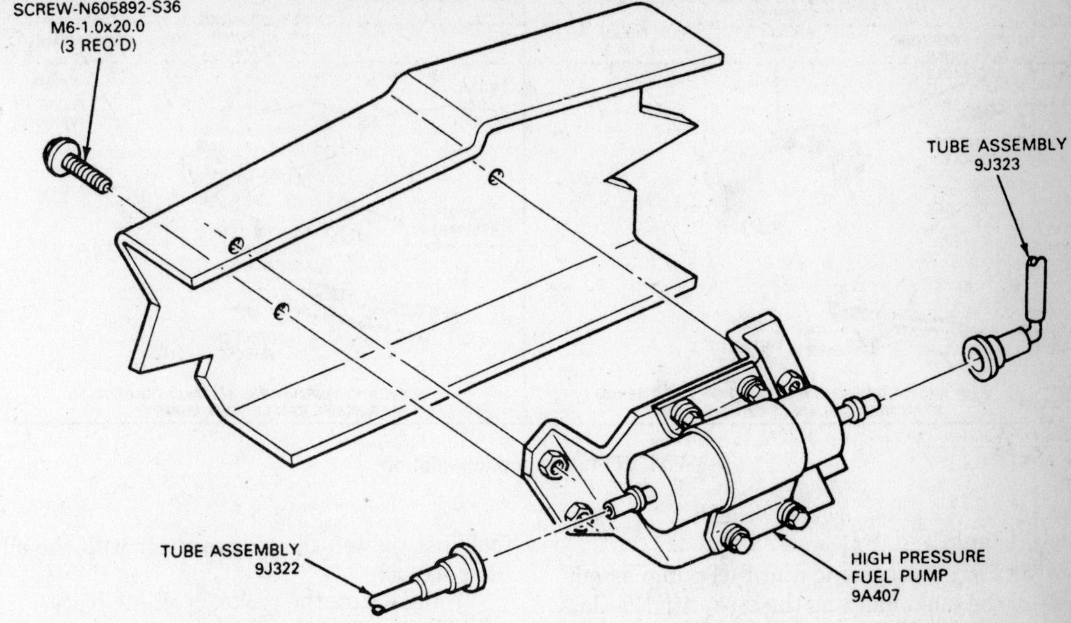

High pressure EFI fuel pump

1987–89 Fuel Injected Engines

Two electric pumps are used on fuel injected models; a low pressure boost pump mounted in the fuel tank and a high pressure pump mounted on the vehicle frame.

On injected models the low pressure pump is used to provide pressurized fuel to the inlet of the high pressure pump and helps prevent noise and heating problems. The externally mounted high pressure pump is capable of supplying 15.9 gallons of fuel an hour. System pressure is controlled by a pressure regulator mounted on the engine.

1990 Engines

These trucks employ a single, high pressure pump which is part of the modular, in-tank reservoir assembly (ITR). Besides the pump, the ITR consists of a venturi jet pump, a supply check valve and a shuttle selector valve. All this is mounted on the fuel gauge sender flange. The sending unit is separate from the ITR module.

NOTE: *On internal fuel tank mounted pumps, tank removal is required. Frame mounted models can be accessed from under the vehicle. Prior to servicing release system pressure (see Fuel Supply Manifold details). Disconnect the negative battery cable prior to pump removal.*

REMOVAL AND INSTALLATION

In-Tank Pump

1. Remove the fuel tank as described below.
2. On steel tanks:
   a. Disconnect the wiring at the connector.
   b. Remove all dirt from the area of the sender.
   c. Disconnect the fuel lines.
   d. Turn the locking ring counterclockwise to remove it. There is a wrench designed for this purpose. If the wrench is not available, you can loosen the locking ring by placing a WOOD dowel against the tabs on the locking ring and hammering it loose. NEVER USE A METAL DRIFT! Use of metal will result in sparks which could cause an explosion! Lift out the fuel pump and sending unit. Discard the gasket.
3. On plastic tanks:
   a. Disconnect the wiring at the connector.
   b. Remove all dirt from the area of the sender.
   c. Disconnect the fuel lines.
   d. Turn the locking ring counterclockwise to remove it. A band-type oil filter wrench is ideal for this purpose. Lift out the fuel pump and sending unit. Discard the gasket.
4. Place a new gasket in position in the groove

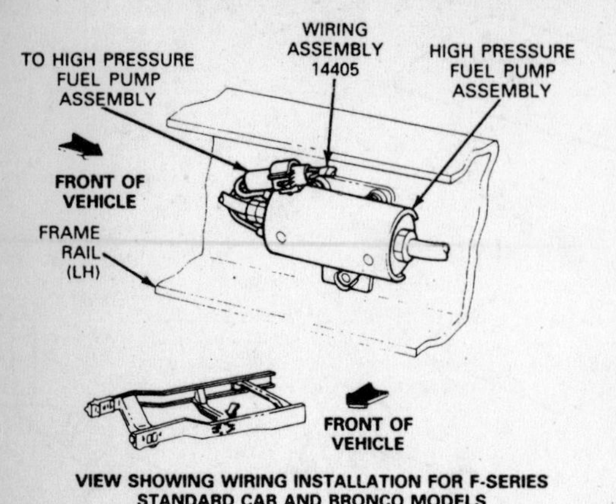

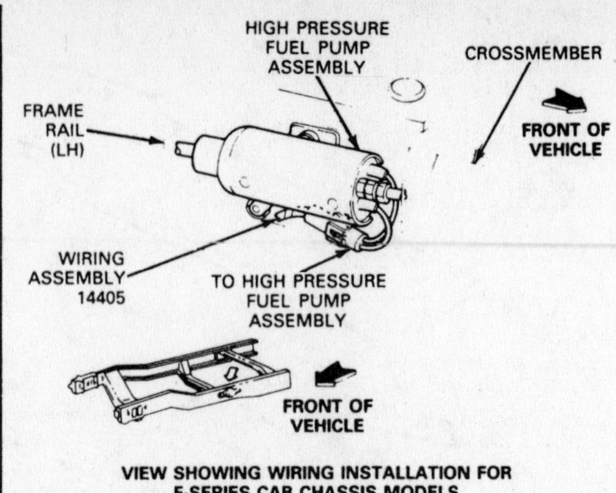

8–7.5L EFI fuel pump installation

in the tank.

5. Place the sending unit/fuel pump assembly in the tank, indexing the tabs with the slots in the tank. Make sure the gasket stays in place.

6. Hold the assembly in place and position the locking ring.

- On steel tanks, turn the locking ring clockwise until the stop is against the retainer ring tab.
- On plastic tanks, turn the retaining ring clockwise until hand-tight. There is a special too available to set the tightening torque for the locking ring. If you have this tool, torque the ring to 40–55 ft. lbs. If you don't have the tool, just tighten the ring securely with the oil filter wrench.

7. Make sure the gasket is still in place.
8. Connect the fuel lines and wiring.
9. Install the tank.

External Pump

1. Disconnect the negative battery cable.

CAUTION: *Never smoke when working around gasoline! Avoid all sources of sparks or ignition. Gasoline vapors are EXTREMELY volatile!*

2. Depressurize the fuel system.
3. Raise and support the rear of the vehicle on jackstands.
4. Disconnect the inlet and outlet fuel lines.

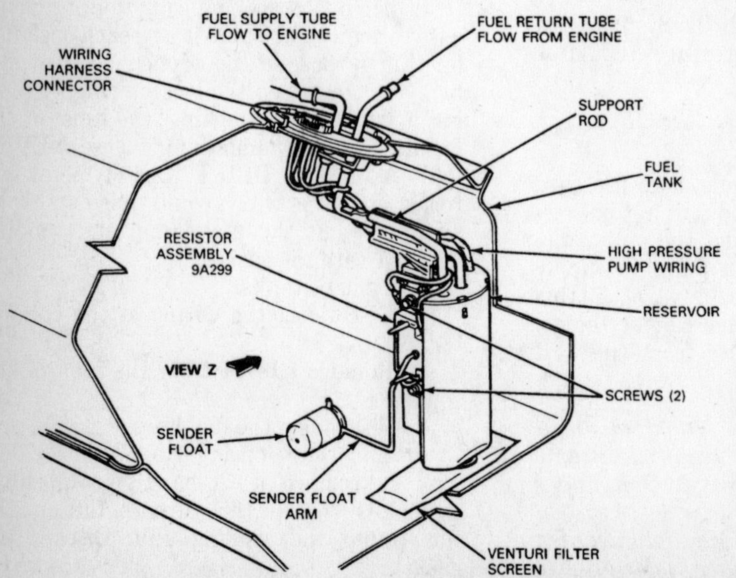

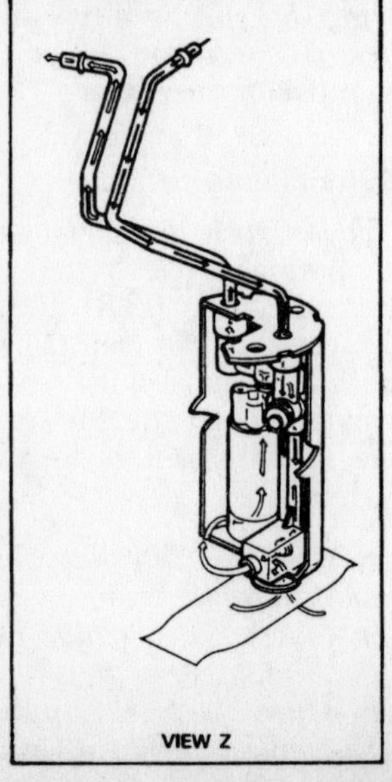

ITR fuel pump assembly

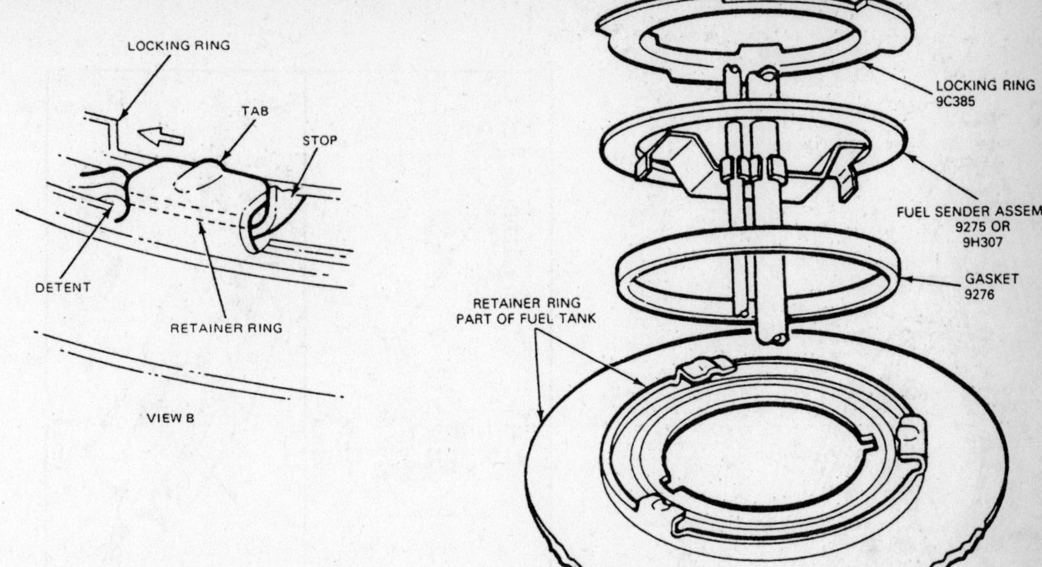

Steel tank type fuel sending unit/pump locking ring

5. Remove the pump from the mounting bracket.

6. Install in reverse order, make sure the pump is indexed correctly in the mounting bracket Insulator.

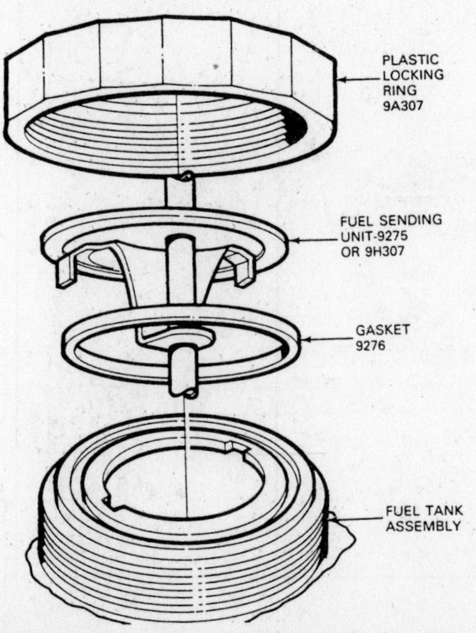

Plastic tank type fuel sending unit/pump locking ring

7. Disconnect the fuel inlet line of the fuel filter at the carburetor. Use care to prevent fire, due to fuel spillage. Place an absorbent cloth under the connection before removing the line to catch any fuel that might flow out of the line.

8. Connect a pressure gauge, a restrictor and flexible hose between the fuel filter and the carburetor.

9. Position the flexible hose and the restrictor so that the fuel can be discharged into a suitable, graduated container.

10. Before taking a pressure reading, operate the Engine at the specified idle rpm and vent the system into the container by opening the hose restrictor momentarily.

11. Close the hose restrictor, allow the pressure to stabilize and note the reading. The pressure should be 5 psi. If the pump pressure is not within 4–6 psi and the fuel lines and filter are in satisfactory condition, the pump is defective and should be replaced. If the pump pressure is within the proper range, perform the test for fuel volume.

VOLUME TEST

1. Operate the engine at the specified idle rpm.

CAUTION: *Never smoke when working around gasoline! Avoid all sources of sparks*

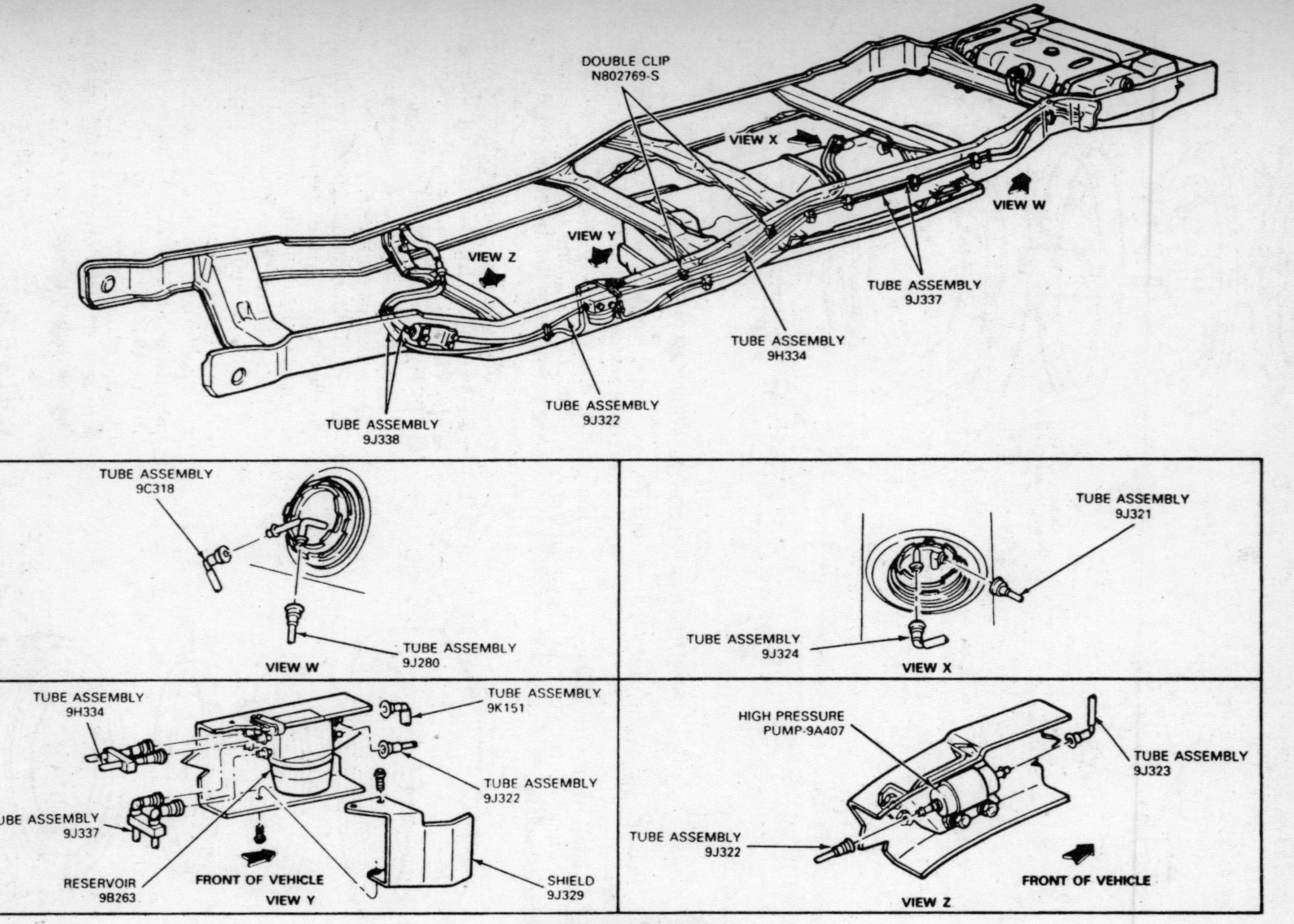

8-302 EFI dual fuel tanks

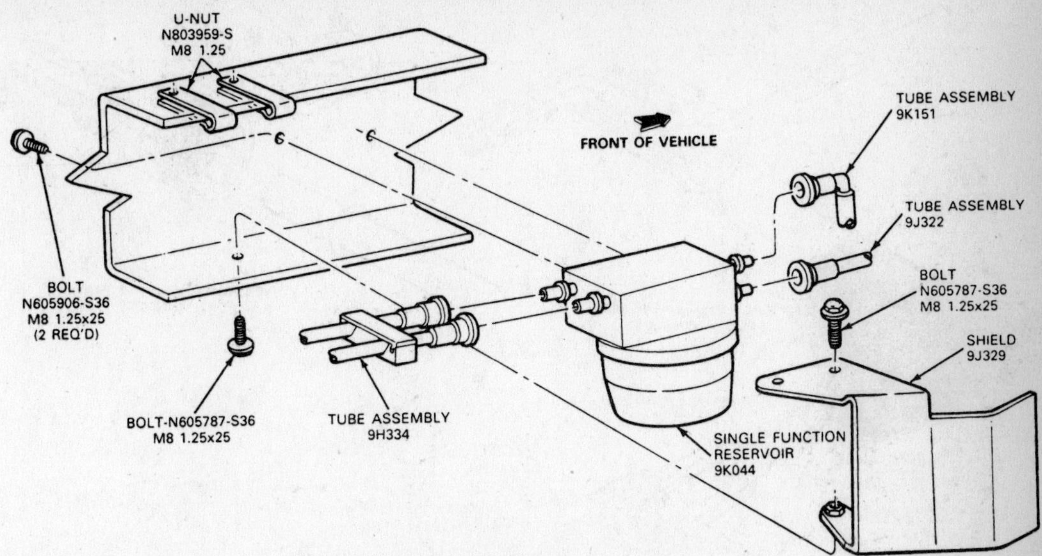

Single function reservoir w/shield

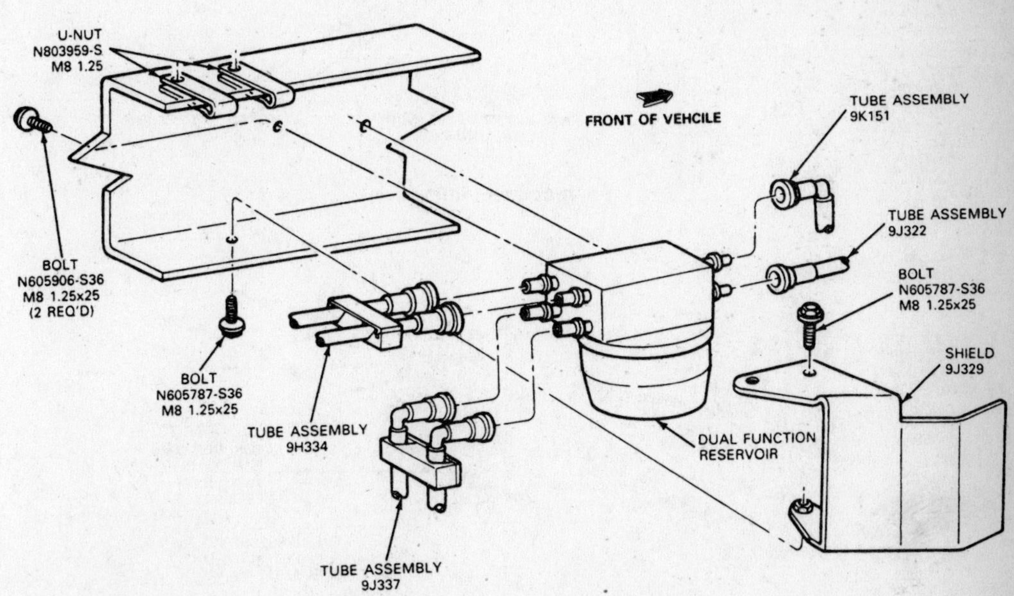

Dual function reservoir w/shield

or ignition. Gasoline vapors are EXTREMELY volatile!

2. Open the hose restrictor and catch the fuel in the container while observing the time it takes to pump 1 pint. 1 pint should be pumped in 20 seconds. If the pump does not pump to specifications, check for proper fuel tank venting or a restriction in the fuel line leading from the fuel tank to the carburetor before replacing the fuel pump.

Quick-Connect Line Fittings

REMOVAL AND INSTALLATION

NOTE: *Quick-Connect (push) type fittings must be disconnected using proper procedures or the fitting may be damaged. Two types of retainers are used on the push connect fittings. Line sizes of $^3/_8$ in. and $^5/_{16}$ in. use a hairpin clip retainer. $^1/_4$ in. line connectors use a Duck bill clip retainer.*

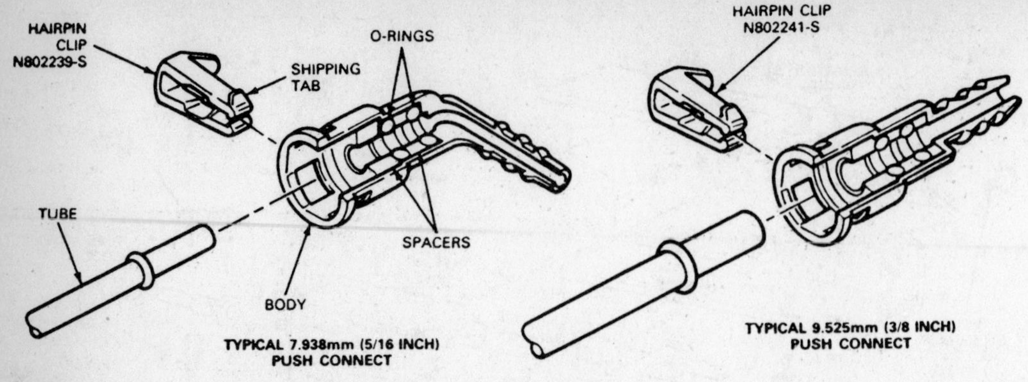

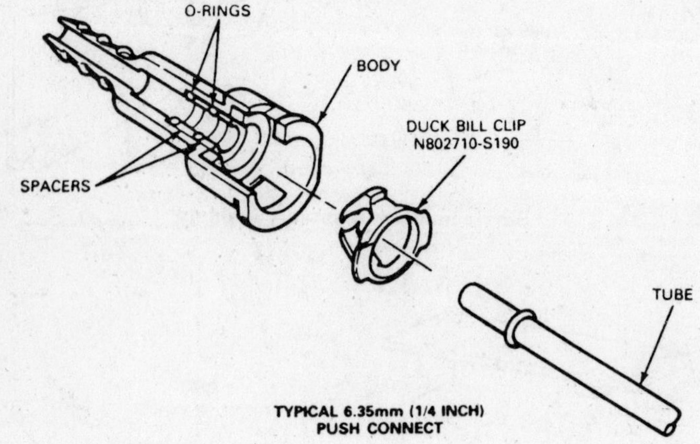

Push-connect fittings

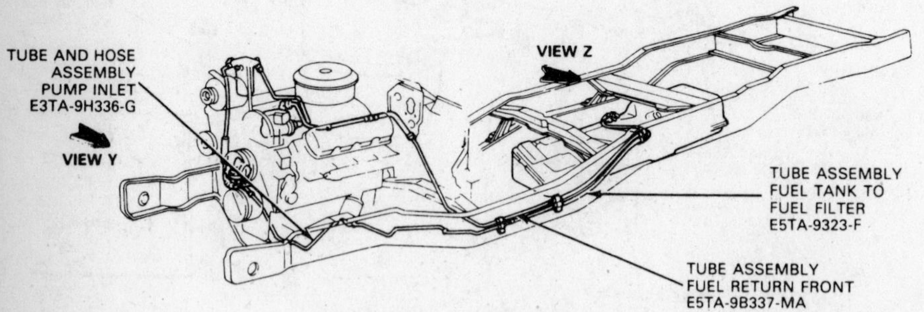

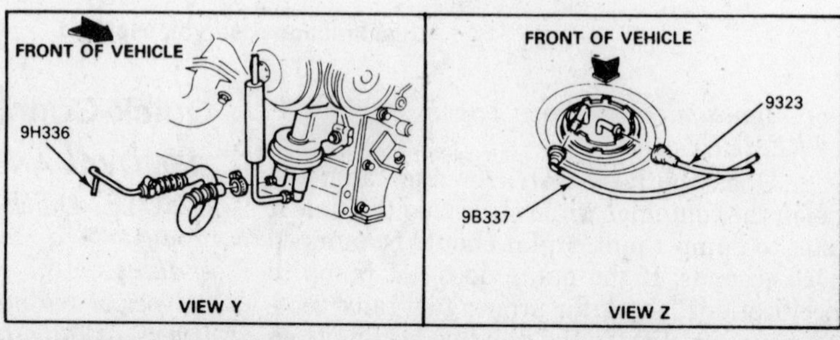

Diesel fuel lines w/midship tank

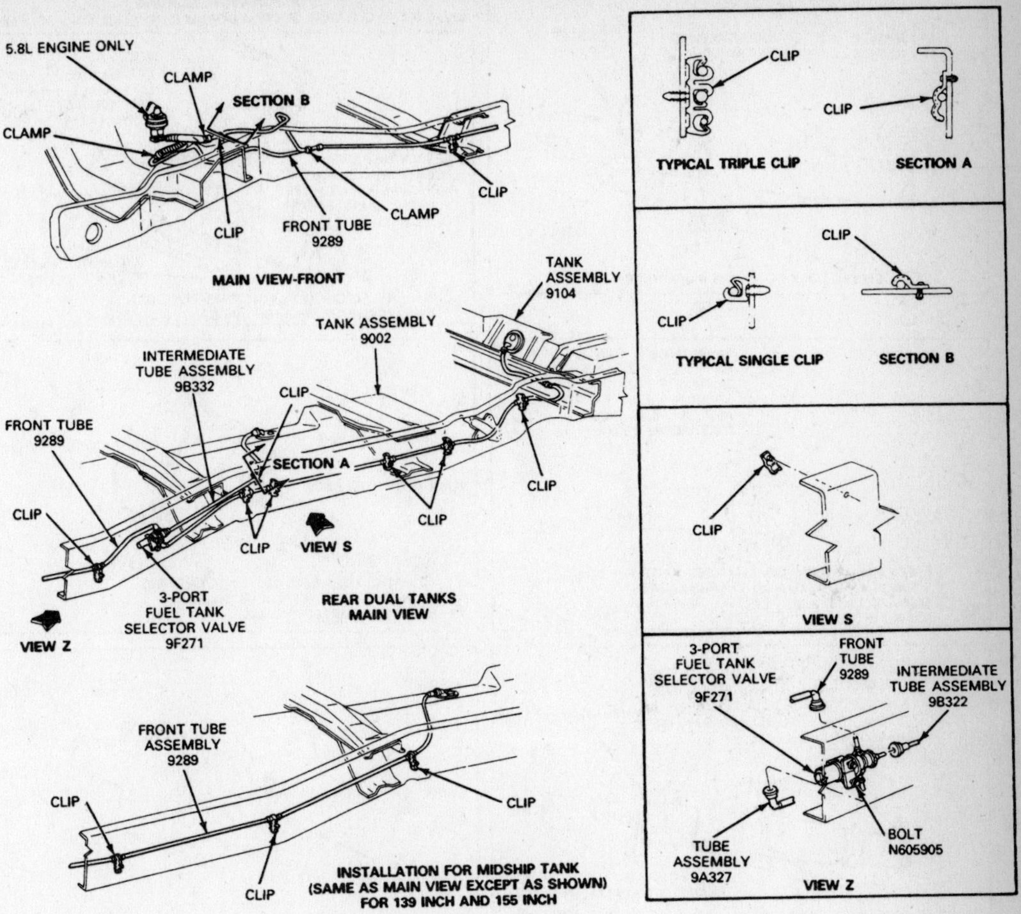

8–5.8L fuel lines

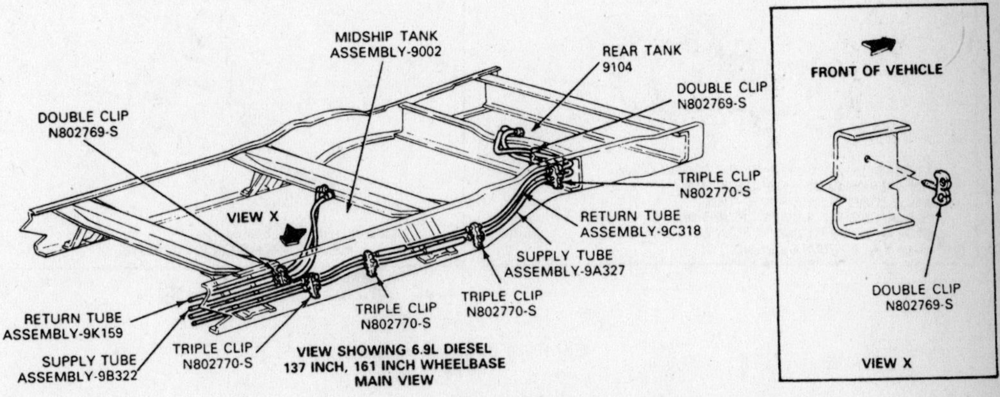

Diesel fuel lines w/dual tanks

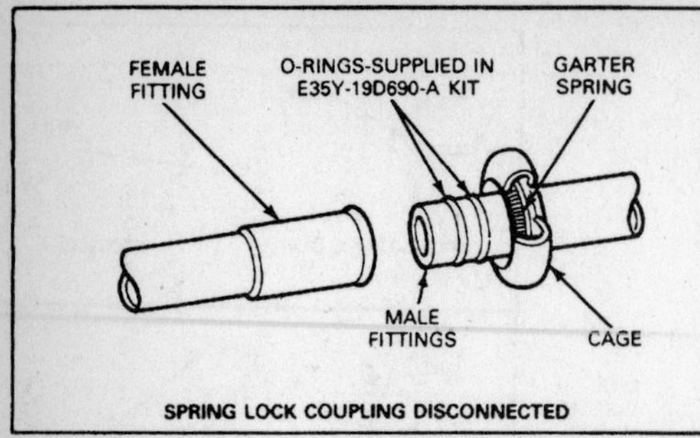

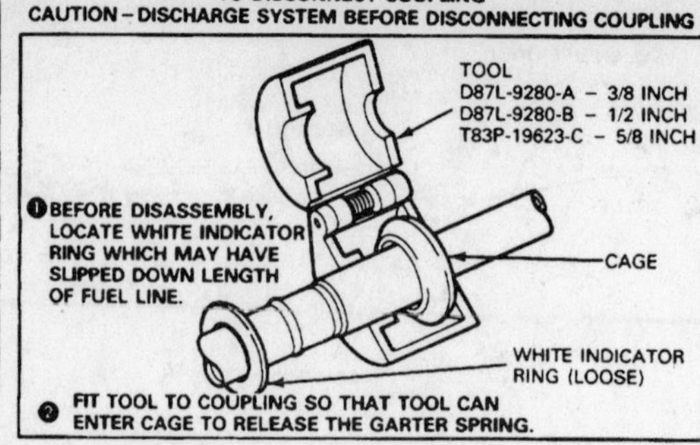

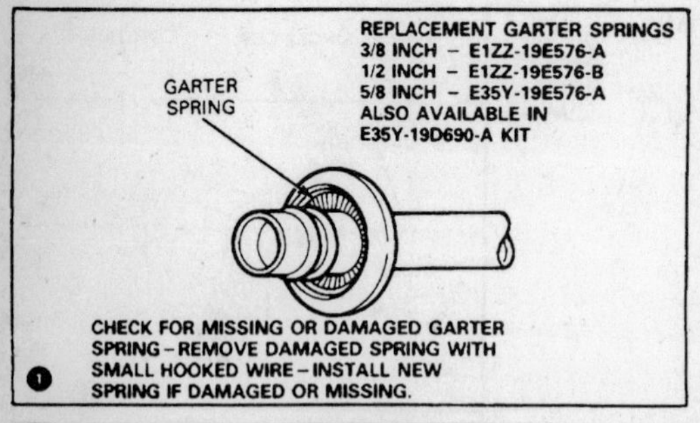

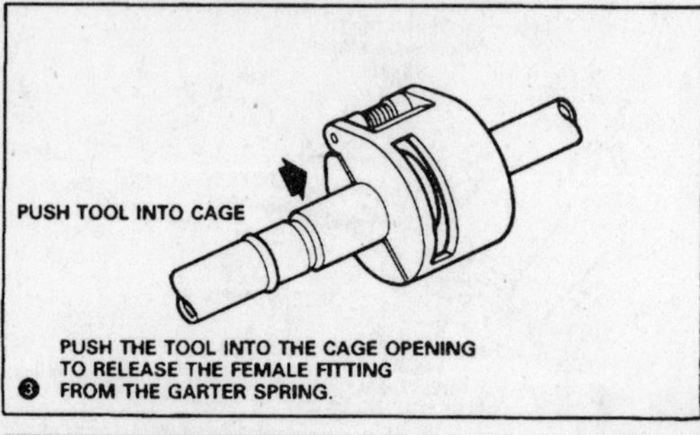

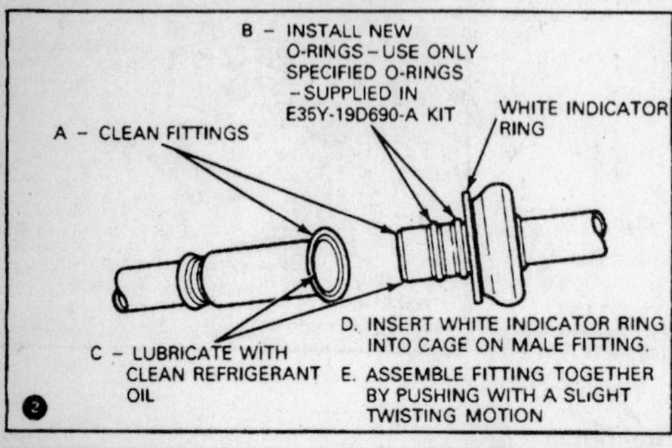

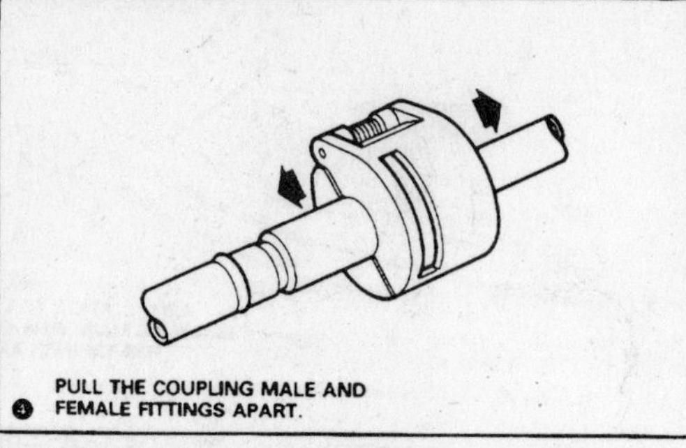

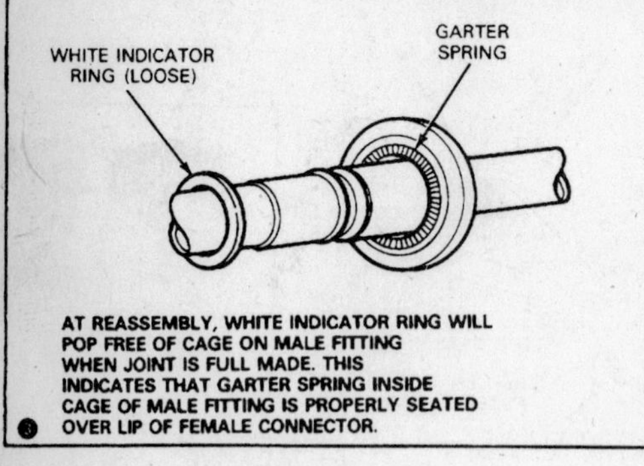

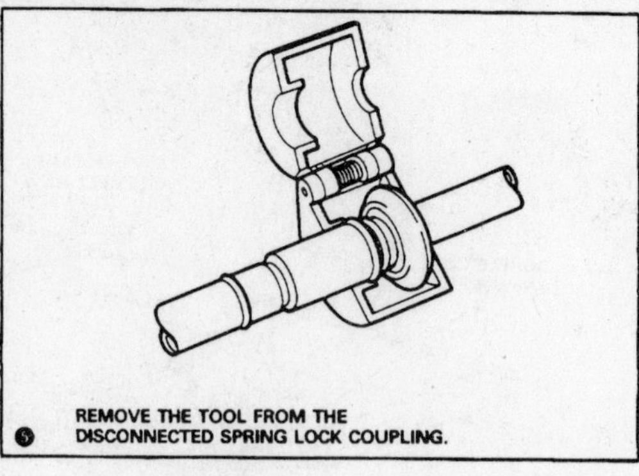

EFI Fuel line connectors

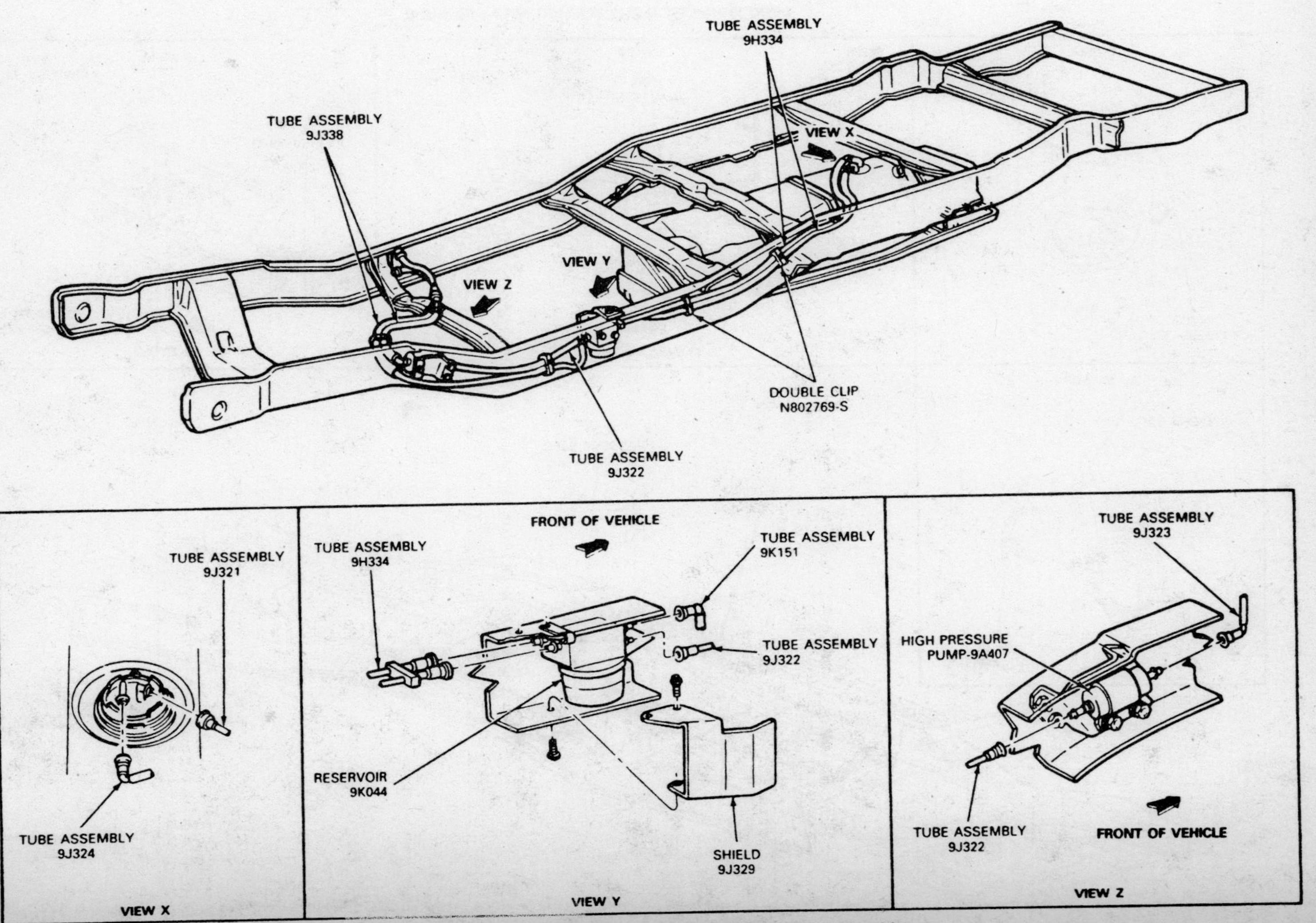

8-302 EFI midships fuel tank w/139 inch and 155 inch wheel base

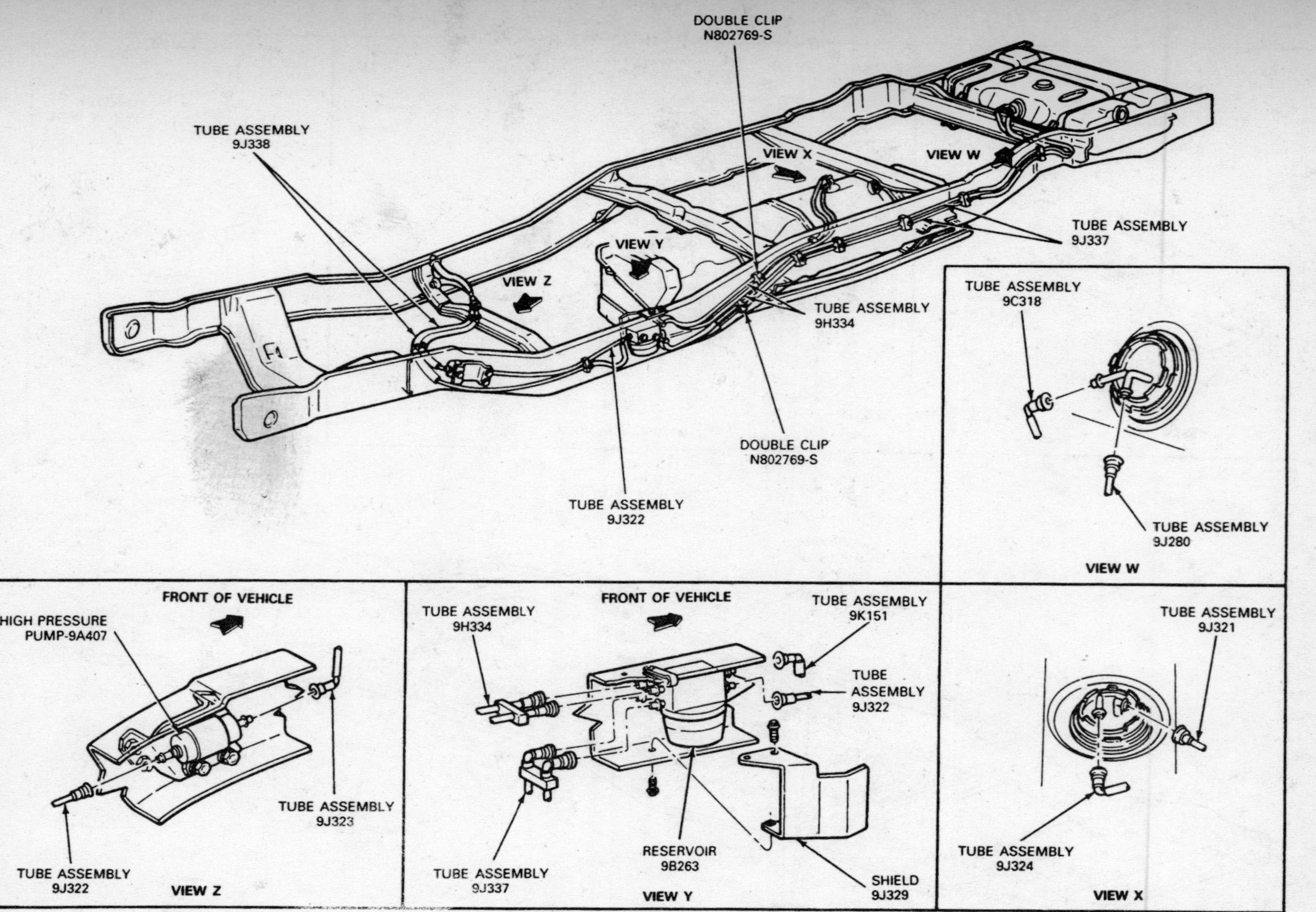

8-302 EFI dual tanks w/133 inch wheel base

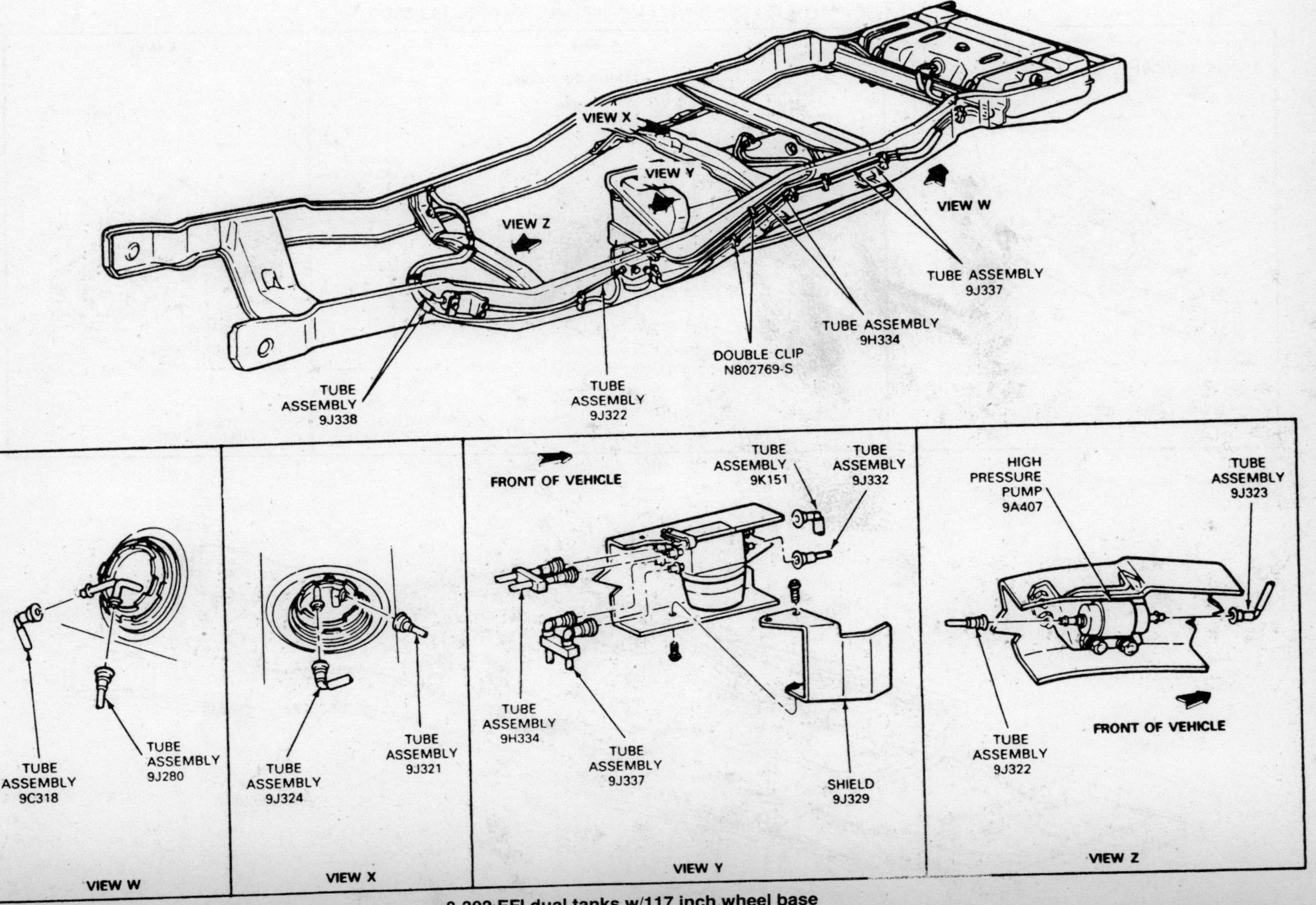

8-302 EFI dual tanks w/117 inch wheel base

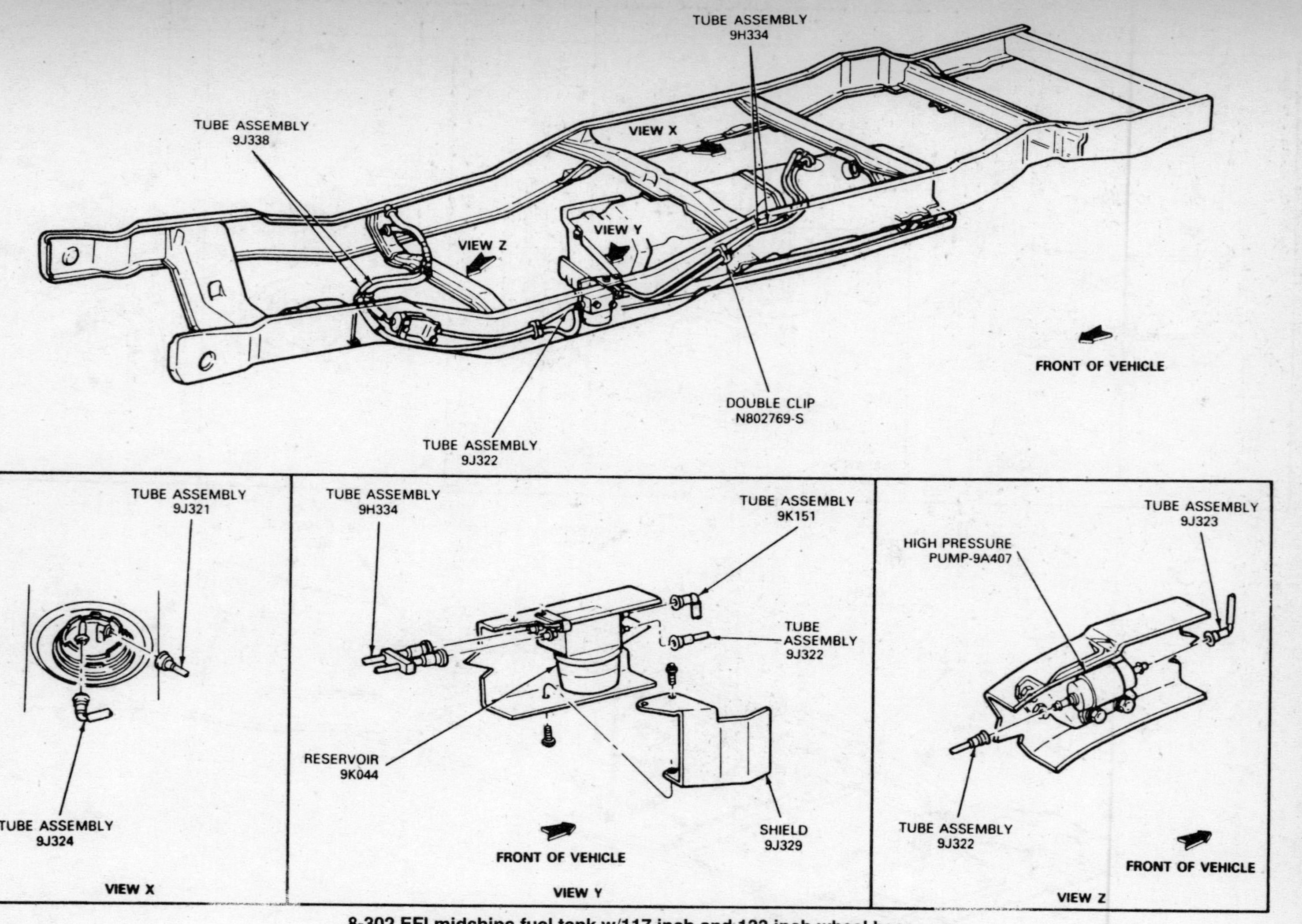

8-302 EFI midships fuel tank w/117 inch and 133 inch wheel base

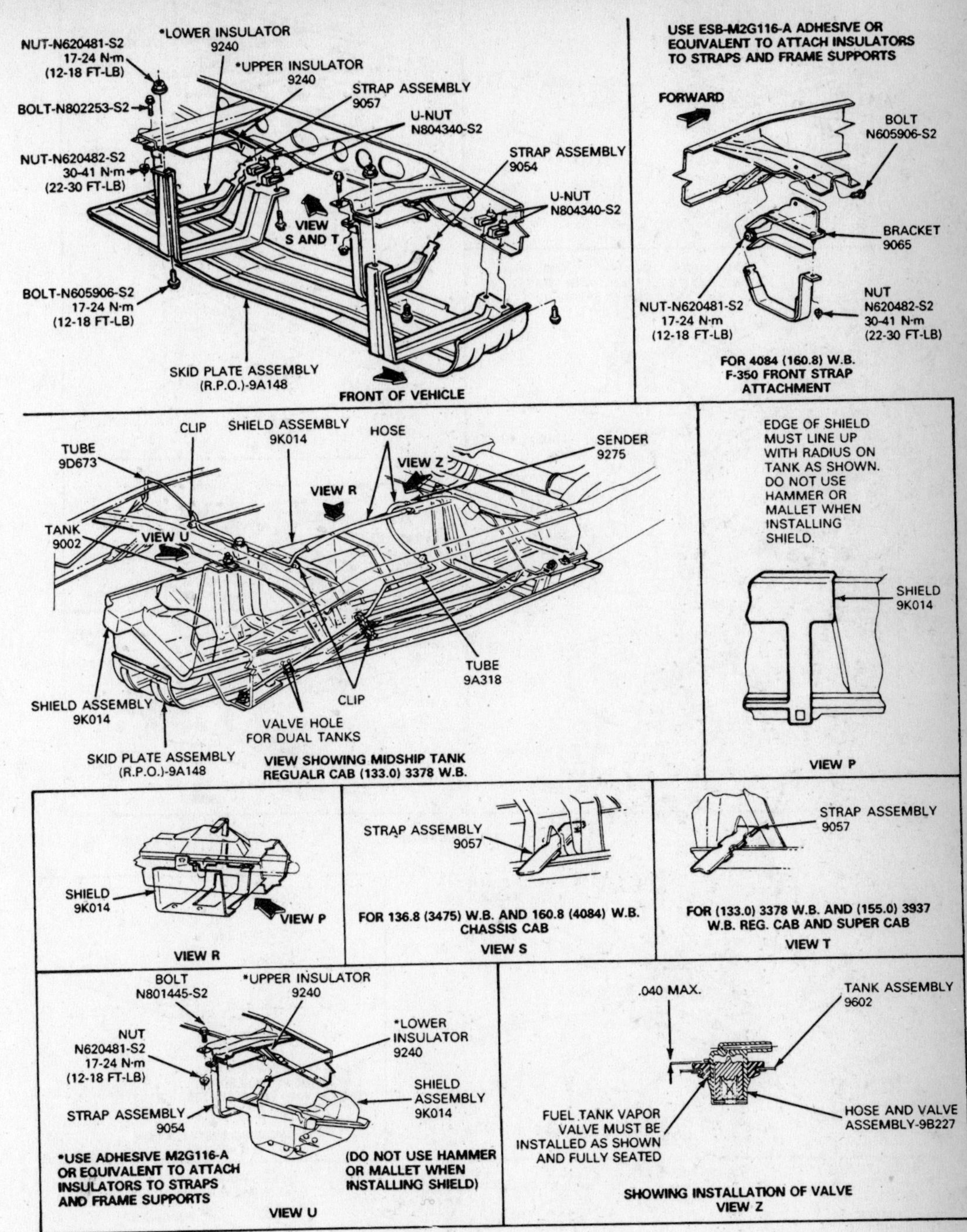

19 gallon midships fuel tank

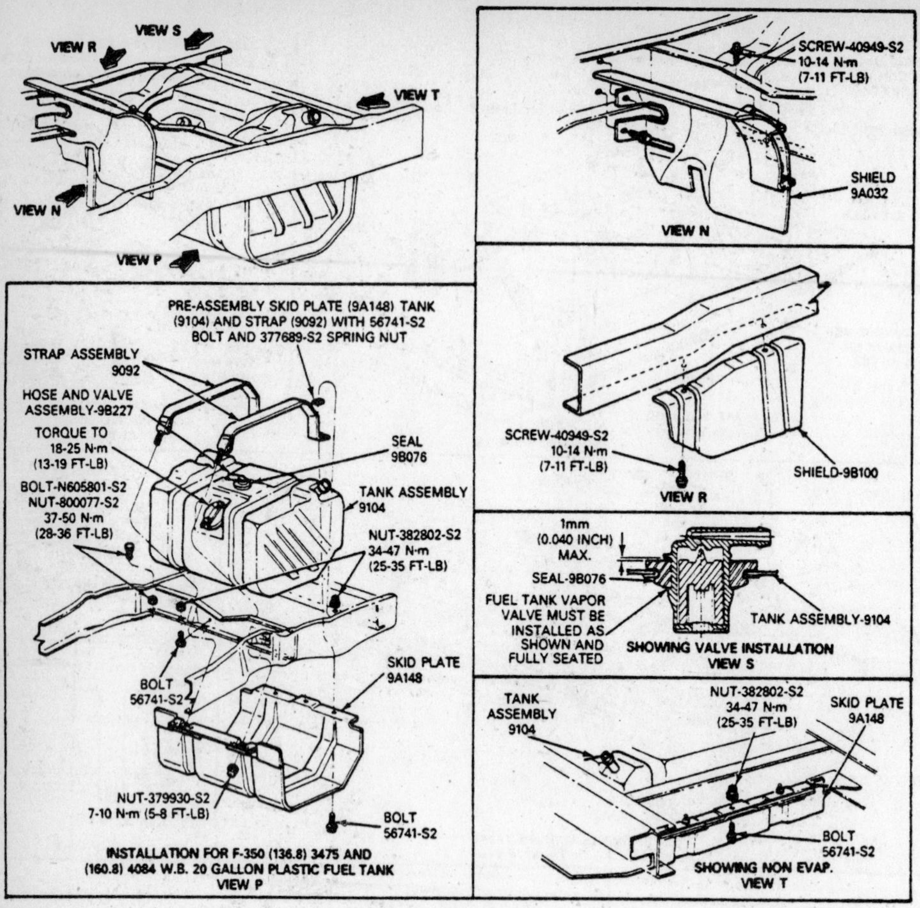

VIEW S
VIEW R
VIEW T
VIEW N
VIEW P
SCREW-40949-S2
10-14 N·m
(7-11 FT-LB)
SHIELD
9A032
VIEW N
PRE-ASSEMBLY SKID PLATE (9A148) TANK
(9104) AND STRAP (9092) WITH 56741-S2
BOLT AND 377689-S2 SPRING NUT
STRAP ASSEMBLY
9092
HOSE AND VALVE
ASSEMBLY-9B227
TORQUE TO
18-25 N·m
(13-19 FT-LB)
BOLT-N605801-S2
NUT-800077-S2
37-50 N·m
(28-36 FT-LB)
SEAL
9B076
TANK ASSEMBLY
9104
NUT-382802-S2
34-47 N·m
(25-35 FT-LB)
SKID PLATE
9A148
BOLT
56741-S2
NUT-379930-S2
7-10 N·m (5-8 FT-LB)
BOLT
56741-S2
INSTALLATION FOR F-350 (136.8) 3475 AND
(160.8) 4084 W.B. 20 GALLON PLASTIC FUEL TANK
VIEW P
SCREW-40949-S2
10-14 N·m
(7-11 FT-LB)
SHIELD-9B100
VIEW R
1mm
(0.040 INCH)
MAX.
SEAL-9B076
FUEL TANK VAPOR
VALVE MUST BE
INSTALLED AS
SHOWN AND
FULLY SEATED
TANK ASSEMBLY-9104
SHOWING VALVE INSTALLATION
VIEW S
TANK
ASSEMBLY
9104
NUT-382802-S2
34-47 N·m
(25-35 FT-LB)
SKID PLATE
9A148
BOLT
56741-S2
SHOWING NON EVAP.
VIEW T

Plastic aft fuel tank

VAPOR TUBE
9D673
CLIPS
351968-S
HOSE AND VALVE
ASSEMBLY
9B227
CLAMP
380882-S100
VIEW S
TANK
ASSEMBLY
9002
VIEW X
HOSE
381110-S150A
FUEL TUBE
9A318
CLIP
388960-S
.040 MAX.
TANK
ASSEMBLY
9002
FUEL TANK VAPOR VALVE
MUST BE INSTALLED AS
SHOWN AND FULLY SEATED
SHOWING INSTALLATION
VIEW S
BOLT
FRONT STRAP
ASSEMBLY
9054
NUT-N620482-S2
TIGHTEN TO
17-24 N·m
(12-18 FT-LB)
DO NOT USE HAMMER
OR MALLET WHEN
INSTALLING SHIELD
SHIELD-9K014
*USE ESB-M2G116-A ADHESIVE
TO ATTACH INSULATORS TO STRAPS
AND FRAME SUPPORTS
SHOWING 116 IN. (2967mm) W.B.
VIEW X
NUT
N620481-S2
ATTACH ON
REAR FLANGE
BOLT
N802253-S2
UPPER
INSULATOR
9240
REAR STRAP
ASSEMBLY
9057
U-NUT
N804340-S2
NUT-N620482-S2
30-41 N·m
(22-30 FT-LB)
BOLT
N802253-S2
LOWER INSULATOR
9240
U-NUT
N804340-S2
NUT
N620481-S2
BOLT-N605906-S2
17-24 N·m
(12-18 FT-LB)
FRONT STRAP
ASSEMBLY
9054
SKID PLATE ASSEMBLY
9A148
NUT-N620482-S2
30-41 N·m
(22-30 FT-LB)
F-150 (4×4) 116.0 IN W.B. ONLY
SHOWING 116 IN (2967mm) W.B.
VIEW X
FRONT OF VEHICLE

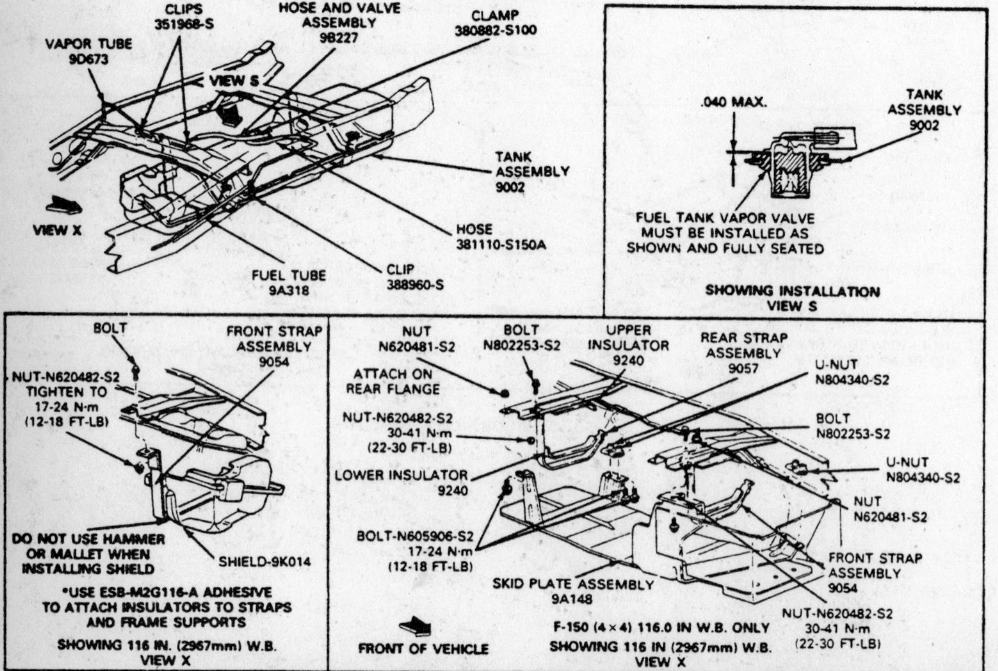

Fuel pump and filter on the 6–4.9L, 8–5.0L and 8–7.5L EFI engines

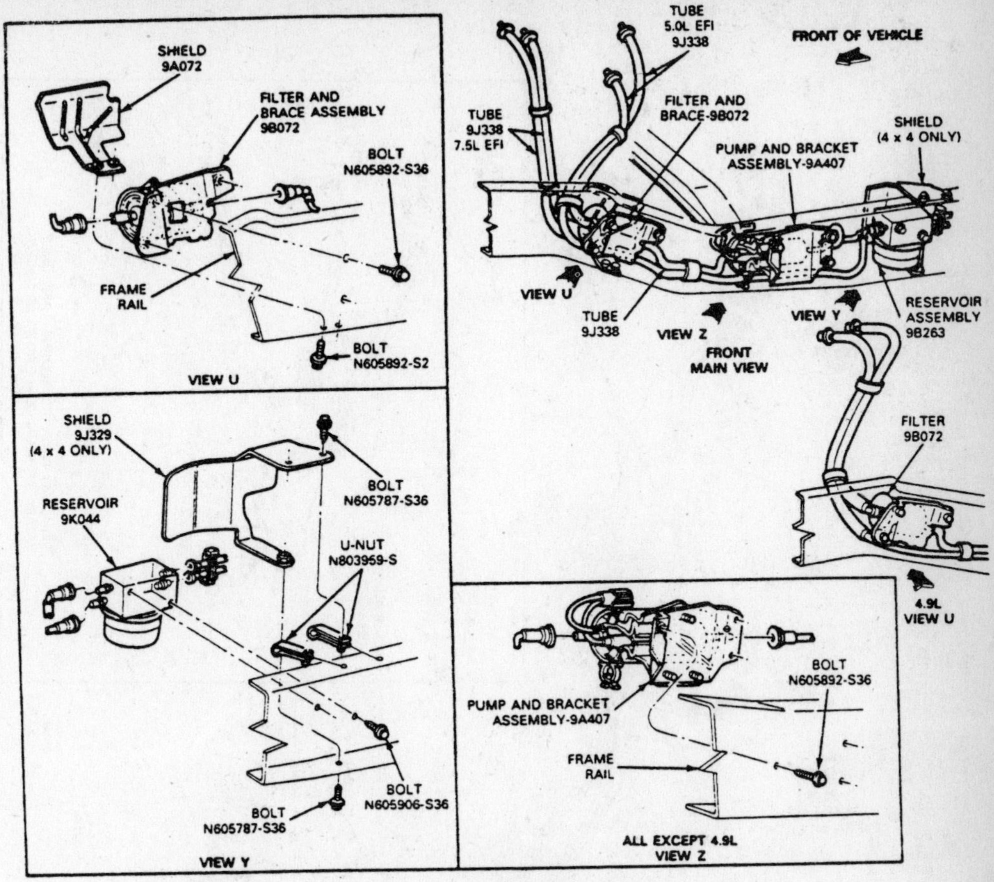

SHIELD
9A072
FILTER AND
BRACE ASSEMBLY
9B072
BOLT
N605892-S36
FRAME
RAIL
BOLT
N605892-S2
VIEW U
TUBE
5.0L EFI
9J338
FRONT OF VEHICLE
TUBE
9J338
7.5L EFI
FILTER AND
BRACE-9B072
SHIELD
(4 x 4 ONLY)
PUMP AND BRACKET
ASSEMBLY-9A407
VIEW U
TUBE
9J338
VIEW Z
VIEW Y
RESERVOIR
ASSEMBLY
9B263
FRONT
MAIN VIEW
SHIELD
9J329
(4 x 4 ONLY)
BOLT
N605787-S36
RESERVOIR
9K044
U-NUT
N803959-S
BOLT
N605906-S36
BOLT
N605787-S36
VIEW Y
FILTER
9B072
4.9L
VIEW U
BOLT
N605892-S36
PUMP AND BRACKET
ASSEMBLY-9A407
FRAME
RAIL
ALL EXCEPT 4.9L
VIEW Z

Fuel pump and filter on the 6–4.9L, 8–5.0L and 8–7.5L EFI engines

STRAP
ASSEMBLY
9092
INSULATORS
9240
BOLT WITH
THREAD
ADHESIVE
N801380-S100
WASHER
382873-S2
WASHER
382873-S2
STONE SHIELD
9K076
(4 x 4) ONLY (RPO)
INSULATORS
9240
NUT-34976-S36
TIGHTEN TO 7-9 N·m
(5-7 FT-LB)
SUPPORT
ASSEMBLY
9A017
STONE SHIELD
9K077
NUT-N620482-S2
TIGHTEN TO 37-50 N·m
(27-37 FT-LB)

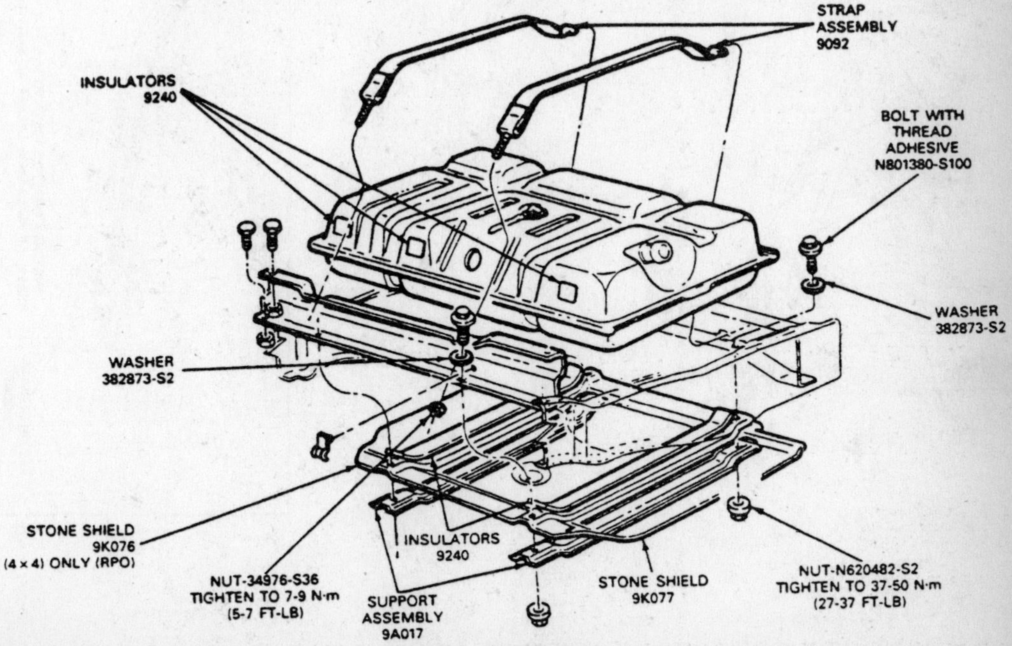

Steel aft fuel tank

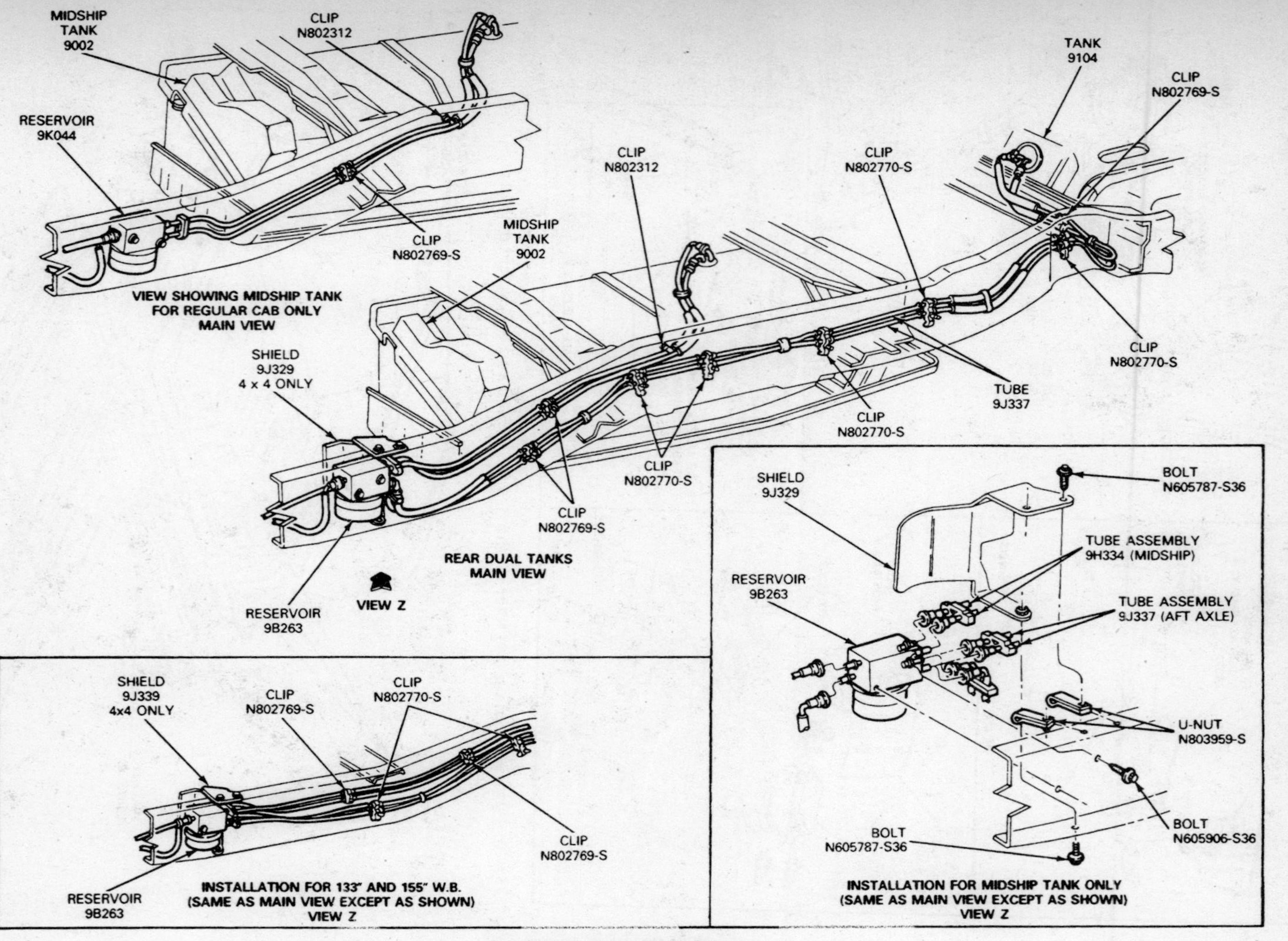

Fuel lines on the EFI engines

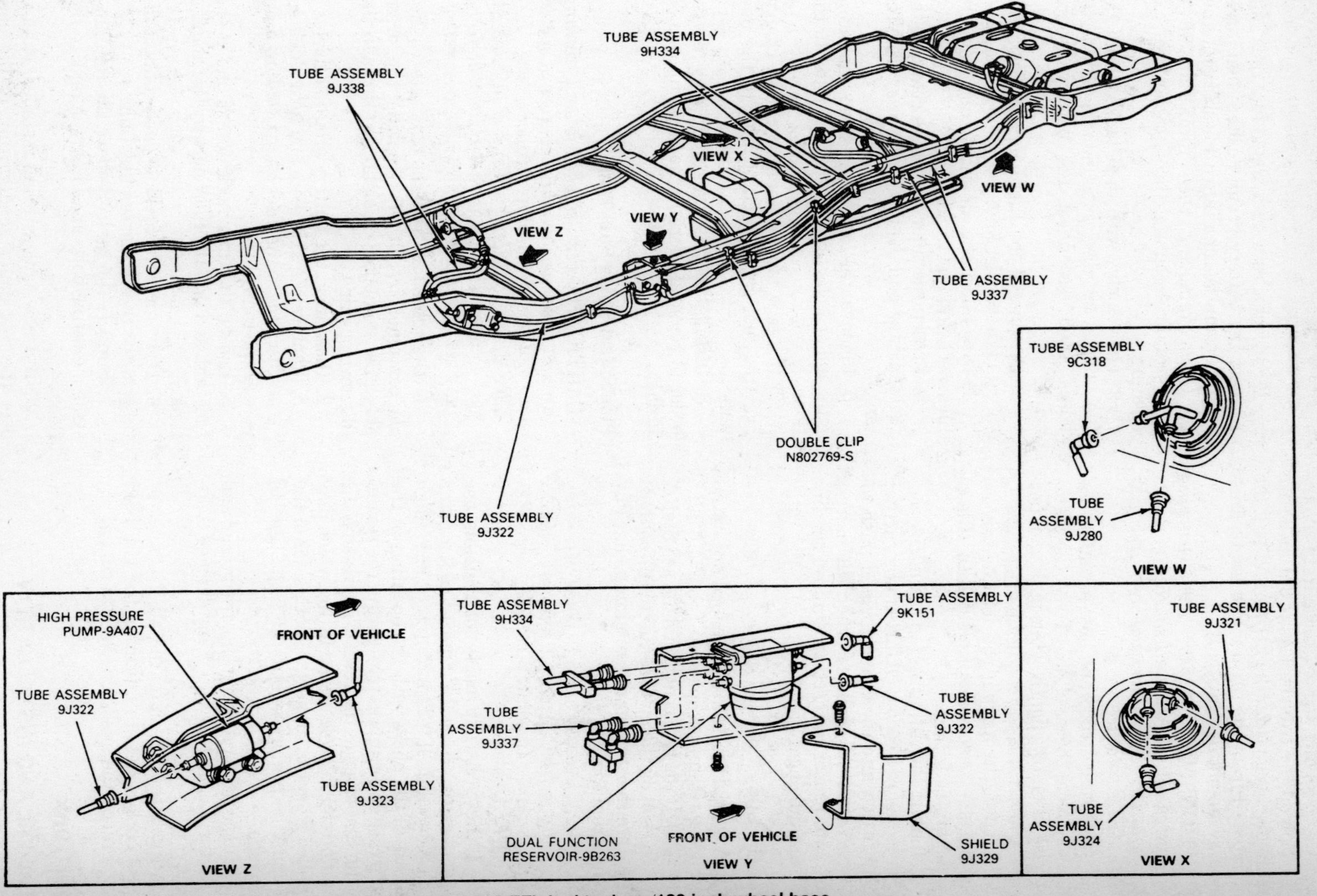

8-302 EFI dual tanks w/139 inch wheel base

Hairpin Clip

1. Clean all dirt and/or grease from the fittings. Spread the two clip legs about an 1/8 in. each to disengage from the fitting and pull the clip outward from the fitting. Use finger pressure only, do not use any tools.

CAUTION: *Never smoke when working around gasoline! Avoid all sources of sparks or ignition. Gasoline vapors are EXTREMELY volatile!*

2. Grasp the fittings and hose assembly and pull away from the steel line. Twist the fitting and hose assembly slightly while pulling, if necessary, when a sticking condition exists.
3. Inspect the hairpin clip for damage, replace the clip if necessary. Reinstall the clip in position on the fitting.
4. Inspect the fitting and inside of the connector to insure freedom Of dirt or obstruction. Install fitting into the connector and push together. A click will be heard when the hairpin snaps into proper connection. Pull on the line to insure full engagement.

Duck Bill Clip

1. A special tool is available for Ford for removing the retaining clip (Ford Tool No. T82L–9500–AH). If the tool is not on hand see Step 2. Align the slot on the push connector disconnect tool with either tab on the retaining clip. Pull the line from the connector.

CAUTION: *Never smoke when working around gasoline! Avoid all sources of sparks or ignition. Gasoline vapors are EXTREMELY volatile!*

2. If the special clip tool is not available, use a pair of narrow 6 in. (152mm) locking pliers with a jaw width of 0.2 in. (5mm) or less. Align the jaws of the pliers with the openings of the fitting case and compress the part of the retaining clip that engages the case. Compressing the retaining clip will release the fitting which may be pulled from the connector. Both sides of the clip must be compressed at the same time to disengage.
3. Inspect the retaining clip, fitting end and connector. Replace the clip if any damage is apparent.
4. Push the line into the steel connector until a click is heard, indicating the clip is in place. Pull on the line to check engagement.

Fuel Tank

REMOVAL AND INSTALLATION

Steel Mid-Ships Fuel Tank(s)

CAUTION: *Never smoke when working around gasoline! Avoid all sources of sparks or ignition. Gasoline vapors are EXTREMELY volatile! On fuel injected engines, depressurize the fuel system. Refer to the Fuel Injection System procedures, below.*

1. On vehicles with a single fuel tank, disconnect the battery ground cable, then, drain the fuel from the tank into a suitable container by either removing the drain plug, if so equipped, or siphoning through the filler cap opening.
2. On vehicles with dual tanks, drain the fuel tanks by disconnecting the connector hoses, then disconnect the battery ground cable.
3. Disconnect the fuel gauge sending unit wire and fuel outlet line.
4. Disconnect the air relief tube from the filler neck and fuel tank.
5. Loosen the filler neck hose clamp at the fuel tank and pull the filler neck away from the tank.
6. Remove the retaining strap mounting nuts and/or bolts and lower the tank(s) to the floor.
7. If a new tank is being installed, change over the fuel gauge sending unit to the new tank.
8. Install the fuel tank(s) in the reverse order of removal. Torque the strap nuts to 30 ft. lbs.

Plastic Mid-Ships Fuel Tank

CAUTION: *Never smoke when working around gasoline! Avoid all sources of sparks or ignition. Gasoline vapors are EXTREMELY volatile! On fuel injected engines, depressurize the fuel system. Refer to the Fuel Injection System procedures, below.*

1. Drain the fuel from the tank into a suitable container by either removing the drain plug, if so equipped, or siphoning through the filler cap opening.
2. Disconnect the battery ground cable(s).
3. Remove the skid plate and heat shields.
4. Disconnect the fuel gauge sending unit wire at the tank.
5. Loosen the filler neck hose clamp at the fuel tank and pull the filler neck away from the tank.
6. Disconnect the fuel line push-connect fittings at the fuel gauge sending unit.
7. Support the tank. Remove the retaining strap mounting bolts and lower the tank to the floor.
8. If a new tank is being installed, change over the fuel gauge sending unit to the new tank.
9. Install the fuel tank(s) in the reverse order of removal. Torque the strap bolts to 12–18 ft. lbs.

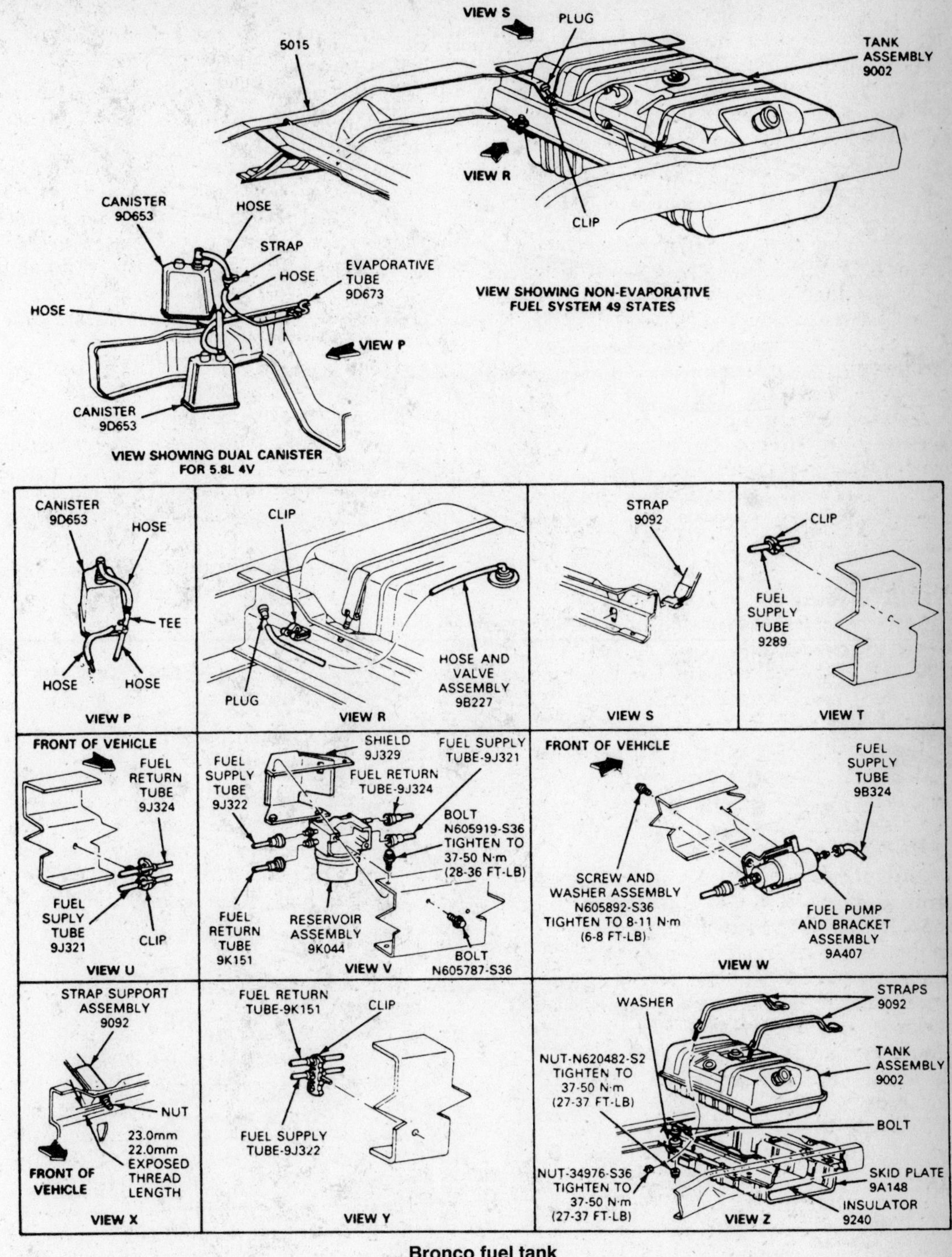

Bronco fuel tank

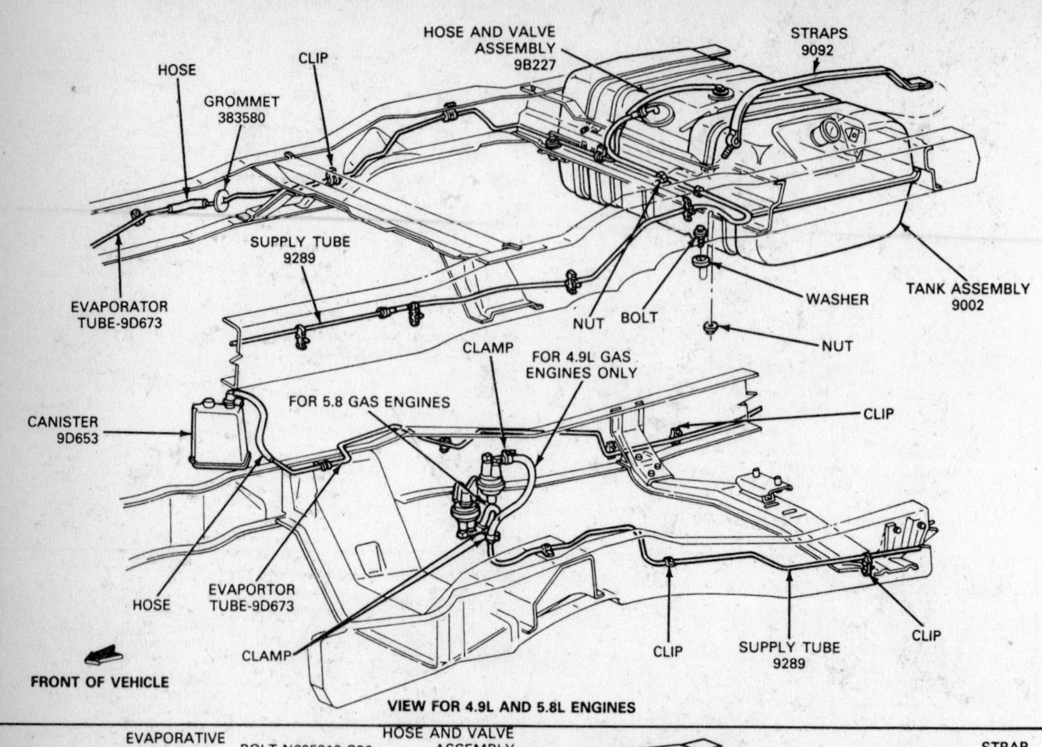

VIEW FOR 4.9L AND 5.8L ENGINES

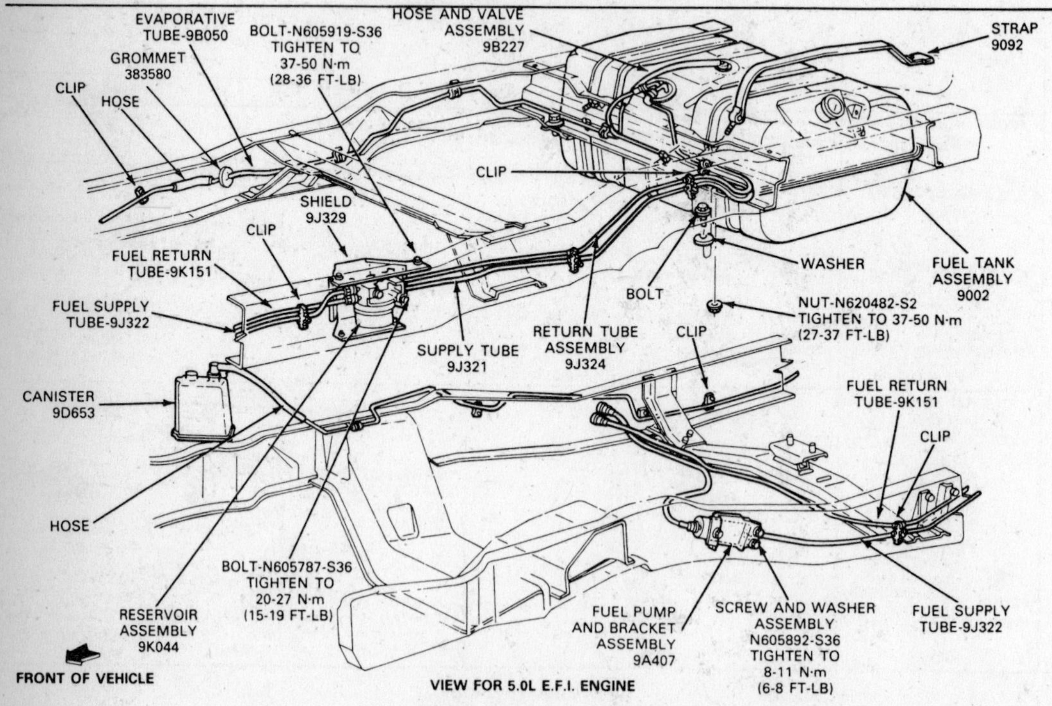

VIEW FOR 5.0L E.F.I. ENGINE

Bronco fuel tank, cont.

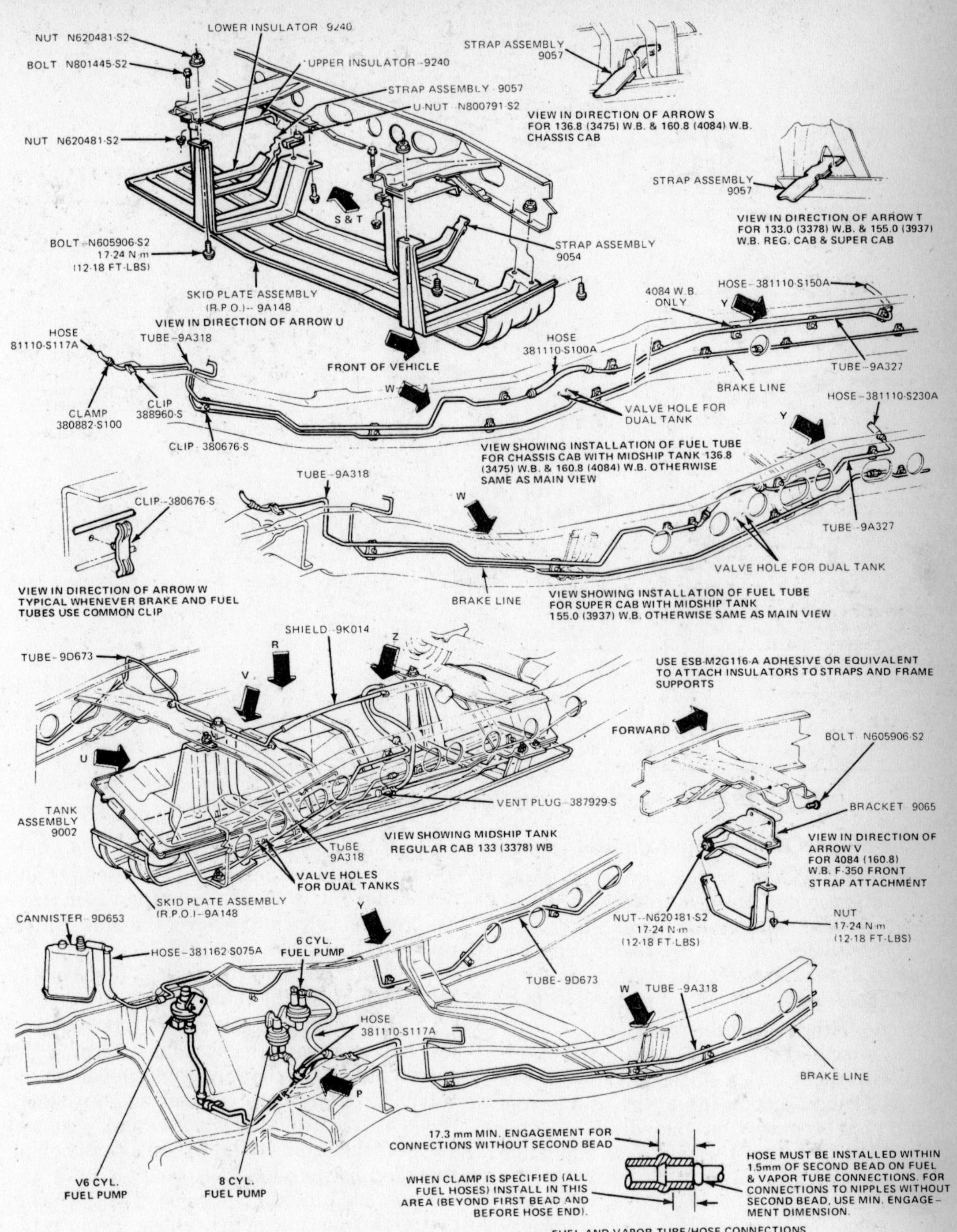

1987 midships fuel tank installation

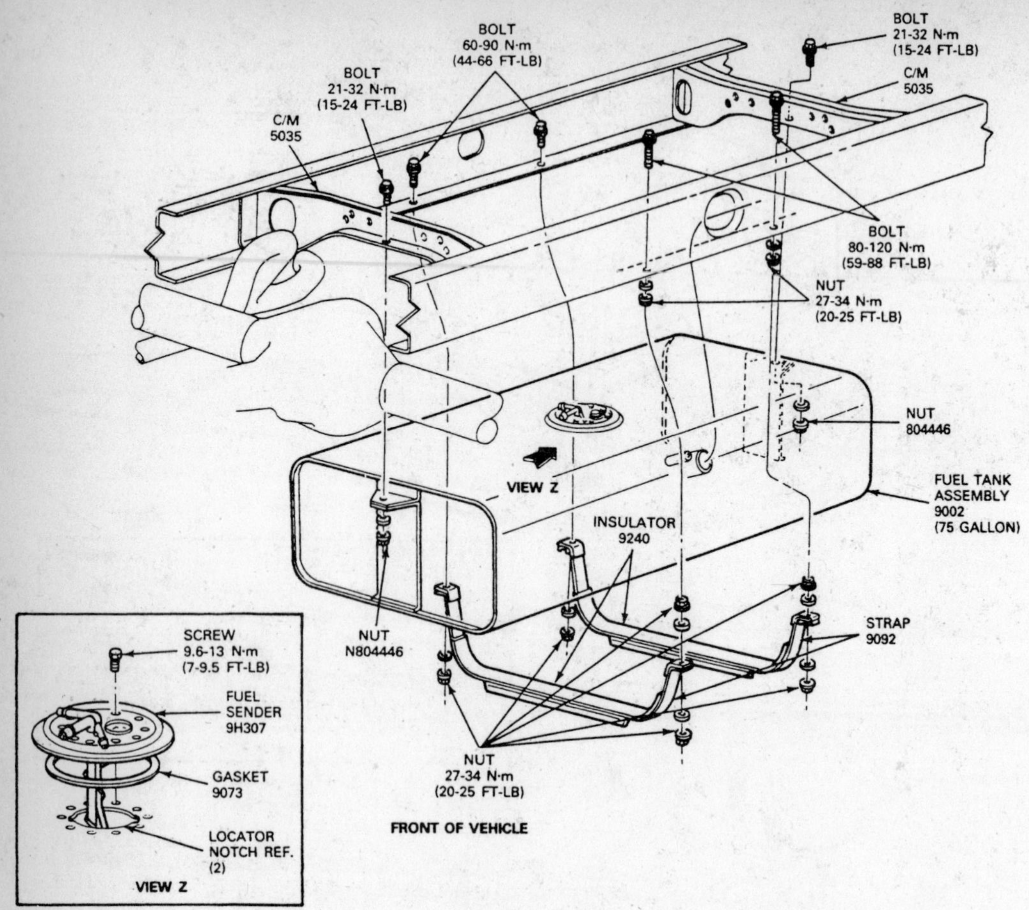

75 gallon aft-of-axle fuel tank used on the motor home chassis

Plastic or Steel Behind-The-Axle Fuel Tank

CAUTION: *Never smoke when working around gasoline! Avoid all sources of sparks or ignition. Gasoline vapors are EXTREMELY volatile! On fuel injected engines, depressurize the fuel system. Refer to the Fuel Injection System procedures, below.*

1. Raise the rear of the truck.
2. Disconnect the negative battery cable.
3. On trucks with a single tank, disconnect the fuel gauge sending unit wire at the fuel tank, then, remove the fuel drain plug or siphon the fuel from the tank into a suitable container.
4. On vehicles with dual tanks, drain the fuel tanks by disconnecting the connector hoses, then disconnect the battery ground cable.
5. Disconnect the fuel line push-connect fittings at the fuel gauge sending unit.
6. Loosen the clamps on the fuel filler pipe and vent hose as necessary and disconnect the filler pipe hose and vent hose from the tank.
7. If the tank is the metal type, support the tank and remove the bolts attaching the tank support or skid plate to the frame. Carefully lower the tank or tank/skid plate assembly and disconnect the vent tube from the vapor emission control valve in the top of the tank. Finish removing the filler pipe and filler pipe vent hose if not possible previously. Remove the tank from under the vehicle.
8. If the tank is the plastic type, support the tank and remove the bolts attaching the combination skid plate and tank support to the frame. Carefully lower the tank and disconnect the vent tube from the vapor emission control valve in the top of the tank. Finish removing the filler pipe and filler pipe vent hose if it was not possible previously. Remove the skid plate and tank from under the vehicle. Remove the skid plate from the tank.
9. If the sending unit is to be removed, turn the unit retaining ring counterclockwise and remove the sending unit, retaining ring and gasket. Discard the gasket.
10. Install the tank in the reverse order of removal. With metal tanks, use thread adhesive such as Loctite® on the bolt threads. Torque these bolts to 27–37 ft. lbs. With plas-

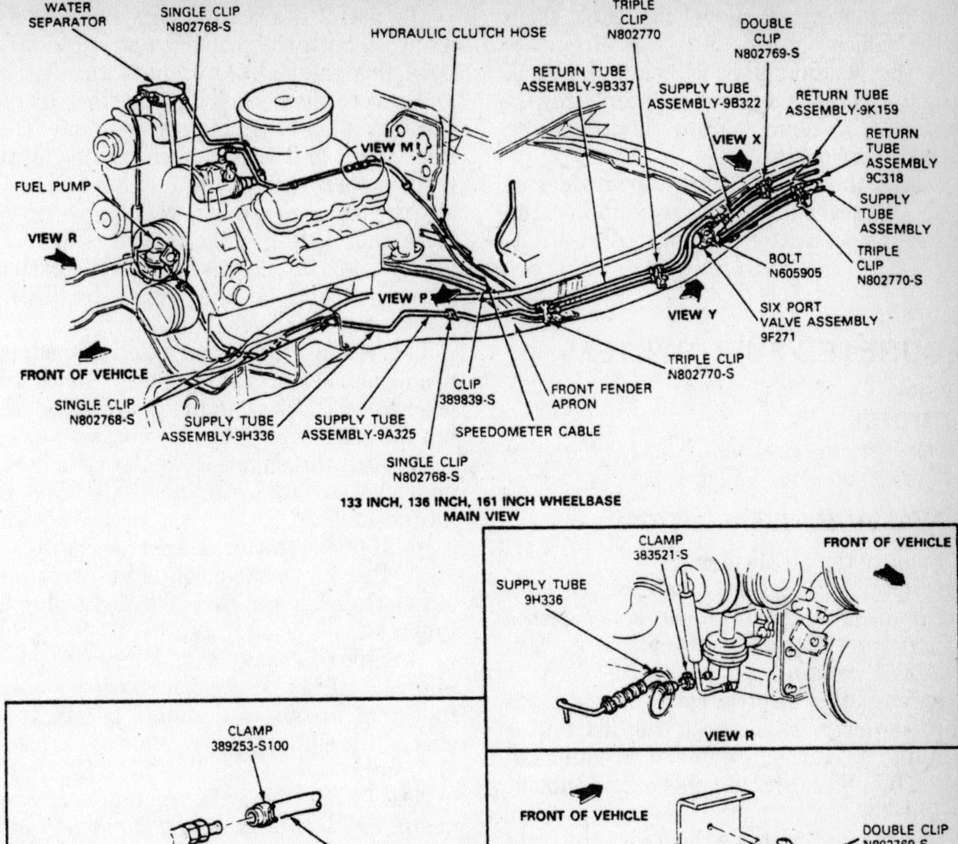

Diesel fuel line installation w/aft fuel tank and 133 in. (337.8cm) wheel base

tic tanks, DO NOT use thread adhesive. Torque the bolts to 25–35 ft. lbs.

Bronco Fuel Tank

CAUTION: *Never smoke when working around gasoline! Avoid all sources of sparks or ignition. Gasoline vapors are EXTREMELY volatile!*

1. Raise and support the rear end on jackstands.
2. Disconnect the negative battery cable.
3. Disconnect the fuel gauge sending unit wire at the fuel tank.
4. Remove the fuel drain plug or siphon the fuel from the tank into a suitable container.
5. Loosen the fuel line hose clamps, slide the clamps forward and disconnect the fuel one at the fuel gauge sending unit.
6. Loosen the clamps on the fuel filler pipe and vent hose as necessary and disconnect the filler pipe hose and vent hose from the tank.
7. Support the tank and remove the bolts lower attaching bolts or skid plate bolts supporting the tank to the frame. Carefully lower the tank or tank/skid plate assembly and disconnect the vent tube from the vapor emission control valve in the top of the tank. Finish removing the filler pipe and filler pipe vent hose if not

possible previously. Remove the tank from under the vehicle.

8. If the sending unit is being removed, turn the unit's retaining ring counterclockwise and remove the sending unit, retaining ring and gasket. Discard the gasket.

9. Install the tank in the reverse order of removal. Use thread locking compound on the bolt threads and torque the bolts to 27–37 ft. lbs.

CARBURETED FUEL SYSTEM

Carburetor

NOTE: *The only carburetor used is the 4-bbl Holley 4180 on some V8 engines.*

REMOVAL AND INSTALLATION

1. Remove the air cleaner.

CAUTION: *Never smoke when working around gasoline! Avoid all sources of sparks or ignition. Gasoline vapors are EXTREMELY volatile!*

2. Remove the throttle cable or rod from the throttle lever. Disconnect the distributor vacuum line, EGR vacuum line, if so equipped, the inline fuel filter and the choke heat tube at the carburetor.

3. Disconnect the choke clean air tube from the air horn. Disconnect the choke actuating cable, if so equipped.

4. Remove the carburetor retaining nuts then remove the carburetor. Remove the carburetor mounting gasket, spacer (if so equipped), and the lower gasket from the intake manifold.

5. Before installing the carburetor, clean the gasket mounting surfaces of the spacer and carburetor. Place the spacer between two new gaskets and position the spacer and gaskets on the intake manifold. Position the carburetor body flange, snug the nuts, then alternately tighten each nut in a criss-cross pattern.

6. Connect the inline fuel filter, throttle cable, choke heat tube, distributor vacuum line, EGR vacuum line, and choke cable.

7. Connect the choke clean air line to the air horn.

8. Adjust the engine idle speed, the idle fuel mixture and anti-stall dashpot (if so equipped). Install the air cleaner.

FLOAT AND FUEL LEVEL ADJUSTMENT

CAUTION: *Never smoke when working around gasoline! Avoid all sources of sparks or ignition. Gasoline vapors are EXTREMELY volatile!*

To perform a preliminary dry float adjustment on both the primary and secondary fuel bowl float assemblies, remove the fuel bowls and invert them allowing the float to rest on the fuel inlet valve and set assembly. the fuel inlet valve and seat can be rotated until the float is parallel with the fuel bowl floor (actually the top of the fuel bowl chamber inverted). Note that this is an initial dry float setting which must be rechecked with the carburetor assembled and on the engine to obtain the proper wet fuel level.

This carburetor has an externally adjustable needle and seat assembly which allows the fuel level to be checked and adjust without removing the carburetor from the engine.

1. Run the engine with the vehicle resting on a level surface until the engine temperature has normalized.

2. Remove the air cleaner assembly.

3. Place a suitable container or an absorbent cloth below the fuel level sight plug in the fuel bowl.

4. Stop the engine and remove the sight plug and gasket on the primary float bowl. The fuel level in the bowl should be at the lower edge of the sight plug hole, plus or minus $^{1}/_{16}$ in. (1.5mm).

CAUTION: *Never loosen the lock screw or nut, or attempt to adjust the fuel level with the sight plug removed or the engine running, since fuel will spray out creating a fire hazard!*

5. To adjust the fuel level, install the sight plug and gasket, loosen one on the lower fuel bowl retaining screws and drain the fuel from the bowl only if the level is too high. Loosen the lock screw on top of the fuel bowl just enough to allow the adjusting nut to be turned. Turn the adjusting nut about $^{1}/_{2}$ of a turn in to lower the fuel level and out to raise the fuel level. By

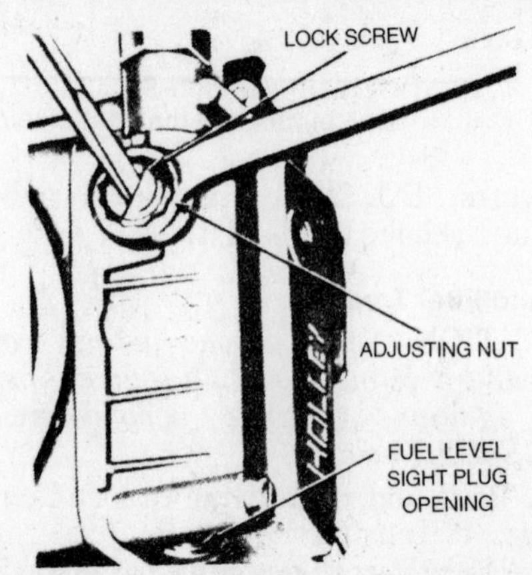

4180 float level adjustment

turning the adjusting nut $^5/_{32}$ of a turn, the fuel level will change $^1/_{32}$ in. (0.8mm) at the sight plug.

6. Start the engine and allow the fuel level to stabilize. Check the fuel level as outlined in Step 4.

7. Repeat the procedure for the secondary float bowl adjustment.

8. Install the air cleaner assembly if no further adjustments are necessary.

SECONDARY THROTTLE PLATE ADJUSTMENT

1. Remove the carburetor.

CAUTION: *Never smoke when working around gasoline! Avoid all sources of sparks or ignition. Gasoline vapors are EXTREMELY volatile!*

2. Hold the secondary throttle plates closed.

3. Turn the secondary throttle shaft lever stop screw out until the secondary throttle plates seat in the throttle bores.

4. Turn the screw back in until the screw just touches the lever, then $^3/_8$ turn more.

FAST IDLE ADJUSTMENT

1. Remove the spark delay valve, if so equipped, from the Distributor vacuum advance line, and route the vacuum line directly to the advance side of the distributor.

CAUTION: *Never smoke when working around gasoline! Avoid all sources of sparks or ignition. Gasoline vapors are EXTREMELY volatile!*

2. Trace the EGR signal vacuum line from the EGR valve to the carburetor and if there is EGR/PVS valve or temperature vacuum switch located in the vacuum line routing, disconnect the EGR vacuum line at the EGR valve and plug the line.

3. If not equipped with an EGR/PVS valve or temperature vacuum switch do not detach the EGR vacuum line.

4. Trace the purge valve vacuum line from the purge valve located on the canister, to the first point where the vacuum line can be detached from the underhood hose routing. Disconnect the vacuum line at that point, cap the open port, and plug the vacuum line.

WARNING: *To prevent damage to the purge valve do not disconnect the vacuum line at the purge valve.*

5. With the engine running at normal operating temperature, the choke plate fully opened and the manual transmission in Neutral and the automatic transmission in Park, place the fast idle level on the 2nd or kickdown step of the fast idle cam.

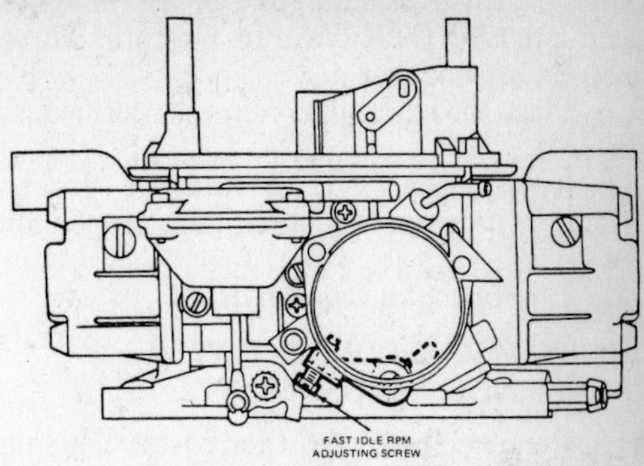

Holley 4180C 4–bbl fast idle adjustment

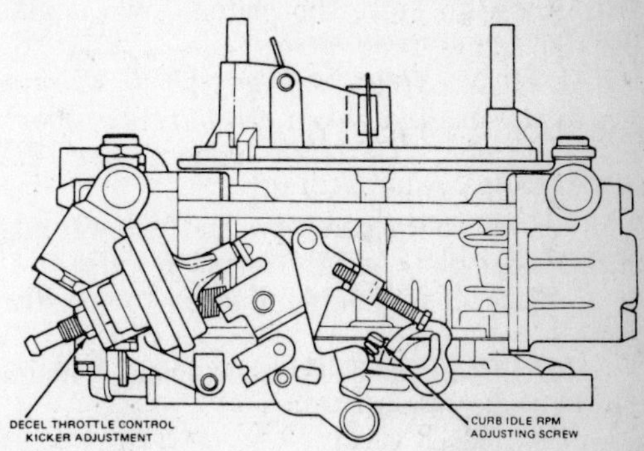

Holley 4180C 4–bbl curb idle and VOTM kicker adjustments location

6. Adjust the fast idle screw to within 100 rpm of the specified speed given on the Vehicle Emission Control Decal.

7. Reconnect all vacuum lines.

VACUUM OPERATED THROTTLE MODULATOR ADJUSTMENT

1. Set the parking brake, put the transmission in Park or Neutral and run the engine up to operating temperature.

CAUTION: *Never smoke when working around gasoline! Avoid all sources of sparks or ignition. Gasoline vapors are EXTREMELY volatile!*

2. Turn off the air conditioning and heater controls.

3. Disconnect and plug the vacuum hoses at the air control valve and EGR valve and purge control valve.

4. Place the transmission in the position specified on the underhood decal.

5. If necessary, check and adjust the curb idle rpm.

6. Place the transmission in Neutral or Park and rev the engine. Place the transmission in the specified position according to the underhood decal and recheck the curb idle rpm. Readjust if necessary.

7. Connect an external vacuum source

which provides a minimum of 10 in.Hg of vacuum to the VOTM (Vacuum Operated Throttle Modulator) kicker.

8. Place the transmission in the specified position.

9. Adjust the VOTM (throttle kicker) locknut if necessary to obtain the proper idle rpm.

10. Reconnect all vacuum hoses.

CHOKE PLATE PULL-DOWN CLEARANCE ADJUSTMENT

1. Remove the choke thermostat housing, gasket and retainer.

2. Insert a piece of wire into the choke piston bore to move the piston down against the stop screw.

CAUTION: *Never smoke when working around gasoline! Avoid all sources of sparks or ignition. Gasoline vapors are EXTREMELY volatile!*

3. Measure the gap between the lower edge of the choke plate and the air horn wall.

4. Turn the adjustment screw to specifications.

5. Reinstall the choke thermostat housing, gasket and retainer.

AUTOMATIC CHOKE HOUSING ADJUSTMENT

This adjustment is present and should not be changed.

ACCELERATOR PUMP LEVER ADJUSTMENT

1. Hold the primary throttle plates in the wide open position.

CAUTION: *Never smoke when working around gasoline! Avoid all sources of sparks or ignition. Gasoline vapors are EXTREMELY volatile!*

2. Using a feeler gauge, check the clearance accelerator pump operating lever adjustment screw head and the pump arm while depressing the pump arm with your finger. The clearance should be $\frac{1}{64}$ in. (0.38mm).

3. To make an adjustment, hold the adjusting screw locknut and turn the adjusting screw inward to increase, or outward to decrease, the adjustment. $\frac{1}{2}$ turn will change the clearance by $\frac{1}{64}$ in. (0.4mm).

ACCELERATOR PUMP STROKE ADJUSTMENT

This adjustment is preset and should not be changed.

CARBURETOR TROUBLESHOOTING

The best way to diagnose a bad carburetor is to eliminate all other possible sources of the problem. If the carburetor is suspected to be the problem, first perform all of the adjustments given in this Section. If this doesn't correct the difficulty, then check the following. Check the ignition system to make sure that the spark plugs, breaker points, and condenser are in good condition and adjusted to the proper specifications. Examine the emission control equipment to make sure that all the vacuum lines are connected and none are blocked or clogged. See the first half of this Chapter. Check the ignition timing adjustment. Check all of the vacuum lines on the engine for loose connections, slips or breaks. Torque the carburetor and intake manifold attaching bolts to the proper specifications. If, after performing all of these checks and adjustments, the problem is still not solved, then you can safely assume that the carburetor is the source of the problem.

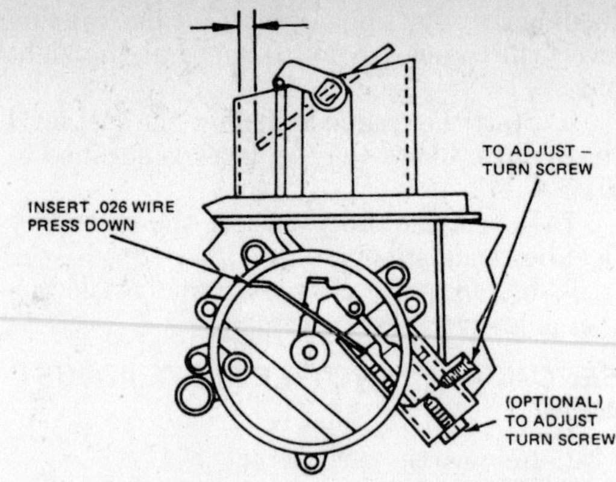

Holley 4180 4–bbl choke pulldown adjustment

OVERHAUL

CAUTION: *Never smoke when working around gasoline! Avoid all sources of sparks or ignition. Gasoline vapors are EXTREMELY volatile!*

Efficient carburetion depends greatly on careful cleaning and inspection during overhaul since dirt, gum, water or varnish in or on the carburetor parts are often responsible for poor performance.

Overhaul the carburetor in a clean, dust free area. Carefully disassembly the carburetor, referring often to the exploded views. Keep all similar and look-alike parts segregated during disassembly and cleaning to avoid accidental interchange during assembly. Make a note of all jet sizes.

When the carburetor is disassembled, wash all parts (except diaphragms, electric choke units, pump plunger and any other plastic, leather, fiber, or rubber parts) in clean carburetor solvent. Do not leave the parts in the solvent any longer than is necessary to sufficiently loosen the dirt and deposits. Excessive cleaning may remove the special finish from the float bowl and choke valve bodies, leaving these parts unfit for service. Rinse all parts in clean solvent and blow them dry with compressed air or allow them to air dry, while resting on clean, lintless paper. Wipe clean all cork, plastic, leather and fiber parts with clean, lint free cloth.

Blow out all passages and jets with compressed air and be sure that there are no restrictions or blockages. Never use wire or similar tools to clean jets, fuel passages or air bleeds. Clean all jets and valves separately to avoid accidental interchange.

Examine all parts for wear or damage. If wear or damage is found, replace the defective parts. Especially, inspect the following:

1. Check the float needle and seat for wear. If wear is found, replace the complete assembly.

2. Check the float hinge pin for wear and the float(s) for dents or distortion. replace the float if fuel has leaked into it.

3. Check the throttle and choke shaft bores for wear or an out-of-round condition. Damage or wear to the throttle arm, shaft or shaft bore will often require replacement of the throttle body. These parts require a close tolerance of fit; wear may allow air leakage, which could affect starting and idling.

NOTE: *Throttle shaft and bushings are not normally included in overhaul kits. They can be purchased separately.*

4. Inspect the idle mixture adjusting needles for burrs and grooves. Any such condition requires replacement of the needle, since you will not be able to obtain a satisfactory idle.

5. Test the accelerator pump check valves. They should pass air one way, but not the other. Test for proper seating by blowing and sucking on the valve. Replace the valve as necessary. If the valve is satisfactory, wash the valve again to remove moisture.

6. Check the bowl cover for warped surfaces with a straightedge.

7. Closely inspect the valves and seats for wear and damage, replacing as necessary.

8. After the carburetor is assembled, check the choke valve for freedom of operation.

Carburetor overhaul kits are recommended for each overhaul. these kits contain all gaskets and new parts to replace those which deteriorate most rapidly. Failure to replace all of the parts supplied with the kit (especially gaskets) can result in poor performance later.

Most carburetor manufacturers supply overhaul kits of three basic types: minor repair; major repair; and gasket kits.

After cleaning and checking all components, reassemble the carburetor, using new parts and referring to the exploded view. When reassembling, make sure that all screws and jets are right in their seat, but do not overtighten, as the tip will be distorted. Tighten all screws gradually, in rotation. Do not tighten needle valves into their seats; uneven jetting will result. Always use new gaskets. Be sure to adjust the float level.

NOTE: *Most carburetor rebuilding kits contain a sheet of specific instructions pertaining to the carburetor the kit is for.*

GASOLINE FUEL INJECTION 6–4.9L ENGINE

Relieving Fuel System Pressure

NOTE: *A special tool is necessary for this procedure.*

1. Make sure the ignition switch is in the OFF position.

CAUTION: *Never smoke when working around gasoline! Avoid all sources of sparks or ignition. Gasoline vapors are EXTREMELY volatile!*

2. Disconnect the battery ground.
3. Remove the fuel filler cap.
4. Using EFI Pressure Gauge T80L–9974–A, or equivalent, at the fuel pressure relief valve (located in the fuel line in the upper right corner of the engine compartment) relieve the fuel system pressure. A valve cap must first be removed to gain access to the pressure relief valve.

Fuel Charging Assembly

REMOVAL AND INSTALLATION

1. Relieve the fuel system pressure.

CAUTION: *Never smoke when working around gasoline! Avoid all sources of sparks or ignition. Gasoline vapors are EXTREMELY volatile!*

2. Disconnect the battery ground cable and drain the cooling system.

CAUTION: *When draining the coolant, keep in mind that cats and dogs are attracted by the ethylene glycol antifreeze, and are quite likely to drink any that is left in an uncovered container or in puddles on the ground. This will prove fatal in sufficient quantity. Always drain the coolant into a sealable container. Coolant should be reused unless it is contaminated or several years old.*

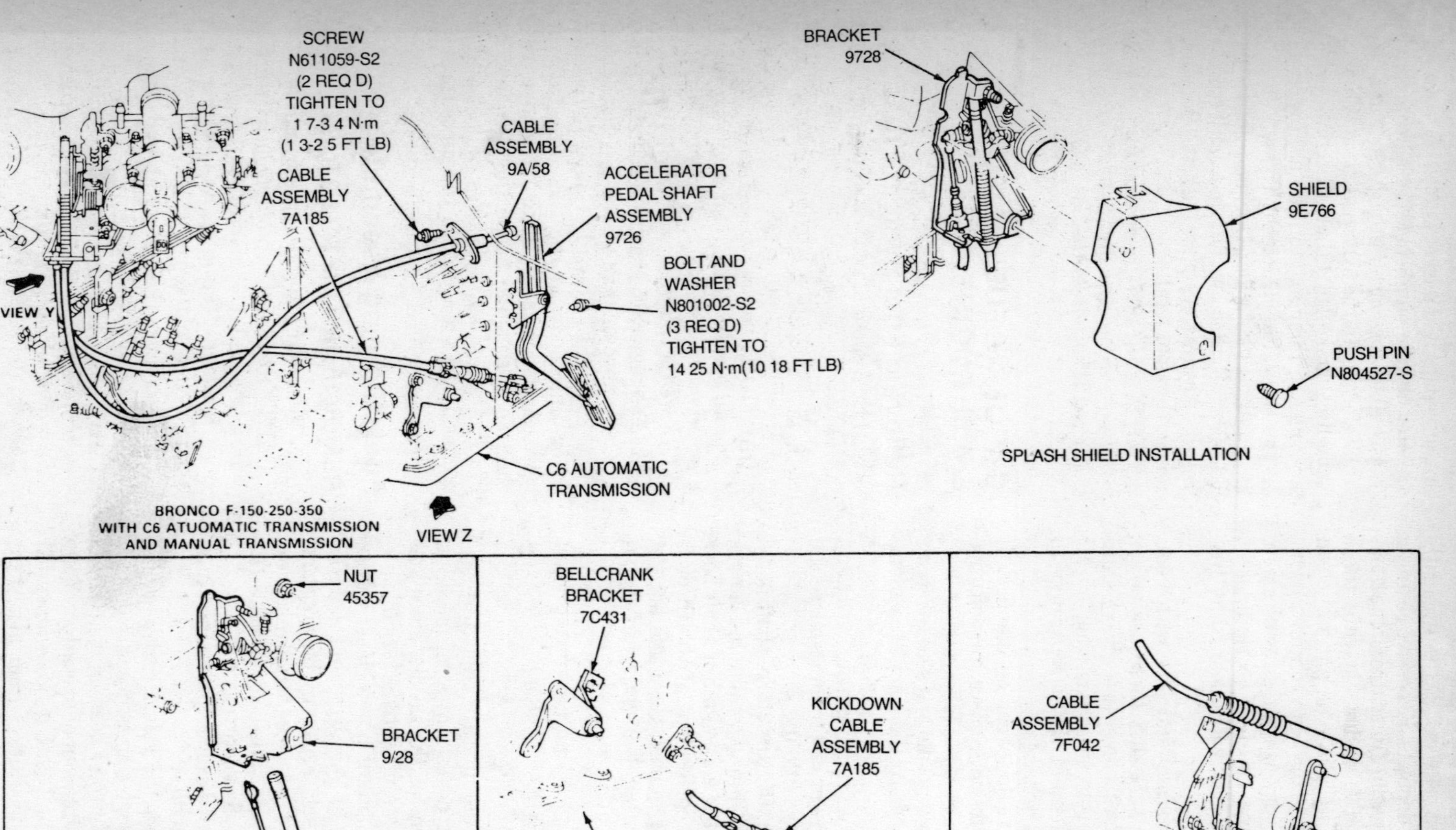

6-300 EFI throttle linkage

55 WAYS TO IMPROVE FUEL ECONOMY

CHILTON'S FUEL ECONOMY & TUNE-UP TIPS

Tune-up • Spark Plug Diagnosis • Emission Controls

Fuel System • Cooling System • Tires and Wheels

General Maintenance

CHILTON'S FUEL ECONOMY & TUNE-UP TIPS

Fuel economy is important to everyone, no matter what kind of vehicle you drive. The maintenance-minded motorist can save both money and fuel using these tips and the periodic maintenance and tune-up procedures in this Repair and Tune-Up Guide.

There are more than 130,000,000 cars and trucks registered for private use in the United States. Each travels an average of 10-12,000 miles per year, and, and in total they consume close to 70 billion gallons of fuel each year. This represents nearly ⅔ of the oil imported by the United States each year. The Federal government's goal is to reduce consumption 10% by 1985. A variety of methods are either already in use or under serious consideration, and they all affect you driving and the cars you will drive. In addition to "down-sizing", the auto industry is using or investigating the use of electronic fuel delivery, electronic engine controls and alternative engines for use in smaller and lighter vehicles, among other alternatives to meet the federally mandated Corporate Average Fuel Economy (CAFE) of 27.5 mpg by 1985. The government, for its part, is considering rationing, mandatory driving curtailments and tax increases on motor vehicle fuel in an effort to reduce consumption. The government's goal of a 10% reduction could be realized — and further government regulation avoided — if every private vehicle could use just 1 less gallon of fuel per week.

How Much Can You Save?

Tests have proven that almost anyone can make at least a 10% reduction in fuel consumption through regular maintenance and tune-ups. When a major manufacturer of spark plugs sur-

TUNE-UP

1. Check the cylinder compression to be sure the engine will really benefit from a tune-up and that it is capable of producing good fuel economy. A tune-up will be wasted on an engine in poor mechanical condition.

2. Replace spark plugs regularly. New spark plugs alone can increase fuel economy 3%.

3. Be sure the spark plugs are the correct type (heat range) for your vehicle. See the Tune-Up Specifications.

Heat range refers to the spark plug's ability to conduct heat away from the firing end. It must conduct the heat away in an even pattern to avoid becoming a source of pre-ignition, yet it must also operate hot enough to burn off conductive deposits that could cause misfiring.

The heat range is usually indicated by a number on the spark plug, part of the manufacturer's designation for each individual spark plug. The numbers in bold-face indicate the heat range in each manufacturer's identification system.

Manufacturer	Typical Designation
AC	R **45** TS
Bosch (old)	WA **145** T30
Bosch (new)	HR **8** Y
Champion	RBL **15** Y
Fram/Autolite	41**5**
Mopar	P-**62** PR
Motorcraft	BRF-**42**
NGK	BP **5** ES-15
Nippondenso	W **16** EP
Prestolite	14GR **5** 2A

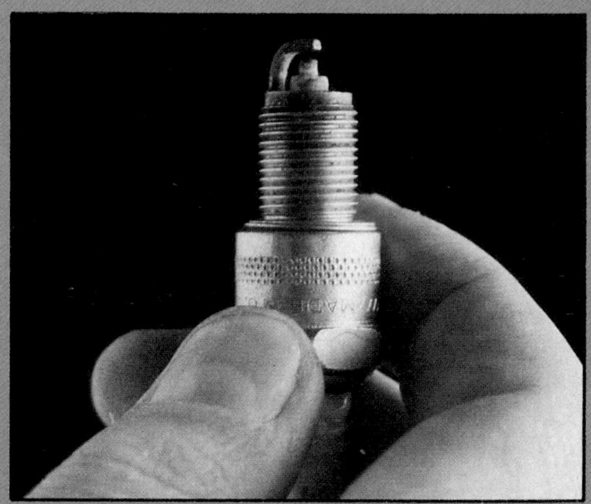

Periodically, check the spark plugs to be sure they are firing efficiently. They are excellent indicators of the internal condition of your engine.

On AC, Bosch (new), Champion, Fram/Autolite, Mopar, Motorcraft and Prestolite, a higher number indicates a hotter plug. On Bosch (old), NGK and Nippondenso, a higher number indicates a colder plug.

4. Make sure the spark plugs are properly gapped. See the Tune-Up Specifications in this book.

5. Be sure the spark plugs are firing efficiently. The illustrations on the next 2 pages show you how to "read" the firing end of the spark plug.

6. Check the ignition timing and set it to specifications. Tests show that almost all cars have incorrect ignition timing by more than 2°.

veyed over 6,000 cars nationwide, they found that a tune-up, on cars that needed one, increased fuel economy over 11%. Replacing worn plugs alone, accounted for a 3% increase. The same test also revealed that 8 out of every 10 vehicles will have some maintenance deficiency that will directly affect fuel economy, emissions or performance. Most of this mileage-robbing neglect could be prevented with regular maintenance.

Modern engines require that all of the functioning systems operate properly for maximum efficiency. A malfunction anywhere wastes fuel. You can keep your vehicle running as efficiently and economically as possible, by being aware of your vehicle's operating and performance characteristics. If your vehicle suddenly develops performance or fuel economy problems it could be due to one or more of the following:

PROBLEM	POSSIBLE CAUSE
Engine Idles Rough	Ignition timing, idle mixture, vacuum leak or something amiss in the emission control system.
Hesitates on Acceleration	Dirty carburetor or fuel filter, improper accelerator pump setting, ignition timing or fouled spark plugs.
Starts Hard or Fails to Start	Worn spark plugs, improperly set automatic choke, ice (or water) in fuel system.
Stalls Frequently	Automatic choke improperly adjusted and possible dirty air filter or fuel filter.
Performs Sluggishly	Worn spark plugs, dirty fuel or air filter, ignition timing or automatic choke out of adjustment.

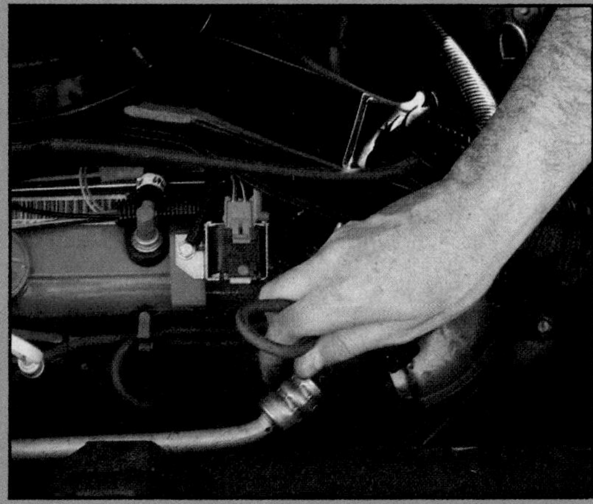

Check spark plug wires on conventional point type ignition for cracks by bending them in a loop around your finger.

Be sure that spark plug wires leading to adjacent cylinders do not run too close together. (Photo courtesy Champion Spark Plug Co.)

7. If your vehicle does not have electronic ignition, check the points, rotor and cap as specified.

8. Check the spark plug wires (used with conventional point-type ignitions) for cracks and burned or broken insulation by bending them in a loop around your finger. Cracked wires decrease fuel efficiency by failing to deliver full voltage to the spark plugs. One misfiring spark plug can cost you as much as 2 mpg.

9. Check the routing of the plug wires. Misfiring can be the result of spark plug leads to adjacent cylinders running parallel to each other and too close together. One wire tends to pick up voltage from the other causing it to fire "out of time".

10. Check all electrical and ignition circuits for voltage drop and resistance.

11. Check the distributor mechanical and/or vacuum advance mechanisms for proper functioning. The vacuum advance can be checked by twisting the distributor plate in the opposite direction of rotation. It should spring back when released.

12. Check and adjust the valve clearance on engines with mechanical lifters. The clearance should be slightly loose rather than too tight.

SPARK PLUG DIAGNOSIS

Normal

APPEARANCE: This plug is typical of one operating normally. The insulator nose varies from a light tan to grayish color with slight electrode wear. The presence of slight deposits is normal on used plugs and will have no adverse effect on engine performance. The spark plug heat range is correct for the engine and the engine is running normally.
CAUSE: Properly running engine.
RECOMMENDATION: Before reinstalling this plug, the electrodes should be cleaned and filed square. Set the gap to specifications. If the plug has been in service for more than 10-12,000 miles, the entire set should probably be replaced with a fresh set of the same heat range.

Oil Deposits

APPEARANCE: The firing end of the plug is covered with a wet, oily coating.
CAUSE: The problem is poor oil control. On high mileage engines, oil is leaking past the rings or valve guides into the combustion chamber. A common cause is also a plugged PCV valve, and a ruptured fuel pump diaphragm can also cause this condition. Oil fouled plugs such as these are often found in new or recently overhauled engines, before normal oil control is achieved, and can be cleaned and reinstalled.
RECOMMENDATION: A hotter spark plug may temporarily relieve the problem, but the engine is probably in need of work.

Incorrect Heat Range

APPEARANCE: The effects of high temperature on a spark plug are indicated by clean white, often blistered insulator. This can also be accompanied by excessive wear of the electrode, and the absence of deposits.
CAUSE: Check for the correct spark plug heat range. A plug which is too hot for the engine can result in overheating. A car operated mostly at high speeds can require a colder plug. Also check ignition timing, cooling system level, fuel mixture and leaking intake manifold.
RECOMMENDATION: If all ignition and engine adjustments are known to be correct, and no other malfunction exists, install spark plugs one heat range colder.

Photos Courtesy Fram Corporation

Carbon Deposits

APPEARANCE: Carbon fouling is easily identified by the presence of dry, soft, black, sooty deposits.
CAUSE: Changing the heat range can often lead to carbon fouling, as can prolonged slow, stop-and-start driving. If the heat range is correct, carbon fouling can be attributed to a rich fuel mixture, sticking choke, clogged air cleaner, worn breaker points, retarded timing or low compression. If only one or two plugs are carbon fouled, check for corroded or cracked wires on the affected plugs. Also look for cracks in the distributor cap between the towers of affected cylinders.
RECOMMENDATION: After the problem is corrected, these plugs can be cleaned and reinstalled if not worn severely.

MMT Fouled

APPEARANCE: Spark plugs fouled by MMT (Methycyclopentadienyl Maganese Tricarbonyl) have reddish, rusty appearance on the insulator and side electrode.
CAUSE: MMT is an anti-knock additive in gasoline used to replace lead. During the combustion process, the MMT leaves a reddish deposit on the insulator and side electrode.
RECOMMENDATION: No engine malfunction is indicated and the deposits will not affect plug performance any more than lead deposits (see Ash Deposits). MMT fouled plugs can be cleaned, regapped and reinstalled.

Ash (Lead) Deposits

APPEARANCE: Ash deposits are characterized by light brown or white colored deposits crusted on the side or center electrodes. In some cases it may give the plug a rusty appearance.
CAUSE: Ash deposits are normally derived from oil or fuel additives burned during normal combustion. Normally they are harmless, though excessive amounts can cause misfiring. If deposits are excessive in short mileage, the valve guides may be worn.
RECOMMENDATION: Ash-fouled plugs can be cleaned, gapped and reinstalled.

High Speed Glazing

APPEARANCE: Glazing appears as shiny coating on the plug, either yellow or tan in color.
CAUSE: During hard, fast acceleration, plug temperatures rise suddenly. Deposits from normal combustion have no chance to fluff-off; instead, they melt on the insulator forming an electrically conductive coating which causes misfiring.
RECOMMENDATION: Glazed plugs are not easily cleaned. They should be replaced with a fresh set of plugs of the correct heat range. If the condition recurs, using plugs with a heat range one step colder may cure the problem.

Detonation

APPEARANCE: Detonation is usually characterized by a broken plug insulator.
CAUSE: A portion of the fuel charge will begin to burn spontaneously, from the increased heat following ignition. The explosion that results applies extreme pressure to engine components, frequently damaging spark plugs and pistons.

Detonation can result by over-advanced ignition timing, inferior gasoline (low octane) lean air/fuel mixture, poor carburetion, engine lugging or an increase in compression ratio due to combustion chamber deposits or engine modification.
RECOMMENDATION: Replace the plugs after correcting the problem.

Photos Courtesy Champion Spark Plug Co.

EMISSION CONTROLS

13. Be aware of the general condition of the emission control system. It contributes to reduced pollution and should be serviced regularly to maintain efficient engine operation.

14. Check all vacuum lines for dried, cracked or brittle conditions. Something as simple as a leaking vacuum hose can cause poor performance and loss of economy.

15. Avoid tampering with the emission control system. Attempting to improve fuel econ-

FUEL SYSTEM

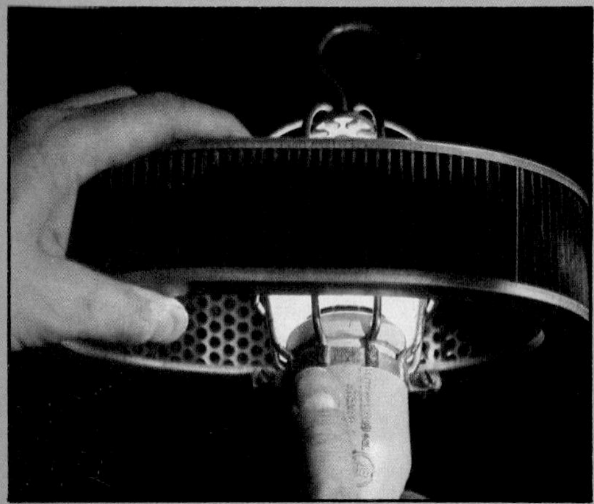

Check the air filter with a light behind it. If you can see light through the filter it can be reused.

Extremely clogged filters should be discarded and replaced with a new one.

18. Replace the air filter regularly. A dirty air filter richens the air/fuel mixture and can increase fuel consumption as much as 10%. Tests show that ⅓ of all vehicles have air filters in need of replacement.

19. Replace the fuel filter at least as often as recommended.

20. Set the idle speed and carburetor mixture to specifications.

21. Check the automatic choke. A sticking or malfunctioning choke wastes gas.

22. During the summer months, adjust the automatic choke for a leaner mixture which will produce faster engine warm-ups.

COOLING SYSTEM

29. Be sure all accessory drive belts are in good condition. Check for cracks or wear.

30. Adjust all accessory drive belts to proper tension.

31. Check all hoses for swollen areas, worn spots, or loose clamps.

32. Check coolant level in the radiator or expansion tank.

33. Be sure the thermostat is operating properly. A stuck thermostat delays engine warm-up and a cold engine uses nearly twice as much fuel as a warm engine.

34. Drain and replace the engine coolant at least as often as recommended. Rust and scale

TIRES & WHEELS

38. Check the tire pressure often with a pencil type gauge. Tests by a major tire manufacturer show that 90% of all vehicles have at least 1 tire improperly inflated. Better mileage can be achieved by over-inflating tires, but never exceed the maximum inflation pressure on the side of the tire.

39. If possible, install radial tires. Radial tires deliver as much as ½ mpg more than bias belted tires.

40. Avoid installing super-wide tires. They only create extra rolling resistance and decrease fuel mileage. Stick to the manufacturer's recommendations.

41. Have the wheels properly balanced.

omy by tampering with emission controls is more likely to worsen fuel economy than improve it. Emission control changes on modern engines are not readily reversible.

16. Clean (or replace) the EGR valve and lines as recommended.

17. Be sure that all vacuum lines and hoses are reconnected properly after working under the hood. An unconnected or misrouted vacuum line can wreak havoc with engine performance.

---

23. Check for fuel leaks at the carburetor, fuel pump, fuel lines and fuel tank. Be sure all lines and connections are tight.

24. Periodically check the tightness of the carburetor and intake manifold attaching nuts and bolts. These are a common place for vacuum leaks to occur.

25. Clean the carburetor periodically and lubricate the linkage.

26. The condition of the tailpipe can be an excellent indicator of proper engine combustion. After a long drive at highway speeds, the inside of the tailpipe should be a light grey in color. Black or soot on the insides indicates an overly rich mixture.

27. Check the fuel pump pressure. The fuel pump may be supplying more fuel than the engine needs.

28. Use the proper grade of gasoline for your engine. Don't try to compensate for knocking or "pinging" by advancing the ignition timing. This practice will only increase plug temperature and the chances of detonation or pre-ignition with relatively little performance gain.

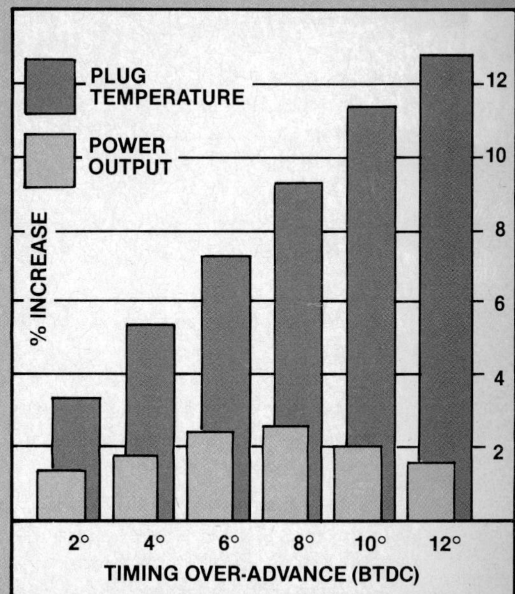

Increasing ignition timing past the specified setting results in a drastic increase in spark plug temperature with increased chance of detonation or preignition. Performance increase is considerably less. (Photo courtesy Champion Spark Plug Co.)

---

that form in the engine should be flushed out to allow the engine to operate at peak efficiency.

35. Clean the radiator of debris that can decrease cooling efficiency.

36. Install a flex-type or electric cooling fan, if you don't have a clutch type fan. Flex fans use curved plastic blades to push more air at low speeds when more cooling is needed; at high speeds the blades flatten out for less resistance. Electric fans only run when the engine temperature reaches a predetermined level.

37. Check the radiator cap for a worn or cracked gasket. If the cap does not seal properly, the cooling system will not function properly.

---

42. Be sure the front end is correctly aligned. A misaligned front end actually has wheels going in differed directions. The increased drag can reduce fuel economy by .3 mpg.

43. Correctly adjust the wheel bearings. Wheel bearings that are adjusted too tight increase rolling resistance.

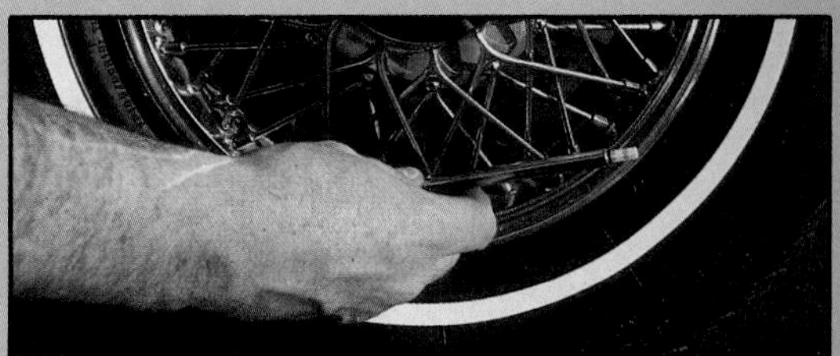
Check tire pressures regularly with a reliable pocket type gauge. Be sure to check the pressure on a cold tire.

GENERAL MAINTENANCE

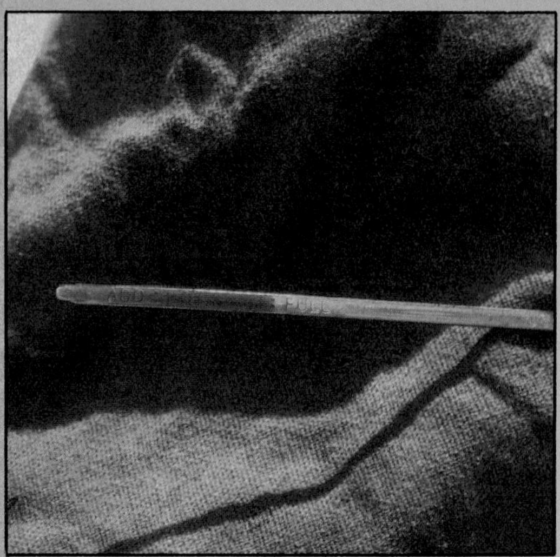

Check the fluid levels (particularly engine oil) on a regular basis. Be sure to check the oil for grit, water or other contamination.

A vacuum gauge is another excellent indicator of internal engine condition and can also be installed in the dash as a mileage indicator.

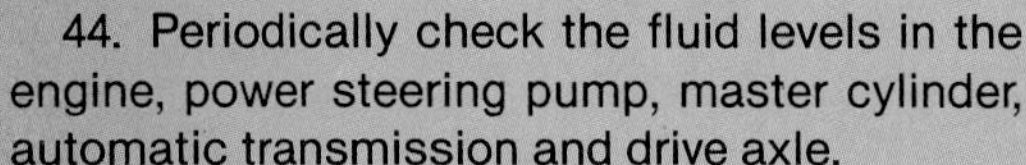

44. Periodically check the fluid levels in the engine, power steering pump, master cylinder, automatic transmission and drive axle.

45. Change the oil at the recommended interval and change the filter at every oil change. Dirty oil is thick and causes extra friction between moving parts, cutting efficiency and increasing wear. A worn engine requires more frequent tune-ups and gets progressively worse fuel economy. In general, use the lightest viscosity oil for the driving conditions you will encounter.

46. Use the recommended viscosity fluids in the transmission and axle.

47. Be sure the battery is fully charged for fast starts. A slow starting engine wastes fuel.

48. Be sure battery terminals are clean and tight.

49. Check the battery electrolyte level and add distilled water if necessary.

50. Check the exhaust system for crushed pipes, blockages and leaks.

51. Adjust the brakes. Dragging brakes or brakes that are not releasing create increased drag on the engine.

52. Install a vacuum gauge or miles-per-gallon gauge. These gauges visually indicate engine vacuum in the intake manifold. High vacuum = good mileage and low vacuum = poorer mileage. The gauge can also be an excellent indicator of internal engine conditions.

53. Be sure the clutch is properly adjusted. A slipping clutch wastes fuel.

54. Check and periodically lubricate the heat control valve in the exhaust manifold. A sticking or inoperative valve prevents engine warm-up and wastes gas.

55. Keep accurate records to check fuel economy over a period of time. A sudden drop in fuel economy may signal a need for tune-up or other maintenance.

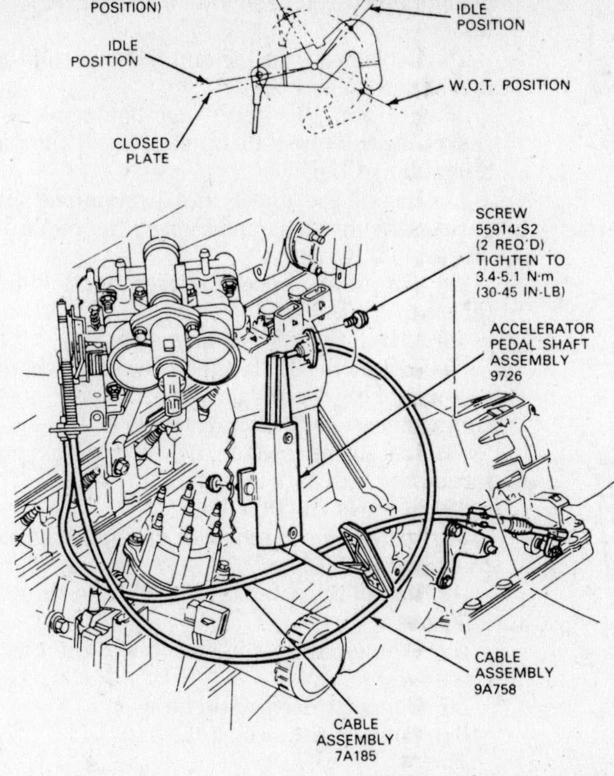

C6 AUTOMATIC TRANSMISSION KICKDOWN CABLE INSTALLATION AND ADJUSTMENT

1. SELECT KICKDOWN CABLE. INSERT CONDUIT FITTING INTO ENGINE BRACKET AND SLIDE CABLE END FITTING ONTO NAILHEAD STUD ON THROTTLE LEVER. ENSURE THAT THROW-AWAY RED SPACER IS SECURED ON CABLE END FITTING. IF SPACER IS MISSING, REUSE A DISCARDED ONE.
2. ROUTE CABLE DOWN TO TRANSMISSION AND INSERT CONDUIT FITTING INTO BRACKET, THEN SNAP CABLE END ONTO BALL STUD ON TRANSMISSION LEVER.
3. RATCHET CABLE ADJUSTING MECHANISM TO CORRECT SETTING BY ROTATING TO WIDE OPEN THROTTLE POSITION, WITH TOOL NO. 52F-23415 OR BY HAND. REMOVE RED SPACER.

AOD AUTOMATIC TRANSMISSION TV CABLE INSTALLATION AND ADJUSTMENT

1. SELECT TV CABLE. INSERT CONDUIT FITTING INTO ENGINE BRACKET. SLIDE CABLE END FITTING OVER NAILHEAD STUD ON THROTTLE LEVER.
2. ROUTE CABLE DOWN TO TRANSMISSION. INSERT CONDUIT FITTING INTO BRACKET ON TRANSMISSION. SNAP CABLE END OVER BALL STUD ON TRANSMISSION LEVER. ENSURE SPRING IS ON TRANSMISSION TO HOLD TV LEVER IN FULL CLOCKWISE POSITION.
3. PUSH DOWN LOCKING TAB AT ENGINE END OF CONDUIT FITTING TO LOCK CONDUIT AT CORRECT LENGTH. TAB TO BE FLUSH WITH CIRCULAR PROFILE OF FITTING.
4. REMOVE SPRING.

6–4.9L EFI throttle linkage, cont.

3. Label and disconnect the wiring at the:
- Throttle position sensor
- Air bypass valve
- EVP sensor at the EGR valve
- Injection wiring harness
- Engine coolant temperature sensor

4. Label and disconnect the following vaccum connectors:
- EGR valve
- Thermactor air bypass valve
- Throttle body
- Fuel pressure regulator
- Upper intake manifold vacuum tree

5. Disconnect the PCV hose at the upper intake manifold.
6. Remove the throttle linkage shield.
7. Disconnect the throttle linkage and speed control cables.
8. Unbolt the accelerator cable from its bracket and position it out of the way.
9. Disconnect the air inlet hoses from the throttle body.
10. Remove the EGR tube.
11. Remove the Thermactor tube from the lower intake manifold.
12. Remove the nut attaching the Thermactor bypass valve bracket to the lower intake manifold.
13. Remove the injector heat shield (2 clips).
14. Remove the 7 studs which retain the upper intake manifold.
15. Remove the screw and washer which retains the upper intake manifold support bracket to the upper intake manifold.
16. Remove the upper intake manifold assembly from the lower intake manifold.
17. Move the vacuum harness away from the lower intake manifold.
18. Remove the injector cooling manifold from the lifting eye attachment.
19. Disconnect the fuel supply and return lines at the quick disconnect couplings using tools T81P–19623–G or T81P–19623–G1.
20. Remove the 16 attaching bolts that the lower intake manifold and exhaust manifolds have in common. DON'T REMOVE THE BOLTS THAT ATTACH ONLY THE EXHAUST MANIFOLDS!
21. Remove the lower intake manifold from the head.
22. Clean and inspect all mating surfaces. All surfaces MUST be flat and free from debris or damage!

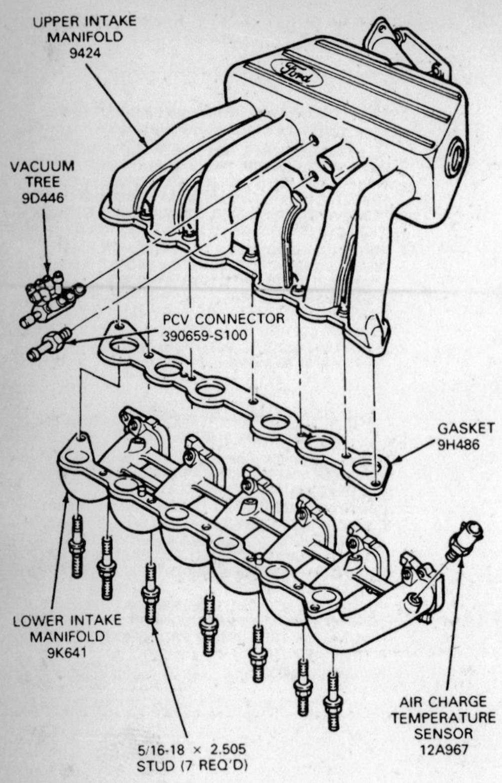

6–4.9L upper intake manifold removal

23. Clean and oil all fastener threads.
24. Position the lower manifold on the head using a new gasket. Tighten the bolts to 30 ft. lbs.
25. Reconnect the vacuum lines at the fuel pressure regulator.
26. Position the upper manifold and new gasket on the lower manifold. Install the fasteners finger tight.
27. Install the upper intake manifold support on the manifold and tighten the retaining screw to 30 ft. lbs.
28. Torque the upper-to-lower manifold fasteners to 18 ft. lbs.
29. Install the injector heat shield.
30. Install the EGR tube. The tube should be routed between the no. 4 and 5 lower intake runners. Torque the fittings to 35 ft. lbs.
31. Install the injector cooling manifold and torque the fasteners to 12 ft. lbs.
32. Connect the PCV hose.
33. Install the Thermactor tube and tighten the nuts to 12 ft. lbs.
34. Install the accelerator cable and throttle linkages.
35. Connect the air inlet hoses to the throttle body.
36. Connect the vacuum hoses.
37. Connect the electrical wiring.

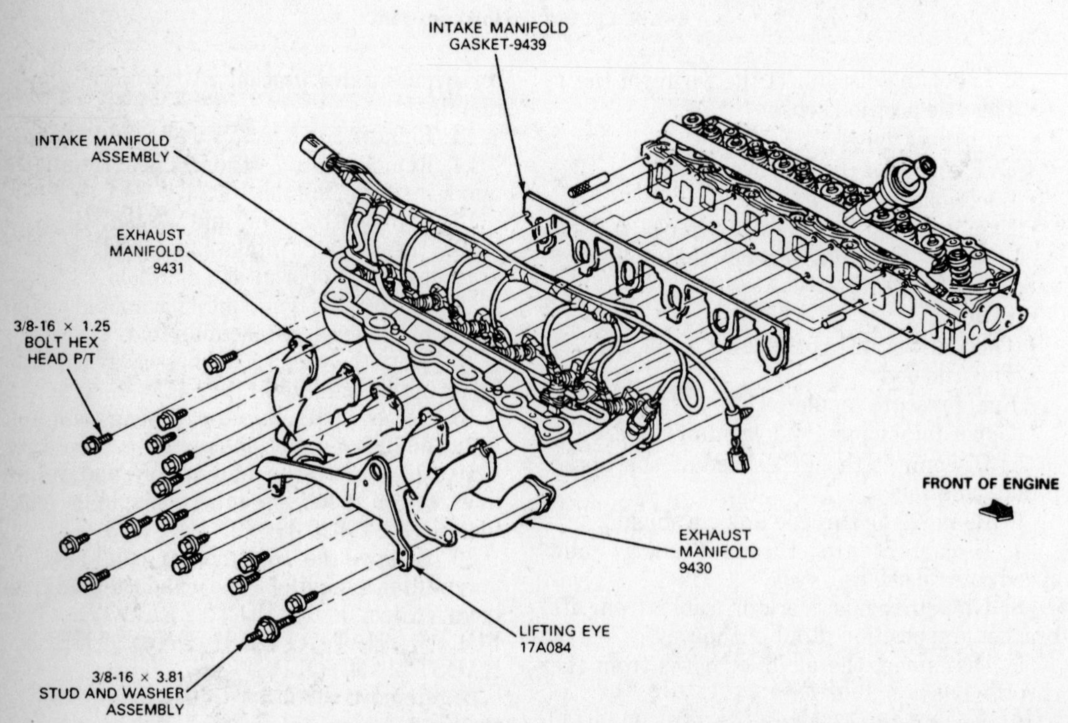

6–4.9L EFI lower intake manifold removal

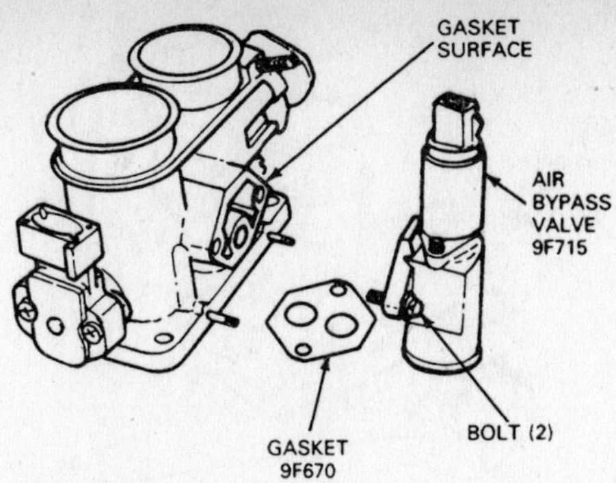

6–4.9L EFI air bypass valve

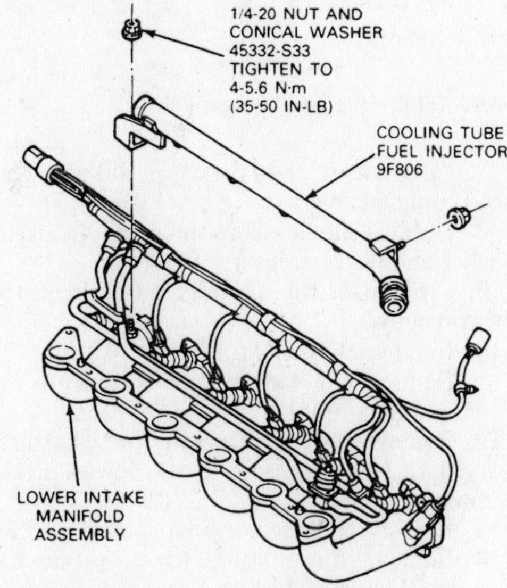

6–4.9L injector cooling manifold removal

38. Connect the air intake hose, air bypass hose and crankcase vent hose.
39. Connect the battery ground.
40. Refill the cooling system.
41. Install the fuel pressure relief cap. Turn the ignition switch from **OFF** to **ON** at least half a dozen times, **WITHOUT STARTING THE ENGINE**, leaving it in the ON position for about 5 seconds each time. This will build up fuel pressure in the system.
42. Start the engine and allow it to run at idle until normal operating temperature is reached. Check for leaks.

Fuel Injector

REMOVAL AND INSTALLATION

1. Relieve the fuel system pressure.

CAUTION: *Never smoke when working around gasoline! Avoid all sources of sparks or ignition. Gasoline vapors are EXTREMELY volatile!*

2. Remove the upper intake manifold assembly.
3. Remove the fuel supply manifold.
4. Disconnect the wiring at each injector.
5. Pull upward on the injector body while gently rocking it from side-to-side.
6. Inspect the O-rings on the injector for any sign of leakage or damage. Replace any suspected O-rings.
7. Inspect the plastic cap at the top of each injector and replace it if any sign of deterioration is noticed.
8. Lubricate the O-rings with clean engine oil ONLY!.
9. Install the injectors by pushing them in with a gentle rocking motion.
10. Install the fuel supply manifold.
11. Connect the electrical wiring.
12. Install the upper intake manifold.

Fuel Pressure Regulator

REMOVAL AND INSTALLATION

1. Relieve the fuel system pressure.

CAUTION: *Never smoke when working around gasoline! Avoid all sources of sparks or ignition. Gasoline vapors are EXTREMELY volatile!*

2. Disconnect the vacuum line at the regulator.
3. Remove the 3 allen screws from the regulator housing.
4. Remove the regulator.
5. Inspect the regulator O-ring for signs of deterioration or damage. Discard the gasket.
6. Lubricate the O-ring with clean engine oil ONLY!
7. Make sure that the mounting surfaces are clean.
8. Using a new gasket, install the regulator. Tighten the retaining screws to 40 inch lbs.
9. Connect the vacuum line.

Pressure Relief Valve

REMOVAL AND INSTALLATION

1. Relieve the fuel system pressure.

CAUTION: *Never smoke when working around gasoline! Avoid all sources of sparks or ignition. Gasoline vapors are EXTREMELY volatile!*

2. Unscrew the valve from the fuel line.
3. When installing the valve, tighten it to 80 inch lbs.
4. Tighten the cap to 5 inch lbs.

Throttle Position Sensor

REMOVAL AND INSTALLATION

1. Disconnect the wiring harness from the TPS.

2. Matchmark the sensor and throttle body for installation reference.

CAUTION: *Never smoke when working around gasoline! Avoid all sources of sparks or ignition. Gasoline vapors are EXTREMELY volatile!*

3. Remove the 2 retaining screws and remove the TPS.

4. Install the TPS so that the wiring harness is parallel with the venturi bores, then, rotate the TPS clockwise to align the scribe marks.

CAUTION: *Slide the rotary tanks into position over the throttle shaft blade, then rotate the TPS CLOCKWISE ONLY to the installed position. FAILURE TO INSTALL THE TPS IN THIS MANNER WILL RESULT IN EXCESSIVE IDLE SPEEDS!*

5. Tighten the retaining screws to 16 inch lbs.

NOTE: *When correctly installed, the TPS wiring harness should be pointing directly at the air bypass valve.*

6. Connect the wiring.

Upper Intake Manifold

REMOVAL AND INSTALLATION

1. Relieve the fuel system pressure.

CAUTION: *Never smoke when working around gasoline! Avoid all sources of sparks or ignition. Gasoline vapors are EXTREMELY volatile!*

2. Disconnect the battery ground cable and drain the cooling system.

CAUTION: *When draining the coolant, keep in mind that cats and dogs are attracted by the ethylene glycol antifreeze, and are quite likely to drink any that is left in an uncovered container or in puddles on the ground. This will prove fatal in sufficient quantity. Always drain the coolant into a sealable container. Coolant should be reused unless it is contaminated or several years old.*

3. Label and disconnect the wiring at the:
- Throttle position sensor
- Air bypass valve
- EVP sensor at the EGR valve
- Injection wiring harness
- Engine coolant temperature sensor

4. Label and disconnect the following vacuum connectors:
- EGR valve
- Thermactor air bypass valve
- Throttle body
- Fuel pressure regulator
- Upper intake manifold vacuum tree

5. Disconnect the PCV hose at the upper intake manifold.

6. Remove the throttle linkage shield.

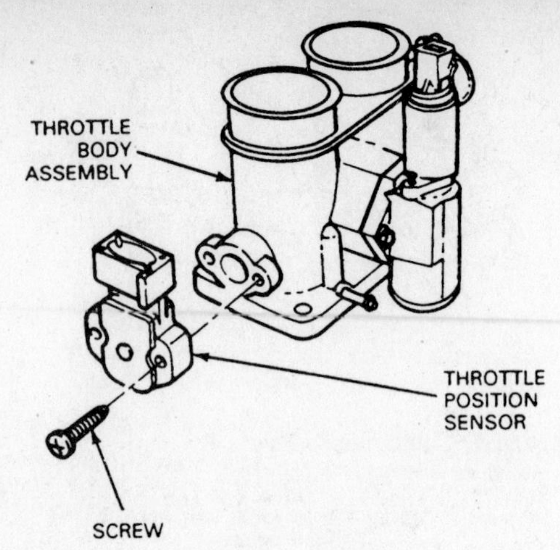

6–4.9L EFI throttle position sensor

7. Disconnect the throttle linkage and speed control cables.

8. Unbolt the accelerator cable from its bracket and position it out of the way.

9. Disconnect the air inlet hoses from the throttle body.

10. Remove the EGR tube.

11. Remove the Thermactor tube from the lower intake manifold.

12. Remove the nut attaching the Thermactor bypass valve bracket to the lower intake manifold.

13. Remove the injector heat shield (2 clips).

14. Remove the 7 studs which retain the upper intake manifold.

15. Remove the screw and washer which retains the upper intake manifold support bracket to the upper intake manifold.

16. Remove the upper intake manifold assembly from the lower intake manifold.

17. Clean and inspect all mating surfaces. All surfaces MUST be flat and free from debris or damage!

18. Clean and oil all fastener threads.

19. Position the upper manifold and new gasket on the lower manifold. Install the fasteners finger tight.

20. Install the upper intake manifold support on the manifold and tighten the retaining screw to 30 ft. lbs.

21. Torque the upper-to-lower manifold fasteners to 18 ft. lbs.

22. Install the injector heat shield.

23. Install the EGR tube. The tube should be routed between the no. 4 and 5 lower intake runners. Torque the fittings to 35 ft. lbs.

24. Install the injector cooling manifold and torque the fasteners to 12 ft. lbs.

25. Connect the PCV hose.

26. Install the Thermactor tube and tighten the nuts to 12 ft. lbs.

27. Install the accelerator cable and throttle linkages.

28. Connect the air inlet hoses to the throttle body.

29. Connect the vacuum hoses.

30. Connect the electrical wiring.

31. Connect the air intake hose, air bypass hose and crankcase vent hose.

32. Connect the battery ground.

33. Refill the cooling system.

34. Install the fuel pressure relief cap. Turn the ignition switch from **OFF** to **ON** at least half a dozen times, **WITHOUT STARTING THE ENGINE**, leaving it in the ON position for about 5 seconds each time. This will build up fuel pressure in the system.

35. Start the engine and allow it to run at idle until normal operating temperature is reached. Check for leaks.

Air Intake Throttle Body

REMOVAL AND INSTALLATION

1. Disconnect the air intake hose.

CAUTION: *Never smoke when working around gasoline! Avoid all sources of sparks or ignition. Gasoline vapors are EXTREMELY volatile!*

2. Disconnect the throttle position sensor and air by-pass valve connectors.

3. Remove the four throttle body mounting nuts and carefully separate the air throttle body from the upper intake manifold.

4. Remove and discard the mounting gasket. Clean all mounting surfaces using care not to damage the gasket surfaces of the throttle body and manifold. Do not allow any material to drop into the intake manifold.

5. Install the throttle body in the reverse order of removal. The mounting nuts are tightened to 12–15 ft. lbs.

Fuel Supply Manifold

REMOVAL AND INSTALLATION

CAUTION: *Never smoke when working around gasoline! Avoid all sources of sparks or ignition. Gasoline vapors are EXTREMELY volatile!*

1. Remove the fuel tank fill cap. Relieve fuel system pressure by locating and disconnecting the electrical connection to either the fuel pump relay, the inertia switch or the in line high pressure fuel pump. Crank the engine for about ten seconds. If the engine starts, crank for an additional five seconds after the engine stalls. Reconnect the connector. Disconnect the negative battery cable. Remove the upper intake manifold assembly.

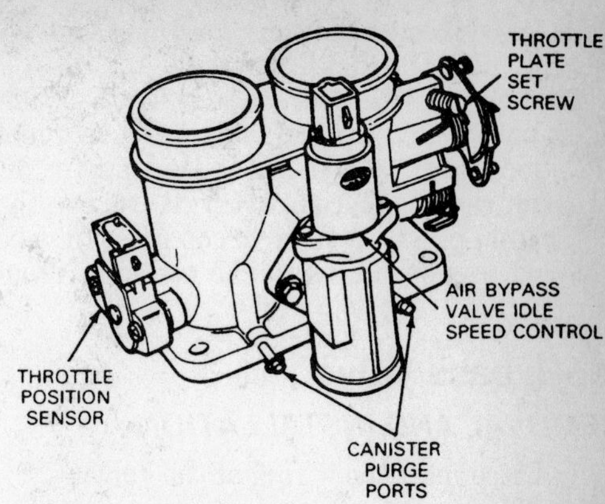

6-4.9L EFI throttle body

NOTE: *Special tool T81P–19623–G or equivalent is necessary to release the garter springs that secure the fuel line/hose connections.*

2. Disconnect the fuel crossover hose from the fuel supply manifold. Disconnect the fuel supply and return line connections at the fuel supply manifold.

3. Remove the two fuel supply manifold retaining bolts. Carefully disengage the manifold from the fuel injectors and remove the manifold.

4. When installing: make sure the injector caps are clean and free of contamination. Place the fuel supply manifold over each injector and seat the injectors into the manifold. Make sure the caps are seated firmly.

5. Torque the fuel supply manifold retaining bolts to 15–22 ft.lbs. Install the remaining components in the reverse order of removal.

NOTE: *Fuel injectors may be serviced after the fuel supply manifold is removed. Grasp the injector and pull up on it while gently rocking injector from side to side. Inspect the mounting O-rings and replace any that show deterioration.*

GASOLINE FUEL INJECTION 8–5.0L ENGINE 8–5.8L ENGINE

Relieving Fuel System Pressure

NOTE: *A special tool is necessary for this procedure.*

1. Make sure the ignition switch is in the OFF position.

CAUTION: *Never smoke when working around gasoline! Avoid all sources of sparks or ignition. Gasoline vapors are EXTREMELY volatile!*

2. Disconnect the battery ground.
3. Remove the fuel filler cap.
4. Using EFI Pressure Gauge T80L–9974–A, or equivalent, at the fuel pressure relief valve (located in the fuel line in the upper right corner of the engine compartment) relieve the fuel system pressure. A valve cap must first be removed to gain access to the pressure relief valve.

Air Bypass Valve

REMOVAL AND INSTALLATION

1. Disconnect the wiring at the valve.

CAUTION: *Never smoke when working around gasoline! Avoid all sources of sparks or ignition. Gasoline vapors are EXTREMELY volatile!*

2. Remove the 2 retaining screws and lift off the valve.
3. Discard the gasket and clean and inspect the mating surfaces.
4. Install the valve with a new gasket, tightening the screws to 102 inch lbs.
5. Connect the wiring.

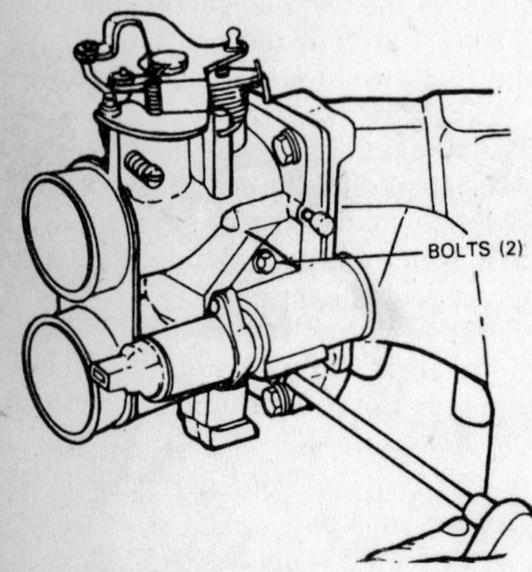

8–5.0L, 5.8L EFI air bypass valve

Air Intake Throttle Body

REMOVAL AND INSTALLATION

1. Disconnect the air intake hose.

CAUTION: *Never smoke when working around gasoline! Avoid all sources of sparks or ignition. Gasoline vapors are EXTREMELY volatile!*

2. Disconnect the throttle position sensor and air by-pass valve connectors.
3. Remove the four throttle body mounting nuts and carefully separate the air throttle body from the upper intake manifold.
4. Remove and discard the mounting gasket. Clean all mounting surfaces using care not to damage the gasket surfaces of the throttle body and manifold. Do not allow any material to drop into the intake manifold.

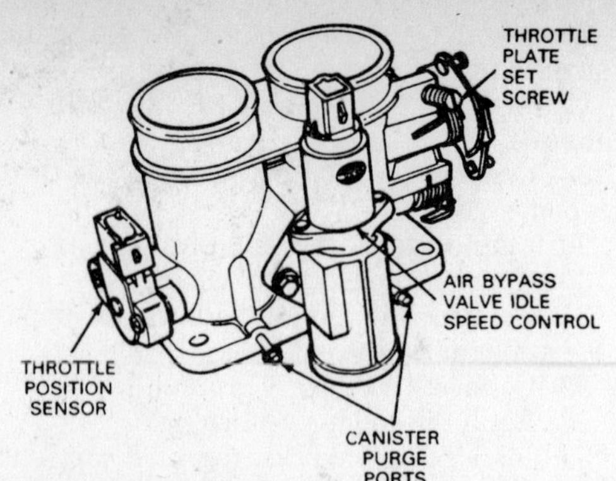

8–5.0L, 5.8L air throttle body

5. Install the throttle body in the reverse order of removal. The mounting nuts are tightened to 12–18 ft. lbs.

Fuel Charging Assembly

REMOVAL AND INSTALLATION

1. Relieve the fuel system pressure.

CAUTION: *Never smoke when working around gasoline! Avoid all sources of sparks or ignition. Gasoline vapors are EXTREMELY volatile!*

2. Disconnect the battery ground cable and drain the cooling system.

CAUTION: *When draining the coolant, keep in mind that cats and dogs are attracted by the ethylene glycol antifreeze, and are quite likely to drink any that is left in an uncovered container or in puddles on the ground. This will prove fatal in sufficient quantity. Always drain the coolant into a sealable container. Coolant should be reused unless it is contaminated or several years old.*

3. Label and disconnect the wiring at the:
- Throttle position sensor
- Air bypass valve
- EGR sensor

4. Label and disconnect the following vacuum connectors:
- EGR valve
- Fuel pressure regulator
- Upper intake manifold vacuum tree

5. Disconnect the PCV hose at the upper intake manifold.
6. Remove the throttle linkage at the throttle ball and AOD transmission linkage at the throttle body.
7. Unbolt the cable bracket from the manifold and position the cables and bracket away from the engine.
8. Disconnect the 2 canister purge lines at the throttle body.

VIEW X
BRACKET
FRONT OF VEHICLE
MAIN VIEW
VIEW Z
SHIELD
9E766
ACCELERATOR
CABLE ASSEMBLY
9A758
ACCELERATOR
CABLE BRACKET
9728
VIEW Y
SCREW
N611038-S2
(2 REQ'D)
TIGHTEN TO
4.7-9.5 N·m
(3.5-7 FT-LB)
VIEW X
CABLE
UPPER INTAKE MANIFOLD
BRACKET
VIEW Y
SCREW
14-28 N·m
(10-20 FT-LB)
SCREW
6-8 N·m
(4-6 FT-LB)
CABLE
SCREW
14-19 N·m (10-14 FT-LB)
PEDAL
ASSEMBLY
DASH PANEL
VIEW Z

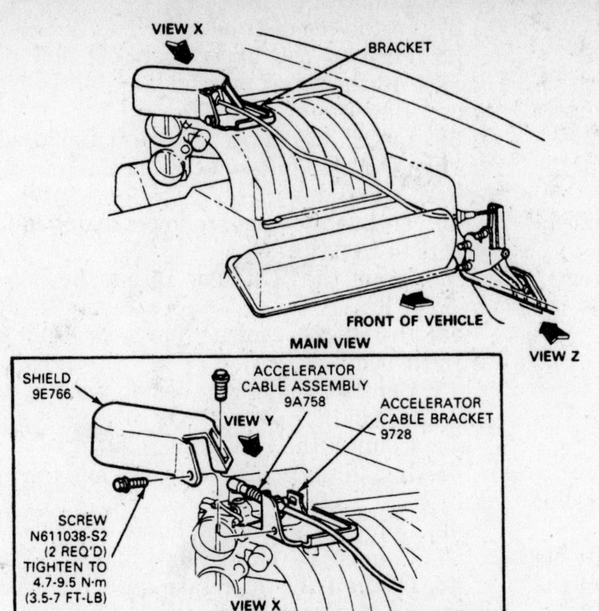

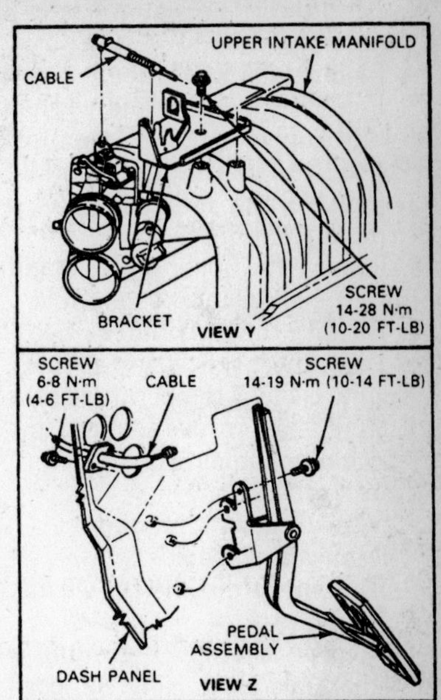

8–5.0L, 8–5.8L EFI throttle linkage

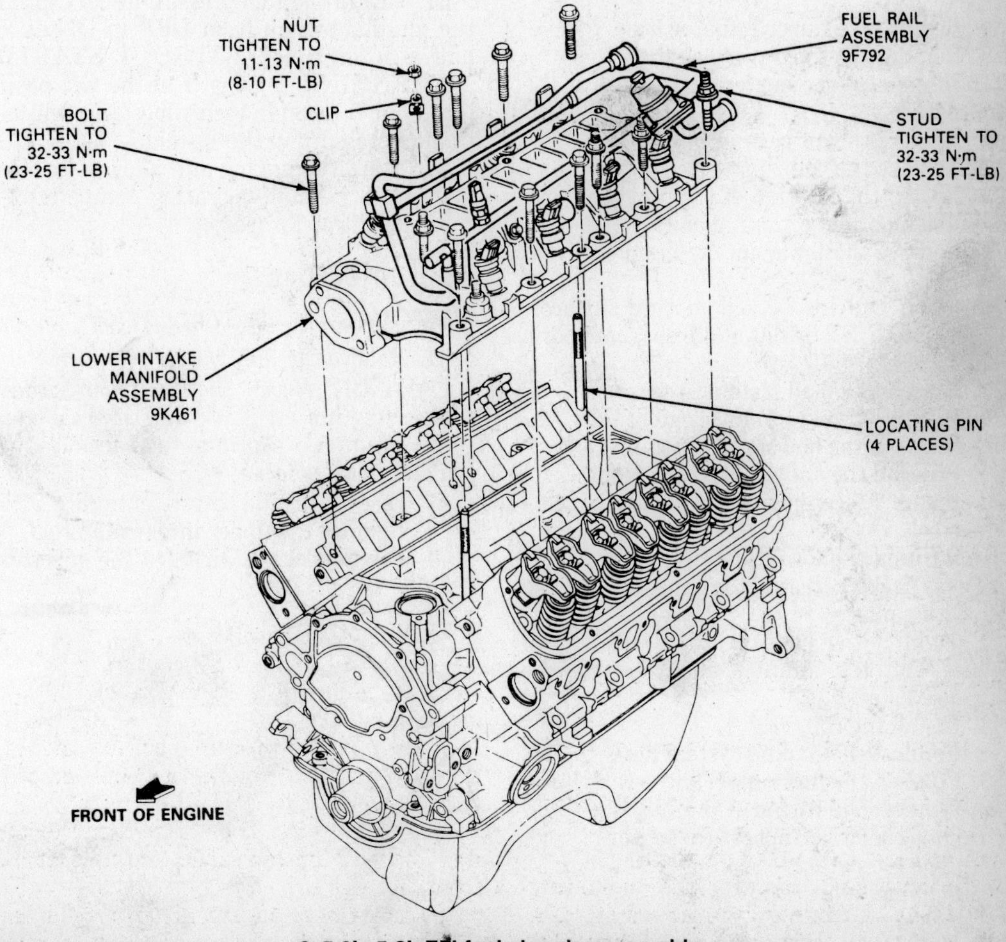

NUT
TIGHTEN TO
11-13 N·m
(8-10 FT-LB)
CLIP
BOLT
TIGHTEN TO
32-33 N·m
(23-25 FT-LB)
FUEL RAIL
ASSEMBLY
9F792
STUD
TIGHTEN TO
32-33 N·m
(23-25 FT-LB)
LOWER INTAKE
MANIFOLD
ASSEMBLY
9K461
LOCATING PIN
(4 PLACES)
FRONT OF ENGINE

8–5.0L, 5.8L EFI fuel charging assembly

9. Disconnect the water heater lines from the throttle body.
10. Remove the EGR tube.
11. Remove the screw and washer which retains the upper intake manifold support bracket to the upper intake manifold.
12. Remove the 6 bolts which retain the upper intake manifold.
13. Remove the upper intake manifold assembly from the lower intake manifold.
14. Remove the distributor. (See Chapter 3).
15. Disconnect the wiring at the:
- Engine coolant temperature sensor.
- Engine temperature sending unit.
- Air charge temperature sensor.
- Knock sensor.
- Electrical vacuum regulator.
- Thermactor solenoids.

16. Disconnect the injector wiring harness at the main harness.
17. Remove the EGO ground wire at its intake manifold stud. Note the position of the stud and ground wire for installation.
18. Disconnect the fuel supply and return lines from the fuel rails using tool T81P–19623–G or G1.
19. Remove the upper radiator hose.
20. Remove the coolant bypass hose.
21. Disconnect the heater outlet hose at the manifold.
22. Remove the air cleaner bracket.
23. Remove the coil.
24. Noting the location of each bolt, remove the intake manifold retaining bolts.
25. Remove the lower intake manifold from the head.
26. Clean and inspect all mating surfaces. All surfaces MUST be flat and free from debris or damage!
27. Clean and oil all fastener threads.
28. Place a $\frac{1}{16}$ in. (1.5mm) bead of RTV silicone sealant to the end seals' junctions.
29. Position the end seals on the block.
30. Install 2 locator pins at opposite corners of the block.
31. Position the lower manifold on the head using new gaskets. Install the bolts and remove the locating pins.
32. Tighten the bolts to 25 ft. lbs. in sequence. Wait ten minutes and retorque the bolts in sequence.
33. Install the coil.
34. Connect the cooling system hoses.
35. Connect the fuel supply and return lines.
36. Connect the wiring at the:
- Engine coolant temperature sensor.
- Engine temperature sending unit.
- Air charge temperature sensor.
- Knock sensor.
- Electrical vacuum regulator.
- Thermactor solenoids.

37. Install the distributor.
38. Position the upper manifold and new gasket on the lower manifold. Install the fasteners finger tight.
39. Install the upper intake manifold support on the manifold and tighten the retaining screw to 30 ft. lbs.
40. Torque the upper-to-lower manifold fasteners to 18 ft. lbs.
41. Install the EGR tube. Torque the fittings to 35 ft. lbs.
42. Install the canister purge lines at the throttle body.
43. Connect the water heater lines at the throttle body.
44. Connect the PCV hose.
45. Install the accelerator cable and throttle linkages.
46. Connect the vacuum hoses.
47. Connect the electrical wiring.
48. Connect the air intake hose, air bypass hose and crankcase vent hose.
49. Connect the battery ground.
50. Refill the cooling system.
51. Install the fuel pressure relief cap. Turn the ignition switch from **OFF** to **ON** at least half a dozen times, **WITHOUT STARTING THE ENGINE**, leaving it in the ON position for about 5 seconds each time. This will build up fuel pressure in the system.
52. Start the engine and allow it to run at idle until normal operating temperature is reached. Check for leaks.

Fuel Injectors

REMOVAL AND INSTALLATION

1. Relieve the fuel system pressure.

CAUTION: *Never smoke when working around gasoline! Avoid all sources of sparks or ignition. Gasoline vapors are EXTREMELY volatile!*

2. Disconnect the battery ground.
3. Remove the upper intake manifold.
4. Disconnect the wiring at the injectors.

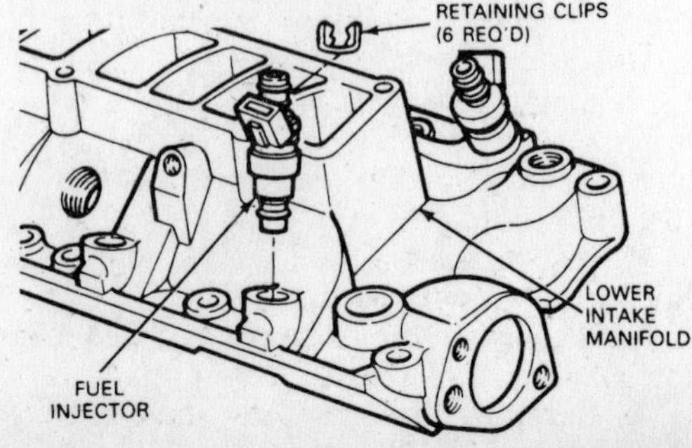

8–5.0L, 5.8L EFI fuel injector

5. Pull upward on the injector body while gently rocking it from side-to-side.

6. Inspect the O-rings on the injector for any sign of leakage or damage. Replace any suspected O-rings.

7. Inspect the plastic cap at the top of each injector and replace it if any sign of deterioration is noticed.

8. Lubricate the O-rings with clean engine oil ONLY!

9. Install the injectors by pushing them in with a gentle rocking motion.

10. Install the fuel supply manifold.

11. Connect the electrical wiring.

12. Install the upper intake manifold.

Fuel Pressure Regulator

REMOVAL AND INSTALLATION

1. Relieve the fuel system pressure.

CAUTION: *Never smoke when working around gasoline! Avoid all sources of sparks or ignition. Gasoline vapors are EXTREMELY volatile!*

2. Disconnect the vacuum line at the regulator.

3. Remove the 3 allen screws from the regulator housing.

4. Remove the regulator.

5. Inspect the regulator O-ring for signs of deterioration or damage. Discard the gasket.

6. Lubricate the O-ring with clean engine oil ONLY!

7. Make sure that the mounting surfaces are clean.

8. Using a new gasket, install the regulator. Tighten the retaining screws to 40 inch lbs.

9. Connect the vacuum line.

Fuel Supply Manifold

REMOVAL AND INSTALLATION

1. Relieve the fuel system pressure.

CAUTION: *Never smoke when working around gasoline! Avoid all sources of sparks or ignition. Gasoline vapors are EXTREMELY volatile!*

2. Remove the upper manifold.

3. Disconnect the chassis fuel inlet and outlet lines at the fuel supply manifold using tool T81P–19623–G or G1.

4. Disconnect the fuel supply and return lines at the fuel supply manifold.

5. Remove the 4 fuel supply manifold retaining bolts.

6. Carefully disengage the manifold from the injectors and lift it off.

7. Inspect all components for signs of damage. Make sure that the injector caps are clean.

8. Place the fuel supply manifold over the injectors and seat the injectors carefully in the manifold.

9. Install the 4 bolts and torque them to 20 ft. lbs.

10. Connect the fuel lines.

11. Install the upper manifold.

Lower Intake Manifold

REMOVAL AND INSTALLATION

1. Relieve the fuel system pressure.

CAUTION: *Never smoke when working around gasoline! Avoid all sources of sparks or ignition. Gasoline vapors are EXTREMELY volatile!*

2. *Disconnect the battery ground cable and drain the cooling system.*

CAUTION: *When draining the coolant, keep in mind that cats and dogs are attracted by the ethylene glycol antifreeze, and are quite likely to drink any that is left in an uncovered container or in puddles on the ground. This will prove fatal in sufficient quantity. Always drain the coolant into a sealable container. Coolant should be reused unless it is contaminated or several years old.*

3. Label and disconnect the wiring at the:

- Throttle position sensor

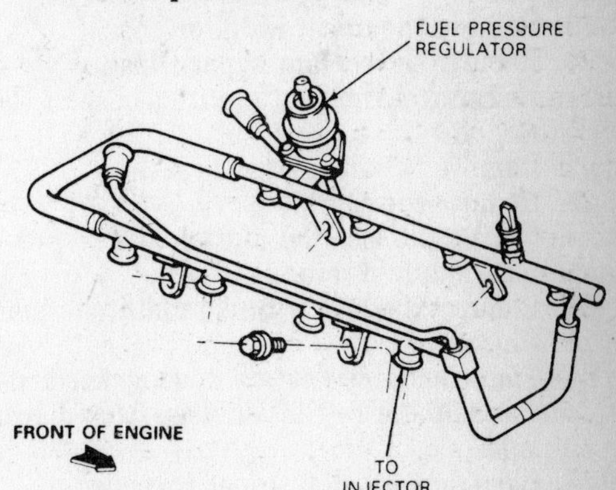

8–5.0L, 5.8L fuel pressure regulator

- Air bypass valve
- EGR sensor

4. Label and disconnect the following vacuum connectors:

- EGR valve
- Fuel pressure regulator
- Upper intake manifold vacuum tree

5. Disconnect the PCV hose at the upper intake manifold.

6. Remove the throttle linkage at the throttle ball and AOD transmission linkage at the throttle body.

7. Unbolt the cable bracket from the manifold and position the cables and bracket away from the engine.

8. Disconnect the 2 canister purge lines at the throttle body.

9. Disconnect the water heater lines from the throttle body.

10. Remove the EGR tube.

11. Remove the screw and washer which retains the upper intake manifold support bracket to the upper intake manifold.

12. Remove the 6 bolts which retain the upper intake manifold.

13. Remove the upper intake manifold assembly from the lower intake manifold.

14. Remove the distributor. (See Chapter 3).

15. Disconnect the wiring at the:

- Engine coolant temperature sensor.
- Engine temperature sending unit.
- Air charge temperature sensor.
- Knock sensor.
- Electrical vacuum regulator.
- Thermactor solenoids.

16. Disconnect the injector wiring harness at the main harness.

17. Remove the EGO ground wire at its intake manifold stud. Note the position of the stud and ground wire for installation.

18. Disconnect the fuel supply and return lines from the fuel rails using tool T81P–19623–G or G1.

19. Remove the upper radiator hose.

20. Remove the coolant bypass hose.

21. Disconnect the heater outlet hose at the manifold.

22. Remove the air cleaner bracket.

23. Remove the coil.

24. Noting the location of each bolt, remove the intake manifold retaining bolts.

25. Remove the lower intake manifold from the head.

26. Clean and inspect all mating surfaces. All surfaces MUST be flat and free from debris or damage!

27. Clean and oil all fastener threads.

28. Place a $\frac{1}{16}$ in. (1.5mm) bead of RTV silicone sealant to the end seals' junctions.

29. Position the end seals on the block.

30. Install 2 locator pins at opposite corners of the block.

31. Position the lower manifold on the head using new gaskets. Install the bolts and remove the locating pins.

32. Tighten the bolts to 25 ft. lbs. in sequence. Wait ten minutes and retorque the bolts in sequence.

33. Install the coil.

34. Connect the cooling system hoses.

35. Connect the fuel supply and return lines.

36. Connect the wiring at the:

- Engine coolant temperature sensor.
- Engine temperature sending unit.
- Air charge temperature sensor.
- Knock sensor.
- Electrical vacuum regulator.
- Thermactor solenoids.

37. Install the distributor.

38. Position the upper manifold and new gasket on the lower manifold. Install the fasteners finger tight.

39. Install the upper intake manifold support on the manifold and tighten the retaining screw to 30 ft. lbs.

40. Torque the upper-to-lower manifold fasteners to 18 ft. lbs.

41. Install the EGR tube. Torque the fittings to 35 ft. lbs.

42. Install the canister purge lines at the throttle body.

43. Connect the water heater lines at the throttle body.

44. Connect the PCV hose.

45. Install the accelerator cable and throttle linkages.

46. Connect the vacuum hoses.

47. Connect the electrical wiring.

48. Connect the air intake hose, air bypass hose and crankcase vent hose.

49. Connect the battery ground.

50. Refill the cooling system.

51. Install the fuel pressure relief cap. Turn the ignition switch from **OFF** to **ON** at least half a dozen times, **WITHOUT STARTING THE ENGINE**, leaving it in the ON position for about 5 seconds each time. This will build up fuel pressure in the system.

52. Start the engine and allow it to run at idle until normal operating temperature is reached. Check for leaks.

Throttle Position Sensor

REMOVAL AND INSTALLATION

1. Disconnect the wiring harness from the TPS.

CAUTION: *Never smoke when working around gasoline! Avoid all sources of sparks or ignition. Gasoline vapors are EXTREMELY volatile!*

2. Matchmark the sensor and throttle body for installation reference.

3. Remove the 2 retaining screws and remove the TPS.

4. Install the TPS so that the wiring harness is parallel with the venturi bores, then, rotate the TPS clockwise to align the scribe marks.

CAUTION: *Slide the rotary tangs into position over the throttle shaft blade, then rotate*

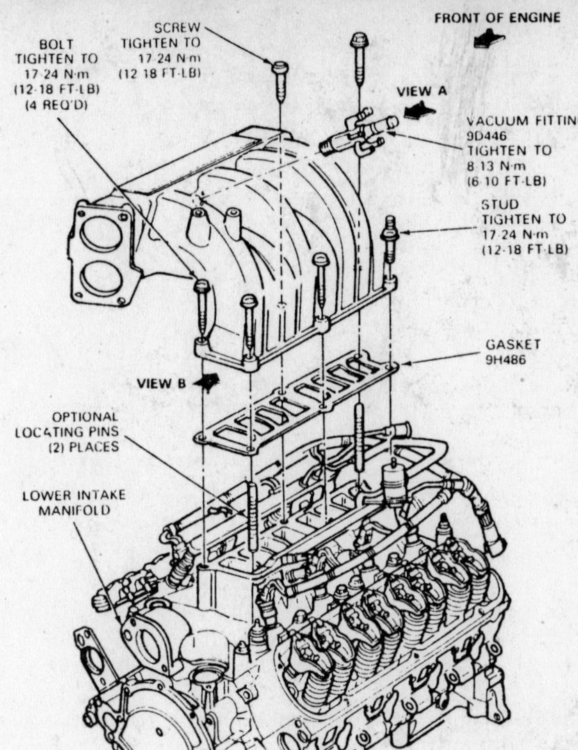

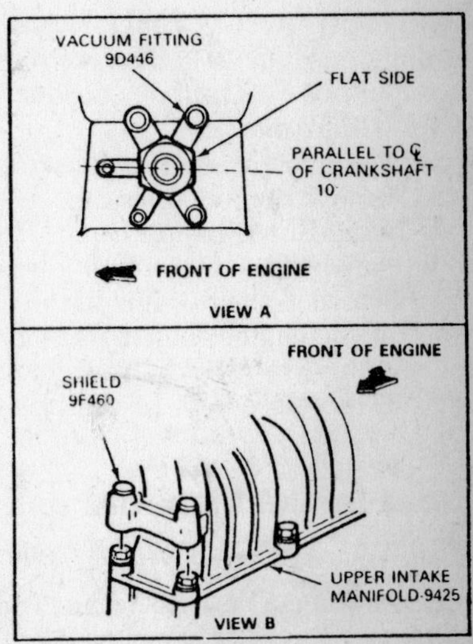

8–5.0L, 5.8L EFI upper intake manifold

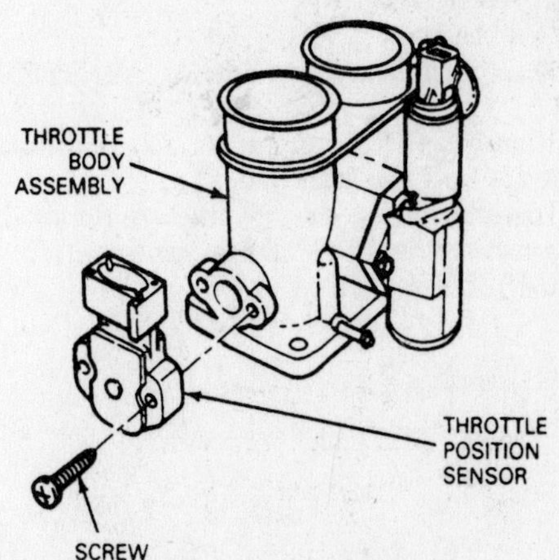

8–5.0L, 5.8L throttle position sensor

the TPS CLOCKWISE ONLY to the installed position. FAILURE TO INSTALL THE TPS IN THIS MANNER WILL RESULT IN EXCESSIVE IDLE SPEEDS!

5. Tighten the retaining screws to 16 inch lbs.

NOTE: *When correctly installed, the TPS wiring harness should be pointing directly at the air bypass valve.*

1. Screw and washer assembly—M4 × 22
2. Throttle position sensor
3. Bolt—5 16-18 × 1.25
4. Gasket—air intake charge throttle
5. Manifold—intake upper
6. Plug—throttle plate set screw locking
7. Spring—throttle plate set screw
8. Screw—10.32 × ¹⁄₅₀ hex head slotted
9. Cap—throttle plate set screw
10. Bolt—M6 × 20
11. Air bypass valve assembly
12. Gasket—air bypass

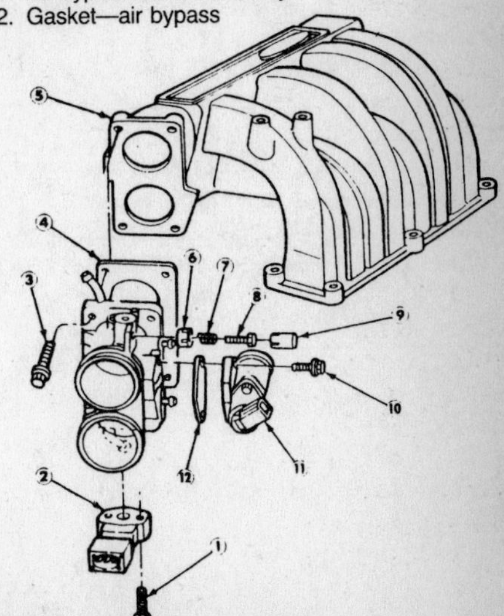

8–5.0L, 5.8L throttle body removal

GASOLINE FUEL INJECTION 8–7.5L ENGINE

Relieving Fuel System Pressure

NOTE: *A special tool is necessary for this procedure.*

1. Make sure the ignition switch is in the OFF position.

CAUTION: *Never smoke when working around gasoline! Avoid all sources of sparks or ignition. Gasoline vapors are EXTREMELY volatile!*

2. Disconnect the battery ground.
3. Remove the fuel filler cap.
4. Using EFI Pressure Gauge T80L–9974–A, or equivalent, at the fuel pressure relief valve (located in the fuel line in the upper right corner of the engine compartment) relieve the fuel system pressure. A valve cap must first be removed to gain access to the pressure relief valve.

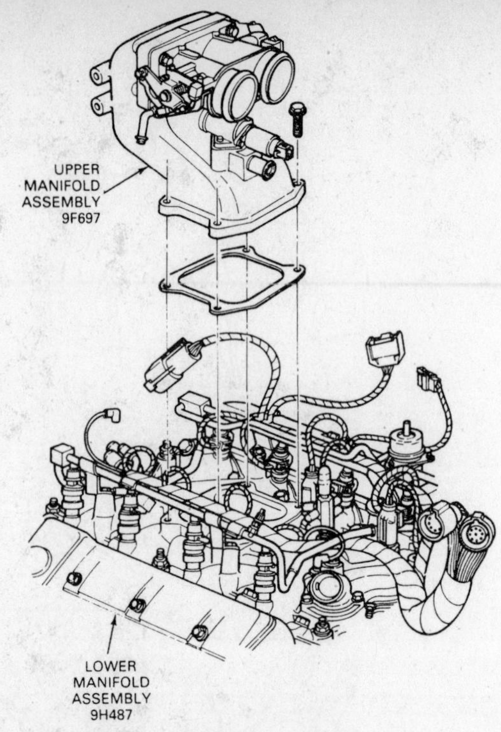

8–7.5L upper intake manifold removal

Upper Intake Manifold

REMOVAL AND INSTALLATION

1. Disconnect the throttle and transmission linkages at the throttle body.

CAUTION: *Never smoke when working around gasoline! Avoid all sources of sparks or ignition. Gasoline vapors are EXTREMELY volatile!*

2. Remove the two canister purge lines from the throttle body.
3. Tag and disconnect the:

- throttle bypass valve wire
- throttle position sensor wire
- EGR position sensor wire
- MAP sensor vacuum line
- EGR vacuum line
- fuel pressure regulator vacuum line
- EGR valve flange nut
- PCV hose

4. Disconnect the water lines at the throttle body.
5. Remove the 4 upper intake manifold bolts and lift off the manifold.
6. Installation is the reverse of removal. Always use new gaskets. Torque the manifold bolts to 18 ft. lbs.

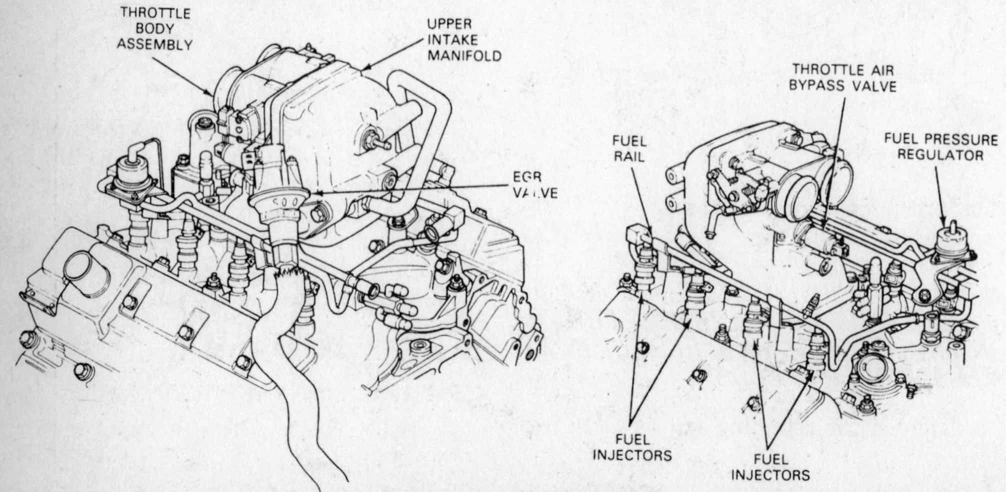

8–7.5L EFI system components

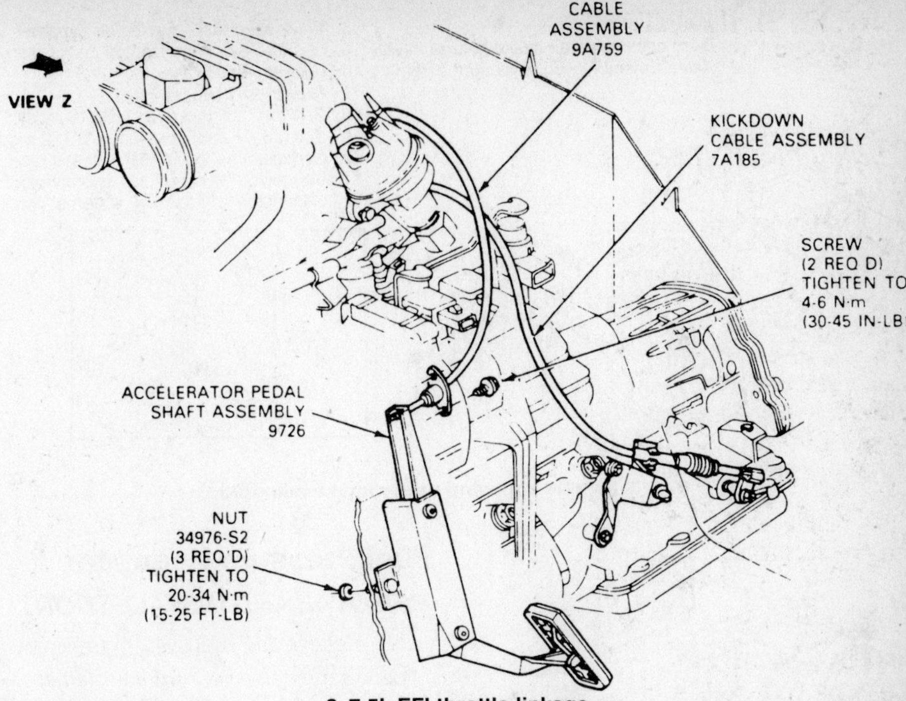

8–7.5L EFI throttle linkage

Throttle Body

REMOVAL AND INSTALLATION

1. Relieve the fuel system pressure.

CAUTION: *Never smoke when working around gasoline! Avoid all sources of sparks or ignition. Gasoline vapors are EXTREMELY volatile!*

2. Disconnect the throttle position sensor wire.
3. Disconnect the water lines at the throttle body.
4. Remove the 4 throttle body bolts and carefully lift off the throttle body. Discard the gasket.
5. Installation is the reverse of removal. Torque the bolts to 18 ft. lbs.

Throttle Position Sensor

REMOVAL AND INSTALLATION

1. Disconnect the wiring harness from the TPS.

CAUTION: *Never smoke when working around gasoline! Avoid all sources of sparks or ignition. Gasoline vapors are EXTREMELY volatile!*

2. Matchmark the sensor and throttle body for installation reference.
3. Remove the 2 retaining screws and remove the TPS.
4. Install the TPS so that the wiring harness is parallel with the venturi bores, then, rotate the TPS clockwise to align the scribe marks.
5. Tighten the retaining screws to 16 inch lbs.

NOTE: *When correctly installed, the TPS wiring harness should be pointing directly at the air bypass valve.*

6. Connect the wiring.

Air Bypass Valve

REMOVAL AND INSTALLATION

1. Disconnect the wiring at the valve.

CAUTION: *Never smoke when working around gasoline! Avoid all sources of sparks or ignition. Gasoline vapors are EXTREMELY volatile!*

2. Remove the 2 retaining screws and lift off the valve.
3. Discard the gasket and clean and inspect the mating surfaces.
4. Install the valve with a new gasket, tightening the screws to 102 inch lbs.
5. Connect the wiring.

Fuel Supply Manifold

REMOVAL AND INSTALLATION

1. Relieve the fuel system pressure.

CAUTION: *Never smoke when working around gasoline! Avoid all sources of sparks or ignition. Gasoline vapors are EXTREMELY volatile!*

1. Manifold assembly—intake
2. Body assembly—air intake charge throttle
3. Valve assembly—EGR vacuum external
4. Valve assembly—throttle air bypass
5. Gasket—air charge control intake manifold
6. Gasket—EGR valve
7. Gasket—air bypass valve
8. Bolt $5/16 \times 1.5$ hex head UBS (6 reqd)
9. Bolt M6 × 25mm hex head UBS (2 reqd)
10. Connector 3/8″ hose × 3/8″ external pipe
11. Connector 3/8″ hose × 3/8″ external pipe
12. Connector 1/4″ hose × 3/8″ external pipe

8–7.5L throttle body and upper intake manifold

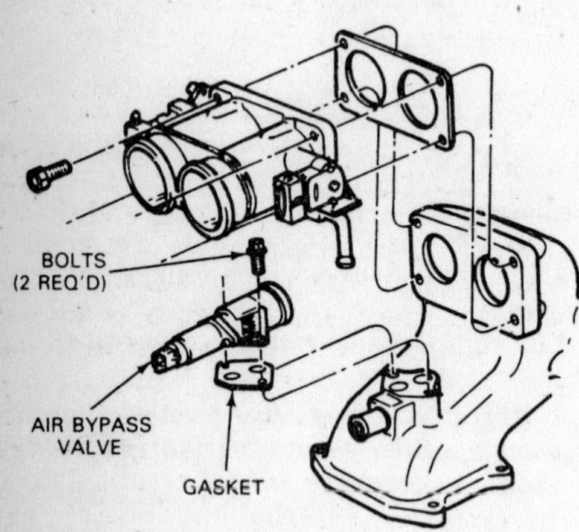

8–7.5L air bypass valve removal

2. Remove the upper manifold.
3. Disconnect the chassis fuel inlet and outlet lines at the fuel supply manifold using tool T81P–19623–G or G1.
4. Disconnect the fuel supply and return lines at the fuel supply manifold.
5. Remove the 4 fuel supply manifold retaining bolts.
6. Carefully disengage the manifold from the injectors and lift it off.
7. Inspect all components for signs of damage. Make sure that the injector caps are clean.
8. Place the fuel supply manifold over the injectors and seat the injectors carefully in the manifold.
9. Install the 4 bolts and torque them to 20 ft. lbs.
10. Connect the fuel lines.
11. Install the upper manifold.

Fuel Pressure Regulator

REMOVAL AND INSTALLATION

1. Relieve the fuel system pressure.

CAUTION: *Never smoke when working around gasoline! Avoid all sources of sparks or ignition. Gasoline vapors are EXTREMELY volatile!*

2. Disconnect the vacuum line at the regulator.
3. Remove the 3 allen screws from the regulator housing.
4. Remove the regulator.
5. Inspect the regulator O-ring for signs of deterioration or damage. Discard the gasket.
6. Lubricate the O-ring with clean engine oil ONLY!
7. Make sure that the mounting surfaces are clean.
8. Using a new gasket, install the regulator. Tighten the retaining screws to 40 inch lbs.
9. Connect the vacuum line.

Fuel Injectors

REMOVAL AND INSTALLATION

1. Relieve the fuel system pressure.

CAUTION: *Never smoke when working around gasoline! Avoid all sources of sparks or ignition. Gasoline vapors are EXTREMELY volatile!*

2. Disconnect the battery ground.
3. Remove the fuel supply manifold.
4. Disconnect the wiring at the injectors.
5. Pull upward on the injector body while gently rocking it from side-to-side.
6. Inspect the O-rings (2 per injector) on the injector for any sign of leakage or damage. Replace any suspected O-rings.
7. Inspect the plastic cap at the top of each

injector and replace it if any sign of deterioration is noticed.

8. Lubricate the O-rings with clean engine oil ONLY!.

9. Install the injectors by pushing them in with a gentle rocking motion.

10. Install the fuel supply manifold.

11. Connect the electrical wiring.

DIESEL ENGINE FUEL SYSTEM

Fuel Pump

REMOVAL

1. Loosen the threaded connections with the proper size wrench (a flare nut wrench is preferred) and retighten snugly. Do not remove the lines at this time.

2. Loosen the mounting bolts, one to two turns. Apply force with your hand to loosen the fuel pump if the gasket is stuck. Rotate the engine by nudging the starter, until the fuel pump cam lobe is at the low position. At this position, spring tension against the fuel pump bolts will be greatly reduced.

3. Disconnect the fuel supply pump inlet, outlet and fuel return line.

CAUTION: *Use care to prevent combustion of the spilled fuel.*

4. Remove the fuel pump attaching bolts and remove the pump and gasket. Discard the old gasket.

INSTALLATION

1. Remove the remaining fuel pump gasket material from the engine and from the fuel pump if you are reinstalling the old pump. Make sure both mounting surfaces are clean.

2. Install the attaching bolts into the fuel supply pump and install a new gasket on the bolts. Position the fuel pump onto the mounting pad. Turn the attaching bolts alternately and evenly and tighten the bolts to the specifications according to the size bolts used on the pump. See the accompanying standard torque chart for reference.

NOTE: *The cam must be at its low position before attempting to install the fuel supply pump. If it is difficult to start the mounting bolts, remove the pump and reinstall with a lever on the bottom side of the cam.*

3. Install the fuel outlet line. Start the fitting by hand to avoid crossthreading.

4. Install the inlet line and the fuel return line.

5. Start the engine and observe all connections for fuel leaks for two minutes.

6. Stop the engine and check all fuel supply pump fuel line connections. Check for oil leaks at the pump mounting pad.

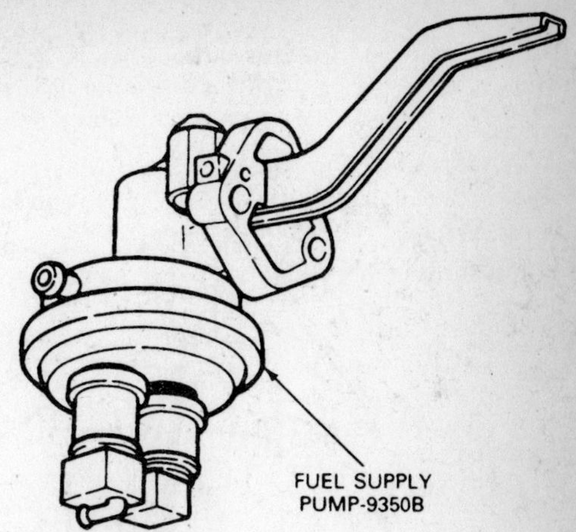

Diesel fuel supply pump

Glow Plug System

The diesel engine utilizes an electric glow plug system to aid in the start of the engine. The function of this stem is to pre-heat the combustion chamber to aid ignition of the fuel.

The system consists of eight glow plugs (one for each cylinder), control switch, power relay, after glow relay, wait lamp latching relay, wait lamp and the eight fusible links located between the harness and the glow plug terminal.

On initial start with cold engine, the glow plug system operates as follows: The glow plug control switch energizes the power relay (which is a magnetic switch) and the power relay contacts close. Battery current energizes the glow plugs. Current to the glow plugs and a wait lamp will be shut off when the glow plugs are hot enough. This takes from 2 to 10 second after the key is first turned on. When the wait lamp goes off, the engine is ready to start. After the engine is started the glow plugs begin an on-off cycle for about 40 to 90 seconds. This cycle helps to clear start-up smoke. The control switch (the brain of the operation) is threaded into the left cylinder head coolant jacket. the control unit senses engine coolant temperature. Since the control unit senses temperature and glow plug operation the glow plug system will not be activated unless needed. On a restart (warm engine) the glow plug system will not be activated unless the coolant temperature drops before 165°F (91°C).

Since the fast start system utilizes 6 volt glow plugs in a 12 volt system to achieve rapid heating of the glow plug, a cycling device is required in the circuit.

CAUTION: *Never bypass the power relay of the glow plug system. Constant battery cur-*

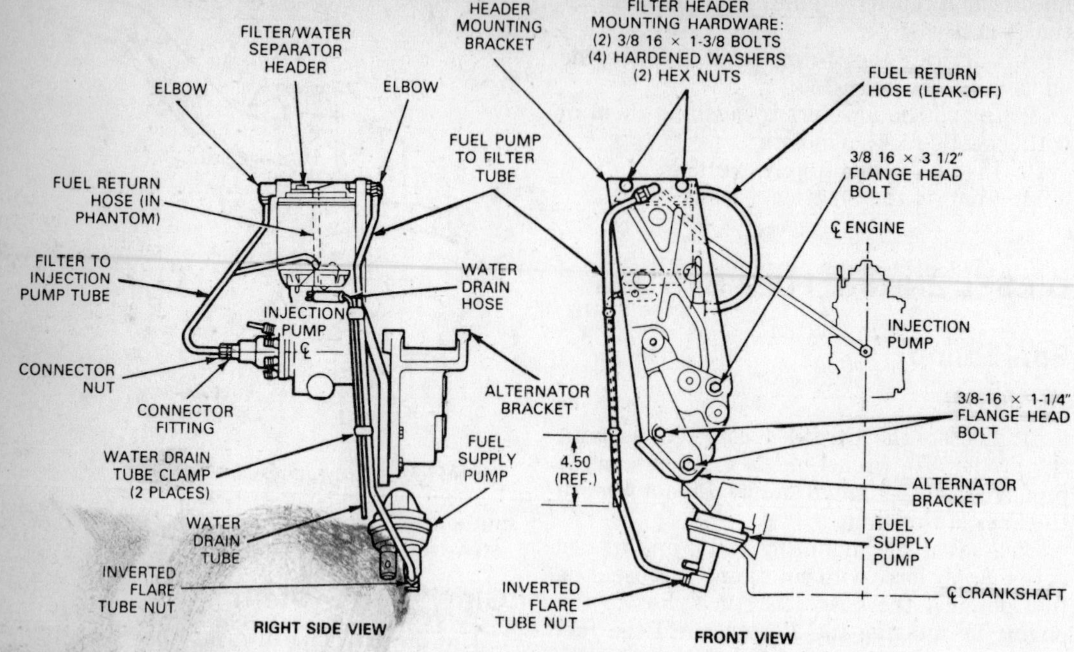

Diesel fuel supply lines

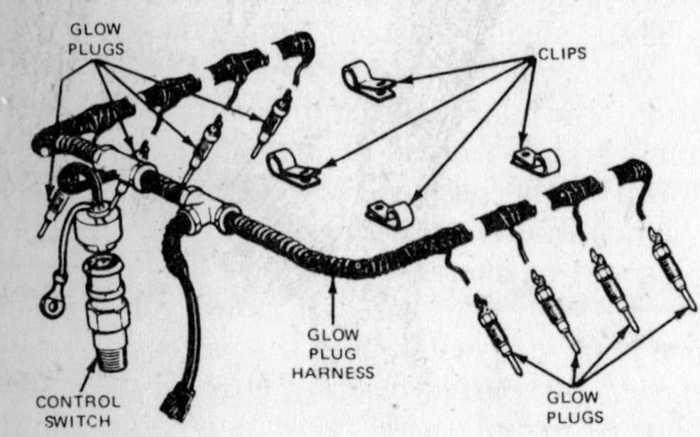

Diesel glow plug system

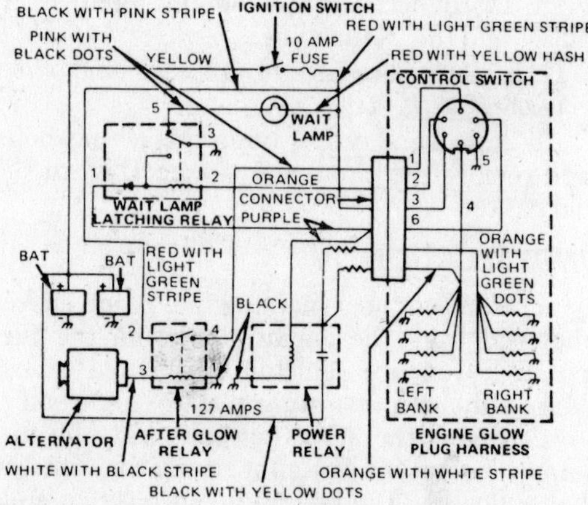

6.9L diesel glow plug wiring schematic

rent (12 volts) to glow plugs will cause them to overheat and fail.

Injection Nozzles

REMOVAL

NOTE: *Before removing the nozzle assemblies, clean the exterior of each nozzle assembly and the surrounding area with clean fuel oil or solvent to prevent entry of dirt into the engine when nozzle assemblies are removed. Also, clean the fuel inlet and fuel leak-off piping connections. Blow dry with compressed air.*

1. Remove the fuel line retaining clamp(s) from the nozzle lines that are to be removed.
2. Disconnect the nozzle fuel inlet (high pressure) and fuel leak-off tees from each nozzle assembly and position out of the way. Cover the open ends of the fuel inlet and outlet or nozzles with protective caps, to prevent dirt from entering.
3. Remove the injection nozzles by turning them counterclockwise. Pull the nozzle assembly with the copper washer attached from the engine. Cover the nozzle fuel opening and spray tip, with plastic caps, to prevent the entry of dirt.

NOTE: *Remove the copper injector nozzle gasket from the nozzle bore with special tool, T71P–19703–C, or equivalent, whenever the gasket does not come out with the nozzle.*

4. Place the nozzle assemblies in a fabricated holder as they are removed from the

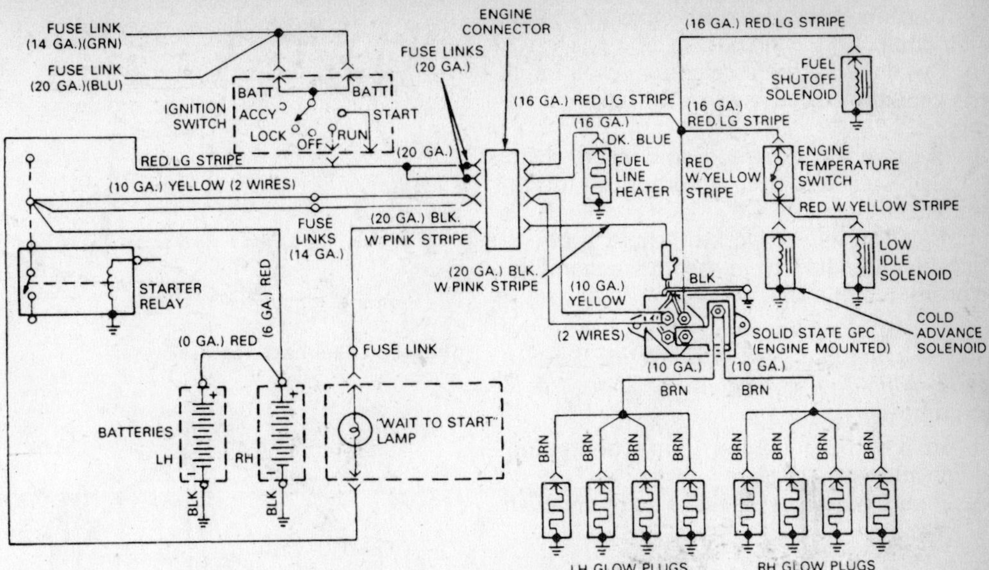

7.3L diesel glow plug wiring schematic

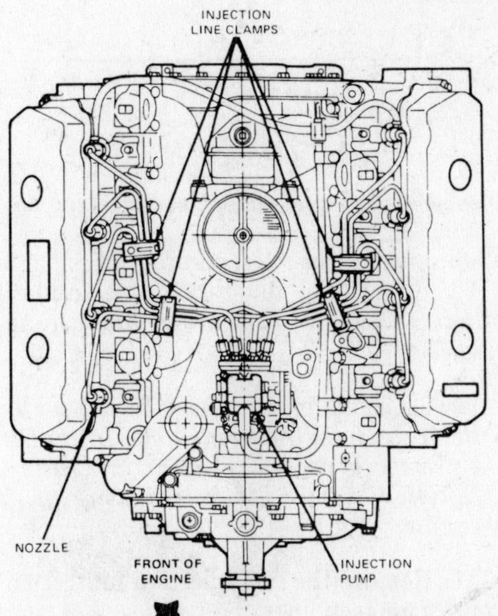

Injection line clamps, Diesel V8. Injection also shown

heads. The holder should be marked with numbers corresponding to the cylinder numbering of the engine. This will allow for reinstallation of the nozzle in the same ports from which they were removed.

INSTALLATION

1. Thoroughly clean the nozzle bore in cylinder head before reinserting the nozzle assembly with nozzle seat cleaner, special tool T83T–9527–A or equivalent. Make certain that no small particles of metal or carbon remain on the seating surface. Blow out the particles with compressed air.

2. Remove the protective cap and install a new copper gasket on the nozzle assembly, with a small dab of grease.

NOTE: *Anti-seize compound or equivalent should be used on nozzle threads to aid in installation and future removal.*

3. Install the nozzle assembly into the cylinder head nozzle bore.

4. Tighten the nozzle assembly to 33 ft. lbs.

5. Remove the protective caps from nozzle assemblies and fuel lines.

6. Install the leak-off tees to the nozzle assemblies.

NOTE: *Install two new O-ring seals for each fuel return tee.*

7. Connect the high pressure fuel line and tighten, using a flare nut wrench.

8. Install the fuel line retainer clamps.

9. Start the engine and check for leaks.

Injection Pump

WARNING: *Before removing the fuel lines, clean the exterior with clean fuel oil or solvent to prevent entry of dirt into the engine when the fuel lines are removed. Do not wash or steam clean engine while engine is running. Serious damage to injection pump could occur.*

REMOVAL

1. Disconnect battery ground cables from both batteries.

2. Remove the engine oil filler neck.

3. Remove the bolts attaching injection pump to drive gear.

4. Disconnect the electrical connectors to injection pump.

5. Disconnect the accelerator cable and speed control cable from throttle lever, if so equipped.

6. Remove the air cleaner and install clean rags to prevent dirt from entering the intake manifold.

7. Remove the accelerator cable bracket, with cables attached, from the intake manifold and position out of the way.

NOTE: *All fuel lines and fittings must be capped using Fuel System Protective Cap Set T83T–9395–A or equivalent, to prevent fuel contamination.*

8. Remove the fuel filter-to-injection pump fuel line and cap fittings.

9. Remove and cap the injection pump inlet elbow and the injection pump fitting adapter.

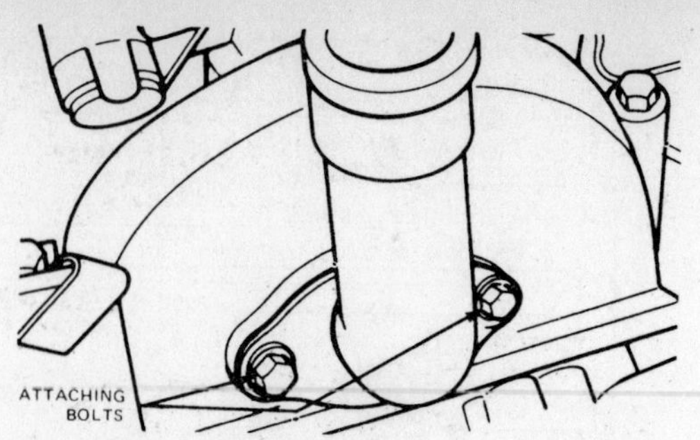

Diesel oil filter neck removal

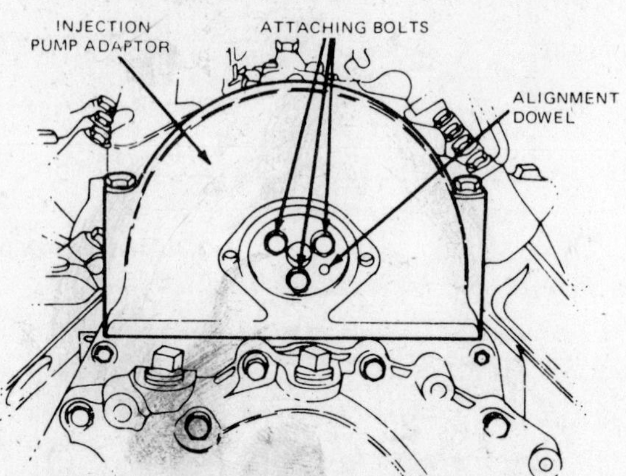

Diesel injection pump drive gear attaching bolts

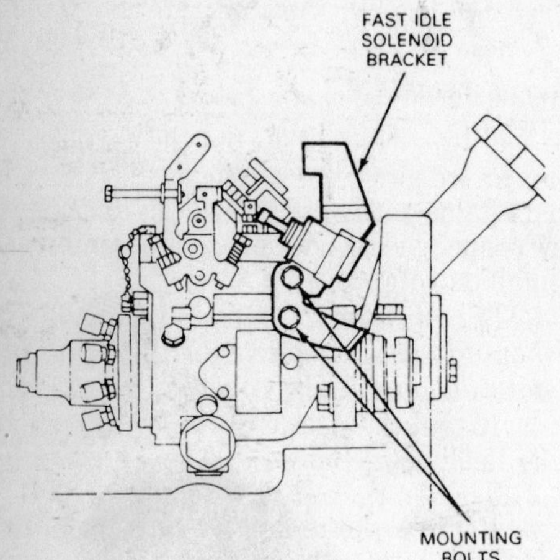

Diesel fast idle solenoid bracket

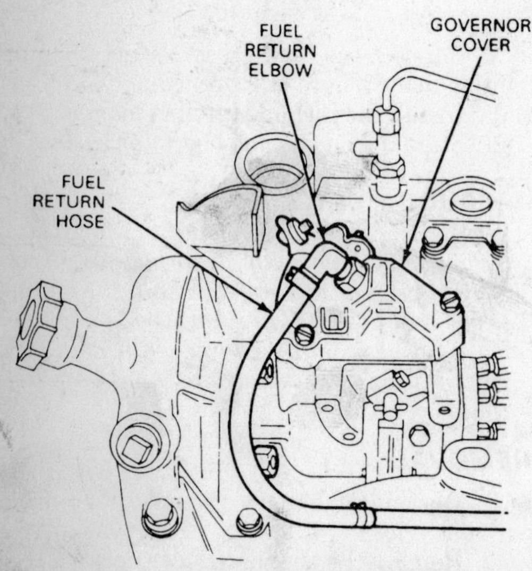

Removing the diesel fuel return line

10. Remove the fuel return line on injection pump, rotate out of the way, And cap all fittings.

NOTE: *It is not necessary to remove injection lines from injection pump. If lines are to be removed, loosen injection line fittings at injection pump before removing it from engine.*

11. Remove the fuel injection lines from the nozzles and cap lines and nozzles.

12. Remove the three nuts attaching the Injection pump to injection pump adapter using Tool T83T–9000–B.

13. If the injection pump is to be replaced, loosen the injection line retaining clips and the injection nozzle fuel lines with Tool T83T–9396–A and cap all fittings at this time with protective cap set T83T–9395–A or equivalent. Do not install the injection nozzle fuel lines until the new pump is installed in the engine.

14. Lift the Injection pump, with the nozzle lines attached, up and out of the engine compartment.

WARNING: *Do not carry injection pump by Injection nozzle fuel lines as this could cause lines to bend or crimp.*

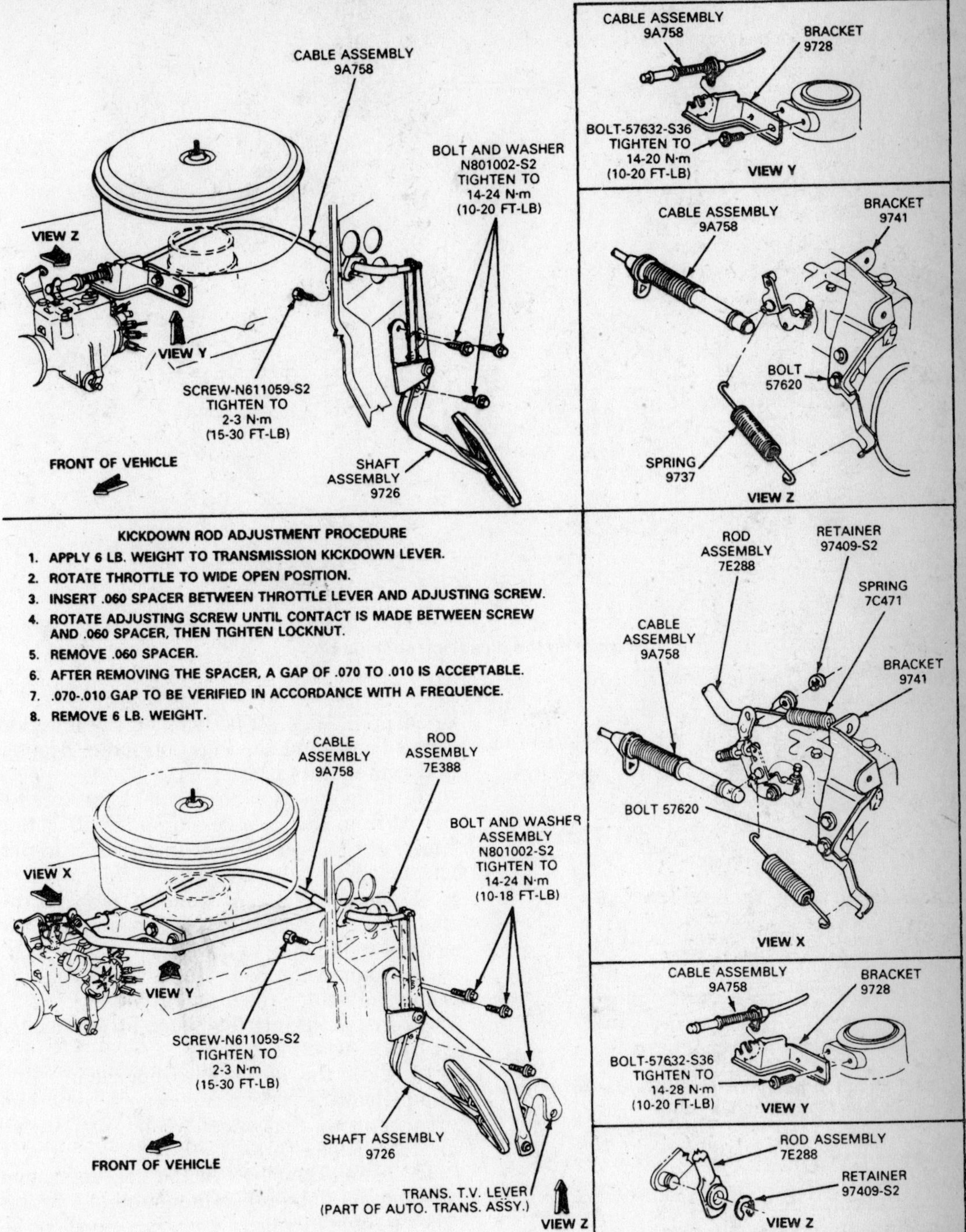

7.3L diesel throttle linkage

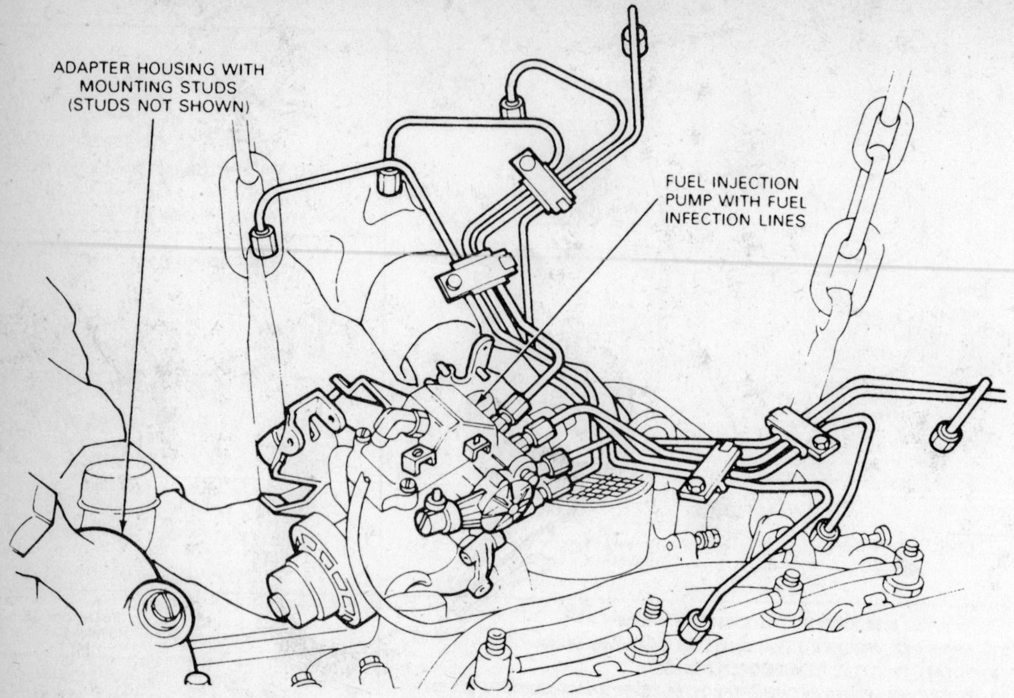

Removing the diesel injection pump

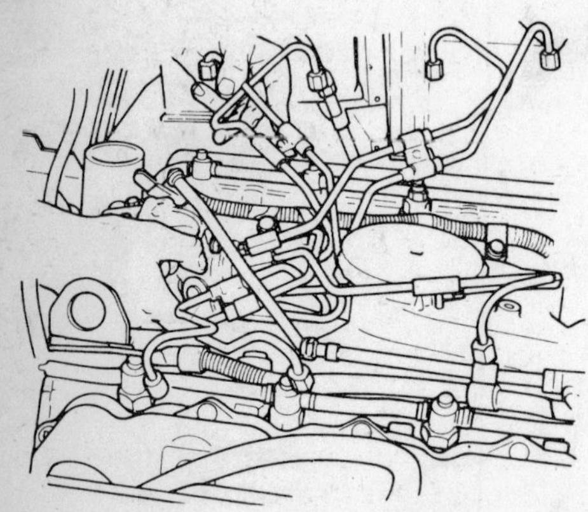

Diesel injection pump removal. Be careful not to crimp or bend the fuel lines

INSTALLATION

1. Install a new O-ring on the drive gear end of the injection pump.

2. Move the injection pump down and into position.

3. Position the alignment dowel on injection pump into the alignment hole on Drive gear.

4. Install the bolts attaching the injection pump to drive gear and tighten.

5. Install the nuts attaching injection pump to adapter. Align scribe lines on the injection pump flange and the injection pump adapter and tighten to 14 ft.lbs.

6. If the injection nozzle fuel lines were removed from the injection pump install at this time, refer to Fuel Lines – Installation, in this chapter.

7. Remove the caps from nozzles and the fuel lines and install the fuel line nuts on the nozzles and tighten to 22 ft. lbs.

8. Connect the fuel return line to injection pump and tighten the nuts.

9. Install the injection pump fitting adapter with a new O-ring.

10. Clean the old sealant from the injection pump elbow threads, using clean solvent, and dry thoroughly. Apply a light coating of pipe sealant to the elbow threads.

11. Install the elbow in the injection pump adapter and tighten to a minimum of 6 ft. lbs. Then tighten further, if necessary, to align the elbow with the injection pump fuel inlet line, but do not exceed 360 degrees of rotation or 10 ft. lbs.

12. Remove the caps and connect the fuel filter-to-Injection pump fuel line.

13. Install the accelerator cable bracket to the intake manifold.

14. Remove the rags from the intake manifold and install the air cleaner.

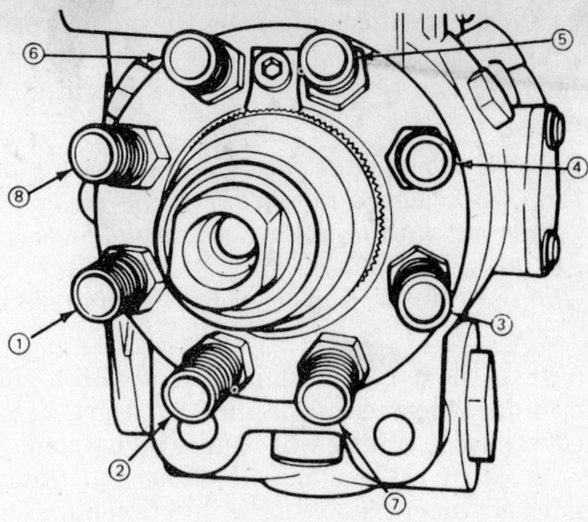

Injection pump cylinder numbering sequence

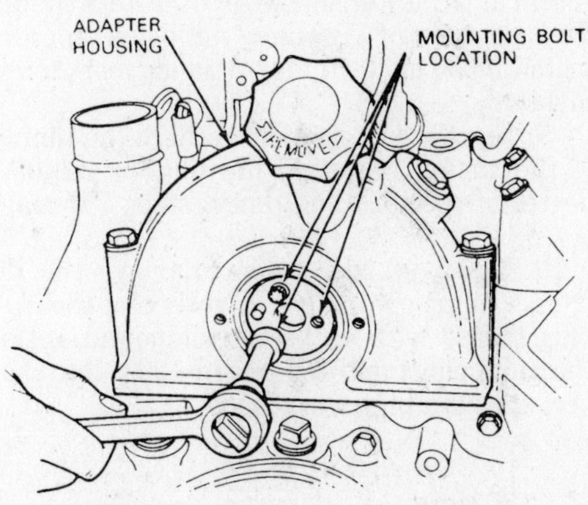

Diesel injection pump drive gear attaching bolts

15. Connect the accelerator and speed control cable, if so equipped, to throttle lever.

16. Install the electrical connectors on injection pump.

17. Clean the injection pump adapter and oil filler neck sealing surfaces.

18. Apply a 1/8 in. (3mm) bead of RTV sealant on the adapter housing.

19. Install the oil filler neck and tighten the bolts.

20. Connect the battery ground cables to both batteries.

21. Run the engine and check for fuel leaks.

22. If necessary, purge high pressure fuel lines of air by loosening connector one half to one turn and cranking engine until solid fuel, free from bubbles flows from connection.

CAUTION: *Keep eyes and hands away from nozzle spray. Fuel spraying from the nozzle under high pressure can penetrate the skin.*

23. Check and adjust injection pump timing as described in this chapter.

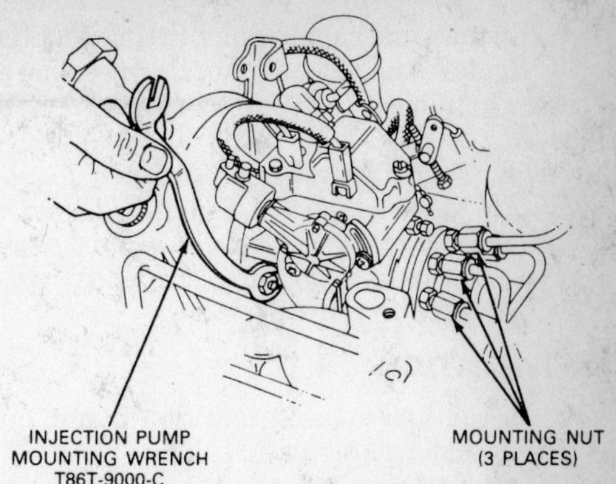

Removing the diesel injection pump mounting nuts

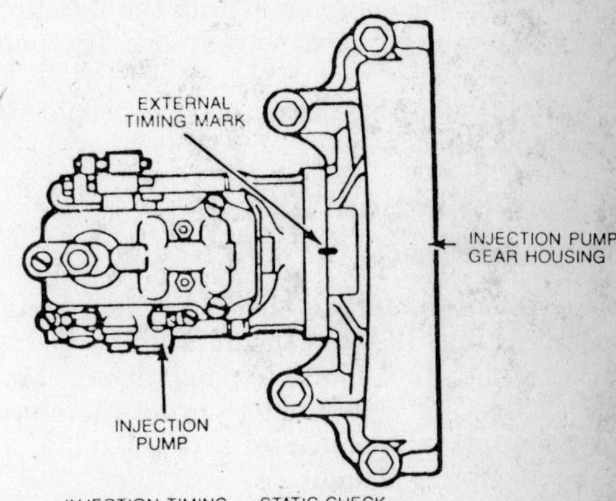

Diesel injection pump static timing marks

Fuel Lines

REMOVAL

NOTE: *Before removing any fuel lines, clean the exterior with clean fuel oil, or solvent to prevent entry of dirt into fuel system when the fuel lines are removed. Blow dry with compressed air.*

1. Disconnect the battery ground cables from both batteries.

2. Remove the air cleaner and cap intake manifold opening with clean rags.

3. Disconnect the accelerator cable and speed control cable, if so equipped, from the injection pump.

4. remove the accelerator cable bracket from the intake manifold and position out of the way with cable(s) attached.

WARNING: *To prevent fuel system contamination, cap all fuel lines and fittings.*

5. Disconnect the fuel line from the fuel filter to injection pump and cap all fittings.

6. Disconnect and cap the nozzle fuel lines at nozzles.

7. Remove the fuel line clamps from the fuel lines to be removed.

8. Remove and cap the injection pump inlet elbow.

9. Remove and cap the inlet fitting adapter.

10. Remove the injection nozzle lines, one at a time, from injection pump using Tool T83T–9396–A.

NOTE: *Fuel lines must be removed following this sequence: 5–6–4–8–3–1–7–2. Install caps on each end of each fuel line and pump fittings as it is removed and identify each fuel line accordingly.*

INSTALLATION

1. Install fuel lines on injection pump, one at a time, and Tighten to 22 ft.lbs.

NOTE: *Fuel lines must be installed in the sequence: 2–7–1–3–8–4–6–5.*

2. Clean the old sealant from the injection pump elbow, using clean solvent, and dry thoroughly.

3. Apply a light coating of pipe sealant on the elbow threads.

Diesel Injection Timing

STATIC TIMING

1. Break the torque of the injection pump mounting nuts (keeping the nuts snug).

2. Rotate the injection pump using Tool T83–9000–C or equivalent to bring the mark on the pump into alignment with the mark on pump mounting adapter.

3. Visually recheck the alignment of the timing marks and tighten injection pump mounting nuts.

DYNAMIC TIMING

1. Bring the engine up to normal operating temperature.

2. Stop the engine and install a dynamic timing meter, Rotunda 78–0100 or equivalent, by placing the magnetic probe pick-up into the probe hole.

3. Remove the no. 1 glow plug wire and remove the glow plug, install the luminosity probe and tighten to 12 ft.lbs. Install the photocell over the probe.

4. Connect the dynamic timing meter to the battery and adjust the offset of the meter.

5. Set the transmission in neutral and raise the rear wheels off the ground. Using Rotunda 14–0302, throttle control, set the engine speed to 1,400 rpm with no accessory load. Observe the injection timing on the dynamic timing meter.

NOTE: *Obtain the fuel sample from the vehicle and check the cetane value using the tester supplied with the Ford special tools 78–0100 or equivalent. Refer to the dynamic timing chart to find the correct timing in degrees.*

6. If the dynamic timing is not within plug or minus 2 degrees of specification, then the injection pump timing will require adjustment.

7. Turn the engine off. Note the timing mark alignment. Loosen the injection pump-to-adapter nuts.

8. Rotate the injection pump clockwise (when viewed from the front of the engine) to retard and counterclockwise to advance timing. Two degrees of dynamic timing is approximately 0.030 in. (0.76mm) of timing mark movement.

9. Start the engine and recheck the timing. If the timing is not within plus or minus 1 degree of specification, repeat steps 7 through 9.

10. Turn off the engine. Remove the dynamic timing equipment. Lightly coat the glow plug thread with anti-seize compound, install the glow plugs and tighten to 12 ft. lbs. Connect the glow plug wires.

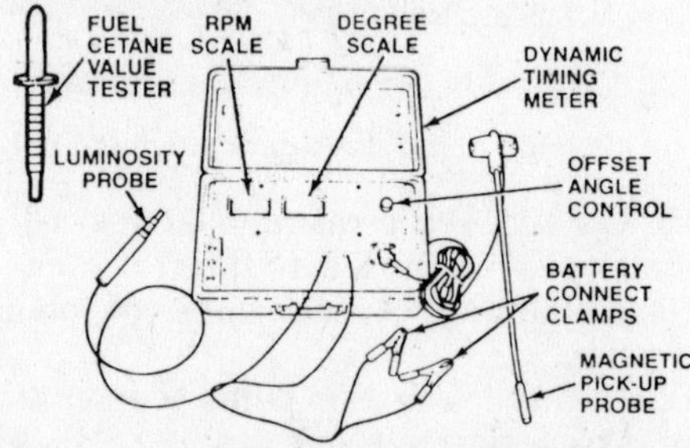

Rotunda dynamic timing meter used for diesel injection timing. Cetane tester, magnetic pick-up probe and luminosity probe also shown

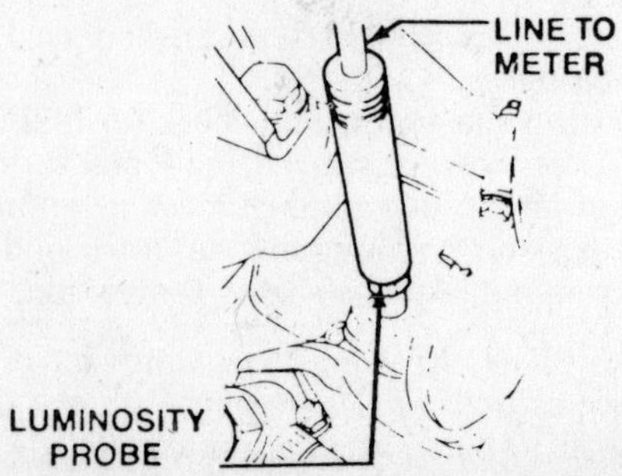

Luminosity probe used for diesel injection timing

Dynamic Timing Specifications

	Altitude	
Fuel Cetane Value	0-3000 Ft ①	Above 3000 Ft ①
38–42	6° ATDC	7° ATDC
43–46	5° ATDC	6° ATDC
47–50	4° ATDC	5° ATDC

① Installation of resetting tolerance for dynamic timing is ± 1°. Service limit is ± 2°.

Chassis Electrical

6

UNDERSTANDING AND TROUBLESHOOTING ELECTRICAL SYSTEMS

At the rate which both import and domestic manufacturers are incorporating electronic control systems into their production lines, it won't be long before every new vehicle is equipped with one or more on-board computer, like the unit installed on the truck. These electronic components (with no moving parts) should theoretically last the life of the vehicle, provided nothing external happens to damage the circuits or memory chips.

While it is true that electronic components should never wear out, in the real world malfunctions do occur. It is also true that any computer-based system is extremely sensitive to electrical voltages and cannot tolerate careless or haphazard testing or service procedures. An inexperienced individual can literally do major damage looking for a minor problem by using the wrong kind of test equipment or connecting test leads or connectors with the ignition switch ON. When selecting test equipment, make sure the manufacturers instructions state that the tester is compatible with whatever type of electronic control system is being serviced. Read all instructions carefully and double check all test points before installing probes or making any test connections.

The following section outlines basic diagnosis techniques for dealing with computerized automotive control systems. Along with a general explanation of the various types of test equipment available to aid in servicing modern electronic automotive systems, basic repair techniques for wiring harnesses and connectors is given. Read the basic information before attempting any repairs or testing on any computerized system, to provide the background of information necessary to avoid the most common and obvious mistakes that can cost both time and money. Although the replacement and testing procedures are simple in themselves, the systems are not, and unless one has a thorough understanding of all components and their function within a particular computerized control system, the logical test sequence these systems demand cannot be followed. Minor malfunctions can make a big difference, so it is important to know how each component affects the operation of the overall electronic system to find the ultimate cause of a problem without replacing good components unnecessarily. It is not enough to use the correct test equipment; the test equipment must be used correctly.

Safety Precautions

CAUTION: *Whenever working on or around any computer based microprocessor control system, always observe these general precautions to prevent the possibility of personal injury or damage to electronic components.*

• Never install or remove battery cables with the key ON or the engine running. Jumper cables should be connected with the key OFF to avoid power surges that can damage electronic control units. Engines equipped with computer controlled systems should avoid both giving and getting jump starts due to the possibility of serious damage to components from arcing in the engine compartment when connections are made with the ignition ON.

• Always remove the battery cables before charging the battery. Never use a high output charger on an installed battery or attempt to use any type of "hot shot" (24 volt) starting aid.

• Exercise care when inserting test probes into connectors to insure good connections without damaging the connector or spreading the pins. Always probe connectors from the rear (wire) side, NOT the pin side, to avoid accidental shorting of terminals during test procedures.

• Never remove or attach wiring harness connectors with the ignition switch ON, especially to an electronic control unit.

• Do not drop any components during service procedures and never apply 12 volts directly to any component (like a solenoid or relay) unless instructed specifically to do so. Some component electrical windings are designed to safely handle only 4 or 5 volts and can be destroyed in seconds if 12 volts are applied directly to the connector.

• Remove the electronic control unit if the vehicle is to be placed in an environment where temperatures exceed approximately 176°F (80°C), such as a paint spray booth or when arc or gas welding near the control unit location in the car.

ORGANIZED TROUBLESHOOTING

When diagnosing a specific problem, organized troubleshooting is a must. The complexity of a modern automobile demands that you approach any problem in a logical, organized manner. There are certain troubleshooting techniques that are standard:

1. Establish when the problem occurs. Does the problem appear only under certain conditions? Were there any noises, odors, or other unusual symptoms?

2. Isolate the problem area. To do this, make some simple tests and observations; then eliminate the systems that are working properly. Check for obvious problems such as broken wires, dirty connections or split or disconnected vacuum hoses. Always check the obvious before assuming something complicated is the cause.

3. Test for problems systematically to determine the cause once the problem area is isolated. Are all the components functioning properly? Is there power going to electrical switches and motors? Is there vacuum at vacuum switches and/or actuators? Is there a mechanical problem such as bent linkage or loose mounting screws? Doing careful, systematic checks will often turn up most causes on the first inspection without wasting time checking components that have little or no relationship to the problem.

4. Test all repairs after the work is done to make sure that the problem is fixed. Some causes can be traced to more than one component, so a careful verification of repair work is important to pick up additional malfunctions that may cause a problem to reappear or a different problem to arise. A blown fuse, for example, is a simple problem that may require more than another fuse to repair. If you don't look for a problem that caused a fuse to blow, for example, a shorted wire may go undetected.

Experience has shown that most problems tend to be the result of a fairly simple and obvious cause, such as loose or corroded connectors or air leaks in the intake system; making careful inspection of components during testing essential to quick and accurate troubleshooting. Special, hand held computerized testers designed specifically for diagnosing the EEC-IV system are available from a variety of aftermarket sources, as well as from the vehicle manufacturer, but care should be taken that any test equipment being used is designed to diagnose that particular computer controlled system accurately without damaging the control unit (ECU) or components being tested.

NOTE: *Pinpointing the exact cause of trouble in an electrical system can sometimes only be accomplished by the use of special test equipment. The following describes commonly used test equipment and explains how to put it to best use in diagnosis. In addition to the information covered below, the manufacturer's instructions booklet provided with the tester should be read and clearly understood before attempting any test procedures.*

TEST EQUIPMENT

Jumper Wires

Jumper wires are simple, yet extremely valuable, pieces of test equipment. Jumper wires are merely wires that are used to bypass sections of a circuit. The simplest type of jumper wire is merely a length of multi-strand wire with an alligator clip at each end. Jumper wires are usually fabricated from lengths of standard automotive wire and whatever type of connector (alligator clip, spade connector or pin connector) that is required for the particular vehicle being tested. The well equipped tool box will have several different styles of jumper wires in several different lengths. Some jumper wires are made with three or more terminals coming from a common splice for special purpose testing. In cramped, hard-to-reach areas it is advisable to have insulated boots over the jumper wire terminals in order to prevent accidental grounding, sparks, and possible fire, especially when testing fuel system components.

Jumper wires are used primarily to locate open electrical circuits, on either the ground (–) side of the circuit or on the hot (+) side. If an electrical component fails to operate, connect the jumper wire between the component and a good ground. If the component operates only with the jumper installed, the ground circuit is open. If the ground circuit is good, but the component does not operate, the circuit between the power feed and component is open. You can sometimes connect the jumper wire directly from the battery to the hot terminal of the component, but first make sure the component uses 12 volts in operation. Some electrical components, such as fuel injectors, are designed to operate on about 4 volts and running 12 volts directly to the injector terminals can burn out the wiring. By inserting an inline fuse holder between a set of test leads, a fused jumper wire can be used for bypassing open circuits. Use a 5 amp fuse to provide protection against voltage spikes. When in doubt, use a voltmeter to check the voltage input to the component and measure how much voltage is being applied normally. By moving the jumper wire successively back from the lamp toward the power source, you can isolate the area of the circuit where the open is located. When the component stops functioning, or the power is cut off, the open is in the segment of wire between the jumper and the point previously tested.

CAUTION: *Never use jumpers made from wire that is of lighter gauge than used in the circuit under test. If the jumper wire is of too small gauge, it may overheat and possibly melt. Never use jumpers to bypass high resistance loads (such as motors) in a circuit. Bypassing resistances, in effect, creates a short circuit which may, in turn, cause damage and fire. Never use a jumper for anything other than temporary bypassing of components in a circuit.*

12 Volt Test Light

The 12 volt test light is used to check circuits and components while electrical current is flowing through them. It is used for voltage and ground tests. Twelve volt test lights come in different styles but all have three main parts; a ground clip, a probe, and a light. The most commonly used 12 volt test lights have pick-type probes. To use a 12 volt test light, connect the ground clip to a good ground and probe wherever necessary with the pick. The pick should be sharp so that it can penetrate wire insulation to make contact with the wire, without making a large hole in the insulation. The wrap-around light is handy in hard to reach areas or where it is difficult to support a wire to push a probe pick into it. To use the wrap around light, hook the wire to probed with the hook and pull the trigger. A small pick will be forced through the wire insulation into the wire core.

CAUTION: *Do not use a test light to probe electronic ignition spark plug or coil wires. Never use a pick-type test light to probe wiring on computer controlled systems unless specifically instructed to do so. Any wire insulation that is pierced by the test light probe should be taped and sealed with silicone after testing.*

Like the jumper wire, the 12 volt test light is used to isolate opens in circuits. But, whereas the jumper wire is used to bypass the open to operate the load, the 12 volt test light is used to locate the presence of voltage in a circuit. If the test light glows, you know that there is power up to that point; if the 12 volt test light does not glow when its probe is inserted into the wire or connector, you know that there is an open circuit (no power). Move the test light in successive steps back toward the power source until the light in the handle does glow. When it does glow, the open is between the probe and point previously probed.

NOTE: *The test light does not detect that 12 volts (or any particular amount of voltage) is present; it only detects that some voltage is present. It is advisable before using the test light to touch its terminals across the battery posts to make sure the light is operating properly.*

Self-Powered Test Light

The self-powered test light usually contains a 1.5 volt penlight battery. One type of self-powered test light is similar in design to the 12 volt test light. This type has both the battery and the light in the handle and pick-type probe tip. The second type has the light toward the open tip, so that the light illuminates the contact point. The self-powered test light is dual purpose piece of test equipment. It can be used to test for either open or short circuits when power is isolated from the circuit (continuity test). A powered test light should not be used on any computer controlled system or component unless specifically instructed to do so. Many engine sensors can be destroyed by even this small amount of voltage applied directly to the terminals.

Open Circuit Testing

To use the self-powered test light to check for open circuits, first isolate the circuit from the vehicle's 12 volt power source by disconnecting the battery or wiring harness connector. Connect the test light ground clip to a good ground and probe sections of the circuit sequentially with the test light. (start from either end of the circuit). If the light is out, the open is between the probe and the circuit ground. If the light is on, the open is between the probe and end of the circuit toward the power source.

Short Circuit Testing

By isolating the circuit both from power and from ground, and using a self-powered test light, you can check for shorts to ground in the circuit. Isolate the circuit from power and ground. Connect the test light ground clip to a good ground and probe any easy-to-reach test point in the circuit. If the light comes on, there is a short somewhere in the circuit. To isolate the short, probe a test point at either end of the isolated circuit (the light should be on). Leave the test light probe connected and open connectors, switches, remove parts, etc., sequentially, until the light goes out. When the light goes out, the short is between the last circuit component opened and the previous circuit opened.

NOTE: *The 1.5 volt battery in the test light does not provide much current. A weak battery may not provide enough power to illuminate the test light even when a complete circuit is made (especially if there are high resistances in the circuit). Always make sure that the test battery is strong. To check the battery, briefly touch the ground clip to the probe; if the light glows brightly the battery is strong enough for testing. Never use a self-powered test light to perform checks for opens or shorts when power is applied to the electrical system under test. The 12 volt vehicle power will quickly burn out the 1.5 volt light bulb in the test light.*

Voltmeter

A voltmeter is used to measure voltage at any point in a circuit, or to measure the voltage drop across any part of a circuit. It can also be used to check continuity in a wire or circuit by indicating current flow from one end to the other. Voltmeters usually have various scales on the meter dial and a selector switch to allow the selection of different voltages. The voltmeter has a positive and a negative lead. To avoid damage to the meter, always connect the negative lead to the negative (–) side of circuit (to ground or nearest the ground side of the circuit) and connect the positive lead to the positive (+) side of the circuit (to the power source or the nearest power source). Note that the negative voltmeter lead will always be black and that the positive voltmeter will always be some color other than black (usually red). Depending on how the voltmeter is connected into the circuit, it has several uses.

A voltmeter can be connected either in parallel or in series with a circuit and it has a very high resistance to current flow. When connected in parallel, only a small amount of current will flow through the voltmeter current path; the rest will flow through the normal circuit current path and the circuit will work normally. When the voltmeter is connected in series with a circuit, only a small amount of current can flow through the circuit. The circuit will not work properly, but the voltmeter reading will show if the circuit is complete or not.

Available Voltage Measurement

Set the voltmeter selector switch to the 20V position and connect the meter negative lead to the negative post of the battery. Connect the positive meter lead to the positive post of the battery and turn the ignition switch ON to provide a load. Read the voltage on the meter or digital display. A well charged battery should register over 12 volts. If the meter reads below 11.5 volts, the battery power may be insufficient to operate the electrical system properly. This test determines voltage available from the battery and should be the first step in any electrical trouble diagnosis procedure. Many electrical problems, especially on computer controlled systems, can be caused by a low state of charge in the battery. Excessive corrosion at the battery cable terminals can cause a poor contact that will prevent proper charging and full battery current flow.

Normal battery voltage is 12 volts when fully charged. When the battery is supplying current to one or more circuits it is said to be "under load". When everything is off the electrical system is under a "no-load" condition. A fully charged battery may show about 12.5 volts at no load; will drop to 12 volts under medium load; and will drop even lower under heavy load. If the battery is partially discharged the voltage decrease under heavy load may be excessive, even though the battery shows 12 volts or more at no load. When allowed to discharge further, the battery's available voltage under load will decrease more severely. For this reason, it is important that the battery be fully charged during all testing procedures to avoid errors in diagnosis and incorrect test results.

Voltage Drop

When current flows through a resistance, the voltage beyond the resistance is reduced (the larger the current, the greater the reduction in voltage). When no current is flowing, there is no voltage drop because there is no current flow. All points in the circuit which are connected to the power source are at the same voltage as the power source. The total voltage drop always equals the total source voltage. In a long circuit with many connectors, a series of small, unwanted voltage drops due to corrosion at the connectors can add up to a total loss of voltage which impairs the operation of the normal loads in the circuit.

INDIRECT COMPUTATION OF VOLTAGE DROPS

1. Set the voltmeter selector switch to the 20 volt position.

2. Connect the meter negative lead to a good ground.

3. Probe all resistances in the circuit with the positive meter lead.

4. Operate the circuit in all modes and observe the voltage readings.

DIRECT MEASUREMENT OF VOLTAGE DROPS

1. Set the voltmeter switch to the 20 volt position.

2. Connect the voltmeter negative lead to the ground side of the resistance load to be measured.

3. Connect the positive lead to the positive side of the resistance or load to be measured.

4. Read the voltage drop directly on the 20 volt scale.

Too high a voltage indicates too high a resistance. If, for example, a blower motor runs too slowly, you can determine if there is too high a resistance in the resistor pack. By taking voltage drop readings in all parts of the circuit, you can isolate the problem. Too low a voltage drop indicates too low a resistance. If, for example, a blower motor runs too fast in the MED and/or LOW position, the problem can be isolated in the resistor pack by taking voltage drop readings in all parts of the circuit to locate a possibly shorted resistor. The maximum allowable voltage drop under load is critical, especially if there is more than one high resistance problem in a circuit because all voltage drops are cumulative. A small drop is normal due to the resistance of the conductors.

HIGH RESISTANCE TESTING

1. Set the voltmeter selector switch to the 4 volt position.

2. Connect the voltmeter positive lead to the positive post of the battery.

3. Turn on the headlights and heater blower to provide a load.

4. Probe various points in the circuit with the negative voltmeter lead.

5. Read the voltage drop on the 4 volt scale. Some average maximum allowable voltage drops are:

FUSE PANEL – 7 volts
IGNITION SWITCH – 5 volts
HEADLIGHT SWITCH – 7 volts
IGNITION COIL (+) – 5 volts
ANY OTHER LOAD – 1.3 volts

NOTE: *Voltage drops are all measured while a load is operating; without current flow, there will be no voltage drop.*

Ohmmeter

The ohmmeter is designed to read resistance (ohms) in a circuit or component. Although there are several different styles of ohmmeters, all will usually have a selector switch which permits the measurement of different ranges of resistance (usually the selector switch allows the multiplication of the meter reading by 10, 100, 1000, and 10,000). A calibration knob allows the meter to be set at zero for accurate measurement. Since all ohmmeters are powered by an internal battery (usually 9 volts), the ohmmeter can be used as a self-powered test light. When the ohmmeter is connected, current from the ohmmeter flows through the circuit or component being tested. Since the ohmmeter's internal resistance and voltage are known values, the amount of current flow through the meter depends on the resistance of the circuit or component being tested.

The ohmmeter can be used to perform continuity test for opens or shorts (either by observation of the meter needle or as a self-powered test light), and to read actual resistance in a circuit. It should be noted that the ohmmeter is used to check the resistance of a component or wire while there is no voltage applied to the circuit. Current flow from an outside voltage source (such as the vehicle battery) can damage the ohmmeter, so the circuit or component should be isolated from the vehicle electrical system before any testing is done. Since the ohmmeter uses its own voltage source, either lead can be connected to any test point.

NOTE: *When checking diodes or other solid state components, the ohmmeter leads can only be connected one way in order to measure current flow in a single direction. Make sure the positive (+) and negative (–) terminal connections are as described in the test procedures to verify the one-way diode operation.*

In using the meter for making continuity checks, do not be concerned with the actual resistance readings. Zero resistance, or any resistance readings, indicate continuity in the circuit. Infinite resistance indicates an open in the circuit. A high resistance reading where there should be none indicates a problem in the circuit. Checks for short circuits are made in the same manner as checks for open circuits except that the circuit must be isolated from both power and normal ground. Infinite resistance indicates no continuity to ground, while zero resistance indicates a dead short to ground.

RESISTANCE MEASUREMENT

The batteries in an ohmmeter will weaken with age and temperature, so the ohmmeter must be calibrated or "zeroed" before taking measurements. To zero the meter, place the selector switch in its lowest range and touch the two ohmmeter leads together. Turn the calibration knob until the meter needle is exactly on zero.

NOTE: *All analog (needle) type ohmmeters must be zeroed before use, but some digital ohmmeter models are automatically calibrated when the switch is turned on. Self-calibrating digital ohmmeters do not have an adjusting knob, but its a good idea to check for a zero readout before use by touching the leads together. All computer controlled systems require the use of a digital ohmmeter with at least 10 megohms impedance for testing. Before any test procedures are attempted, make sure the ohmmeter used is compatible with the electrical system or damage to the on-board computer could result.*

To measure resistance, first isolate the circuit from the vehicle power source by disconnecting the battery cables or the harness connector. Make sure the key is OFF when disconnecting any components or the battery. Where necessary, also isolate at least one side of the circuit to be checked to avoid reading parallel resistances. Parallel circuit resistances will always give a lower reading than the actual resistance of either of the branches. When measuring the resistance of parallel circuits, the total resistance will always be lower than the smallest resistance in the circuit. Connect the meter leads to both sides of the circuit (wire or component) and read the actual measured ohms on the meter scale. Make sure the selector switch is set to the proper ohm scale for the circuit being tested to avoid misreading the ohmmeter test value.

CAUTION: *Never use an ohmmeter with power applied to the circuit. Like the self-powered test light, the ohmmeter is designed to operate on its own power supply. The normal 12 volt automotive electrical system current could damage the meter.*

Ammeters

An ammeter measures the amount of current flowing through a circuit in units called amperes or amps. Amperes are units of electron flow which indicate how fast the electrons are flowing through the circuit. Since Ohms Law dictates that current flow in a circuit is equal to the circuit voltage divided by the total circuit resistance, increasing voltage also increases the current level (amps). Likewise, any decrease in resistance will increase the amount of amps in a circuit. At normal operating voltage, most circuits have a characteristic amount of amperes, called "current draw" which can be measured using an ammeter. By referring to a specified current draw rating, measuring the amperes, and comparing the two values, one can determine what is happening within the circuit to aid in diagnosis. An open circuit, for example, will not allow any current to flow so the ammeter reading will be zero. More current flows through a heavily loaded circuit or when the charging system is operating.

An ammeter is always connected in series with the circuit being tested. All of the current that normally flows through the circuit must also flow through the ammeter; if there is any other path for the current to follow, the ammeter reading will not be accurate. The ammeter itself has very little resistance to current flow and therefore will not affect the circuit, but it will measure current draw only when the circuit is closed and electricity is flowing. Excessive current draw can blow fuses and drain the battery, while a reduced current draw can cause motors to run slowly, lights to dim and other components to not operate properly. The ammeter can help diagnose these conditions by locating the cause of the high or low reading.

Multimeters

Different combinations of test meters can be built into a single unit designed for specific tests. Some of the more common combination test devices are known as Volt/Amp testers, Tach/Dwell meters, or Digital Multimeters. The Volt/Amp tester is used for charging system, starting system or battery tests and consists of a voltmeter, an ammeter and a variable resistance carbon pile. The voltmeter will usually have at least two ranges for use with 6, 12 and 24 volt systems. The ammeter also has more than one range for testing various levels of battery loads and starter current draw and the carbon pile can be adjusted to offer different amounts of resistance. The Volt/Amp tester has heavy leads to carry large amounts of current and many later models have an inductive ammeter pickup that clamps around the wire to simplify test connections. On some models, the ammeter also has a zero-center scale to allow testing of charging and starting systems without switching leads or polarity. A digital multimeter is a voltmeter, ammeter and ohmmeter combined in an instrument which gives a digital readout. These are often used when testing solid state circuits because of their high input impedance (usually 10 megohms or more).

The tach/dwell meter combines a tachometer and a dwell (cam angle) meter and is a specialized kind of voltmeter. The tachometer scale is marked to show engine speed in rpm and the dwell scale is marked to show degrees of distributor shaft rotation. In most electronic ignition systems, dwell is determined by the control unit, but the dwell meter can also be used to check the duty cycle (operation) of some electronic engine control systems. Some tach/dwell meters are powered by an internal battery, while others take their power from the car battery in use. The battery powered testers usually require calibration much like an ohmmeter before testing.

Special Test Equipment

A variety of diagnostic tools are available to help troubleshoot and repair computerized engine control systems. The most sophisticated of these devices are the console type engine analyzers that usually occupy a garage service bay, but there are several types of aftermarket electronic testers available that will allow quick circuit tests of the engine control system by plugging directly into a special connector located in the engine compartment or under the dashboard. Several tool and equipment manufacturers offer simple, hand held testers that measure various circuit voltage levels on command to check all system components for proper operation. Although these testers usually cost about $300–500, consider that the average computer control unit (or ECM) can cost just as much and the money saved by not replacing perfectly good sensors or components in an attempt to correct a problem could justify the purchase price of a special diagnostic tester the first time it's used.

These computerized testers can allow quick and easy test measurements while the engine is operating or while the car is being driven. In addition, the on-board computer memory can be read to access any stored trouble codes; in effect allowing the computer to tell you where it hurts and aid trouble diagnosis by pinpointing exactly which circuit or component is malfunctioning. In the same manner, repairs can be tested to make sure the problem has been corrected. The biggest advantage these special testers have is their relatively easy hookups that minimize or eliminate the chances of making the wrong connections and getting false voltage readings or damaging the computer accidentally.

NOTE: *It should be remembered that these testers check voltage levels in circuits; they don't detect mechanical problems or failed components if the circuit voltage falls within the preprogrammed limits stored in the tester PROM unit. Also, most of the hand held testers are designed to work only on one or two systems made by a specific manufacturer.*

A variety of aftermarket testers are available to help diagnose different computerized control systems. Owatonna Tool Company (OTC), for example, markets a device called the OTC Monitor which plugs directly into the assembly line diagnostic link (ALDL). The OTC tester makes diagnosis a simple matter of pressing the correct buttons and, by changing the internal PROM or inserting a different diagnosis cartridge, it will work on any model from full size to subcompact, over a wide range of years. An adapter is supplied with the tester to allow connection to all types of ALDL links, regardless of the number of pin terminals used. By inserting an updated PROM into the OTC tester, it can be easily updated to diagnose any new modifications of computerized control systems.

Wiring Harnesses

The average automobile contains about 1/2 mile of wiring, with hundreds of individual connections. To protect the many wires from damage and to keep them from becoming a confusing tangle, they are organized into bundles, enclosed in plastic or taped together and called wire harnesses. Different wiring harnesses serve different parts of the vehicle. Individual wires are color coded to help trace them through a harness where sections are hidden from view.

A loose or corroded connection or a replacement wire that is too small for the circuit will add extra resistance and an additional voltage drop to the circuit. A ten percent voltage drop can result in slow or erratic motor operation, for example, even though the circuit is complete. Automotive wiring or circuit conductors can be in any one of three forms:

1. Single strand wire
2. Multi-strand wire
3. Printed circuitry

Single strand wire has a solid metal core and is usually used inside such components as alternators, motors, relays and other devices. Multi-strand wire has a core made of many small strands of wire twisted together into a single conductor. Most of the wiring in an automotive electrical system is made up of multi-strand wire, either as a single conductor or grouped together in a harness. All wiring is color coded on the insulator, either as a solid color or as a colored wire with an identification stripe. A printed circuit is a thin film of copper or other conductor that is printed on an insulator backing. Occasionally, a printed circuit is sandwiched between two sheets of plastic for more protection and flexibility. A complete printed circuit, consisting of conductors, insulating material and connectors for lamps or other components is called a printed circuit board. Printed circuitry is used in place of individual wires or harnesses in places where space is limited, such as behind instrument panels.

Wire Gauge

Since computer controlled automotive electrical systems are very sensitive to changes in resistance, the selection of properly sized wires is critical when systems are repaired. The wire gauge number is an expression of the cross section area of the conductor. The most common system for expressing wire size is the American Wire Gauge (AWG) system.

Wire cross section area is measured in circular mils. A mil is $^{1}/_{1000}$ in. (0.001 in.); a circular mil is the area of a circle one mil in diameter. For example, a conductor $^{1}/_{4}$ in. in diameter is 0.250 in. or 250 mils. The circular mil cross section area of the wire is 250 squared (250^2)or 62,500 circular mils. Imported car models usually use metric wire gauge designations, which is simply the cross section area of the conductor in square millimeters (mm^2).

Gauge numbers are assigned to conductors of various cross section areas. As gauge number increases, area decreases and the conductor becomes smaller. A 5 gauge conductor is smaller than a 1 gauge conductor and a 10 gauge is smaller than a 5 gauge. As the cross section area of a conductor decreases, resistance increases and so does the gauge number. A conductor with a higher gauge number will carry less current than a conductor with a lower gauge number.

NOTE: *Gauge wire size refers to the size of the conductor, not the size of the complete wire. It is possible to have two wires of the same gauge with different diameters because one may have thicker insulation than the other.*

12 volt automotive electrical systems generally use 10, 12, 14, 16 and 18 gauge wire. Main power distribution circuits and larger accessories usually use 10 and 12 gauge wire. Battery cables are usually 4 or 6 gauge, although 1 and 2 gauge wires are occasionally used. Wire length must also be considered when making repairs to a circuit. As conductor length increases, so does resistance. An 18 gauge wire, for example, can carry a 10 amp load for 10 feet without excessive voltage drop; however if a 15 foot wire is required for the same 10 amp load, it must be a 16 gauge wire.

An electrical schematic shows the electrical current paths when a circuit is operating properly. It is essential to understand how a circuit works before trying to figure out why it doesn't. Schematics break the entire electrical system down into individual circuits and show only one particular circuit. In a schematic, no attempt is made to represent wiring and components as they physically appear on the vehicle; switches and other components are shown as simply as possible. Face views of harness connectors show the cavity or terminal locations in all multi-pin connectors to help locate test points.

If you need to backprobe a connector while it is on the component, the order of the terminals must be mentally reversed. The wire color code can help in this situation, as well as a keyway, lock tab or other reference mark.

NOTE: *Wiring diagrams are not included in this book. As trucks have become more complex and available with longer option lists, wiring diagrams have grown in size and complexity. It has become almost impossible to provide a readable reproduction of a wiring diagram in a book this size. Information on ordering wiring diagrams from the vehicle manufacturer can be found in the owner's manual.*

WIRING REPAIR

Soldering is a quick, efficient method of joining metals permanently. Everyone who has the occasion to make wiring repairs should know how to solder. Electrical connections that are soldered are far less likely to come apart and will conduct electricity much better than connections that are only "pig-tailed" together. The most popular (and preferred) method of soldering is with an electrical soldering gun. Soldering irons are available in many sizes and wattage ratings. Irons with higher wattage ratings deliver higher temperatures and recover lost heat faster. A small soldering iron rated for no more than 50 watts is recommended, especially on electrical systems where excess heat can damage the components being soldered.

There are three ingredients necessary for successful soldering; proper flux, good solder and sufficient heat. A soldering flux is necessary to clean the metal of tarnish, prepare it for soldering and to enable the solder to spread into tiny crevices. When soldering, always use a resin flux or resin core solder which is non-corrosive and will not attract moisture once the job is finished. Other types of flux (acid core) will leave a residue that will attract moisture and cause the wires to corrode. Tin is a unique metal with a low melting point. In a molten state, it dissolves and alloys easily with many metals. Solder is made by mixing tin with lead. The most common proportions are 40/60, 50/50 and 60/40, with the percentage of tin listed first. Low priced solders usually contain less tin, making them very difficult for a beginner to use because more heat is required to melt the solder. A common solder is 40/60 which is well suited for all-around general use, but 60/40 melts easier, has more tin for a better joint and is preferred for electrical work.

Soldering Techniques

Successful soldering requires that the metals to be joined be heated to a temperature that will melt the solder—usually 360–460°F (182–238°C). Contrary to popular belief, the purpose of the soldering iron is not to melt the solder itself, but to heat the parts being soldered to a temperature high enough to melt the solder when it is touched to the work. Melting flux-cored solder on the soldering iron will usually destroy the effectiveness of the flux.

NOTE: *Soldering tips are made of copper for good heat conductivity, but must be "tinned" regularly for quick transference of heat to the project and to prevent the solder from sticking to the iron. To "tin" the iron, simply heat it and touch the flux-cored solder to the tip; the solder will flow over the hot tip. Wipe the excess off with a clean rag, but be careful as the iron will be hot.*

After some use, the tip may become pitted. If so, simply dress the tip smooth with a smooth file and "tin" the tip again. An old saying holds that "metals well cleaned are half soldered." Flux-cored solder will remove oxides but rust, bits of insulation and oil or grease must be removed with a wire brush or emery cloth. For maximum strength in soldered parts, the joint must start off clean and tight. Weak joints will result in gaps too wide for the solder to bridge.

If a separate soldering flux is used, it should be brushed or swabbed on only those areas that are to be soldered. Most solders contain a core of flux and separate fluxing is unnecessary. Hold the work to be soldered firmly. It is best to solder on a wooden board, because a metal vise will only rob the piece to be soldered of heat and make it difficult to melt the solder. Hold the soldering tip with the broadest face against the work to be soldered. Apply solder under the tip close to the work, using enough solder to give a heavy film between the iron and the piece being soldered, while moving slowly and making sure the solder melts properly. Keep the work level or the solder will run to the lowest part and favor the thicker parts, because these require more heat to melt the solder. If the soldering tip overheats (the solder coating on the face of the tip burns up), it should be retinned. Once the soldering is completed, let the soldered joint stand until cool. Tape and seal all soldered wire splices after the repair has cooled.

Wire Harness and Connectors

The on-board computer (ECM) wire harness electrically connects the control unit to the various solenoids, switches and sensors used by the control system. Most connectors in the engine compartment or otherwise exposed to the elements are protected against moisture and dirt which could create oxidation and deposits on the terminals. This protection is important because of the very low voltage and current levels used by the computer and sensors. All connectors have a lock which secures the male and female terminals together, with a secondary lock holding the seal and terminal into the connector. Both terminal locks must be released when disconnecting ECM connectors.

These special connectors are weather-proof and all repairs require the use of a special terminal and the tool required to service it. This tool is used to remove the pin and sleeve terminals. If removal is attempted with an ordinary pick, there is a good chance that the terminal will be bent or deformed. Unlike standard blade type terminals, these terminals cannot be straightened once they are bent. Make certain that the connectors are properly seated and all of the sealing rings in place when connecting leads. On some models, a hinge-type flap provides a backup or secondary locking feature for the terminals. Most secondary locks are used to improve the connector reliability by retaining the terminals if the small terminal lock tangs are not positioned properly.

Molded-on connectors require complete replacement of the connection. This means splicing a new connector assembly into the harness. All splices in on-board computer systems should be soldered to insure proper contact. Use care when probing the connections or replacing terminals in them as it is possible to short between opposite terminals. If this happens to the wrong terminal pair, it is possible to damage certain components. Always use jumper wires between connectors for circuit checking and never probe through weatherproof seals.

Open circuits are often difficult to locate by sight because corrosion or terminal misalignment are hidden by the connectors. Merely wiggling a connector on a sensor or in the wiring harness may correct the open circuit condition. This should always be considered when an open circuit or a failed sensor is indicated. Intermittent problems may also be caused by oxidized or loose connections. When using a circuit tester for diagnosis, always probe connections from the wire side. Be careful not to damage sealed connectors with test probes.

All wiring harnesses should be replaced with identical parts, using the same gauge wire and connectors. When signal wires are spliced into a harness, use wire with high temperature insulation only. With the low voltage and current levels found in the system, it is important that the best possible connection at all wire splices be made by soldering the splices together. It is seldom necessary to replace a complete harness. If replacement is necessary, pay close attention to insure proper harness routing. Secure the harness with suitable plastic wire clamps to prevent vibrations from causing the harness to wear in spots or contact any hot components.

NOTE: *Weatherproof connectors cannot be replaced with standard connectors. Instructions are provided with replacement connector and terminal packages. Some wire harnesses have mounting indicators (usually pieces of colored tape) to mark where the harness is to be secured.*

In making wiring repairs, it's important that you always replace damaged wires with wires that are the same gauge as the wire being replaced. The heavier the wire, the smaller the gauge number. Wires are color-coded to aid in identification and whenever possible the same color coded wire should be used for replacement. A wire stripping and crimping tool is necessary to install solderless terminal connectors. Test all crimps by pulling on the wires; it should not be possible to pull the wires out of a good crimp.

Wires which are open, exposed or otherwise damaged are repaired by simple splicing. Where possible, if the wiring harness is accessible and the damaged place in the wire can be located, it is best to open the harness and check for all possible damage. In an inaccessible harness, the wire must be bypassed with a new insert, usually taped to the outside of the old harness.

When replacing fusible links, be sure to use fusible link wire, NOT ordinary automotive wire. Make sure the fusible segment is of the same gauge and construction as the one being replaced and double the stripped end when crimping the terminal connector for a good contact. The melted (open) fusible link segment of the wiring harness should be cut off as close to the harness as possible, then a new segment spliced in as described. In the case of a damaged fusible link that feeds two harness wires, the harness connections should be replaced with two fusible link wires so that each circuit will have its own separate protection.

NOTE: *Most of the problems caused in the wiring harness are due to bad ground connections. Always check all vehicle ground connections for corrosion or looseness before performing any power feed checks to eliminate the chance of a bad ground affecting the circuit.*

Repairing Hard Shell Connectors

Unlike molded connectors, the terminal contacts in hard shell connectors can be replaced. Weatherproof hard-shell connectors with the leads molded into the shell have non-replaceable terminal ends. Replacement usually involves the use of a special terminal removal tool that depress the locking tangs (barbs) on the connector terminal and allow the connector to be removed from the rear of the shell. The connector shell should be replaced if it shows any evidence of burning, melting, cracks, or breaks. Replace individual terminals that are burnt, corroded, distorted or loose.

NOTE: *The insulation crimp must be tight to prevent the insulation from sliding back on the wire when the wire is pulled. The insulation must be visibly compressed under the crimp tabs, and the ends of the crimp should be turned in for a firm grip on the insulation.*

The wire crimp must be made with all wire strands inside the crimp. The terminal must be fully compressed on the wire strands with the ends of the crimp tabs turned in to make a firm grip on the wire. Check all connections with an ohmmeter to insure a good contact. There should be no measurable resistance between the wire and the terminal when connected.

Mechanical Test Equipment

Vacuum Gauge

Most gauges are graduated in inches of mercury (in.Hg), although a device called a manometer reads vacuum in inches of water (in. H_2O). The normal vacuum reading usually varies between 18 and 22 in.Hg at sea level. To test engine vacuum, the vacuum gauge must be connected to a source of manifold vacuum. Many engines have a plug in the intake manifold which can be removed and replaced with an adapter fitting. Connect the vacuum gauge to the fitting with a suitable rubber hose or, if no manifold plug is available, connect the vacuum gauge to any device using manifold vacuum, such as EGR valves, etc. The vacuum gauge can be used to determine if enough vacuum is reaching a component to allow its actuation.

Hand Vacuum Pump

Small, hand-held vacuum pumps come in a variety of designs. Most have a built-in vacuum gauge and allow the component to be tested without removing it from the vehicle. Operate the pump lever or plunger to apply the correct amount of vacuum required for the test specified in the diagnosis routines. The level of vacuum in inches of Mercury (in.Hg) is indicated on the pump gauge. For some testing, an additional vacuum gauge may be necessary.

Intake manifold vacuum is used to operate various systems and devices on late model vehi-

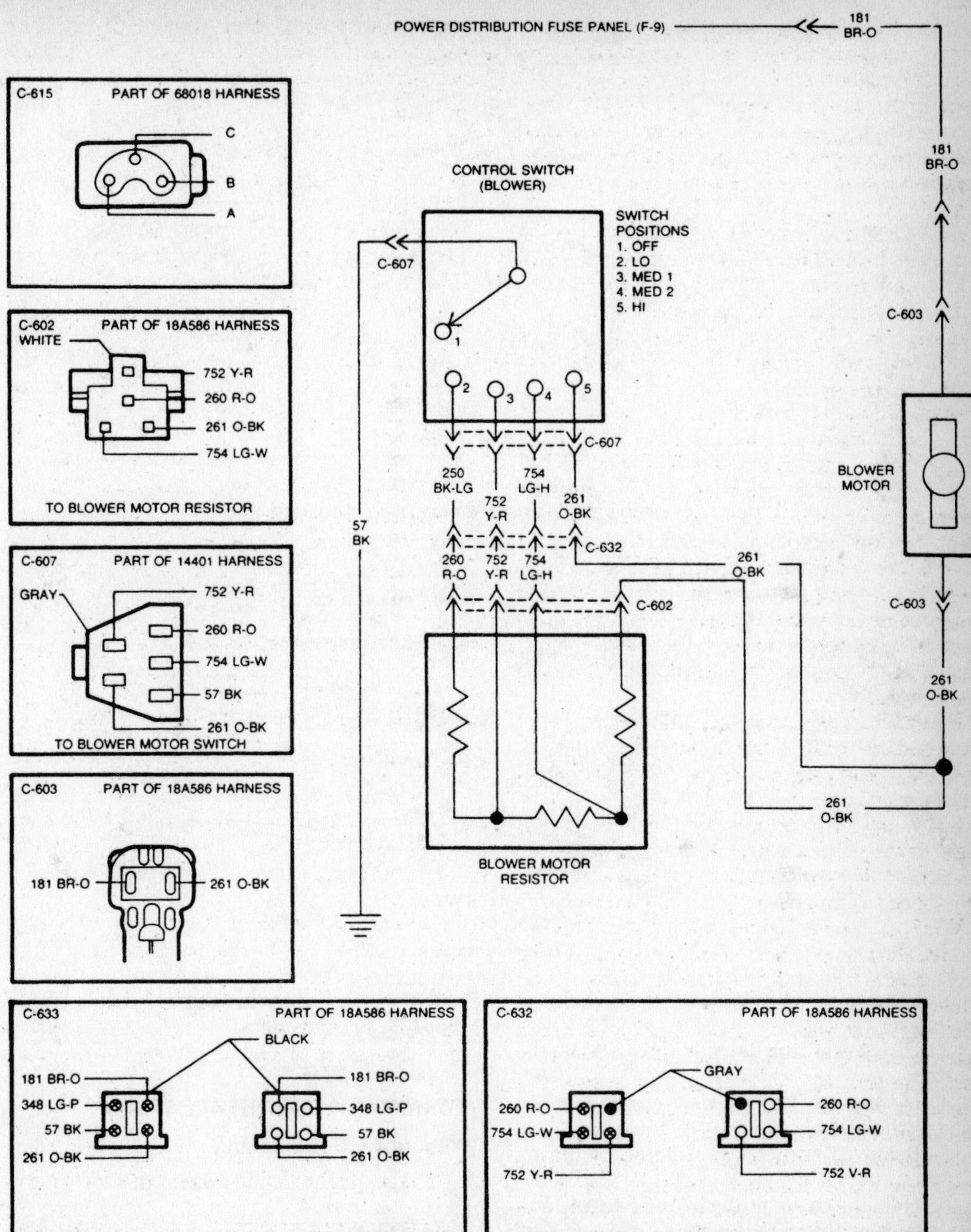

Heater electrical schematic

cles. To correctly diagnose and solve problems in vacuum control systems, a vacuum source is necessary for testing. In some cases, vacuum can be taken from the intake manifold when the engine is running, but vacuum is normally provided by a hand vacuum pump. These hand vacuum pumps have a built-in vacuum gauge that allow testing while the device is still attached to the component. For some tests, an additional vacuum gauge may be necessary.

HEATING AND AIR CONDITIONING

Blower

REMOVAL AND INSTALLATION

Without Air Conditioning

1. Disconnect the battery ground.
2. On trucks built for sale in California,

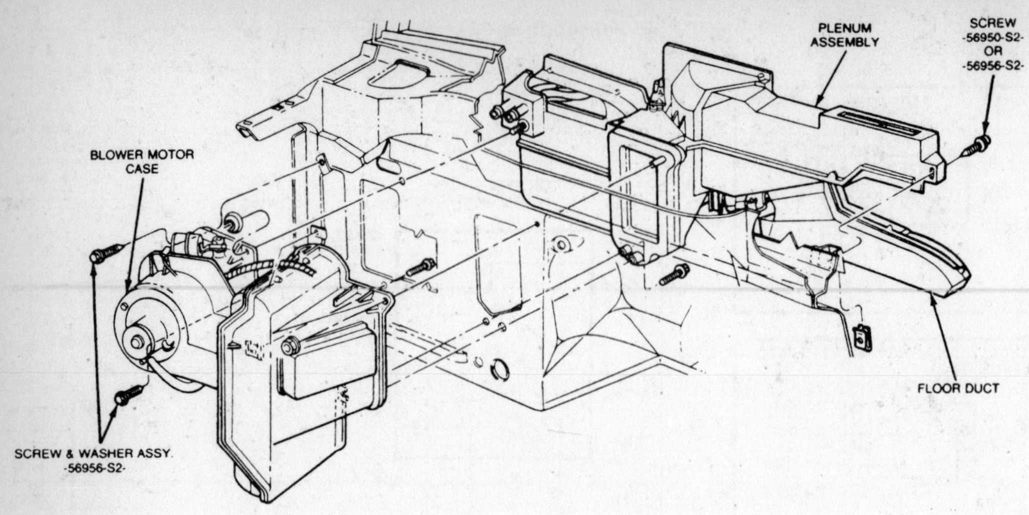

Heater assembly and plenum removal wo/air conditioning

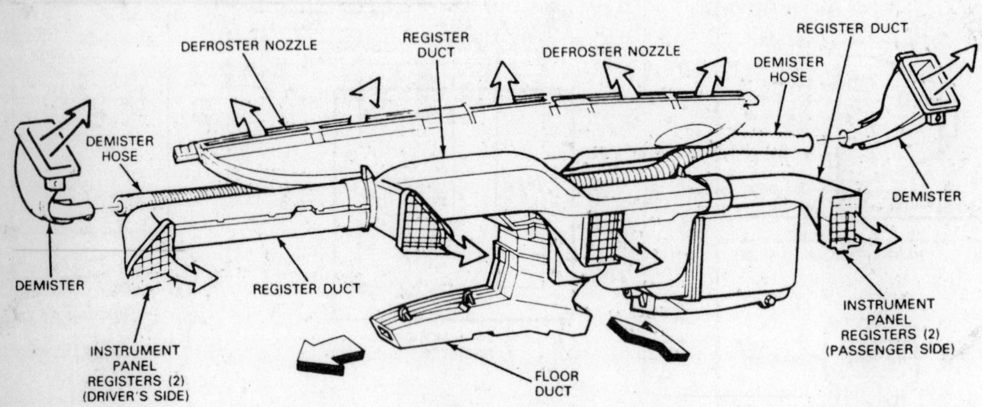

Heater/vent ducts

remove the emission module located in front of the blower.

3. Disconnect the wiring harness at the blower.

4. Disconnect the blower motor cooling tube at the blower.

5. Remove the 3 blower motor mounting screws.

6. Hold the cooling tube to one side and pull the blower motor from the housing.

7. Installation is the reverse of removal.

With Air Conditioning

1. Disconnect the blower motor wiring at the blower.

2. Disconnect the cooling tube at the blower.

3. Remove the 4 mounting screws and pull the motor from the housing.

4. Installation is the reverse of removal. Cement the cooling tube on the nipple at the housing using Liquid Butyl Sealer D9AZ–19554–A, or equivalent.

Heater Core

REMOVAL AND INSTALLATION

Without Air Conditioning

1. Drain the cooling system to a level below the heater core.

CAUTION: *When draining the coolant, keep in mind that cats and dogs are attracted by the ethylene glycol antifreeze, and are quite likely to drink any that is left in an uncovered container or in puddles on the ground. This will prove fatal in sufficient quantity. Always drain the coolant into a sealable container. Coolant should be reused unless it is contaminated or several years old.*

2. Disconnect the coolant hoses at the heater core tubes.

3. From inside the passenger compartment, remove the 7 screws that secure the heater core

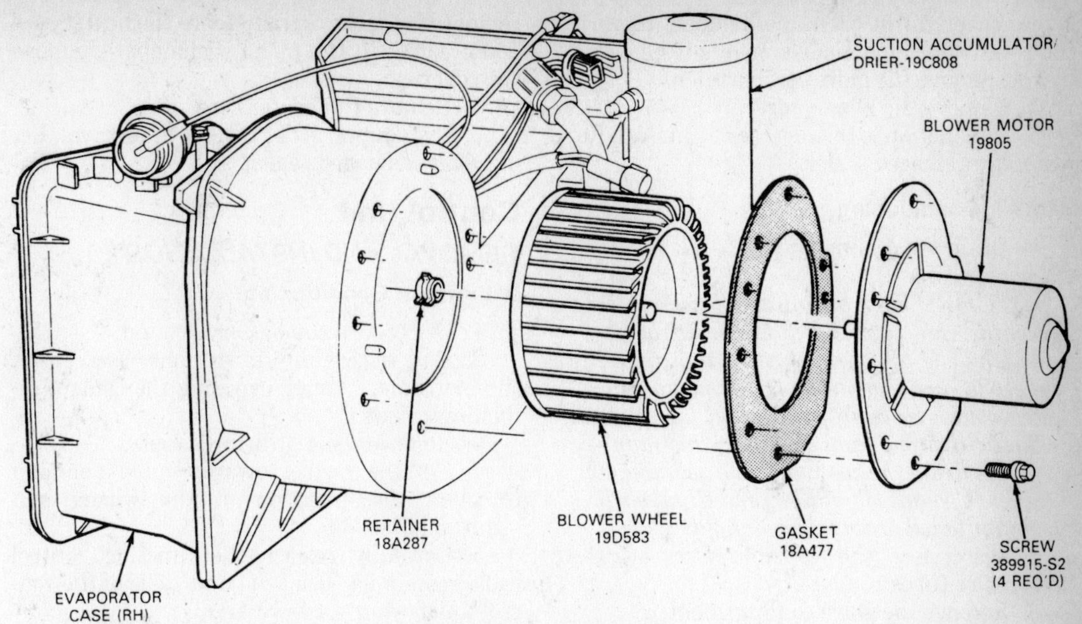

Blower motor and wheel disassembly

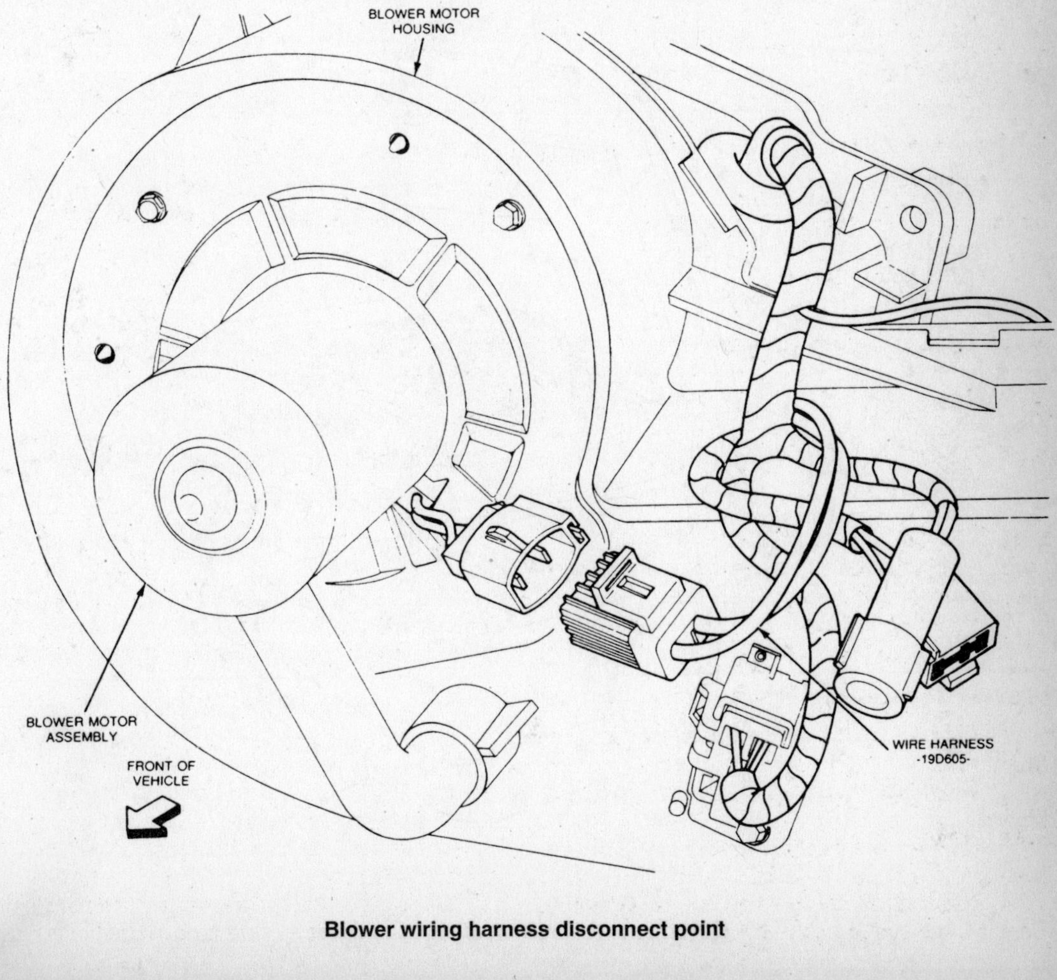

BLOWER MOTOR
HOUSING
BLOWER MOTOR
ASSEMBLY
FRONT OF
VEHICLE
WIRE HARNESS
-19D605-

Blower wiring harness disconnect point

access cover to the plenum chamber. Remove the cover. On some models, it might be easier to first remove the glove compartment.

4. Remove the heater core.

5. Installation is the reverse of removal. Replace any damaged sealer.

With Air Conditioning

1. Drain the cooling system to a level below the heater core.

CAUTION: *When draining the coolant, keep in mind that cats and dogs are attracted by the ethylene glycol antifreeze, and are quite likely to drink any that is left in an uncovered container or in puddles on the ground. This will prove fatal in sufficient quantity. Always drain the coolant into a sealable container. Coolant should be reused unless it is contaminated or several years old.*

2. Disconnect the coolant hoses at the heater core tubes.

3. Remove the glove compartment.

4. Disconnect the temperature and function cables.

5. From inside the passenger compartment, remove the 7 screws that secure the heater core access cover to the plenum chamber. Remove the cover.

6. Remove the heater core.

7. Installation is the reverse of removal. Replace any damaged sealer.

Control Unit

REMOVAL AND INSTALLATION

Without Air Conditioning

1. Disconnect the battery ground.

2. Pull the center finish panel away from the instrument panel, exposing the control attaching screws.

3. Remove the 4 attaching screws.

4. Pull the control towards you just enough to allow disconnection of the wiring and vacuum hoses.

5. Carefully release the function control cable snap-in flag from the underside of the control unit, using a screwdriver.

6. Pull enough cable through the instrument panel to allow the cable to be held vertical to the control unit.

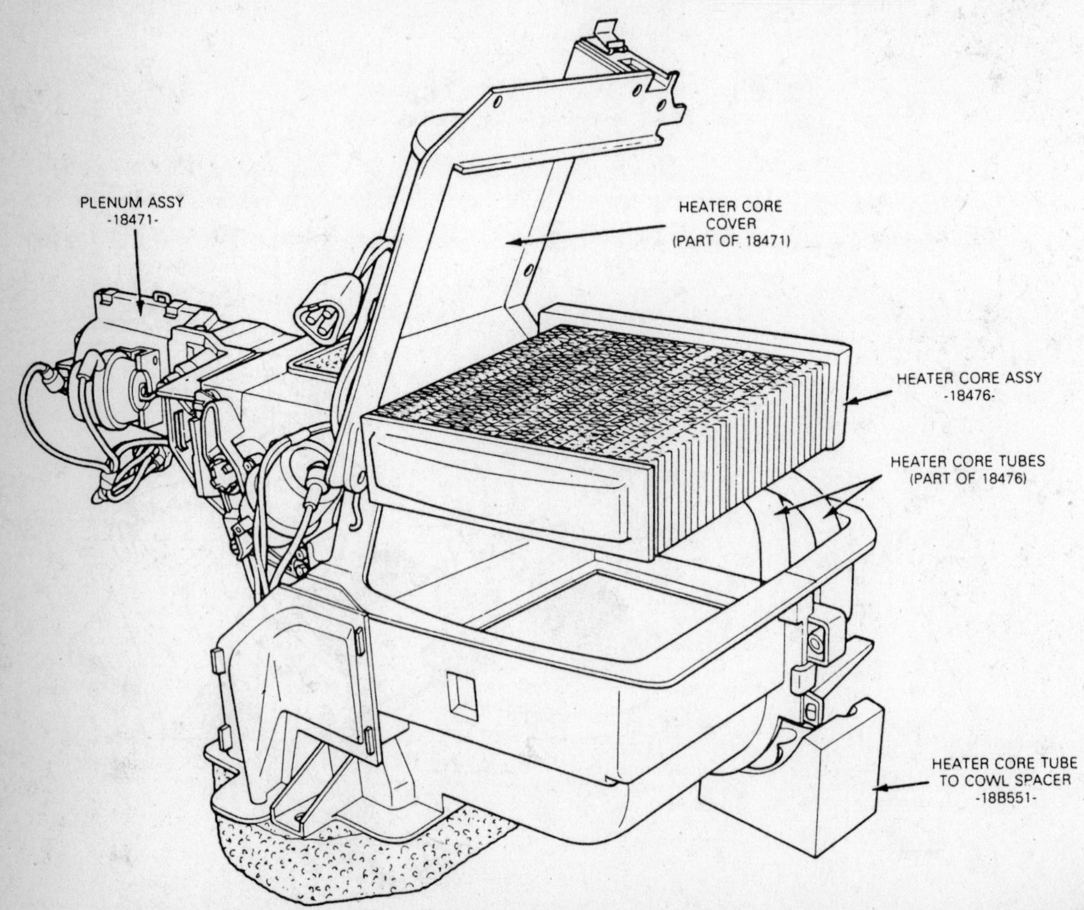

Heater core removal for 1989–90 models

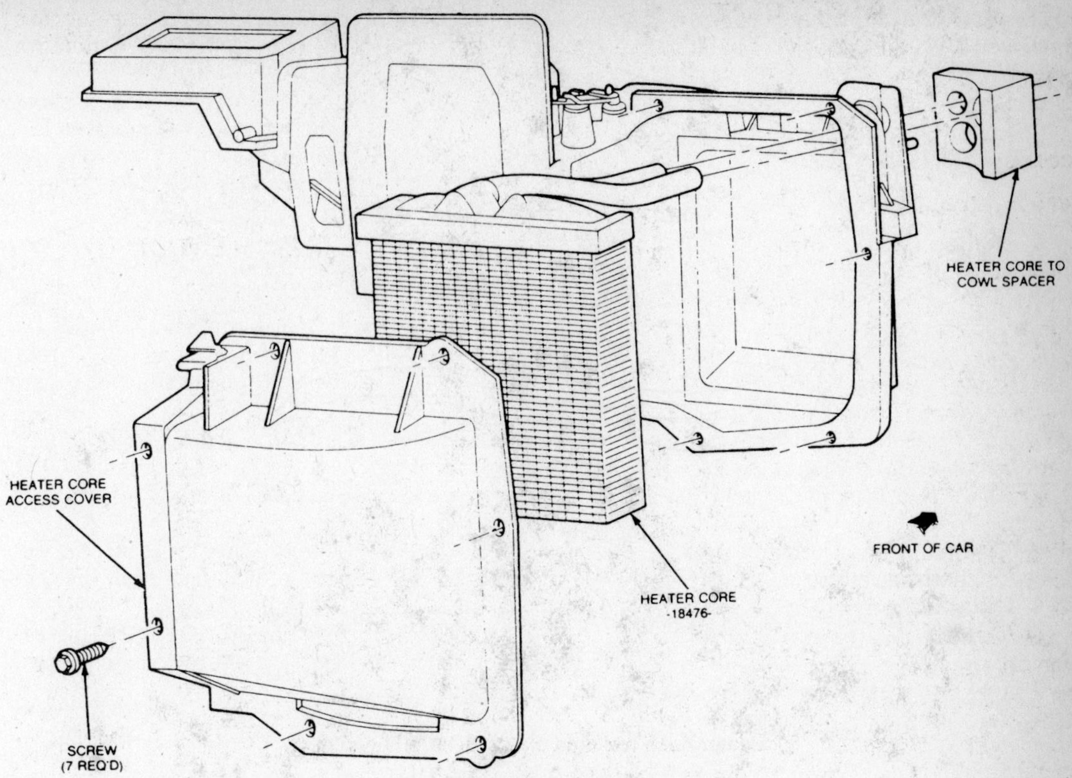

HEATER CORE TO
COWL SPACER
HEATER CORE
ACCESS COVER
FRONT OF CAR
HEATER CORE
-18476-
SCREW
(7 REQ'D)

Heater core removal for 1987–88 models

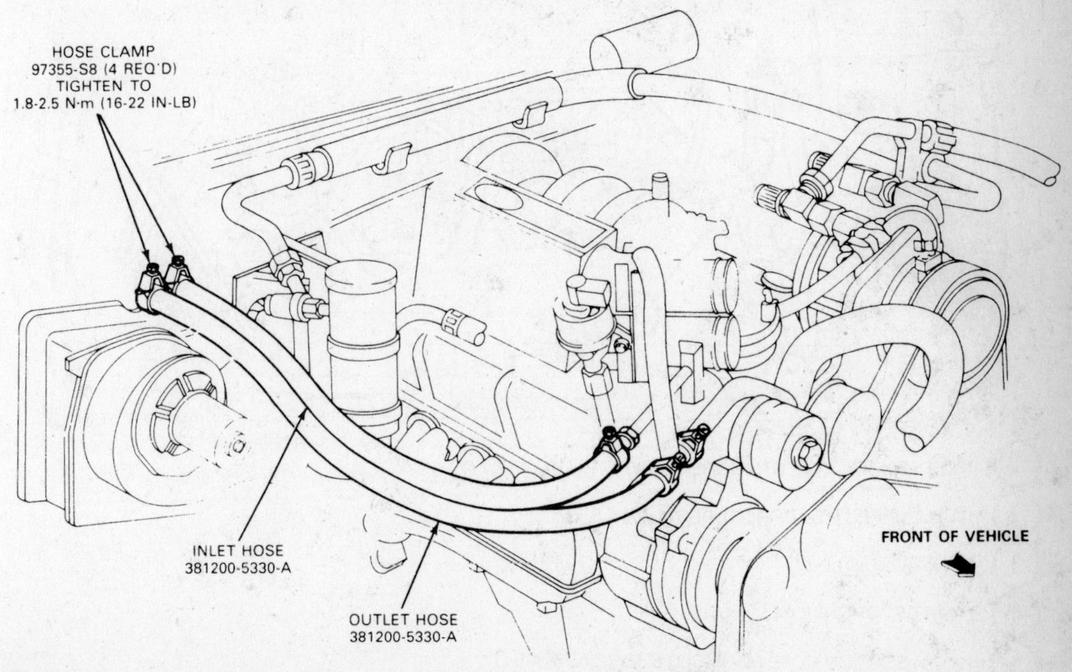

Heater hose routings on the 8-302 EFI engine

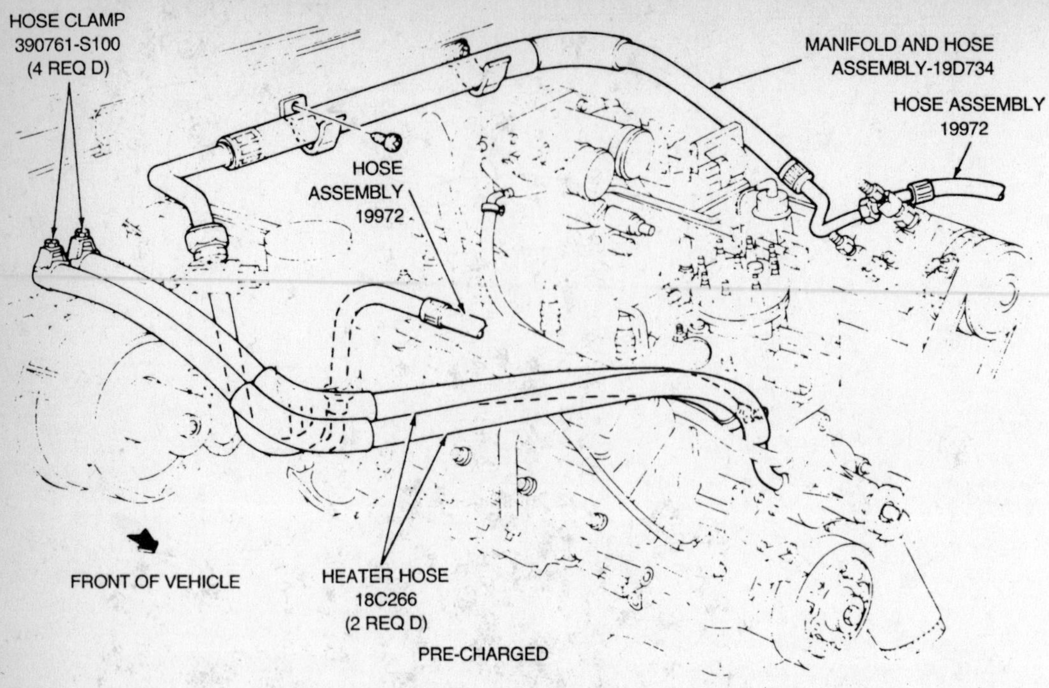

Heater hose routings on the 8-460 EFI engine

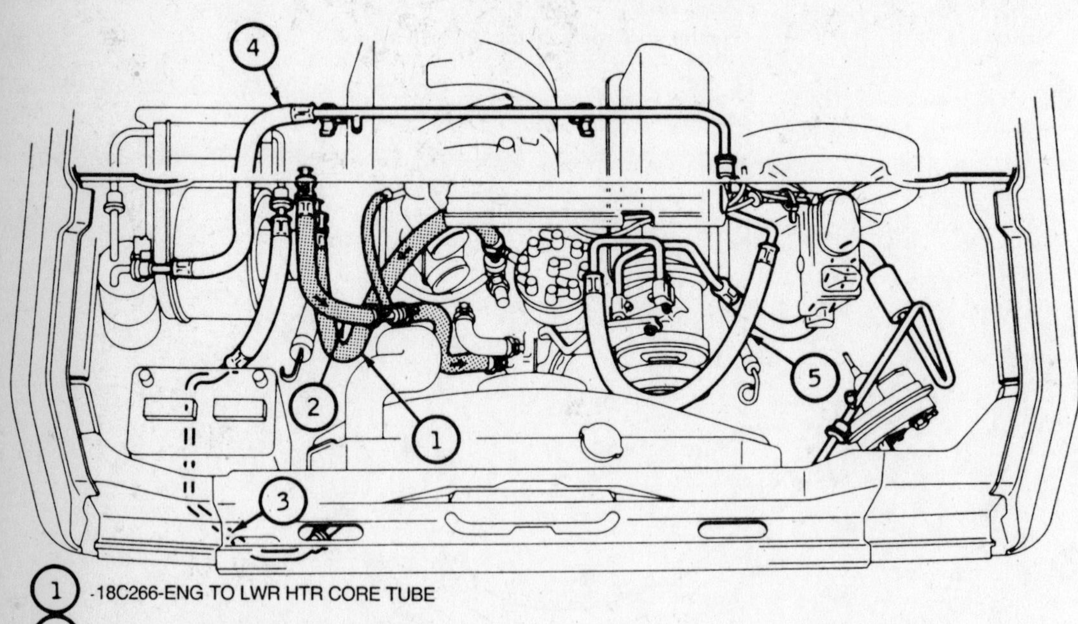

Heater hose routings on the 8-351 EFI engine

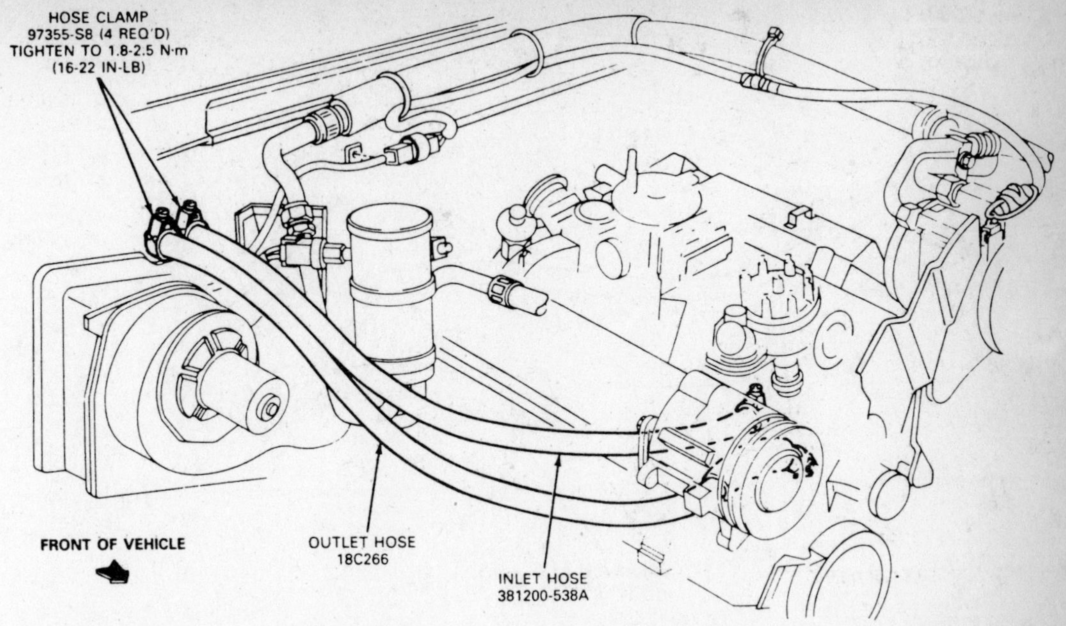

Heater hose routings on the 8-460 4-bbl engine

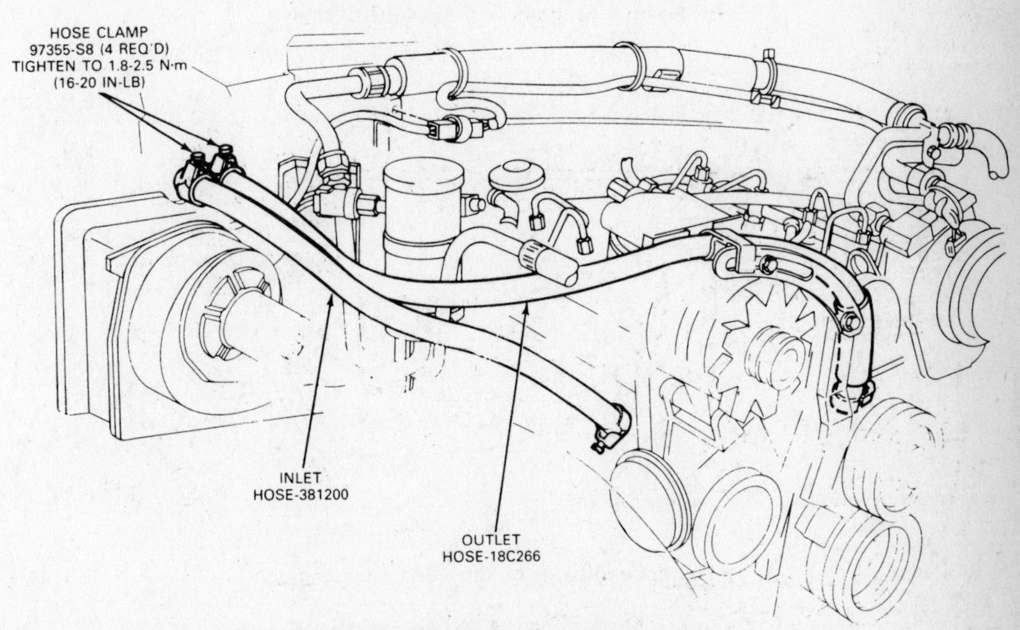

Heater hose routings on the diesel engine

7. Carefully release the temperature control cable snap-in flag from the topside of the control unit, using a screwdriver.
8. Rotate the control unit 90° and disconnect the temperature control cable from the temperature control lever.
9. Pull out the control unit.
10. Installation is the reverse of removal. Check the operation of the unit.

With Air Conditioning

1. Remove the instrument panel center finish panel.
2. Remove the control unit knobs by prying on the spring retainer while pulling out on the knob.
3. Remove the 4 control unit attaching screws.

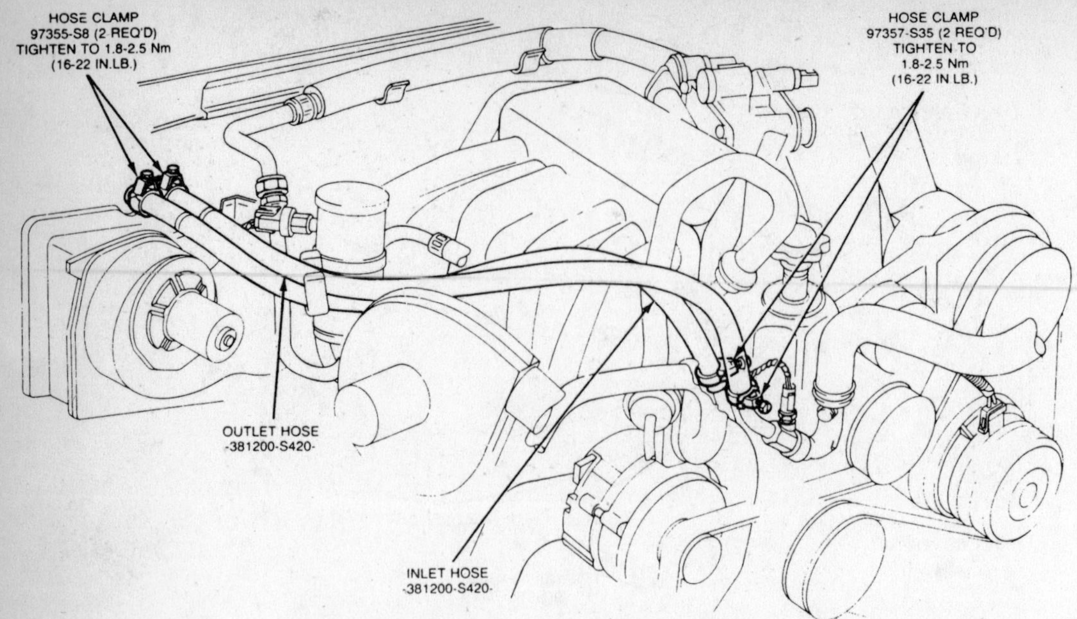

Heater hose routings on the 6-300 EFI engine

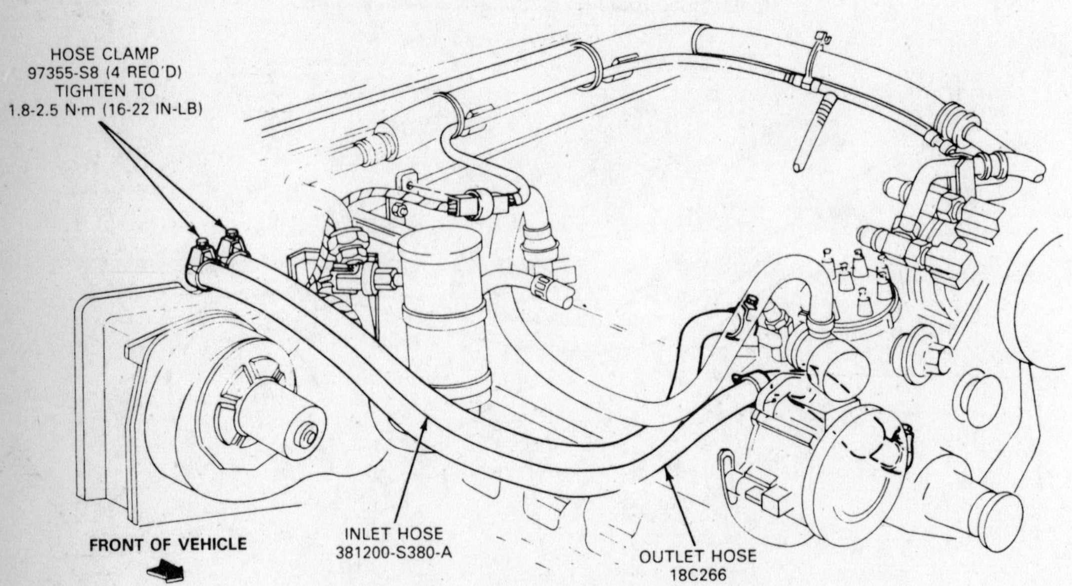

Heater hose routings on the 8-351 4-bbl engine

4. Disconnect the wiring and vacuum lines from the control unit.

5. Disengage the temperature cable by depressing the locking tabs on the connector.

6. Rotate the control unit 180° and disconnect the function cable from the control assembly. Remove the control assembly by compressing the locking tabs on the connector.

7. Installation is the reverse of removal. Check the operation of the unit.

Evaporator Core

REMOVAL AND INSTALLATION

1987–88

1. Discharge the refrigerant system. See Chapter 1.
2. Disconnect the wiring from the pressure switch on the side of the suction accumulator.
3. Remove the pressure switch.
4. Disconnect the suction hose from the suc-

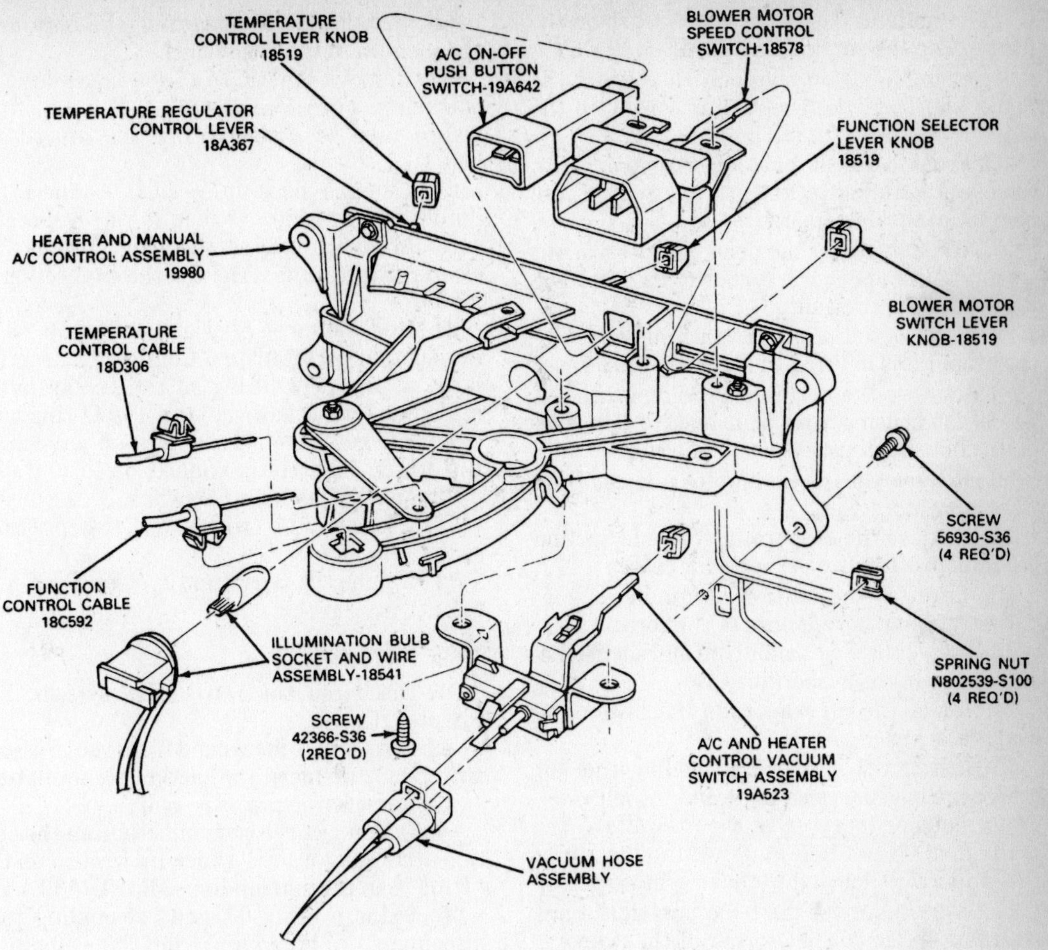

TEMPERATURE CONTROL LEVER KNOB 18519
A/C ON-OFF PUSH BUTTON SWITCH-19A642
BLOWER MOTOR SPEED CONTROL SWITCH-18578
TEMPERATURE REGULATOR CONTROL LEVER 18A367
FUNCTION SELECTOR LEVER KNOB 18519
HEATER AND MANUAL A/C CONTROL ASSEMBLY 19980
BLOWER MOTOR SWITCH LEVER KNOB-18519
TEMPERATURE CONTROL CABLE 18D306
SCREW 56930-S36 (4 REQ'D)
FUNCTION CONTROL CABLE 18C592
SPRING NUT N802539-S100 (4 REQ'D)
ILLUMINATION BULB SOCKET AND WIRE ASSEMBLY-18541
SCREW 42366-S36 (2REQ'D)
A/C AND HEATER CONTROL VACUUM SWITCH ASSEMBLY 19A523
VACUUM HOSE ASSEMBLY

Control unit disassembled

HEATER CONTROL ASSY -19980-
SCREW -56930-S36- (4 REQ'D)
BLOWER MOTOR CONTROL SWITCH -18578-
ILLUMINATION LIGHT WIRE ASSY. -18541-
FUNCTION CONTROL CABLE -18C592-
TEMPERATURE CONTROL CABLE -18D306-

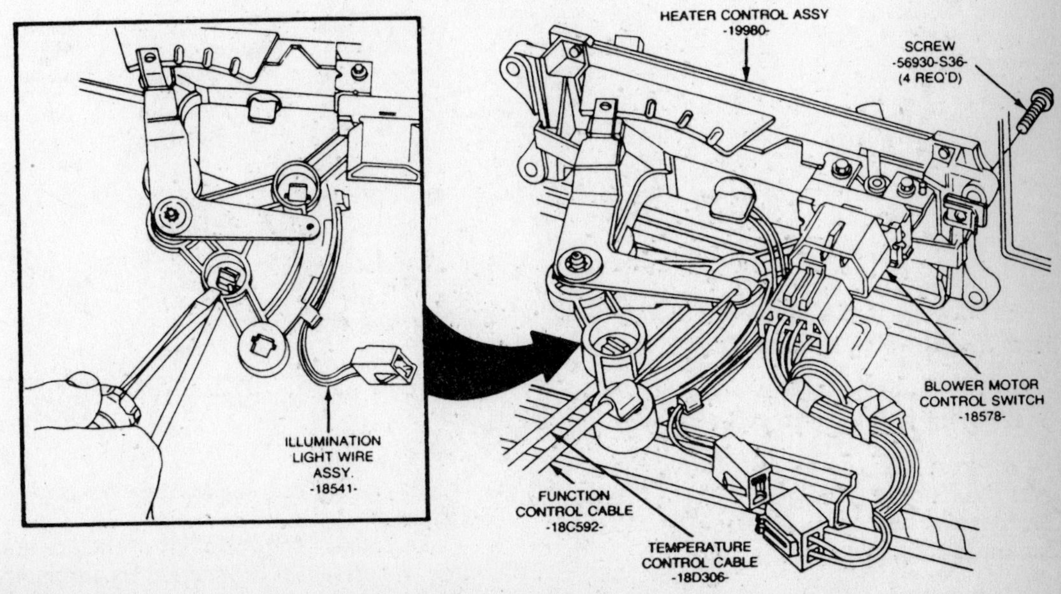

Control unit removal

tion accumulator. Use a back-up wrench on the fitting. Cap the suction line IMMEDIATELY!

5. Using a back-up wrench, disconnect the liquid line from the evaporator core. Cap the liquid line IMMEDIATELY!

6. From inside the passenger compartment, remove 1 screw attaching the bottom of the plenum to the dash panel.

7. Working under the hood, remove the nut retaining the upper left corner of the evaporator case to the firewall.

8. Remove the 6 screws attaching the left of the evaporator housing to the evaporator case.

9. Remove the spring clip holding the left side of the housing cover plate and the left evaporator housing together, at the firewall.

10. Remove the left evaporator housing from the evaporator case.

11. Remove the evaporator core and suction accumulator from the evaporator case.

12. Transfer the suction accumulator support straps and spring nuts to the core.

13. Install the evaporator core and suction accumulator in the evaporator case.

14. Install the left evaporator housing on the evaporator case.

15. Install the spring clip holding the left side of the housing cover plate and the left evaporator housing together, at the firewall.

16. Install the 6 screws attaching the left of the evaporator housing to the evaporator case.

17. Working under the hood, install the nut retaining the upper left corner of the evaporator case to the firewall.

18. From inside the passenger compartment, install 1 screw attaching the bottom of the plenum to the dash panel.

19. Remove the cap from the liquid line. At this point, Ford recommends that a new fixed orifice tube be installed. See the procedures below.

20. Using a back-up wrench, connect the liquid line, with new O-ring, to the evaporator core. Always lubricate the new O-ring with clean refrigerant oil. Tighten the connection to 20 ft. lbs.

21. Add 3 ounces of clean refrigerant oil to the suction accumulator. Connect the suction hose, with a new O-ring, at the suction accumulator. Always lubricate the new O-ring with clean refrigerant oil. Use a back-up wrench on the fitting. Tighten the connection to 20 ft. lbs.

22. Install the pressure switch.

23. Connect the wiring at the pressure switch.

24. Charge the refrigerant system. See Chapter 1.

1989–90

1. Discharge the refrigerant system. See Chapter 1.

2. Disconnect the wiring from the pressure switch on the side of the suction accumulator.

3. Remove the pressure switch.

4. Disconnect the suction hose from the suction accumulator. Use a back-up wrench on the fitting. Cap the suction line IMMEDIATELY!

5. Using a quick-disconnect coupling tool, disconnect the liquid line from the evaporator core. Cap the liquid line IMMEDIATELY!

6. Remove the nut holding the MAP sensor

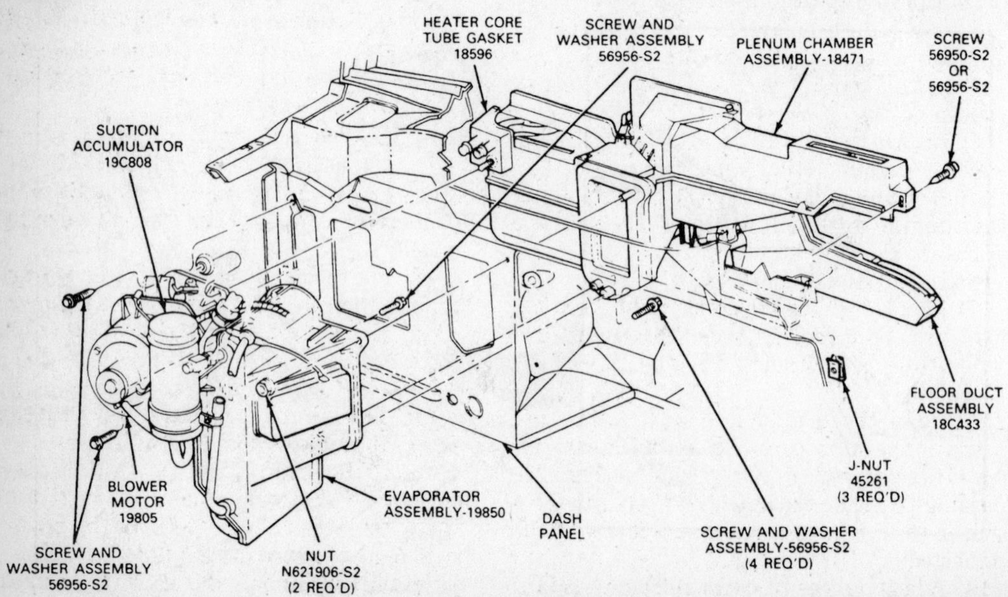

1987–88 evaporator case components

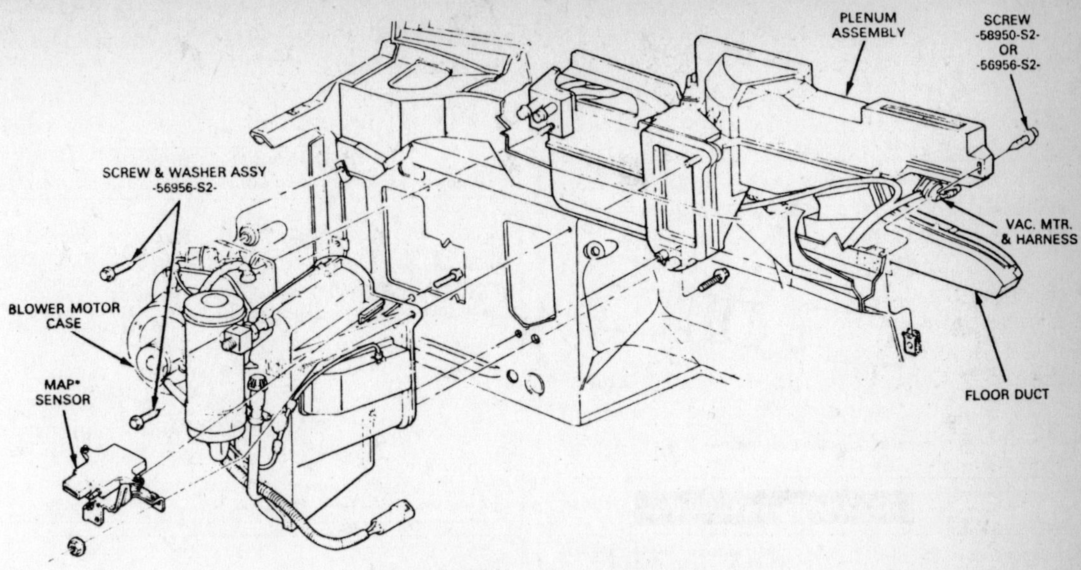

1989–90 evaporator case components

to the left corner of the evaporator case. Remove the spring clip and left the sensor away from the case.

7. Working under the hood, remove the nut retaining the upper left corner of the evaporator case to the firewall.

8. Remove the 6 screws attaching the left of the evaporator housing to the evaporator case.

9. Remove the left evaporator cover from the evaporator case.

10. Remove the evaporator core and suction accumulator from the evaporator case.

To install:

11. Transfer the suction accumulator support straps and spring nuts to the core.

12. Install the evaporator core and suction accumulator in the evaporator case.

13. Install the left evaporator cover on the evaporator case.

14. Install the 6 screws attaching the left evaporator cover to the evaporator case.

15. Working under the hood, install the nut retaining the upper left corner of the evaporator case to the firewall.

16. Install the MAP sensor.

17. Remove the cap from the liquid line. At this point, Ford recommends that a new fixed orifice tube be installed. See the procedures below.

18. Connect the liquid line, with new O-ring, to the evaporator core. Always lubricate the new O-ring with clean refrigerant oil. Push the coupling together until it snaps securely. Pull back on the coupling to make sure it is correctly connected.

19. Add 3 ounces of clean refrigerant oil to the suction accumulator.

20. Connect the suction hose, with a new O-ring, at the suction accumulator. Always lubricate the new O-ring with clean refrigerant oil. Use a back-up wrench on the fitting. Tighten the connection to 20 ft. lbs.

21. Install the pressure switch using a new O-ring coated with clean refrigerant oil.

22. Connect the wiring at the pressure switch.

23. Charge the refrigerant system. See Chapter 1.

Fixed Orifice Tube

REPLACEMENT

NOTE: *Do not attempt to remove the tube with pliers or to twist or rotate the tube in the evaporator. To do so will break the tube in the evaporator core. Use only the tools recommended in the procedure.*

1. Discharge the system. See Chapter 1.

2. Using back-up wrenches (1987–88) or a quick-disconnect coupling tool (1989–90), disconnect the liquid line. Cap all openings at once!

3. Pour a small amount of clean refrigerant oil into the core inlet tube to ease removal.

4. Using remover tool T83L-19990-A, engage the 2 tangs on the orifice tube. DO NOT TWIST OR ROTATE THE TUBE!

5. Tighten the nut on the tool until the orifice tube is withdrawn from the core.

6. If the orifice tube breaks in the core, it must be extracted using tool T83L-1990-B. Thread the end of the tool into the brass tube end of the orifice tube. Pull the orifice tube from the core. If only the brass tube comes out, thread the tool back into the orifice body and pull that out.

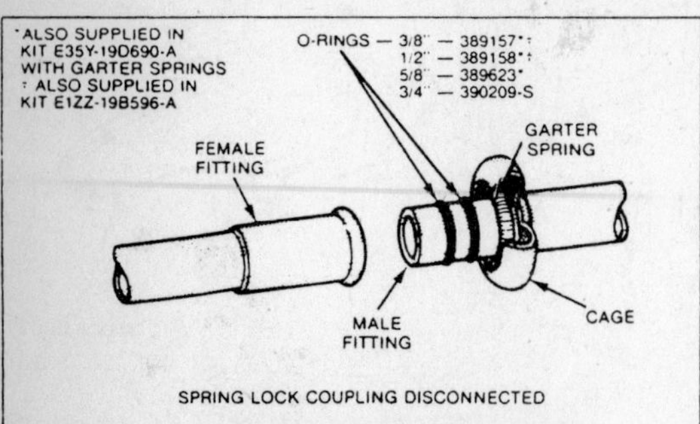

TO CONNECT COUPLING

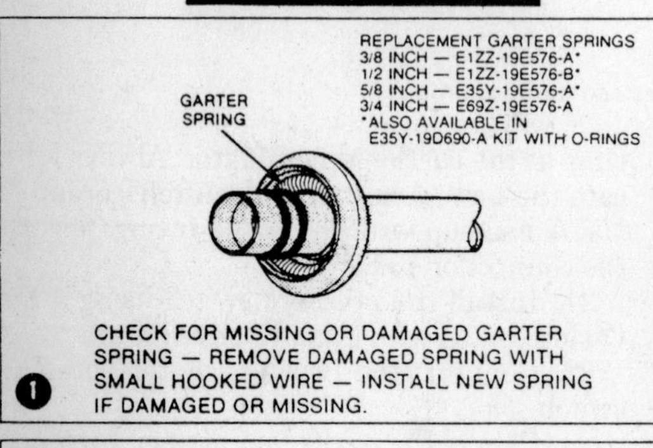

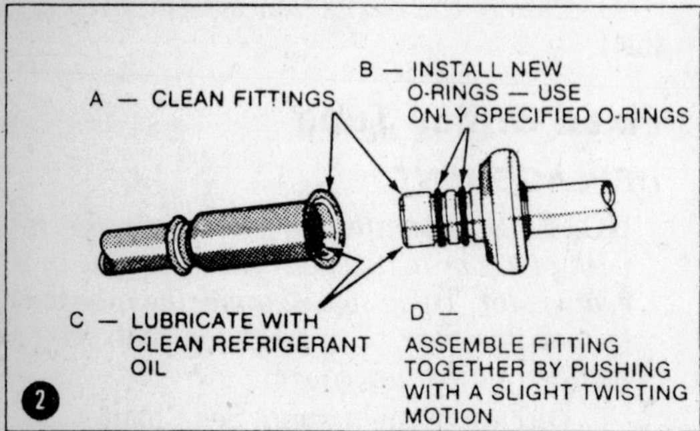

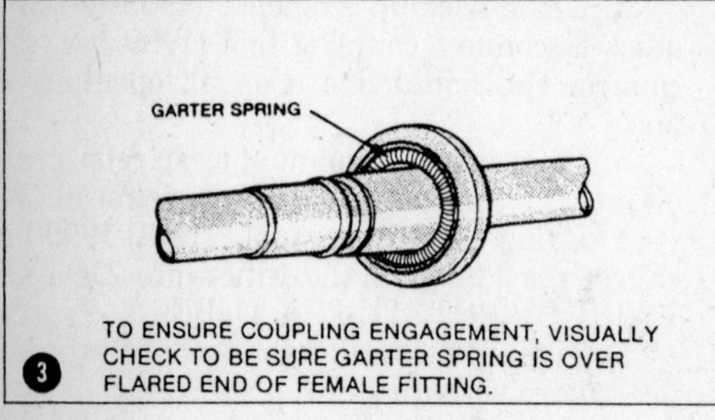

TO DISCONNECT COUPLING

CAUTION — DISCHARGE SYSTEM BEFORE DISCONNECTING COUPLING

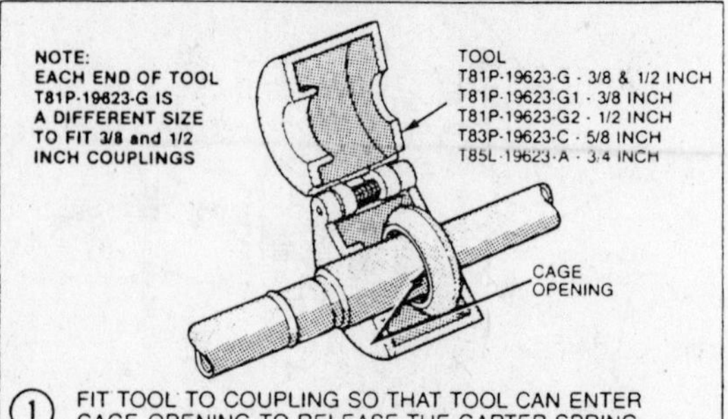

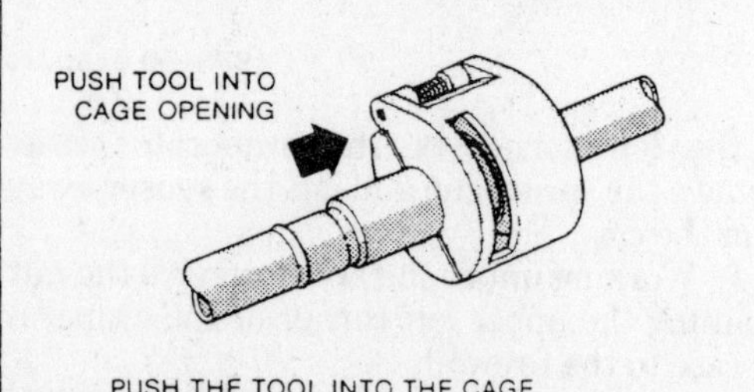

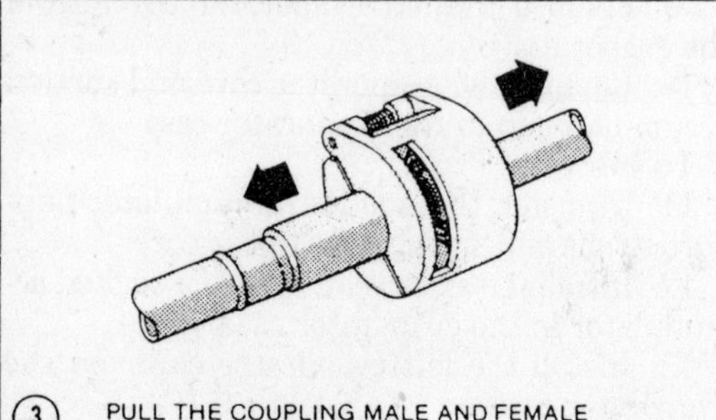

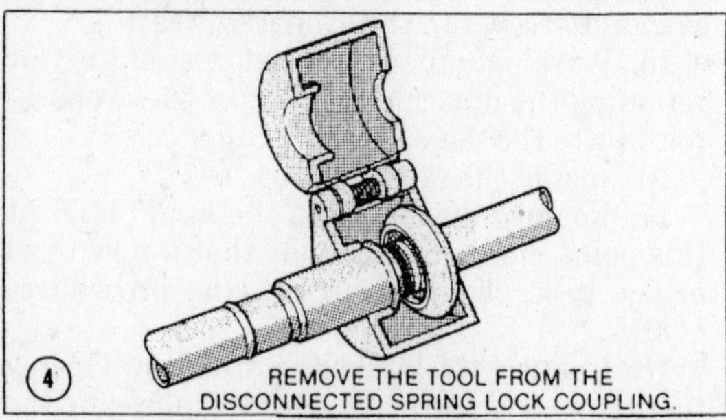

Wiper motor installation

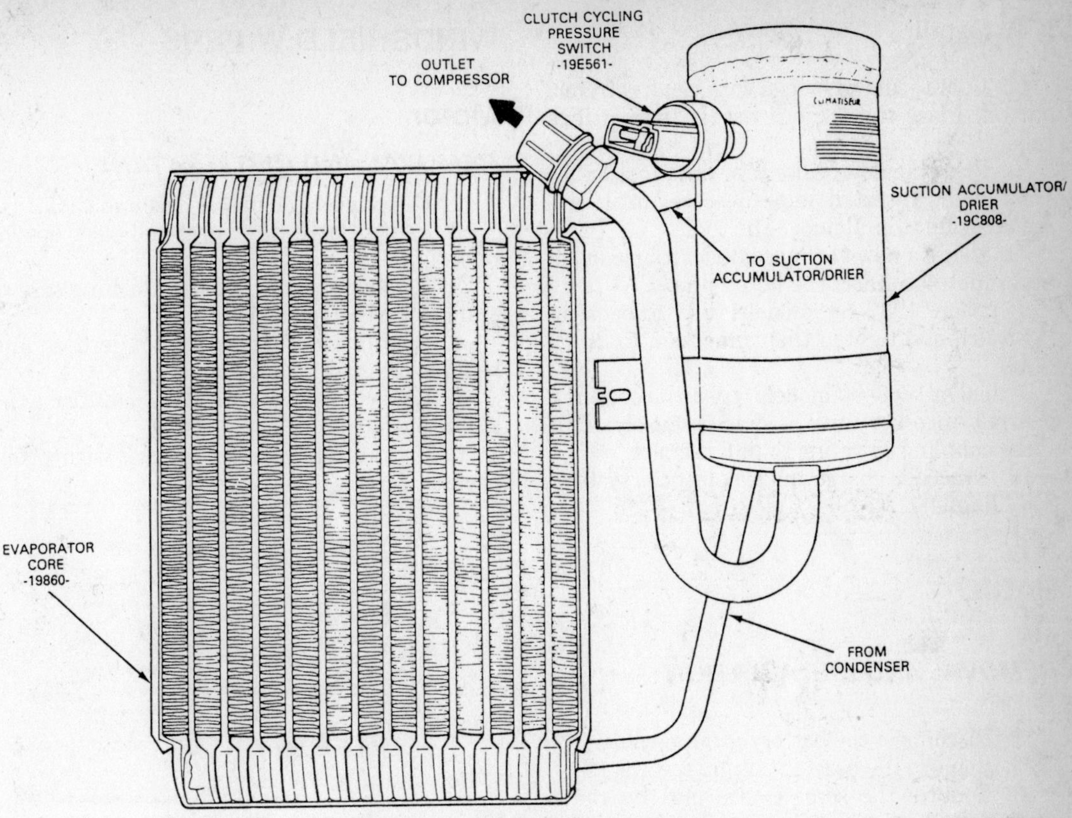

Evaporator core and accumulator/drier

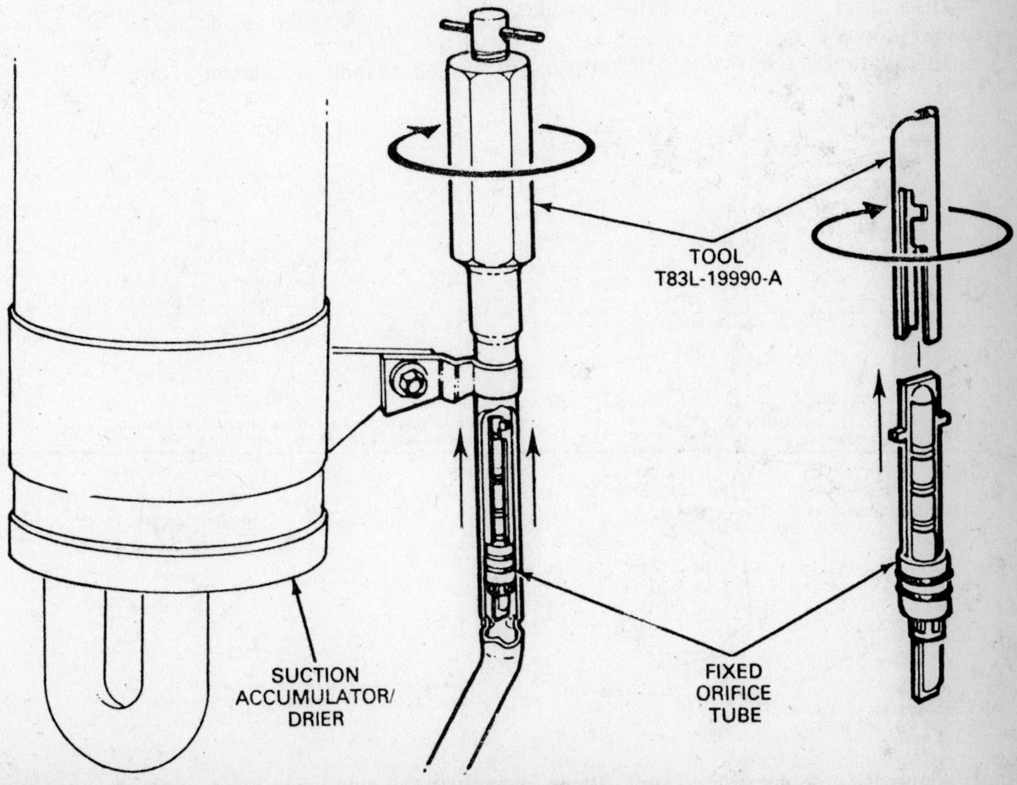

Fixed orifice tube removal

To install:

7. Coat the new O-rings with clean refrigerant oil. Place the O-rings on the new orifice tube.
8. Place the new orifice tube onto tool T83L-1990-A and insert it into the core until it is seated at its stop. Remove the tool.
9. Using a new O-ring coated with clean refrigerant oil, connect the liquid line.
   a. On 1987–88 models, use a back-up wrench and tighten the connection to 20 ft. lbs.
   b. On 1989–90 models, push the coupling firmly together until is snaps securely. Test the coupling by trying to pull it apart.
10. Evacuate, charge and leak test the system. See Chapter 1.

RADIO

REMOVAL AND INSTALLATION

1. Disconnect the battery ground cable.
2. Remove the bezel retaining screws.
3. Remove the screws securing the radio mounting plate to the instrument panel and pull out the radio.
4. Disconnect the antenna cable, speaker wires and power wire.
5. Installation is the reverse of removal.

WINDSHIELD WIPERS

Motor

REMOVAL AND INSTALLATION

1. Disconnect the battery ground cable.
2. Remove both wiper arm and blade assemblies.
3. Remove the cowl grille attaching screws and lift the cowl grille slightly.
4. Disconnect the washer nozzle hose and remove the cowl grille assembly.
5. Remove the wiper linkage clip from the motor output arm.
6. Disconnect the wiper motor's wiring connector.

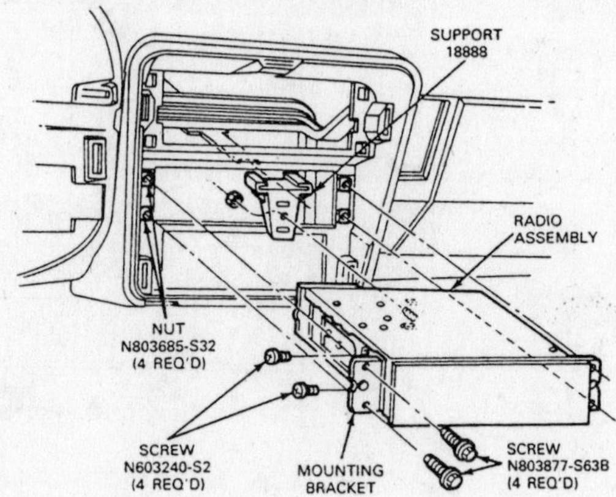

1988–90 radio installation

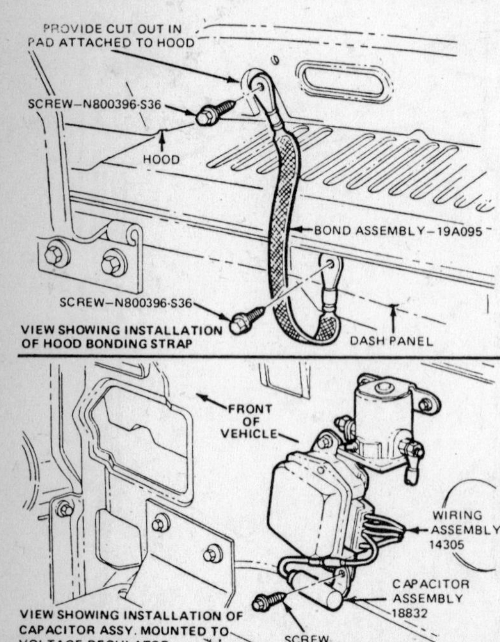

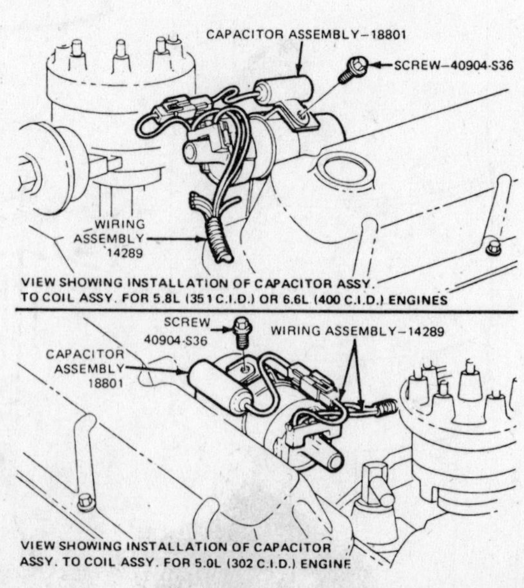

Radio suppression equipment, pickups. These, along with the spark plug wires and radio itself, are the areas to check when radio reception becomes poor

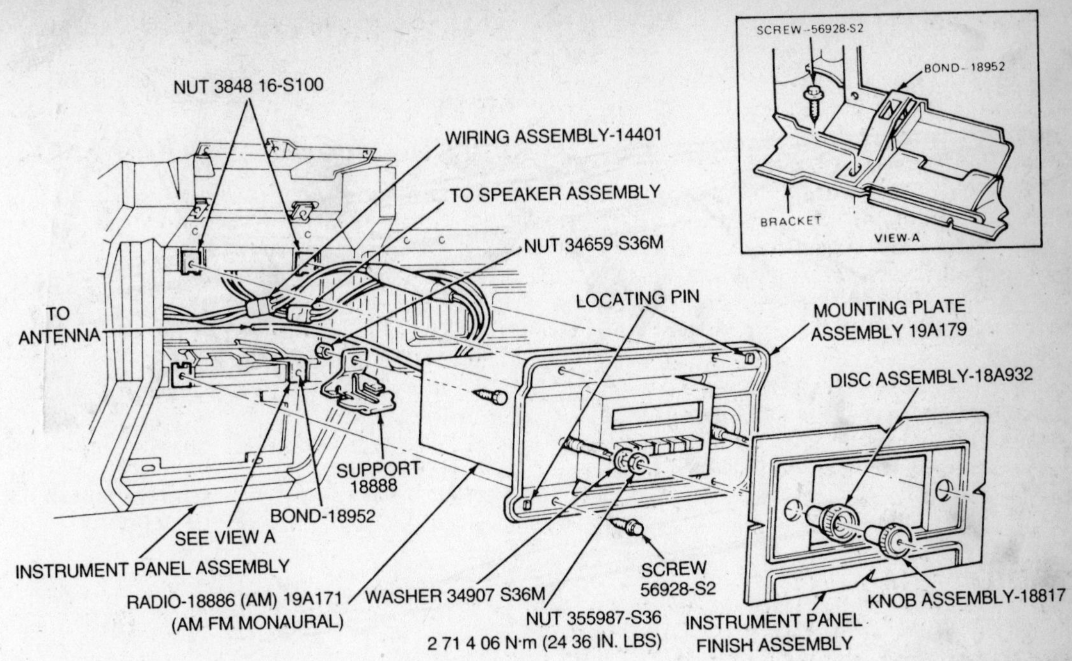

Radio installation

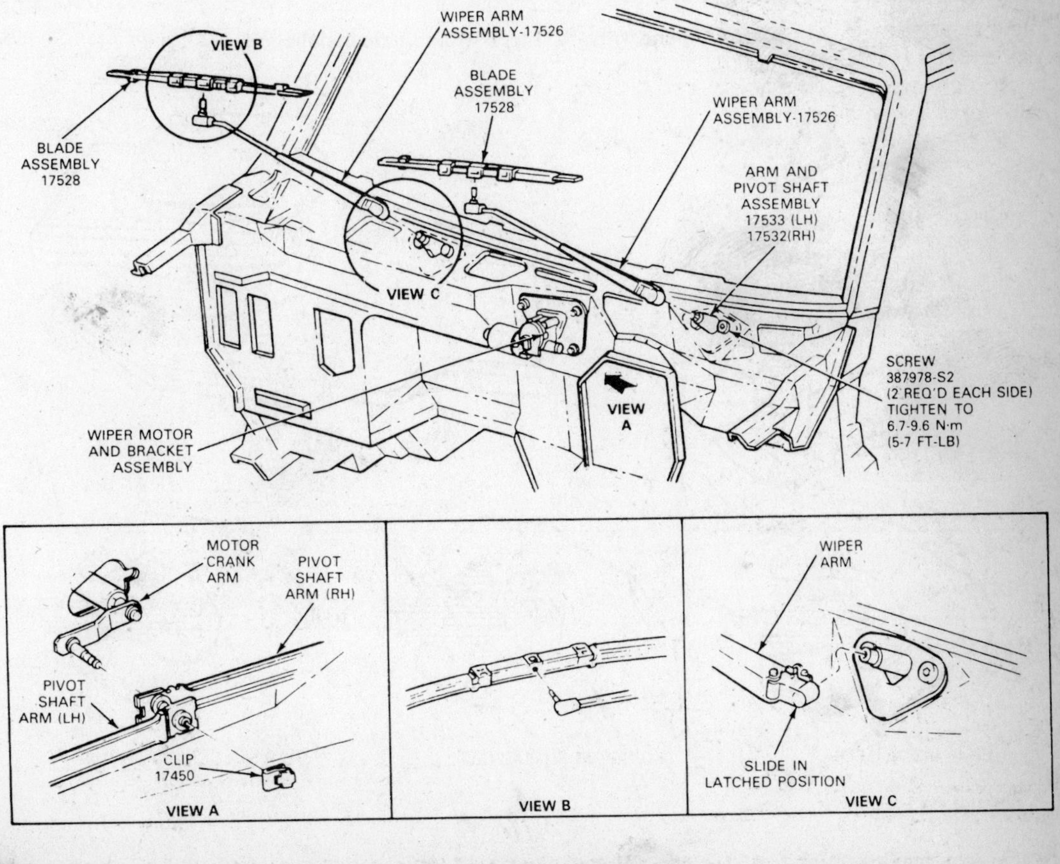

Wiper motor installation

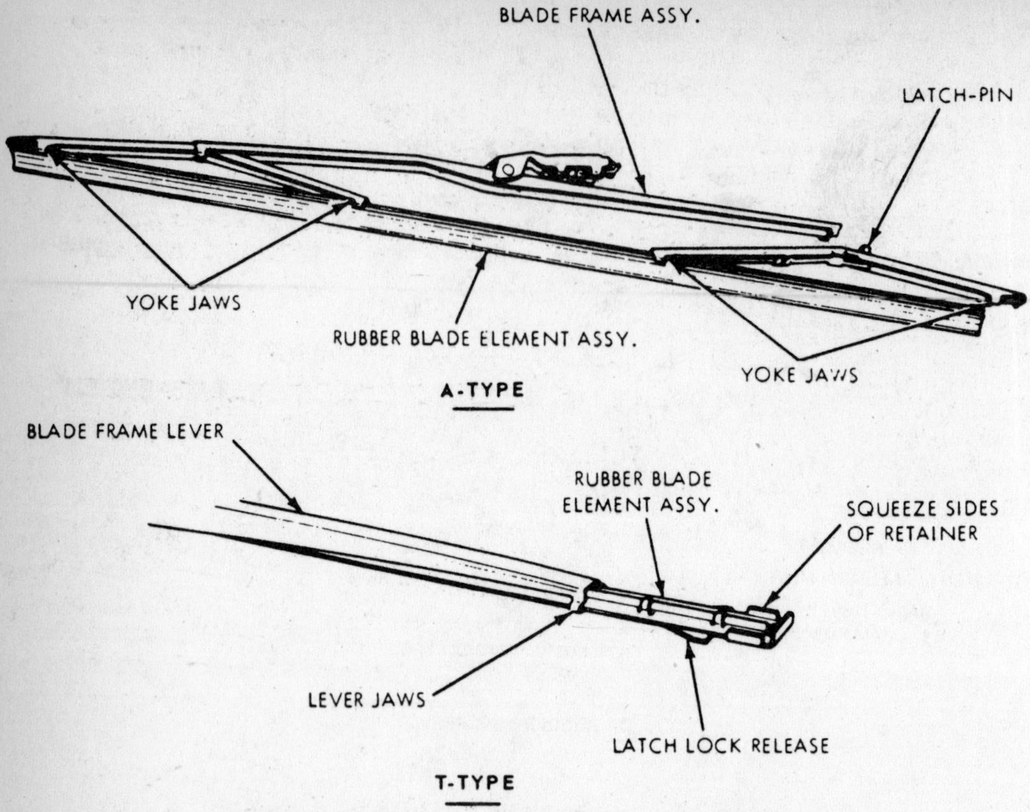

BLADE FRAME ASSY.
LATCH-PIN
YOKE JAWS
RUBBER BLADE ELEMENT ASSY.
YOKE JAWS
A-TYPE
BLADE FRAME LEVER
RUBBER BLADE ELEMENT ASSY.
SQUEEZE SIDES OF RETAINER
LEVER JAWS
LATCH LOCK RELEASE
T-TYPE

Anco® (A) and Trico® (T) type wiper blade installation

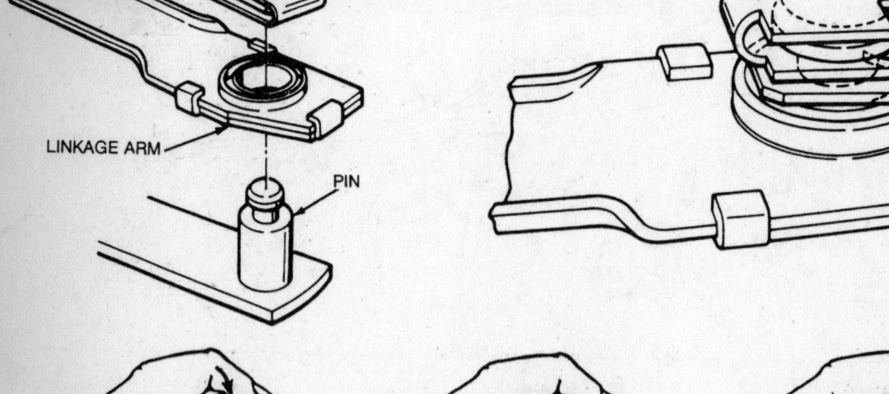

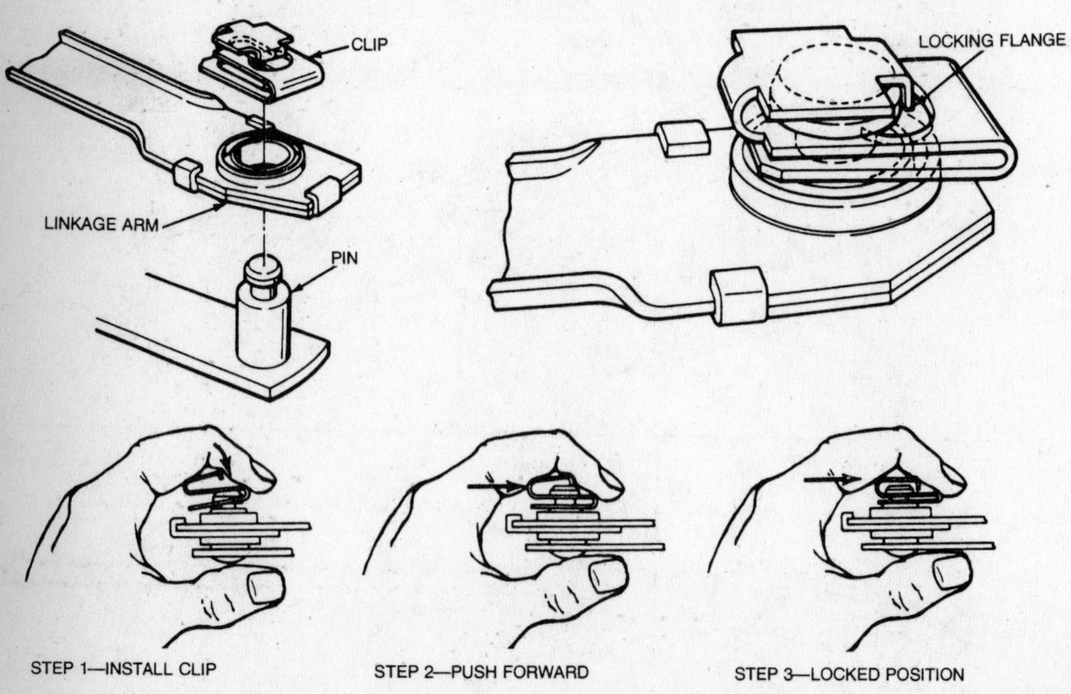

CLIP
LOCKING FLANGE
LINKAGE ARM
PIN
STEP 1—INSTALL CLIP
STEP 2—PUSH FORWARD
STEP 3—LOCKED POSITION

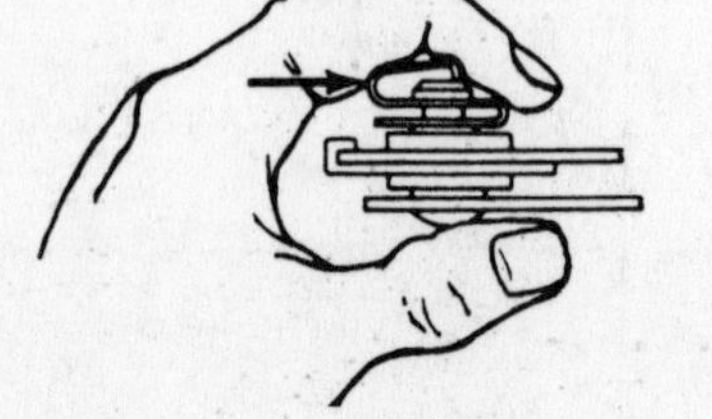

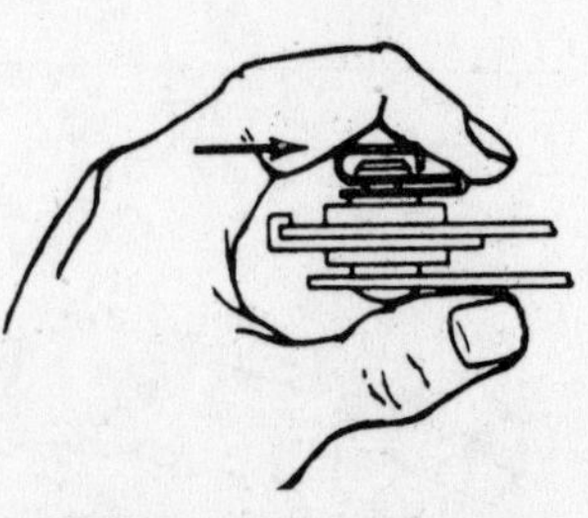

Installing the wiper arm connecting clip

7. Remove the wiper motor's three attaching screws and remove the motor.

8. Install the motor and attach the three attaching screws. Tighten to 60–85 inch lbs.

9. Connect wiper motor's wiring connector.

10. Install wiper linkage clip to the motor's output arm.

11. Connect the washer nozzle hose and install the cowl assembly and attaching screws.

12. Install both wiper arm assemblies.

13. Connect battery ground cable.

Linkage

REMOVAL AND INSTALLATION

1. Disconnect the battery ground cable.
2. Remove both wiper arm assemblies.

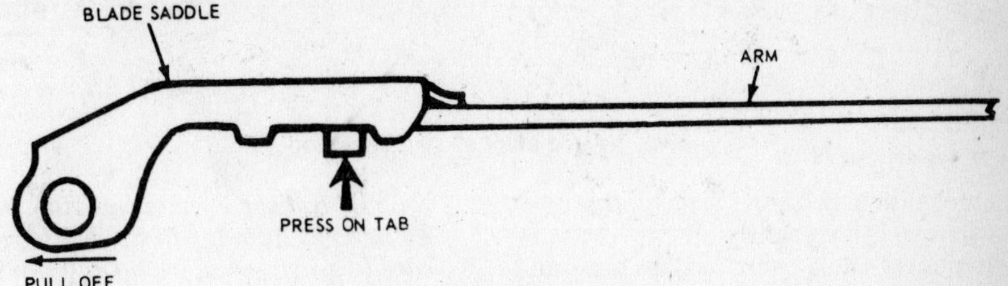

Anco® type wiper arm removal

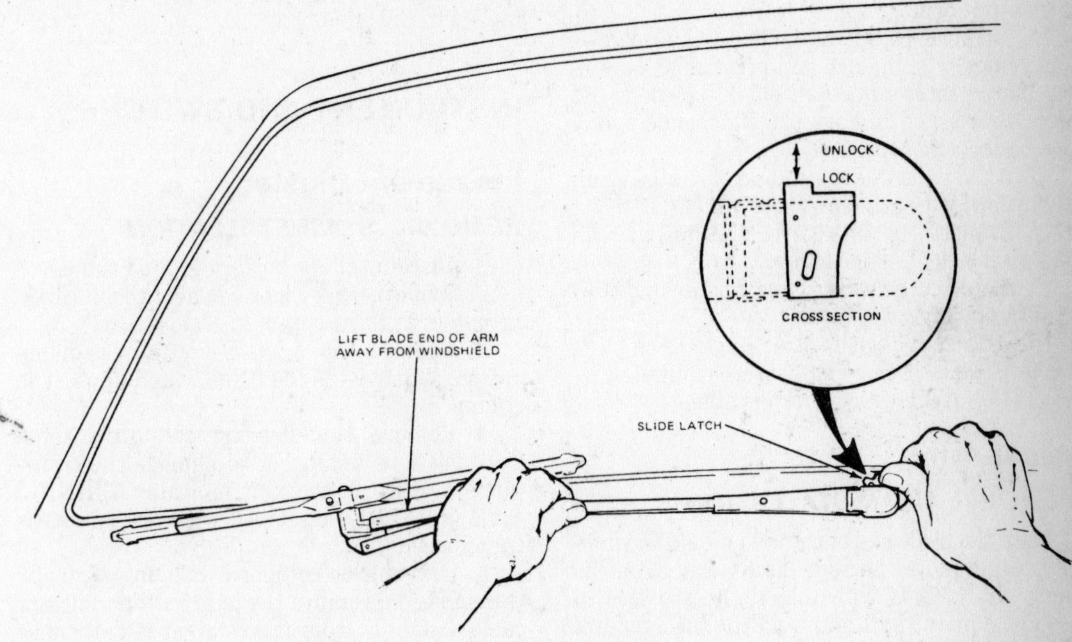

Wiper arm installation

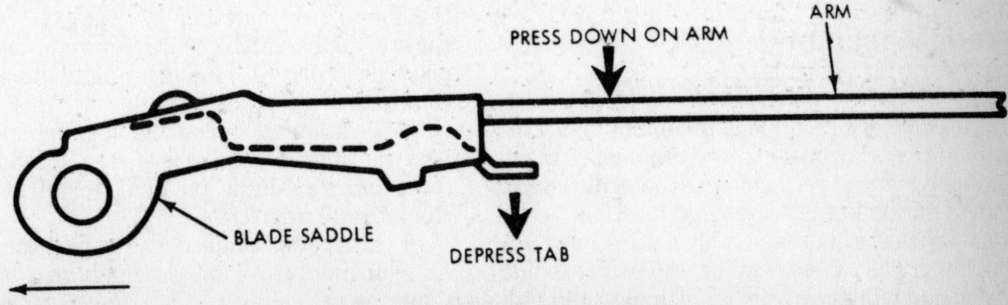

Removal of a Trico® wiper blade

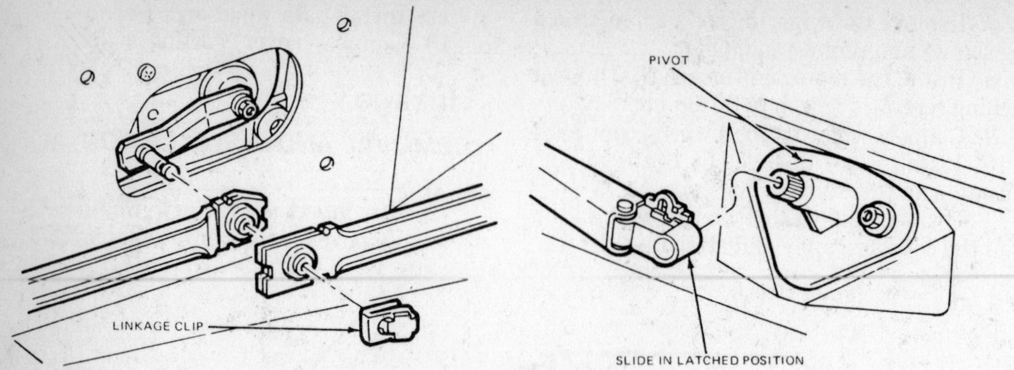

Linkage and pivot shaft installation

3. Remove the cowl grille attaching screws and lift the cowl grille slightly.
4. Disconnect the washer nozzle hose and remove the cowl grille assembly.
5. Remove the wiper linkage clip from the motor output arm and pull the linkage from the output arm.
6. Remove the pivot body to cowl screws and remove the linkage and pivot shaft assembly (three screws on each side). The left and right pivots and linkage are independent and can be serviced separately.
7. Attach the linkage and pivot shaft assembly to cowl with attaching screws.
8. Replace the linkage to the output arm and attach the linkage clip.
9. Connect the washer nozzle hose and cowl grills assembly.
10. Attach cowl grille attaching screws.
11. Replace both wiper arm assemblies.
12. Connect battery ground cable.

Wiper Arm

REMOVAL AND INSTALLATION

Raise the blade end of the arm off of the windshield and move the slide latch away from the pivot shaft. This will unlock the wiper arm from the pivot shaft and hold the blade end of the arm off of the glass at the same time. The wiper arm can now be pulled off of the pivot shaft without the aid of any tools.

Blade Assembly

REMOVAL AND INSTALLATION

1. Cycle arm and blade assembly to a position on the windshield where removal of blade assembly can be performed without difficulty. Turn ignition key off at desired position.
2. With the blade assembly resting on windshield, grasp either end of the wiper blade frame and pull away from windshield, then pull blade assembly from pin.

NOTE: *Rubber element extends past frame. To prevent damage to the blade element, be sure to grasp blade frame and not the end of the blade element.*

3. To install, push blade assembly onto pin until fully seated. Be sure blade is securely attached to the wiper arm.

INSTRUMENT AND SWITCHES

Instrument Cluster

REMOVAL AND INSTALLATION

1. Disconnect the battery ground cable.
2. Remove the wiper-washer knob. Use a hook tool to release each knob lock tab.
3. Remove the knob from the headlamp switch. Remove the fog lamp switch knob, if so equipped.
4. Remove the steering column shroud. Care must be taken not to damage the transmission control selector indicator (PRNDL) cable on vehicles equipped with an automatic transmission.
5. On vehicles equipped with an automatic transmission, remove the loop on the indicator cable assembly from the retainer pin. Remove the bracket screw from the cable bracket and slide the bracket out of the slot in the tube.
6. Remove the cluster trim cover. Remove the four cluster attaching screws, disconnect the speedometer cable, wire connector from the printed circuit, 4 x 4 indicator light and remove the cluster.
7. Position cluster at the opening and connect the multiple connector, the speedometer cable and 4 x 4 indicator light. Install the four cluster retaining screws.
8. If so equipped, place the loop on the transmission indicator cable assembly over the retainer on the column.
9. Position the tab on the steering column

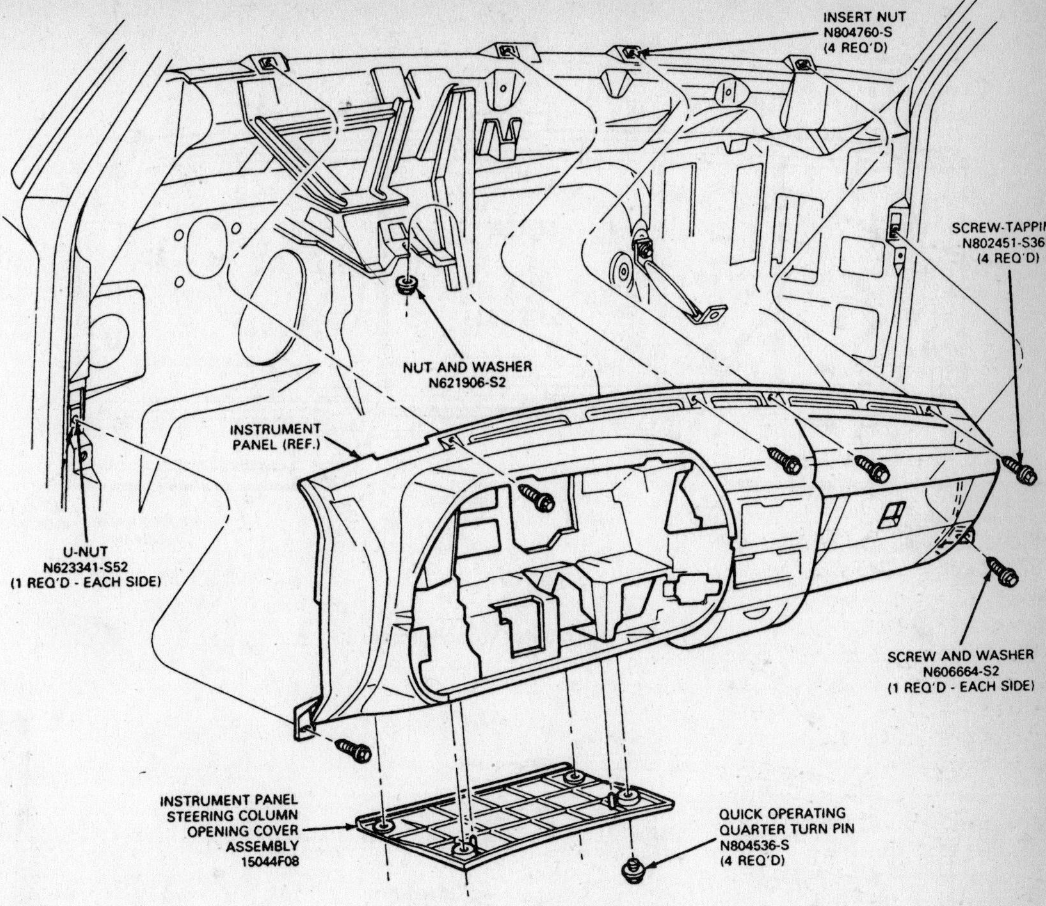

INSERT NUT
N804760-S
(4 REQ'D)
SCREW-TAPPING
N802451-S36B
(4 REQ'D)
NUT AND WASHER
N621906-S2
INSTRUMENT
PANEL (REF.)
U-NUT
N623341-S52
(1 REQ'D - EACH SIDE)
SCREW AND WASHER
N606664-S2
(1 REQ'D - EACH SIDE)
INSTRUMENT PANEL
STEERING COLUMN
OPENING COVER
ASSEMBLY
15044F08
QUICK OPERATING
QUARTER TURN PIN
N804536-S
(4 REQ'D)

Instrument panel disassembly

SCREW
N804988-S2
(7 REQ'D)
TIGHTEN TO 0.8-1.4 N·m
(7.0-12.4 IN-LB)
NORMAL
BRAKE
MPH
km/h
NORMAL
UNLEADED FUEL ONLY
FRONT VIEW
LH TURN
INDICATOR
CHECK
ENGINE
NOT
USED
AMP
INDICATOR
ANTI-LOCK
INDICATOR
4 x 4
INDICATOR
LOW RANGE
INDICATOR
RH TURN
INDICATOR

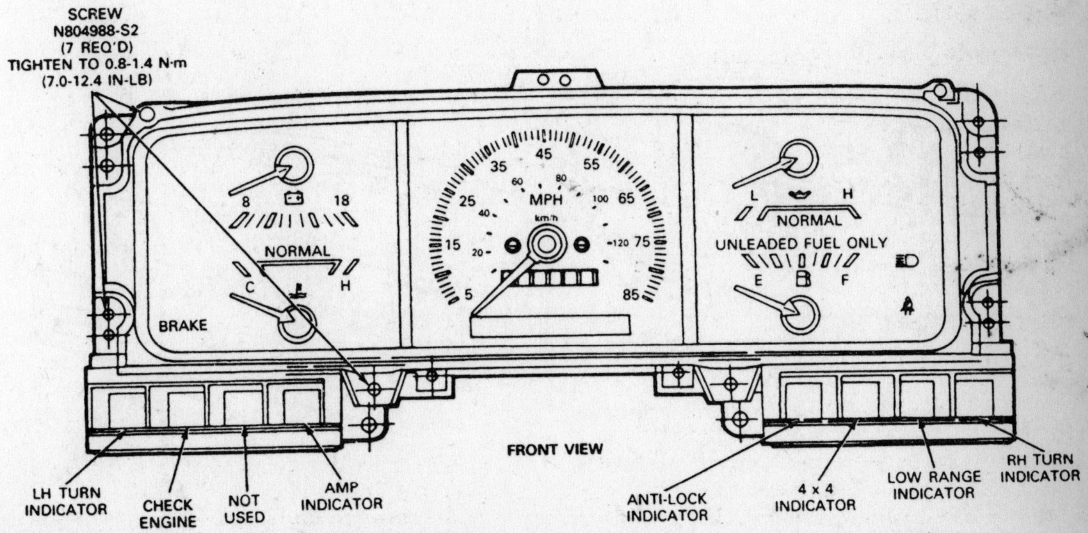

Instrument cluster without tachometer

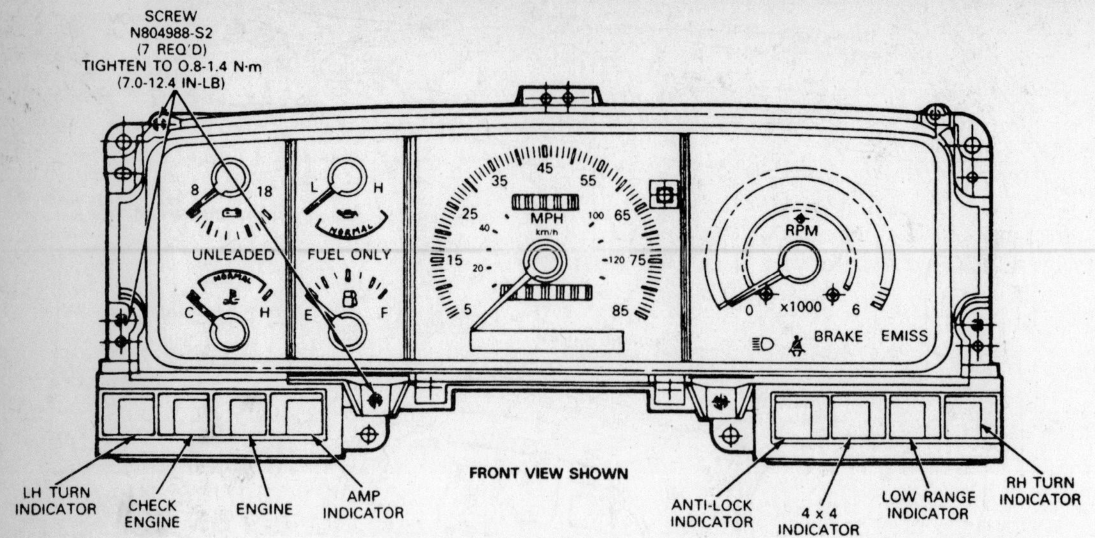

SCREW
N804988-S2
(7 REQ'D)
TIGHTEN TO 0.8-1.4 N·m
(7.0-12.4 IN-LB)
UNLEADED
FUEL ONLY
MPH
km/h
RPM
x1000
BRAKE
EMISS
FRONT VIEW SHOWN
LH TURN INDICATOR
CHECK ENGINE
ENGINE
AMP INDICATOR
ANTI-LOCK INDICATOR
4 x 4 INDICATOR
LOW RANGE INDICATOR
RH TURN INDICATOR

Instrument cluster w/tachometer

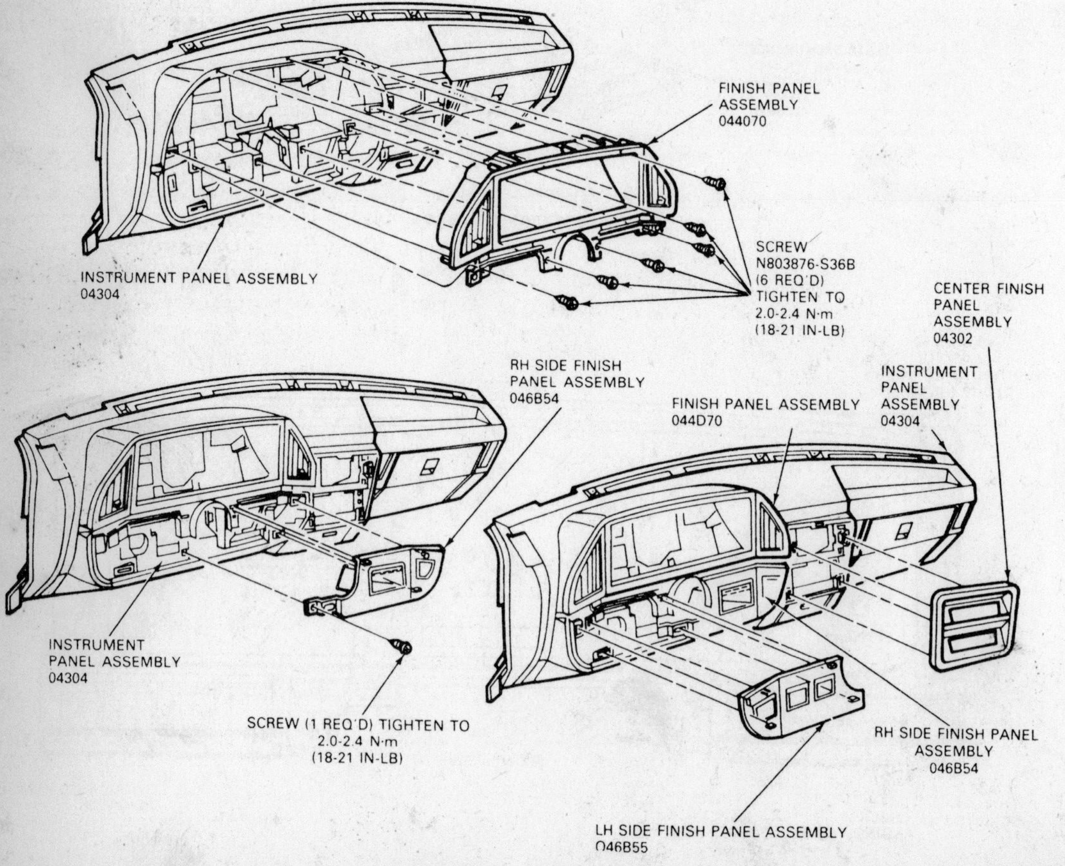

FINISH PANEL ASSEMBLY 044070
INSTRUMENT PANEL ASSEMBLY 04304
SCREW N803876-S36B (6 REQ'D) TIGHTEN TO 2.0-2.4 N·m (18-21 IN-LB)
CENTER FINISH PANEL ASSEMBLY 04302
RH SIDE FINISH PANEL ASSEMBLY 046B54
FINISH PANEL ASSEMBLY 044D70
INSTRUMENT PANEL ASSEMBLY 04304
INSTRUMENT PANEL ASSEMBLY 04304
SCREW (1 REQ'D) TIGHTEN TO 2.0-2.4 N·m (18-21 IN-LB)
RH SIDE FINISH PANEL ASSEMBLY 046B54
LH SIDE FINISH PANEL ASSEMBLY 046B55

Instrument cluster removal

bracket into the slot on the column. Align and attach the screw.

10. Place the transmission selector lever on the steering column into **D** position.

11. Adjust the slotted bracket so the pin is within the letter band.

12. Install the trim cover.

13. Install the headlamp switch knob. If so equipped, install the fog lamp switch.

14. Install the wiper washer control knobs.

15. Connect the battery cable, and check the operation of all gauges, lights and signals.

Speedometer Cable Core

REMOVAL AND INSTALLATION

1. Reach up behind the cluster and disconnect the cable by depressing the quick disconnect tab and pulling the cable away.

2. Remove the cable from the casing. If the cable is broken, raise the vehicle on a hoist and disconnect the cable from the transmission.

3. Remove the cable from the casing.

4. To remove the casing from the vehicle pull it through the floor pan.

5. To replace the cable, slide the new cable into the casing and connect it at the transmission.

6. Route the cable through the floor pan and position the grommet in its groove in the floor.

7. Push the cable onto the speedometer head.

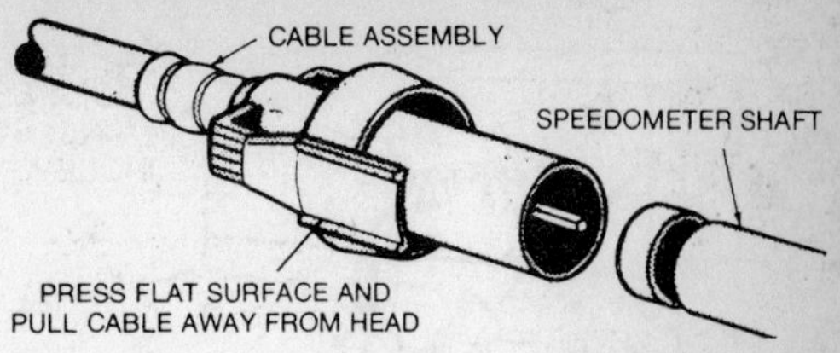

Speedometer cable quick-disconnect

Clock

REMOVAL AND INSTALLATION

1. Disconnect the battery ground.

2. Remove the 3 clock retaining screws.

3. Pull the clock from the dash slowly and disconnect the wiring.

4. Installation is the reverse of removal.

Windshield Wiper Switch

REMOVAL AND INSTALLATION

1. Disconnect the battery ground.

2. Remove the switch knob, bezel nut and bezel.

3. Pull the switch out from under the panel and unplug the wiring.

4. Installation is the reverse of removal.

Headlight Switch

REMOVAL AND INSTALLATION

1. Disconnect the battery ground cable.

2. Depending on the year and model remove the wiper-washer and fog lamp switch knob if they will interfere with the headlight switch knob removal. Check the switch body (behind dash, see Step 3) for a release button.

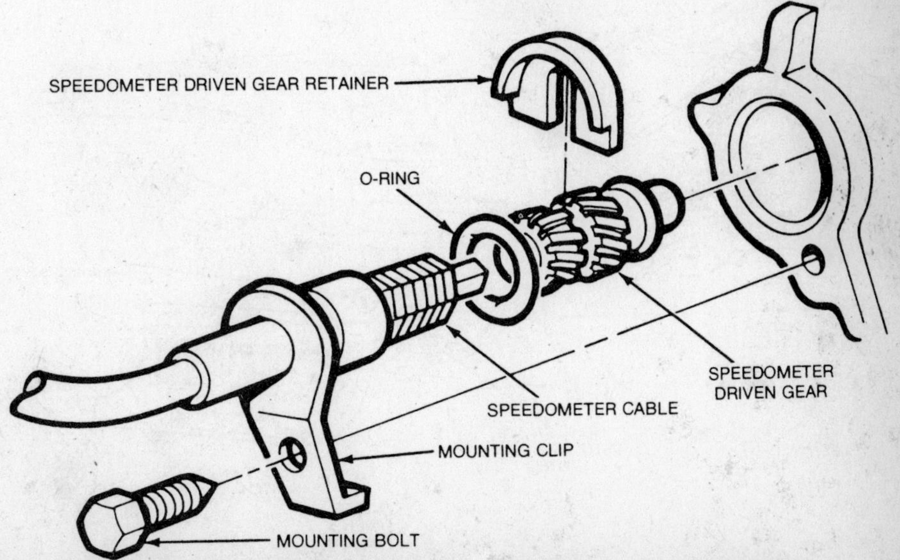

Speedometer driven gear to-transmission installation, all models similar

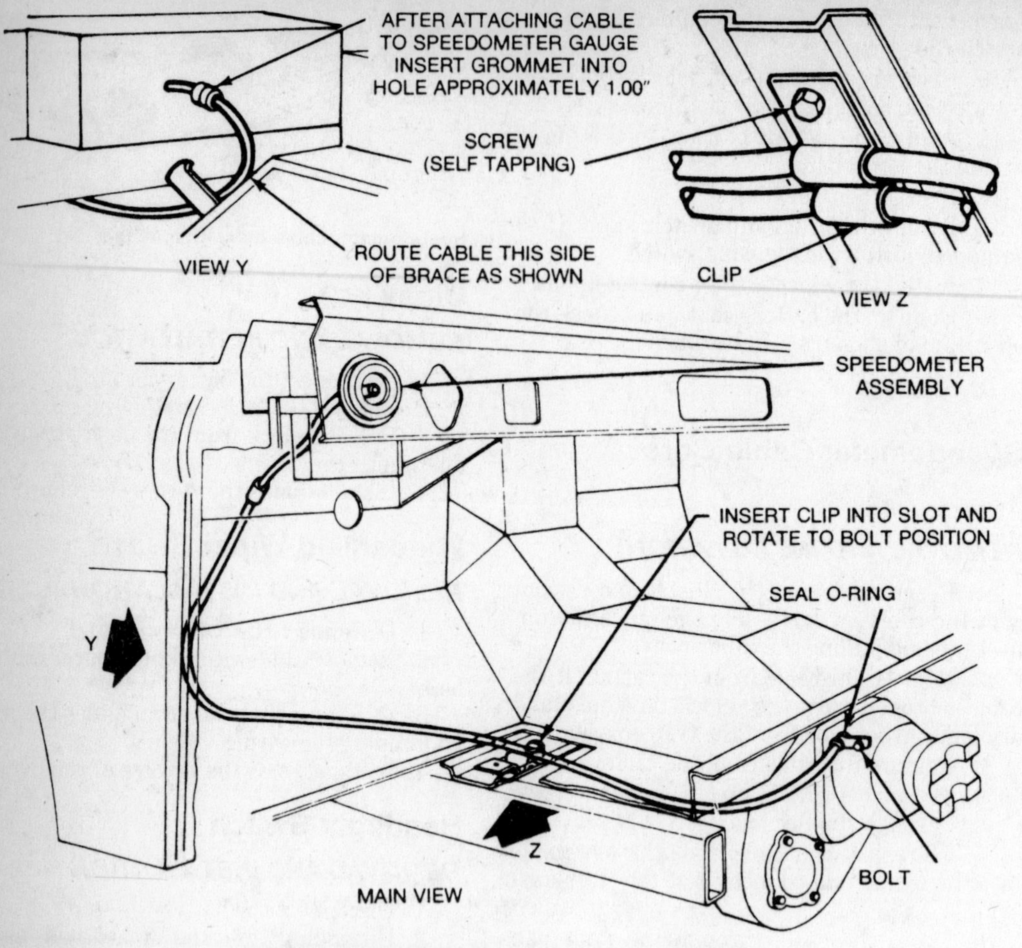

AFTER ATTACHING CABLE TO SPEEDOMETER GAUGE INSERT GROMMET INTO HOLE APPROXIMATELY 1.00"
SCREW (SELF TAPPING)
VIEW Y
ROUTE CABLE THIS SIDE OF BRACE AS SHOWN
CLIP
VIEW Z
SPEEDOMETER ASSEMBLY
INSERT CLIP INTO SLOT AND ROTATE TO BOLT POSITION
SEAL O-RING
Y
Z
BOLT
MAIN VIEW

Speedometer cable installation, 4 × 4 model shown

WINDSHIELD WIPER SWITCH-17A553
INTERVAL WINDSHIELD WIPER SWITCH-17A553
LIGHTING SWITCH ASSEMBLY-11654
NUT 3501038-S2
WINDSHIELD WIPER CONTROL KNOB ASSEMBLY-17513
INSTRUMENT PANEL
LIGHT SWITCH NUT ASSEMBLY 11650
LIGHT KNOB SWITCH-11666
CLUSTER FINISH PANEL

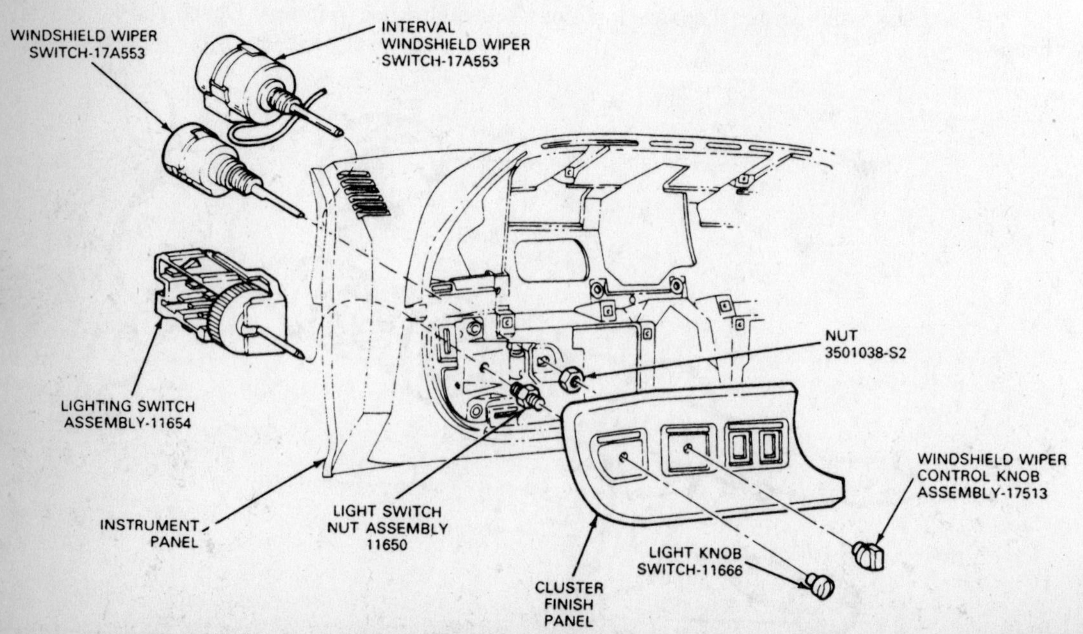

Headlamp switch

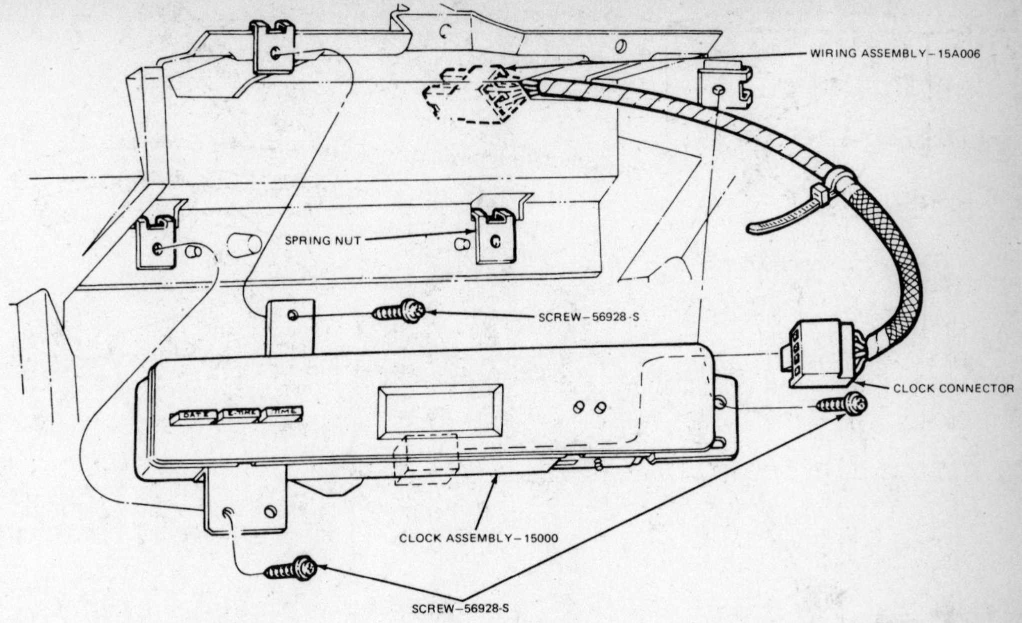

Clock removal

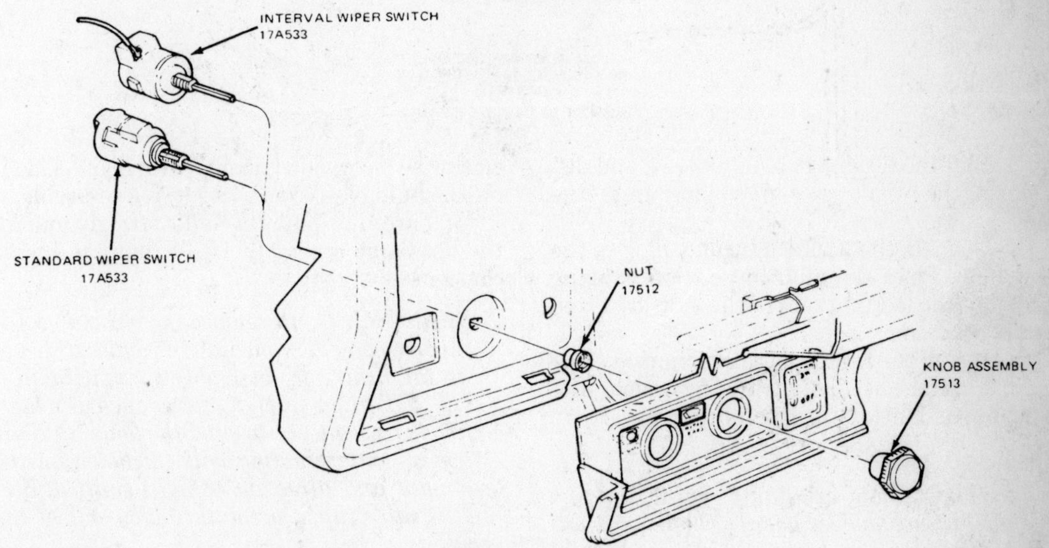

Wiper control switch

Press in on the button and remove the knob and shaft assembly. If not equipped with a release button, a hook tool may be necessary for knob removal.

3. Remove the steering column shrouds and cluster panel finish panel if they interfere with the required clearance for working behind the dash.

4. Unscrew the switch mounting nut from the front of the dash. Remove the switch from the back of the dash and disconnect the wiring harness.

5. Install in reverse order.

LIGHTING

Headlights

REMOVAL AND INSTALLATION

1987

1. Remove the attaching screws and remove the headlamp door attaching screw and remove the headlamp door.

2. Remove the headlight retaining ring screws, and remove the retaining ring. Do not disturb the adjusting screw settings.

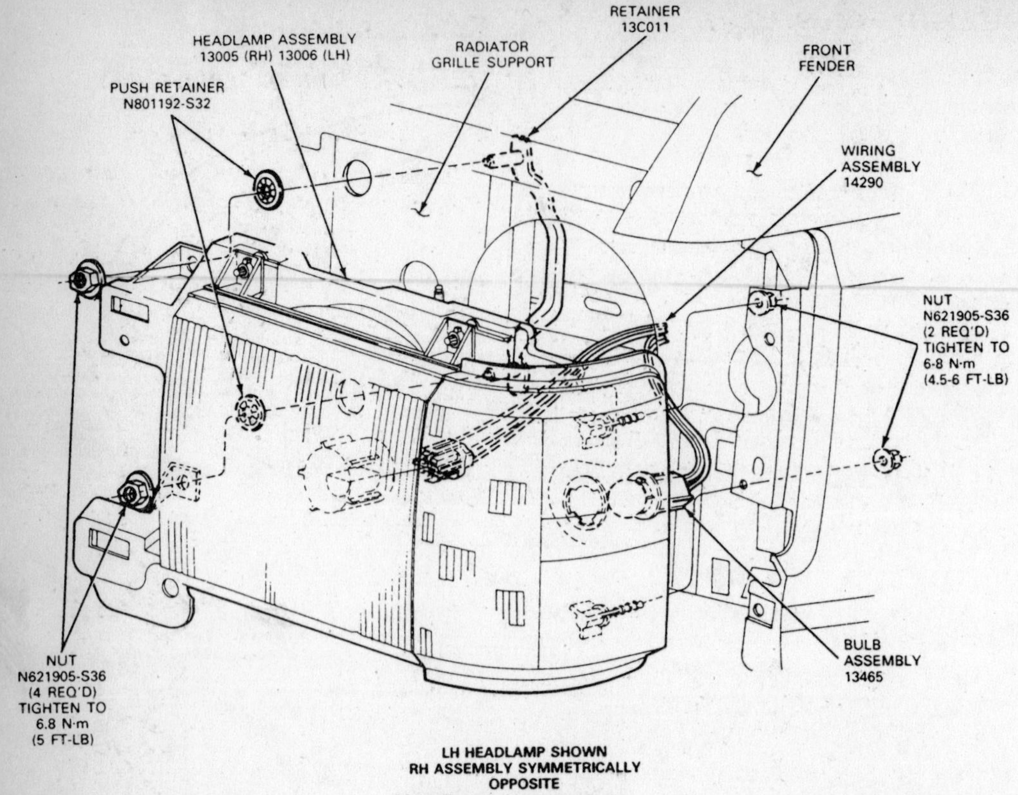

Headlamp components

3. Pull the headlight bulb forward and disconnect the wiring assembly plug from the bulb.

4. Connect the wiring assembly plug to the new bulb. Place the bulb in position, making sure that the locating tabs of the bulb are fitted in the positioning slots.

5. Install the headlight retaining ring.

6. Place the headlight trim ring or door into position, and install the retaining screws.

1988–90

CAUTION: *The headlamp bulb contains high pressure halogen gas. The bulb may shatter if scratched or dropped! Hold the bulb by its plastic base only. If you touch the glass portion with your fingers, or if any dirt or oily deposits are found on the glass, it must be wiped clean with an alcohol soaked paper towel. Even the oil from your skin will cause the bulb to burn out prematurely due to hot-spotting.*

1. Make sure that the headlight switch is **OFF**.

2. Raise the hood and find the bulb base protruding from the back of the headlamp assembly

3. Disconnect the wiring by grasping the connector and snapping it rearward firmly.

4. Rotate the bulb retaining ring counterclockwise (rear view) about $^1/_8$ turn and slide it off the bulb base. Don't lose it; it's re-usable.

5. Carefully pull the bulb straight out of the headlamp assembly. Don't rotate it during removal.

WARNING: *Don't remove the old bulb until you are ready to immediately replace it! Leaving the headlamp assembly open, without a bulb, will allow foreign matter such as water, dirt, leaves, oil, etc. to enter the housing. This type of contamination will cut down on the amount and direction of light emitted, and eventually cause premature blow-out of the bulb.*

To install:

6. With the flat side of the bulb base facing upward, insert it into the headlamp assembly. You may have to turn the bulb slightly to align the locating tabs. Once aligned, push the bulb firmly into place until the bulb base contacts the mounting flange in the socket.

7. Place the retaining ring over the bulb base, against the mounting flange and rotate it clockwise to lock it. It should lock against a definite stop when fully engaged.

8. Snap the electrical connector into place. A definite snap will be felt.

9. Turn the headlights on a check that everything works properly.

HEADLIGHT ADJUSTMENT

NOTE: *Before making any headlight adjustments, preform the following steps for preparation:*

1. Make sure all tires are properly inflated.
2. Take into consideration any faulty wheel alignment or improper rear axle tracking.
3. Make sure there is no load in the truck other than the driver.
4. Make sure all lenses are clean.

Each headlight is adjusted by means of two screws located at the 12 o'clock and 9 o'clock positions on the headlight underneath the trim ring. Always bring each beam into final position by turning the adjusting screws clockwise so that the headlight will be held against the tension springs when the operation is completed.

Parking Lamps

REMOVAL AND INSTALLATION

1. Remove the headlamp assembly attaching screws.
2. Pull the headlamp assembly out and disconnect the parking lamp socket from the headlamp body.
3. Replace the bulb.
4. Installation is the reverse of removal.

Rear Lamps

REMOVAL AND INSTALLATION

Style Side Pick-Ups and Bronco

1. Remove the screws that attach the combination lamp lens assembly and remove the lens.
2. Turn the affected bulb socket counterclockwise to remove the bulb; clockwise to install a new bulb.

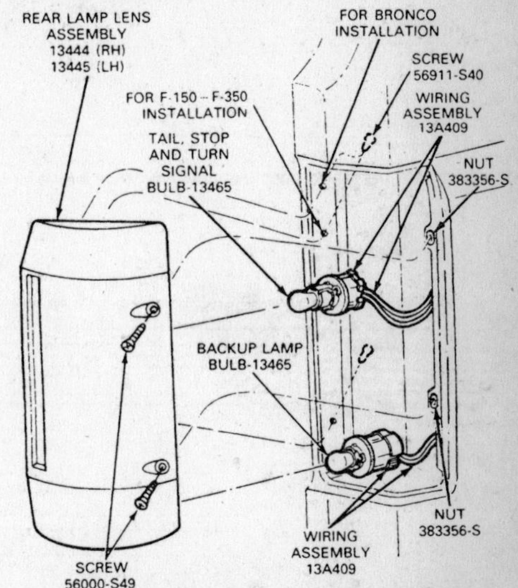

Rear lamps on the Bronco, F-series Styleside and F-Super Duty

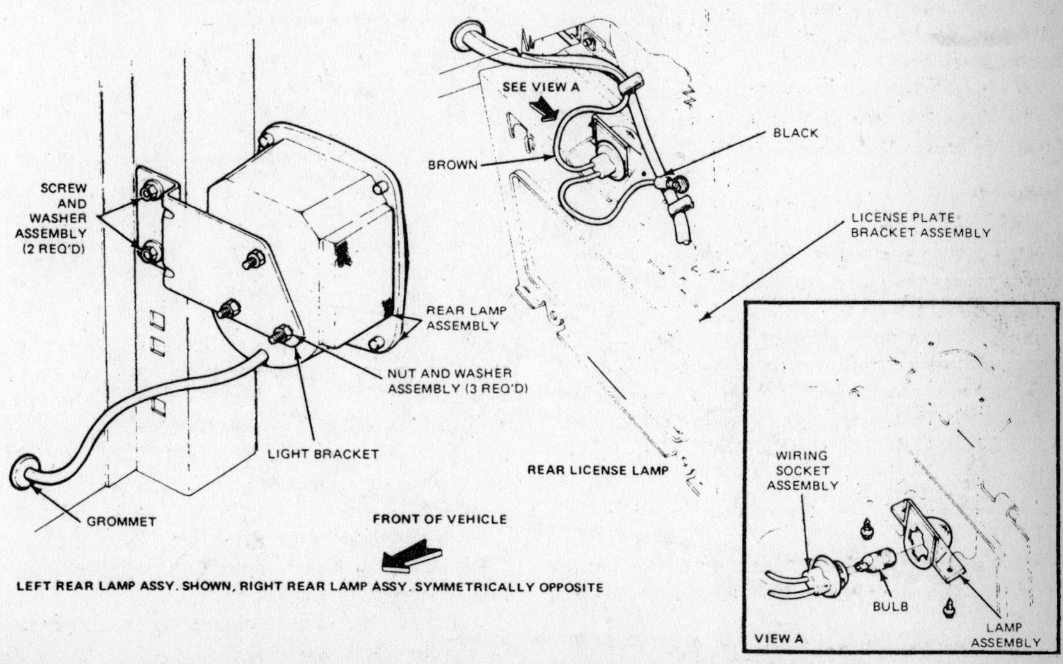

Rear side marker lights and license plate lamps on Flare Side pick-ups

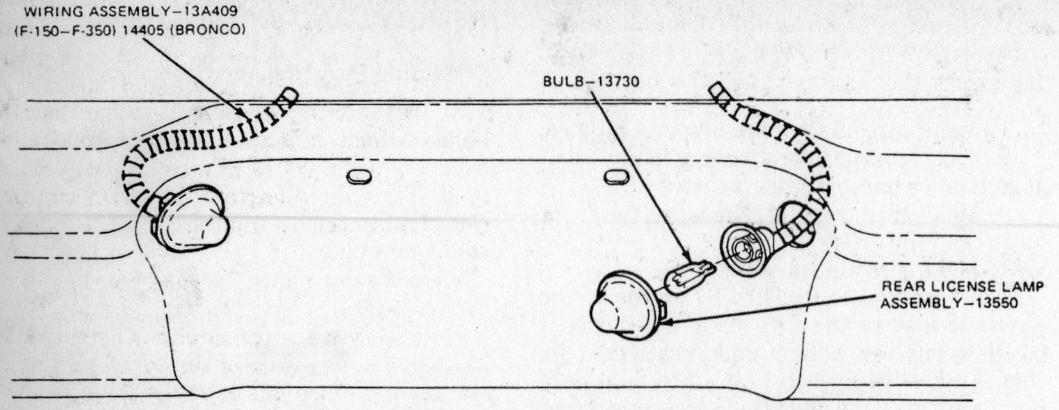

VIEW SHOWING INSTALLATION OF LICENSE LAMP ASSY. WITH STRAIGHT BUMPER FOR BRONCO

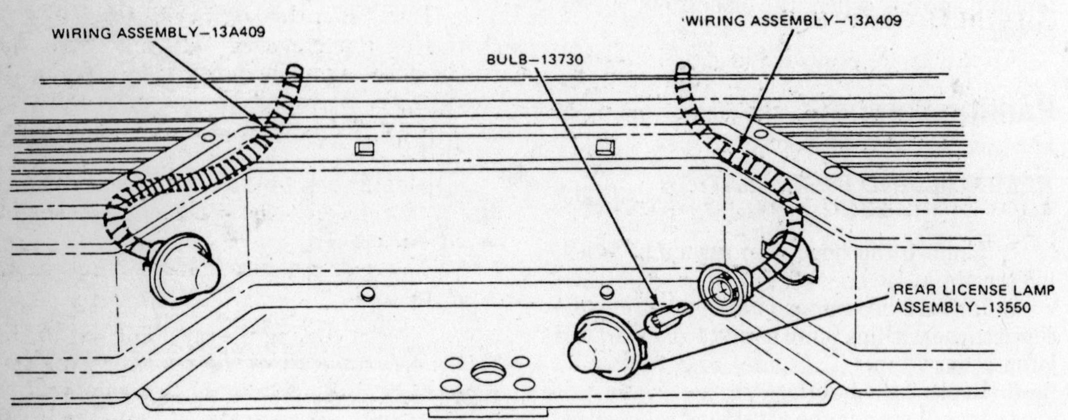

VIEW SHOWING INSTALLATION OF LICENSE LAMP ASSY. WITH STEP-UP BUMPER

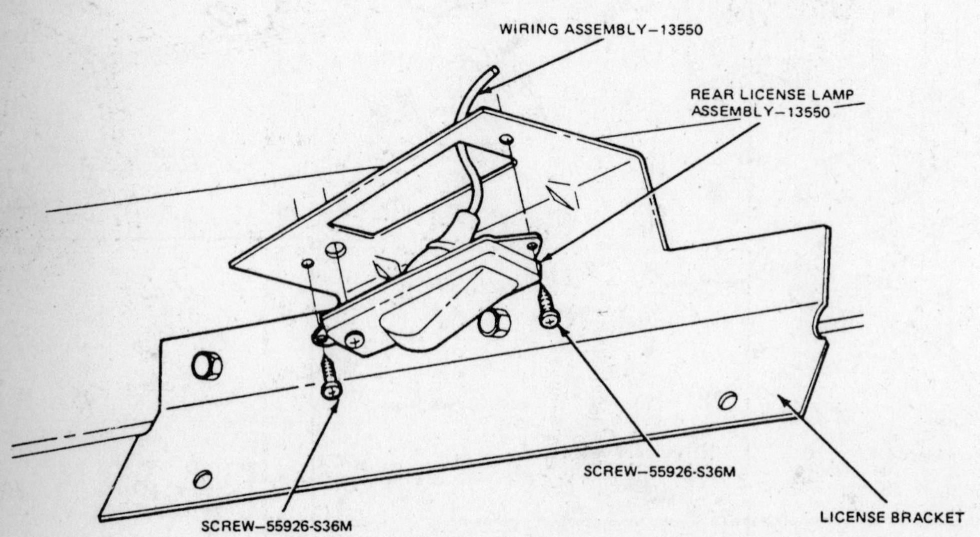

F-150—F-350 STYLESIDE WITHOUT BUMPER

License plate lamps for F-150, 250, 350, and Bronco

Flare Side

The bulbs can be replaced by removing the lens (4 screws). To replace the lamp assembly, remove the 3 nuts from the mounting studs, disconnect the wiring inside the frame rail, unhook the wiring from the retaining clip, pull out the wires and remove the lamp assembly.

Installation is the reverse of removal.

CIRCUIT PROTECTION

Fuses

The fuse panel is located on the firewall above the driver's left foot.

Circuit Breakers

Two circuit are protected by circuit breakers located in the fuse panel: the power windows (20 amp) and the power door locks (30 amp). The breakers are self-resetting.

Turn Signal and Hazard Flasher Locations

Both the turn signal flasher and the hazard warning flasher are mounted on the fuse panel. The turn signal flasher is mounted on the front of the fuse panel, and the hazard warning flasher is mounted on the rear of the fuse panel.

Fuse Link

The fuse link is a short length of special, Hypalon (high temperature) insulated wire, integral with the engine compartment wiring harness and should not be confused with standard wire. It is several wire gauges smaller than the circuit which it protects. Under no circumstances should a fuse link replacement repair be made using a length of standard wire cut from bulk stock or from another wiring harness.

To repair any blown fuse link use the following procedure:

1. Determine which circuit is damaged, its location and the cause of the open fuse link. If the damaged fuse link is one of three fed by a common No. 10 or 12 gauge feed wire, determine the specific affected circuit.
2. Disconnect the negative battery cable.
3. Cut the damaged fuse link from the wiring harness and discard it. If the fuse link is one of three circuits fed by a single feed wire, cut it out of the harness at each splice end and discard it.
4. Identify and procure the proper fuse link and butt connectors for attaching the fuse link to the harness.
5. To repair any fuse link in a 3-link group with one feed:

   a. After cutting the open link out of the harness, cut each of the remaining undamaged fuse links close to the feed wire weld.

   b. Strip approximately ½ in. (13mm) of

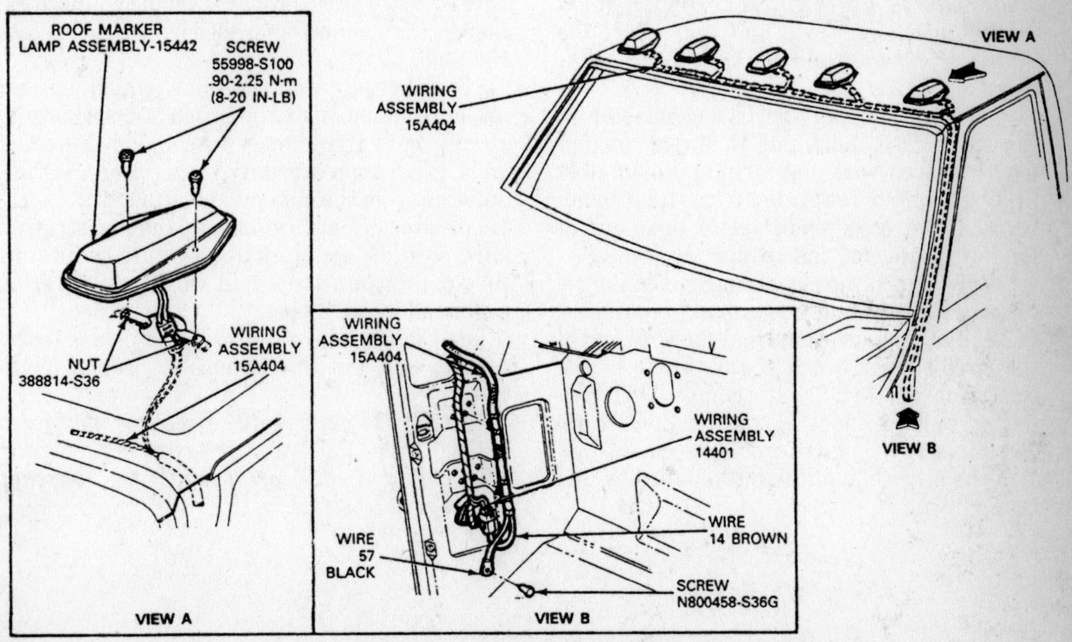

Roof marker lamps for all models

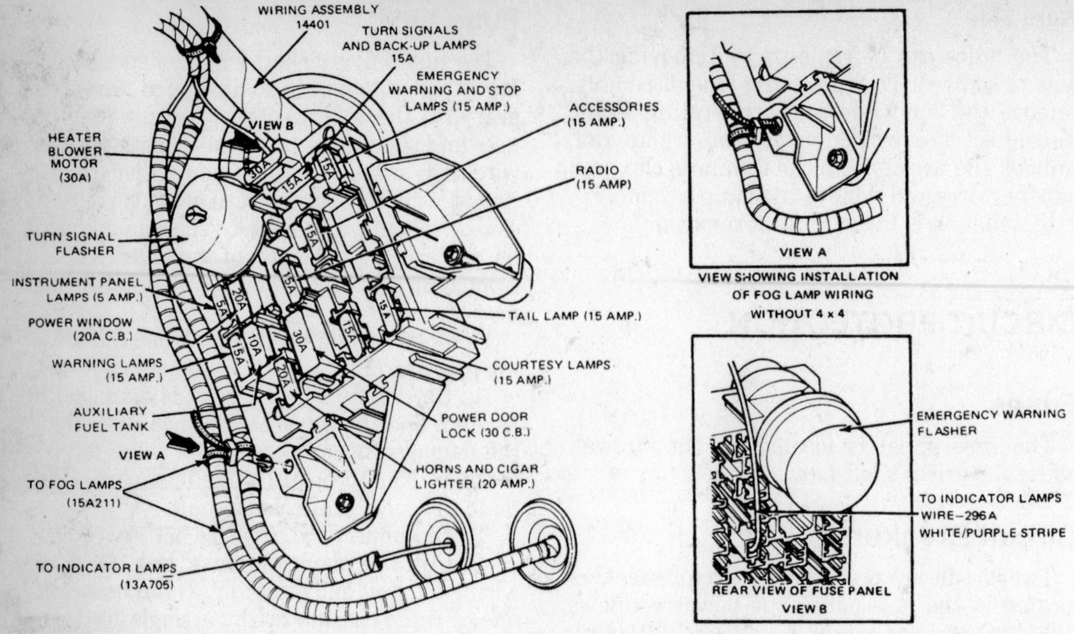

Fuse box, turn signal and hazard flashers

insulation from the detached ends of the two good fuse links. Then insert two wire ends into one end of a butt connector and carefully push one stripped end of the replacement fuse link into the same end of the butt connector and crimp all three firmly together.

NOTE: *Care must be taken when fitting the three fuse links into the butt connector as the internal diameter is a snug it for three wires. Make sure to use a proper crimping tool. Pliers, side cutters, etc. will not apply the proper crimp to retain the wires and withstand a pull test.*

c. After crimping the butt connector to the three fuse links, cut the weld portion from the feed wire and strip approximately $1/2$ in. (13mm) of insulation from the cut end. Insert the stripped end into the open end of the butt connector and crimp very firmly.

d. To attach the remaining end of the replacement fuse link, strip approximately $1/2$ in. (13mm) of insulation from the wire end of the circuit from which the blown fuse link was removed, and firmly crimp a butt connector or equivalent to the stripped wire. Then, insert the end of the replacement link into the other end of the butt connector and crimp firmly.

e. Using rosin core solder with a consistency of 60 percent tin and 40 percent lead, solder the connectors and the wires at the repairs and insulate with electrical tape.

6. To replace any fuse link on a single circuit in a harness, cut out the damaged portion, strip approximately $1/2$ in. (13mm) of insulation from the two wire ends and attach the appropriate replacement fuse link to the stripped wire ends with two proper size butt connectors. Solder the connectors and wires and insulate the tape.

7. To repair any fuse link which has an eyelet terminal on one end such as the charging circuit, cut off the open fuse link behind the weld, strip approximately $1/2$ in. (13mm) of insulation from the cut end and attach the appropriate new eyelet fuse link to the cut stripped wire with an appropriate size butt connector. Solder the connectors and wires at the repair and insulate with tape.

8. Connect the negative battery cable to the battery and test the system for proper operation.

NOTE: *Do not mistake a resistor wire for a fuse link. The resistor wire is generally longer and has print stating, "Resistor: don't cut or splice."*

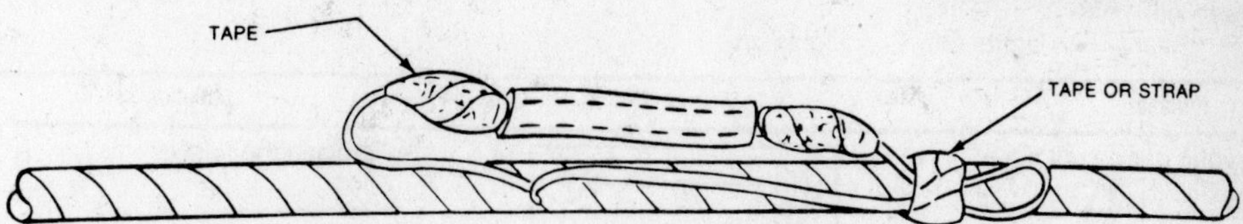

TYPICAL REPAIR USING THE SPECIAL #17 GA. (9.00" LONG-YELLOW) FUSE LINK REQUIRED FOR THE AIR/COND. CIRCUITS (2) #687E and #261A LOCATED IN THE ENGINE COMPARTMENT

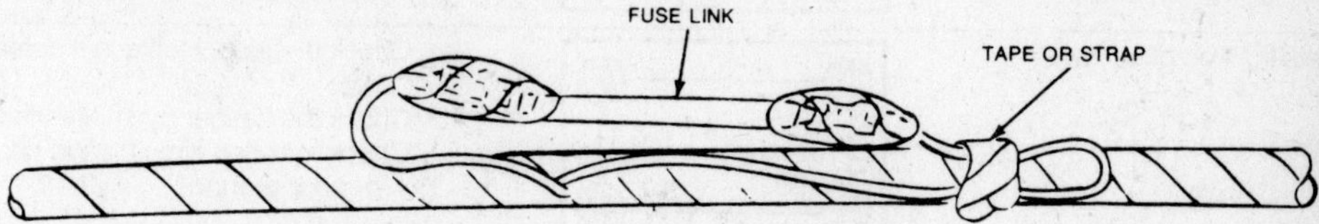

TYPICAL REPAIR FOR ANY IN-LINE FUSE LINK USING THE SPECIFIED GAUGE FUSE LINK FOR THE SPECIFIC CIRCUIT

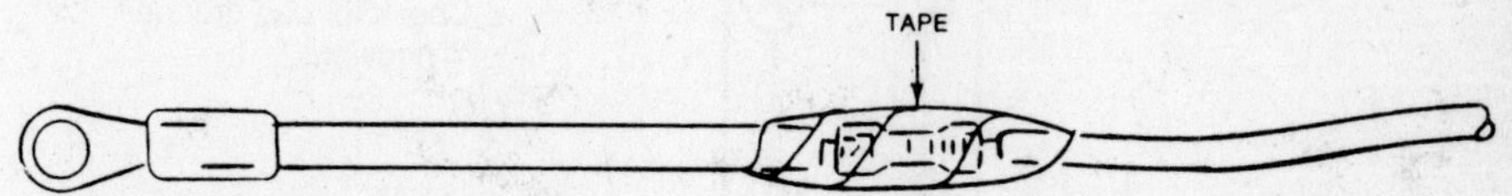

TYPICAL REPAIR USING THE EYELET TERMINAL FUSE LINK OF THE SPECIFIED GAUGE FOR ATTACHMENT TO A CIRCUIT WIRE END

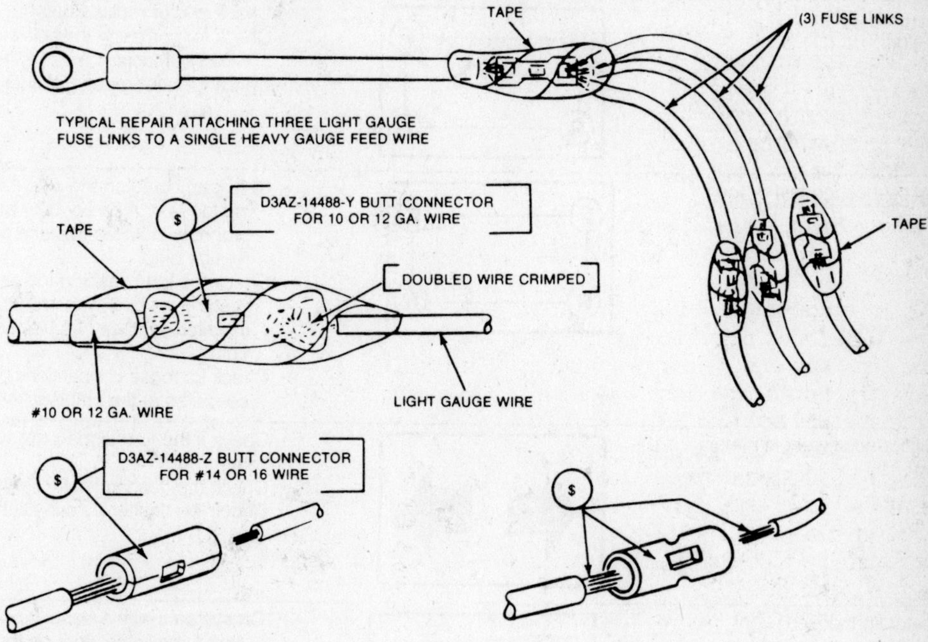

FUSIBLE LINK REPAIR PROCEDURE

General fuse link repair procedure

Troubleshooting Basic Turn Signal and Flasher Problems

Most problems in the turn signals or flasher system can be reduced to defective flashers or bulbs, which are easily replaced. Occasionally, problems in the turn signals are traced to the switch in the steering column, which will require professional service.

F = Front R = Rear • = Lights off ○ = Lights on

Problem		Solution
Turn signals light, but do not flash	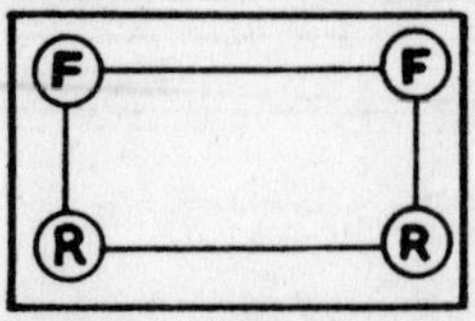 F F / R R	• Replace the flasher
No turn signals light on either side	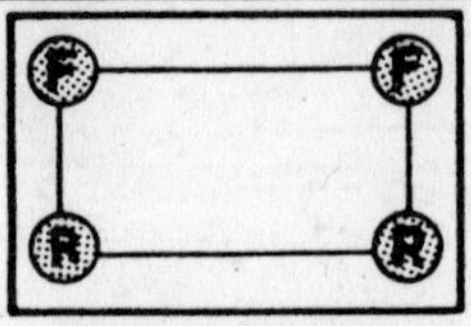 F F / R R	• Check the fuse. Replace if defective. • Check the flasher by substitution • Check for open circuit, short circuit or poor ground
Both turn signals on one side don't work	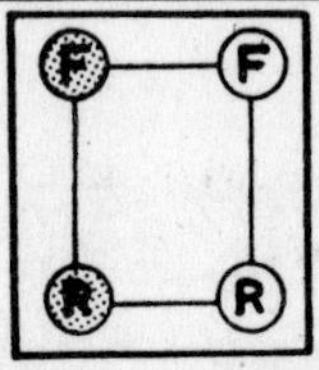 F F / R R	• Check for bad bulbs • Check for bad ground in both housings
One turn signal light on one side doesn't work	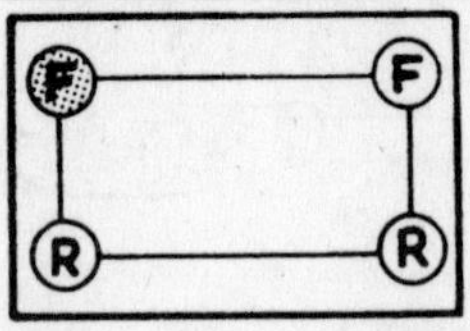 F F / R R	• Check and/or replace bulb • Check for corrosion in socket. Clean contacts. • Check for poor ground at socket
Turn signal flashes too fast or too slow	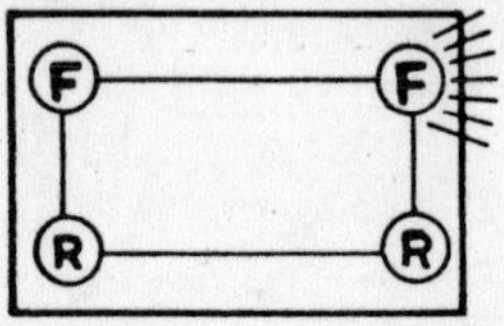 F F / R R	• Check any bulb on the side flashing too fast. A heavy-duty bulb is probably installed in place of a regular bulb. • Check the bulb flashing too slow. A standard bulb was probably installed in place of a heavy-duty bulb. • Check for loose connections or corrosion at the bulb socket
Indicator lights don't work in either direction		• Check if the turn signals are working • Check the dash indicator lights • Check the flasher by substitution
One indicator light doesn't light		• On systems with 1 dash indicator: See if the lights work on the same side. Often the filaments have been reversed in systems combining stoplights with taillights and turn signals. Check the flasher by substitution • On systems with 2 indicators: Check the bulbs on the same side Check the indicator light bulb Check the flasher by substitution

Troubleshooting Basic Lighting Problems

Problem	Cause	Solution
Lights		
One or more lights don't work, but others do	• Defective bulb(s) • Blown fuse(s) • Dirty fuse clips or light sockets • Poor ground circuit	• Replace bulb(s) • Replace fuse(s) • Clean connections • Run ground wire from light socket housing to car frame
Lights burn out quickly	• Incorrect voltage regulator setting or defective regulator • Poor battery/alternator connections	• Replace voltage regulator • Check battery/alternator connections
Lights go dim	• Low/discharged battery • Alternator not charging • Corroded sockets or connections • Low voltage output	• Check battery • Check drive belt tension; repair or replace alternator • Clean bulb and socket contacts and connections • Replace voltage regulator
Lights flicker	• Loose connection • Poor ground • Circuit breaker operating (short circuit)	• Tighten all connections • Run ground wire from light housing to car frame • Check connections and look for bare wires
Lights "flare"—Some flare is normal on acceleration—if excessive, see "Lights Burn Out Quickly"	• High voltage setting	• Replace voltage regulator
Lights glare—approaching drivers are blinded	• Lights adjusted too high • Rear springs or shocks sagging • Rear tires soft	• Have headlights aimed • Check rear springs/shocks • Check/correct rear tire pressure
Turn Signals		
Turn signals don't work in either direction	• Blown fuse • Defective flasher • Loose connection	• Replace fuse • Replace flasher • Check/tighten all connections
Right (or left) turn signal only won't work	• Bulb burned out • Right (or left) indicator bulb burned out • Short circuit	• Replace bulb • Check/replace indicator bulb • Check/repair wiring
Flasher rate too slow or too fast	• Incorrect wattage bulb • Incorrect flasher	• Flasher bulb • Replace flasher (use a variable load flasher if you pull a trailer)
Indicator lights do not flash (burn steadily)	• Burned out bulb • Defective flasher	• Replace bulb • Replace flasher
Indicator lights do not light at all	• Burned out indicator bulb • Defective flasher	• Replace indicator bulb • Replace flasher

Troubleshooting Basic Dash Gauge Problems

Problem	Cause	Solution
Coolant Temperature Gauge		
Gauge reads erratically or not at all	• Loose or dirty connections • Defective sending unit	• Clean/tighten connections • Bi-metal gauge: remove the wire from the sending unit. Ground the wire for an instant. If the gauge registers, replace the sending unit.
	• Defective gauge	• Magnetic gauge: disconnect the wire at the sending unit. With ignition ON gauge should register COLD. Ground the wire; gauge should register HOT.
Ammeter Gauge—Turn Headlights ON (do not start engine). Note reaction		
Ammeter shows charge	• Connections reversed on gauge	• Reinstall connections
Ammeter shows discharge	• Ammeter is OK	• Nothing
Ammeter does not move	• Loose connections or faulty wiring • Defective gauge	• Check/correct wiring • Replace gauge
Oil Pressure Gauge		
Gauge does not register or is inaccurate	• On mechanical gauge, Bourdon tube may be bent or kinked	• Check tube for kinks or bends preventing oil from reaching the gauge
	• Low oil pressure	• Remove sending unit. Idle the engine briefly. If no oil flows from sending unit hole, problem is in engine.
	• Defective gauge	• Remove the wire from the sending unit and ground it for an instant with the ignition ON. A good gauge will go to the top of the scale.
	• Defective wiring	• Check the wiring to the gauge. If it's OK and the gauge doesn't register when grounded, replace the gauge.
	• Defective sending unit	• If the wiring is OK and the gauge functions when grounded, replace the sending unit
All Gauges		
All gauges do not operate	• Blown fuse • Defective instrument regulator	• Replace fuse • Replace instrument voltage regulator
All gauges read low or erratically	• Defective or dirty instrument voltage regulator	• Clean contacts or replace
All gauges pegged	• Loss of ground between instrument voltage regulator and car • Defective instrument regulator	• Check ground • Replace regulator
Warning Lights		
Light(s) do not come on when ignition is ON, but engine is not started	• Defective bulb • Defective wire	• Replace bulb • Check wire from light to sending unit
	• Defective sending unit	• Disconnect the wire from the sending unit and ground it. Replace the sending unit if the light comes on with the ignition ON.
Light comes on with engine running	• Problem in individual system • Defective sending unit	• Check system • Check sending unit (see above)

Troubleshooting the Heater

Problem	Cause	Solution
Blower motor will not turn at any speed	• Blown fuse • Loose connection • Defective ground • Faulty switch • Faulty motor • Faulty resistor	• Replace fuse • Inspect and tighten • Clean and tighten • Replace switch • Replace motor • Replace resistor
Blower motor turns at one speed only	• Faulty switch • Faulty resistor	• Replace switch • Replace resistor
Blower motor turns but does not circulate air	• Intake blocked • Fan not secured to the motor shaft	• Clean intake • Tighten security
Heater will not heat	• Coolant does not reach proper temperature • Heater core blocked internally • Heater core air-bound • Blend-air door not in proper position	• Check and replace thermostat if necessary • Flush or replace core if necessary • Purge air from core • Adjust cable
Heater will not defrost	• Control cable adjustment incorrect • Defroster hose damaged	• Adjust control cable • Replace defroster hose

Troubleshooting Basic Windshield Wiper Problems

Problem	Cause	Solution
Electric Wipers		
Wipers do not operate— Wiper motor heats up or hums	• Internal motor defect • Bent or damaged linkage • Arms improperly installed on linking pivots	• Replace motor • Repair or replace linkage • Position linkage in park and reinstall wiper arms
Wipers do not operate— No current to motor	• Fuse or circuit breaker blown • Loose, open or broken wiring • Defective switch • Defective or corroded terminals • No ground circuit for motor or switch	• Replace fuse or circuit breaker • Repair wiring and connections • Replace switch • Replace or clean terminals • Repair ground circuits
Wipers do not operate— Motor runs	• Linkage disconnected or broken	• Connect wiper linkage or replace broken linkage
Vacuum Wipers		
Wipers do not operate	• Control switch or cable inoperative • Loss of engine vacuum to wiper motor (broken hoses, low engine vacuum, defective vacuum/fuel pump) • Linkage broken or disconnected • Defective wiper motor	• Repair or replace switch or cable • Check vacuum lines, engine vacuum and fuel pump • Repair linkage • Replace wiper motor
Wipers stop on engine acceleration	• Leaking vacuum hoses • Dry windshield • Oversize wiper blades • Defective vacuum/fuel pump	• Repair or replace hoses • Wet windshield with washers • Replace with proper size wiper blades • Replace pump

Drive Train 7

UNDERSTANDING THE MANUAL TRANSMISSION

Because of the way an internal combustion engine breathes, it can produce torque, or twisting force, only within a narrow speed range. Most modern, overhead valve engines must turn at about 2,500 rpm to produce their peak torque. By 4,500 rpm they are producing so little torque that continued increases in engine speed produce no power increases.

The torque peak on overhead camshaft engines is, generally, much higher, but much narrower.

The manual transmission and clutch are employed to vary the relationship between engine speed and the speed of the wheels so that adequate engine power can be produced under all circumstances. The clutch allows engine torque to be applied to the transmission input shaft gradually, due to mechanical slippage. The car can, consequently, be started smoothly from a full stop.

The transmission changes the ratio between the rotating speeds of the engine and the wheels by the use of gears. 4-speed or 5-speed transmissions are most common. The lower gears allow full engine power to be applied to the rear wheels during acceleration at low speeds.

The clutch drive plate is a thin disc, the center of which is splined to the transmission input shaft. Both sides of the disc are covered with a layer of material which is similar to brake lining and which is capable of allowing slippage without roughness or excessive noise.

The clutch cover is bolted to the engine flywheel and incorporates a diaphragm spring which provides the pressure to engage the clutch. The cover also houses the pressure plate. The driven disc is sandwiched between the pressure plate and the smooth surface of the flywheel when the clutch pedal is released, thus forcing it to turn at the same speed as the engine crankshaft.

The transmission contains a mainshaft which passes all the way through the transmission, from the clutch to the driveshaft. This shaft is separated at one point, so that front and rear portions can turn at different speeds.

Power is transmitted by a countershaft in the lower gears and reverse. The gears of the countershaft mesh with gears on the mainshaft, allowing power to be carried from one to the other. All the countershaft gears are integral with that shaft, while several of the mainshaft gears can either rotate independently of the shaft or be locked to it. Shifting from one gear to the next causes one of the gears to be freed from rotating with the shaft and locks another to it. Gears are locked and unlocked by internal dog clutches which slide between the center of the gear and the shaft. The forward gears usually employ synchronizers; friction members which smoothly bring gear and shaft to the same speed before the toothed dog clutches are engaged.

The clutch is operating properly if:

1. It will stall the engine when released with the vehicle held stationary.

2. The shift lever can be moved freely between first and reverse gears when the vehicle is stationary and the clutch disengaged.

A clutch pedal free-play adjustment is incorporated in the linkage. If there is about 1–2 in. (25–50mm) of motion before the pedal begins to release the clutch, it is adjusted properly. Inadequate free-play wears all parts of the clutch releasing mechanisms and may cause slippage. Excessive free-play may cause inadequate release and hard shifting of gears.

Some clutches use a hydraulic system in place of mechanical linkage. If the clutch fails to release, fill the clutch master cylinder with

Troubleshooting the Manual Transmission

Problem	Cause	Solution
Transmission shifts hard	• Clutch adjustment incorrect	• Adjust clutch
	• Clutch linkage or cable binding	• Lubricate or repair as necessary
	• Shift rail binding	• Check for mispositioned selector arm roll pin, loose cover bolts, worn shift rail bores, worn shift rail, distorted oil seal, or extension housing not aligned with case. Repair as necessary.
	• Internal bind in transmission caused by shift forks, selector plates, or synchronizer assemblies	• Remove, dissemble and inspect transmission. Replace worn or damaged components as necessary.
	• Clutch housing misalignment	• Check runout at rear face of clutch housing
	• Incorrect lubricant	• Drain and refill transmission
	• Block rings and/or cone seats worn	• Blocking ring to gear clutch tooth face clearance must be 0.030 inch or greater. If clearance is correct it may still be necessary to inspect blocking rings and cone seats for excessive wear. Repair as necessary.
Gear clash when shifting from one gear to another	• Clutch adjustment incorrect	• Adjust clutch
	• Clutch linkage or cable binding	• Lubricate or repair as necessary
	• Clutch housing misalignment	• Check runout at rear of clutch housing
	• Lubricant level low or incorrect lubricant	• Drain and refill transmission and check for lubricant leaks if level was low. Repair as necessary.
	• Gearshift components, or synchronizer assemblies worn or damaged	• Remove, disassemble and inspect transmission. Replace worn or damaged components as necessary.
Transmission noisy	• Lubricant level low or incorrect lubricant	• Drain and refill transmission. If lubricant level was low, check for leaks and repair as necessary.
	• Clutch housing-to-engine, or transmission-to-clutch housing bolts loose	• Check and correct bolt torque as necessary
	• Dirt, chips, foreign material in transmission	• Drain, flush, and refill transmission
	• Gearshift mechanism, transmission gears, or bearing components worn or damaged	• Remove, disassemble and inspect transmission. Replace worn or damaged components as necessary.
	• Clutch housing misalignment	• Check runout at rear face of clutch housing
Jumps out of gear	• Clutch housing misalignment	• Check runout at rear face of clutch housing
	• Gearshift lever loose	• Check lever for worn fork. Tighten loose attaching bolts.
	• Offset lever nylon insert worn or lever attaching nut loose	• Remove gearshift lever and check for loose offset lever nut or worn insert. Repair or replace as necessary.
	• Gearshift mechanism, shift forks, selector plates, interlock plate, selector arm, shift rail, detent plugs, springs or shift cover worn or damaged	• Remove, disassemble and inspect transmission cover assembly. Replace worn or damaged components as necessary.
	• Clutch shaft or roller bearings worn or damaged	• Replace clutch shaft or roller bearings as necessary

Troubleshooting the Manual Transmission

Problem	Cause	Solution
Jumps out of gear (cont.)	• Gear teeth worn or tapered, synchronizer assemblies worn or damaged, excessive end play caused by worn thrust washers or output shaft gears	• Remove, disassemble, and inspect transmission. Replace worn or damaged components as necessary.
	• Pilot bushing worn	• Replace pilot bushing
Will not shift into one gear	• Gearshift selector plates, interlock plate, or selector arm, worn, damaged, or incorrectly assembled	• Remove, disassemble, and inspect transmission cover assembly. Repair or replace components as necessary.
	• Shift rail detent plunger worn, spring broken, or plug loose	• Tighten plug or replace worn or damaged components as necessary
	• Gearshift lever worn or damaged	• Replace gearshift lever
	• Synchronizer sleeves or hubs, damaged or worn	• Remove, disassemble and inspect transmission. Replace worn or damaged components.
Locked in one gear—cannot be shifted out	• Shift rail(s) worn or broken, shifter fork bent, setscrew loose, center detent plug missing or worn	• Inspect and replace worn or damaged parts
	• Broken gear teeth on countershaft gear, clutch shaft, or reverse idler gear	• Inspect and replace damaged part
	Gearshift lever broken or worn, shift mechanism in cover incorrectly assembled or broken, worn damaged gear train components	• Disassemble transmission. Replace damaged parts or assemble correctly.

fluid to the proper level and pump the clutch pedal to fill the system with fluid. Bleed the system in the same way as a brake system. If leaks are located, tighten loose connections or overhaul the master or slave cylinder as necessary.

MANUAL TRANSMISSION

Back-Up Light Switch

REMOVAL AND INSTALLATION

The back-up light switch is mounted on the transmission extension housing. this switch is not adjustable. To remove, place the transmission shift lever in any gear but neutral, and disconnect the electrical connector from the switch. Remove the switch assembly from the transmission and install a new switch in the reverse order of removal.

LINKAGE ADJUSTMENT

Ford TOD 4-Speed Overdrive

1. Attach the shift rods in the levers.
2. Rotate the output shaft to determine that the transmission is in neutral.
3. Insert a alignment pin into the shift control assembly alignment hole.
4. Attach the slotted end of the shift rods over the flats of the studs in the shift control assembly.
5. Install the lock nuts and remove the alignment pin.

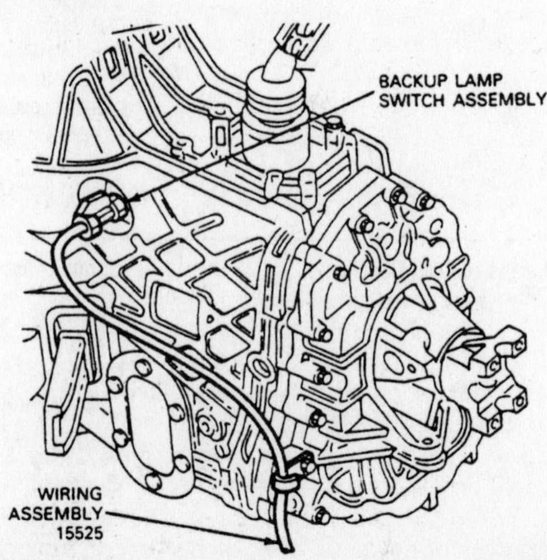

1988–90 back-up lamp switch

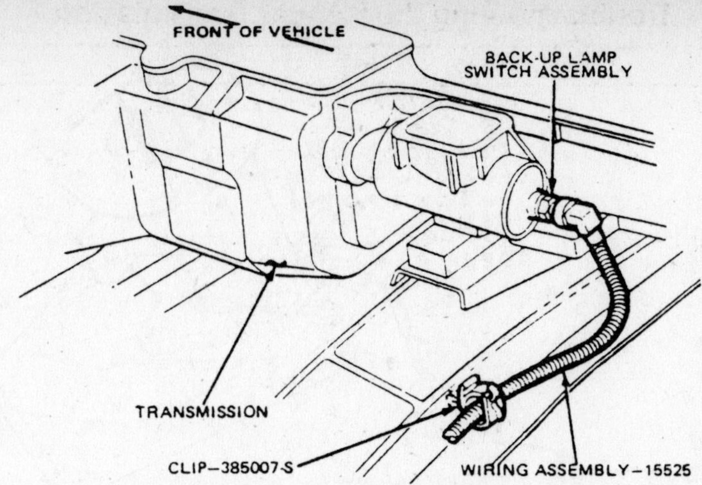

1987 back-up lamp switch

REMOVAL AND INSTALLATION

CAUTION: *The clutch driven disc contains asbestos, which has been determined to be a cancer causing agent. Never clean clutch surfaces with compressed air! Avoid inhaling any dust from any clutch surface! When cleaning clutch surfaces, use a commercially available brake cleaning fluid.*

Warner T-18, T-19A, T-19C 4-Speed

2-WHEEL DRIVE

1. Remove the rubber boot, floor mat, and the body floor pan cover. Remove the gearshift lever. Remove the weather pad.
2. Disconnect the back-up light switch at the rear of the gearshift housing cover.
3. Raise the vehicle and support it with jackstands. Position a transmission jack under the transmission and disconnect the speedometer cable.
4. Disconnect the driveshaft from the transmission and wire it up to one side.
5. Remove the rear transmission support.
6. Remove the transmission attaching bolts.
7. Move the transmission to the rear until the input shaft clears the flywheel housing and lower the transmission.
8. Before installing the transmission, apply a light film of grease to the inner hub surface of the clutch release bearing, the release lever fulcrum and the front bearing retainer of the transmission. do not apply excessive grease because it will fly off onto the clutch disc.
9. Install the transmission in the reverse order of removal. It may be necessary to turn the output shaft with the transmission in gear to align the input shaft splines with the splines in the clutch disc. Fill the transmission with lubricant if it was drained. Observe the following torque specifications:

- Back-up light switch: 25 ft. lbs.
- Transmission-to-clutch housing bolts: 65 ft. lbs.
- Drain plug: 50 ft. lbs.
- Fill plug: 50 ft. lbs.
- Transmission to rear support: 80 ft. lbs.
- Rear support-to-frame: 55 ft. lbs.

4-WHEEL DRIVE

1. Remove the rubber boot, floor mat, and the body floor pan cover. Remove the gearshift lever. Remove the weather pad.
2. Remove the transfer case shift lever, shift ball and boot as an assembly.
3. Disconnect the back-up light switch at the rear of the gearshift housing cover.
4. Raise the vehicle and support it with jackstands. Remove the drain and fill plugs and drain the lubricant.
5. Position a transmission jack under the transfer case and disconnect the speedometer cable.
6. Matchmark the flanges and disconnect the rear driveshaft from the transfer case. Wire it up and out of the way.
7. Matchmark and disconnect the front driveshaft at the transfer case. Wire it up and out of the way.
8. Remove the shift link from the transfer case.
9. Unbolt the transfer case from the transmission (6 bolts) and lower the transfer case from the vehicle.
10. Position the transmission jack under the transmission.
11. Remove the 8 rear transmission support-to-transmission bolts.

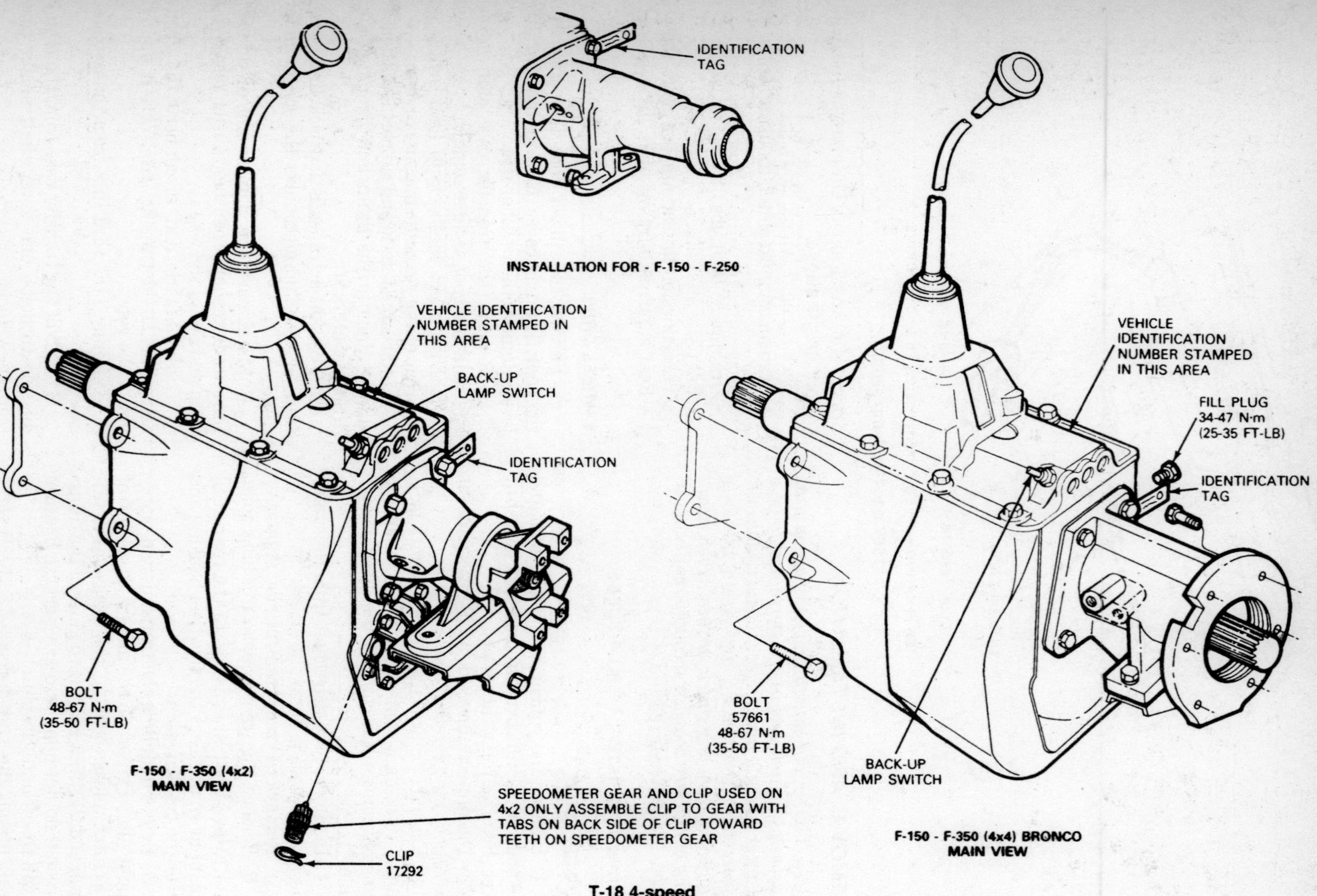
IDENTIFICATION TAG
INSTALLATION FOR - F-150 - F-250
VEHICLE IDENTIFICATION NUMBER STAMPED IN THIS AREA
BACK-UP LAMP SWITCH
IDENTIFICATION TAG
BOLT 48-67 N·m (35-50 FT-LB)
F-150 - F-350 (4x2) MAIN VIEW
SPEEDOMETER GEAR AND CLIP USED ON 4x2 ONLY ASSEMBLE CLIP TO GEAR WITH TABS ON BACK SIDE OF CLIP TOWARD TEETH ON SPEEDOMETER GEAR
CLIP 17292
VEHICLE IDENTIFICATION NUMBER STAMPED IN THIS AREA
FILL PLUG 34-47 N·m (25-35 FT-LB)
IDENTIFICATION TAG
BOLT 57661 48-67 N·m (35-50 FT-LB)
BACK-UP LAMP SWITCH
F-150 - F-350 (4x4) BRONCO MAIN VIEW

T-18 4-speed

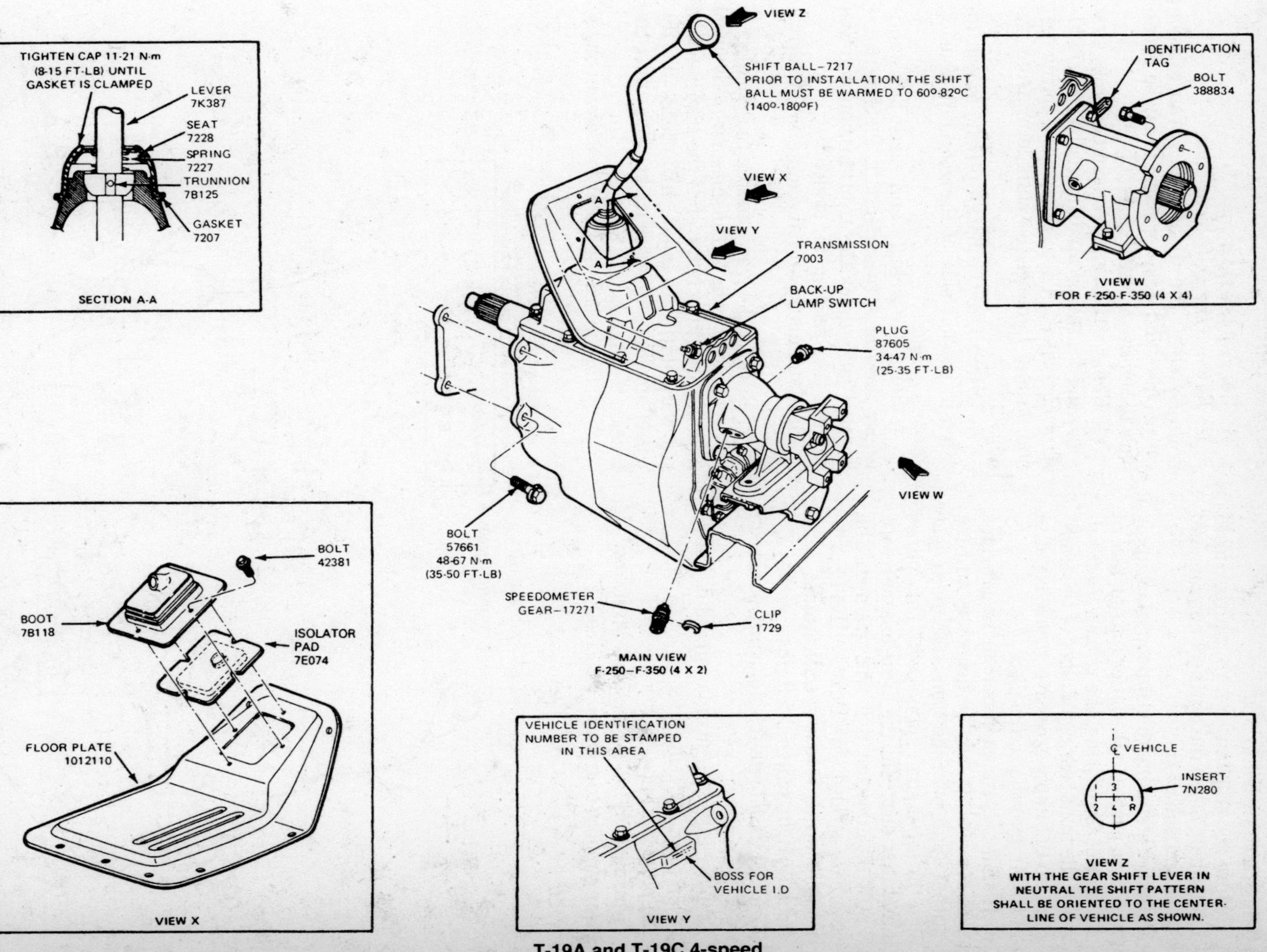

T-19A and T-19C 4-speed

12. Remove the rear transmission support.

13. Remove the 4 transmission-to-clutch housing attaching bolts.

14. Move the transmission to the rear until the input shaft clears the flywheel housing and lower the transmission.

15. Before installing the transmission, apply a light film of grease to the inner hub surface of the clutch release bearing, the release lever fulcrum and the front bearing retainer of the transmission. do not apply excessive grease because it will fly off onto the clutch disc.

16. Install the transmission in the reverse order of removal. It may be necessary to turn the output shaft with the transmission in gear to align the input shaft splines with the splines in the clutch disc. Fill the transmission with SAE 80W/90 lubricant if it was drained. The transfer case is filled with Dexron®II ATF. Observe the following torque specifications:

- Back-up light switch: 25 ft. lbs.
- Transmission-to-clutch housing bolts: 65 ft. lbs.
- Transfer case-to-transmission: 40 ft. lbs.
- Drain plug: 50 ft. lbs.
- Fill plug: 50 ft. lbs.
- Transmission to rear support: 80 ft. lbs.
- Rear support-to-frame: 55 ft. lbs.

New Process 435 4-Speed

2-WHEEL DRIVE

1. Remove the floor mat.

2. Remove the shift lever boot.

3. Remove the floor pan, transmission cover plate, and weather pad. It may be necessary to remove the seat assembly.

4. Remove the shift lever and knob by first removing the inner cap using tool T73T–7220–A, or equivalent. Then, remove the spring seat and spring. Remove the shift lever from the housing.

5. Disconnect the back-up light switch located in the left side of the gearshift housing cover.

4. Raise the vehicle and place jackstands under the frame to support it. Place a transmission jack under the transmission and disconnect the speedometer cable.

6. Matchmark and disconnect the driveshaft.

7. Remove the transmission rear support.

8. Remove the transmission-to-flywheel housing attaching bolts, slide the transmission rearward until the input shaft clears the flywheel housing and lower it out from under the truck.

9. Before installing the transmission, apply

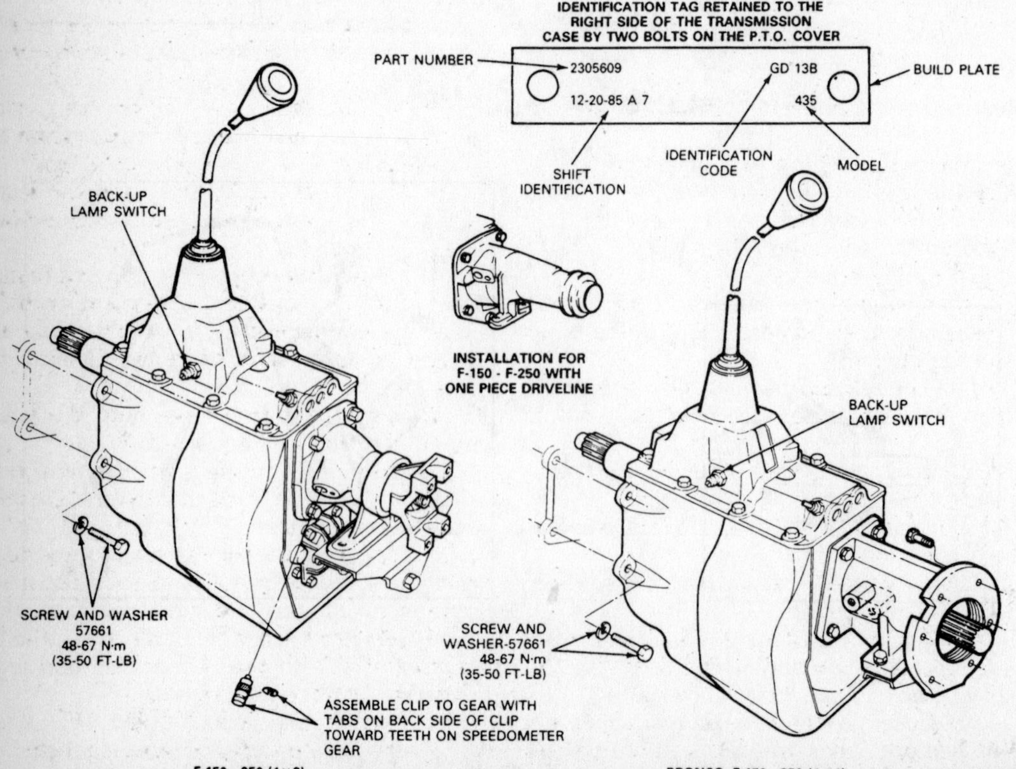

NP-435 4-speed

a light film of grease of the inner hub surface of the clutch release bearing, release lever fulcrum and fork, and the front bearing retainer of the transmission. Do not apply excessive grease because if will fly off and contaminate the clutch disc.

10. Install the transmission in the reverse order of removal. It may be necessary to turn the output shaft with the transmission in gear to align the input shaft splines with the splines in the clutch disc. The front bearing retainer is installed through the clutch release bearing. Observe the following torques:

- Transmission-to-clutch housing bolts: 65 ft. lbs.
- Back-up light switch: 25 ft. lbs.
- Drain and fill plugs: 30 ft. lbs.
- Transmission-to-support: 80 ft. lbs.
- Support-to-frame: 55 ft. lbs.

4-WHEEL DRIVE

1. Remove the transmission lever rubber boot and floor mat.
2. Remove the transfer case shift lever, boot and ball as an assembly.
3. Remove the floor pan, transmission cover plate, and weather pad. It may be necessary to remove the seat assembly.
4. Remove the shift lever and knob by first removing the inner cap using tool T73T–7220–A, or equivalent. Then, remove the spring seat and spring. Remove the shift lever from the housing.
5. Disconnect the back-up light switch located in the left side of the gearshift housing cover.
6. Raise the vehicle and place jackstands under the frame to support it. Place a transmission jack under the transfer case and disconnect the speedometer cable.
7. Drain the transfer case.
8. Matchmark and disconnect the front driveshaft from the transfer case. Wire is up out of the way.
9. Matchmark and disconnect the rear driveshaft from the transfer case. Wire it up out of the way.
10. Disconnect the shift link from the transfer case.
11. Remove the 3 bolts securing the transfer case to the support bracket.
12. Remove the 6 bolts securing the transfer case to the transmission.
13. Lower the transfer case from the truck.
14. Place the transmission jack under the transmission.
15. Remove the transmission rear support.
16. Remove the transmission-to-flywheel housing attaching bolts, slide the transmission rearward until the input shaft clears the flywheel housing and lower it out from under the truck.
17. Before installing the transmission, apply a light film of grease of the inner hub surface of the clutch release bearing, release lever fulcrum and fork, and the front bearing retainer of the transmission. Do not apply excessive grease because if will fly off and contaminate the clutch disc.
18. Install the transmission in the reverse order of removal. It may be necessary to turn the output shaft with the transmission in gear to align the input shaft splines with the splines in the clutch disc. The front bearing retainer is installed through the clutch release bearing. Observe the following torques:

- Back-up light switch: 25 ft. lbs.
- Transmission-to-clutch housing bolts: 65 ft. lbs.
- Drain and fill plugs: 30 ft. lbs.
- Transmission-to-support: 80 ft. lbs.
- Support-to-frame: 55 ft. lbs.
- Transfer case-to-transmission: 40 ft. lbs.

Ford TOD 4-Speed Overdrive

2-WHEEL DRIVE

1. Raise the truck and support it on jackstands. Drain the transmission.
2. Mark the driveshaft so that it can be installed in the same position.
3. Disconnect the driveshaft at the rear U-joint and slide it off the transmission output shaft.
4. Disconnect the speedometer cable, back-up light switch and high gear switch from the transmission.
5. Remove the shift rods from the levers and the shift control from the extension housing.
6. Support the engine on a jack and remove the extension housing-to-crossmember bolts. Raise the engine just high enough to take the weight off the rear crossmenber. Remove the crossmember.
7. Support the transmission on a jack and unbolt it from the clutch housing.
8. Move the transmission and jack rearward until clear. If necessary, lower the engine enough for clearance.
9. Installation is the reverse of removal. It is a good idea to install and snug down the upper transmission-to-engine bolts first, then the lower. For linkage adjustment, see the beginning of this chapter. check the fluid level. Observe the following torques:

- Back-up light switch: 25 ft. lbs.
- Transmission-to-clutch housing bolts: 65 ft. lbs.
- Drain and fill plugs: 30 ft. lbs.

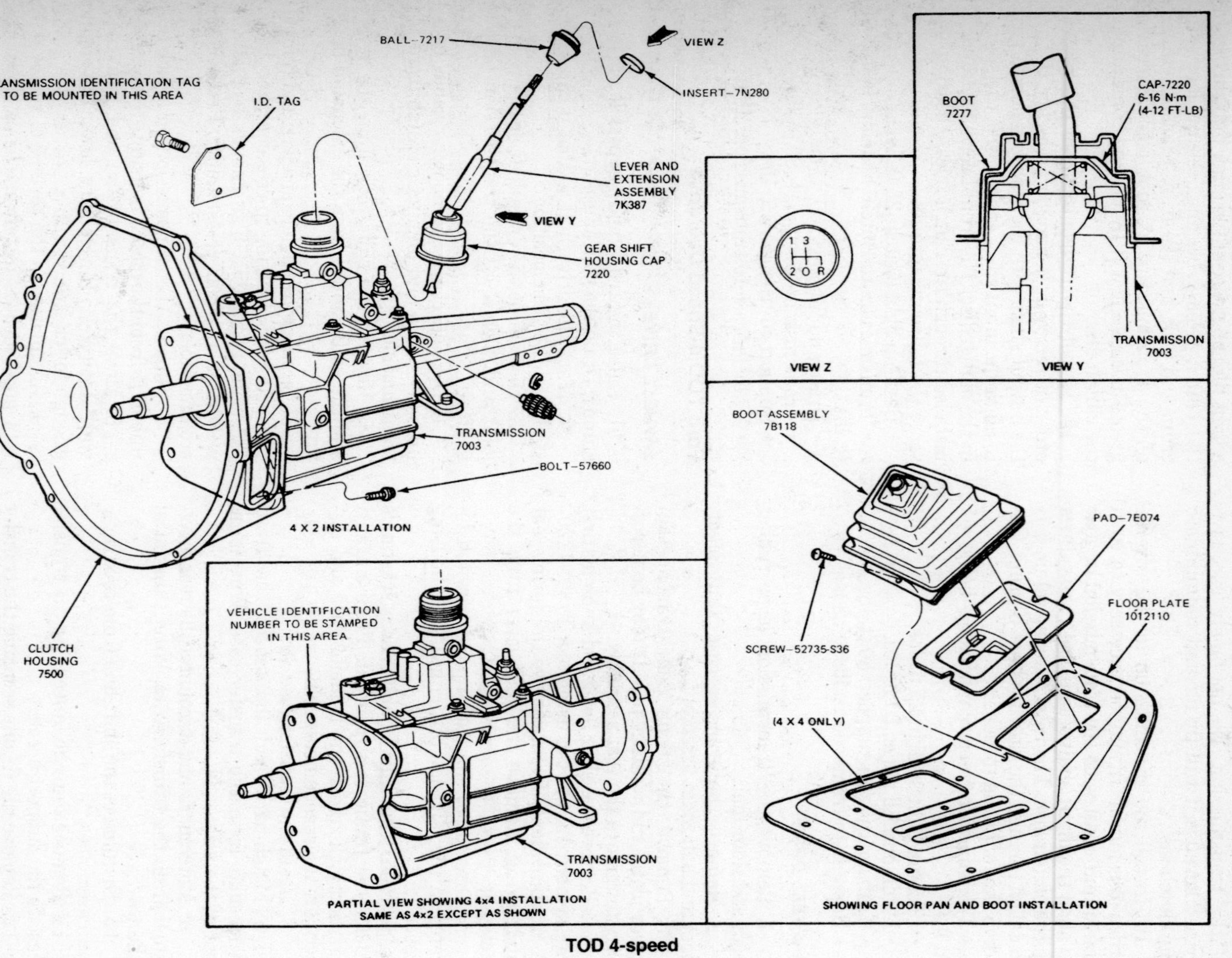

BALL-7217
VIEW Z
TRANSMISSION IDENTIFICATION TAG TO BE MOUNTED IN THIS AREA
I.D. TAG
INSERT-7N280
LEVER AND EXTENSION ASSEMBLY 7K387
VIEW Y
GEAR SHIFT HOUSING CAP 7220
TRANSMISSION 7003
BOLT-57660
4 X 2 INSTALLATION
CLUTCH HOUSING 7500
1 3
2 O R
VIEW Z
BOOT 7277
CAP-7220 6-16 N·m (4-12 FT-LB)
TRANSMISSION 7003
VIEW Y
BOOT ASSEMBLY 7B118
PAD-7E074
SCREW-52735-S36
FLOOR PLATE 1012110
(4 X 4 ONLY)
SHOWING FLOOR PAN AND BOOT INSTALLATION
VEHICLE IDENTIFICATION NUMBER TO BE STAMPED IN THIS AREA
TRANSMISSION 7003
PARTIAL VIEW SHOWING 4x4 INSTALLATION SAME AS 4x2 EXCEPT AS SHOWN

TOD 4-speed

- Transmission-to-support: 80 ft. lbs.
- Support-to-frame: 55 ft. lbs.

4-WHEEL DRIVE

1. Raise the truck and support it on jackstands. Drain the transmission and transfer case.
2. Mark the driveshaft so that it can be installed in the same position.
3. Matchmark and disconnect the front and rear driveshafts at the transfer case.
4. Disconnect the speedometer cable and 4-wheel drive indicator switch from the transfer case; the back-up light switch and high gear switch from the transmission.
5. Remove the skid plate.
6. Disconnect the shift link from the transfer case.
7. Remove the shift lever from the transmission.
8. Support the transmission on a jack and remove the transmission housing rear support bracket.
9. Raise the transmission just high enough to take the weight off the rear crossmember.
10. Remove the 2 nuts securing the upper gusset to the frame on both sides of the frame.
11. Remove the nut and bolt connecting the gusset to the support. Remove the gusset on the left side.
12. Remove the transmission-to-support plate bolts.
13. Remove the support plate and right gusset.
14. Remove the crossmember.
15. Remove the transfer case heat shield. Be very careful if the catalytic converter is hot!
16. Support the transfer case on a jack and unbolt it from the transmission.
17. Move the transfer case and jack rearward until clear and lower it. Discard the adapter gasket.
18. Support the transmission on a jack and unbolt it from the clutch housing.
19. Move the transmission and jack rearward until clear. If necessary, lower the engine for clearance.
20. Installation is the reverse of removal. It is a good idea to install and snug down the upper transmission-to-clutch housing bolts first, then the lower. For linkage adjustment, see the beginning of this chapter. Check the fluid level. Observe the following torques:

- Back-up light switch: 25 ft. lbs.
- Transmission-to-clutch housing bolts: 65 ft. lbs.
- Transfer case-to-transmission: 40 ft. lbs.
- Rear driveshaft-to-yoke: 25 ft. lbs.
- Front driveshaft-to-yoke: 15 ft. lbs.
- Drain and fill plugs: 30 ft. lbs.
- Transmission-to-support: 80 ft. lbs.
- Support-to-frame: 55 ft. lbs.

Mazda M5OD 5-Speed

1. Raise and support the truck on jackstands. Prop the clutch pedal in the full up position with a block of wood.
2. Matchmark the driveshaft-to-flange relation.
3. Disconnect the driveshaft at the rear axle and slide it off of the transmission output shaft. Lubricant will leak out of the transmission so be prepared to catch it, or plug the opening with rags or a seal installation tool.
4. Disconnect the speedometer cable at the transmission.
5. Disconnect the shift rods from the shift levers.
6. Remove the shift control from the extension housing and transmission case.
7. On 4-wheel drive models, remove the transfer case.
8. Remove the extension housing-to-rear support bolts.
9. Take up the weight of the transmission with a transmission jack. Chain the transmission to the jack.
10. Raise the transmission just enough to take the weight off of the No.3 crossmember.
11. Unbolt the crossmember from the frame rails and remove it.
12. Place a jackstand under the rear of the engine at the bellhousing.
13. Lower the jack and allow the jackstand to take the weight of the engine. The engine should be angled slightly downward to allow the transmission to roll backward.
14. Remove the transmission-to bellhousing bolts.
15. Roll the jack rearward until the input shaft clears the bellhousing. Lower the jack and remove the transmission.

WARNING: *Do not depress the clutch pedal with the transmission removed.*

To install:

16. Clean all machined mating surfaces thoroughly.
17. Install a guide pin in each lower bolt hole. Position the spacer plate on the guide pins.
18. Raise the transmission and start the input shaft through the clutch release bearing.
19. Align the input shaft splines with the clutch disc splines. Roll the transmission forward so that the input shaft will enter the clutch disc. If the shaft binds in the release bearing, work the release arm back and forth.
20. Once the transmission is all the way in, install the 2 upper retaining bolts and washers

and remove the lower guide pins. Install the lower bolts. Torque the bolts to 50 ft. lbs.

21. Raise the transmission just enough to allow installation of the No.3 crossmember.
22. Install the crossmember on the frame rails. Torque the bolts to 80 ft. lbs.
23. Lower the transmission onto the crossmember and install the nuts. Torque the nuts to 70 ft. lbs.
24. Remove the transmission jack.
25. Install the transfer case.
26. Install the shift control on the extension housing and transmission case.
27. Connect the shift rods at the shift levers.
28. Connect the speedometer cable at the transmission.
29. Slide the driveshaft onto the output shaft and connect the driveshaft at the rear axle, aligning the matchmarks.

ZF S5-42 5-Speed

1. Place the transmission in neutral.
2. Remove the carpet or floor mat.
3. Remove the ball from the shift lever.
4. Remove the boot and bezel assembly from the floor.
5. Remove the 2 bolts and disengage the upper shift lever from the lower shift lever.
6. Raise and support the tuck on jackstands.
7. Disconnect the speedometer cable.
8. Disconnect the back-up switch wire.
9. Place a drain pan under the case and drain the case through the drain plug.
10. Position a transmission jack under the case and safety-chain the case to the jack.
11. Remove the driveshaft.
12. Disconnect the clutch linkage.
13. On F-Super Duty models, remove the transmission-mounted parking brake. See Chapter 9.
14. On 4-wheel drive models, remove the transfer case.
15. Remove the transmission rear insulator and lower retainer.
16. Unbolt and remove the crossmember.
17. Remove the transmission-to-engine block bolts.
18. Roll the transmission rearward until the input shaft clears, lower the jack and remove the transmission.
19. Install 2 guide studs into the lower bolt holes.
20. Raise the transmission until the input shaft splines are aligned with the clutch disc splines. The clutch release bearing and hub must be properly positioned in the release lever fork.
21. Roll the transmission forward and into position on the front case.
22. Install the bolts and torque them to 50 ft. lbs. Remove the guide studs and install and tighten the 2 remaining bolts.
23. Install the crossmember and torque the bolts to 55 ft. lbs.
24. Install the transmission rear insulator and lower retainer. Torque the bolts to 60 ft. lbs.
25. On 4-wheel drive models, install the transfer case.
26. On F-Super Duty models, install the transmission-mounted parking brake. See Chapter 9.
27. Connect the clutch linkage.
28. Install the driveshaft.
29. Remove the transmission jack.
30. Fill the transmission.
31. Connect the back-up switch wire.
32. Connect the speedometer cable.

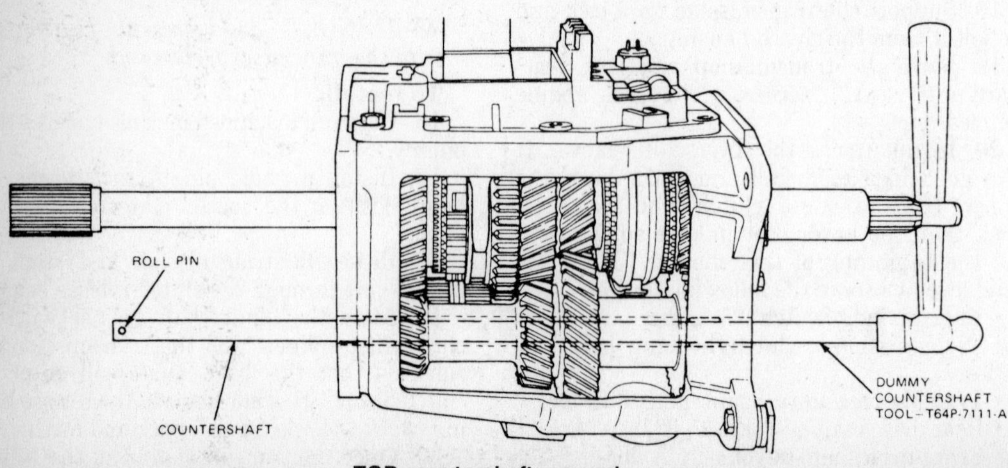

TOD countershaft removal

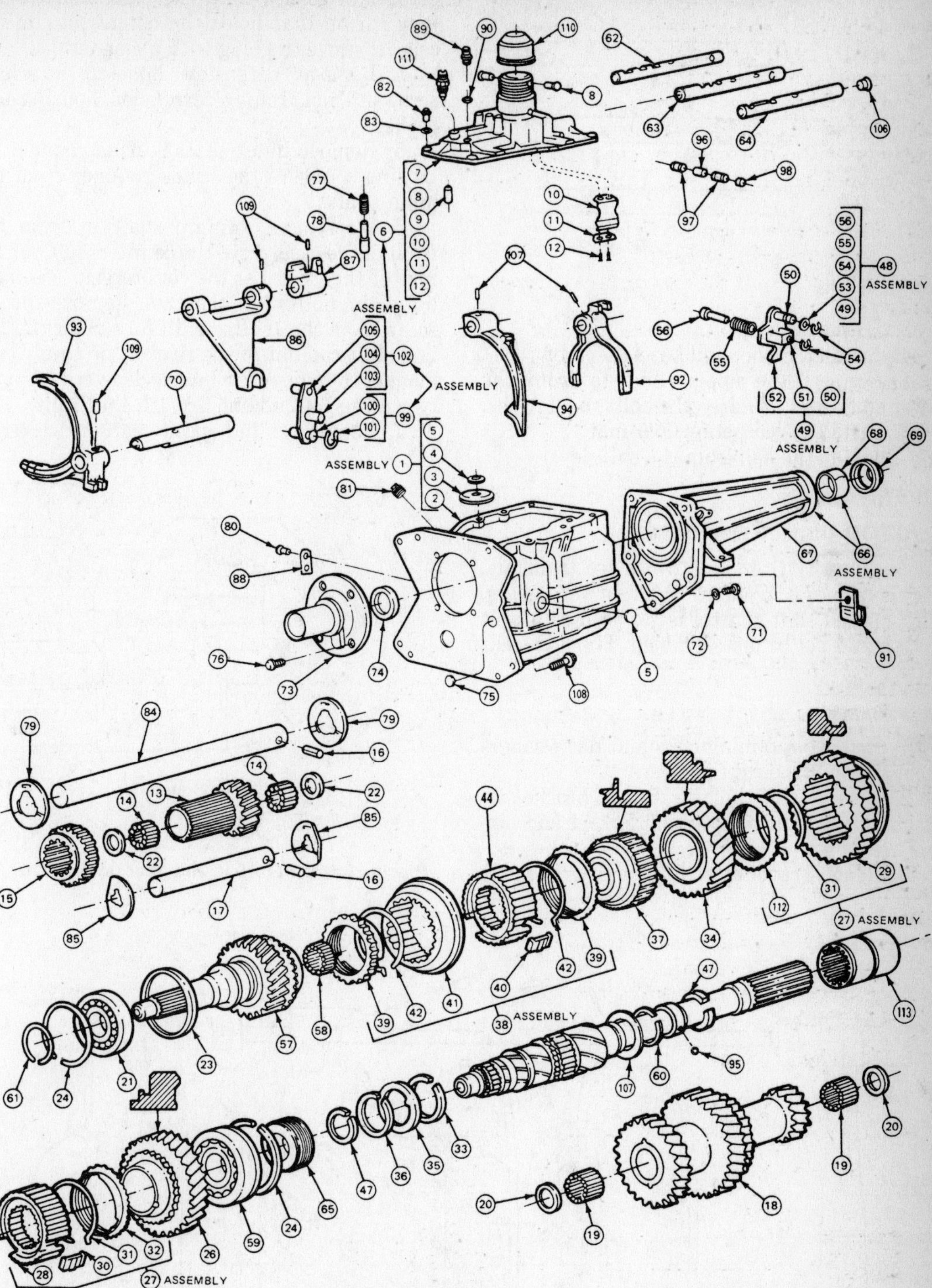

1. Transmission case assy.
2. Transmission case
3. Chip magnet
4. Spring push-on nut
5. Expansion cup plug
6. Gearshift housing assy.
7. Gearshift housing
8. Gearshift lever pin
9. Dowel
10. Third/overdrive shift bias spring
11. Spring retainer plate
12. Rivet
13. Reverse idler gear
14. Idler shaft roller bearings (44)
15. Reverse idler sliding gear
16. Pin
17. Reverse idler gear shaft
18. Countershaft gear

TOD 4-speed exploded view

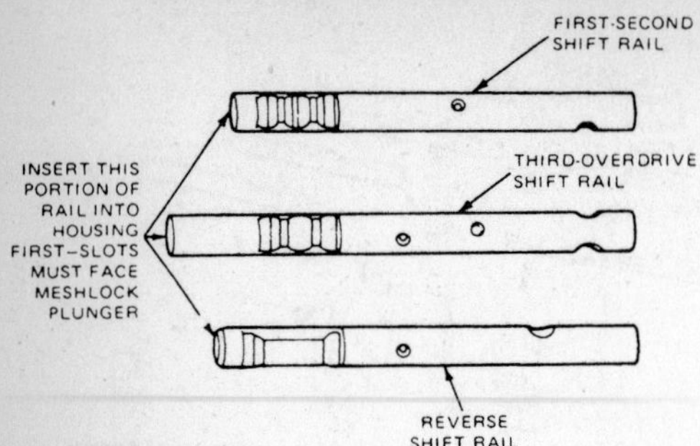

TOD shift rails

33. Lower the van.
34. Install the boot and bezel assembly.
35. Connect the upper shift to from the lower shift lever. Tighten the bolts to 20 ft. lbs.
36. Install the carpet or floor mat.
37. Install the ball from the shift lever.

OVERHAUL

Ford TOD 4-Speed Overdrive

The Ford TOD 4-speed overdrive transmission is fully synchronized in all forward gears. The 4-speed shift control is serviced as a unit and should not be disassembled. The lubricant capacity is 4.5 pints.

DISASSEMBLY

1. Remove retaining clips and flat washers from the shift rods at the levers.
2. Remove shift linkage control bracket attaching screws and remove shift linkage and control brackets.
3. Remove cover attaching screws. Then lift cover and gasket from the case. Remove the long spring that holds the detent plug in the case. Remove the plug with a magnet.
4. Remove extension housing attaching screws. Then, remove extension housing and gasket.
5. Remove input shaft bearing retainer attaching screws. Then, slide retainer from the input shaft.
6. Working a dummy shaft in from the front of the case, drive the countershaft out the rear of the case. Let the countergear assembly lie in the bottom of the case. Remove the set screw from the 1st/2nd shift fork. Slide the 1st/2nd shift rail out of the rear of the case. Use a magnet to remove the interlock detent from between the 1st/2nd and 3rd/4th shift rails.
7. Locate 1st/2nd speed gear shift lever in

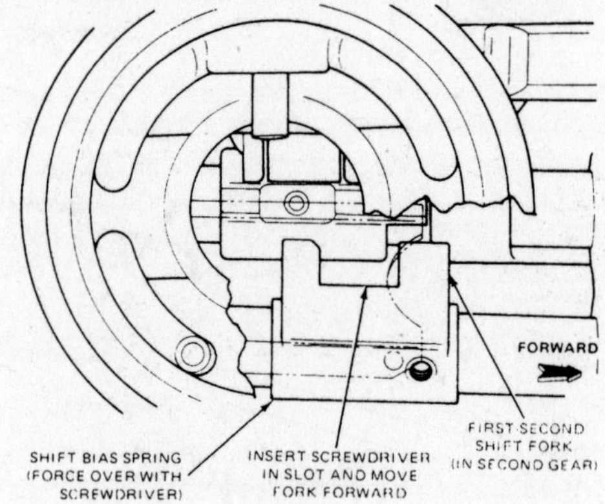

Placing the shift fork in 2nd gear on the TOD

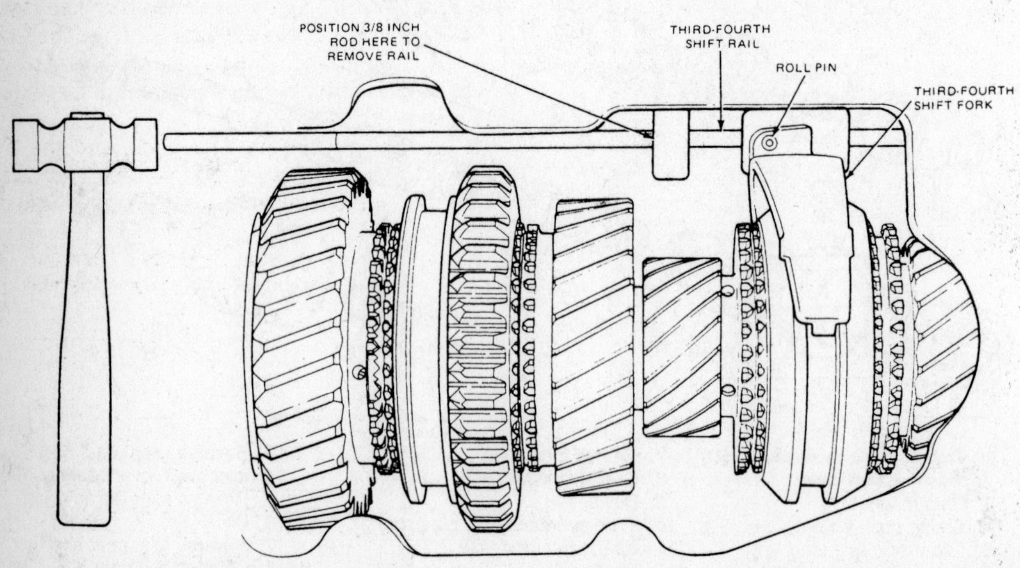

TOD 3rd/4th shift rail removal

neutral. Locate 3rd/4th speed gear shift lever in 3rd speed position.

NOTE: *On overdrive transmissions, locate 3rd/4th speed gear shift lever in the 4th speed position.*

8. Remove the lockbolt that holds the 3rd/4th speed shift rail detent spring and plug in the left side of the case. Remove spring and plug with a magnet.

9. Remove the detent mechanism set screw from top of case. Then, remove the detent spring and plug with a small magnet.

10. Remove attaching screw from the 3rd/4th speed shift fork. Tap lightly on the inner end of the shift rail to remove the expansion plug from front of case. Then, withdraw the 3rd/4th speed shift rail from the front. Do not lose the interlock pin from rail.

11. Remove attaching screw from the 1st and 2nd speed shift fork. Slide the 1st/2nd shift rail from the rear of case.

12. Remove the interlock and detent plugs from the top of the case with a magnet.

13. Remove the snapring or disengage retainer that holds the speedometer drive gear to the output shaft, then remove speedometer gear drive ball.

14. Remove the snapring used to hold the output shaft bearing to the shaft. Pull out the output shaft bearing.

15. Remove the input shaft bearing snaprings. Use a press to remove the input shaft bearing. Remove the input shaft and blocking ring from the front of the case.

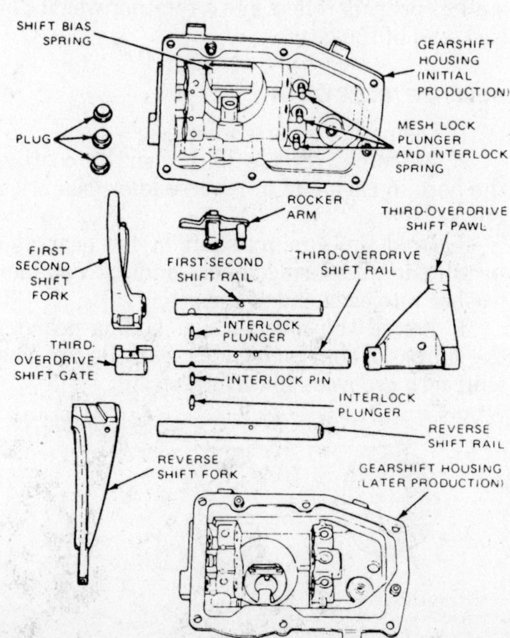

TOD shift housing exploded view

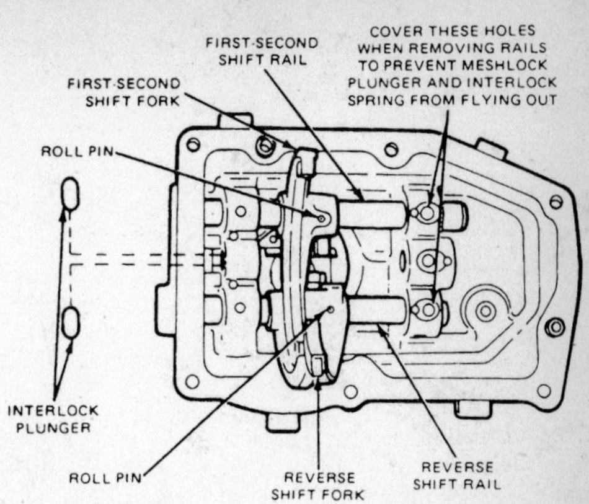

TOD 1st/2nd and reverse shift rail removal

16. Move output shaft to the right side of the case. Then, maneuver the forks to permit lifting them from the case.

17. Support the thrust washer and 1st speed gear to prevent sliding from the shaft, then lift output shaft from the case.

18. Remove reverse gear shift fork attaching screw. Rotate the reverse shift rail 90°, then, slide the shift rail out the rear of the case. Lift out the reverse shift fork.

19. Remove the reverse detent plug and spring from the case with a magnet.

20. Using a dummy shaft, remove the reverse idler shaft from the case.

21. Lift reverse idler gear and thrust washers from the case. Be careful not to drop the bearing rollers or the dummy shaft from the gear.

22. Lift the countergear, thrust washers, rollers and dummy shaft assembly from the case.

23. Remove the next snapring from the front of the output shaft. Then, slide the 3rd/4th synchronizer blocking ring and the 3rd speed gear from the shaft.

24. Remove the next snapring and the 2nd speed gear thrust washer from the shaft. Slide the 2nd speed gear and the blocking ring from the shaft.

25. Remove the snapring, then slide the 1st/2nd synchronizer, blocking ring and the 1st speed gear from the shaft.

26. Remove the thrust washer from rear of the shaft.

CAM & SHAFT SEALS

1. Remove attaching nut and washers from each shift lever, then remove the three levers.

2. Remove the three cams and shafts from inside the case.

3. Replace the old O-rings with new ones that have been well lubricated.

4. Slide each cam and shaft into its respective bore in the transmission.

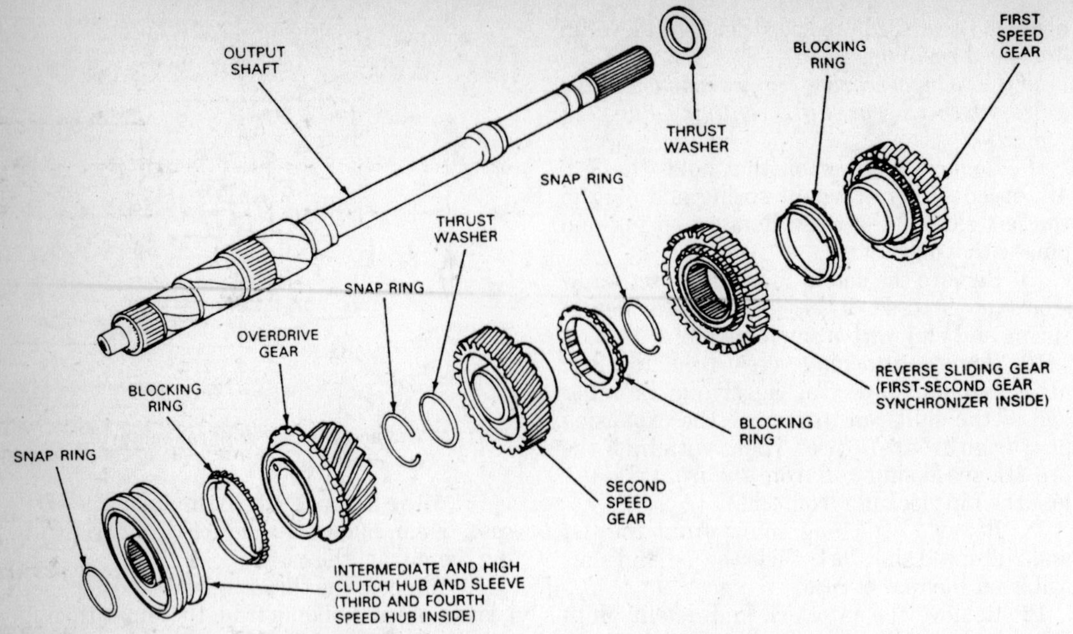

TOD output shaft and gears, exploded view

5. Install the levers and secure them with their respective washers and nuts.

SYNCHRONIZERS

1. Push the synchronizer hub from each synchronizer sleeve.
2. Separate the inserts and springs from the hubs. Do not mix parts of the 1st/2nd with parts of 3rd/4th synchronizers.
3. To assemble, position the hub in the sleeve. Be sure the alignment marks are properly indexed.
4. Place the three inserts into place on the hub. Install the insert springs so that the irregular surface (hump) is seated in one of the inserts. Do not stagger the springs.

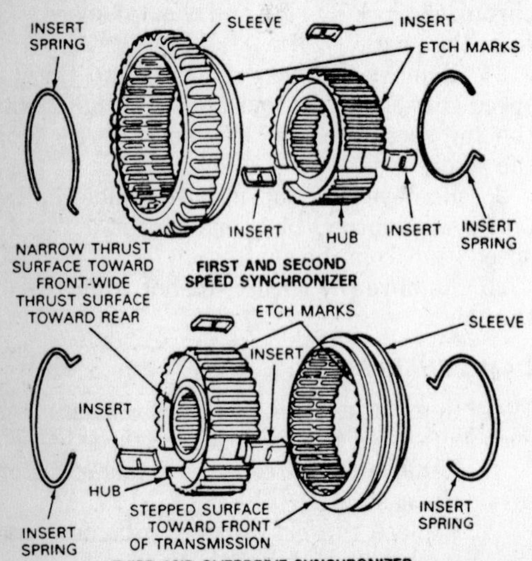

TOD synchronizers, exploded view

COUNTERSHAFT GEAR

1. Dismantle the countershaft gear assembly.
2. Assemble the gear by coating each end of the countershaft gear bore with grease.
3. Install dummy shaft in the gear. Then install 21 bearing rollers and a retainer washer in each end of the gear.

REVERSE IDLER GEAR

1. Dismantle reverse idler gear.
2. Assemble reverse idler gear by coating the bore in each end of reverse idler gear with grease.
3. Hold the dummy shaft in the gear and install the 22 bearing rollers and the retainer washer into each end of the gear.
4. Install the reverse idler sliding gear on the splines of the reverse idler gear. Be sure the shift fork groove is toward the front.

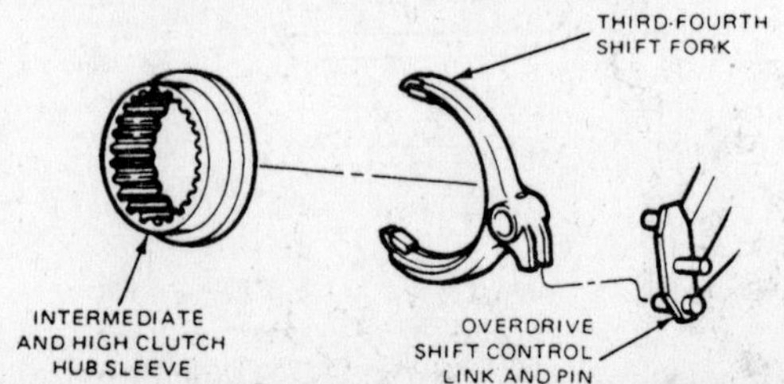

TOD 3rd/4th shift fork installation

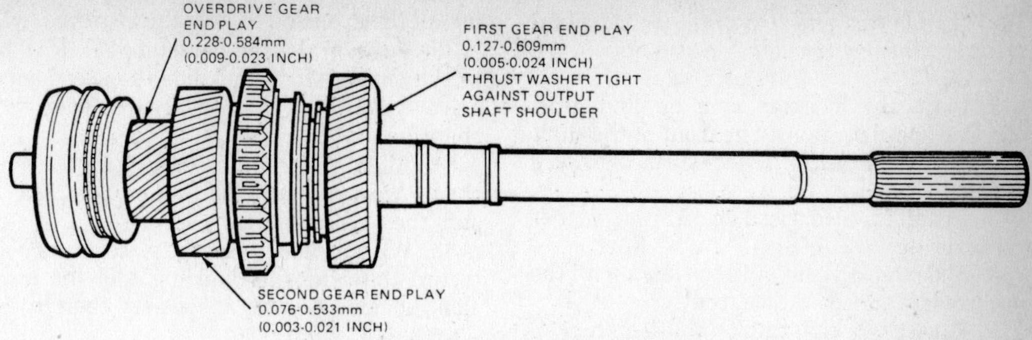

Measuring gear train endplay on the TOD

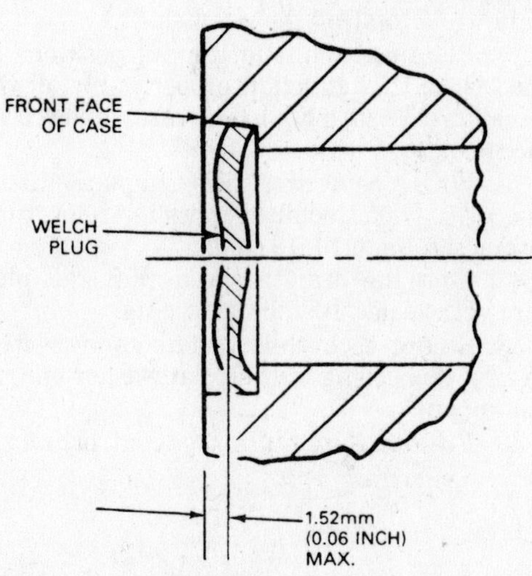

TOD welch plug installation

INPUT SHAFT SEAL

1. Remove the seal from the input shaft bearing retainer.
2. Coat the sealing surface of a new seal with lubricant, then press the new seal into the input shaft bearing retainer.

ASSEMBLY

1. Grease the countershaft gear thrust surfaces in the case. Then, position a thrust washer at each end of the case.
2. Position the countershaft gear, dummy shaft, and roller bearings in the case.
3. Align the gear bore and thrust washers with the bores in the case. Install the countershaft.
4. With the case in a horizontal position, countershaft gear end-play should be from 0.004–0.018 in. (0.10–0.25mm). Use thrust washers to obtain play within these limits.
5. After establishing correct endplay, place the dummy shaft in the countershaft gear and allow the gear assembly to remain on the bottom of the case.
6. Grease the reverse idler gear thrust surfaces in the case, and position the two thrust washers.
7. Position the reverse idler gear, sliding gear, dummy, etc., in place. Make sure that the shift fork groove in the sliding gear is toward the front.
8. Align the gear bore and thrust washers with the case bores and install the reverse idler shaft.
9. Reverse idler gear end-play should be 0.004–0.018 in. (0.10–0.25mm). Use selective thrust washers to obtain play within these limits.
10. Position reverse gear shift rail detent spring and detent plug in the case. Hold the reverse shift fork in place on the reverse idler sliding gear and install the shift rail from the rear of the case. Lock the fork to the rail with the Allen head set screws.
11. Install the 1st/2nd synchronizer onto the output shaft. The 1st and reverse synchronizer hub are a press fit and should be installed with gear teeth facing the rear of the shaft.

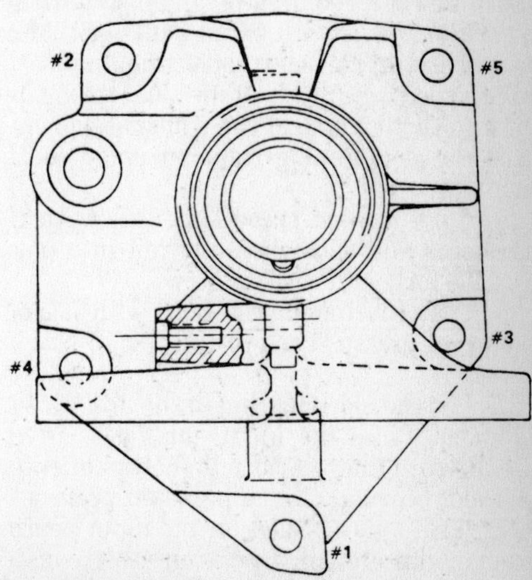

TOD extension housing bolt torque sequence

NOTE: *On overdrive transmissions, 1st and reverse synchronizer hub is a slip fit.*

12. Place the blocking ring on 2nd gear. Slide 2nd speed gear onto the front of the shaft with the synchronizer coned surface toward the rear.
13. Install the 2nd speed gear thrust washer and snapring.
14. Slide the 4th gear onto the shaft with the synchronizer coned surface front.
15. Place a blocking ring on the 4th gear.
16. Slide the 3rd/4th speed gear synchronizer onto the shaft. Be sure that the inserts in the synchronizer engage the notches in the blocking ring. Install the snapring onto the front of the output shaft.
17. Put the blocking ring on the 1st gear.
18. Slide the 1st gear onto the rear of the output shaft. Be sure that the inserts engage the notches in the blocking ring and that the shift fork groove is toward the rear.
19. Install heavy thrust washer onto the rear of the output shaft.
20. Lower the output shaft assembly into the case.
21. Position the 1st/2nd speed shift fork and the 3rd/4th speed shift fork in place on their respective gears. Rotate them into place.
22. Place a spring and detent plug in the detent bore. Place the reverse shift rail into neutral position.
23. Coat the 3rd/4th speed shift rail interlock pin (tapered ends) with grease, then position it in the shift rail.
24. Align the 3rd/4th speed shift fork with the shift rail bores and slide the shift rail into place. Be sure that the three detents are facing the outside of the case. Place the front synchronizer into 4th speed position and install the set screw into the 3rd/4th speed shift fork. Move the synchronizer to neutral position. Install the 3rd/4th speed shift rail detent plug, spring and bolt into the left side of the transmission case. Place the detent plug (tapered ends) in the detent bore.
25. Align 1st/2nd speed shift fork with the case bores and slide the shift rail into place. Lock the fork with the set screw.
26. Coat the input gear bore with a small amount of grease. Then install the 15 bearing rollers.
27. Put the blocking ring in the 3rd/4th synchronizer. Place the input shaft gear in the case. Be sure that the output shaft pilot enters the roller bearing of the input shaft gear.
28. With a new gasket on the input bearing retainer, dip attaching bolts in sealer, install bolts and torque to 30–36 ft. lbs.
29. Press on the output shaft bearing, then install the snapring to hold the bearing.
30. Position the speedometer gear drive ball in the output shaft and slide the speedometer drive gear into place. Secure gear with snapring.
31. Align the countershaft gear bore and thrust washers with the bore in the case. Install the countershaft.
32. With a new gasket in place, install and secure the extension housing. Dip the extension housing screws in sealer, then torque screws to 42–50 ft. lbs.
33. Install the filler plug and the drain plug.
34. Pour E.P. gear oil over the entire gear train while rotating the input shaft.
35. Place each shift fork in all positions to make sure they function properly. Install the remaining detent plug in the case, followed by the spring.
36. With a new cover gasket in place, install the cover. Dip attaching screws in sealer, then torque screws to 14–19 ft. lbs.
37. Coat the 3rd/4th speed shift rail plug bore with sealer. Install a new plug.
38. Secure each shift rod to its respective lever with a spring washer, flat washer and retaining pin.
39. Position the shift linkage control bracket

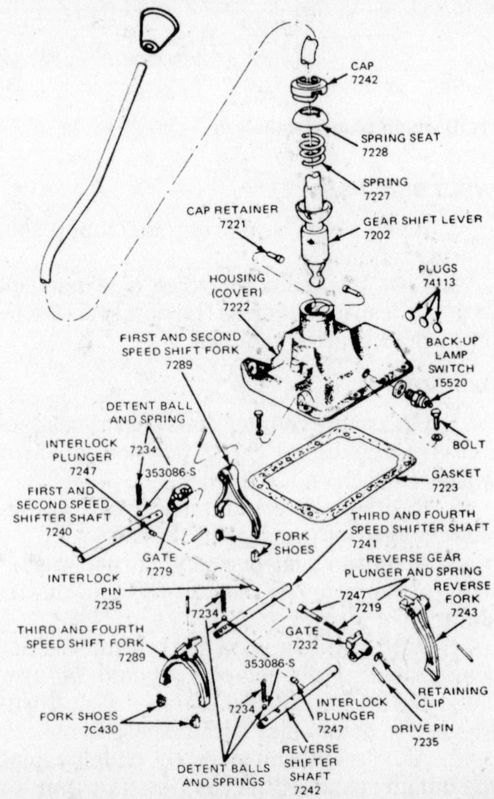

NP-435 shift housing exploded view

to the extension housing. Install and torque the attaching screws to 12–15 ft. lbs.

NP-435 4-Speed

DISASSEMBLY

1. Mount the transmission in a holding fixture. Remove the parking brake assembly, if one is installed.

2. Shift the gears into neutral by replacing the gear shift lever temporarily, or by using a bar or screw driver.

3. Remove the cover screws, the 2nd screw from the front on each side is shouldered with a split washer for installation alignment.

4. While lifting the cover, rotate slightly counterclockwise to provide clearance for the shift levers. Remove the cover.

5. Lock the transmission in two gears and

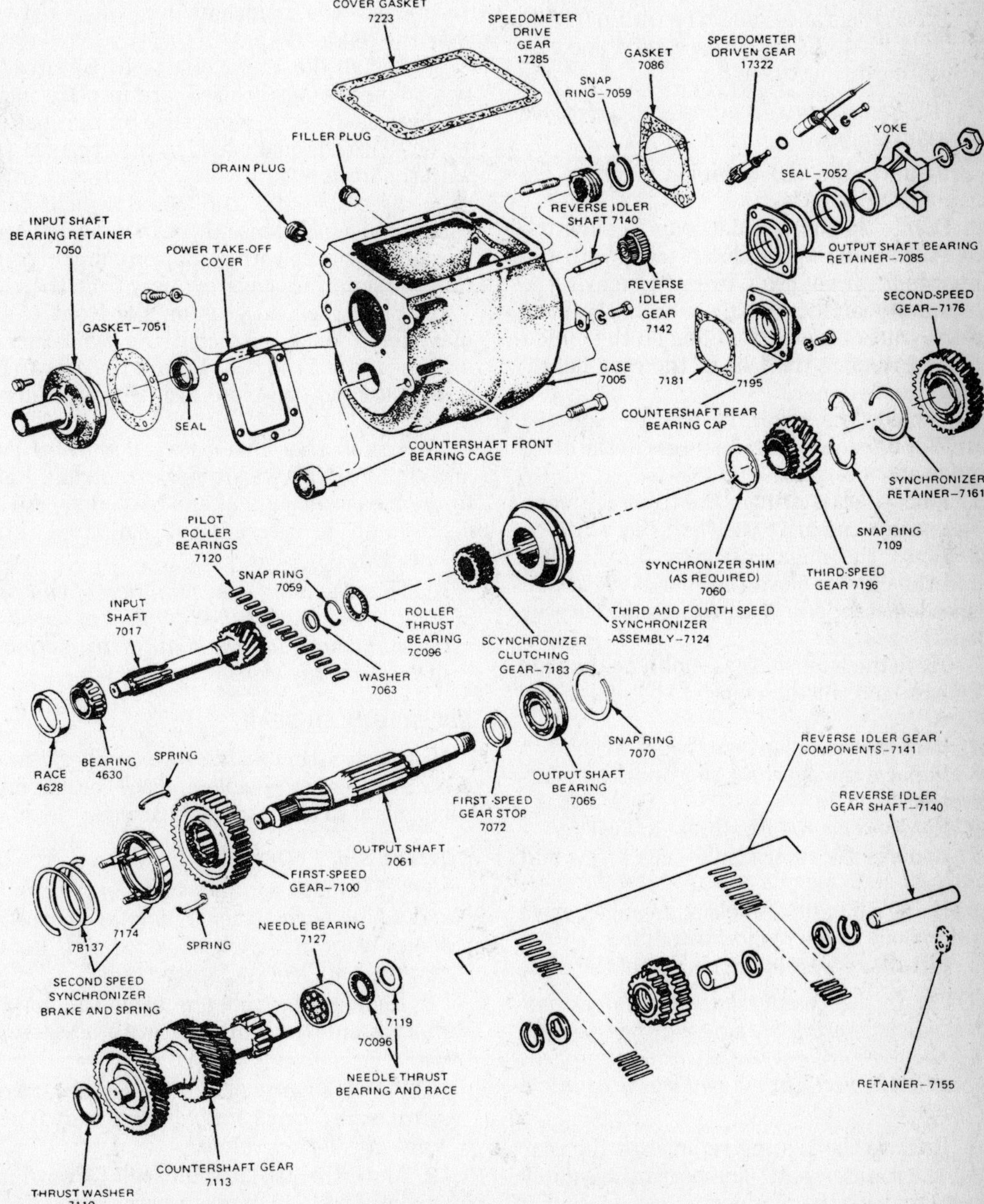

NP-435 4-speed exploded view

remove the output flange nut, the yoke, and the parking brake drum as a unit assembly.

NOTE: *The drum and yoke are balanced and unless replacement of parts are required, it is recommended that the drum and yoke be removed as a assembly.*

6. Remove the speedometer drive gear pinion and the mainshaft rear bearing retainer.

7. Before removal and disassembly of the drive pinion and mainshaft, measure the end play between the synchronizer stop ring and the 3rd gear. Clearance should be within 0.050–0.070 in. (1.27–1.78mm). If necessary, add corrective shims during assembly.

NOTE: *Record this reading for reference during assembly.*

8. Remove the drive pinion bearing retainer.

9. Rotate the drive pinion gear to align the space in the pinion gear clutch teeth with the countershaft drive gear teeth. Remove the drive pinion gear and the tapered roller bearing from the transmission by pulling on the pinion shaft, and rapping the face of the case lightly with a brass hammer.

10. Remove the snapring, washer, and the pilot roller bearings from the recess in the drive pinion gear.

11. Place a brass drift in the front center of the mainshaft and drive the shaft rearward.

12. When the mainshaft rear bearing has cleared the case, remove the rear bearing and the speedometer drive gear with a suitable gear puller.

13. Move the mainshaft assembly to the rear of the case and tilt the front of the mainshaft upward.

14. Remove the roller type thrust washer.

15. Remove the synchronizer and stop rings separately.

16. Remove the mainshaft assembly.

17. Remove the reverse idler lock screw and lock plate.

18. Using a brass drift held at an angle, drive the idler shaft to the rear while pulling.

19. Lift the reverse idler gear out of the case.

NOTE: *If the countershaft gear does not show signs of excessive side play or end play and the teeth are not badly worn or chipped, it may not be necessary to replace the countershaft gear.*

20. Remove the bearing retainer at the rear end of the countershaft. The bearing assembly will remain with the retainer.

21. Tilt the cluster gear assembly and work it out of the transmission case.

22. Remove the front bearings from the case with a suitable driver.

MAINSHAFT

1. Remove the clutch gear snapring.

2. Remove the clutch gear, the synchronizer outer stop ring to 3rd gear shim, and the 3rd gear.

3. Remove the special split lock ring with two screw drivers. Remove the 2nd gear and synchronizer.

4. Remove the 1st/reverse sliding gear.

5. Drive the old seal out of the bearing retainer.

6. Place the mainshaft in a soft-jawed vise with the rear end up.

7. Install the 1st/reverse gear. Be sure the two spline springs, if used, are in place inside the gear as the gear is installed on the shaft.

8. Place the mainshaft in a soft-jawed vise with the front end up.

9. Assemble the 2nd speed synchronizer spring and synchronizer brake on the 2nd gear. Secure the brake with a snapring making sure that the snapring tangs are away from the gear.

10. Slide the 2nd gear on the front of the mainshaft. Make sure that the synchronizer brake is toward the rear. Secure the gear to the shaft with the two piece lock ring. Install the 3rd gear.

11. Install the shim between the 3rd gear and the 3rd/4th synchronizer stop ring. Refer to the measurements of end play made during disassembly to determine if additional shims are needed.

NOTE: *The exact determination of end-play must be made after the complete assembly of the mainshaft and the main drive pinion is installed in the transmission case.*

REVERSE IDLER GEAR

Do not disassemble the reverse idler gear. If it is no longer serviceable, replace the assembly complete with the integral bearings.

COVER & SHIFT FORK UNIT

NOTE: *The cover and shift fork assembly should be disassembled only if inspection shows worn or damaged parts, or if the assembly is not working properly.*

1. Remove the roll pin from the 1st/2nd shift fork and the shift gate with a screw extractor.

NOTE: *A square type or a closely wound spiral screw extractor mounted in a tap is preferable for this operation.*

2. Move the 1st/2nd shift rail forward and force the expansion plug out of the cover. Cover the detent ball access hole in the cover with a cloth to prevent it from flying out. Remove the rail, fork, and gate from the cover.

3. Remove the 3rd/4th shift rail, then the

reverse rail in the manner outlined in Steps 1 and 2 above.

4. Compress the reverse gear plunger and remove the retaining clip. Remove the plunger and spring from the gate.

5. Install the spring on the reverse gear plunger and hold it in the reverse shift gate. Compress the spring in the shift gate and install the retaining clip.

6. Insert the reverse shift rail in the cover and place the detent ball and spring in position. Depress the ball and slide the shift rail over it.

7. Install the shift gate and fork on the reverse shift rail. Install a new roll pin in the gate and the fork.

8. Place the reverse fork in the neutral position.

9. Install the two interlock plungers in their bores.

10. Insert the interlock pin in the 3rd/4th shift rail. Install the shift rail in the same manner as the reverse shift rail.

11. Install the 1st/2nd shift rail in the same manner as outlined above. Make sure the interlock plunger is in place.

12. Check the interlocks by shifting the reverse shift rail into the Reverse position. It should be impossible to shift the other rails with the reverse rail in this position.

13. If the shift lever is to be installed at this point, lubricate the spherical ball seat and place the cap in place.

14. Install the back-up light switch.

15. Install new expansion plugs in the bores of the shift rail holes in the cover. Install the rail interlock hole plug.

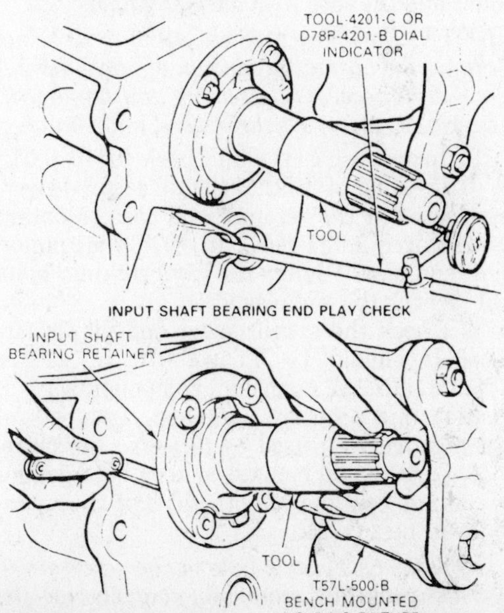

Checking input shaft endplay on the NP-435

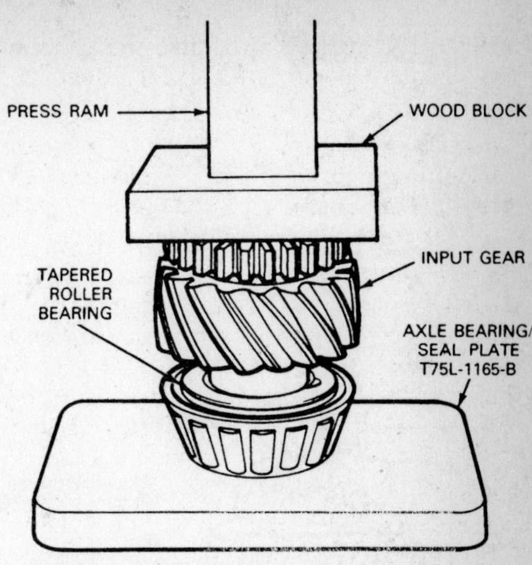

NP-435 input shaft bearing installation

DRIVE PINION & BEARING RETAINER

1. Remove the tapered roller bearing from the pinion shaft with a suitable tool.

2. Remove the snapring, washer, and the pilot rollers from the gear bore, if they have not been previously removed.

3. Pull the bearing race from the front bearing retainer with a suitable puller.

4. Remove the pinion shaft seal with a suitable tool.

5. Position the drive pinion in an arbor press.

6. Place a wood block on the pinion gear and press it into the bearing until it contacts the bearing inner race.

7. Coat the roller bearings with a light film of grease to hold the bearings in place, and

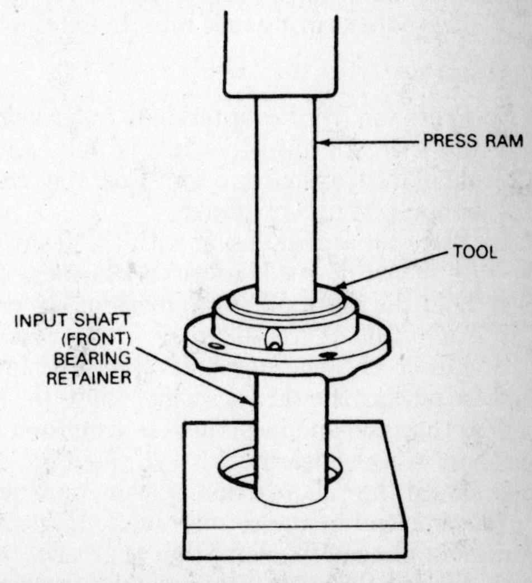

NP-435 front bearing race installation

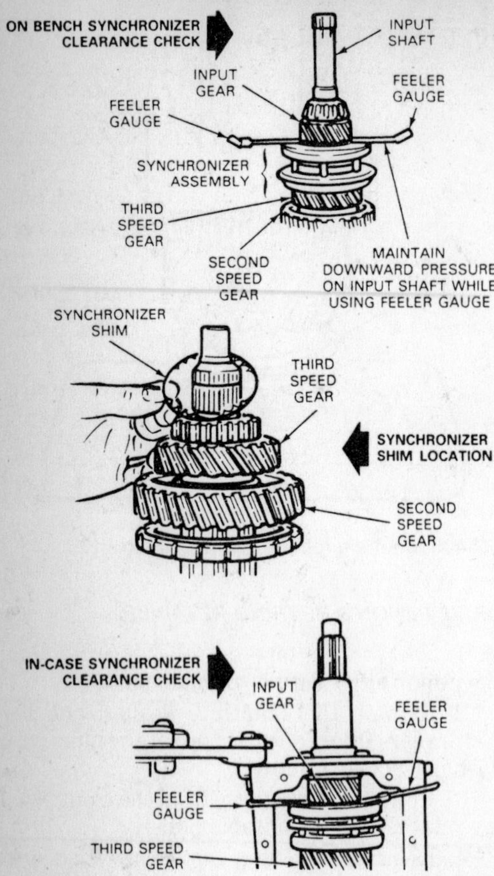

Measuring input shaft-to-synchronizer clearance on the NP-435

insert them in the pocket of the drive pinion gear.

8. Install the washer and snapring.
9. Press a new seal into the bearing retainer. Make sure that the lip of the seal is toward the mounting surface.
10. Press the bearing race into the retainer.

ASSEMBLY

1. Press the front countershaft roller bearings into the case until the cage is flush with the front of the transmission case. Coat the bearings with a light film of grease.
2. Place the transmission with the front of the case facing down. If uncaged bearings are used, hold the loose rollers in place in the cap with a light film of grease.
3. Lower the countershaft assembly into the case placing the thrust washer tangs in the slots in the case, and inserting the front end of the shaft into the bearing.
4. Place the roller thrust bearing and race on the rear end of the countershaft. Hold the bearing in place with a light film of grease.
5. While holding the gear assembly in alignment, install the rear bearing retainer gasket, retainer, and bearing assembly. Install and tighten the cap screws.
6. Position the reverse idler gear and bearing assembly in the case.
7. Align the idler shaft so that the lock plate groove in the shaft is in position to install the lock plate.
8. Install the lock plate, washer, and cap screw.
9. Make sure the reverse idler gear turns freely.
10. Lower the rear end of the mainshaft assembly into the case, holding the 1st gear on the shaft. Maneuver the shaft through the rear bearing opening.

NOTE: *With the mainshaft assembly moved to the rear of the case, be sure the 3rd/4th synchronizer and shims remain in position.*

11. Install the roller type thrust bearing.
12. Place a wood block between the front of the case and the front of the mainshaft.
13. Install the rear bearing on the mainshaft by carefully driving the bearing onto the shaft and into the case, snapring flush against the case.
14. Install the drive pinion shaft and bearing assembly. Make sure that the pilot rollers remain in place.
15. Install the spacer and speedometer drive gear.
16. Install the rear bearing retainer and gasket.
17. Place the drive pinion bearing retainer over the pinion shaft, without the gasket.
18. Hold the retainer tight against the bearing and measure the clearance between the retainer and the case with a feeler gauge.

NOTE: *End play in Steps 19 and 20 below allows for normal expansion of parts during operation, preventing seizure and damage to bearings, gears, synchronizers, and shafts.*

19. Install a gasket shim pack 0.010–0.015 in. (0.25–0.38mm) thicker than measured clearance between the retainer and case to obtain the required 0.007–0.017 in. (0.43mm) pinion shaft end play. Tighten the front retainer bolts and recheck the end play.
20. Check the synchronizer end play clearance. It should be 0.050–0.070 in. (1.27–1.78mm) after all mainshaft components are in position and properly tightened. Two sets of feeler gauges are used to measure the clearance. Care should be used to keep both gauges as close as possible to both sides of the mainshaft for best results.

NOTE: *In some cases, it may be necessary to disassemble the mainshaft and change the thickness of the shims to keep the end play clearance within the specified limits, 0.050–*

0.070 in. (1.27–1.78mm). Shims are available in two thicknesses.

21. Install the speedometer drive pinion.

22. Install the yoke flange, drum, and drum assembly.

23. Place the transmission in two gears at once, and tighten the yoke flange nut.

24. Shift the gears and/or synchronizers into all gear positions and check for free rotation.

25. Cover all transmissions components with a film of transmission oil to prevent damage during start up after initial lubricant fill-up.

26. Move the gears to the neutral position.

27. Place a new cover gasket on the transmission case, and lower the cover over the transmission.

28. Carefully engage the shift forks into their proper gears. Align the cover.

29. Install a shouldered alignment screw with split washer in the screw hole 2nd from the front of the cover. Try out gear operation by shifting through all ranges. Make sure everything moves freely.

30. Install the remaining cover screws.

T-18, T-19A & T-19C 4-Speed

The Warner T-18, T-19A and T-19C transmissions have four forward speeds and one reverse. A power take-off opening is provided on certain transmissions, depending upon the models and applications and can be located on either the right or left sides of the case. The

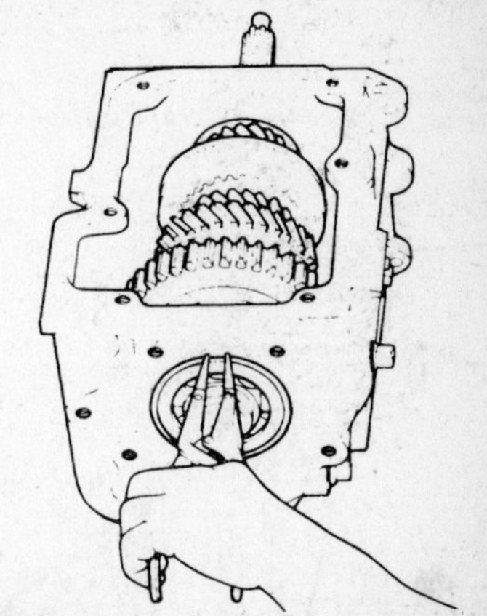

Removing the output shaft bearing snapring on the T-18

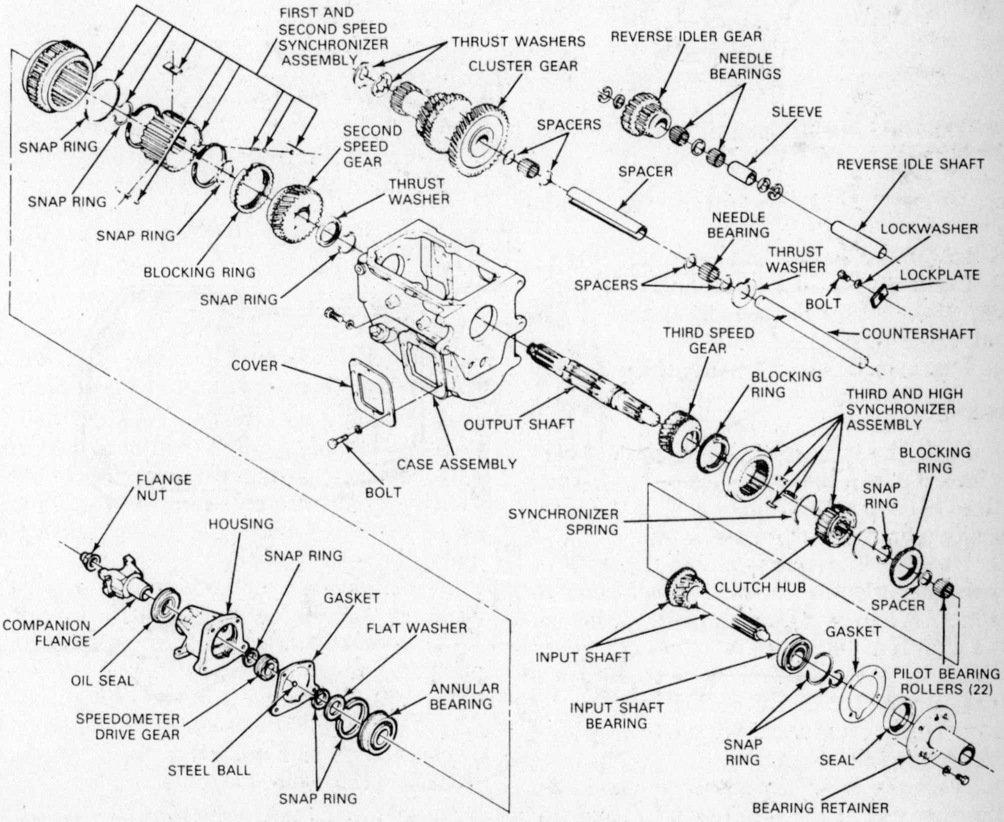

T-18 4-speed exploded view

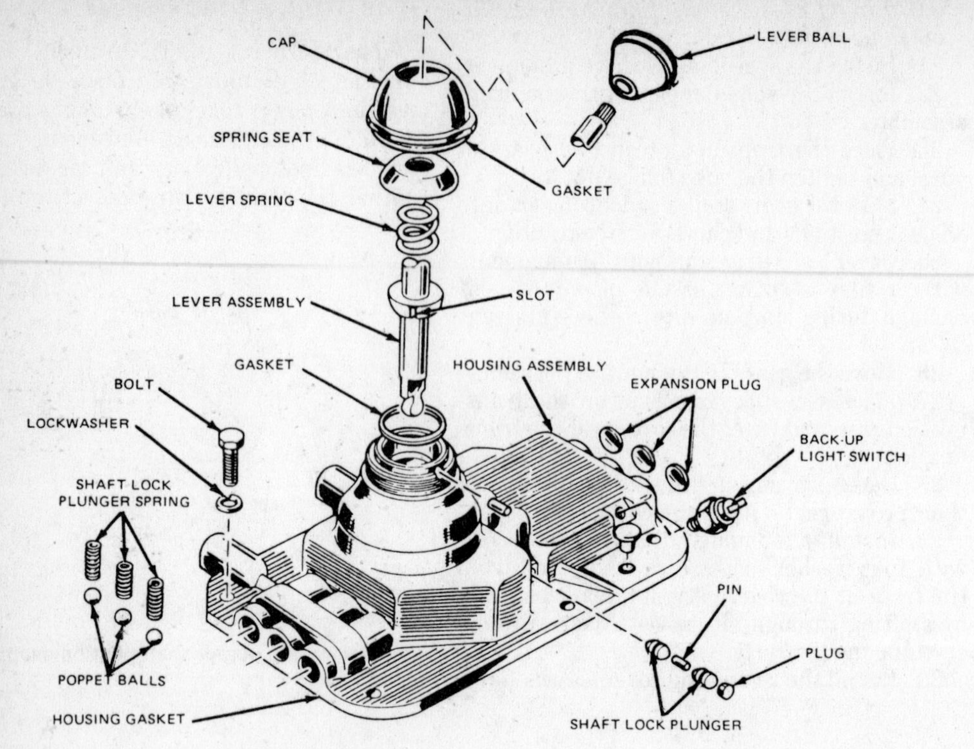

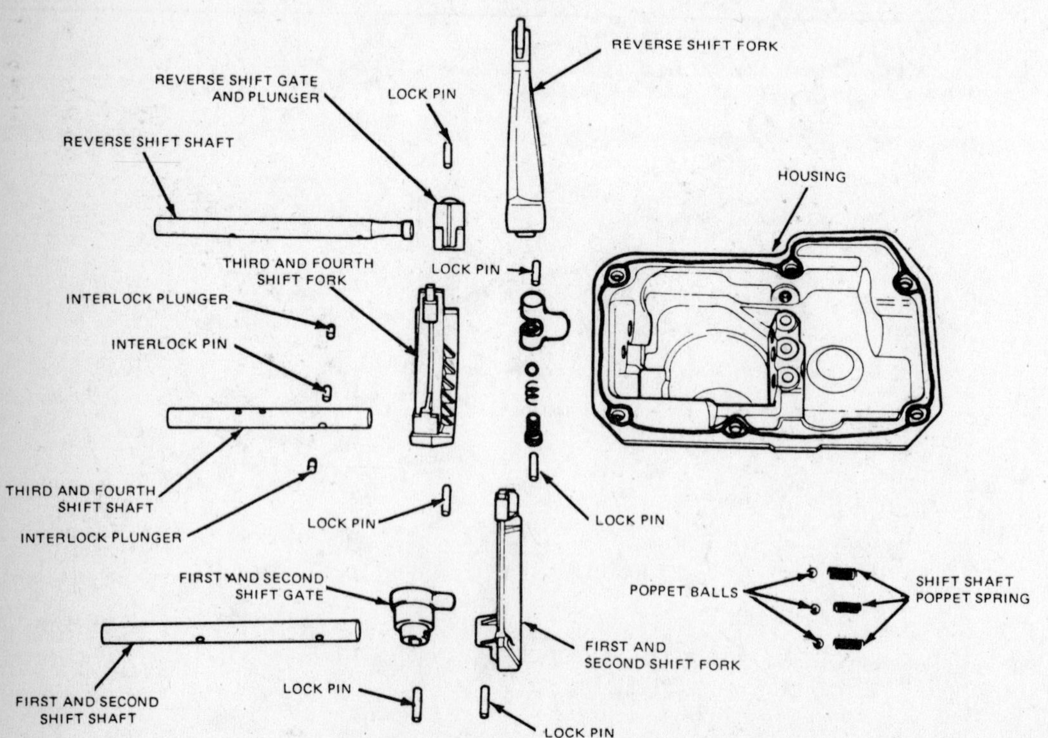

T-18 shift housing exploded view

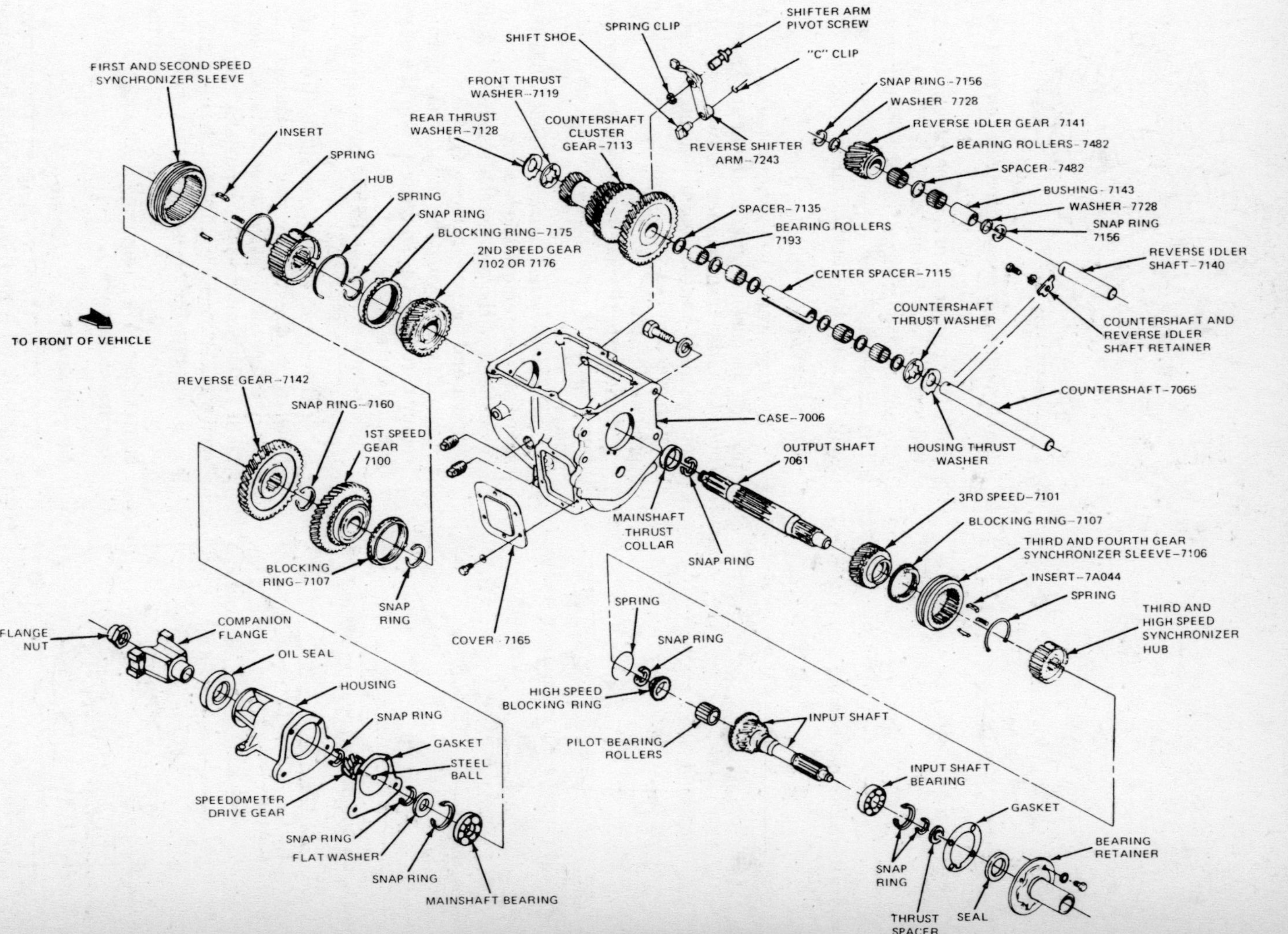

T-19A and T-19C 4-speed exploded view

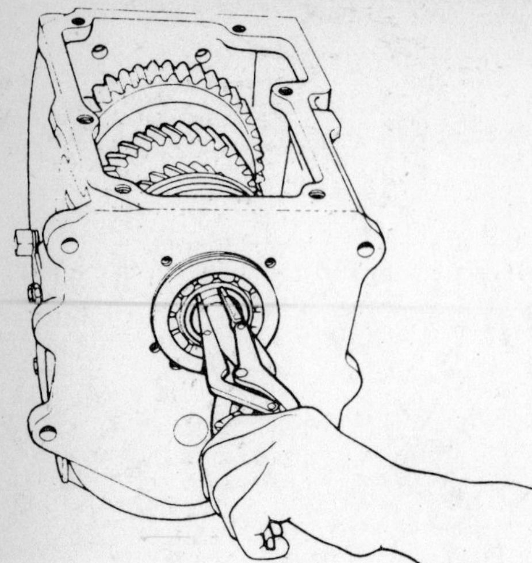

Removing the input shaft bearing snapring on the T-18

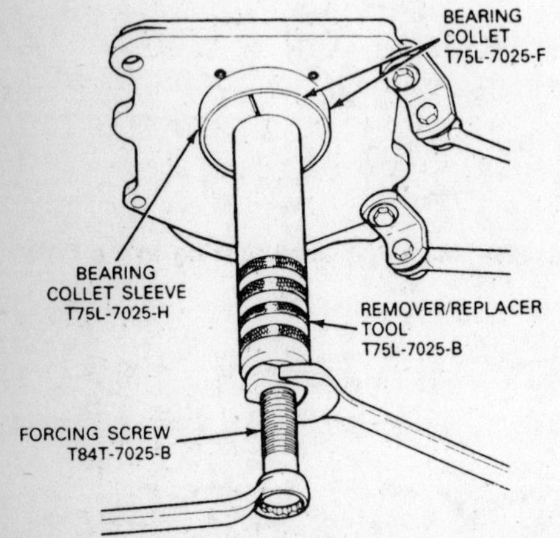

Removing the output shaft bearing on the T-18

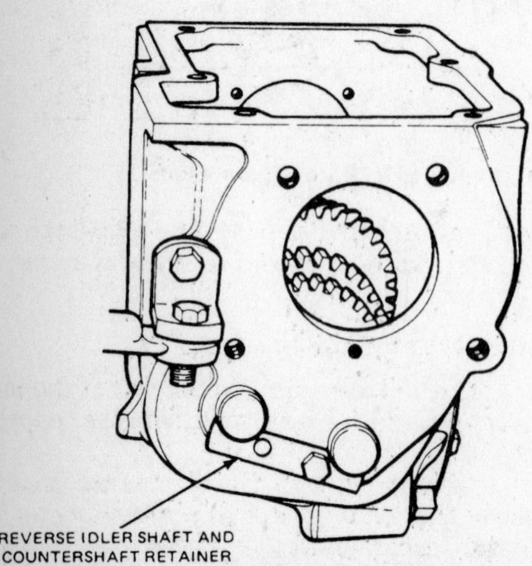

T-18 reverse idler gear shaft and countershaft retainer

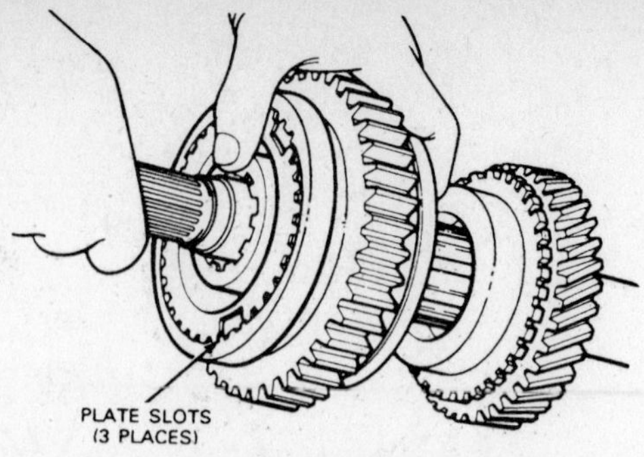

Removing the 2nd gear synchronizer on the T-18

T-18 transmissions are synchronized in 2nd, 3rd and 4th speeds only, while the T-19 transmission is synchronized in all forward gears. The disassembly and assembly remains basically the same for the transmission models.

DISASSEMBLY

1. After draining the transmission and removing the parking brake drum (or shoe assembly), lock the transmission in two gears and remove the U-joint flange, oil seal, speedometer driven gear and bearing assembly. Lubricant capacity is $6^1/_2$ pints.
2. Remove the output shaft bearing retainer and the speedometer drive gear and spacer.
3. Remove the output shaft bearing snapring, and remove the bearing.
4. Remove the countershaft and idler shaft retainer and the power take-off cover.
5. After removing the input shaft bearing retainer, remove the snaprings from the bearing and the shaft.
6. Remove the input shaft bearing and oil baffle.
7. Drive out the countershaft (from the front). Keep the dummy shaft in contact with the countershaft to avoid dropping any rollers.
8. After removing the input shaft and the synchronizer blocking ring, pull the idler shaft.
9. Remove the reverse gear shifter arm, the output shaft assembly, the idler gear, and the cluster gear. When removing the cluster, do not lose any of the rollers.

OUTPUT SHAFT

1. Remove the 3rd/4th speed synchronizer hub snapring from the output shaft, and slide the 3rd/4th speed synchronizer assembly and the 3rd speed gear off the shaft. Remove the synchronizer sleeve and the inserts from the hub. Before removing the two snaprings from the ends of the hub, check the end play of the 2nd speed gear. It should be 0.005–0.024 in. (0.127–0.610mm).
2. Remove the 2nd speed synchronizer

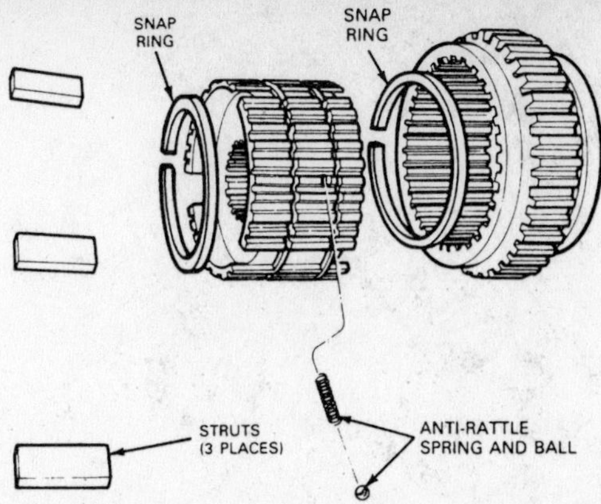

2nd gear synchronizer disassembled on the T-18

snapring. Slide the 2nd speed synchronizer hub gear off the hub. Do not lose any of the balls, springs, or plates.

3. Pull the hub off the shaft, and remove the 2nd speed synchronizer from the 2nd speed gear. Remove the snapring from the rear of the 2nd speed gear, and remove the gear, spacer, roller bearings, and thrust washer from the output shaft. Remove the remaining snapring from the shaft.

CLUSTER GEAR

Remove the dummy shaft, pilot bearing rollers, bearing spacers, and center spacer from the cluster gear.

REVERSE IDLER GEAR

Rotate the reverse idler gear on the shaft, and if it turns freely and smoothly, disassembly of the unit is not necessary. If any roughness is noticed, disassemble the unit.

GEAR SHIFT HOUSING

1. Remove the housing cap and lever. Be sure all shafts are in neutral before disassembly.

2. Tap the shifter shafts out of the housing while holding one hand over the holes in the housing to prevent loss of the springs and balls. Remove the two shaft lock plungers from the housing.

CLUSTER GEAR ASSEMBLY

Slide the long bearing spacer into the cluster gear bore, and insert the dummy shaft in the spacer. Hold the cluster gear in a vertical position, and install one of the bearing spacers. Position the 22 pilot bearing rollers in the cluster gear bore. Place a spacer on the rollers, and install 22 more rollers and another spacer. Hold a large thrust washer against the end of cluster gear and turn the assembly over. Install the rollers and spacers in the other end of the gear.

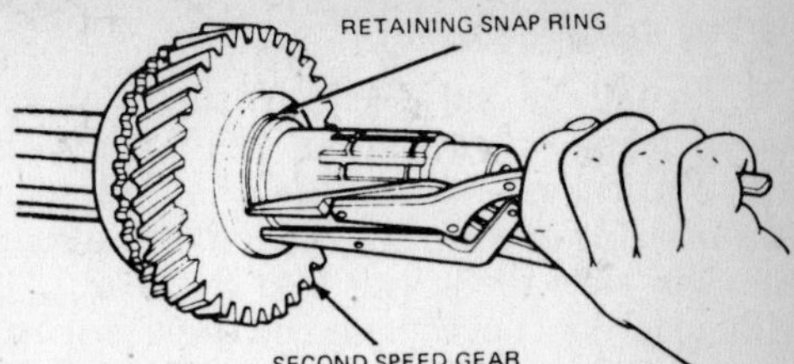

Removing the 2nd gear snapring on the T-18

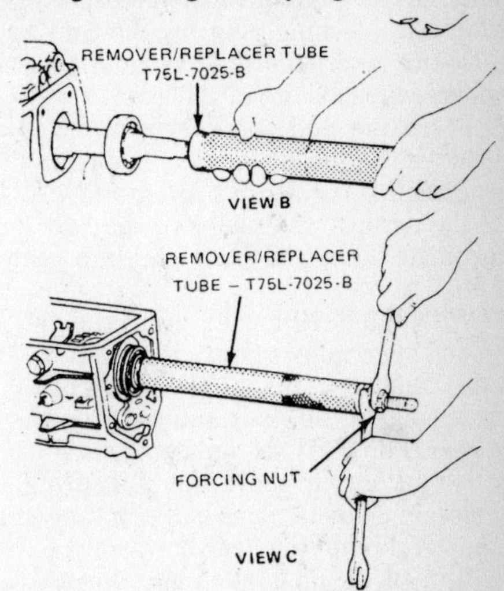

Installing the output shaft bearing on the T-18

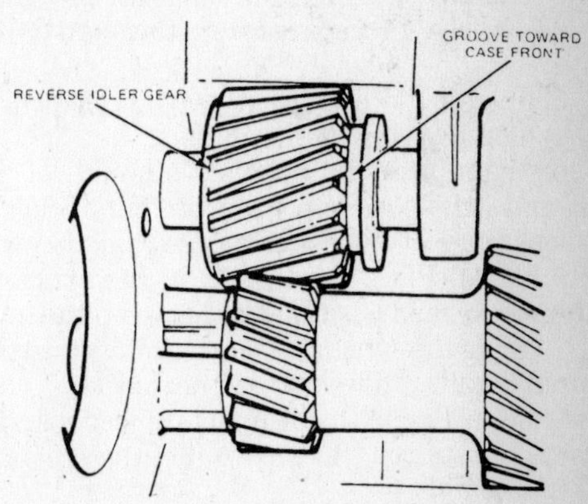

T-19 reverse idler gear installation

REVERSE IDLER GEAR ASSEMBLY

1. Install a snapring in one end of the idler gear, and set the gear on end, with the snapring at the bottom.

2. Position a thrust washer in the gear on top of the snapring. Install the bushing on top of the washer, insert the 37 bearing rollers, and then a spacer followed by 37 more rollers. Place the remaining thrust washer on the rollers, and install the other snapring.

OUTPUT SHAFT ASSEMBLY

1. Install the 2nd speed gear thrust washer and snapring on the output shaft. Hold the shaft vertically, and slide on the 2nd speed gear. Insert the bearing rollers in the 2nd speed gear, and slide the spacer into the gear. (The T-18 model does not contain 2nd speed gear rollers or spacer). Install the snapring on the output shaft at the rear of the 2nd speed gear. Position the blocking ring on the 2nd speed gear. Do not invert the shaft because the bearing rollers will slide out of the gear.

2. Press the 2nd speed synchronizer hub onto the shaft, and install the snapring. Position the shaft vertically in a soft-jawed vise. Position the springs and plates in the 2nd speed synchronizer hub, and place the hub gear on the hub.

3. With the T-19 model, press the 1st and 2nd speed synchronizer onto the shaft and install the snapring. Install the 1st speed gear and snapring on the shaft and press on the reverse gear. For the T-19, ignore Steps 2 and 4.

4. Hold the gear above the hub spring and ball holes, and position one ball at a time in the hub, and slide the hub gear downward to hold the ball in place. Push the plate upward, and insert a small block to hold the plate in position, thereby holding the ball in the hub. Follow these procedures for the remaining balls.

5. Install the 3rd speed gear and synchronizer blocking ring on the shaft.

6. Install the snaprings at both ends of the 3rd and 4th speed synchronizer hub. Stagger the openings of the snaprings so that they are not aligned. Place the inserts in the synchronizer sleeve, and position the sleeve on the hub.

7. Slide the synchronizer assembly onto the output shaft. The slots in the blocking ring must be in line with the synchronizer inserts. Install the snapring at the front of the synchronizer assembly.

GEAR SHIFT HOUSING

1. Place the spring on the reverse gear shifter shaft gate plunger, and install the spring and plunger in the reverse gate. Press the plunger through the gate, and fasten it with the clip. Place the spring and ball in the reverse gate poppet hole. Compress the spring and install the cotter pin.

2. Place the spring and ball in the reverse shifter shaft hole in the gear shift housing. Press down on the ball, and position the reverse shifter shaft so that the reverse shifter arm notch does not slide over the ball. Insert the shaft part way into the housing.

3. Slide the reverse gate onto the shaft, and

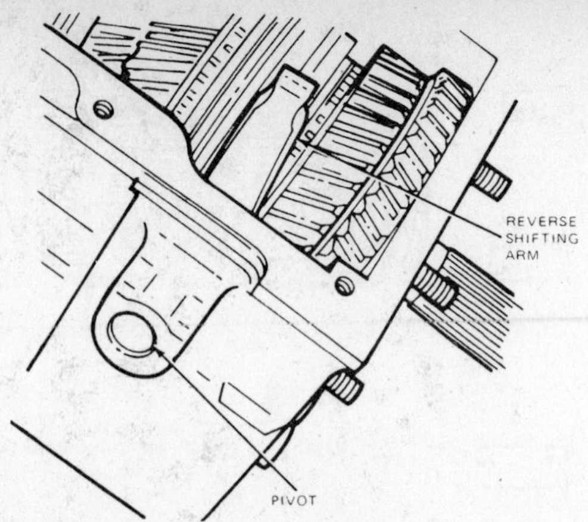

T-19 reverse shift arm installation

drive the shaft into the housing until the ball snaps into the groove of the shaft. Install the lock screw lock wire to the gate.

4. Insert the two interlocking plungers in the pockets between the shifter shaft holes. Place the spring and ball in the low and 2nd shifter shaft hole. Press down on the ball, and insert the shifter shaft part way into the housing.

5. Slide the low and 2nd shifter shaft gate onto the shaft, and install the corresponding shifter fork on the shaft so that the offset of the fork is toward the rear of the housing. Push the shaft all the way into the housing until the ball engages the shaft groove. Install the lock screw and wire that fastens the fork to the shaft. Install the 3rd and high shifter shaft in the same manner. Check the interlocking system. Install new expansion plugs in the shaft bores.

CASE ASSEMBLY

1. Coat all parts, especially the bearings, with transmission lubricant to prevent scoring during initial operation.

2. Position the cluster gear assembly in the case. Do not lose any rollers.

3. Place the idler gear assembly in the case, and install the idler shaft. Position the slot in

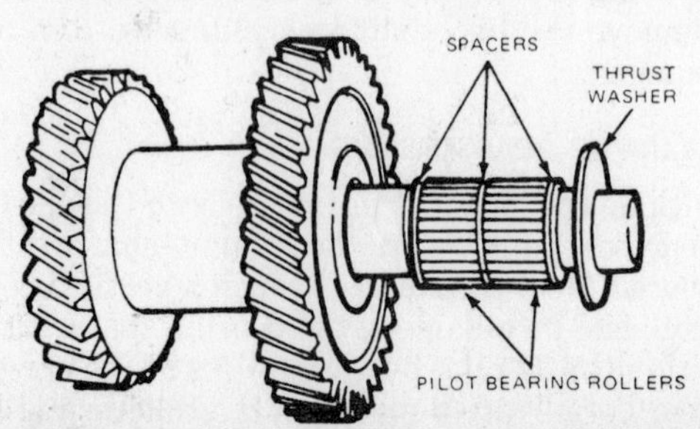

T-19 countershaft bearing rollers installation

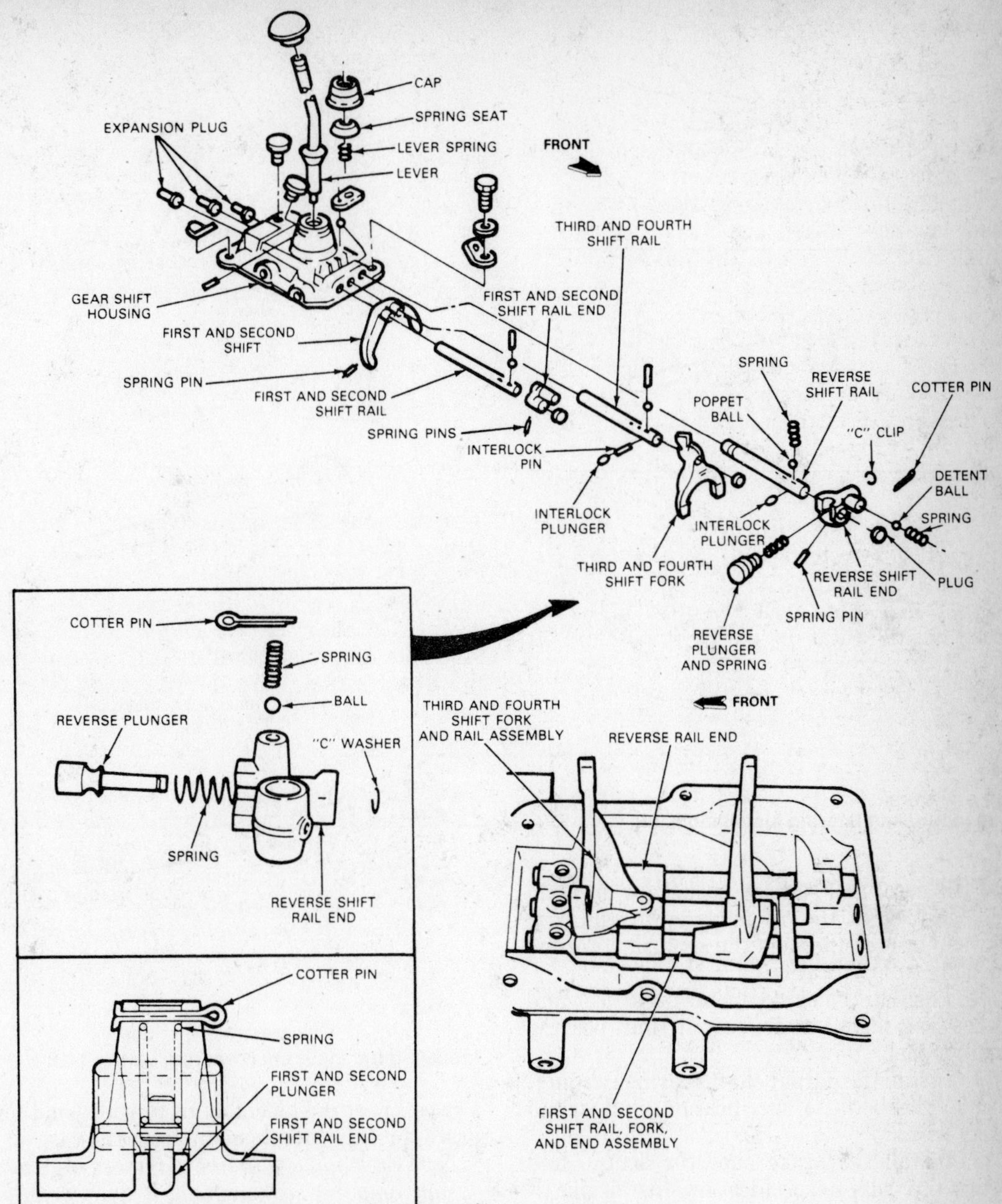

T-19 shift housing, exploded view

the rear of the shaft so that it can engage the retainer. Install the reverse shifter arm.

4. Drive out the cluster gear dummy shaft by installing the countershaft from the rear. Position the slot in the rear of the shaft so that it can engage the retainer. Use thrust washers as required to get 0.006–0.020 in. (0.152–0.508mm) cluster gear end play. Install the countershaft and idler shaft retainer.

5. Position the input shaft pilot rollers and the oil baffle, so that the baffle will not rub the bearing race. Install the input shaft and the blocking ring in the case.

6. Install the output shaft assembly in the case, and use a special tool to prevent jamming the blocking ring when the input shaft bearing is installed.

7. Drive the input shaft bearing onto the shaft. Install the thickest select-fit snapring that will fit on the bearing. Install the input shaft snapring.

8. Install the output shaft bearing.

9. Install the input shaft bearing without a gasket, and tighten the bolts only enough to bottom the retainer on the bearing snapring. Measure the clearance between the retainer

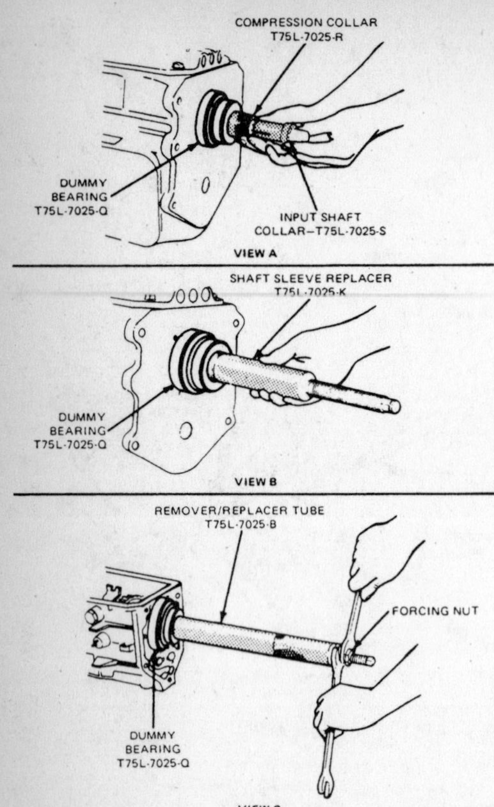

T-19 input shaft bearing installation

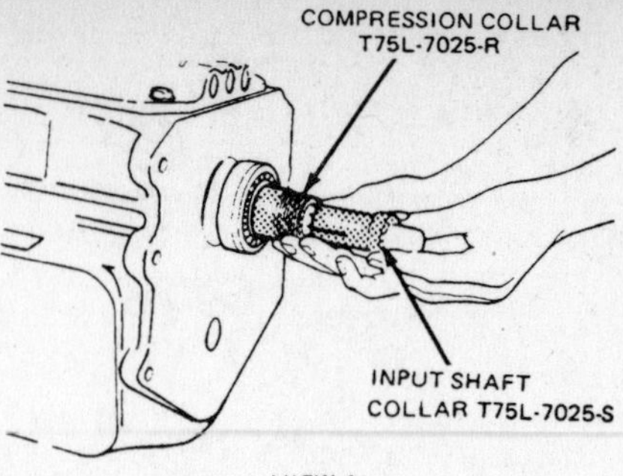

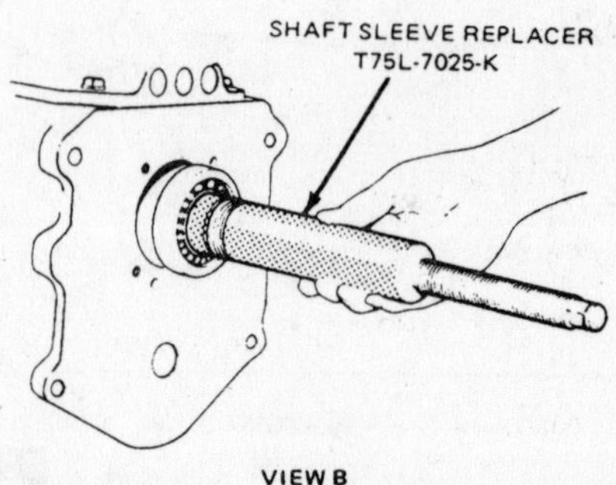

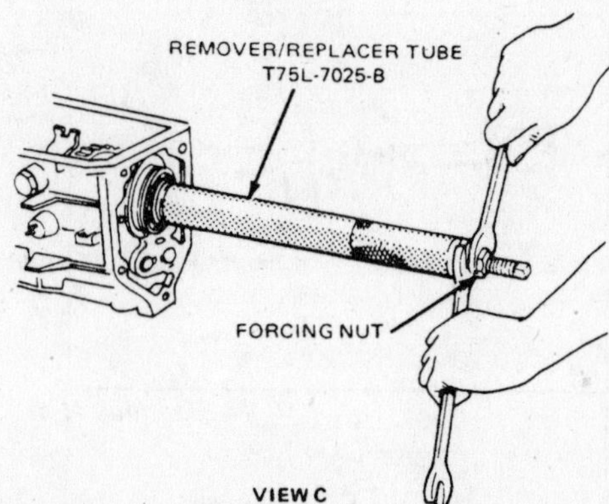

Installing the input shaft bearing on the T-18

and the case, and select a gasket (or gaskets) that will seal in the oil and prevent end play between the retainer and the snapring. Torque the bolts to specification.

10. Position the speedometer drive gear and spacer, and install a new output shaft bearing retainer seal.

11. Install the output shaft bearing retainer. Torque the bolts to specification, and install safety wire.

12. Install the brake shoe (or drum), and torque the bolts to specification. Install the U-joint flange. Lock the transmission in two gears and torque the nut to specification.

13. Install the power take-off cover plates with new gaskets. Fill the transmission according to specifications.

Mazda M5OD 5-Speed

CASE DISASSEMBLY

1. Remove the drain plug.
2. Remove the shift lever from the top cover.
3. Remove the 10 top cover bolts and lift off the cover. Discard the gasket.
4. Remove the 9 extension housing bolts. Pry gently at the indentations provided and separate the extension housing from the case.

NOTE: *If you would like to remove the extension housing seal, remove it with a puller BEFORE separating the extension housing from the case.*

5. Remove the rear oil passage from the extension housing using a 10mm socket.
6. Remove and discard the anti-spill seal from the output shaft.
7. Remove the speedometer drive gear and ball. If you're going to replace the gear, replace it with one of the same color.
8. Lock the transmission into 1st and 3rd gears.
9. Using a hammer and chisel, release the staked areas securing the output shaft and countershaft locknuts.
10. Using a 32mm socket, remove and discard the countershaft rear bearing locknut.

11. Remove the countershaft bearing and thrust washer.

12. Using Mainshaft Locknut Wrench T88T–7025–A and Remover Tube T75L–7025–B, or equivalents, remove and discard the output shaft locknut.

13. Using a 17mm wrench, remove the reverse idler shaft bolt.

14. Remove the reverse idler gear assembly by pulling it rearward.

15. Remove the output shaft rear bearing from the output shaft using Remover/Replacer Tube T75L–7025–B, TOD Forcing Screw T84T–7025–B, Bearing Puller T77J–7025–H and Puller Ring T77J–7025–J, or equivalents.

16. Using a brass drift, drive the reverse gear from the output shaft.

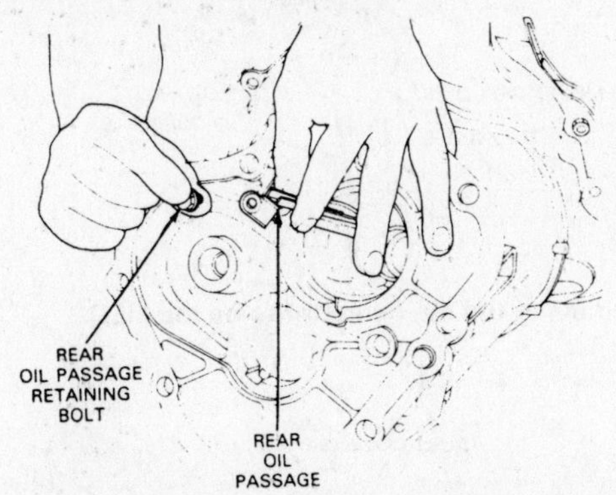

Rear oil passage removal from the M5OD 5-speed

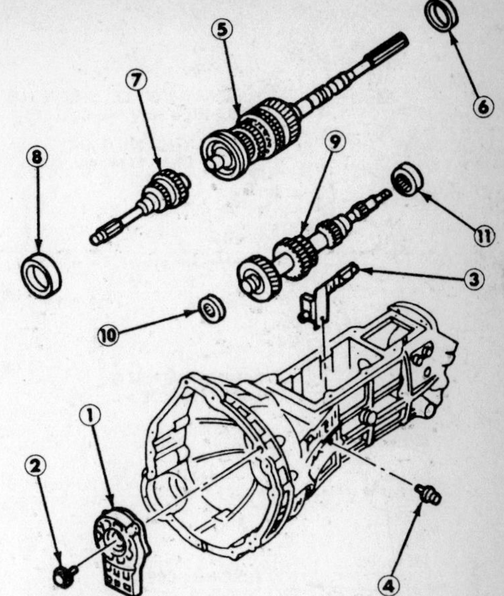

1. Front bearing cover
2. Front cover retaining bolt
3. Oil trough
4. Retaining bolt—oil trough
5. Output shaft assembly
6. Output shaft center bearing outer race
7. Input shaft assembly
8. Input shaft bearing outer race
9. Counter shaft assembly
10. Countershaft front bearing outer race
11. Countershaft rear bearing outer race

M5OD main case exploded view

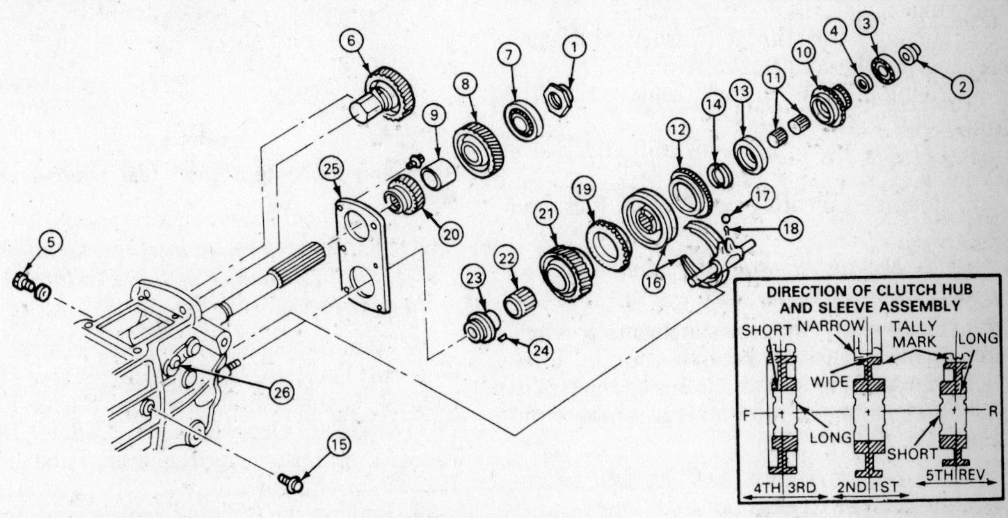

1. Locknut—output shaft
2. Locknut—countershaft
3. Countershaft rear bearing
4. Thrust washer
5. Fixing bolt—reverse idler gear
6. Reverse idle gear assembly
7. Bearing—output shaft rear
8. Reverse gear—output shaft
9. Sleeve—output shaft
10. Countershaft reverse gear
11. Needle bearings
12. Synchronizer ring—reverse
13. Thrust washer
14. Split washer (2 pcs)
15. Fixing bolt—shift rod
16. Shift rail/fork/hub/sleeve assembly
17. Lock ball (steel) shift rail
18. Spring—shift rail
19. Synchronizer ring—5th gear
20. 5th gear—output shaft
21. 5th gear—countershaft
22. Needle bearing—5th gear

M5OD rear housing components, exploded view

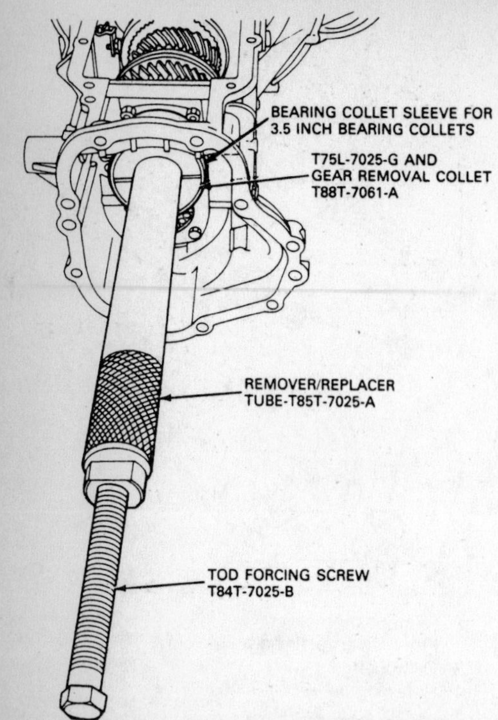

Removing 5th gear from the output shaft on the M5Od

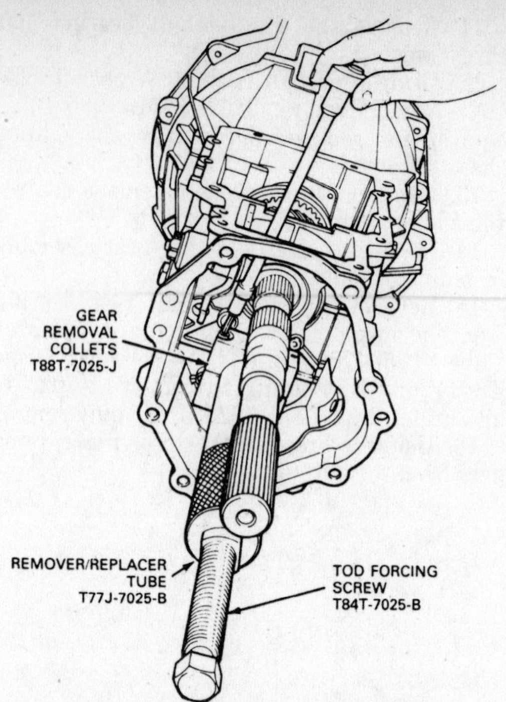

Removing the 5th gear sleeve on the M5OD

17. Remove the sleeve from the output shaft.

18. Remove the counter/reverse gear with two needle bearings and the reverse synchronizer ring.

19. Remove the thrust washer and split washer from the countershaft.

20. Using a 12mm wrench, remove the 5th/reverse shift rod fixing bolt.

21. Remove the 5th/reverse hub and sleeve assembly.

22. Remove the 5th/reverse shift fork and rod.

NOTE: *Do not separate the steel ball and spring unless necessary.*

23. Remove the 5th gear synchronizer ring.

24. Remove the 5th/reverse counter lever lockplate retaining bolt and inner circlip.

25. Remove the counter lever assembly from the case.

NOTE: *Do not remove the Torx® nut retaining the counter lever pin at this time.*

26. Remove the 5th gear counter with the needle bearing.

27. Remove the 5th gear from the output shaft using the Bearing Collet Sleeve for the 3½ in. (89mm). Bearing Collets T75L–7025–G, Remover/Replacer Tube T85T–7025–A, TOD Forcing Screw T84T–7025–B and Gear Remover Collet T88T–7061–A, or equivalents.

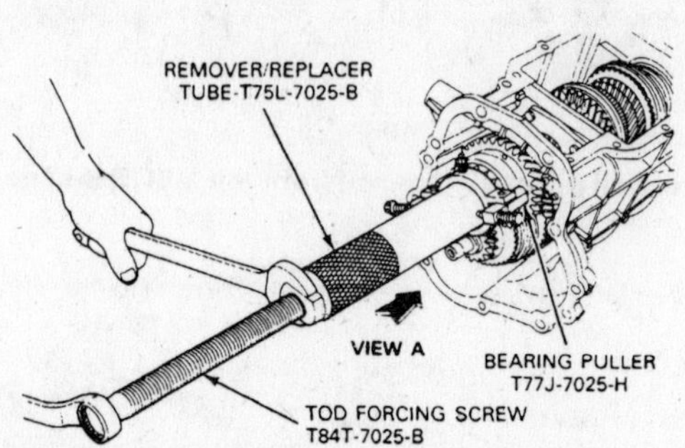

Removing the output shaft rear bearing on the M5OD

NOTE: *For reference during assembly, observe that the longer of the 2 collars on the 5th gear faces forward.*

28. Remove the 5th gear sleeve and Woodruff key using TOD Forcing Screw T84T–7025–B, Countershaft 5th Gear Sleeve Puller T88T–7025–J, Gear Removal Collets T88T–7025–J1 and Remover/Replacer Tube T77J–7025–B, or equivalents.

29. Remove the 6 center bearing cover retaining bolts and lift off the cover.

NOTE: *There is a reference arrow on the cover which points upward.*

30. Remove the 6 front bearing cover bolts.

31. Remove the front bearing cover by threading 2 of the retaining bolts back into the cover at the service bolt locations (9 and 3 o'clock).

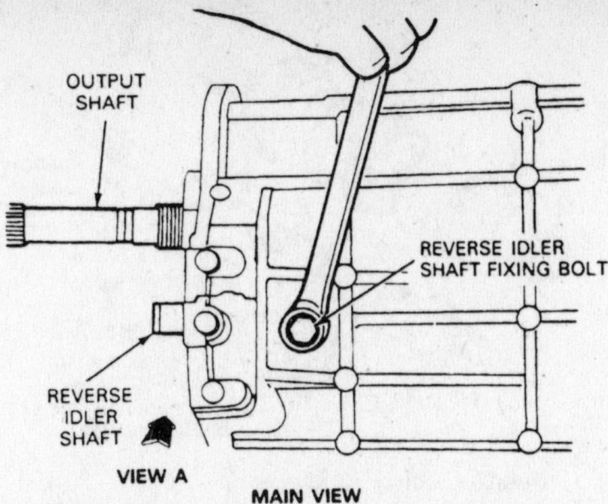

Removing the reverse idler gear shaft retaining bolt on the M5OD

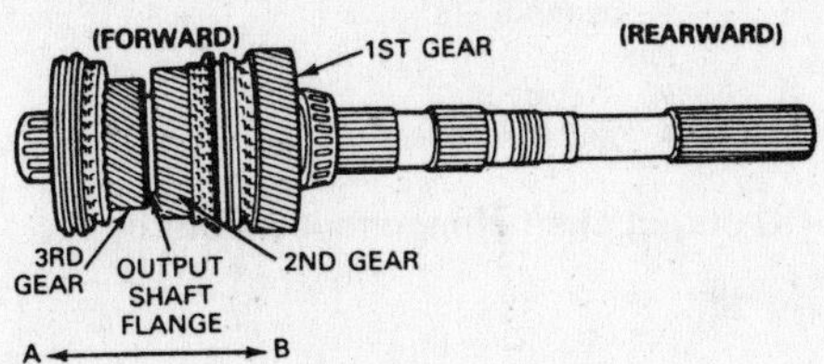

M5OD output shaft

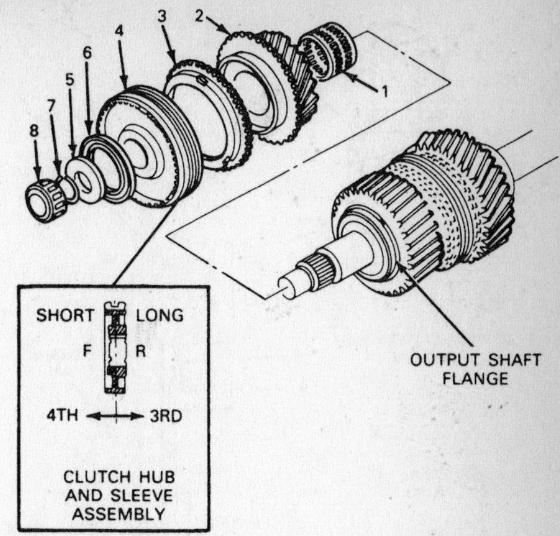

1. Needle bearing—3rd gear
2. Third gear
3. Synchronizer ring—3rd gear
4. Clutch hub and sleeve assembly—3rd/4th
5. Spacer
6. Needle bearing (plain)
7. Retaining ring
8. Roller bearing—pilot bearing

M5OD output shaft exploded view

Alternately tighten the bolts until the cover pops off. Discard the front bearing oil baffle.

NOTE: *Don't remove the plastic scoop ring from the input shaft at this time.*

32. Remove the oil trough retaining bolt and lift out the oil trough from the upper case.

33. Pull the input shaft forward and remove the input bearing outer race. Pull the output shaft rearward.

34. Pull the input shaft forward and separate it from the output shaft.

35. Incline the output shaft upward and lift it from the case.

36. Remove the input shaft from the case.

37. Remove the countershaft bearing outer races (front and center) by moving the countershaft forward and rearward.

38. Pull the countershaft rearward far enough to permit tool clearance behind the front countershaft bearing. Using Bearing Race Puller T88T–7120–A and Slide Hammer T50T–100–A, or equivalents, remove the front countershaft bearing.

WARNING: *Tap gently during bearing removal. A forceful blow can cause damage to the bearing and/or case.*

39. Remove the countershaft through the upper opening of the case.

40. Input Shaft Disassembly and Assembly:

a. Remove and discard the plastic scoop ring.

b. Press the tapered roller bearing from the input shaft using Bearing Cone Remover T71P–4621–b, or equivalent, and an arbor press.

c. Install the input shaft tapered roller bearing onto the input shaft using a press and Bearing Cone Replacer T88T–7025–B, or equivalent.

d. Install the plastic scoop ring onto the input shaft. Manually rotate the ring clockwise to ensure that the input shaft oil holes properly engage the scoop ring. A click should be heard as the scoop ring notches align with the input shaft holes.

41. Output Shaft Disassembly and Assembly:

a. Remove the pilot bearing needle roller, snapring, needle bearing and spacer from the front (short side) of the output shaft.

b. Position the front (short side) of the shaft upward and lift off the 3rd/4th clutch hub and sleeve assembly, 3rd gear synchronizing ring, 3rd gear, and needle bearing.

c. Turn the shaft so that the long end faces upward.

d. Place the output shaft into a press with the press cradle contacting the lower part of the 2nd gear.

NOTE: *Make sure that the output shaft flange doesn't contact or ride up on the press cradle.*

e. Press off the following as a unit:

- center bearing,
- 1st gear sleeve,
- 1st gear,
- needle bearing,

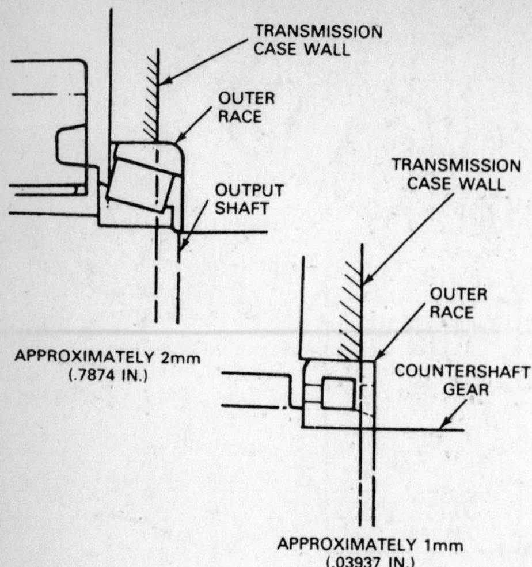

Installing the output shaft center bearing on the M5OD

- 1st/2nd clutch hub and sleeve,
- 1st/2nd synchronizer rings,
- 2nd gear, and
- needle bearing using Bearing Replacer T53T–4621–B and Bearing Cone Replacer T88T–7025–B, or equivalents. Use T53T–4621–B as a press plate, and Bearing Cone Replacer T88T–7025–B to protect the inner race rollers.

f. Position the output shaft so the rear (long end) faces upward and press on the following parts, in the order listed, using T53T–4621–B and T75L–1165–B, or equivalents:

- 2nd gear needle bearing
- 2nd gear
- 2nd gear synchronizer ring
- 1st/2nd clutch hub and sleeve
- 1st gear synchronizer ring
- 1st gear needle bearing
- 1st gear
- 1st gear sleeve
- center bearing

NOTE: *Make sure that the center bearing race ins installed in the case. When install-*

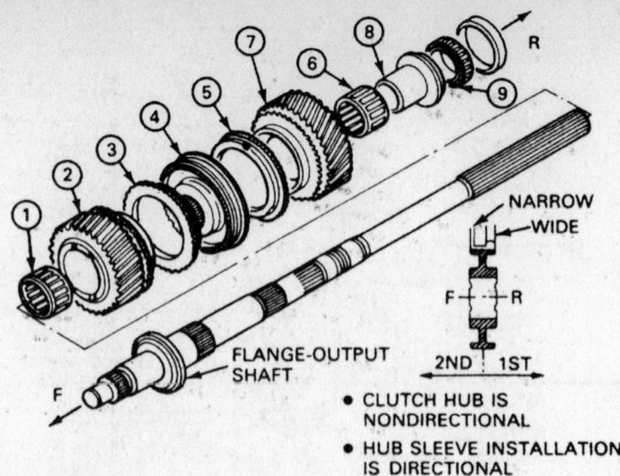

1. Needle bearing—2nd gear
2. 2nd gear
3. Synchronizer ring—2nd gear
4. Clutch hub and sleeve assembly—1st and 2nd
5. Synchronizer ring—1st gear
6. Needle bearing—1st gear
7. 1st gear
8. Sleeve—1st gear
9. Center bearing—inner

M5OD output shaft component assembly

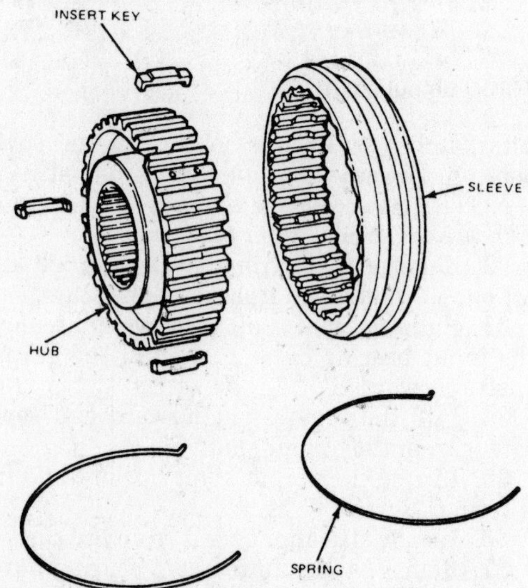

M5OD synchronizer exploded view

ing the 1st/2nd clutch hub and sleeve make sure that the smaller width sleeve faces the 2nd gear side. Make sure that the reference marks face the rear of the transmission.

g. Install the center bearing on the output shaft.

h. Position the output shaft so that the front of the shaft flange faces upward. Install the 3rd gear needle bearing, 3rd gear and 3rd gear synchronizer ring.

i. Install the 3rd/4th clutch hub and sleeve:

- Mate the clutch hub synchronizer key groove with the reference mark on the clutch hub sleeve. The mark should face rearward.

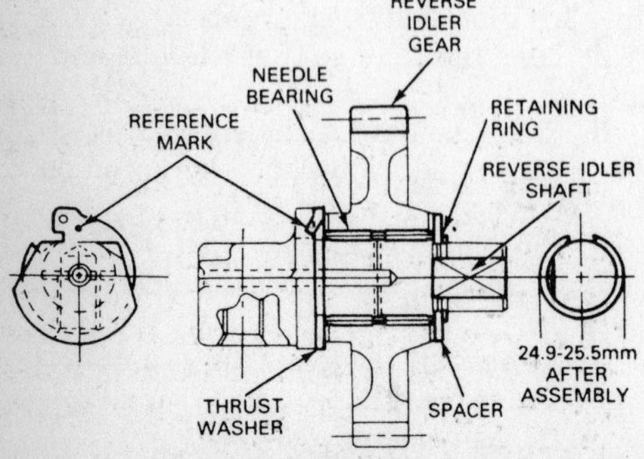

M5OD reverse idler gear shaft

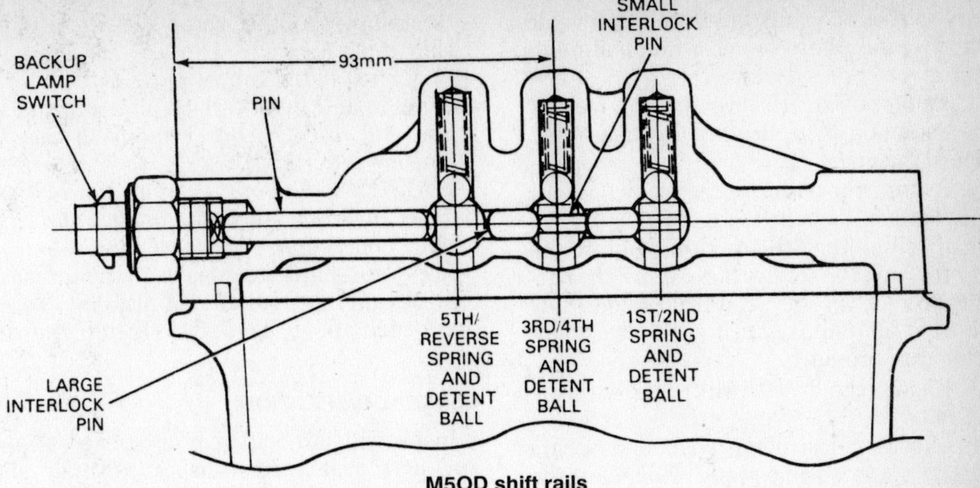

M5OD shift rails

• Install the longer flange on the clutch hub sleeve towards the 3rd gear side.

NOTE: *The front and rear sides of the clutch hub are identical, except for the reference mark.*

j. Install the spacer, needle bearing (with rollers upward), retaining ring, and pilot bearing roller.

k. Install the original retaining ring. Using a feeler gauge, check the clutch hub endplay. Endplay should be 0–0.05mm (0–0.0019 in.). If necessary, adjust the endplay by using a new retaining ring. Retaining ring are available in 0.05mm increments in sizes ranging from 1.5mm to 1.95mm.

42. Countershaft Disassembly and Assembly:

a. Place the countershaft in a press with Bearing Cone Remover T71P–4621–B, or equivalent, and remove the countershaft bearing inner race.

b. Using a press and bearing splitter D84L–1123–A, or equivalent, remove the countershaft front bearing inner race.

c. Assemble the shaft in the press in the reverse order of disassembly.

43. Reverse Idler Gear Shaft Disassembly and Assembly:

a. Remove the following parts:

• Retaining ring
• Spacer
• Idler gear
• Needle bearings
• Thrust washer

b. Install the thrust washer making sure that the tab mates with the groove in the shaft.

c. Install the needle bearings, idler gear and spacer.

d. Install the original retaining ring onto the shaft.

e. Insert a flat feeler gauge between the retaining ring and the reverse idler gear to measure the reverse idler gear endplay. Endplay should be 0.1–0.2mm. If not, use a new retaining ring. Retaining rings are available in 0.5mm increments in thicknesses ranging from 1.5 to 1.9mm.

44. Top Cover Disassembly and Assembly:

a. Remove the dust cover (3 allen screws). Note that the grooves in the bushing align with the slots in the lower shift lever ball and the notch in the lower shift lever faces forward.

b. Remove the back-up lamp switch from the cover.

c. Drive out the spring pins retaining the shift forks to the shift rails. Discard the pins.

d. Place the 5th/reverse shift rail in the fully forward position.

Remove the spring pin from the end of the 5th/reverse rail.

e. Remove the 3 rubber plugs from the shift rod service bores.

CAUTION: *Wear safety goggles when performing the shift rail removal procedure! Cover the lock ball bores and friction device and spring seats with a heavy cloth held firmly in place. The ball/friction device and spring can fly out during removal, causing possible personal injury!*

f. Remove the 5th/reverse shift rail from the top cover through the service bore. It may be necessary to rock the shift rail from side-to-side with a $^{5}/_{16}$ in. (8mm) punch while maintaining rearward pressure.

g. Remove the 1st/2nd shift rail from the cover through the service bore. It may be necessary to rock the shift rail from side-to-side with a $^{5}/_{16}$ in. (8mm) punch while maintaining rearward pressure.

h. Remove the 3rd/4th shift rail from the cover through the service bore. It may be necessary to rock the shift rail from side-to-side with a $^5/_{16}$ in. (8mm) punch while maintaining rearward pressure.

i. Remove the 5th/reverse cam lockout plate retaining bolts using a 10mm socket. Remove the plate.

j. Install the 5th/reverse cam lockout plate. Torque the bolts to 72–84 inch lbs.

k. Position the 3rd/4th shift rail into the cover through the service bore. It may be necessary to rock the shift rail from side-to-side with a $^5/_{16}$ in. (8mm) punch, while maintaining forward pressure.

l. Engage the 3rd/4th shift fork with the shift rail.

m. Position the detent ball and spring into the cover spring seats. Compress the detent ball and spring and push the shift rail into position over the detent ball.

n. Position the friction device and spring into the cover spring seats. Compress the friction device and spring and push the shift rail into position over the friction device.

o. Install the spring pins retaining the shift rail to the cover.

p. Install the spring retaining the 3rd/4th shift fork to the shift rail.

q. Position the 1st/2nd shift rail in the cover through the service bore. It may be necessary to rock the shift rail from side-to-side with a $^5/_{16}$ in. (8mm) punch, while maintaining forward pressure.

r. Engage the 1st/2nd shift fork with the shift rail.

s. Position the detent ball and spring into the cover seats.

t. Compress the detent ball and spring and push the shift rail into position over the detent ball.

u. Position the friction device and spring into the cover seats. Compress the friction device and spring and push the shift rail into position over the friction device.

v. Install the spring pins retaining the shift rail to the cover. Install the spring pin retaining the 1st/2nd shift fork to the shift rail.

w. Position the 5th/reverse shift rail in the top cover through the service bore. It may be necessary to rock the shift rail from side-to-side with a $^5/_{16}$ in. (8mm) punch, while maintaining forward pressure. Engage the 5th/reverse shift fork with the shift rail. Position the detent ball and spring into the cover seats. Compress the detent ball and spring and push the shift rail into position over the detent ball.

x. Install the spring pins retaining the shift rail to the cover. Install the spring pin retaining the 5th/reverse shift fork to the shift rail.

y. Install the rubber plugs.

z. Install the interlock pins into the 1st/2nd and 3rd/4th shift rails. Note that the pins are different sizes.

WARNING: *Use of the wrong size pins will affect neutral start and/or back-up light switch operation.*

Apply non-hardening sealer to the threads of the back-up light switch and install it. Torque the switch to 18–26 ft. lbs. Install the dust cover.

GENERAL INSPECTION

Inspect all parts for wear or damage. Replace any part that seems suspect. Output shaft runout must not exceed 0.05mm. Replace the shaft is it does. Synchronizer-to-gear clearance must not exceed 0.8mm. Replace the synchronizer ring or gear if necessary. Shift fork-to-clutch hub clearance must not exceed 0.8mm.

GENERAL CASE ASSEMBLY

1. Place the countershaft assembly into the case.
2. Place the input shaft in the case. Make sure that the needle roller bearing is on the shaft.
3. Place the output shaft assembly in the case. Mate the input and out shafts. Make sure that the 4th gear synchronizer is installed.
4. Drive the output shaft center bearing into place with a brass drift.
5. Install the countershaft center bearing. Make sure that the center bearing outer races are squarely seated in their bores.
6. Position the center bearing cover on the case with the arrow upwards. Torque the cover bolts to 14–19 ft. lbs. Use only bolts marked with a grade **8** on the bolt head.
7. Position the transmission on end with the input end up. Make sure that the input shaft front bearing outer race is squarely positioned in its bore. Install the front cover oil seal with a seal driver.
8. Install the countershaft front bearing.
9. Check and record the following dimensions:
   a. Check and record the height of the input shaft bearing outer race above the transmission front bearing cover mating surface.
   b. Check and record the depth of the front cover outer race bore at the input shaft.
   c. Check and record the depth of the countershaft front bearing race (case-to-cover mating surface).
   d. Check and record the depth of the front cover outer race bore at the output shaft.

10. Select the proper shims using the following formulae:

• Dimension b – (dimension a + the shim thickness) = 0.05–0.15mm

• Dimension c + (dimension d – the shim thickness) = 0.15–0.25mm

Shims are available in 0.1mm increments ranging from 1.4mm to 3.0mm thick.

11. Clean the mating surfaces of the transmission and front cover.

12. Wrap the input shaft splines with masking tape.

13. Apply a light coat of oil to the front cover oil seal lip. Position the bearing shim and baffle into the cover. The shim groove should be visible.

14. Install the spacer in the case countershaft front bearing bore. You may want to apply a coating of chassis grease to parts to hold them in place during assembly.

15. Apply a 1/8 in. (3mm) wide bead of silicone RTV sealant to the front cover mating surface and the bolt threads. Install the cover and torque the bolts to 9–12 ft. lbs. Always us bolts marked grade **6** on the bolt head.

16. Lay the transmission down and install the woodruff key and 5th gear sleeve.

NOTE: *Install the 5th gear sleeve using the nut, Shaft Adapter T75L–7025–L, Adapter T88T–7025–J2 and Remover/Replacer Tube T75L–7025–B, or equivalents.*

17. Install the 5th gear needle bearing onto the countershaft 5th gear.

18. Install the 5th gear onto the output shaft using Gear Installation Spacers T88T–7025–F, and –G, Shaft Adapter T75L–7025–P, Shaft Adapter Screw T75L–7025–K, Remover/Replacer Tube T75L–7025–B (2-wheel drive only) or Remover/Replacer Tube T85T–7025–A (4-wheel drive models), nut and washer, or

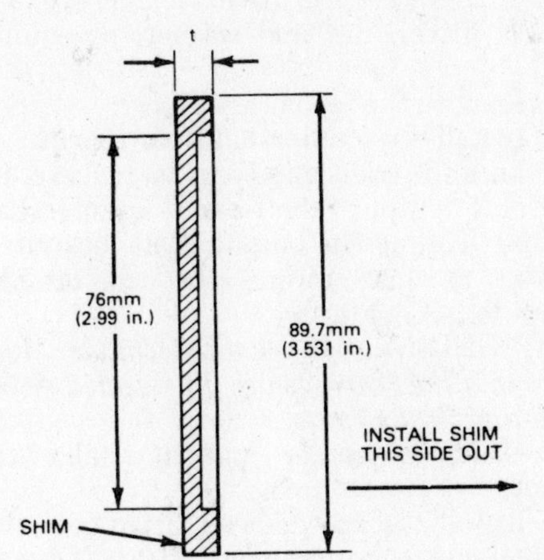

SHIM SELECT CHART — M50D R2

Part Number	Thickness (t)
E8TZ-7029-FA	1.4mm (0.0551 in.)
E8TZ-7029-GA	1.5mm (0.0590 in.)
E8TZ-7029-Ha	1.6mm (0.0629 in.)
E8TZ-7029-Ja	1.7mm (0.0669 in.)
E8TZ-7029-S	1.8mm (0.0708 in.)
E8TZ-7029-T	1.9mm (0.0748 in.)
E8TZ-7029-U	2.0mm (0.0787 in.)
E8TZ-7029-V	2.1mm (0.0826 in.)
E8TZ-7029-W	2.2mm (0.0866 in.)
E8TZ-7029-X	2.3mm (0.0905 in.)
E8TZ-7029-Y	2.4mm (0.0944 in.)
E8TZ-7029-Z	2.5mm (0.0984 in.)
E8TZ-7029-AA	2.6mm (0.1023 in.)
E8TZ-7029-BA	2.7mm (0.1062 in.)
E8TZ-7029-CA	2.8mm (0.1102 in.)
E8TZ-7029-DA	2.9mm (0.1141 in.)
E8TZ-7029-EA	3.0mm (0.1181 in.)

M5OD shim selection chart

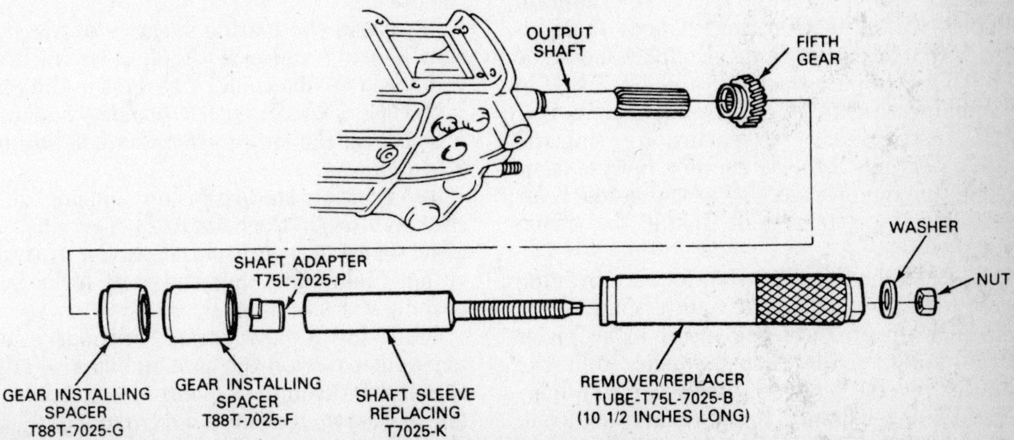

Installing 5th gear on the M5OD

equivalents. Make sure that the long flange on the 5th gear faces forward.

19. On 2-wheel drive models: install T88T–7025–F. When the tool bottoms, add T88T–7025–G and press the 5th gear assembly all the way into position. On 4-wheel drive models: follow the procedure for 2-wheel drive, except use T85T–7025–A and T84T–7025–A.

20. Position counterlever assembly in the transmission and install the thrust washer and retaining ring. Apply sealant on the counterlever fixing bolt threads. Install the counterlever fixing bolt and torque it to 72–84 inch lbs.

21. Position the 5th/reverse shift fork and shift rail in the top cover. Insert the 5th/reverse shift rail through the top cover bore and the 5th/reverse shift fork. Install the spring and detent ball on the lower part of the rod.

22. Assemble the 5th/reverse synchronizer hub, sleeve and 5th gear synchronizer ring on the 5th/reverse shift fork and rod. The longer flange faces front. The reference mark on the synchronizer sleeve faces the reverse gear side.

23. Install the 5th/reverse shift fork and rail assembly on the countershaft. Mate the shift fork gate to the 5th/reverse counterlever end. Install the 5th/reverse fork and shift rail with the threaded fixing bolt bores aligned.

NOTE: *It's easier if you place the 5th/reverse shift fork into the rear most of the three detent positions. Return the shift fork to the neutral position after assembly.*

24. Apply sealant to the 5th/reverse shift rail fixing bolt threads. Install the 5th/reverse shift rail fixing bolt in the case. Torque the 5th/reverse shift rail bolt to 16–22 ft. lbs.

25. Apply sealant to the oil passage retaining bolt. Position the oil passage in the case and torque the bolt to 72–84 inch lbs.

26. Install the split washer and thrust washer onto the countershaft. If the clutch hub and/or counter reverse gear have been replaced, new split washers must be selected to maintain endplay within specifications. Check the endplay with a flat feeler gauge. Endplay should be 0.2–0.3mm. Split washers are provided in 0.1mm increments ranging from 3.0–3.5mm.

27. Install the reverse synchronizer ring and needle bearings into the counter reverse gear. Install the counter reverse gear and needle bearings onto the countershaft. Install the thrust washer.

28. Push the thrust washer forward by hand against the shoulder on the countershaft. Maintain forward pressure and insert a flat feeler gauge between the thrust washer and the counter reverse gear. Counter reverse endplay should be 0.2–0.3mm. Thrust washers are available in 0.2mm increments ranging from 7.4–7.8mm thicknesses.

29. Temporarily install a spacer, with an inner bore larger than 21mm and an outer diameter smaller than 36mm, 15–20mm overall length, in place of the countershaft bearing. Loosely install the locknut.

30. Install the reverse idler gear assembly. Apply sealant to the threads of the reverse idler gear fixing bolt. Torque the bolt to 58–86 ft. lbs.

31. Drive the sleeve and reverse gear assembly into place on the output shaft using Gear Installation Spacer T88T–7025–G, Shaft Adapter T75L–7025–P, Shaft Adapter Screw T75L–7025–P, Shaft Adapter Screw T75L–7025–K, Remover/Replacer Tube T75L–7025–B (2-wheel drive), Remover/Replacer Tube T85T–7025–A (4-wheel drive), nut and washer, or equivalents. Install the reverse gear with the longer flange facing forward.

32. Install the output shaft rear bearing using Gear Installation Spacer T88T–7025–G, Shaft Adapter T75L–7025–P, Shaft Adapter Screw T75L–7025–K, Remover/Replacer Tube T75L–7025–B (2-wheel drive) or T85T–7025–A (4-wheel drive), nut and washer, or equivalents.

33. Remove the temporary spacer.

34. Install the countershaft rear bearing.

35. Lock the transmission in 1st and 3rd. Install new output shaft and countershaft locknuts. Torque the output shaft locknut to 160–200 ft. lbs.; torque the countershaft locknut to 94–144 ft. lbs.

WARNING: *Always use new locknuts. Make sure that the bearings are fully seated before torquing the locknuts.*

36. Using a center punch, stake the locknuts.

37. Install the speedometer drive gear and steel ball on the output shaft. The ball can be installed in any of the three detents. Make sure, if you are installing a new speedometer gear, make sure that it is the same color code as the old one.

38. Clean the mating surfaces of the extension housing and case. Apply a 1/8 in. (3mm) wide bead of silicone RTV sealant to the case.

NOTE: *If the extension housing bushing is defective, the entire extension housing must be replaced.*

39. Position the extension housing on the case and torque the bolts to 24–34 ft. lbs.

40. Place the synchronizers in the neutral position. Make sure that the shift forks in the cover are also in neutral.

41. Using a new gasket, without sealant, place the cover on the case and careful engage the shift forks in the synchronizers. Apply sealant to the two rear most cover bolts and install them. Install the remaining bolts without sealant. Torque the bolts to 12–16 ft. lbs.

42. Install the drain plug. Torque it to 40 ft. lbs.

43. Install the rear oil seal into the extension housing. Make sure that the drain hole faces downward.

44. Fill the case with Dexron®II fluid.

ZF S5-42 5-Speed Overdrive

MAIN COMPONENT DISASSEMBLY

1. Place the transmission face downward on a clean work surface.

2. Using a hammer and chisel, bend back the tab on the output shaft flange locknut.

3. Install a holding tool on the flange and loosen, but don't remove, the output shaft locknut.

4. Remove 15 of the 17 bolts holding the rear case cover to the case. Leave 2 bolts at opposite corners.

5. Remove any power take-off (pto) equipment.

6. Remove the shift tower assembly from the case.

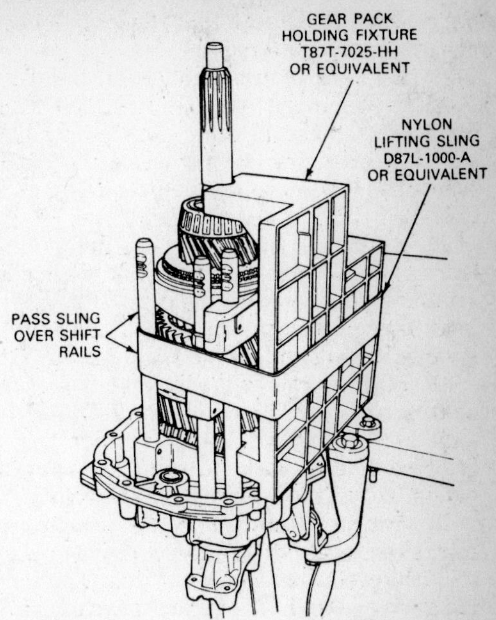

Lifting sling and holding fixture in place on the ZF

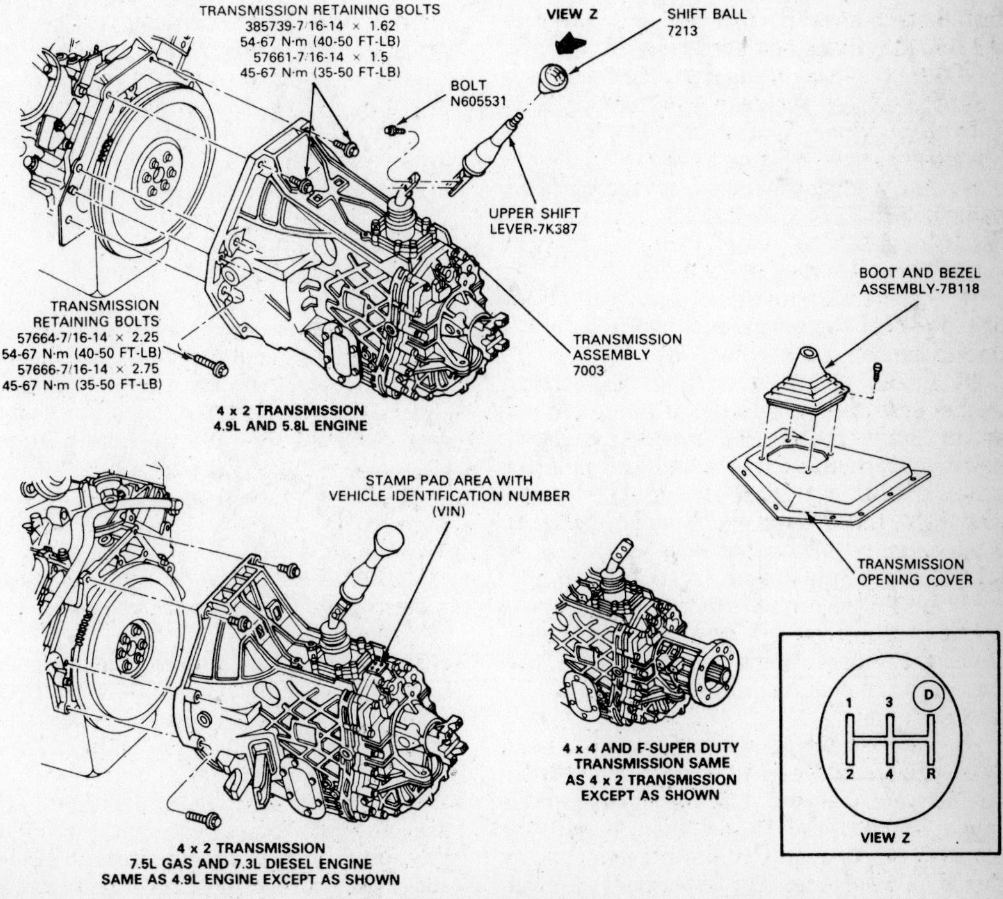

S5-42 ZF 5-speed

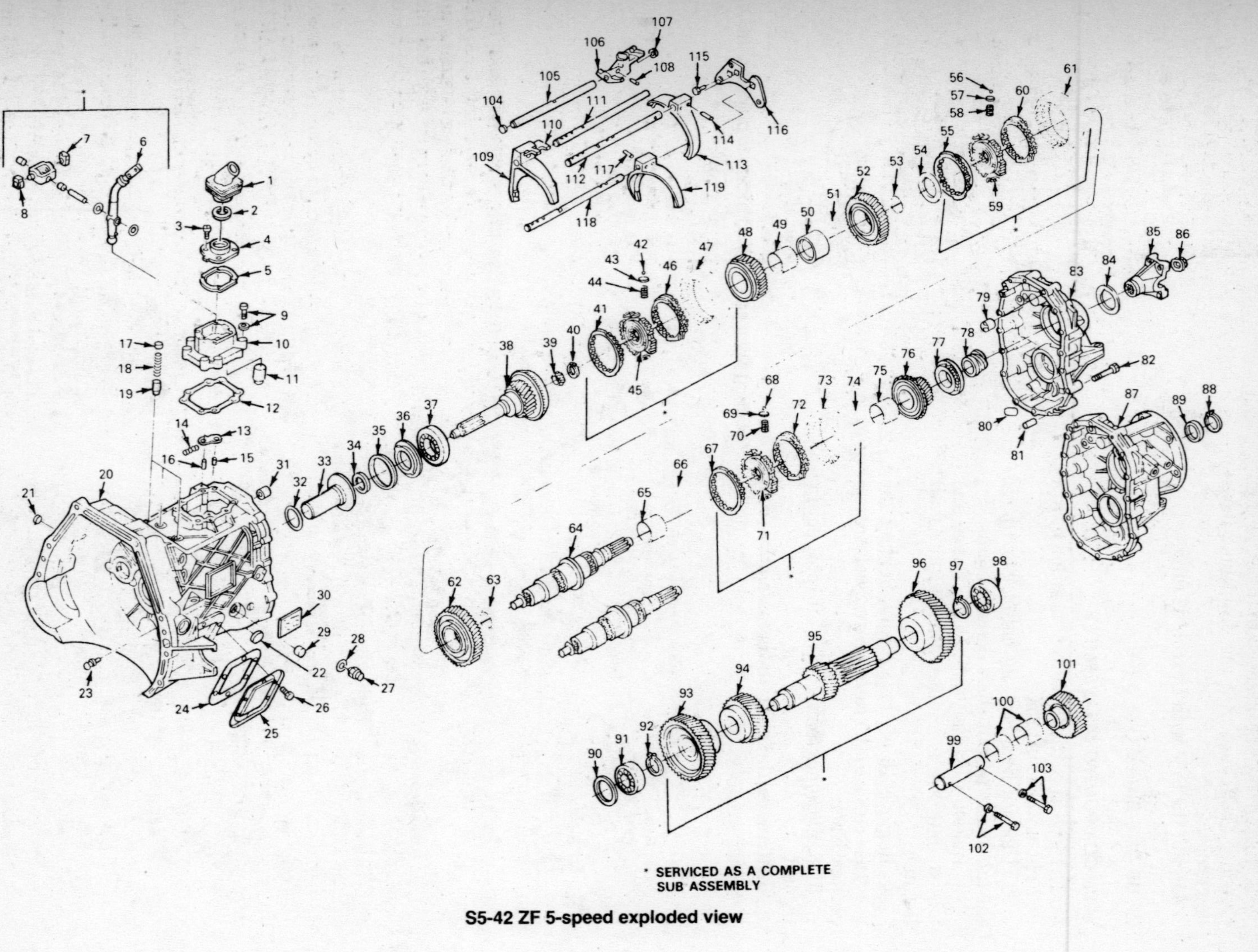

S5-42 ZF 5-speed exploded view

1. Shift lever boot
2. Snap ring
3. Capscrew
4. Shift tower cover
5. Gasket
6. Lower shift lever
7. Guide piece
8. Guide piece
9. Hex bolts
10. Shift housing
11. Shift detent
12. Gasket
13. 5th-reverse interlock
14. Interlock spring
15. Interlock roll pin
16. Interlock roll pin
17. Sealing cap
18. Spring
19. Shift rail detent
20. Front case
21. Sealing cap
22. Plug—drain
23. Bolt
24. Gasket
25. PTO cover
26. Bolt
27. Backup lamp switch
28. Sealing ring
29. Plug—filler
30. ID plate
31. Central shift rail bearing
32. O-ring
33. Quill
34. Oil seal
35. Shim
36. Baffle
37. Input shaft bearing
38. Input shaft
39. Mainshaft bearing
40. Snap ring
41. 4th gear synchronizer ring
42. Ball
43. Pressure piece
44. Spring
45. 3rd-4th synchronizer body
46. 3rd gear synchronizer ring
47. 3rd-4th sliding sleeve
48. 3rd gear
49. Caged needle rollers
50. Bearing race
51. Thrust washer
52. 2nd gear
53. Caged needle rollers
54. Snap ring
55. 2nd gear synchronizer ring
56. Ball
57. Pressure piece
58. Spring
59. 1st-2nd synchronizer body
60. 1st gear synchronizer ring
61. 1st-2nd sliding sleeve
62. 1st gear
63. Needle rollers
64. Mainshaft
65. Caged needle rollers
66. Reverse gear
67. Reverse gear synchronizer ring
68. Ball
69. Pressure piece
70. Spring
71. 5th-reverse synchronizer body
72. 5th gear syncrhonizer ring
73. 5th-reverse sliding sleeve
74. Snap ring
75. Caged needle rollers
76. 5th gear
77. Mainshaft bearing
78. Speedometer drive gear (4×2 only)
79. Central shift rail bearing
80. Magnet
81. Dowel
82. Bolt
83. Rear case (4×2)
84. Rear oil seal (4×2)
85. Output yoke (4×2)
86. Locknut (4×2)
87. Rear case (4×4)
88. Snap ring (4×4)
89. Oil seal (4×4)
90. Shim
91. Front countershaft bearing
92. Snap ring
93. Countershaft drive gear
94. Countershaft 3rd gear
95. Countershaft
96. Countershaft 5th gear
97. Snap ring
98. Countershaft rear bearing
99. Reverse idler shaft
100. Caged needle rollers
101. Reverse idler gear
102. Screw and sealing ring
103. Screw and sealing ring
104. Plug
105. Central shift rail
106. Shift finger
107. Plug
108. Roll pin
109. Roll pin
110. Shift fork
111. Shift rail
112. Shift rail
113. Shift fork
114. Roll pin
115. Bolt
116. Interlock plate
117. Roll pin
118. Shift rail
119. Shift fork

S5-42 ZF 5-speed exploded view

7. Remove the interlock plate and compression spring which serves as a reverse gear interlock.

NOTE: *Be careful...these parts tend to fall into the case.*

8. Place a punch against the detent bolt cap, at an angle and slightly off center. Drive the cap inward until spring pressure against its underside forces the cap out of its hole. Repeat this procedure for the other two detent bolt sealing caps in the front case.

CAUTION: *Always wear goggles! The cap is under spring pressure.*

9. Remove the springs from the sealing cap holes.

10. Drive out the sealing caps from the two reverse idler shaft cap screws. Remove the screws.

11. Remove the back-up light switch and switch sealing ring.

12. Using a punch remove the two dowel pins from the two upper corners of the rear case mating surface. Drive them out towards the rear.

13. Remove the two remaining hex bolts from the rear case.

14. Carefully separate the front and rear cases. It may be necessary to push the central shift rail inwards to prevent it from hanging up on the front case. Be careful to ensure that the central shift rail is not lifted off with the front case.

WARNING: *The case mating surfaces are sealed with RTV sealant in place of a gasket. If you experience difficulty in separating the case sections DON'T PRY THEM APART! Tap around the rear case section to break it loose with a rubber or plastic mallet.*

15. Remove the central shift rail and shift finger assembly.

16. Lift the shaft out of the reverse idler gear and remove the gear and two caged roller bearings from the rear case.

17. Remove the three capscrews that retain the shift interlock to the rear case.

18. With the transmission on end, front up, install the Gear Pack Holding Fixture T87T–7025–HH using sling D87L–1000–A on the mainshaft and output shaft assemblies. Pass the sling over the shift rails.

19. Place Shift Rod Support T87T–7025–JH over the ends of the shift rails.

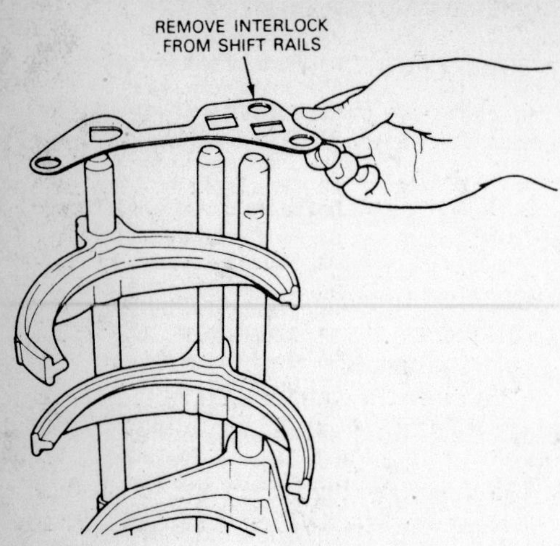

Removing the ZF shift interlock

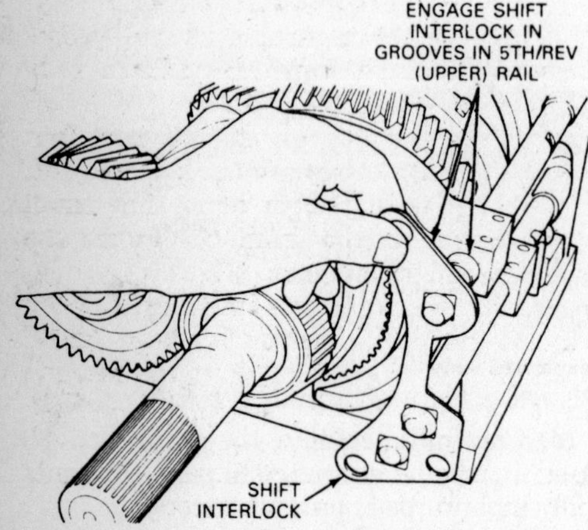

Installing the interlock on the ZF shift rails

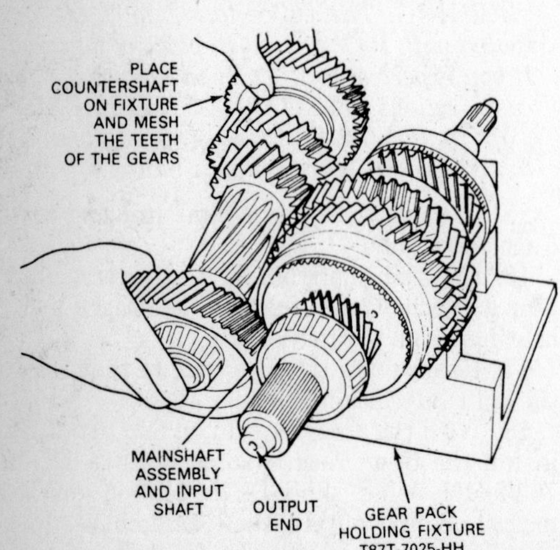

Using the gear pack holding fixture on the ZF

20. Turn the transmission to the horizontal position with the holding fixture under the gear pack.

21. Remove the output shaft flange retaining nut.

22. Remove the flange. If it's hard to get off, tap it off with a hammer.

23. Carefully pull the gearpack and shift rails, along with their holding fixtures, forward to dislodge them from the rear case.

24. Remove the speedometer drive gear from the mainshaft.

25. Remove the sling from around the shift rails, gearpack and fixture.

26. Turn the shift rails 45° to release them from the shift hubs.

27. Lift the shift rails, forks and interlock, together with the Support Tool from the mainshaft.

28. Using the shift rod support tool as a base, set the shift rail assembly on a work bench with the shift rails in a vertical position. Remove the interlock.

29. Make identifying marks on each shift

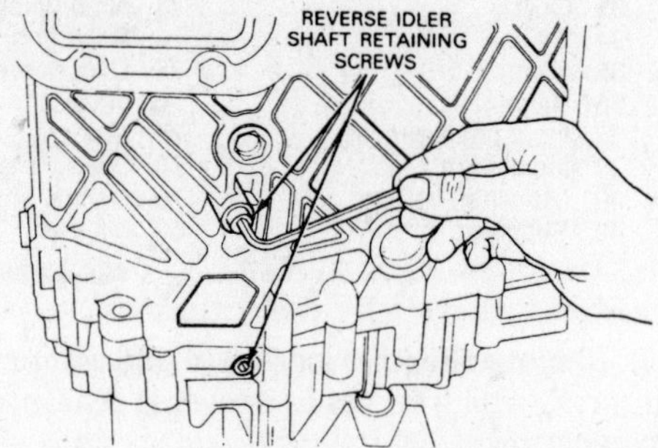

Removing the reverse idler shaft cap screws on the ZF

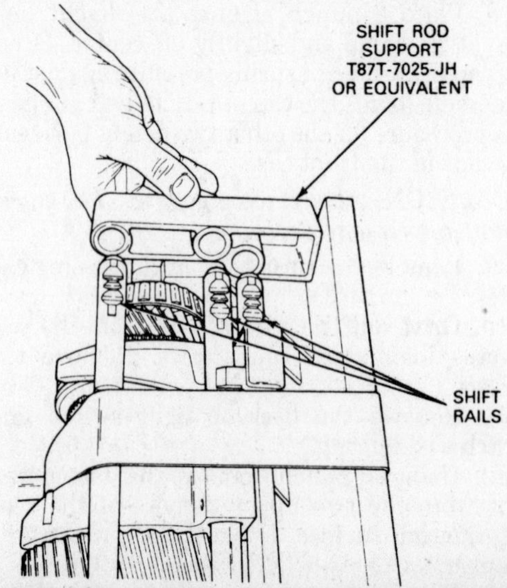

Installing the shift rod support on the ZF shift rails

fork and shift rail and position them in the holding fixture. Lift the shift rails from the support tool.

30. Lift the countershaft off of the workbench stand. Separate the input shaft from the mainshaft. Lift the mainshaft and output shaft from the stand.

31. Remove the rear cover from the holding fixture.

SUBASSEMBLIES

1. Shift Tower:

a. Remove the lever cover from the shift housing.

b. Lift the lever, boot, cover and attached parts off the housing.

c. Slide the two pieces off the cardan joint.

d. Slide the boot and cover off the top of the gearshift lever.

e. Invert the cover and remove the boot snapring.

f. Assemble the parts in reverse order of disassembly.

2. Shift Rails:

a. Install each shift rail in a soft-jawed vise and drive the roll pins out of the shift forks with a punch.

b. Assembly is the reverse of disassembly.

3. Rear Case:

a. Drive the two dowel pins out of the rear case.

b. Using a slide hammer and internal puller, remove the mainshaft rear bearing outer race from the rear case.

c. Using a drift, drive the mainshaft rear seal out of the rear cover. Discard the seal.

d. Using a slide hammer and bearing cup puller, remove the countershaft rear bearing outer race from the rear case.

e. Remove the central shift rail bearing from the rear cover using Blind Hole Puller D80L–100–Q and Slide Hammer T50T–100–A.

f. To install the central shift rail bearing, heat the rear case bore area to 320°F (160°C) with a heat gun. Insert the ball sleeve and drive the bearing in until it seats against its stop using Needle Bearing Replacer T87T–7025–DH.

g. Heat the rear case in the area around the countershaft rear bearing outer race to 320°F (160°C) with a heat gun. Install the countershaft bearing outer race with a driver until it seats against its stop.

h. Heat the case in the area of the mainshaft outer race to 320°F (160°C) with a heat gun. Drive the bearing cup into its bore with a driver and cup tool, until it seats against its stop.

4. Front Case:

a. Using a slide hammer and cup puller, remove the input shaft bearing outer race from the front case.

b. Remove the baffle and shims. Discard the baffle.

c. Using a punch, drive out the input shaft oil seal from the base of the quill.

d. Remove the O-ring from the quill. Remove the oil seal.

e. Remove the countershaft front bearing outer race using a slide hammer and internal puller.

f. Remove the fluid drain and fill plugs.

g. Remove the sealing caps and three shift rail detents from the case.

h. Remove the roll pins that hold the 5th/reverse interlock plate from their bores in the case, just below the shift housing.

i. Remove the central shift rail needle bearings from the front case with a slide hammer and blind hole puller.

j. Install the 5th/reverse roll pins into their bores until the bigger one bottoms out. It should stick out about 8mm. The small one sticks out about 4–5mm. Don't allow the small one to bottom out.

k. Heat the front case in the area of the central shift rail bearing bore to 320°F (160°C) with a heat gun. Drive the bearing sleeve in with a driver until it is flush with the surface of the bore.

l. Install the drain and fill plugs. Torque them to 44 ft. lbs.

m. Insert the three shift rail detent bolts into their bores. They must seat in the detents and must move freely when installed.

n. Place a new O-ring on the input shaft quill.

o. Position the seal in the front case.

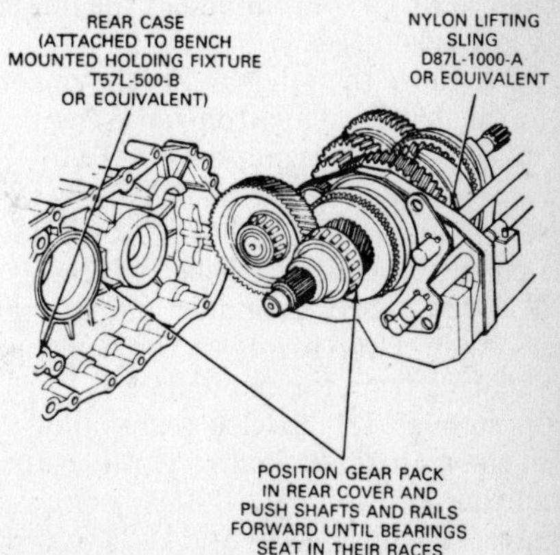

Assembling the ZF rear case to the main case

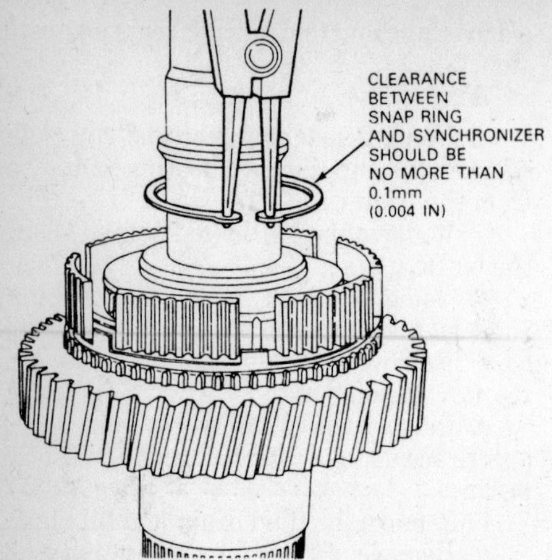

5th/reverse synchronizer snapring on the ZF

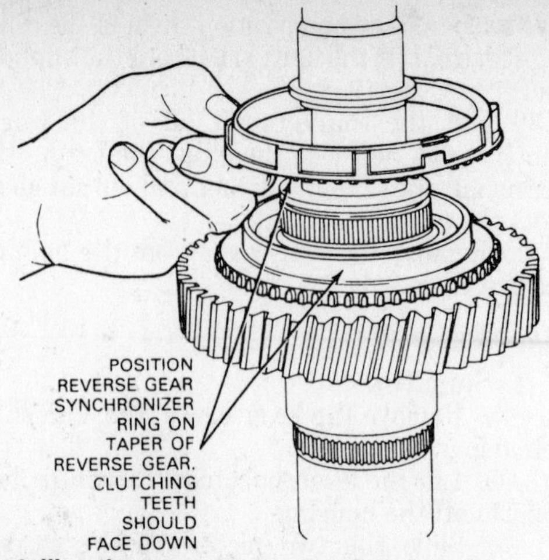

Installing the reverse gear synchronizer ring on the ZF

Drive it in with a seal driver until it seats against its stop in the quill.

NOTE: *If the countershaft, input shaft, mainshaft or any tapered roller bearing is replaced, it will be necessary to adjust the tapered roller bearings to obtain a preload of 0.02–0.11mm. See the ADJUSTMENTS section below.*

p. Heat the mounting bore in the front case for the tapered roller bearing outer race of the countershaft to 320°F (160°C) with a heat gun. Position the proper thickness shim in the bore. Using a bearing driver, drive the race in until it seats against the stop in the case.

q. Heat the front case in the area of the input shaft tapered roller bearing outer race to 320°F (160°C) with a heat gun.

r. Using the ADJUSTMENT procedures below, position the correct shim pack in the bore for the input shaft bearing outer race. Using a driver, drive the bearing cup into place until it seats against its stop in the bore.

5. Mainshaft:

a. Clamp the output end of the mainshaft in a soft-jawed vise.

b. Remove the 4th gear synchronizer ring from the 3rd/4th synchronizer assembly.

c. Place the bearing collets T87T–7025–FH on either side of the mainshaft front bearing. Position Puller Tube T77J –7025–B in the collets. Pass the Collet Retaining Ring T75L–7025–G over the puller and into the collets so they clamp firmly on the bearing. Pull the bearing from the mainshaft.

d. Remove the 3rd/4th gear sliding sleeve from the mainshaft. Place a cloth around the synchronizer to catch the compression springs, pressure pieces and balls that will be released when the sliding sleeves are removed.

e. Remove the cap ring that retains the 3rd/4th synchronizer body to the mainshaft.

f. Place the Collet Retaining ring T87T–7025–OH over the mainshaft and let it rest on the mainshaft 1st gear.

g. Position the two collet halves T87T–7025–NH on the 3rd/4th synchronizer body and slide the collet retaining ring over the collet halves to hold them in place on the synchronizer body.

h. Place the Shaft Protector D80L–625–4 on the end of the mainshaft. Place a 3-jawed puller on the collet halves and retaining ring, and pull the synchronizer body from the mainshaft.

i. Remove the synchronizer ring from the mainshaft 3rd gear.

j. Remove the 3rd gear from the mainshaft.

k. Remove the 3rd gear caged needle rollers from the mainshaft.

l. Lift the 1st/2nd gear sliding sleeve up as far as it will go. Position Collet Retaining Ring T87T–7025–OH over the mainshaft and let it rest on the 1st gear.

m. Position the two Collet Halves T87T–7025–MH so they seat in the groove in the 1st/2nd sliding sleeve. Pass the retaining ring from below over the two halves and secure them to the sliding sleeve.

n. Position the shaft protector D80L–625–4 on the end of the mainshaft. Position a 3-jawed puller on the collet retaining ring and pull off the 1st/2nd sliding sleeve, 2nd gear, thrust washer, and 3rd gear bearing inner race from the mainshaft.

CAUTION: *Wrap a heavy cloth around the 1st/2nd synchronizer body to catch the springs, pressure pieces and balls.*

o. Remove the snapring retaining the 1st/2nd synchronizer to the mainshaft.

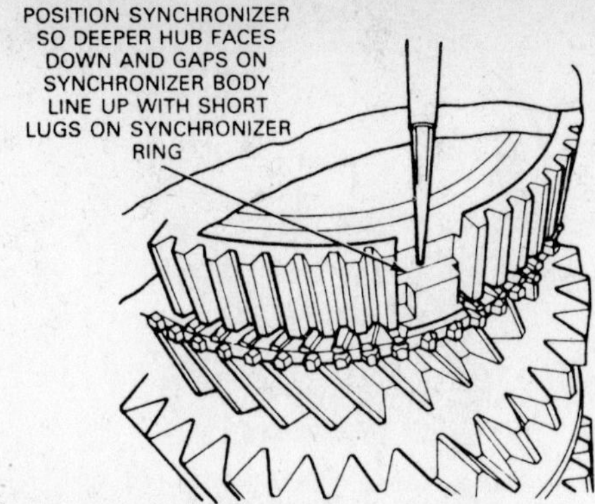

Installing the synchronizer body on the ZF mainshaft

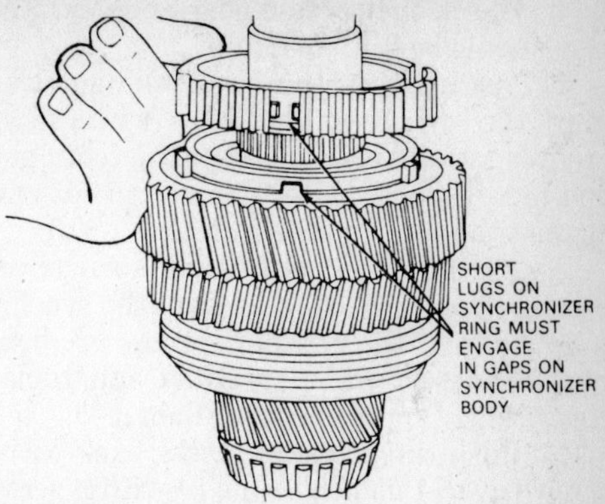

Synchronizer ring installation showing engaging lugs, on the ZF

p. Reposition the mainshaft in the vise so that the output end is facing upward.

q. On 4-wheel drive and F-Super Duty models, a snapring retaining the tapered roller bearing inner race should be removed.

r. Place a bearing gripper on the mainshaft rear tapered roller bearing. The gripper must be used to back the bearing during removal. Place a 3-jawed puller over the mainshaft and onto the gripper. Pull the bearing from the mainshaft.

s. Remove 5th gear from the mainshaft along with its caged needle rollers.

t. Remove the synchronizer ring from the 5th/reverse synchronizer.

u. Remove the snapring from the 5th/ reverse synchronizer body. Remove the 5th/reverse sliding sleeve.

CAUTION: *Wrap a heavy cloth around the 1st/2nd synchronizer body to catch the springs, pressure pieces and balls.*

v. Position Collet Retaining Ring T87T–7025–OH over the mainshaft and let it rest on the 1st gear. Position the two Collet Halves T87T–7025–NH so the ridge rests between the synchronizer body and the synchronizer ring. Slide the retaining ring upwards around the collets to secure them in position.

w. Position a 3-jawed puller on the collet retaining ring and pull the 5th/reverse synchronizer body from the mainshaft. Remove the synchronizer ring from the reverse gear. Remove the reverse gear from the mainshaft along with the caged needle bearings.

x. Remove the mainshaft from the vise. Position the mainshaft in a press and press off the 1st gear and 1st/2nd synchronizer body.

y. Remove the 1st gear caged needle rollers.

To assemble the mainshaft:

a. Clamp the input end of the mainshaft in a soft-jawed vise.

b. Place the reverse gear caged needle roller on the mainshaft.

c. Place the reverse gear on the mainshaft over the needle rollers. The clutch teeth must face upwards.

NOTE: *Before installing the original synchronizer ring and body, check them for excessive wear.*

d. Position the reverse gear synchronizer ring on the taper of the first gear.

e. Using a heat gun, heat the 5th/reverse synchronizer body to 320°F (160°C).

WARNING: *Don't heat the synchronizer body for more than 15 minutes.*

f. Position the synchronizer body on the mainshaft splines so that the side with the deeper hub faces downwards and the short lugs on the synchronizer ring engage the gaps in the synchronizer body. Push or lightly tap the synchronizer body down until it stops.

g. Install the snapring on the mainshaft next to the 5th/reverse synchronizer body. The clearance between the snapring and the synchronizer body should be 0–0.1mm, with 0 preferable.

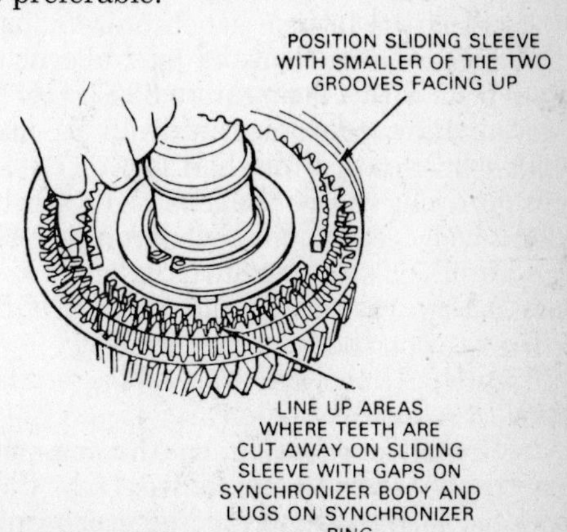

5th/reverse sliding sleeve installation on the ZF

h. Check the reverse gear endplay. Endplay should be 0.15–0.35mm.

i. Position the 5th/reverse sliding sleeve over the synchronizer body with the 2 grooves facing upwards. Align the tooth gaps and lugs. Slide the sleeve down until it rests against the reverse gear clutching teeth.

j. Insert the 3 compression springs and pressure pieces in the recesses of the synchronizer body. If the original springs are being reused, inspect them carefully and replace them if they appear worn or damaged.

k. Push the pressure pieces back with a screwdriver. Push the balls in with a screwdriver and slide the pressure piece against the ball.

l. Place the 5th gear synchronizer ring on the synchronizer body. The short lugs on the synchronizer ring should be located over the gaps in the 5th/reverse synchronizer body.

m. Push the 5th gear synchronizer ring downwards while pulling the sliding sleeve into the center position.

n. Pace the 5th gear caged needle rollers on the mainshaft. Install the 5th gear on the mainshaft over the caged needle rollers.

o. Heat the inner race of the mainshaft rear tapered roller bearing to 320°F (160°C) with a heat gun. Place it on the mainshaft and drive it until it seats against its stop.

WARNING: *Don't heat the bearing for more than 15 minutes.*

p. Check the 5th gear endplay. Endplay should be 0.15–0.35mm. On 4-wheel drive and F-Super Duty models, fit an additional retaining ring in the groove next to the tapered roller bearing inner race. It should have an endplay of 0–0.1mm, with 0 preferred.

q. Turn the mainshaft over and clamp it on the input end. Place the 1st gear caged needle rollers on the shaft. Place 1st gear over the rollers with the taper facing upward.

r. Place the 1st gear synchronizer ring on the 1st gear taper. Heat the 1st/2nd synchronizer body with a heat gun to 320°F (160°C). Position the synchronizer body on the mainshaft splines so that the short lugs on the synchronizer ring engage the gaps in the synchronizer body. Push the synchronizer body down until it stops against the ring. If the installation was correct, the word ENGINE will appear on the synchronizer body.

WARNING: *Don't heat the bearing for more than 15 minutes.*

s. Install a snapring on the mainshaft next to the 1st/2nd synchronizer body. Clearance between the snapring and synchronizer body should be 0–0.1mm. 1st gear endplay should be 0.15–0.35mm.

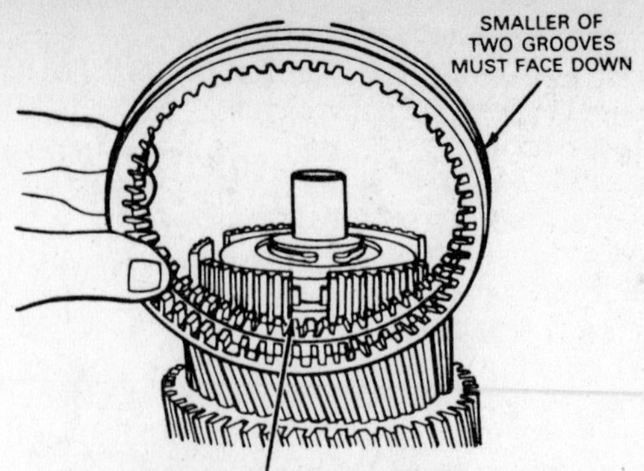

3rd gear sliding sleeve installation on the ZF

t. Position the sliding sleeve over the synchronizer body with its tapered collar facing downward. Align the lugs and tooth gaps, and push the sleeve down until it rests against 1st gear.

u. Insert the three compression springs and pressure pieces in the recesses of the synchronizer body. Push the pressure pieces back with a screwdriver. Push the balls in with a screwdriver and slide the pressure piece against the ball.

v. Place the 2nd gear synchronizer ring on the synchronizer body. The short lugs on the synchronizer ring should be located over the gaps in the 1st/2nd synchronizer body.

w. Push the 2nd gear synchronizer ring downwards while pulling the sliding sleeve into the center position. Pace the 2nd gear caged needle rollers on the mainshaft. Install the 2nd gear on the mainshaft over the caged needle rollers.

x. Heat the thrust washer to 320°F (160°C) with a heat gun. Place it on the mainshaft and drive it until it seats against its stop.

WARNING: *Don't heat the washer for more than 15 minutes.*

y. Heat the 3rd gear bearing inner race to 320°F (160°C) with a heat gun. Place the race on the mainshaft and push it down until it seats against its stop. Check the 2nd gear endplay. Endplay should be 0.15–0.45mm. After the 3rd gear has cooled, place the 3rd gear caged needle rollers over it. Place the 3rd gear over the needle rollers with the taper upwards. Place the 3rd gear synchronizer ring on the 3rd gear taper. Heat the 3rd/4th synchronizer body with a heat gun to 320°F (160°C). Position the body on the mainshaft splines so that the short lugs on the synchronizer ring engage the gaps in the body. Push the body down until it stops against the ring. The recess in the body must face upwards.

z. Install a snapring on the mainshaft next to the 1st/2nd synchronizer body. Clearance between the snapring and synchronizer body should be 0–0.1mm. 1st gear endplay should be 0.15–0.35mm. Position the sliding sleeve over the synchronizer body with its tapered collar facing downward. Align the lugs and tooth gaps, and push the sleeve down until it rests against 1st gear. Insert the three compression springs and pressure pieces in the recesses of the synchronizer body. Push the pressure pieces back with a screwdriver. Push the balls in with a screwdriver and slide the pressure piece against the ball. Place the 2nd gear synchronizer ring on the synchronizer body. The short lugs on the synchronizer ring should be located over the gaps in the 1st/2nd synchronizer body. Push the 2nd gear synchronizer ring downwards while pulling the sliding sleeve into the center position. Pace the 2nd gear caged needle rollers on the mainshaft. Install the 2nd gear on the mainshaft over the caged needle rollers. Heat the thrust washer to 320°F (160°C) with a heat gun. Place it on the mainshaft and drive it until it seats against its stop.

WARNING: *Don't heat the washer for more than 15 minutes.*

6. Input Shaft Disassembly and Assembly:

a. Position the two Collet Halves (44803 and 44797) of Universal Bearing Remover Set D81L–4220–A around the input shaft bearing cone. Install the pulling tube and pull the bearing from the shaft.

b. Inspect the bearing and shaft thoroughly. Replace any worn or damaged parts.

c. Place the bearing on the shaft.

d. Place the Bearing Cone Replacer T85T–4621–AH over the bearing.

e. Position the shaft, bearing and tool in Press Plate T75L–1165–B.

f. Press the bearing on until it seats against its stop.

INPUT SHAFT AND MAINSHAFT TAPERED ROLLER BEARING PRELOAD MEASUREMENT

This adjustment is necessary whenever a major, related component is replaced.

1. Place the transmission on a holding fixture with the output shaft facing upward.

2. Attach a dial indicator with a magnetic base so that the measurement bar rests on the output end of the mainshaft.

3. Zero the indicator and pry up on the input shaft and mainshaft with a prybar. Note the indicator reading. The shim and shaft seal must have a combined thickness equal to the indicator reading plus 0.02–0.11mm.

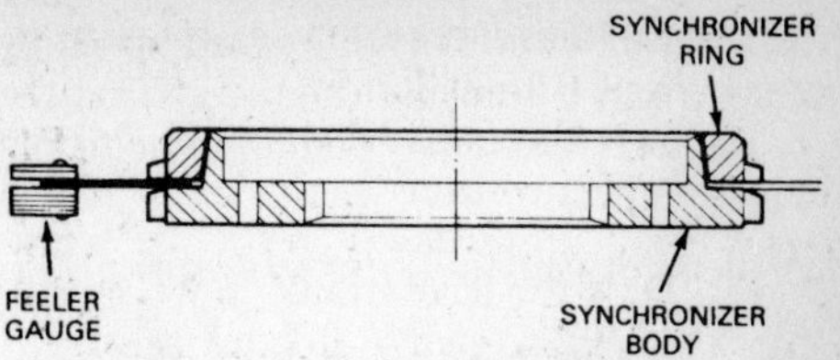

GEARS	CLEARANCE
1	0.6 mm (0.024 inch)
2	0.6 mm (0.024 inch)
3	0.6 mm (0.024 inch)
4	0.6 mm (0.024 inch)
5	0.6 mm (0.024 inch)
Reverse	0.2 mm (0.008 inch)

ZF synchronizer ring-to-body wear check

COUNTERSHAFT TAPERED ROLLER BEARING PRELOAD MEASUREMENT

1. Using two 10mm hex screws, attach the magnetic mount dial indicator near the pto opening on the front case. Position the dial indicator gauge on the support in such a way that the measurement bar rests against the flat face of the 5th speed helical gear on the countershaft. Zero the gauge.

2. Insert prybars through each of the two pto openings and position them beneath the 5th speed helical gear on the countershaft. Pry upward gently. Preload should be 0.0–0.11mm. Use shims to correct the preload.

MAINSHAFT AND INPUT SHAFT TAPERED ROLLER BEARING PRELOAD ADJUSTMENT

1. Position the transmission with the input shaft facing upwards.

2. Drive the two dowel pins out of their holes in the front and rear cases, and lift the front case off of the rear case.

3. Using a slide hammer and internal puller, remove the countershaft and mainshaft tapered roller bearing outer races from the front case.

4. Fit each race with a shim, or shim and shaft seal, to obtain the required preload determined above. The countershaft preload is set with shims alone. The input shaft and mainshaft preload is set using shims and a baffle. In both cases, parts are installed under the outer race of the tapered roller bearing which seats in the front case.

5. Apply Loctite 574® to the mating surfaces of the front and rear cases.

WARNING: *Do not use silicone type sealer.*

6. Join the case sections and torque the bolts to 16 ft. lbs.

SYNCHRONIZER RING AND SYNCHRONIZER BODY WEAR CHECK

1. Install the ring on the body.

2. Insert a feeler gauge and measure the clearance at two opposite positions. If clearance

is less than 0.6mm for the forward speed synchronizers and 0.2mm for the reverse synchronizer, replace the ring and/or synchronizer body as required.

SYNCHRONIZER COMPRESSION SPRING TENSION CHECK

The length of all springs should be 14.8mm; the outer diameter should be 5.96mm and the wire diameter should be 0.95mm. Replace any spring that is not to specifications.

MAIN COMPONENT ASSEMBLY

1. Place the input shaft and synchronizer ring assembly over the tapered roller bearing on the input end of the mainshaft.
2. Place the mainshaft and input shaft on Gear Pack Holding Fixture T87T–7025–HH. Place the countershaft on the fixture and mesh the gears of the two shafts.
3. Place the three shift rails and fork assemblies into Shift Rod Support Tool T87T–7025–JH in the same position from which they were removed during disassembly.
4. Position the three shift rail together with the shift rod support tool and interlock, so that the shift forks engage in the correct mainshaft sliding sleeves.
5. Place the shift interlock on the three gearshift rails and engage it in the interlock grooves in the 5th/reverse upper rail.
6. Slide the speedometer worm gear onto the mainshaft until it seats against its stop.
7. Secure the rear cover on the holding fixture T57L–500–B.
8. Position nylon lifting sling D87L–1000–A around the shift rails, holding fixture and mainshaft and countershaft.
9. Position the gear pack into the rear cover and push the shafts and rails forward until the bearings seat in their races and the gearshift rails slide into their retaining holes.

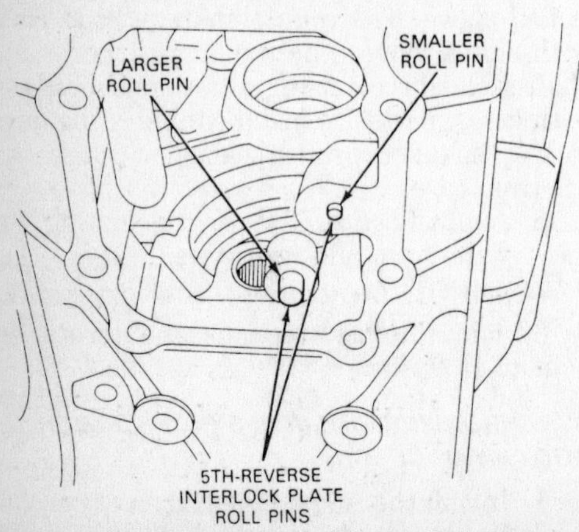

5th/reverse interlock plate roll pins on the ZF

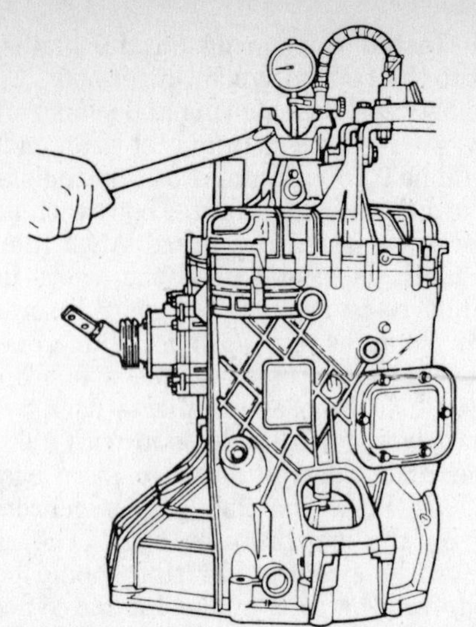

Measuring the preload on the ZF input shaft and mainshaft roller bearings

10. Rotate the gear pack and rear case upwards so that the input shaft faces up.
11. Slide the output shaft flange onto the output end of the mainshaft so that it seats against its stop. Screw the hex nut onto the shaft finger-tightly.

NOTE: *Make sure that the mainshaft bearing is not pushed off its race when the flange is installed.*

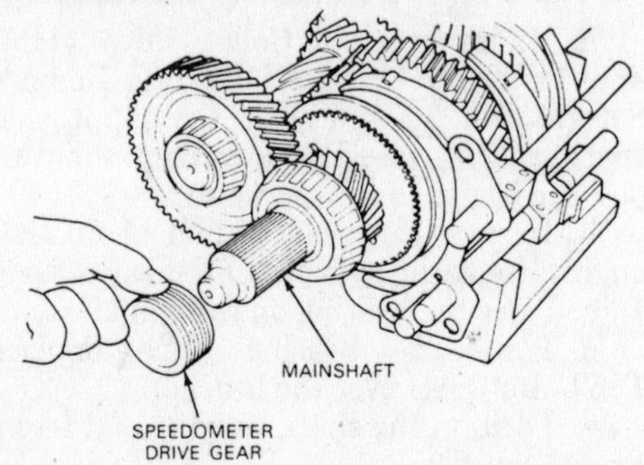

Installing the speedometer gear on the ZF mainshaft

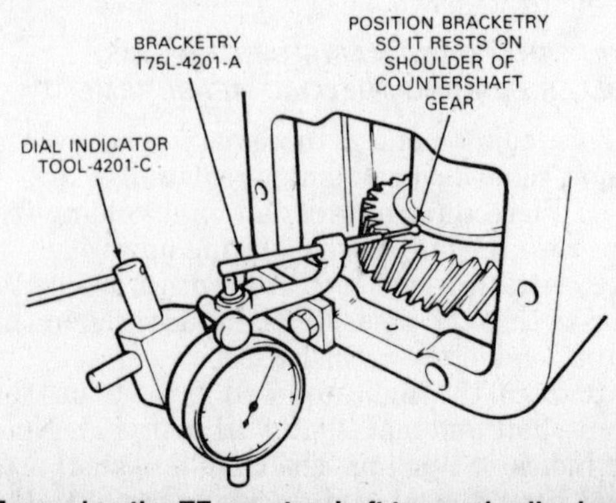

Measuring the ZF countershaft tapered roller bearing preload

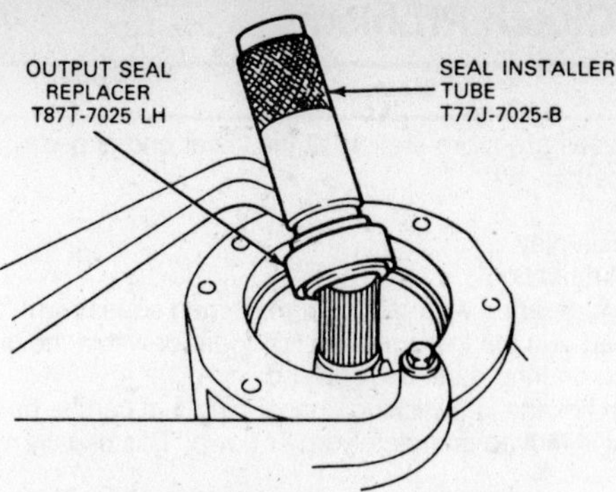

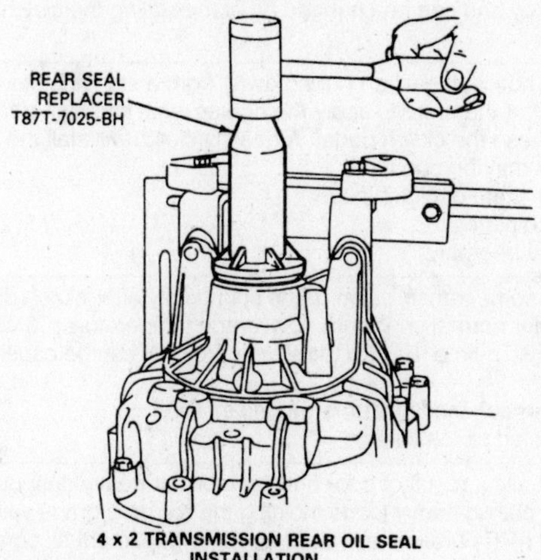

ZF rear oil seal installation

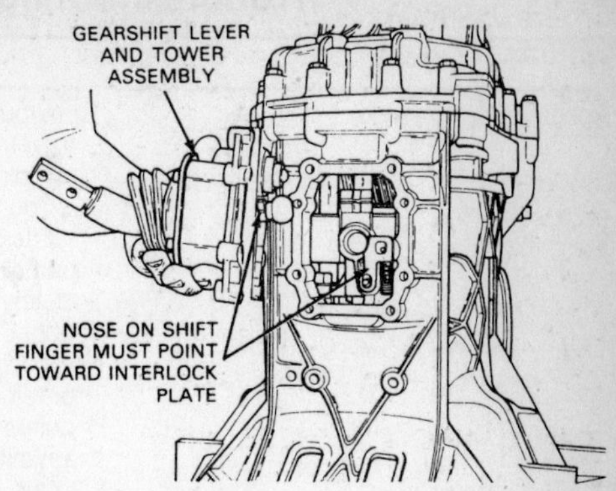

Installing the ZF shift tower assembly

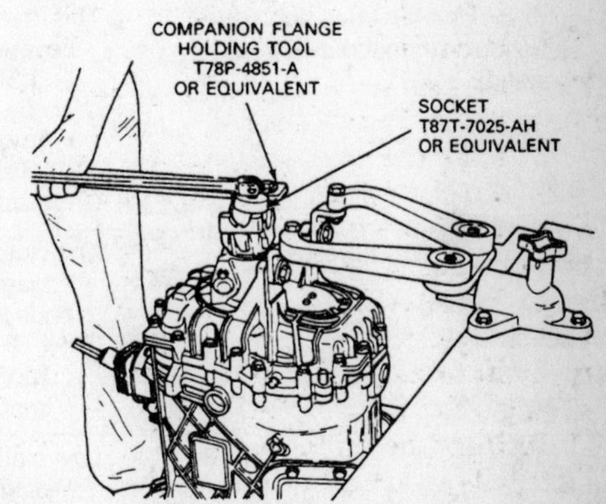

Installing the output flange on the ZF

12. Remove the shift rod support tool from the ends of the shift rails.

13. Remove the strap and gear pack holding fixture.

14. Attach the three capscrews that secure the shift interlock to the rear housing. Torque them to 84 inch lbs. Make sure that the interlock still moves freely.

15. Mesh the reverse idler gear and reverse gear. Slide the reverse idler shaft downward through the bearings and into the rear case. Tighten the bolt finger-tightly.

16. Insert the central shift rail and finger assembly into its bore in the rear case.

17. If the tapered roller bearings on the mainshaft or countershaft do not need adjustment, place a thin coating of Loctite 574® on the rear case mating surface. If the bearings need adjustment, do it at this time, then, apply sealer.

NOTE: *Do not use silicone type sealers.*

18. Push the three shift rail detents back into their holes in the front case.

19. Carefully place the front case half over the shafts and gearshift rails until it rests on the mating surface of the rear case. It may be necessary to push the central shift rail inward to clear the inner surfaces of the front case.

20. Drive in the two dowels that align the rear case and front case. Insert the two hex screws and tighten them finger-tightly.

21. Screw to additional hex screws into the rear case and make them finger tight.

22. If shaft preload adjustment is not necessary, install all the hex screws and torque all of them to 18 ft. lbs. If adjustment is necessary, do it at this time, then install and tighten all the hex screws.

23. Insert the reverse idler shaft screws and torque them to 16 ft. lbs. Push the sealing cover into the screw heads.

24. Turn the transmission so that the input shaft is facing down.

25. Install the speedometer drive gear on the mainshaft.

26. On 2-wheel drive vehicles, remove the hex nut that secures the output shaft flange to the mainshaft. Position the output shaft seal on the Output Shaft Seal Replacer Tool T87T–7025–BH. Position the seal and tool in the opening in the rear case. using a plastic or rubber mallet tap the seal in until it seats in the opening.

Troubleshooting Basic Clutch Problems

Problem	Cause
Excessive clutch noise	Throwout bearing noises are more audible at the lower end of pedal travel. The usual causes are: • Riding the clutch • Too little pedal free-play • Lack of bearing lubrication A bad clutch shaft pilot bearing will make a high pitched squeal, when the clutch is disengaged and the transmission is in gear or within the first 2″ of pedal travel. The bearing must be replaced. Noise from the clutch linkage is a clicking or snapping that can be heard or felt as the pedal is moved completely up or down. This usually requires lubrication. Transmitted engine noises are amplified by the clutch housing and heard in the passenger compartment. They are usually the result of insufficient pedal free-play and can be changed by manipulating the clutch pedal.
Clutch slips (the car does not move as it should when the clutch is engaged)	This is usually most noticeable when pulling away from a standing start. A severe test is to start the engine, apply the brakes, shift into high gear and SLOWLY release the clutch pedal. A healthy clutch will stall the engine. If it slips it may be due to: • A worn pressure plate or clutch plate • Oil soaked clutch plate • Insufficient pedal free-play
Clutch drags or fails to release	The clutch disc and some transmission gears spin briefly after clutch disengagement. Under normal conditions in average temperatures, 3 seconds is maximum spin-time. Failure to release properly can be caused by: • Too light transmission lubricant or low lubricant level • Improperly adjusted clutch linkage
Low clutch life	Low clutch life is usually a result of poor driving habits or heavy duty use. Riding the clutch, pulling heavy loads, holding the car on a grade with the clutch instead of the brakes and rapid clutch engagement all contribute to low clutch life.

On 4-wheel drive models, use Output Shaft Seal Replacer T87T–7025–LH and Installer Tube T77J–7025–B to install the output shaft oil seal.

27. On 2-wheel drive models, install the output shaft flange on the shaft. Hold the flange with a holding fixture and torque the shaft nut to 184 ft. lbs.

28. Lock the nut by bending the lock tabs.

29. Using new gaskets, install the pto covers and torque the bolts 28 ft. lbs.

30. Place the 5th/reverse gear interlock plate into position. Place the gasket over the shift tower mating surface on the front case. Make sure that the stop plate moves freely. Make sure that the plate and spring do not drop into the case.

31. Place the spring above the nose on the interlock plate and move both parts into their proper positions.

WARNING: *Follow this sequence exactly to ensure proper interlock function!*

32. Install the shift tower. The nose on the gearshift finger must point towards the interlock plate. Install the spring washers and torque the screws to 18 ft. lbs.

33. Check the interlock operation.

34. Install the compression springs over each detent bolt.

35. Drive the sealing caps over the springs and detent bolts. Each cap should seat $^{3}/_{64}$ in. (1.2mm) below the case surface. If you install them any deeper it will cause increased shift effort.

36. Install the back-up lamp switch and new sealing ring. Torque the switch to 15 ft. lbs.

CLUTCH

Understanding the Clutch

The purpose of the clutch is to disconnect and connect engine power from the transmission. A car at rest requires a lot of engine torque to get all that weight moving. An internal combustion engine does not develop a high starting torque (unlike steam engines), so it must be allowed to operate without any load until it builds up enough torque to move the car. Torque increases with engine rpm. The clutch allows the engine to build up torque by

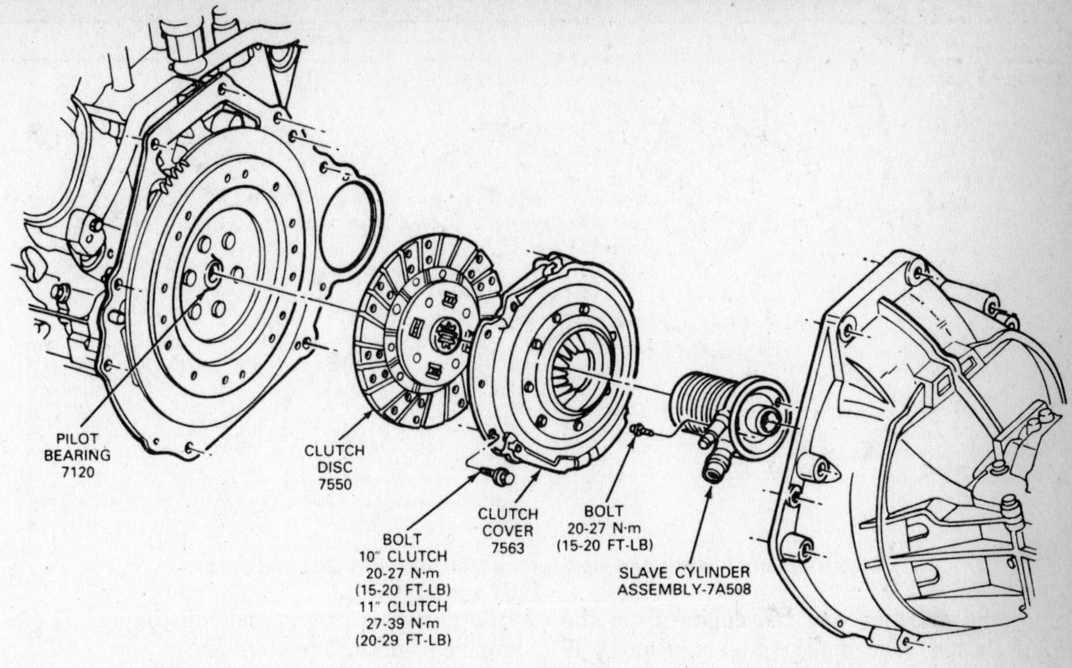

Clutch assembly exploded view for the 1988–90 6–300, 8–302 and 8–351

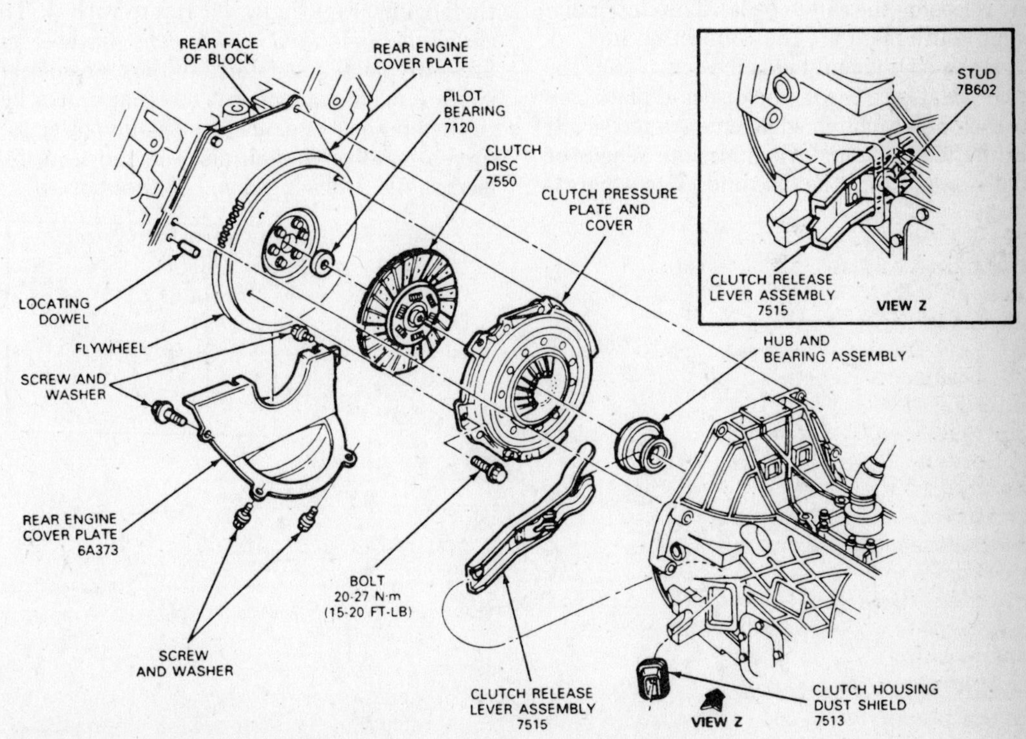

Clutch assembly exploded view for the 1987 8–460 and 7.3L diesel

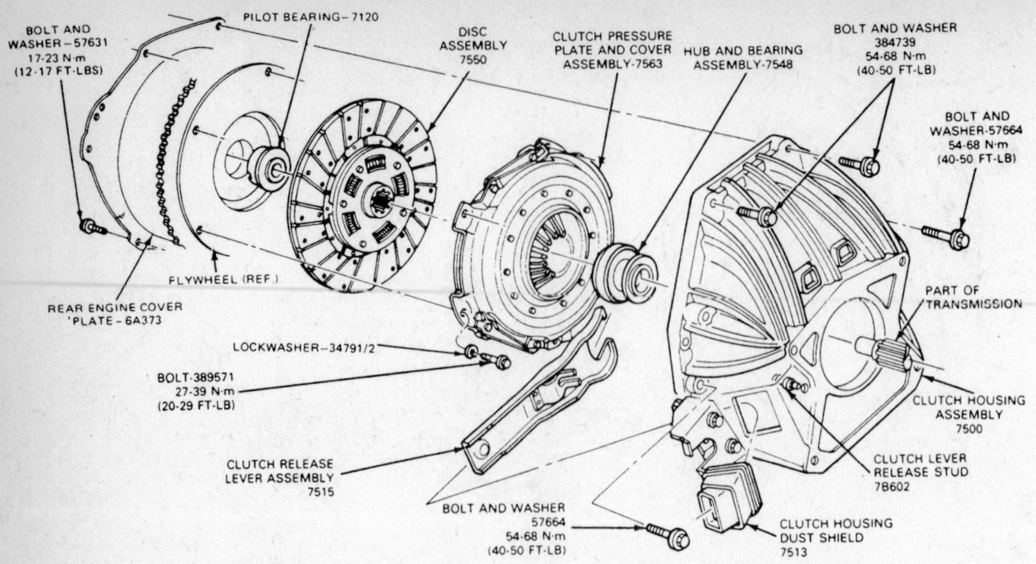

Clutch assembly exploded view for the 1987 6–300, 8–302 and 8–351

physically disconnecting the engine from the transmission, relieving the engine of any load or resistance. The transfer of engine power to the transmission (the load) must be smooth and gradual; if it weren't, drive line components would wear out or break quickly. This gradual power transfer is made possible by gradually releasing the clutch pedal. The clutch disc and pressure plate are the connecting link between the engine and transmission. When the clutch pedal is released, the disc and plate contact each other (clutch engagement), physically joining the engine and transmission. When the pedal is pushed in, the disc and plate separate (the clutch is disengaged), disconnecting the engine from the transmission.

The clutch assembly consists of the flywheel, the clutch disc, the clutch pressure plate, the throwout bearing and fork, the actuating linkage and the pedal. The flywheel and clutch pressure plate (driving members) are connected to the engine crankshaft and rotate with it. The clutch disc is located between the flywheel and pressure plate, and splined to the transmission shaft. A driving member is one that is attached to the engine and transfers engine power to a driven member (clutch disc) on the transmission shaft. A driving member (pressure plate)

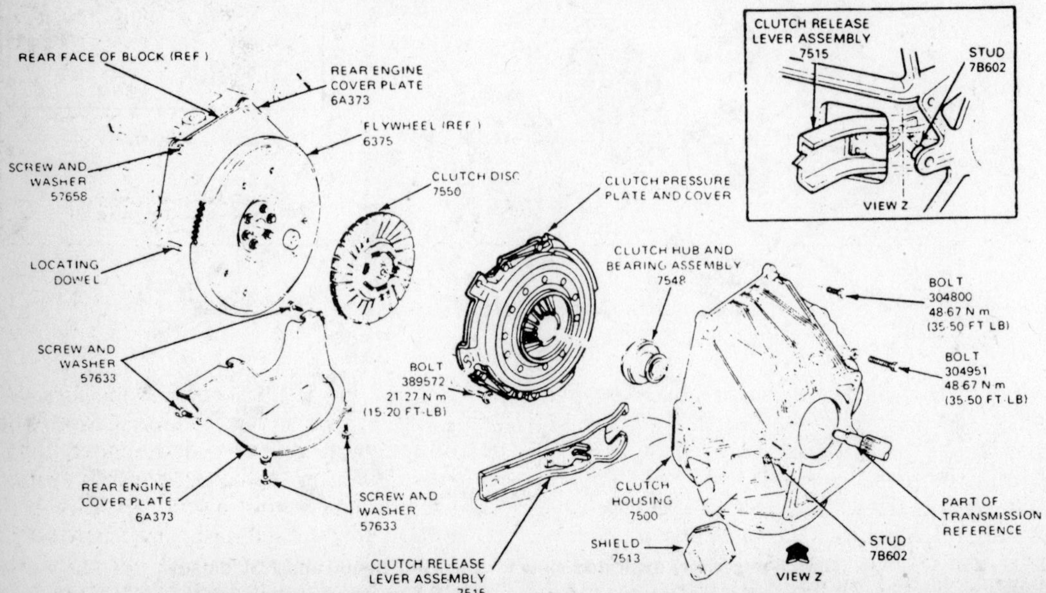

Clutch assembly exploded view for the 1987 8–460 and 6.9L diesel

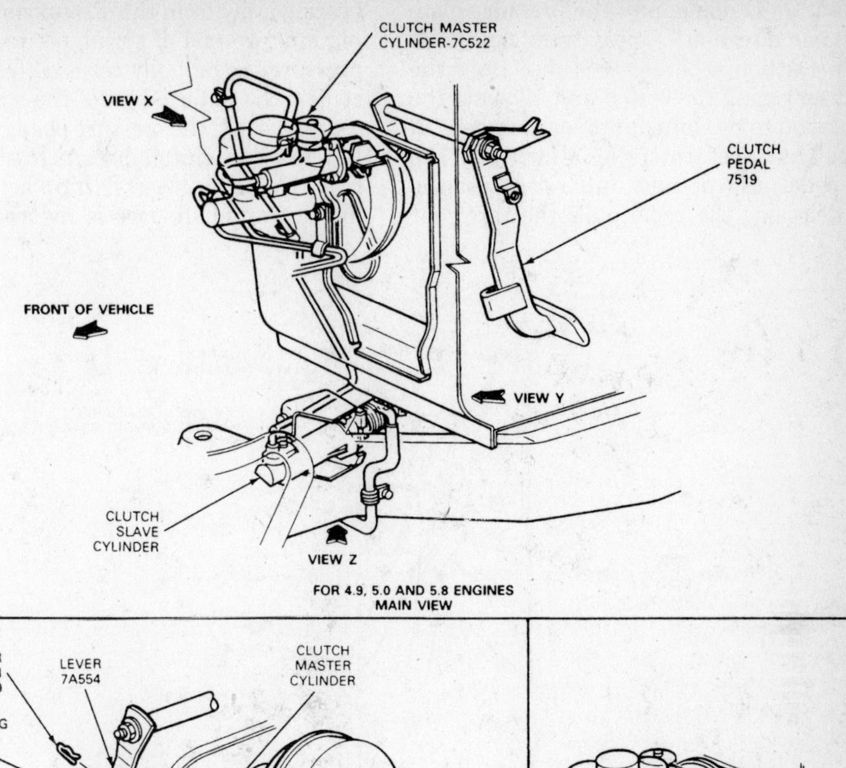

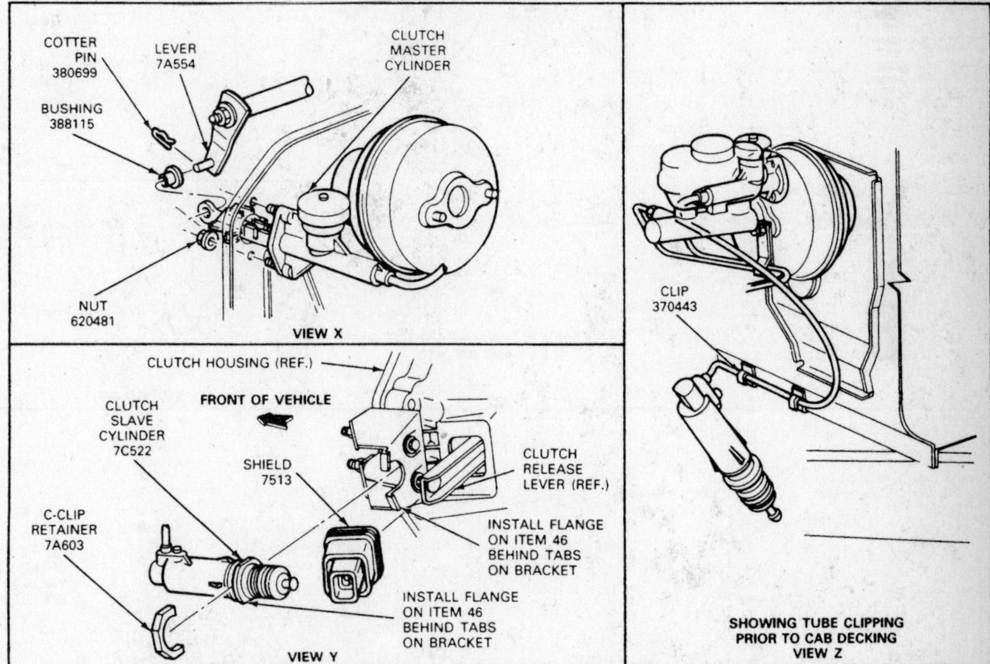

1987 hydraulic clutch system used on the 6–300, 8–302, and 8–351

rotates (drives) a driven member (clutch disc) on contact and, in so doing, turns the transmission shaft. There is a circular diaphragm spring within the pressure plate cover (transmission side). In a relaxed state (when the clutch pedal is fully released), this spring is convex; that is, it is dished outward toward the transmission. Pushing in the clutch pedal actuates an attached linkage rod. Connected to the other end of this rod is the throwout bearing fork. The throwout bearing is attached to the fork. When the clutch pedal is depressed, the clutch linkage pushes the fork and bearing forward to contact the diaphragm spring of the pressure plate. The outer edges of the spring are secured to the pressure plate and are pivoted on rings so that when the center of the spring is compressed by the throwout bearing, the outer edges bow outward and, by so doing, pull the pressure plate in the same direction – away from the clutch disc. This action separates the disc from the plate, disengaging the clutch and allowing the transmission to be shifted into another gear. A coil type clutch return spring attached to the clutch pedal arm permits full release of the pedal. Releasing the pedal pulls the throwout bearing away from the diaphragm spring resulting in a reversal of spring position. As bearing pressure is gradually released from the spring center, the outer edges of the spring bow outward, pushing the pressure plate into closer contact with the clutch disc. As the disc and plate move closer together, friction between the two increases and slippage is reduced until, when

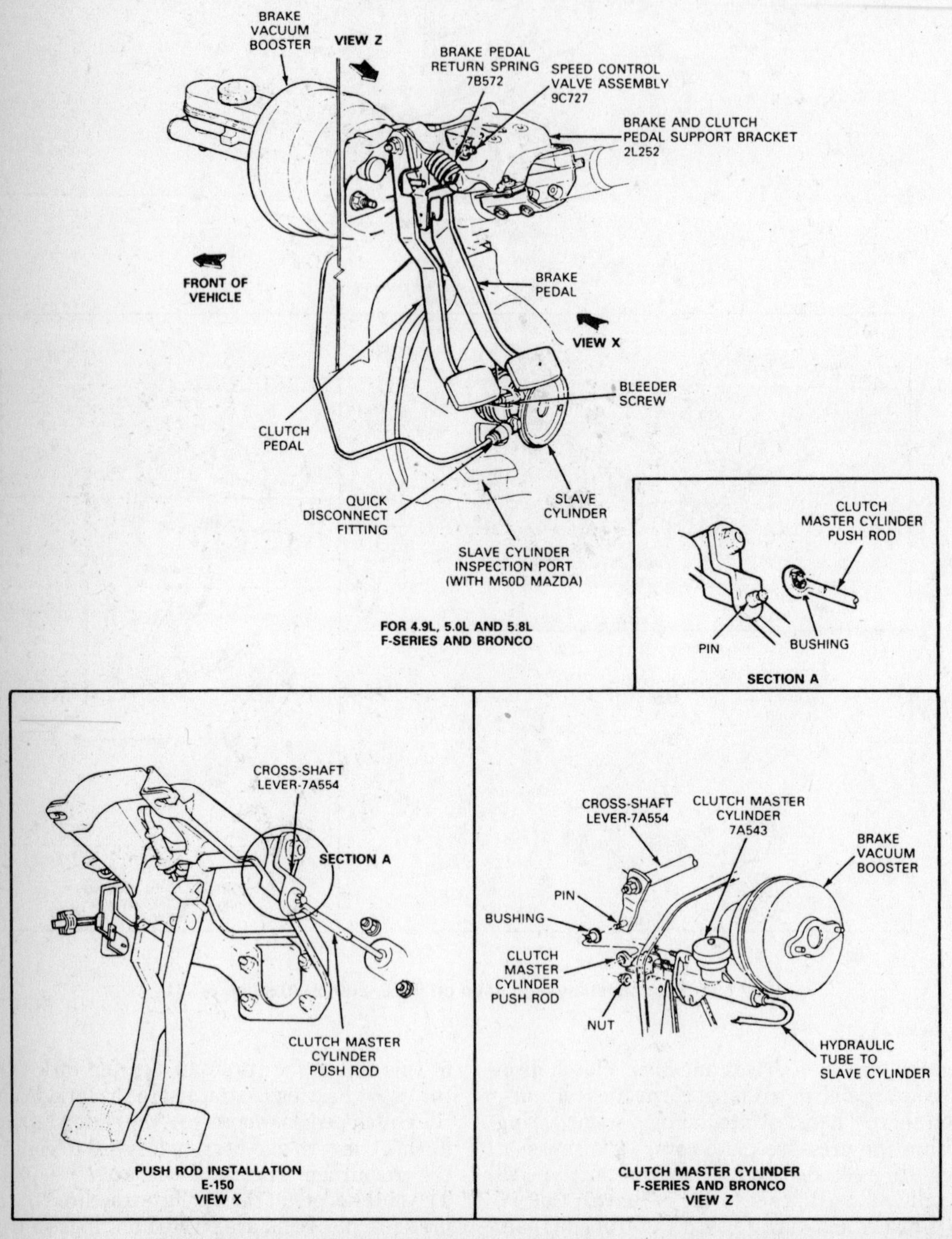

1988–90 hydraulic clutch system used on the 6–300, 8–302, and 8–351

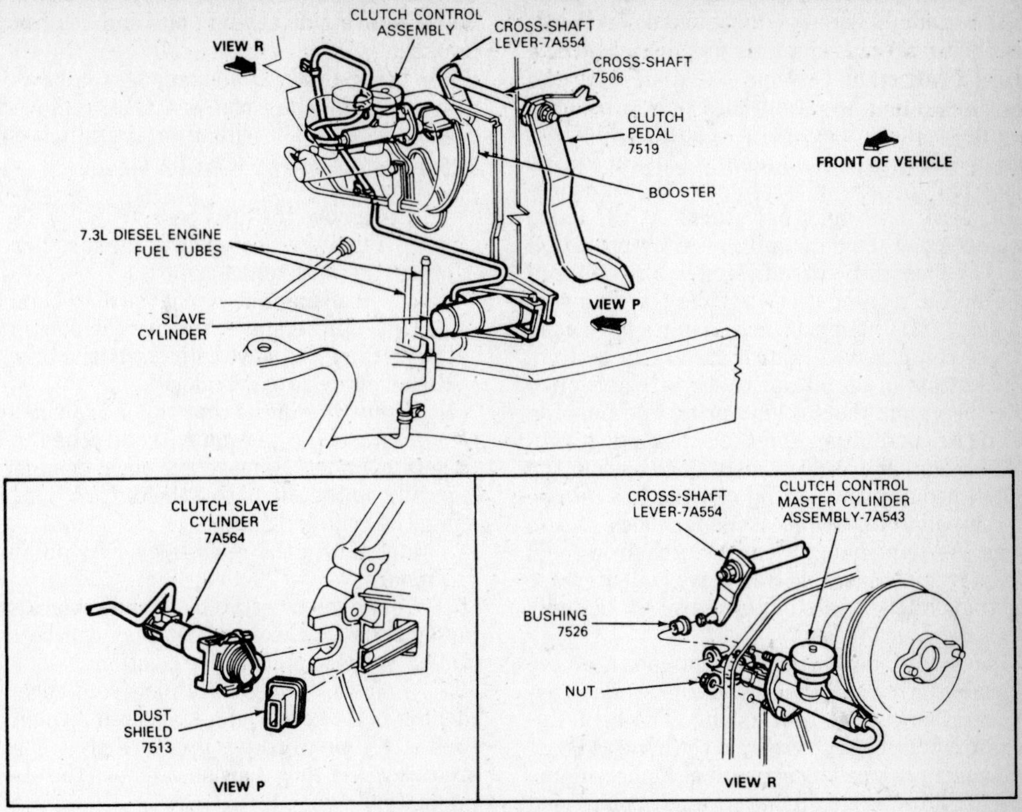

CLUTCH CONTROL ASSEMBLY
CROSS-SHAFT LEVER-7A554
VIEW R
CROSS-SHAFT 7506
CLUTCH PEDAL 7519
FRONT OF VEHICLE
BOOSTER
7.3L DIESEL ENGINE FUEL TUBES
VIEW P
SLAVE CYLINDER
CLUTCH SLAVE CYLINDER 7A564
DUST SHIELD 7513
VIEW P
CROSS-SHAFT LEVER-7A554
CLUTCH CONTROL MASTER CYLINDER ASSEMBLY-7A543
BUSHING 7526
NUT
VIEW R

1988–90 hydraulic clutch system used on the 8–460 and 7.3L diesel

CLUTCH CONTROL ASSEMBLY--7C522
CLUTCH PEDAL LEVER-7A554
RESERVOIR
BOOSTER 2005
VIEW Z
6.9L DIESEL ENG. FUEL TUBES
VIEW V
SLAVE CYLINDER
FRONT OF VEHICLE
CLUTCH CONTROL ASSEMBLY 7C522
CLUTCH CONTROL ASSEMBLY-7C522 (SLAVE CYLINDER)
DUST SHIELD 7513
VIEW V
CLUTCH PEDAL LEVER-7A554
CLUTCH CONTROL ASSEMBLY-7C522
COTTER PIN 380699
BUSHING 388115
NUT-N620481
RESERVOIR
MASTER CYLINDER
VIEW Z

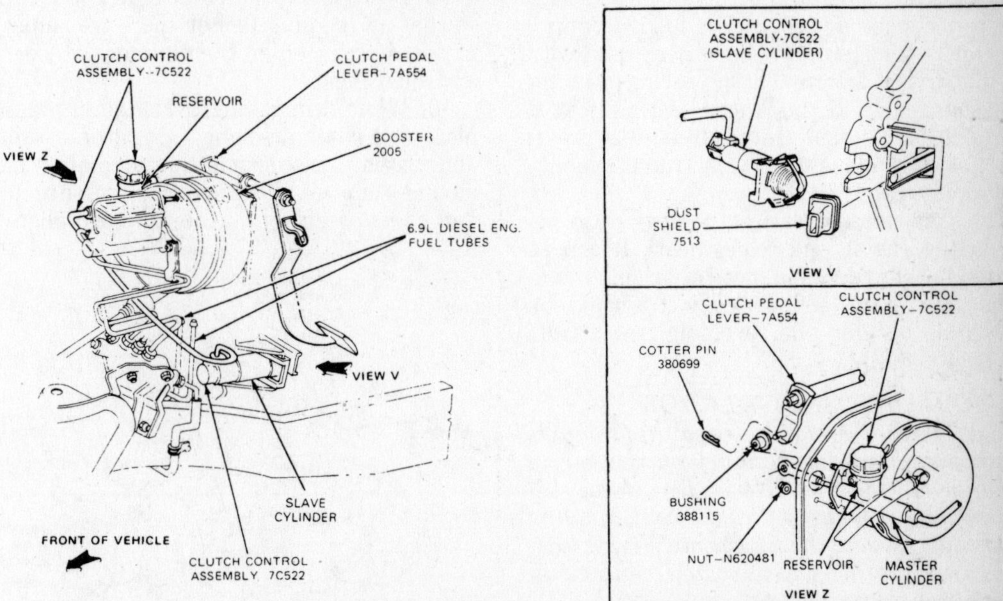

1987 hydraulic clutch system used on the 8–460 and 6.9L diesel

full spring pressure is applied (by fully releasing the pedal), The speed of the disc and plate are the same. This stops all slipping, creating a direct connection between the plate and disc which results in the transfer of power from the engine to the transmission. The clutch disc is now rotating with the pressure plate at engine speed and, because it is splined to the transmission shaft, the shaft now turns at the same engine speed. Understanding clutch operation can be rather difficult at first; if you're still confused after reading this, consider the following analogy. The action of the diaphragm spring can be compared to that of an oil can bottom. The bottom of an oil can is shaped very much like the clutch diaphragm spring and pushing in on the can bottom and then releasing it produces a similar effect. As mentioned earlier, the clutch pedal return spring permits full release of the pedal and reduces linkage slack due to wear. As the linkage wears, clutch free-pedal travel will increase and free-travel will decrease as the clutch wears. Free-travel is actually throwout bearing lash.

The diaphragm spring type clutches used are available in two different designs: flat diaphragm springs or bent spring. The bent fingers are bent back to create a centrifugal boost ensuring quick re-engagement at higher engine speeds. This design enables pressure plate load to increase as the clutch disc wears and makes low pedal effort possible even with a heavy-duty clutch. The throwout bearing used with the bent finger design is $1^1/_4$ in. (31.75mm) long and is shorter than the bearing used with the flat finger design. These bearings are not interchangeable. If the longer bearing is used with the bent finger clutch, free-pedal travel will not exist. This results in clutch slippage and rapid wear.

The transmission varies the gear ratio between the engine and rear wheels. It can be shifted to change engine speed as driving conditions and loads change. The transmission allows disengaging and reversing power from the engine to the wheels.

REMOVAL AND INSTALLATION

CAUTION: *The clutch driven disc contains asbestos, which has been determined to be a cancer causing agent. Never clean clutch surfaces with compressed air! Avoid inhaling any dust from any clutch surface! When cleaning clutch surfaces, use a commercially available brake cleaning fluid.*

1. Raise and support the truck end on jackstands.
2. Remove the clutch slave cylinder.
3. Remove the transmission.
4. If the clutch housing does not have a dust cover, remove the starter. Remove the flywheel housing attaching bolts and remove the housing.
5. If the flywheel housing does have a dust cover, remove the cover and then remove the release lever and bearing from the clutch housing. To remove the release lever:

   a. Remove the dust boot.

   b. Push the release lever forward to compress the slave cylinder.

   c. On all engines except the diesel and the 7.5L gasoline engines, remove the plastic clip that retains the slave cylinder to the bracket. Remove the slave cylinder.

   d. On the diesel and the 7.5L, the steel retaining clip is permanently attached to the slave cylinder. Remove the slave cylinder by prying on the clip to free the tangs while pulling the cylinder clear.

   e. Remove the release lever by pulling it outward.

6. Mark the pressure plate and cover assembly and the flywheel so that they can be reinstalled in the same relative position.
7. Loosen the pressure plate and cover attaching bolts evenly in a staggered sequence a turn at a time until the pressure plate springs are relieved of their tension. Remove the attaching bolts.
8. Remove the pressure plate and cover assembly and the clutch disc from the flywheel.
9. Position the clutch disc on the flywheel so that an aligning tool or spare transmission mainshaft can enter the clutch pilot bearing and align the disc.
10. When reinstalling the original pressure plate and cover assembly, align the assembly and flywheel according to the marks made during removal. Position the pressure plate and cover assembly on the flywheel, align the

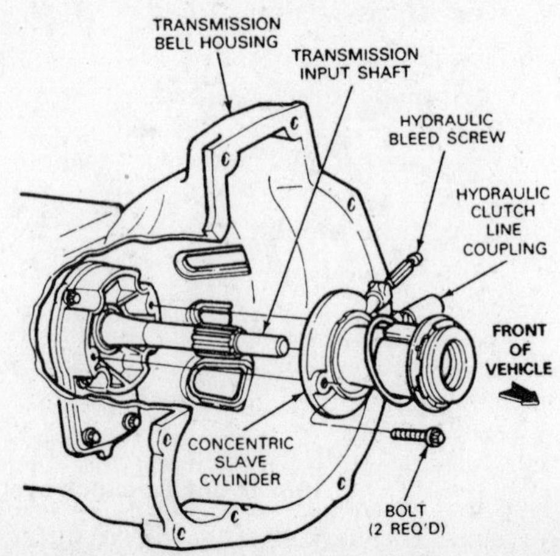

Slave cylinder removal

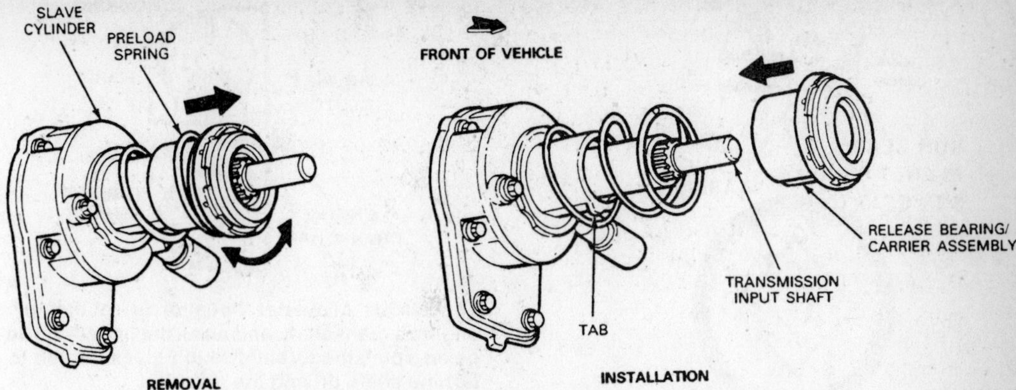

Clutch release bearing removal on systems with a concentric slave cylinder

pressure plate and disc, and install the retaining bolts. Tighten the bolts in an alternating sequence a few turns at a time until 15–20 ft. lbs. is reached.

11. Remove the tool used to align the clutch disc.

12. With the clutch fully released, apply a light coat of grease on the sides of the driving lugs.

13. Position the clutch release bearing and the bearing hub on the release lever. Install the release lever on the fulcrum in the flywheel housing. Apply a light coating of grease to the release lever fingers and the fulcrum. Fill the groove of the release bearing hub with grease.

14. If the flywheel housing has been removed, position it against the rear engine cover plate and install the attaching bolts and tighten them to 40–50 ft. lbs.

15. Install the starter motor.

16. Install the transmission.

17. Install the salve cylinder and bleed the system.

Hydraulic System

The hydraulic clutch system operates much like a hydraulic brake system. When you push down (disengage) the clutch pedal, the mechanical clutch pedal movement is converted into hydraulic fluid movement, which is then converted back into mechanical movement by the slave cylinder to actuate the clutch release lever.

The system consists of a combination clutch fluid reservoir/master cylinder assembly, a slave cylinder mounted on the bellhousing, and connecting tubing.

Fluid level is checked at the master cylinder reservoir. The hydraulic clutch system continually remains in adjustment, like a hydraulic disc brake system, so not clutch linkage or pedal adjustment is necessary.

REMOVAL

The clutch hydraulic system is serviced as a complete assembly and is pre-filled and bled. Individual components are not available.

WARNING: *Prior to any vehicle service that requires removal of the slave cylinder, such as transmission and/or clutch housing removal, the clutch master cylinder pushrod must be disconnected from the clutch pedal. Failure to do this may damage the slave cylinder if the clutch pedal is depressed while the slave cylinder is disconnected.*

1. From inside the truck cab, remove the cotter pin retaining the clutch master cylinder pushrod to the clutch pedal lever. Disconnect the pushrod and remove the bushing.

2. Remove the two nuts retaining the clutch reservoir and master cylinder assembly to the firewall.

3. From the engine compartment, remove the clutch reservoir and master cylinder assembly from the firewall. Note here how the clutch tubing routes to the slave cylinder.

4. Push the release lever forward to compress the slave cylinder.

5. On all engines except the diesel and the 7.5L gasoline engines, remove the plastic clip that retains the slave cylinder to the bracket. Remove the slave cylinder.

6. On the diesel and the 7.5L, the steel retaining clip is permanently attached to the slave cylinder. Remove the slave cylinder by prying on the clip to free the tangs while pulling the cylinder clear.

7. Remove the release lever by pulling it outward.

8. Remove the clutch hydraulic system from the truck.

INSTALLATION

1. Position the clutch pedal reservoir and master cylinder assembly into the firewall from

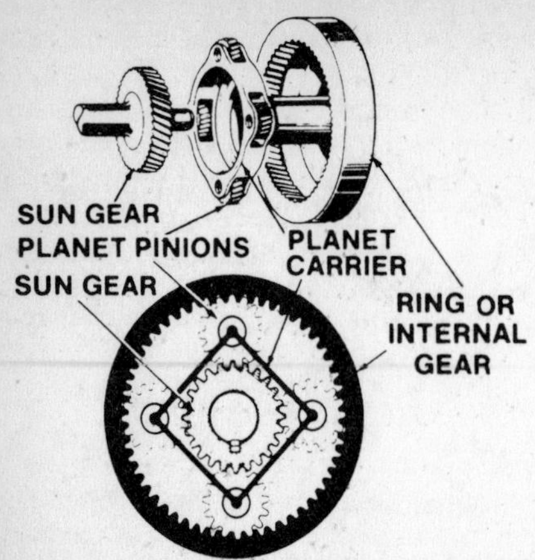

Planetary gears are similar to manual transmission gears but are composed of three parts

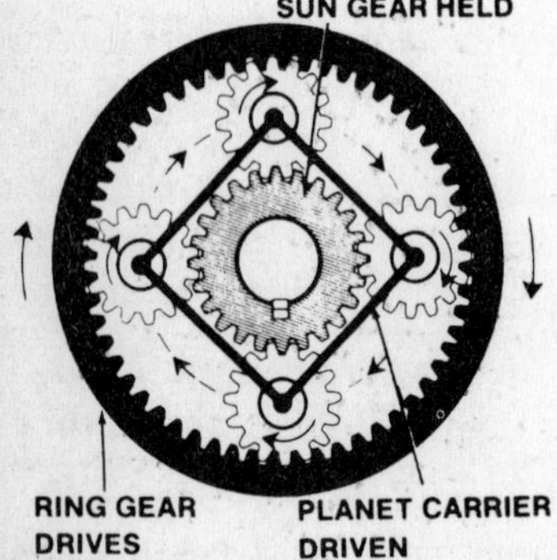

Planetary gears in the minimum reduction (drive) range. The ring gear is allowed to revolve, providing a higher gear ratio

inside the cab, and install the two nuts and tighten.

2. Route the clutch tubing and slave cylinder to the bell housing, taking care that the nylon lines are kept away from any hot exhaust system components.

3. Install the slave cylinder by pushing the slave cylinder pushrod into the cylinder. Engage the pushrod into the release lever and slide the slave cylinder into the bell housing lugs. Seat the cylinder into the recess in the lugs.

NOTE: *When installing a new hydraulic system, you'll notice that the slave cylinder contains a shipping strap that propositions the pushrod for installation, and also provides a bearing insert. Following installation of the new slave cylinder, the first actuation of the clutch pedal will break the shipping strap and give normal clutch action.*

4. Clean the master cylinder pushrod bearing and apply a light film of SAE 30 engine oil.

5. From inside the cab, install the bushing on the clutch pedal lever. Connect the clutch master cylinder pushrod to the clutch pedal lever and install the cotter pin.

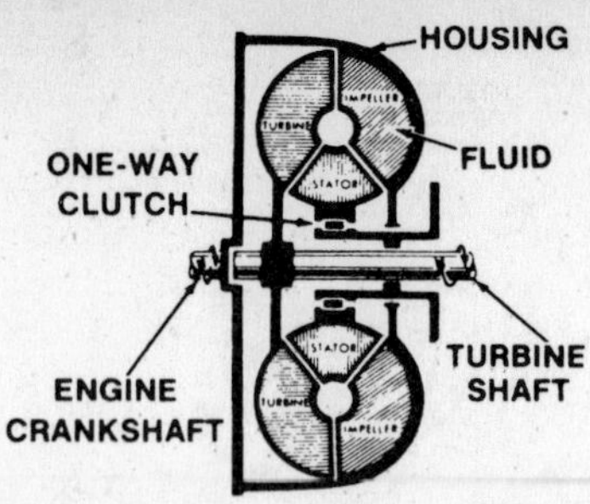

The torque converter housing is rotated by the engine's crankshaft, and turns the impeller. The impeller spins the turbine, which gives motion to the turbine shaft, driving the gears.

6. Check the clutch reservoir and add fluid if required. Depress the clutch pedal at least ten times to verify smooth operation and proper clutch release.

AUTOMATIC TRANSMISSION

Understanding Automatic Transmissions

The automatic transmission allows engine torque and power to be transmitted to the rear wheels within a narrow range of engine operating speeds. The transmission will allow the engine to turn fast enough to produce plenty of power and torque at very low speeds, while keeping it at a sensible rpm at high vehicle speeds. The transmission performs this job entirely without driver assistance. The transmission uses a light fluid as the medium for the transmission of power. This fluid also works in the operation of various hydraulic control circuits and as a lubricant. Because the transmission fluid performs all of these three functions, trouble within the unit can easily travel from one part to another. For this reason, and because of the complexity and unusual operating principles of the transmission, a very sound understanding of the basic principles of operation will simplify troubleshooting.

THE TORQUE CONVERTER

The torque converter replaces the conventional clutch. It has three functions:

1. It allows the engine to idle with the vehicle at a standstill, even with the transmission in gear.

2. It allows the transmission to shift from range to range smoothly, without requiring that the driver close the throttle during the shift.

3. It multiplies engine torque to an increasing extent as vehicle speed drops and throttle opening is increased. This has the effect of

making the transmission more responsive and reduces the amount of shifting required.

The torque converter is a metal case which is shaped like a sphere that has been flattened on opposite sides. It is bolted to the rear end of the engine's crankshaft. Generally, the entire metal case rotates at engine speed and serves as the engine's flywheel.

The case contains three sets of blades. One set is attached directly to the case. This set forms the torus or pump. Another set is directly connected to the output shaft, and forms the turbine. The third set is mounted on a hub which, in turn, is mounted on a stationary shaft through a one-way clutch. This third set is known as the stator.

A pump, which is driven by the converter hub at engine speed, keeps the torque converter full of transmission fluid at all times. Fluid flows continuously through the unit to provide cooling.

Under low speed acceleration, the torque converter functions as follows:

The torus is turning faster than the turbine. It picks up fluid at the center of the converter and, through centrifugal force, slings it outward. Since the outer edge of the converter moves faster than the portions at the center, the fluid picks up speed.

The fluid then enters the outer edge of the turbine blades. It then travels back toward the center of the converter case along the turbine blades. In impinging upon the turbine blades, the fluid loses the energy picked up in the torus.

If the fluid were now to immediately be returned directly into the torus, both halves of the converter would have to turn at approximately the same speed at all times, and torque input and output would both be the same.

In flowing through the torus and turbine, the fluid picks up two types of flow, or flow in two separate directions. It flows through the turbine blades, and it spins with the engine. The stator, whose blades are stationary when the vehicle is being accelerated at low speeds, converts one type of flow into another. Instead of allowing the fluid to flow straight back into the torus, the stator's curved blades turn the fluid almost 90° toward the direction of rotation of the engine. Thus the fluid does not flow as fast toward the torus, but is already spinning when the torus picks it up. This has the effect of allowing the torus to turn much faster than the turbine. This difference in speed may be compared to the difference in speed between the smaller and larger gears in any gear train. The result is that engine power output is higher, and engine torque is multiplied.

As the speed of the turbine increases, the fluid spins faster and faster in the direction of engine rotation. As a result, the ability of the stator to redirect the fluid flow is reduced. Under cruising conditions, the stator is eventually forced to rotate on its one-way clutch in the direction of engine rotation. Under these conditions, the torque converter begins to behave almost like a solid shaft, with the torus and turbine speeds being almost equal.

THE PLANETARY GEARBOX

The ability of the torque converter to multiply engine torque is limited. Also, the unit tends to be more efficient when the turbine is rotating at relatively high speeds. Therefore, a planetary gearbox is used to carry the power output of the turbine to the driveshaft.

Planetary gears function very similarly to conventional transmission gears. However, their construction is different in that three elements make up one gear system, and, in that all three elements are different from one another. The three elements are: an outer gear that is shaped like a hoop, with teeth cut into the inner surface; a sun gear, mounted on a shaft and located at the very center of the outer gear; and a set of three planet gears, held by pins in a ring-like planet carrier, meshing with both

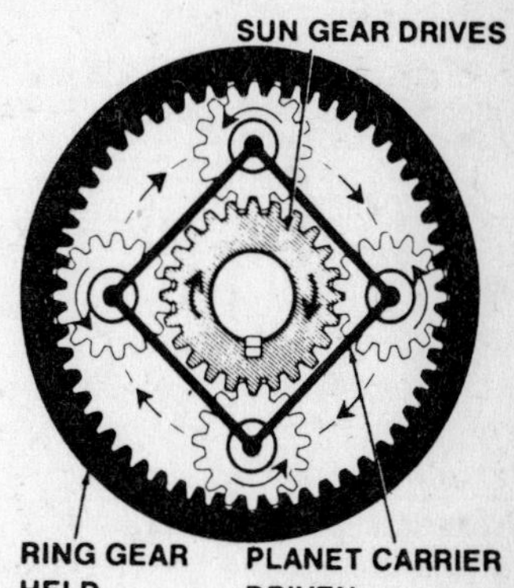

Planetary gears in the maximum reduction (low) range. The ring gear is held and a lower gear ration is obtained

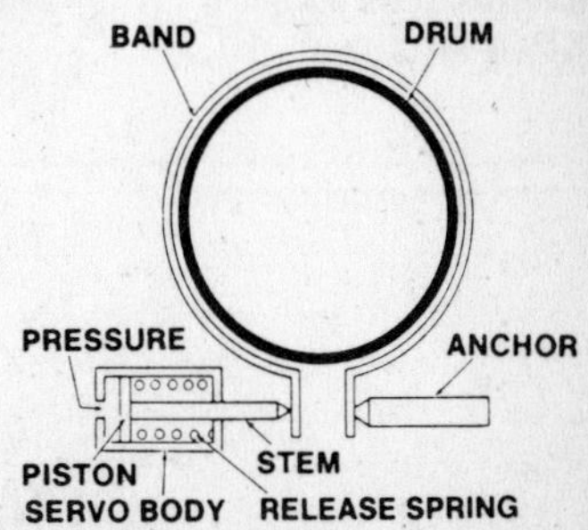

Servos, operated by pressure, are used to apply or release the bands, to either hold the ring gear or allow it to rotate

Lockup Torque Converter Service Diagnosis

Problem	Cause	Solution
No lockup	· Faulty oil pump · Sticking governor valve · Valve body malfunction (a) Stuck switch valve (b) Stuck lockup valve (c) Stuck fail-safe valve · Failed locking clutch · Leaking turbine hub seal · Faulty input shaft or seal ring	· Replace oil pump · Repair or replace as necessary · Repair or replace valve body or its internal components as necessary · Replace torque converter · Replace torque converter · Repair or replace as necessary
Will not unlock	· Sticking governor valve · Valve body malfunction (a) Stuck switch valve (b) Stuck lockup valve (c) Stuck fail-safe valve	· Repair or replace as necessary · Repair or replace valve body or its internal components as necessary
Stays locked up at too low a speed in direct	· Sticking governor valve · Valve body malfunction (a) Stuck switch valve (b) Stuck lockup valve (c) Stuck fail-safe valve	· Repair or replace as necessary · Repair or replace valve body or its internal components as necessary
Locks up or drags in low or second	· Faulty oil pump · Valve body malfunction (a) Stuck switch valve (b) Stuck fail-safe valve	· Replace oil pump · Repair or replace valve body or its internal components as necessary
Sluggish or stalls in reverse	· Faulty oil pump · Plugged cooler, cooler lines or fittings · Valve body malfunction (a) Stuck switch valve (b) Faulty input shaft or seal ring	· Replace oil pump as necessary · Flush or replace cooler and flush lines and fittings · Repair or replace valve body or its internal components as necessary
Loud chatter during lockup engagement (cold)	· Faulty torque converter · Failed locking clutch · Leaking turbine hub seal	· Replace torque converter · Replace torque converter · Replace torque converter
Vibration or shudder during lockup engagement	· Faulty oil pump · Valve body malfunction · Faulty torque converter · Engine needs tune-up	· Repair or replace oil pump as necessary · Repair or replace valve body or its internal components as necessary · Replace torque converter · Tune engine
Vibration after lockup engagement	· Faulty torque converter · Exhaust system strikes underbody · Engine needs tune-up · Throttle linkage misadjusted	· Replace torque converter · Align exhaust system · Tune engine · Adjust throttle linkage
Vibration when revved in neutral Overheating: oil blows out of dip stick tube or pump seal	· Torque converter out of balance · Plugged cooler, cooler lines or fittings · Stuck switch valve	· Replace torque converter · Flush or replace cooler and flush lines and fittings · Repair switch valve in valve body or replace valve body
Shudder after lockup engagement	· Faulty oil pump · Plugged cooler, cooler lines or fittings · Valve body malfunction · Faulty torque converter · Fail locking clutch · Exhaust system strikes underbody · Engine needs tune-up · Throttle linkage misadjusted	· Replace oil pump · Flush or replace cooler and flush lines and fittings · Repair or replace valve body or its internal components as necessary · Replace torque converter · Replace torque converter · Align exhaust system · Tune engine · Adjust throttle linkage

Transmission Fluid Indications

The appearance and odor of the transmission fluid can give valuable clues to the overall condition of the transmission. Always note the appearance of the fluid when you check the fluid level or change the fluid. Rub a small amount of fluid between your fingers to feel for grit and smell the fluid on the dipstick.

If the fluid appears:	It indicates:
Clear and red colored	• Normal operation
Discolored (extremely dark red or brownish) or smells burned	• Band or clutch pack failure, usually caused by an overheated transmission. Hauling very heavy loads with insufficient power or failure to change the fluid, often result in overheating. Do not confuse this appearance with newer fluids that have a darker red color and a strong odor (though not a burned odor).
Foamy or aerated (light in color and full of bubbles)	• The level is too high (gear train is churning oil) • An internal air leak (air is mixing with the fluid). Have the transmission checked professionally.
Solid residue in the fluid	• Defective bands, clutch pack or bearings. Bits of band material or metal abrasives are clinging to the dipstick. Have the transmission checked professionally.
Varnish coating on the dipstick	• The transmission fluid is overheating

Troubleshooting Basic Automatic Transmission Problems

Problem	Cause	Solution
Fluid leakage	• Defective pan gasket • Loose filler tube • Loose extension housing to transmission case • Converter housing area leakage	• Replace gasket or tighten pan bolts • Tighten tube nut • Tighten bolts • Have transmission checked professionally
Fluid flows out the oil filler tube	• High fluid level • Breather vent clogged • Clogged oil filter or screen • Internal fluid leakage	• Check and correct fluid level • Open breather vent • Replace filter or clean screen (change fluid also) • Have transmission checked professionally
Transmission overheats (this is usually accompanied by a strong burned odor to the fluid)	• Low fluid level • Fluid cooler lines clogged • Heavy pulling or hauling with insufficient cooling • Faulty oil pump, internal slippage	• Check and correct fluid level • Drain and refill transmission. If this doesn't cure the problem, have cooler lines cleared or replaced. • Install a transmission oil cooler • Have transmission checked professionally
Buzzing or whining noise	• Low fluid level • Defective torque converter, scored gears	• Check and correct fluid level • Have transmission checked professionally
No forward or reverse gears or slippage in one or more gears	• Low fluid level • Defective vacuum or linkage controls, internal clutch or band failure	• Check and correct fluid level • Have unit checked professionally
Delayed or erratic shift	• Low fluid level • Broken vacuum lines • Internal malfunction	• Check and correct fluid level • Repair or replace lines • Have transmission checked professionally

the sun gear and the outer gear. Either the outer gear or the sun gear may be held stationary, providing more than one possible torque multiplication factor for each set of gears. Also, if all three gears are forced to rotate at the same speed, the gearset forms, in effect, a solid shaft.

Most modern automatics use the planetary gears to provide either a single reduction ratio of about 1.8:1, or two reduction gears: a low of about 2.5:1, and an intermediate of about 1.5:1. Bands and clutches are used to hold various portions of the gearsets to the transmission case or to the shaft on which they are mounted. Shifting is accomplished, then, by changing the portion of each planetary gearset which is held to the transmission case or to the shaft.

THE SERVOS AND ACCUMULATORS

The servos are hydraulic pistons and cylinders. They resemble the hydraulic actuators used on many familiar machines, such as bulldozers. Hydraulic fluid enters the cylinder, under pressure, and forces the piston to move to engage the band or clutches.

The accumulators are used to cushion the engagement of the servos. The transmission fluid must pass through the accumulator on the way to the servo. The accumulator housing contains a thin piston which is sprung away from the discharge passage of the accumulator. When fluid passes through the accumulator on the way to the servo, it must move the piston against spring pressure, and this action smooths out the action of the servo.

THE HYDRAULIC CONTROL SYSTEM

The hydraulic pressure used to operate the servos comes from the main transmission oil pump. This fluid is channeled to the various servos through the shift valves. There is generally a manual shift valve which is operated by the transmission selector lever and an automatic shift valve for each automatic upshift the transmission provides: i.e., 2-speed automatics have a low/high shift valve, while 3-speeds have a 1–2 valve, and a 2–3 valve.

There are two pressures which effect the operation of these valves. One is the governor pressure which is affected by vehicle speed. The other is the modulator pressure which is affected by intake manifold vacuum or throttle position. Governor pressure rises with an increase in vehicle speed, and modulator pressure rises as the throttle is opened wider. By responding to these two pressures, the shift valves cause the upshift points to be delayed with increased throttle opening to make the best use of the engine's power output.

Most transmissions also make use of an auxiliary circuit for down shifting. This circuit may be actuated by the throttle linkage or the vacuum line which actuates the modulator, or by a cable or solenoid. It applies pressure to a special downshift surface on the shift valve or valves.

The transmission modulator also governs the line pressure, used to actuate the servos. In this way, the clutches and bands will be actuated with a force matching the torque output of the engine.

Transmission

REMOVAL AND INSTALLATION

C6

1. From in the engine compartment, remove the two upper converter housing-to-engine bolts.
2. Disconnect the neutral switch wire at the inline connector.
3. Remove the bolt securing the fluid filler tube to the engine cylinder head.
4. Raise and support the truck on jackstands.
5. Place the drain pan under the transmission fluid pan. Starting at the rear of the pan and working toward the front, loosen the attaching bolts and allow the fluid to drain. Finally remove all of the pan attaching bolts except two at the front, to allow the fluid to further drain. With fluid drained, install two bolts on the rear side of the pan to temporarily hold it in place.
6. Remove the converter drain plug access cover from the lower end of the converter housing.
7. Remove the converter-to-flywheel attaching nuts. Place a wrench on the crankshaft pulley attaching bolt to turn the converter to gain access to the nuts.
8. With the wrench on the crankshaft pulley attaching bolt, turn the converter to gain access to the converter drain plug. Place a drain pan under the converter to catch the fluid and remove the plug. After the fluid has been drained, reinstall the plug.
9. On 2-wheel drive models, disconnect the driveshaft from the rear axle and slide shaft rearward from the transmission. Install a seal installation tool in the extension housing to prevent fluid leakage.
10. Disconnect the speedometer cable from the extension housing.
11. Disconnect the downshift and manual linkage rods from the levers at the transmission.
12. Disconnect the oil cooler lines from the transmission.
13. Remove the vacuum hose from the

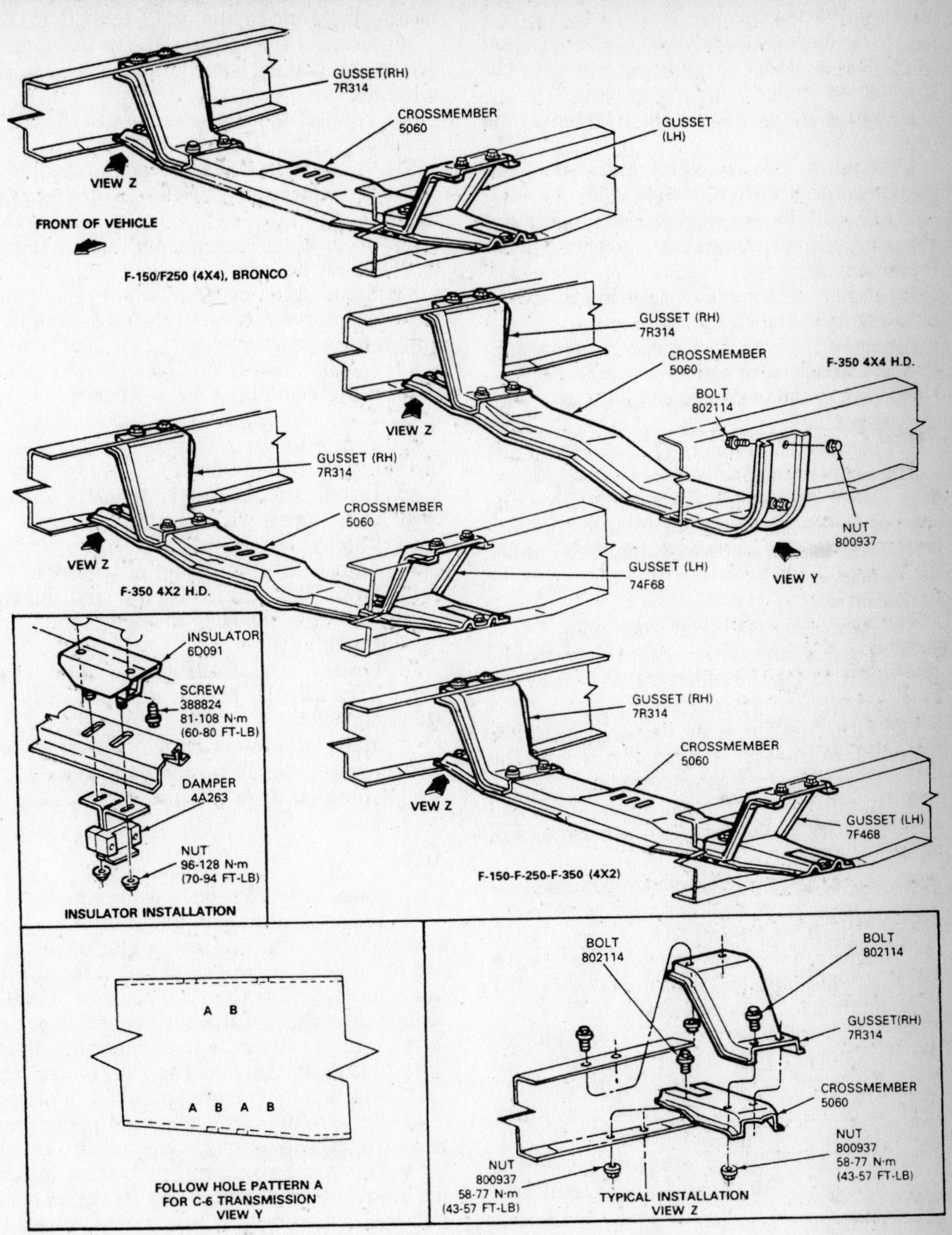

C6 mounting points

vacuum diaphragm unit. Remove the vacuum line retaining clip.

14. Disconnect the cable from the terminal on the starter motor. Remove the three attaching bolts and remove the starter motor.

15. On 4-wheel drive models remove the transfer case.

16. Remove the two engine rear support and insulator assembly-to-attaching bolts.

17. Remove the two engine rear support and insulator assembly-to-extension housing attaching bolts.

18. Remove the six bolts securing the No. 2 crossmember to the frame side rails.

19. Raise the transmission with a transmission jack and remove both crossmembers.

20. Secure the transmission to the jack with the safety chain.

21. Remove the remaining converter housing-to-engine attaching bolts.

22. Move the transmission away from the engine. Lower the jack and remove the converter and transmission assembly from under the vehicle.

To install:

23. Tighten the converter drain plug.

24. Position the converter on the transmission making sure the converter drive flats are fully engaged in the pump gear.

25. With the converter properly installed, place the transmission on the jack. Secure the transmission on the jack with the chain.

26. Rotate the converter until the studs and drain plug are in alignment with their holes in the flywheel.

27. Move the converter and transmission assembly forward into position, using care not to damage the flywheel and the converter pilot. The converter must rest squarely against the flywheel. This indicates that the converter pilot is not binding in the engine crankshaft.

28. Install the converter housing-to-engine attaching bolts and torque them to 65 ft. lbs. for the diesel; 50 ft. lbs. for gasoline engines.

29. Remove the transmission jack safety chain from around the transmission.

30. Position the No. 2 crossmember to the frame side rails. Install and tighten the attaching bolts.

31. Install transfer case on 4-wheel drive models.

32. Position the engine rear support and insulator assembly above the crossmember. Install the rear support and insulator assembly-to-extension housing mounting bolts and tighten the bolts to 45 ft. lbs.

33. Lower the transmission and remove the jack.

34. Secure the engine rear support and insulator assembly to the crossmember with the attaching bolts and tighten them to 80 ft. lbs.

35. Connect the vacuum line to the vacuum diaphragm making sure that the line is in the retaining clip.

36. Connect the oil cooler lines to the transmission.

37. Connect the downshift and manual linkage rods to their respective levers on the transmission.

38. Connect the speedometer cable to the extension housing.

39. Secure the starter motor in place with the attaching bolts. Connect the cable to the terminal on the starter.

40. Install a new O-ring on the lower end of the transmission filler tube and insert the tube in the case.

41. Secure the converter-to-flywheel attaching nuts and tighten them to 30 ft. lbs.

42. Install the converter housing access cover and secure it with the attaching bolts.

43. Connect the driveshaft.

44. Adjust the shift linkage as required.

45. Lower the vehicle. Then install the two upper converter housing-to-engine bolts and tighten them.

46. Position the transmission fluid filler tube to the cylinder head and secure with the attaching bolts.

47. Make sure the drain pan is securely attached, and fill the transmission to the correct level with the Dexron®II fluid.

AOD

1. Raise the vehicle on hoist or stands.

2. Place the drain pan under the transmission fluid pan. Starting at the rear of the pan and working toward the front, loosen the attaching bolts and allow the fluid to drain. Finally remove all of the pan attaching bolts except two at the front, to allow the fluid to further drain. With fluid drained, install two bolts on the rear side of the pan to temporarily hold it in place.

3. Remove the converter drain plug access cover from the lower end of the converter.

4. Remove the converter-to-flywheel attaching nuts. Place a wrench on the crankshaft pulley attaching bolt to turn the converter to gain access to the nuts.

5. Place a drain pan under the converter to catch the fluid. With the wrench on the crankshaft pulley attaching bolt, turn the converter to gain access to the converter drain plug and remove the plug. After the fluid has been drained, reinstall the plug.

6. On 2-wheel drive models, matchmark and disconnect the driveshaft from the rear axle and slide shaft rearward from the trans-

mission. Install a seal installation tool in the extension housing to prevent fluid leakage.

7. Disconnect the cable from the terminal on the starter motor. Remove the three attaching bolts and remove the starter motor. Disconnect the neutral start switch wires at the plug connector.

8. Remove the rear mount-to-crossmember attaching bolts and the two crossmember-to-frame attaching bolts.

9. Remove the two engine rear support-to-extension housing attaching bolts.

10. Disconnect the TV linkage rod from the transmission TV lever. Disconnect the manual rod from the transmission manual lever at the transmission.

11. Remove the two bolts securing the bellcrank bracket to the converter housing.

12. On 4-wheel drive models, remove the transfer case.

13. Raise the transmission with a transmission jack to provide clearance to remove the crossmember. Remove the rear mount from the crossmember and remove the crossmember from the side supports.

14. Lower the transmission to gain access to the oil cooler lines.

15. Disconnect each oil line from the fittings on the transmission.

16. Disconnect the speedometer cable from the extension housing.

17. Remove the bolt that secures the transmission fluid filler tube to the cylinder block. Lift the filler tube and the dipstick from the transmission.

18. Secure the transmission to the jack with the chain.

19. Remove the converter housing-to-cylinder block attaching bolts.

20. Carefully move the transmission and con-

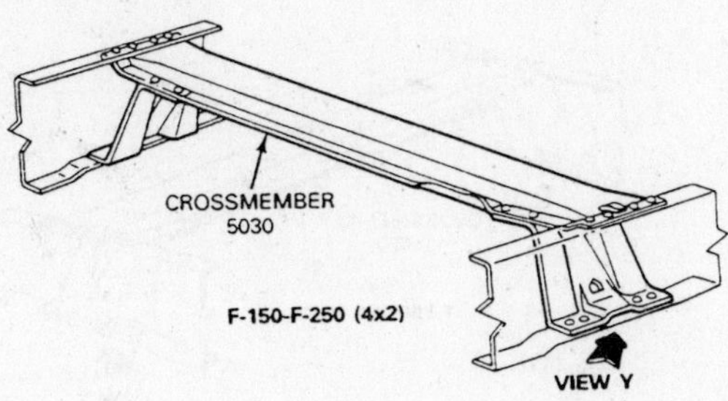

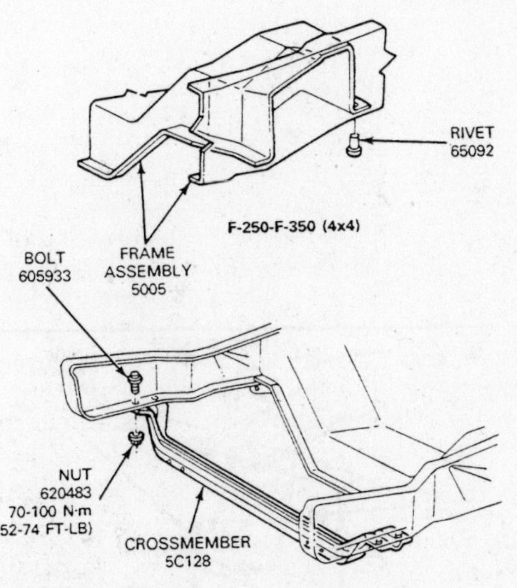

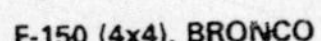

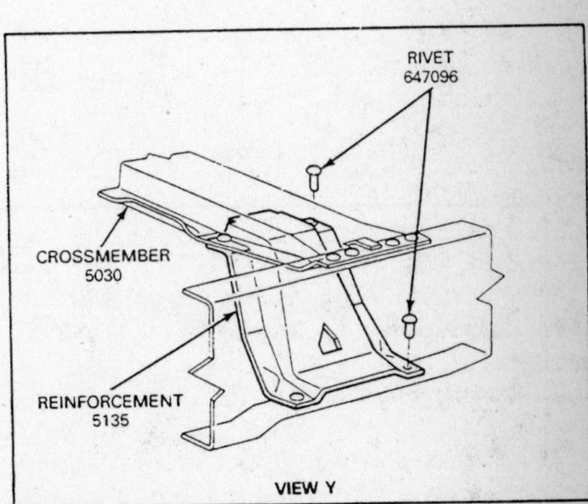

AOD mounting points

verter assembly away from the engine and, at the same time, lower the jack to clear the underside of the vehicle.

21. Remove the converter and mount the transmission in a holding fixture.

22. Tighten the converter drain plug.

23. To install, position the converter on the transmission, making sure the converter drive flats are fully engaged in the pump gear by rotating the converter.

24. With the converter properly installed, place the transmission on the jack. Secure the transmission to the jack with a chain.

25. Rotate the converter until the studs and drain plug are in alignment with the holes in the flywheel.

26. Move the converter and transmission assembly forward into position, using care not to damage the flywheel and the converter pilot. The converter must rest squarely against the flywheel. This indicates that the converter pilot is not binding in the engine crankshaft.

27. Install and tighten the converter housing-to-engine attaching bolts to 40–50 ft. lbs.

28. Remove the safety chain from around the transmission.

29. Install a new O-ring on the lower end of the transmission filler tube. Insert the tube in the transmission case and secure the tube to the engine with the attaching bolt.

30. Connect the speedometer cable to the extension housing.

31. Connect the oil cooler lines to the right side of transmission case.

32. Position the crossmember on the side supports. Torque the bolts to 55 ft. lbs. Position the rear mount on the crossmember and install the attaching nuts to 90 ft. lbs.

33. On 4-wheel drive models, install the transfer case.

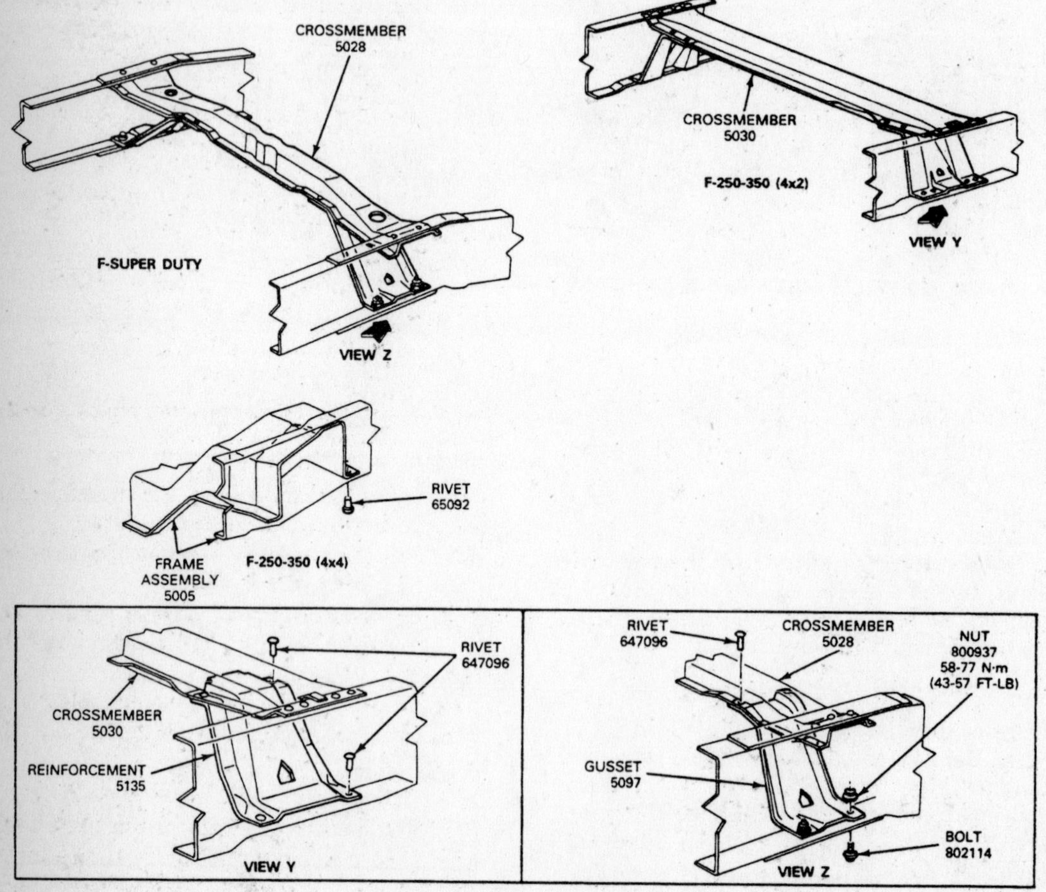

E4OD mounting points

4x2 Vehicles

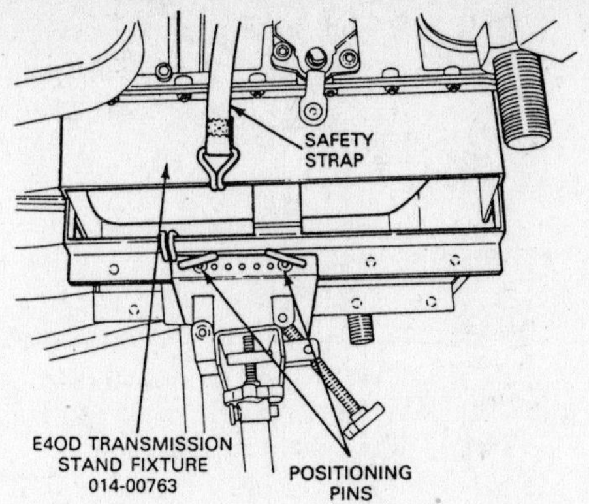

4x4 Vehicles

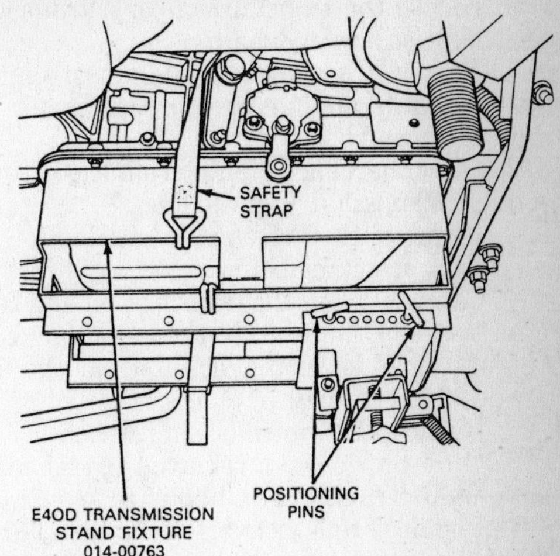

Placement of transmission holding fixture for the E4OD

34. Secure the rear support to the extension housing and tighten the bolts to 80 ft. lbs.

35. Lower the transmission and remove the jack.

E4OD

1. Raise and support the truck on jackstands.

2. Place the drain pan under the transmission fluid pan. Starting at the rear of the pan and working toward the front, loosen the attaching bolts and allow the fluid to drain. Finally remove all of the pan attaching bolts except two at the front, to allow the fluid to further drain. With fluid drained, install two bolts on the rear side of the pan to temporarily hold it in place.

3. Remove the dipstick from the transmission.

4. On 4-wheel drive models, matchmark and remove the front driveshaft.

5. Matchmark and remove the rear driveshaft. Install a seal installation tool in the extension housing to prevent fluid leakage.

6. Disconnect the linkage from the transmission.

7. On 4-wheel drive models, disconnect the transfer case linkage.

8. Remove the heat shield and remove the manual lever position sensor connector by squeezing the tabs and pulling on the connector. NEVER ATTEMPT TO PRY THE CONNECTOR APART!

9. Remove the solenoid body heat shield.

10. Remove the solenoid body connector by pushing on the center tab and pulling on the wiring harness. NEVER ATTEMPT TO PRY APART THE CONNECTOR!

11. On 4-wheel drive models, remove the

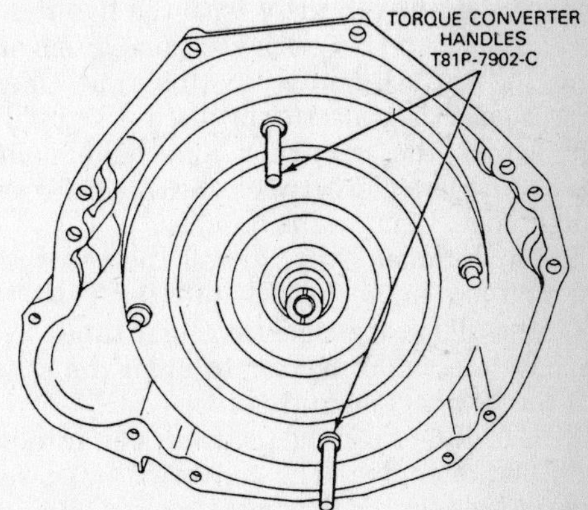

Installation of the torque converter handles on the E4OD

4×4 switch connector from the transfer case. Be careful not to over-extend the tabs.

12. Pry the harness connector from the extension housing wire bracket.

13. On 4-wheel drive models, remove the wiring harness locators from the left side of the connector.

14. Disconnect the speedometer cable.

15. On 4-wheel drive models, remove the transfer case.

16. Remove the converter cover bolts.

17. Remove the rear engine cover plate bolts.

18. Disconnect the cable from the terminal on the starter motor. Remove the three attaching bolts and remove the starter motor. Disconnect the neutral start switch wires at the plug connector.

19. Remove the converter-to-flywheel attaching nuts. Place a wrench on the crankshaft

pulley attaching bolt to turn the converter to gain access to the nuts.

20. Secure the transmission to a transmission jack. Use a safety chain.

21. Remove the rear mount-to-crossmember attaching nuts and the two crossmember-to-frame attaching bolts.

22. Disconnect each oil line from the fittings on the transmission. Cap the lines.

23. Remove the 6 converter housing-to-cylinder block attaching bolts.

24. Carefully move the transmission and converter assembly away from the engine and, at the same time, lower the jack to clear the underside of the vehicle.

25. Remove the transmission filler tube.

26. On F-Super Duty, remove the transmission-mounted brake. See Chapter 9.

27. Install Torque Converter Handles T81P-7902-C, or equivalent, at the 12 o'clock and 6 o'clock positions.

To install:

28. Install the converter with the handles at the 12 o'clock and 6 o'clock positions. Push and rotate the converter until it bottoms out. Check the seating of the converter by placing a straightedge across the converter and bellhousing. There must be a gap between the converter and straightedge. Remove the handles.

29. On F-Super Duty, install the transmission-mounted brake. See Chapter 9.

30. Install the transmission filler tube.

31. Rotate the converter to align the studs with the flywheel mounting holes.

32. Carefully raise the transmission into position at the engine. The converter must rest squarely against the flywheel.

33. Install the 6 converter housing-to-cylinder block attaching bolts. Snug them alternately and evenly, then, tighten them alternately and evenly to 40-50 ft. lbs.

34. Install the converter drain plug cover.

35. Connect each oil line at the fittings on the transmission.

36. Install the rear mount-to-crossmember attaching nuts and the two crossmember-to-frame attaching bolts. Torque the nuts and bolts to 50 ft. lbs.

37. Remove the transmission jack.

38. Install the converter-to-flywheel attaching nuts. Place a wrench on the crankshaft pulley attaching bolt to turn the converter to gain access to the nuts. Torque the nuts to 20–30 ft. lbs.

39. Install the starter motor. Connect the cable at the terminal on the starter motor. Connect the neutral start switch wires at the plug connector.

40. Install the rear engine cover plate bolts.

41. Install the converter cover bolts.

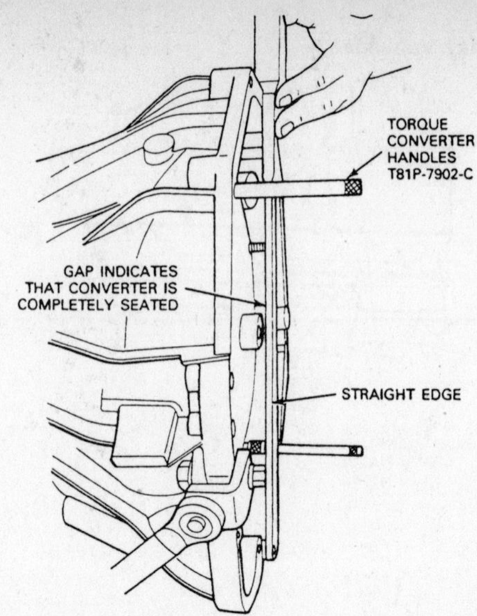

Check torque converter installation with a straightedge

42. On 4-wheel drive models, install the transfer case.

43. Connect the speedometer cable.

44. On 4-wheel drive models, install the wiring harness locators at the left side of the connector.

45. Connect the harness connector at the extension housing wire bracket.

46. On 4-wheel drive models, install the 4×4 switch connector at the transfer case.

47. Install the solenoid body connector. An audible click indicates connection.

48. Install the solenoid body heat shield.

49. Install the manual lever position sensor connector and the heat shield.

50. On 4-wheel drive models, connect the transfer case linkage.

51. Connect the linkage at the transmission.

52. Install the rear driveshaft.

53. On 4-wheel drive models, install the front driveshaft.

54. Install the dipstick.

55. Install the drain pan using a new gasket and sealer.

56. Lower the truck.

57. Refill the transmission and check for leaks.

Fluid Pan

REMOVAL AND INSTALLATION

1. Raise the truck on a hoist or jackstands.
2. Place a drain pan under the transmission.
3. Loosen the pan attaching bolts and drain the fluid from the transmission.
4. When the fluid has drained to the level of

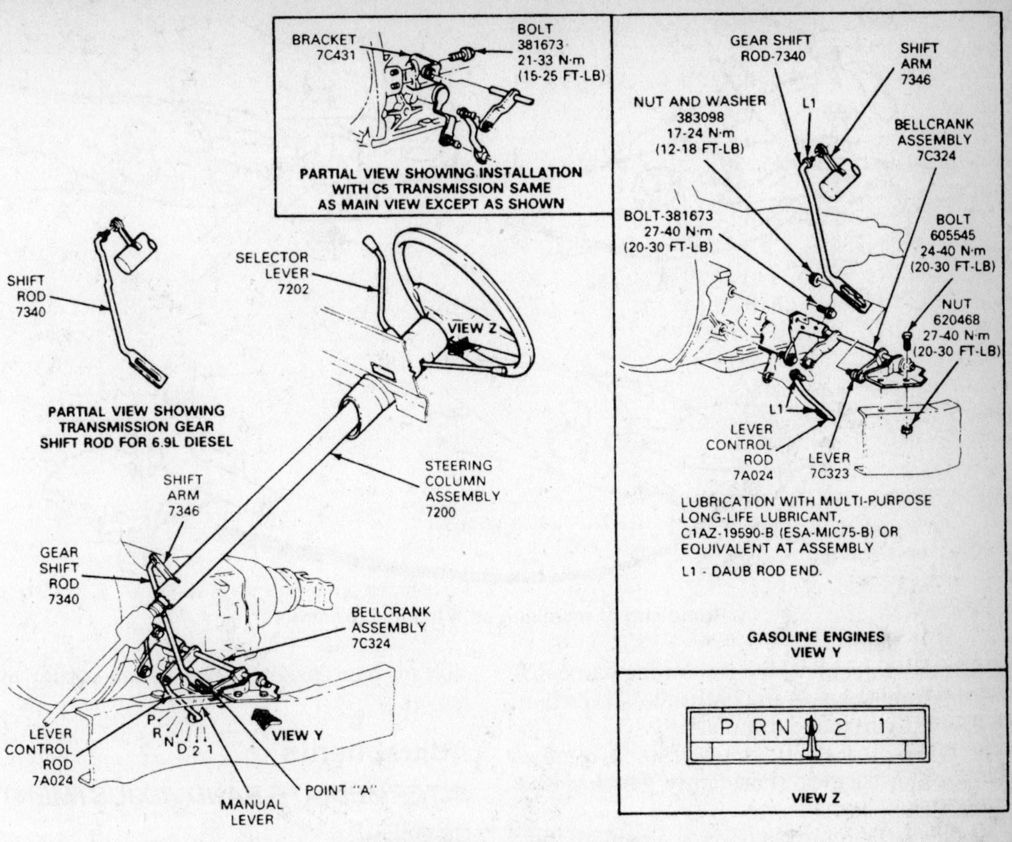

BRACKET
7C431
BOLT
381673
21-33 N·m
(15-25 FT-LB)
PARTIAL VIEW SHOWING INSTALLATION
WITH C5 TRANSMISSION SAME
AS MAIN VIEW EXCEPT AS SHOWN
SHIFT
ROD
7340
PARTIAL VIEW SHOWING
TRANSMISSION GEAR
SHIFT ROD FOR 6.9L DIESEL
SELECTOR
LEVER
7202
VIEW Z
STEERING
COLUMN
ASSEMBLY
7200
SHIFT
ARM
7346
GEAR
SHIFT
ROD
7340
BELLCRANK
ASSEMBLY
7C324
P
R
N
D
2
1
VIEW Y
LEVER
CONTROL
ROD
7A024
POINT "A"
MANUAL
LEVER
GEAR SHIFT
ROD-7340
SHIFT
ARM
7346
NUT AND WASHER
383098
17-24 N·m
(12-18 FT-LB)
L1
BELLCRANK
ASSEMBLY
7C324
BOLT-381673
27-40 N·m
(20-30 FT-LB)
BOLT
605545
24-40 N·m
(20-30 FT-LB)
NUT
620468
27-40 N·m
(20-30 FT-LB)
L1
LEVER
CONTROL
ROD
7A024
LEVER
7C323
LUBRICATION WITH MULTI-PURPOSE
LONG-LIFE LUBRICANT,
C1AZ-19590-B (ESA-MIC75-B) OR
EQUIVALENT AT ASSEMBLY
L1 - DAUB ROD END.
GASOLINE ENGINES
VIEW Y
P R N D 2 1
VIEW Z

C6 shift linkage adjustment points

P R N D D 1
VIEW A
SELECTOR
LEVER
7202
VIEW A
STEERING
COLUMN
ASSEMBLY
7200
SHIFT ARM
7346
GEAR SHIFT
ROD-7340
BELLCRANK
ASSEMBLY
7C324
POINT "A"
LEVER
CONTROL
ROD
7A024
P
R
N
D
D
1
MANUAL
LEVER
VIEW B
MAIN VIEW
NUT AND WASHER
383098
17-24 N·m
(12-18 FT-LB)
SHIFT LEVER
ASSEMBLY
7346
BOLT
381673
27-40 N·m
(20-30 FT-LB)
SHIFT ROD
7340
POINT "A"
BELLCRANK
ASSEMBLY
7C324
BOLT
605545
CONTROL
ROD
7A024
BELLCRANK
LEVER
7C323
NUT-620468
27-40 N·m (20-30 FT-LB)
VIEW B
LUBRICATION AT ASSEMBLY WITH MULTI-PURPOSE LONG-LIFE
LUBRICANT C1AZ-19590-B (ESA-M1C75-B) OR EQUIVALENT

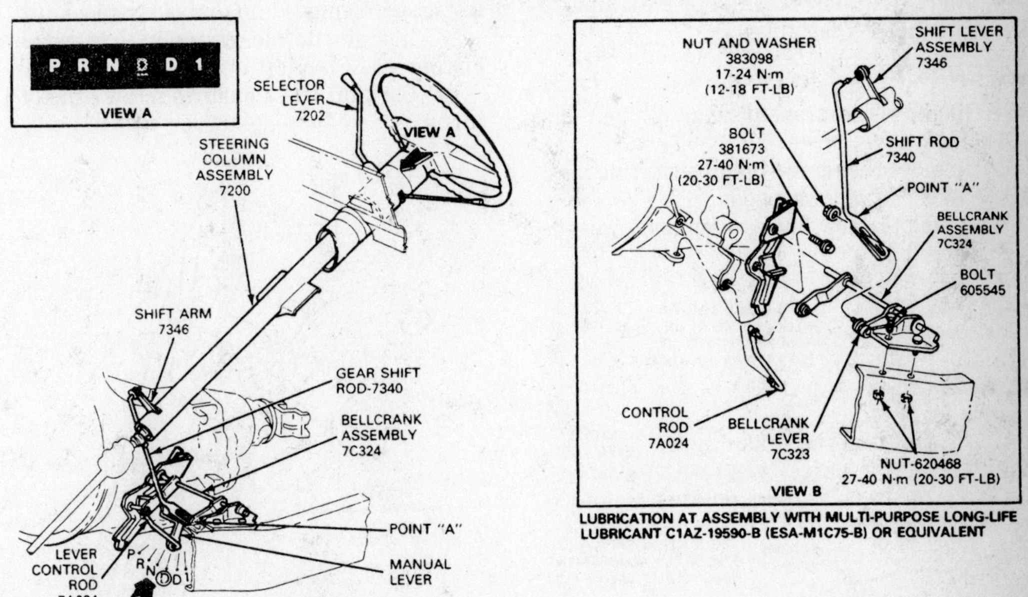

AOD shift linkage adjustment on 2-wheel drive models

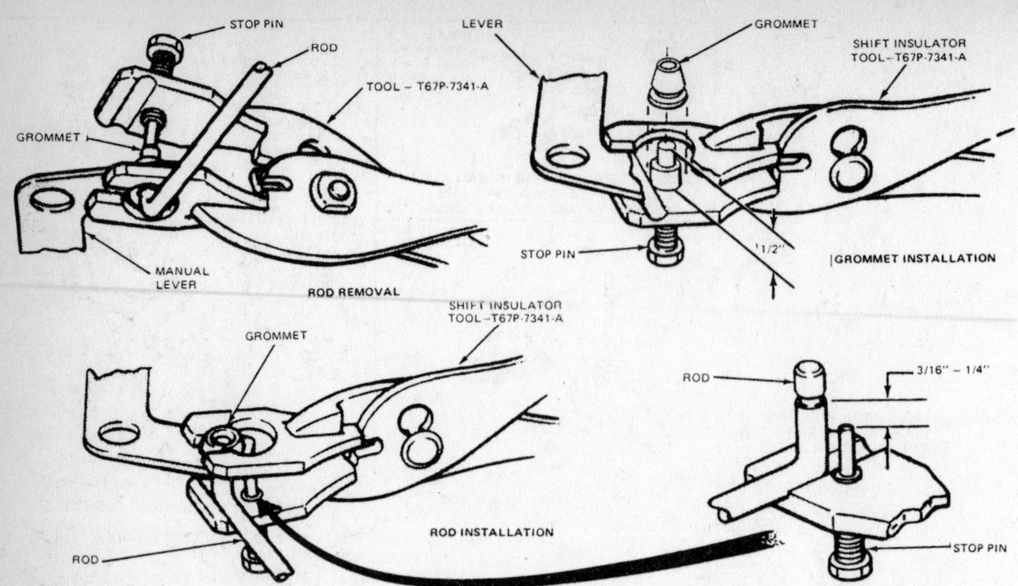

Removing or installing shift linkage grommets

the pan flange, remove the remaining pan bolts working from the rear and both sides of the pan to allow it to drop and drain slowly.

5. When all of the fluid has drained, remove the pan and clean it thoroughly, Discard the pan gasket.

6. Place the new gasket on the pan, and install the pan on the transmission. Tighten the attaching bolts to 12–16 ft. lbs.

7. Add three quarts of fluid to the transmission through the filler tube.

FILTER SERVICE

1. Remove the transmission oil pan and gasket.

2. Remove the screws holding the fine mesh screen to the lower valve body.

3. Install the new filter screen and transmission oil pan gasket in the reverse order of removal.

Adjustments

INTERMEDIATE BAND ADJUSTMENT

C6 Only

1. Raise the truck on a hoist or jackstands.

2. Clean all dirt away from the band adjusting screw. Remove and discard the locknut.

3. Install a new locknut and tighten the adjusting screw to 10 ft. lbs.

4. Back off the adjusting screw exactly $1^1/_2$ turns.

Throttle valve control cable adjustment

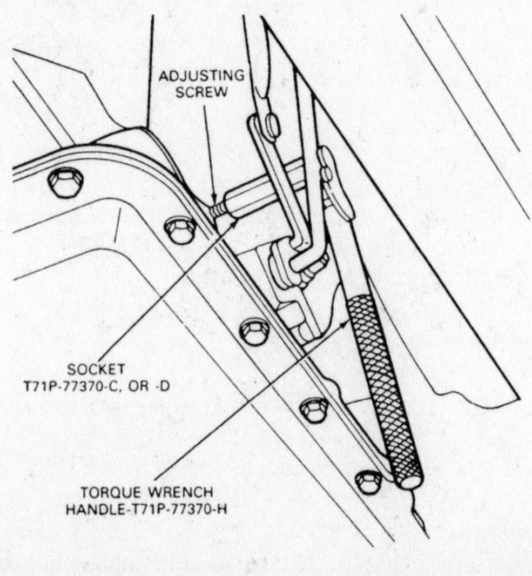

Adjusting the C6 intermediate band

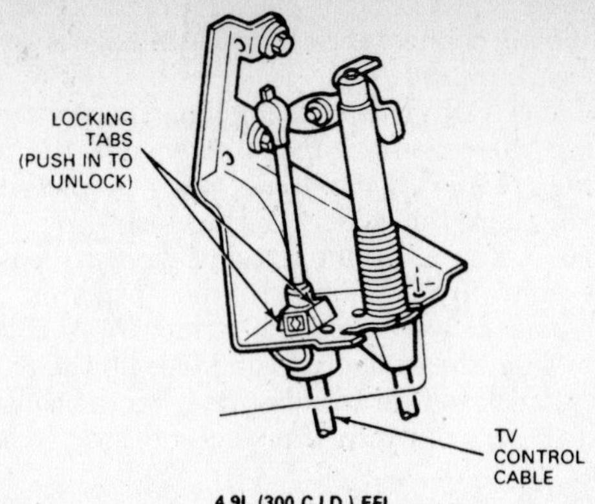

AOD throttle valve control cable locking tab installation

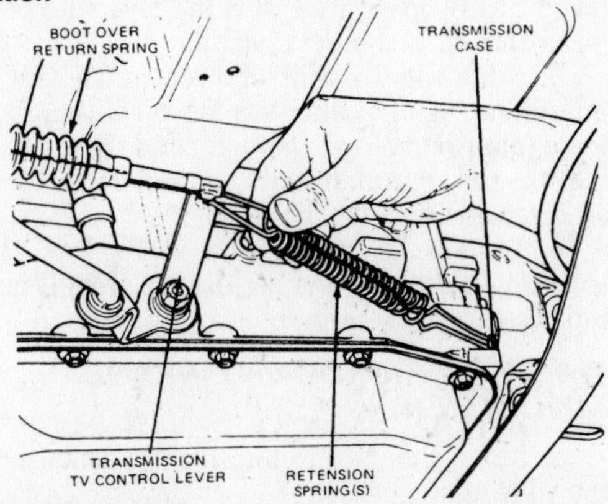

Throttle valve lever retention spring on the 6–300 EFI and 8–302 EFI

5. Hold the adjusting screw from turning and tighten the locknut to 35–40 ft. lbs.

6. Remove the jackstands and lower the vehicle.

SHIFT LINKAGE ADJUSTMENT

1. With the engine stopped, place the transmission selector lever at the steering column in the D position for the C6 or the D overdrive position for the AOD and E4OD, and hold the lever against the stop by hanging an 8 lb. weight from the lever handle.

2. Loosen the shift rod adjusting nut at the transmission lever.

3. Shift the manual lever at the transmission to the **D** position, two detents from the rear. On the F-150 with 4WD and Bronco, move the bellcrank lever.

4. With the selector lever and transmission manual lever in the D or D overdrive position, tighten the adjusting nut to 12–18 ft. lbs. Do not allow the rod or shift lever to move while tightening the nut. Remove the weight.

5. Check the operation of the shift linkage.

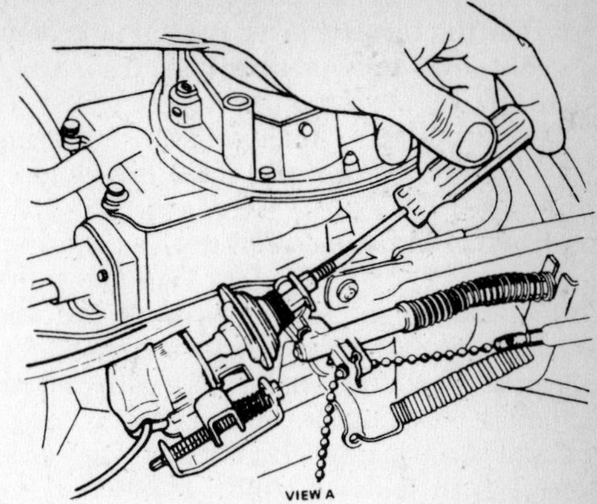

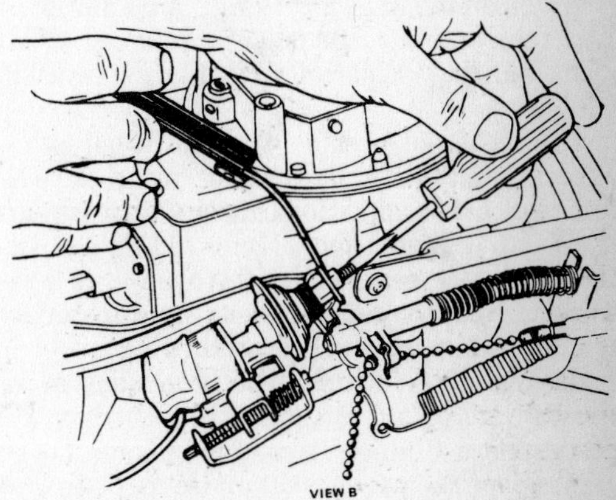

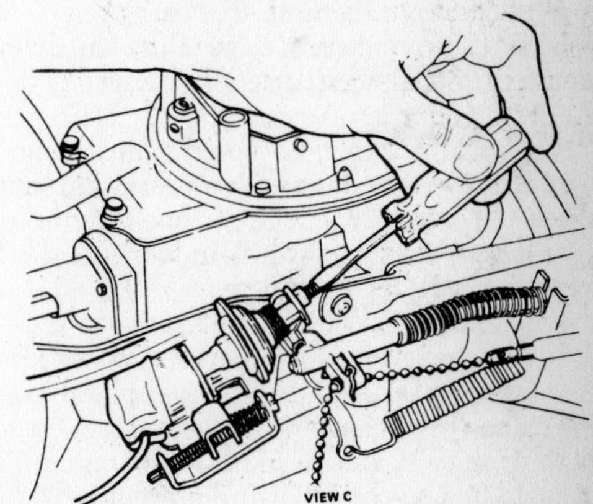

Automatic overdrive throttle linkage adjustment

THROTTLE VALVE LINKAGE ADJUSTMENT

Automatic Overdrive

ADJUSTMENT AT THE CARBURETOR

The TV control linkage may be adjusted at the carburetor using the following procedure:

1. Check that engine idle speed is set at the specification.

2. De-cam the fast idle cam on the carbure-

tor so that the throttle lever is at its idle stop. Place shift lever in N (neutral), set park brake (engine off).

3. Back out the linkage lever adjusting screw all the way (screw end if flush with lever face).

4. Turn in adjusting screw until a thin shim (0.005 in. max.) or piece of writing paper fits snugly between end of screw and Throttle Lever. To eliminate effect of friction, push linkage lever forward (tending to close gap) and release before checking clearance between end of screw and throttle lever. Do not apply any load on levers with tools or hands while checking gap.

5. Turn in adjusting screw an additional four turns. (Four turns are preferred. Two turns minimum is permissible if screw travel is limited).

6. If it is not possible to turn in adjusting screw at least two addition turns or if there was sufficient screw adjusting capacity to obtain an initial gap in Step 2 above, refer to Linkage Adjustment at Transmission. Whenever it is required to adjust idle speed by more than 50 rpm, the adjustment screw on the linkage lever at the carburetor should also be readjusted as shown.

Idle Speed Change/Turns on Linkage Lever Adjustment Screw

- Less than 50 rpm: No change required
- 50 to 100 rpm increase: $1^1/_2$ turns out
- 50 to 100 rpm decrease: $1^1/_2$ turns in
- 100 to 150 rpm increase: $2^1/_2$ turns out
- 100 to 150 rpm decrease: $2^1/_2$ turns in

After making any idle speed adjustments, always verify the linkage lever and throttle lever are in contact with the throttle lever at its idle stop and the shift lever is in N (neutral).

ADJUSTMENT AT TRANSMISSION

The linkage lever adjustment screw has limited adjustment capability. It is not possible to adjust the TV linkage using this screw, the length of the TV control rod assembly must be readjusted using the following procedure. This procedure must also be followed whenever a new TV control rod assembly is installed.

This procedure requires placing the vehicle on jackstands to give access to the linkage components at the transmission TV control lever.

1. Set the engine curb idle speed to specification.

2. With engine off, de-cam the fast idle cam on the carburetor so that the throttle lever is against the idle stop. Place shift lever in Neutral and set park brake (engine off).

3. Set the linkage lever adjustment screw at its approximately mid-range.

4. If a new TV control rod assembly is being installed, connect the rod to the linkage lever at the carburetor.

CAUTION: *The following steps involve working in proximity to the exhaust system. Allow the exhaust system to cool before proceeding.*

5. Raise the vehicle on the hoist.

6. Using a 13mm box end wrench, loosen the bolt on the sliding trunnion block on the TV control rod assembly. Remove any corrosion from the control rod and free-up the trunnion block so that it slides freely on the control rod. Insert pin into transmission lever grommet.

7. Push up on the lower end of the control rod to insure that the linkage lever at carburetor is firmly against the throttle lever. Release force on rod. Rod must stay up.

8. Push the TV control lever on the transmission up against its internal stop with a firm force (approximately 5 pounds) and tighten the bolt on the trunnion block. do not relax force on lever until nut is tightened.

9. Lower the vehicle and verify that the throttle lever is still against the idle stop. If not, repeat steps 2 through 9.

THROTTLE KICKDOWN LINKAGE ADJUSTMENT

1. Move the carburetor throttle linkage to the wide open position.

2. Insert a 0.060 in. thick spacer between the throttle lever and the kickdown adjusting screw.

3. Rotate the transmission kickdown lever until the lever engages the transmission internal stop. Do not use the kickdown rod to turn the transmission lever.

4. Turn the adjusting screw until it contacts the 0.060 in. spacer.

5. Remove the spacer.

Neutral Safety Switch

REMOVAL AND INSTALLATION

C6

1. Remove the downshift linkage rod return spring at the low-reverse servo cover.

2. Coat the outer lever attaching nut with penetrating oil. Remove the nut and lever.

3. Remove the 2 switch attaching bolts, disconnect the wiring at the connectors and remove the switch.

4. Installation is the reverse of removal. Adjust the switch and torque the bolts to 55–75 inch lbs.

AOD

1. Disconnect the wiring from the switch.

2. Using a deep socket, unscrew the switch.

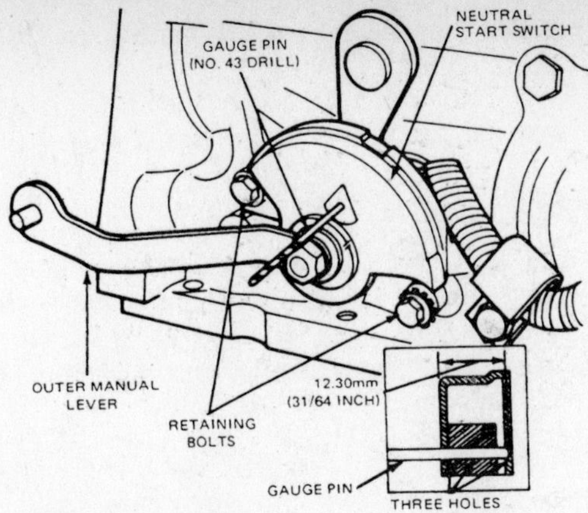

C6 neutral start switch

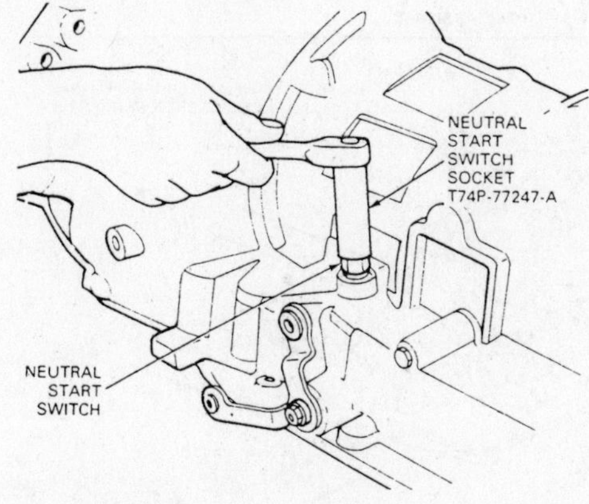

Removing the AOD neutral start switch

3. Installation is the reverse of removal. Torque the switch to 10 ft. lbs.

ADJUSTMENT

1. Hold the steering column transmission selector lever against the Neutral stop.
2. Move the sliding block assembly on the neutral switch to the neutral position and insert a 0.091 in. (2.3mm) gauge pin in the alignment hole on the terminal side of the switch.
3. Move the switch assembly housing so that the sliding block contacts the actuating pin lever. Secure the switch to the outer tube of the steering column and remove the gauge pin.
4. Check the operation of the switch. The engine should only start in Neutral and Park.

TRANSFER CASE

REMOVAL AND INSTALLATION

Borg-Warner Model 13–45

1. Raise and support the truck on jackstands.
2. Drain the fluid from the transfer case.
3. Disconnect the four wheel drive indicator switch wire connector at the transfer case.
4. Remove the skid plate from the frame, if so equipped.
5. Matchmark and disconnect the front driveshaft from the front output yoke.
6. Matchmark and disconnect the rear driveshaft from the rear output shaft yoke.
7. Disconnect the speedometer driven gear from the transfer case rear bearing retainer.
8. Remove the retaining rings and shift rod from the transfer case shift lever.
9. Disconnect the vent hose from the transfer case.
10. Remove the heat shield from the frame.
11. Support the transfer case with a transmission jack.
12. Remove the bolts retaining the transfer case to the transmission adapter.
13. Lower the transfer case from the vehicle.
14. When installing place a new gasket between the transfer case and the adapter.
15. Raise the transfer case with the transmission jack so that the transmission output shaft aligns with the splined transfer case input shaft. Install the bolts retaining the transfer case to the adapter.
16. Remove the transmission jack from the transfer case.
17. Connect the rear driveshaft to the rear output shaft yoke. Torque the bolts to 15 ft. lbs.
18. Install the shift lever to the transfer case and install the retaining nut.
19. Connect the speedometer driven gear to the transfer case.
20. Connect the four wheel drive indicator switch wire connector at the transfer case.
21. Connect the front driveshaft to the front output yoke. Torque the bolts to 15 ft. lbs.
22. Position the heat shield to the frame crossmember and the mounting lug on the transfer case. Install and tighten the retaining bolts.
23. Install the skid plate to the frame.
24. Install the drain plug. Remove the filler plug and install six pints of Dexron®II type transmission fluid or equivalent.
25. Lower the vehicle.

Borg-Warner 13–56 Manual Shift

1. Raise and support the truck on jackstands.
2. Drain the fluid from the transfer case.
3. Disconnect the four wheel drive indicator switch wire connector at the transfer case.
4. Remove the skid plate from the frame, if so equipped.
5. Matchmark and disconnect the front driveshaft from the front output yoke.

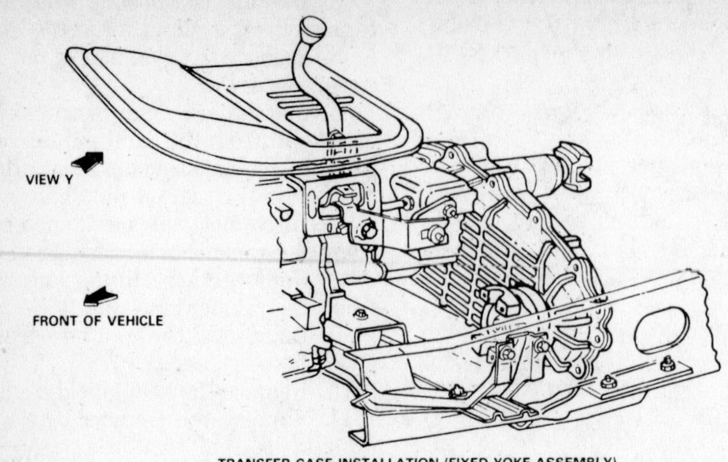

TRANSFER CASE INSTALLATION (FIXED YOKE ASSEMBLY)

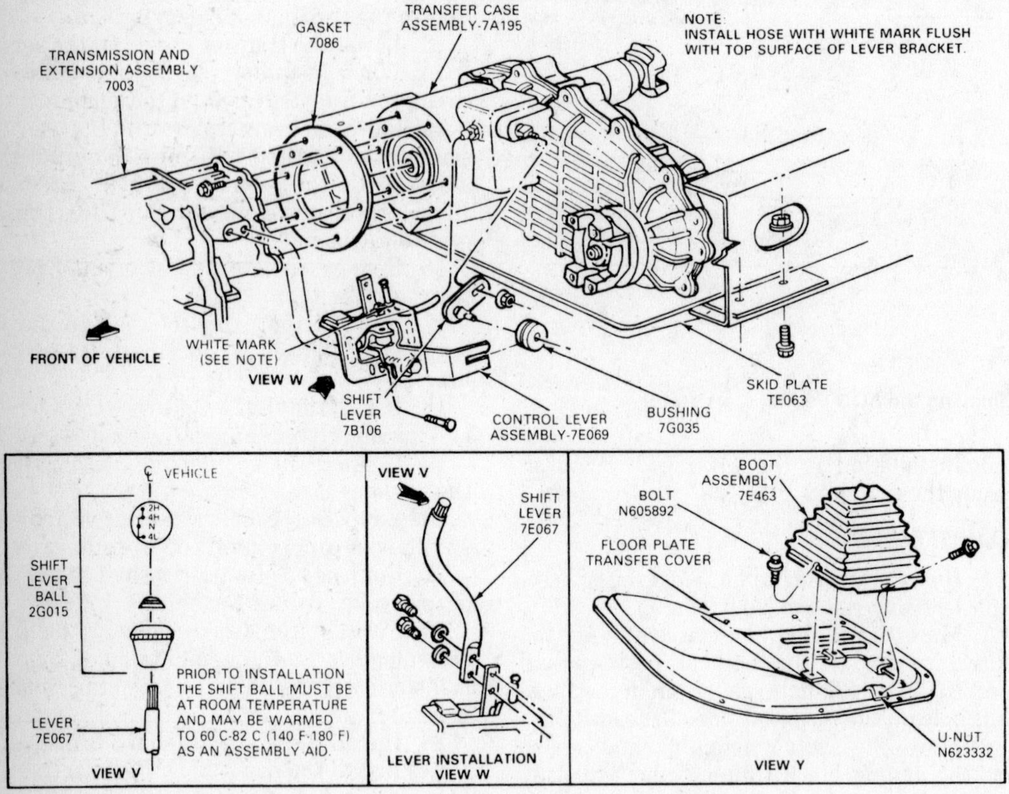

TRANSMISSION AND EXTENSION ASSEMBLY 7003
GASKET 7086
TRANSFER CASE ASSEMBLY-7A195
NOTE: INSTALL HOSE WITH WHITE MARK FLUSH WITH TOP SURFACE OF LEVER BRACKET.
FRONT OF VEHICLE
WHITE MARK (SEE NOTE)
VIEW W
SHIFT LEVER 7B106
CONTROL LEVER ASSEMBLY-7E069
BUSHING 7G035
SKID PLATE TE063

℄ VEHICLE
2H 4H N 4L
SHIFT LEVER BALL 2G015
PRIOR TO INSTALLATION THE SHIFT BALL MUST BE AT ROOM TEMPERATURE AND MAY BE WARMED TO 60 C-82 C (140 F-180 F) AS AN ASSEMBLY AID.
LEVER 7E067
VIEW V

VIEW V
SHIFT LEVER 7E067
LEVER INSTALLATION VIEW W

BOOT ASSEMBLY 7E463
BOLT N605892
FLOOR PLATE TRANSFER COVER
U-NUT N623332
VIEW Y

Borg-Warner 13–56 manual shift transfer case installation

6. Matchmark and disconnect the rear driveshaft from the rear output shaft yoke.

7. Disconnect the speedometer driven gear from the transfer case rear bearing retainer.

8. Remove the retaining rings and shift rod from the transfer case shift lever.

9. Disconnect the vent hose from the transfer case.

10. Remove the heat shield from the frame.

11. Support the transfer case with a transmission jack.

12. Remove the bolts retaining the transfer case to the transmission adapter.

13. Lower the transfer case from the vehicle.

14. When installing place a new gasket between the transfer case and the adapter.

15. Raise the transfer case with the transmission jack so that the transmission output shaft

aligns with the splined transfer case input shaft. Install the bolts retaining the transfer case to the adapter. Torque the bolts to 40 ft. lbs. in the pattern shown.

16. Remove the transmission jack from the transfer case.

17. Connect the rear driveshaft to the rear output shaft yoke. Torque the bolts to 15 ft. lbs.

18. Install the shift lever to the transfer case and install the retaining nut.

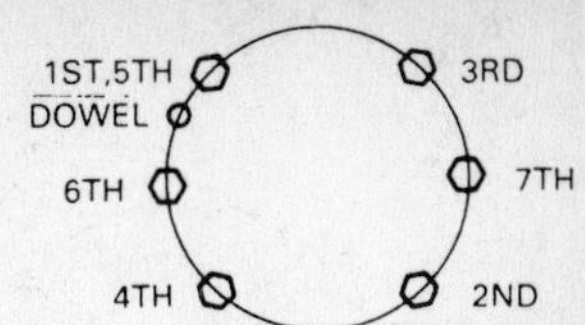

TIGHTEN CASE TO EXTENSION BOLTS IN THIS SEQUENCE

13–56 electronic shift transfer case extension bolt torque sequence

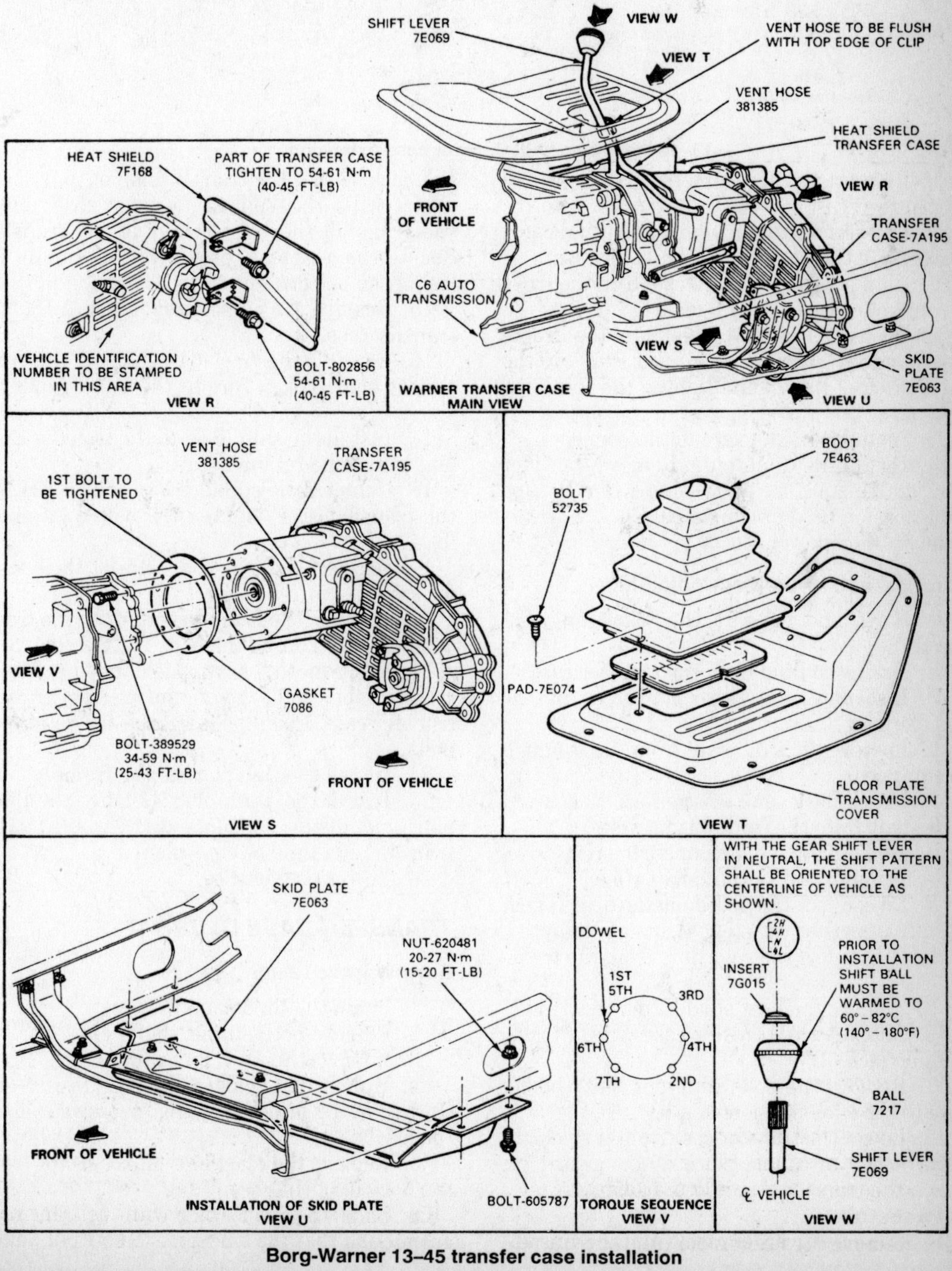

Borg-Warner 13–45 transfer case installation

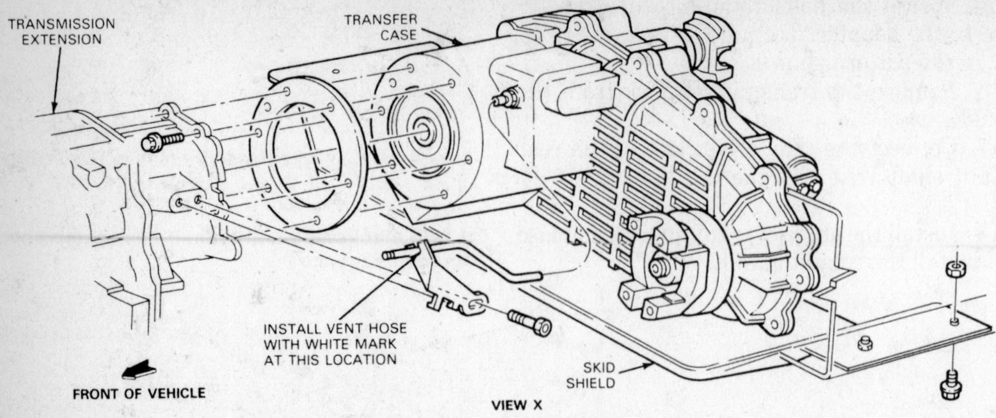

13–56 electronic shift transfer case extension

19. Connect the speedometer driven gear to the transfer case.

20. Connect the four wheel drive indicator switch wire connector at the transfer case.

21. Connect the front driveshaft to the front output yoke. Torque the bolts to 15 ft. lbs.

22. Position the heat shield to the frame crossmember and the mounting lug on the transfer case. Install and tighten the retaining bolts.

23. Install the skid plate to the frame.

24. Install the drain plug. Remove the filler plug and install six pints of Dexron®II type transmission fluid or equivalent.

25. Lower the vehicle.

Borg-Warner 13–56 Electronic Shift

1. Raise and support the truck on jackstands.

2. Drain the fluid from the transfer case.

3. Disconnect the wire connector at the transfer case.

4. Remove the skid plate from the frame, if so equipped.

5. Matchmark and disconnect the front driveshaft from the front output yoke.

6. Matchmark and disconnect the rear driveshaft from the rear output shaft yoke.

7. Disconnect the speedometer driven gear from the transfer case rear bearing retainer.

8. Disconnect the vent hose from the transfer case.

9. Remove the heat shield from the frame.

10. Support the transfer case with a transmission jack.

11. Remove the bolts retaining the transfer case to the transmission adapter.

12. Lower the transfer case from the vehicle.

13. When installing place a new gasket between the transfer case and the adapter.

To install:

14. Raise the transfer case with the transmission jack so that the transmission output shaft aligns with the splined transfer case input shaft. Install the bolts retaining the transfer case to the adapter. Torque the bolts to 40 ft. lbs. in the pattern illustrated.

15. Remove the transmission jack from the transfer case.

16. Connect the rear driveshaft to the rear output shaft yoke. Torque the bolts to 28 ft. lbs.

17. Install the shift lever to the transfer case and install the retaining nut.

18. Connect the speedometer driven gear to the transfer case. Tighten the bolt to 25 inch lbs.

19. Connect the wire connector at the transfer case.

20. Connect the front driveshaft to the front output yoke. Torque the bolts to 15 ft. lbs.

21. Position the heat shield to the frame crossmember and the mounting lug on the transfer case. Install and tighten the retaining bolts.

22. Install the skid plate to the frame.

23. Install the drain plug. Remove the filler plug and install six pints of Dexron®II type transmission fluid or equivalent.

24. Lower the vehicle.

TRANSFER CASE OVERHAUL

Borg-Warner 13–45

1. Drain the fluid from the case.

2. Remove both output shaft yokes.

3. Remove the 4WD indicator switch.

4. Unbolt and remove the case cover. The cover may be pried off using a screwdriver in the pry bosses.

5. Remove the magnetic chip collector from the bottom of the case.

6. Slide the shift collar hub off the rear output shaft.

7. Compress the shift fork spring and remove the upper and lower spring retainers from the shaft.

8. Lift the four wheel drive lockup fork and lockup shift collar assembly from the case.

9. Remove the thrust washer being careful not to lose the nylon wear pads on the lockup fork.

10. Remove the snap ring and thrust washer from the front output shaft.

11. Grip the chain and both sprockets and lift them straight up to remove the drive sprocket, driven sprocket and chain from the output shafts.

12. Lift the front output shaft from the case.

13. Remove the four oil pump attaching screws and remove the oil pump rear cover, pickup tube, filter and pump body, two pump pins, pump spring and oil pump front cover from the rear output shaft.

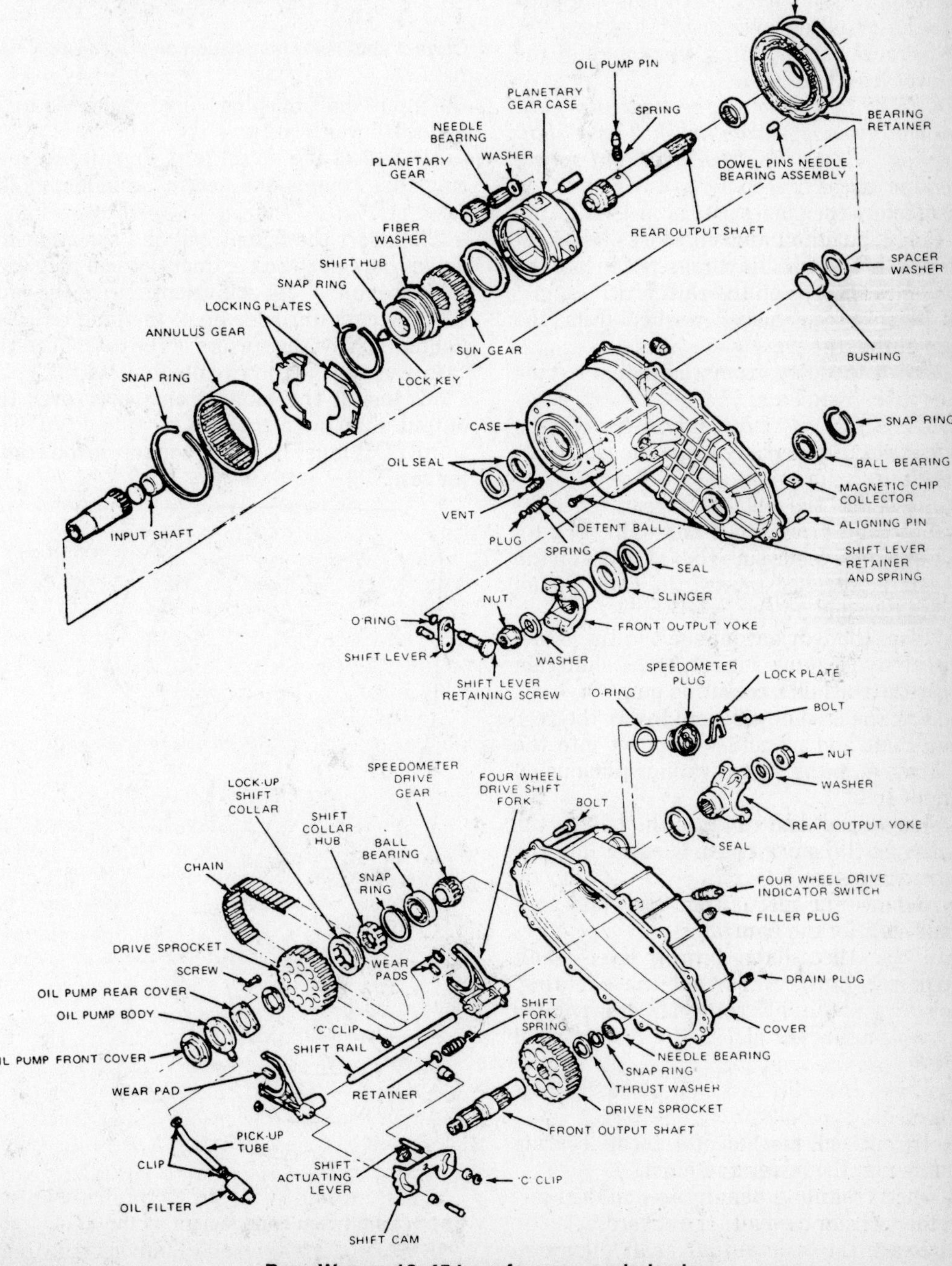

Borg-Warner 13–45 transfer case explode view

14. Remove the snapring that holds the bearing retainer inside the case. Lift the rear output shaft while tapping on the bearing retainer with a plastic hammer.

NOTE: *Two dowel pins will fall into the case when the retainer is removed.*

15. Lift the rear output shaft and bearing retainer from the case. Remove the rear output shaft from the bearing retainer. If necessary, press the needle bearing assembly out of the retainer.

16. Remove the C-clip that holds the shift cam to the actuating lever inside the case.

17. Remove the retaining screw and lift the shift lever from the case.

NOTE: *When removing the lever, the shift cam will disengage from the shift lever shaft and may release the detent ball and spring from the case.*

18. Remove the planetary gear set, shift rail, shift cam, input shaft and shift forks, as an assembly, from the case. Be careful not to lose the two nylon wear pads on the shift fork.

19. Remove the spacer washer from the bottom of the case.

20. Drive the plug from the detent spring bore.

NOTE: *Before assembly, lubricate all parts with clean Dexron®II automatic transmission fluid.*

21. Assemble the planetary gear set, shift rail, shift cam, input shaft and shift fork together as a unit. Make sure that the boss on the shift cam is installed toward the case. Install the spacer washer on the input shaft.

22. Place the rear output shaft in the planetary gear set, making sure that the shift cam engages the shift fork actuating pin.

23. Lay the case on its side. Insert the rear output shaft and planetary gear set into the case. Make sure the spacer washer remains on the input shaft.

24. Install the shift rail into the hole in the case. Install the outer roller bushing into the guide in the case.

25. Remove the rear output shaft and position the shift fork in neutral.

26. Place the shift control lever shaft through the cam, and install the clip ring. Make sure that the shift control lever is pointed downward and is parallel to the front face of the case.

27. Check the shift fork and planetary gear engagement.

28. If removed, press a new needle bearing assembly into the bearing retainer.

29. Insert the output shaft through the bearing retainer from the bottom outward.

30. Insert the rear output shaft pilot into the input shaft bushing. Align the dowel holes and the lower bearing.

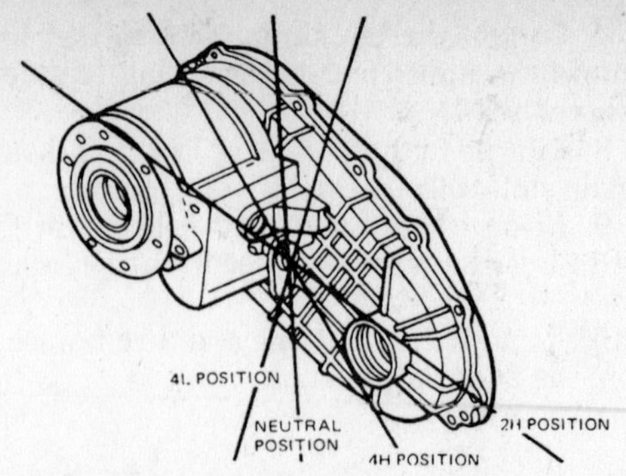

Correct shift lever installation on the 13–45

31. Install the dowel pins. Install the snap ring that retains the bearing retainer in the case.

32. Insert the detent ball and spring in the detent bore in the case. Coat the seal plug with RTV sealant or its equivalent. Drive the plug into the case until the lip of the plug is $\frac{1}{32}$ in. (0.8mm) below the surface of the case. Peen the case over the plug in two places.

33. Install the pump front cover over the output shaft with the flanged side down. The word **TOP** must be facing the top of the transfer case.

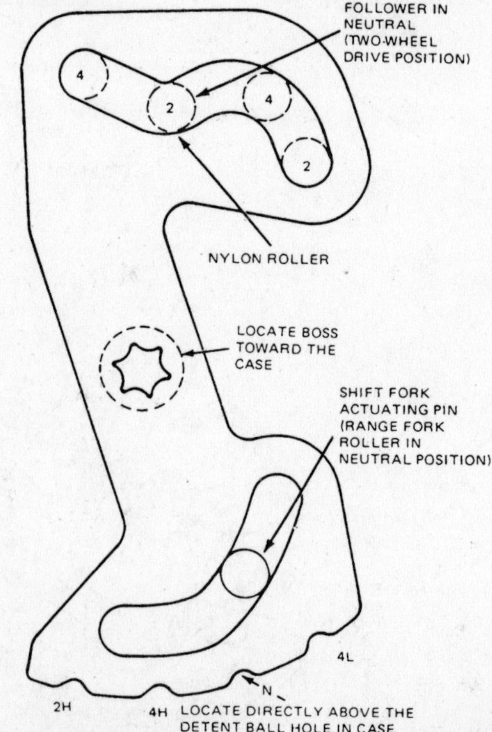

Correct shift cam engagement on the 13–45 transfer case

34. Install the oil pump spring and two pump pins with the flat side outward in the hole in the output shaft. Push both pins in to install the oil pump body, pickup tube and filter.

35. Place the oil pump rear cover on the output shaft with the flanged side outward. The word **TOP** must be positioned toward the

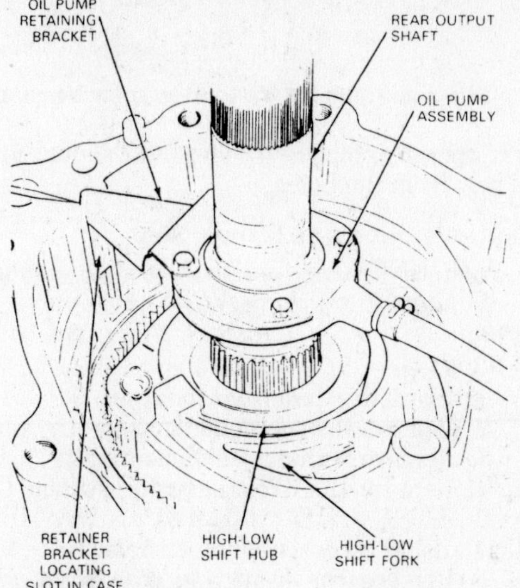

Removing the output shaft and oil pump from the 13–56 manual shift

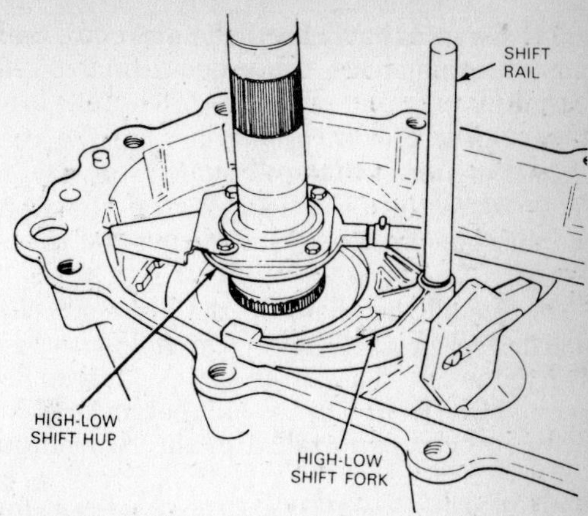

High/low shift fork and rail on the 13–56 manual shift

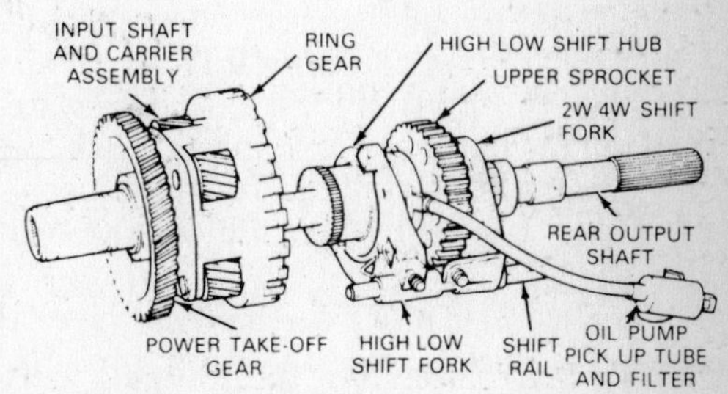

13–56 manual shift drive train components, exploded view

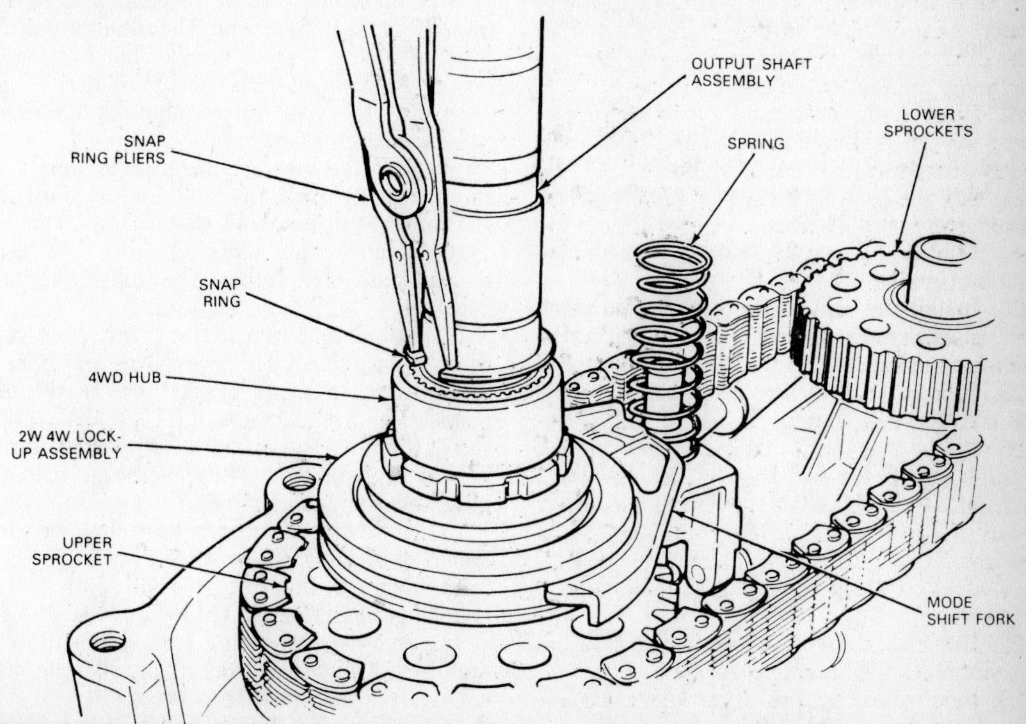

2W/4W sprockets, 2W/4W lock-up assembly, chain and upper and lower sprockets on the 13–56 manual shift

top of the case. Apply Loctite® or its equivalent to the oil pump bolts and torque them to 36–40 inch lbs.

36. Install the thrust washer on the rear output shaft nest to the oil pump.

37. Place the drive sprocket on the front output shaft. Install the snap ring and thrust washer.

38. Install the chain on the drive sprocket and driven sprocket. Lower the chain into position in the case. The driven sprocket is installed through the front output shaft bearing and the drive sprocket is installed in the rear output shaft.

39. Engage the 4WD shift fork on the shift collar. Slide the shift fork over the shift shaft and the shift collar over the rear output shaft. Make sure the nylon wear pads are installed on the shift fork tips and the necked-down part of the shift collar is facing downward.

40. Push the 4WD shift spring downward and install the upper spring retainer. Push the spring upward and install the lower retainer.

41. Install the shift collar hub on the rear output shaft.

42. Apply a bead of RTV sealant on the case mounting surface. Lower the cover over the rear output shaft. Align the shift rail with its blind hole in the cover. Make sure the front output shaft is fully seated in its support bearing. Install and tighten the bolts to 40–45 ft. lbs. Allow one hour curing time for the RTV sealant prior to using the case.

43. Install the 4WD indicator switch. Torque to 8–12 ft. lbs.

44. Press the oil slinger on the front yoke. Install the front and rear output shaft yokes. Coat the nuts with Loctite® or equivalent and torque to 100–130 ft. lbs.

45. Fill the unit with 6 pints of Dexron® II. Tighten the fill plug to 18 ft. lbs.

46. Install the unit in the vehicle and start the engine. Remove the level plug. If the fluid is flowing from the hole in a stream, the pump is not operating properly. The fluid should drip slowly from the hole.

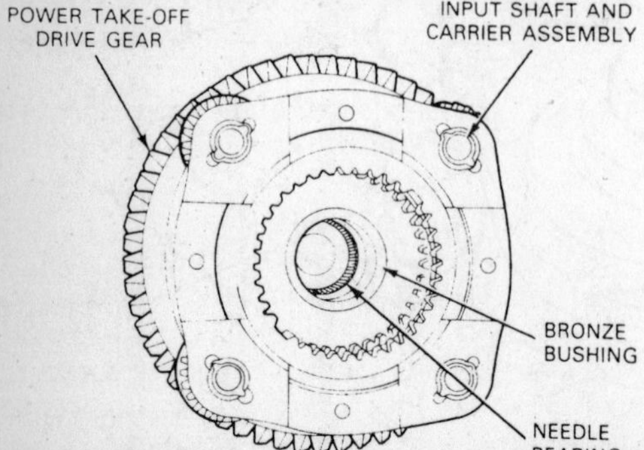

13–56 manual shift front input shaft and carrier assembly

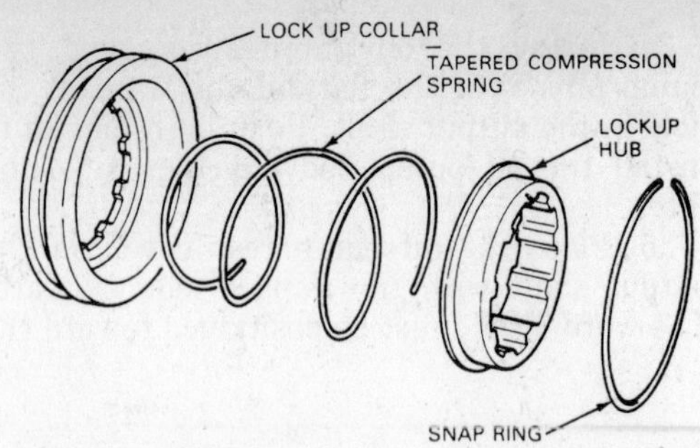

13–56 manual shift 2W/4W lock-up collar assembly

Borg-Warner 13–56 Manual Shift

WARNING: *The transfer case shell is made of magnesium. It is VERY susceptible to damage, such a scratches, nicks and chipping!*

1. Drain the fluid from the case.
2. Remove the speedometer cover.
3. Remove both output shaft yokes.
4. Remove the 4WD indicator switch. DO NOT LOSE THE ALUMINUM WASHER! This washer controls switch operation.
5. Remove the front and rear yoke seals using tools T74P–77248–A and T50L–100–A.
6. Using the same tools, remove the input shaft seal.
7. Unbolt and remove the rear bearing retainer from the case cover. The retainer may be pried off using a 1/2 in. breaker bar in the pry bosses. Remove all traces of RTV sealer.
8. Lift the rear output shaft and remove the speedometer gear retaining clip.
9. Slide the speedometer gear forward and remove the ball with a small magnet. Pull the gear off the output shaft.
10. Remove the snapring from the rear output shaft that retains the upper rear ball bearing.
11. Unbolt and remove front case cover from the rear case cover. The case halves may be separated using a 1/2 in. breaker bar in the pry bosses. Remove all traces of RTV sealer.
12. Remove the front output shaft inner needle bearing from the rear cover using a puller-type slidehammer.
13. Drive out the rear output shaft bearing from the inside of the case.
14. Remove the output shaft clutch hub snapring. Slide the 4WD hub off of the shaft.
15. Remove the spring from the shift rail and lift the mode shift fork along with the shift collar, from the upper sprocket spline.
16. Disassemble the 2WD-4WD lockup assembly by removing the internal snapring and pull the lockup hub and spring from the collar.

17. Remove the snapring retaining the lower sprocket to the lower output shaft. Grasp the upper and lower sprocket along with the chain, and lift them, simultaneously, from the upper and lower shafts.

18. Remove the shift rail by sliding it straight out of the shift fork.

19. Remove the high/low shift fork by first rotating it until the roller is free from the cam, then sliding it out of engagement from the shift hub.

20. Remove the magnetic chip collector from the bottom of the case.

21. Lift the pump screen and remove the output shaft assembly with the pump assembled on it. If you are going to disassemble the pump, remove the 4 bolts from the pump body. Note the position of the pump front body, pins, spring, rear cover and pump retainer before disassembly.

22. Remove the high/low shift hub.

23. Remove the front output shaft from the case.

24. Turn the front case over and remove the front oil seal with a puller.

25. Expand the snapring on the input shaft and allow it to drop out of the bearing. If either the bearing or bushing is defective, both must be replaced as a unit. Drive them out together.

26. Remove the ring gear by prying out the internal snapring and lift out the gear.

27. Remove the PTO drive gear from the input shaft carrier assembly.

28. Remove the internal snapring holding the input shaft bearing and drive out the bearing from the outside.

29. Remove the internal snapring holding the front output shaft bearing and drive out the bearing from the front of the case.

30. Remove the shift cam by removing the retaining clip and sliding the shift shaft out of the case.

31. Remove the shift shaft seal by carefully prying it out of the case, being careful to avoid damaging the magnesium surfaces.

32. Remove the shift cam, assist spring and assist spring bushing.

NOTE: *Before assembly, lubricate all parts with clean Dexron®II automatic transmission fluid. Remove any chips from the bolt holes or the case cover.*

33. Install the input shaft and front output shaft bearings in the case using drivers.

34. Install the internal snaprings.

35. Drive the front output shaft seal into the case until it is fully seated.

36. Install the front output shaft through the lower bearing.

37. Install the front yoke assembly onto the shaft, followed by the rubber seal, flat washer and 30mm locknut. Torque the nut to 130–180 ft. lbs.

38. Press the PTO drive gear onto the input shaft.

39. Press the needle bearing and bronze bushing into the input shaft.

40. Install the ring gear into the slots in the case and retain it with the large internal snapring, making certain that it is fully seated.

41. Install the input shaft and carrier in the case through the input shaft bearing bore, carefully aligning the gear teeth.

42. Support the carrier assembly and install a new snapring on the front side of the input shaft bearing, making sure that it is fully seated in the groove.

43. Install the upper input shaft oil seal in the case.

44. Install a new shifter shaft seal in the case.

45. Assemble the shift cam assembly in the case by sliding the shift shaft and lever assembly through the case and seal into engagement with the shift cam. Secure the cam with the retaining clip.

46. Install the shift cam assist spring into position in the bushing of the shift cam in the recess of the case.

47. Assemble the pump and output shaft as follows:

a. Install the oil pump cover with the word FRONT facing the front of the case.

b. Install the two pins, with the flats facing upward, with the springs between the pins, and place the assembly in the oil pump bore in the output shaft.

c. Place the oil pump body and pick-up tube over the shaft, and make certain that the pins are riding against the inside of the pump body.

d. Place the oil pump rear cover, with the words TOP REAR facing the rear of the case.

e. Install the pump retainer with the tabs facing the front of the case.

f. Install the 4 retaining bolts and rotate the output shaft while tightening the bolts to prevent the pump from binding. Torque the bolts to 40 inch lbs.

g. Lubricate the whole assembly with clean transmission fluid. The output shaft should turn freely. If not, loosen and retorque the bolts.

48. Install the high/low shift hub.

49. Install the shift rail through the high/low fork bore and into the rail bore in the case.

50. Install the output shaft and oil pump assembly in the input shaft. Make certain that the external splines of the output shaft engage the internal splines of the high/low shift hub. Make sure that the oil pump retainer and oil

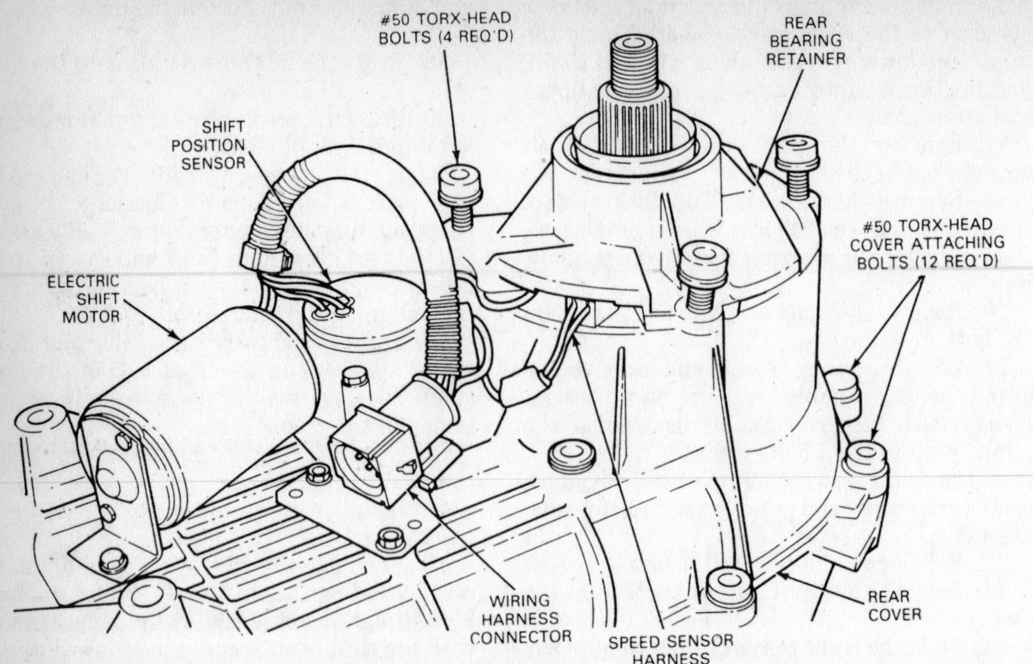

Removing rear bearing retainer on the 13–56 electronic shift

filter leg are in the groove and notch of the front case.

51. Install the collector magnet.

52. Assemble the upper and lower sprockets with the chain, and place them on the upper and lower shafts. Install the washer and snapring that retain the lower sprocket.

53. Assemble the 2WD/4WD lock-up assembly:

a. Install the tapered compression spring in the lock-up collar with the small end installed first.

b. Place the lock-up hub over the spring and compress the spring while installing the internal snapring which holds the assembly together.

54. Install the lock-up assembly and its shift fork over the external splines of the upper sprocket and the shift rail, with the long boss of the shift rail facing forward.

55. Assemble the 4WD return spring over the shift rail and against the shift fork.

56. Place the 4WD hub over the external splines of the output shaft. Install the snapring.

57. Press the lower output needle bearing into its bore in the rear cover.

58. Press the rear output shaft bearing into the cover. Install the snapring.

59. Install the rear output shaft seal in the bearing retainer.

60. Coat the mating surface of the front case with a non-acidic silicone rubber gasket material.

61. Place the cover on the case making sure that the shafts and shift rail are all aligned. Torque the bolts to 36 ft. lbs.

62. Install the rear bearing snapring on the output shaft.

63. Place the speedometer drive gear over the shaft aligning the slot with the drive ball hole. The gear should go completely against the snapring retaining the output shaft. Place the ball in the hole and pull the gear over the ball. Snap the retaining clip between the snapring and speedometer gear.

64. Apply a bead of non-acidic silicone rubber gasket material on the face of the rear bearing retainer.

65. Place the retainer in position and torque the 4 bolts to 36 ft. lbs.

66. If the case has a slip yoke rear bearing retainer housing, remove the extension yoke oil seal and bushing and install a new bushing and seal. Use puller and drivers for this operation.

67. Install the rear output shaft yoke and slinger. Install the rubber seal, flat washer and locking nut. Torque the nut to 150–180 ft. lbs.

68. Install the drain plug.

69. Install the 4WD indicator light switch and aluminum washer.

70. Fill the case with 64 ounces of Dexron®II fluid and install the fill plug.

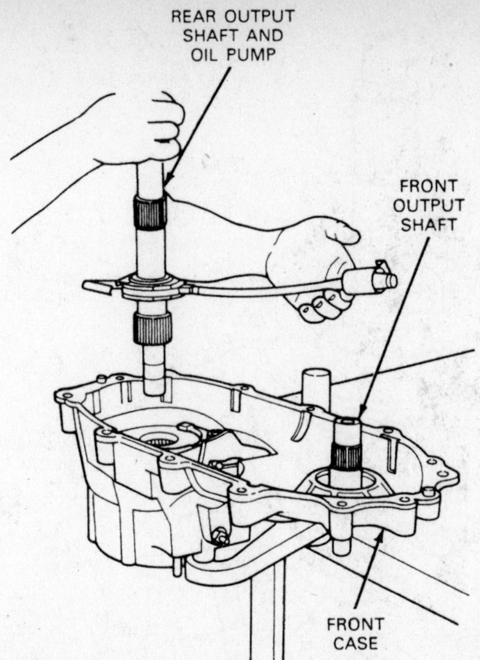

Rear output shaft and oil pump installation on the 13–56 electronic shift

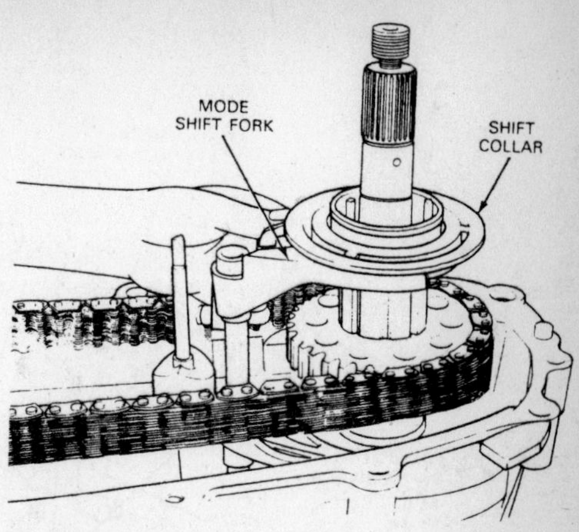

Removing the mode shift fork and shift collar on the 13–56 electronic shift

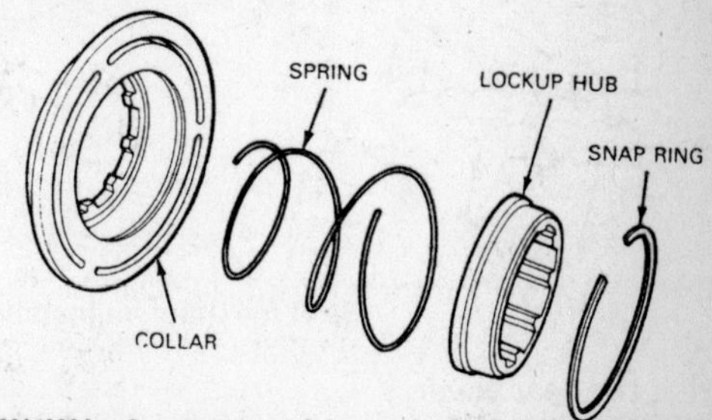

2W/4W lock-up assembly exploded view for the 13–56 electronic shift

Borg-Warner 13–56 Electronic Shift

WARNING: *The transfer case shell is made of magnesium. It is VERY susceptible to damage, such a scratches, nicks and chipping!*

1. Drain the fluid from the case.
2. Remove the speedometer cover and the wire connector assembly from the mounting bracket on the rear cover. If necessary, remove the bracket.
3. Remove both output shaft yokes.
4. Remove the 4WD indicator switch. DO NOT LOSE THE ALUMINUM WASHER! This washer controls switch operation.
5. Bend a paper clip to form a small hook. Remove the locking sleeve from the wire connector by hooking it with the paper clip and pull it up from the bottom. Take care not to damage the locking sleeve.
6. Remove the brown wire from the No.1 center position in the connector. If required, remove the speed sensor green wire from the No.4 connector position and the blue wire from the No.5 position.
7. Remove the front and rear yoke seals using tools T74P–77248–A and T50L–100–A.
8. Using the same tools, remove the input shaft seal.
9. Unbolt and remove the rear bearing retainer from the case cover. The retainer may be pried off using a $^{1}/_{2}$ in. breaker bar in the pry bosses. Remove all traces of RTV sealer.
10. Lift the rear output shaft and remove the speedometer gear retaining clip.
11. Slide the speedometer gear forward and remove the ball with a small magnet. Pull the gear off the output shaft.
12. Remove the speed sensor from the rear cover.
13. Remove the 3 bolts attaching the shift motor to the rear cover and remove the shift motor. Note the position of the triangular shaft extending out of the rear cover and the triangular slot in the motor.

NOTE: *Don't disassemble the motor!*

14. Remove the snapring from the rear output shaft that retains the upper rear ball bearing.
15. Unbolt and remove front case cover from the rear case cover. The case halves may be separated using a $^{1}/_{2}$ in. breaker bar in the pry bosses. Remove all traces of RTV sealer.
16. Remove the front output shaft inner needle bearing from the rear cover using a puller-type slidehammer.
17. Drive out the rear output shaft bearing from the inside of the case.
18. Remove the nuts retaining the clutch coil assembly to the rear cover. Pull the assembly, along with the O-rings and brown wire, from the cover.
19. Remove the shift shaft bushing and seal

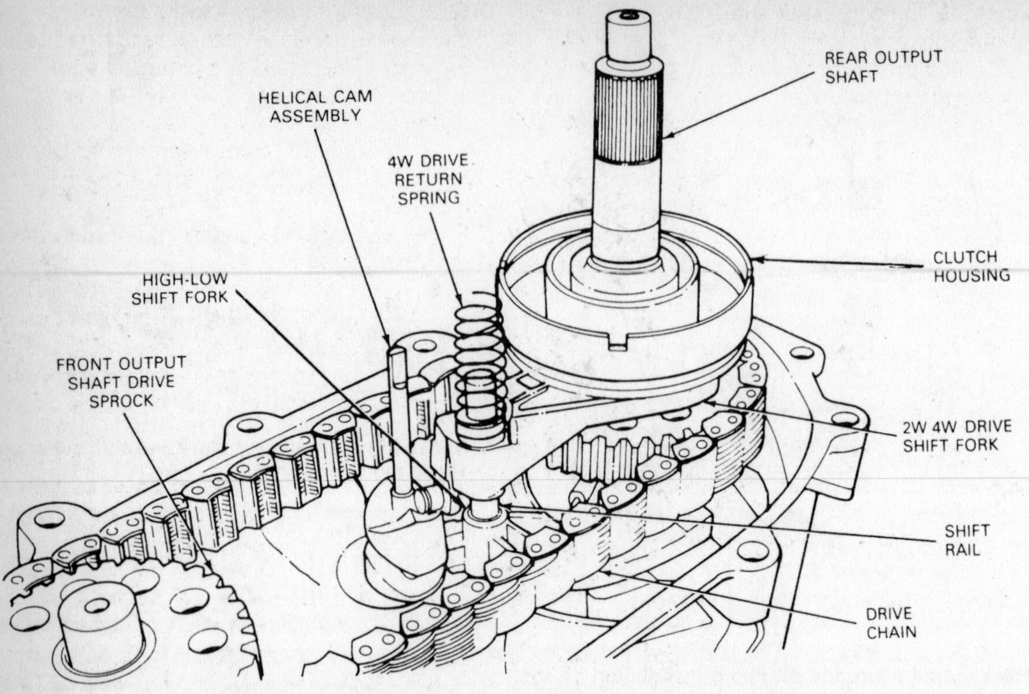

Shift mechanism installation on the 13–56 electronic shift

from the rear cover.

20. Remove the output shaft clutch hub snapring. Slide the 4WD hub off of the shaft.

21. Remove the spring from the shift shaft and lift the mode shift fork along with the shift collar, from the upper rear output shaft sprocket splines.

22. Disassemble the 2WD-4WD lockup assembly by removing the internal snapring and pull the lockup hub and spring from the collar.

23. Remove the snapring retaining the lower sprocket to the lower output shaft. Grasp the upper and lower sprocket along with the chain, and lift them, simultaneously, from the upper and lower shafts.

24. Remove the shift rail by sliding it straight out of the shift fork.

25. Remove the high/low shift fork by first rotating it until the roller is free from the cam, then sliding it out of engagement from the shift hub.

26. Remove the helical cam assembly from the front case. If you are going to disassemble the helical cam assembly, be careful when the cam is slid rearward to disengage it from the spring. The spring is energized and can fly out with considerable force. The spring must be removed from the helical cam and the shift finger. Don't get your fingers in the way. It will

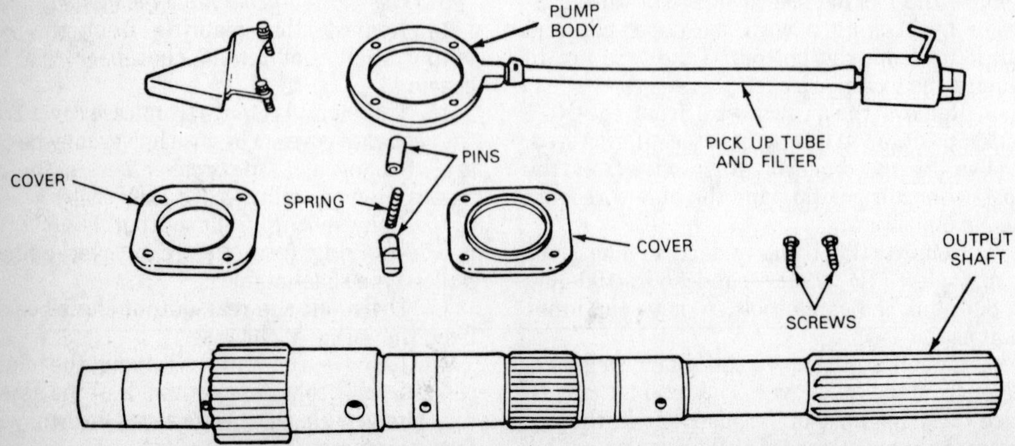

Rear output shaft and oil pump exploded view the 13–56 electronic shift

rotate to the point that the spring ends will be about 180° apart.

27. Remove the magnetic chip collector from the bottom of the case.

28. Lift the pump screen and remove the output shaft assembly with the pump assembled on it. If you are going to disassemble the pump, remove the 4 bolts from the pump body. Note the position of the pump front body, pins, spring, rear cover and pump retainer before disassembly.

29. Remove the high/low shift hub.

30. Remove the front output shaft from the case.

31. Turn the front case over and remove the front oil seal with a puller.

32. Expand the snapring on the input shaft and allow it to drop out of the bearing. If either the bearing or bushing is defective, both must be replaced as a unit. Drive them out together.

33. Remove the ring gear by prying out the internal snapring and lift out the gear.

34. Remove the internal snapring holding the input shaft bearing and drive out the bearing from the outside.

35. Remove the internal snapring holding the front output shaft bearing and drive out the bearing from the front of the case.

NOTE: *Before assembly, lubricate all parts with clean Dexron®II automatic transmission fluid. Remove any chips from the bolt holes or the case cover.*

36. Install the input shaft and front output shaft bearings in the case using drivers.

37. Install the internal snaprings.

38. Drive the front output shaft seal into the case until it is fully seated.

39. Install the front output shaft through the lower bearing.

40. Install the front yoke assembly onto the shaft, followed by the rubber seal, flat washer and 30mm locknut. Torque the nut to 150–180 ft. lbs.

41. Press the needle bearing and bronze bushing into the input shaft.

42. Install the ring gear into the slots in the case and retain it with the large internal snapring, making certain that it is fully seated.

43. Install the input shaft and carrier in the case through the input shaft bearing bore, carefully aligning the gear teeth.

44. Support the carrier assembly and install a new snapring on the front side of the input shaft bearing, making sure that it is fully seated in the groove.

45. Install the upper input shaft oil seal in the case.

46. Reassemble the helical cam by engaging one end of the spring on the shaft finger and the other end of the spring on the cam finger. With the shaft finger secured carefully in a soft-jawed vise, turn the cam to wind up the spring until the fingers of the cam and shaft are in alignment, and slide the cam forward to lock the spring in the cocked position.

47. Install the cam assembly in the small hole of the case with the shaft in a vertical position.

48. Assemble the pump and output shaft as follows:

a. Install the oil pump cover with the word FRONT facing the front of the case.

b. Install the two pins, with the flats facing upward, with the springs between the pins, and place the assembly in the oil pump bore in the output shaft.

c. Place the oil pump body and pick-up tube over the shaft, and make certain that the pins are riding against the inside of the pump body.

d. Place the oil pump rear cover, with the words TOP REAR facing the rear of the case.

e. Install the pump retainer with the tabs facing the front of the case.

f. Install the 4 retaining bolts and rotate the output shaft while tightening the bolts to prevent the pump from binding. Torque the bolts to 40 inch lbs.

g. Lubricate the whole assembly with clean transmission fluid. The output shaft should turn freely. If not, loosen and retorque the bolts.

49. Install the high/low shift hub.

50. Install the high/low shift fork by engaging it with the shift hub flange and rotating it until the roller is engaged with the lower groove of the helical cam.

51. Install the shift rail through the high/low fork bore and into the rail bore in the case.

52. Install the output shaft and oil pump assembly in the input shaft. Make certain that the external splines of the output shaft engage the internal splines of the high/low shift hub. Make sure that the oil pump retainer and oil filter leg are in the groove and notch of the front case.

53. Install the collector magnet.

54. Assemble the upper and lower sprockets with the chain, and place them on the upper and lower shafts. Install the washer and snapring that retain the lower sprocket.

55. Assemble the 2WD/4WD lock-up assembly:

a. Install the tapered compression spring in the lock-up collar with the small end installed first.

b. Place the lock-up hub over the spring and compress the spring while installing the internal snapring which holds the assembly together.

Troubleshooting Basic Driveshaft and Rear Axle Problems

When abnormal vibrations or noises are detected in the driveshaft area, this chart can be used to help diagnose possible causes. Remember that other components such as wheels, tires, rear axle and suspension can also produce similar conditions.

BASIC DRIVESHAFT PROBLEMS

Problem	Cause	Solution
Shudder as car accelerates from stop or low speed	• Loose U-joint • Defective center bearing	• Replace U-joint • Replace center bearing
Loud clunk in driveshaft when shifting gears	• Worn U-joints	• Replace U-joints
Roughness or vibration at any speed	• Out-of-balance, bent or dented driveshaft • Worn U-joints • U-joint clamp bolts loose	• Balance or replace driveshaft • Replace U-joints • Tighten U-joint clamp bolts
Squeaking noise at low speeds	• Lack of U-joint lubrication	• Lubricate U-joint; if problem persists, replace U-joint
Knock or clicking noise	• U-joint or driveshaft hitting frame tunnel • Worn CV joint	• Correct overloaded condition • Replace CV joint

56. Install the lock-up assembly and its shift fork over the external splines of the upper sprocket and the shift rail, with the long boss of the shift rail facing forward.

57. Assemble the 4WD return spring over the shift rail and against the shift fork.

58. Place the 4WD hub over the external splines of the output shaft. Install the snapring.

59. Place the clutch housing over the splines on the output shaft and secure it with a snapring.

60. Press the lower output needle bearing into its bore in the rear cover.

61. Press the rear output shaft bearing into the cover. Install the snapring.

62. Install the rear output shaft seal in the bearing retainer.

63. Install a new shift shaft bushing and seal into the cover.

64. Install new O-rings on the clutch coil assembly studs and grommet.

65. Install the clutch coil assembly from inside the rear cover until the wire and studs extend through the cover. Torque the nuts to 72–96 inch lbs. Take care to avoid kinking the wires.

66. Coat the mating surface of the front case with a non-acidic silicone rubber gasket material.

67. Place the cover on the case making sure that the shafts and shift rail are all aligned. Torque the bolts to 36 ft. lbs.

68. Install the rear bearing snapring on the output shaft.

69. Place the speedometer drive gear over the shaft aligning the slot with the drive ball hole. The gear should go completely against the snapring retaining the output shaft. Place the ball in the hole and pull the gear over the ball. Snap the retaining clip between the snapring and speedometer gear.

70. Install the speed sensor in the cover.

71. Apply a bead of non-acidic silicone rubber gasket material on the face of the rear bearing retainer.

72. Place the retainer in position and torque the 4 bolts to 36 ft. lbs.

WARNING: *Be careful to avoid trapping the brown wire beneath the retainer.*

73. Install the rear output shaft yoke and slinger. Install the rubber seal, flat washer and locking nut. Torque the nut to 150–180 ft. lbs.

74. Using soft-jawed pliers, rotate the triangular shift shaft so that it is aligned with the triangular slot in the motor. Install the motor. Torque the retaining screws to 72–96 inch lbs.

NOTE: *If the shaft will not stay in the 4H position, rotate the shaft to the 2H position. Install the motor and rotate it counterclockwise until the motor is aligned with the mounting holes.*

75. Install the brown clutch coil wire to the No.1 center terminal.

76. Connect the speed sensor green wire to the No.4 connector.

77. Connect the blue wire to the No.5 connector.

78. Install the locking sleeve.

79. Install the wire connector mounting

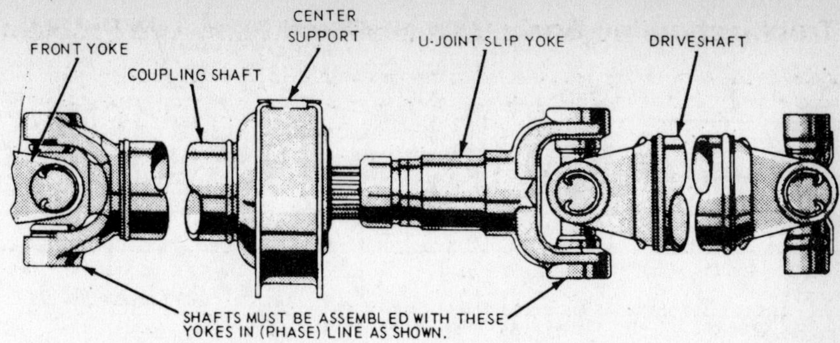

Two-piece driveshaft with a slip yoke at the transmission end

bracket and torque the bolts to 72–96 inch lbs.

80. Install the wire connector on the mounting bracket.

81. Install the drain plug. Torque it to 20 ft. lbs.

82. Fill the case with Dexron®II fluid and install the fill plug. Torque the fill plug to 20 ft. lbs.

DRIVELINE

Driveshaft

REMOVAL AND INSTALLATION

4-Wheel Drive

1. To remove the rear driveshaft, disconnect the double Cardan joint from the flange at the transfer case and the single U-joint from the flange at the rear axle. Remove the driveshaft.

2. To remove the front driveshaft, disconnect the double Cardan joint from the flange at the transfer case and the single U-joint from the front axle. remove the driveshaft.

3. Installation is the reverse of removal. Torque driveshaft-to-transfer case bolts to 20–25 ft. lbs.; driveshaft to axle bolts to 8–15 ft. lb.

2-Wheel Drive

1. Unscrew the nuts attaching the U-bolts to the flange at the rear axle. Remove the U-bolts and allow the rear of the driveshaft to drop down. Slide the front of the driveshaft out of the rear of the transmission or the center support bearing. Remove the driveshaft from the vehicle.

2. On those vehicles equipped with a two-piece driveshaft and a center support bearing,

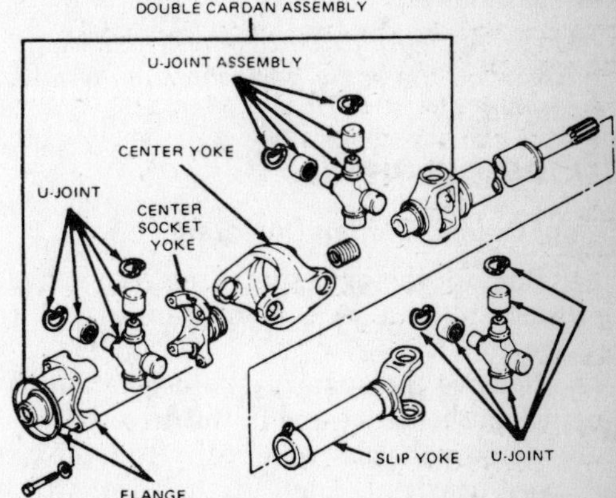

Rear driveshaft components on the Bronco and F-350 4×4

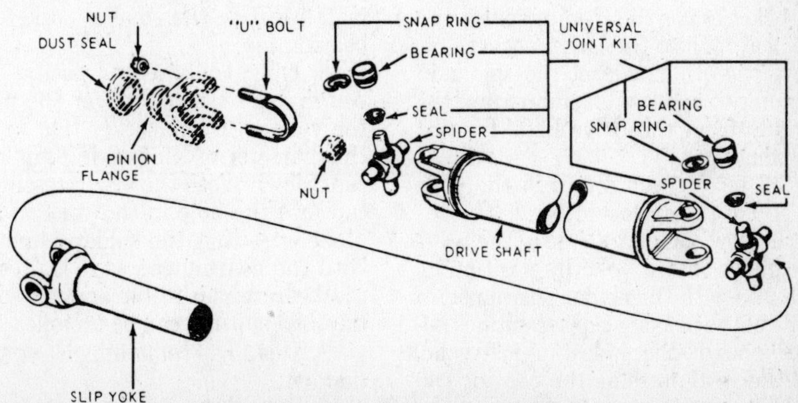

One-piece driveshaft with a slip yoke

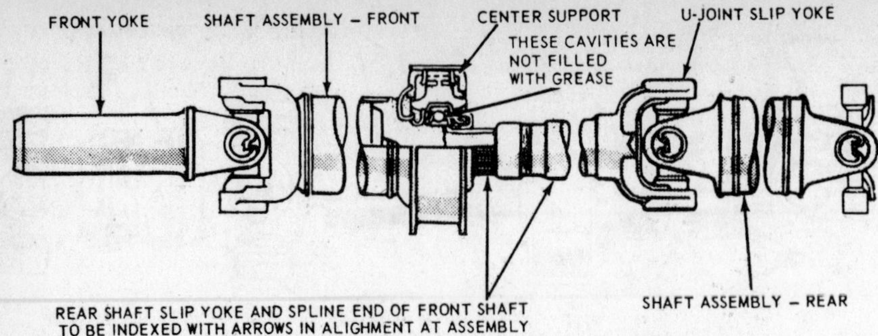

Two-piece driveshaft with a fixed yoke at the transmission end

unscrew the attaching bolts holding the center support bearing to the frame. if equipped with a sliding yoke at the transmission, slide the coupling shaft out of the rear of the extension housing. Otherwise, remove the nuts from the U-bolts holding the front of the coupling shaft to the flange on the rear of the transmission while supporting the center bearing. Remove the U-bolts from the front flange and remove the coupling shaft assembly together with the center support bearing.

3. Install the driveshaft(s) in the reverse order of removal.

NOTE: *All U-joints on two-piece driveshafts must be on the same horizontal plane when installed.*

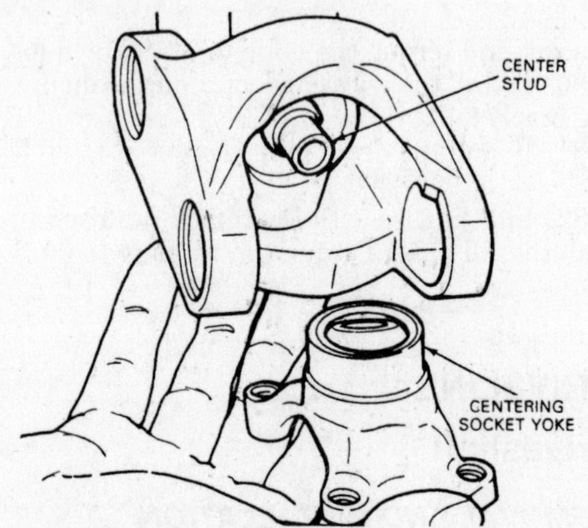

Removing the center socket yoke

U-JOINT OVERHAUL

Except Double Cardan Universal

1. Remove the driveshaft from the vehicle and place it in a vise, being careful not to damage it.

2. Remove the snaprings which retain the bearings in the flange and in the driveshaft.

3. Remove the driveshaft tube from the vise and position the U-joint in the vise with a socket smaller than the bearing cap on one side and a socket larger than the bearing cap on the other side.

4. Slowly tighten the jaws of the vise so that the smaller socket forces the U-joint spider and the opposite bearing into the larger socket.

5. Remove the other side of the spider in the same manner (if applicable) and remove the spider assembly from the driveshaft. Discard the spider assemblies.

6. Clean all foreign matter from the yoke areas at the end of the driveshaft(s).

7. Start the new spider and one of the bearing cap assemblies into a yoke by positioning the yoke in a vise with the spider positioned in place with one of the bearing cap assemblies positioned over one of the holes in the yoke. Slowly close the vise, pressing the bearing cap assembly in the yoke. Press the cap in far enough so that the retaining snapring can be installed. Use the smaller socket to recess the bearing cap.

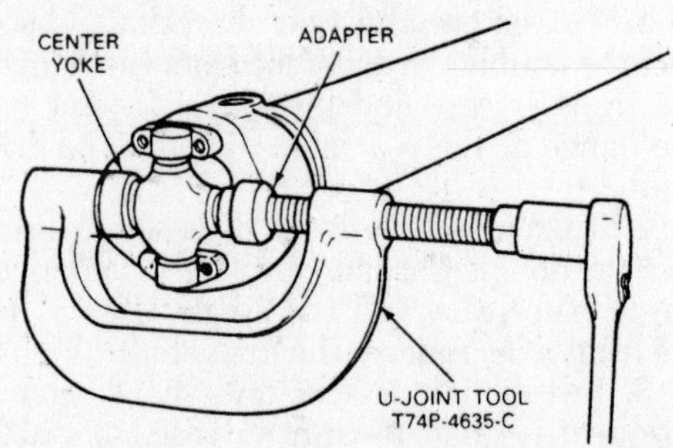

Partially pressing the bearing from the center yoke

8. Open the vise and position the opposite bearing cap assembly over the proper hole in the yoke with the socket that is smaller than the diameter of the bearing cap located on the cap. Slowly close the vise, pressing the bearing cap into the hole in the yoke with the socket. Make sure that the spider assembly is in line with the bearing cap as it is pressed in. Press the bearing cap in far enough so that the retaining snapring can be installed.

9. Install all remaining U-joints in the same manner.

10. Install the driveshaft and grease the new U-joints.

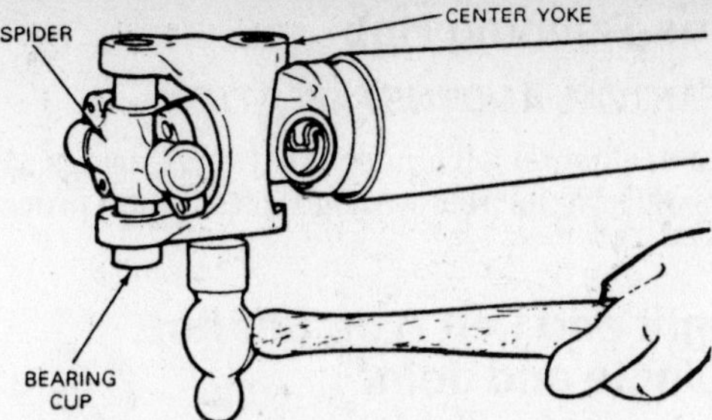

Removing the bearing from the center yoke

9. Remove the spider from the center yoke.

10. Remove the bearings from the driveshaft yoke as outlined above and remove the spider from the yoke.

11. Insert a suitable tool into the centering ball socket located in the companion flange and pry out the rubber seal. Remove the retainer, three piece ball seat, washer and spring from the ball socket.

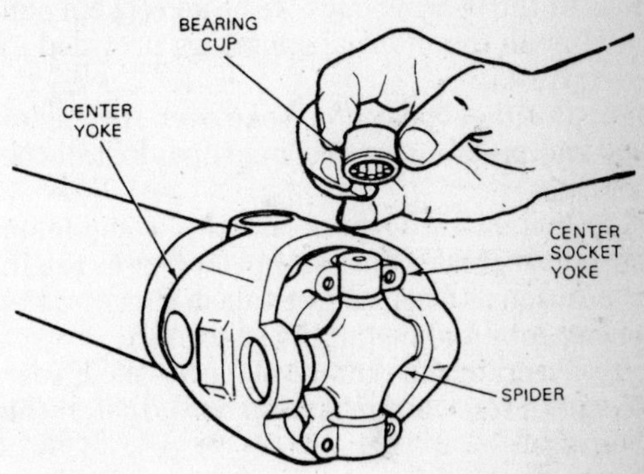

Removing the bearing cup from the center yoke socket

Double Cardan Joint

1. Working at the rear axle end of the shaft, mark the position of the spiders, the center yoke, and the centering socket yoke as related to the companion flange. The spiders must be assembled with the bosses in their original position to provide proper clearances.

2. Using a large vise or an arbor press and a socket smaller than the bearing cap on one side and a socket larger than the bearing cap on the other side, drive one of the bearings in toward the center of the universal joint, which will force the opposite bearing out.

3. Remove the driveshaft from the vise.

4. Tighten the bearing in the vise and tap on the yoke to free the bearing from the center yoke. Do not tap on the driveshaft tube.

5. Reposition the sockets on the yoke and force the opposite bearing outward and remove it.

6. Position the sockets on one of the remaining bearings and force it outward approximately $^{3}/_{8}$ in. (9.5mm).

7. Grip the bearing in the vise and tap on the weld yoke to free the bearing from the center yoke. Do not tap on the driveshaft tube.

8. Reposition the sockets on the yoke to press out the remaining bearing.

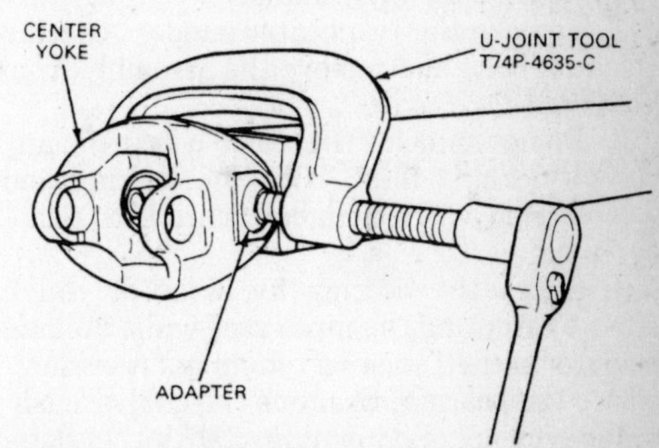

Removing the bearing from the rear of the center yoke

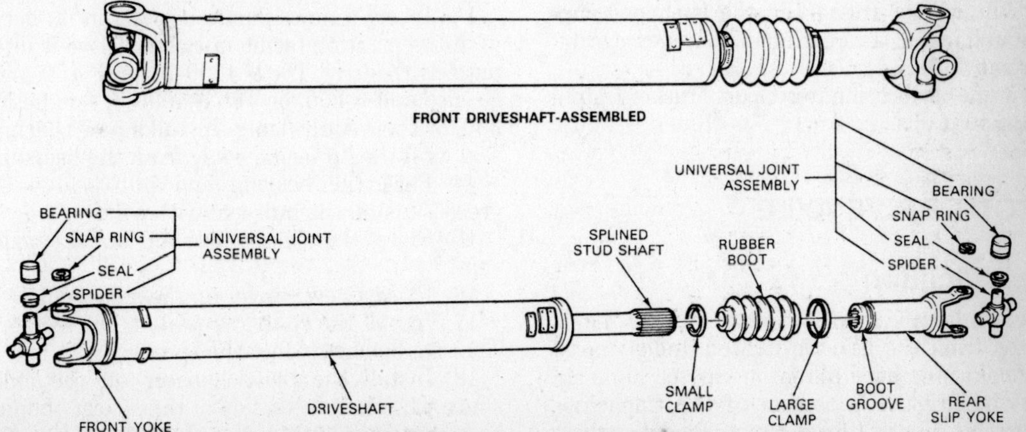

Front driveshaft exploded view

12. Inspect the centering ball socket assembly for worn or damaged parts. If any damage is evident replace the entire assembly.
13. Insert the spring, washer, three piece ball seat and retainer into the ball socket.
14. Using a suitable tool, install the centering ball socket seal.
15. Position the spider in the driveshaft yoke. Make sure the spider bosses are in the same position as originally installed. Press in the bearing cups with the sockets and vise. Install the internal snaprings provided in the repair kit.
16. Position the center yoke over the spider ends and press in the bearing cups. Install the snaprings.
17. Install the spider in the companion flange yoke. Make sure the spider bosses are in the position as originally installed. Press on the bearing cups and install the snaprings.
18. Position the center yoke over the spider ends and press on the bearing cups. Install the snaprings.

Center Bearing

REMOVAL AND INSTALLATION

1. Remove the driveshafts.
2. Remove the two center support bearing attaching bolts and remove the assembly from the vehicle.
3. Do not immerse the sealed bearing in any type of cleaning fluid. Wipe the bearing and cushion clean with a cloth dampened with cleaning fluid.
4. Check the bearing for wear or rough action by rotating the inner race while holding the outer race. If wear or roughness is evident, replace the bearing. Examine the rubber cushion for evidence of hardening, cracking, or deterioration. Replace it if it is damaged in any way.
5. Place the bearing in the rubber support and the rubber support in the U-shaped support and install the bearing in the reverse order of removal.

Torque the bearing to support bracket fasteners to 50 ft. lbs.

FRONT DRIVE AXLE

Identification

Axle identification and ratio can be determined from the I.D. tag located under one of the bolts on the differential carrier housing. See the drive axle section of the Capacities Chart in Chapter 1 for complete model application.

Free-Running Hub

REMOVAL AND INSTALLATION

See Chapter 1 under Wheel Bearings 4-Wheel Drive for removal and installation procedures.

Right and Left Axle Shafts, Spindle and Joint

REMOVAL AND INSTALLATION

Dana 44 IFS
Dana 44 IFS-HD
Dana 50 IFS

1. Raise and support the front end on jackstands.
2. Remove the front wheels.
3. Remove the calipers.
4. Remove the hub/rotor assemblies.
5. Remove the nuts retaining the spindle to the steering knuckle. Tap the spindle with a plastic mallet to remove it from the knuckle.
6. Remove the splash shield.
7. On the left side, pull the shaft from the carrier, through the knuckle.
8. On the right side, remove and discard the keystone clamp from the shaft and joint assembly and the stub shaft. Slide the rubber boot onto the shaft and pull the shaft and joint assembly from the splines of the stub shaft.
9. Place the spindle in a soft-jawed vise clamped on the second step of the spindle.
10. Using a slidehammer and bearing puller, remove the needle bearing from the spindle.
11. Inspect all parts. If the spindle is excessively corroded or pitted it must be replaced. If the U-joints are excessively loose or don't move freely, they must be replaced. If any shaft is bent, it must be replaced.
12. Clean all dirt and grease from the spindle bearing bore. The bore must be free of nicks and burrs.
13. Insert a new spindle bearing in its bore with the printing facing outward. Drive it into place with drive T80T–4000–S for F-150 and Bronco and F-250, or T80T–4000–R for the F-350, or their equivalents. Install a new bearing seal with the lip facing away from the bearing.
14. Pack the bearing and hub seal with grease. Install the hub seal with a driver.
15. Place the thrust washer on the axle shaft.
16. Place a new slinger on the axle shaft.
17. Install the rubber V-seal on the slinger. The seal lip should face the spindle.
18. Install the plastic spacer on the axle shaft. The chamfered side of the spacer should be inboard against the axle shaft.
19. Pack the thrust face of the seal in the

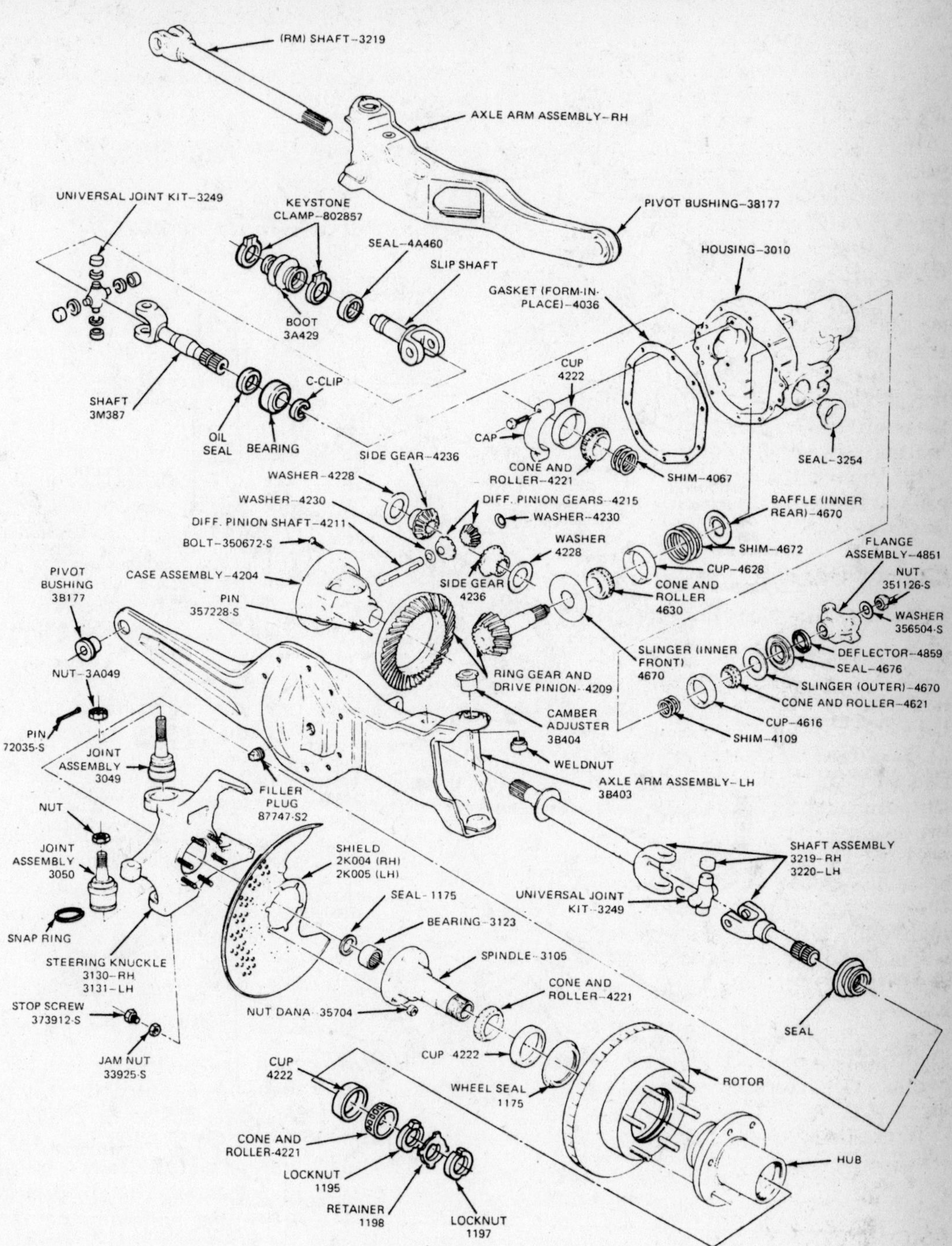

Dana 44-IFS front drive axle with automatic locking hubs

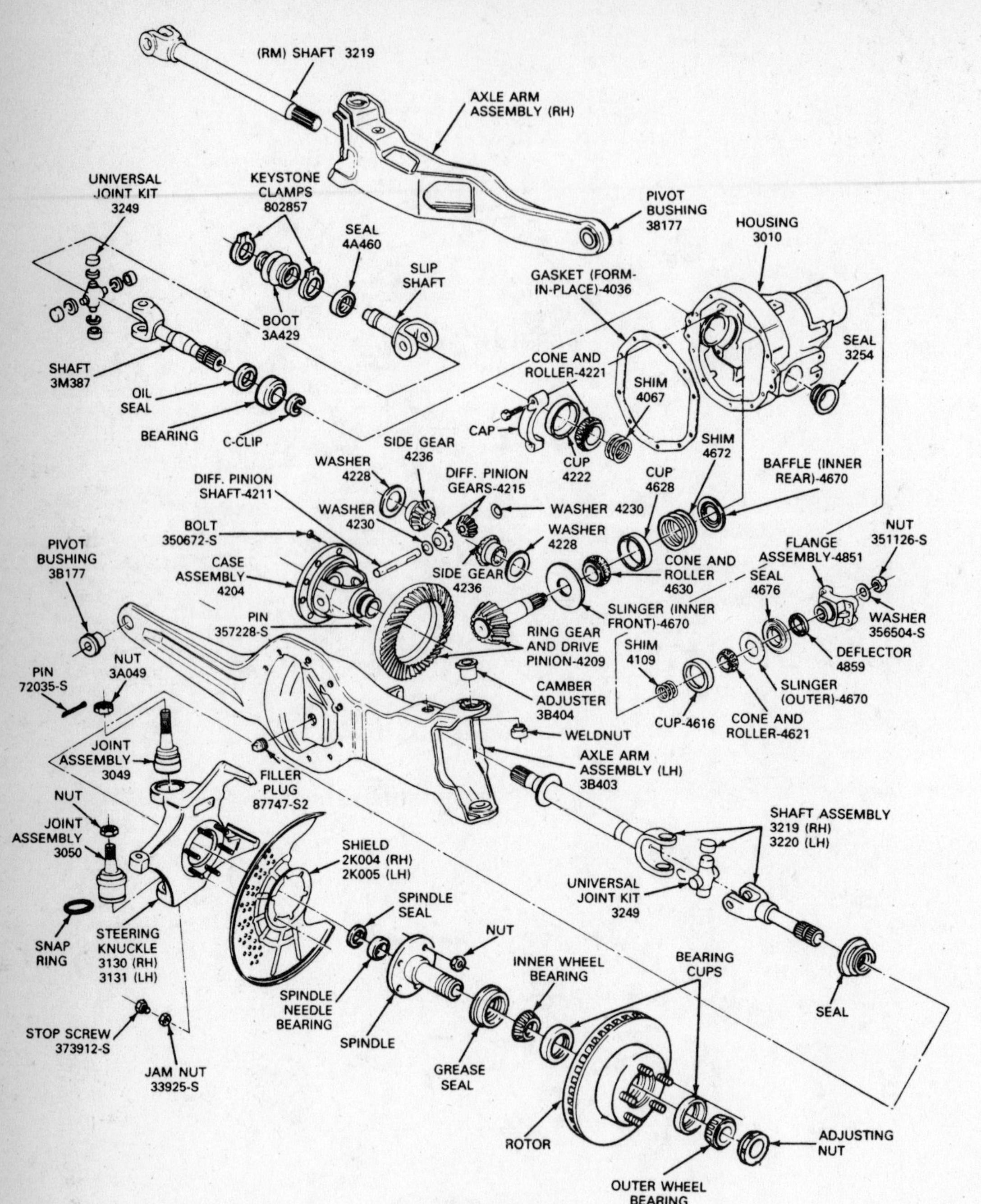

Dana 44-IFS front drive axle with manual locking hubs

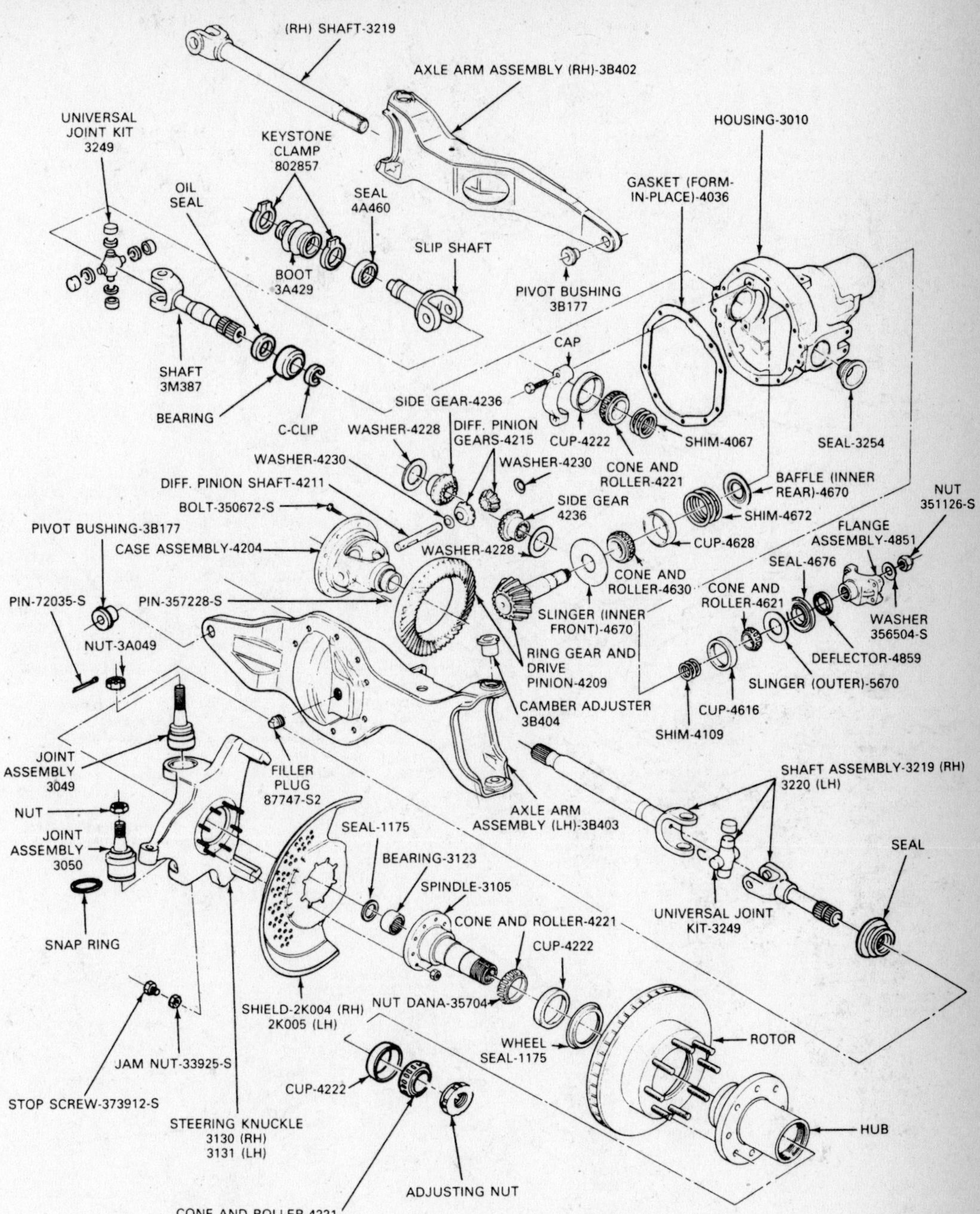

Dana 44-IFS-HD front drive axle

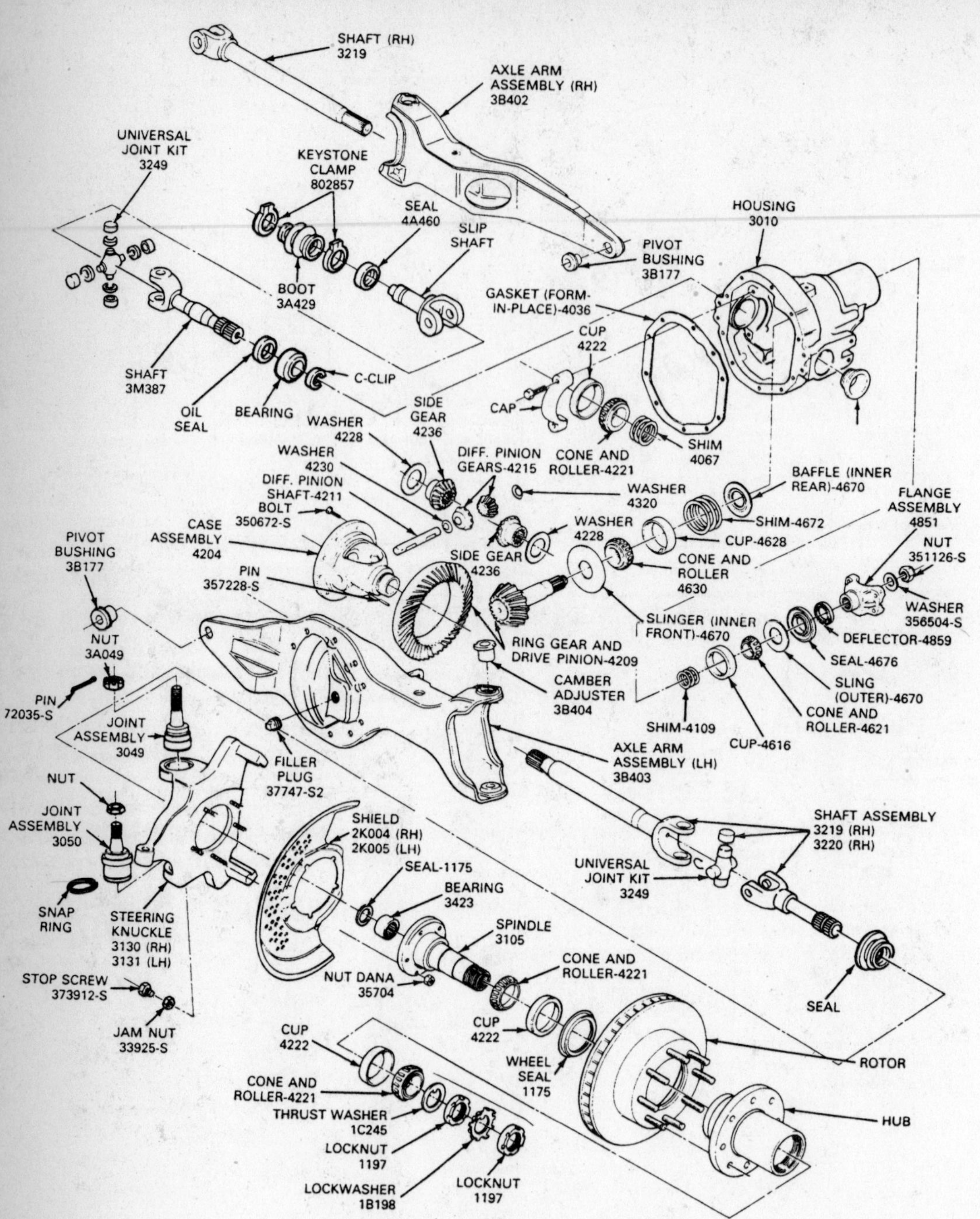

Dana 50-IFS front drive axle

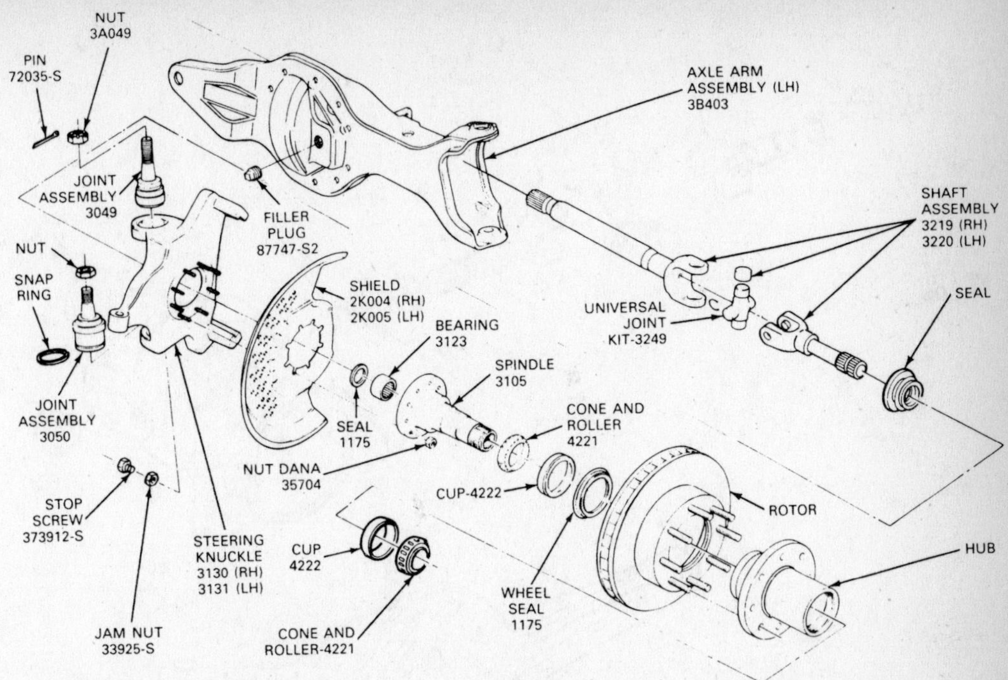

Spindle and left shaft and joint installation for the Dana 44 and 50 front axles

spindle bore and the V-seal on the axle shaft with heavy duty, high temperature, waterproof wheel bearing grease.

20. On the right side, install the rubber boot and new keystone clamps on the stub shaft and slip yoke. The splines permit only one way of meshing so you'll have to properly align the missing spline in the slip yoke with the gapless male spline on the shaft. Slide the right shaft and joint assembly into the slip yoke, making sure that the splines are fully engaged. Slide the boot over the assembly and crimp the keystone clamp.

21. On the left side, slide the shaft and joint assembly through the knuckle and engage the splines in the carrier.

22. Install the splash shield and spindle on the knuckle. Tighten the spindle nuts to 60 ft. lbs.

23. Install the rotor on the spindle. Install the outer wheel bearing into the cup. Make sure that the grease seal lip totally encircles the spindle.

24. Install the wheel bearing, locknut, thrust bearing, snapring and locking hubs. See Chapter 1.

25. Install the caliper.

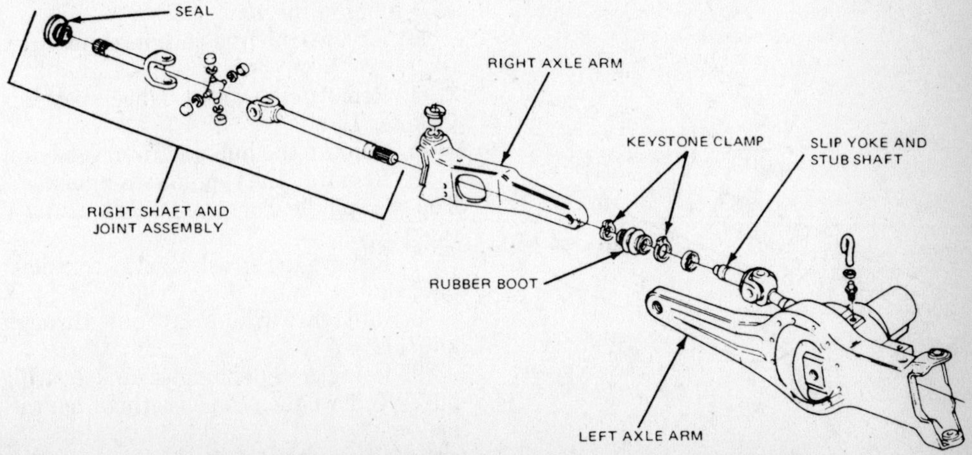

Right shaft and joint installation for the Dana 44 and 50 front axles

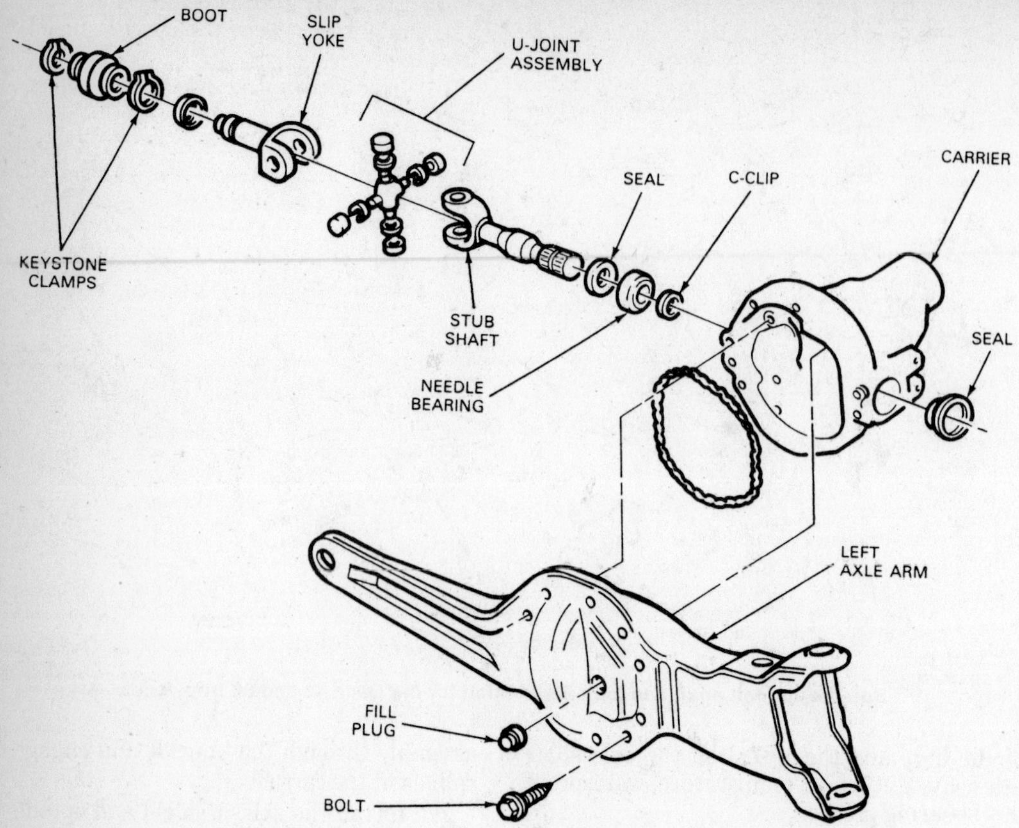

Carrier and slip yoke, and stub shaft installation on the Dana 44 and 50 IFS

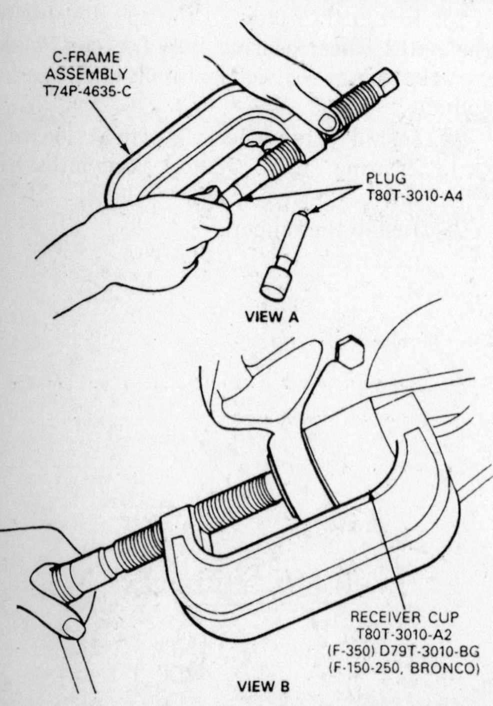

Upper ball joint removal on the Dana 44 and 50 IFS

Spindle and Front Axle Shaft

REMOVAL AND INSTALLATION

Dana 60 Monobeam

1. Raise and support the front end on jackstands.
2. Remove the caliper from the knuckle and wire it out of the way.
3. Remove the free-running hub. See Chapter 1.
4. Remove the front wheel bearing. See Chapter 1.
5. Remove the hub and rotor assembly.
6. Remove the spindle-to-knuckle bolts. Tap the spindle from the knuckle using a plastic mallet.
7. Remove the splash shield and caliper support.
8. Pull the axle shaft out through the knuckle.
9. Using a slidehammer and bearing cup puller, remove the needle bearing from the spindle.
10. Clean the spindle bore thoroughly and make sure that it is free of nicks and burrs. If

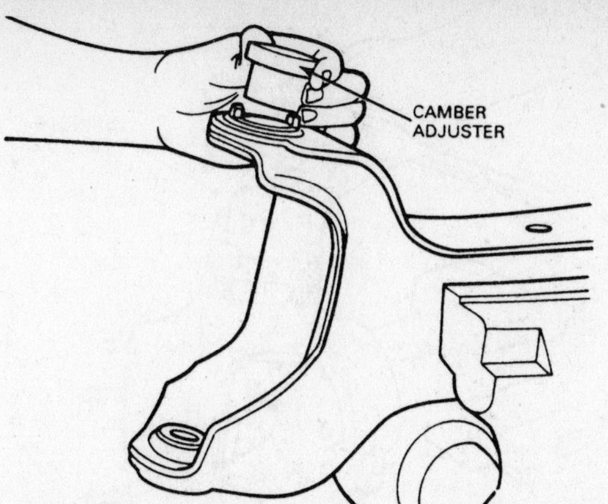

Removing the camber adjuster on the Dana 44 and 50 IFS

the bore is excessively pitted or scored, the spindle must be replaced.

11. Insert a new spindle bearing in its bore with the printing facing outward. Drive it into place with driver T80T–4000–R, or its equivalent. Install a new bearing seal with the lip facing away from the bearing.

12. Pack the bearing with waterproof wheel bearing grease.

13. Pack the thrust face of the seal in the spindle bore and the V-seal on the axle shaft with waterproof wheel bearing grease.

14. Carefully guide the axle shaft through the knuckle and into the housing. Align the splines and fully seat the shaft.

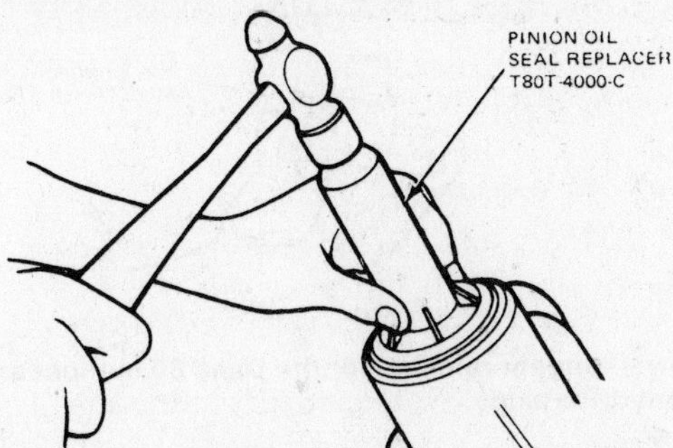

Pinion oil seal installation on the Dana 44 and 50 IFS

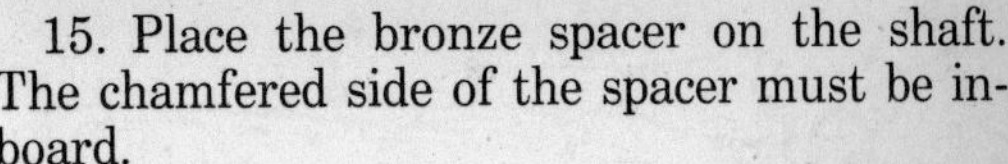

15. Place the bronze spacer on the shaft. The chamfered side of the spacer must be inboard.

16. Install the splash shield and caliper support.

17. Place the spindle on the knuckle and install the bolts. Torque the bolts to 50–60 ft. lbs.

18. Install the hub/rotor assembly on the spindle.

19. Assemble the wheel bearings.

20. Assemble the free-running hub.

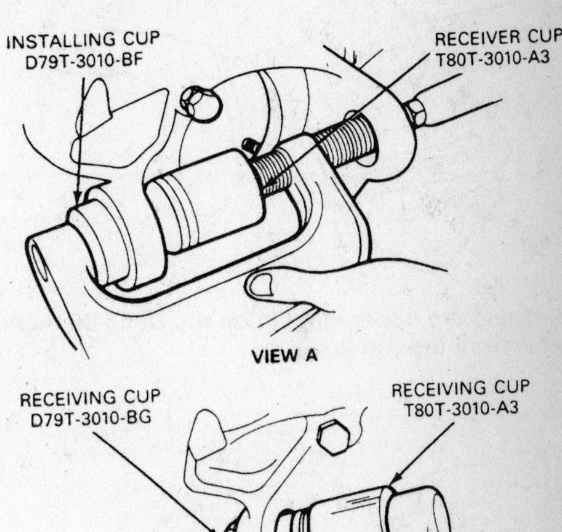

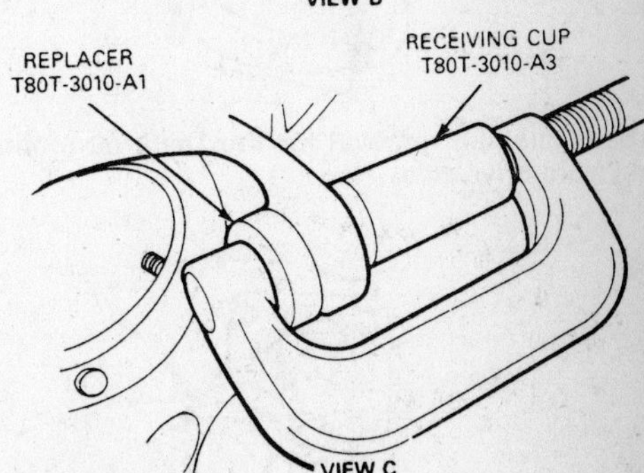

Ball joint installation on the Dana 44 and 50 IFS

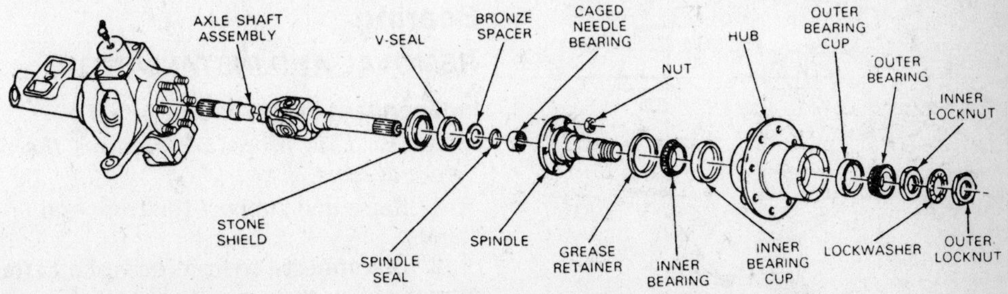

Axle shaft components for the Dana 60 monobeam front drive axle

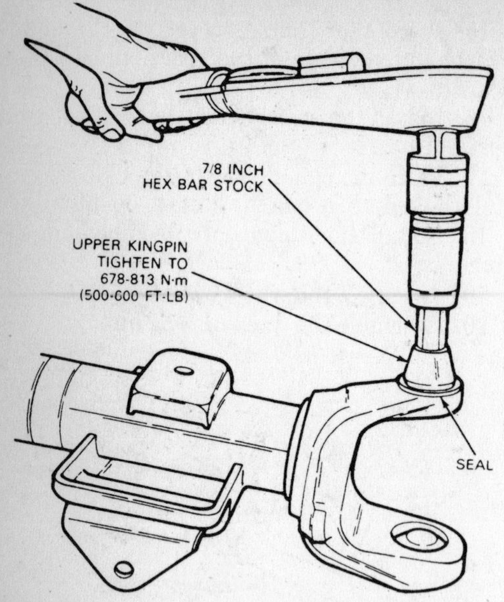

Installing the upper kingpin on the Dana 60 monobeam front drive axle

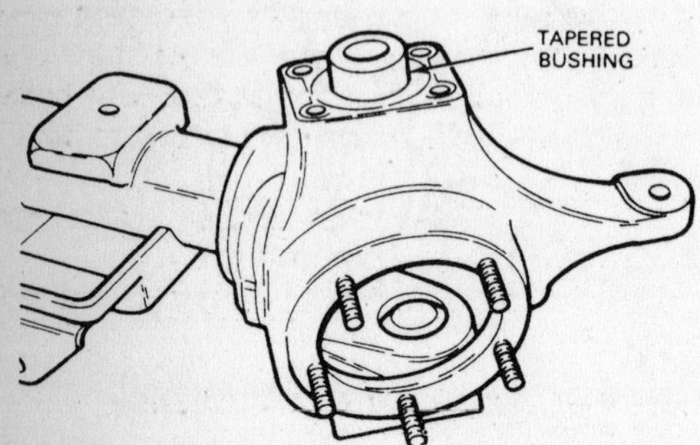

Tapered bushing removal for the Dana 60 monobeam front drive axle

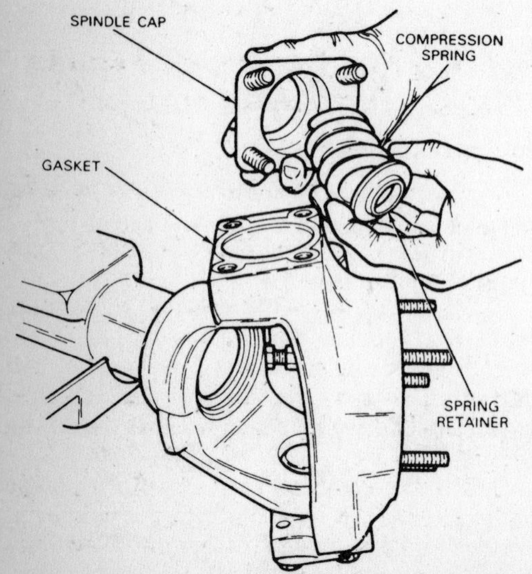

Compression spring removal for the Dana 60 monobeam front drive axle

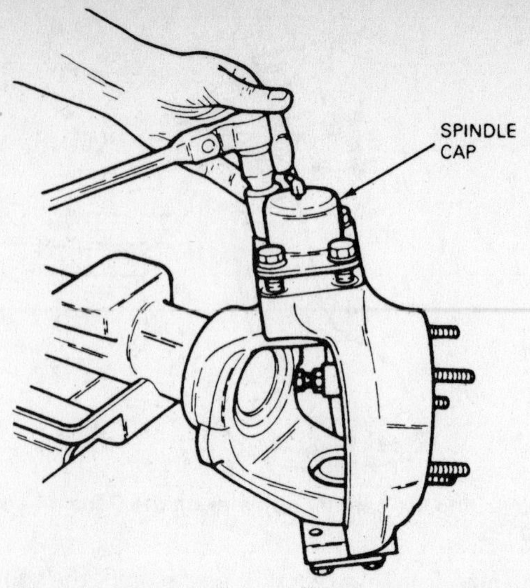

Spindle cap removal for the Dana 60 monobeam front drive axle

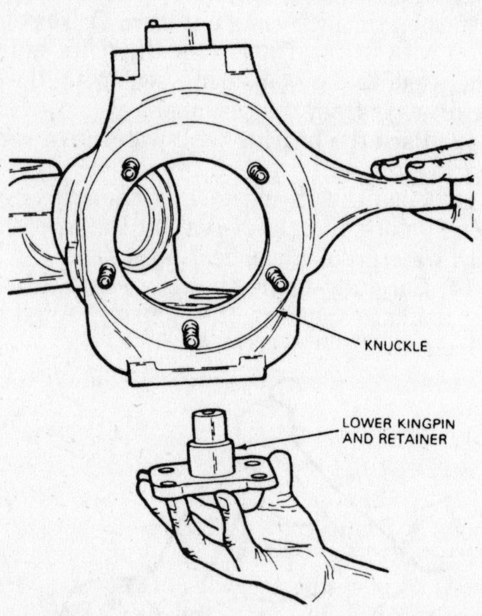

Lower kingpin removal for the Dana 60 monobeam front drive axle

Right Side Slip Yoke and Stub Shaft, Carrier, Carrier Oil Seal and Bearing

REMOVAL AND INSTALLATION

Independent Front Axles

NOTE: *This procedure requires the use of special tools.*

1. Raise and support the front end on jackstands.
2. Disconnect the front driveshaft from the carrier and wire it up out of the way.
3. Remove the left and right axle shafts and both spindles.

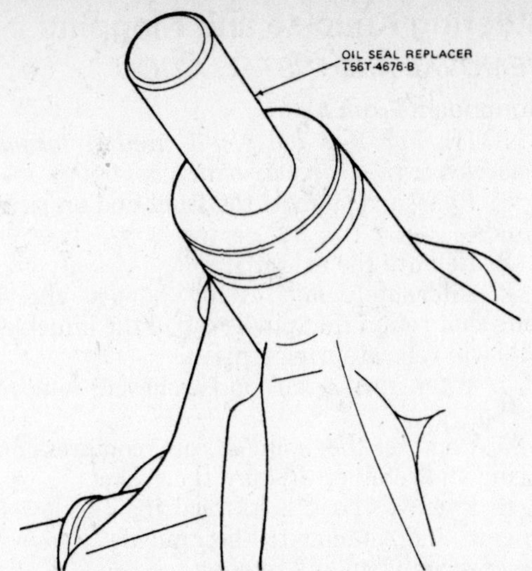

Pinion oil seal installation on the Dana 60 monobeam front drive axle

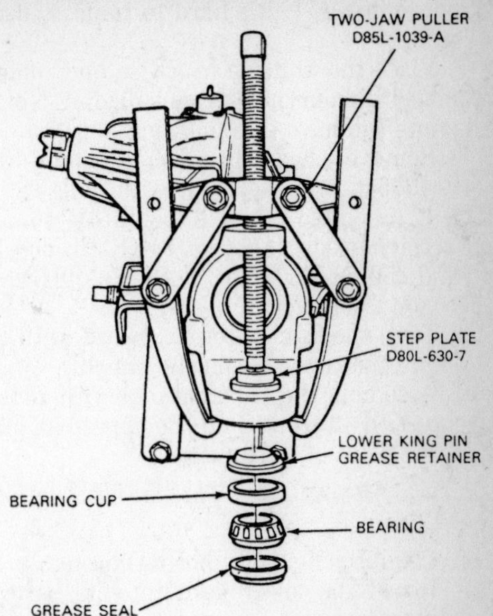

Removing the lower kingpin on the Dana 60 monobeam front drive axle

4. Support the carrier with a floor jack and unbolt the carrier from the support arm.
5. Place a drain pan under the carrier, separate the carrier from the support arm and drain the carrier.
6. Remove the carrier from the truck.
7. Place the carrier in holding fixture T57L–500–B with adapters T80T–4000–B.
8. Rotate the slip yoke and shaft assembly from the carrier.
9. Using a slidehammer/puller remove the caged needle bearing and oil seal as a unit. Discard the oil seal and bearing.
10. Clean the bearing bore thoroughly and make sure that it is free of nicks and burrs.
11. Insert a new bearing in its bore with the printing facing outward. Drive it into place with driver T83T–1244–A, or its equivalent. Install a new bearing seal with the lip facing away from the bearing. Coat the bearing and seal with waterproof wheel bearing grease.
12. Install the slip yoke and shaft assembly into the carrier so that the groove in the shaft is visible in the differential case.
13. Install the snapring in the groove in the shaft. It may be necessary to force the snapring into place with a small prybar. Don't strike the snapring!
14. Remove the carrier from the holding fixture.
15. Clean all traces of sealant from the carrier and support arm. Make sure the mating surfaces are clean. Apply a 1/4 in. (6mm) wide bead of RTV sealant to the mating surface of the carrier. The bead must be continuous and should not pass through or outside of the holes. Install the carrier with 5 minutes of applying the sealer.
16. Position the carrier on the jack and raise it into position using guide pins to align it if you'd like. Install and hand-tighten the bolts. Torque the bolts in a circular pattern to 30–40 ft. lbs.
17. Install the support arm tab bolts and torque them to 85–100 ft. lbs.
18. Install all other parts in reverse order of removal.

AXLE SHAFT U-JOINT OVERHAUL

Follow the procedures outlined under Axle Shaft Removal and Installation to gain access to the U-joints. Overhaul them as described under U-joints.

Steering Knuckle and Ball Joints

REMOVAL AND INSTALLATION

Independent Front Axles

1. Raise and support the front end on jackstands.
2. Remove the spindles and left and right shafts and joint.
3. Remove the tie rod nut and disconnect the tie rod from the steering arm.
4. Remove the cotter pin from the top ball joint stud. Remove the nut from the top stud and loosen the nut on the lower stud inside the knuckle.
5. Hit the top stud sharply with a plastic mallet to free the knuckle from the axle arm. Remove and discard the bottom nut. New nuts should be used at assembly.
6. Note the positioning of the camber adjuster carefully for reassembly. Remove the

camber adjuster. If it's hard to remove, use a puller.

7. Place the knuckle in a vise and remove the snapring from the bottom ball joint. Not all ball joints will have this snapring.

8. Remove the plug from C-frame tool T74P–4635–C and replace it with plug T80T–3010–A. Assemble C-frame tool T74P–4635–C and receiving cup D79T–3010–G (Bronco, F-150 and 250) or T80T–3010–A2 (F-250HD and F-350). on the knuckle.

9. Turn the forcing screw inward until the ball joint is separated from the knuckle.

10. Assemble the C-frame tool with receiving cup D79P–3010–BG on the upper ball joint and force it out of the knuckle.

NOTE: *Always force out the bottom ball joint first.*

11. Clean the ball joint bores thoroughly.

12. Insert the lower joint into its bore as straight as possible.

13. On the Bronco, F-150 and F-250, assemble the C-frame tool, receiving cup T80T–3010–A3 and installing cup D79T–3010–BF onto the lower ball joint. On the F-250HD and F-350, assemble the C-frame tool, receiving cup T80T–3010–A3 and receiving cup D79T–3010–BG on the lower ball joint.

14. Turn the screw clockwise until the ball joint is firmly seated.

NOTE: *If the ball joint cannot be installed to the correct depth, you'll have to realign the receiving cup on the tool.*

15. On all models, assemble the C-frame, receiving cup T80T–3010–A3 and replacer T80T–3010–A1 on the upper ball joint.

16. Turn the screw clockwise until the ball joint is firmly seated.

NOTE: *If the ball joint cannot be installed to the correct depth, you'll have to realign the receiving cup on the tool.*

17. Place the knuckle into position on the axle arm. Install the camber adjuster on the upper ball joint stud with the arrow point to positive or negative as noted before disassembly.

18. Install a new nut on the bottom stud, finger tight. Install a new nut on the top stud finger tight.

19. Tighten the bottom nut to 80 ft. lbs.

20. Tighten the top nut to 100 ft. lbs., then, (tighten) advance the nut until the cotter pin hole align with the castellations. Install a new cotter pin.

21. Again tighten the bottom nut, this time to 110 ft. lbs.

22. Install all other parts as described elsewhere in this chapter.

Steering Knuckle and Kingpins

REMOVAL AND INSTALLATION

Monobeam Front Axle

NOTE: *For this job you'll need a torque wrench with a capacity of at least 600 ft. lbs.*

1. Raise and support the front end on jackstands.

2. Remove the axle shafts.

3. Alternately and evenly remove the 4 bolts that retain the spindle cap to the knuckle. This will relieve spring tension.

4. When spring tension is relieved, remove the bolts.

5. Remove the spindle cap, compression spring and retainer. Discard the gasket.

6. Remove the 4 bolts securing the lower kingpin and retainer to the knuckle. Remove the lower kingpin and retainer.

7. Remove the tapered bushing from the top of the upper kingpin.

8. Remove the knuckle from the axle yoke.

9. Remove the upper kingpin from the axle yoke with a piece of 7/8 in. hex-shaped case hardened metal bar stock, or, with a 7/8 in. hex socket. Discard the upper kingpin and seal.

NOTE: *The upper kingpin is tightened to 500–600 ft. lbs.*

10. Using a 2-jawed puller and step plate, press out the lower kingpin grease retainer, bearing cup, bearing and seal from the axle yoke lower bore. Discard the grease seal and retainer, and the lower bearing cup.

11. Coat the mating surfaces of a new lower kingpin grease retainer with RTV silicone sealer.

12. Install the retainer in the axle yoke bore so that the concave portion of the retainer faces the upper kingpin.

13. Using a bearing driver, drive a new bearing cup in the lower kingpin bore until it bottoms against the grease retainer.

14. Pack the lower kingpin bearing and the yoke bore with waterproof wheel bearing grease.

15. Using a driver, drive a new seal into the lower kingpin bore.

16. Install a new seal and upper kingpin into the yoke using tool T86T–3110–AH. Tighten the kingpin to 500–600 ft. lbs.

17. Install the knuckle on the yoke.

18. Place the tapered bushing over the upper kingpin in the knuckle bore.

19. Place the lower kingpin and retainer in the knuckle and axle yoke. Install the 4 bolts and tighten them, alternately and evenly, to 90 ft. lbs.

20. Place the retainer and compression spring on the tapered bushing.

21. Install a new gasket on the knuckle. Po-

sition the spindle cap on the gasket and knuckle. Install the 4 bolts and tighten them, alternately and evenly, to 90 ft. lbs.

22. Install the axle shafts and lubricate the upper kingpin through the zerk fitting and the lower fitting through the flush fitting. The lower fitting may be lubricated with Alemite adapter #6783, or equivalent.

Pinion Seal

REMOVAL AND INSTALLATION

Independent Front Axle

NOTE: *A torque wrench capable of at least 225 ft. lbs. is required for pinion seal installation.*

1. Raise and safely support the vehicle with jackstands under the frame rails. Allow the axle to drop to rebound position for working clearance.
2. Mark the companion flanges and U-joints for correct reinstallation position.
3. Remove the driveshaft. Use a suitable tool to hold the companion flange. Remove the pinion nut and companion flange.
4. Use a slide hammer and hook or sheet metal screw to remove the oil seal.
5. Install a new pinion seal after lubricating the sealing surfaces. Use a suitable seal driver. Install the companion flange and pinion nut. Tighten the nut to 200–220 ft. lbs.

Monobeam Front Axle

NOTE: *A torque wrench capable of at least 300 ft. lbs. is required for pinion seal installation.*

1. Raise and support the truck on jackstands.
2. Allow the axle to hang freely.
3. Matchmark and disconnect the driveshaft from the front axle.
4. Using a tool such as T75T–4851–B, or equivalent, hold the pinion flange while removing the pinion nut.
5. Using a puller, remove the pinion flange.
6. Use a puller to remove the seal, or punch the seal out using a pin punch.
7. Thoroughly clean the seal bore and make sure that it is not damaged in any way. Coat the sealing edge of the new seal with a small amount of 80W/90 oil and drive the seal into the housing using a seal driver.
8. Coat the inside of the pinion flange with clean 80W/90 oil and install the flange onto the pinion shaft.
9. Install the nut on the pinion shaft and tighten it to 250–300 ft. lbs.
10. Connect the driveshaft.

Axle Unit

REMOVAL AND INSTALLATION

Independent Front Axles

1. Raise and support the front end on jackstands placed under the radius arms.
2. Remove the wheels.
3. Remove the calipers and wire them out of the way. Don't disconnect the brake lines.
4. Support the axle arm with a jack and remove the upper coil spring retainers.
5. Lower the jack and remove the coil springs, spring cushions and lower spring seats.
6. Disconnect the shock absorbers at the radius arms and upper mounting brackets.
7. Remove the studs and spring seats at the radius arms and axle arms.
8. Remove the bolts securing the upper attachment to the axle arm and the lower attachment to the axle arm.
9. Disconnect the vent tube at the housing. Remove the vent fitting and install a 1/8 in. pipe plug.
10. Remove the pivot bolt securing the right side axle arm to the crossmember. Remove and discard the boot clamps and remove the boot from the shaft. Remove the right drive axle assembly and pull the axle shaft from the slip shaft.
11. Support the housing with a floor jack. Remove the bolt securing the left side axle assembly to the crossmember. Remove the left side drive axle assembly.
12. Installation is, basically, a reversal of the removal procedure. Always use new boot clamps. Observe the following torques:
    - Left and right drive axles-to-crossmember: 120–150 ft. lbs.
    - Axle arm-to-radius arm: 180–240 ft. lbs.
    - Coil spring insulator: 30–70 ft. lbs.
    - Upper spring retainer: 13–18 ft. lbs.

Monobeam Axle

1. Raise and support the front end on jackstands placed under the frame.
2. Remove the wheels.
3. Remove the calipers and wire them out of the way. Don't disconnect the brake lines.
4. Disconnect the stabilizer links at the stabilizer bar.
5. Remove the U-bolts securing the stabilizer bar and mounting brackets to the axle.
6. Remove the cotter pins and nuts securing the spindle connecting rod to the steering knuckles. Separate the connecting rod to the steering knuckles. Separate the connecting rods from the knuckles with a pitman arm puller. Wire the steering linkage to the spring.

7. Matchmark and disconnect the driveshaft from the front axle.

8. Disconnect the vent tube at the axle and plug the fitting.

9. On the right side, disconnect the track bar from the right spring cap.

10. Raise the front end and position jackstands under front springs at a point about half way between the axle and spring rear hanger. Remove the jackstands from the front of the frame and lower the truck onto the stands under the springs. Make sure that the truck is securely supported.

11. Support the axle with a floor jack.

12. Remove the U-bolts securing the springs to the axle.

13. Lower the axle from the truck.

14. Installation is the reverse of removal. Observe the following torques:

- Driveshaft-to-flange: 15–20 ft. lbs.
- Track bar nut and bolt: 160–200 ft. lbs.
- Stabilizer link nut: 20–30 ft. lbs.
- Stabilizer bar U-bolt: 50–65 ft. lbs.
- Spindle connecting rod-to-knuckle: 70–100 ft. lbs.
- Front spring U-bolts: 85–100 ft. lbs.

REAR AXLE

Understanding Drive Axles

The drive axle is a special type of transmission that reduces the speed of the drive from the engine and transmission and divides the power to the wheels. Power enters the axle from the driveshaft via the companion flange. The flange is mounted on the drive pinion shaft. The drive pinion shaft and gear which carry the power into the differential turn at engine speed. The gear on the end of the pinion shaft drives a large ring gear the axis of rotation of which is 90 degrees away from the of the pinion. The pinion and gear reduce the gear ratio of the axle, and change the direction of rotation to turn the axle shafts which drive both wheels. The axle gear ratio is found by dividing the number of pinion gear teeth into the number of ring gear teeth.

The ring gear drives the differential case. The case provides the two mounting points for the ends of a pinion shaft on which are mounted two pinion gears. The pinion gears drive the two side gears, one of which is located on the inner end of each axle shaft.

By driving the axle shafts through the arrangement, the differential allows the outer drive wheel to turn faster than the inner drive wheel in a turn.

The main drive pinion and the side bearings, which bear the weight of the differential case, are shimmed to provide proper bearing preload, and to position the pinion and ring gears properly.

WARNING: *The proper adjustment of the relationship of the ring and pinion gears is critical. It should be attempted only by those with extensive equipment and/or experience.*

Limited-slip differentials include clutches which tend to link each axle shaft to the differential case. Clutches may be engaged either by spring action or by pressure produced by the torque on the axles during a turn. During turning on a dry pavement, the effects of the clutches are overcome, and each wheel turns at the required speed. When slippage occurs at either wheel, however, the clutches will transmit some of the power to the wheel which has the greater amount of traction. Because of the presence of clutches, limited-slip units require a special lubricant.

Determining Axle Ratio

The drive axle is said to have a certain axle ratio. This number (usually a whole number and a decimal fraction) is actually a comparison of the number of gear teeth on the ring gear and the pinion gear. For example, a 4.11 rear means that theoretically, there are 4.11 teeth on the ring gear and one tooth on the pinion gear or, put another way, the driveshaft must turn 4.11 times to turn the wheels once. Actually, on a 4.11 rear, there might be 37 teeth on the ring gear and 9 teeth on the pinion gear. By dividing the number of teeth on the pinion gear into the number of teeth on the ring gear, the numerical axle ratio (4.11) is obtained. This also provides a good method of ascertaining exactly what axle ratio one is dealing with.

Another method of determining gear ratio is to jack up and support the car so that both rear wheels are off the ground. Make a chalk mark on the rear wheel and the driveshaft. Put the transmission in neutral. Turn the rear wheel one complete turn and count the number of turns that the driveshaft makes. The number of turns that the driveshaft makes in one complete revolution of the rear wheel is an approximation of the rear axle ratio.

Differential Overhaul

A differential overhaul is a complex, highly technical, and time-consuming operation, which requires a great many tools, extensive knowledge of the unit and the way it works, and a high degree of mechanical experience and ability. It is highly advisable that the amateur mechanic not attempt any work on the differential unit.

Improved Traction Differentials

Ford calls their improved traction differential Traction-Lok®. In this assembly, a multiple-disc clutch is employed to control differential action. Repair procedures are the same as for conventional axles (within the scope of this book).

Identification

Four types of rear axles used on Ford F-150 and Bronco, F-250 and F-350 pick-ups:

1. The Ford integral carrier type semi-floating 8.8 in. (223.5mm) ring gear axle used on F-150 and Bronco models.
2. The Ford integral carrier type semi-floating 10.25 in. (260.35mm) ring gear axle used on F-250 Light Duty models.
3. The Ford integral carrier type full-floating 10.25 in. (260.35mm) ring gear axle used on F-250 Heavy Duty models and F-350 models.
4. The Dana 80 integral carrier full-floating 11.25 in. (285.75mm) ring gear rear axle used on F-Super Duty models.

On a full floating rear axle, the weight of the vehicle is support by the axle housing. The axle shafts can be removed without disturbing the wheel bearings.

On a semi-floating axle, the outboard end of the axle shaft is supported by the bearing which is mounted in a recess in the end of the axle housing.

The axle shaft on a full-floating rear axle is held in place by a flange and bolts attaching it to the hub on the outboard side. The hub is held to the rear spindle by nuts which are also used to adjust the preload of the rear axle bearings.

The axle shaft on the semi-floating rear axle is held in position by C-locks in the differential housing.

Axle Identification and Ratio are found on an I.D. tag located under one of the bolts on the

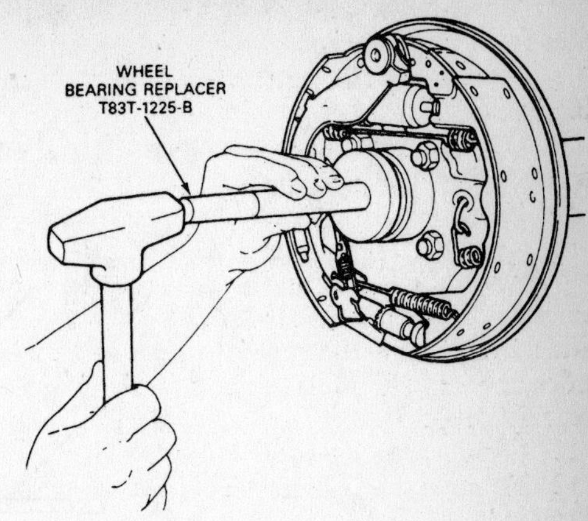

Ford 8.8 inch rear axle bearing installation

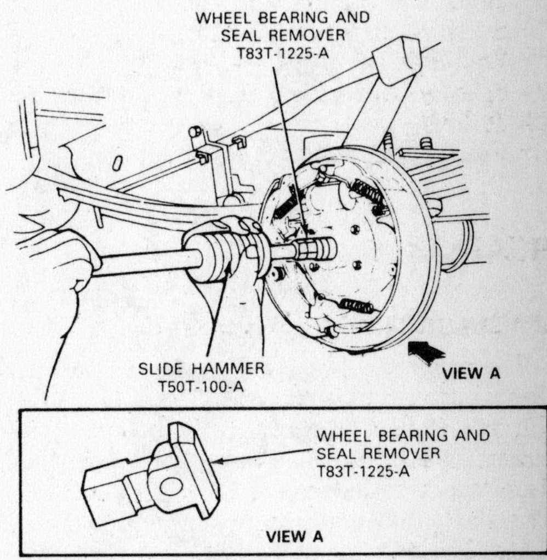

Rear axle bearing and seal removal for the Ford 8.8 inch axle

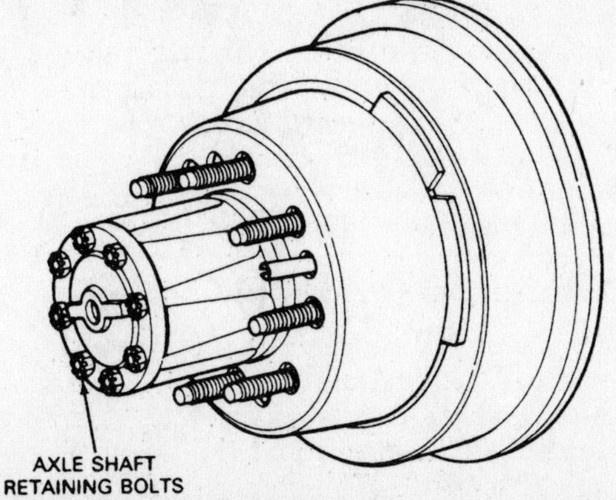

Rear axle shaft retaining bolts on the Ford 10.25 inch full-floating rear axle

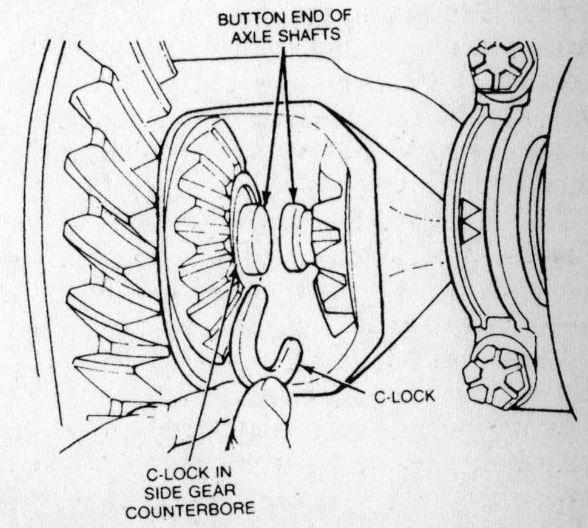

Installing the C-locks

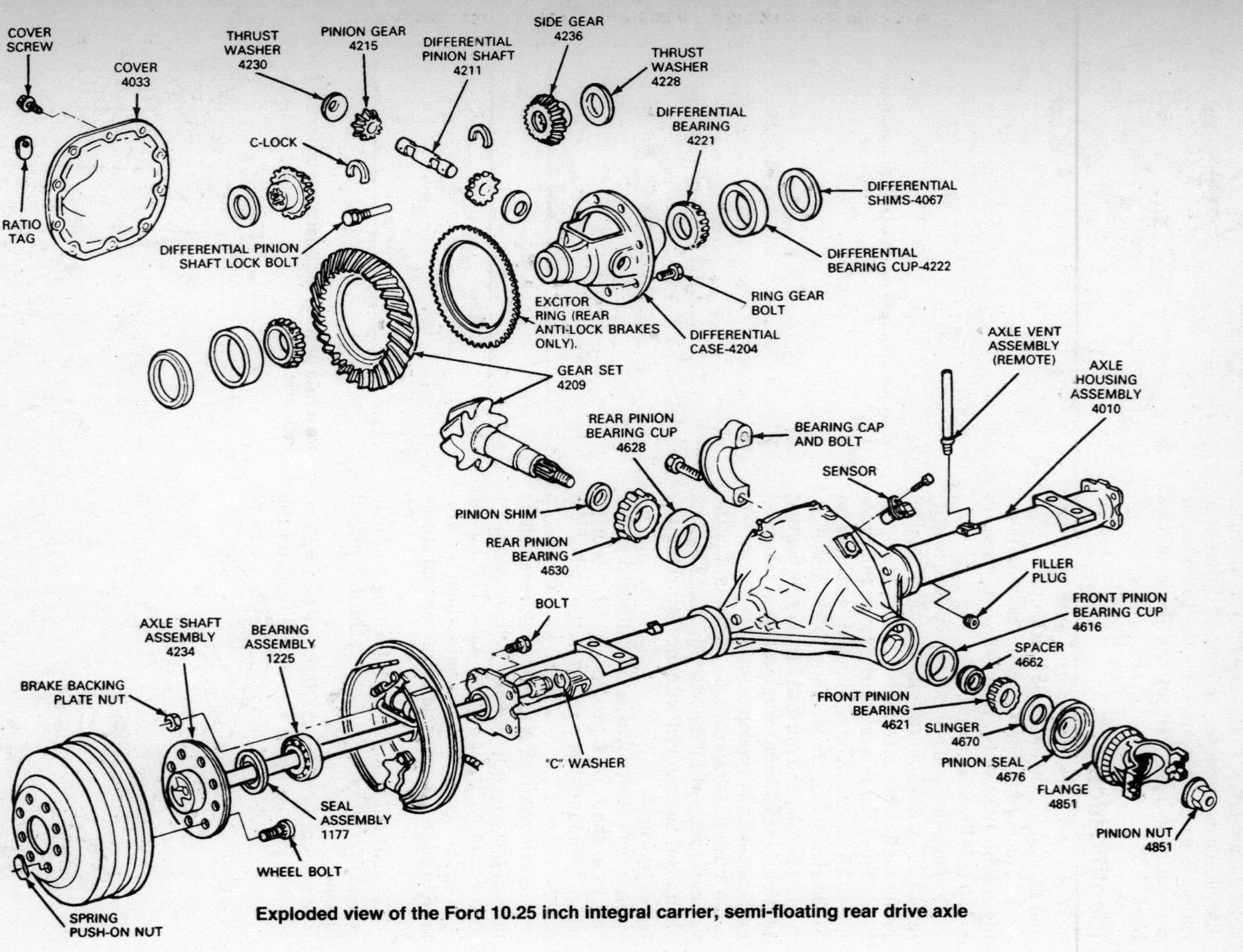

Exploded view of the Ford 10.25 inch integral carrier, semi-floating rear drive axle

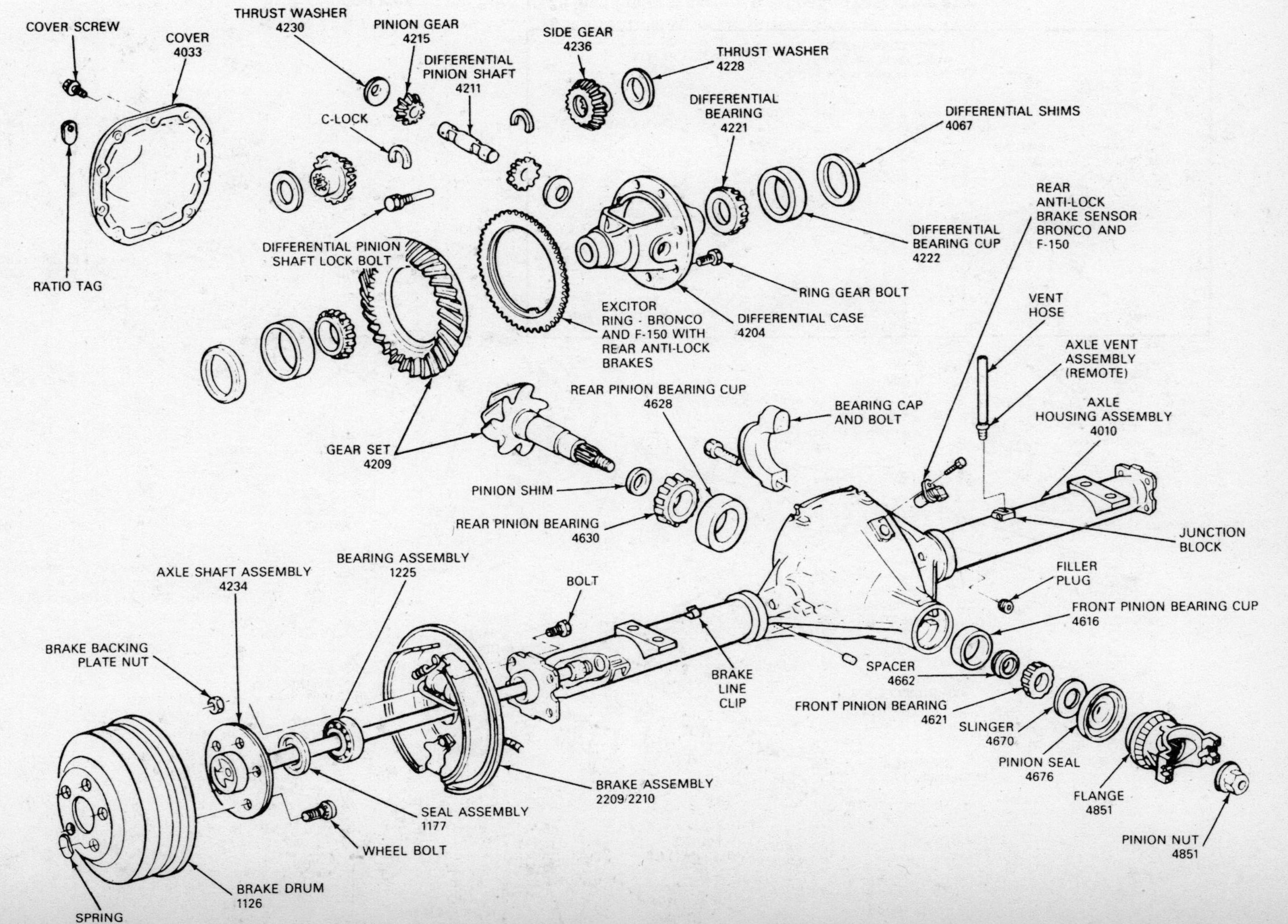

Exploded view of the Ford 8.8 inch integral carrier rear drive axle

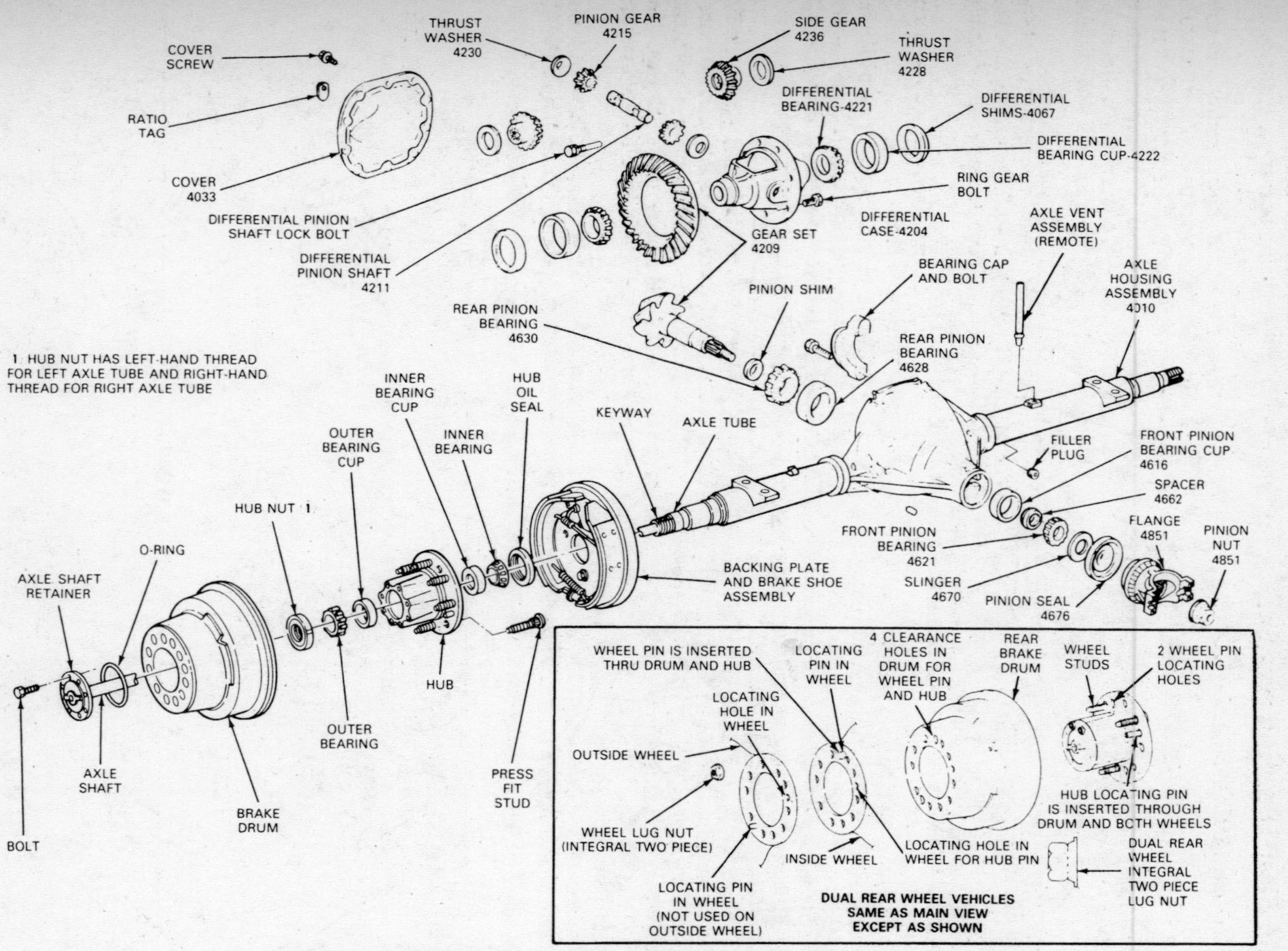

Exploded view of the Ford 10.25 inch integral carrier, full-floating rear drive axle

differential housing. Also refer to the Drive Axle Section of the Capacities Chart in Chapter 1 for complete model application.

Axle Shaft, Bearing and Seal

REMOVAL AND INSTALLATION

Ford 8.8 in. (223.5mm) Ring Gear Integral Carrier
Ford 10.25 in. (260.35mm) Ring Gear, Semi-floating Integral Carrier

1. Raise and safely support the vehicle on jackstands.
2. Remove the wheels from the brake drums.
3. Place a drain pan under the housing and drain the lubricant by loosening the housing cover.
4. Remove the locks securing the brake drums to the axle shaft flanges and remove the drums.
5. Remove the housing cover and gasket.
6. Remove the side gear pinion shaft lockbolt and the side gear pinion shaft.
7. Push the axle shafts inward and remove the C-locks from the inner end of the axle shafts. Temporarily replace the shaft and lockbolt to retain the differential gears in position.
8. Remove the axle shafts with a slide hammer. Be sure the seal is not damaged by the splines on the axle shaft.
9. Remove the bearing and oil seal from the housing. Both the seal and bearing can be removed with a slide hammer
10. Two types of bearings are used on some axles, one requiring a press fit and the other a loose fit. A loose fitting bearing does not necessarily indicate excessive wear.
11. Inspect the axle shaft housing and axle shafts for burrs or other irregularities. Replace any work or damaged parts. A light yellow color on the bearing journal of the axle shaft is normal, and does not require replacement of the axle shaft. Slight pitting and wear is also normal.
12. Lightly coat the wheel bearing rollers with axle lubricant. Install the bearings in the axle housing until the bearing seats firmly against the shoulder.
13. Wipe all lubricant from the oil seal bore, before installing the seal.
14. Inspect the original seals for wear. If necessary, these may be replaced with new seals, which are prepacked with lubricant and do not require soaking.
15. Install the oil seal.
16. Remove the lockbolt and pinion shaft. Carefully slide the axle shafts into place. Be careful that you do not damage the seal with the splined end of the axle shaft. Engage the splined end of the shaft with the differential side gears.
17. Install the axle shaft C-locks on the inner end of the axle shafts and seat the C-

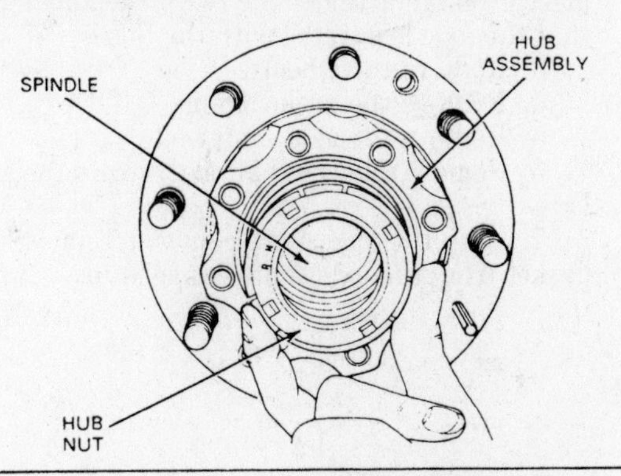

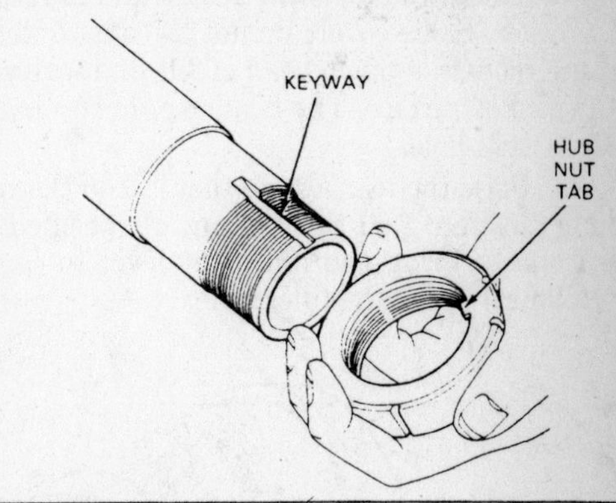

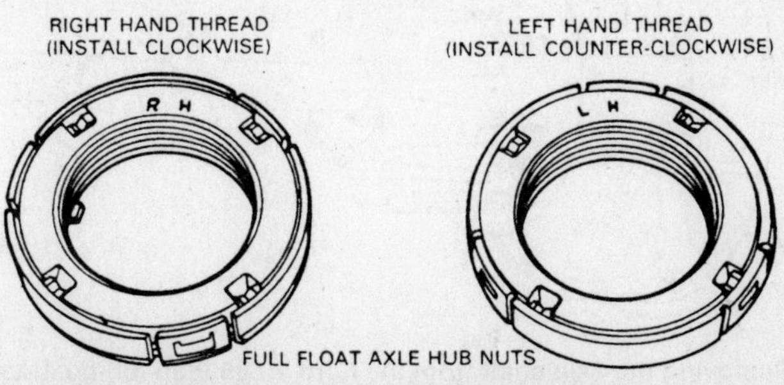

Hub nuts for the 10.25 inch full-floating axle

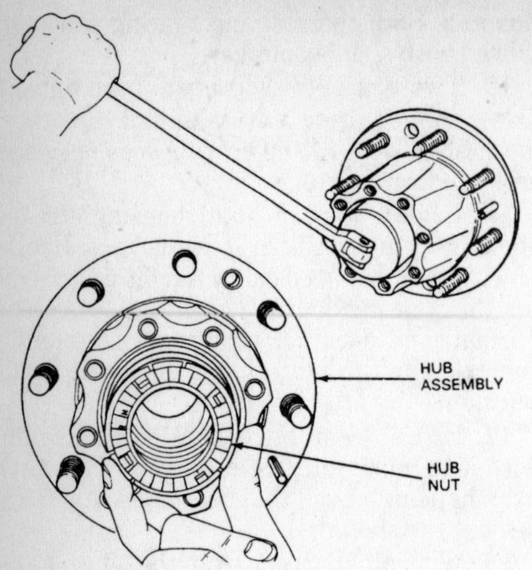

Hub nut removal on the 10.25 inch full-floating axle

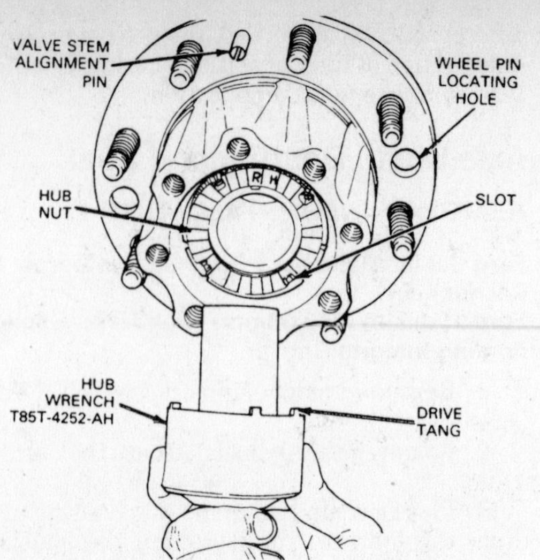

Using a hub wrench to remove the hub nuts on the 10.25 inch full-floating axle

locks in the counterbore of the differential side gears.

18. Rotate the differential pinion gears until the differential pinion shaft can be installed. Install the differential pinion shaft lockbolt. Tighten to 15–22 ft. lbs.

19. Install the brake drum on the axle shaft flange.

20. Install the wheel and tire on the brake drum and tighten the attaching nuts.

21. Clean the gasket surface of the rear housing and install a new cover gasket and the housing cover. Some covers do not use a gasket. On these models, apply a bead of silicone sealer on the gasket surface. The bead should run inside of the bolt holes.

22. Raise the rear axle so that it is in the running position. Add the amount of specified lubricant to bring the lubricant level to 1/2 in. (12.7mm) below the filler hole.

Ford 10.25 in. (260.35mm) Ring Gear, Full Floating Integral Carrier

The wheel bearings on the full floating rear axle are packed with wheel bearing grease. Axle lubricant can also flow into the wheel hubs and bearings, however, wheel bearing grease is the primary lubricant. The wheel bearing grease provides lubrication until the axle lubricant reaches the bearings during normal operation.

1. Set the parking brake and loosen the axle shaft bolts.
2. Raise the rear wheels off the floor and place jackstands under the rear axle housing so that the axle is parallel with the floor.
3. Remove the wheels.
4. Remove the brake drums.
5. Remove the axle shaft bolts.
6. Remove the axle shaft and discard the gaskets.
7. With the axle shaft removed, remove the gasket from the axle shaft flange studs.

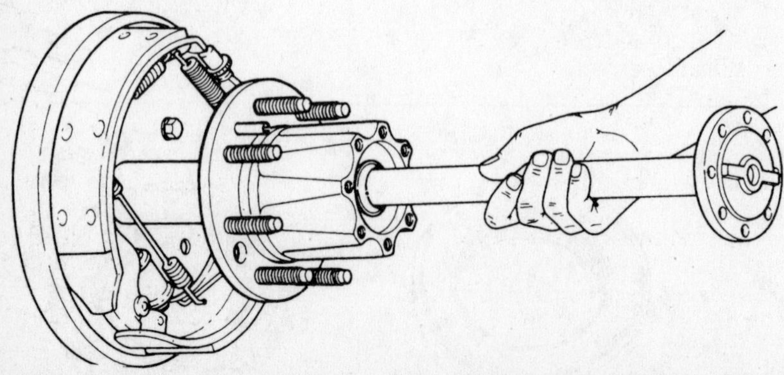
Removing the axle shaft from the Ford 10.25 inch full-floating rear axle

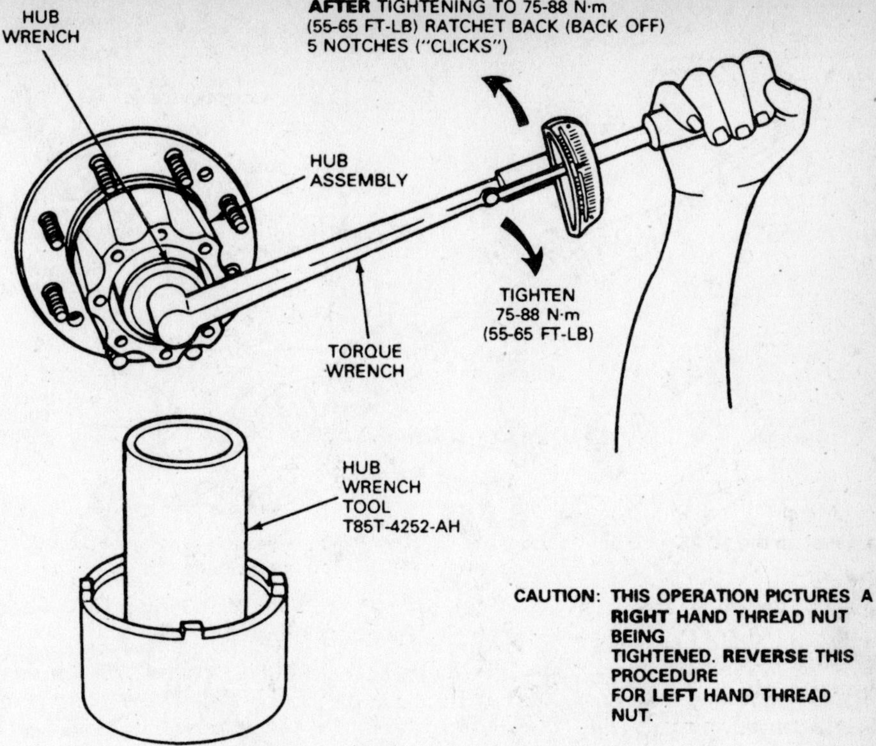

Installing the hub nuts for the 10.25 inch full-floating axle

8. Install Hub Wrench T85T–4252–AH, or equivalent, so that the drive tangs on the tool engage the slots in the hub nut.

NOTE: *The hub nuts are right hand thread on the right hub and left hand thread on the left hub. The hub nuts should be stamped RH and LH. Never use power or impact tools on these nuts! The nuts will ratchet during removal.*

9. Remove the hub nut.
10. Install step plate adapter tool D80L–630–7, or equivalent, in the hub.
11. Install puller D80L–1002–L, or equivalent and loosen the hub to the point of removal. Remove the puller and step plate.
12. Remove the hub, taking care to catch the outer bearing as the hub comes off.
13. Install the hub in a soft-jawed vise and pry out the hub seal.
14. Lift out the inner bearing.
15. Drive out the inner and outer bearing races with a drift.
16. Wash all the old grease or axle lubricant out of the wheel hub, using a suitable solvent.
17. Wash the bearing races and rollers and inspect them for pitting, galling, and uneven wear patterns. Inspect the roller for end wear. Replace any bearing and race that appears in any way damaged. Always replace the bearings and races as a set.

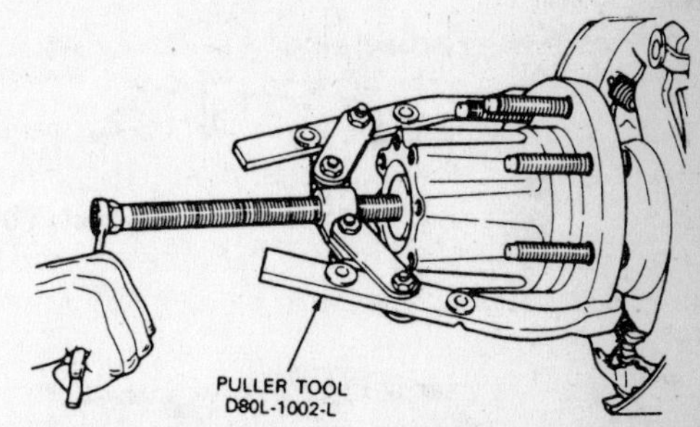

Loosening the hub on the 10.25 inch full-floating axle

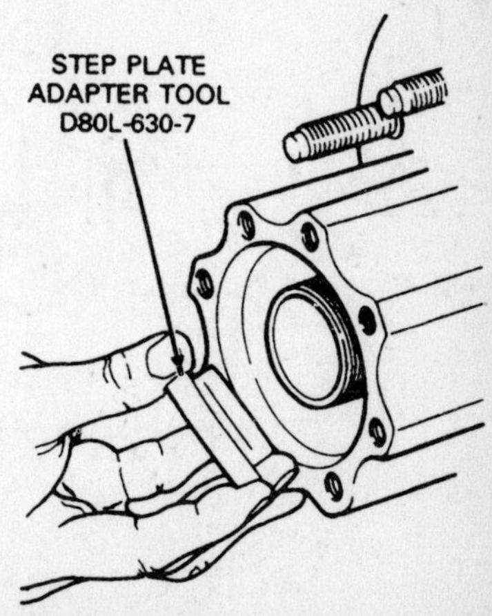

Installing the step plate adapter tool on the 10.25 inch full-floating axle

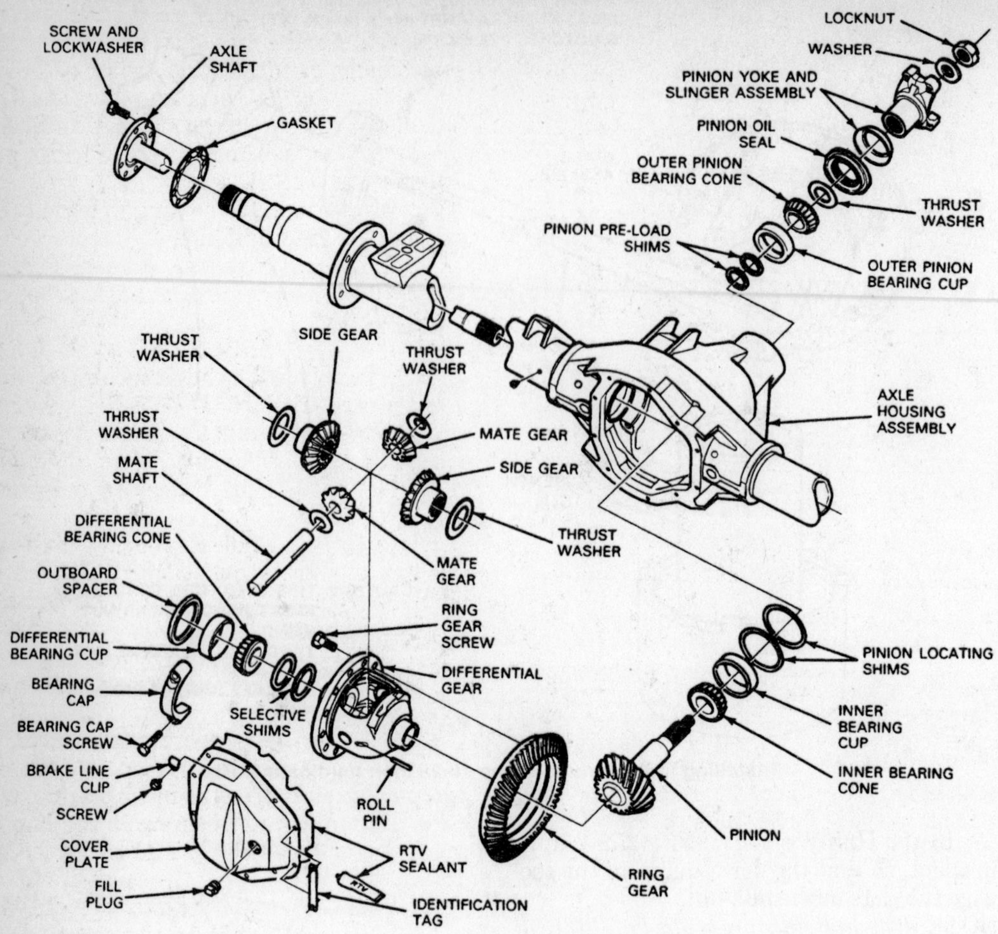

Dana 80 exploded view

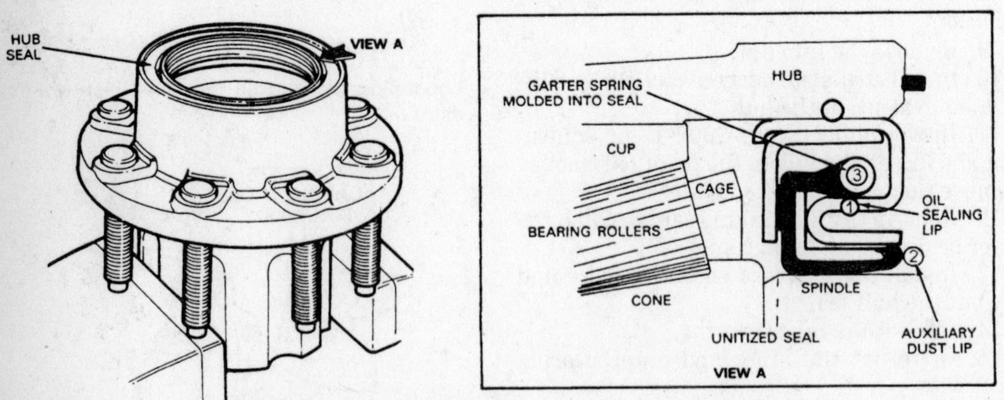

Unitized rear wheel seals on the 10.25 inch full-floating axle

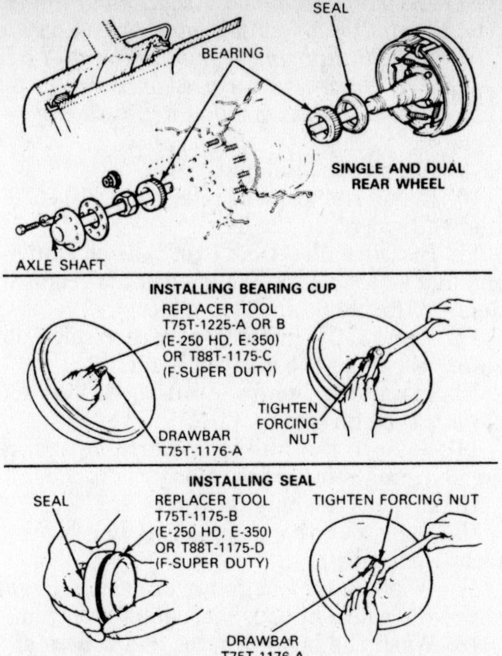

Installation of the rear wheel bearings and seal on the Dana 80 rear axle

18. Coat the race bores with a light coat of clean, waterproof wheel bearing grease and drive the races squarely into the bores until they are fully seated. A good indication that the race is seated is when you notice the grease from the bore squishing out under the race when it contact the shoulder. Another indication is a definite change in the metallic tone when you seat the race. Just be very careful to avoid damaging the bearing surface of the race!

19. Pack each bearing cone and roller with a bearing packer or in the manner outlined in Chapter 1 for the front wheel bearings on 2-Wheel Drive trucks.

20. Place the inner bearing cone and roller assembly in the wheel hub.

NOTE: *When installing the new seal, the words OIL SIDE must go inwards towards the bearing!*

21. Place the seal squarely in the hub and drive it into place. The best tool for the job is a seal driver such as T85T–1175–AH, which will stop when the seal is at the proper depth.

NOTE: *If the seal is misaligned or damaged during installation, a new seal must be installed.*

22. Clean the spindle thoroughly. If the spindle is excessively pitted, damaged or has a predominately bluish tint (from overheating), it must be replaced.

23. Coat the spindle with 80W/90 oil.

24. Pack the hub with clean, waterproof wheel bearing grease.

25. Pack the outer bearing with clean, waterproof wheel bearing grease in the same manner as you packed the inner bearing.

26. Place the outer bearing in the hub and install the hub and bearing together on the spindle.

27. Install the hub nut on the spindle. Make sure that the nut tab is located in the keyway

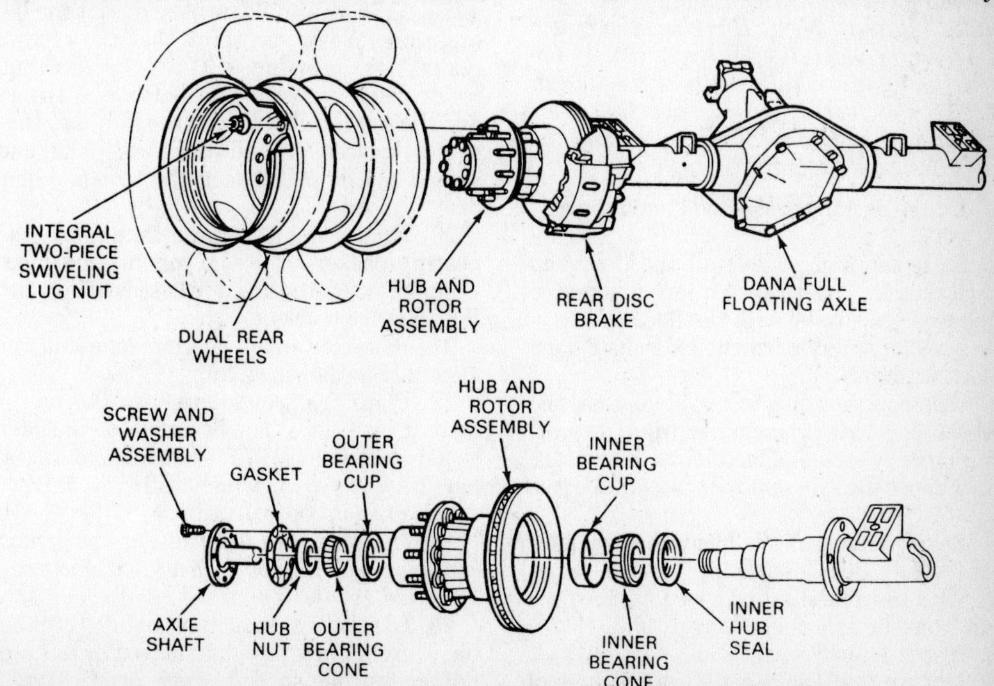

Rear wheel hub on the Dana full-floating used on the F-Super Duty

prior to thread engagement. Turn the hub nut onto the threads as far as you can by hand, noting the thread direction.

28. Install the hub wrench tool and tighten the nut to 55–65 ft. lbs. Rotate the hub occasionally during nut tightening.

29. Ratchet the nut back 5 teeth. **Make sure that you hear 5 clicks!**

30. Inspect the axle shaft O-ring seal and replace it if it looks at all bad.

31. Install the axle shaft.

32. Coat the axle shaft bolt threads with waterproof seal and install them by hand until they seat. **Do not tighten them with a wrench at this time!**

33. Check the diameter across the center of the brake shoes. Check the diameter of the brake drum. Adjust the brake shoes so that their diameter is 0.030 in. (0.76mm) less than the drum diameter.

34. Install the brake drum

36. Install the wheel.

37. Loosen the differential filler plug. If lubricant starts to run out, retighten the plug. If not, remove the plug and fill the housing with 80W/90 gear oil.

38. Lower the truck to the floor.

39. Tighten the wheel lugs to 140 ft. lbs.

40. Now tighten the axle shaft bolts. Torque them to 60–80 ft. lbs.

Dana Model 80

CAUTION: *New Dual Rear Wheel models have flat-faced lug nut replacing the old cone-shaped lug nuts. NEVER replace these new nuts with the older design! Never replace the newer designed wheels with older design wheels! The newer wheels have lug holes with special shoulders to accommodate the newly designed lug nuts.*

1. Set the parking brake and loosen the axle shaft bolts.

2. Raise the rear wheels off the floor and place jackstands under the rear axle housing so that the axle is parallel with the floor.

3. Remove and discard the axle shaft bolts and lock washers.

4. Using a heavy duty wheel dolly, raise the wheels until all weight is removed from the bearings. If no dolly is available, remove the wheels.

5. Remove the axle shaft and discard the gaskets.

6. Remove the brake caliper and suspend it out of the way. See Chapter 9.

7. With the axle shaft removed, remove the gasket from the axle shaft flange studs.

8. Install Hub Wrench T85T–4252–AH, or equivalent, so that the drive tangs on the tool engage the slots in the hub nut.

NOTE: *The hub nuts are right hand thread on the right hub and left hand thread on the left hub. The hub nuts should be stamped RH and LH. Never use power or impact tools on these nuts! The nuts will ratchet during removal.*

9. Remove the hub nut.

10. Install step plate adapter tool D80L–630–7, or equivalent, in the hub.

11. Install puller D80L–1002–L, or equivalent and loosen the hub to the point of removal. Remove the puller and step plate.

12. Remove the hub, taking care to catch the outer bearing as the hub comes off.

13. Install the hub in a soft-jawed vise and pry out the hub seal.

14. Remove the hub-to-brake rotor attaching bolts and remove the rotor.

15. Lift out the inner bearing.

16. Drive out the inner and outer bearing races with a drift.

17. Wash all the old grease or axle lubricant out of the wheel hub, using a suitable solvent.

18. Wash the bearing races and rollers and inspect them for pitting, galling, and uneven wear patterns. Inspect the roller for end wear. Replace any bearing and race that appears in any way damaged. Always replace the bearings and races as a set.

19. Coat the race bores with a light coat of clean, waterproof wheel bearing grease and drive the races squarely into the bores until they are fully seated. A special tool, such as bearing cup replacer T75T–1225–A and drawbar T75T–1176–A, should be used to seat the bearing races. When you think that the races are seated, try inserting a 0.0015 in. (0.038mm) feeler gauge between the bottom of the race and the seating shoulder in the hub. Try this at several places around the race. The gauge should not enter between the race and shoulder.

20. Pack each bearing cone and roller with a bearing packer or in the manner outlined in Chapter 1 for the front wheel bearings on 2-Wheel Drive trucks.

21. Place the inner bearing cone and roller assembly in the wheel hub.

22. Place the seal squarely in the hub and drive it into place. The best tool for the job is a seal driver such as T75T–1175–B and threaded bar T75T–1176–A, which will stop when the seal is at the proper depth.

NOTE: *If the seal is misaligned or damaged during installation, a new seal must be installed.*

23. Clean the spindle thoroughly. If the spindle is excessively pitted, damaged or has a predominately bluish tint (from overheating), it must be replaced.

24. Coat the spindle with 80W/90 oil.
25. Pack the hub with clean, waterproof wheel bearing grease.
26. Pack the outer bearing with clean, waterproof wheel bearing grease in the same manner as you packed the inner bearing.
27. Install the rotor. Coat the bolts with thread locking compound and torque them to 74–89 ft. lbs.
28. Install the hub on the spindle, taking great care to avoid damaging the spindle threads.
29. Install the outer bearing in the hub.
30. Install the hub nut on the spindle. Make sure that the nut tab is located in the keyway prior to thread engagement. Turn the hub nut onto the threads as far as you can by hand, noting the thread direction.
31. Install the hub wrench tool and tighten the nut to 55–65 ft. lbs. Rotate the hub occasionally during nut tightening.
32. Ratchet the nut back 5 teeth. **Make sure that you hear 5 clicks!**
33. Inspect the axle shaft O-ring seal and replace it if it looks at all bad.
34. Install the axle shaft.
35. Coat the axle shaft bolt threads with waterproof seal and install them by hand until they seat. **Do not tighten them with a wrench at this time!**
36. Install the wheel.
37. Loosen the differential filler plug. If lubricant starts to run out, retighten the plug. If not, remove the plug and fill the housing with 80W/90 gear oil.
38. Lower the truck to the floor.
38. Tighten the wheel lugs to 140 ft. lbs.
39. Now tighten the axle shaft bolts. Torque them to 40–55 ft. lbs.
40. Adjust the brakes.

Pinion Seal

REMOVAL AND INSTALLATION

Ford 8.8 in. (223.5mm) Ring Gear Integral Carrier Axle

NOTE: *A torque wrench capable of at least 225 ft. lbs. is required for pinion seal installation.*

1. Raise and safely support the vehicle with jackstands under the frame rails. Allow the axle to drop to rebound position for working clearance.
2. Remove the rear wheels and brake drums. No drag must be present on the axle.
3. Mark the companion flanges and U-joints for correct reinstallation position.
4. Remove the driveshaft.
5. Using an inch pound torque wrench and socket on the pinion yoke nut measure the amount of torque needed to maintain differential rotation through several clockwise revolutions. Record the measurement.

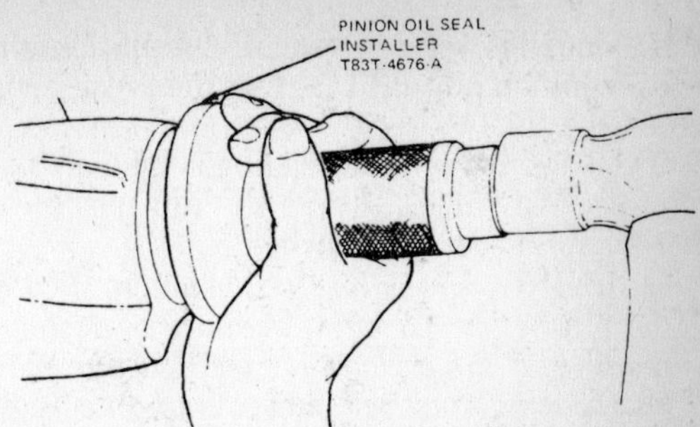

Pinion seal installation for the Ford 8.8 inch rear axle

6. Use a suitable tool to hold the companion flange. Remove the pinion nut.
7. Place a drain pan under the differential, clean the area around the seal, and mark the yoke-to-pinion relation.
8. Use a 2-jawed puller to remove the pinion.
9. Remove the seal with a small prybar.
10. Thoroughly clean the oil seal bore.

NOTE: *If you are not absolutely certain of the proper seal installation depth, the proper seal driver must be used. If the seal is misaligned or damaged during installation, it must be removed and a new seal installed.*

11. Drive the new seal into place with a seal driver such as T83T–4676–A. Coat the seal lip with clean, waterproof wheel bearing grease.
12. Coat the splines with a small amount of wheel bearing grease and install the yoke, aligning the matchmarks. Never hammer the yoke onto the pinion!
13. Install a NEW nut on the pinion.
14. Hold the yoke with a holding tool. Tighten the pinion nut to at least 160 ft. lbs., taking frequent turning torque readings until the original preload reading is attained.

If the original preload reading, that you noted before disassembly, is lower than the specified reading of 8–14 inch lbs. for used bearings;

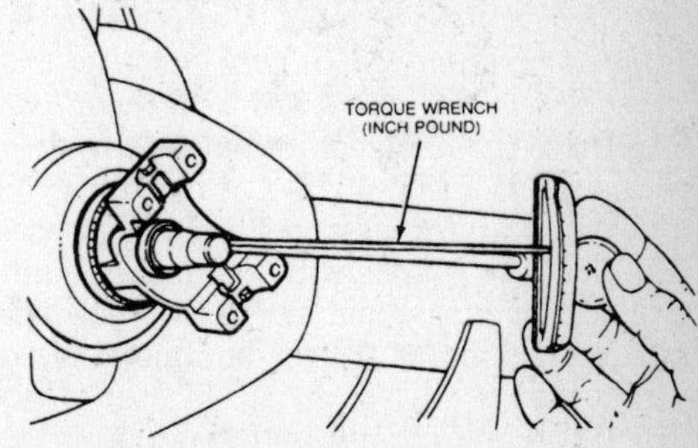

Measuring pinion bearing preload

16–29 inch lbs. for new bearings, keep tightening the pinion nut until the specified reading is reached.

If the original preload reading is higher than the specified values, torque the nut just until the original reading is reached.

WARNING: *Under no circumstances should the nut be backed off to reduce the preload reading! If the preload is exceeded, the yoke and bearing must be removed and a new collapsible spacer must be installed. The entire process of preload adjustment must be repeated.*

15. Install the driveshaft using the matchmarks. Torque the nuts to 15 ft. lbs.

Ford 10.25 in. (260.35mm) Ring Gear Integral Carrier Axle

NOTE: *A torque wrench capable of at least 225 ft. lbs. is required for pinion seal installation.*

1. Raise and safely support the vehicle with jackstands under the frame rails. Allow the axle to drop to the rebound position for working clearance.
2. Remove the rear wheels and brake drums. No drag must be present on the axle.
3. Mark the companion flanges and U-joints for correct reinstallation position.
4. Remove the driveshaft.
5. Using an inch pound torque wrench and socket on the pinion yoke nut measure the amount of torque needed to maintain differential rotation through several clockwise revolutions. Record the measurement.
6. Use a suitable tool to hold the companion flange. Remove the pinion nut.
7. Place a drain pan under the differential, clean the area around the seal, and mark the yoke-to-pinion relation.
8. Use a 2-jawed puller to remove the pinion.
9. Remove the seal with a small prybar.
10. Thoroughly clean the oil seal bore.

NOTE: *If you are not absolutely certain of the proper seal installation depth, the proper seal driver must be used. If the seal is misaligned or damaged during installation, it must be removed and a new seal installed.*

11. Drive the new seal into place with a seal driver such as T83T–4676–A. Coat the seal lip with clean, waterproof wheel bearing grease.
12. Coat the splines with a small amount of wheel bearing grease and install the yoke, aligning the matchmarks. Never hammer the yoke onto the pinion!
13. Install a NEW nut on the pinion.
14. Hold the yoke with a holding tool. Tighten the pinion nut to at least 160 ft. lbs., taking frequent turning torque readings until the original preload reading is attained.

If the original preload reading, that you noted before disassembly, is lower than the specified reading of 8–14 inch lbs. for used bearings; 16–29 inch lbs. for new bearings, keep tightening the pinion nut until the specified reading is reached.

If the original preload reading is higher than the specified values, torque the nut just until the original reading is reached.

WARNING: *Under no circumstances should the nut be backed off to reduce the preload reading! If the preload is exceeded, the yoke and bearing must be removed and a new collapsible spacer must be installed. The entire process of preload adjustment must be repeated.*

15. Install the driveshaft using the matchmarks. Torque the nuts to 15 ft. lbs.

Dana 80

NOTE: *A torque wrench capable of at least 275 ft. lbs. is required for pinion seal installation.*

1. Raise and safely support the vehicle with jackstands under the frame rails. Allow the axle to drop to the rebound position for working clearance.
2. Remove the rear wheels and brake drums. No drag must be present on the axle.
3. Mark the companion flanges and U-joints for correct reinstallation position.
4. Remove the driveshaft.
5. Use a suitable tool to hold the companion flange. Remove the pinion nut.
6. Place a drain pan under the differential, clean the area around the seal, and mark the yoke-to-pinion relation.
7. Use a 2-jawed puller to remove the pinion.
8. Remove the seal with a small prybar.
9. Thoroughly clean the oil seal bore.

NOTE: *If you are not absolutely certain of the proper seal installation depth, the proper seal driver must be used. If the seal is misaligned or damaged during installation, it must be removed and a new seal installed.*

10. Coat the new oil seal with wheel bearing grease. Install the seal using oil seal driver T56T–4676–B. After the seal is installed, make sure that the seal garter spring has not become dislodged. If it has, remove and replace the seal.
11. Install the yoke, using flange replacer

tool D81T–4858–A if necessary to draw the yoke into place.

12. Install a new pinion nut and washer. Torque the nut to 250–270 ft. lbs.

13. Connect the driveshaft. Torque the fasteners to 15–20 ft. lbs.

Axle Housing

REMOVAL AND INSTALLATION

Ford 8.8 in. (223.5mm) Ring Gear Integral Carrier
Ford 10.25 in. (260.35mm) Ring Gear Semi-Floating Integral Carrier

1. Raise and support the rear end on jackstands under the rear frame members, and support the housing with a floor jack.

2. Matchmark and disconnect the driveshaft at the axle.

3. Remove the wheels and brake drums.

4. Disengage the brake line from the clips that retain the line to the housing.

5. Disconnect the vent tube from the housing.

6. Remove the axle shafts.

7. Remove the brake backing plate from the housing, and support them with wire. Do not disconnect the brake line.

8. Disconnect each rear shock absorber from the mounting bracket stud on the housing.

9. Lower the axle slightly to reduce some of the spring tension. At each rear spring, remove the spring clip (U-bolt) nuts, spring clips, and spring seat caps.

10. Remove the housing from under the vehicle.

To Install:

1. Position the axle housing under the rear springs. Install the spring clips (U-bolts), spring seat clamps and nuts. Tighten the spring clamps evenly to 115 ft. lbs.

2. If a new axle housing is being installed, remove the bolts that attach the brake backing plate and bearing retainer from the old housing flanges. Position the bolts in the new housing flanges to hold the brake backing plates in position. Torque the bolts to 40 ft. lbs.

3. Install the axle shafts.

4. Connect the vent tube to the housing.

5. Position the brake line to the housing, and secure it with the retaining clips.

6. Raise the axle housing and springs enough to allow connecting the rear shock absorbers to the mounting bracket studs on the housing. Torque the nuts to 60 ft. lbs.

7. Connect the driveshaft to the axle. Torque the nuts to 8-15 ft. lbs.

8. Install the brake drums and wheels.

Ford 10.25 in. (260.35mm) Ring Gear Full Floating Integral Carrier

1. Raise and support the rear end on jackstands under the rear frame members, and support the housing with a floor jack.

2. Matchmark and disconnect the driveshaft at the axle.

3. Remove the wheels and brake drums.

4. Disengage the brake line from the clips that retain the line to the housing.

5. Disconnect the vent tube from the housing.

6. Remove the hubs.

7. Remove the brake backing plate from the housing, and support them with wire. Do not disconnect the brake line.

8. Disconnect each rear shock absorber from the mounting bracket stud on the housing.

9. Lower the axle slightly to reduce some of the spring tension. At each rear spring, remove the spring clip (U-bolt) nuts, spring clips, and spring seat caps.

10. Remove the housing from under the vehicle.

To Install:

1. Position the axle housing under the rear springs. Install the spring clips (U-bolts), spring seat clamps and nuts. Tighten the spring clamps evenly to 200 ft. lbs.

2. If a new axle housing is being installed, remove the bolts that attach the brake backing plate and bearing retainer from the old housing flanges. Position the bolts in the new housing flanges to hold the brake backing plates in position. Torque the bolts to 40 ft. lbs.

3. Connect the vent tube to the housing.

4. Position the brake line to the housing, and secure it with the retaining clips.

5. Raise the axle housing and springs enough to allow connecting the rear shock absorbers to the mounting bracket studs on the housing. Torque the nuts to 60 ft. lbs.

6. Connect the driveshaft to the axle. Torque the nuts to 20 ft. lbs.

7. Install the brake drums and wheels.

Dana Axles

1. Disconnect the shock absorbers from the rear axle.

2. Loosen the rear axle shaft nuts.

3. Raise and support the rear end on jackstands placed under the frame.

4. Remove the rear wheels.

5. Disconnect the rear stabilizer bar.

6. Disconnect the brake hose at the frame.

7. Disconnect the parking brake cable at the equalizer and remove the cables from the support brackets.

8. Matchmark the driveshaft-to-axle flange position.

9. Disconnect the driveshaft from the rear axle and move it out of the way.

10. Take up the weight of the axle with a floor jack.

11. Remove the nuts from the spring U-bolts and remove the spring seat caps.

12. Lower the axle and roll it from under the van.

13. Installation is the reverse of removal. Torque the spring U-bolt nuts to 160 ft. lbs. Bleed the brake system.

Suspension and Steering

WHEELS

CAUTION: *Some aftermarket wheels may not be compatible with these vehicles. The use of incompatible wheels may result in equipment failure and possible personal injury! Use only approved wheels!*

Front or Rear Wheels

REMOVAL AND INSTALLATION

Bronco
F-150 and 250
F-350 with Single Rear Wheels

1. Set the parking brake and block the opposite wheel.
2. On trucks with an automatic transmission, place the selector lever in **P**. On trucks with a manual transmission, place the transmission in reverse.
3. If equipped, remove the wheel cover.
4. Break loose the lug nuts.
5. Raise the truck until the tire is clear of the ground.
6. Remove the lug nuts and remove the wheel.

To install:

7. Clean the wheel lugs and brake drum or hub of all foreign material.
8. Position the wheel on the hub or drum and hand-tighten the lug nuts. Make sure that the coned ends face inward.
9. Using the lug wrench, tighten all the lugs, in a criss-cross fashion until they are snug.
10. Lower the truck. Tighten the nuts, in the sequence shown, to 100 ft. lbs. for 5-lug wheels; 140 ft. lbs. for 8-lug wheels.

Front Wheels

REMOVAL AND INSTALLATION

F-350 with Dual Rear Wheels
F-Super Duty

CAUTION: *Use only integral 2-piece, swiveling lug nuts. Do not attempt to use cone-shaped, one-piece lugs. The use of cone-shaped nuts will cause the nuts to come loose during vehicle operation!*
Do not attempt to use older-style wheels that use cone-shaped lug nuts. This practice will also cause the wheels to come loose!

1. Set the parking brake and block the opposite wheel.
2. On trucks with an automatic transmission, place the selector lever in **P**. On trucks with a manual transmission, place the transmission in reverse.

Wheel Alignment Specifications
F-Super Duty
(Caster and camber angles are not adjustable)

Ride Height (mm)	Caster (deg.) Range	Caster (deg.) Pref.	Camber (deg.) Range	Camber (deg.) Pref.	Toe-in (in.)	Front Wheel Angle (deg.)
108.0	—	5 1/4P	—	3/5P	1/32	9.6

For the F-Super Duty, ride height is the measured distance between the bottom of the metal rebound stop to the top of the front spring plate spacer.

Troubleshooting Basic Steering and Suspension Problems

Problem	Cause	Solution
Hard steering (steering wheel is hard to turn)	• Low or uneven tire pressure • Loose power steering pump drive belt • Low or incorrect power steering fluid • Incorrect front end alignment • Defective power steering pump • Bent or poorly lubricated front end parts	• Inflate tires to correct pressure • Adjust belt • Add fluid as necessary • Have front end alignment checked/adjusted • Check pump • Lubricate and/or replace defective parts
Loose steering (too much play in the steering wheel)	• Loose wheel bearings • Loose or worn steering linkage • Faulty shocks • Worn ball joints	• Adjust wheel bearings • Replace worn parts • Replace shocks • Replace ball joints
Car veers or wanders (car pulls to one side with hands off the steering wheel)	• Incorrect tire pressure • Improper front end alignment • Loose wheel bearings • Loose or bent front end components • Faulty shocks	• Inflate tires to correct pressure • Have front end alignment checked/adjusted • Adjust wheel bearings • Replace worn components • Replace shocks
Wheel oscillation or vibration transmitted through steering wheel	• Improper tire pressures • Tires out of balance • Loose wheel bearings • Improper front end alignment • Worn or bent front end components	• Inflate tires to correct pressure • Have tires balanced • Adjust wheel bearings • Have front end alignment checked/adjusted • Replace worn parts
Uneven tire wear	• Incorrect tire pressure • Front end out of alignment • Tires out of balance	• Inflate tires to correct pressure • Have front end alignment checked/adjusted • Have tires balanced

Wheel Alignment Specifications
F-250 and F-350 4x2

Ride Height (mm)	Caster (deg.)		Camber (deg.)		Toe-in (in.)	Front Wheel Angle (deg.)
	Range	Pref.	Range	Pref.		
70–80	—	—	$2\frac{7}{10}$N to $\frac{1}{2}$N	$\frac{3}{4}$N	$\frac{1}{32}$	12.5
80–90	$7\frac{1}{2}$P to $10\frac{1}{2}$P	9P	$1\frac{1}{2}$N to $\frac{1}{2}$P	$\frac{1}{2}$N	$\frac{1}{32}$	12.5
90–100	$6\frac{1}{2}$P to 10P	$8\frac{1}{4}$P	2N to $\frac{1}{2}$P	$1\frac{1}{2}$N	$\frac{1}{32}$	12.5
100–110	$5\frac{3}{4}$P to $8\frac{3}{4}$P	$7\frac{1}{4}$P	$\frac{1}{4}$P to $2\frac{1}{2}$P	$1\frac{3}{8}$P	$\frac{1}{32}$	12.5
110–120	$4\frac{3}{4}$P to $7\frac{3}{4}$P	$6\frac{1}{4}$P	1P to 4P	$2\frac{1}{2}$P	$\frac{1}{32}$	12.5
120–130	$3\frac{1}{2}$P to $6\frac{3}{4}$P	$4\frac{7}{8}$P	$2\frac{1}{2}$P to 5P	$3\frac{3}{4}$P	$\frac{1}{32}$	12.5
130–140	$2\frac{3}{4}$P to $5\frac{1}{2}$P	$4\frac{1}{8}$P	—	—	$\frac{1}{32}$	12.5

Caster and Camber are determined based on ride height.
For all 2-wheel drive models, ride height is the measured distance between the bottom of the front spring tower and the top of the front axle beam, measured at the rebound bumper.

Wheel Alignment Specifications
F-150 4x4 and Bronco

Ride Height (mm)	Caster (deg.)		Camber (deg.)		Toe-in (in.)	Front Wheel Angle (deg.)
	Range	Pref.	Range	Pref.		
80–90	5P to 8P	6 1/2P	1 1/2N to 1/2P	1/2N	1/32	13.0
90–100	4P to 7P	5 1/2P	3/4N to 1 3/4P	1/2P	1/32	13.0
100–110	3P to 6P	4 1/2P	1/4P to 2 1/2P	1 1/2P	1/32	13.0
110–120	2P to 5P	3 1/2P	1 1/4P to 3 1/2P	2 3/8P	1/32	13.0

Caster and Camber are determined based on ride height.
For the F-150 4x4, ride height is the measured distance between the bottom of the front spring tower and the top of the front axle tube, measured at the rebound bumper.

Wheel Alignment Specifications
F-150 4x2

Ride Height (mm)	Caster (deg.)		Camber (deg.)		Toe-in (in.)	Front Wheel Angle (deg.)
	Range	Pref.	Range	Pref.		
80–90	5 1/2P to 7 1/2P	6 1/4P	1 1/8N to 1 1/4P	0	1/32	12.5
90–100	4 1/4P to 7 1/4P	5 3/4P	1/2N to 2P	3/4P	1/32	12.5
100–110	3 1/4P to 6 1/4P	4 3/4P	1/2P to 3P	1 3/4P	1/32	12.5
110–120	2 3/8P to 5 3/8P	3 7/8P	1 1/2P to 3 1/2P	2 3/4P	1/32	12.5
120–130	1 1/2P to 4 1/2P	3P	2 3/8P to 4 3/8P	3 3/8P	1/32	12.5
130–140	3/8P to 3 3/8P	1 7/8P	3 3/8P to 5 1/2P	4 7/16P	1/32	12.5

Caster and Camber are determined based on ride height.
For all 2-wheel drive models, ride height is the measured distance between the bottom of the front spring tower and the top of the front axle beam, measured at the rebound bumper.

Wheel Alignment Specifications
F-250 4x4

Ride Height (mm)	Caster (deg.)		Camber (deg.)		Toe-in (in.)	Front Wheel Angle (deg.)
	Range	Pref.	Range	Pref.		
125–140	3 1/16P to 5 1/8P	4 1/8P	1 3/4N to 5/8P	9/16P	1/32	13.0
140–150	3 1/4P to 5 1/4P	4 1/4P	3/4N to 1 3/4P	1/2P	1/32	13.0
150–160	3 3/8P to 5 3/8P	4 3/8P	3/8P to 3P	1 11/16P	1/32	13.0
160–175	3 7/16P to 5 1/2P	4 19/23P	1 1/2P to 4 1/4P	2 3/4P	1/32	13.0

Caster and Camber are determined based on ride height.
For the F-250 4x4, ride height is the measured distance between the bottom of the frame and the top of the front axle tube, measured at the rebound bumper.

Wheel Alignment Specifications
F-350 4x4

Ride Height (mm)	Caster (deg.) Range	Caster (deg.) Pref.	Camber (deg.) Range	Camber (deg.) Pref.	Toe-in (in.)	Front Wheel Angle (deg.)
95.25–111.75	6 1/4P to 10P	8 1/8P	3/4N to 1 1/2P	3/4P	1/32	8
111.75–124.5	5P to 8 1/4P	6 5/8P	1/4P to 2 1/2P	1 3/8P	1/32	8
124.5–137.2	3 3/4P to 7P	5 1/4P	1 1/4P to 3 1/2P	2 3/8P	1/32	8
137.2–146.0	3 1/4P to 5 3/4P	4 1/2P	2 3/8P to 4 1/8P	3 1/4P	1/32	8

Caster and Camber are determined based on ride height.
For the F-350 4x4, ride height is the measured distance between the bottom of the metal rebound stop to the top of the front spring plate spacer.

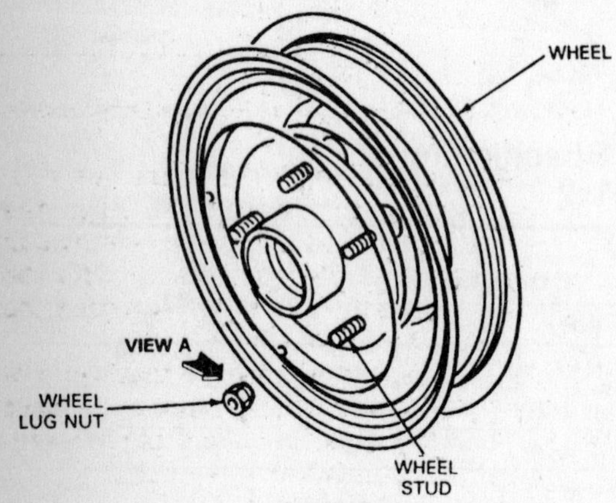

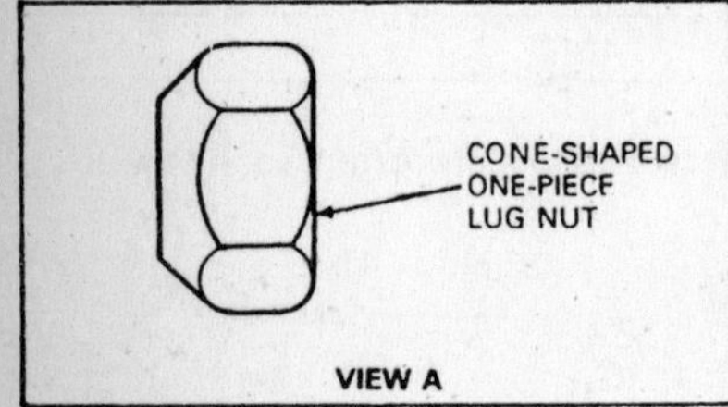

5-lug wheel installation

3. If equipped, remove the wheel cover.
4. Break loose the lug nuts.
5. Raise the truck until the tire is clear of the ground.
6. Remove the lug nuts and remove the wheel.

To install:

7. Clean the wheel lugs and brake drum or hub of all foreign material.
8. Position the wheel on the hub or drum and hand-tighten the lug nuts.
9. Using the lug wrench, tighten all the lugs, in a criss-cross fashion until they are snug.
10. Lower the truck. Tighten the nuts, in the sequence shown, to 140 ft. lbs.

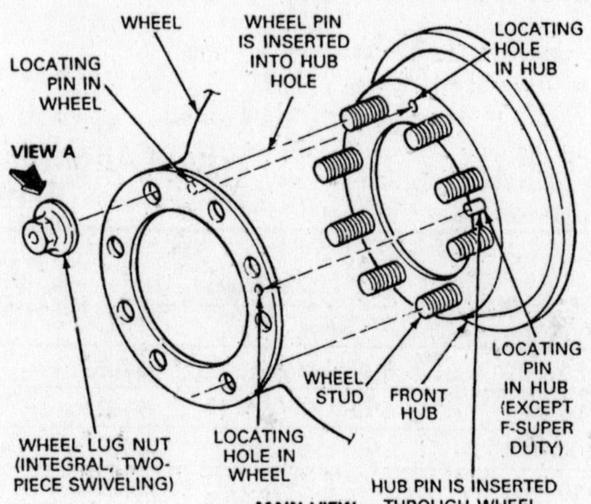

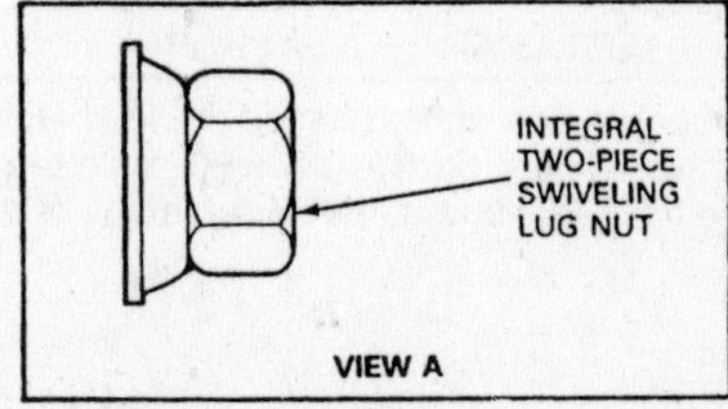

Front wheel installation for F-350 w/dual rear wheels and F-Super Duty. The 10-lug wheel is identical except for the number of wheel lugs

Dual Rear Wheels

REMOVAL AND INSTALLATION

CAUTION: *Use only integral 2-piece, swiveling lug nuts. Do not attempt to use cone-shaped, one-piece lugs. The use of cone-shaped nuts will cause the nuts to come loose during vehicle operation!*
Do not attempt to use older-style wheels that use cone-shaped lug nuts. This practice will also cause the wheels to come loose!

NOTE: *F-Super Duty models require the use of center-pilot type wheels.*

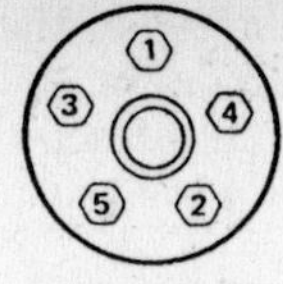

5 LUG WHEEL

TIGHTEN LUG NUTS
IN THIS SEQUENCE

8 LUG WHEEL

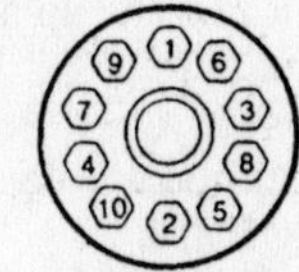

10 LUG WHEEL
(F-SUPER DUTY P40/P45)

Wheel lug torque sequence

1. Set the parking brake and block the opposite wheel.
2. On trucks with an automatic transmission, place the selector lever in **P**. On trucks with a manual transmission, place the transmission in reverse.
3. If equipped, remove the wheel cover.
4. Break loose the lug nuts.
5. Raise the truck until the tire is clear of the ground.
6. Remove the lug nuts and remove the wheel(s).

To install:

7. Clean the wheel lugs and brake drum or hub of all foreign material.

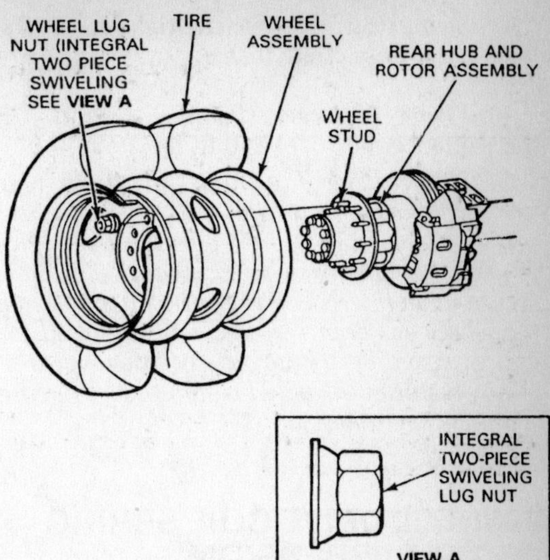

Rear wheel installation for all F-Super Duty models

8. Mount the inner wheel on the hub with the dished (concave) side inward. Align the wheel with the small indexing hole – located in the wheel between the stud holes – with the alignment pin on the hub. Make sure that the wheel is flush against the hub.
9. Install the outer wheel so that the protruding (convex) side is flush against the inner wheel. Make sure that the alignment pin is protruding through the wheel index hole.
10. Hand-tighten the lug nuts.

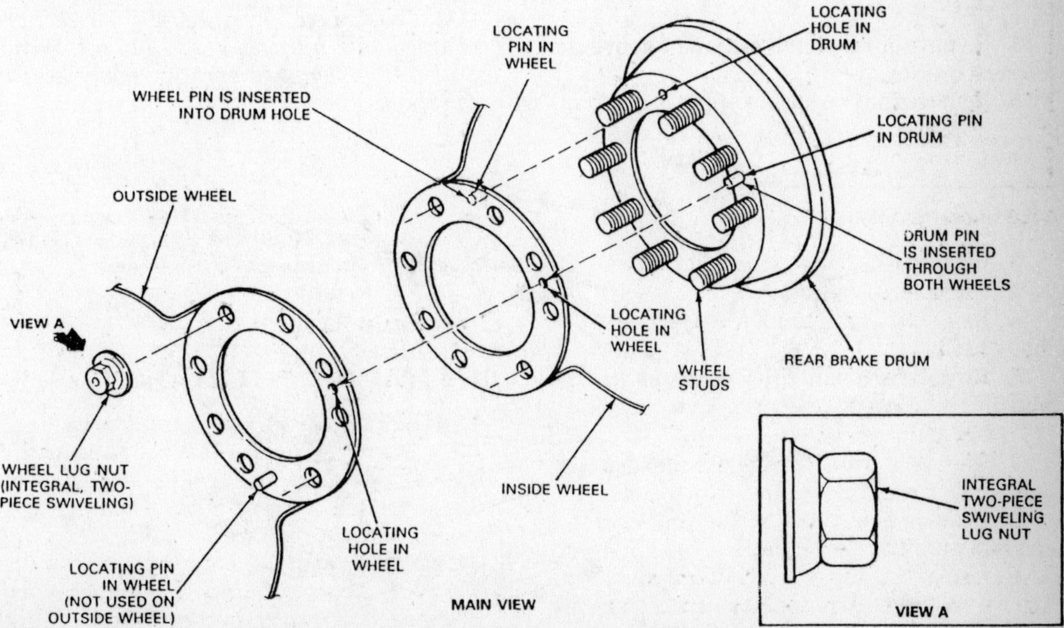

Rear wheel installation for F-350 w/dual rear wheels

11. Using the lug wrench, tighten all the lugs, in a criss-cross fashion until they are snug.

10. Lower the truck. Tighten the nuts, in the sequence shown, to 140 ft. lbs.

CAUTION: *The lug nuts on dual rear wheels should be retightened after the first 100 miles of new-vehicle operation. The lug nuts on dual rear wheels should be retightened at an interval of 500 miles after anytime a wheel has been removed and installed for any reason! Failure to observe this procedure may result in the wheel coming loose during vehicle operation!*

2-WHEEL DRIVE COIL SPRING FRONT SUSPENSION

Trucks with 2-Wheel Drive and coil springs use two I-beam type front axles; one for each wheel. One end of each axle is attached to the spindle and a radius arm, and the other end is attached to a frame pivot bracket on the opposite side of the truck.

Springs

REMOVAL AND INSTALLATION

1. Raise the front of the vehicle and place jackstands under the frame and a jack under the axle.
2. Remove the wheels.
3. Disconnect the shock absorber from the lower bracket.
4. Remove one bolt and nut and remove the rebound bracket.
5. Remove the two spring upper retainer attaching bolts from the top of the spring upper seat and remove the retainer.
6. Remove the nut attaching the spring lower retainer to the lower seat and axle and remove the retainer.
7. Place a safety chain through the spring to prevent it from suddenly coming loose. Slowly lower the axle and remove the spring.

To install:

8. Place the spring in position and raise the front axle.
9. Position the spring lower retainer over the stud and lower seat, and install the two attaching bolts.
10. Position the upper retainer over the spring coil and against the spring upper seat, and install the two attaching bolts.
11. Tighten the upper retaining bolts to 13–18 ft. lbs.; the lower retainer attaching nuts to 70–100 ft. lbs.
12. Connect the shock absorber to the lower bracket. Torque the bolt and nut to 40–60 ft. lbs. Install the rebound bracket.
13. Remove the jack and safety stands.

Shock Absorbers

Most of these trucks are equipped with hydraulic shock absorbers as standard equipment. Some, however, are equipped with low pressure gas shock absorbers as standard equipment and all are available with gas shocks as optional equipment.

CAUTION: *Low pressure gas shocks are charged with nitrogen gas to 135 psi. Do not puncture, attempt to open, or apply heat to the shock absorbers.*

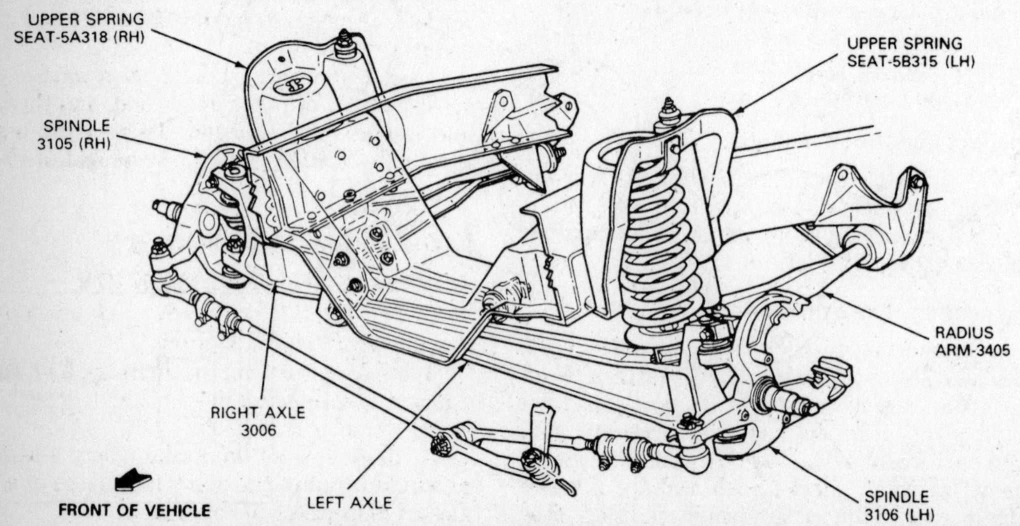

2-wheel drive Twin I-Beam front suspension, w/ball joints

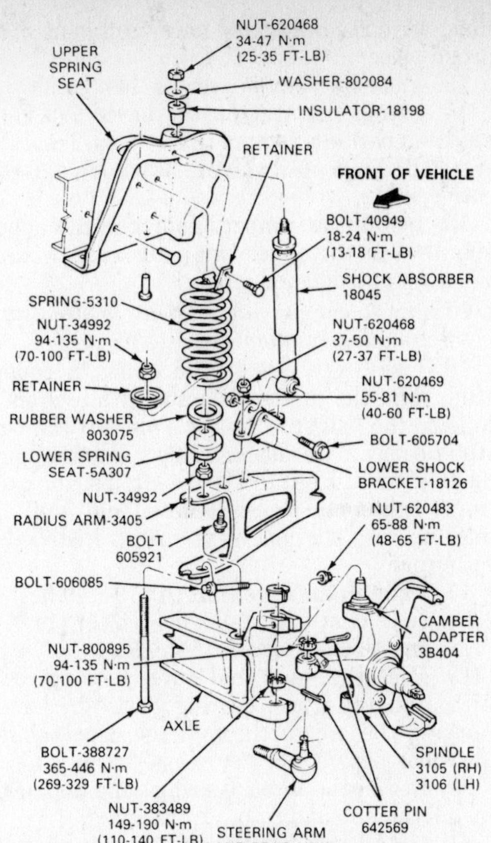

Front spring and shock absorber installation for the 2-wheel drive F-150, 250, and 350, w/ball joints

TESTING

Bounce Test

Each shock absorber can be tested by bouncing the corner of the truck until maximum up and down movement is obtained. Let go of the truck. It should stop bouncing in 1–2 bounces. If not, the shock should be inspected for damage and possibly replaced.

Inspect the Shock Mounts

Check the shock mountings for worn or defective grommets, loose mounting nuts, interference or missing bump stops. If no apparent defects are noted, continue testing.

Inspecting Hydraulic Shocks for Leaks

Disconnect each shock lower mount and pull down on the shock until it is fully extended. inspect for leaks in the seal area. Shock absorber fluid is very thin and has a characteristic odor and dark brown color. Don't confuse the glossy paint on some shocks with leaking fluid. A slight trace of fluid is a normal condition; they are designed to seep a certain amount of fluid past the seals for lubrication. If you are in doubt as to whether the fluid on the shock is coming from the shock itself or from some other source, wipe the seal area clean and manually operate the shock (see the following procedure). Fluid will appear if the unit is leaking.

Manually Operating the Shocks

It may be necessary to fabricate a holding fixture for certain types of shock absorbers. If a suspected problem is in the front shocks, disconnect both front shock lower mountings.

NOTE: *When manually operating air shocks, the air line must be disconnected at the shock.*

Grip the lower end of the shock and pull down (rebound stroke) and then push up (compression stroke). The control arms will limit the movement of front shocks during the compression stroke. Compare the rebound resistance of both shocks and compare the compression resistance. Usually any shock showing a noticeable difference will be the one at fault.

If the shock has internal noises, extend the shock fully then exert an extra pull. If a small additional movement is felt, this usually means a loose piston and the shock should be replaced. Other noises that are cause for replacing shocks are a squeal after a full stroke in both directions, a clicking noise on fast reverse and a lag at reversal near mid-stroke.

REMOVAL AND INSTALLATION

To replace the front shock absorber, remove the self-locking nut, steel washer, and rubber bushings at the upper end of the shock absorber. Remove the bolt and nut at the lower end and remove the shock absorber.

When installing a new shock absorber, use new rubber bushings. Position the shock absorber on the mounting brackets with the stud end at the top.

Install the rubber bushing, steel washer and self-locking nut at the upper end, and the bolt and nut at the lower end. Tighten the upper end to 25–35 ft. lbs. and the lower end to 40–60 ft. lbs.

Front Wheel Spindle

REMOVAL AND INSTALLATION

NOTE: *All 2-Wheel Drive pick-ups utilize upper and lower ball joints.*

1. Jack up the front of the truck and safely support it with jackstands.
2. Remove the wheels.
3. Remove the front brake caliper assembly and hold it out of the way with a piece of wire. Do not disconnect the brake line.
4. Remove the brake rotor from the spindle.

5. Remove the inner bearing cone and seal. discard the seal, as you'll be fitting a new one during installation.

6. Remove the brake dust shield.

7. Disconnect the steering linkage from the spindle arm using a tie rod removal tool.

8. Remove the cotter from the upper and lower ball joint stud nuts. Discard the cotter pins, as new ones should be installed during reassembly.

9. Remove the upper ball joint nut and loosen the lower ball joint nut to the end of the threads.

10. Strike the inside area or the spindle as shown in the illustration to pop the ball joints loose from the spindle.

WARNING: *Do not use a forked ball joint removal tool to separate the ball joints as this damage the seal and ball joint socket.*

11. Remove the nut. Remove the spindle.

12. Before reassembly, note that new cotter pins should be used on the ball joints, and that new bearing seal(s) should also be used. Also, make sure the upper and lower ball joint seals are in place.

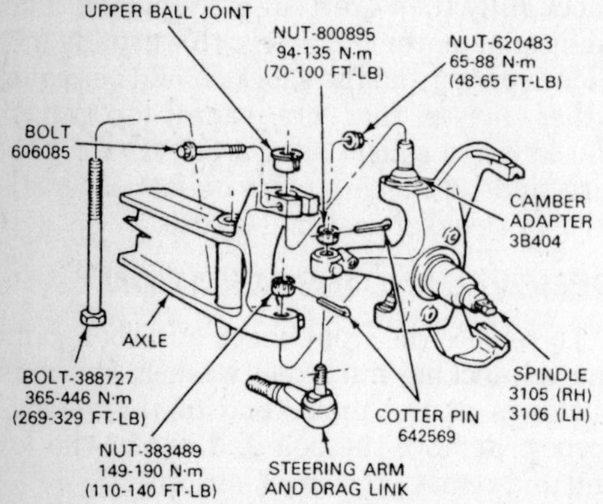

Front wheel spindle installation for the 2-wheel drive F-150, 250 and 350 with ball joints

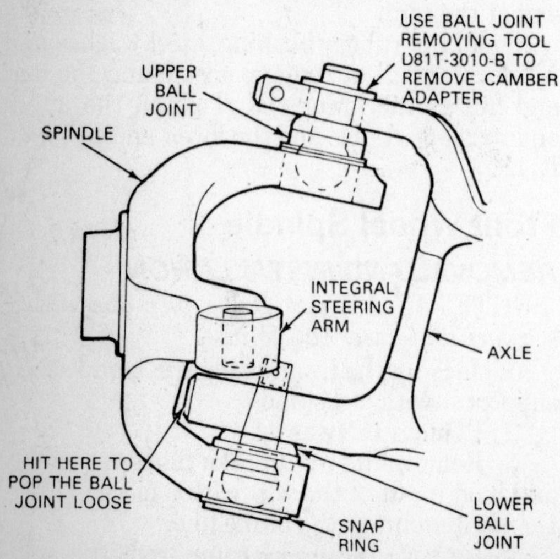

Spindle removal

13. Place the spindle over the ball joints.

14. Install the nuts on the lower ball joint stud and partially tighten to 35 ft. lbs. Turn the castellated nut until you are able to install the cotter pin.

15. Install the camber adapter in the upper spindle over the upper ball joint stud. Be sure the adapter is aligned properly.

NOTE: *If camber adjustment is necessary special adapters must be installed.*

16. Install the nut on the upper ball joint stud. Hold the camber adapter with a wrench to keep the ball stud from turning. If the ball stud turns, tap the adapter deeper into the spindle. Tighten the nut to 110–140 ft. lbs. and continue tightening the castellated nut until it lines up with the hole in the stud. Install the cotter pin.

17. Tighten the lower nut to 110–140 ft. lbs. Advance the nut to install a new cotter pin.

18. Install the brake dust shield.

19. Pack the inner and outer bearing cone with a quality wheel bearing grease by hand, working the grease through the cage behind the roller.

20. Install the inner bearing cone and seal. Install the hub and rotor on the spindle.

21. Install the outer bearing cone, washer, and nut. Adjust the bearing end-play and install the nut retainer, cotter pin and dust cap.

22. Install the brake caliper. connect the steering linkage to the spindle. Tighten the nut to 70–100 ft. lbs. and advance the nut as far necessary to install the cotter pin.

23. Install the wheels. Lower the truck and adjust toe-in if necessary.

Upper and Lower Ball Joints

INSPECTION

1. Before an inspection of the ball joints, make sure the front wheel bearings are properly packed and adjusted.

2. Jack up the front of the truck and safely support it with jackstands, placing the stands under the I-beam axle beneath the spring as shown in the accompanying illustration.

3. Have a helper grab the lower edge of the tire and move the wheel assembly in and out.

4. While the wheel is being moved, observe the lower spindle arm and the lower part of the axle jaw (the end of the axle to which the spindle assembly attaches). If there is $\frac{1}{32}$ in. (0.8mm) or greater movement between the lower part of the axle jaw and the lower spindle arm, the lower ball must be replaced.

5. To check upper ball joints, grab the upper edge of the tire and move the wheel in

and out. If there is $\frac{1}{32}$ in. (0.8mm) or greater movement between the upper spindle arm and the upper part of the jaw, the upper ball joint must be replaced.

REMOVAL

1. Remove the spindle as previously described.
2. Remove the snapring from the ball joints. Assemble the C-frame assembly T74P–4635–C and receiver cup D81T–3010–A, or equivalents, on the upper ball joint. Turn the forcing screw clockwise until the ball joint is removed from the axle.
3. Repeat step 2 on the lower ball joint.

NOTE: *The upper ball joint must always be removed first. DO NOT heat the ball joint or spindle!*

INSTALLATION

NOTE: *The lower ball joint must be installed first.*

1. To install the lower ball joint, assemble the C-frame with ball joint receiver cup D81T–3010–A5 and installation cup D81T–3010–A1, and turn the forcing screw clockwise until the ball joint is seated. DO NOT heat the ball joint to aid in installation!
2. Install the snapring onto the ball joint.
3. Install the upper ball joint in the same manner as the lower ball joint.
4. Install the spindle assembly.

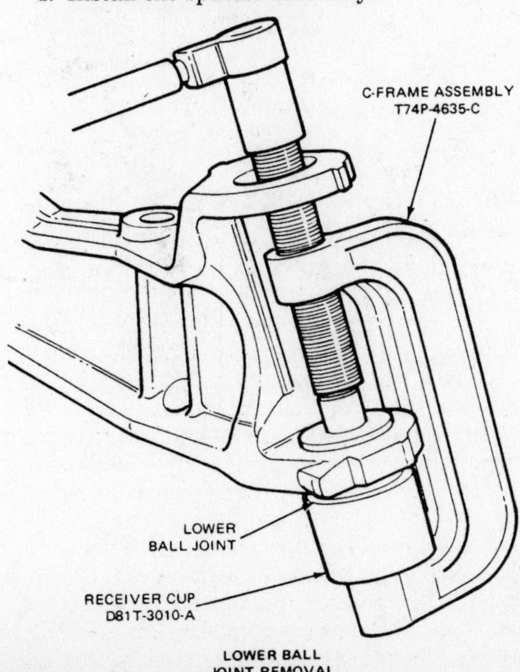

Lower ball joint removal

Radius Arm

REMOVAL AND INSTALLATION

NOTE: *A torque wrench with a capacity of at least 350 ft. lbs. is necessary, along with other special tools, for this procedure.*

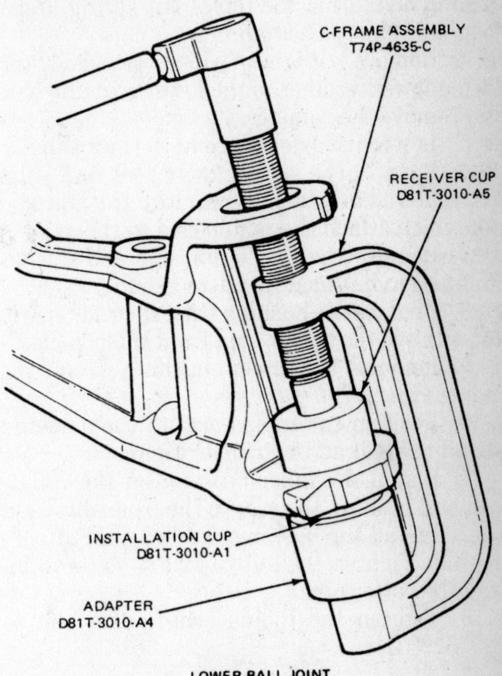

Lower ball joint installation

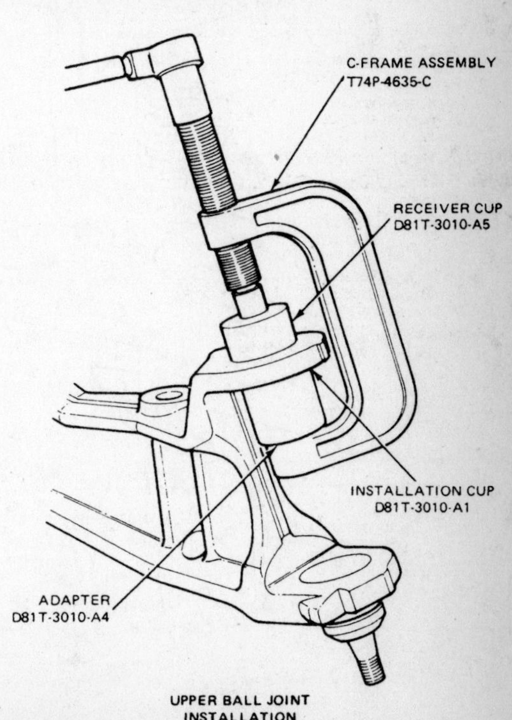

Upper ball joint installation

1. Raise the front of the vehicle and place safety stands under the frame and a jack under the wheel or axle. Remove the wheels.

2. Disconnect the shock absorber from the radius arm bracket.

3. Remove the two spring upper retainer attaching bolts from the top of the spring upper seat and remove the retainer.

4. Remove the nut which attached the spring lower retainer to the lower seat and axle and remove the retainer.

5. Lower the axle and remove the spring.

6. Remove the spring lower seat and shim from the radius arm. The, remove the bolt and nut which attach the radius arm to the axle.

7. Remove the cotter pin, nut and washer from the radius arm rear attachment.

8. Remove the bushing from the radius arm and remove the radius arm from the vehicle.

9. Remove the inner bushing from the radius arm.

10. Position the radius arm to the axle and install the bolt and nut finger-tight.

11. Install the inner bushing on the radius arm and position the arm to the frame bracket.

12. Install the bushing, washer, and attaching nut. Tighten the nut to 120 ft. lbs. and install the cotter pin.

13. Tighten the radius arm-to-axle bolt to 269–329 ft. lbs.

14. Install the spring seat and insulator on the radius arm so that the hole in the seat fits over the arm-to-axle nut.

15. Install the spring.

16. Connect the shock absorber. Torque the nut and bolt to 40–60 ft. lbs.

17. Install the wheels.

Stabilizer Bar

REMOVAL AND INSTALLATION

1. Raise and support the front end on jackstands.

2. Disconnect the right and left stabilizer bar ends from the link assembly.

3. Disconnect the retainer bolts and remove the stabilizer bar.

4. Disconnect the stabilizer link assemblies by loosening the right and left locknuts from their respective brackets. on the I-beams.

To install:

5. Loosely install the entire assembly. The links are marked with an **R** and **L** for identification.

6. Tighten the link-to-stabilizer bar and axle bracket fasteners to 70 ft. lbs.

7. Check to make sure that the insulators are properly seated and the stabilizer bar is centered.

8. On the F-150, torque the 6 stabilizer bar

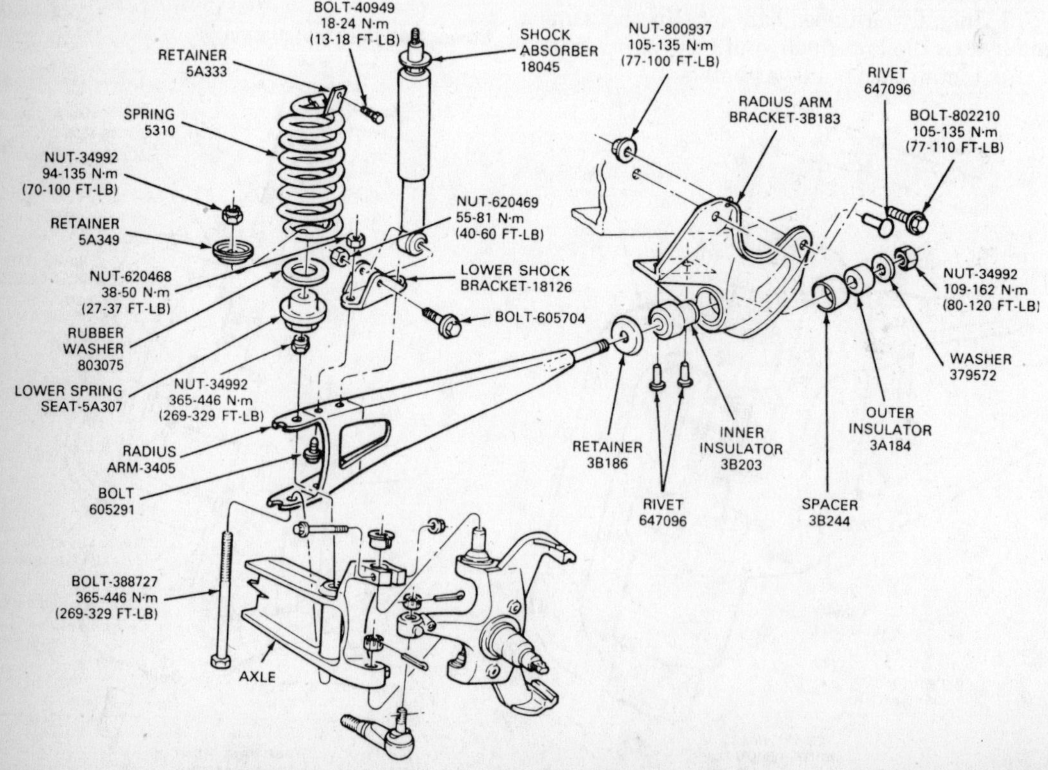

Radius arm installation for the 2-wheel drive F-150, 250, 350

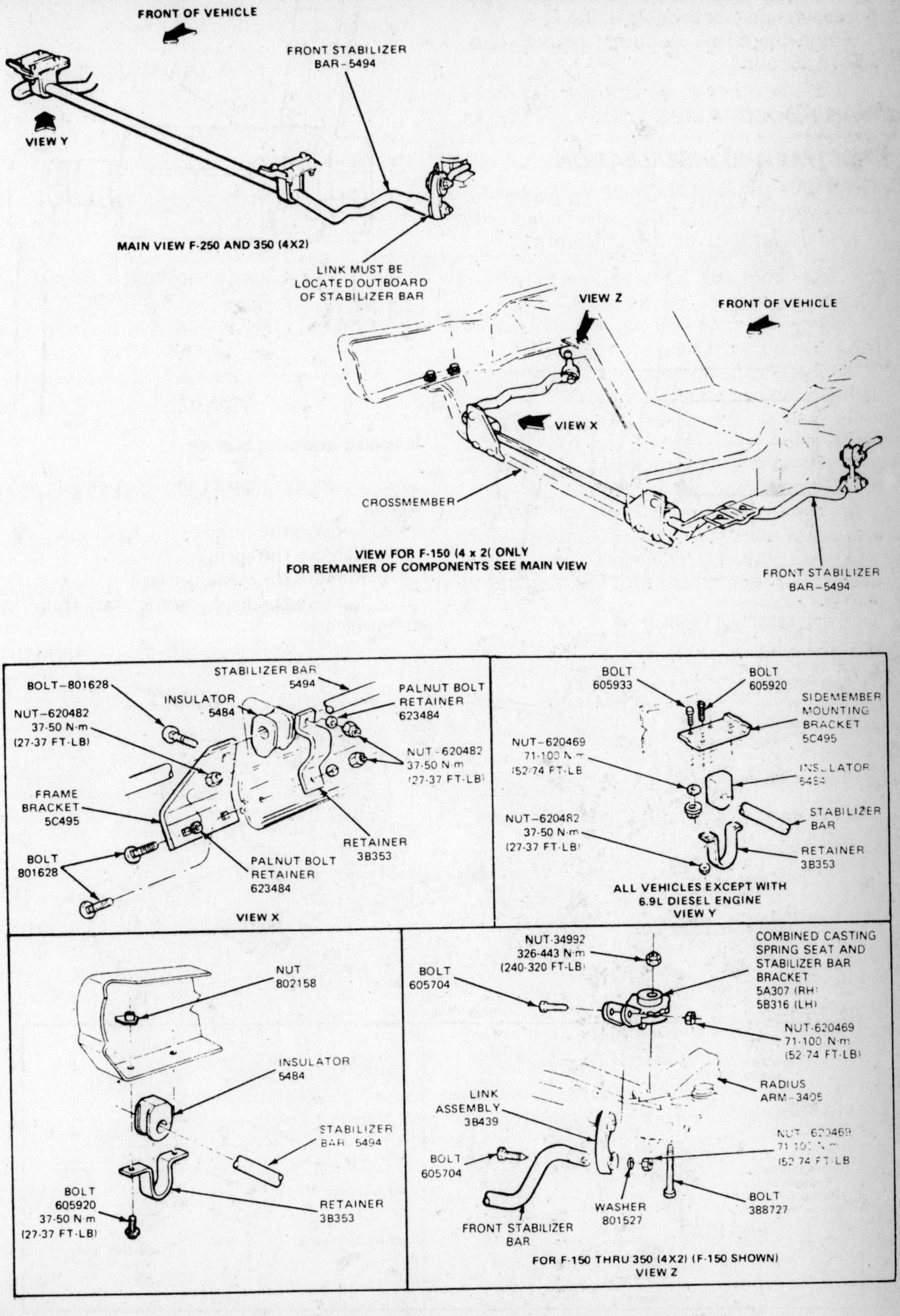

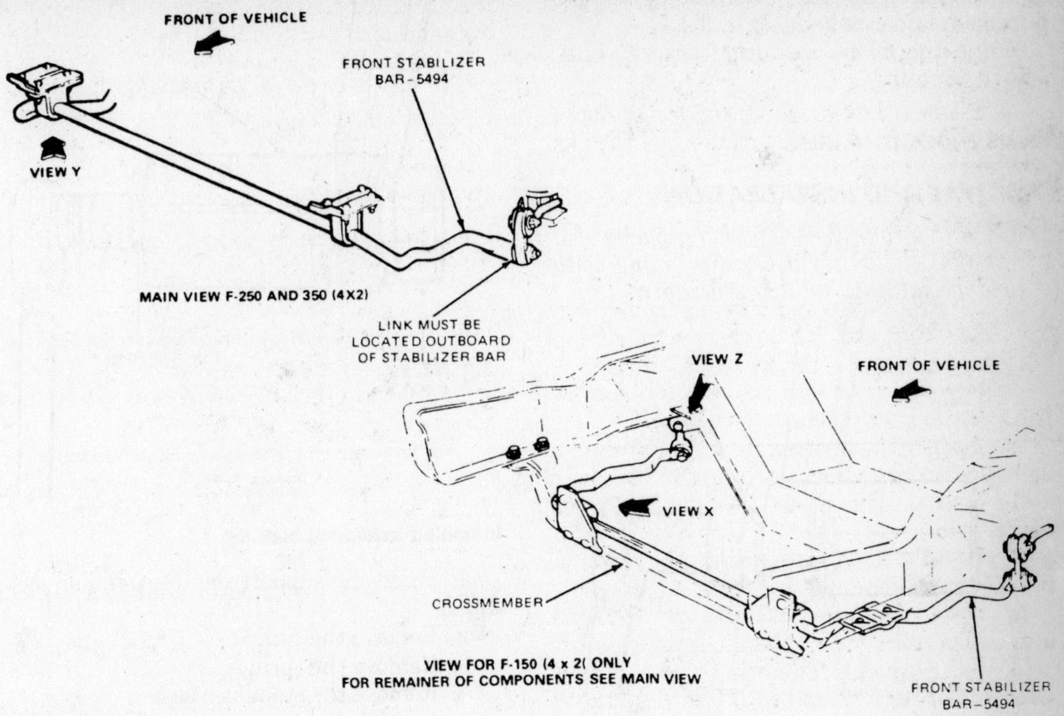

Front stabilizer bar installation for the 2-wheel drive F-150, 250, 350

to crossmember attaching bolts to 35 ft. lbs. On the F-250 and F-350, torque the stabilizer bar-to-frame retainer bolts to 35 ft. lbs.

Torque the frame mounting bracket nuts/bolts to 65 ft. lbs.

Twin I-Beam Axles

REMOVAL AND INSTALLATION

NOTE: *A torque wrench with a capacity of at least 350 ft. lbs. is necessary, along with other special tools, for this procedure.*

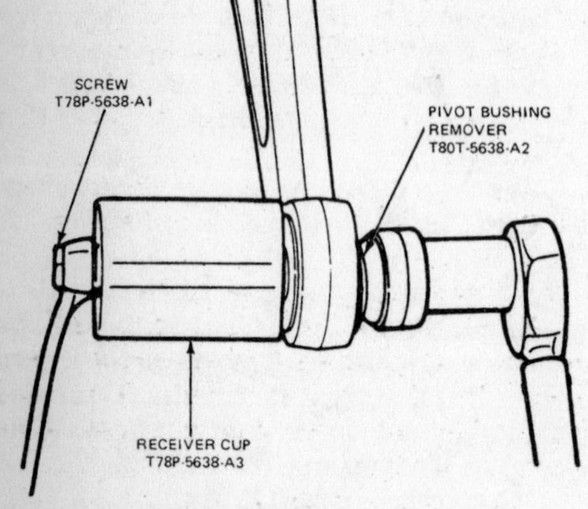

Removing axle pivot bushing

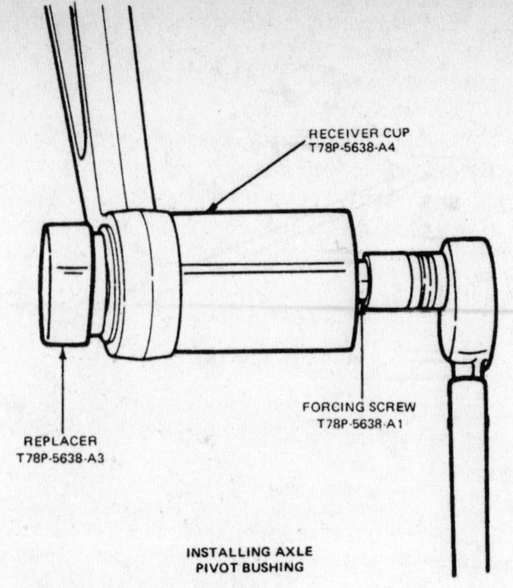

Installing axle pivot bushing

1. Raise and support the front end on jackstands.
2. Remove the spindles.
3. Remove the springs.
4. Remove the stabilizer bar.
5. Remove the lower spring seats from the radius arms.

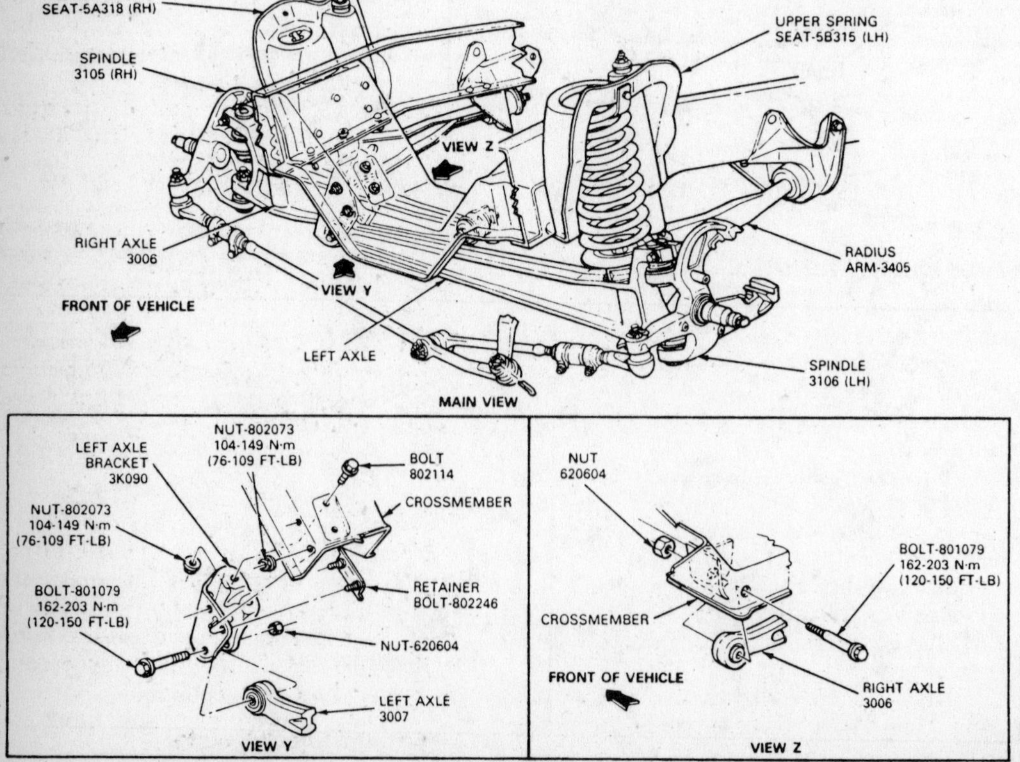

Axle pivot bracket and axle arm installation for the 2-wheel drive F-150, 250, 350

6. Remove the radius arm-to-axle bolts.

7. Remove the axle-to-frame pivot bolts and remove the axles.

To install:

8. Position the axle on the pivot bracket and loosely install the bolt/nut.

9. Position the other end on the radius arm and install the bolt. Torque the bolt to 269–329 ft. lbs.

10. Install the spring seats.

11. Install the springs.

12. Torque the axle pivot bolts to 120–150 ft. lbs.

13. Install the spindles.

14. Install the stabilizer bar.

2-WHEEL DRIVE LEAF SPRING FRONT SUSPENSION

The F-Super Duty chassis/cab utilizes leaf springs attached to a solid, I-beam type front axle. The springs are mounted on the axle with U-bolts and attached to the frame side rails by a fixed bracket at the rear and movable shackles at the front.

The F-Super Duty stripped chassis and motor home chassis utilize leaf springs attached to a solid, I-beam type front axle. The springs are mounted on the axle with U-bolts and attached to the frame side rails by a fixed bracket at the front and movable shackles at the rear.

Chassis/cab models also utilize a tracking bar between the left side of the No.1 crossmember and the right side of the axle beam, inboard of the right spring pad.

Springs

REMOVAL AND INSTALLATION

1. Raise and support the front end on jackstands with the tires still touching the ground.

2. Using jacks, take up the weight of the axle, off the U-bolts.

3. Disconnect the lower end of each shock absorber.

4. Disconnect the spring from the front bracket or shackle.

5. Disconnect the spring from the rear bracket or shackle.

6. Remove the U-bolt nuts.

7. Remove the U-bolts.

8. Disconnect the jack bracket or stabilizer bar as necessary.

9. Lower the axle slightly and remove the spring. Take note of the position of the spring spacer.

To install

10. Position the spring on its seat on the axle and raise it to align the front of the spring with the bracket or shackle.

11. Coat the bushing with silicone grease.

12. Carefully guide the attaching bolt through the bracket or shackle, and the bushing.

13. Install the nut and, depending on model or which bolts you removed, torque it to:

• chassis/cab spring-to-shackle: 120–150 ft. lbs.

• chassis/cab shackle-to-frame: 150–210 ft. lbs.

• stripped chassis or motor home chassis spring-to-bracket: 148–207 ft. lbs.

14. In a similar fashion, attach the rear of the spring. The torques are:

• chassis/cab spring-to-bracket: 150–210 ft. lbs.

• stripped chassis or motor home chassis spring-to-shackle or shackle-to-bracket: 74–110 ft. lbs.

15. Position the spacer on the spring.

16. Install the U-bolts. Install the jack bracket or stabilizer bar bracket on the forward U-bolt. Install the U-bolt nuts. Torque the nuts, evenly and in gradual increments, in a criss-cross fashion, to:

• chassis/cab: 150–210 ft. lbs.

• stripped chassis and motor home chassis: 220–300 ft. lbs.

17. Connect the shock absorbers. Torque them to:

• chassis/cab models, shock absorber-to-bracket nuts to 52–74 ft. lbs.

• stripped chassis or motor home chassis models, lower attaching bolt to 220–300 ft. lbs.

Shock Absorbers

These trucks are equipped with either hydraulic shock absorbers or with low pressure gas shock absorbers depending on equipment ordered.

CAUTION: *Low pressure gas shocks are charged with nitrogen gas to 135 psi. Do not puncture, attempt to open, or apply heat to the shock absorbers.*

TESTING

Bounce Test

Each shock absorber can be tested by bouncing the corner of the truck until maximum up and down movement is obtained. Let go of the truck. It should stop bouncing in 1–2 bounces. If not, the shock should be inspected for damage and possibly replaced.

Inspect the Shock Mounts

Check the shock mountings for worn or defective grommets, loose mounting nuts, inter-

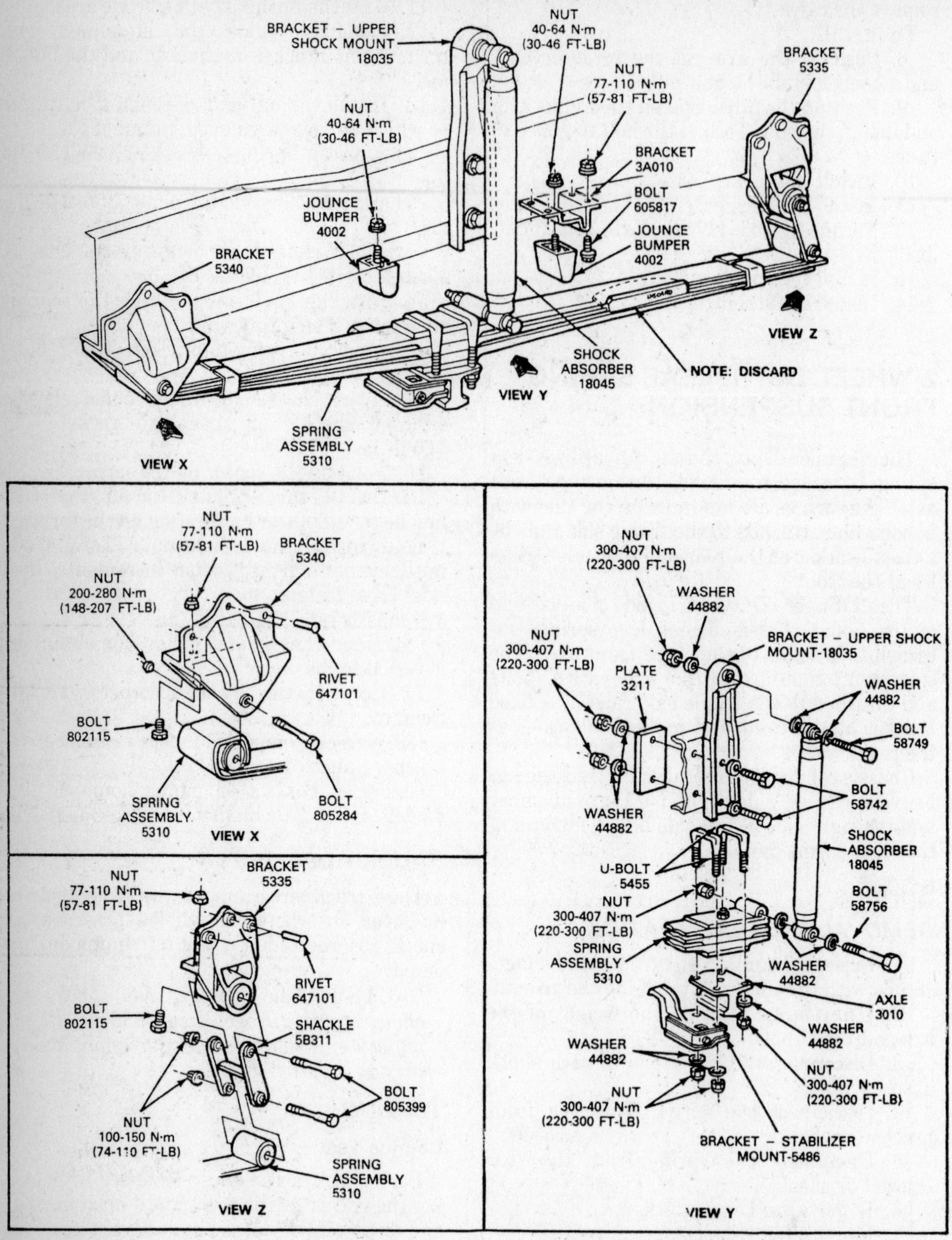

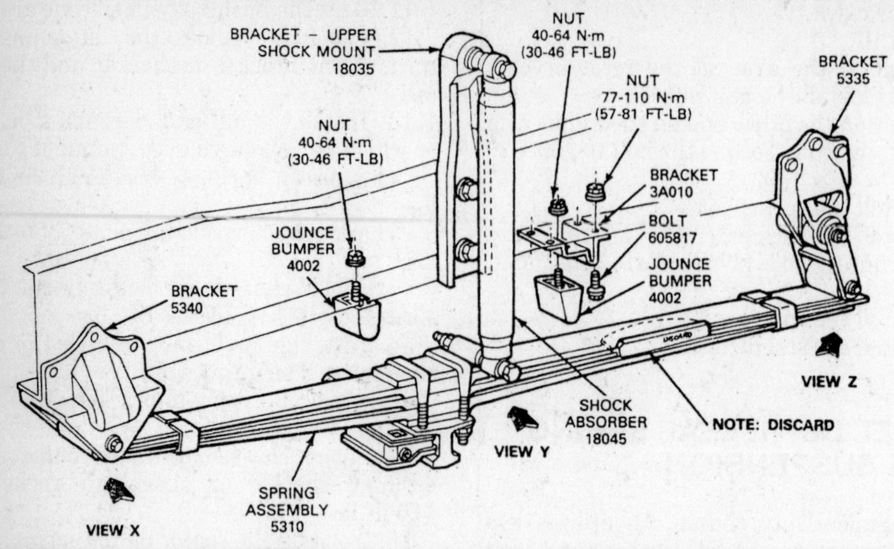

Front spring and shock absorber installation for F-Super Duty stripped chassis or motor home chassis models

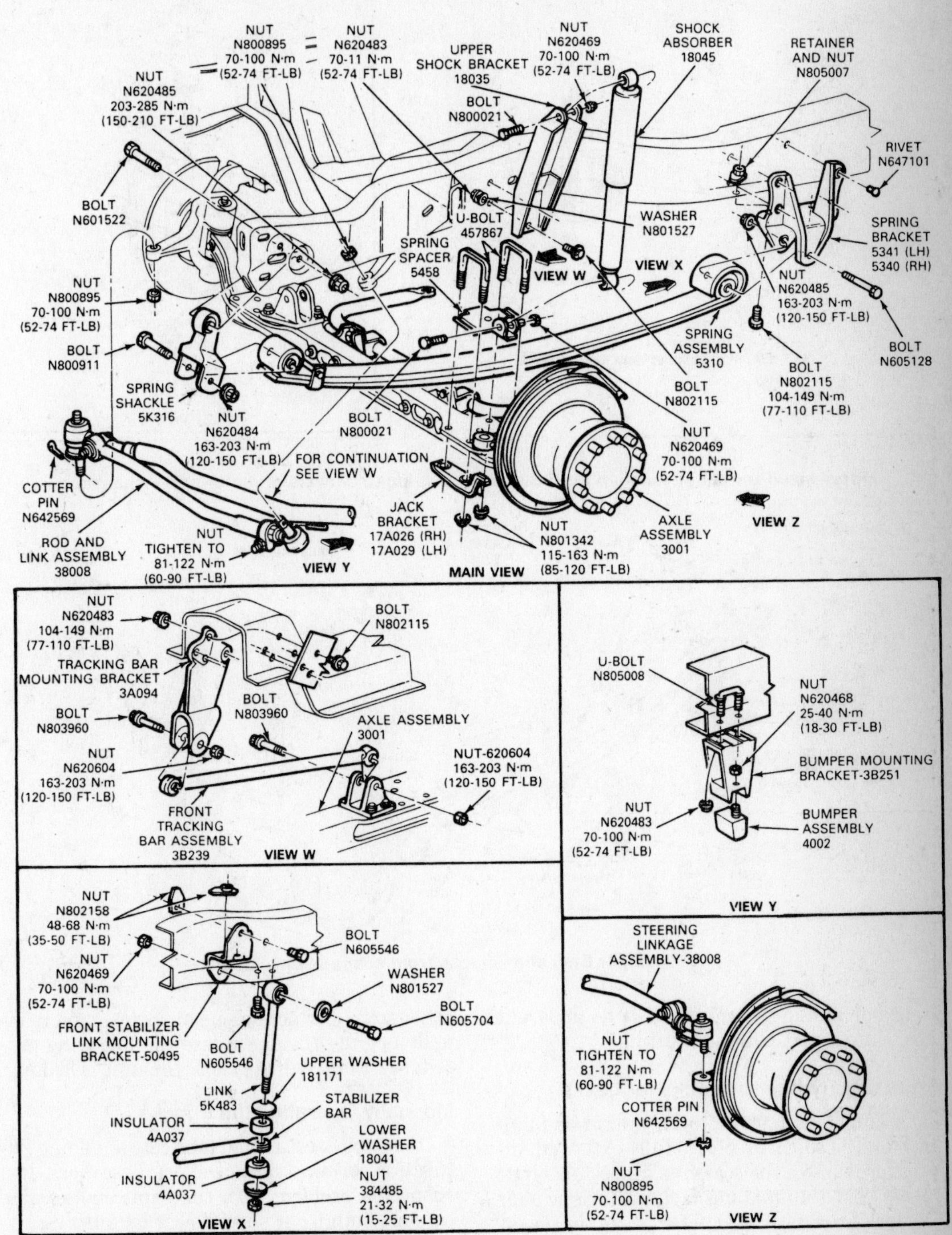

Front spring and shock absorber installation for F-Super Duty chassis/cab

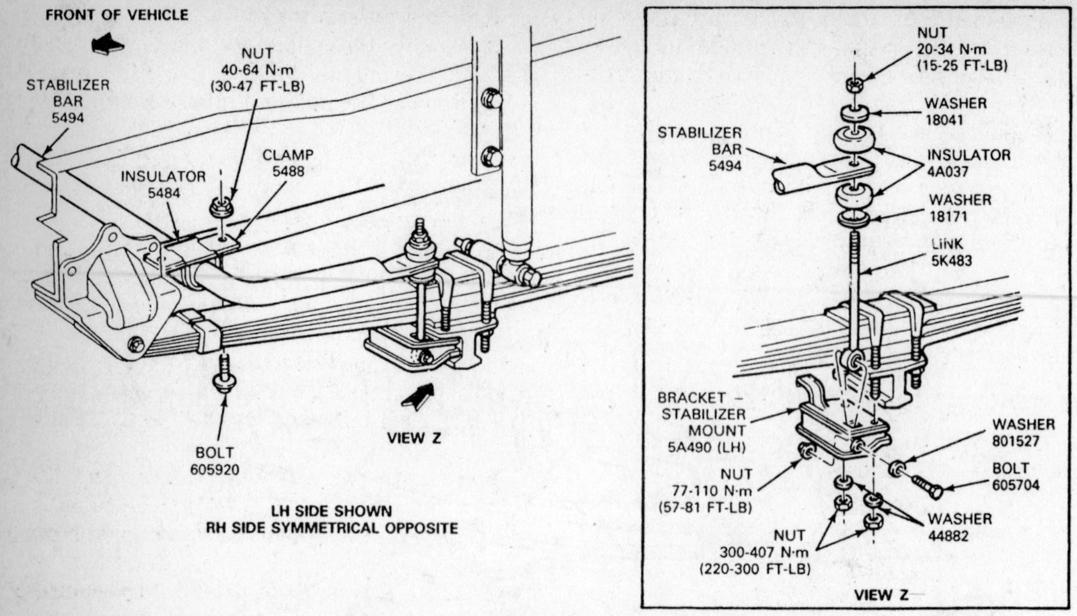

Front stabilizer bar installation for F-Super Duty stripped chassis or motor home chassis

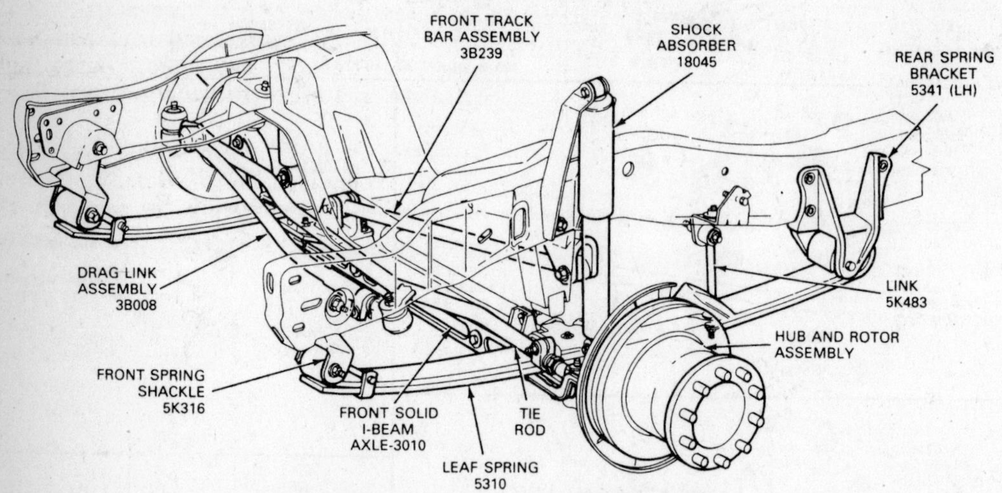

F-Super Duty chassis/cab front suspension

ference or missing bump stops. If no apparent defects are noted, continue testing.

Inspecting Hydraulic Shocks for Leaks

Disconnect each shock lower mount and pull down on the shock until it is fully extended. inspect for leaks in the seal area. Shock absorber fluid is very thin and has a characteristic odor and dark brown color. Don't confuse the glossy paint on some shocks with leaking fluid. A slight trace of fluid is a normal condition; they are designed to seep a certain amount of fluid past the seals for lubrication. If you are in doubt as to whether the fluid on the shock is coming from the shock itself or from some other source, wipe the seal area clean and manually operate the shock (see the following procedure). Fluid will appear if the unit is leaking.

Manually Operating the Shocks

It may be necessary to fabricate a holding fixture for certain types of shock absorbers. If a suspected problem is in the front shocks, disconnect both front shock lower mountings.

NOTE: *When manually operating air shocks, the air line must be disconnected at the shock.*

Grip the lower end of the shock and pull down (rebound stroke) and then push up (compression stroke). The control arms will limit the movement of front shocks during the compression stroke. Compare the rebound resistance of both shocks and compare the compression resistance. Usually any shock showing a noticeable difference will be the one at fault.

If the shock has internal noises, extend the shock fully then exert an extra pull. If a small additional movement is felt, this usually means a loose piston and the shock should be replaced. Other noises that are cause for replacing shocks are a squeal after a full stroke in both directions, a clicking noise on fast reverse and a lag at reversal near mid-stroke.

REMOVAL AND INSTALLATION

1. Remove the nut and bolt which retains the shock to the upper bracket.

2. Remove the nut (chassis/cab) or nut and bolt (stripped chassis and motor home chassis) that retains the lower end of the shock at the spring.

3. Installation is the reverse of removal. It's a good idea to lubricate the bushings with silicone grease prior to installation. Torque the fasteners as follows:

- chassis/cab upper and lower: 52–74 ft. lbs.
- stripped cab and motor home chassis upper and lower: 220–300 ft. lbs.

Spindles

REMOVAL AND INSTALLATION

1. Raise and support the front end on jackstands.

2. Remove the wheels.

3. Remove the caliper and suspend it out of the way. See Chapter 9.

4. Remove the hub and rotor assembly. See Chapter 9.

5. Remove the inner bearing and seal. Discard the seal.

6. Remove the dust shield.

7. Remove the cotter pin and nut, and, using a ball joint separator – the forcing screw type, not the fork type – disconnect the tie rod end from the spindle arm.

8. On stripped chassis and motor home models, disconnect the drag link from the steering arm using a forcing type ball joint separator.

9. Remove the nut and washer from the spindle bolt lock pin and remove the lock pin.

10. Remove the upper and lower spindle pin plugs.

11. Using a brass drift, drive out the spindle pin from the top and remove the spindle and thrust bearing.

12. Remove the thrust bearing and seal.

To install:

13. Clean the spindle pin bore and make sure it is free of corrosion, nicks or burrs. Light corrosion and other irregularities can be removed.

14. Lightly coat the bore with lithium based grease meeting ESA-M1C75-B rating.

15. Install a new spindle pin seal with the metal side facing up into the spindle. Gently

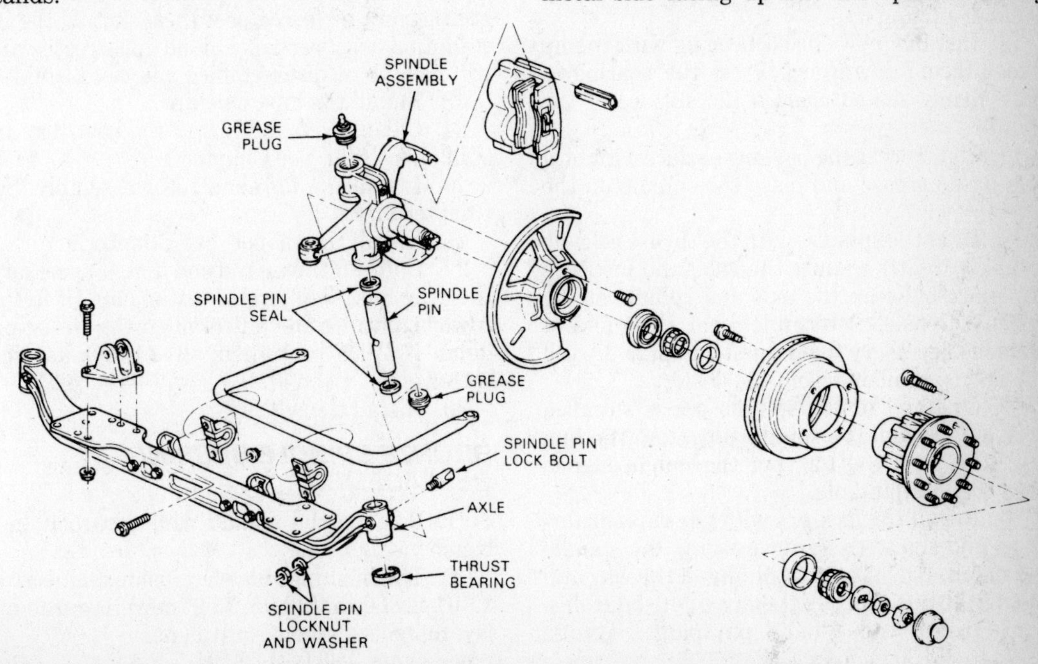

Front wheel spindle installation for F-Super Duty chassis/cab models

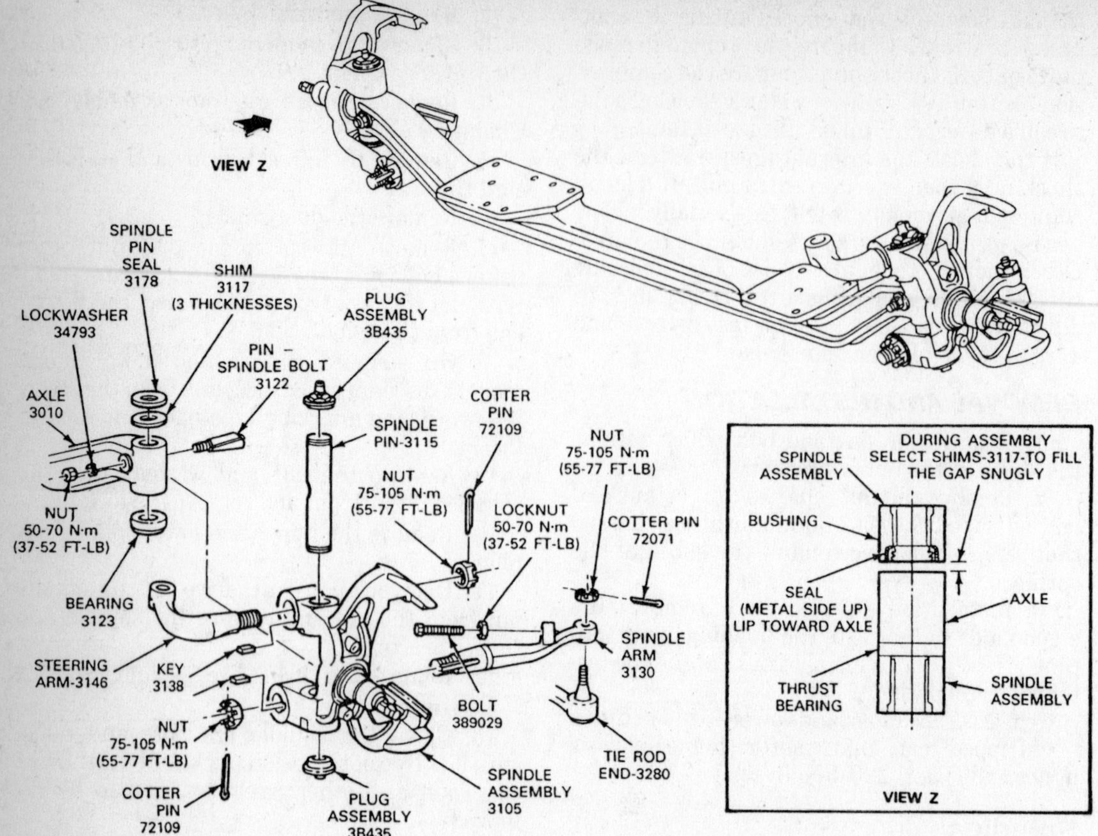

Front wheel spindle installation for F-Super Duty stripped chassis or motor home chassis models

press the seal into position being careful to avoid distorting it.

16. Install a new thrust bearing with the lip flange facing downward. Press the bearing in until firmly seated against the surface of the spindle.

17. Lightly coat the bushing surface with lithium based grease and place the spindle on the axle.

18. Hold the spindle, with the thrust bearing in place, tightly against the axle, and measure the space between the axle and spindle at the top of the axle. Determine what thickness of shims is necessary to eliminate all play. Install the shims, available from the dealer.

19. One end of the spindle pin is stamped with a **T**. Install the spindle pin, from the top, with the **T** at the top and the notch aligned with the lock pin hole.

20. Install the lock pin with the threads forward and the wedge groove facing the spindle pin notch. Drive the lock pin in all the way and install the nut. Torque the nut to 40–50 ft. lbs.

21. Install the spindle pin plugs. Torque them to 35–50 ft. lbs.

22. Lubricate the spindle pin through the fittings until grease seeps past the upper seal and the thrust bearing slip joint at the bottom. If grease can't be forced past these points, the installation was probably done incorrectly and will have to be disassembled and re-assembled.

23. Install the dust shield.

24. Clean, pack and install the bearings. Install a new seal. See Chapter 1.

25. Install the hub and rotor assembly. See Chapter 9.

26. Install the caliper. See Chapter 9.

27. Connect the tie rod end and, if necessary, the drag link. Tighten the nuts to 50–70 ft. lbs. Always advance the nut to align the cotter pin holes. NEVER back them off! Always use new cotter pins!

28. Install the wheels.

BRONZE SPINDLE BUSHING REPLACEMENT

1. Remove the spindle and secure it in a bench vise.

2. The bushings have an inside diameter of 1.301–1.302 in. (33.05–33.07mm). Use the following tools or their equivalents:

- Reamer T88T-3110-BH
- Bushing Remover/Installer T88T-3110-AH

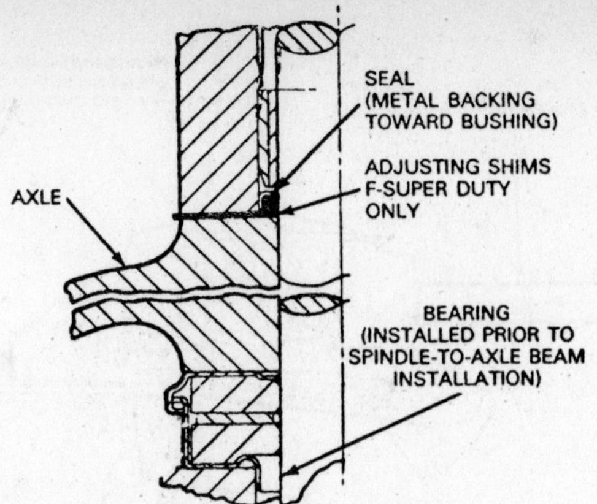

Bearing seal installation on F-Super Duty

- Driver Handle T80T-4000-W

One side of the Remover/Installer is marked with a **T**; the other side with a **B**. The **T** side is used on the top bushing; the **B** side is for the bottom bushing.

3. Remove and discard the seal from the upper bushing bore.

4. Working on the upper bushing first, install the driver handle through the bottom bore. Position a new bushing on the **T** side of the tool. The bushing must be positioned so that the open end grooves will face outward when installed. Position the bushing and tool over the old bushing, insert the handle and drive out the old bushing while driving in the new bushing. Continue driving until the tool is fully seated. The new bushing should then be seated at the proper depth of 0.08 in. (2.03mm) minimum from the bottom of the upper spindle boss.

5. Working on the bottom bushing, position the driver handle through the top bushing bore. Position a new bushing on the **B** side of the tool. The bushing must be positioned so that the open end grooves will face outward when installed. Position the bushing and tool over the old bushing, insert the handle and drive out the old bushing while driving in the new bushing. Continue driving until the tool is fully seated. The new bushing should then be seated at the proper depth of 0.13 in. (3.3mm) minimum from the top of the lower spindle boss.

6. Ream the new bushings to 0.001–0.003 in. (0.025–0.076mm) larger than the diameter of the new spindle pin. Ream the top bushing first. Install the smaller diameter of the reamer through the top bore and into the bottom bore until the threads are in position is the top bush-

'T' STAMPING
USE FOR TOP
BUSHING INSTALLATION
REAMER
T53T-3110-DA (E-150)
D82T-3110-A
(E-250 — E-350)
T88T-3110-BH
(F-SUPER DUTY)
BUSHING REMOVER/
INSTALLER DRIVER
D82T-3110-G (E-150)
D82T-3110-B (E-350 — E-350)
T88T-3110-AH
(F-SUPER DUTY)
'B' STAMPING
USE FOR BOTTOM
BUSHING INSTALLATION
DRIVER HANDLE
D82T-3110-C
T80T-4000-W
(FOR F-SUPER DUTY)

Spindle bushing replacement tools for solid front axles

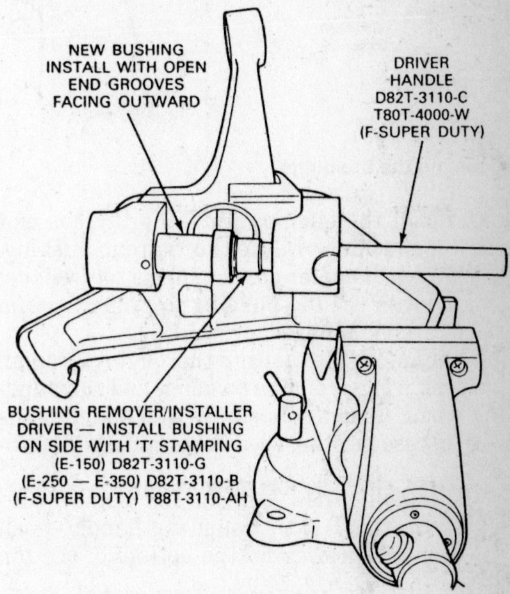

Top spindle bushing replacement

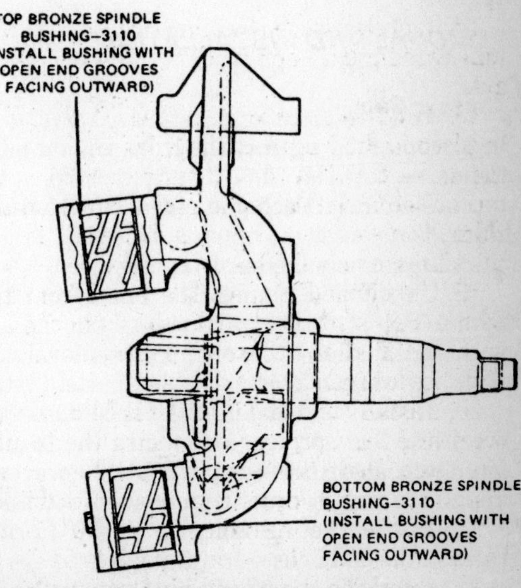

Solid front axle spindle bushing installation

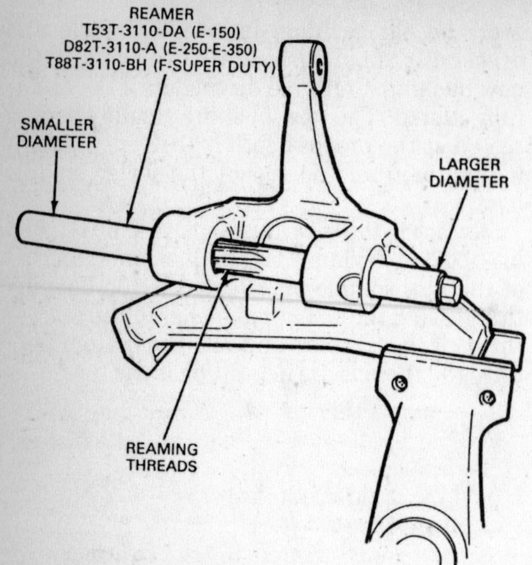

Reaming the bushings

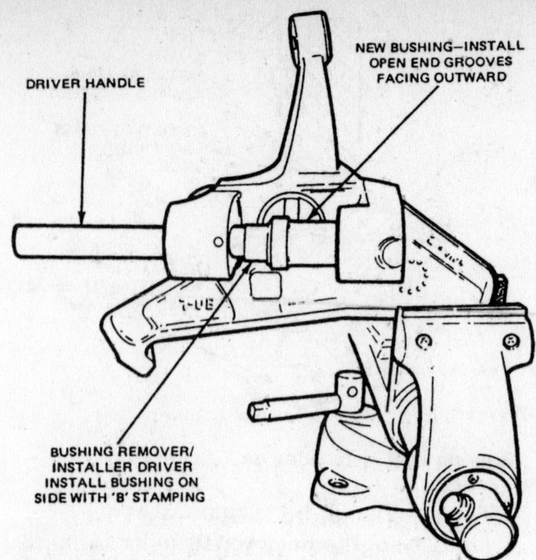

Bottom spindle bushing replacement

ing. Ream the bushing until the threads exit the top bushing. Ream the bottom bushing. The larger diameter portion of the tool will act as a pilot in the top bushing to properly ream the bottom bushing.

7. Remove the tool and thoroughly clean all metal shavings from the bushings and surrounding parts. Coat the bushings and spindle pins with grease meeting specification ESA-M1C75-B.

8. Install a new seal on the Remover/Installer on the **T** side. Using the handle, push the seal into position in the bottom of the top bore.

Stabilizer Bar

REMOVAL AND INSTALLATION

Chassis/Cab

1. Raise and support the front end on jackstands.
2. Disconnect each end of the bar from the links.
3. Disconnect the bar from the axle.
4. Unbolt and remove the links from the frame.
5. Installation is the reverse of removal. Replace any worn or cracked rubber parts. Install the bar loosely and make sure it is centered between the leaf springs. Make sure the insulators are seated in the retainers. When everything is in proper order, tighten the stabilizer bar-to-axle mounting bolts to 35–50 ft. lbs. Tighten the end link-to-frame bolts to 52–74 ft. lbs. Tighten the bar-to-end link nuts to 15–25 ft. lbs.

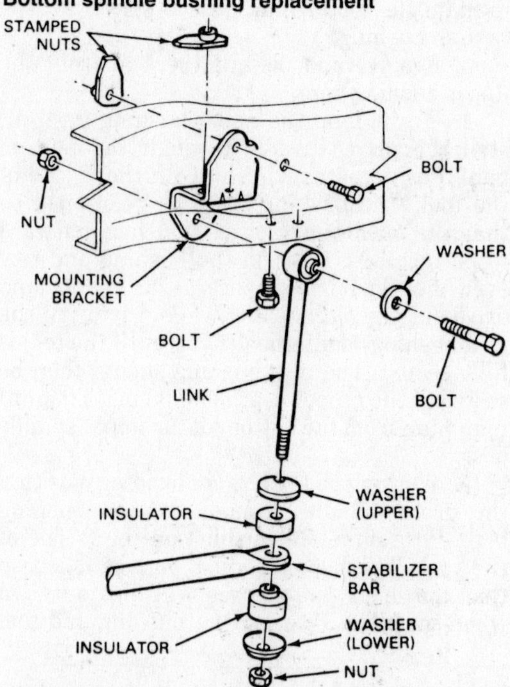

Front stabilizer bar installation for F-Super Duty chassis/cab

Stripped Chassis or Motor Home Chassis

1. Raise and support the front end on jackstands.
2. Disconnect the stabilizer bar ends from the links attached to the axle.
3. Remove the bar-to-frame bolts and remove the bar.
4. Remove the links from the axle brackets.
5. Installation is the reverse of removal. Re-

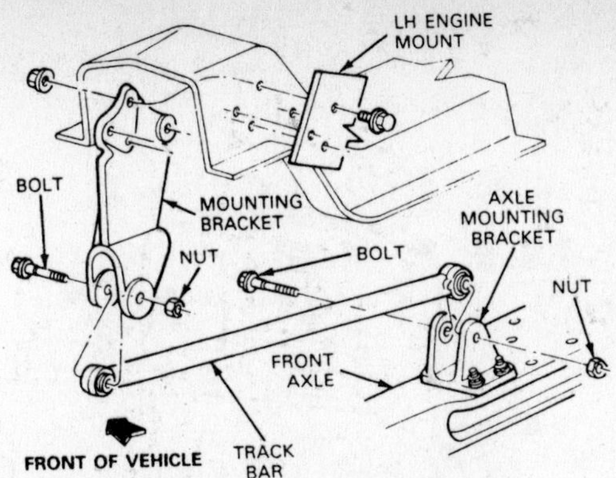

Track bar installation for the F-Super Duty

place any worn or cracked rubber parts. Assemble all parts loosely and make sure the assembly is centered on the frame. make sure that the insulators are seated in the retainers. When everything is in proper order, tighten the bar-to-frame brackets bolts to 30–47 ft. lbs. Tighten the link-to-axle bracket bolts to 57–81 ft. lbs. Tighten the bar-to-link nuts to 15–25 ft. lbs.

Track Bar

REMOVAL AND INSTALLATION

Chassis/Cab Models

1. Raise and support the front end on jackstands.
2. Unbolt the track bar from the crossmember bracket.
3. Unbolt the track bar fro the axle bracket.
4. Installation is the reverse of removal. Torque the bolts at each end to 120–150 ft. lbs.

Axle

REMOVAL AND INSTALLATION

1. Raise and support the front end on jackstands positioned under the frame.
2. Remove the wheels.
3. Remove the brake calipers and suspend them out of the way. See Chapter 9.
4. Install the wheels with a few lug nuts finger-tight.
5. Adjust the height of the truck on the stands so that the weight is off the front springs, but the tires still touch the ground.
6. Disconnect the stabilizer bar from the axle.
7. Disconnect the tie rod end and, if applicable, the drag link, from the spindle.
8. On chassis/cab models, disconnect the track bar from the axle.
9. Remove the spring U-bolt nuts and remove the stabilizer bar brackets or jack brackets.
10. Remove the U-bolts.
11. Raise the truck and roll the axle from underneath.

To install:

12. Roll the axle into position under the truck and align it so that the spring seats align with the locating boss on each spring.
13. Install the U-bolts and jack brackets or stabilizer bar brackets. Install the U-bolt nuts and tighten them evenly, gradually and in a criss-cross fashion, to 150–210 ft. lbs. for chassis/cab models, or, 220–300 ft. lbs. for stripped chassis or motor home models.
14. Connect the tie rod ends and drag link.
15. Install the track bar on chassis/cab models.
16. Connect the stabilizer bar.
17. Install the calipers.
18. Install and tighten all the lug nuts.

4-WHEEL DRIVE FRONT SUSPENSION

The suspension of an F-150 and Bronco 4-Wheel Drive consists of a Dana 44-IFS independent driving axle attached to the frame with two coil springs, two radius arms, and a stabilizer bar.

The front suspension on an F-250 4-Wheel Drive consists of a Dana 44-or 50-IFS independent driving axle attached to the frame with two semi-elliptic leaf springs. Each spring is clamped to the axle with two U-bolts. The front of the spring rests in a front shackle bracket and the rear is attached to a frame bracket.

The front suspension on an F-350 4-Wheel Drive consists of a Dana 60 Monobeam one piece driving axle attached to the frame with two semi-elliptic leaf springs. Each spring is clamped to the axle with two U-bolts. The front of the spring rests in a front shackle bracket and the rear is attached to a frame bracket. On the right spring cap a track bar is attached with the other end mounted on the crossmember.

Springs

REMOVAL AND INSTALLATION

F-150 and Bronco

1. Raise and support the front end on jackstands.
2. Remove the shock absorber lower attaching bolt and nut.
3. Remove the spring lower retainer nuts from inside of the spring coil.
4. Remove the upper spring retainer by removing the attaching screw.
5. Position safety stands under the frame

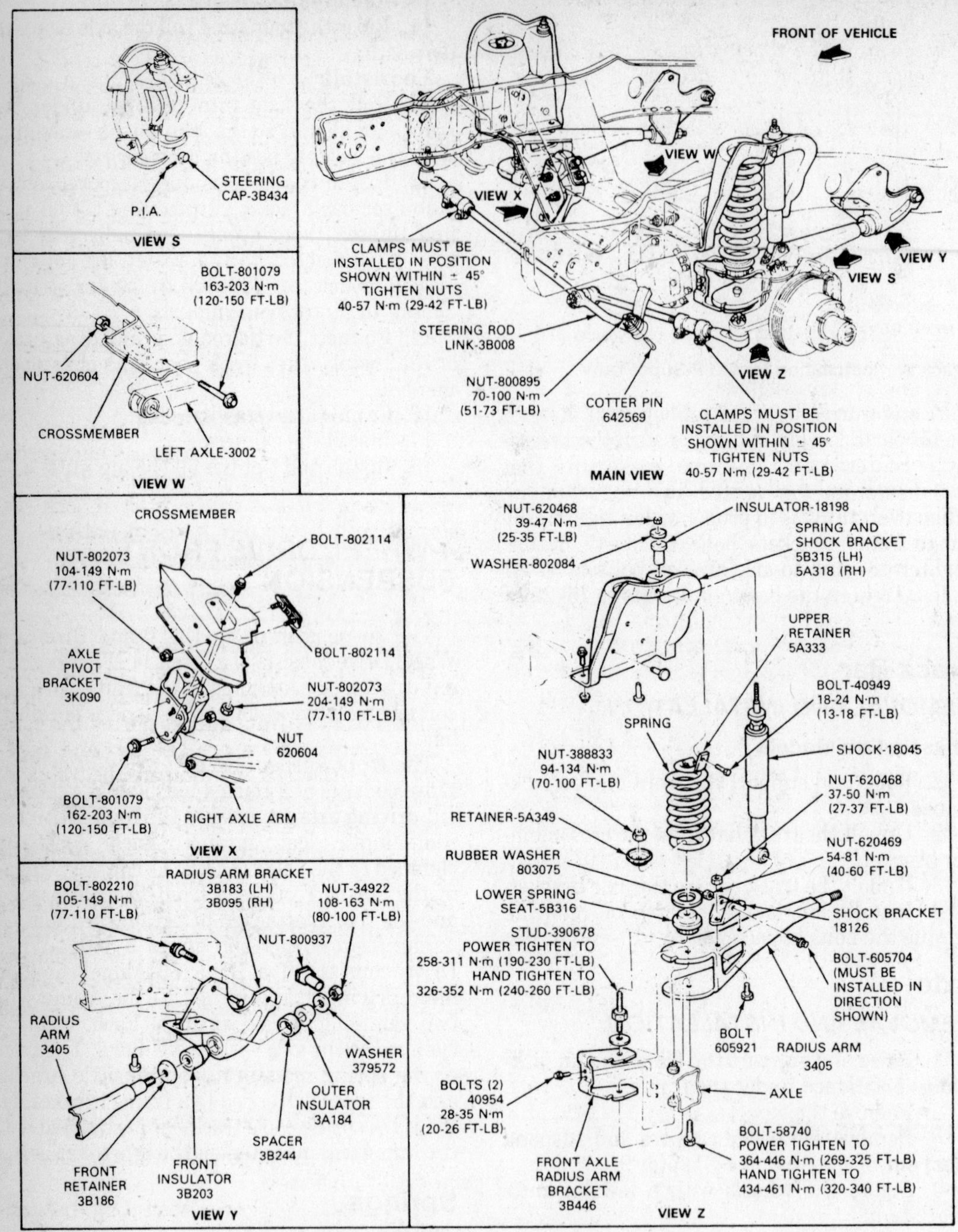

Bronco and 4-wheel drive F-150 front suspension

side rails and lower the axle on a floor jack just enough to relieve tension from the spring.

NOTE: *The axle must be supported on the jack throughout spring removal, and must not be permitted to hang from the brake hose. If the length of the brake hose does not provide sufficient clearance it may be necessary to remove and support the brake caliper.*

6. Remove the spring lower retainer and lower the spring from the vehicle.
7. To install place the spring in position and slowly raise the front axle. Make sure the springs are positioned correctly in the upper spring seats.
8. Install the lower spring retainer and torque the nut to 100 ft. lbs.
9. Position the upper retainer over the

spring coil and tighten the attaching screws to 13–18 ft. lbs.

10. Position the shock absorber to the lower bracket and torque the attaching bolt and nut to 65 ft. lbs.

11. Remove the safety stands and lower the vehicle.

F-250, F-350

1. Raise the vehicle frame until the weight is off the front spring with the wheels still touching the floor. Support the axle to prevent rotation.

2. Disconnect the lower end of the shock absorber from the U-bolt spacer. Remove the U-bolts, U-bolt cap and spacer.

On F-350 models, remove the 2 bolts retaining the track bar to the spring cap and the track bar bracket.

3. Remove the nut from the hanger bolt retaining the spring at the rear and drive out the hanger bolt.

4. Remove the nut connecting the front shackle and spring eye and drive out the shackle bolt and remove the spring.

5. To install position the spring on the spring seat. Install the shackle bolt through the shackle and spring. Torque the nuts to 150 ft. lbs.

6. Position the rear of the spring and install the hanger bolt. Torque the nut to 150 ft. lbs.

7. Position the U-bolt spacer and place the U-bolts in position through the holes in the spring seat cap. Install but do not tighten the U-bolt nut.

On the F-350, install the track bar. Torque the track bar-to-bracket bolts to 200 ft. lbs.

8. Connect the lower end of the shock absorber to the U-bolt spacer. Torque the fasteners to 60 ft. lbs. on the F-250; 70 ft. lbs. on the F-350.

9. Lower the vehicle and tighten the U-bolt nuts to 120 ft. lbs.

Shock Absorbers

TESTING

Bounce Test

Each shock absorber can be tested by bouncing the corner of the truck until maximum up and down movement is obtained. Let go of the truck. It should stop bouncing in 1–2 bounces. If not, the shock should be inspected for damage and possibly replaced.

Inspect the Shock Mounts

Check the shock mountings for worn or defective grommets, loose mounting nuts, interference or missing bump stops. If no apparent defects are noted, continue testing.

Inspecting Shocks for Leaks

Disconnect each shock lower mount and pull down on the shock until it is fully extended. inspect for leaks in the seal area. Shock absorber fluid is very thin and has a characteristic odor and dark brown color. Don't confuse the glossy paint on some shocks with leaking fluid. A slight trace of fluid is a normal condition; they are designed to seep a certain amount of fluid past the seals for lubrication. If you are in doubt as to whether the fluid on the shock is coming from the shock itself or from some other source, wipe the seal area clean and manually operate the shock (see the following procedure). Fluid will appear if the unit is leaking.

Manually Operating the Shocks

It may be necessary to fabricate a holding fixture for certain types of shock absorbers. If a suspected problem is in the front shocks, disconnect both front shock lower mountings.

NOTE: *When manually operating air shocks, the air line must be disconnected at the shock.*

Grip the lower end of the shock and pull down (rebound stroke) and then push up (compression stroke). The control arms will limit the movement of front shocks during the compression stroke. Compare the rebound resistance of both shocks and compare the compression resistance. Usually any shock showing a noticeable difference will be the one at fault.

If the shock has internal noises, extend the shock fully then exert an extra pull. If a small additional movement is felt, this usually means a loose piston and the shock should be replaced. Other noises that are cause for replacing shocks are a squeal after a full stroke in both directions, a clicking noise on fast reverse and a lag at reversal near mid-stroke.

REMOVAL AND INSTALLATION

F-150 and Bronco, except Quad Shocks

1. Remove the upper nut while holding the shock absorber stem.

2. Remove the lower mounting bolt/nut from the bracket.

3. Compress the shock and remove it.

4. Installation is the reverse of removal. Hold the stud while tightening the upper nut to 30 ft. lbs. Torque the lower bolt/nut to 60 ft. lbs.

F-150 and Bronco w/Quad Shocks

1. Remove the upper nut while holding the shock absorber stem on both forward and rearward shocks.

2. Remove the lower mounting bolt/nut

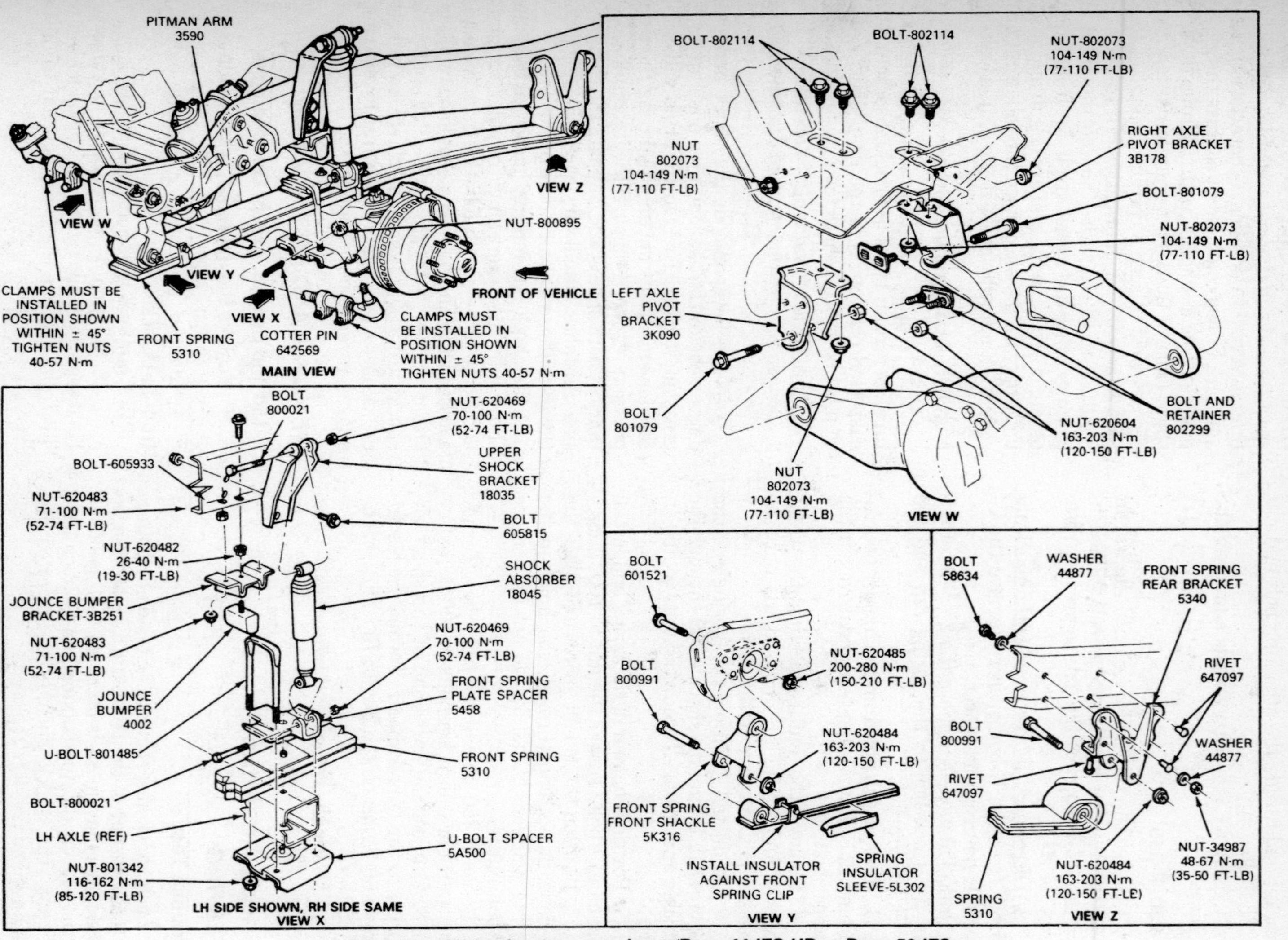

F-250 4-wheel drive front suspension w/Dana 44-IFS-HD or Dana 50-IFS

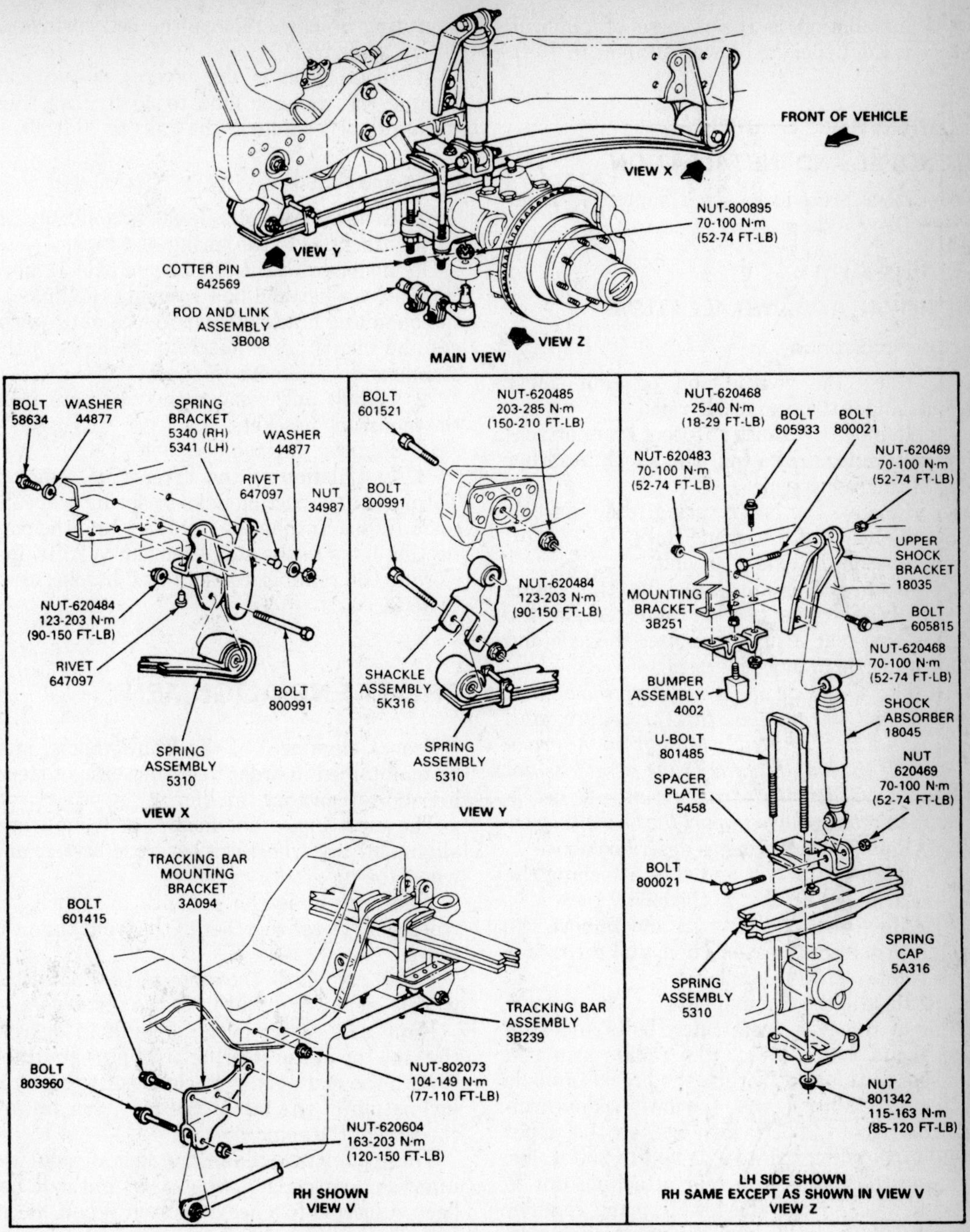

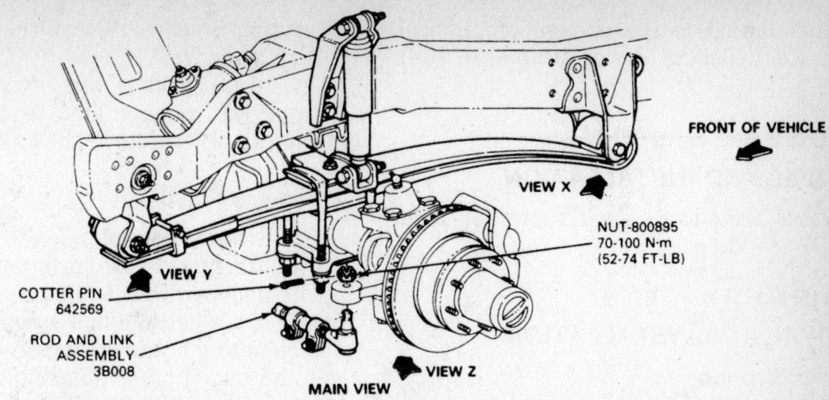

F-350 4-wheel drive front suspension

from the rearward shock bracket; the nut and washer from the forward shock bracket.

3. Compress the shocks and remove them.

4. Cut the insulators from the upper spring seat.

5. Install new one piece insulators into the top surface of the upper spring seat. Coat them with a soap solution to aid in installation.

6. Installation of the shocks is the reverse of removal. Use a new steel washer under the upper nut. Hold the stud while tightening the upper nut to 30 ft. lbs. Torque the lower bolt/nut to 60 ft. lbs.

F-250, F-350

1. Remove the nut/bolt retaining the shock to the upper bracket.

2. Remove the lower mounting bolt/nut from the bracket.

3. Compress the shock and remove it.

4. Installation is the reverse of removal. Tighten the upper and lower nut/bolt to 70 ft. lbs.

Front Wheel Spindle

REMOVAL AND INSTALLATION

For this procedure, see Chapter 7 under Front Drive Axle.

Radius Arm

REMOVAL AND INSTALLATION

F-150 and Bronco

1. Raise the vehicle and position safety stands under the frame side rails.
2. Remove the shock absorber lower attaching bolt and nut and pull the shock absorber free of the radius arm.
3. Remove the lower spring retaining bolt from the inside of the spring coil.
4. Loosen the axle pivot bolt.
5. Remove the nut attaching the radius arm to the frame bracket and remove the radius arm rear insulator. Lower the axle and allow the axle to move forward.

NOTE: *The axle must be supported on a floor jack throughout this procedure, and must not be permitted to hang from the brake hose. If the length of the brake hose does not provide sufficient clearance it may be necessary to remove and support the brake caliper.*

6. Remove the spring as described above.
7. Remove the bolt and stud attaching the radius arm and bracket to the axle.
8. Move the axle forward and remove the radius arm from the axle. Then, pull the radius arm from the frame bracket.
9. Install the components in the reverse order of removal. Install new bolts and stud type bolts which attach the radius arm and bracket to the axle. Torque the bracket-to-axle bolts to 25 ft. lbs. Torque the lower radius arm-to-axle bolt to 330 ft. lbs. Tighten the upper stud-type radius arm-to-axle bolt to 250 ft. lbs. Torque the radius arm rear attaching nut to 120 ft. lbs. Torque the lower spring retainer nut to 100 ft. lbs. Torque the upper spring retainer bolts to 15 ft. lbs. Torque the axle pivot bolt to 150 ft. lbs. Torque the lower shock absorber bolt to 60 ft. lbs.

Stabilizer Bar

REMOVAL AND INSTALLATION

F-150 and Bronco

1. Unbolt the stabilizer bar from the connecting links.
2. Unbolt the stabilizer bar retainers.
3. If you have to remove the stabilizer bar mounting bracket, remove the coil springs as described above.
4. Installation is the reverse of removal. Torque the retainer nuts to 35 ft. lbs., then torque all other nuts at the links to 70 ft. lbs.

F-250 and F-350

1. Remove the bolts, washers and nuts securing the links to the spring seat caps.

On models with the Monobeam axle, remove the nut, washer and bolt securing the links to the mounting brackets. Remove the nuts, washers and insulators connecting the links to the stabilizer bar. Remove the links.

2. Unbolt and remove the retainers from the mounting brackets.
3. Remove the stabilizer bar.
4. Installation is the reverse of removal. Torque the connecting links-to-spring seat caps to 70 ft. lbs. Torque the nuts securing the connecting links to the stabilizer bar to 25 ft. lbs. Torque the retainer-to-mounting bracket nuts to 35 ft. lbs.

FRONT END ALIGNMENT

Proper alignment of the front wheels must be maintained in order to ensure ease of steering and satisfactory tire life.

The most important factors of front wheel alignment are wheel camber, axle caster, and wheel toe-in.

Wheel toe-in is the distance by which the wheels are closer together at the front than the rear.

Wheel camber is the amount the top of the wheels incline in or out from the vertical.

From axle caster is the amount in degrees that the top of the steering pivot pins are tilted toward the rear of the vehicle. Positive caster is inclination of the top of the pivot pin toward the rear of the vehicle.

These points should be checked at regulator intervals, particularly when the front axle has been subjected to a heavy impact. When checking wheel alignment, it is important that the wheel bearings and knuckle bearings be in proper adjustment. Loose bearings will affect instrument readings when checking the camber and toe-in.

If you start to notice abnormal tire wear patterns and handling characteristics (steering wheel is hard to return to the straight ahead position after negotiating a turn), then front end misalignment can be suspected. However, toe-in alignment maladjustment, rather than cast or camber, is more likely to be the cause of excessive or uneven tire wear on vehicles with

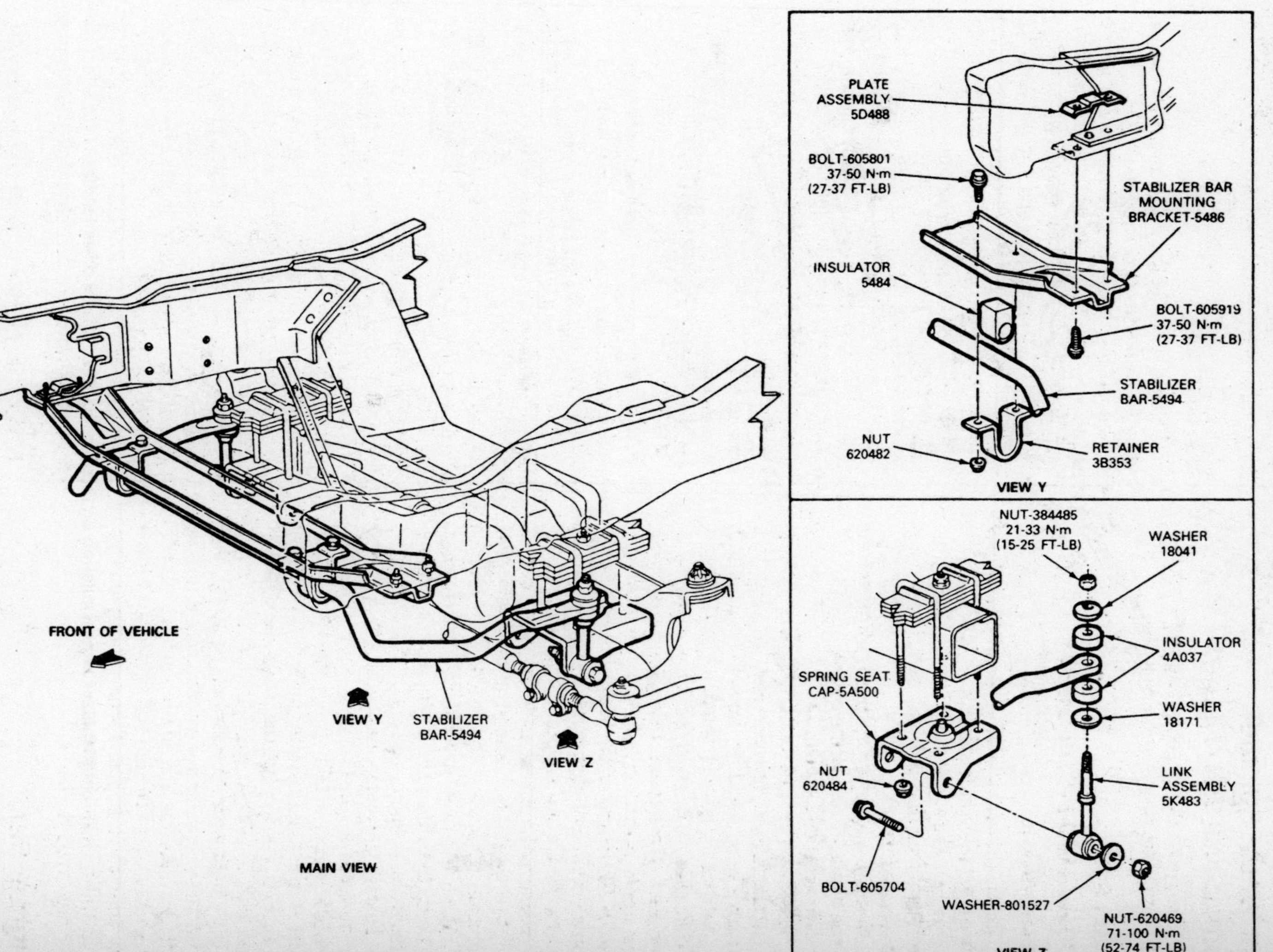

Front stabilizer bar installation on the F-250 4-wheel drive

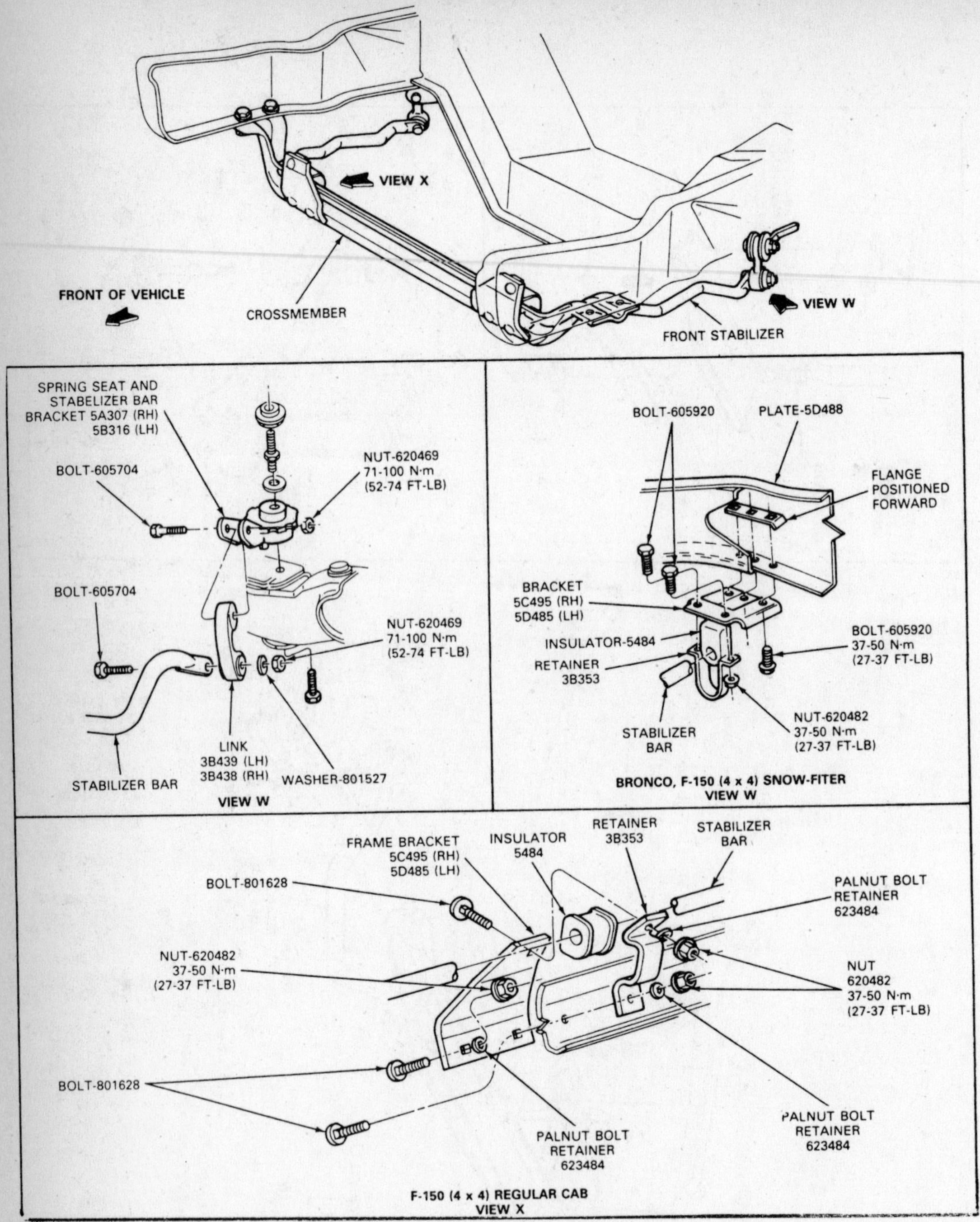

Front stabilizer bar installation on the Bronco and 4-wheel drive F-150

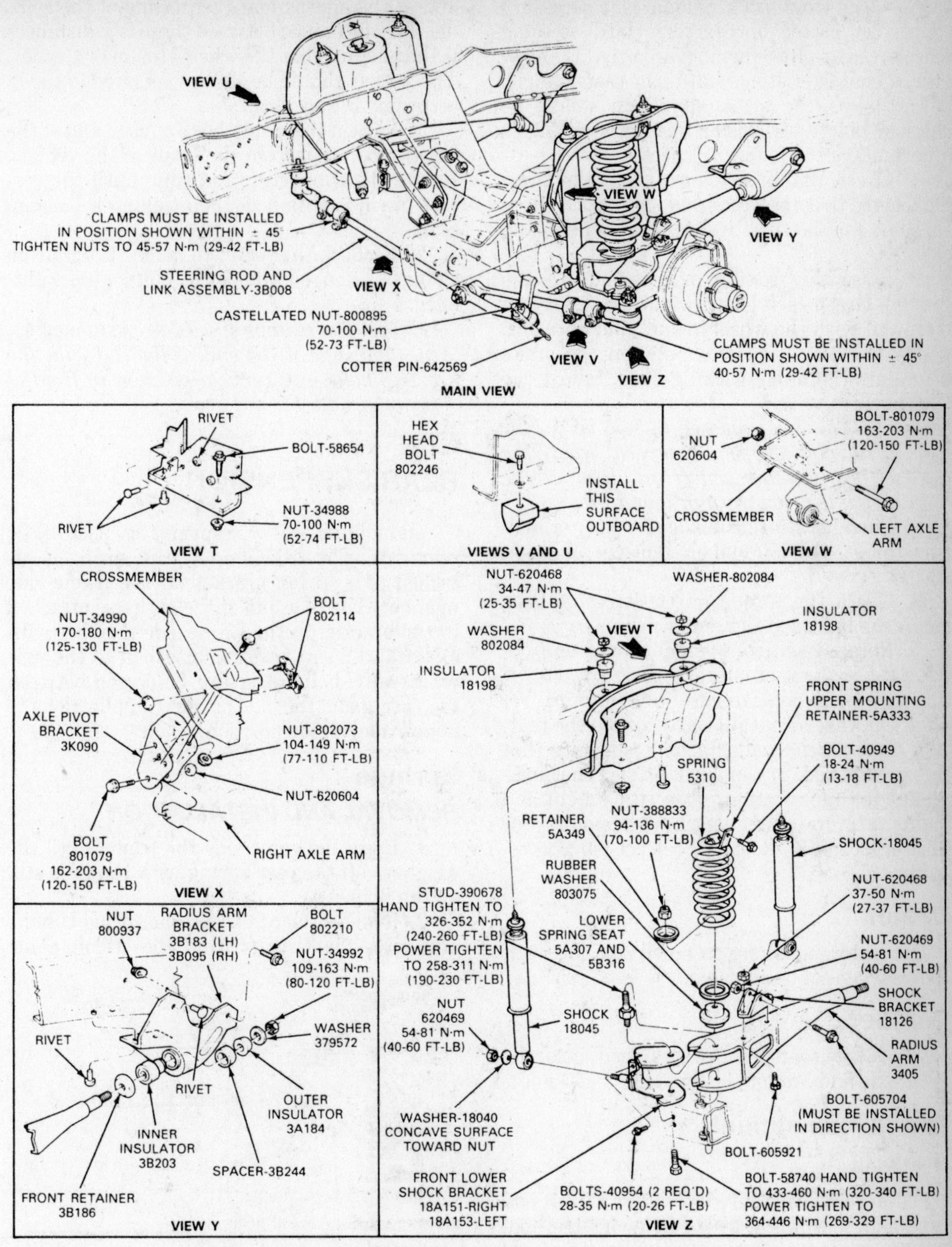

Quad shock installation on the Bronco and 4-wheel drive F-150

twin I-beam front axles. Seldom is it necessary to correct caster or camber. Hard steering wheel return after turning a corner is, however, a characteristic of improper caster angle. Nevertheless, the toe-in alignment should be checked before the caster and camber angles after making the following checks:

1. Check the air pressure in all the tires. Make sure that the pressures agree with those specified for the tires and vehicle model being checked.

2. Raise the front of the vehicle off the ground. Grasp each front tire at the front and rear, and push the wheel inward and outward. If any free-play is noticed between the brake drum and the brake backing plate, adjust the wheel bearings.

NOTE: *There is supposed to be a very, very small amount of free-play present where the wheel bearings are concerned. Replace the bearing if they are worn or damaged.*

3. Check all steering linkage for wear or maladjustment. Adjust and/or replace all worn parts.

4. Check the torque on the steering gear mounting bolts and tighten as necessary.

5. Rotate each front wheel slowly, and observe the amount of lateral or side run-out. If the wheel run-out exceeds $^1/_8$ in. (3mm), replace the wheel or install the wheel on the rear.

6. Inspect the radius arms to be sure that they are not bent or damaged. Inspect the bushings at the radius arm-to-axle attachment and radius arm-to-frame attachment points for wear or looseness. Repair or replace parts as required.

Caster

The caster angles are designed into the front axle and cannot be adjusted.

Camber

The camber angles are designed into the front axle and cannot be adjusted.

Toe-in Adjustment

All Models

Toe-in can be measured by either a front end alignment machine or by the following method:

With the front wheels in the straight ahead position, measure the distance between the extreme front and the extreme rear of the front wheels. In other words, measure the distance across the undercarriage of the vehicle between the two front edges and the two rear edges of the two front wheels. Both of these measurements (front and rear of the two wheels) must be taken at an equal distance from the floor and at the approximate centerline of the spindle. The difference between these two distances is the amount that the wheels toe-in or toe-out. The wheels should be always adjusted to toe-in according to specifications.

1. Loosen the clamp bolts at each end of the left tie rod, seen from the front of the vehicle. Rotate the connecting rod tube until the correct toe-in is obtained, then tighten the clamp bolts.

2. Recheck the toe-in to make sure that no changes occurred when the bolts were tightened.

NOTE: *The clamps should be positioned $^3/_{16}$ in. (5mm) from the end of the rod with the clamp bolts in a vertical position in front of the tube, with the nut down.*

REAR SUSPENSION

Semi-elliptic, leaf type springs are used at the rear axle. The front end of the spring is attached to a spring bracket on the frame side member. The rear end of the spring is attached to the bracket on the frame side member with a shackle. Each spring is attached to the axle with two U-bolts. A spacer is located between the spring and the axle on some applications to obtain a level ride position.

Springs

REMOVAL AND INSTALLATION

1. Raise the vehicle by the frame until the weight is off the rear spring with the tires still on the floor.

2. Remove the nuts from the spring U-bolts and drive the U-bolts from the U-bolt plate.

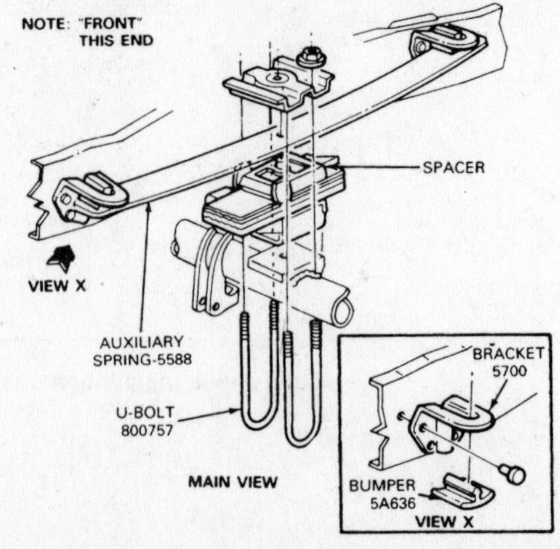

Rear spring installation with auxiliary spring for the 4-wheel drive F-150, 250, 350

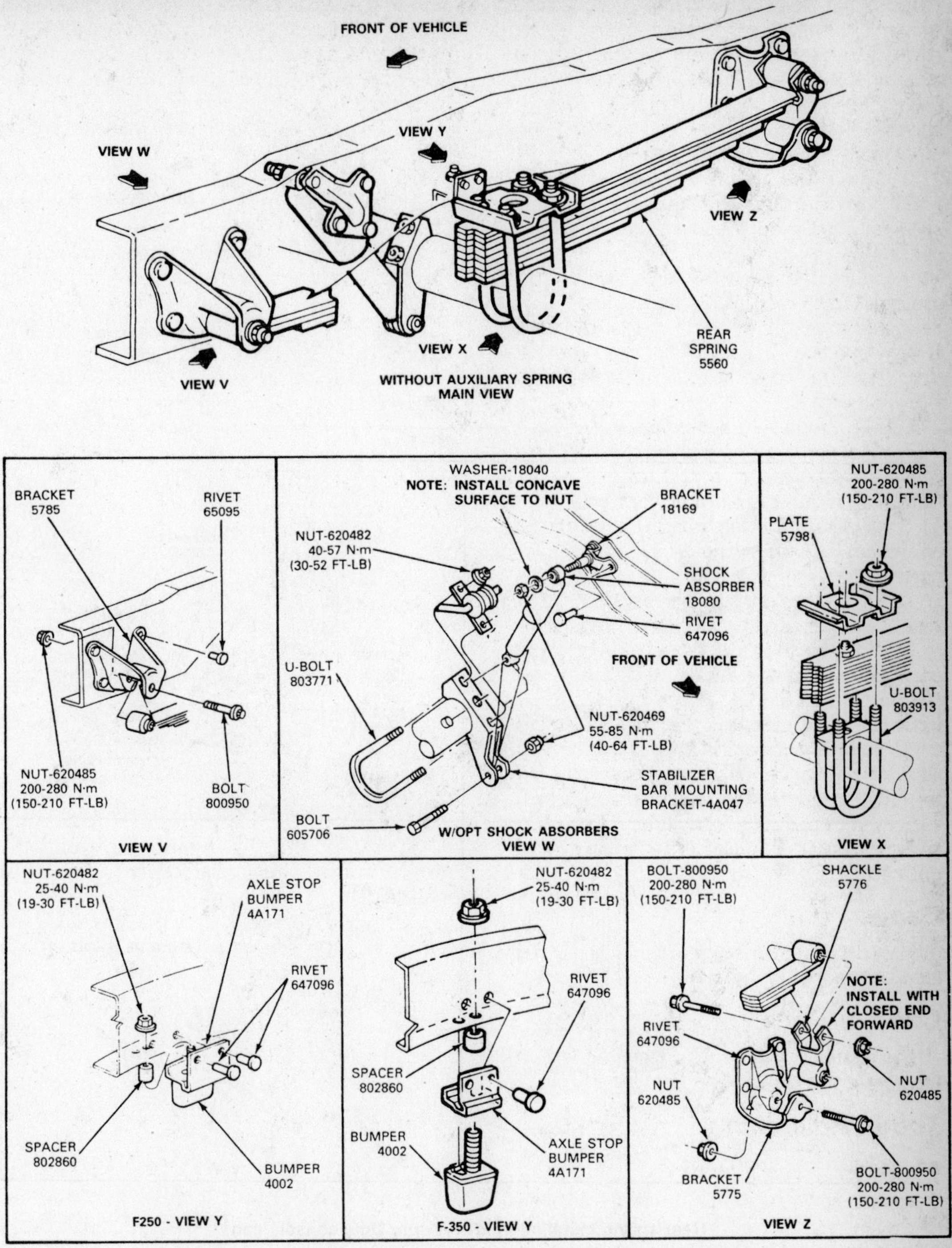

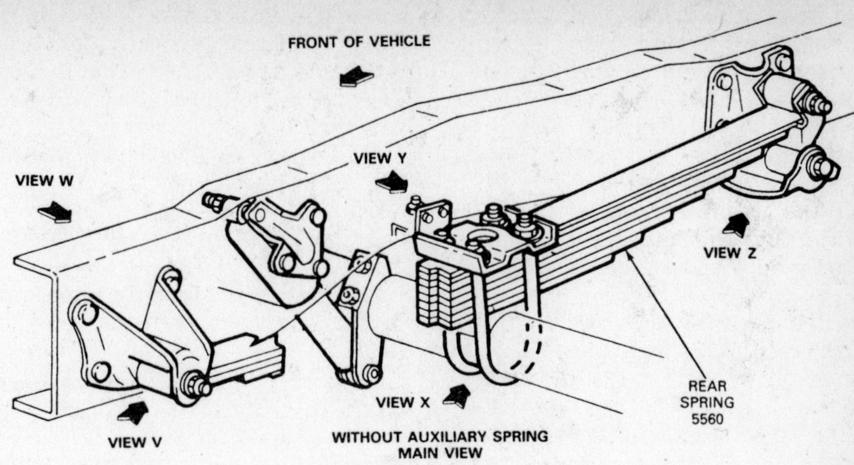

Rear spring installation for F-250, 350 2-wheel Chasis Cab w/Dana axles

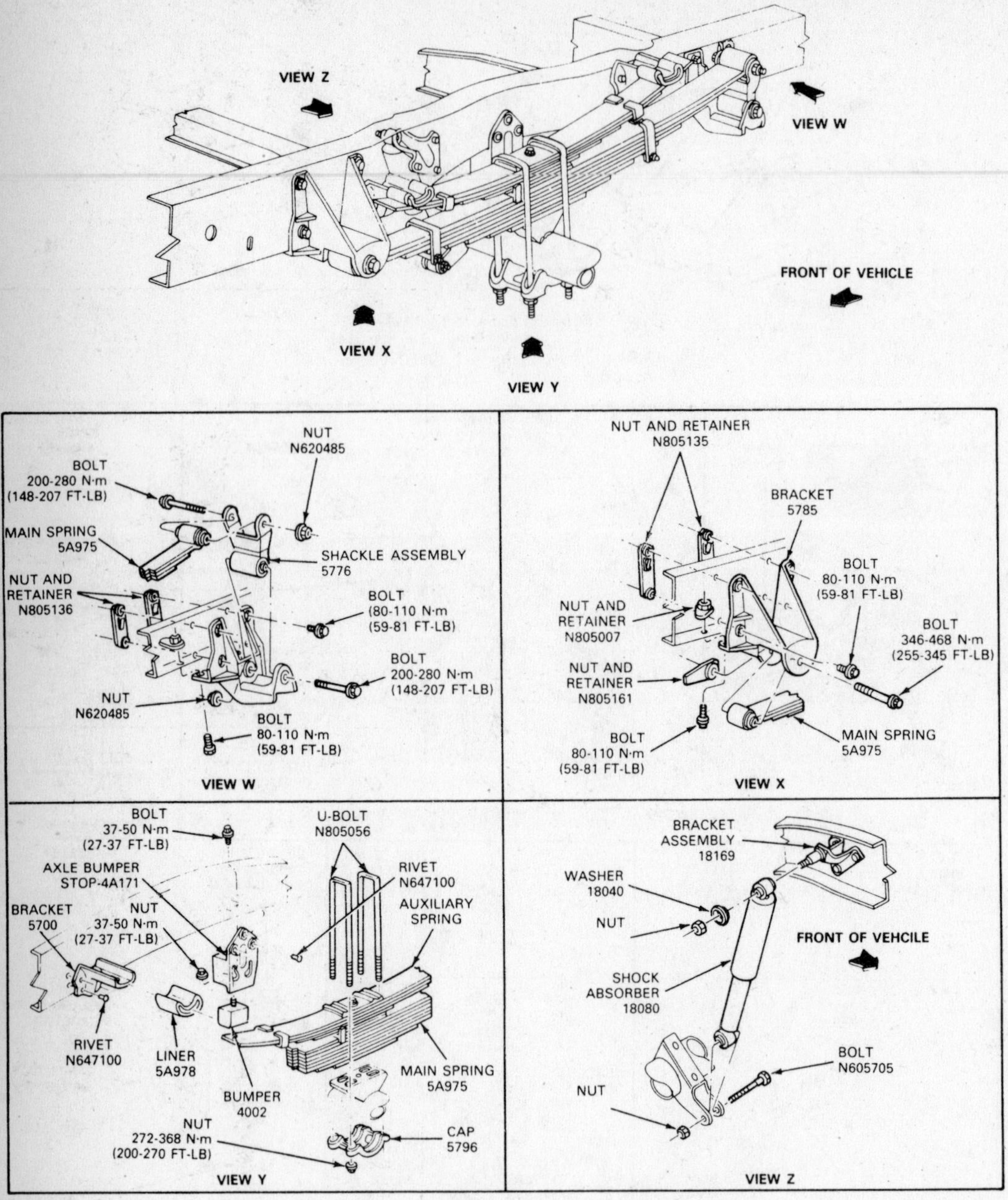

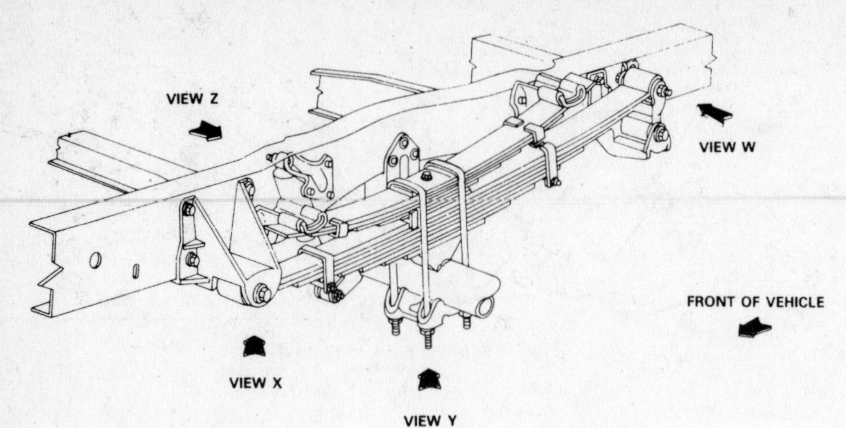

NUT
N620485
BOLT
200-280 N·m
(148-207 FT-LB)
MAIN SPRING
5A975
SHACKLE ASSEMBLY
5776
NUT AND
RETAINER
N805136
BOLT
(80-110 N·m
(59-81 FT-LB)
BOLT
200-280 N·m
(148-207 FT-LB)
NUT
N620485
BOLT
80-110 N·m
(59-81 FT-LB)
VIEW W

NUT AND RETAINER
N805135
BRACKET
5785
BOLT
80-110 N·m
(59-81 FT-LB)
NUT AND
RETAINER
N805007
BOLT
346-468 N·m
(255-345 FT-LB)
NUT AND
RETAINER
N805161
BOLT
80-110 N·m
(59-81 FT-LB)
MAIN SPRING
5A975
VIEW X

BOLT
37-50 N·m
(27-37 FT-LB)
U-BOLT
N805056
AXLE BUMPER
STOP-4A171
RIVET
N647100
AUXILIARY
SPRING
BRACKET
5700
NUT
37-50 N·m
(27-37 FT-LB)
RIVET
N647100
LINER
5A978
BUMPER
4002
MAIN SPRING
5A975
NUT
272-368 N·m
(200-270 FT-LB)
CAP
5796
VIEW Y

BRACKET
ASSEMBLY
18169
WASHER
18040
NUT
FRONT OF VEHCILE
SHOCK
ABSORBER
18080
BOLT
N605705
NUT
VIEW Z

Rear spring installation for F-Super Duty chassis/cab

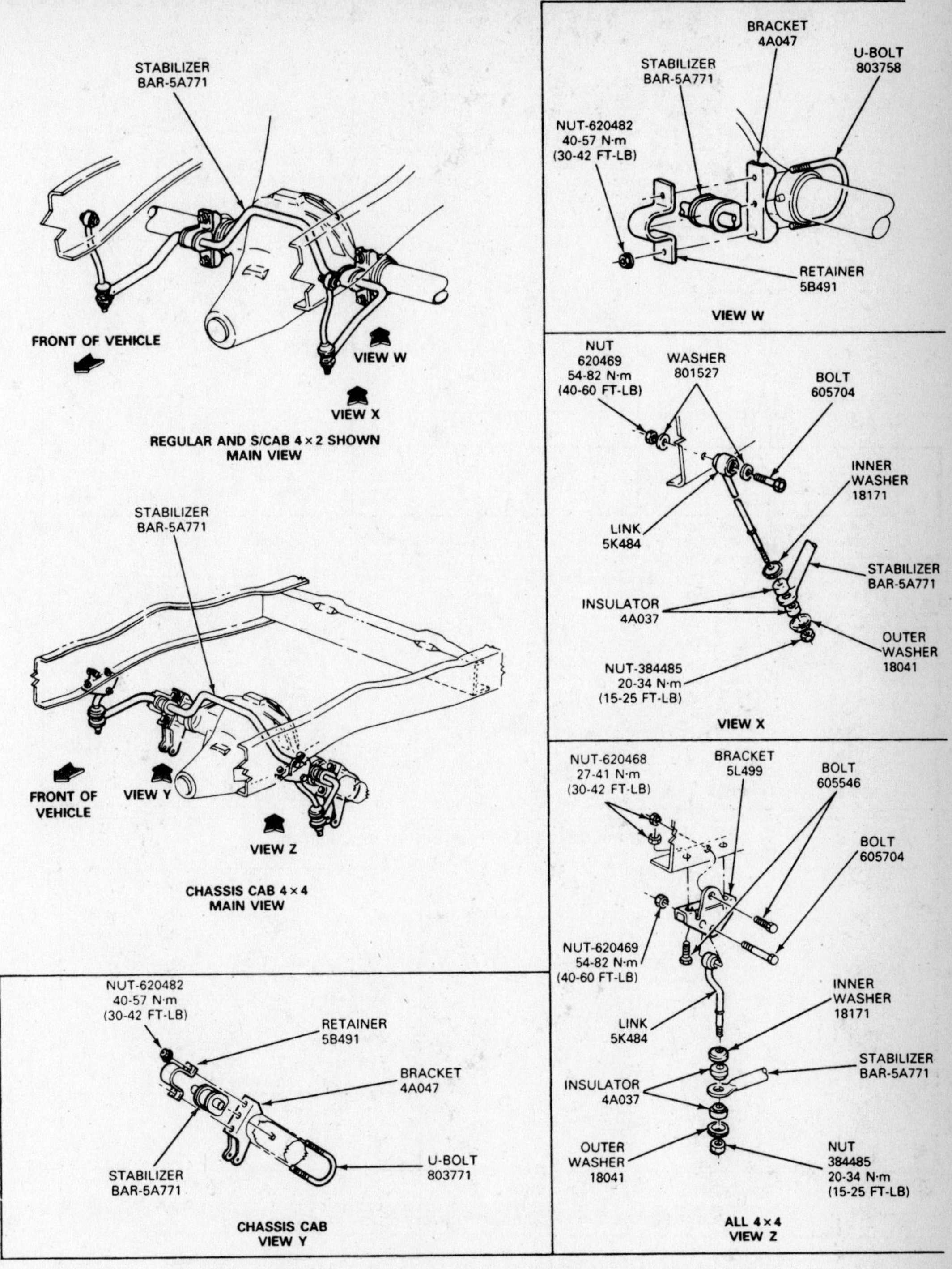

Rear stabilizer bar installation for the F-250, 350 w/Ford rear axles

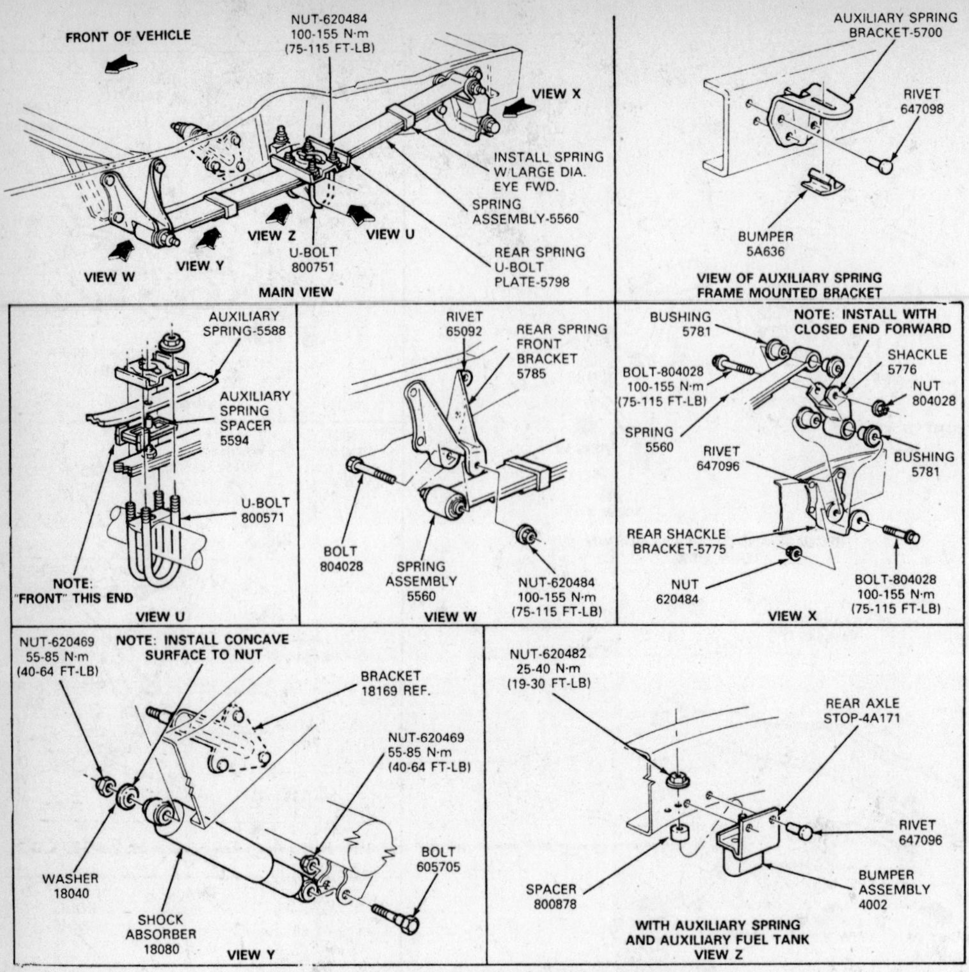

FRONT OF VEHICLE
NUT-620484
100-155 N·m
(75-115 FT-LB)
VIEW X
INSTALL SPRING
W/LARGE DIA.
EYE FWD.
SPRING
ASSEMBLY-5560
VIEW Z
VIEW U
U-BOLT
800751
REAR SPRING
U-BOLT
PLATE-5798
VIEW W
VIEW Y
MAIN VIEW
AUXILIARY SPRING
BRACKET-5700
RIVET
647098
BUMPER
5A636
VIEW OF AUXILIARY SPRING
FRAME MOUNTED BRACKET
AUXILIARY
SPRING-5588
AUXILIARY
SPRING
SPACER
5594
U-BOLT
800571
NOTE:
"FRONT" THIS END
VIEW U
RIVET
65092
REAR SPRING
FRONT
BRACKET
5785
BOLT
804028
SPRING
ASSEMBLY
5560
NUT-620484
100-155 N·m
(75-115 FT-LB)
VIEW W
BUSHING
5781
NOTE: INSTALL WITH
CLOSED END FORWARD
SHACKLE
5776
BOLT-804028
100-155 N·m
(75-115 FT-LB)
NUT
804028
SPRING
5560
RIVET
647096
BUSHING
5781
REAR SHACKLE
BRACKET-5775
NUT
620484
BOLT-804028
100-155 N·m
(75-115 FT-LB)
VIEW X
NUT-620469
55-85 N·m
(40-64 FT-LB)
NOTE: INSTALL CONCAVE
SURFACE TO NUT
BRACKET
18169 REF.
NUT-620469
55-85 N·m
(40-64 FT-LB)
BOLT
605705
WASHER
18040
SHOCK
ABSORBER
18080
VIEW Y
NUT-620482
25-40 N·m
(19-30 FT-LB)
REAR AXLE
STOP-4A171
RIVET
647096
BUMPER
ASSEMBLY
4002
SPACER
800878
WITH AUXILIARY SPRING
AND AUXILIARY FUEL TANK
VIEW Z

2-wheel drive F-150 rear spring installation

STABILIZER
BAR
5A771
FRONT OF
VEHICLE
VIEWS Y
AND Z
RETAINER
5B491
BRACKET
BOLT
37-50 N·m
(27-37 FT-LB)
STABILIZER
BAR
5A771
VIEW Y
WASHER
BOLT
NUT
54-82 N·m
(40-61 FT-LB)
WASHER
LINK
5K484
INNER
WASHER
18171
STABILIZER
BAR
5A771
INSULATOR
4A037
OUTER
WASHER
18041
NUT
20-34 N·m
(15-25 FT-LB)
VIEW Z

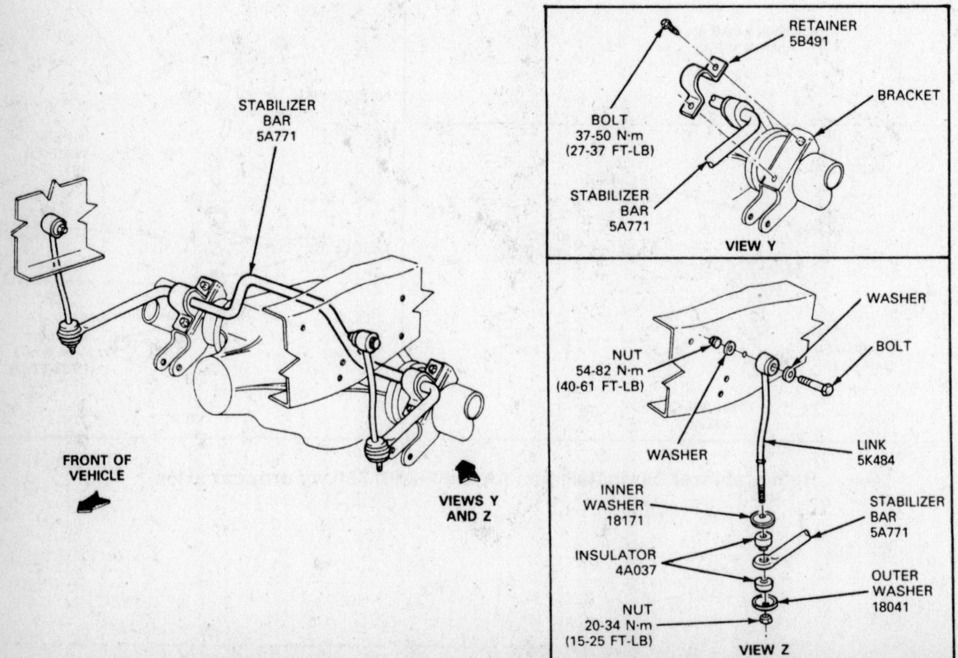

Rear stabilizer bar installation for F-Super Duty chassis/cab

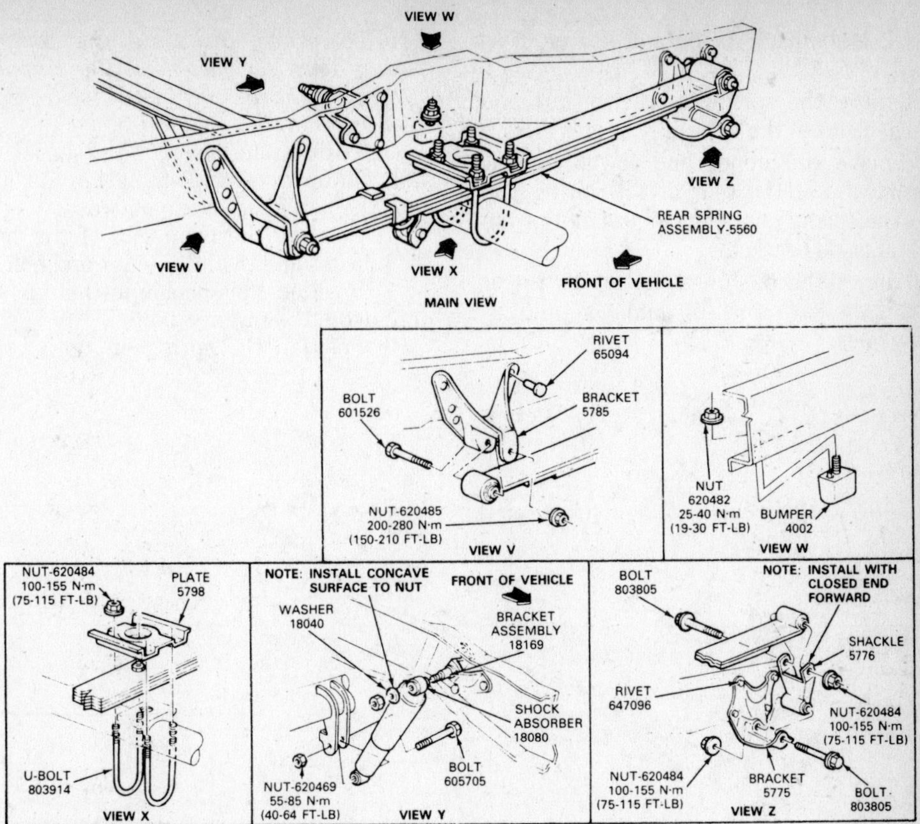

Conventional rear spring installation for F-250, 350 2-wheel drive regular cab and Super Cab

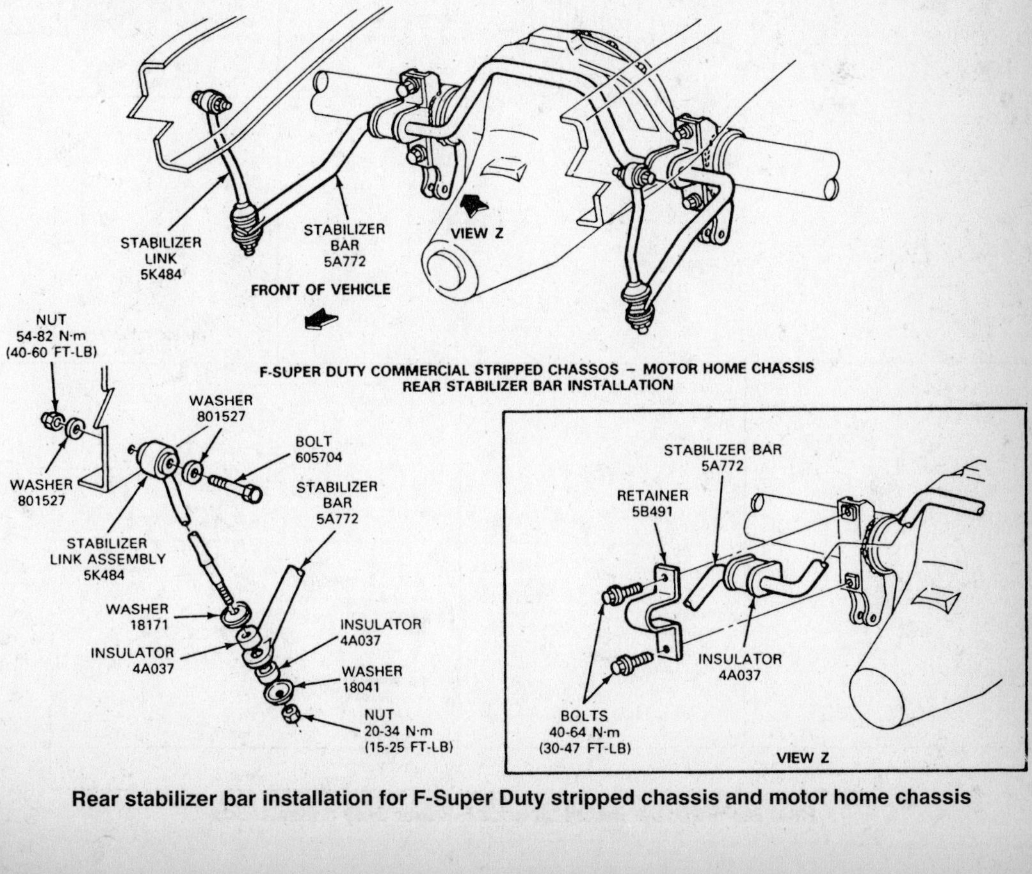

STABILIZER LINK 5K484

STABILIZER BAR 5A772

VIEW Z

FRONT OF VEHICLE

NUT 54-82 N·m (40-60 FT-LB)

F-SUPER DUTY COMMERCIAL STRIPPED CHASSOS – MOTOR HOME CHASSIS REAR STABILIZER BAR INSTALLATION

WASHER 801527

BOLT 605704

WASHER 801527

STABILIZER BAR 5A772

STABILIZER LINK ASSEMBLY 5K484

WASHER 18171

INSULATOR 4A037

INSULATOR 4A037

WASHER 18041

NUT 20-34 N·m (15-25 FT-LB)

STABILIZER BAR 5A772

RETAINER 5B491

INSULATOR 4A037

BOLTS 40-64 N·m (30-47 FT-LB)

VIEW Z

Rear stabilizer bar installation for F-Super Duty stripped chassis and motor home chassis

Remove the auxiliary spring and spacer, if so equipped.

3. Remove the spring-to-bracket nut and bolt at the front of the spring.

4. Remove the upper and lower shackle nuts and bolts at the rear of the spring and remove the spring and shackle assembly from the rear shackle bracket.

5. Remove the bushings in the spring or shackle, if they are worn or damaged, and install new ones.

NOTE: *When installing the components, snug down the fasteners. Don't apply final torque to the fasteners until the truck is back on the ground.*

6. Position the spring in the shackle and install the upper shackle-to-spring nut and bolt with the bolt head facing outward.

7. Position the front end of the spring in the bracket and install the nut and bolt.

8. Position the shackle in the rear bracket and install the nut and bolt.

9. Position the spring on top of the axle

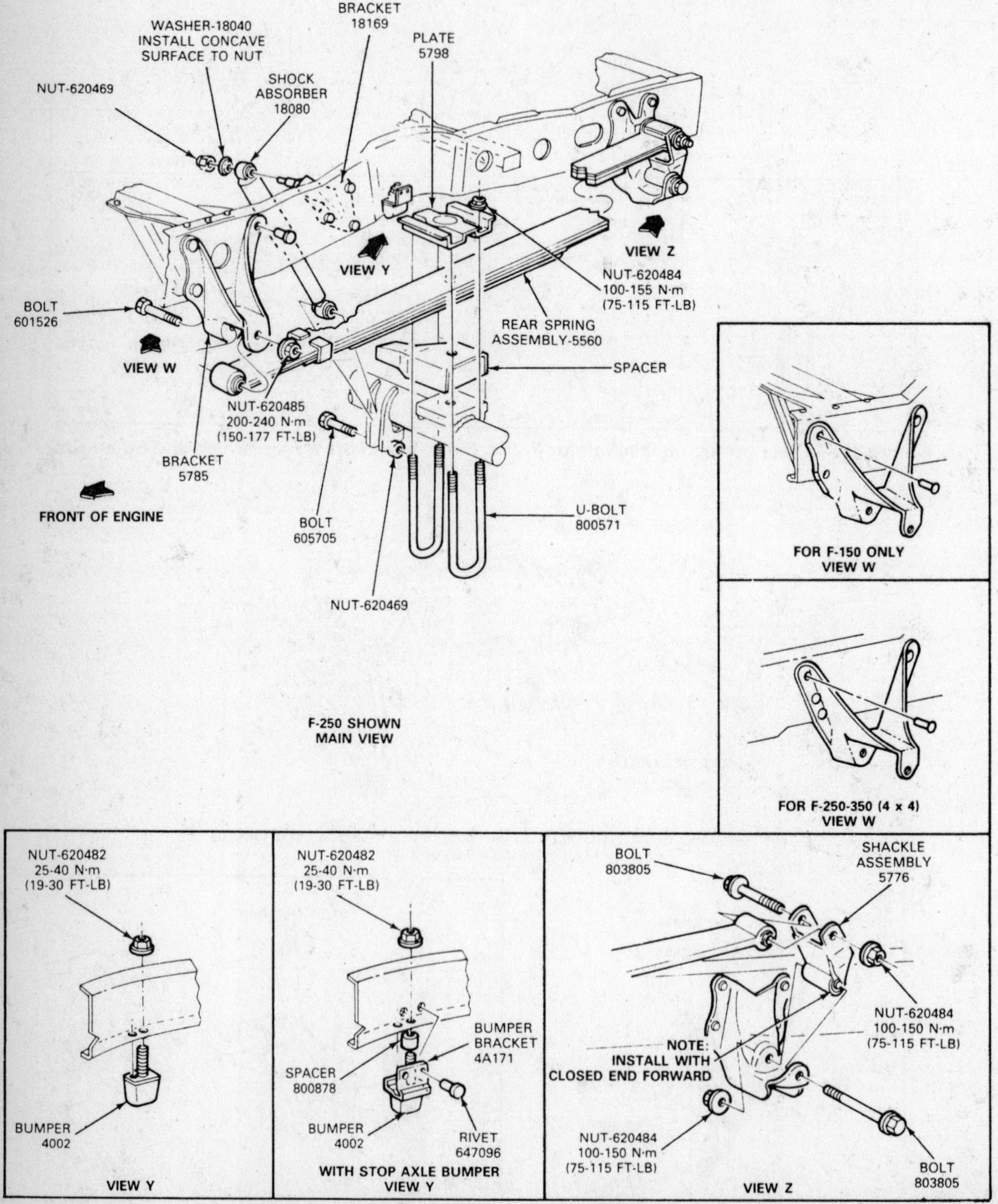

Rear spring installation for the 4-wheel drive F-150, 250, 350

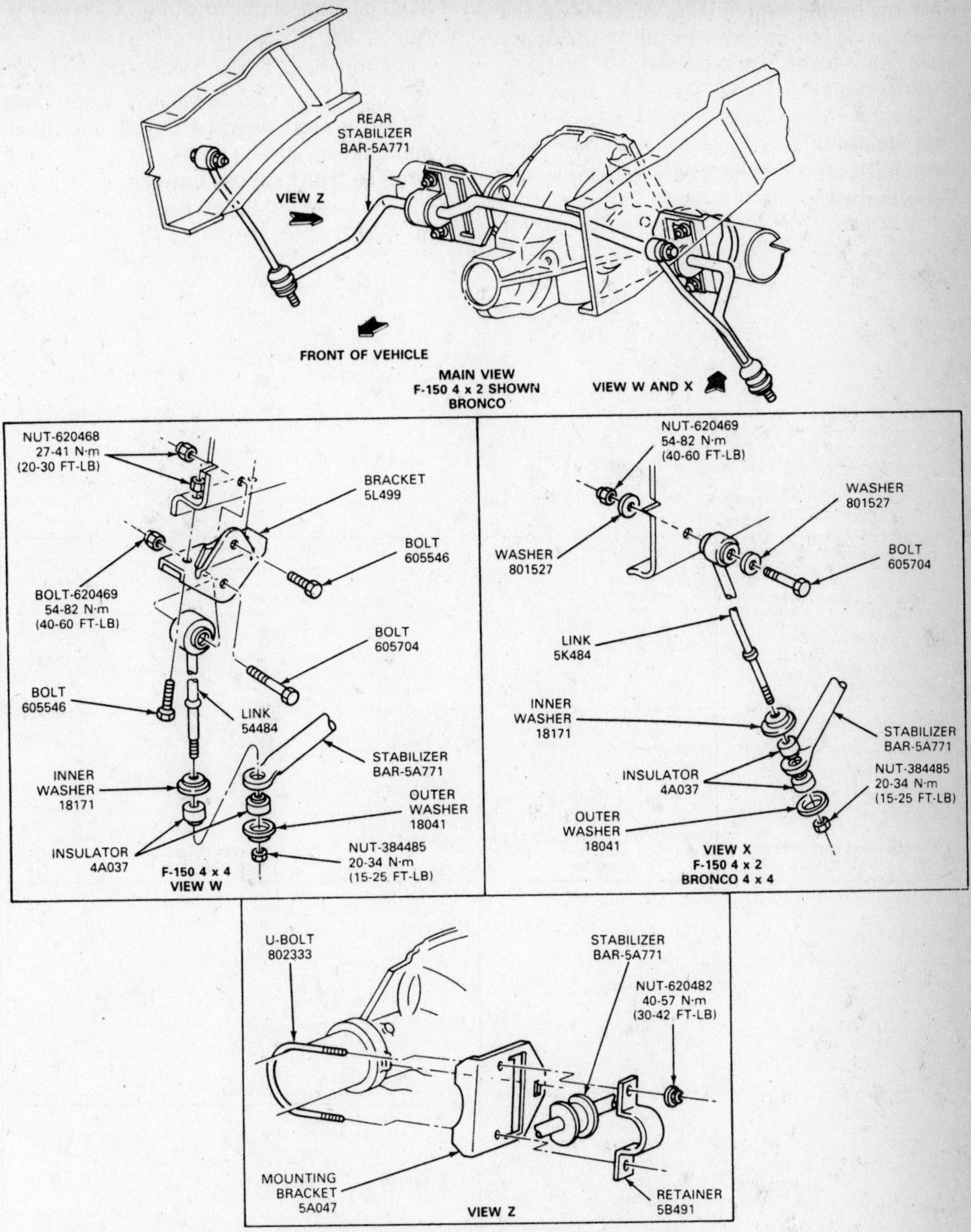

REAR
STABILIZER
BAR-5A771
VIEW Z
FRONT OF VEHICLE
MAIN VIEW
F-150 4 x 2 SHOWN
BRONCO
VIEW W AND X
NUT-620468
27-41 N·m
(20-30 FT-LB)
BRACKET
5L499
BOLT
605546
BOLT-620469
54-82 N·m
(40-60 FT-LB)
BOLT
605704
BOLT
605546
LINK
54484
STABILIZER
BAR-5A771
INNER
WASHER
18171
OUTER
WASHER
18041
INSULATOR
4A037
NUT-384485
20-34 N·m
(15-25 FT-LB)
F-150 4 x 4
VIEW W
NUT-620469
54-82 N·m
(40-60 FT-LB)
WASHER
801527
WASHER
801527
BOLT
605704
LINK
5K484
INNER
WASHER
18171
STABILIZER
BAR-5A771
INSULATOR
4A037
NUT-384485
20-34 N·m
(15-25 FT-LB)
OUTER
WASHER
18041
VIEW X
F-150 4 x 2
BRONCO 4 x 4
U-BOLT
802333
STABILIZER
BAR-5A771
NUT-620482
40-57 N·m
(30-42 FT-LB)
MOUNTING
BRACKET
5A047
VIEW Z
RETAINER
5B491

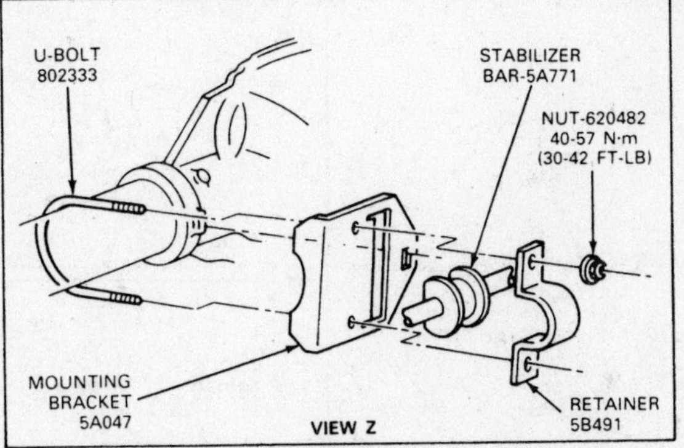

Rear stabilizer bar for the Bronco and F-150

with the spring center bolts centered in the hole provided in the seat. Install the auxiliary spring and spacer, if so equipped.

10. Install the spring U-bolts, plate and nuts.

11. Lower the vehicle to the floor and tighten the attaching hardware as follows:

U-bolts nuts:

- Bronco, F-150 and F-250 under 8,500 lb. GVW: 75–115 ft. lbs.
- F-250 HD and F-350: 150–210 ft. lbs.
- F-Super Duty chassis/cab: 200–270 ft. lbs.
- F-Super Duty stripped chassis and motor home chassis: 220–300 ft. lbs.

Spring to front spring hanger:

- F-150 2-wd: 75–115 ft. lbs.

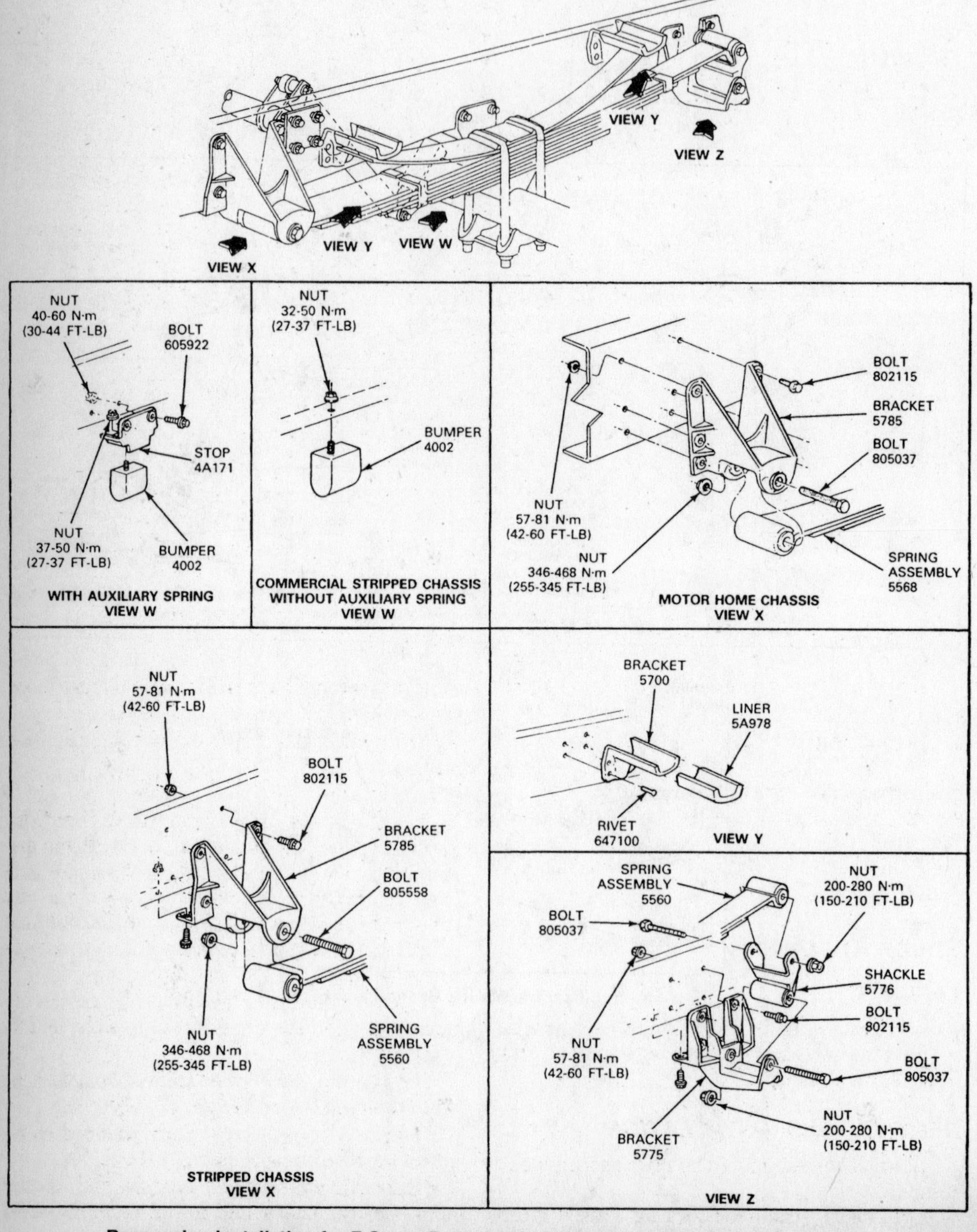

Rear spring installation for F-Super Duty stripped chassis and motor home chassis

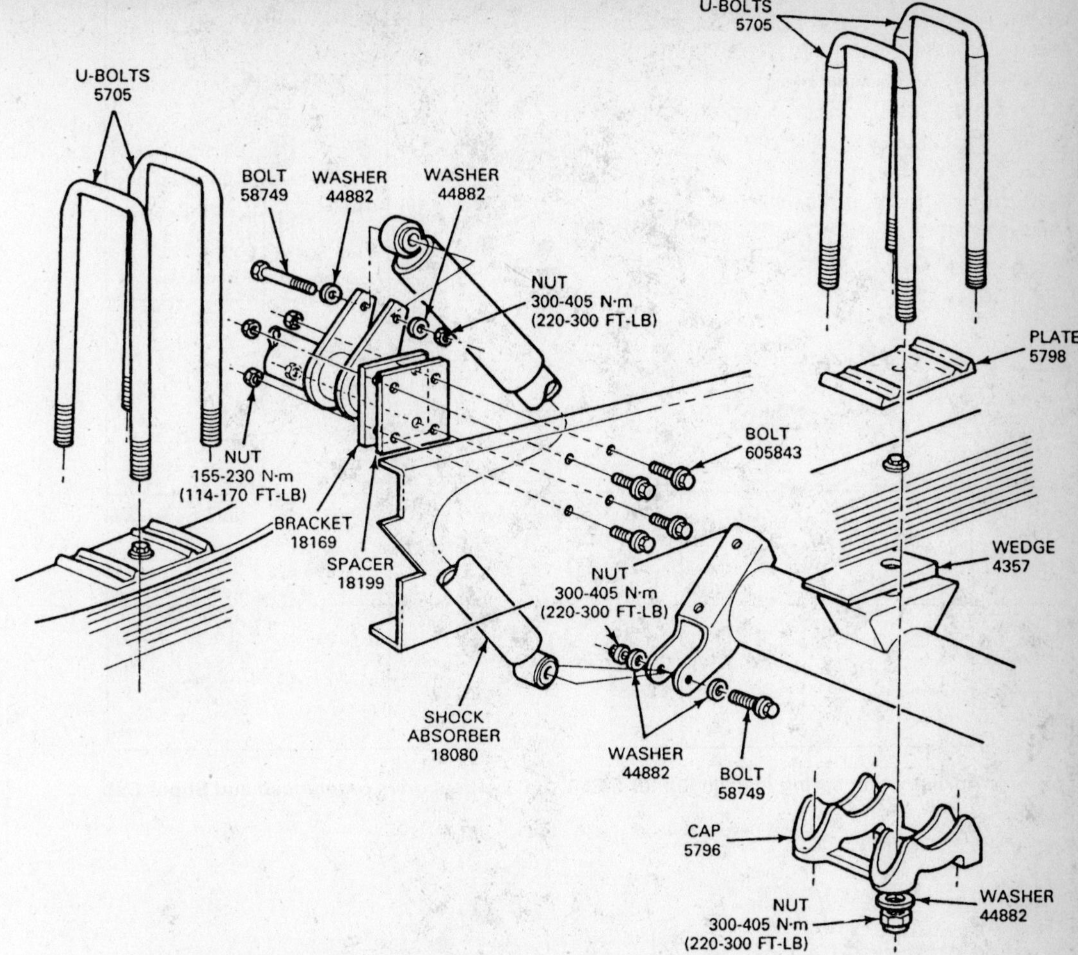

Rear shock absorber for F-Super Duty stripped chassis and motor home chassis

- F-250 2-wd, F-350 2-wd and Bronco: 150–210 ft. lbs.
- F-150, 250, 350 4-wd: 150–175 ft. lbs.
- F-Super Duty: 255–345 ft. lbs.

Spring to rear spring hanger:

- All except F-250 and F-350 2-wd Chassis Cab: 75–115 ft. lbs.
- F-250 and F-350 2-wd Chassis Cab; F-Super Duty: 150–210 ft. lbs.

Shock Absorbers

TESTING

Check, inspect and test the rear shock absorbers in the same manner as outlined for the front shock absorbers.

REMOVAL AND INSTALLATION

1. Raise and support the rear end on jackstands.
2. Remove the self-locking nut, steel washer and bolt from the lower end of the shock absorber. Swing the lower end away from the bracket.
3. Remove the upper mounting nut and washer.

To install:

4. Attach the upper end first, then the lower end; don't tighten the nuts yet. If you are installing new gas shocks, attach the upper end loosely, aim the lower end at its bracket and cut the strap holding the shock compressed. Once extended, these shocks are very difficult to compress by hand!
5. Once the upper and lower ends are attached, tighten the nuts, for all models, as follows:

- Lower end, exc. Super Duty stripped chassis and motor home chassis: 52–74 ft. lbs.
- Upper end, exc. Super Duty stripped chassis and motor home chassis: 40–60 ft. lbs.
- Super Duty stripped chassis and motor home chassis upper and lower ends: 220–300 ft. lbs.

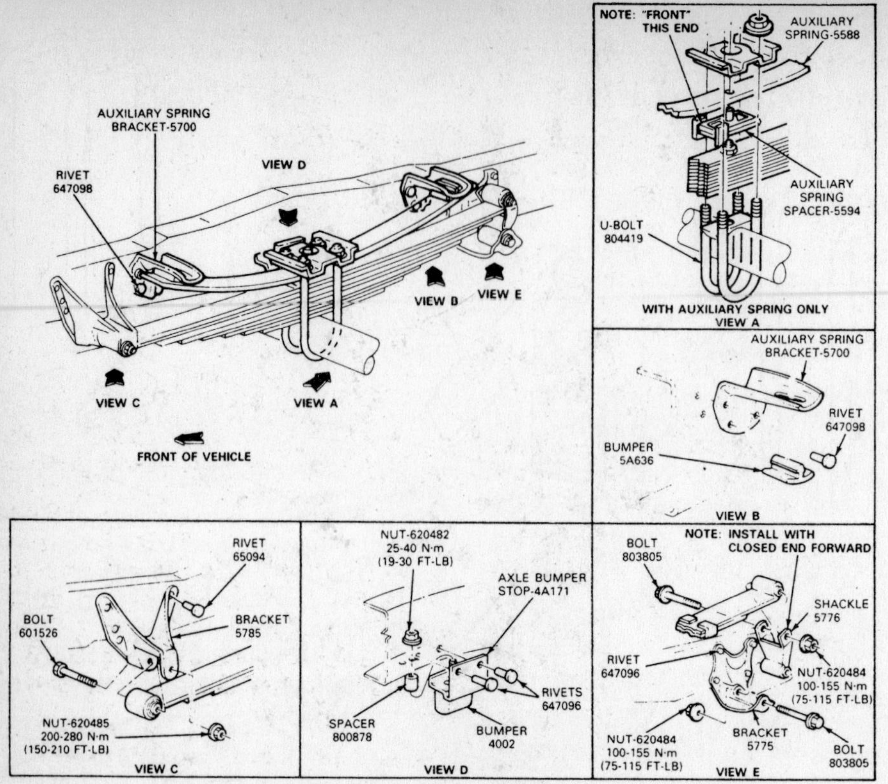

Auxiliary rear spring installation for F-250, 350 2-wheel drive regular cab and Super Cab

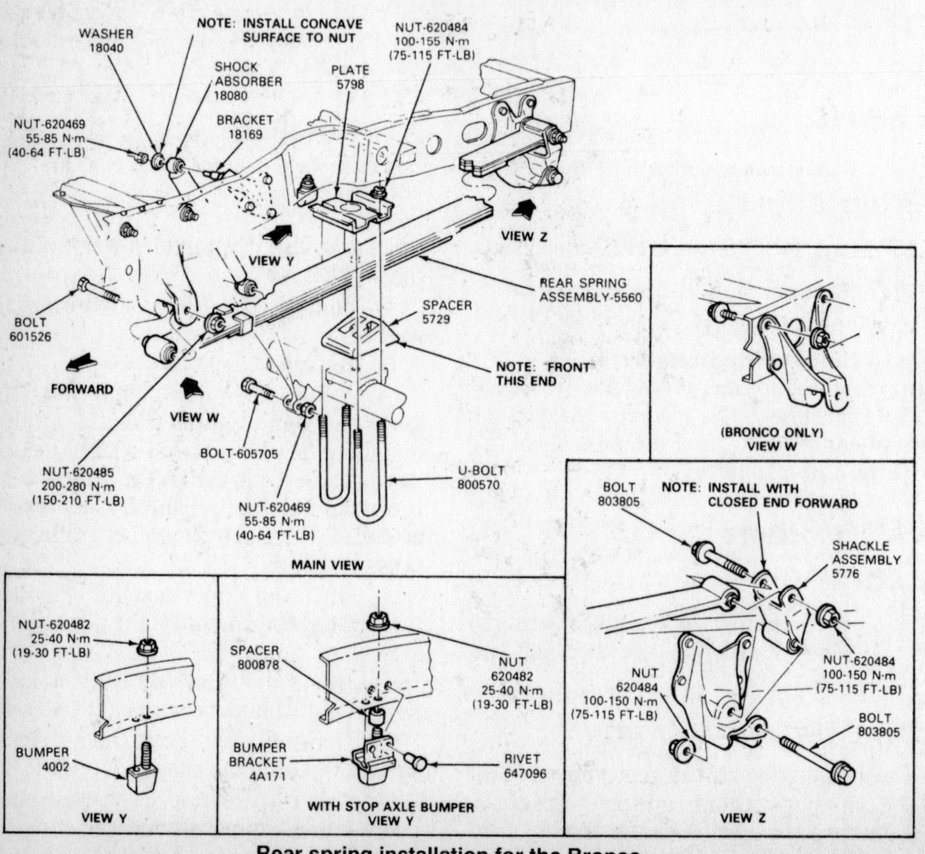

Rear spring installation for the Bronco

Stabilizer Bar

REMOVAL AND INSTALLATION

1. Remove the nuts from the lower ends of the stabilizer bar link.
2. Remove the outer washers and insulators.
3. Disconnect the bar from the links.
4. Remove the inner insulators and washers.
5. Unbolt the link from the frame.
6. Remove the U-bolts, brackets and retainers.
7. Installation is the reverse of removal. Replace all worn or cracked rubber parts. Coat all new rubber parts with silicone grease. Assemble all parts loosely and make sure the bar assembly is centered before tightening the fasteners. Observe the following torque figures:

• Stabilizer bar-to-axle nut, exc. Super Duty: 30–42 ft. lbs.
• Stabilizer bar-to-axle bolt, Super Duty chassis/cab: 27–37 ft. lbs.
• Stabilizer bar-to-axle bolt, Super Duty stripped chassis and motor home chassis: 30–47 ft. lbs.
• Link bracket-to-frame nut, 4-wd: 30–42 ft. lbs.
• Link-to-bracket nut, 4-wd: 60 ft. lbs.
• Link-to-frame nut, 2-wd: 60 ft. lbs.
• Stabilizer bar-to-link: 15–25 ft. lbs.

STEERING

Steering Wheel

REMOVAL AND INSTALLATION

All Except F-Super Duty Stripped Chassis models and Motor Home Chassis Models

1. Set the front wheel in the straight ahead position and make chalk marks on the column and steering wheel hub for alignment purposes during installation.
2. Disconnect the negative battery cable.
3. Remove the one screw from the underside of each steering wheel spoke, and lift the horn switch assembly (steering wheel pad) from the steering wheel. On vehicles equipped with the sport steering wheel option, pry the button cover off with a screwdriver.
4. Disconnect the horn switch wires at the connector and remove the switch assembly. On trucks equipped with speed control, squeeze the J-clip ground wire terminal firmly and pull it out of the hole in the steering wheel. Don't pull the wire out without squeezing the clip.
5. Remove the horn switch assembly.

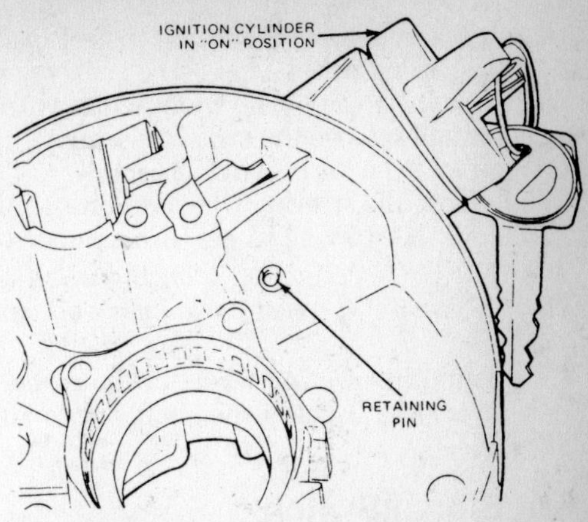

Lock retaining pin access slot on non-tilt column

6. Remove the steering wheel retaining nut and remove the steering wheel with a puller.

WARNING: *Never hammer on the wheel or shaft to remove it! Never use a knock-off type puller.*

7. Install the steering wheel in the reverse order of removal. Tighten the shaft nut to 40 ft. lbs.

F-Super Duty Stripped Chassis Motor Home Chassis

1. Set the front wheel in the straight ahead position and make chalk marks on the column and steering wheel hub for alignment purposes during installation.
2. Disconnect the negative battery cable.
3. Remove the one screw from the underside of each steering wheel spoke, and lift the

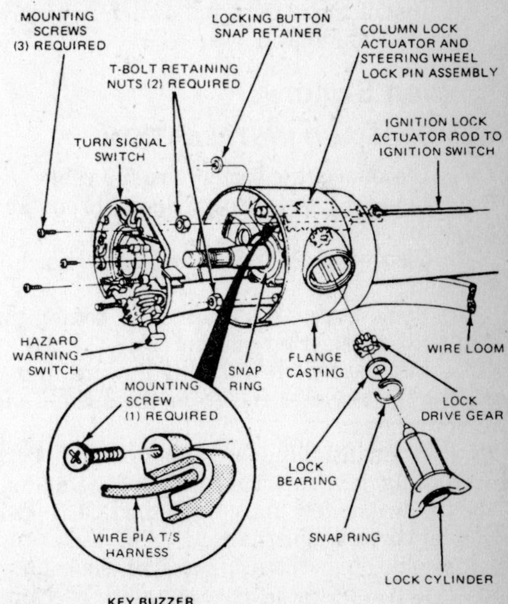

Non-tilting column mechanism

horn switch assembly (steering wheel pad) from the steering wheel.

4. Disconnect the horn switch wires at the connector and remove the switch assembly.

5. Remove the horn switch assembly.

6. Remove the steering wheel retaining nut and remove the steering wheel with a puller.

WARNING: *Never hammer on the wheel or shaft to remove it! Never use a knock-off type puller.*

7. Install the steering wheel in the reverse order of removal. Tighten the shaft nut to 30–42 ft. lbs.

Turn Signal Switch

REMOVAL AND INSTALLATION

1. Disconnect the battery ground cable.
2. Remove the steering wheel.
3. Remove the turn signal lever by unscrewing it from the steering column.
4. Disconnect the turn signal indicator switch wiring connector plug by lifting up the tabs on the side of the plug and pulling it apart.
5. Remove the switch assembly attaching screws.
6. On trucks with a fixed column, lift the switch out of the column and guide the connector plug through the opening in the shift socket.
7. On trucks with a tilt column, remove the connector plug before removing the switch from the column. The shift socket opening is not large enough for the plug connector to pass through.
8. Install the turn signal switch in the reverse order of removal.

Ignition Switch

REMOVAL AND INSTALLATION

1. Disconnect the battery ground cable.
2. Remove the steering column shroud and lower the steering column.
3. Disconnect the switch wiring at the multiple plug.
4. Remove the two nuts that retain the switch to the steering column.
5. Lift the switch vertically upward to disengage the actuator rod from the switch and remove the switch.
6. When installing the ignition switch, both the locking mechanism at the top of the column and the switch itself must be in the LOCK position for correct adjustment.

To hold the mechanical parts of the column in the LOCK position, move the shift lever into PARK (with automatic transmissions) or REVERSE (with manual transmissions), turn the key to the LOCK position, and remove the key.

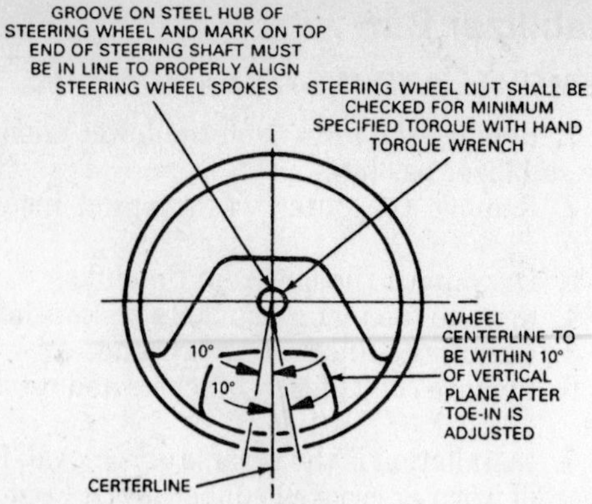

Correct steering wheel installation

New replacement switches, when received, are already pinned in the LOCK position by a metal shipping pin inserted in a locking hole on the side of the switch.

7. Engage the actuator rod in the switch.
8. Position the switch on the column and install the retaining nuts, but do not tighten them.
9. Move the switch up and down along the column to locate the mid-position of rod lash, and then tighten the retaining nuts.
10. Remove the locking pin, connect the battery cable, and check for proper start in PARK or NEUTRAL.

Also check to make certain that the start circuit cannot be actuated in the DRIVE and REVERSE position.

11. Raise the steering column into position at instrument panel. Install steering column shroud.

Ignition Lock Cylinder

REMOVAL AND INSTALLATION

With Key

1. Disconnect the battery ground.
2. On tilt columns, remove the upper extension shroud by unsnapping the shroud from the retaining clip at the 9 o'clock position.
3. Remove the trim shroud halves.
4. Unplug the wire connector at the key warning switch.
5. Place the shift lever in PARK and turn the key to ON.
6. Place a 1/8 in. (3mm) wire pin in the hole in the casting surrounding the lock cylinder and depress the retaining pin while pulling out on the cylinder.
7. When installing the cylinder, turn the lock cylinder to the RUN position and depress the retaining pin, then insert the lock cylinder into its housing in the flange casting. Assure that the cylinder is fully seated and aligned in

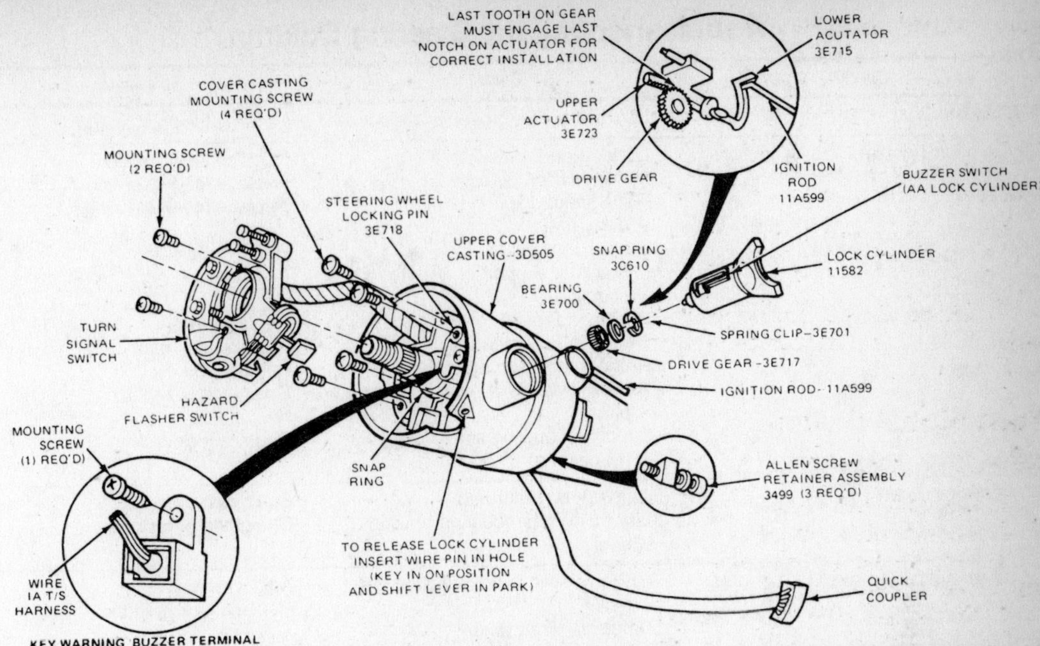

Tilt column mechanism

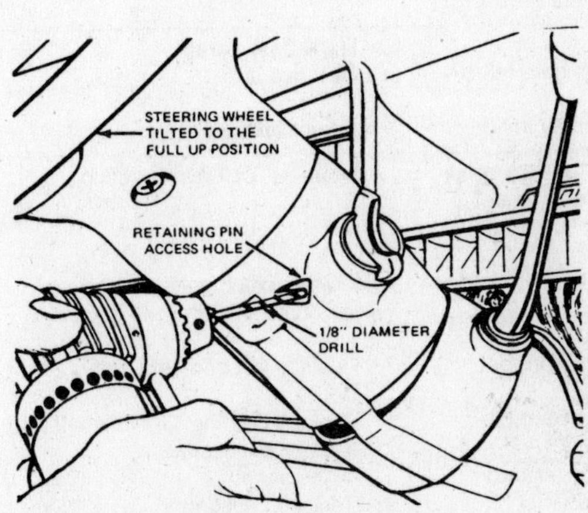

Drilling out the lock retaining pin

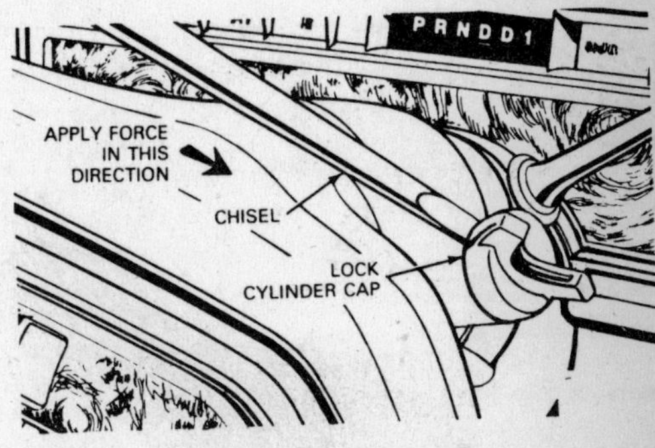

Breaking the cap away from the lock cylinder

the interlocking washer before turning the key to the OFF position. This will allow the cylinder retaining pin to extend into the cylinder cast housing hole.

8. The remainder of installation is the reverse of removal.

Non-Functioning Cylinder or No Key Available

FIXED COLUMNS

1. Disconnect the battery ground.
2. Remove the steering wheel.
3. Remove the turn signal lever.
4. Remove the column trim shrouds.
5. Unbolt the steering column and lower it carefully.
6. Remove the ignition switch and warning buzzer and pin the switch in the LOCK position.
7. Remove the turn signal switch.
8. Remove the snapring and T-bolt nuts that retain the flange casting to the column outer tube.
9. Remove the flange casting, upper shaft bearing, lock cylinder, ignition switch actuator and the actuator rod by pulling the entire assembly over the end of the steering column shaft.
10. Remove the lock actuator insert, the T-bolts and the automatic transmission indicator insert, or, with manual transmissions, the key release lever.
11. Upon reassembly, the following parts must be replaced with new parts:

Troubleshooting the Steering Column

Problem	Cause	Solution
Will not lock	• Lockbolt spring broken or defective	• Replace lock bolt spring
High effort (required to turn ignition key and lock cylinder)	• Lock cylinder defective • Ignition switch defective • Rack preload spring broken or deformed • Burr on lock sector, lock rack, housing, support or remote rod coupling • Bent sector shaft • Defective lock rack • Remote rod bent, deformed • Ignition switch mounting bracket bent • Distorted coupling slot in lock rack (tilt column)	• Replace lock cylinder • Replace ignition switch • Replace preload spring • Remove burr • Replace shaft • Replace lock rack • Replace rod • Straighten or replace • Replace lock rack
Will stick in "start"	• Remote rod deformed • Ignition switch mounting bracket bent	• Straighten or replace • Straighten or replace
Key cannot be removed in "off-lock"	• Ignition switch is not adjusted correctly • Defective lock cylinder	• Adjust switch • Replace lock cylinder
Lock cylinder can be removed without depressing retainer	• Lock cylinder with defective retainer • Burr over retainer slot in housing cover or on cylinder retainer	• Replace lock cylinder • Remove burr
High effort on lock cylinder between "off" and "off-lock"	• Distorted lock rack • Burr on tang of shift gate (automatic column) • Gearshift linkage not adjusted	• Replace lock rack • Remove burr • Adjust linkage
Noise in column	• One click when in "off-lock" position and the steering wheel is moved (all except automatic column) • Coupling bolts not tightened • Lack of grease on bearings or bearing surfaces • Upper shaft bearing worn or broken • Lower shaft bearing worn or broken • Column not correctly aligned • Coupling pulled apart • Broken coupling lower joint • Steering shaft snap ring not seated • Shroud loose on shift bowl. Housing loose on jacket—will be noticed with ignition in "off-lock" and when torque is applied to steering wheel.	• Normal—lock bolt is seating • Tighten pinch bolts • Lubricate with chassis grease • Replace bearing assembly • Replace bearing. Check shaft and replace if scored. • Align column • Replace coupling • Repair or replace joint and align column • Replace ring. Check for proper seating in groove. • Position shroud over lugs on shift bowl. Tighten mounting screws.
High steering shaft effort	• Column misaligned • Defective upper or lower bearing • Tight steering shaft universal joint • Flash on I.D. of shift tube at plastic joint (tilt column only) • Upper or lower bearing seized	• Align column • Replace as required • Repair or replace • Replace shift tube • Replace bearings
Lash in mounted column assembly	• Column mounting bracket bolts loose • Broken weld nuts on column jacket • Column capsule bracket sheared	• Tighten bolts • Replace column jacket • Replace bracket assembly

Troubleshooting the Steering Column (cont.)

Problem	Cause	Solution
Lash in mounted column assembly (cont.)	• Column bracket to column jacket mounting bolts loose • Loose lock shoes in housing (tilt column only) • Loose pivot pins (tilt column only) • Loose lock shoe pin (tilt column only) • Loose support screws (tilt column only)	• Tighten to specified torque • Replace shoes • Replace pivot pins and support • Replace pin and housing • Tighten screws
Housing loose (tilt column only)	• Excessive clearance between holes in support or housing and pivot pin diameters • Housing support-screws loose	• Replace pivot pins and support • Tighten screws
Steering wheel loose—every other tilt position (tilt column only)	• Loose fit between lock shoe and lock shoe pivot pin	• Replace lock shoes and pivot pin
Steering column not locking in any tilt position (tilt column only)	• Lock shoe seized on pivot pin • Lock shoe grooves have burrs or are filled with foreign material • Lock shoe springs weak or broken	• Replace lock shoes and pin • Clean or replace lock shoes • Replace springs
Noise when tilting column (tilt column only)	• Upper tilt bumpers worn • Tilt spring rubbing in housing	• Replace tilt bumper • Lubricate with chassis grease
One click when in "off-lock" position and the steering wheel is moved	• Seating of lock bolt	• None. Click is normal characteristic sound produced by lock bolt as it seats.
High shift effort (automatic and tilt column only)	• Column not correctly aligned • Lower bearing not aligned correctly • Lack of grease on seal or lower bearing areas	• Align column • Assemble correctly • Lubricate with chassis grease
Improper transmission shifting—automatic and tilt column only	• Sheared shift tube joint • Improper transmission gearshift linkage adjustment • Loose lower shift lever	• Replace shift tube • Adjust linkage • Replace shift tube

Troubleshooting the Ignition Switch

Problem	Cause	Solution
Ignition switch electrically inoperative	• Loose or defective switch connector • Feed wire open (fusible link) • Defective ignition switch	• Tighten or replace connector • Repair or replace • Replace ignition switch
Engine will not crank	• Ignition switch not adjusted properly	• Adjust switch
Ignition switch wil not actuate mechanically	• Defective ignition switch • Defective lock sector • Defective remote rod	• Replace switch • Replace lock sector • Replace remote rod
Ignition switch cannot be adjusted correctly	• Remote rod deformed	• Repair, straighten or replace

Troubleshooting the Turn Signal Switch

Problem	Cause	Solution
Turn signal will not cancel	• Loose switch mounting screws • Switch or anchor bosses broken • Broken, missing or out of position detent, or cancelling spring	• Tighten screws • Replace switch • Reposition springs or replace switch as required
Turn signal difficult to operate	• Turn signal lever loose • Switch yoke broken or distorted • Loose or misplaced springs • Foreign parts and/or materials in switch • Switch mounted loosely	• Tighten mounting screws • Replace switch • Reposition springs or replace switch • Remove foreign parts and/or material • Tighten mounting screws
Turn signal will not indicate lane change	• Broken lane change pressure pad or spring hanger • Broken, missing or misplaced lane change spring • Jammed wires	• Replace switch • Replace or reposition as required • Loosen mounting screws, reposition wires and retighten screws
Turn signal will not stay in turn position	• Foreign material or loose parts impeding movement of switch yoke • Defective switch	• Remove material and/or parts • Replace switch
Hazard switch cannot be pulled out	• Foreign material between hazard support cancelling leg and yoke	• Remove foreign material. No foreign material impeding function of hazard switch—replace turn signal switch.
No turn signal lights	• Inoperative turn signal flasher • Defective or blown fuse • Loose chassis to column harness connector • Disconnect column to chassis connector. Connect new switch to chassis and operate switch by hand. If vehicle lights now operate normally, signal switch is inoperative • If vehicle lights do not operate, check chassis wiring for opens, grounds, etc.	• Replace turn signal flasher • Replace fuse • Connect securely • Replace signal switch • Repair chassis wiring as required
Instrument panel turn indicator lights on but not flashing	• Burned out or damaged front or rear turn signal bulb • If vehicle lights do not operate, check light sockets for high resistance connections, the chassis wiring for opens, grounds, etc. • Inoperative flasher • Loose chassis to column harness connection • Inoperative turn signal switch • To determine if turn signal switch is defective, substitute new switch into circuit and operate switch by hand. If the vehicle's lights operate normally, signal switch is inoperative.	• Replace bulb • Repair chassis wiring as required • Replace flasher • Connect securely • Replace turn signal switch • Replace turn signal switch
Stop light not on when turn indicated	• Loose column to chassis connection • Disconnect column to chassis connector. Connect new switch into system without removing old.	• Connect securely • Replace signal switch

Troubleshooting the Turn Signal Switch (cont.)

Problem	Cause	Solution
Stop light not on when turn indicated (cont.)	Operate switch by hand. If brake lights work with switch in the turn position, signal switch is defective. • If brake lights do not work, check connector to stop light sockets for grounds, opens, etc.	• Repair connector to stop light circuits using service manual as guide
Turn indicator panel lights not flashing	• Burned out bulbs • High resistance to ground at bulb socket • Opens, ground in wiring harness from front turn signal bulb socket to indicator lights	• Replace bulbs • Replace socket • Locate and repair as required
Turn signal lights flash very slowly	• High resistance ground at light sockets • Incorrect capacity turn signal flasher or bulb • If flashing rate is still extremely slow, check chassis wiring harness from the connector to light sockets for high resistance • Loose chassis to column harness connection • Disconnect column to chassis connector. Connect new switch into system without removing old. Operate switch by hand. If flashing occurs at normal rate, the signal switch is defective.	• Repair high resistance grounds at light sockets • Replace turn signal flasher or bulb • Locate and repair as required • Connect securely • Replace turn signal switch
Hazard signal lights will not flash—turn signal functions normally	• Blow fuse • Inoperative hazard warning flasher • Loose chassis-to-column harness connection • Disconnect column to chassis connector. Connect new switch into system without removing old. Depress the hazard warning lights. If they now work normally, turn signal switch is defective. • If lights do not flash, check wiring harness "K" lead for open between hazard flasher and connector. If open, fuse block is defective	• Replace fuse • Replace hazard warning flasher in fuse panel • Conect securely • Replace turn signal switch • Repair or replace brown wire or connector as required

Troubleshooting the Manual Steering Gear

Problem	Cause	Solution
Hard or erratic steering	• Incorrect tire pressure	• Inflate tires to recommended pressures
	• Insufficient or incorrect lubrication	• Lubricate as required (refer to Maintenance Section)
	• Suspension, or steering linkage parts damaged or misaligned	• Repair or replace parts as necessary
	• Improper front wheel alignment	• Adjust incorrect wheel alignment angles
	• Incorrect steering gear adjustment	• Adjust steering gear
	• Sagging springs	• Replace springs
Play or looseness in steering	• Steering wheel loose	• Inspect shaft spines and repair as necessary. Tighten attaching nut and stake in place.
	• Steering linkage or attaching parts loose or worn	• Tighten, adjust, or replace faulty components
	• Pitman arm loose	• Inspect shaft splines and repair as necessary. Tighten attaching nut and stake in place
	• Steering gear attaching bolts loose	• Tighten bolts
	• Loose or worn wheel bearings	• Adjust or replace bearings
	• Steering gear adjustment incorrect or parts badly worn	• Adjust gear or replace defective parts
Wheel shimmy or tramp	• Improper tire pressure	• Inflate tires to recommended pressures
	• Wheels, tires, or brake rotors out-of-balance or out-of-round	• Inspect and replace or balance parts
	• Inoperative, worn, or loose shock absorbers or mounting parts	• Repair or replace shocks or mountings
	• Loose or worn steering or suspension parts	• Tighten or replace as necessary
	• Loose or worn wheel bearings	• Adjust or replace bearings
	• Incorrect steering gear adjustments	• Adjust steering gear
	• Incorrect front wheel alignment	• Correct front wheel alignment
Tire wear	• Improper tire pressure	• Inflate tires to recommended pressures
	• Failure to rotate tires	• Rotate tires
	• Brakes grabbing	• Adjust or repair brakes
	• Incorrect front wheel alignment	• Align incorrect angles
	• Broken or damaged steering and suspension parts	• Repair or replace defective parts
	• Wheel runout	• Replace faulty wheel
	• Excessive speed on turns	• Make driver aware of conditions
Vehicle leads to one side	• Improper tire pressures	• Inflate tires to recommended pressures
	• Front tires with uneven tread depth, wear pattern, or different cord design (i.e., one bias ply and one belted or radial tire on front wheels)	• Install tires of same cord construction and reasonably even tread depth, design, and wear pattern
	• Incorrect front wheel alignment	• Align incorrect angles
	• Brakes dragging	• Adjust or repair brakes
	• Pulling due to uneven tire construction	• Replace faulty tire

Troubleshooting the Power Steering Gear

Problem	Cause	Solution
Hissing noise in steering gear	• There is some noise in all power steering systems. One of the most common is a hissing sound most evident at standstill parking. There is no relationship between this noise and performance of the steering. Hiss may be expected when steering wheel is at end of travel or when slowly turning at standstill.	• Slight hiss is normal and in no way affects steering. Do not replace valve unless hiss is extremely objectionable. A replacement valve will also exhibit slight noise and is not always a cure. Investigate clearance around flexible coupling rivets. Be sure steering shaft and gear are aligned so flexible coupling rotates in a flat plane and is not distorted as shaft rotates. Any metal-to-metal contacts through flexible coupling will transmit valve hiss into passenger compartment through the steering column.
Rattle or chuckle noise in steering gear	• Gear loose on frame	• Check gear-to-frame mounting screws. Tighten screws to 88 N·m (65 foot pounds) torque.
	• Steering linkage looseness	• Check linkage pivot points for wear. Replace if necessary.
	• Pressure hose touching other parts of car	• Adjust hose position. Do not bend tubing by hand.
	• Loose pitman shaft over center adjustment **NOTE:** A slight rattle may occur on turns because of increased clearance off the "high point." This is normal and clearance must not be reduced below specified limits to eliminate this slight rattle.	• Adjust to specifications
	• Loose pitman arm	• Tighten pitman arm nut to specifications
Squawk noise in steering gear when turning or recovering from a turn	• Damper O-ring on valve spool cut	• Replace damper O-ring
Poor return of steering wheel to center	• Tires not properly inflated	• Inflate to specified pressure
	• Lack of lubrication in linkage and ball joints	• Lube linkage and ball joints
	• Lower coupling flange rubbing against steering gear adjuster plug	• Loosen pinch bolt and assemble properly
	• Steering gear to column misalignment	• Align steering column
	• Improper front wheel alignment	• Check and adjust as necessary
	• Steering linkage binding	• Replace pivots
	• Ball joints binding	• Replace ball joints
	• Steering wheel rubbing against housing	• Align housing
	• Tight or frozen steering shaft bearings	• Replace bearings
	• Sticking or plugged valve spool	• Remove and clean or replace valve
	• Steering gear adjustments over specifications	• Check adjustment with gear out of car. Adjust as required.
	• Kink in return hose	• Replace hose
Car leads to one side or the other (keep in mind road condition and wind. Test car in both directions on flat road)	• Front end misaligned	• Adjust to specifications
	• Unbalanced steering gear valve **NOTE:** If this is cause, steering effort will be very light in direction of lead and normal or heavier in opposite direction	• Replace valve

Troubleshooting the Power Steering Gear (cont.)

Problem	Cause	Solution
Momentary increase in effort when turning wheel fast to right or left	• Low oil level • Pump belt slipping • High internal leakage	• Add power steering fluid as required • Tighten or replace belt • Check pump pressure. (See pressure test)
Steering wheel surges or jerks when turning with engine running especially during parking	• Low oil level • Loose pump belt • Steering linkage hitting engine oil pan at full turn • Insufficient pump pressure • Pump flow control valve sticking	• Fill as required • Adjust tension to specification • Correct clearance • Check pump pressure. (See pressure test). Replace relief valve if defective. • Inspect for varnish or damage, replace if necessary
Excessive wheel kickback or loose steering	• Air in system • Steering gear loose on frame • Steering linkage joints worn enough to be loose • Worn poppet valve • Loose thrust bearing preload adjustment • Excessive overcenter lash	• Add oil to pump reservoir and bleed by operating steering. Check hose connectors for proper torque and adjust as required. • Tighten attaching screws to specified torque • Replace loose pivots • Replace poppet valve • Adjust to specification with gear out of vehicle • Adjust to specification with gear out of car
Hard steering or lack of assist	• Loose pump belt • Low oil level **NOTE:** Low oil level will also result in excessive pump noise • Steering gear to column misalignment • Lower coupling flange rubbing against steering gear adjuster plug • Tires not properly inflated	• Adjust belt tension to specification • Fill to proper level. If excessively low, check all lines and joints for evidence of external leakage. Tighten loose connectors. • Align steering column • Loosen pinch bolt and assemble properly • Inflate to recommended pressure
Foamy milky power steering fluid, low fluid level and possible low pressure	• Air in the fluid, and loss of fluid due to internal pump leakage causing overflow	• Check for leak and correct. Bleed system. Extremely cold temperatures will cause system aeriation should the oil level be low. If oil level is correct and pump still foams, remove pump from vehicle and separate reservoir from housing. Check welsh plug and housing for cracks. If plug is loose or housing is cracked, replace housing.
Low pressure due to steering pump	• Flow control valve stuck or inoperative • Pressure plate not flat against cam ring	• Remove burrs or dirt or replace. Flush system. • Correct
Low pressure due to steering gear	• Pressure loss in cylinder due to worn piston ring or badly worn housing bore • Leakage at valve rings, valve body-to-worm seal	• Remove gear from car for disassembly and inspection of ring and housing bore • Remove gear from car for disassembly and replace seals

Troubleshooting the Power Steering Pump

Problem	Cause	Solution
Chirp noise in steering pump	• Loose belt	• Adjust belt tension to specification
Belt squeal (particularly noticeable at full wheel travel and stand still parking)	• Loose belt	• Adjust belt tension to specification
Growl noise in steering pump	• Excessive back pressure in hoses or steering gear caused by restriction	• Locate restriction and correct. Replace part if necessary.
Growl noise in steering pump (particularly noticeable at stand still parking)	• Scored pressure plates, thrust plate or rotor • Extreme wear of cam ring	• Replace parts and flush system • Replace parts
Groan noise in steering pump	• Low oil level • Air in the oil. Poor pressure hose connection.	• Fill reservoir to proper level • Tighten connector to specified torque. Bleed system by operating steering from right to left—full turn.
Rattle noise in steering pump	• Vanes not installed properly • Vanes sticking in rotor slots	• Install properly • Free up by removing burrs, varnish, or dirt
Swish noise in steering pump	• Defective flow control valve	• Replace part
Whine noise in steering pump	• Pump shaft bearing scored	• Replace housing and shaft. Flush system.
Hard steering or lack of assist	• Loose pump belt • Low oil level in reservoir **NOTE:** Low oil level will also result in excessive pump noise • Steering gear to column misalignment • Lower coupling flange rubbing against steering gear adjuster plug • Tires not properly inflated	• Adjust belt tension to specification • Fill to proper level. If excessively low, check all lines and joints for evidence of external leakage. Tighten loose connectors. • Align steering column • Loosen pinch bolt and assemble properly • Inflate to recommended pressure
Foaming milky power steering fluid, low fluid level and possible low pressure	• Air in the fluid, and loss of fluid due to internal pump leakage causing overflow	• Check for leaks and correct. Bleed system. Extremely cold temperatures will cause system aeriation should the oil level be low. If oil level is correct and pump still foams, remove pump from vehicle and separate reservoir from body. Check welsh plug and body for cracks. If plug is loose or body is cracked, replace body.
Low pump pressure	• Flow control valve stuck or inoperative • Pressure plate not flat against cam ring	• Remove burrs or dirt or replace. Flush system. • Correct
Momentary increase in effort when turning wheel fast to right or left	• Low oil level in pump • Pump belt slipping • High internal leakage	• Add power steering fluid as required • Tighten or replace belt • Check pump pressure. (See pressure test)
Steering wheel surges or jerks when turning with engine running especially during parking	• Low oil level • Loose pump belt • Steering linkage hitting engine oil pan at full turn • Insufficient pump pressure	• Fill as required • Adjust tension to specification • Correct clearance • Check pump pressure. (See pressure test). Replace flow control valve if defective.

Troubleshooting the Power Steering Pump (cont.)

Problem	Cause	Solution
Steering wheel surges or jerks when turning with engine running especially during parking (cont.)	• Sticking flow control valve	• Inspect for varnish or damage, replace if necessary
Excessive wheel kickback or loose steering	• Air in system	• Add oil to pump reservoir and bleed by operating steering. Check hose connectors for proper torque and adjust as required.
Low pump pressure	• Extreme wear of cam ring	• Replace parts. Flush system.
	• Scored pressure plate, thrust plate, or rotor	• Replace parts. Flush system.
	• Vanes not installed properly	• Install properly
	• Vanes sticking in rotor slots	• Freeup by removing burrs, varnish, or dirt
	• Cracked or broken thrust or pressure plate	• Replace part

- Flange
- Lock cylinder assembly
- Steering column lock gear
- Steering column lock bearing
- Steering column upper bearing retainer
- Lock actuator assembly

12. Assembly is a reversal of the disassembly procedure. It is best to install a new upper bearing. Check that the truck starts only in PARK and NEUTRAL.

TILT COLUMNS

1. Disconnect the battery ground.
2. Remove the steering column shrouds.
3. Using masking tape, tape the gap between the steering wheel hub and the cover casting. Cover the entire circumference of the casting. Cover the seat and floor area with a dropcloth.
4. Pull out the hazard switch and tape it in a downward position.
5. The lock cylinder retaining pin is located on the outside of the steering column cover casting adjacent to the hazard flasher button.
6. Tilt the steering column to the full up position and prepunch the lock cylinder retaining pin with a sharp punch.
7. Using a $^{1}/_{8}$ in. (3mm) drill bit, mounted in a right angle drive drill adapter, drill out the retaining pin, going no deeper than $^{1}/_{2}$ in. (13mm).
8. Tilt the column to the full down position. Place a chisel at the base of the ignition lock cylinder cap and using a hammer break away the cap from the lock cylinder.
9. Using a $^{3}/_{8}$ in. (10mm) drill bit, drill down the center of the ignition lock cylinder key slot about $1^{3}/_{4}$ in. (44mm), until the lock cylinder breaks loose from the steering column cover casting.
10. Remove the lock cylinder and the drill shavings.
11. Remove the steering wheel.
12. Remove the turn signal lever.
13. Remove the turn signal switch attaching screws.
14. Remove the key buzzer attaching screw.
15. Remove the turn signal switch up and over the end of the column, but don't disconnect the wiring.
16. Remove the 4 attaching screws from the cover casting and lift the casting over the end of the steering shaft, allowing the turn signal switch to pass through the casting. The removal of the casting cover will expose the upper actuator. Remove the upper actuator.
17. Remove the drive gear, snapring and washer from the cover casting along with the upper actuator.
18. Clean all components and replace any that appear damaged or worn.
19. Installation is the reverse of removal.

Steering Column

REMOVAL AND INSTALLATION

All Models Except F-Super Duty Stripped Chassis and Motor Home Chassis

1. Set the parking brake.
2. Disconnect the battery ground cable.
3. Unbolt the intermediate shaft from the steering column.
4. Disconnect the shift linkage rod(s) from the column.

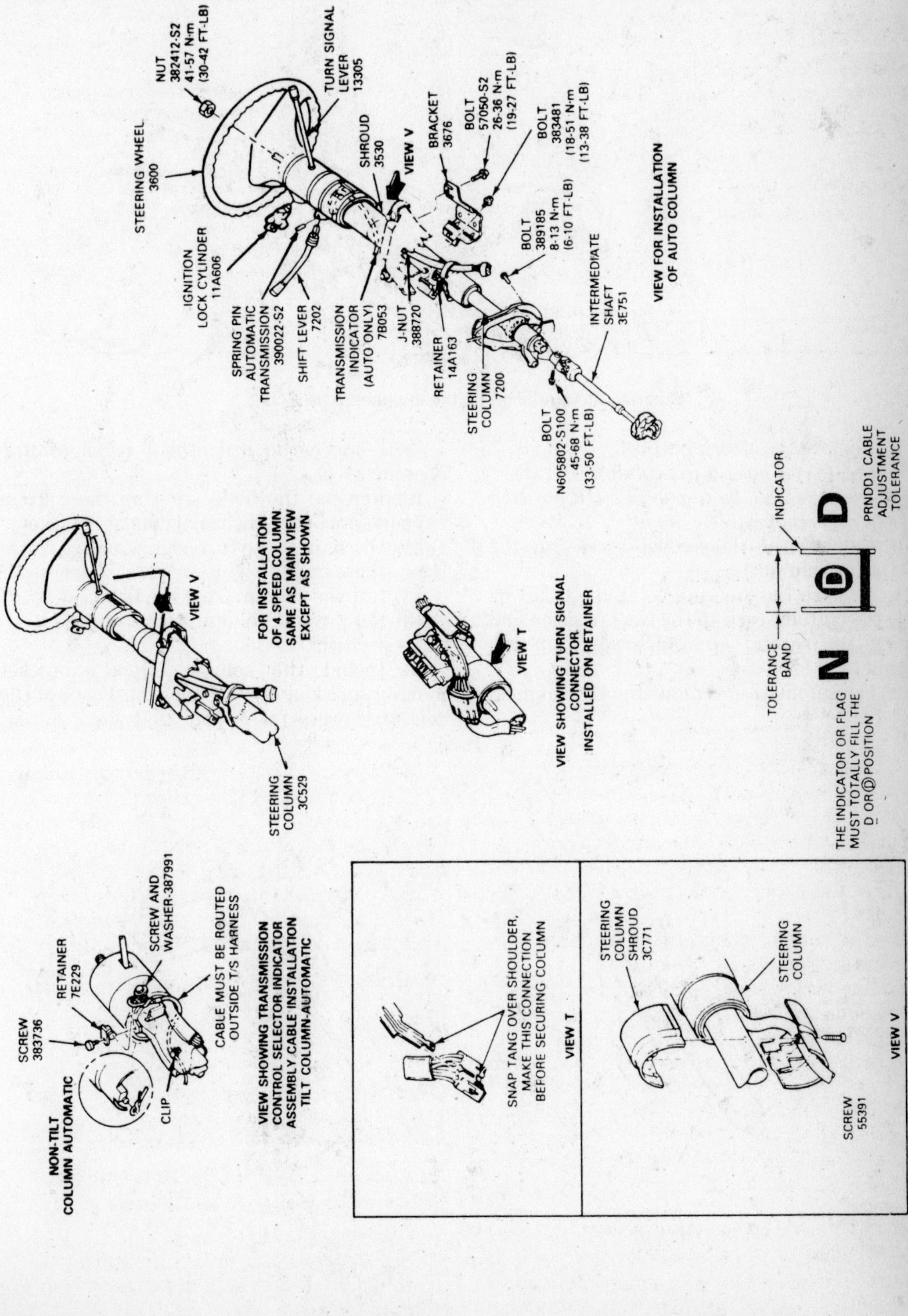

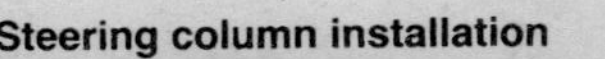

Steering column installation

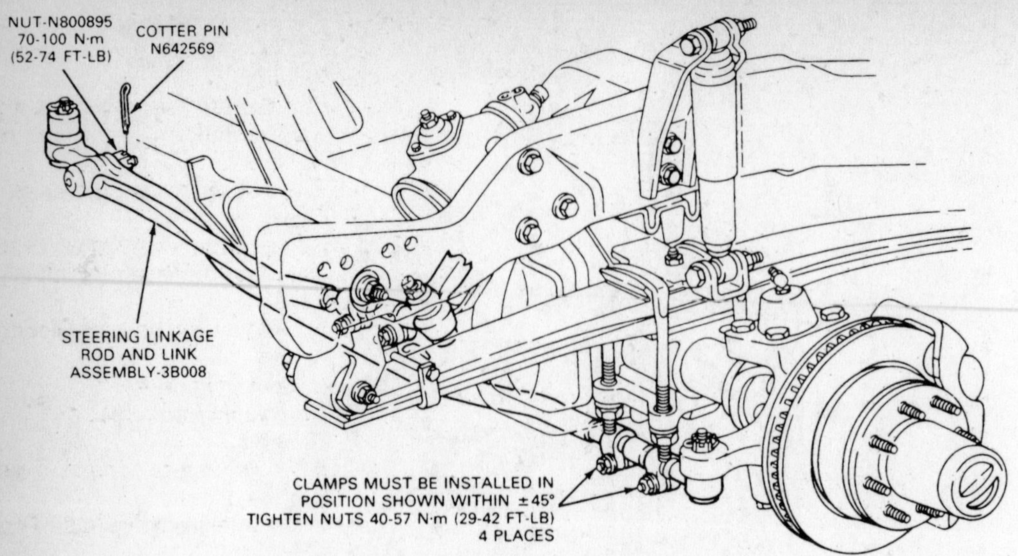

Steering linkage used on the 4-wheel drive F-350

5. Remove the steering wheel.

NOTE: *If you have a tilt column, the steering wheel MUST be in the full UP position when it is removed.*

6. Remove the floor cover screws at the base of the column.

7. Remove the steering column shroud by place the bottom screw in the No.1 position and pulling the shroud up and away from the column.

8. On automatics, remove the shift indicator cable.

9. Remove the instrument panel column opening cover.

10. Remove the bolts securing the column support bracket to the pedal support bracket.

11. Disconnect the turn signal/hazard warning harness and the ignition switch harness.

12. Lift the column from the truck.

13. Remove the column support bracket

To install:

14. Install the column support bracket making sure that the wiring is outboard of the column. Torque the nuts to 35 ft. lbs.

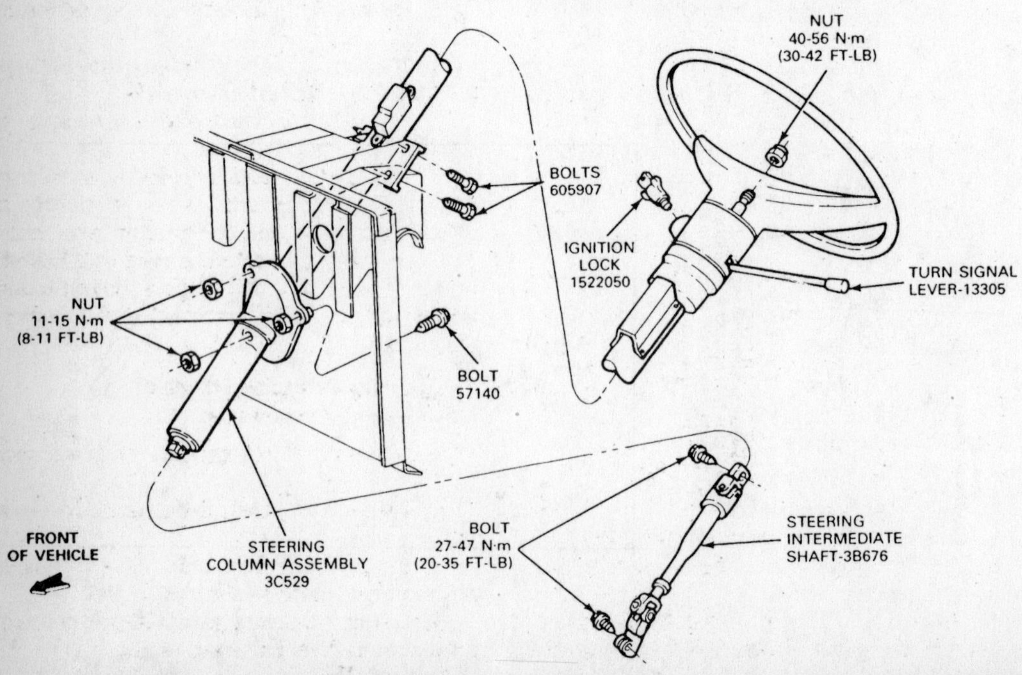

Steering column installation in F-Super Duty stripped chassis and motor home chassis

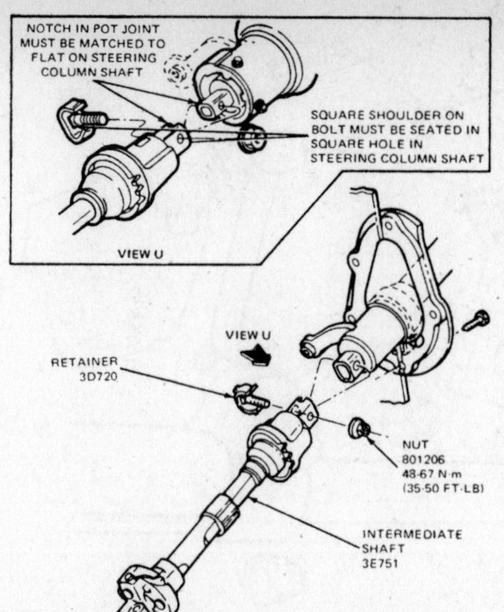

Pot joint alignment for all models, except F-Super Duty stripped chassis and motor home chassis

15. Start the floor cover clamp bolt and press the plate until the clamp flats touch the stops on the column outer tube.
16. Install the column through the floor opening.
17. Connect the turn signal/hazard warning and ignition harnesses.
18. Raise the column and install the 2 support bolts.
19. Tighten the floor cover bolts to 10 ft. lbs.
20. Torque the support bracket bolts to 25 ft. lbs.
21. Torque the cover plate clamp bolt to 18 ft. lbs.
22. Install and adjust the shift indicator cable, on automatics.
23. Install the instrument panel column opening cover.
24. Install the column shroud.
25. Torque the shroud bottom screw to 15 inch lbs.
26. Connect the shifter rod(s).
27. Connect the intermediate shaft. Torque the bolt to 50 ft. lbs.

F-Super Duty Stripped Chassis Motor Home Chassis

1. Set the parking brake.
2. Disconnect the battery ground cable.
3. Unbolt the intermediate shaft from the steering column.
4. On trucks with automatic transmission, disconnect the shift linkage rod(s) from the column.
5. Remove the steering wheel.

NOTE: *If you have a tilt column, the steering wheel MUST be in the full UP position when it is removed.*

6. Disconnect the turn signal/hazard warning harness and the ignition switch and horn harnesses.
7. Remove the floor cover screws at the base of the column.
8. Remove the column-to-support bracket bolts and lift the column from the truck.

To install:

9. Install the column through the floor opening.
10. Connect the wiring harnesses.
11. Raise the column and install the 2 support bolts.
12. Torque the column-to-support bracket bolts to 19–27 ft. lbs.
13. Connect the intermediate shaft. Torque the bolt to 20–35 ft. lbs.
14. Tighten the floor cover bolts to 10 ft. lbs.
15. Connect the shifter rod(s).
16. Install the steering wheel.

Pitman Arm

REMOVAL AND INSTALLATION

All Models Except F-Super Duty Stripped Chassis and Motor Home Chassis.

1. Place the wheels in a straight-ahead position.
2. Disconnect the drag link at the pitman arm. You'll need a puller such as a tie rod end remover.
3. Remove the pitman arm-to-gear nut and washer.
4. Matchmark the pitman arm and gear housing for installation purposes.
5. Using a 2-jawed puller, remove the pitman arm from the gear.
6. Installation is the reverse of removal. Align the matchmarks when installing the pitman arm. Torque the pitman arm nut to 170–230 ft. lbs.; torque the drag link ball stud nut to 50–75 ft. lbs., advancing the nut to align the cotter pin hole. Never back off the nut to align the hole.

F-Super Duty Stripped Chassis Motor Home Chassis

1. Matchmark the pitman arm and sector shaft.
2. Disconnect the drag link from the pitman arm.
3. Remove the bolt and nut securing the pitman arm to the sector shaft.
4. Using a 2-jawed gear puller, remove the pitman arm from the sector shaft.

To install:

5. Aligning the matchmarks, slide the

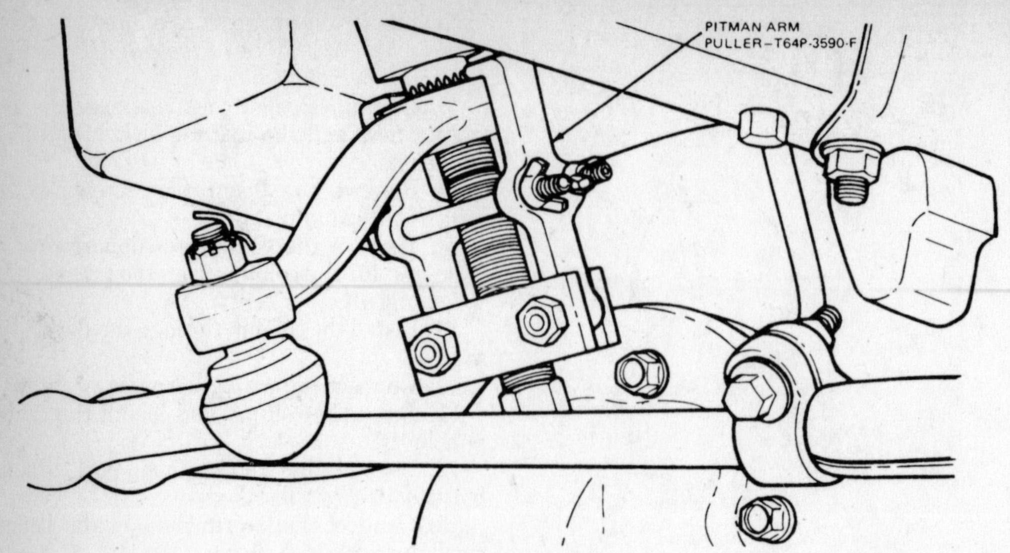

Pitman arm removal

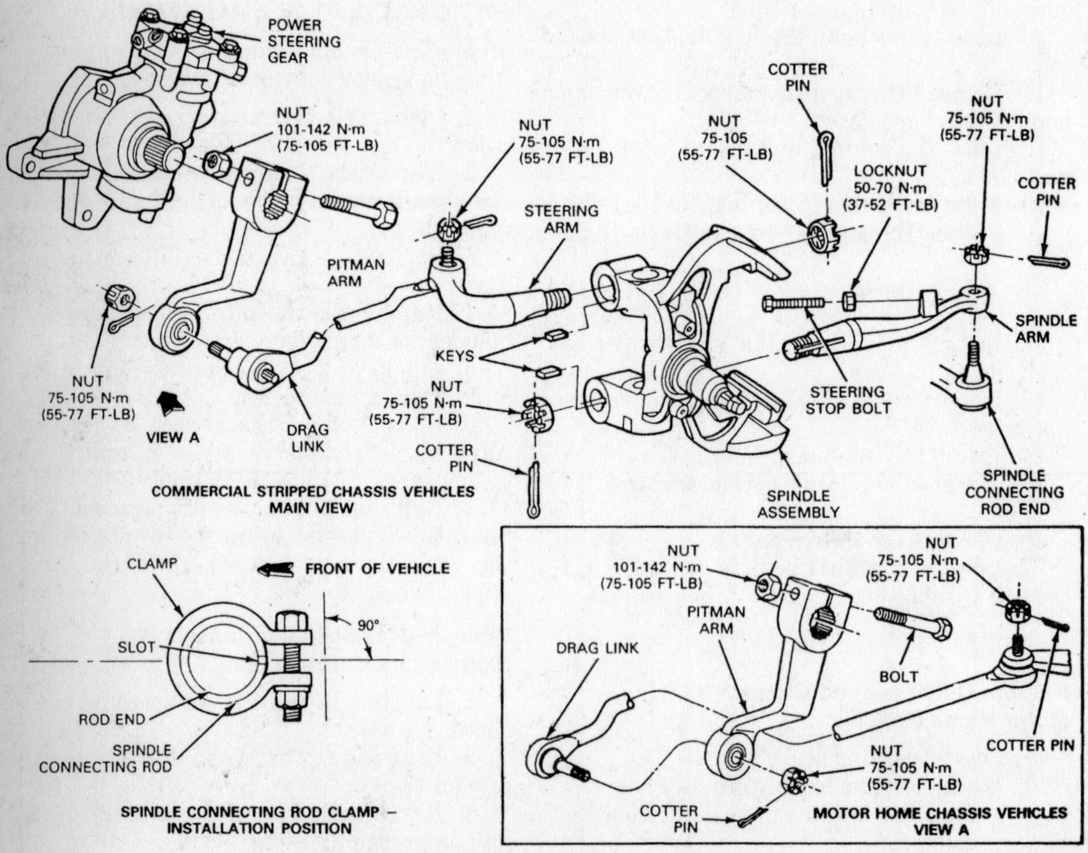

Steering linkage for F-Super Duty stripped chassis and motor home chassis

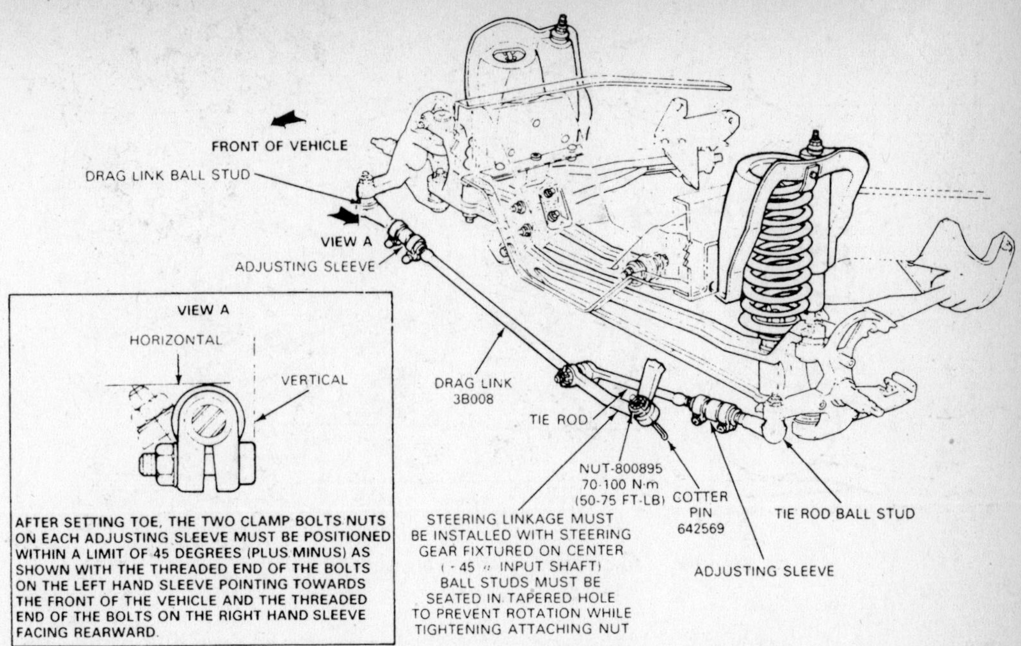

Steering linkage used on the 2-wheel drive F-150, 250, 350

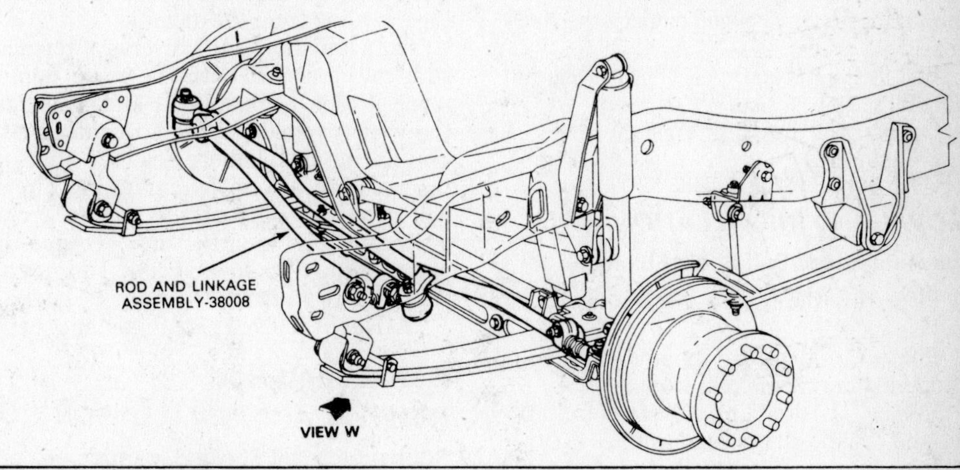

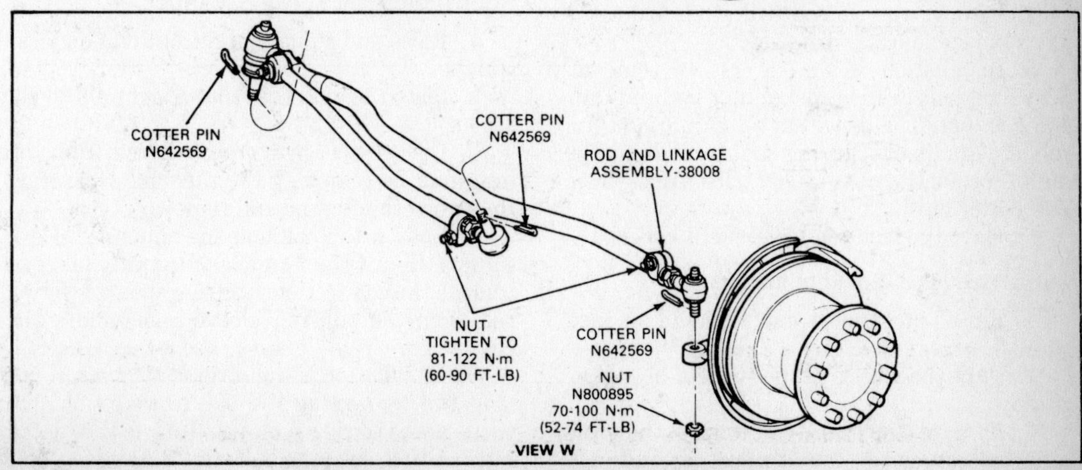

Steering linkage used on F-Super Duty chassis/cab

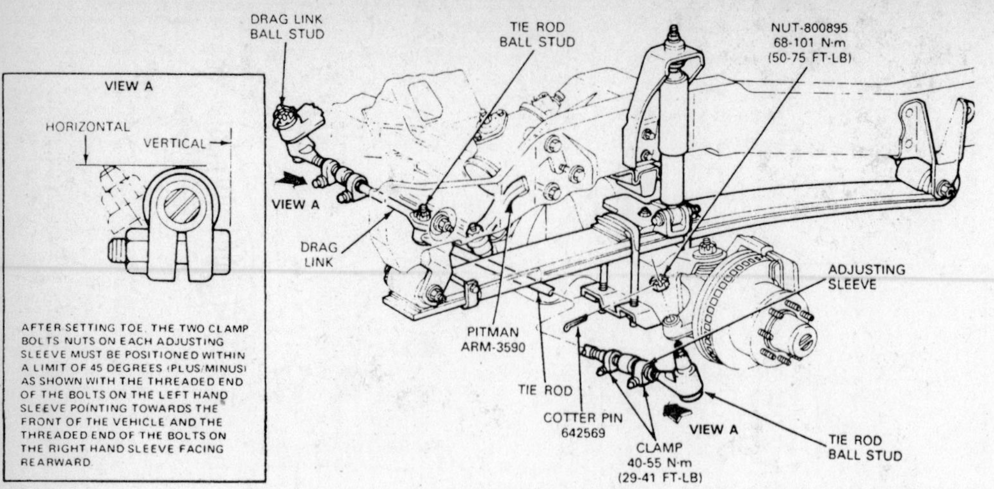

Steering linkage used on the 4-wheel drive F-250

pitman arm onto the sector shaft. If the arm won't slide on easily, use a cold chisel to spread the separation. NEVER HAMMER THE ARM ONTO THE SHAFT!

Hammering on the arm will damage the steering gear!

6. Install the nut and bolt. Torque the nut to 220–300 ft. lbs.

7. Connect the drag link.

Tie Rod and Drag Link

REMOVAL AND INSTALLATION

Except Rubberized Ball Socket Linkage

1. Place the wheels in a straight-ahead position.

2. Remove the cotter pins and nuts from the drag link and tie rod ball studs.

3. Remove the drag link ball studs from the right hand spindle and pitman arm.

4. Remove the tie rod ball studs from the left hand spindle and drag link.

5. Installation is the reverse of removal. Seat the studs in the tapered hole before tightening the nuts. This will avoid wrap-up of the rubber grommets during tightening of the nuts. Torque the nuts to 70 ft. lbs. Always use new cotter pins.

6. Have the front end alignment checked.

Rubberized Ball Socket Linkage

1. Raise and support the front end on jackstands.

2. Place the wheels in the straight-ahead position.

3. Remove the nuts connecting the drag link ball studs to the connecting rod and pitman arm.

4. Disconnect the drag link using a tie rod end remover.

5. Loosen the bolts on the adjuster clamp. Count the number of turns it take to remove the drag link from the adjuster.

6. Installation is the reverse of removal. Install the drag link with the same number of turns it took to remove it. Make certain that the wheels remain in the straight-ahead position during installation. Seat the studs in the tapered hole before tightening the nuts. This will avoid wrap-up of the rubber grommets during tightening of the nuts. Torque the adjuster clamp nuts to 40 ft. lbs. Torque the ball stud nuts to 75 ft. lbs.

7. Have the front end alignment checked.

Connecting Rod

REMOVAL AND INSTALLATION

Rubberized Ball Socket Linkage

1. Raise and support the front end on jackstands.

2. Place the wheels in the straight-ahead position.

3. Disconnect the connecting rod from the drag link by removing the nut and separating the two with a tie rod end remover.

4. Loosen the bolts on the adjusting sleeve clamps. Count the number of turns it takes to remove the connecting rod from the connecting rod from the adjuster sleeve and remove the rod.

5. Installation is the reverse of removal. Install the connecting rod the exact number of turns noted during removal. Torque the tie rod nuts to 40 ft. lbs.; the ball stud nut to 75 ft. lbs.

6. Have the front end alignment checked.

Measuring steering gear preload

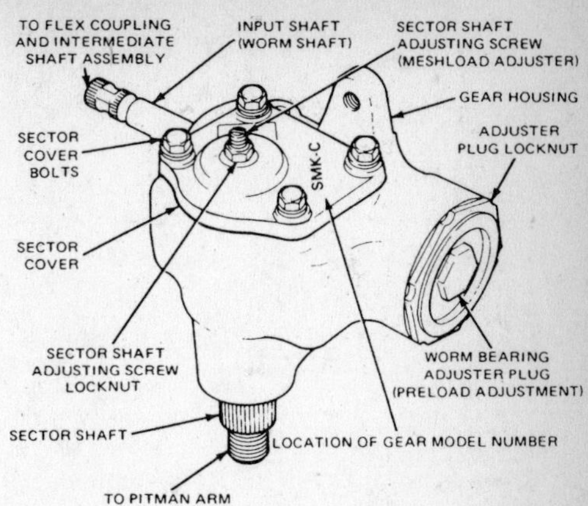

Manual steering gear

Tie Rod Ends

REMOVAL AND INSTALLATION

Rubberized Ball Socket Linkage

1. Raise and support the front end on jackstands.
2. Place the wheels in a straight-ahead position.
3. Remove the ball stud from the pitman arm using a tie rod end remover.
4. Loosen the nuts on the adjusting sleeve clamp. Remove the ball stud from the adjuster, or the adjuster from the tie rod. Count the number of turns it takes to remove the sleeve from the tie rod or ball stud from the sleeve.
5. Install the sleeve on the tie rod, or the ball in the sleeve the same number of turns noted during removal. Make sure that the adjuster clamps are in the correct position, illustrated, and torque the clamp bolts to 40 ft. lbs.
6. Keep the wheels straight ahead and install the ball studs. Torque the nuts to 75 ft. lbs. Use new cotter pins.
7. Install the drag link and connecting rod.
8. Have the front end alignment checked.

Manual Steering Gear

NOTE: *Manual steering is found only on 1987 F-150 2-wheel drive models.*

ADJUSTMENTS

Preload and Meshload Check

1. Raise and support the front end on jackstands.
2. Disconnect the drag link from the pitman arm.
3. Lubricate the wormshaft seal with a drop of automatic transmission fluid.
4. Remove the horn pad from the steering wheel.
5. Turn the steering wheel slowly to one stop.
6. Using an inch-pound torque wrench on the steering wheel nut, check the amount of torque needed to rotate the steering wheel through a 1$^1/_2$ turn cycle. The preload should be 5–9 inch lbs. If not, proceed with the rest of the steps.
7. Rotate the steering wheel from stop-to-stop, counting the total number of turns. Using that figure, center the steering wheel ($^1/_2$ the total turns).
8. Using the inch-pound torque wrench, rotate the steering wheel 90° to either side of center, noting the highest torque reading over center. The meshload should be 9–14 inch lbs., or at least 2 inch lbs. more than the preload figure.

Preload and Meshload Adjustment

1. Remove the steering gear.
2. Torque the sector cover bolts on the gear to 40 ft. lbs.
3. Loosen the preload adjuster nut and tighten the worm bearing adjuster nut until all endplay has been removed. Lubricate the wormshaft seal with a few drops of automatic transmission fluid.
4. Using an $^{11}/_{16}$ in., 12-point socket and an inch-pound torque wrench, carefully turn the wormshaft all the way to the right.
5. Turn the shaft back to the left and measure the torque over a 1$^1/_2$ turn cycle. This is the preload reading.
6. Tighten or loosen the adjuster nut to bring the preload into range (7–9 inch lbs.).
7. Hold the adjuster nut while torquing the locknut to 187 ft. lbs.
8. Rotate the wormshaft stop-to-stop count-

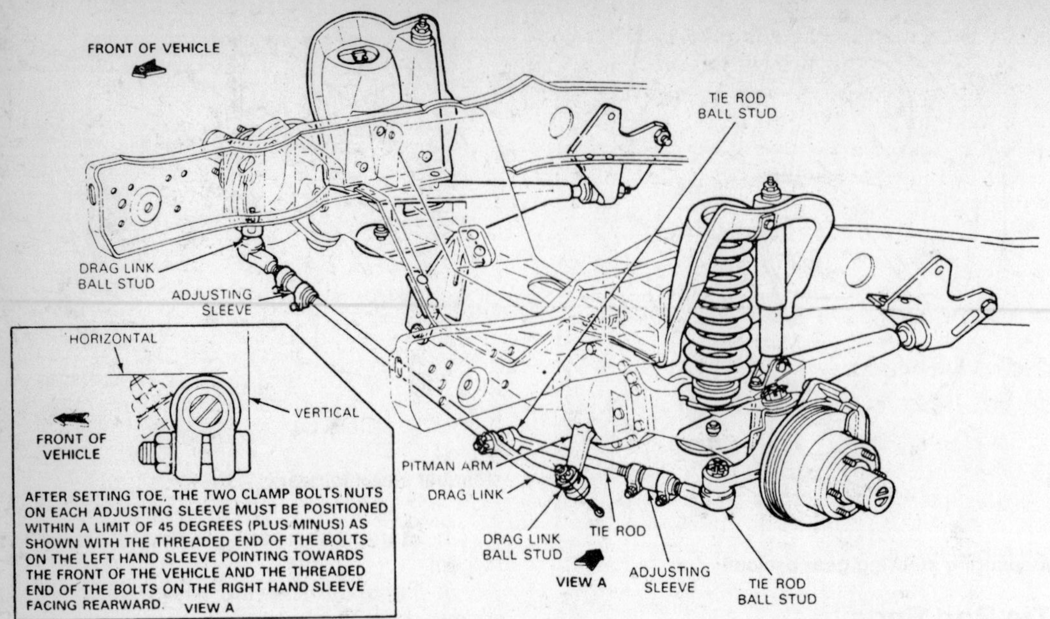

Steering linkage used on the Bronco and 4-wheel drive F-150

ing the total number of turns and center the shaft (1/2 the total turns).

9. Using the torque wrench and socket, measure the torque required to turn the shaft 90° to either side of center.

10. Turn the sector shaft adjusting screw as needed to bring the meshload torque within the 12–14 inch lbs. range, or at least 4 inch lbs. higher than the preload torque.

11. Hold the adjusting screw while tightening the locknut to 25 ft. lbs.

12. Install the gear.

REMOVAL AND INSTALLATION

1. Raise and support the front end on jackstands.

2. Place the wheels in a straight-ahead position.

Disengage the flex coupling shield from the steering gear input shaft shield and slide it up the intermediate shaft.

3. Disconnect the flexible coupling from the steering shaft flange by removing the 2 nuts.

4. Disconnect the drag link from the pitman arm.

5. Matchmark and remove the pitman arm.

6. Support the steering gear and remove the attaching bolts.

7. Remove the coupling-to-gear attaching bolt and remove the coupling from the gear.

To install:

8. Install the flex coupling on the input shaft. Make sure that the flat on the gear is facing upward and aligns with the flat on the coupling. Install a new coupling-to-gear bolt and torque it to 30 ft. lbs.

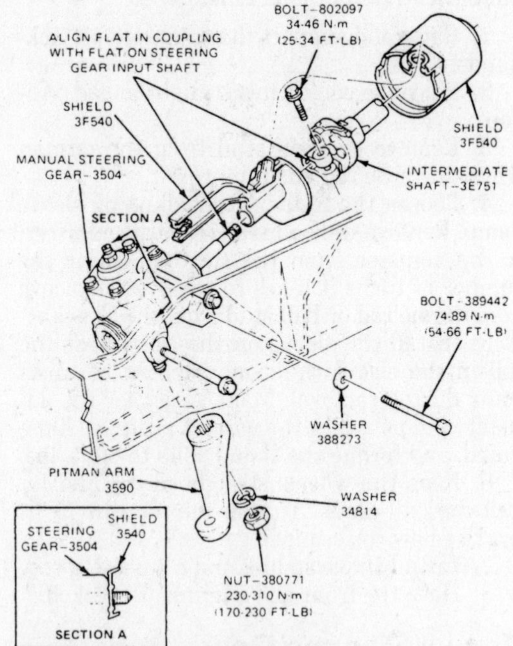

Manual steering gear installation

9. Center the input shaft.

10. Place the steering gear into position. Make sure that all bolts and holes align.

11. Install the gear mounting bolts and torque them to 65 ft. lbs.

CAUTION: *If you are using new mounting bolts they* **MUST** be grade 9!

12. Connect the drag link to the pitman arm and hand-tighten the nut.

13. Install the pitman arm on the sector

shaft. Torque the sector shaft nut to 230 ft. lbs.

14. Make sure that the wheels are still in the straight-ahead position and tighten the drag link stud nut to 70 ft. lbs. Install a new cotter pin, advancing the nut to align the hole.

15. Torque the sector shaft-to-flex coupling nuts to 20 ft. lbs.

16. Snap the flex coupling shield into place.

17. Make sure that the steering system moves freely and that the steering wheel is straight with the wheels straight-ahead.

Ford Integral Power Steering Gear

The Ford Integral Power Steering Gear is used on all models except the F-Super Duty stripped chassis and motor home chassis

ADJUSTMENTS

Meshload

1. Raise and support the front end on jackstands.
2. Matchmark the pitman arm and gear housing.
3. Set the wheels in a straight-ahead position.
4. Disconnect the pitman arm from the sector shaft.
5. Disconnect the fluid RETURN line at the pump reservoir and cap the reservoir nipple.
6. Place the end of the return line in a clean container and turn the steering wheel lock-to-lock a few times to expel the fluid from the gear.
7. Turn the steering wheel all the way to the right stop. Place a small piece of masking tape on the steering wheel rim as a reference

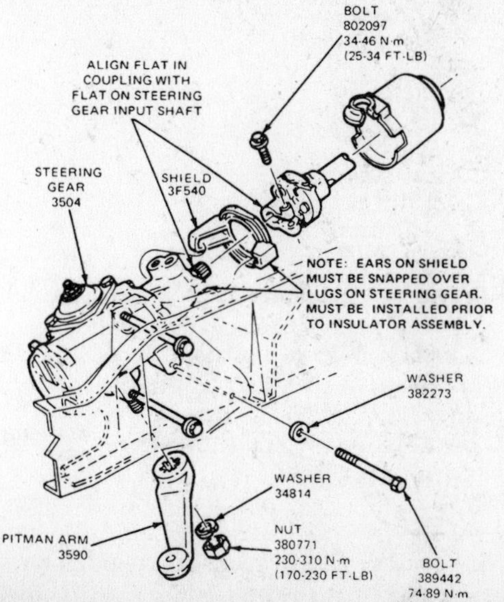

Power steering gear installation

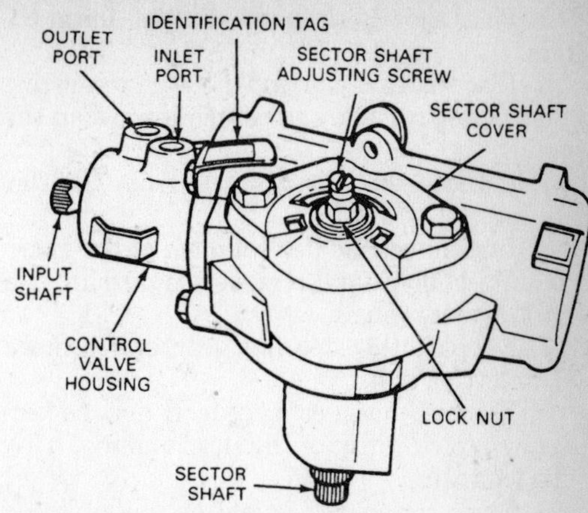

Ford integral power steering gear

and rotate the steering wheel 45° from the right stop.

8. Disconnect the battery ground.
9. Remove the horn pad.
10. Using an inch-pound torque wrench on the steering wheel nut, record the amount of torque needed to turn the steering wheel 1/8 turn counterclockwise. The preload reading should be 4–9 inch lbs.
11. Center the steering wheel (1/2 the total lock-to-lock turns) and record the torque needed to turn the steering wheel 90° to either side of center. On a truck with fewer than 5,000 miles, the meshload should be 15–25 inch lbs. On a truck with 5,000 or more miles, the meshload should be 7 inch lbs. more than the preload torque.

On trucks with fewer than 5,000 miles, if the meshload is not within specifications, it should be reset to a figure 14–18 inch lbs. greater than the recorded preload torque.

On trucks with 5,000 or more miles, if the meshload is not within specifications, it should be reset to a figure 10–14 inch lbs. greater than the recorded preload torque.

12. If an adjustment is required, loosen the adjuster locknut and turn the sector shaft adjuster screw until the necessary torque is achieved.
13. Once adjustment is completed. hold the adjuster screw and tighten the locknut to 45 ft. lbs.
14. Recheck the adjustment readings and reset if necessary.
15. Connect the return line and refill the reservoir.
16. Install the pitman arm.
17. Install the horn pad.

REMOVAL AND INSTALLATION

1. Raise and support the front end on jackstands.

2. Place the wheels in the straight-ahead position.

3. Place a drain pan under the gear and disconnect the pressure and return lines. Cap the openings.

4. Remove the splash shield from the flex coupling.

5. Disconnect the flex coupling at the gear.

6. Matchmark and remove the pitman arm from the sector shaft.

7. Support the steering gear and remove the mounting bolts.

8. Remove the steering gear. It may be necessary to work it free of the flex coupling.

To install:

9. Place the splash shield on the steering gear lugs.

10. Slide the flex coupling into place on the steering shaft. Make sure the steering wheel spokes are still horizontal.

11. Center the steering gear input shaft with the indexing flat facing downward.

12. Slide the steering gear input shaft into the flex coupling and into place on the frame side rail. Install the flex coupling bolt and torque it to 30 ft. lbs.

13. Install the gear mounting bolts and torque them to 65 ft. lbs.

14. Make sure that the wheels are still straight ahead and install the pitman arm. Torque the nut to 230 ft. lbs.

15. Connect the pressure, then, the return lines. Torque the pressure line to 25 ft. lbs.

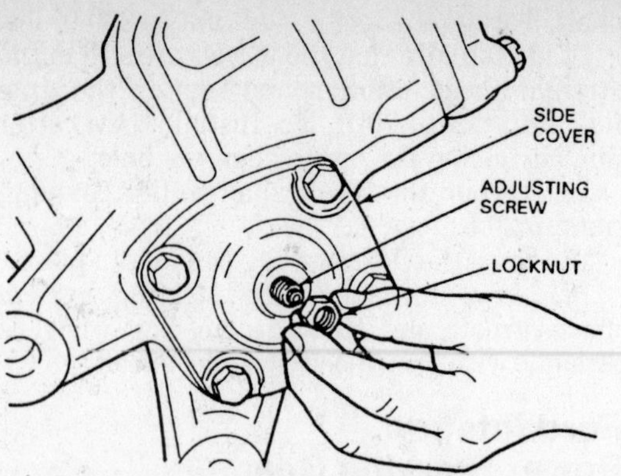

C-300N power steering gear adjustment point

16. Snap the flex coupling shield into place.

17. Fill the steering reservoir.

18. Run the engine and turn the steering wheel lock-to-lock several times to expel air. Check for leaks.

Bendix C-300N Power Steering Gear

The Bendix gear is used on F-Super Duty stripped chassis models and motor home chassis models.

ADJUSTMENTS

Adjustments must be made with the steering gear removed and mounted in a vise.

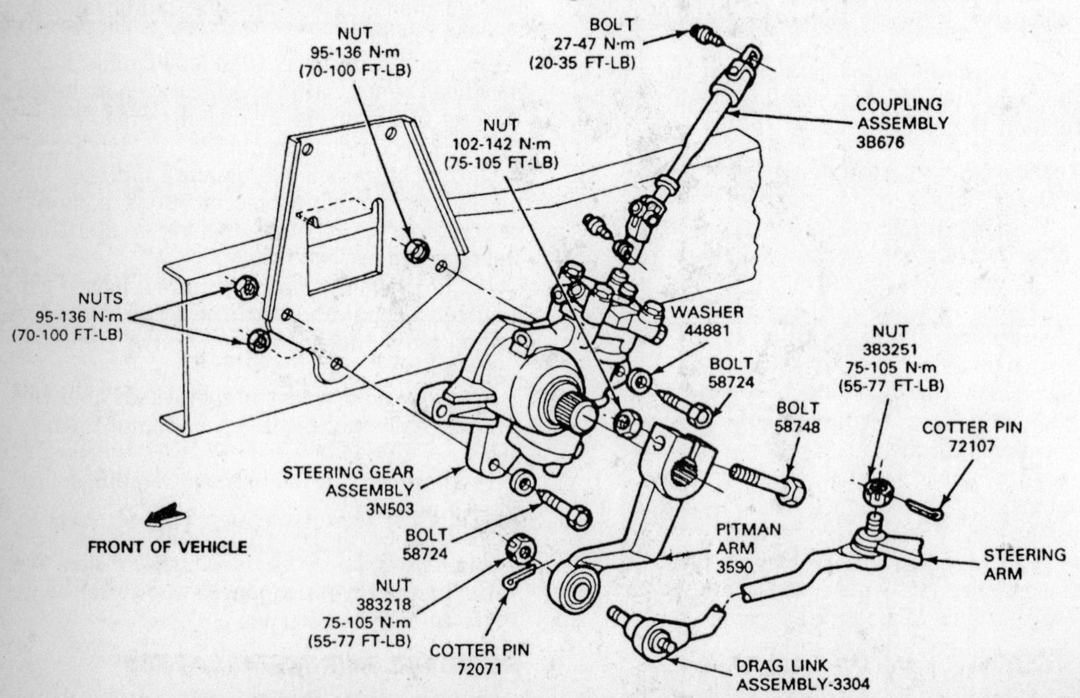

Steering gear installation on F-Super Duty stripped chassis models

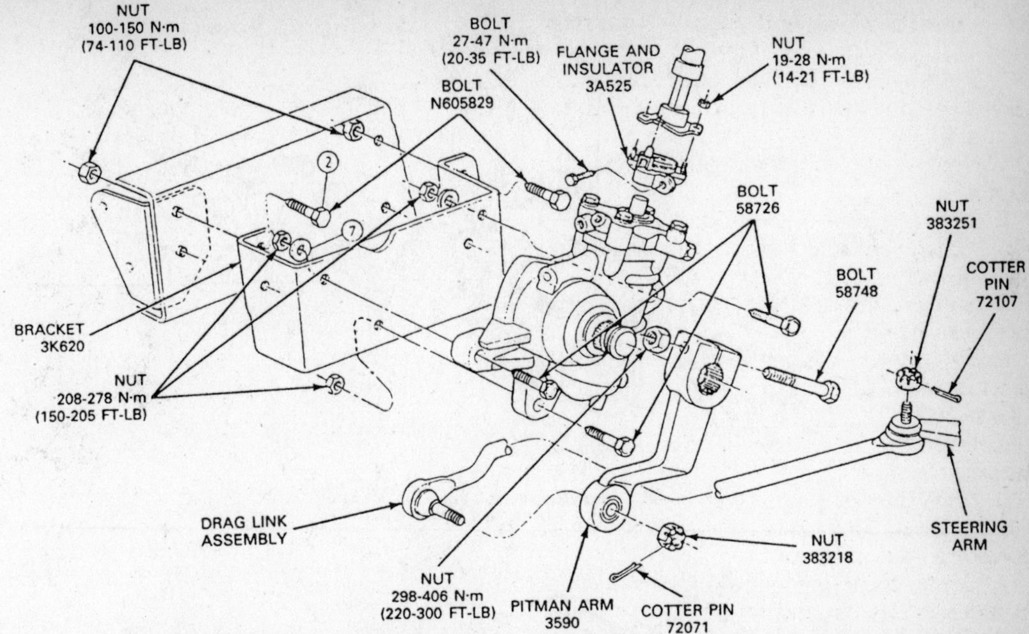

Steering gear installation on F-Super Duty motor home chassis models

Piston-to-Output Shaft Gear Backlash Adjustment

NOTE: *Backlash is correct when a 4–18 inch lb. increase in rotational torque is noted at the input shaft as it is rotated and the piston passes the mid-point of its total travel in the housing. The torque increase should occur only at mid-point and should disappear after mid-point.*

1. Loosen the locknut and turn the adjusting screw counterclockwise as far as it will go.
2. Using an inch-pound torque wrench, rotate the input shaft as far as it will go in one direction, then, counting the number of full turns and noting the rotational torque, rotate it to the opposite stop.
3. Turn the shaft back $1/2$ the total number of turns to the mid-point.
4. Rotate the shaft 180° to both sides of the mid-point, noting the change in rotational torque. Turn the adjusting screw $1/8$–$1/4$ turn at a time until the proper reading of 4–18 inch lb. increase in torque is noted over the mid-point. This increase in torque must be plus the total rotational torque.
5. When the adjustment is correct, hold the adjusting screw and, using a crow's foot adapter, torque the locknut to 74–88 ft. lbs.
6. Check the adjustment to make sure it hasn't changed. Rotate the shaft through its entire travel. It must rotate smoothly.

REMOVAL AND INSTALLATION

1. Raise and support the front end on jackstands.
2. Thoroughly clean all connections.
3. Place a drain pan under the area.
4. Disconnect the hydraulic lines at the gear. Cap all openings at once.
5. Remove the retaining bolt and nut and disconnect the pitman arm from the sector shaft.
6. Remove the bolt and nut securing the input shaft and U-joint.
7. Support the gear and remove the gear-to-frame bolts and nuts.

To install:

8. Position the gear on the frame and install the bolts and nuts. Torque the nuts to 150–200 ft. lbs.
9. Install the U-joint bolt and nut. Torque the nut to 50–70 ft. lbs.
10. Install the pitman arm.

CAUTION: *Never hammer the pitman shaft onto the sector shaft! Hammering will damage the gear. Use a cold chisel to separate the pitman arm opening.*

11. Install the bolt and nut. Torque the nut to 220–300 ft. lbs.
12. Connect the hydraulic lines, fill the reservoir, run the engine and check for leaks.

Ford C-II Power Steering Pump

This pump is used by all models except the F-Super Duty stripped chassis and motor home models.

REMOVAL AND INSTALLATION

1. Disconnect the return line at the pump and drain the fluid into a container.

PULLEY-3D673
PULLEY WITH PULL OFF GROOVE
FACING FRONT TO BE PRESSED ON
FLUSH WITH END OF SHAFT
WITHIN ± 0.254 mm (± 0.010 INCH)
ENGINE
MOUNTING
BRACKET
3A732
PUMP
SUPPORT
3C511
BOLT
56576
61-88 N·m
(45-65 FT-LB)
SPACER
3642
BOLT
56561
61-88 N·m
(45-65 FT-LB)
POWER
STEERING
PUMP
3A674
BOLT
370608
41-61 N·m
(30-45 FT-LB)
ADJUSTING
BOLT
370608
41-61 N·m
(30-45 FT-LB)
BOLT
800199
41-61 N·m
(30-45 FT-LB)
POWER STEERING PUMP INSTALLATION
WITHOUT AIR CONDITIONING
A/C
COMPRESSOR
19D629
STUD
389716
40-67 N·m
(30-50 FT-LB)
BRACE
19D896
SPACER
386107
BOLT
801179
41-61 N·m
(30-45 FT-LB)
NUT
34988
41-61 N·m
(30-45 FT-LB)
SUPPORT
19E557
BOLT
802090
41-61 N·m
(30-45 FT-LB)
FRONT OF VEHICLE
BOLT
370608
34-40 N·m
(25-35 FT-LB)
A/C COMPRESSOR
MOUNTING BRACKET
19D624
POWER
STEERING
PUMP
3A674
BOLT-56576
61-81 N·m
(45-65 FT-LB)
ADJUSTING
BOLT-370608
41-61 N·m
(30-45 FT-LB)
BOLT-56561
61-88 N·m
(45-65 FT-LB)
POWER STEERING PUMP INSTALLATION
WITH AIR CONDITIONING

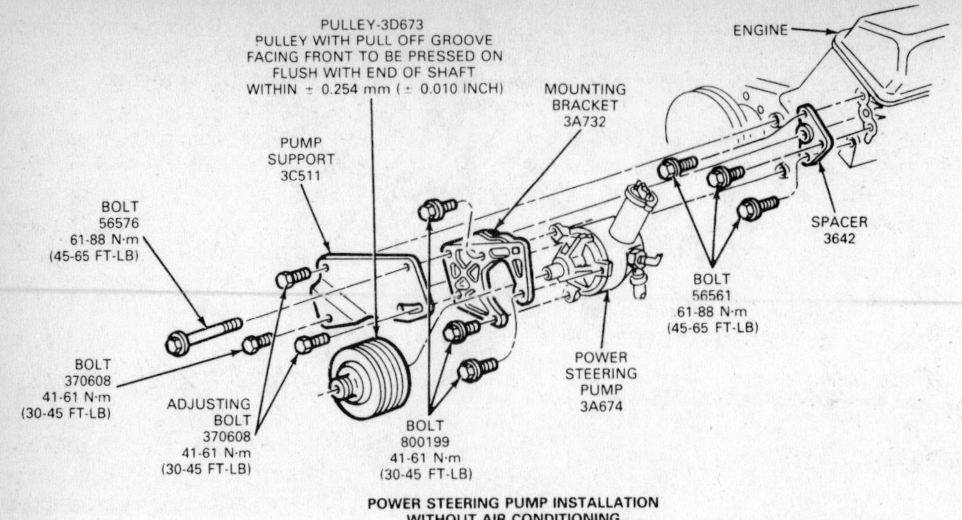

Power steering pump installation on the 8–7.5L 4–bbl

2. Disconnect the pressure line from the pump.

3. Loosen the pump bracket nuts and remove the drive belt. On the 6-4.9L and 8-5.0L with a serpentine drive belt, remove belt tension by lifting the tensioner out of position.

4. Remove the nuts and lift out the pump/bracket assembly.

5. If a new pump or bracket is being installed, you'll have to remove the pulley from the present pump. This is best done with a press and adapters.

6. Installation is the reverse of removal. Note the following torques:

- Pivot bolt (6-4.9L and 8-5.0L): 45 ft. lbs.
- Pump-to-adjustment bracket: 45 ft. lbs.
- Support bracket-to-engine (8-5.8L):65 ft. lbs.

• Support bracket-to-water pump housing (6-4.9L): 17 ft. lbs.
• Support bracket-to-water pump housing (8-5.0L, 5.8L): 45 ft. lbs.
• Pressure line-to-fitting: 29 ft. lbs.
• Adjustment bracket-to-support bracket:
6-4.9L, 8-5.0L, 8-5.8L: 45 ft. lbs.
8-7.5L and Diesel:
Long bolt – 65 ft. lbs.
Short bolt – 45 ft. lbs.

ZF Power Steering Pump

This pump is used on the F-Super Duty stripped chassis and motor home models.

REMOVAL AND INSTALLATION

1. Place a drain pan under the pump, remove the return hose and drain the reservoir.

2. Disconnect the pressure line from the pump and tie up the ends of both hoses in a raised position. Cap the openings.

3. Loosen the pump pivot and adjusting bolts and remove the drive belt.

4. Remove the bolts and lift out the pump.

5. Installation is the reverse of removal. Adjust the belt tension. Tighten the bolts to 30–45 ft. lbs. Connect the hoses. Refill the reservoir. Run the engine and check for leaks.

Quick-Connect Pressure Line

Some pumps will have a quick-connect fitting for the pressure line. This fitting may, under certain circumstances, leak and/or be improperly engaged resulting in unplanned disconnection.

The leak is usually caused by a cut O-ring,

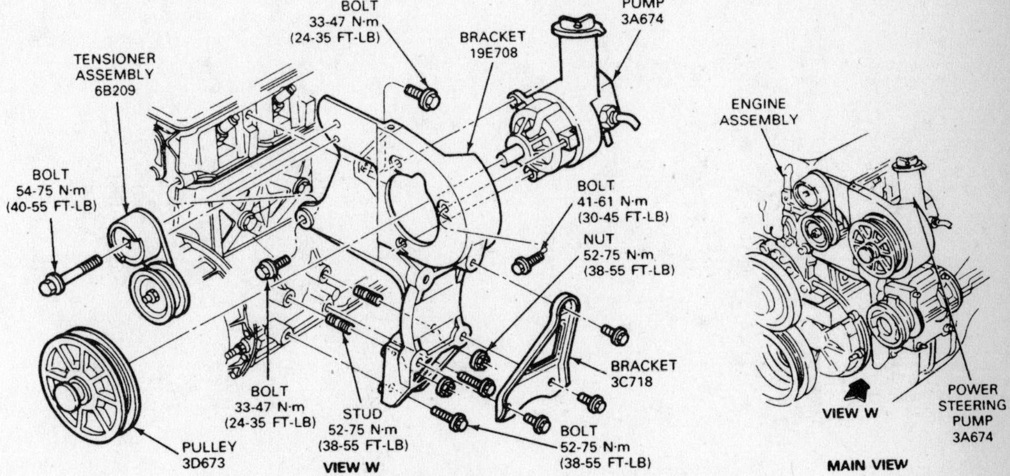

Power steering pump installation on the 1988–90 6–4.9L EFI

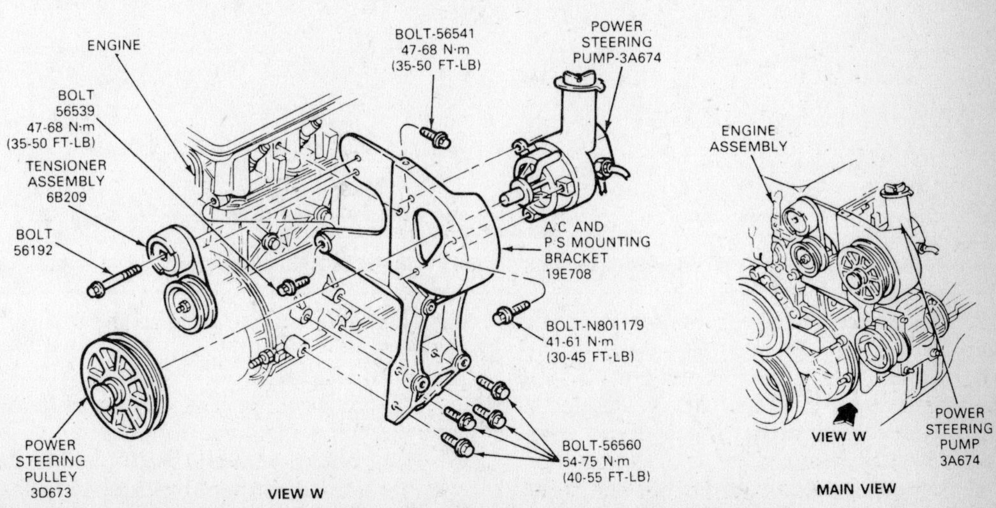

Power steering pump installation on the 1987 6–4.9L EFI

imperfections in the outlet fitting inside diameter, or an improperly machined O-ring groove.

Improper engagement can be caused by an improperly machined tube end, tube nut, snapring, outlet fitting or gear port.

If a leak occurs, the O-ring should be replaced with new O-rings. Special O-rings are made for quick-disconnect fittings. Standard O-rings should never be used in their place. If the new O-rings do not solve the leak problem, replace the outlet fitting. If that doesn't work, replace the pressure line.

Improper engagement due to a missing or bent snapring, or improperly machined tube nut, may be corrected with a Ford snapring kit made for the purpose. If that doesn't work, replace the pressure hose.

When tightening a quick-connect tube nut, always use a tube nut wrench; never use an open-end wrench! Use of an open-end wrench will result in deformation of the nut! Tighten quick-connect tube nuts to 15 ft. lbs. maximum.

Swivel and/or endplay of quick-connect fittings is normal.

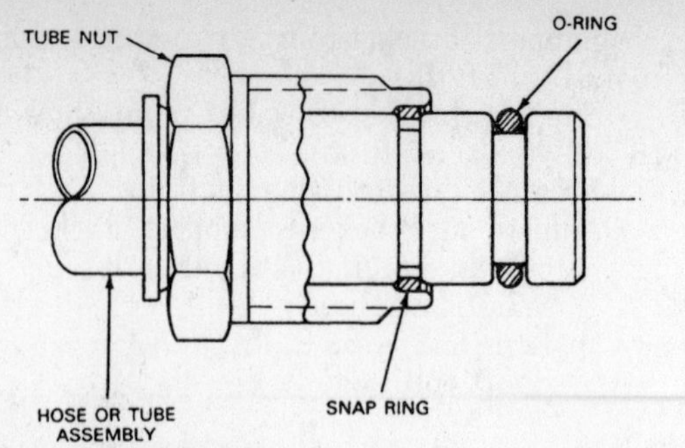

Quick-connect fittings

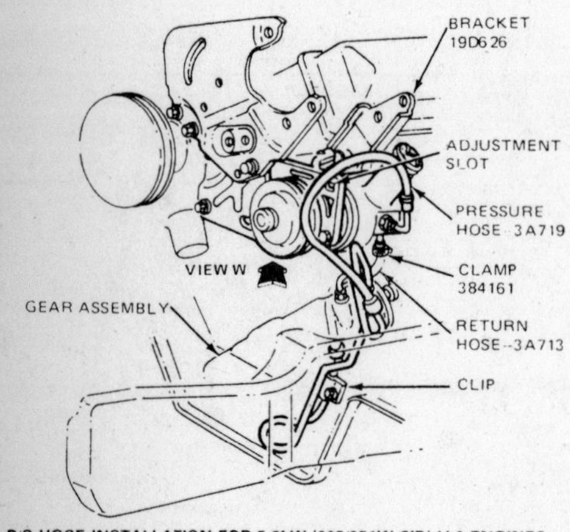

P/S HOSE INSTALLATION FOR 5.8LW (302/351W CID) V-8 ENGINES WITHOUT P/S COOLER, WITH A/C

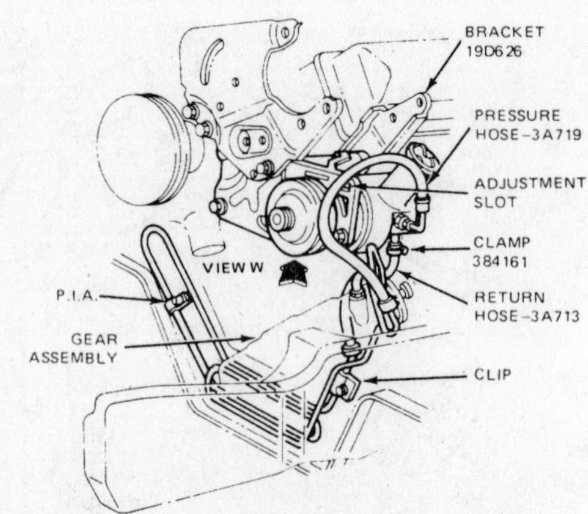

P/S HOSE INSTALLATION FOR 5.8LW (302/351W CID) V-8 ENGINES WITH P/S COOLER, WITH A/C

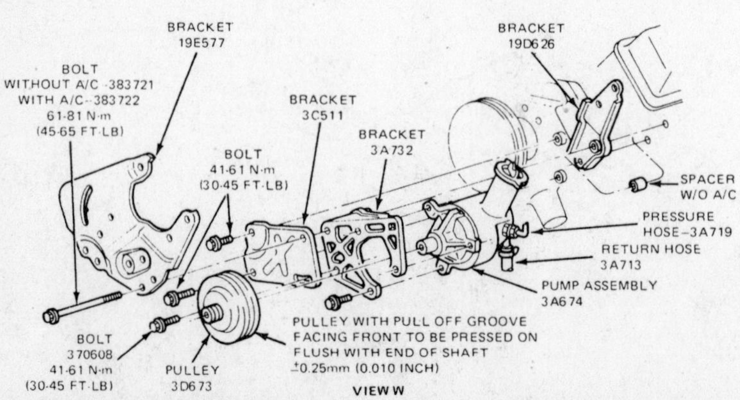

Power steering pump installation on the 1987 8–5.8L 4–bbl

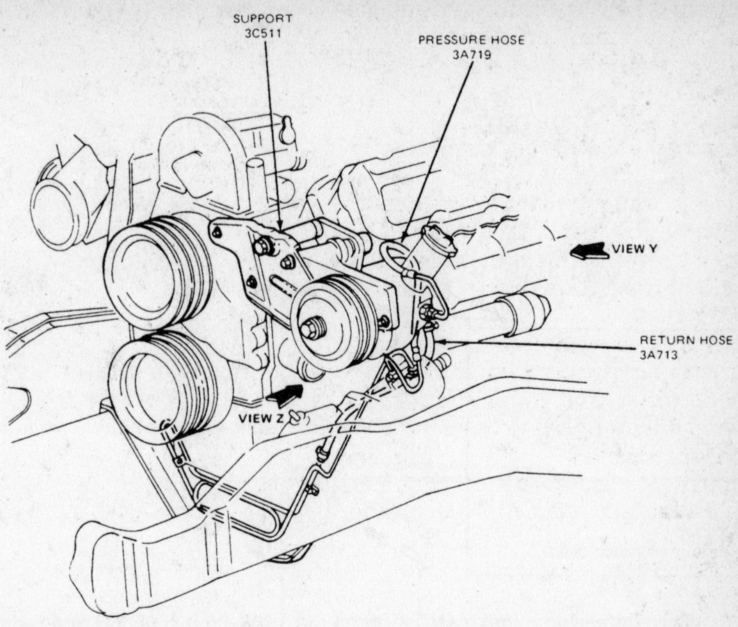

P/S HOSE INSTALLATION
WITH P/S COOLER

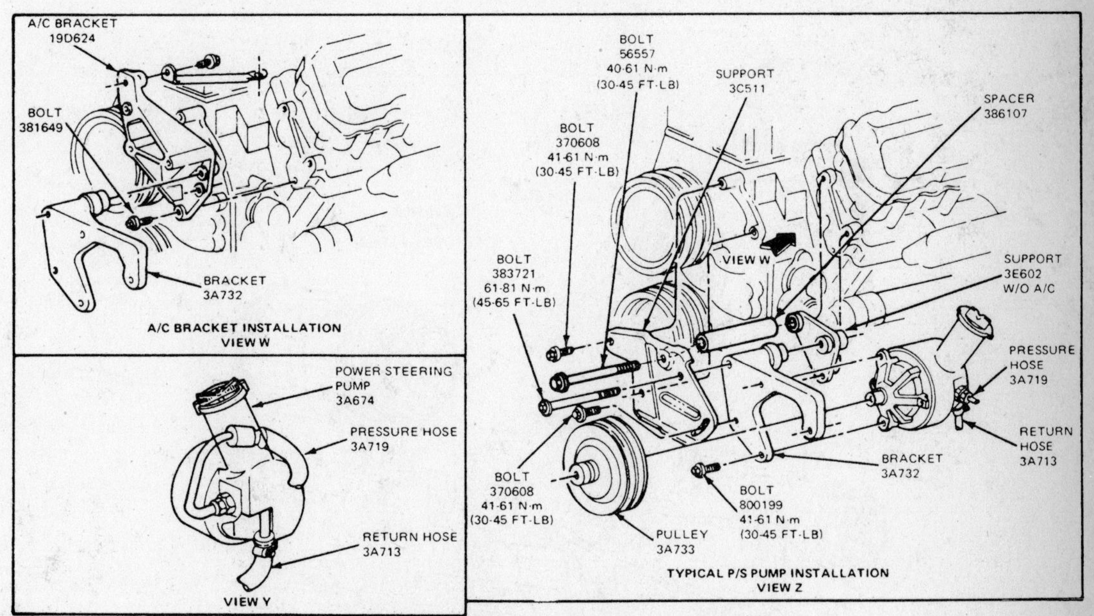

Power steering pump installation on the diesel

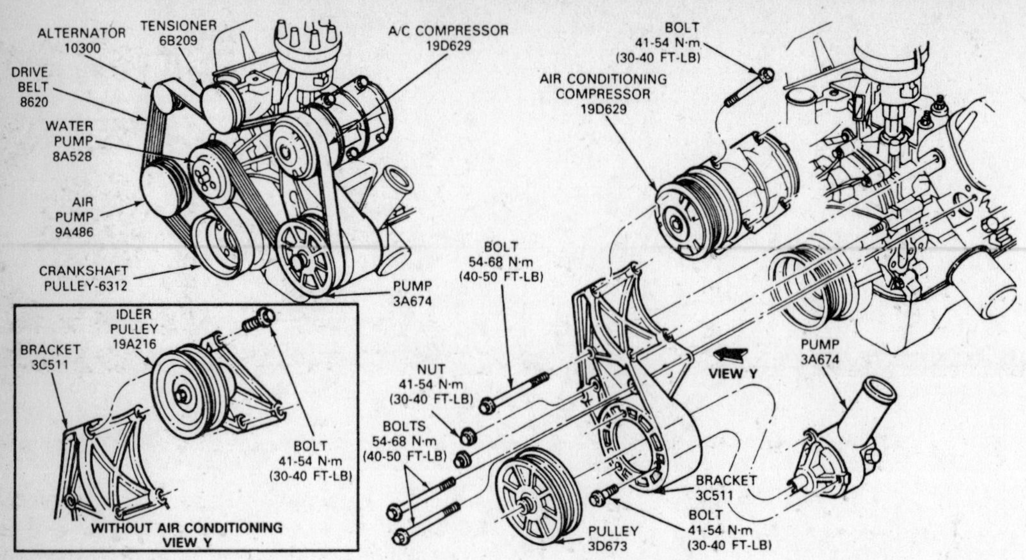

Power steering pump installation on the 1988–90 8–5.0L EFI and 8–5.8L EFI

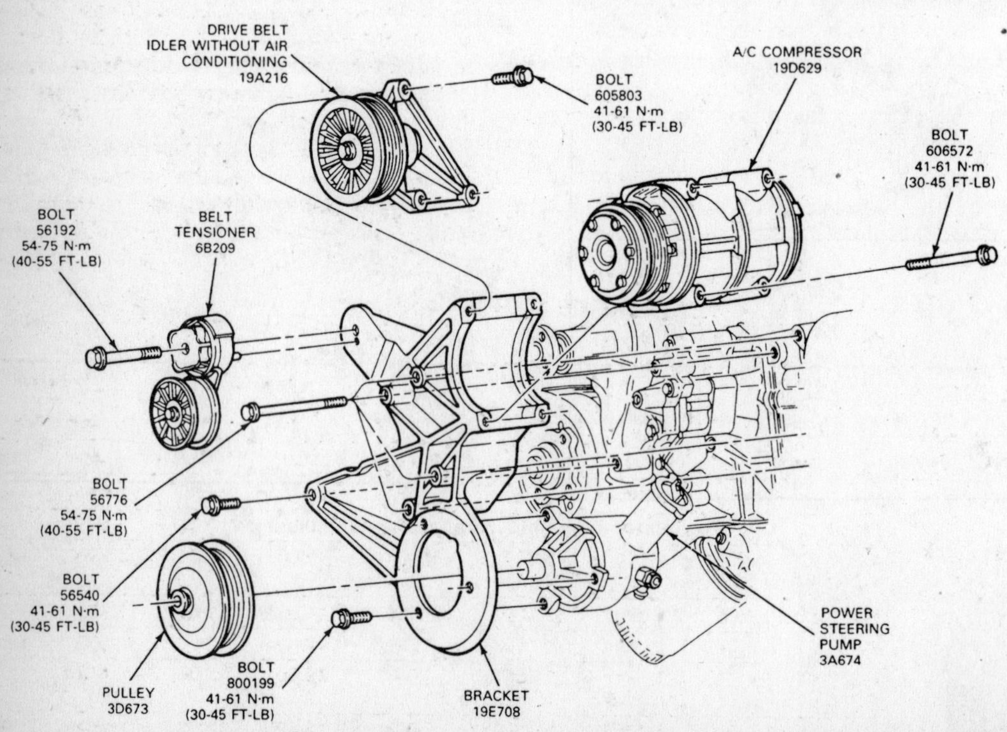

Power steering pump installation on the 8–7.5L EFI

Brakes

9

BASIC OPERATING PRINCIPLES

Hydraulic systems are used to actuate the brakes of all automobiles. The system transports the power required to force the frictional surfaces of the braking system together from the pedal to the individual brake units at each wheel. A hydraulic system is used for two reasons.

First, fluid under pressure can be carried to all parts of an automobile by small pipes and flexible hoses without taking up a significant amount of room or posing routing problems.

Second, a great mechanical advantage can be given to the brake pedal end of the system, and the foot pressure required to actuate the brakes can be reduced by making the surface area of the master cylinder pistons smaller than that of any of the pistons in the wheel cylinders or calipers.

The master cylinder consists of a fluid reservoir and a double cylinder and piston assembly. Double type master cylinders are designed to separate the front and rear braking systems hydraulically in case of a leak.

Steel lines carry the brake fluid to a point on the vehicle's frame near each of the vehicle's wheels. The fluid is then carried to the calipers and wheel cylinders by flexible tubes in order to allow for suspension and steering movements.

In drum brake systems, each wheel cylinder contains two pistons, one at either end, which push outward in opposite directions.

In disc brake systems, the cylinders are part of the calipers. One cylinder in each caliper is used to force the brake pads against the disc.

All pistons employ some type of seal, usually made of rubber, to minimize fluid leakage. A rubber dust boot seals the outer end of the cylinder against dust and dirt. The boot fits around the outer end of the piston on disc brake calipers, and around the brake actuating rod on wheel cylinders.

The hydraulic system operates as follows: When at rest, the entire system, from the piston(s) in the master cylinder to those in the wheel cylinders or calipers, is full of brake fluid.

Brake Specifications

All specifications in inches

Years	Models	Master Cyl. Bore	Brake Disc		Brake Drum		Wheel Cyl. or Caliper Bore	
			Minimum Thickness	Maximum Run-out	Orig. Inside Dia.	Max. Wear Limit	Front	Rear
1987	F-150 and Bronco	1.000	1.120	0.003	11.03	11.09	2.875	1.000
	F-250	1.062	1.180	0.003	12.00	12.06	2.180	1.000
	F-250HD F-350	1.125	1.180	0.003	12.00	12.06	2.180	1.063
1988–90	F-150 and Bronco	1.000	1.120	0.003	11.03	11.09	2.875	1.000
	F-250	1.062	1.180	0.003	12.00	12.06	2.180	1.000
	F-250HD F-350	1.125	1.180	0.005	12.00	12.06	2.180	1.063
	F-Super Duty	1.125	1.430	0.008	12.00	12.06	2.180	1.000

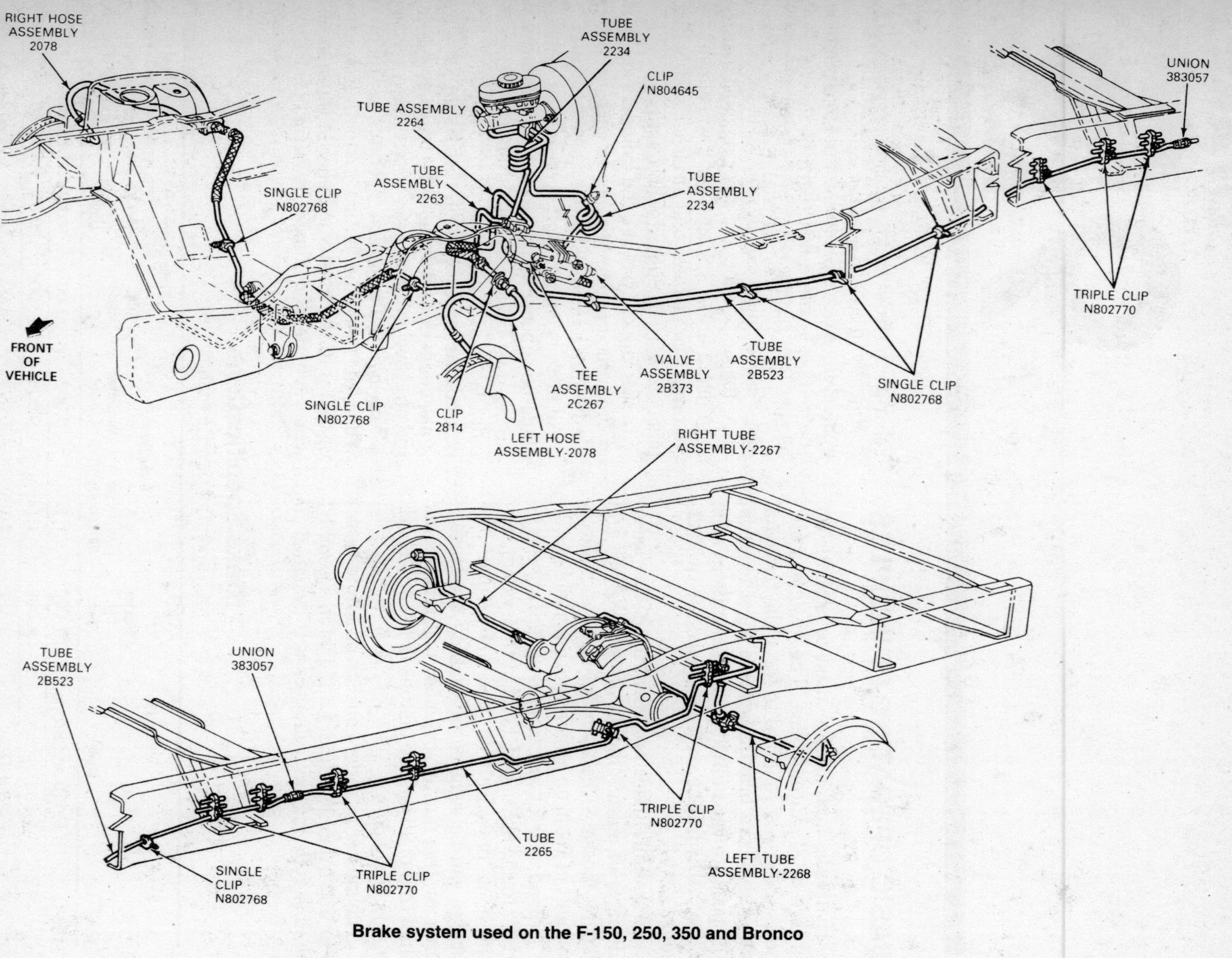

Brake system used on the F-150, 250, 350 and Bronco

Troubleshooting the Brake System

Problem	Cause	Solution
Low brake pedal (excessive pedal travel required for braking action.)	• Excessive clearance between rear linings and drums caused by inoperative automatic adjusters	• Make 10 to 15 alternate forward and reverse brake stops to adjust brakes. If brake pedal does not come up, repair or replace adjuster parts as necessary.
	• Worn rear brakelining	• Inspect and replace lining if worn beyond minimum thickness specification
	• Bent, distorted brakeshoes, front or rear	• Replace brakeshoes in axle sets
	• Air in hydraulic system	• Remove air from system. Refer to Brake Bleeding.
Low brake pedal (pedal may go to floor with steady pressure applied.)	• Fluid leak in hydraulic system	• Fill master cylinder to fill line; have helper apply brakes and check calipers, wheel cylinders, differential valve tubes, hoses and fittings for leaks. Repair or replace as necessary.
	• Air in hydraulic system	• Remove air from system. Refer to Brake Bleeding.
	• Incorrect or non-recommended brake fluid (fluid evaporates at below normal temp).	• Flush hydraulic system with clean brake fluid. Refill with correct-type fluid.
	• Master cylinder piston seals worn, or master cylinder bore is scored, worn or corroded	• Repair or replace master cylinder
Low brake pedal (pedal goes to floor on first application—o.k. on subsequent applications.)	• Disc brake pads sticking on abutment surfaces of anchor plate. Caused by a build-up of dirt, rust, or corrosion on abutment surfaces	• Clean abutment surfaces
Fading brake pedal (pedal height decreases with steady pressure applied.)	• Fluid leak in hydraulic system	• Fill master cylinder reservoirs to fill mark, have helper apply brakes, check calipers, wheel cylinders, differential valve, tubes, hoses, and fittings for fluid leaks. Repair or replace parts as necessary.
	• Master cylinder piston seals worn, or master cylinder bore is scored, worn or corroded	• Repair or replace master cylinder
Decreasing brake pedal travel (pedal travel required for braking action decreases and may be accompanied by a hard pedal.)	• Caliper or wheel cylinder pistons sticking or seized	• Repair or replace the calipers, or wheel cylinders
	• Master cylinder compensator ports blocked (preventing fluid return to reservoirs) or pistons sticking or seized in master cylinder bore	• Repair or replace the master cylinder
	• Power brake unit binding internally	• Test unit according to the following procedure: (a) Shift transmission into neutral and start engine (b) Increase engine speed to 1500 rpm, close throttle and fully depress brake pedal (c) Slow release brake pedal and stop engine (d) Have helper remove vacuum check valve and hose from power unit. Observe for backward movement of brake pedal. (e) If the pedal moves backward, the power unit has an internal bind—replace power unit

Troubleshooting the Brake System (cont.)

Problem	Cause	Solution
Spongy brake pedal (pedal has abnormally soft, springy, spongy feel when depressed.)	• Air in hydraulic system	• Remove air from system. Refer to Brake Bleeding.
	• Brakeshoes bent or distorted	• Replace brakeshoes
	• Brakelining not yet seated with drums and rotors	• Burnish brakes
	• Rear drum brakes not properly adjusted	• Adjust brakes
Hard brake pedal (excessive pedal pressure required to stop vehicle. May be accompanied by brake fade.)	• Loose or leaking power brake unit vacuum hose	• Tighten connections or replace leaking hose
	• Incorrect or poor quality brakelining	• Replace with lining in axle sets
	• Bent, broken, distorted brakeshoes	• Replace brakeshoes
	• Calipers binding or dragging on mounting pins. Rear brakeshoes dragging on support plate.	• Replace mounting pins and bushings. Clean rust or burrs from rear brake support plate ledges and lubricate ledges with molydisulfide grease. **NOTE:** If ledges are deeply grooved or scored, do not attempt to sand or grind them smooth—replace support plate.
	• Caliper, wheel cylinder, or master cylinder pistons sticking or seized	• Repair or replace parts as necessary
	• Power brake unit vacuum check valve malfunction	• Test valve according to the following procedure: (a) Start engine, increase engine speed to 1500 rpm, close throttle and immediately stop engine (b) Wait at least 90 seconds then depress brake pedal (c) If brakes are not vacuum assisted for 2 or more applications, check valve is faulty
	• Power brake unit has internal bind	• Test unit according to the following procedure: (a) With engine stopped, apply brakes several times to exhaust all vacuum in system (b) Shift transmission into neutral, depress brake pedal and start engine (c) If pedal height decreases with foot pressure and less pressure is required to hold pedal in applied position, power unit vacuum system is operating normally. Test power unit. If power unit exhibits a bind condition, replace the power unit.
	• Master cylinder compensator ports (at bottom of reservoirs) blocked by dirt, scale, rust, or have small burrs (blocked ports prevent fluid return to reservoirs).	• Repair or replace master cylinder **CAUTION:** Do not attempt to clean blocked ports with wire, pencils, or similar implements. Use compressed air only.
	• Brake hoses, tubes, fittings clogged or restricted	• Use compressed air to check or unclog parts. Replace any damaged parts.
	• Brake fluid contaminated with improper fluids (motor oil, transmission fluid, causing rubber components to swell and stick in bores	• Replace all rubber components, combination valve and hoses. Flush entire brake system with DOT 3 brake fluid or equivalent.
	• Low engine vacuum	• Adjust or repair engine

Troubleshooting the Brake System (cont.)

Problem	Cause	Solution
Grabbing brakes (severe reaction to brake pedal pressure.)	• Brakelining(s) contaminated by grease or brake fluid	• Determine and correct cause of contamination and replace brakeshoes in axle sets
	• Parking brake cables incorrectly adjusted or seized	• Adjust cables. Replace seized cables.
	• Incorrect brakelining or lining loose on brakeshoes	• Replace brakeshoes in axle sets
	• Caliper anchor plate bolts loose	• Tighten bolts
	• Rear brakeshoes binding on support plate ledges	• Clean and lubricate ledges. Replace support plate(s) if ledges are deeply grooved. Do not attempt to smooth ledges by grinding.
	• Incorrect or missing power brake reaction disc	• Install correct disc
	• Rear brake support plates loose	• Tighten mounting bolts
Dragging brakes (slow or incomplete release of brakes)	• Brake pedal binding at pivot	• Loosen and lubricate
	• Power brake unit has internal bind	• Inspect for internal bind. Replace unit if internal bind exists.
	• Parking brake cables incorrrectly adjusted or seized	• Adjust cables. Replace seized cables.
	• Rear brakeshoe return springs weak or broken	• Replace return springs. Replace brakeshoe if necessary in axle sets.
	• Automatic adjusters malfunctioning	• Repair or replace adjuster parts as required
	• Caliper, wheel cylinder or master cylinder pistons sticking or seized	• Repair or replace parts as necessary
	• Master cylinder compensating ports blocked (fluid does not return to reservoirs).	• Use compressed air to clear ports. Do not use wire, pencils, or similar objects to open blocked ports.
Vehicle moves to one side when brakes are applied	• Incorrect front tire pressure	• Inflate to recommended cold (reduced load) inflation pressure
	• Worn or damaged wheel bearings	• Replace worn or damaged bearings
	• Brakelining on one side contaminated	• Determine and correct cause of contamination and replace brakelining in axle sets
	• Brakeshoes on one side bent, distorted, or lining loose on shoe	• Replace brakeshoes in axle sets
	• Support plate bent or loose on one side	• Tighten or replace support plate
	• Brakelining not yet seated with drums or rotors	• Burnish brakelining
	• Caliper anchor plate loose on one side	• Tighten anchor plate bolts
	• Caliper piston sticking or seized	• Repair or replace caliper
	• Brakelinings water soaked	• Drive vehicle with brakes lightly applied to dry linings
	• Loose suspension component attaching or mounting bolts	• Tighten suspension bolts. Replace worn suspension components.
	• Brake combination valve failure	• Replace combination valve
Chatter or shudder when brakes are applied (pedal pulsation and roughness may also occur.)	• Brakeshoes distorted, bent, contaminated, or worn	• Replace brakeshoes in axle sets
	• Caliper anchor plate or support plate loose	• Tighten mounting bolts
	• Excessive thickness variation of rotor(s)	• Refinish or replace rotors in axle sets
Noisy brakes (squealing, clicking, scraping sound when brakes are applied.)	• Bent, broken, distorted brakeshoes	• Replace brakeshoes in axle sets
	• Excessive rust on outer edge of rotor braking surface	• Remove rust

Troubleshooting the Brake System (cont.)

Problem	Cause	Solution
Noisy brakes (squealing, clicking, scraping sound when brakes are applied.) (cont.)	• Brakelining worn out—shoes contacting drum of rotor	• Replace brakeshoes and lining in axle sets. Refinish or replace drums or rotors.
	• Broken or loose holdown or return springs	• Replace parts as necessary
	• Rough or dry drum brake support plate ledges	• Lubricate support plate ledges
	• Cracked, grooved, or scored rotor(s) or drum(s)	• Replace rotor(s) or drum(s). Replace brakeshoes and lining in axle sets if necessary.
	• Incorrect brakelining and/or shoes (front or rear).	• Install specified shoe and lining assemblies
Pulsating brake pedal	• Out of round drums or excessive lateral runout in disc brake rotor(s)	• Refinish or replace drums, re-index rotors or replace

Upon application of the brake pedal, fluid trapped in front of the master cylinder piston(s) is forced through the lines to the wheel cylinders. Here, it forces the pistons outward, in the case of drum brakes, and inward toward the disc, in the case of disc brakes. The motion of the pistons is opposed by return springs mounted outside the cylinders in drum brakes, and by spring seals, in disc brakes.

Upon release of the brake pedal, a spring located inside the master cylinder immediately returns the master cylinder pistons to the normal position. The pistons contain check valves and the master cylinder has compensating ports drilled in it. These are uncovered as the pistons reach their normal position. The piston check valves allow fluid to flow toward the wheel cylinders or calipers as the pistons withdraw. Then, as the return springs force the brake pads or shoes into the released position, the excess fluid reservoir through the compensating ports. It is during the time the pedal is in the released position that any fluid that has leaked out of the system will be replaced through the compensating ports.

Dual circuit master cylinders employ two pistons, located one behind the other, in the same cylinder. The primary piston is actuated directly by mechanical linkage from the brake pedal through the power booster. The secondary piston is actuated by fluid trapped between the two pistons. If a leak develops in front of the secondary piston, it moves forward until it bottoms against the front of the master cylinder, and the fluid trapped between the pistons will operate the rear brakes. If the rear brakes develop a leak, the primary piston will move forward until direct contact with the secondary piston takes place, and it will force the secondary piston to actuate the front brakes. In either case, the brake pedal moves farther when the brakes are applied, and less braking power is available.

All dual circuit systems use a switch to warn the driver when only half of the brake system is operational. This switch is located in a valve body which is mounted on the firewall or the frame below the master cylinder. A hydraulic piston receives pressure from both circuits, each circuit's pressure being applied to one end of the piston. When the pressures are in balance, the piston remains stationary. When one circuit has a leak, however, the greater pressure in that circuit during application of the brakes will push the piston to one side, closing the switch and activating the brake warning light.

In disc brake systems, this valve body also contains a metering valve and, in some cases, a proportioning valve. The metering valve keeps pressure from traveling to the disc brakes on the front wheels until the brake shoes on the rear wheels have contacted the drums, ensuring that the front brakes will never be used alone. The proportioning valve controls the pressure to the rear brakes to lessen the chance of rear wheel lock-up during very hard braking.

Warning lights may be tested by depressing the brake pedal and holding it while opening one of the wheel cylinder bleeder screws. If this does not cause the light to go on, substitute a new lamp, make continuity checks, and, finally, replace the switch as necessary.

The hydraulic system may be checked for leaks by applying pressure to the pedal gradually and steadily. If the pedal sinks very slowly to the floor, the system has a leak. This is not to be confused with a springy or spongy feel due to the compression of air within the lines. If the system leaks, there will be a gradual change in the position of the pedal with a constant pressure.

Check for leaks along all lines and at wheel cylinders. If no external leaks are apparent, the problem is inside the master cylinder.

Disc Brakes

BASIC OPERATING PRINCIPLES

Instead of the traditional expanding brakes that press outward against a circular drum, disc brake systems utilize a disc (rotor) with brake pads positioned on either side of it. Braking effect is achieved in a manner similar to the way you would squeeze a spinning phonograph record between your fingers. The disc (rotor) is a casting with cooling fins between the two braking surfaces. This enables air to circulate between the braking surfaces making them less sensitive to heat buildup and more resistant to fade. Dirt and water do not affect braking action since contaminants are thrown off by the centrifugal action of the rotor or scraped off the by the pads. Also, the equal clamping action of the two brake pads tends to ensure uniform, straight line stops. Disc brakes are inherently self-adjusting. There are three general types of disc brake:

1. A fixed caliper.
2. A floating caliper.
3. A sliding caliper.

The fixed caliper design uses two pistons mounted on either side of the rotor (in each side of the caliper). The caliper is mounted rigidly and does not move.

The sliding and floating designs are quite similar. In fact, these two types are often lumped together. In both designs, the pad on the inside of the rotor is moved into contact with the rotor by hydraulic force. The caliper, which is not held in a fixed position, moves slightly, bringing the outside pad into contact with the rotor. There are various methods of attaching floating calipers. Some pivot at the bottom or top, and some slide on mounting bolts. In any event, the end result is the same.

All the cars covered in this book employ the sliding caliper design.

Drum Brakes

BASIC OPERATING PRINCIPLES

Drum brakes employ two brake shoes mounted on a stationary backing plate. These shoes are positioned inside a circular drum which rotates with the wheel assembly. The shoes are held in place by springs. This allows them to slide toward the drums (when they are applied) while keeping the linings and drums in alignment. The shoes are actuated by a wheel cylinder which is mounted at the top of the backing plate. When the brakes are applied, hydraulic pressure forces the wheel cylinder's actuating links outward. Since these links bear directly against the top of the brake shoes, the tops of the shoes are then forced against the inner side of the drum. This action forces the bottoms of the two shoes to contact the brake drum by rotating the entire assembly slightly (known as servo action). When pressure within the wheel cylinder is relaxed, return springs pull the shoes back away from the drum.

Most modern drum brakes are designed to self-adjust themselves during application when the vehicle is moving in reverse. This motion causes both shoes to rotate very slightly with the drum, rocking an adjusting lever, thereby causing rotation of the adjusting screw.

Power Boosters

Power brakes operate just as non-power brake systems except in the actuation of the master cylinder pistons. A vacuum diaphragm is located on the front of the master cylinder and assists the driver in applying the brakes, reducing both the effort and travel he must put into moving the brake pedal.

The vacuum diaphragm housing is connected to the intake manifold by a vacuum hose. A check valve is placed at the point where the hose enters the diaphragm housing, so that during periods of low manifold vacuum brake assist vacuum will not be lost.

Depressing the brake pedal closes off the vacuum source and allows atmospheric pressure to enter on one side of the diaphragm. This causes the master cylinder pistons to move and apply the brakes. When the brake pedal is released, vacuum is applied to both sides of the diaphragm, and return springs return the diaphragm and master cylinder pistons to the released position. If the vacuum fails, the brake pedal rod will butt against the end of the master cylinder actuating rod, and direct mechanical application will occur as the pedal is depressed.

The hydraulic and mechanical problems that apply to conventional brake systems also apply to power brakes, and should be checked for if the tests below do not reveal the problem. **Test for a system vacuum leak as described below:**

1. Operate the engine at idle without touching the brake pedal for at least one minute.
2. Turn off the engine, and wait one minute.
3. Test for the presence of assist vacuum by depressing the brake pedal and releasing it several times. Light application will produce less and less pedal travel, if vacuum was present. If

there is no vacuum, air is leaking into the system somewhere.

Test for system operation as follows:

1. Pump the brake pedal (with engine off) until the supply vacuum is entirely gone.
2. Put a light, steady pressure on the pedal.
3. Start the engine, and operate it at idle. If the system is operating, the brake pedal should fall toward the floor if constant pressure is maintained on the pedal.

Power brake systems may be tested for hydraulic leaks just as ordinary systems are tested.

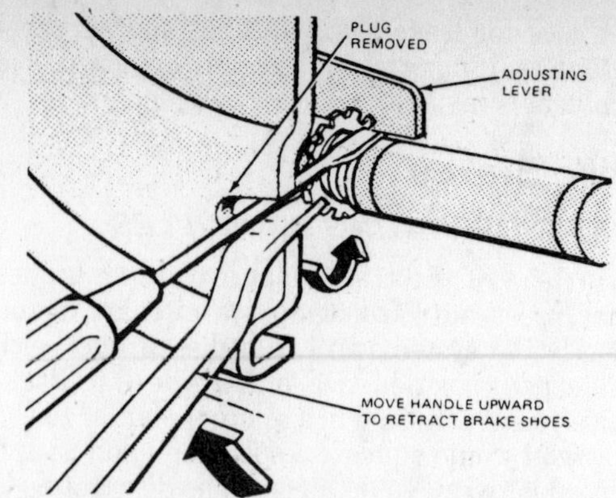

F-150 and Bronco rear brake adjustment

BRAKE SYSTEM

WARNING: *Clean, high quality brake fluid is essential to the safe and proper operation of the brake system. You should always buy the highest quality brake fluid that is available. If the brake fluid becomes contaminated, drain and flush the system and fill the master cylinder with new fluid.*
Never reuse any brake fluid. Any brake fluid that is removed from the system should be discarded.

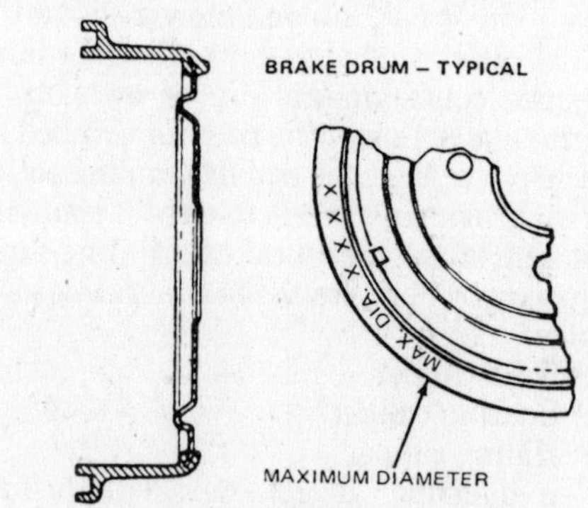

Brake drum maximum diamter location

Adjustments

DRUM BRAKES

The drum brakes are self-adjusting and require a manual adjustment only after the brake shoes have been replaced, or when the length of the adjusting screw has been changed while performing some other service operation, as i.e., taking off brake drums.

To adjust the brakes, follow the procedures given below:

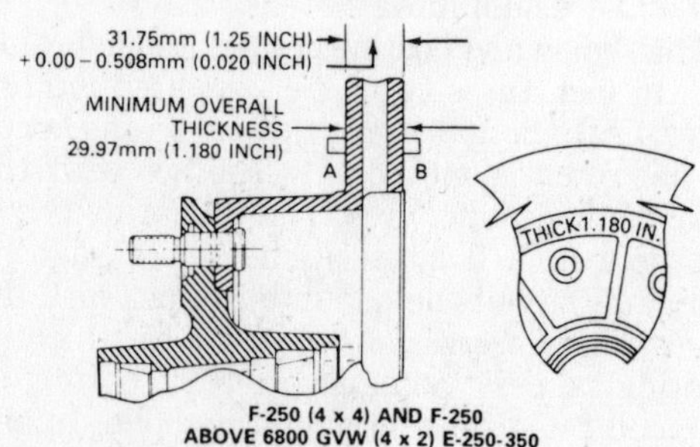

Brake rotor service limits

Drum Installed

1. Raise and support the rear end on jackstands.
2. Remove the rubber plug from the adjusting slot on the backing plate.
3. Insert a brake adjusting spoon into the slot and engage the lowest possible tooth on the starwheel. Move the end of the brake spoon downward to move the starwheel upward and expand the adjusting screw. Repeat this operation until the brakes lock the wheels.
4. Insert a small screwdriver or piece of firm wire (coat hanger wire) into the adjusting slot and push the automatic adjusting lever out and free of the starwheel on the adjusting screw and hold it there.
5. Engage the topmost tooth possible on the starwheel with the brake adjusting spoon. Move the end of the adjusting spoon upward to move the adjusting screw starwheel downward and contract the adjusting screw. Back off the

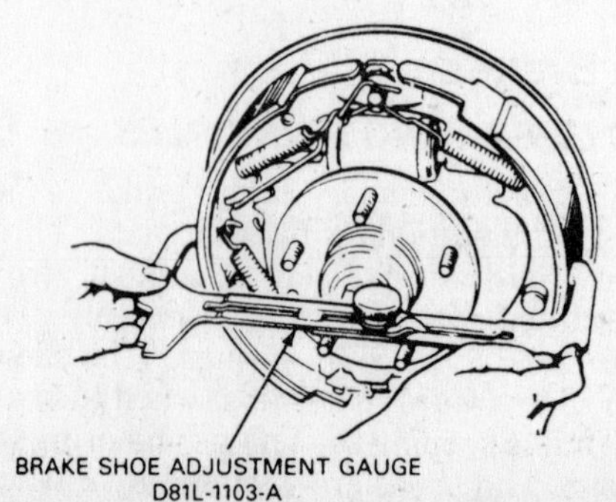

Measuring shoes

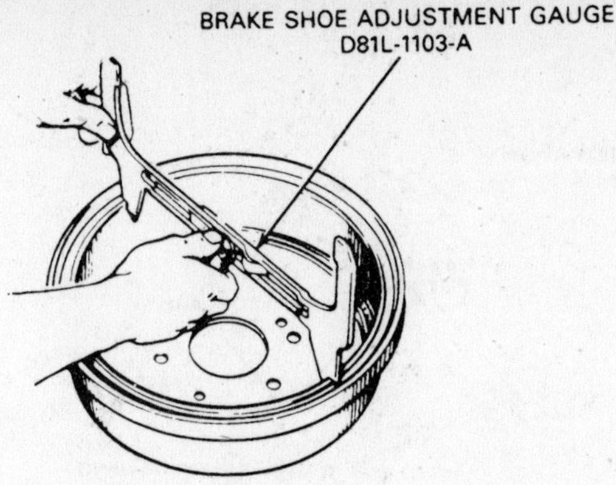

Measuring drum

adjusting screw starwheel until the wheel spins freely with a minimum of drag. Keep track of the number of turns that the starwheel is backed off, or the number of strokes taken with the brake adjusting spoon.

6. Repeat this operation for the other side. When backing off the brakes on the other side, the starwheel adjuster must be backed off the same number of turns to prevent side-to-side brake pull.

7. When the brakes are adjusted make several stops while backing the vehicle, to equalize the brakes at both of the wheels.

8. Remove the safety stands and lower the vehicle. Road test the vehicle.

Drum Removed

CAUTION: *Brake shoes contain asbestos, which has been determined to be a cancer causing agent. Never clean the brake surfaces with compressed air! Avoid inhaling any dust from any brake surface! When cleaning brake surfaces, use a commercially available brake cleaning fluid.*

1. Make sure that the shoe-to-contact pad areas are clean and properly lubricated.

2. Using and inside caliper check the inside diameter of the drum. Measure across the diameter of the assembled brake shoes, at their widest point.

3. Turn the adjusting screw so that the diameter of the shoes is 0.030 in. (0.76mm) less than the brake drum inner diameter.

4. Install the drum.

Brake Light Switch

REMOVAL AND INSTALLATION

1. Lift the locking tab on the switch connector and disconnect the wiring.

2. Remove the hairpin retainer, slide the

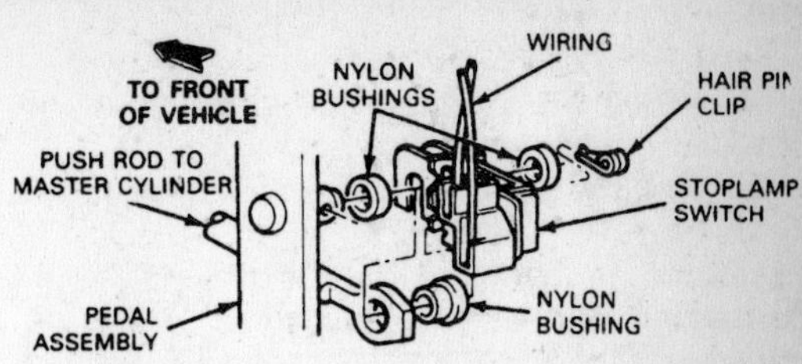

Brake light switch installation

stop lamp switch, pushrod and nylon washer off of the pedal. Remove the washer, then the switch by sliding it up or down.

NOTE: *On trucks equipped with speed control, the spacer washer is replaced by the dump valve adapter washer.*

3. To install the switch, position it so that the U-shaped side is nearest the pedal and directly over/under the pin.

4. Slide the switch up or down, trapping the master cylinder pushrod and bushing between the switch side plates.

5. Push the switch and pushrod assembly firmly towards the brake pedal arm. Assemble the outside white plastic washer to the pin and install the hairpin retainer.

CAUTION: *Don't substitute any other type of retainer. Use only the Ford specified hairpin retainer.*

6. Assemble the connector on the switch.

7. Check stop lamp operation.

CAUTION: *Make sure that the stop lamp switch wiring has sufficient travel during a full pedal stroke!*

Master Cylinder

REMOVAL AND INSTALLATION

1. Disconnect the hydraulic system brake lines at the master cylinder.

2. Disconnect the brake warning light indicator wire from the reservoir socket.

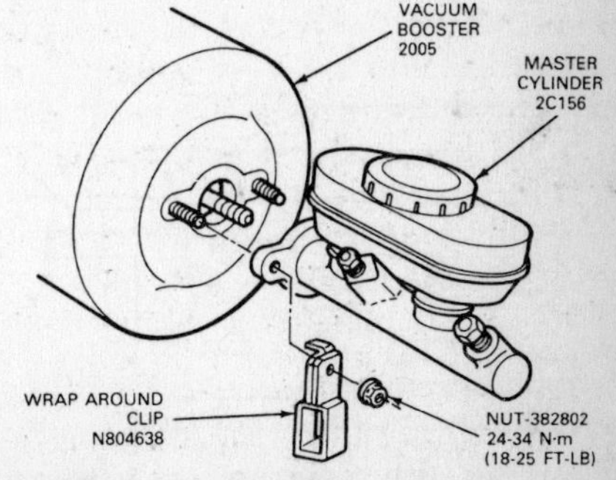

Master cylinder installation on 1988–90 F-150, 250, 350 and Bronco

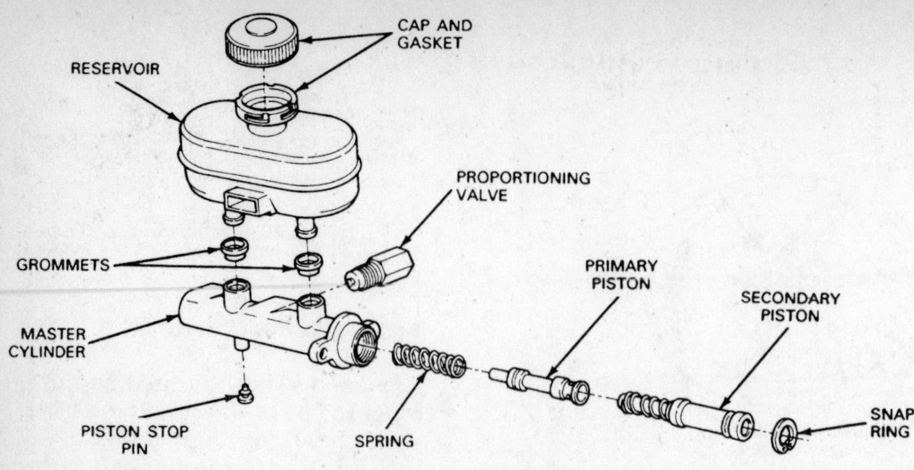

1988–90 master cylinder

3. Drain the reservoir.

4. Using a large screwdriver, pry between the master cylinder body and reservoir to remove the reservoir.

5. Remove the master cylinder retaining nuts and remove the master cylinder.

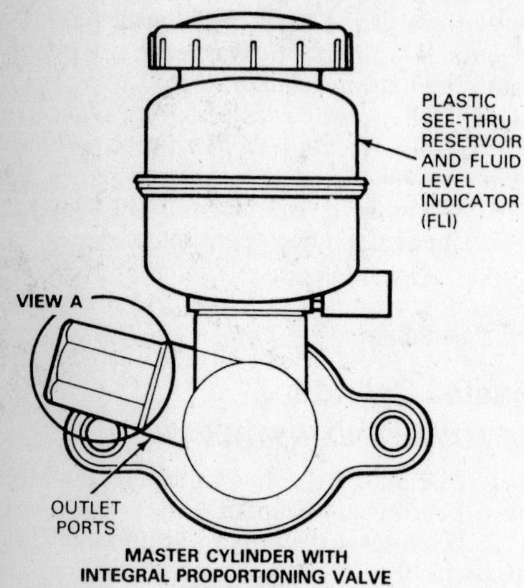

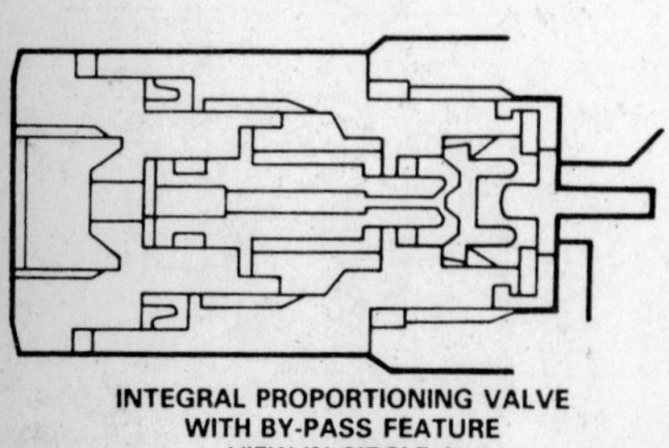

Master cylinder with integral proportioning valve front view

To install the master cylinder:

6. Lubricate 2 new grommets with clean brake fluid and install them in the master cylinder body.

7. Press the reservoir into the grommets with the indicator socket facing inboard. The reservoir should snap into place.

8. Position the master cylinder assembly on the booster and install the retaining nuts.

9. Connect the hydraulic brake system lines to the master cylinder.

10. Connect the wiring.

11. Bleed the master cylinder as described below.

OVERHAUL

The most important thing to remember when rebuilding the master cylinder is cleanliness. Work in clean surroundings with clean tools and clean cloths or paper for drying purposes. Have plenty of clean alcohol and brake fluid on hand to clean and lubricate the internal components. There are service repair kits available for overhauling the master cylinder.

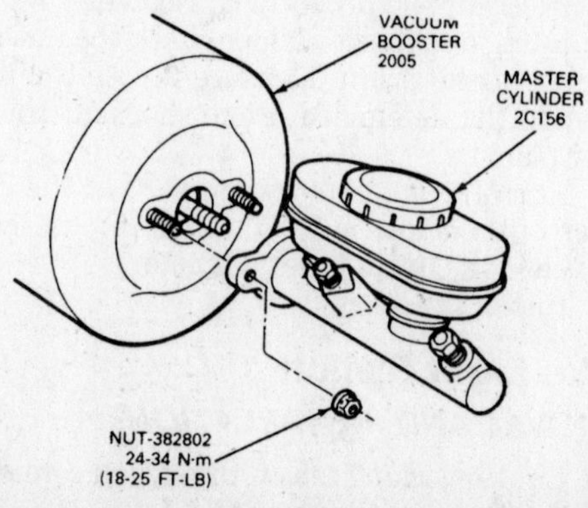

Master cylinder installation on 1987 F-150, 250, 350 and Bronco

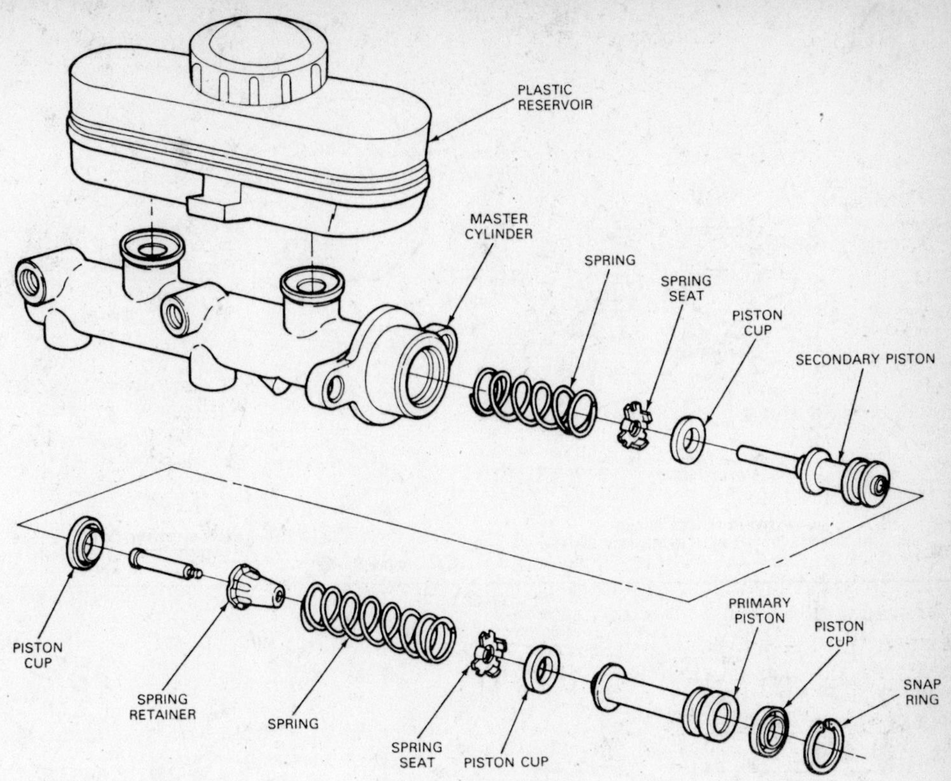

1987 master cylinder

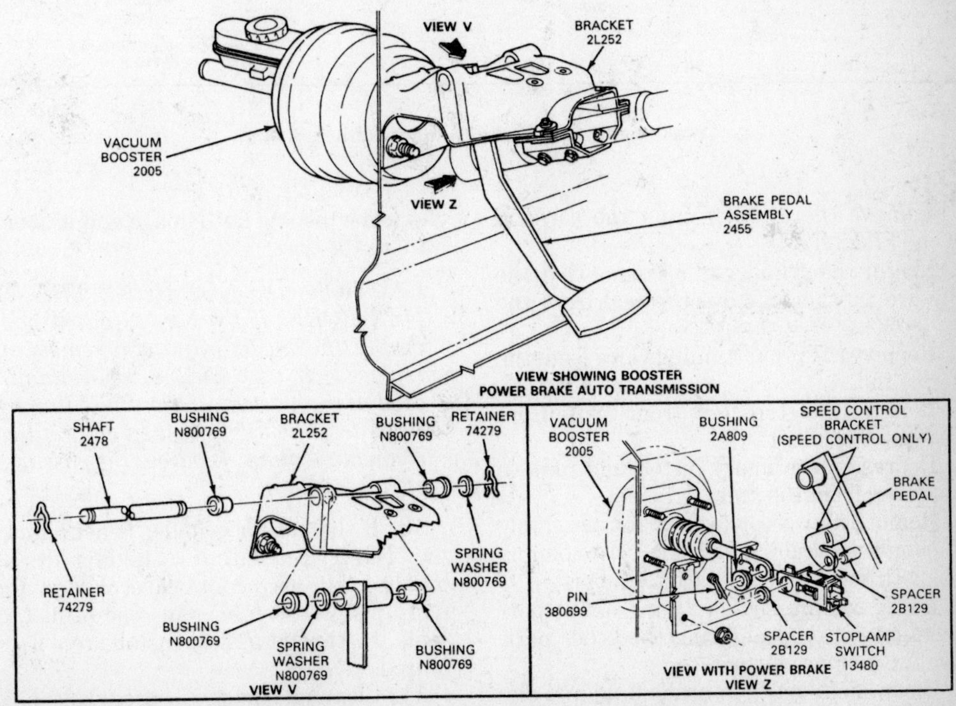

Brake pedal installation w/automatic transmission

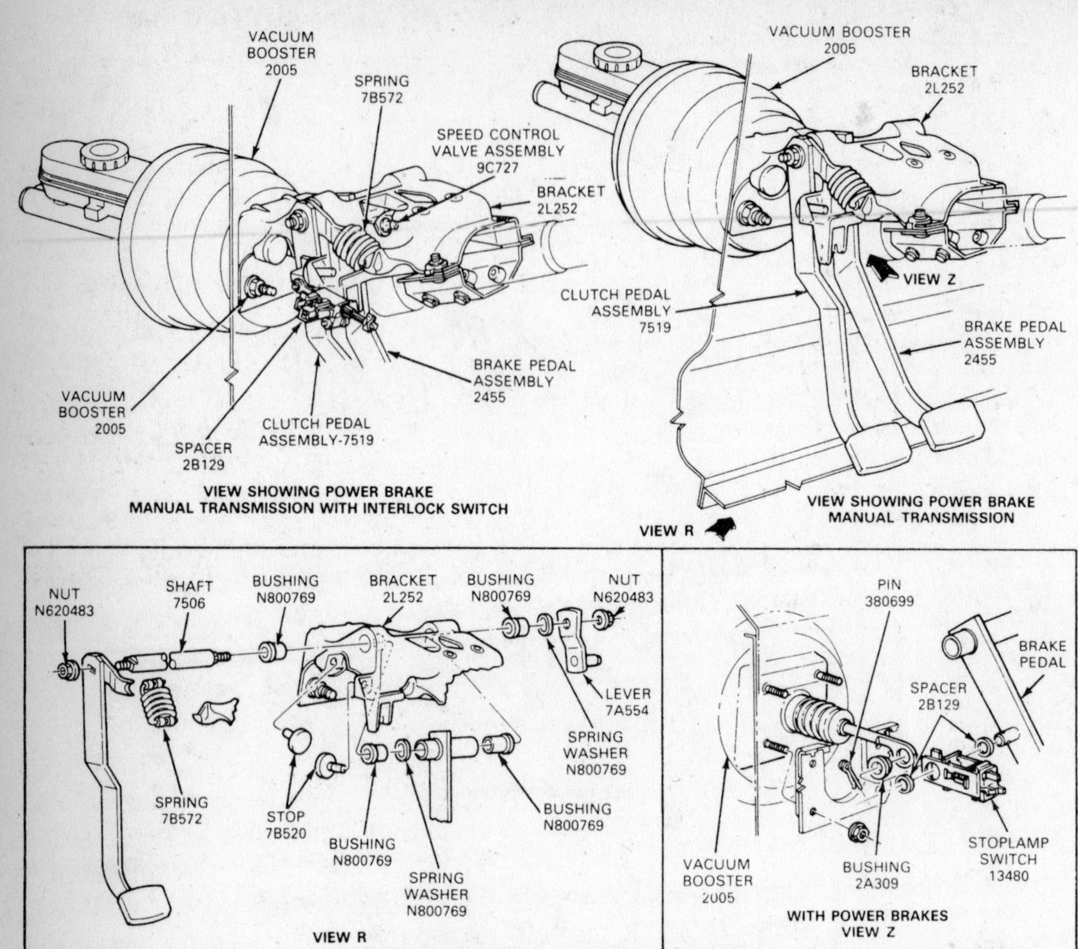

Brake pedal installation w/manual transmission

1. Remove the cylinder from the car and drain the brake fluid.
2. Mount the cylinder in a vise so that the outlets are up then remove the seal from the hub.
3. Remove the proportioning valve from the master cylinder.
4. Remove the stopscrew from the bottom of the master cylinder.
5. Depress the primary piston and remove the snapring from the rear of the bore.
6. Remove the secondary piston assembly using compressed air. Cover the bore opening with a cloth to prevent damage to the piston.
7. Using compressed air in the outlet port at the blind end and plugging the other port, remove the primary piston.
8. Clean metal parts in brake fluid and discard the rubber parts.
9. Inspect the bore for damage or wear, and check the pistons for damage and proper clearance in the bore.

CAUTION: *DO NOT HONE THE CYLINDER BORE! If the bore is pitted or scored deeply, the master cylinder assembly must be replaced. If any evidence of contamination exist in the master cylinder, the entire hydraulic system should be flushed and refilled with clean brake fluid. Blow out the passages with compressed air.*

10. If the master cylinder is not damaged, it may be serviced with a rebuilding kit. The rebuilding kit may contain secondary and primary piston assemblies instead of just rubber seals. In this case, seal installation is not required.
11. Clean all parts in isopropyl alcohol.
12. Install new secondary seals in the two grooves in the flat end of the front piston. The

lips of the seals will be facing away from each other.

13. Install a new primary seal and the seal protector on the opposite end of the front piston with the lips of the seal facing outward.

14. Coat the seals with brake fluid. Install the spring on the front piston with the spring retainer in the primary seal.

15. Insert the piston assembly, spring end first, into the bore and use a wooden rod to seat it.

16. Coat the rear piston seals with brake fluid and install them into the piston grooves with the lips facing the spring end.

17. Assemble the spring onto the piston and install the assembly into the bore spring first. Install the snapring.

18. Hold the piston train at the bottom of the bore and install the stopscrew. Install a new seal on the hub. Bench-bleed the cylinder or install and bleed the cylinder on the car.

Pressure Differential Valve

REMOVAL AND INSTALLATION

1. Disconnect the electrical leads from the valve.
2. Unscrew the valve from the master cylinder.
3. Install the valve in the reverse order of removal.
4. Bleed the master cylinder.

Height Sensing Proportioning Valve

REMOVAL AND INSTALLATION

F-Super Duty Only

NOTE: *If the linkage is disconnected from the valve, the proper setting of the valve will be lost and a new valve will have to be installed. The new valve will have the shaft preset and secured internally. If the shaft of the new valve turns freely, DO NOT USE IT!*

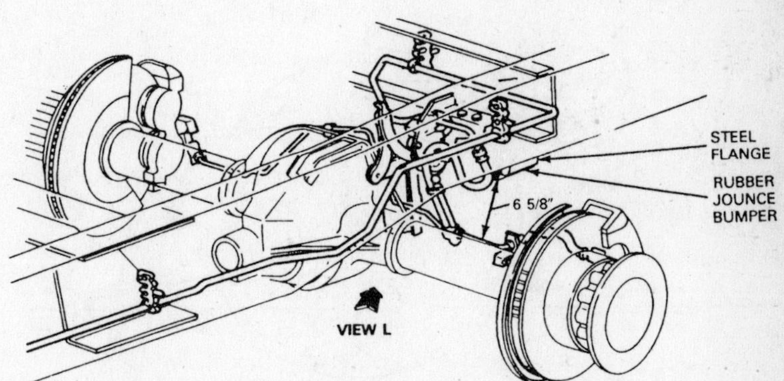

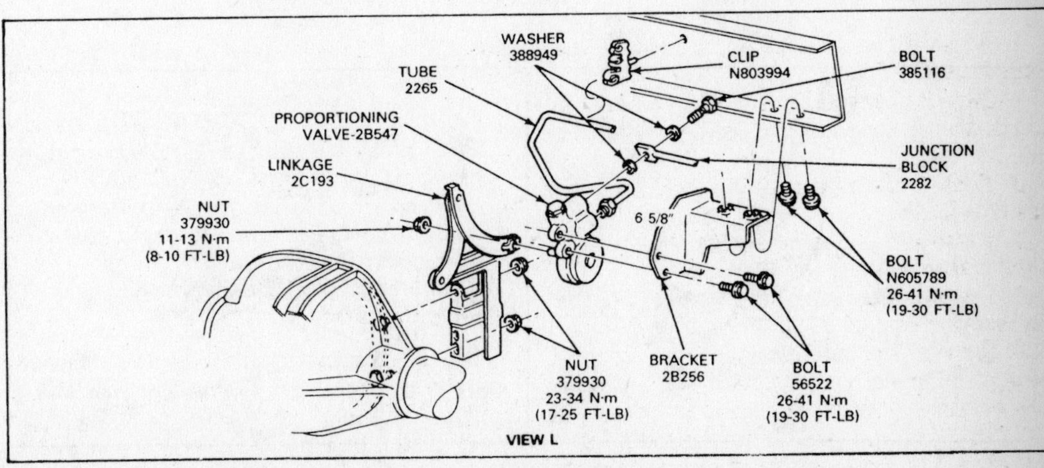

Height sensing proportioning valve installation on F-Super Duty

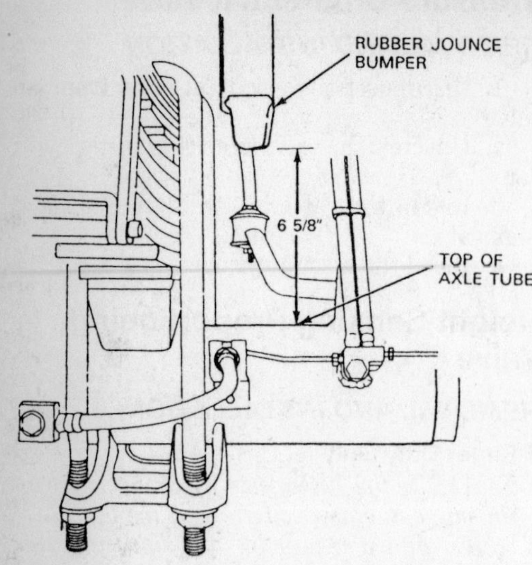

Setting the correct indexing height for the height sensing proportioning valve

The valve cannot be repaired or disassembled. It is to be replaced as a unit.

If the linkage is damaged or broken and requires replacement, a new sensing valve will also be required.

1. Raise and support the rear end on jackstands.
2. Raise the frame to obtain a clearance of $6^5/_8$ in. (168.3mm) between the bottom edge of the rubber jounce bumper and the top of the axle tube – on BOTH sides of the axle. The is the correct indexing height for the valve.
3. Remove the nut holding the linkage arm to the valve and disconnect the arm.
4. Remove the bolt holding the flexible brake hose to the valve.
5. Disconnect the brake line from the valve.
6. Remove the 2 mounting bolts and remove the valve from its bracket.

To install:

7. Place the new valve on the bracket and tighten the mounting bolts to 12–18 ft. lbs.

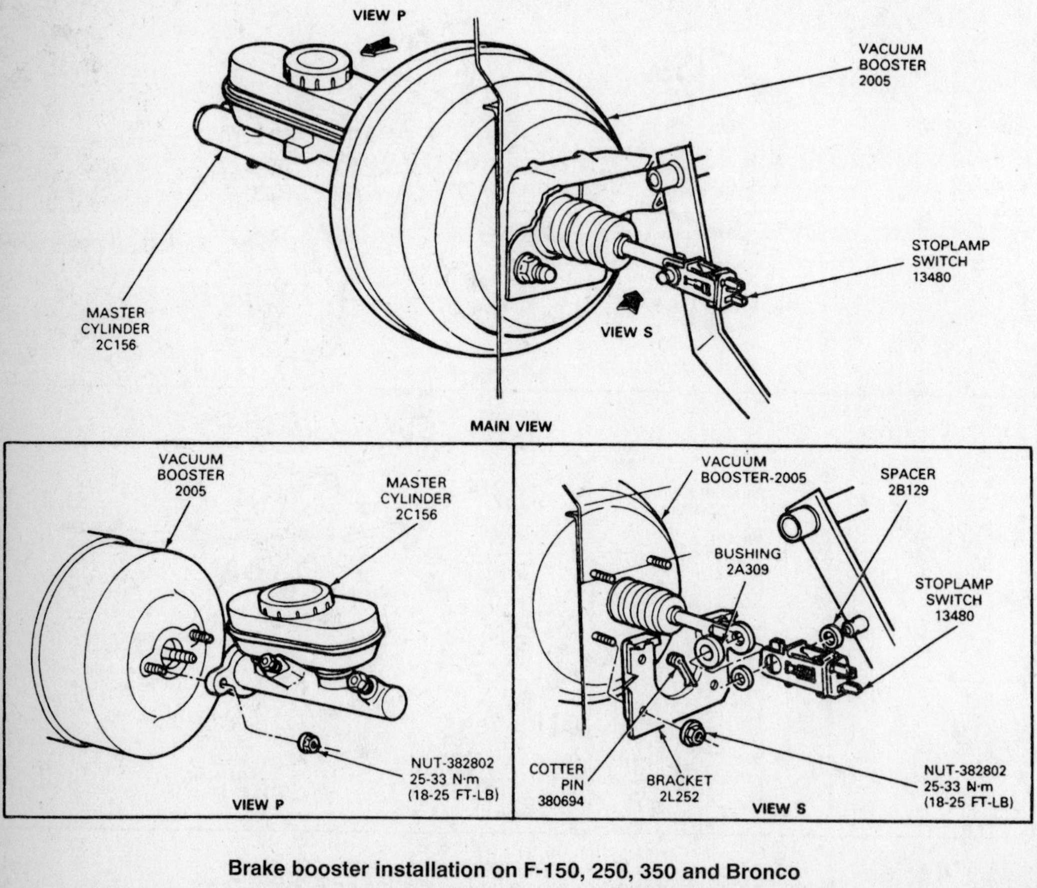

Brake booster installation on F-150, 250, 350 and Bronco

VACUUM
MANIFOLD
9C490
1/4" PORT TO
AUTO. TRANS.
TO LOW VACUUM
INDICATOR SWITCH
5/16" PORT TO
SPEED CONTROL
TO BRAKE
BOOSTER
1/4" PORT TO
CLIMATE
CONTROL
FROM
VACUUM
PUMP
SCREWS-N802658
VIEW X
HOSE
381298
TO BRAKE
BOOSTER
VIEW X
HOSE
381377-S26
JUNCTION
BLOCK
HOSE CLAMP
382984-S32
FRONT OF VEHICLE
LOW VACUUM
INDICATOR
SWITCH-12A182
VACUUM
PUMP-2A451
VACUUM
PUMP PULLEY
2L487
F-250-F-350 INSTALLATION

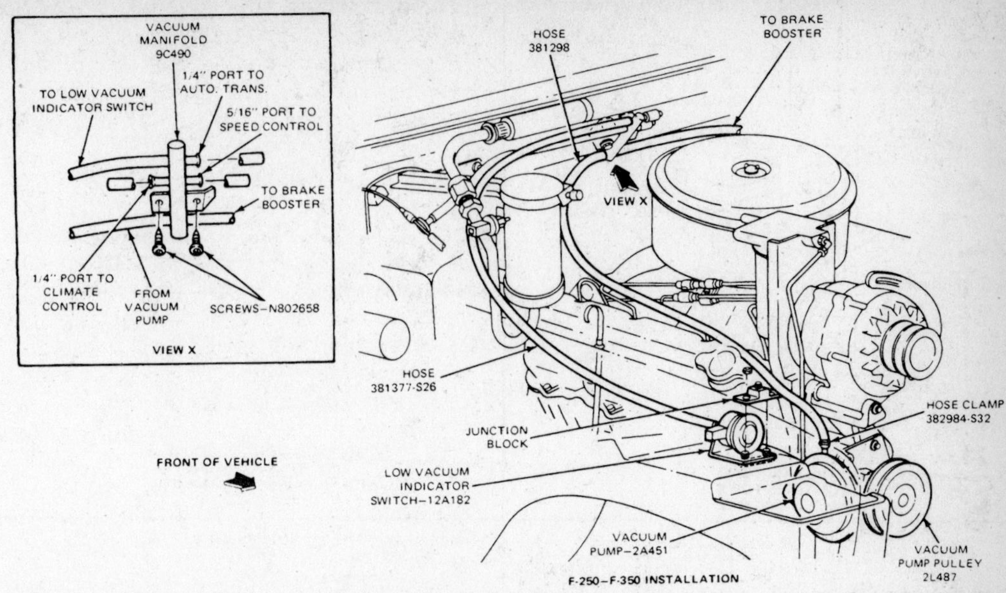

Brake booster vacuum pump for the diesel

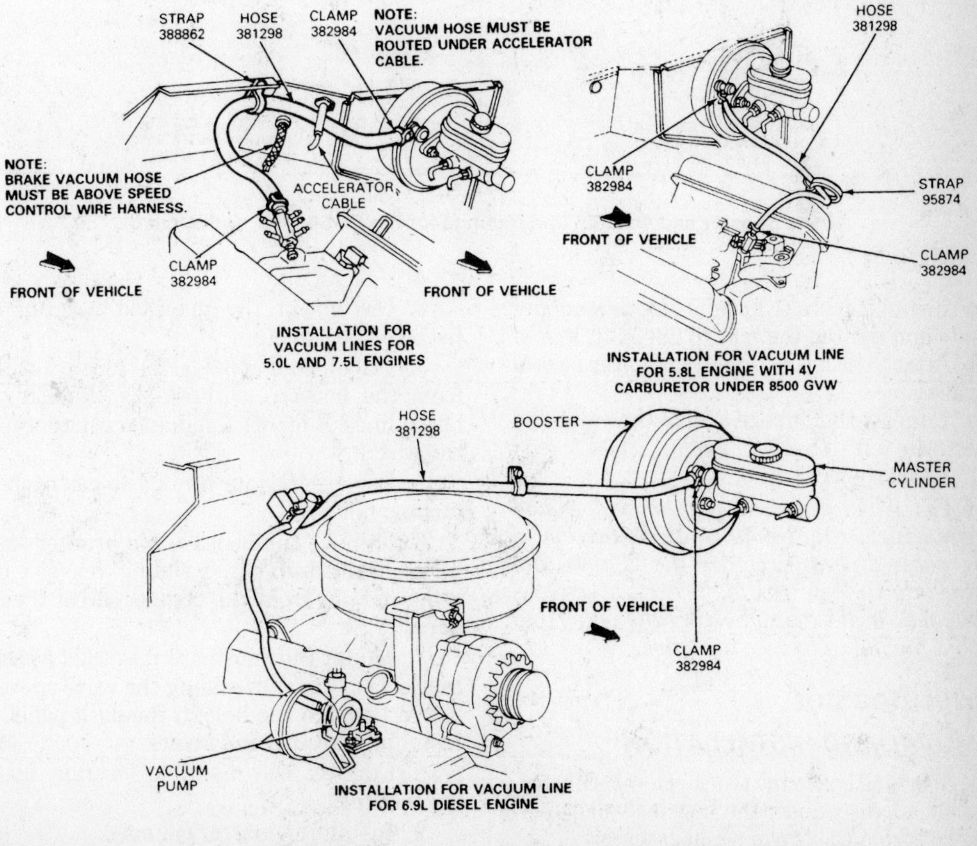

STRAP
388862
HOSE
381298
CLAMP
382984
NOTE:
VACUUM HOSE MUST BE
ROUTED UNDER ACCELERATOR
CABLE.
NOTE:
BRAKE VACUUM HOSE
MUST BE ABOVE SPEED
CONTROL WIRE HARNESS.
ACCELERATOR
CABLE
CLAMP
382984
FRONT OF VEHICLE
FRONT OF VEHICLE
INSTALLATION FOR
VACUUM LINES FOR
5.0L AND 7.5L ENGINES
HOSE
381298
CLAMP
382984
STRAP
95874
FRONT OF VEHICLE
CLAMP
382984
INSTALLATION FOR VACUUM LINE
FOR 5.8L ENGINE WITH 4V
CARBURETOR UNDER 8500 GVW
HOSE
381298
BOOSTER
MASTER
CYLINDER
FRONT OF VEHICLE
CLAMP
382984
VACUUM
PUMP
INSTALLATION FOR VACUUM LINE
FOR 6.9L DIESEL ENGINE

Brake booster and vacuum line routings for the F-250 and F-350

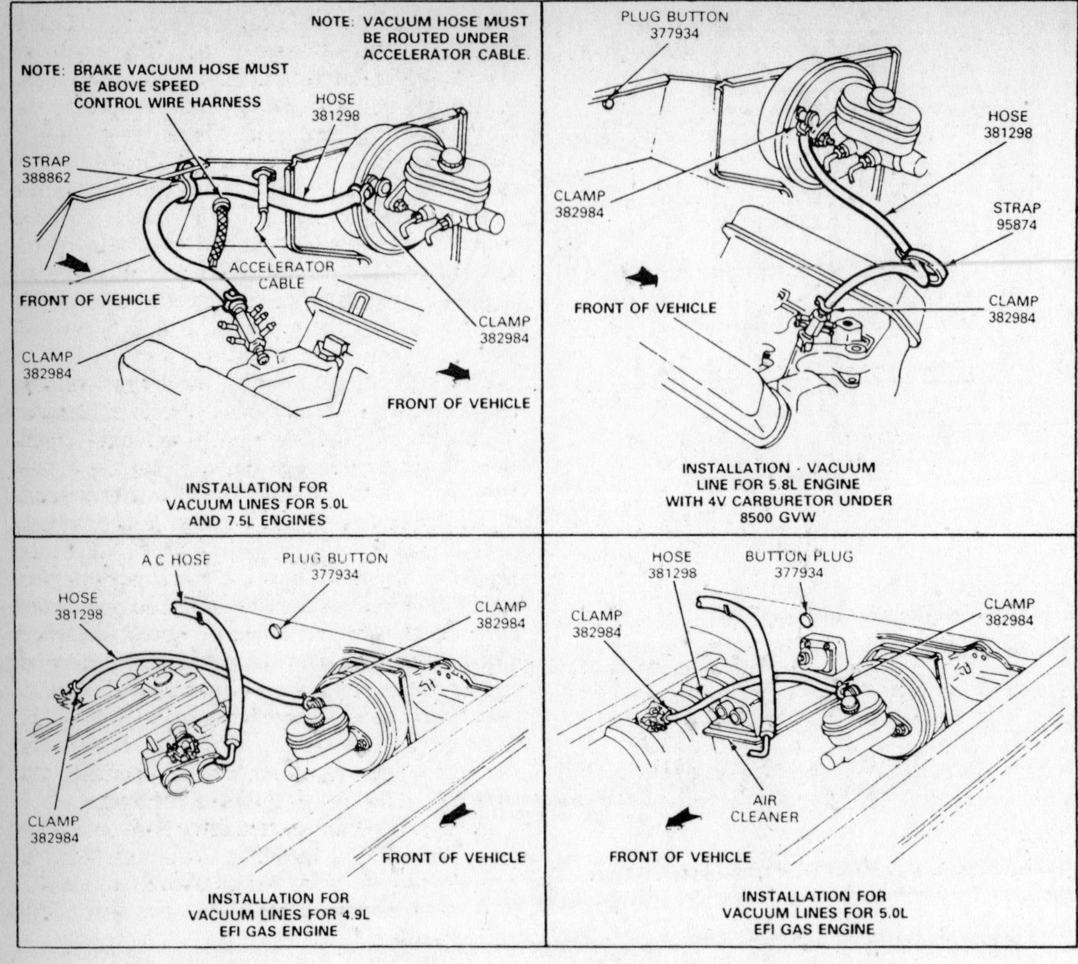

Brake booster and vacuum line routings for the F-150, 250, and Bronco

8. Install the brake hose, using new copper gaskets and tighten the bolt to 28–34 ft. lbs.
9. Attach the brake line to the lower part of the valve.
10. Connect the linkage arm to the valve and tighten the nut to 8–10 ft. lbs.
11. Bleed the brakes.

NOTE: *When servicing axle or suspension parts which would require disconnection of the valve, instead, remove the 2 nuts that attach the linkage arm to the axle cover plate. This will avoid disconnecting the valve and avoid having to replace the valve.*

Power Booster

REMOVAL AND INSTALLATION

1. Working inside the truck below the instrument panel, disconnect the booster valve operating rod from the brake pedal assembly.
2. Disconnect the wires from the stoplight switch.
3. Disconnect the manifold vacuum hose from the booster unit.
4. Unbolt and remove the master cylinder from the booster, without disconnecting the brake lines. Support the master cylinder out of the way.
5. Remove the four bracket-to-dash panel attaching bolts.
6. Remove the booster and bracket assembly from the dash panel, sliding the valve operating rod out from the engine side of the dash panel.
7. Mount the booster and bracket assembly to the dash panel by sliding the valve operating rod in through the hole in the dash panel, and installing the attaching bolts.
8. Connect the manifold vacuum hose to the booster.
9. Install the master cylinder.
10. Connect the stop light switch wires.
11. Working inside the truck below the in-

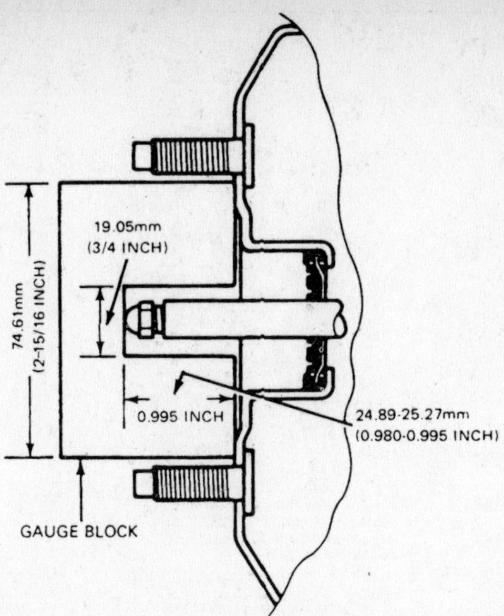

Bendix booster pushrod adjustment

strument panel, install the rubber boot on the valve operating rod at the passenger side of the dash panel.

12. Connect the valve operating rod to the brake pedal with the bushings, eccentric shoulder bolt, and nut.

BRAKE BOOSTER PUSHROD ADJUSTMENT

The pushrod has an adjustment screw to maintain the correct relationship between the booster control valve plunger and the master cylinder piston. If the plunger is too long it will prevent the master cylinder piston from completely releasing hydraulic pressure, causing the brakes to drag. If the plunger is too short it will cause excessive pedal travel and an undesirable clunk in the booster area. Remove the master cylinder for access to the booster pushrod.

To check the alignment of the screw, fabricate a gauge (from cardboard, following the dimensions in the illustration) and place it against the master cylinder mounting surface of the booster body. Adjust the pushrod screw by turning it until the end of the screw just touches the inner edge of the slot in the gauge. Install the master cylinder and bleed the system.

Brake Hoses and Lines

HYDRAULIC BRAKE LINE CHECK

The hydraulic brake lines and brake linings are to be inspected at the recommended intervals in the maintenance schedule. Follow the steel tubing from the master cylinder to the flexible hose fitting at each wheel. If a section of the tubing is found to be damaged, replace the entire section with tubing of the same type (steel, not copper), size, shape, and length. When installing a new section of brake tubing, flush clean brake fluid or denatured alcohol through to remove any dirt or foreign material from the line. Be sure to flare both ends to provide sound, leak-proof connections. When bending the tubing to fit the underbody contours, be careful not to kink or crack the line. Torque all hydraulic connections to 10–15 lbs.

Check the flexible brake hoses that connect the steel tubing to each wheel cylinder. Replace the hose if it shows any signs of softening, cracking, or other damage. When installing a new front brake hose, position the hose to avoid contact with other chassis parts. Place a new copper gasket over the hose fitting and thread the hose assembly into the front wheel cylinder. A new rear brake hose must be positioned clear of the exhaust pipe or shock absorber. Thread the hose into the rear brake tube connector. When installing either a new front or rear brake hose, engage the opposite end of the hose to the bracket on the frame. Install the horseshoe type retaining clip and connect the tube to the hose with the tube fitting nut.

Always bleed the system after hose or line replacement. Before bleeding, make sure that the master cylinder is topped up with high temperature, extra heavy duty fluid of at least SAE 70R3 quality.

Diesel Brake Booster Vacuum Pump

Unlike gasoline engines, diesel engines have little vacuum available to power brake booster systems. The diesel is thus equipped with a vacuum pump, which is driven by a single belt off of the alternator. This pump is located on the top right side of the engine.

Diesel pick-ups are also equipped with a low

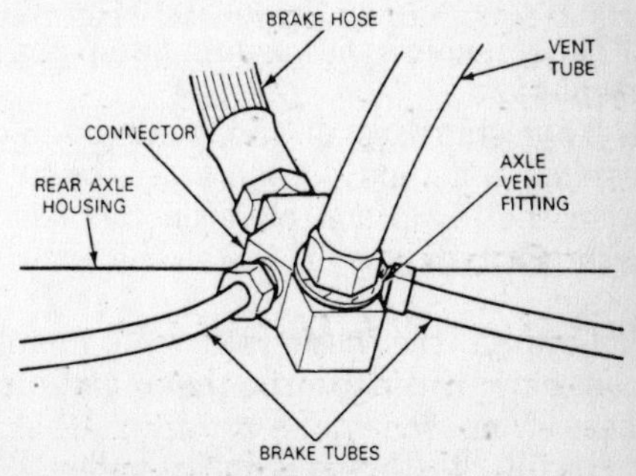

Rear brake line connector

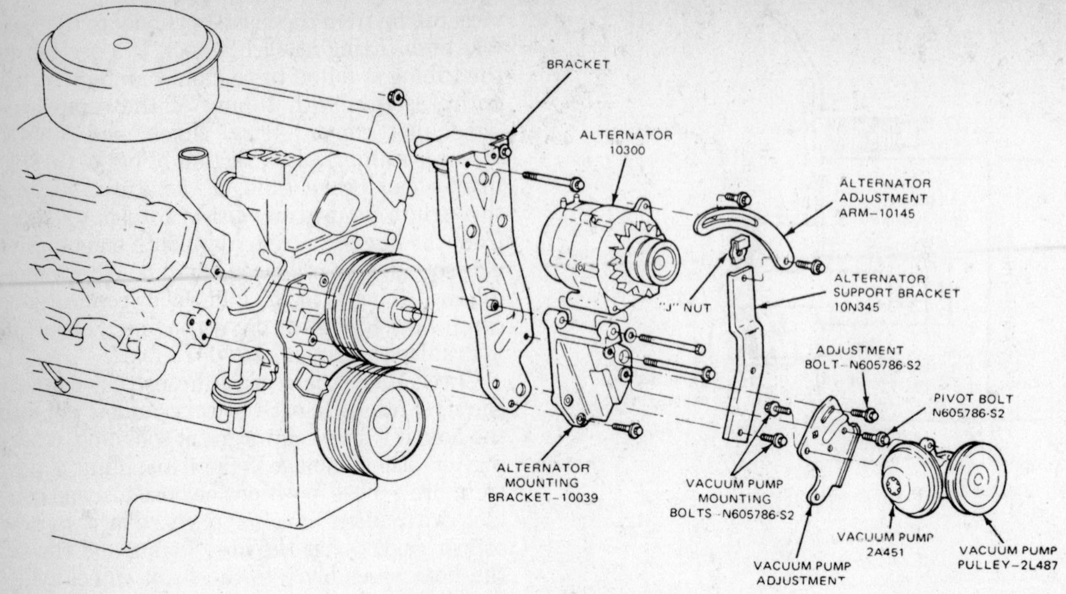

Vacuum pump installation

vacuum indicator switch which actuates the BRAKE warning lamp when available vacuum is below a certain level. The switch senses vacuum through a fitting in the vacuum manifold that intercepts the vacuum flow from the pump. The low vacuum switch is mounted on the right side of the engine compartment, adjacent to the vacuum pump on F-250 and F-350 models.

NOTE: *The vacuum pump cannot be disassembled. It is only serviced as a unit (the pulley is separate).*

REMOVAL AND INSTALLATION

1. Remove the hose clamp and disconnect the pump from the hose on the manifold vacuum outlet fitting.
2. Loosen the vacuum pump adjustment bolt and the pivot bolt. Slide the pump downward and remove the drive belt from the pulley.
3. Remove the pivot and adjustment bolts and the bolts retaining the pump to the adjustment plate. Remove the vacuum pump and adjustment plate.
4. To install, install the pump-to-adjustment plate bolts and tighten to 11–18 ft. lbs. Position the pump and plate on the vacuum pump bracket and loosely install the pivot and adjustment bolts.
5. Connect the hose from the manifold vacuum outlet fitting to the pump and install the hose clamp.
6. Install the drive belt on the pulley. Place a $^{3}/_{8}$ in. drive breaker bar or ratchet into the slot on the vacuum pump adjustment plate. Lift up on the assembly until the proper belt tension is obtained. Tighten the pivot and adjustment bolts to 11–18 ft. lbs.
7. Start the engine and make sure the brake system functions properly.

NOTE: *The BRAKE light will glow until brake vacuum builds up to the normal level.*

F-Super Duty Hydro-Boost Brake Booster

A hydraulically powered brake booster is used on the F-Super Duty truck. The power steering pump provides the fluid pressure to operate both the brake booster and the power steering gear.

The hydro-boost assembly contains a valve which controls pump pressure while braking, a lever to control the position of the valve and a boost piston to provide the force to operate a conventional master cylinder attached to the front of the booster. The hydro-boost also has a reserve system, designed to store sufficient pressurized fluid to provide at least 2 brake applications in the event of insufficient fluid flow from the power steering pump. The brakes can also be applied unassisted if the reserve system is depleted.

WARNING: *Before removing the hydro-boost, discharge the accumulator by making several brake applications until a hard pedal is felt.*

REMOVAL AND INSTALLATION

CAUTION: *Do not depress the brake pedal with the master cylinder removed!*

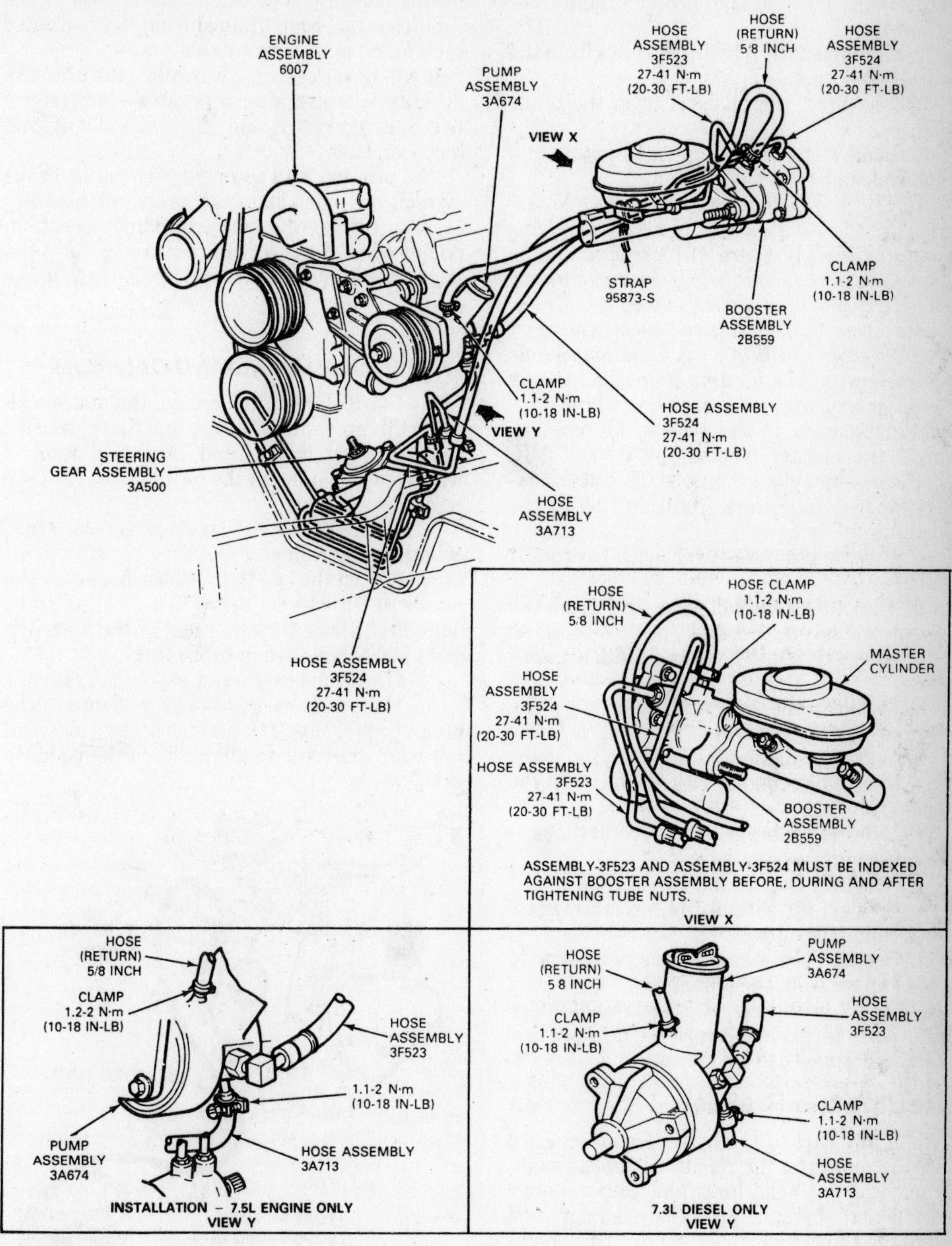

Hydro-boost installation

1. Remove the master cylinder from the Hydro-Boost unit. DO NOT DISCONNECT THE BRAKE LINES FROM THE MASTER CYLINDER! Position the master cylinder out of the way.

2. Disconnect the 3 hydraulic lines from the Hydro-Boost unit.

3. Disconnect the pushrod from the brake pedal.

4. Remove the booster mounting nuts and lift the booster from the firewall.

CAUTION: *The booster should never be carried by the accumulator. The accumulator contains high pressure nitrogen and can be dangerous if mishandled! If the accumulator is to be disposed of, do not expose it to fire or other forms of incineration! Gas pressure can be relieved by drilling a $\frac{1}{16}$ in. (1.5mm) hole in the end of the accumulator can. Always wear safety goggles during the drilling!*

5. Installation is the reverse of removal. Torque the booster mounting nuts to 25 ft. lbs.; the master cylinder nuts to 25 ft. lbs.; connect the hydraulic lines, refill and bleed the booster as follows:

a. Fill the pump reservoir with Dexron®II ATF.

b. Disconnect the coil wires and crank the engine for several seconds.

c. Check the fluid level and refill, if necessary.

d. Connect the coil wires and start the engine.

e. With the engine running, turn the steering wheel lock-to-lock twice. Shut off the engine.

f. Depress the brake pedal several times to discharge the accumulator.

g. Start the engine and repeat Step e.

h. If foam appears in the reservoir, allow the foam to dissipate.

i. Repeat Step e as often as necessary to expel all air from the system.

NOTE: *The system is, in effect, self-bleeding and normal vehicle operation will expel any further trapped air.*

Bleeding the Brakes

When any part of the hydraulic system has been disconnected for repair or replacement, air may get into the lines and cause spongy pedal action (because air can be compressed and brake fluid cannot). To correct this condition, it is necessary to bleed the hydraulic system after it has been properly connected to be sure that all air is expelled from the brake cylinders and lines.

When bleeding the brake system, bleed one brake cylinder at a time, beginning at the cylinder with the longest hydraulic line (farthest from the master cylinder) first. keep the master cylinder reservoir filled with brake fluid during bleeding operation. Never use brake fluid that has been drained from the hydraulic system, no matter how clean it is.

It will be necessary to centralize the pressure differential valve after a brake system failure has been corrected and the hydraulic system has been bled.

The primary and secondary hydraulic brake systems are individual systems and are bled separately. During the entire bleeding operation, do not allow the reservoir to run dry. Keep the master cylinder reservoirs filled with brake fluid.

WHEEL CYLINDERS AND CALIPERS

1. Clean all dirt from around the master cylinder fill cap, remove the cap and fill the master cylinder with brake fluid until the level is within $\frac{1}{4}$ in. (6mm) of the top of the edge of the reservoir.

2. Clean off the bleeder screws at the wheel cylinders and calipers.

3. Attach the length of rubber hose over the nozzle of the bleeder screw at the wheel to be done first. Place the other end of the hose in a glass jar, submerged in brake fluid.

4. Open the bleed screw valve $\frac{1}{2}$–$\frac{3}{4}$ turn.

5. Have an assistant slowly depress the brake pedal. Close the bleeder screw valve and tell your assistant to allow the brake pedal to

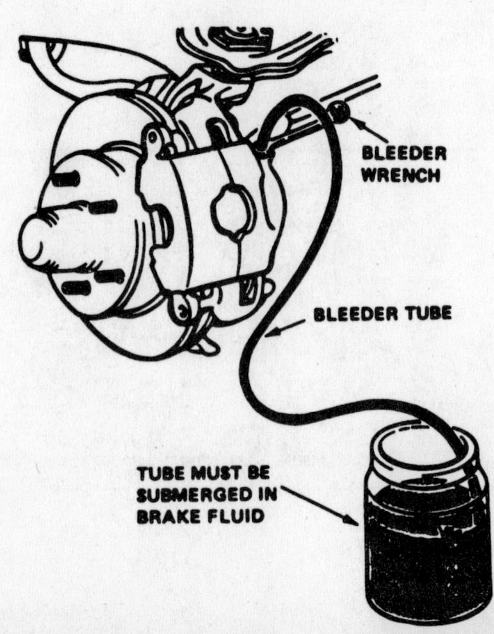

Brake bleeding equipment

return slowly. Continue this pumping action to force any air out of the system. When bubbles cease to appear at the end of the bleeder hose, close the bleed valve and remove the hose.

6. Check the master cylinder fluid level and add fluid accordingly. Do this after bleeding each wheel.

7. Repeat the bleeding operation at the remaining 3 wheels, ending with the one closest to the master cylinder. Fill the master cylinder reservoir.

MASTER CYLINDER

1. Fill the master cylinder reservoirs.
2. Place absorbent rags under the fluid lines at the master cylinder.
3. Have an assistant depress and hold the brake pedal.
4. With the pedal held down, slowly crack open the hydraulic line fitting, allowing the air to escape. Close the fitting and have the pedal released.
5. Repeat Steps 3 and 4 for each fitting until all the air is released.

FRONT DISC BRAKES

CAUTION: *Brake shoes contain asbestos, which has been determined to be a cancer causing agent. Never clean the brake surfaces with compressed air! Avoid inhaling any dust from any brake surface! When cleaning brake surfaces, use a commercially available brake cleaning fluid.*

There are two types of sliding calipers, the LD sliding caliper unit is operated by one piston per caliper. The caliper and steering arm are cast as one piece and combined with the spindle stem to form an integral spindle assembly.

The light duty system is used on all F-150 and Bronco models.

The HD slider caliper unit contains two pistons on the same side of the rotor. The caliper slides on the support assembly and is retained by a key and spring.

The heavy duty system is used on all F-250, F-350 and F-Super Duty models.

Disc Brake Pads

INSPECTION

Remove the brake pads as described below and measure the thickness of the lining. If the

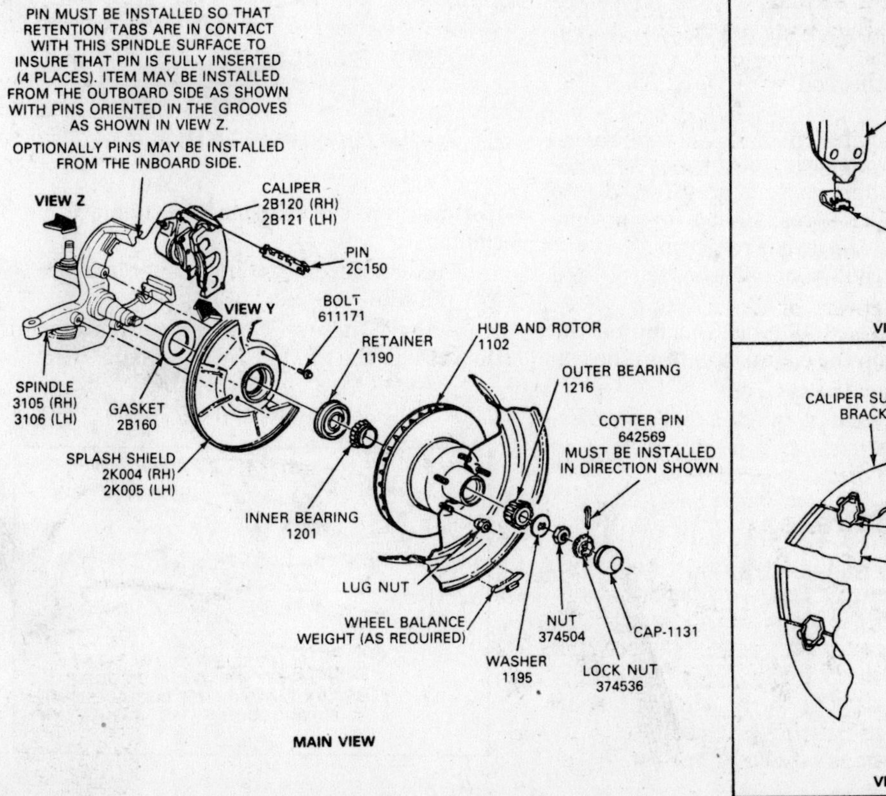

F-150 sliding caliper disc brake installation

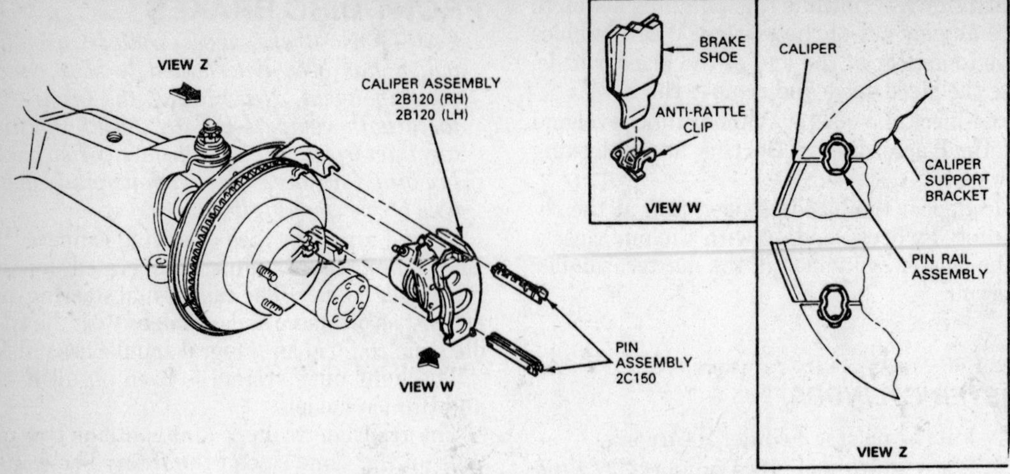

Disc brake used on the 4-wheel drive F-150 and Bronco

lining at any point on the pad assembly is less $\frac{1}{16}$ in. (1.5mm) for LD brakes or $\frac{1}{32}$ in. (0.8mm) for HD brakes, thick (above the backing plate or rivets), or there is evidence of the lining being contaminated by brake fluid or oil, replace the brake pad.

REMOVAL AND INSTALLATION

NOTE: *NEVER REPLACE THE PADS ON ONE SIDE ONLY! ALWAYS REPLACE PADS ON BOTH WHEELS AS A SET!*

LD Sliding Caliper (Single Piston)

1. To avoid overflowing of the master cylinder when the caliper pistons are pressed into the caliper cylinder bores, siphon or dip some brake fluid out of the larger reservoir.
2. Jack up the front of the truck and remove the wheels.
3. Place an 8 in. (203mm) C-clamp on the caliper and tighten the clamp to bottom the caliper piston in the cylinder bore. Remove the C-clamp.
4. Clean the excess dirt from around the caliper pin tabs.
5. Drive the upper caliper pin inward until the tabs on the pin touch the spindle.

Compressing the pin tabs on LD calipers

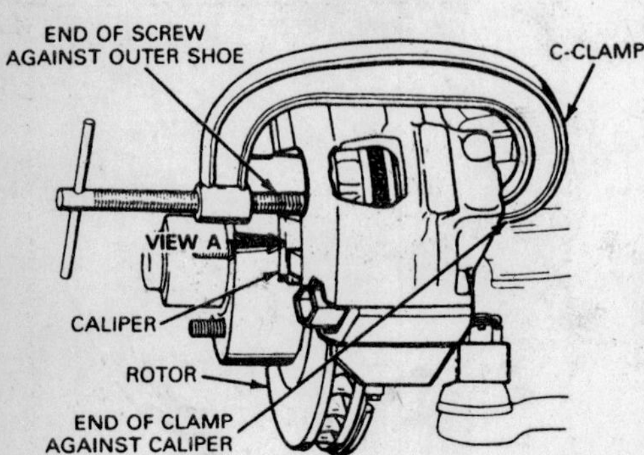

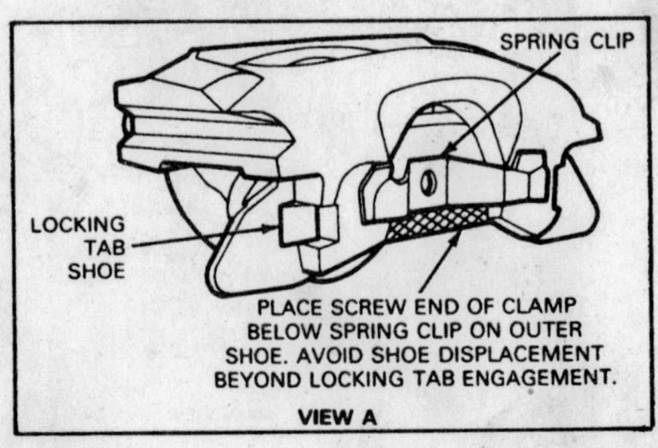

Bottoming the caliper piston on LD calipers

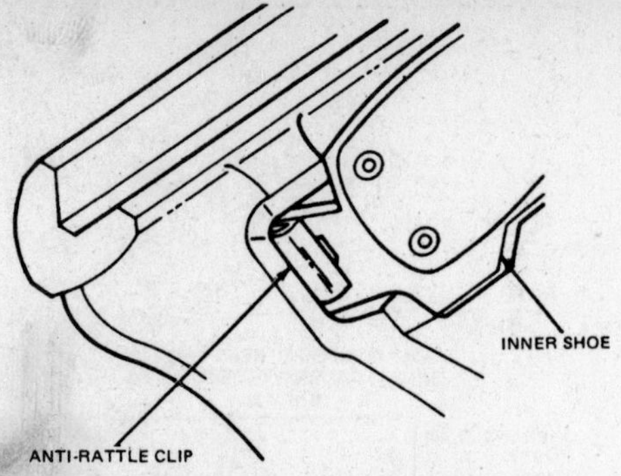

Inner shoe installation on LD calipers

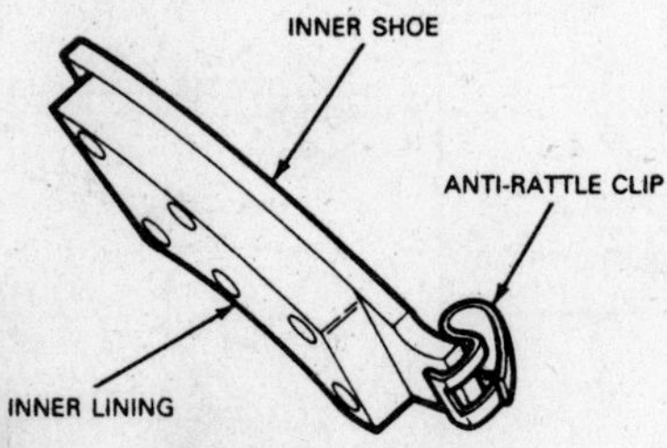

Installing the inner shoe anti-rattle clip on LD calipers

6. Insert a small prybar into the slot provided behind the pin tabs on the inboard side of the pin.

7. Using needle nosed pliers, compress the outboard end of the pin while, at the same time, prying with the prybar until the tabs slip into the groove in the spindle.

8. Place the end of a $^{7}/_{16}$ in. (11mm) punch against the end of the caliper pin and drive the pin out of the caliper slide groove.

9. Repeat this procedure for the lower pin.

10. Lift the caliper off of the rotor.

11. Remove the brake pads and anti-rattle spring.

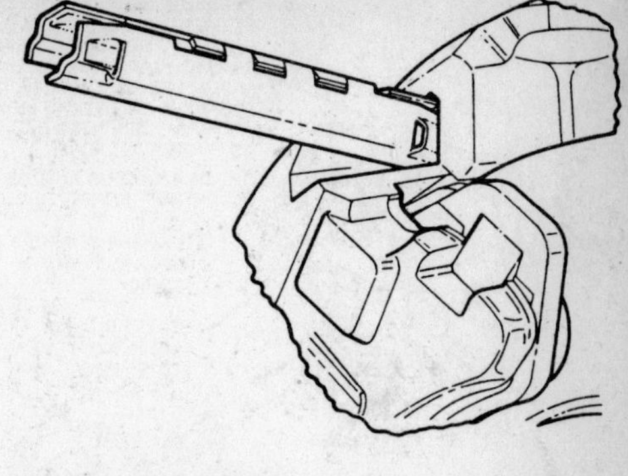
Caliper pin installation

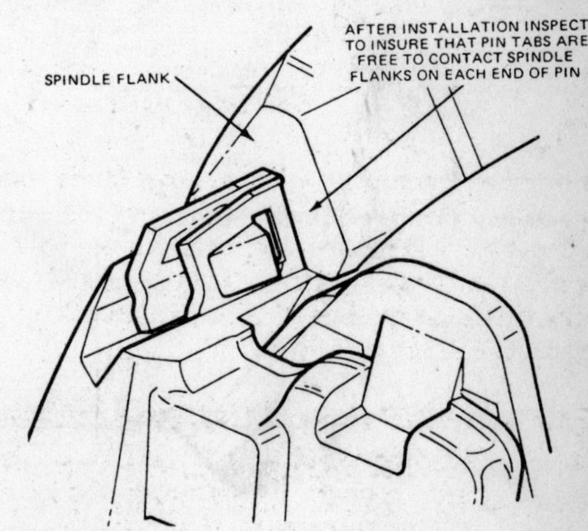

Correct caliper pin installation

NOTE: *Do not allow the caliper to hang by the brake hose.*

12. Thoroughly clean the areas of the caliper and spindle assembly which contact each other during the sliding action of the caliper.

13. Place a new anti-rattle clip on the lower end of the inboard shoe. Make sure that the tabs on the clip are positioned correctly and the loop-type spring is away from the rotor.

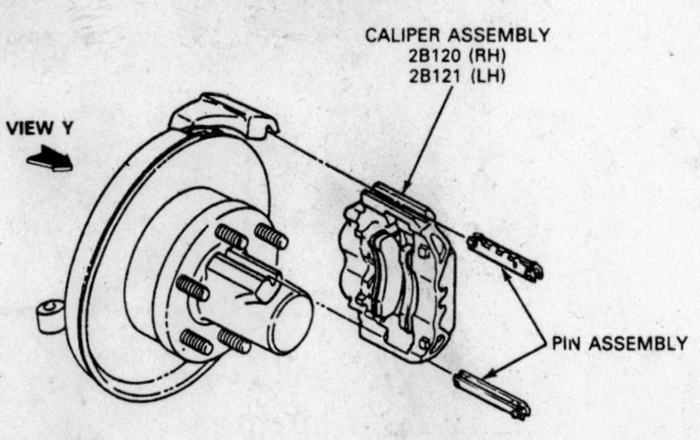

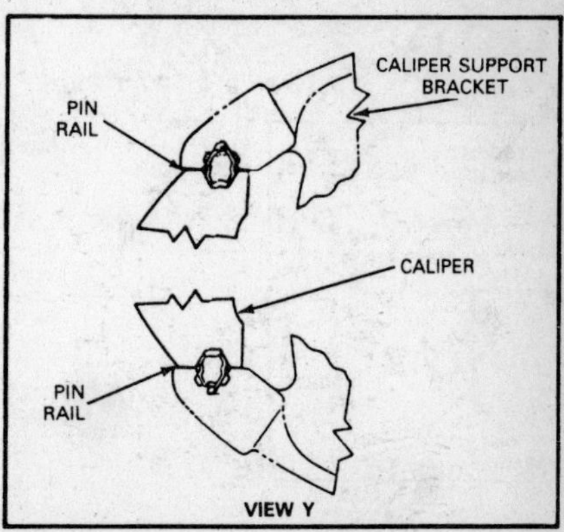

Disc brake used on the 4-wheel drive F-250 and F-350

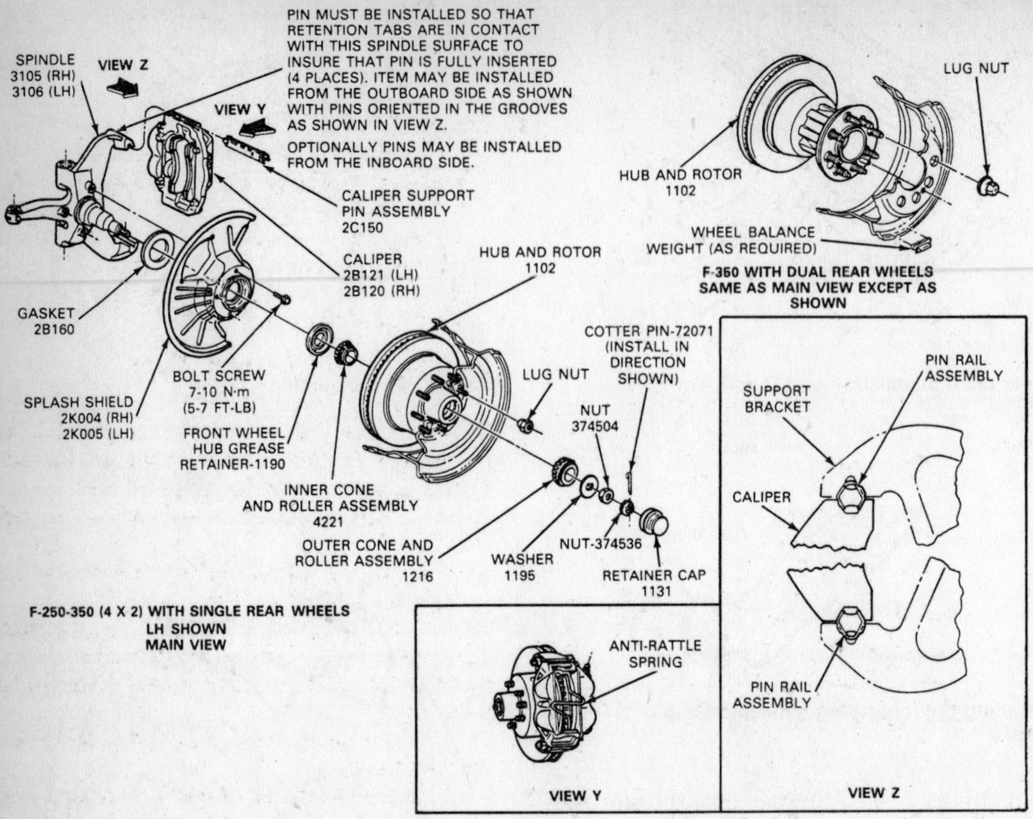

PIN MUST BE INSTALLED SO THAT RETENTION TABS ARE IN CONTACT WITH THIS SPINDLE SURFACE TO INSURE THAT PIN IS FULLY INSERTED (4 PLACES). ITEM MAY BE INSTALLED FROM THE OUTBOARD SIDE AS SHOWN WITH PINS ORIENTED IN THE GROOVES AS SHOWN IN VIEW Z.
OPTIONALLY PINS MAY BE INSTALLED FROM THE INBOARD SIDE.
SPINDLE 3105 (RH) 3106 (LH)
VIEW Z
VIEW Y
CALIPER SUPPORT PIN ASSEMBLY 2C150
CALIPER 2B121 (LH) 2B120 (RH)
GASKET 2B160
HUB AND ROTOR 1102
SPLASH SHIELD 2K004 (RH) 2K005 (LH)
BOLT SCREW 7-10 N·m (5-7 FT-LB)
FRONT WHEEL HUB GREASE RETAINER-1190
LUG NUT
COTTER PIN-72071 (INSTALL IN DIRECTION SHOWN)
NUT 374504
INNER CONE AND ROLLER ASSEMBLY 4221
OUTER CONE AND ROLLER ASSEMBLY 1216
WASHER 1195
NUT-374536
RETAINER CAP 1131
F-250-350 (4 X 2) WITH SINGLE REAR WHEELS LH SHOWN MAIN VIEW
LUG NUT
HUB AND ROTOR 1102
WHEEL BALANCE WEIGHT (AS REQUIRED)
F-350 WITH DUAL REAR WHEELS SAME AS MAIN VIEW EXCEPT AS SHOWN
PIN RAIL ASSEMBLY
SUPPORT BRACKET
CALIPER
PIN RAIL ASSEMBLY
VIEW Z
ANTI-RATTLE SPRING
VIEW Y

Disc brake used on the 2-wheel drive F-250 (above 6,900 lb. GVWR) and F-350

CALIPER ASSEMBLY
PIN ASSEMBLY
VIEW Z
SPINDLE
GREASE RETAINER
SCREW 100-120 N·m (136-162 FT-LB)
SCREW 6.8-10.2 N·m (5-7.5 FT-LB)
SHIELD
INNER BEARING
WHEEL LUG NUT STUD
INNER BEARING RACE
ROTOR
HUB ASSEMBLY
OUTER BEARING RACE
OUTER BEARING RETAINER WASHER
NUT RETAINER
CAP
OUTER BEARING
NUT
SUPPORT BRACKET
PIN RAIL ASSEMBLY
CALIPER
PIN RAIL ASSEMBLY
VIEW Z

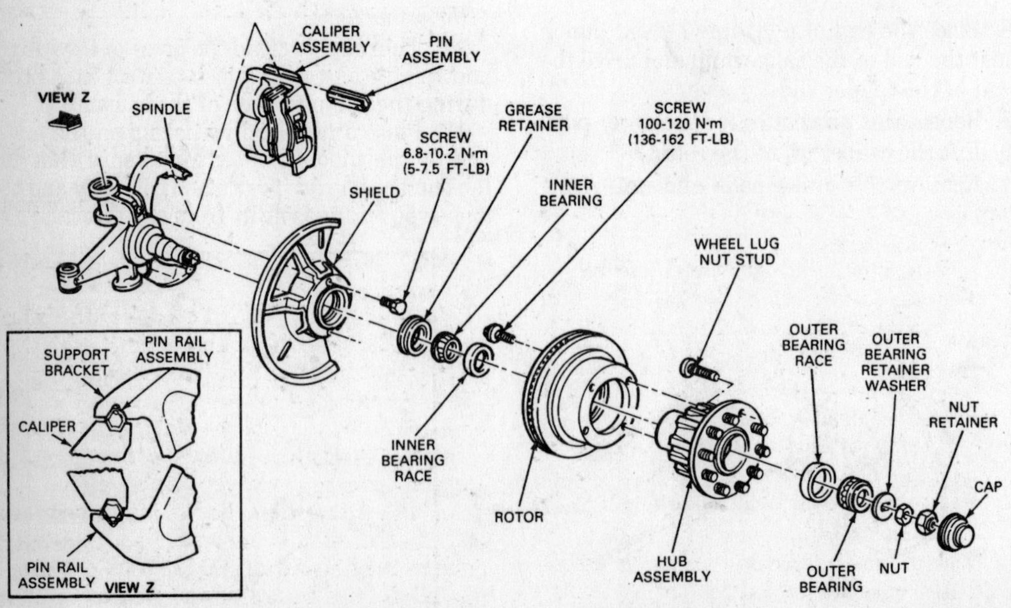

Disc brake used on the F-Super Duty

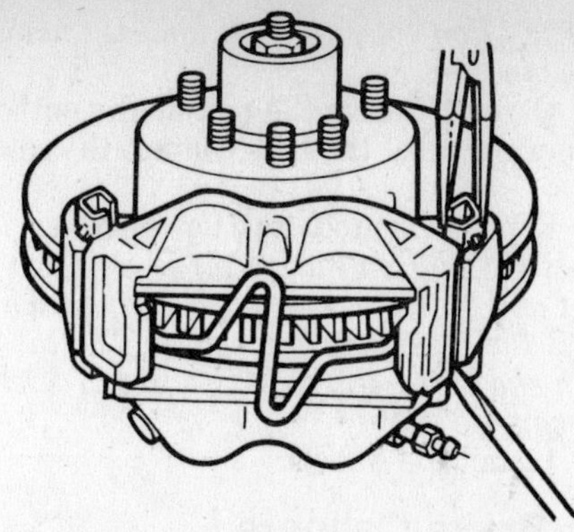

Compressing the spring tabs on HD calipers

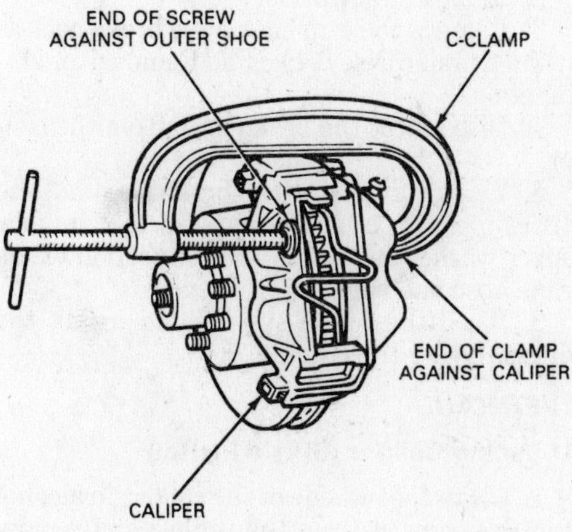

Bottoming the caliper piston on HD calipers

14. Place the lower end of the inner brake pad in the spindle assembly pad abutment, against the anti-rattle clip, and slide the upper end of the pad into position. Be sure that the clip is still in position.

15. Check and make sure that the caliper piston is fully bottomed in the cylinder bore. Use a large C-clamp to bottom the piston, if necessary.

16. Position the outer brake pad on the caliper, and press the pad tabs into place with your fingers. If the pad cannot be pressed into place by hand, use a C-clamp. Be careful not to damage the lining with the clamp. Bend the tabs to prevent rattling.

17. Position the caliper on the spindle assembly. Lightly lubricate the caliper sliding grooves with caliper pin grease.

18. Position the a new upper pin with the retention tabs next to the spindle groove.

NOTE: *Don't use the bolt and nut with the new pin.*

19. Carefully drive the pin, at the outboard end, inward until the tabs contact the spindle face.

20. Repeat the procedure for the lower pin.

WARNING: *Don't drive the pins in too far, or it will be necessary to drive them back out until the tabs snap into place. The tabs on each end of the pin MUST be free to catch on the spindle sides!*

21. Install the wheels.

HD Sliding Caliper (Two Piston)

1. To avoid overflowing of the master cylinder when the caliper pistons are pressed into the caliper cylinder bores, siphon or dip some brake fluid out of the larger reservoir.

2. Raise and support the front end on jackstands.

3. Jack up the front of the truck and remove the wheels.

4. Place an 8 in. (203mm) C-clamp on the caliper and tighten the clamp to bottom the caliper pistons in the cylinder bores. Remove the C-clamp.

5. Clean the excess dirt from around the caliper pin tabs.

6. Drive the upper caliper pin inward until the tabs on the pin touch the spindle.

7. Insert a small prybar into the slot provided behind the pin tabs on the inboard side of the pin.

8. Using needle nosed pliers, compress the outboard end of the pin while, at the same time, prying with the prybar until the tabs slip into the groove in the spindle.

9. Place the end of a $\frac{7}{16}$ in. (11mm) punch against the end of the caliper pin and drive the pin out of the caliper slide groove.

10. Repeat this procedure for the lower pin.

11. Lift the caliper off of the rotor.

12. Remove the brake pads and anti-rattle spring.

NOTE: *Do not allow the caliper to hand by the brake hose.*

13. Thoroughly clean the areas of the caliper and spindle assembly which contact each other during the sliding action of the caliper.

14. Place a new anti-rattle clip on the lower end of the inboard shoe. Make sure that the tabs on the clip are positioned correctly and the loop-type spring is away from the rotor.

15. Place the lower end of the inner brake pad in the spindle assembly pad abutment, against the anti-rattle clip, and slide the upper end of the pad into position. Be sure that the clip is still in position.

16. Check and make sure that the caliper piston is fully bottomed in the cylinder bore.

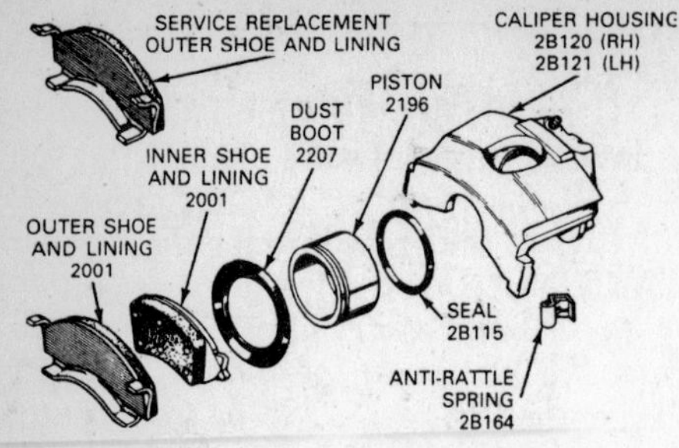

LD caliper disassembled

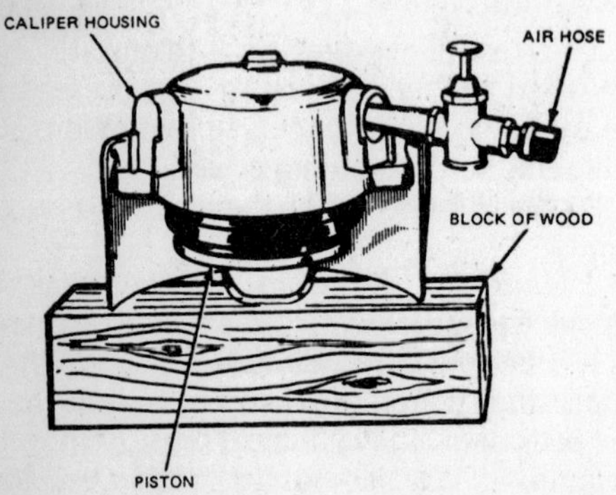

Removing the piston

Use a large C-clamp to bottom the piston, if necessary.

17. Position the outer brake pad on the caliper, and press the pad tabs into place with your fingers. If the pad cannot be pressed into place by hand, use a C-clamp. Be careful not to damage the lining with the clamp. Bend the tabs to prevent rattling.

18. Position the caliper on the spindle assembly. Lightly lubricate the caliper sliding grooves with caliper pin grease.

19. Position the a new upper pin with the retention tabs next to the spindle groove.

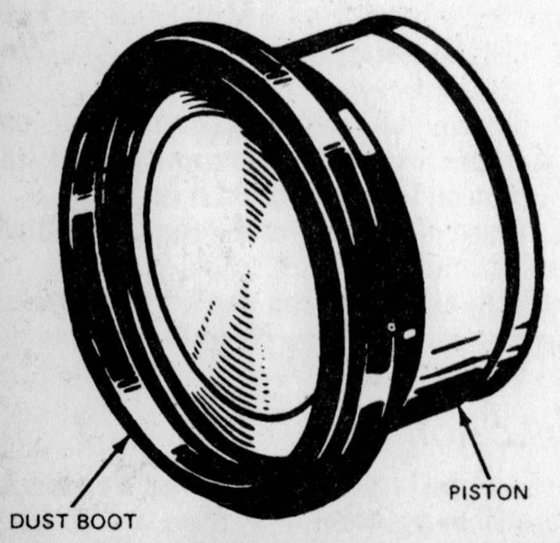

Piston and dust boot

NOTE: *Don't use the bolt and nut with the new pin.*

20. Carefully drive the pin, at the outboard end, inward until the tabs contact the spindle face.

21. Repeat the procedure for the lower pin.

WARNING: *Don't drive the pins in too far, or it will be necessary to drive them back out until the tabs snap into place. The tabs on each end of the pin MUST be free to catch on the spindle sides!*

22. Install the wheels.

Disc Brake Calipers

REMOVAL AND INSTALLATION

1. Raise and support the front end on jackstands.
2. Remove the wheels.
3. Remove the caliper and the brake pads as outlined under Disc Brake Pad Removal and Installation.
4. Disconnect the brake hose from the caliper.
5. When connecting the brake fluid hose to the caliper, it is recommended that a new copper washer be used at the connection of the brake hose and caliper.
6. Bleed the brake system and install the wheels. Lower the truck.

OVERHAUL

LD Sliding Caliper (Single Piston)

1. Clean the outside of the caliper in alcohol after removing it from the vehicle and removing the brake pads.
2. Drain the caliper through the inlet port.
3. Roll some thick shop cloths or rags and place them between the piston and the outer legs of the caliper.
4. Apply compressed air to the caliper inlet port until the piston comes out of the caliper bore. Use low air pressure to avoid having the piston pop out too rapidly and possible causing injury.
5. If the piston becomes cocked in the cylinder bore and will not come out, remove the air pressure and tap the piston with a soft hammer to try and straighten it. Do not use a sharp tool or pry the piston out of the bore. Reapply the air pressure.
6. Remove the boot from the piston and seal from the caliper cylinder bore.
7. Clean the piston and caliper in alcohol.
8. Lubricate the piston seal with clean brake fluid, and position the seal in the groove in the cylinder bore.
9. Coat the outside of the piston and both of the beads of dust boot with clean brake fluid. Insert the piston through the dust boot until

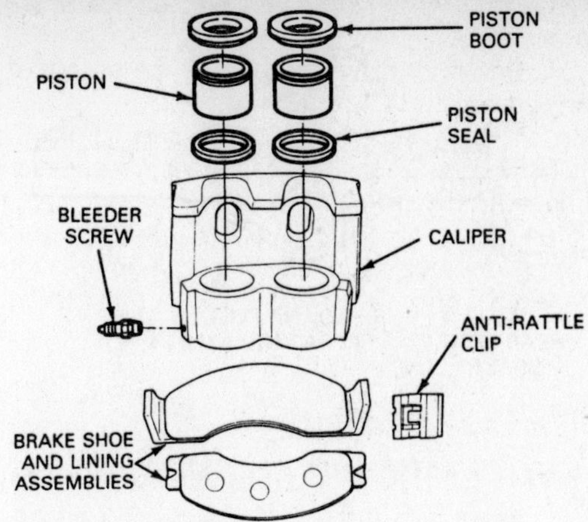

F-Super Duty disc brake caliper, front or rear

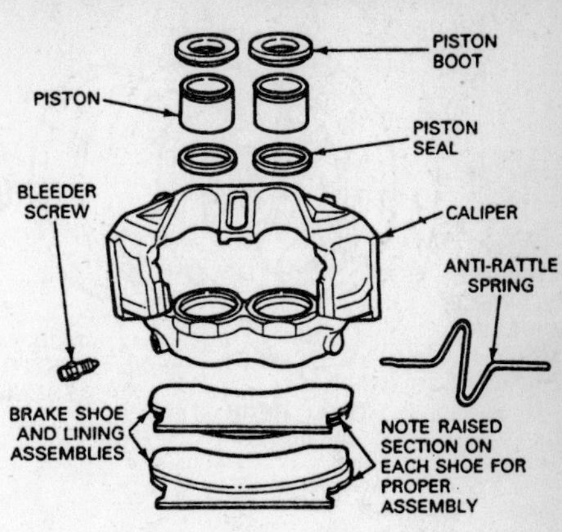

HD caliper disassembled

the boot is around the bottom (closed end) of the piston.

10. Hold the piston and dust boot directly above the caliper cylinder bore, and use your fingers to work the bead of dust boot into the groove near the top of the cylinder bore.

11. After the bead is seated in the groove, press straight down on the piston until it bottoms in the bore. Be careful not to cock the piston in the bore. Be careful not to cock the piston in the bore. Use a C-clamp with a block of wood inserted between the clamp and the piston to bottom the piston, if necessary.

12. Install the brake pads and install the caliper. Bleed the brake hydraulic system and recenter the pressure differential valve. Do not drive the vehicle until a firm brake pedal is obtained.

HD Sliding Caliper (Two Piston)

1. Disconnect and plug the flexible brake hose.

2. Remove the front shoe and lining assemblies.

3. Drain the fluid from the cylinders.

4. Secure the caliper in a vise and place a block of wood between the caliper bridge and the cylinders.

5. Apply low pressure air to the brake hose inlet and the pistons will be forced out to the wood block.

6. Remove the block of wood and remove the pistons.

7. Remove the piston seals.

8. Lubricate the new piston seals with clean brake fluid and install them in the seal grooves in the cylinder bores.

9. Lubricate the retaining lips of the dust boots with clean brake fluid and install them in the grooves of the cylinder bores.

10. Apply a film of clean brake fluid to the pistons.

11. Insert the pistons into the dust boots and start them into the cylinders by hand until they are beyond the piston seals. Be careful not to dislodge or damage the piston seals.

12. Place a block of wood over one piston and press the piston into the cylinder. Be careful not to cock the piston in the cylinder bore.

13. Install the second piston in the same manner.

14. Install the brake shoe assemblies and anti-rattle clip in the caliper assembly.

15. Install the brake hose. Torque the fitting to 25 ft. lbs.

16. Install the caliper and bleed the system.

Brake Disc (Rotor)

REMOVAL AND INSTALLATION

1. Jack up the front of the truck and support it with jackstands. Remove the front wheel.

2. Remove the caliper assembly and support it to the frame with a piece of wire without disconnecting the brake fluid hose.

3. Remove the hub and rotor assembly as described in Chapter 1.

4. Install the rotor in the reverse order of removal, and adjust the wheel bearing as outlined in Chapter 1.

INSPECTION

If the rotor is deeply scarred or has shallow cracks, it may be refinished on a disc brake rotor lathe. Also, if the lateral run-out exceeds 0.010 in. (0.25mm) within a 6 in. (152mm)

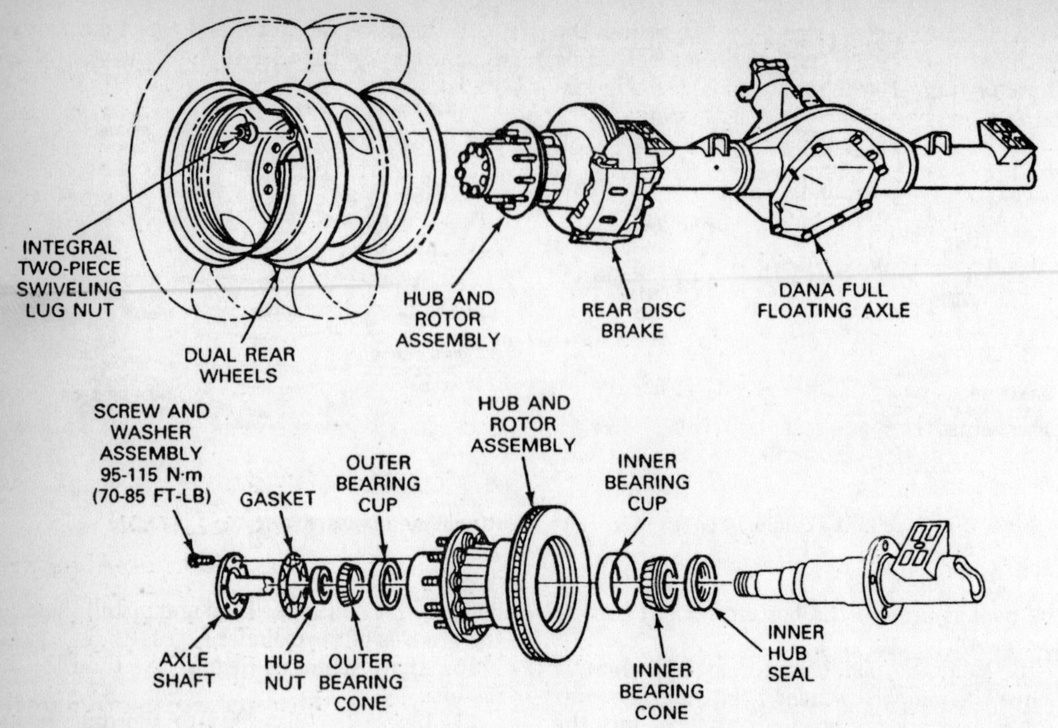

F-Super Duty rear disc brake assembly

radius when measured with a dial indicator, with the stylus 1 in. (25mm) in from the edge of the rotor, the rotor should be refinished or replaced.

A maximum of 0.020 in. (0.5mm) of material may be removed equally from each friction surface of the rotor. If the damage cannot be corrected when the rotor has been machined to the minimum thickness shown on the rotor, it should be replaced.

The finished braking surfaces of the rotor must be parallel within 0.007 in. (0.18mm) and lateral run-out must not be more than 0.003 in. (0.076mm) on the inboard surface in a 5 in. (127mm) radius.

REAR DISC BRAKES

F-Super Duty models are equipped with the heavy duty, sliding 2-piston caliper similar to that used on the front axle.

Disc Brake Pads

INSPECTION

Remove the brake pads as described below and measure the thickness of the lining. If the lining at any point on the pad assembly is less than $\frac{1}{32}$ in. (0.8mm) thick (above the backing plate or rivets), or there is evidence of the lining being contaminated by brake fluid or oil, replace the brake pad.

REMOVAL AND INSTALLATION

NOTE: *NEVER REPLACE THE PADS ON ONE SIDE ONLY! ALWAYS REPLACE PADS ON BOTH WHEELS AS A SET!*

1. To avoid overflowing of the master cylinder when the caliper pistons are pressed into the caliper cylinder bores, siphon or dip some brake fluid out of the larger reservoir.
2. Raise and support the rear end on jackstands.
3. Remove the wheels.
4. Place an 8 in. (203mm) C-clamp on the caliper and tighten the clamp to bottom the caliper pistons in the cylinder bores. Remove the C-clamp.
5. Clean the excess dirt from around the caliper pin tabs.
6. Drive the upper caliper pin inward until the tabs on the pin touch the caliper support.
7. Insert a small prybar into the slot provided behind the pin tabs on the inboard side of the pin.

8. Using needle nosed pliers, compress the outboard end of the pin while, at the same time, prying with the prybar until the tabs slip into the groove in the caliper support.

9. Place the end of a $^7/_{16}$ in. (11mm) punch against the end of the caliper pin and drive the pin out of the caliper slide groove.

10. Repeat this procedure for the lower pin.

11. Lift the caliper off of the rotor.

12. Remove the brake pads and anti-rattle spring.

NOTE: *Do not allow the caliper to hand by the brake hose.*

13. Thoroughly clean the areas of the caliper and caliper support assembly which contact each other during the sliding action of the caliper.

14. Place a new anti-rattle clip on the lower end of the inboard shoe. Make sure that the tabs on the clip are positioned correctly and the loop-type spring is away from the rotor.

15. Place the lower end of the inner brake pad in the caliper support assembly pad abutment, against the anti-rattle clip, and slide the upper end of the pad into position. Be sure that the clip is still in position.

16. Check and make sure that the caliper pistons are fully bottomed in the cylinder bores. Use a large C-clamp to bottom the pistons, if necessary.

17. Position the outer brake pad on the caliper, and press the pad tabs into place with your fingers. If the pad cannot be pressed into place by hand, use a C-clamp. Be careful not to damage the lining with the clamp. Bend the tabs to prevent rattling.

18. Position the caliper on the caliper support. Lightly lubricate the caliper sliding grooves with caliper pin grease.

19. Position the a new upper pin with the retention tabs next to the support groove.

NOTE: *Don't use the bolt and nut with the new pin.*

20. Carefully drive the pin, at the outboard end, inward until the tabs contact the caliper support face.

21. Repeat the procedure for the lower pin.

WARNING: *Don't drive the pins in too far, or it will be necessary to drive them back out until the tabs snap into place. The tabs on each end of the pin MUST be free to catch on the support sides!*

22. Install the wheels.

Disc Brake Calipers

REMOVAL AND INSTALLATION

1. Raise and support the rear end on jackstands.

2. Remove the wheels.

3. Remove the caliper and the brake pads as outlined under Disc Brake Pad Removal and Installation.

4. Disconnect the brake hose from the caliper. Cap the openings at once!

5. When connecting the brake fluid hose to the caliper, it is recommended that a new copper washer be used at the connection of the brake hose and caliper.

6. Bleed the brake system and install the wheels. Lower the truck.

OVERHAUL

See the procedures for heavy duty calipers under Front Disc Brakes.

Brake Disc (Rotor)

REMOVAL AND INSTALLATION

1. Jack up the rear of the truck and support it with jackstands. Remove the wheel.

2. Remove the caliper assembly and support it to the frame with a piece of wire without disconnecting the brake fluid hose.

3. Remove the axle hub and rotor assembly. See Chapter 7 under Dana 80 rear axle.

4. Install the rotor using the procedures found in Chapter 7.

INSPECTION

If the rotor is deeply scarred or has shallow cracks, it may be refinished on a disc brake rotor lathe. Also, if the lateral run-out exceeds 0.008 in. (0.20mm) within a 6 in. (152mm) radius when measured with a dial indicator, with the stylus 1 in. (25mm) in from the edge of the rotor, the rotor should be refinished or replaced.

A maximum of 0.020 in. (0.5mm) of material may be removed equally from each friction surface of the rotor. If the damage cannot be corrected when the rotor has been machined to the minimum thickness shown on the rotor, it should be replaced.

The finished braking surfaces of the rotor must be parallel within 0.0010 in. (0.025mm) and lateral run-out must not be more than 0.008 in. (0.20mm) on the inboard surface in a 5 in. (127mm) radius.

REAR DRUM BRAKES

CAUTION: *Brake shoes contain asbestos, which has been determined to be a cancer causing agent. Never clean the brake surfaces with compressed air! Avoid inhaling any dust from any brake surface! When cleaning brake surfaces, use a commercially available brake cleaning fluid.*

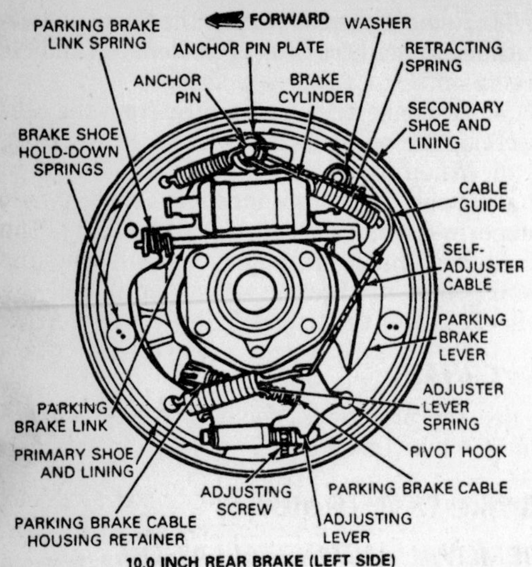

Standard rear brakes used on the F-150 and Bronco

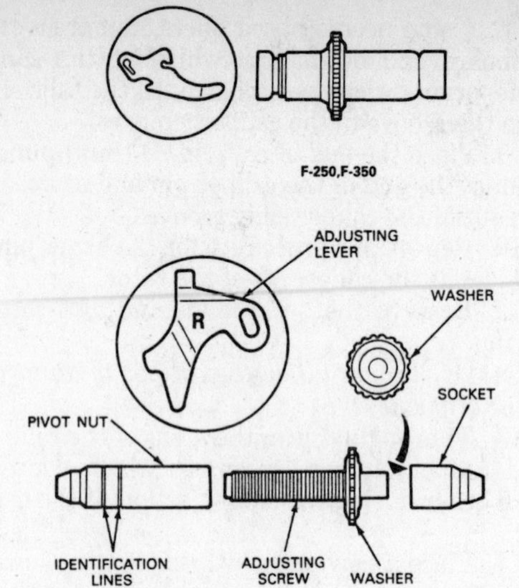

Adjusting screw and lever

Brake Drums

INSPECTION

Check that there are no cracks or chips in the braking surface. Excessive bluing indicates overheating and a replacement drum is needed. The drum can be machined to remove minor damage and to establish a rounded braking surface on a warped drum. Never exceed the maximum oversize of the drum when machining the braking surface. The maximum inside diameter is stamped on the rim of the drum.

REMOVAL AND INSTALLATION

Bronco, F-150, and F-250 Light Duty

1. Raise the vehicle so that the wheel to be worked on is clear of the floor and install jackstands under the vehicle.
2. Remove the wheel. Remove the three retaining nuts and remove the brake drum. It may be necessary to back off the brake shoe adjustment in order to remove the brake drum. This is because the drum might be grooved or worn from being in service for an extended period of time.
3. Before installing a new brake drum, be sure to remove any protective coating with carburetor degreaser.
4. Install the brake drum in the reverse order of removal and adjust the brakes.

F-250HD, F-350

1. Raise the vehicle and install jackstands.
2. Remove the wheel. Loosen the rear brake shoe adjustment.
3. Remove the rear axle retaining bolts and lock washers, axle shaft, and gasket.
4. Remove the wheel bearing locknut, lockwasher, and adjusting nut.
5. Remove the hub and drum assembly from the axle.
6. Remove the brake drum-to-hub retaining screws, bolts or bolts and nut. Remove the brake drum from the hub.
7. Place the drum on the hub and attach it to the hub with the attaching nuts and bolts.
8. Place the hub and drum assembly on the axle and start the adjusting nut.
9. Adjust the wheel bearing nut and install the wheel bearing lockwasher and locknut.
10. Install the axle shaft with a new gasket and install the axle retaining bolts and lock washers.
11. Install the wheel and adjust the brake shoes. Remove the jackstands and lower the vehicle.

Brake Shoes

REMOVAL AND INSTALLATION

Bronco, F-150, F-250 Light Duty

1. Raise and support the vehicle and remove the wheel and brake drum from the wheel to be worked on.

NOTE: *If you have never replaced the brakes on a car before and you are not too familiar with the procedures involved, only dissemble and assemble one side at a time, leaving the other side intact as a reference during reassembly.*

2. Install a clamp over the ends of the wheel cylinder to prevent the pistons of the wheel cylinder from coming out, causing loss of fluid and much grief.

3. Contract the brake shoes by pulling the self-adjusting lever away from the starwheel adjustment screw and turn the starwheel up and back until the pivot nut is drawn onto the starwheel as far as it will come.

4. Pull the adjusting lever, cable and automatic adjuster spring down and toward the rear to unhook the pivot hook from the large hole in the secondary shoe web. Do not attempt to pry the pivot hook from the hole.

5. Remove the automatic adjuster spring and the adjusting lever.

6. Remove the secondary shoe-to-anchor spring with a brake tool. (Brake tools are very common implements and are available to auto parts stores). Remove the primary shoe-to-anchor spring and unhook the cable anchor. Remove the anchor pin plate.

7. Remove the cable guide from the secondary shoe.

8. Remove the shoe holddown springs, shoes, adjusting screw, pivot nut, and socket. Note the color of each holddown spring for assembly. To remove the holddown springs, reach behind the brake backing plate and place one finger on the end of one of the brake holddown spring mounting pins. Using a pair of pliers, grasp the washer type retainer on top of the holddown spring that corresponds to the pin which you are holding. Push down on the pliers and turn them 90 degrees to align the slot in the washer with the head on the spring mounting pin. Remove the spring and washer retainer and repeat this operation on the hold down spring on the other shoe.

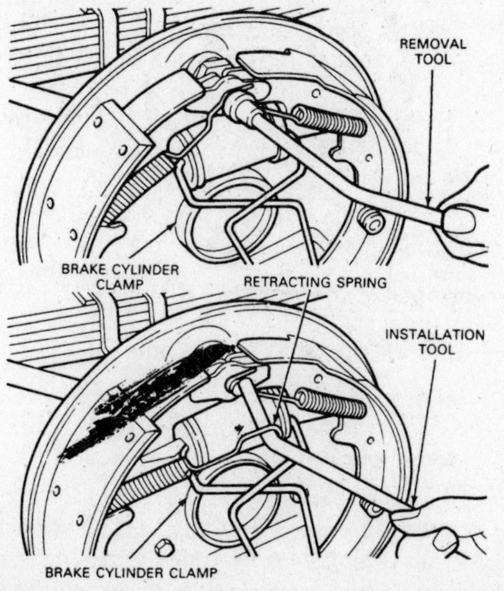

Retracing spring replacement

9. Remove the parking brake link and spring. Disconnect the parking brake cable from the parking brake lever.

10. After removing the rear brake secondary shoe, disassemble the parking brake lever from the shoe by removing the retaining clip and spring washer.

11. Assemble the parking brake lever to the secondary shoe and secure it with the spring washer and retaining clip.

12. Apply a light coating of Lubriplate® at the points where the brake shoes contact the backing plate.

13. Position the brake shoes on the backing plate, and install the holddown spring pins, springs, and spring washer type retainers. On the rear brake, install the parking brake link, spring and washer. Connect the parking brake cable to the parking brake lever.

14. Install the anchor pin plate, and place the cable anchor over the anchor pin with the crimped side toward the backing plate.

15. Install the primary shoe-to-anchor spring with the brake tool.

16. Install the cable guide on the secondary shoe web with the flanged holes fitted into the hole in the secondary shoe web. Thread the cable around the cable guide groove.

17. Install the secondary shoe-to-anchor (long) spring. Be sure that the cable end is not cocked or binding on the anchor pin when installed. All of the parts should be flat on the anchor pin. Remove the wheel cylinder piston clamp.

18. Apply Lubriplate® to the threads and the socket end of the adjusting starwheel screw. Turn the adjusting screw into the adjusting pivot nut to the limit of the threads and then back off $^1/_2$ turn.

NOTE: *Interchanging the brake shoe adjusting screw assemblies from one side of the vehicle to the other would cause the brake shoes to retract rather than expand each time the automatic adjusting mechanism is operated. To prevent this, the socket end of the adjusting screw is stamped with an "R" or an "L" for "RIGHT" or "LEFT". The adjusting pivot nuts can be distinguished by the number of lines machined around the body of the nut; one line indicates left hand nut and two lines indicate a right hand nut.*

19. Place the adjusting socket on the screw and install this assembly between the shoe ends with the adjusting screw nearest to the secondary shoe.

20. Place the cable hook into the hole in the adjusting lever from the backing plate side. The

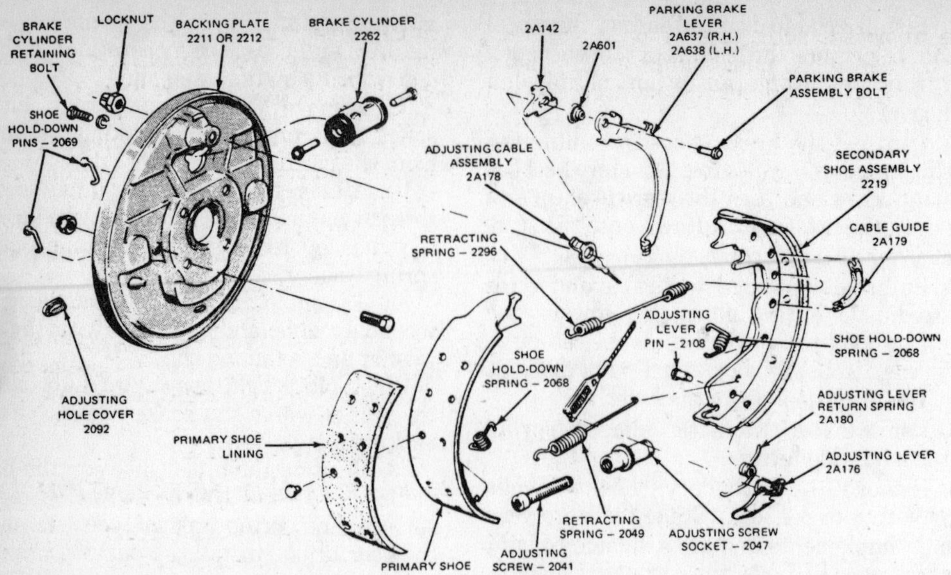

F-250, 350 rear web ledge single anchor brake components

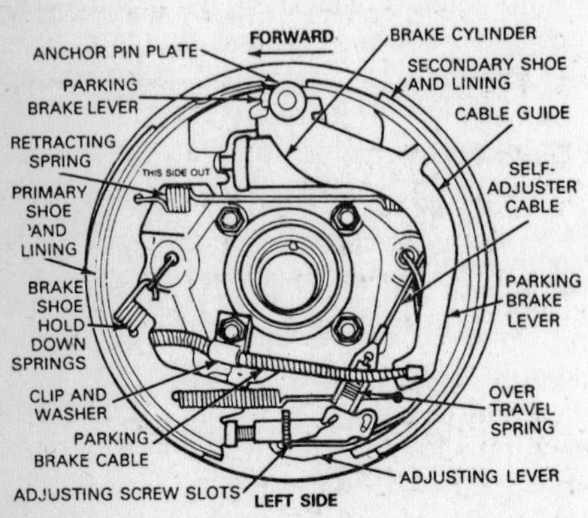

Rear brakes used on the F-250 and F-350

adjusting levers are stamped with an **R** (right) or a **L** (left) to indicate their installation on the right or left hand brake assembly.

21. Position the hooked end of the adjuster spring in the primary shoe web and connect the loop end of the spring to the adjuster lever hole.

22. Pull the adjuster lever, cable and automatic adjuster spring down toward the rear to engage the pivot hook in the large hole in the secondary shoe web.

23. After installation, check the action of the adjuster by pulling the section of the cable guide and the adjusting lever toward the secondary shoe web far enough to lift the lever past a tooth on the adjusting screw starwheel. The lever should snap into position behind the next tooth, and release of the cable should cause the adjuster spring to return the lever to its original position. This return action of the lever will turn the adjusting screw starwheel one tooth. The lever should contact the adjusting screw starwheel one tooth above the centerline of the adjusting screw.

If the automatic adjusting mechanism does not perform properly, check the following:

1. Check the cable and fittings. The cable ends should fill or extend slightly beyond the crimped section of the fittings. If this is not the case, replace the cable.

2. Check the cable guide for damage. The

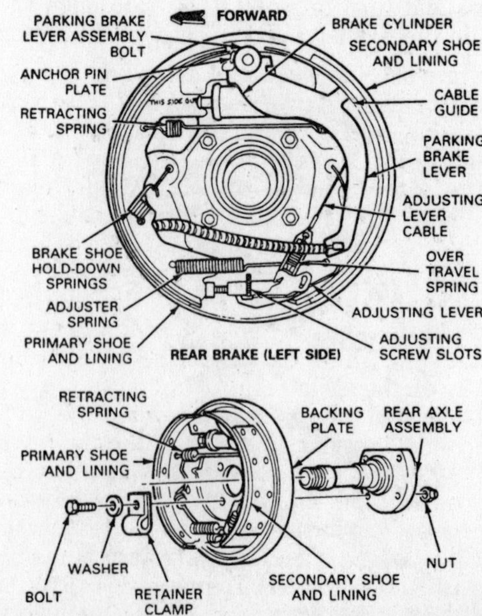

HD rear brakes used on the F-250 and F-350

cable groove should be parallel to the shoe web, and the body of the guide should lie flat against the web. Replace the cable guide if this is not so.

3. Check the pivot hook on the lever. The hook surfaces should be square with the body on the lever for proper pivoting. Repair or replace the hook as necessary.

4. Make sure that the adjusting screw starwheel is properly seated in the notch in the shoe web.

F-250 HD, F-350

1. Raise and support the vehicle.
2. Remove the wheel and drum.
3. Remove the parking brake lever assembly retaining nut from behind the backing plate and remove the parking brake lever assembly.
4. Remove the adjusting cable assembly from the anchor pin, cable guide, and adjusting lever.
5. Remove the brake shoe retracting springs.
6. Remove the brake shoe holddown spring from each shoe.
7. Remove the brake shoes and adjusting screw assembly.
8. Disassemble the adjusting screw assembly.
9. Clean the ledge pads on the backing plate. Apply a light coat of Lubriplate® to the ledge pads (where the brake shoes rub the backing plate).
10. Apply Lubriplate® to the adjusting screw assembly and the holddown and retracting spring contacts on the brake shoes.
11. Install the upper retracting spring on the primary and secondary shoes and position the shoe assembly on the backing plate with the wheel cylinder pushrods in the shoe slots.
12. Install the brake shoe holddown springs.
13. Install the brake shoe adjustment screw assembly with the slot in the head of the adjusting screw toward the primary shoe, lower retracting spring, adjusting lever spring, adjusting lever assembly, and connect the adjusting cable to the adjusting lever. Position the cable in the cable guide and install the cable anchor fitting on the anchor pin.
14. Install the adjusting screw assemblies in the same locations from which they were removed. Interchanging the brake shoe adjusting screws from one side of the vehicle to the other will cause the brake shoes to retract rather than expand each time the automatic adjusting mechanism is operated. To prevent incorrect installation, the socket end of each adjusting screw is stamped with an **R** or an **L** to indicate their installation on the right or left side of the vehicle. The adjusting pivot nuts can be distinguished by the number of lines machined around the body of the nut. Two lines indicate a right hand nut; one line indicates a left hand nut.
15. Install the parking brake assembly in the anchor pin and secure with the retaining nut behind the backing plate.
16. Adjust the brakes before installing the brake drums and wheels. Install the brake drums and wheels.
17. Lower the vehicle and road test the brakes. New brakes may pull to one side or the other before they are seated. Continued pulling or erratic braking should not occur.

Wheel Cylinders

REMOVAL AND INSTALLATION

1. Remove the brake drum.
2. Remove the brake shoes.
3. Loosen the brake line at the wheel cylinder.
4. Remove the wheel cylinder attaching bolt and unscrew the cylinder from the brake line.
5. Installation is the reverse of removal.

OVERHAUL

Purchase a brake cylinder repair kit. Remove and disassemble the wheel cylinder. Follow the instructions in the kit. Never repair only one cylinder. Repair both at the same time.

PARKING BRAKE EXCEPT F-SUPER DUTY

NOTE: *Before making any parking brake adjustment, make sure that the drum brakes are properly adjusted.*

ADJUSTMENT

1. Raise and support the rear end on jackstands.
2. The brake drums should be cold.
3. Make sure that the parking brake pedal is fully released.
4. While holding the tension equalizer, tighten the equalizer nut 6 full turns past its original position.
5. Fully depress the parking brake pedal. Using a cable tension gauge, check rear cable tension. Cable tension should be 350 lbs. minimum.
6. Fully release the parking brake. No drag should be noted at the wheels.
7. If drag is noted on F-250 and F-350 models, you'll have to remove the drums and adjust the clearance between the parking brake lever and cam plate. Clearance should be 0.015

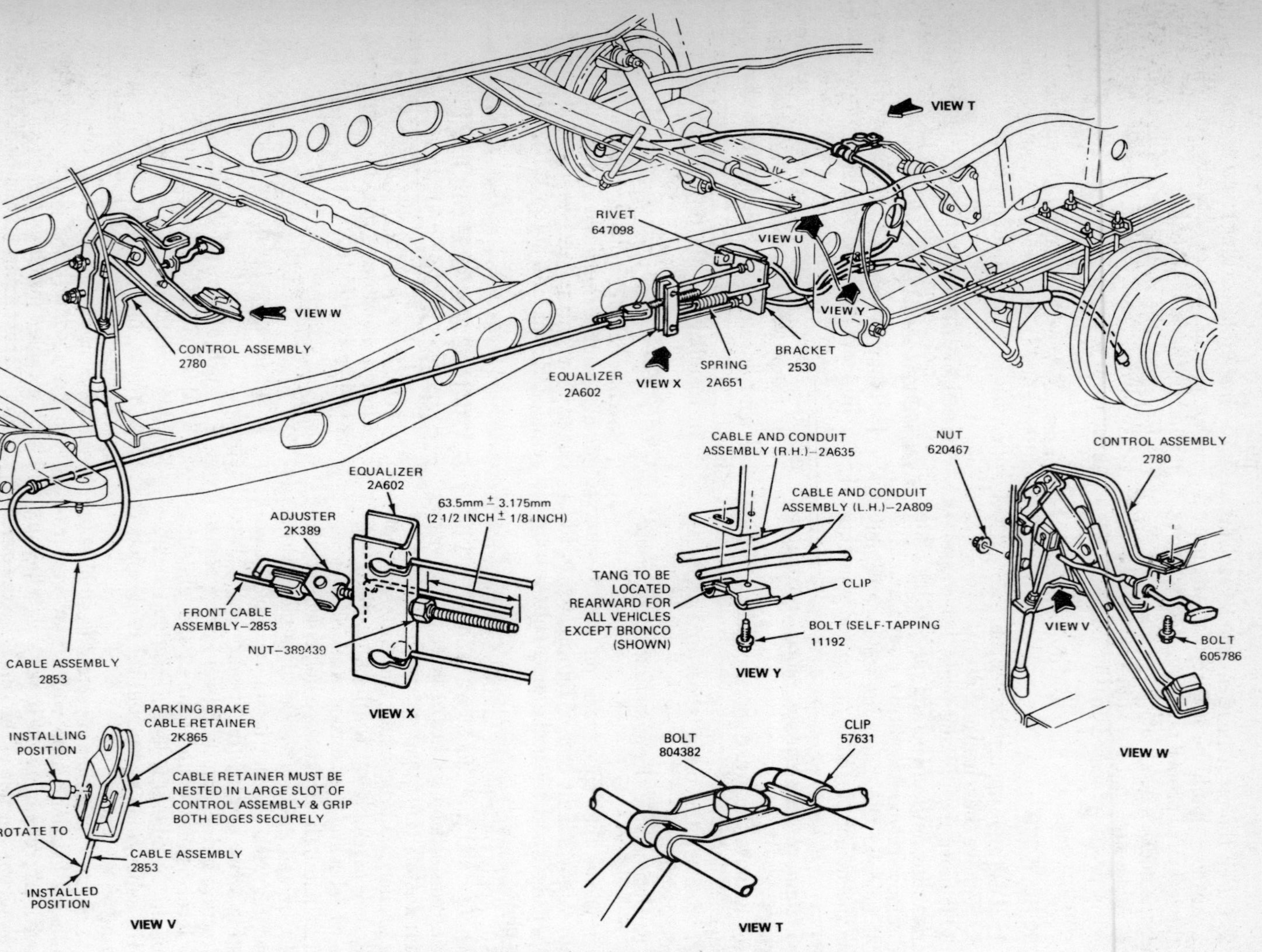

Parking brake cables on the F-150, 250, 350 and Bronco

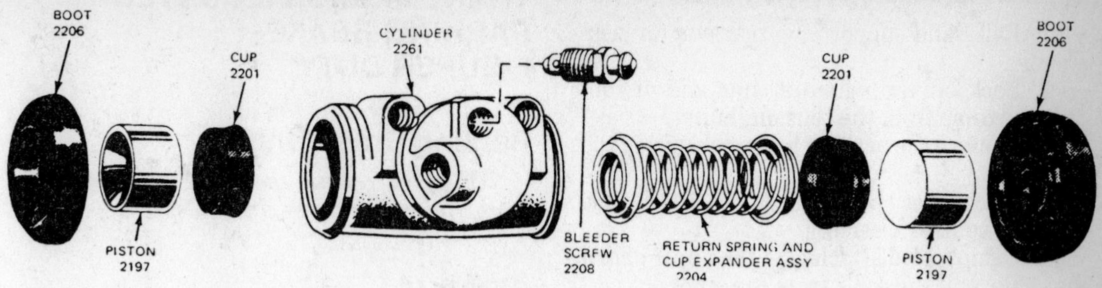

Rear wheel cylinder exploded view

in. (0.38mm). Clearance is adjusted at the parking brake equalizer adjusting nut.

If the tension limiter on the F-150 and Bronco doesn't release the drag, the tension limiter will have to be replaced.

INITIAL ADJUSTMENT WHEN THE TENSION LIMITER HAS BEEN REPLACED

1. Raise and support the front end on jackstands.
2. Depress the parking brake pedal fully.
3. Hold the tension limiter, install the equalizer nut and tighten it to a point $2^1/_2$ in. $\pm$ $^1/_8$ in. (63.5mm $\pm$ 3mm) up the rod.
4. Check to make sure that the cinch strap has $1^3/_8$ in. (35mm) remaining.

REMOVAL AND INSTALLATION

Parking Brake Control

1. Raise and support the rear end on jackstands.
2. Loosen the adjusting nut at the equalizer.
3. Working in the engine compartment, remove the nuts attaching the parking brake control to the firewall.
4. Remove the cable from the control assembly clevis by compressing the conduit end prongs.
5. Installation is the reverse of removal. Torque the attaching nuts to 15 ft. lbs.

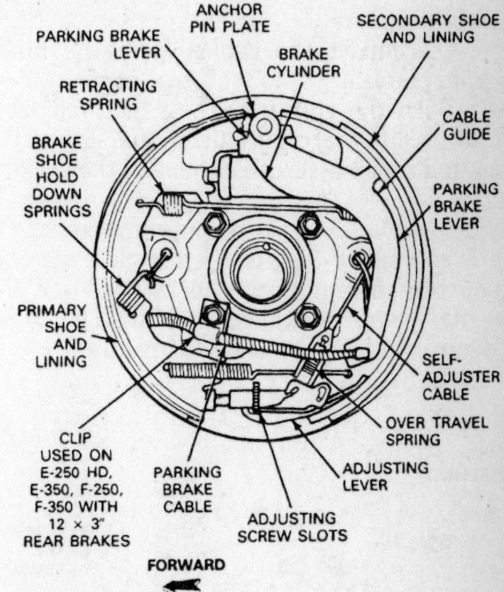

F-250, 350 parking brake

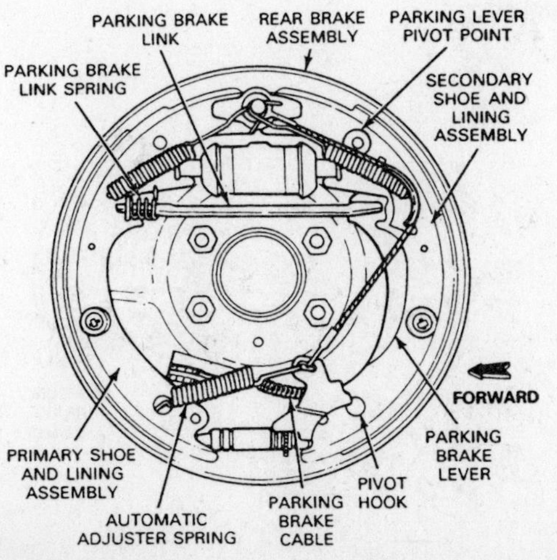

Parking brake cable tension limiters

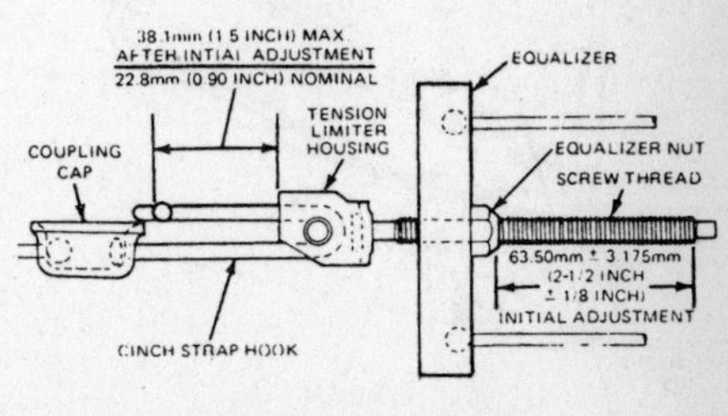

F-150 and Bronco parking brake

Equalizer-to-Control Assembly Cable

1. Raise and support the rear end on jackstands.
2. Back off the equalizer nut and disconnect the cable from the tension limiter.
3. Remove the parking brake cable from the mount.
4. Disconnect the forward end of the cable from the control assembly.
5. Using a cord attached to the upper end of the cable, pull the cable from the truck.
6. Installation is the reverse of removal. Adjust the parking brake.

Equalizer-to-Rear Wheel Cable

1. Raise and support the rear end on jackstands.
2. Remove the wheels and brake drums.
3. Remove the tension limiter.
4. Remove the locknut from the threaded rod and disconnect the cable from the equalizer.
5. Disconnect the cable housing from the frame bracket and pull the cable and housing out of the bracket.
6. Disconnect the cables from the brake backing plates.
7. With the spring tension removed from the lever, lift the cable out of the slot in the lever and remove the cable through the backing plate hole.
8. Installation is the reverse of removal. On the F-250 and F-350, check the clearance between the parking brake operating lever and the cam plate. Clearance should be 0.015 in. (0.38mm) with the brakes fully released.
9. Adjust the brakes.

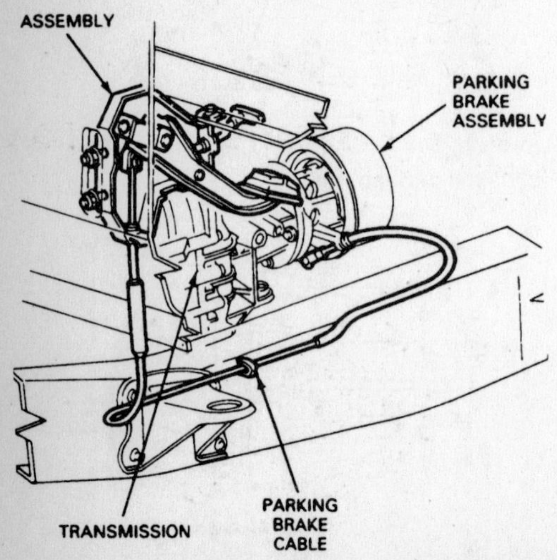

F-Super Duty parking brake cables

TRANSMISSION MOUNTED PARKING BRAKE F-SUPER DUTY

Parking Brake Unit

NOTE: *To replace the brake shoes, or any other component, the unit must be disassembled.*

REMOVAL

1. Place the transmission in gear.
2. Fully release the parking brake pedal.
3. Raise and support the truck on jackstands.
4. Disconnect the speedometer cable.
5. Spray penetrating oil on the adjusting clevis, jam nut and threaded end of the cable.
6. Loosen the jam nut and remove the locking pin from the clevis pin.
7. Remove the clevis pin, clevis and jam nut from the cable.
8. Remove the cable from the bracket on the case.

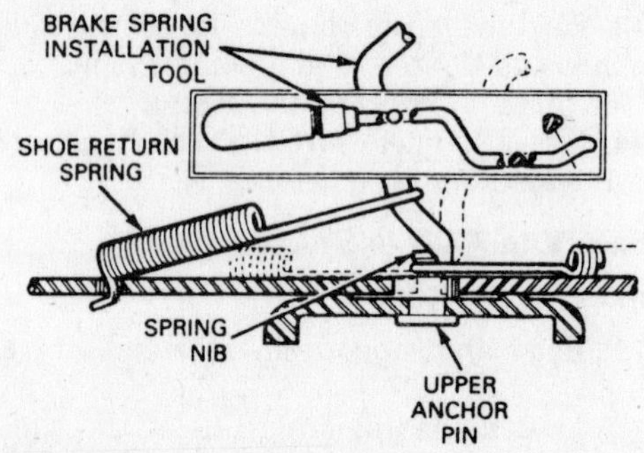

F-Super Duty parking brake shoe return spring installation

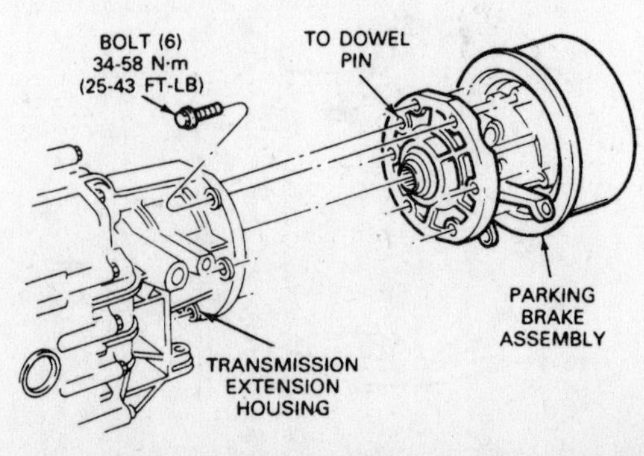

F-Super Duty parking brake unit removal

9. Matchmark the driveshaft and disconnect it from the flange.

10. Remove the 6 hex-head bolts securing the parking brake unit to the transmission extension housing and lift off the unit.

NOTE: *The unit is filled with Ford Type H ATF.*

CAUTION: *Brake shoes contain asbestos, which has been determined to be a cancer causing agent. Never clean the brake surfaces with compressed air! Avoid inhaling any dust from any brake surface! When cleaning brake surfaces, use a commercially available brake cleaning fluid.*

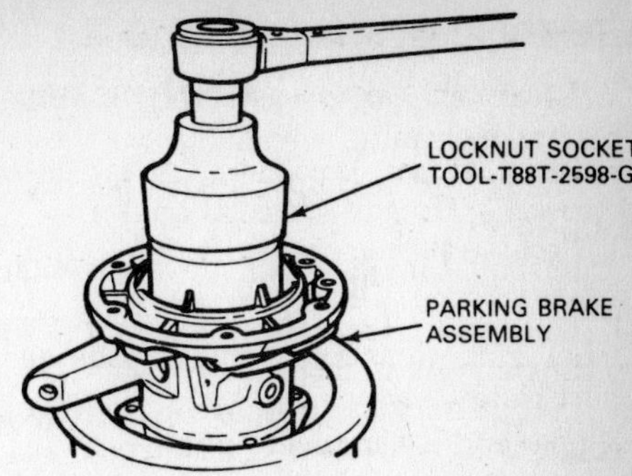

Removing the parking brake mainshaft locknut

DISASSEMBLY

NOTE: *Several special tools and a hydraulic press are necessary.*

1. Remove the unit from the truck.
2. Remove the 4 bolts securing the yoke flange and drum, and remove the flange and drum.
3. Remove the 75mm hex nut from the mainshaft, using tool T88T–2598–G, or equivalent.
4. Press the mainshaft, drum and output flange from the case.
5. Remove the speedometer drive gear from the case.
6. Using tools D80L–1002–2, D79L–4621–A and D80L–630–6, remove the outer bearing cone from the mainshaft.
7. Place the threaded end of the output shaft in a soft-jawed vise.
8. Matchmark the drum, flange/yoke and mainshaft. Remove the 4 nuts securing the flange and drum to the output shaft and remove the flange and drum.
9. Using tool T77F–1102–A, remove the input shaft oil seal, spacer, O-ring, bearing cone and race from the input shaft end of the case.
10. Remove the 4 bolts securing the splash shield and brake assembly from the case. Remove the brake assembly and splash shield.
11. Remove the brake actuating lever and spring from the case.
12. Using tool T77F–1102–A, remove the outer bearing cup and oil seal.
13. Unscrew the vent from the case.
14. Hold the brake assembly securely and remove the 2 brake sure return springs.
15. Spread the free ends of the shoes and remove the shoes from the lower anchor pin. Remove the shoe-to-shoe spring.

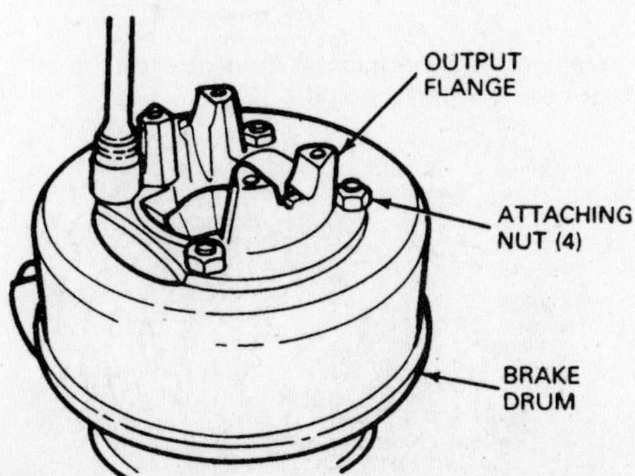

Removing the F-Super Duty parking brake output flange

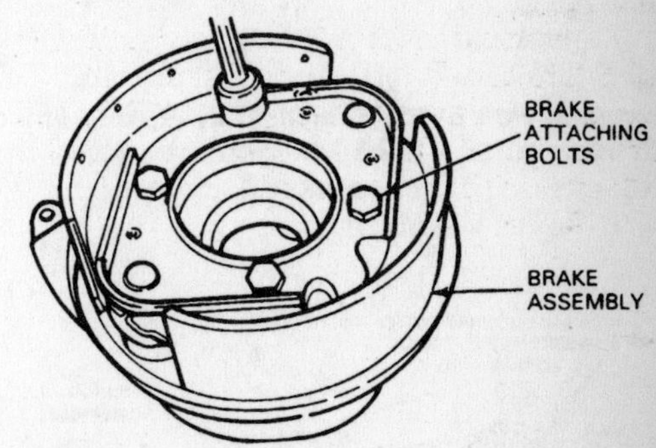

Removing the F-Super Duty parking brake splash shield

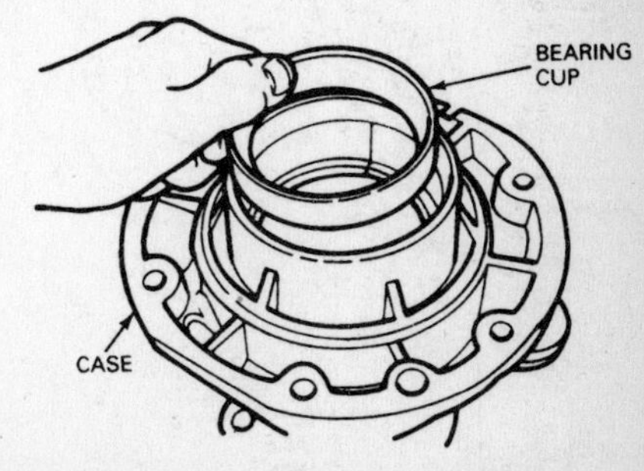

Removing the F-Super Duty parking brake outer bearing cup

ASSEMBLY

1. Clean the brake assembly thoroughly with a brake cleaning solvent.

2. Using a brake caliper grease, place a light coating on:

- Camshaft lugs and ball on the actuating lever
- Shoe guide lugs and support pads on the support plate
- Upper and lower anchor pins
- Brake shoe anchor pin contact points

3. Connect a NEW shoe-to-shoe spring between the brake shoes, spread the shoes and position them on the lower anchor pin.

4. Position the upper ends on the upper anchor pin, inserting the show webs between the shoe guide lugs and the pads on the support plate.

5. Install 2 NEW return springs.

6. Drive a new inner bearing race into place.

7. Drive a new outer bearing race into the case making sure it bottoms evenly.

8. Install a new outer bearing.

9. Coat the outer edge of a new outer oil seal with sealer and drive the seal into place with the lip facing inward. The seal must be flush with the bore surface.

10. Install the actuating lever spring.

11. Apply a light coating of brake grease on the actuating lever ball and install the lever through the coiled end of the spring.

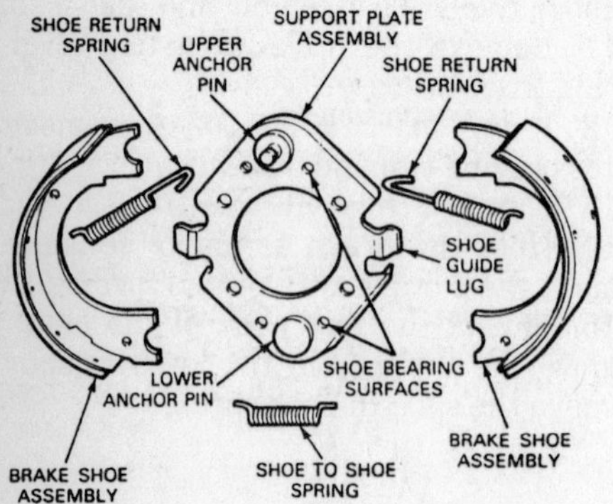

Exploded view of the F-Super Duty parking brake shoes

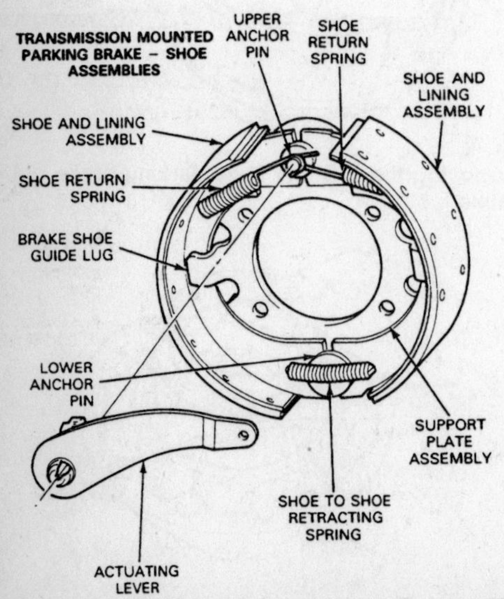

Assembling the F-Super Duty parking brake shoes

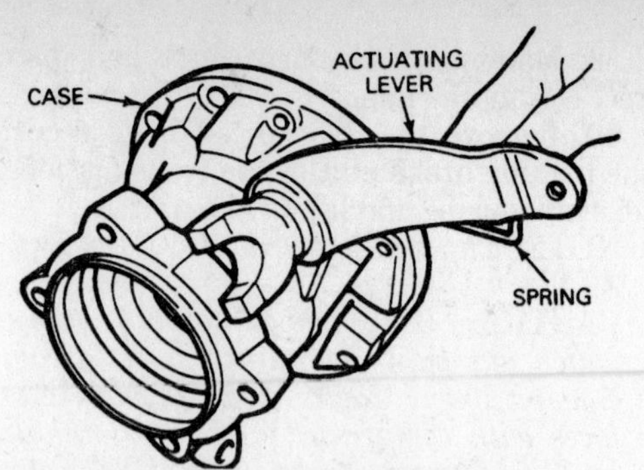

Installing the F-Super Duty parking brake lever

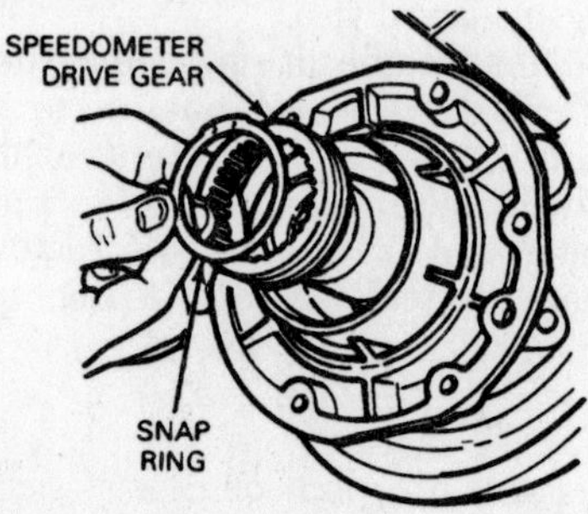

Installing the speedometer drive gear on the F-Super Duty parking brake

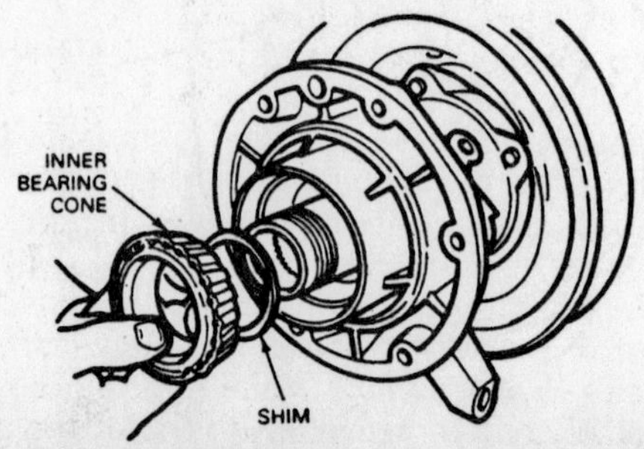

Installing the inner bearing cone and shim on the F-Super Duty parking brake

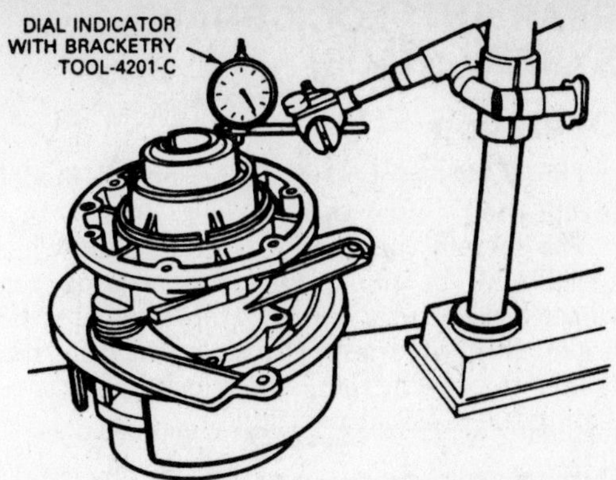

Measuring endplay on the F-Super Duty parking brake

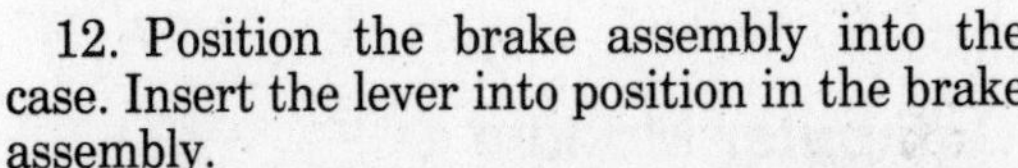

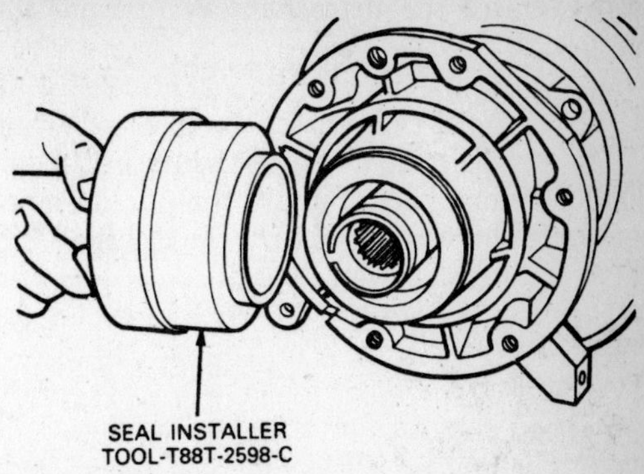

Installing the inner seal on the F-Super Duty parking brake

12. Position the brake assembly into the case. Insert the lever into position in the brake assembly.
13. Torque the 4 brake assembly attaching bolts to 90 ft. lbs.
14. Attach the retracting spring to the actuating lever while bending the long end to snap over the lever.
15. Place the mainshaft in a soft-jawed vise with the flanged end upward.
16. Install the brake drum and output flange onto the mainshaft, being aware of the matchmarks.
17. Install the 4 nuts and torque them to 85 ft. lbs.
18. Turn the mainshaft over and clamp it in the vise.
19. Install the case, with the outer bearing installed loosely on the mainshaft, guiding the mainshaft through the oil seal and bearing cone.
20. Install the outer bearing cone on the mainshaft using tool T88T–2598–F to seat the bearing on the shaft.
21. Install the speedometer gear and snapring.
22. Install the shim on the mainshaft.

NOTE: *This shim determines endplay. It is available in several thicknesses with variations of 0.05mm (0.0019 in.).*

23. Install the inner bearing cone and spacer on the mainshaft.

NOTE: *To check endplay, first install the inner bearing spacer without the O-ring.*

24. Thread the 75mm nut onto the shaft and torque it to 215 ft. lbs.
25. Mount a dial indicator and bracket with the dial indicator between the mainshaft and case to check endplay. While rotating the case assembly on the mainshaft to center the bearings, apply pressure up and down. An endplay reading of 0.05–0.10mm (0.0019–0.0039 in.) is desired. Shim as necessary.
26. Remove the 75mm nut, spacer and bearing to install the shim(s).
27. Install the bearing.
28. Coat the outer edge of a new seal with sealer and seat it in the case bore with the lip facing inward.
29. Install a new O-ring in the spacer and install the spacer on the mainshaft until it butts against the shoulder of the shaft.
30. Install a NEW 75mm nut and torque it to 215 ft. lbs.
31. Install the vent.

INSTALLATION

1. Refill the unit through the filler plug to the bottom of the plug hole. Install the plug and tighten it to 45 ft. lbs.
2. Position the unit on the extension housing using 2 guide pins.
3. Using 6 NEW hex-bolts, attach the unit and torque the bolts to 40 ft. lbs.

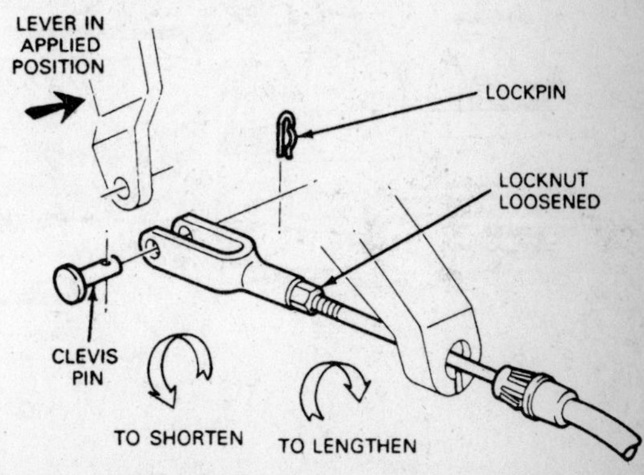

F-Super Duty parking brake adjustment points

4. Connect the driveshaft and torque the bolts to 20 ft. lbs.

5. Assemble the cable components. Screw on the clevis until the pin can be inserted while the lever and cable are held tightly in the applied position. Then, remove the pin, let go of the cable and lever, and turn the clevis 10 full turns counterclockwise (loosen).

6. Install the pin.

ADJUSTMENT

1. Fully release the brake pedal.
2. Spray penetrating oil on the adjusting clevis, jam nut and threaded end of the cable.
3. Loosen the jam nut and remove the locking pin from the clevis.
4. Back off on the clevis until there is slack in the cable.
5. Screw on the clevis until the pin can be inserted while the lever and cable are held tightly in the applied position. Then, remove the pin, let go of the cable and lever, and turn the clevis 10 full turns counterclockwise (loosen).
6. Install the pin.

REAR ANTI-LOCK BRAKE SYSTEM (RABS)

Operation

The RABS system is found on all models except the F-Super Duty.

The system constantly monitors rear wheel speed and, in the event of impending rear wheel lock-up in a sudden stop, regulates the brake fluid hydraulic pressure at the rear brakes to prevent total wheel lock-up, thus reducing the possibility of skidding.

Diagnosis and Service

Diagnosis is lengthy and complex and is best left to qualified service personnel.

Repair is limited to replacement of defective parts. No repairs to the parts are possible.

Computer Module

REMOVAL AND INSTALLATION

The module is located on the firewall just inboard of the master cylinder.

1. Disconnect the wiring harness.
2. Remove the 2 attaching screws and lift out the module.
3. Installation is the reverse of removal.

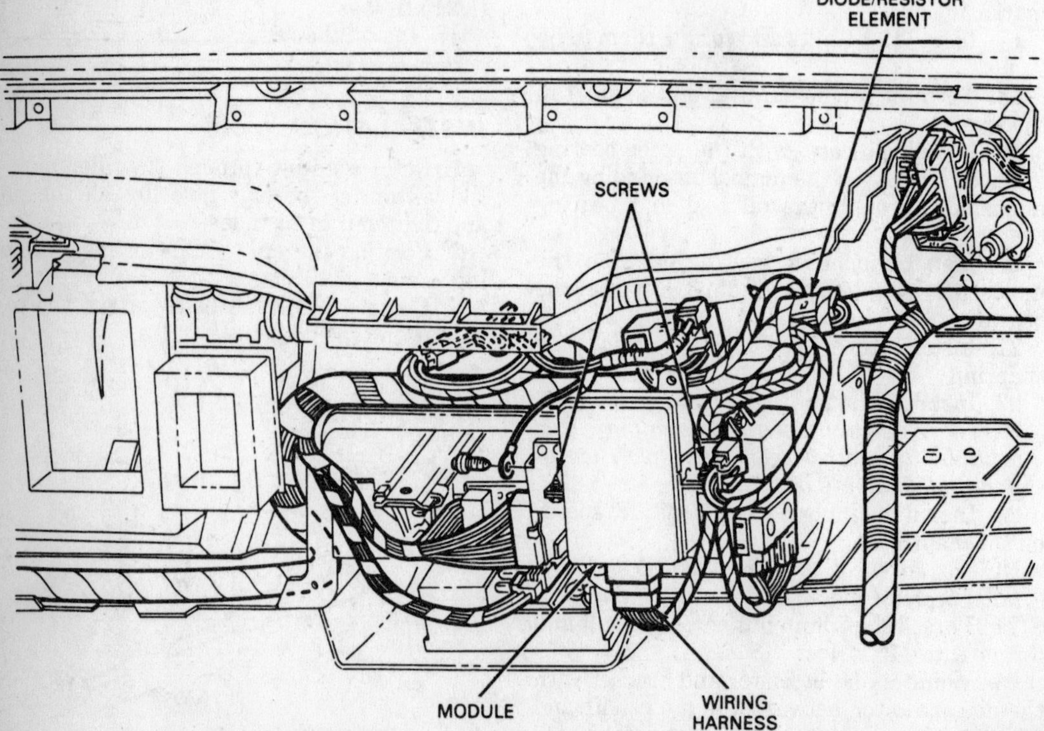

Rear anti-lock braking system module

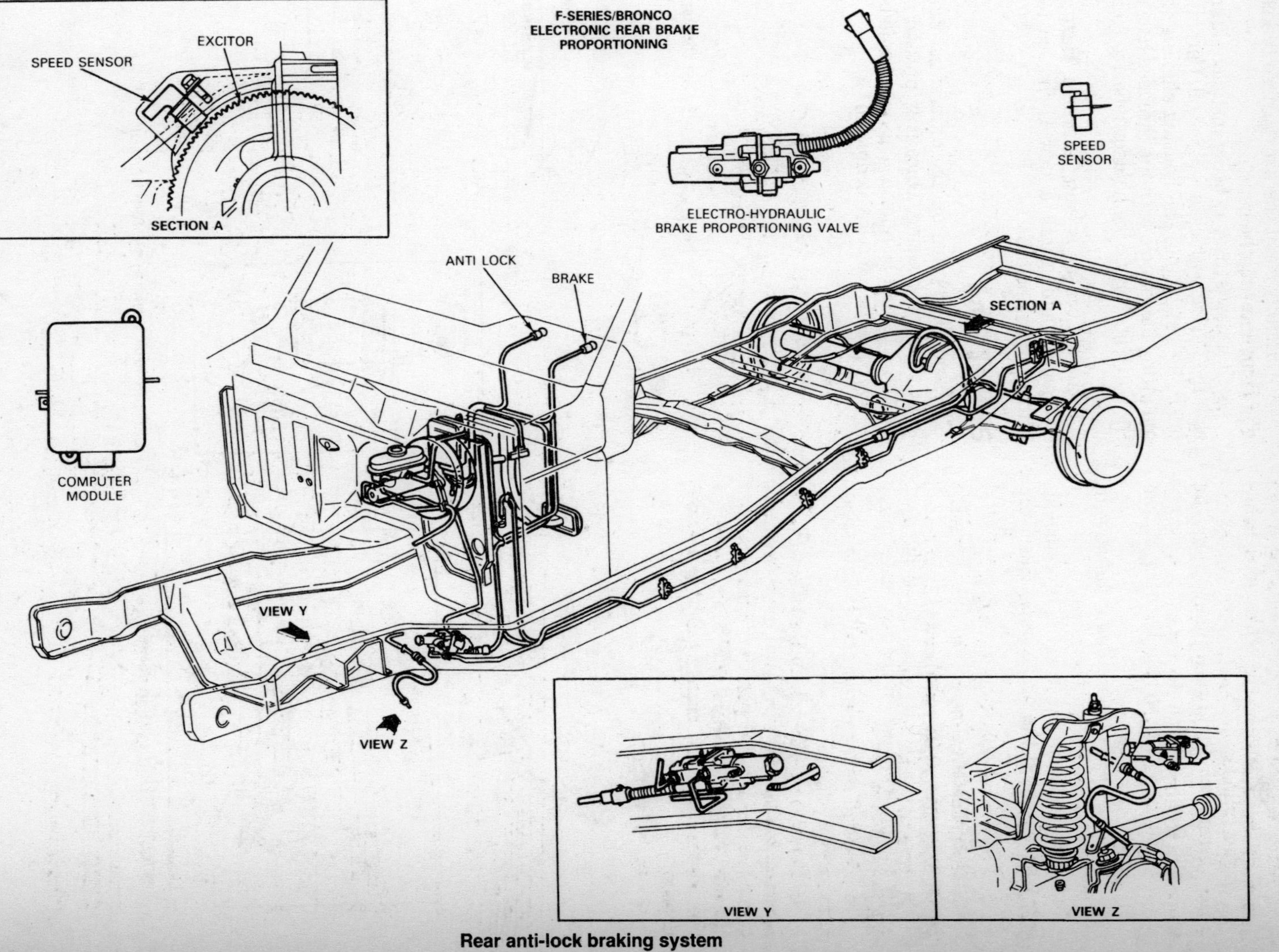

Rear anti-lock braking system

RABS Valve

REMOVAL AND INSTALLATION

The valve is located in the brake lines, below the master cylinder.

1. Disconnect the brake lines from the valve and plug the lines.
2. Disconnect the wiring harness at the valve.
3. Remove the 3 nuts retaining the valve to the frame rail and lift out the valve.
4. Installation is the reverse of removal. Don't over tighten the brake lines. Bleed the brakes.

RABS Sensor

REMOVAL AND INSTALLATION

The sensor is located on the rear axle housing.

1. Remove the sensor holddown bolt.
2. Remove the sensor.
3. Carefully clean the axle surface to keep dirt from entering the housing.
4. If a new sensor is being installed, lubricate the O-ring with clean engine oil. Carefully push the sensor into the housing aligning the mounting flange hole with the threaded hole in the housing. Torque the holddown bolt to 30 ft. lbs.

If the old sensor is being installed, clean it thoroughly and install a new O-ring coated with clean engine oil.

Exciter Ring

The ring is located on the differential case inside the axle housing. Once it is pressed of the case it cannot be reused. This job should be left to a qualified service technician.

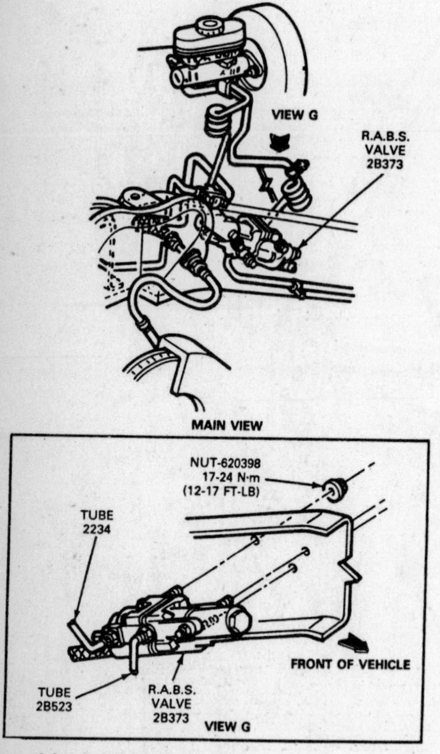

Rear anti-lock braking system valve

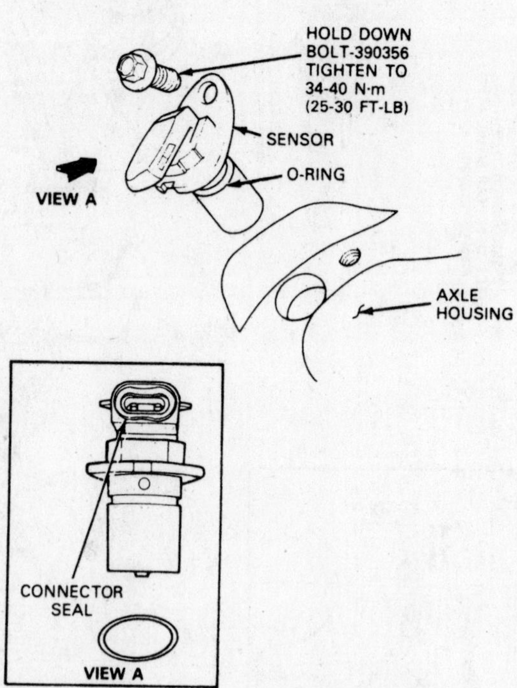

Rear anti-lock braking system sensor

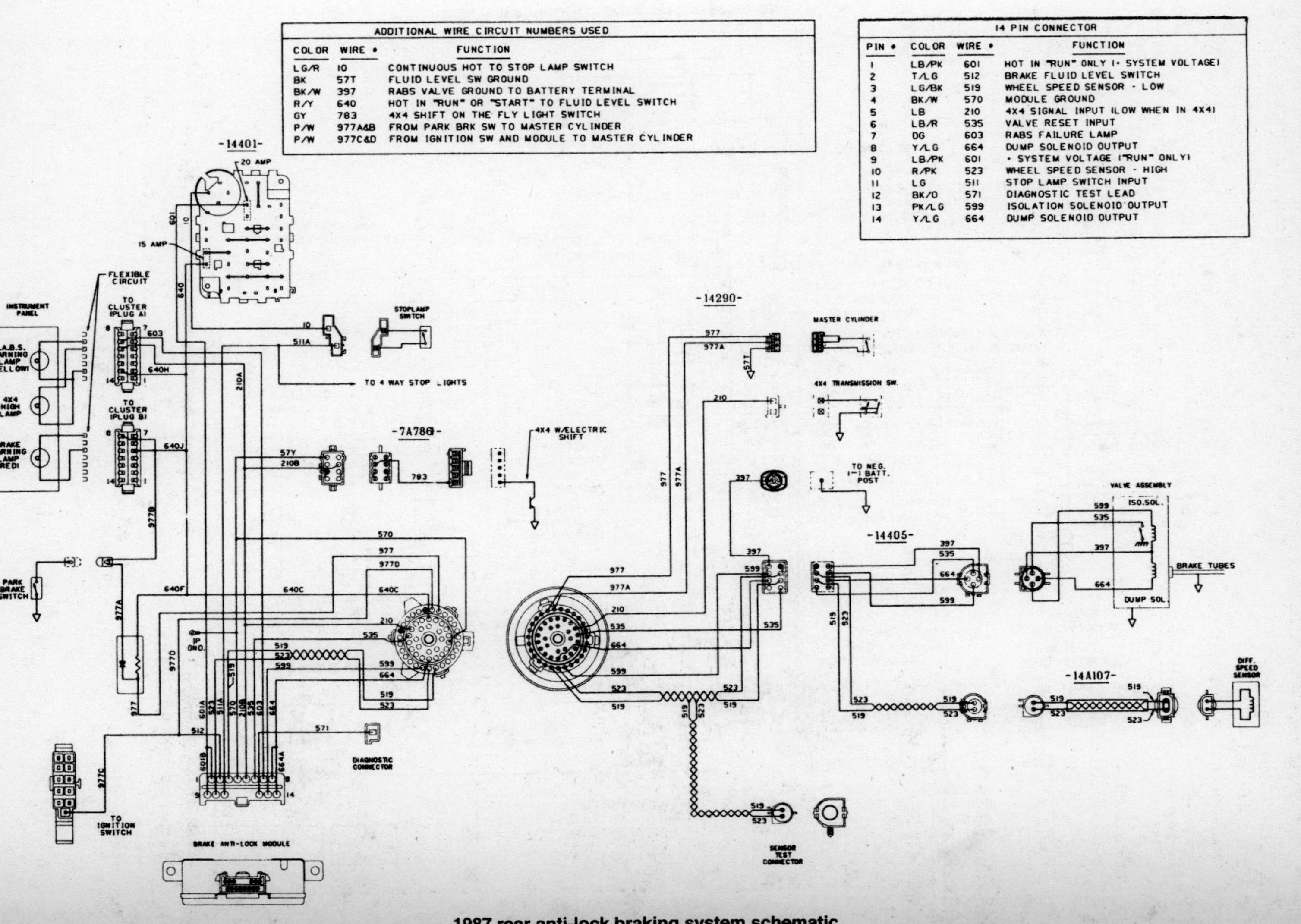

ADDITIONAL WIRE CIRCUIT NUMBERS USED

COLOR	WIRE •	FUNCTION
LG/R	10	CONTINUOUS HOT TO STOP LAMP SWITCH
BK	57T	FLUID LEVEL SW GROUND
BK/W	397	RABS VALVE GROUND TO BATTERY TERMINAL
R/Y	640	HOT IN "RUN" OR "START" TO FLUID LEVEL SWITCH
GY	783	4X4 SHIFT ON THE FLY LIGHT SWITCH
P/W	977A&B	FROM PARK BRK SW TO MASTER CYLINDER
P/W	977C&D	FROM IGNITION SW AND MODULE TO MASTER CYLINDER

14 PIN CONNECTOR

PIN •	COLOR	WIRE •	FUNCTION
1	LB/PK	601	HOT IN "RUN" ONLY (• SYSTEM VOLTAGE)
2	T/LG	512	BRAKE FLUID LEVEL SWITCH
3	LG/BK	519	WHEEL SPEED SENSOR - LOW
4	BK/W	570	MODULE GROUND
5	LB	210	4X4 SIGNAL INPUT (LOW WHEN IN 4X4)
6	LB/R	535	VALVE RESET INPUT
7	DG	603	RABS FAILURE LAMP
8	Y/LG	664	DUMP SOLENOID OUTPUT
9	LB/PK	601	• SYSTEM VOLTAGE ("RUN" ONLY)
10	R/PK	523	WHEEL SPEED SENSOR - HIGH
11	LG	511	STOP LAMP SWITCH INPUT
12	BK/O	571	DIAGNOSTIC TEST LEAD
13	PK/LG	599	ISOLATION SOLENOID OUTPUT
14	Y/LG	664	DUMP SOLENOID OUTPUT

1987 rear anti-lock braking system schematic

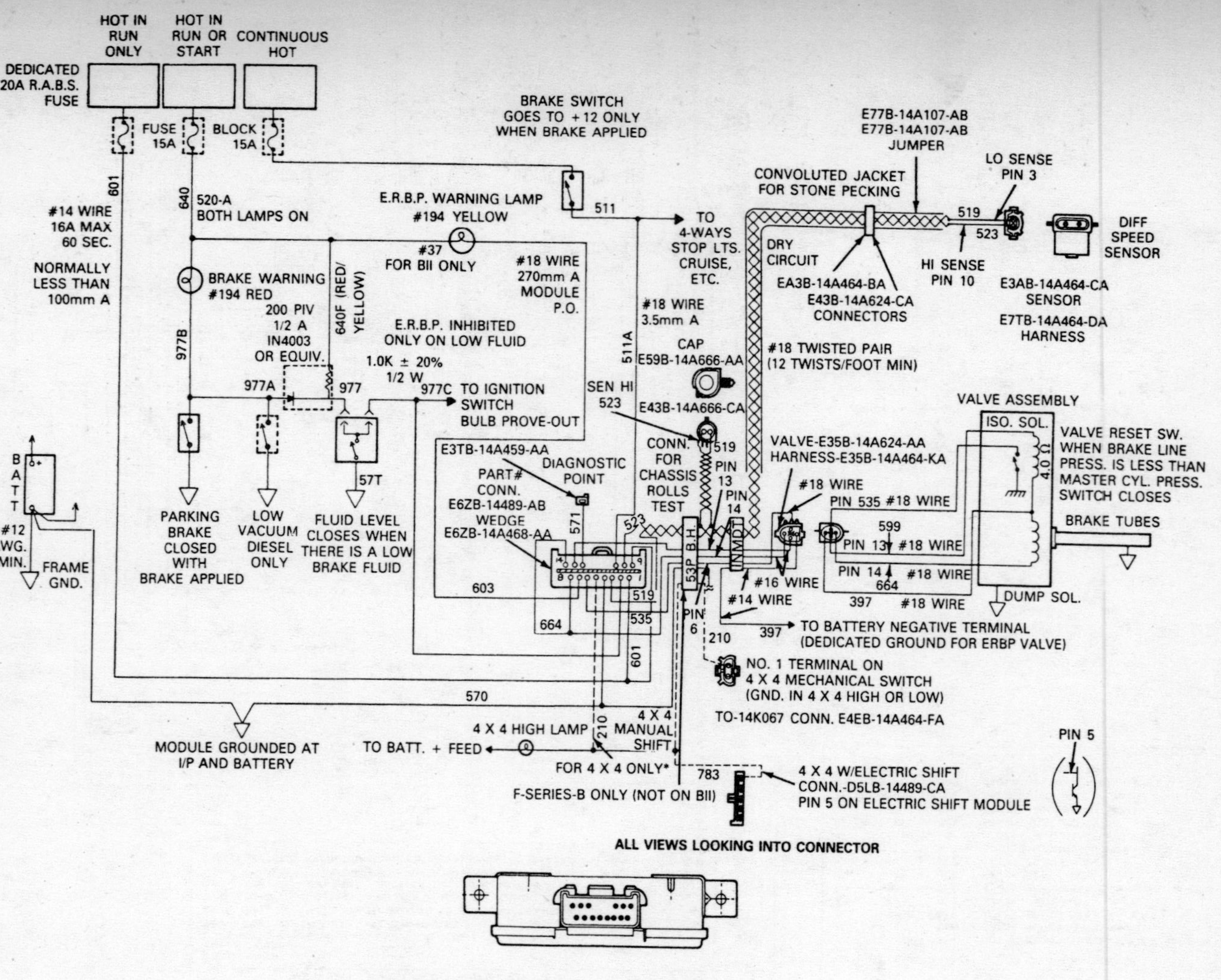

1988 rear anti-lock braking system schematic

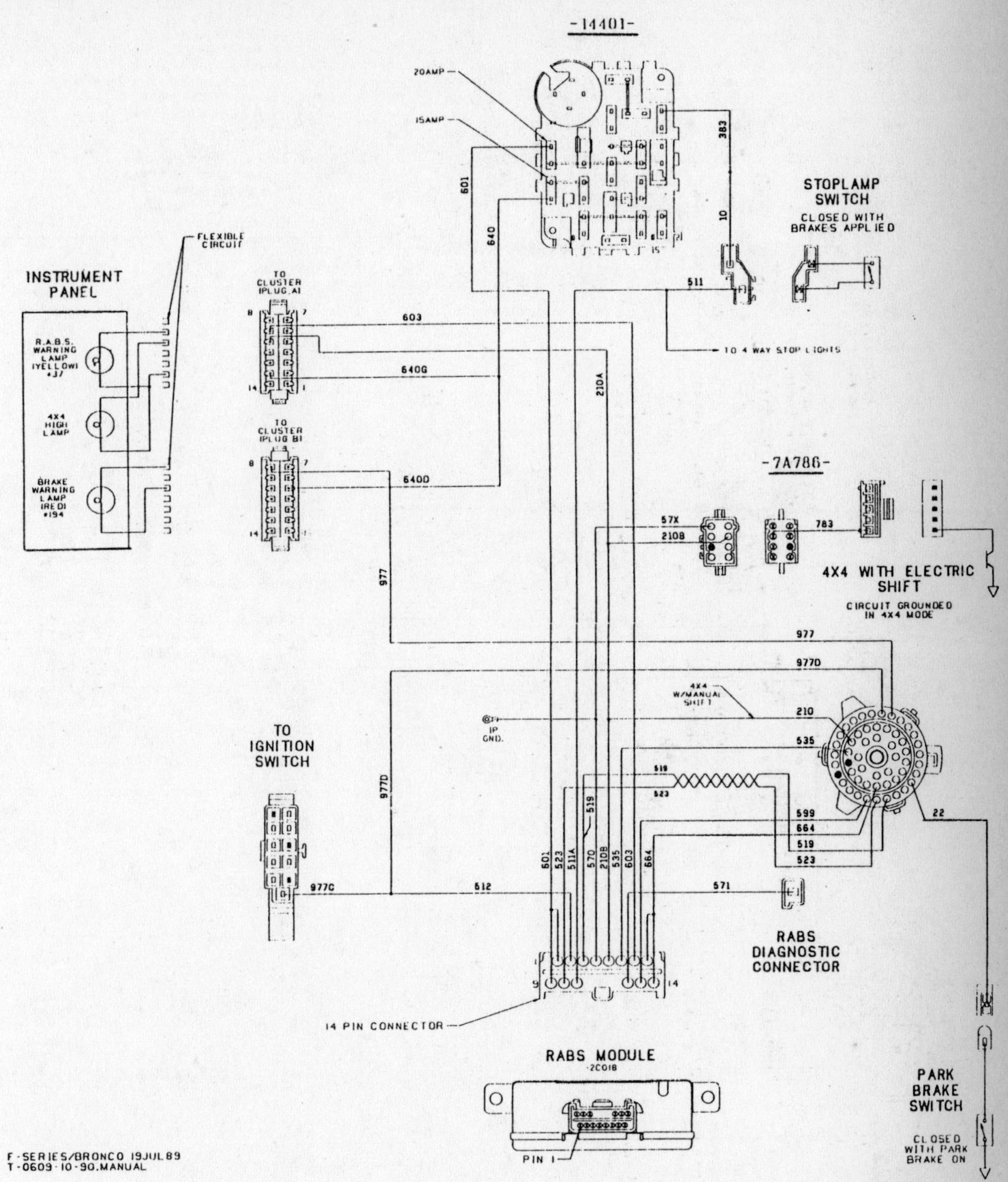

1990 rear wheel anti-lock braking system wiring diagram

ADDITIONAL WIRE CIRCUIT NUMBERS USED		
COLOR	WIRE NO.	FUNCTION
LG/R	10	CONTINUOUS HOT (STOP LAMP SWITCH)
R/LG	16	HOT IN RUN OR START
LB/BK	22	PARKING BRAKE SWITCH
BK	57T	FLUID LEVEL SW GROUND
R/W	383	STOP LIGHT SWITCH AT FUSE BOX
BK/W	397	RABS VALVE GROUND TO BATTERY TERMINAL
R/Y	640	HOT IN "RUN" OR "START"
GY	783	4X4 SHIFT ON THE FLY LIGHT SWITCH
P/W	977A&B	FROM PARK SWITCH TO MASTER CYLINDER
P/W	977C&D	FROM IG SW AND MODULE TO MASTER CYLINDER

14 PIN CONNECTOR			
PIN NO.	COLOR	WIRE NO.	FUNCTION
1	LB/PK	601	HOT IN "RUN" ONLY (• SYSTEM VOLTAGE)
2	T/LG	512	BRAKE FLUID LEVEL SWITCH
3	LG/BK	519	WHEEL SPEED SENSOR - LOW
4	BK/W	570	MODULE GROUND
5	LB	210	4X4 SIGNAL INPUT (LOW WHEN IN 4X4)
6	LB/R	535	VALVE RESET INPUT
7	DG	603	RABS FAILURE LAMP
8	Y/LG	664	DUMP SOLENOID OUTPUT
9	LB/PK	601	• SYSTEM VOLTAGE ("RUN" ONLY)
10	R/PK	523	WHEEL SPEED SENSOR - HIGH
11	LG	511	STOP LAMP SWITCH INPUT
12	BK/O	571	DIAGNOSTIC TEST LEAD
13	PK/LG	599	ISOLATION SOLENOID OUTPUT
14	Y/LG	664	DUMP SOLENOID OUTPUT

NOTE : ALL VIEWS LOOKING INTO CONNECTOR

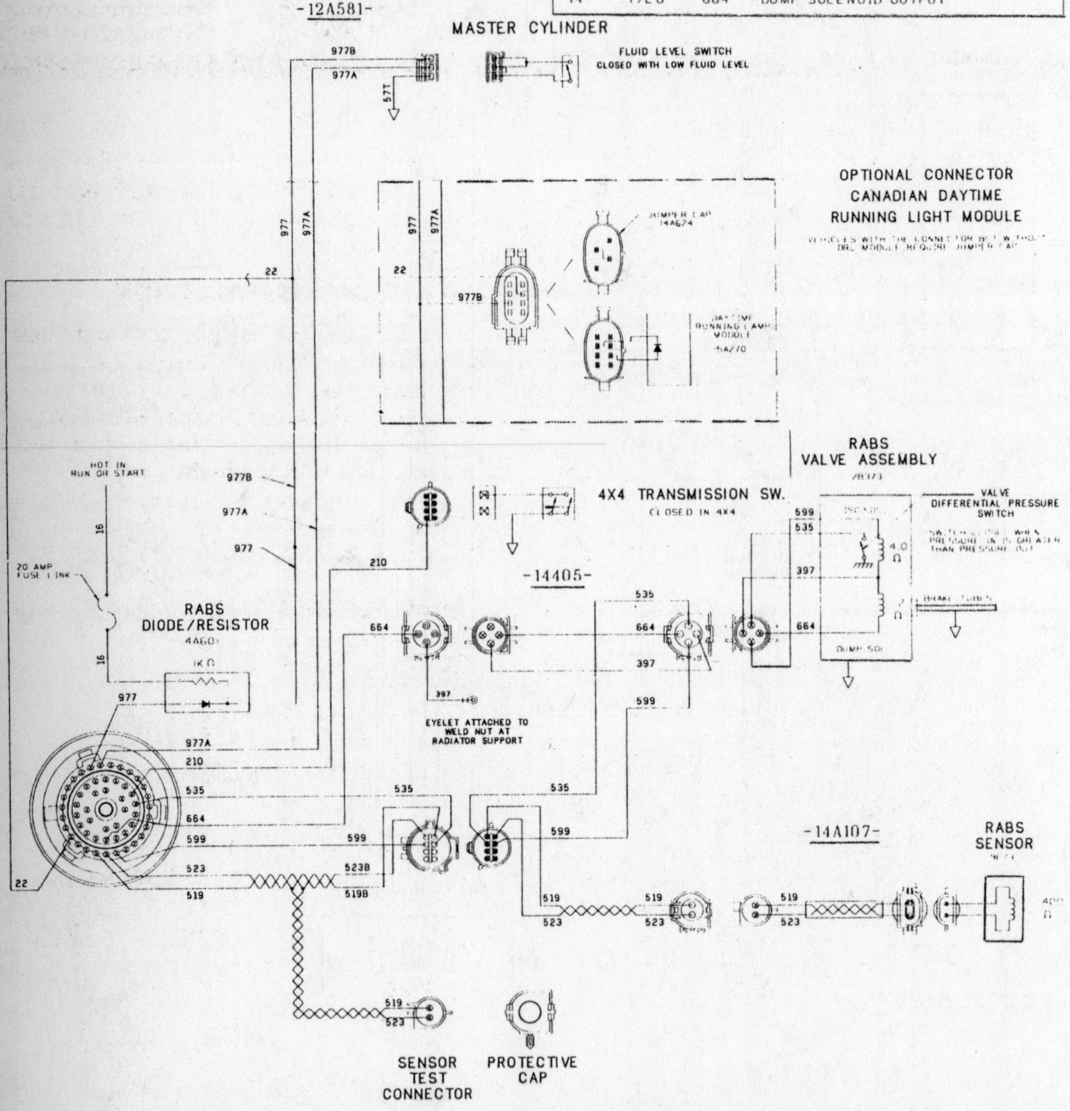

1990 rear wheel anti-lock braking system wiring diagram (cont.)

Body 10

EXTERIOR

Doors

ADJUSTMENT

NOTE: *Loosen the hinge-to-door bolts for lateral adjustment only. Loosen the hinge-to-body bolts for both lateral and vertical adjustment.*

1. Determine which hinge bolts are to be loosened and back them out just enough to allow movement.
2. To move the door safely, use a padded pry bar. When the door is in the proper position, tighten the bolts to 24 ft. lbs. and check the door operation. There should be no binding or interference when the door is closed and opened.
3. Door closing adjustment can also be affected by the position of the lock striker plate. Loosen the striker plate bolts and move the striker plate just enough to permit proper closing and locking of the door.

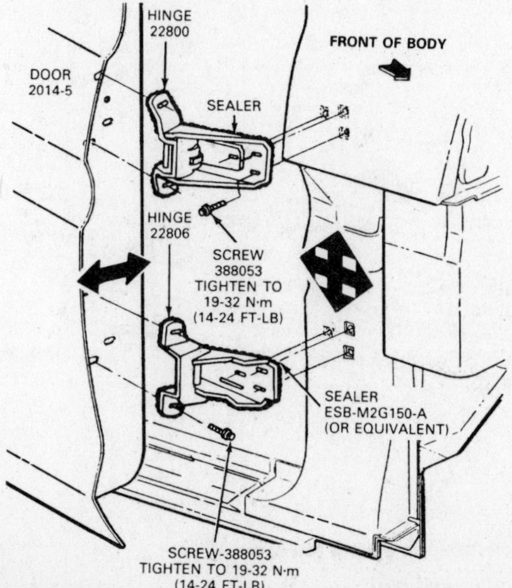

Door hinge adjustment

REMOVAL AND INSTALLATION

1. Matchmark the hinge-to-body and hinge-to-door locations. Support the door either on jackstands or have somebody hold it for you.
2. Remove the lower hinge-to-door bolts.
3. Remove the upper hinge-to-door bolts and lift the door off the hinges.
4. If the hinges are being replaced, remove them from the door pillar.
5. Install the door and hinges with the bolts finger tight.
6. Adjust the door and torque the hinge bolts to 24 ft. lbs.

Hood

REMOVAL AND INSTALLATION

NOTE: *You'll need an assistant for this job.*

1. Open the hood.
2. Remove the 2 link assembly bolts.

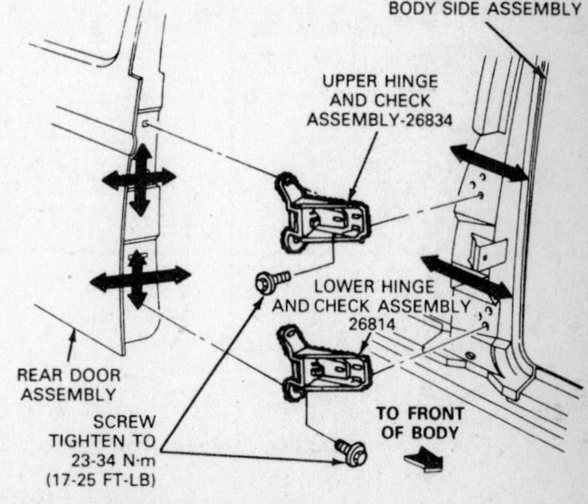

Rear door hinge adjustment, F-350 Crew Cab

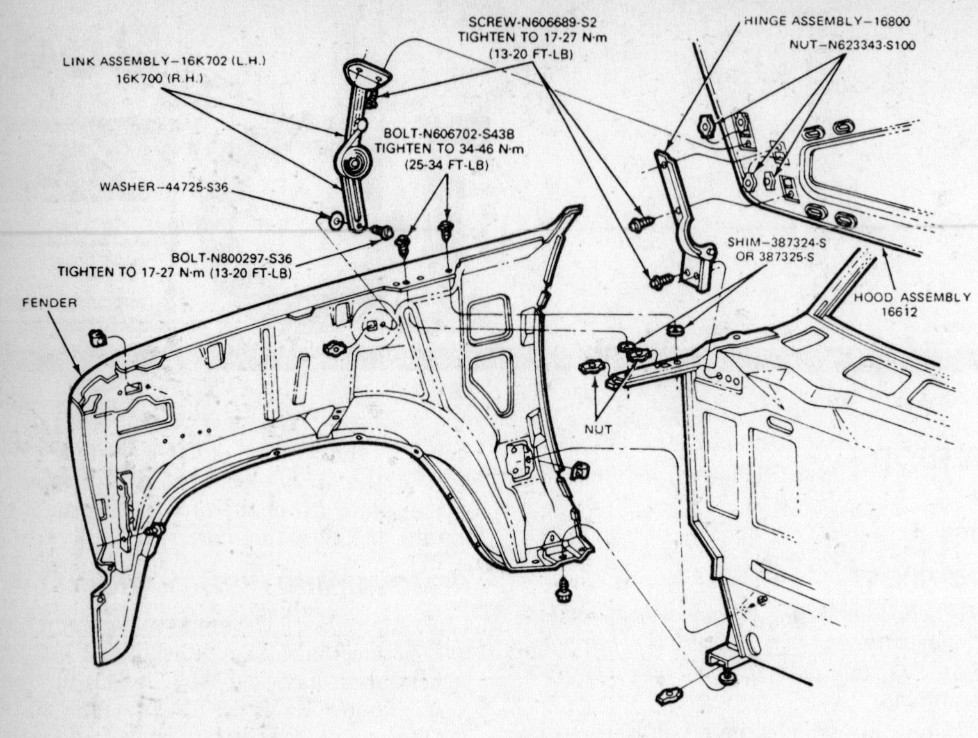

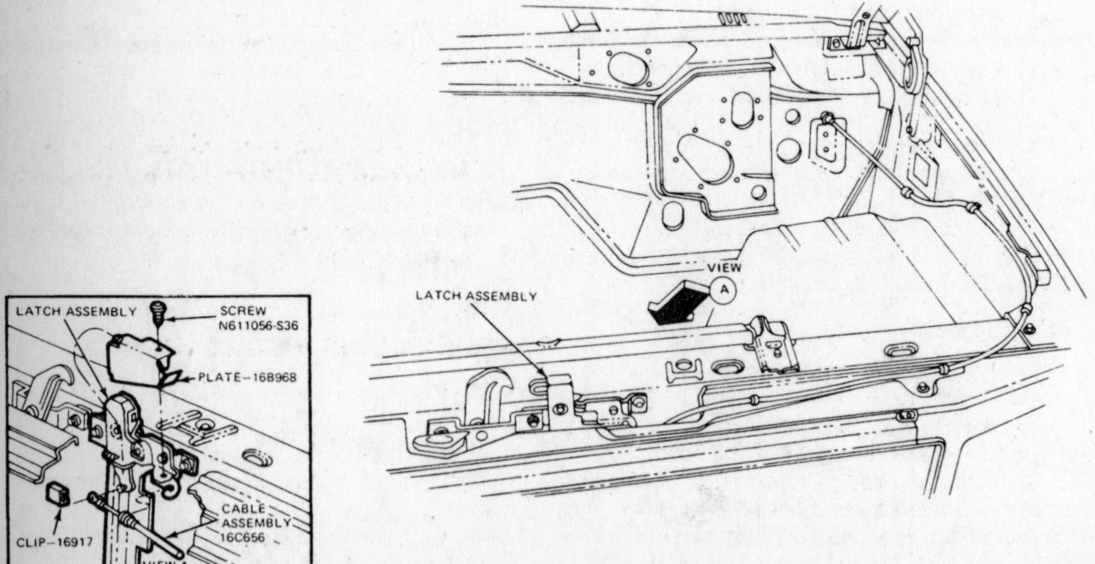

Hood, hinge and latch installation

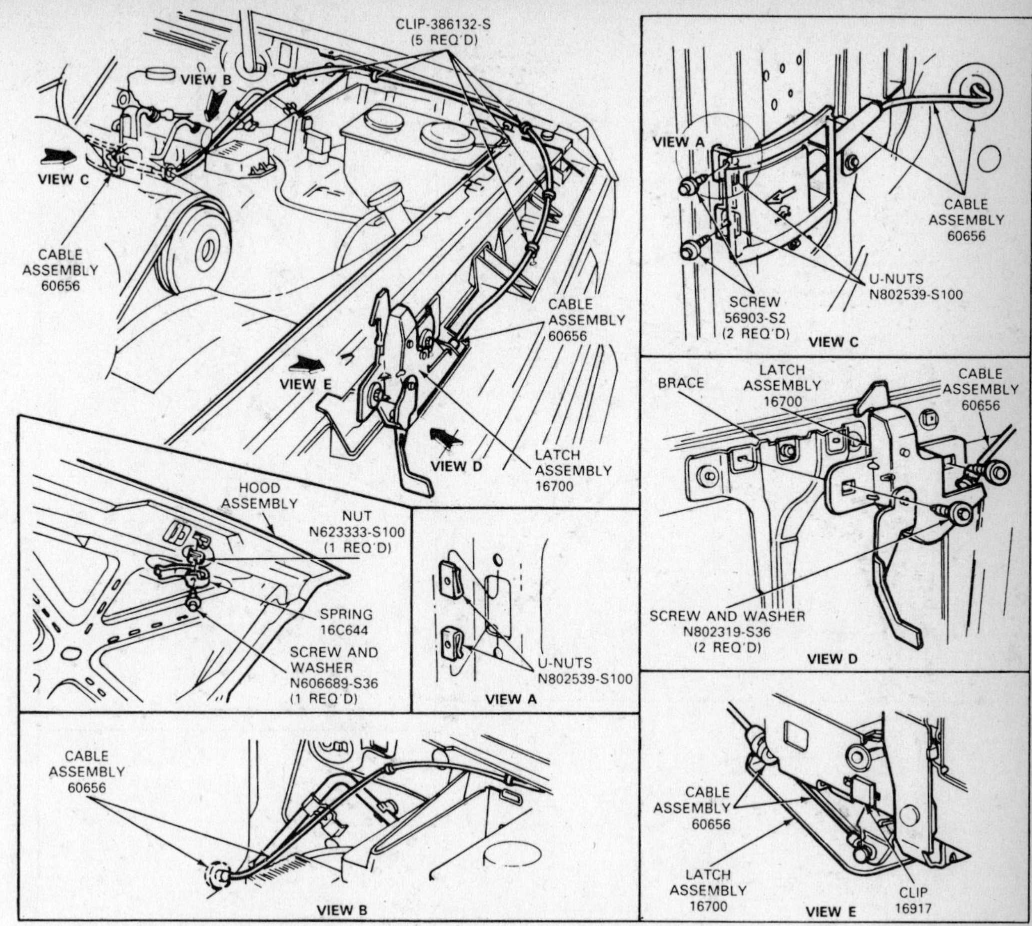

Hood latch cable and lock

3. Matchmark the hood-to-hinge position.
4. Remove the hood-to-hinge bolts and lift off the hood.
5. Installation is the reverse of removal. Loosely install the hood and align the matchmarks. Torque all bolts to 20 ft. lbs.

ADJUSTMENT

1. Open the hood and matchmark the hinge and latch positions.
2. Loosen the hinge-to-fender bolts just enough to allow movement of the hood.
3. Move the hood as required to obtain the proper fit and alignment between the hood and the top of the cowl panel. Tighten the bolts to 34 ft. lbs.
4. Loosen the 2 latch attaching bolts.
5. Loosen the hinge-to-hood bolts just enough to allow movement of the hood.
6. Move the hood forward/backward and/or side-to-side to obtain a proper hood fit.
7. Tighten the hood-to-hinge bolts to 20 ft. lbs.
8. Move the latch from side-to-side to align the latch with the striker. Torque the latch bolts.
9. Lubricate the latch and hinges and check the hood fit several times.

Tailgate

REMOVAL AND INSTALLATION

Bronco

1. Lower the tailgate.
2. Disconnect the cable at each end.
3. Disconnect the tailgate wiring at the connector.
4. Pull the wiring from the tailgate body rail.
5. Have someone support the tailgate and remove the torsion bar retainer from the body.
6. Matchmark the hinge-to-body positions and unbolt the hinges from the body.
7. Installation is the reverse of removal. Torque the hinge bolts to 11 ft. lbs.; the cable bolts to 30 ft. lbs.

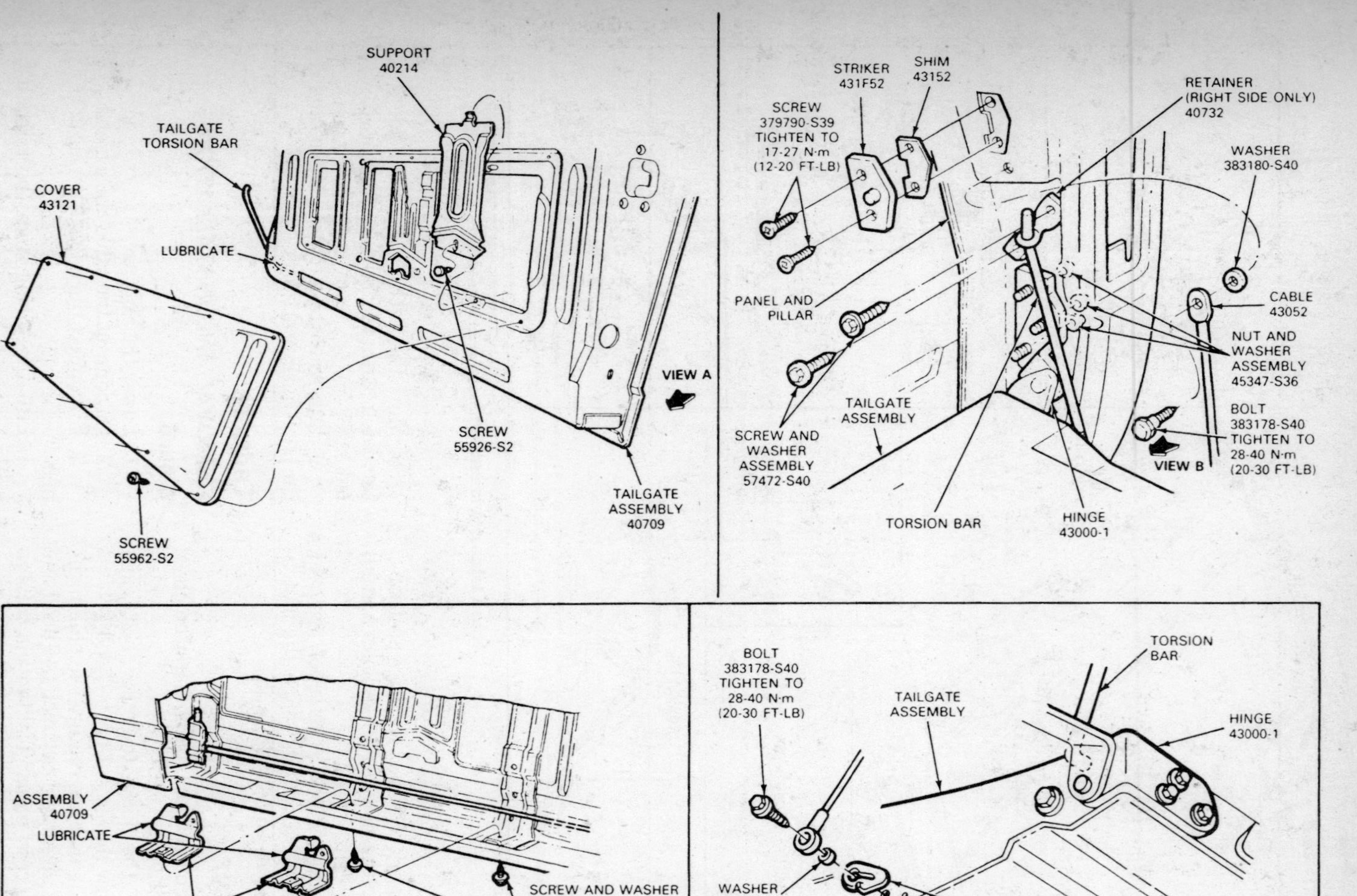

Bronco tailgate installation

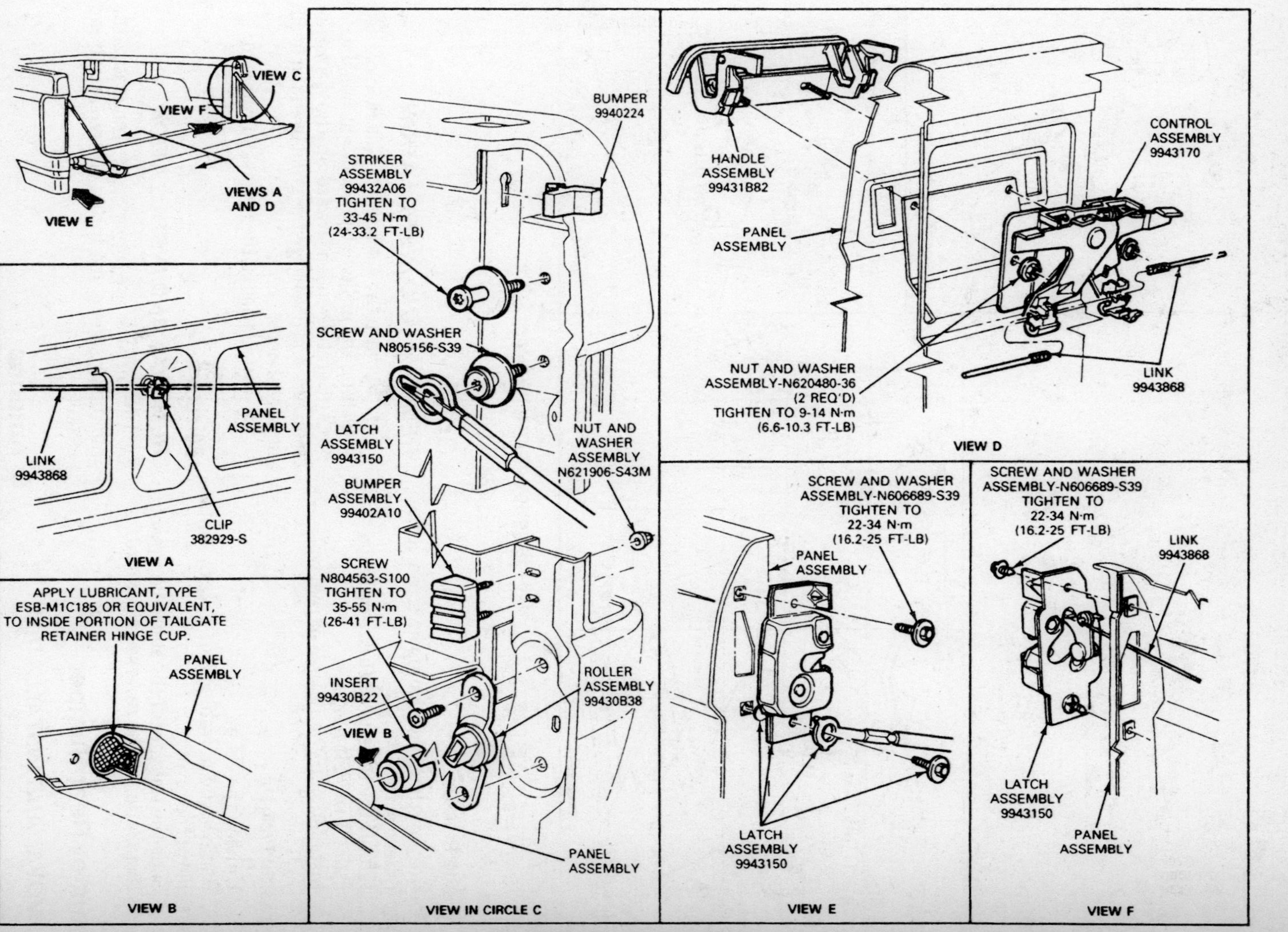

1988 Styleside pick-up tailgate

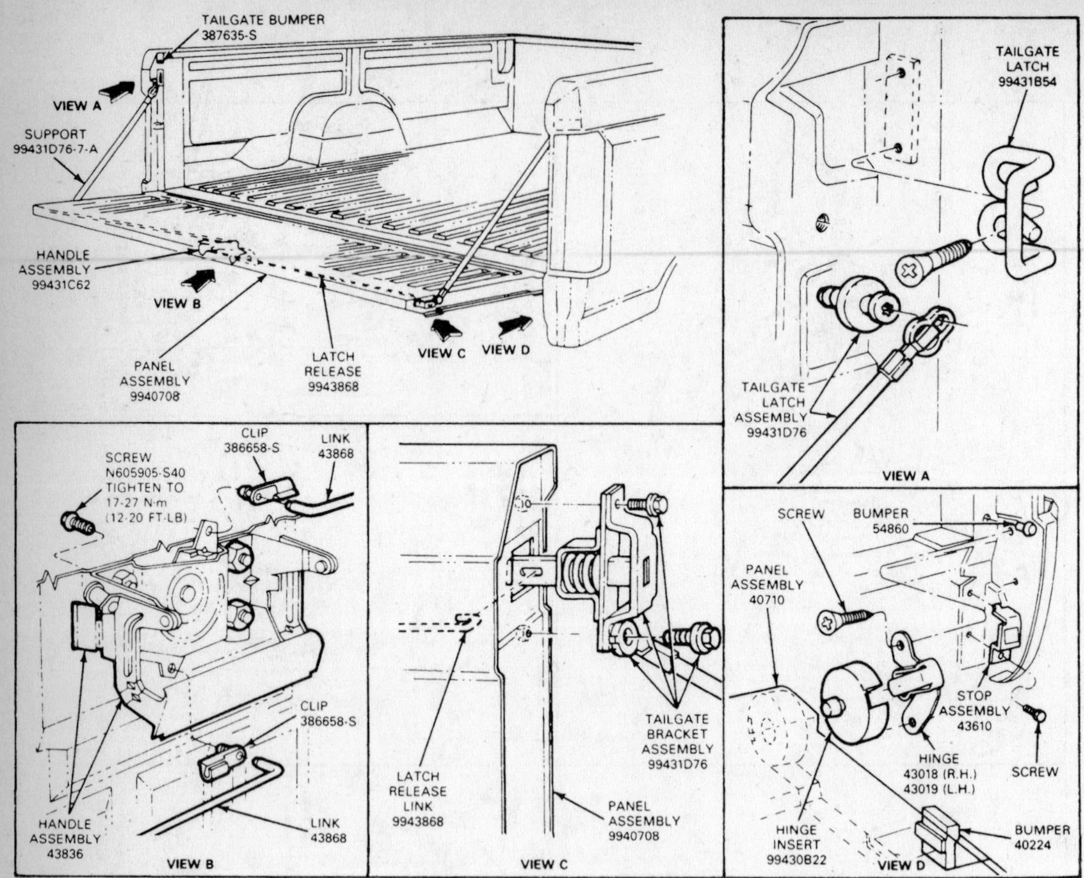

1987 Styleside pick-up tailgate

Styleside Pick-Up

1. Remove the tailgate support strap at the pillar T-head pivot.
2. Lift off the tailgate at the right hinge.
3. Pull off the left hinge.
4. Installation is the reverse of removal.

Flareside Pick-Up

1. Unhook the chain.
2. Remove the movable pivot-to-body bolts and remove the pivot.
3. Slide the tailgate off the stationary pivot.
4. Installation is the reverse of removal.

Front or Rear Bumper

REMOVAL AND INSTALLATION

1. Support the bumper.
2. Remove the nuts and bolts attaching the bumper to the frame.
3. Installation is the reverse of removal. Torque the bracket-to-frame bolts to 100 ft. lbs.

Grille

REMOVAL AND INSTALLATION

1. Remove the 4 screws, one at each corner, attaching the grille to the headlight housings.
2. Carefully push inward on the 4 snap-in retainers and disengage the grille from the headlight housings.
3. Installation is the reverse of removal.

Mirrors

REMOVAL AND INSTALLATION

All mirrors are remove by removing the mounting screws and lifting off the mirror and gasket.

Antenna

REMOVAL AND INSTALLATION

1. Disconnect the antenna cable at the radio by pulling it straight out of the set.
2. Working under the instrument panel, disengage the cable from its retainers.

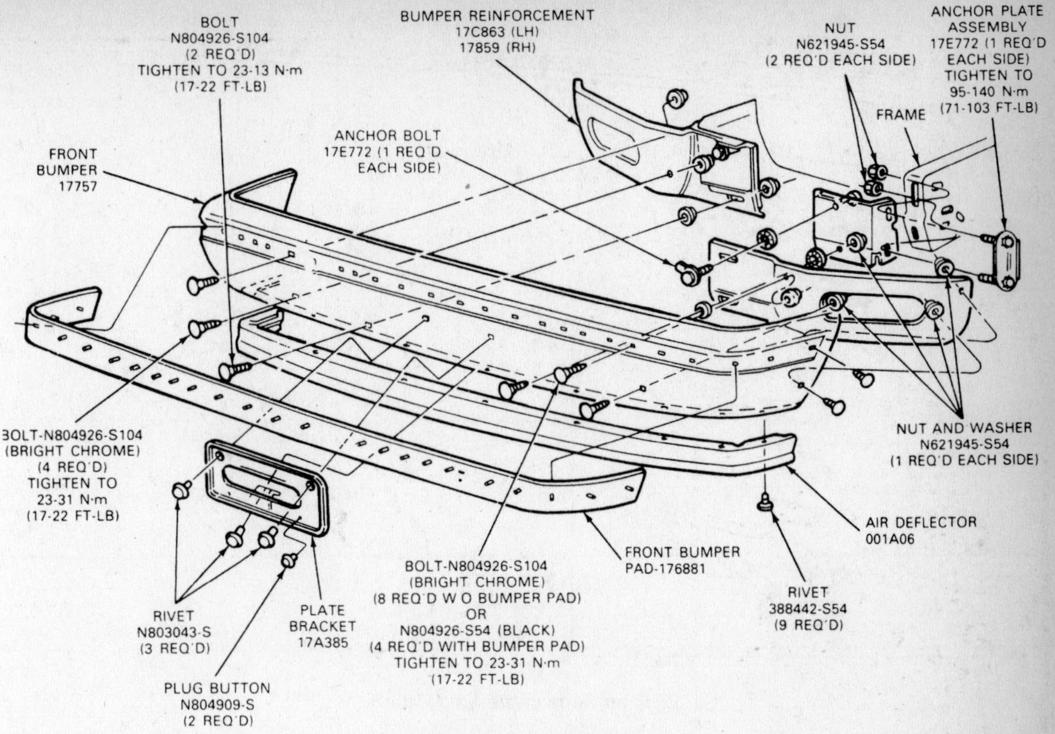

BOLT
N804926-S104
(2 REQ'D)
TIGHTEN TO 23-13 N·m
(17-22 FT-LB)
BUMPER REINFORCEMENT
17C863 (LH)
17859 (RH)
NUT
N621945-S54
(2 REQ'D EACH SIDE)
ANCHOR PLATE
ASSEMBLY
17E772 (1 REQ'D
EACH SIDE)
TIGHTEN TO
95-140 N·m
(71-103 FT-LB)
FRAME
ANCHOR BOLT
17E772 (1 REQ'D
EACH SIDE)
FRONT
BUMPER
17757
BOLT-N804926-S104
(BRIGHT CHROME)
(4 REQ'D)
TIGHTEN TO
23-31 N·m
(17-22 FT-LB)
NUT AND WASHER
N621945-S54
(1 REQ'D EACH SIDE)
AIR DEFLECTOR
001A06
FRONT BUMPER
PAD-176881
BOLT-N804926-S104
(BRIGHT CHROME)
(8 REQ'D W O BUMPER PAD)
OR
N804926-S54 (BLACK)
(4 REQ'D WITH BUMPER PAD)
TIGHTEN TO 23-31 N·m
(17-22 FT-LB)
RIVET
388442-S54
(9 REQ'D)
RIVET
N803043-S
(3 REQ'D)
PLATE
BRACKET
17A385
PLUG BUTTON
N804909-S
(2 REQ'D)

Front bumper installation

U-NUT
N800974-S100
NUT
N620484-S2
SCREW
57030-S43B
NUT-N621945-S2
23-31 N·m
(17-23 FT-LB)
LICENSE PLATE
BRACKET-13418
NUT-N620482-S2
81-122 N·m
(60-90 FT-LB)
REAR BUMPER
BRACKET
17787-C
BOLT
N605827-S2
81-122 N·m
(60-90 FT-LB)
REAR BUMPER
BOLT
N605920-S2
REAR BUMPER
BRACKET
17788-C
BOLT
N800883-S100

REAR BUMPER FLARESIDE

BUMPER
COVER
17D781
NUT AND WASHER
N620484-S2
(2 REQ'D EACH SIDE)
TIGHTEN TO
95-140 N·m
(71-103 FT-LB)
BOLT-N605827-S2
(1 REQ'D EACH SIDE)
TIGHTEN TO
95-140 N·m
(71-103 FT-LB)
NUT
N620484-S2
(3 REQ'D
EACH SIDE)
FRAME
RAIL
BOLT-N605827-S2
(2 REQ'D EACH SIDE)
TIGHTEN TO 95-140 N·m
(71-103 FT-LB)
INNER BUMPER
ARM-17787
NUT AND WASHER
N621945-S2
(1 REQ'D EACH SIDE)
TIGHTEN TO 20-27 N·m
(15-19 FT-LB)
OUTER BUMPER
ARM-17795
BUMPER
PAD
176996
BOLT
N605827-S2
(2 REQ'D EACH SIDE)
REAR BUMPER
ASSEMBLY-17775
BUMPER PAD
17914
CARRAIGE BOLT
N800883-S55
(1 REQ'D EACH SIDE)

STEP BUMPER BRONCO - ALL

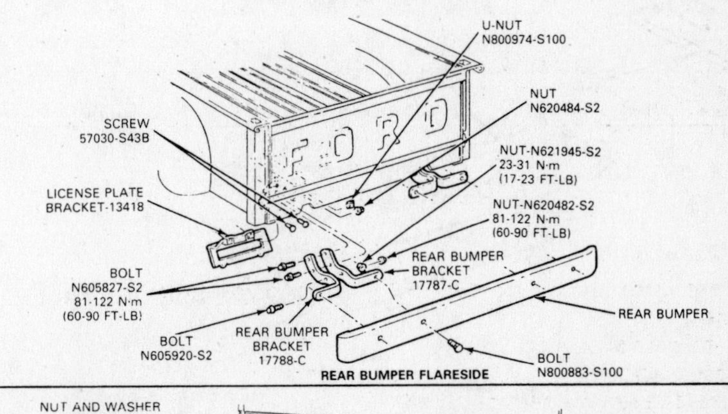

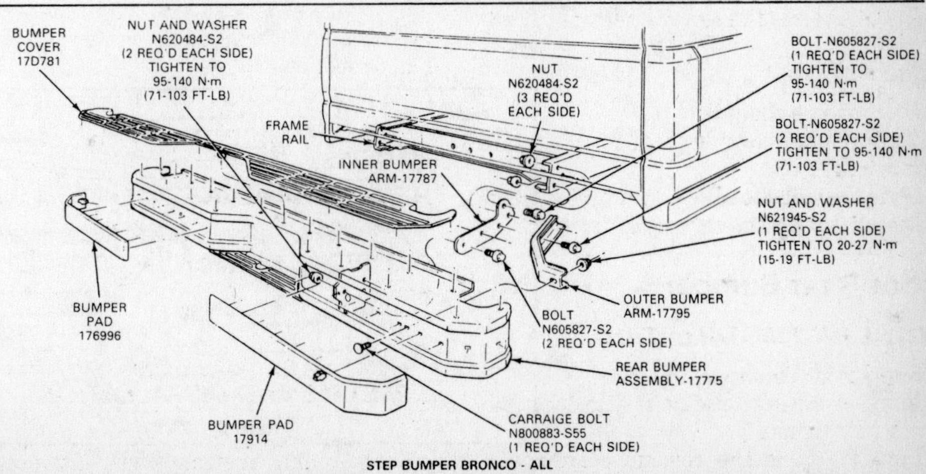

Rear bumper installation

SEE VIEW A
CABLE ASSEMBLY - 18812
ELECTRONIC
RADIO
ANTENNA

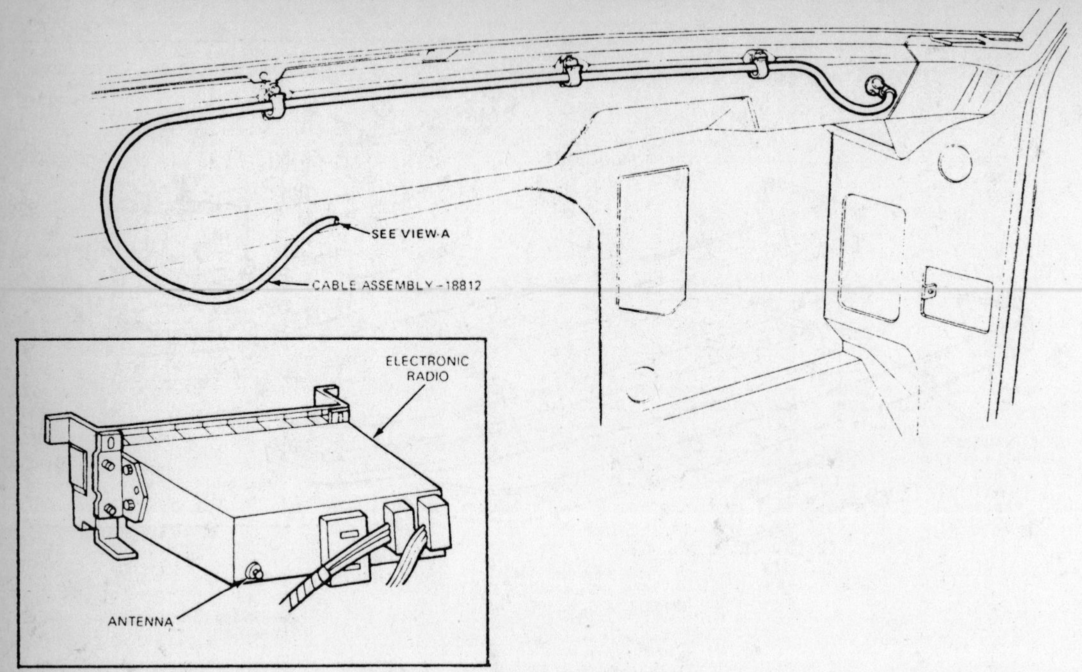

1987 antenna cable installation

PLENUM
18471
CLIP
CABLE
ASSEMBLY
18812
VIEW A
DASH
PANEL
FRONT OF VEHICLE
RADIO
RECEIVER
ASSEMBLY
CABLE
ASSEMBLY
18812
VIEW A

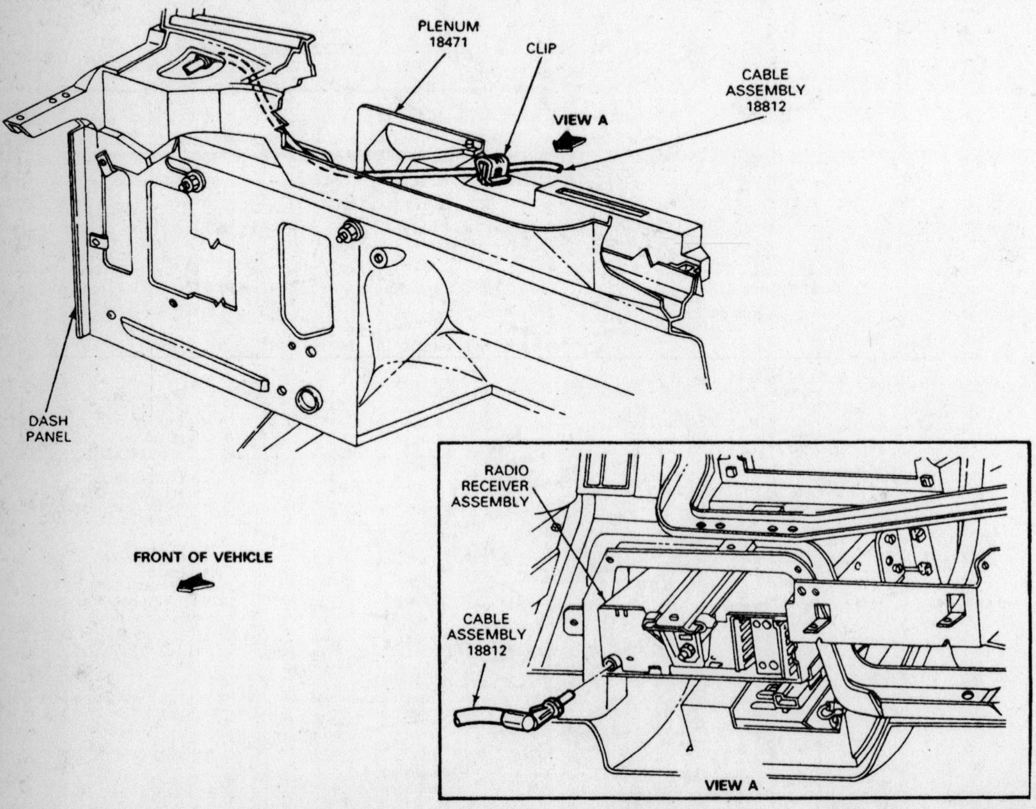

1988–90 antenna cable installation

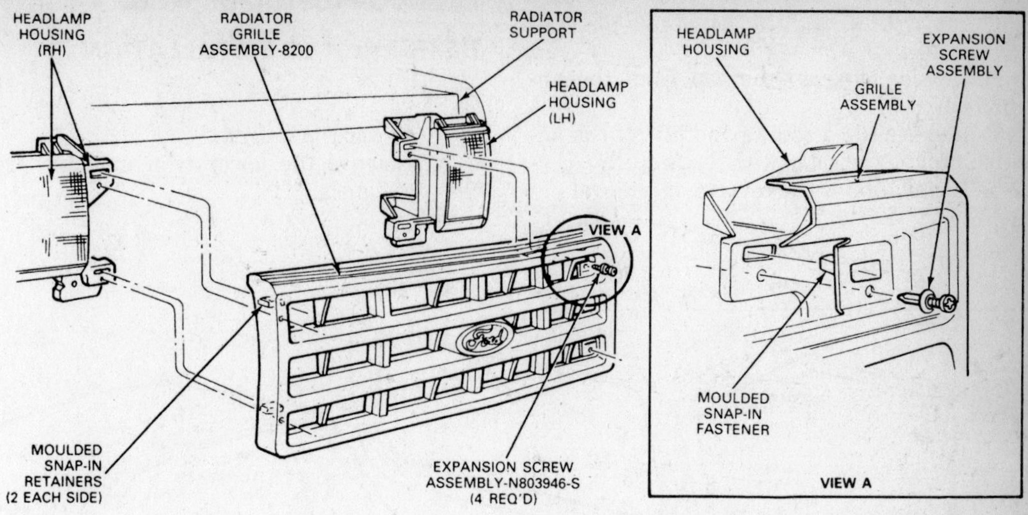

Grille installation

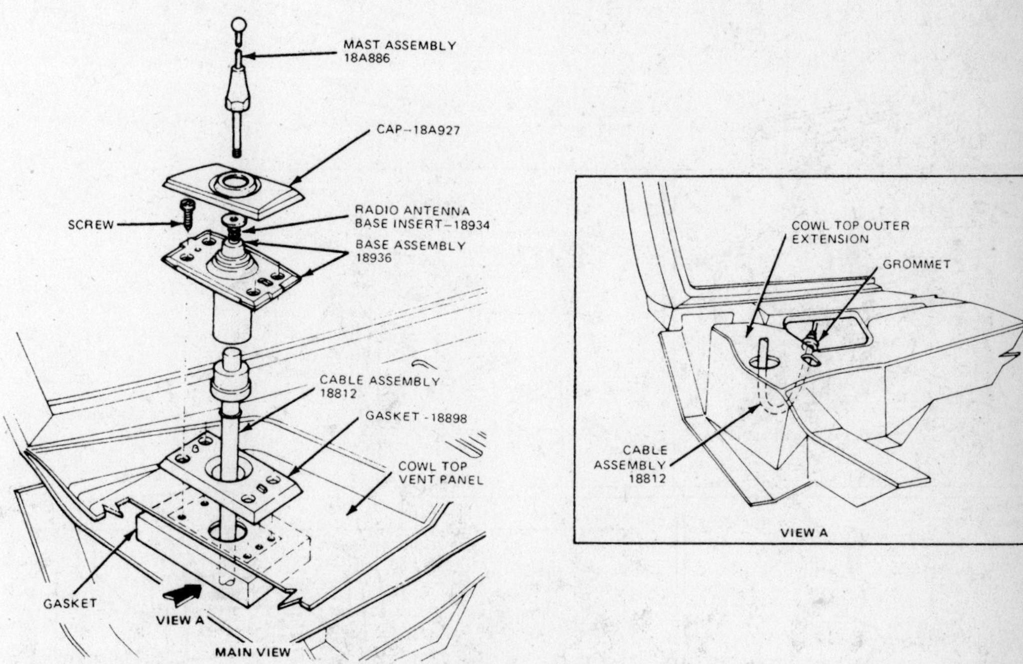

Antenna installation

NOTE: *On some models, it may be necessary to remove the instrument panel pad to get at the cable.*

3. Outside, unsnap the cap from the antenna base.
4. Remove the 4 screws and lift off the antenna, pulling the cable with it, carefully.
5. Installation is the reverse of removal.

Bronco Fiberglass Roof

REMOVAL AND INSTALLATION

Roof

1. Lower the tailgate.
2. Remove the lower trim moldings from the roof panels.

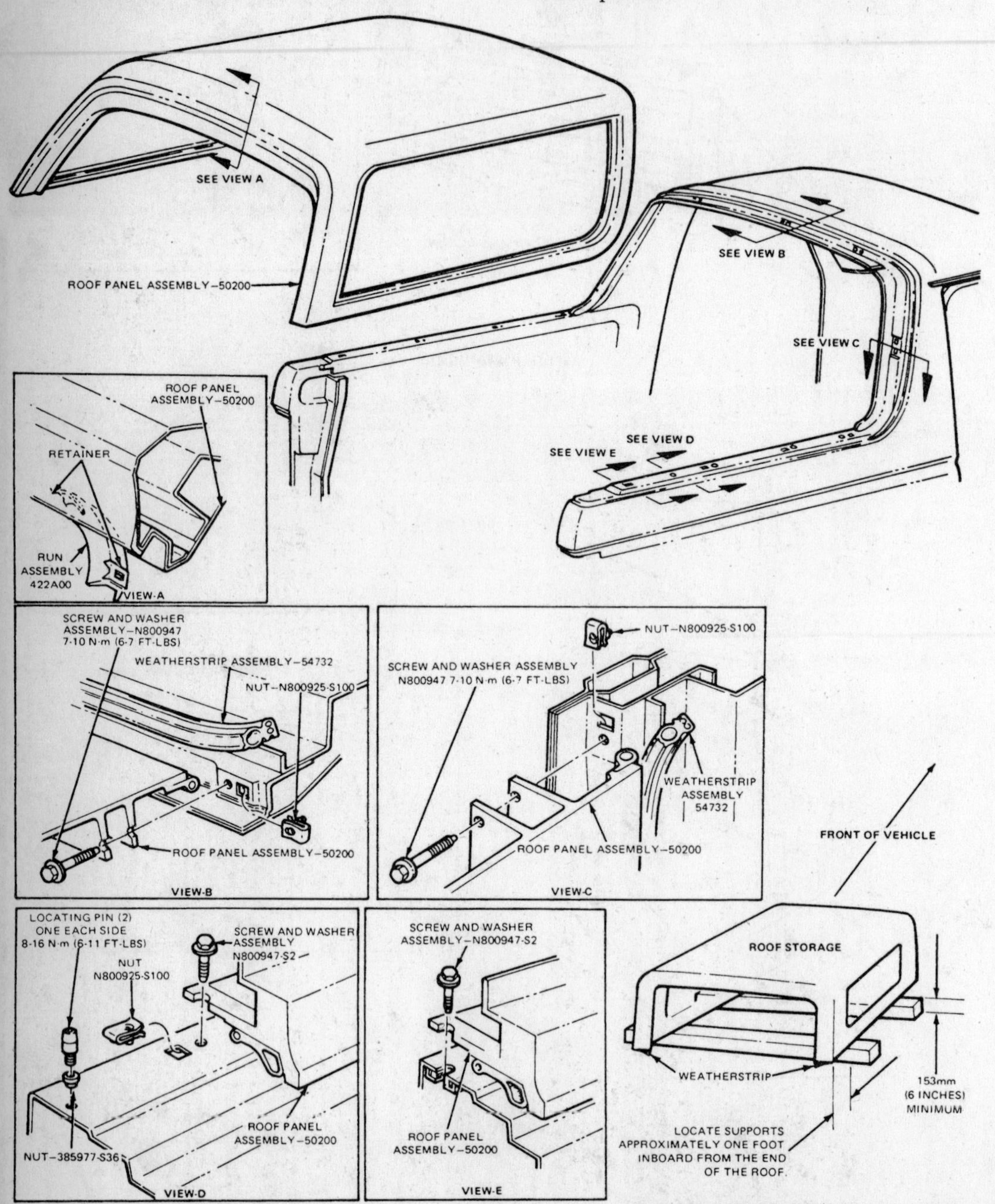

Bronco roof removal

CHILTON'S

AUTO BODY REPAIR TIPS

EASY STEP-BY-STEP TIPS FROM PROS

Tools and Materials • Step-by-Step Illustrated Procedures
How To Repair Dents, Scratches and Rust Holes
Spray Painting and Refinishing Tips

With a little practice, basic body repair procedures can be mastered by any do-it-yourself mechanic. The step-by-step repairs shown here can be applied to almost any type of auto body repair.

TOOLS & MATERIALS

You may already have basic tools, such as hammers and electric drills. Other tools unique to body repair — body hammers, grinding attachments, sanding blocks, dent puller, half-round plastic file and plastic spreaders — are relatively inexpensive and can be obtained wherever auto parts or auto body repair parts are sold. Portable air compressors and paint spray guns can be purchased or rented.

Auto Body Repair Kits

The best and most often used products are available to the do-it-yourselfer in kit form, from major manufacturers of auto body repair products. The same manufacturers also merchandise the individual products for use by pros.

Kits are available to make a wide variety of repairs, including holes, dents and scratches and fiberglass, and offer the advantage of buying the materials you'll need for the job. There is little waste or chance of materials going bad from not being used. Many kits may also contain basic body-working tools such as body files, sanding blocks and spreaders. Check the contents of the kit before buying your tools.

BODY REPAIR TIPS

Safety

Many of the products associated with auto body repair and refinishing contain toxic chemicals. Read all labels before opening containers and store them in a safe place and manner.

- Wear eye protection (safety goggles) when using power tools or when performing any operation that involves the removal of any type of material.
- Wear lung protection (disposable mask or respirator) when grinding, sanding or painting.

Sanding

1 Sand off paint before using a dent puller. When using a non-adhesive sanding disc, cover the back of the disc with an overlapping layer or two of masking tape and trim the edges. The disc will last considerably longer.

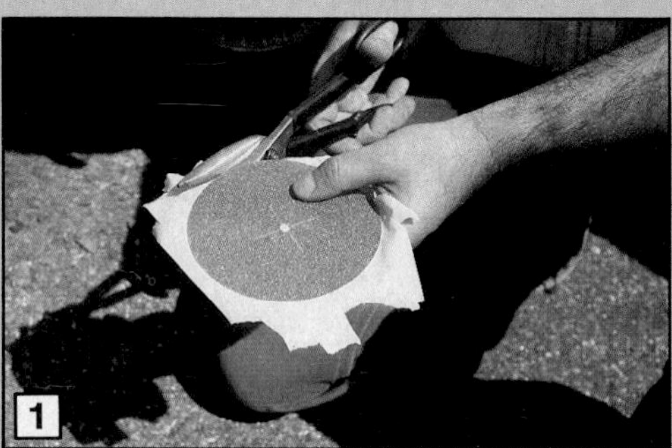
1

2 Use the circular motion of the sanding disc to grind *into* the edge of the repair. Grinding or sanding away from the jagged edge will only tear the sandpaper.

3 Use the palm of your hand flat on the panel to detect high and low spots. Do not use your fingertips. Slide your hand slowly back and forth.

3

WORKING WITH BODY FILLER

Mixing The Filler

Cleanliness and proper mixing and application are extremely important. Use a clean piece of plastic or glass or a disposable artist's palette to mix body filler.

1 Allow plenty of time and follow directions. No useful purpose will be served by adding more hardener to make it cure (set-up) faster. Less hardener means more curing time, but the mixture dries harder; more hardener means less curing time but a softer mixture.

2

2 Both the hardener and the filler should be thoroughly kneaded or stirred before mixing. Hardener should be a solid paste and dispense like thin toothpaste. Body filler should be smooth, and free of lumps or thick spots.

Getting the proper amount of hardener in the filler is the trickiest part of preparing the filler. Use the same amount of hardener in cold or warm weather. For contour filler (thick coats), a bead of hardener twice the diameter of the filler is about right. There's about a 15% margin on either side, but, if in doubt use less hardener.

2

2

3 Mix the body filler and hardener by wiping across the mixing surface, picking the mixture up and wiping it again. Colder weather requires longer mixing times. Do not mix in a circular motion; this will trap air bubbles which will become holes in the cured filler.

3

Applying The Filler

1 For best results, filler should not be applied over 1/4" thick.

Apply the filler in several coats. Build it up to above the level of the repair surface so that it can be sanded or grated down.

The first coat of filler must be pressed on with a firm wiping motion.

Apply the filler in one direction only. Working the filler back and forth will either pull it off the metal or trap air bubbles.

REPAIRING DENTS

Before you start, take a few minutes to study the damaged area. Try to visualize the shape of the panel before it was damaged. If the damage is on the left fender, look at the right fender and use it as a guide. If there is access to the panel from behind, you can reshape it with a body hammer. If not, you'll have to use a dent puller. Go slowly and work the metal a little at a time. Get the panel as straight as possible before applying filler.

1 This dent is typical of one that can be pulled out or hammered out from behind. Remove the headlight cover, headlight assembly and turn signal housing.

2 Drill a series of holes 1/2 the size of the end of the dent puller along the stress line. Make some trial pulls and assess the results. If necessary, drill more holes and try again. Do not hurry.

3 If possible, use a body hammer and block to shape the metal back to its original contours. Get the metal back as close to its original shape as possible. Don't depend on body filler to fill dents.

4 Using an 80-grit grinding disc on an electric drill, grind the paint from the surrounding area down to bare metal. Use a new grinding pad to prevent heat buildup that will warp metal.

5 The area should look like this when you're finished grinding. Knock the drill holes in and tape over small openings to keep plastic filler out.

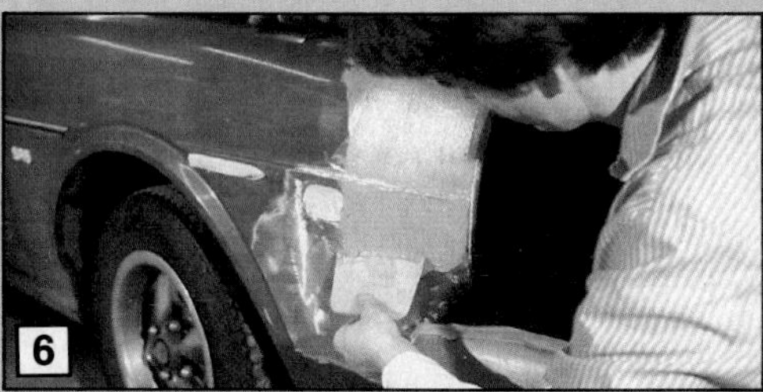

6 Mix the body filler (see Body Repair Tips). Spread the body filler evenly over the entire area (see Body Repair Tips). Be sure to cover the area completely.

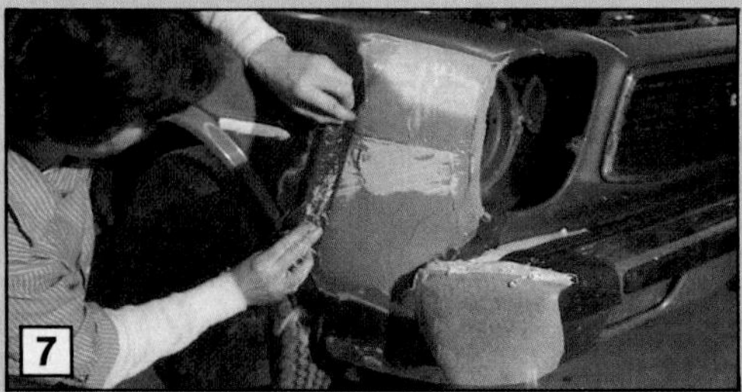

7 Let the body filler dry until the surface can just be scratched with your fingernail. Knock the high spots from the body filler with a body file ("Cheesegrater"). Check frequently with the palm of your hand for high and low spots.

8 Check to be sure that trim pieces that will be installed later will fit exactly. Sand the area with 40-grit paper.

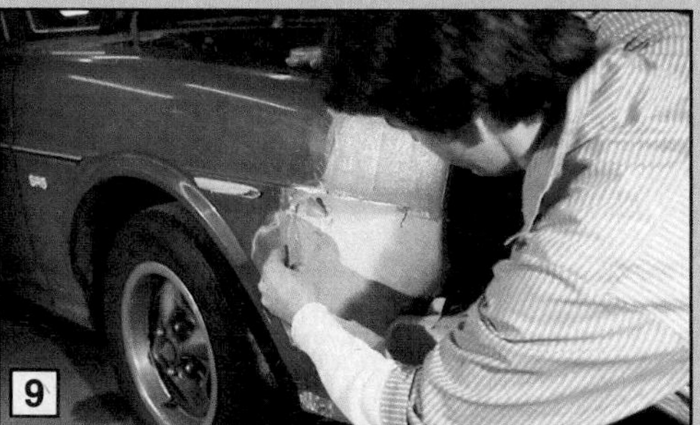

9 If you wind up with low spots, you may have to apply another layer of filler.

10 Knock the high spots off with 40-grit paper. When you are satisfied with the contours of the repair, apply a thin coat of filler to cover pin holes and scratches.

11 Block sand the area with 40-grit paper to a smooth finish. Pay particular attention to body lines and ridges that must be well-defined.

12 Sand the area with 400 paper and then finish with a scuff pad. The finished repair is ready for priming and painting (see Painting Tips).

Materials and photos courtesy of Ritt Jones Auto Body, Prospect Park, PA.

REPAIRING RUST HOLES

There are many ways to repair rust holes. The fiberglass cloth kit shown here is one of the most cost efficient for the owner because it provides a strong repair that resists cracking and moisture and is relatively easy to use. It can be used on large and small holes (with or without backing) and can be applied over contoured areas. Remember, however, that short of replacing an entire panel, no repair is a guarantee that the rust will not return.

1 Remove any trim that will be in the way. Clean away all loose debris. Cut away all the rusted metal. But be sure to leave enough metal to retain the contour or body shape.

2 Grind away all traces of rust with a 24-grit grinding disc. Be sure to grind back 3-4 inches from the edge of the hole down to bare metal and be sure all traces of paint, primer and rust are removed.

3 Block sand the area with 80 or 100 grit sandpaper to get a clear, shiny surface and feathered paint edge. Tap the edges of the hole inward with a ball peen hammer.

4 If you are going to use release film, cut a piece about 2-3″ larger than the area you have sanded. Place the film over the repair and mark the sanded area on the film. Avoid any unnecessary wrinkling of the film.

5 Cut 2 pieces of fiberglass matte to match the shape of the repair. One piece should be about 1″ smaller than the sanded area and the second piece should be 1″ smaller than the first. Mix enough filler and hardener to saturate the fiberglass material (see Body Repair Tips).

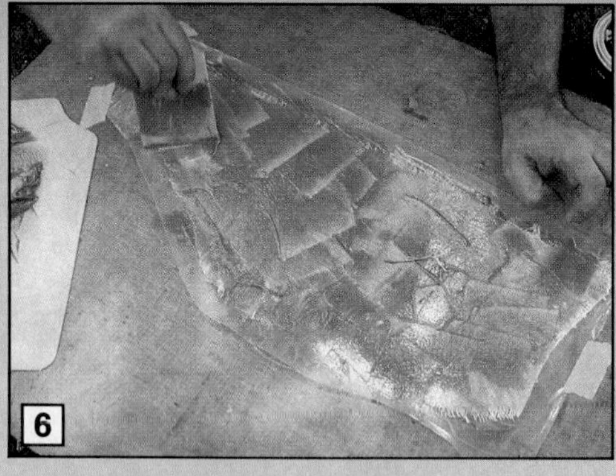

6 Lay the release sheet on a flat surface and spread an even layer of filler, large enough to cover the repair. Lay the smaller piece of fiberglass cloth in the center of the sheet and spread another layer of filler over the fiberglass cloth. Repeat the operation for the larger piece of cloth.

7 Place the repair material over the repair area, with the release film facing outward. Use a spreader and work from the center outward to smooth the material, following the body contours. Be sure to remove all air bubbles.

8 Wait until the repair has dried tack-free and peel off the release sheet. The ideal working temperature is 60°-90° F. Cooler or warmer temperatures or high humidity may require additional curing time. Wait longer, if in doubt.

9

9 Sand and feather-edge the entire area. The initial sanding can be done with a sanding disc on an electric drill if care is used. Finish the sanding with a block sander. Low spots can be filled with body filler; this may require several applications.

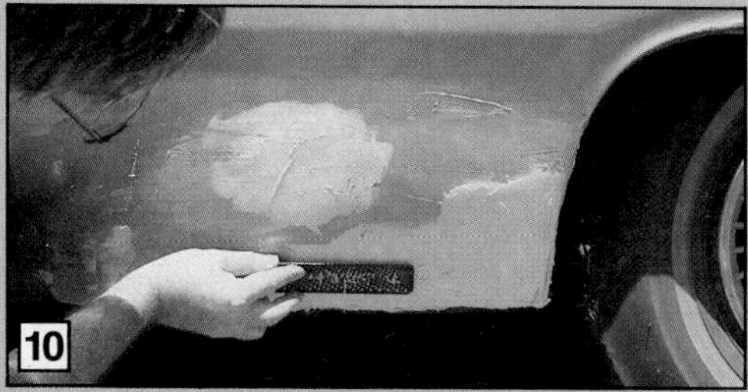

10

10 When the filler can just be scratched with a fingernail, knock the high spots down with a body file and smooth the entire area with 80-grit. Feather the filled areas into the surrounding areas.

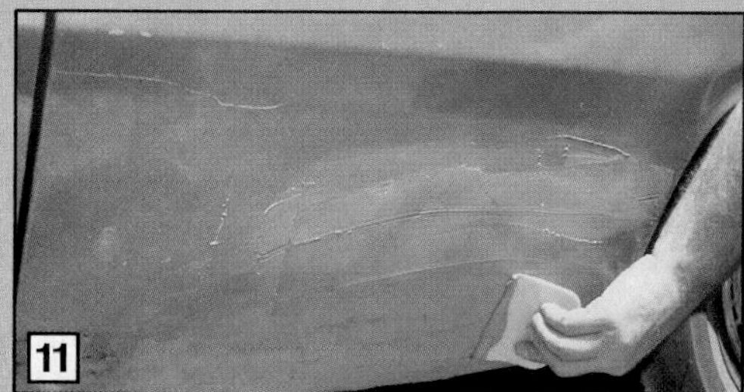

11

11 When the area is sanded smooth, mix some topcoat and hardener and apply it directly with a spreader. This will give a smooth finish and prevent the glass matte from showing through the paint.

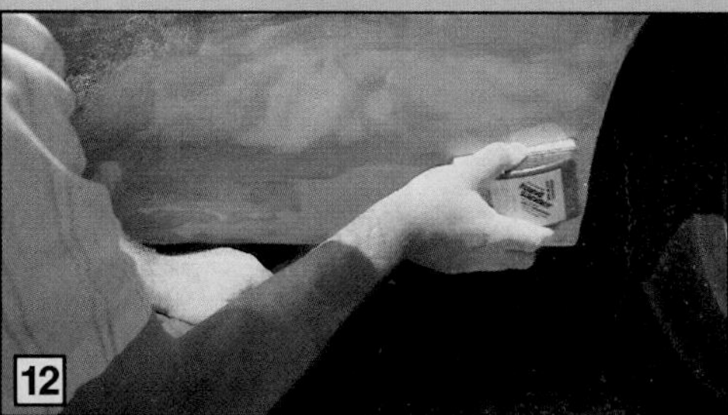

12

12 Block sand the topcoat smooth with finishing sandpaper (200 grit), and 400 grit. The repair is ready for masking, priming and painting (see Painting Tips).

Materials and photos courtesy Marson Corporation, Chelsea, Massachusetts

PAINTING TIPS

Preparation

1 SANDING — Use a 400 or 600 grit wet or dry sandpaper. Wet-sand the area with a 1/4 sheet of sandpaper soaked in clean water. Keep the paper wet while sanding. Sand the area until the repaired area tapers into the original finish.

2 CLEANING — Wash the area to be painted thoroughly with water and a clean rag. Rinse it thoroughly and wipe the surface dry until you're sure it's completely free of dirt, dust, fingerprints, wax, detergent or other foreign matter.

3 MASKING — Protect any areas you don't want to overspray by covering them with masking tape and newspaper. Be careful not get fingerprints on the area to be painted.

4 PRIMING — All exposed metal should be primed before painting. Primer protects the metal and provides an excellent surface for paint adhesion. When the primer is dry, wet-sand the area again with 600 grit wet-sandpaper. Clean the area again after sanding.

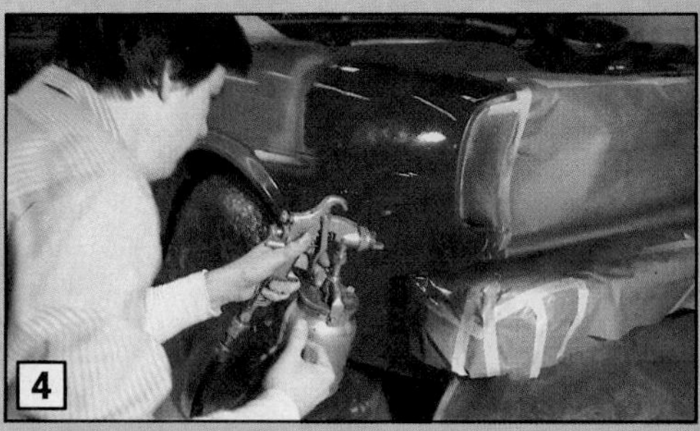

4

Painting Techniques

Paint applied from either a spray gun or a spray can (for small areas) will provide good results. Experiment on an old piece of metal to get the right combination before you begin painting.

SPRAYING VISCOSITY (SPRAY GUN ONLY) — Paint should be thinned to spraying viscosity according to the directions on the can. Use only the recommended thinner or reducer and the same amount of reduction regardless of temperature.

AIR PRESSURE (SPRAY GUN ONLY) — This is extremely important. Be sure you are using the proper recommended pressure.

TEMPERATURE — The surface to be painted should be approximately the same temperature as the surrounding air. Applying warm paint to a cold surface, or vice versa, will completely upset the paint characteristics.

THICKNESS — Spray with smooth strokes. In general, the thicker the coat of paint, the longer the drying time. Apply several thin coats about 30 seconds apart. The paint should remain wet long enough to flow out and no longer; heavier coats will only produce sags or wrinkles. Spray a light (fog) coat, followed by heavier color coats.

DISTANCE — The ideal spraying distance is 8″-12″ from the gun or can to the surface. Shorter distances will produce ripples, while greater distances will result in orange peel, dry film and poor color match and loss of material due to overspray.

OVERLAPPING — The gun or can should be kept at right angles to the surface at all times. Work to a wet edge at an even speed, using a 50% overlap and direct the center of the spray at the lower or nearest edge of the previous stroke.

RUBBING OUT (BLENDING) FRESH PAINT — Let the paint dry thoroughly. Runs or imperfections can be sanded out, primed and repainted.

Don't be in too big a hurry to remove the masking. This only produces paint ridges. When the finish has dried for at least a week, apply a small amount of fine grade rubbing compound with a clean, wet cloth. Use lots of water and blend the new paint with the surrounding area.

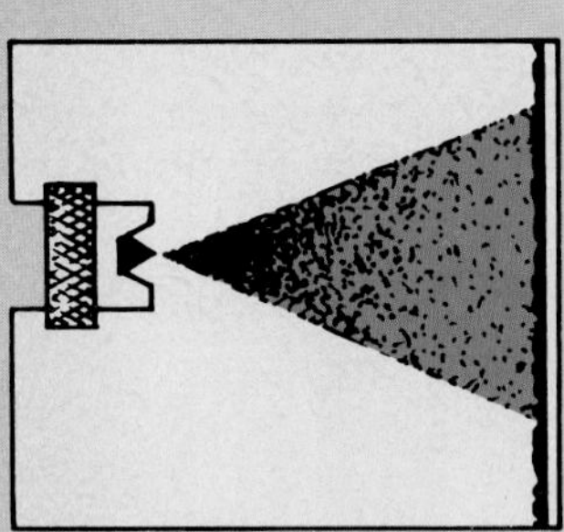

WRONG

Thin coat. Stroke too fast, not enough overlap, gun too far away.

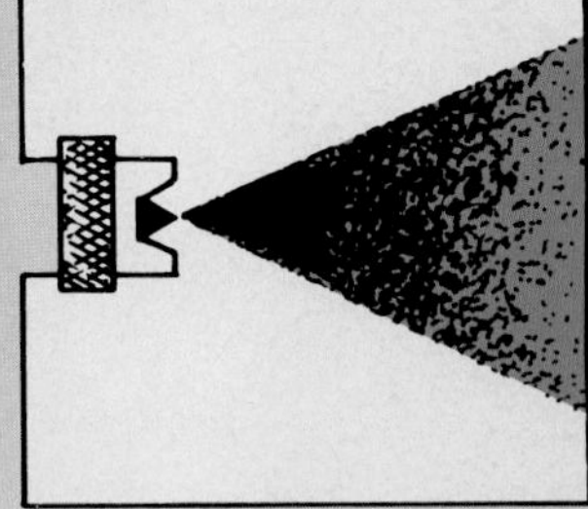

CORRECT

Medium coat. Proper distance, good stroke, proper overlap.

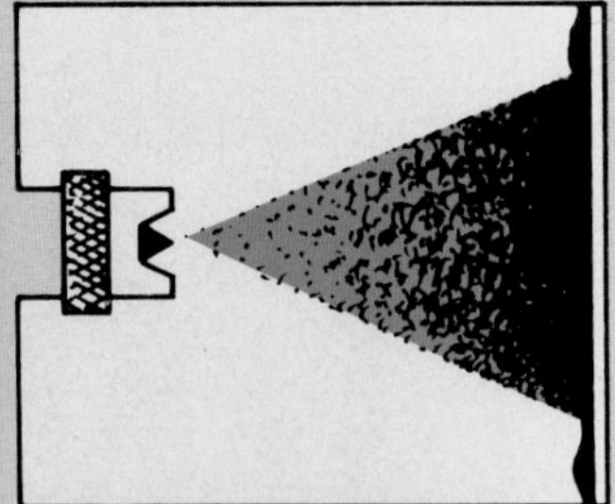

WRONG

Heavy coat. Stroke too slow, too much overlap, gun too close.

3. Scribe the locations of each trim molding bracket and number each bracket as it is removed.

4. Remove all the roof attaching bolts and trim bolts.

5. With at least one other person, carefully lift the roof off of the body. Be careful to avoid tearing the weatherstripping. Be careful to avoid over-flexing the roof. The roof weighs about 120 lb.

6. Installation is the reverse of removal. Torque the roof retaining bolts to 72–84 inch lbs.

Stationary Window

NOTE: *You'll need an assistant for this job.*

1. Have your assistant stand outside and support the glass.

2. Working from the inside truck, start at one upper corner and work the weatherstripping across the top of the glass, pulling the weatherstripping down and pushing outward on the glass until your assistant can grab the glass and lift it out.

3. Remove the moldings.

4. Remove the weatherstripping from the glass.

To install:

5. Clean the weatherstripping, glass and glass opening with solvent to remove all old sealer.

6. Apply liquid butyl sealer C9AZ–19554–B, or equivalent, in the glass channel of the weatherstripping and install the weatherstripping on the glass.

7. Install the moldings.

8. Apply a bead of sealer to the opening flange and in the inner flange crevice of the weatherstripping lip.

9. Place a length of strong cord, such as butcher's twine, in the flange crevice of the weatherstripping. The cord should go all the way around the weatherstripping with the ends, about 18 in. (457mm) long each, hanging down together at the bottom center of the window.

10. Apply soapy water to the weatherstripping lip.

11. Have your assistant position the window assembly in the channel from the outside, applying firm inward pressure.

12. From inside, you guide the lip of the weatherstripping into place using the cord, working each end alternately, until the window is locked in place.

13. Remove the cord, clean the glass and weatherstripping of excess sealer and leak test the window.

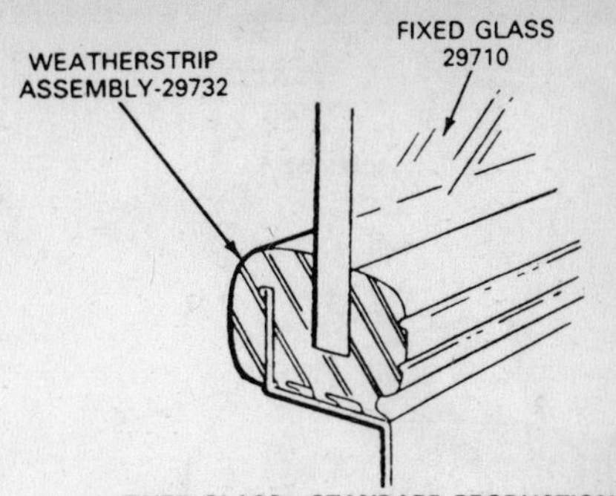

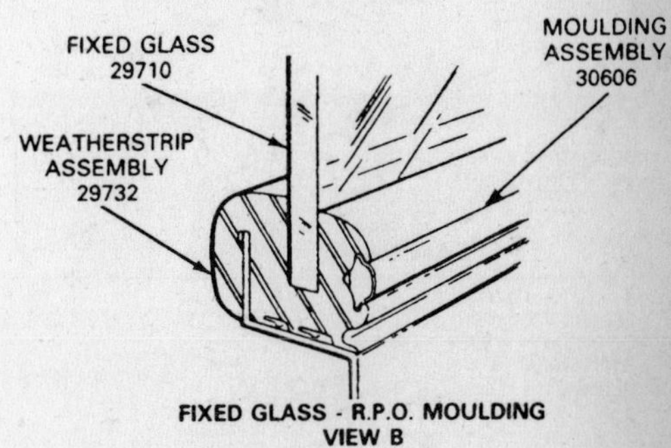

Fixed window installation

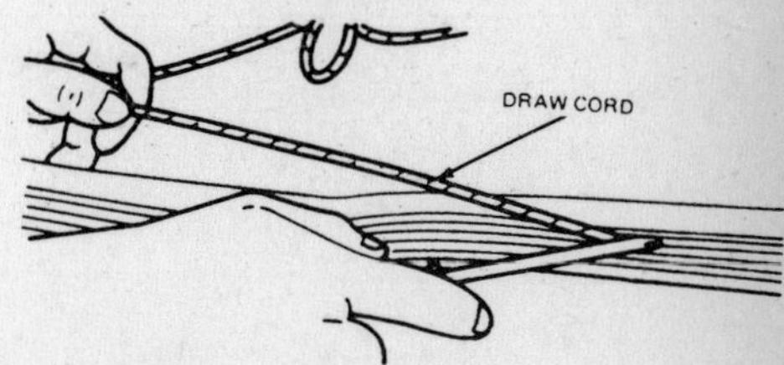

Draw cord use

INTERIOR

Door Trim Panels

REMOVAL AND INSTALLATION

1. Remove the armrest.

2. Remove the door handle screw and pull off the handle.

3. On models with manual windows, remove the window regulator handle screw and pull off the handle.

On models with power windows, remove the power window switch housing.

4. On models with manual door locks, remove the door lock control.

On models with power door locks, remove the power door lock switch housing.

5. On models with electric outside rear view mirrors, remove the power mirror switch housing.

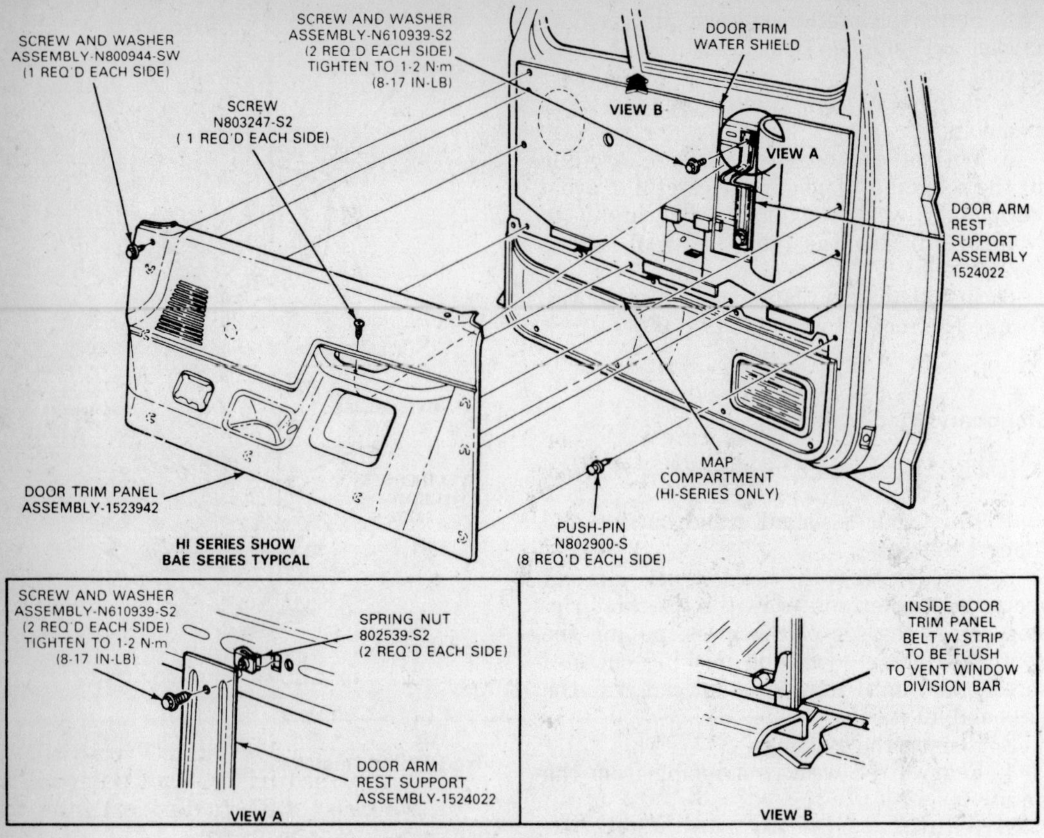

SCREW AND WASHER ASSEMBLY-N800944-SW (1 REQ'D EACH SIDE)
SCREW AND WASHER ASSEMBLY-N610939-S2 (2 REQ D EACH SIDE) TIGHTEN TO 1-2 N·m (8-17 IN-LB)
SCREW N803247-S2 (1 REQ'D EACH SIDE)
DOOR TRIM WATER SHIELD
VIEW B
VIEW A
DOOR ARM REST SUPPORT ASSEMBLY 1524022
MAP COMPARTMENT (HI-SERIES ONLY)
DOOR TRIM PANEL ASSEMBLY-1523942
PUSH-PIN N802900-S (8 REQ'D EACH SIDE)
HI SERIES SHOW BAE SERIES TYPICAL
SCREW AND WASHER ASSEMBLY-N610939-S2 (2 REQ'D EACH SIDE) TIGHTEN TO 1-2 N·m (8-17 IN-LB)
SPRING NUT 802539-S2 (2 REQ'D EACH SIDE)
DOOR ARM REST SUPPORT ASSEMBLY-1524022
VIEW A
INSIDE DOOR TRIM PANEL BELT W STRIP TO BE FLUSH TO VENT WINDOW DIVISION BAR
VIEW B

Door trim panel installation

TO FRONT OF BODY
SCREW 389404-S2
ARM REST ASSEMBLY 24140
CUP–22634
DOOR ARM REST CLIP 24146
REAR DOOR TRIM PANEL 27440
SCREW N800482-S2
VIEW A
PUSH PIN N801925-C
REAR DOOR TRIM PANEL 27440
PUSH PIN N801925-C
VIEW A

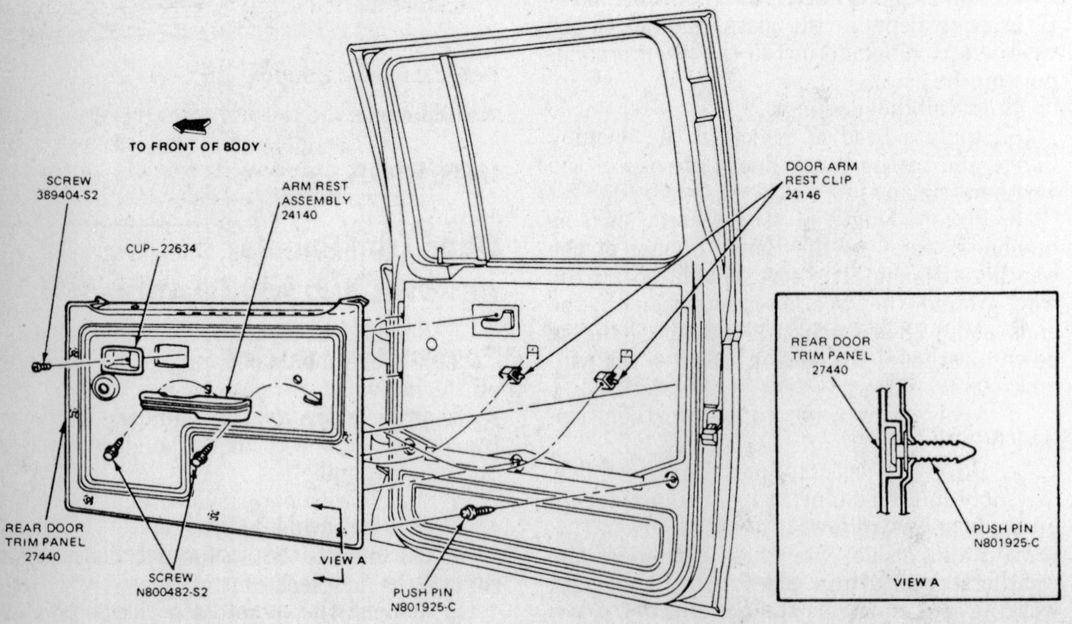

F-350 Crew Cab rear door trim panel installation

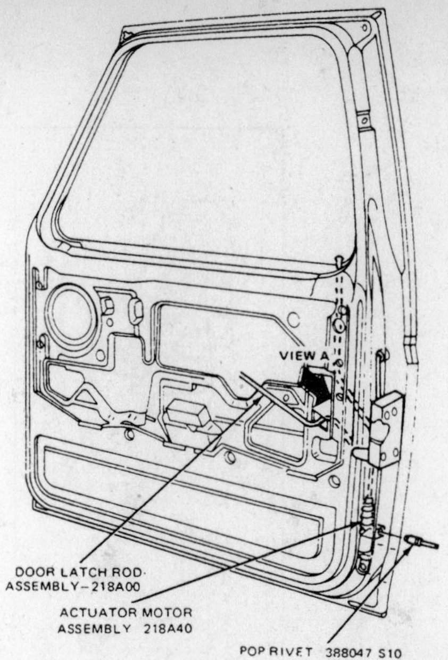

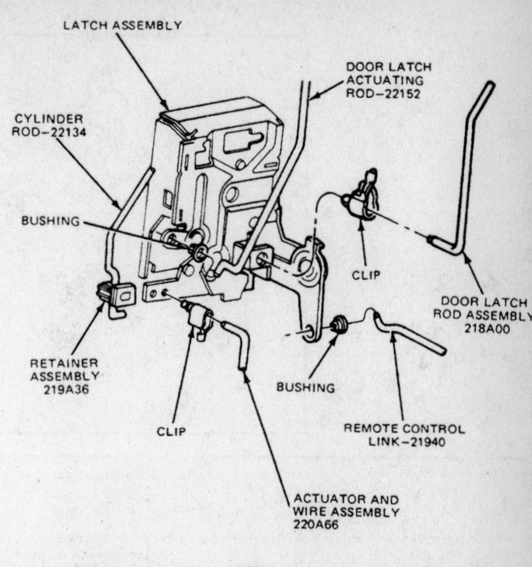

Electric door lock installation

6. Using a flat wood spatula, insert it carefully behind the panel and slide it along to find the push-pins. When you encounter a pin, pry the pin outward. Do this until all the pins are out. NEVER PULL ON THE PANEL TO REMOVE THE PINS!
7. Installation is the reverse of removal.

Manual Door Locks

REMOVAL AND INSTALLATION

Front Door Latch

ALL MODELS

1. Remove the door trim panel and watershield.
2. Disconnect the rods from the handle and lock cylinder, and from the remote control assembly.
3. Remove the latch assembly attaching screws and remove the latch from the door.
4. Installation is the reverse of removal.

Rear Door Latch

F-350 CREW CAB

1. Remove the door trim panel and watershield.
2. Disconnect the rods from the handle and lock cylinder, and from the remote control assembly.
3. Remove the latch assembly attaching screws and remove the latch from the door.
4. Installation is the reverse of removal.

Door Lock Cylinder

1. Place the window in the UP position.
2. Remove the trim panel and watershield.
3. Disconnect the actuating rod from the lock control link clip.
4. Slide the retainer away from the lock cylinder.
5. Pull the cylinder from the door.
6. Installation is the reverse of removal.

Tailgate Lock Cylinder

1. Remove the tailgate access cover.
2. Raise the glass. If the glass can't be raised, remove it as described below.
3. Remove the lock cylinder retainer.
4. Disengage the lock cylinder from the switch and remove it from the tailgate.
5. Installation is the reverse of removal.

Power Door Locks

REMOVAL AND INSTALLATION

Actuator Motor

1. Remove the door trim panel.
2. Disconnect the motor from the door latch.
3. Remove the motor and swivel bracket from the door by drilling out the pop rivet.
4. Disconnect the wiring harness.
5. Installation is the reverse of removal. Make sure that the pop rivet is tight.

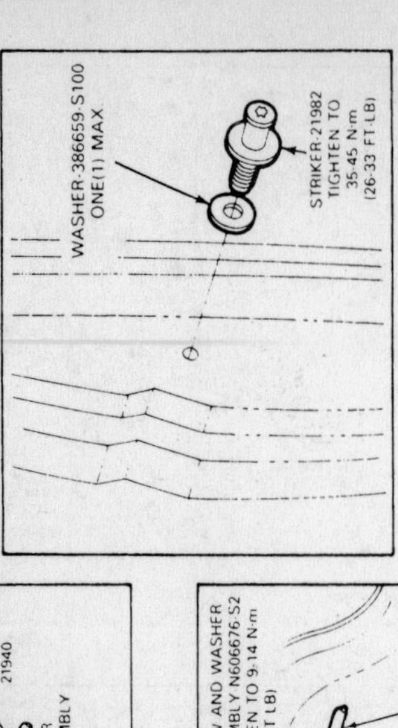

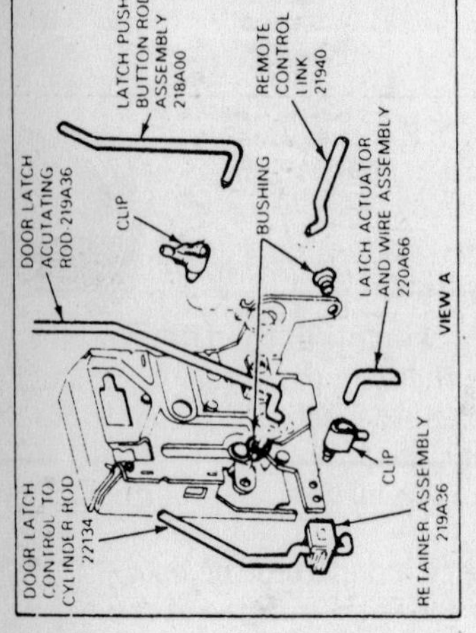

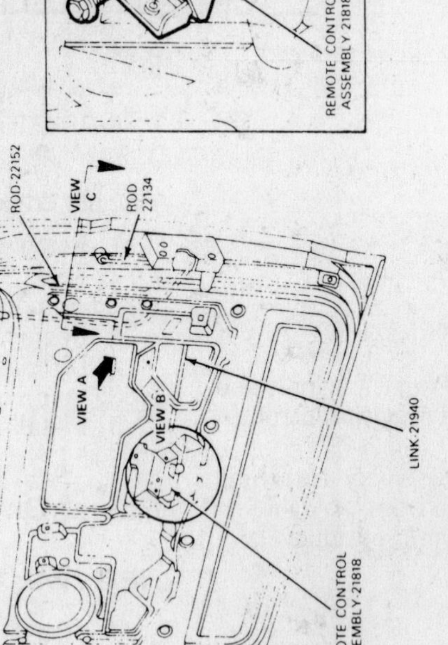

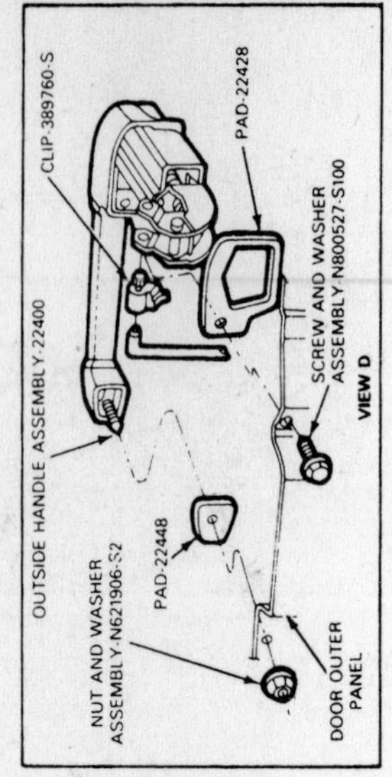

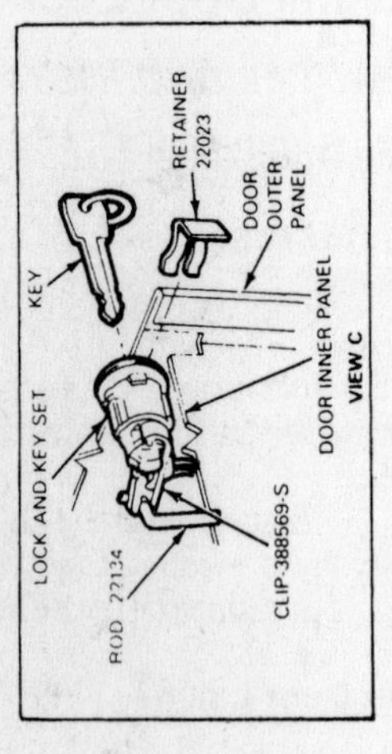

Door latch installation

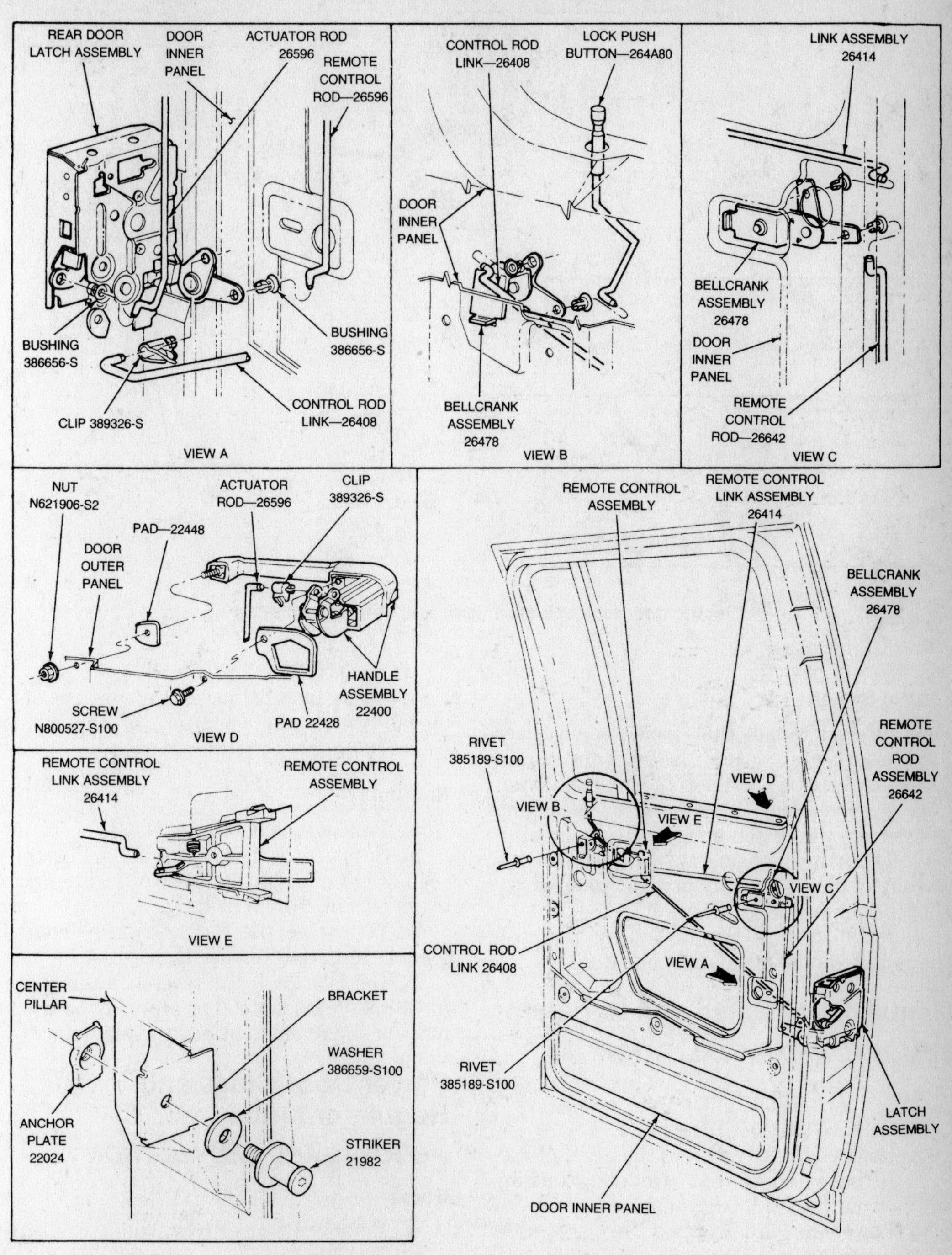

F-350 Crew Cab rear door latch installation

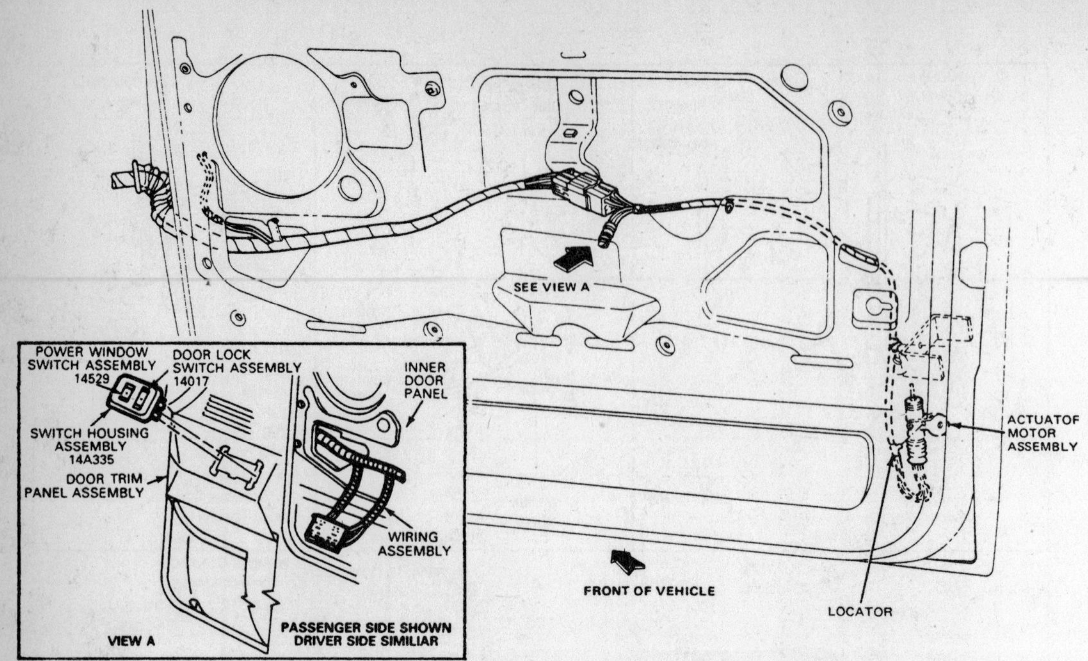

Electric door lock actuator motor and control switch wiring

Control Switch

1. Insert a small, thin-bladed screwdriver into the spring tab slots at the front and rear of the switch housing, and pop the housing out.
2. Remove the 3 connector attaching screws from the switch housing.
3. The switch is held in place by the electrical contact pins. Carefully pry the switch away from the connector to remove it.
4. Installation is the reverse of removal. The switch can be install only one way.

Manual Door Glass and Regulator

REMOVAL AND INSTALLATION

Glass

1. Remove the door trim panel.
2. Remove the screw from the division bar.
3. Remove the 2 vent window attaching screws from the front edge of the door.
4. Lower the glass and pull the glass out of the run retainer near the vent window division bar, just enough to allow the removal of the vent window.
5. Push the front edge of the glass downward and remove it from the door.
6. Remove the glass from the channel using Glass and Channel Removal Tool 2900, made by the Sommer and Mala Glass Machine Co. of Chicago, ILL., or its equivalent.
7. Glass installation is the reverse of removal. Check the operation of the window before installing the trim panel.

Regulator

1. Remove the door trim panel.
2. Support the glass in the full UP position.
3. Drill out the regulator attaching rivets using a $^1/_4$ in. (6mm) drill bit.
4. Disengage the regulator arm from the glass bracket and remove the regulator.
5. Installation is the reverse of removal. $^1/_4$ in.–20 × $^1/_2$ in. bolts and nuts may be used in place of the rivets to attach the regulator.

Power Door Glass and Regulator Motor

REMOVAL AND INSTALLATION

Glass

1. Remove the door trim panel.
2. Remove the screw from the division bar.
3. Remove the 2 vent window attaching screws from the front edge of the door.
4. Lower the glass and pull the glass out of the run retainer near the vent window division bar, just enough to allow the removal of the vent window.
5. Push the front edge of the glass downward and remove it from the door.

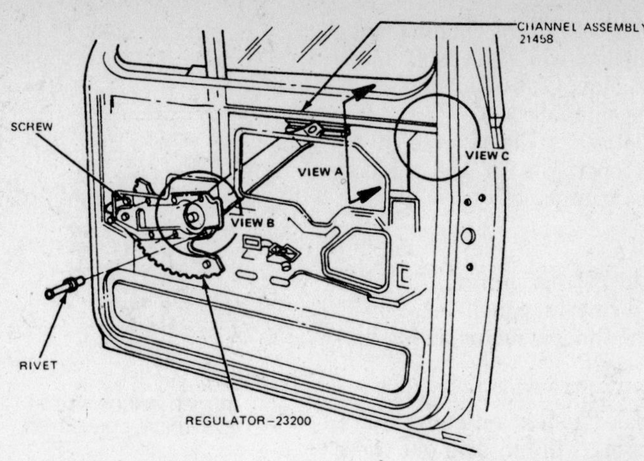

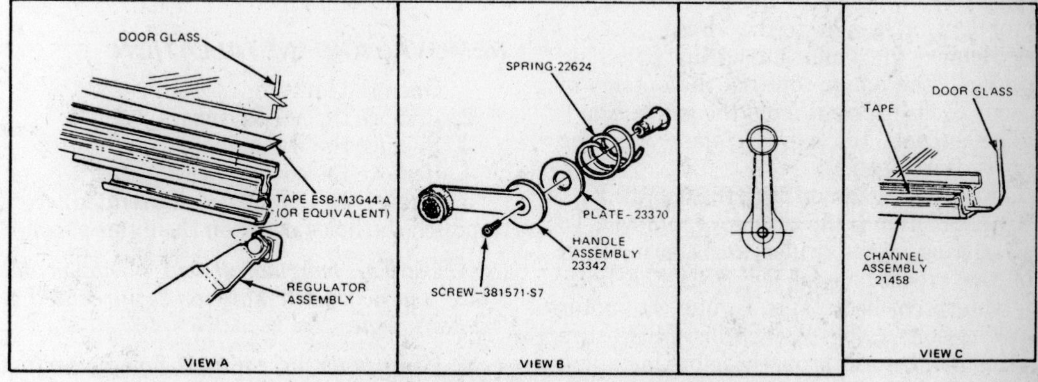

Window regulator replacement

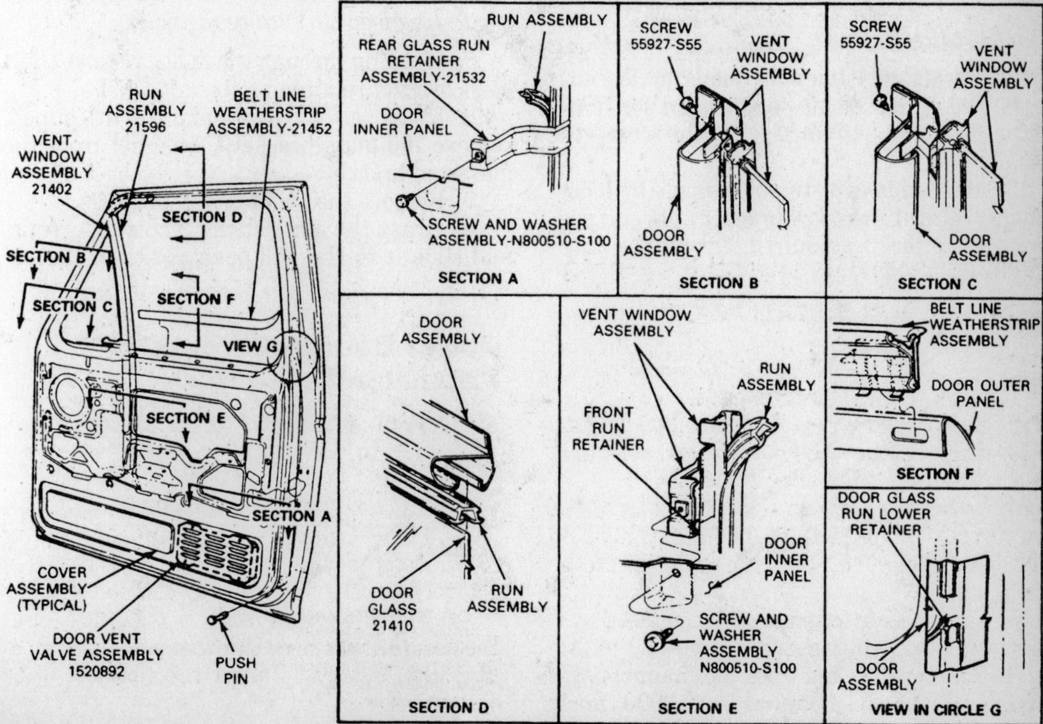

Door glass and vent window installation

6. Remove the glass from the channel using Glass and Channel Removal Tool 2900, made by the Sommer and Mala Glass Machine Co. of Chicago, ILL., or its equivalent.

7. Glass installation is the reverse of removal. Check the operation of the window before installing the trim panel.

Regulator

1. Disconnect the battery ground.
2. Remove the door trim panel.
3. Disconnect the window motor wiring harness.
4. There are 2 dimples in the door panel, opposite the 2 concealed motor retaining bolts. Using a 1/2 in. (13mm) drill bit, drill out these dimples to gain access to the motor bolts. Be careful to avoid damage to the wires.
5. Remove the 3 motor mounting bolts.
6. Push the motor towards the outside of the door to disengage it from the gears. You'll have to support the window glass once the motor is disengaged.
7. Remove the motor from the door.
8. Installation is the reverse of removal. To avoid rusting in the drilled areas, prime and paint the exposed metal, or, cover the holes with waterproof body tape. Torque the motor mounting bolts to 50–85 inch lbs. Make sure that the motor works properly before installing the trim panel.

Bronco Tailgate Window Glass

ADJUSTMENT

1. Fore-aft adjustment is made by loosening the glass run attaching screws and positioning the glass as required. Tighten the screws to 10 ft. lbs.
2. Side-to-side adjustment is made by loosening the glass-to-window bracket nuts and positioning the glass as required. Torque the nuts to 10 ft. lbs.

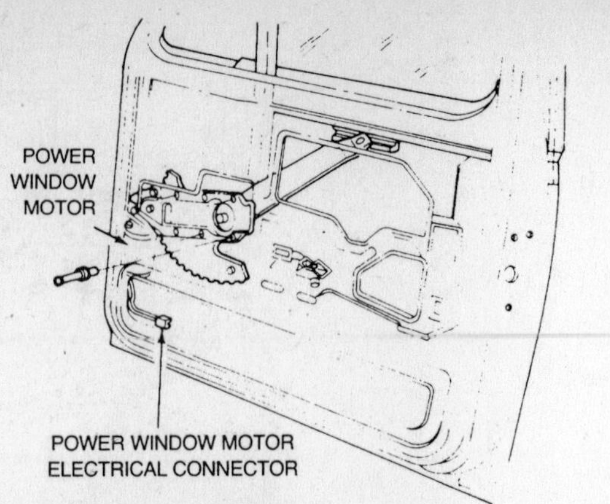

Power window installation

REMOVAL AND INSTALLATION

1. Open the tailgate.
2. Remove the access cover.
3. Remove the watershield.
4. Remove the cover panel support.
5. Using the template illustrated, centerpunch the holes noted on the inner panel.

NOTE: *The template shown is not actual size. The actual template can be purchased at a Ford dealer.*

6. Using a 5/8 in. (16mm) holesaw, cut 4 holes at the template hole location.

WARNING: *Cover the glass with protective padding prior to cutting the holes.*

7. Working through the holes, remove the 4 glass bracket retaining nuts.
8. Using a 5/16 in. (8mm) drift punch, remove the glass bracket C-channel from the glass and bracket.
9. Remove the padding and drillings.
10. Grasp the glass at the 2 bottom cutouts and slide it to the half-open position. Discon-

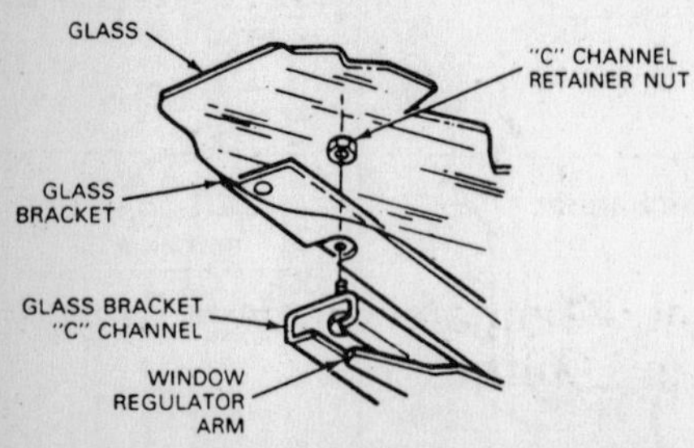

Bronco tailgate glass bracket installation

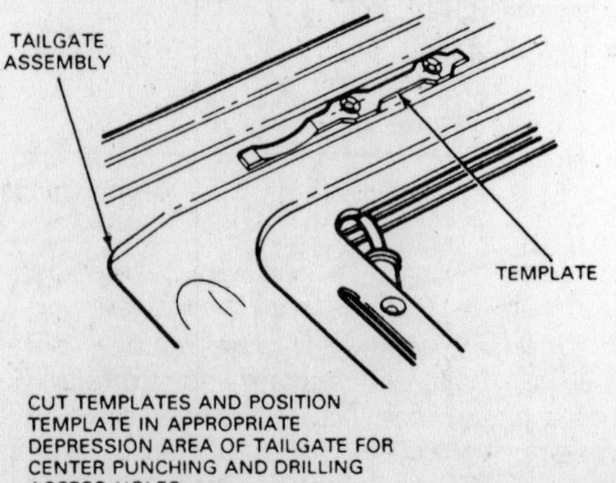

Tailgate template placement

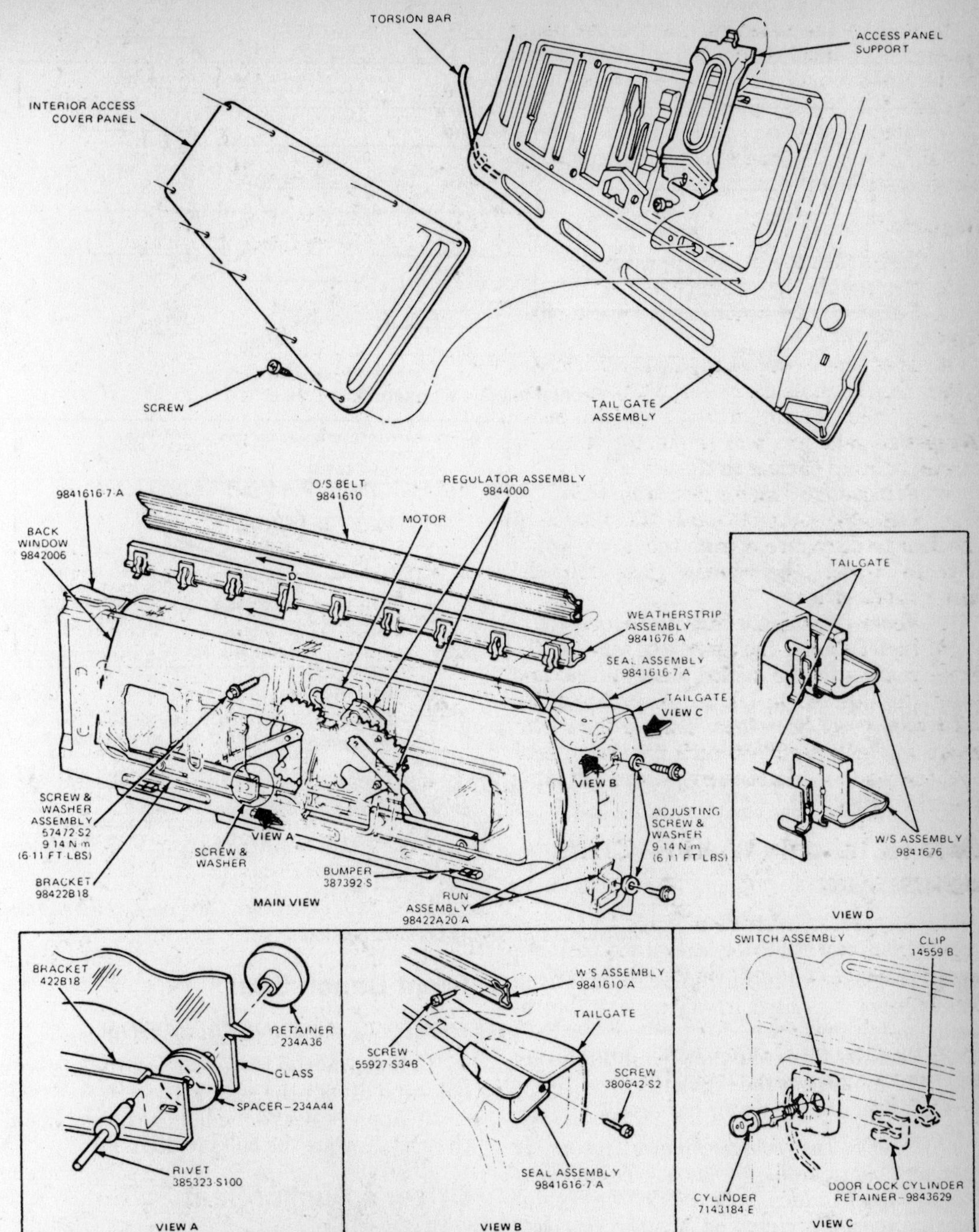

Bronco tailgate window mechanism

nect the rear window grid wire, if so equipped, and remove the glass from the tailgate.

11. Make sure that you remove all the drillings from the tailgate. Vacuuming them out is a good idea. These drillings, if left in the tailgate will lead to rusting of the surrounding metal. Prime and paint the drilled out holes to prevent rusting.

12. Installation is the reverse of removal. Torque the four retaining nuts to 10 ft. lbs.

Bronco Tailgate Window Regulator and Motor

REMOVAL AND INSTALLATION

1. Lower the tailgate and remove the access panel. If the glass cannot be lowered, remove the access panel and depress the lockout rod located in the bottom center of the tailgate.

2. Using a jumper to the tailgate motor,

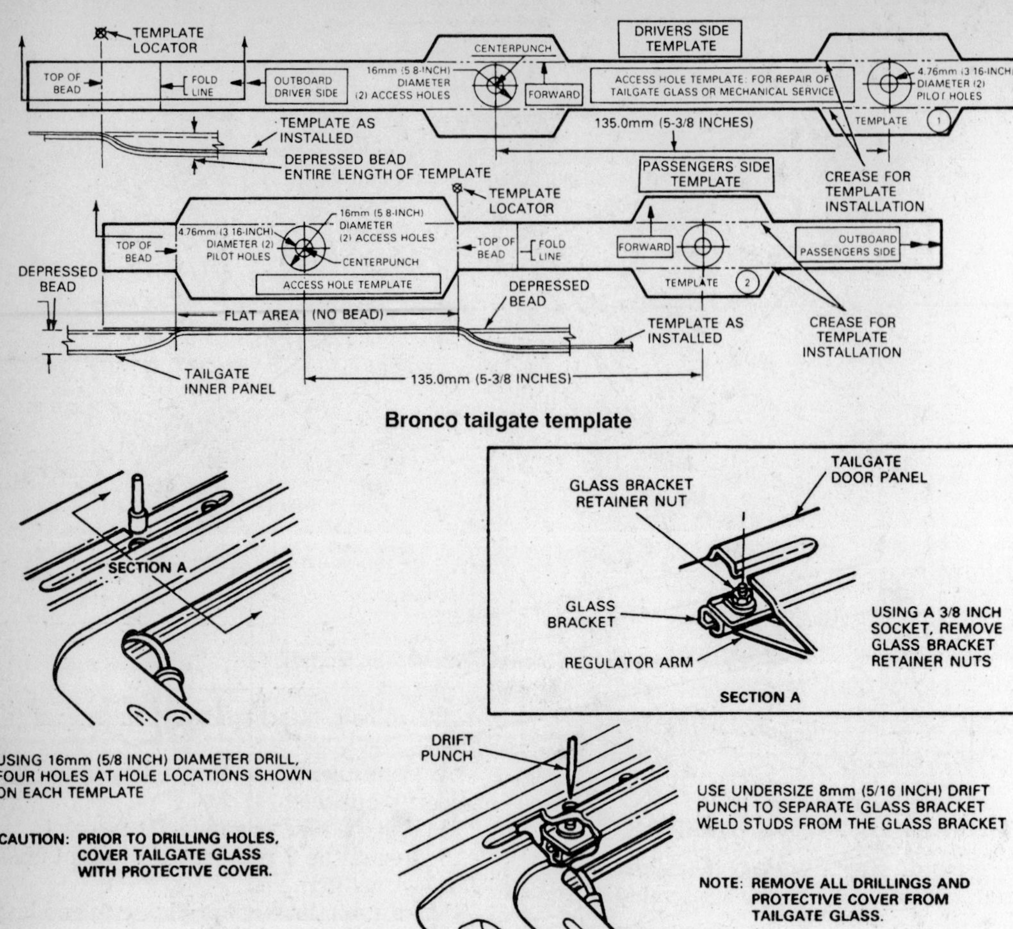

Bronco tailgate template

Bronco tailgate glass bracket installation

raise the glass to the full up position. If the glass cannot be raised it will have to be removed as outlined above.

3. Remove the regulator mounting bolts and nuts and lift out the regulator.
4. Disconnect the motor harness.

CAUTION: *The counterbalance spring is under considerable tension. To prevent injury from sudden movement of the regulator components, clamp or lock the gear sectors prior to removing the components!*

5. Detach the motor from the tailgate and remove it.
6. Installation is the reverse of removal. Torque the regulator mounting bolts to 10 ft. lbs.

Inside Rear View Mirror

The mirror is held in place with a single setscrew. Loosen the screw and lift the mirror off. Repair kit for damaged mirrors are available and most auto parts stores.

Front Bench Seat

REMOVAL AND INSTALLATION

1. Remove the 4 seat track-to-floor pan bolts and lift out the seat.
2. Apply sealer to the hole areas and install the seat. Torque the bolts to 30 ft. lbs.

Driver's Bucket Seat

REMOVAL AND INSTALLATION

1. Remove the 4 seat track-to-floor pan bolts and lift out the seat.
2. Apply sealer to the hole areas and install the seat. Torque the bolts to 30 ft. lbs.

Driver's Captain's Chair

REMOVAL AND INSTALLATION

1. Remove the 4 seat track-to-floor pan bolts and lift out the seat.
2. Apply sealer to the hole areas and install the seat. Torque the bolts to 30 ft. lbs.

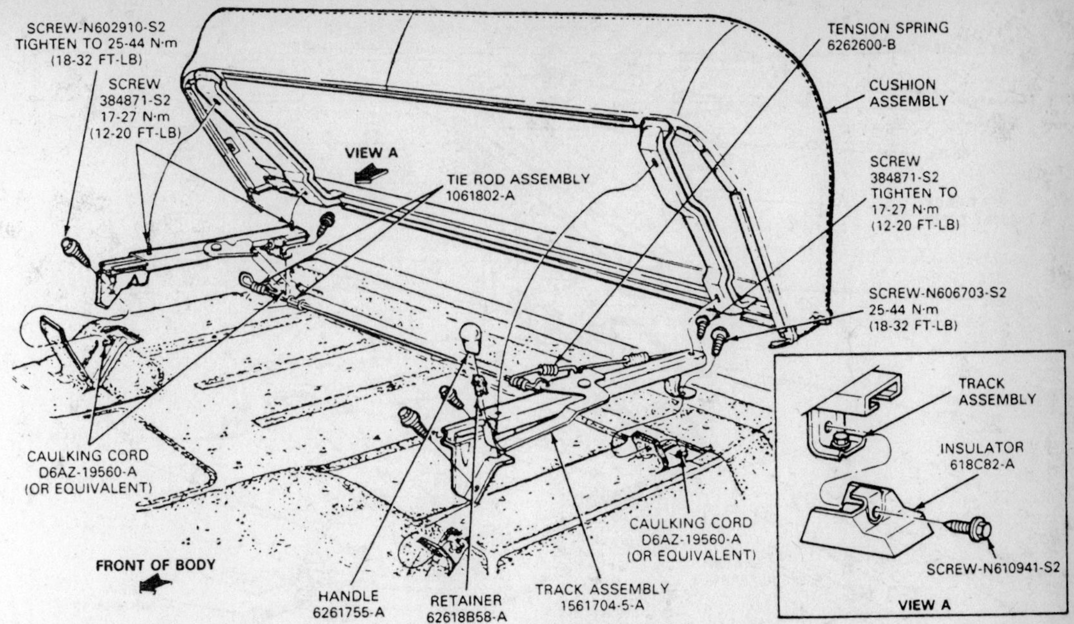

Bench seat and track installation — all models

Passenger's Bucket Seat or Captain's Chair

REMOVAL AND INSTALLATION

1. Remove the 2 front bolts retaining the passenger's seat and support assembly to the floor pan.
2. Move the seat release lever rearward allowing the seat to pop-up and fold forward.
3. Remove the 2 rear seat assembly-to-floor pan bolts.
4. Disengage one end of the passenger's seat support stop cable.
5. Move the seat and support assembly rearward until the seat back clears the instrument panel when folded forward.
6. Fold the seat fully forward and disengage the ends of the 3 assist springs from their retainers. NEVER TRY TO REMOVE THE SEAT WITH THE SPRINGS ATTACHED!
7. Return the seat to the upright position and push the seat back down firmly until the seat is latched.
8. Remove the seat from the truck.

To install:

9. Position the seat in the truck far enough rearward to enable the seat to clear the instrument panel when folded forward.
10. Fold the seat forward.
11. Attach the assist springs to their retainers.
12. Place the seat in the upright position. Push the seat down firmly to latch it.
13. Position the seat and install the 2 front holddown bolt. Hand-tighten them only at this time.
14. Connect the end of the passenger's seat support stop cable.
15. Pop the seat up and fold it forward.
16. Install the 2 rear seat bolts and tighten all 4 bolts to 30 ft. lbs.
17. Position the seat upright again and latch it into place.

WARNING: *To insure that the seat support assembly is in an unlatched position, a measured distance of 102mm, or more, is required between the bumper and the lower support.*

18. For captain's chairs:
    a. Push the seat support release lever rearward.
    b. Make sure that the seat back adjuster is actuated allowing the seat back to fold forward at approximately the same time that the seat support assembly pops up.
    c. If the seat assembly and/or the seat back does not release properly, it will be necessary to adjust the release cable by moving the slotted cable retainer fore or aft as needed.

Rear Bench Seat

REMOVAL AND INSTALLATION

F-350 Crew Cab

1. Remove the seat track-to-floor pan bolts and lift the seat and track out of the truck.
2. Installation is the reverse of removal. Apply sealer to the area of the bolt holes. Torque the bolts to 30 ft. lbs.

SCREW
ACTUATOR HANDLE
BEZEL
SEAT BACK ADJUSTER STEM
SPACER
CABLE RETAINER/ ADJUSTER
SPACER REFERENCE
PASSENGER SEAT SUPPORT ASSEMBLY
CABLE
SCREW N610958-S2
BOLT TIGHTEN TO 16-27 N·m (12-19 FT-LB) (4 REQ'D)
BOLT TIGHTEN TO 16-27 N·m (12-19 FT-LB)
SPACER (CAPTAINS CHAIR ONLY)

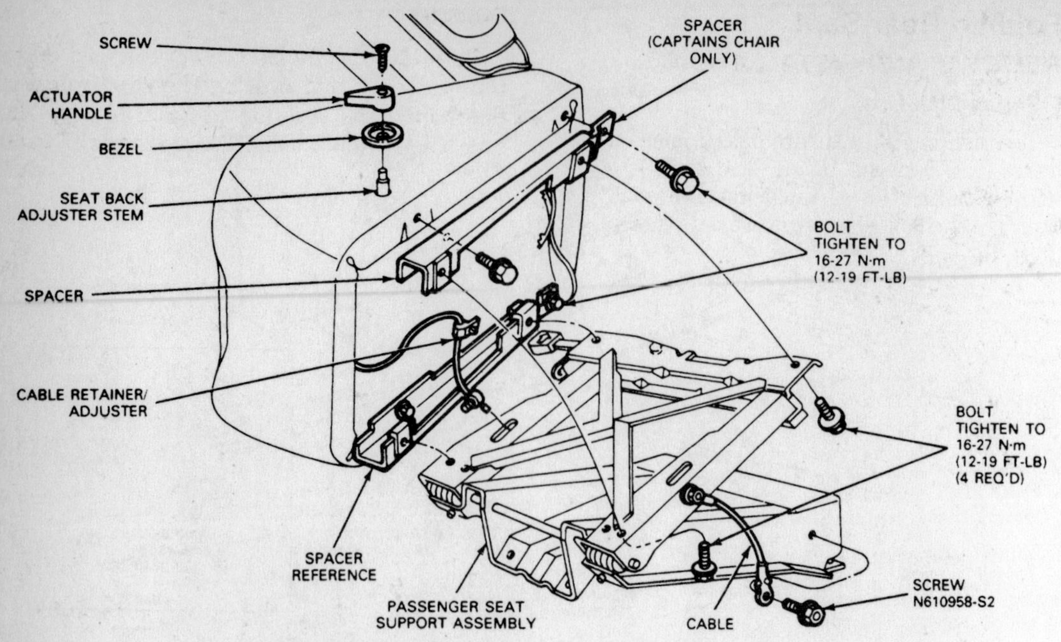

Bronco passenger's bucket seat installation

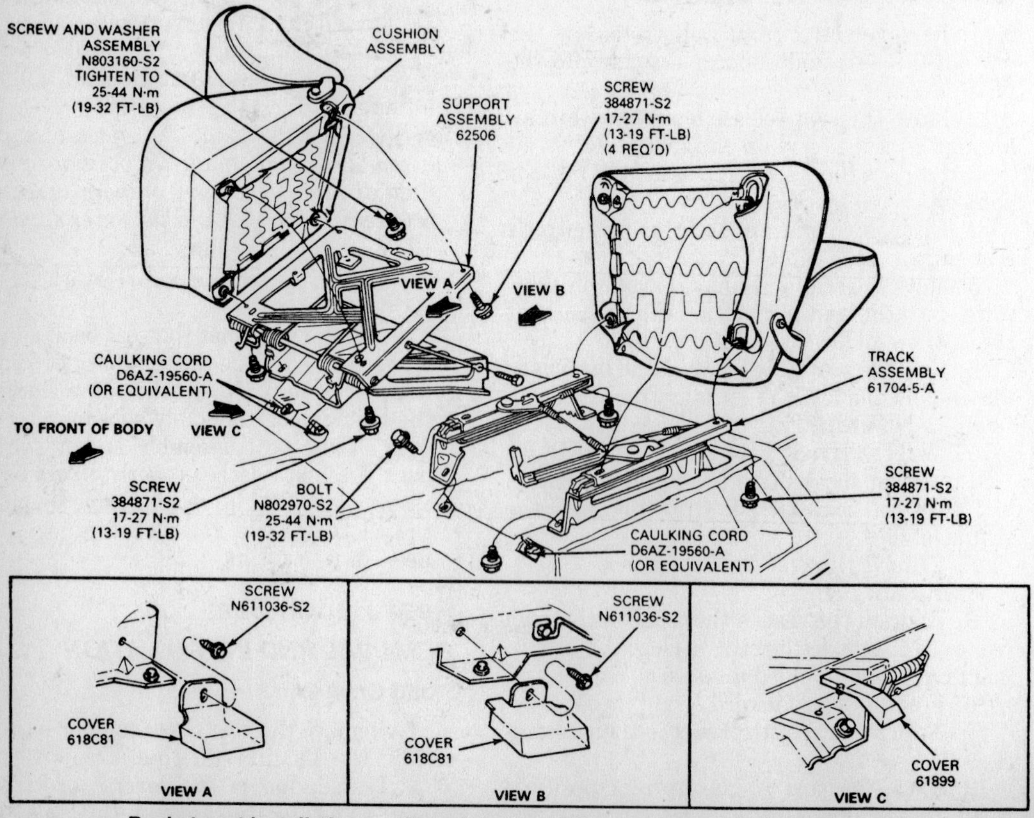

SCREW AND WASHER ASSEMBLY N803160-S2 TIGHTEN TO 25-44 N·m (19-32 FT-LB)
CUSHION ASSEMBLY
SUPPORT ASSEMBLY 62506
SCREW 384871-S2 17-27 N·m (13-19 FT-LB) (4 REQ'D)
VIEW A
VIEW B
CAULKING CORD D6AZ-19560-A (OR EQUIVALENT)
TO FRONT OF BODY
VIEW C
SCREW 384871-S2 17-27 N·m (13-19 FT-LB)
BOLT N802970-S2 25-44 N·m (19-32 FT-LB)
TRACK ASSEMBLY 61704-5-A
SCREW 384871-S2 17-27 N·m (13-19 FT-LB)
CAULKING CORD D6AZ-19560-A (OR EQUIVALENT)
SCREW N611036-S2
COVER 618C81
VIEW A
SCREW N611036-S2
COVER 618C81
VIEW B
COVER 61899
VIEW C

Bucket seat installation — all models except Bronco passenger's seat

Folding Rear Seat

REMOVAL AND INSTALLATION

F-Series Pick-Ups

The side-facing seats are held in place with 2 bolts. The forward facing seat is held down with 4 bolts. When replacing the seat, use sealer in the bolt hole areas. Torque the bolts to 30 ft. lbs.

Bronco

To remove the folding rear seat, fold down the seat back and unlatch the seat from the floor. Fold the seat forward and remove the seat track-to-floor bolts. Torque the bolts to 60 ft. lbs.

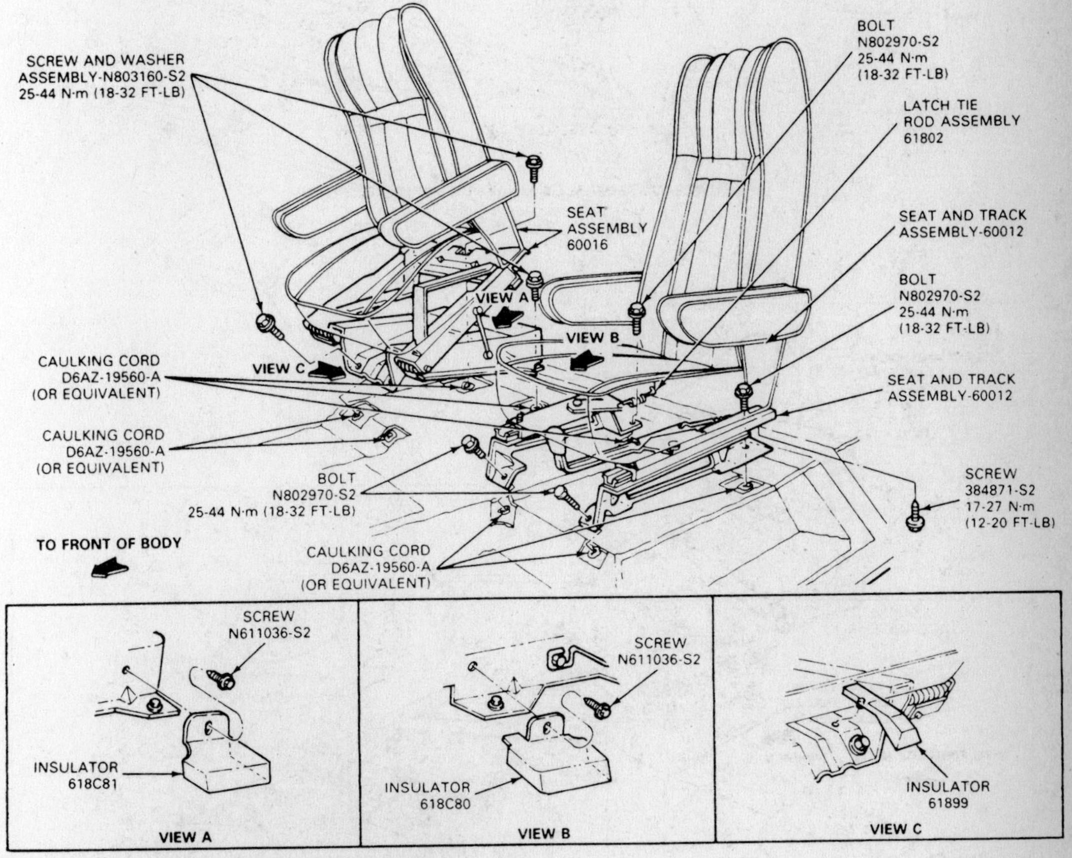

Captain's chairs

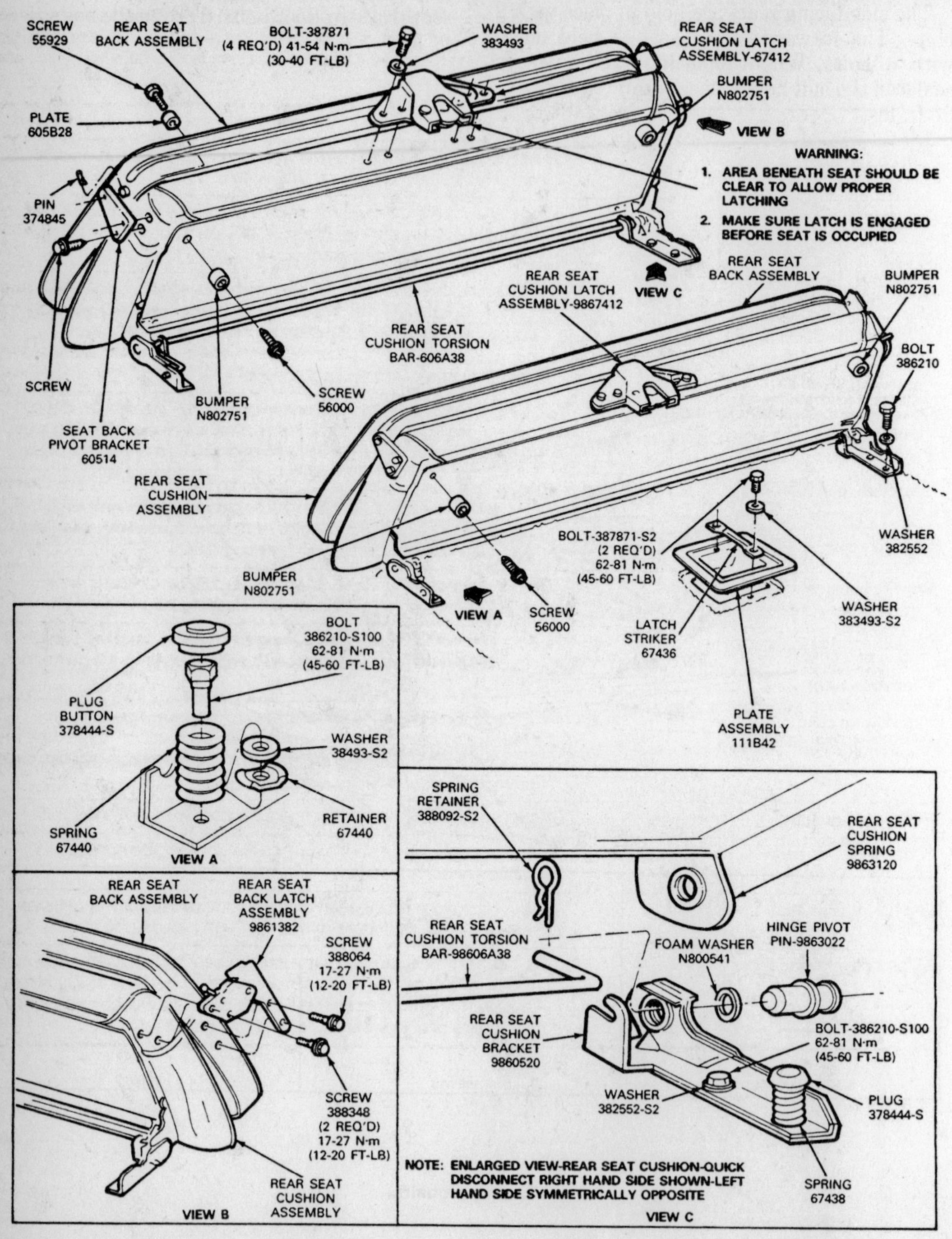

Bronco rear seat

How to Remove Stains from Fabric Interior

For best results, spots and stains should be removed as soon as possible. Never use gasoline, lacquer thinner, acetone, nail polish remover or bleach. Use a 3′ x 3″ piece of cheesecloth. Squeeze most of the liquid from the fabric and wipe the stained fabric from the outside of the stain toward the center with a lifting motion. Turn the cheesecloth as soon as one side becomes soiled. When using water to remove a stain, be sure to wash the entire section after the spot has been removed to avoid water stains. Encrusted spots can be broken up with a dull knife and vacuumed before removing the stain.

Type of Stain	How to Remove It
Surface spots	Brush the spots out with a small hand brush or use a commercial preparation such as K2R to lift the stain.
Mildew	Clean around the mildew with warm suds. Rinse in cold water and soak the mildew area in a solution of 1 part table salt and 2 parts water. Wash with upholstery cleaner.
Water stains	Water stains in fabric materials can be removed with a solution made from 1 cup of table salt dissolved in 1 quart of water. Vigorously scrub the solution into the stain and rinse with clear water. Water stains in nylon or other synthetic fabrics should be removed with a commercial type spot remover.
Chewing gum, tar, crayons, shoe polish (greasy stains)	Do not use a cleaner that will soften gum or tar. Harden the deposit with an ice cube and scrape away as much as possible with a dull knife. Moisten the remainder with cleaning fluid and scrub clean.
Ice cream, candy	Most candy has a sugar base and can be removed with a cloth wrung out in warm water. Oily candy, after cleaning with warm water, should be cleaned with upholstery cleaner. Rinse with warm water and clean the remainder with cleaning fluid.
Wine, alcohol, egg, milk, soft drink (non-greasy stains)	Do not use soap. Scrub the stain with a cloth wrung out in warm water. Remove the remainder with cleaning fluid.
Grease, oil, lipstick, butter and related stains	Use a spot remover to avoid leaving a ring. Work from the outisde of the stain to the center and dry with a clean cloth when the spot is gone.
Headliners (cloth)	Mix a solution of warm water and foam upholstery cleaner to give thick suds. Use only foam—liquid may streak or spot. Clean the entire headliner in one operation using a circular motion with a natural sponge.
Headliner (vinyl)	Use a vinyl cleaner with a sponge and wipe clean with a dry cloth.
Seats and door panels	Mix 1 pint upholstery cleaner in 1 gallon of water. Do not soak the fabric around the buttons.
Leather or vinyl fabric	Use a multi-purpose cleaner full strength and a stiff brush. Let stand 2 minutes and scrub thoroughly. Wipe with a clean, soft rag.
Nylon or synthetic fabrics	For normal stains, use the same procedures you would for washing cloth upholstery. If the fabric is extremely dirty, use a multi-purpose cleaner full strength with a stiff scrub brush. Scrub thoroughly in all directions and wipe with a cotton towel or soft rag.

Mechanic's Data

11

General Conversion Table

Multiply By	To Convert	To	
	LENGTH		
2.54	Inches	Centimeters	.3937
25.4	Inches	Millimeters	.03937
30.48	Feet	Centimeters	.0328
.304	Feet	Meters	3.28
.914	Yards	Meters	1.094
1.609	Miles	Kilometers	.621
	VOLUME		
.473	Pints	Liters	2.11
.946	Quarts	Liters	1.06
3.785	Gallons	Liters	.264
.164	Cubic inches	Liters	61.02
16.39	Cubic inches	Cubic cms.	.061
28.32	Cubic feet	Liters	.0353
	MASS (Weight)		
28.35	Ounces	Grams	.035
.4536	Pounds	Kilograms	2.20
—	To obtain	From	Multiply by

Multiply By	To Convert	To	
	AREA		
6.45	Square inches	Square cms.	.155
.836	Square yds.	Square meters	1.196
	FORCE		
4.448	Pounds	Newtons	.225
.138	Ft. lbs.	Kilogram/meters	7.23
1.356	Ft. lbs.	Newton-meters	.737
.113	In. lbs.	Newton-meters	8.844
	PRESSURE		
.068	Psi	Atmospheres	14.7
6.89	Psi	Kilopascals	.145
	OTHER		
1.104	Horsepower (DIN)	Horsepower (SAE)	.9861
.746	Horsepower (SAE)	Kilowatts (KW)	1.34
1.609	Mph	Km/h	.621
.425	Mpg	Km/L	2.35
—	To obtain	From	Multiply by

Tap Drill Sizes

National Coarse or U.S.S.

Screw & Tap Size	Threads Per Inch	Use Drill Number
No. 5	40	39
No. 6	32	36
No. 8	32	29
No. 10	24	25
No. 12	24	17
1/4	20	8
5/16	18	F
3/8	16	5/16
7/16	14	U
1/2	13	27/64
9/16	12	31/64
5/8	11	17/32
3/4	10	21/32
7/8	9	49/64

National Coarse or U.S.S.

Screw & Tap Size	Threads Per Inch	Use Drill Number
1	8	7/8
1 1/8	7	63/64
1 1/4	7	1 7/64
1 1/2	6	1 11/32

National Fine or S.A.E.

Screw & Tap Size	Threads Per Inch	Use Drill Number
No. 5	44	37
No. 6	40	33
No. 8	36	29
No. 10	32	21

National Fine or S.A.E.

Screw & Tap Size	Threads Per Inch	Use Drill Number
No. 12	28	15
1/4	28	3
6/16	24	1
3/8	28	Q
7/16	20	W
1/2	20	29/64
9/16	18	33/64
5/8	18	37/64
3/4	16	11/16
7/8	14	13/16
1 1/8	12	1 3/64
1 1/4	12	1 11/64
1 1/2	12	1 27/64

Drill Sizes In Decimal Equivalents

Inch	Decimal	Wire	mm	Inch	Decimal	Wire	mm	Inch	Decimal	Wire & Letter	mm	Inch	Decimal	Letter	mm	Inch	Decimal	mm
1/64	.0156		.39		.0730	49			.1614		4.1		.2717		6.9		.4331	11.0
	.0157		.4		.0748		1.9		.1654		4.2		.2720	I		7/16	.4375	11.11
	.0160	78			.0760	48			.1660	19			.2756		7.0		.4528	11.5
	.0165		.42		.0768		1.95		.1673		4.25		.2770	J		29/64	.4531	11.51
	.0173		.44	5/64	.0781		1.98		.1693		4.3		.2795		7.1	15/32	.4688	11.90
	.0177		.45		.0785	47			.1695	18			.2810	K			.4724	12.0
	.0180	77			.0787		2.0	11/64	.1719		4.36	9/32	.2812		7.14	31/64	.4844	12.30
	.0181		.46		.0807		2.05		.1730	17			.2835		7.2		.4921	12.5
	.0189		.48		.0810	46			.1732		4.4		.2854		7.25	1/2	.5000	12.70
	.0197		.5		.0820	45			.1770	16			.2874		7.3		.5118	13.0
	.0200	76			.0827		2.1		.1772		4.5		.2900	L		33/64	.5156	13.09
	.0210	75			.0846		2.15		.1800	15			.2913		7.4	17/32	.5312	13.49
	.0217		.55		.0860	44			.1811		4.6		.2950	M			.5315	13.5
	.0225	74			.0866		2.2		.1820	14			.2953		7.5	35/64	.5469	13.89
	.0236		.6		.0886		2.25		.1850	13		19/64	.2969		7.54		.5512	14.0
	.0240	73			.0890	43			.1850		4.7		.2992		7.6	9/16	.5625	14.28
	.0250	72			.0906		2.3		.1870		4.75		.3020	N			.5709	14.5
	.0256		.65		.0925		2.35	3/16	.1875		4.76		.3031		7.7	37/64	.5781	14.68
	.0260	71			.0935	42			.1890		4.8		.3051		7.75		.5906	15.0
	.0276		.7	3/32	.0938		2.38		.1890	12			.3071		7.8	19/32	.5938	15.08
	.0280	70			.0945		2.4		.1910	11			.3110		7.9	39/64	.6094	15.47
	.0292	69			.0960	41			.1929		4.9	5/16	.3125		7.93		.6102	15.5
	.0295		.75		.0965		2.45		.1935	10			.3150		8.0	5/8	.6250	15.87
	.0310	68			.0980	40			.1960	9			.3160	O			.6299	16.0
1/32	.0312		.79		.0981		2.5		.1969		5.0		.3189		8.1	41/64	.6406	16.27
	.0315		.8		.0995	39			.1990	8			.3228		8.2		.6496	16.5
	.0320	67			.1015	38			.2008		5.1		.3230	P		21/32	.6562	16.66
	.0330	66			.1024		2.6		.2010	7			.3248		8.25		.6693	17.0
	.0335		.85		.1040	37		13/64	.2031		5.16		.3268		8.3	43/64	.6719	17.06
	.0350	65			.1063		2.7		.2040	6		21/64	.3281		8.33	11/16	.6875	17.46
	.0354		.9		.1065	36			.2047		5.2		.3307		8.4		.6890	17.5
	.0360	64			.1083		2.75		.2055	5			.3320	Q		45/64	.7031	17.85
	.0370	63		7/64	.1094		2.77		.2067		5.25		.3346		8.5		.7087	18.0
	.0374		.95		.1100	35			.2087		5.3		.3386		8.6	23/32	.7188	18.25
	.0380	62			.1102		2.8		.2090	4			.3390	R			.7283	18.5
	.0390	61			.1110	34			.2126		5.4		.3425		8.7	47/64	.7344	18.65
	.0394		1.0		.1130	33			.2130	3		11/32	.3438		8.73		.7480	19.0
	.0400	60			.1142		2.9		.2165		5.5		.3445		8.75	3/4	.7500	19.05
	.0410	59			.1160	32		7/32	2188		5.55		.3465		8.8	49/64	.7656	19.44
	.0413		1.05		.1181		3.0		.2205		5.6		.3480	S			.7677	19.5
	.0420	58			.1200	31			.2210	2			.3504		8.9	25/32	.7812	19.84
	.0430	57			.1220		3.1		.2244		5.7		.3543		9.0		.7874	20.0
	.0433		1.1	1/8	.1250		3.17		.2264		5.75		.3580	T		51/64	.7969	20.24
	.0453		1.15		.1260		3.2		.2280	1			.3583		9.1		.8071	20.5
	.0465	56			.1280		3.25		.2283		5.8	23/64	.3594		9.12	13/16	.8125	20.63
3/64	.0469		1.19		.1285	30			.2323		5.9		.3622		9.2		.8268	21.0
	.0472		1.2		.1299		3.3		.2340	A			.3642		9.25	53/64	.8281	21.03
	.0492		1.25		.1339		3.4	15/64	.2344		5.95		.3661		9.3	27/32	.8438	21.43
	.0512		1.3		.1360	29			.2362		6.0		.3680	U			.8465	21.5
	.0520	55			.1378		3.5		.2380	B			.3701		9.4	55/64	.8594	21.82
	.0531		1.35		.1405	28			.2402		6.1		.3740		9.5		.8661	22.0
	.0550	54		9/64	.1406		3.57		.2420	C		3/8	.3750		9.52	7/8	.8750	22.22
	.0551		1.4		.1417		3.6		.2441		6.2		.3770	V			.8858	22.5
	.0571		1.45		.1440	27			.2460	D			.3780		9.6	57/64	.8906	22.62
	.0591		1.5		.1457		3.7		.2461		6.25		.3819		9.7		.9055	23.0
	.0595	53			.1470	26			.2480		6.3		.3839		9.75	29/32	.9062	23.01
	.0610		1.55		.1476		3.75	1/4	.2500	E	6.35		.3858		9.8	59/64	.9219	23.41
1/16	.0625		1.59		.1495	25			.2520		6.		.3860	W			.9252	23.5
	.0630		1.6		.1496		3.8		.2559		6.5		.3898		9.9	15/16	.9375	23.81
	.0635	52			.1520	24			.2570	F		25/64	.3906		9.92		.9449	24.0
	.0650		1.65		.1535		3.9		.2598		6.6		.3937		10.0	61/64	.9531	24.2
	.0669		1.7		.1540	23			.2610	G			.3970	X			.9646	24.5
	.0670	51		5/32	.1562		3.96		.2638		6.7		.4040	Y		31/64	.9688	24.6
	.0689		1.75		.1570	22		17/64	.2656		6.74	13/32	.4062		10.31		.9843	25.0
	.0700	50			.1575		4.0		.2657		6.75		.4130	Z		63/64	.9844	25.0
	.0709		1.8		.1590	21			.2660	H			.4134		10.5	1	1.0000	25.4
	.0728		1.85		.1610	20			.2677		6.8	27/64	.4219		10.71			

AIR/FUEL RATIO: The ratio of air to gasoline by weight in the fuel mixture drawn into the engine.

AIR INJECTION: One method of reducing harmful exhaust emissions by injecting air into each of the exhaust ports of an engine. The fresh air entering the hot exhaust manifold causes any remaining fuel to be burned before it can exit the tailpipe.

ALTERNATOR: A device used for converting mechanical energy into electrical energy.

AMMETER: An instrument, calibrated in amperes, used to measure the flow of an electrical current in a circuit. Ammeters are always connected in series with the circuit being tested.

AMPERE: The rate of flow of electrical current present when one volt of electrical pressure is applied against one ohm of electrical resistance.

ANALOG COMPUTER: Any microprocessor that uses similar (analogous) electrical signals to make its calculations.

ARMATURE: A laminated, soft iron core wrapped by a wire that converts electrical energy to mechanical energy as in a motor or relay. When rotated in a magnetic field, it changes mechanical energy into electrical energy as in a generator.

ATMOSPHERIC PRESSURE: The pressure on the Earth's surface caused by the weight of the air in the atmosphere. At sea level, this pressure is 14.7 psi at 32°F (101 kPa at 0°C).

ATOMIZATION: The breaking down of a liquid into a fine mist that can be suspended in air.

AXIAL PLAY: Movement parallel to a shaft or bearing bore.

BACKFIRE: The sudden combustion of gases in the intake or exhaust system that results in a loud explosion.

BACKLASH: The clearance or play between two parts, such as meshed gears.

BACKPRESSURE: Restrictions in the exhaust system that slow the exit of exhaust gases from the combustion chamber.

BAKELITE: A heat resistant, plastic insulator material commonly used in printed circuit boards and transistorized components.

BALL BEARING: A bearing made up of hardened inner and outer races between which hardened steel balls roll.

BALLAST RESISTOR: A resistor in the primary ignition circuit that lowers voltage after the engine is started to reduce wear on ignition components.

BEARING: A friction reducing, supportive device usually located between a stationary part and a moving part.

BIMETAL TEMPERATURE SENSOR: Any sensor or switch made of two dissimilar types of metal that bend when heated or cooled due to the different expansion rates of the alloys. These types of sensors usually function as an on/off switch.

BLOWBY: Combustion gases, composed of water vapor and unburned fuel, that leak past the piston rings into the crankcase during normal engine operation. These gases are removed by the PCV system to prevent the buildup of harmful acids in the crankcase.

BRAKE PAD: A brake shoe and lining assembly used with disc brakes.

BRAKE SHOE: The backing for the brake lining. The term is, however, usually applied to the assembly of the brake backing and lining.

BUSHING: A liner, usually removable, for a bearing; an anti-friction liner used in place of a bearing.

BYPASS: System used to bypass ballast resistor during engine cranking to increase voltage supplied to the coil.

CALIPER: A hydraulically activated device in a disc brake system, which is mounted straddling the brake rotor (disc). The caliper contains at least one piston and two brake pads. Hydraulic pressure on the piston(s) forces the pads against the rotor.

CAMSHAFT: A shaft in the engine on which are the lobes (cams) which operate the valves. The camshaft is driven by the crankshaft, via a belt, chain or gears, at one half the crankshaft speed.

CAPACITOR: A device which stores an electrical charge.

CARBON MONOXIDE (CO): A colorless, odorless gas given off as a normal byproduct of combustion. It is poisonous and extremely dangerous in confined areas, building up slowly to toxic levels without warning if adequate ventilation is not available.

CARBURETOR: A device, usually mounted on the intake manifold of an engine, which mixes the air and fuel in the proper proportion to allow even combustion.

CATALYTIC CONVERTER: A device installed in the exhaust system, like a muffler, that converts harmful byproducts of combustion into carbon dioxide and water vapor by means of a heat-producing chemical reaction.

CENTRIFUGAL ADVANCE: A mechanical method of advancing the spark timing by using fly weights in the distributor that react to centrifugal force generated by the distributor shaft rotation.

CHECK VALVE: Any one-way valve installed to permit the flow of air, fuel or vacuum in one direction only.

CHOKE: A device, usually a movable valve, placed in the intake path of a carburetor to restrict the flow of air.

CIRCUIT: Any unbroken path through which an electrical current can flow. Also used to describe fuel flow in some instances.

CIRCUIT BREAKER: A switch which protects an electrical circuit from overload by opening the circuit when the current flow exceeds a predetermined level. Some circuit breakers must be reset manually, while most reset automatically

COIL (IGNITION): A transformer in the ignition circuit which steps up the voltage provided to the spark plugs.

COMBINATION MANIFOLD: An assembly which includes both the intake and exhaust manifolds in one casting.

COMBINATION VALVE: A device used in some fuel systems that routes fuel vapors to a charcoal storage canister instead of venting them into the atmosphere. The valve relieves fuel tank pressure and allows fresh air into the tank as the fuel level drops to prevent a vapor lock situation.

COMPRESSION RATIO: The comparison of the total volume of the cylinder and combustion chamber with the piston at BDC and the piston at TDC.

CONDENSER: 1. An electrical device which acts to store an electrical charge, preventing voltage surges.

2. A radiator-like device in the air conditioning system in which refrigerant gas condenses into a liquid, giving off heat.

CONDUCTOR: Any material through which an electrical current can be transmitted easily.

CONTINUITY: Continuous or complete circuit. Can be checked with an ohmmeter.

COUNTERSHAFT: An intermediate shaft which is rotated by a mainshaft and transmits, in turn, that rotation to a working part.

CRANKCASE: The lower part of an engine in which the crankshaft and related parts operate.

CRANKSHAFT: The main driving shaft of an engine which receives reciprocating motion from the pistons and converts it to rotary motion.

CYLINDER: In an engine, the round hole in the engine block in which the piston(s) ride.

CYLINDER BLOCK: The main structural member of an engine in which is found the cylinders, crankshaft and other principal parts.

CYLINDER HEAD: The detachable portion of the engine, fastened, usually, to the top of the cylinder block, containing all or most of the combustion chambers. On overhead valve engines, it contains the valves and their operating parts. On overhead cam engines, it contains the camshaft as well.

DEAD CENTER: The extreme top or bottom of the piston stroke.

DETONATION: An unwanted explosion of the air/fuel mixture in the combustion chamber caused by excess heat and compression, advanced timing, or an overly lean mixture. Also referred to as "ping".

DIAPHRAGM: A thin, flexible wall separating two cavities, such as in a vacuum advance unit.

DIESELING: A condition in which hot spots in the combustion chamber cause the engine to run on after the key is turned off.

DIFFERENTIAL: A geared assembly which allows the transmission of motion between drive axles, giving one axle the ability to turn faster than the other.

DIODE: An electrical device that will allow current to flow in one direction only.

DISC BRAKE: A hydraulic braking assembly consisting of a brake disc, or rotor, mounted on an axle, and a caliper assembly containing, usually two brake pads which are activated by hydraulic pressure. The pads are forced against the sides of the disc, creating friction which slows the vehicle.

DISTRIBUTOR: A mechanically driven device on an engine which is responsible for electrically firing the spark plug at a predetermined point of the piston stroke.

DOWEL PIN: A pin, inserted in mating holes in two different parts allowing those parts to maintain a fixed relationship.

DRUM BRAKE: A braking system which consists of two brake shoes and one or two wheel cylinders, mounted on a fixed backing plate, and a brake drum, mounted on an axle, which revolves around the assembly. Hydraulic action applied to the wheel cylinders forces the shoes outward against the drum, creating friction, slowing the vehicle.

DWELL: The rate, measured in degrees of shaft rotation, at which an electrical circuit cycles on and off.

ELECTRONIC CONTROL UNIT (ECU): Ignition module, amplifier or igniter. See Module for definition.

ELECTRONIC IGNITION: A system in which the timing and firing of the spark plugs is controlled by an electronic control unit, usually called a module. These systems have no points or condenser.

ENDPLAY: The measured amount of axial movement in a shaft.

ENGINE: A device that converts heat into mechanical energy.

EXHAUST MANIFOLD: A set of cast passages or pipes which conduct exhaust gases from the engine.

FEELER GAUGE: A blade, usually metal, of precisely predetermined thickness, used to measure the clearance between two parts. These blades usually are available in sets of assorted thicknesses.

F-HEAD: An engine configuration in which the intake valves are in the cylinder head, while the camshaft and exhaust valves are located in the cylinder block. The camshaft operates the intake valves via lifters and pushrods, while it operates the exhaust valves directly.

FIRING ORDER: The order in which combustion occurs in the cylinders of an engine. Also the order in which spark is distributed to the plugs by the distributor.

FLATHEAD: An engine configuration in which the camshaft and all the valves are located in the cylinder block.

FLOODING: The presence of too much fuel in the intake manifold and combustion chamber which prevents the air/fuel mixture from firing, thereby causing a no-start situation.

FLYWHEEL: A disc shaped part bolted to the rear end of the crankshaft. Around the outer perimeter is affixed the ring gear. The starter drive engages the ring gear, turning the flywheel, which rotates the crankshaft, imparting the initial starting motion to the engine.

FOOT POUND (ft.lb. or sometimes, ft. lbs.): The amount of energy or work needed to raise an item weighing one pound, a distance of one foot.

FUSE: A protective device in a circuit which prevents circuit overload by breaking the circuit when a specific amperage is present. The device is constructed around a strip or wire of a lower amperage rating than the circuit it is designed to protect. When an amperage higher than that stamped on the fuse is present in the circuit, the strip or wire melts, opening the circuit.

GEAR RATIO: The ratio between the number of teeth on meshing gears.

GENERATOR: A device which converts mechanical energy into electrical energy.

HEAT RANGE: The measure of a spark plug's ability to dissipate heat from its firing end. The higher the heat range, the hotter the plug fires. **HUB:** The center part of a wheel or gear.

HYDROCARBON (HC): Any chemical compound made up of hydrogen and carbon. A major pollutant formed by the engine as a byproduct of combustion.

HYDROMETER: An instrument used to measure the specific gravity of a solution.

INCH POUND (in.lb. or sometimes, in. lbs.): One twelfth of a foot pound.

INDUCTION: A means of transferring electrical energy in the form of a magnetic field. Principle used in the ignition coil to increase voltage.

INJECTION PUMP: A device, usually mechanically operated, which meters and delivers fuel under pressure to the fuel injector.

INJECTOR: A device which receives metered fuel under relatively low pressure and is activated to inject the fuel into the engine under relatively high pressure at a predetermined time.

INPUT SHAFT: The shaft to which torque is applied, usually carrying the driving gear or gears.

INTAKE MANIFOLD: A casting of passages or pipes used to conduct air or a fuel/air mixture to the cylinders.

JOURNAL: The bearing surface within which a shaft operates.

KEY: A small block usually fitted in a notch between a shaft and a hub to prevent slippage of the two parts.

MANIFOLD: A casting of passages or set of pipes which connect the cylinders to an inlet or outlet source.

MANIFOLD VACUUM: Low pressure in an engine intake manifold formed just below the throttle plates. Manifold vacuum is highest at idle and drops under acceleration.

MASTER CYLINDER: The primary fluid pressurizing device in a hydraulic system. In automotive use, it is found in brake and hydraulic clutch systems and is pedal activated, either directly or, in a power brake system, through the power booster.

MODULE: Electronic control unit, amplifier or igniter of solid state or integrated design which controls the current flow in the ignition primary circuit based on input from the pick-up coil. When the module opens the primary circuit, the high secondary voltage is induced in the coil.

NEEDLE BEARING: A bearing which consists of a number (usually a large number) of long, thin rollers.

OHM:(Ω) The unit used to measure the resistance of conductor to electrical flow. One ohm is the amount of resistance that limits current flow to one ampere in a circuit with one volt of pressure.

OHMMETER: An instrument used for measuring the resistance, in ohms, in an electrical circuit.

OUTPUT SHAFT: The shaft which transmits torque from a device, such as a transmission.

OVERDRIVE: A gear assembly which produces more shaft revolutions than that transmitted to it.

OVERHEAD CAMSHAFT (OHC): An engine configuration in which the camshaft is mounted on top of the cylinder head and operates the valves either directly or by means of rocker arms.

OVERHEAD VALVE (OHV): An engine configuration in which all of the valves are located in the cylinder head and the camshaft is located in the cylinder block. The camshaft operates the valves via lifters and pushrods.

OXIDES OF NITROGEN (NOx): Chemical compounds of nitrogen produced as a byproduct of combustion. They combine with hydrocarbons to produce smog.

OXYGEN SENSOR: Used with the feedback system to sense the presence of oxygen in the exhaust gas and signal the computer which can reference the voltage signal to an air/fuel ratio.

PINION: The smaller of two meshing gears.

PISTON RING: An open ended ring which fits into a groove on the outer diameter of the piston. Its chief function is to form a seal between the piston and cylinder wall. Most automotive pistons have three rings: two for compression sealing; one for oil sealing.

PRELOAD: A predetermined load placed on a bearing during assembly or by adjustment.

PRIMARY CIRCUIT: Is the low voltage side of the ignition system which consists of the ignition switch, ballast resistor or resistance wire, bypass, coil, electronic control unit and pick-up coil as well as the connecting wires and harnesses.

PRESS FIT: The mating of two parts under pressure, due to the inner diameter of one being smaller than the outer diameter of the other, or vice versa; an interference fit.

RACE: The surface on the inner or outer ring of a bearing on which the balls, needles or rollers move.

REGULATOR: A device which maintains the amperage and/or voltage levels of a circuit at predetermined values.

RELAY: A switch which automatically opens and/or closes a circuit.

RESISTANCE: The opposition to the flow of current through a circuit or electrical device, and is measured in ohms. Resistance is equal to the voltage divided by the amperage.

RESISTOR: A device, usually made of wire, which offers a preset amount of resistance in an electrical circuit.

RING GEAR: The name given to a ring-shaped gear attached to a differential case,or affixed to a flywheel or as part a planetary gear set.

ROLLER BEARING: A bearing made up of hardened inner and outer races between which hardened steel rollers move.

ROTOR: 1. The disc-shaped part of a disc brake assembly, upon which the brake pads bear; also called, brake disc.

2. The device mounted atop the distributor shaft, which passes current to the distributor cap tower contacts.

SECONDARY CIRCUIT: The high voltage side of the ignition system, usually above 20,000 volts. The secondary includes the ignition coil, coil wire, distributor cap and rotor, spark plug wires and spark plugs.

SENDING UNIT: A mechanical, electrical, hydraulic or electromagnetic device which transmits information to a gauge.

SENSOR: Any device designed to measure engine operating conditions or ambient pressures and temperatures. Usually electronic in nature and designed to send a voltage signal to an on-board computer, some sensors may operate as a simple on/off switch or they may provide a variable voltage signal (like a potentiometer) as conditions or measured parameters change.

SHIM: Spacers of precise, predetermined thickness used between parts to establish a proper working relationship.

SLAVE CYLINDER: In automotive use, a device in the hydraulic clutch system which is activated by hydraulic force, disengaging the clutch.

SOLENOID: A coil used to produce a magnetic field, the effect of which is to produce work.

SPARK PLUG: A device screwed into the combustion chamber of a spark ignition engine. The basic construction is a conductive core inside of a ceramic insulator, mounted in an outer conductive base. An electrical charge from the spark plug wire travels along the conductive core and jumps a preset air gap to a grounding point or points at the end of the conductive base. The resultant spark ignites the fuel/air mixture in the combustion chamber.

SPLINES: Ridges machined or cast onto the outer diameter of a shaft or inner diameter of a bore to enable parts to mate without rotation.

TACHOMETER: A device used to measure the rotary speed of an engine, shaft, gear, etc., usually in rotations per minute.

THERMOSTAT: A valve, located in the cooling system of an engine, which is closed when cold and opens gradually in response to engine heating, controlling the temperature of the coolant and rate of coolant flow.

TOP DEAD CENTER (TDC): The point at which the piston reaches the top of its travel on the compression stroke.

TORQUE: The twisting force applied to an object.

TORQUE CONVERTER: A turbine used to transmit power from a driving member to a driven member via hydraulic action, providing changes in drive ratio and torque. In automotive use, it links the driveplate at the rear of the engine to the automatic transmission.

TRANSDUCER: A device used to change a force into an electrical signal.

TRANSISTOR: A semi-conductor component which can be actuated by a small voltage to perform an electrical switching function.

TUNE-UP: A regular maintenance function, usually associated with the replacement and adjustment of parts and components in the electrical and fuel systems of a vehicle for the purpose of attaining optimum performance.

TURBOCHARGER: An exhaust driven pump which compresses intake air and forces it into the combustion chambers at higher than atmospheric pressures. The increased air pressure allows more fuel to be burned and results in increased horsepower being produced.

VACUUM ADVANCE: A device which advances the ignition timing in response to increased engine vacuum.

VACUUM GAUGE: An instrument used to measure the presence of vacuum in a chamber.

VALVE: A device which control the pressure, direction of flow or rate of flow of a liquid or gas.

VALVE CLEARANCE: The measured gap between the end of the valve stem and the rocker arm, cam lobe or follower that activates the valve.

VISCOSITY: The rating of a liquid's internal resistance to flow.

VOLTMETER: An instrument used for measuring electrical force in units called volts. Voltmeters are always connected parallel with the circuit being tested.

WHEEL CYLINDER: Found in the automotive drum brake assembly, it is a device, actuated by hydraulic pressure, which, through internal pistons, pushes the brake shoes outward against the drums.

A: Ampere
AC: Alternating current
A/C: Air conditioning
A–h: Amper hour
AT: Automatic transmission
ATDC: After top dead center
μA: Microampere
bbl: Barrel
BDC: Bottom dead center
bhp: Brake horsepower
BTDC: Before top dead center
BTU: British thermal unit
C: Celsius (Centigrade)
CCA: Cold cranking amps
cd: Candela
cm^2: Square centimeter
cm^3, cc: Cubic centimeter
CO: Carbon monoxide
CO_2: Carbon dioxide
cu.in., in^3: Cubic inch
CV: Constant velocity
Cyl.: Cylinder
DC: Direct current
ECM: Electronic control module
EFE: Early fuel evaporation
EFI: Electronic fuel injection
EGR: Exhaust gas recirculation
Exh.: Exhaust
F: Farenheit
F: Farad
pF: Picofarad
μF: Microfarad
FI: Fuel injection
ft.lb., ft. lb., ft. lbs.: foot pound(s)
gal: Gallon
g: Gram
HC: Hydrocarbon
HEI: High energy ignition
HO: High output
hp: Horsepower
Hyd: Hydraulic
Hz: Hertz
ID: Inside diameter
in.lb; in. lbs.; in. lbs.: inch pound(s)
Int: Intake
K: Kelvin
kg: Kilogram
kHz: Kilohertz
km: Kilometer
km/h: Kilometers per hour
kΩ: Kilohm
kPa: Kilopascal
kV: Kilovolt
kW: Kilowatt
l: Liter
l/s: Liters per second
m: Meter
mA: Milliampere

mg: Milligram

mHz: Megahertz

mm: Millimeter

mm^2: Square millimeter

m^3: Cubic meter

MΩ: Megohm

m/s: Meters per second

MT: Manual transmission

mV: Millivolt

μm: Micrometer

N: Newton

N–m: Newton meter

NOx: Nitrous oxide

OD: Outside diameter

OHC: Over head camshaft

OHV: Over head valve

Ω: Ohm

PCV: Positive crankcase ventilation

psi: Pounds per square inch

pts: Pints

qts: Quarts

rpm: Rotations per minute

rps: Rotations per second

R–12: refrigerant gas (Freon)

SAE: Society of Automotive Engineers

SO_2: Sulfur dioxide

T: Ton

t: Megagram

TBI: Throttle Body Injection

TPS: Throttle Position Sensor

V: 1. Volt; 2. Venturi

μV: Microvolt

W: Watt

∞: Infinity

<: Less than

>: Greater than

A

B

C

F

G

H

I

J

K

L

M

N

O

P

R

S